# Western Sahara

As the Spanish were preparing to leave colonized Western Sahara in 1975, Morocco invaded, sparking a war with the Western Saharan Polisario Front. About 70% of Western Sahara was occupied by Morocco, which stations up to 140,000 soldiers in the territory, primarily along a 1700 kilometre long sand berm that is protected by one of the world's largest fields of landmines. In 1991, Morocco and the Polisario Front agreed to a truce ahead of a referendum on Western Sahara's future. However, Morocco has since refused to allow the referendum to take place, and has begun the extensive exploitation of Western Sahara's non-renewable natural resources. This has both highlighted the plight of the Saharawi people who live in refugee camps in Algeria and in occupied Western Sahara, and pushed the Polisario Front back to a position where it is openly canvassing for a return to war.

This book was originally published as a special issue of *Global Change, Peace & Security*.

**Damien Kingsbury** holds a Personal Chair and is Professor of International Politics in the School of Humanities and Social Sciences at Deakin University, Melbourne, Australia. His research interests include assertions of self-determination, the role of the military in politics, post-colonial political structures, and nation formation. He is the author of *Sri Lanka and the Responsibility to Protect: politics, ethnicity and genocide* (2012), and *East Timor: the price of liberty* (2009).

# Western Sahara

International law, justice and natural resources

*Edited by*
**Damien Kingsbury**

Routledge
Taylor & Francis Group

LONDON AND NEW YORK

First published 2016
by Routledge

2 Park Square, Milton Park, Abingdon, Oxfordshire OX14 4RN
711 Third Avenue, New York, NY 10017

*Routledge is an imprint of the Taylor & Francis Group, an informa business*

First issued in paperback 2017

*British Library Cataloguing in Publication Data*
A catalogue record for this book is available from the British Library

ISBN 13: 978-1-138-95892-0 (hbk)
ISBN 13: 978-1-138-50261-1 (pbk)

Typeset in Times New Roman
by RefineCatch Limited, Bungay, Suffolk

**Publisher's Note**
The publisher accepts responsibility for any inconsistencies that may have
arisen during the conversion of this book from journal articles to book chapters,
namely the possible inclusion of journal terminology.

**Disclaimer**
Every effort has been made to contact copyright holders for their permission to
reprint material in this book. The publishers would be grateful to hear from any
copyright holder who is not here acknowledged and will undertake to rectify
any errors or omissions in future editions of this book.

# Contents

# Citation Information

The chapters in this book were originally published in *Global Change, Peace & Security*, volume 27, issue 3 (October 2015). When citing this material, please use the original page numbering for each article, as follows:

**Chapter 1**
*The role of resources in the resolution of the Western Sahara issue*
Damien Kingsbury
*Global Change, Peace & Security*, volume 27, issue 3 (October 2015), pp. 253–262

**Chapter 2**
*The taking of the Sahara: the role of natural resources in the continuing occupation of Western Sahara*
Jeffrey J. Smith
*Global Change, Peace & Security*, volume 27, issue 3 (October 2015), pp. 263–284

**Chapter 3**
*Western Sahara, resources, and international accountability*
Stephen Zunes
*Global Change, Peace & Security*, volume 27, issue 3 (October 2015), pp. 285–299

**Chapter 4**
*The status of Western Sahara as occupied territory under international humanitarian law and the exploitation of natural resources*
Ben Saul
*Global Change, Peace & Security*, volume 27, issue 3 (October 2015), pp. 301–322

**Chapter 5**
*The hidden cost of phosphate fertilizers: mapping multi-stakeholder supply chain risks and impacts from mine to fork*
Dana Cordell, Andrea Turner and Joanne Chong
*Global Change, Peace & Security*, volume 27, issue 3 (October 2015), pp. 323–344

**Chapter 6**
*The role of natural resources in the building of an independent Western Sahara*
Fadel Kamal
*Global Change, Peace & Security*, volume 27, issue 3 (October 2015), pp. 345–359

For any permission-related enquiries please visit:
http://www.tandfonline.com/page/help/permissions

# Notes on Contributors

**Damien Kingsbury** holds a Personal Chair in the Faculty of Arts and Education at Deakin University, Melbourne, and is Professor of International Politics in the School of Social Sciences and Humanities. Professor Kingsbury is author or editor of more than two dozen books and numerous book chapters and journal articles on political and security issues and has acted as adviser to a number of non-state military organizations seeking settlement of outstanding political claims. His primary research focuses on conflict resolution and political transitions in authoritarian and post-conflict environments.

**Jeffrey J. Smith** is a Canadian law professor (Carleton University), lawyer, and doctoral fellow (McGill University). He was previously counsel for the United Nations Transitional Administration in East Timor, engaged in the international law dimensions of that country's preparation for independence in 2002. Jeffrey has written extensively about Western Sahara, including its fisheries and environmental protection challenges, and the history and status of the Saharawi state-in-exile. His present areas of research include the development of international environmental law within the law of the sea, climate change regulation, human migration, and governance of the Arctic Ocean area. Jeffrey resides in Montreal and Ottawa.

**Stephen Zunes** is a prominent specialist on US Middle East policy. Professor Zunes has presented numerous lectures and conference papers in the United States and over a dozen foreign countries. He has traveled frequently to the Middle East and other conflict regions, meeting with prominent government officials, scholars, and dissidents. He has served as a political analyst for local, national, and international radio and television, and as a columnist for the *National Catholic Reporter*, *Huffington Post*, *Truthout*, *Alternet*, and *Common Dreams*. He has published scores of articles in academic journals, anthologies, magazines, and newspaper op-ed pages on such topics as US foreign policy, Middle Eastern politics, Latin American politics, African politics, human rights, arms control, social movements, and nonviolent action.

**Ben Saul** is Professor of International Law at the University of Sydney and an Australian Research Council Future Fellow. Ben has expertise in general public international law (particularly terrorism, human rights, the law of war, the use of force, international criminal law, environmental law, and the United Nations). He has published 11 books, over 80 scholarly articles, made hundreds of scholarly presentations, been awarded numerous research grants, and his research has been used in international and national courts. His book *Defining Terrorism in International Law* (Oxford, 2006) is the leading work on the subject, and he is lead author of the *Oxford Commentary on the International Covenant on Economic, Social and Cultural Rights* (2014), awarded the 2015 Certificate of Merit by the American Society of International Law. Ben has taught law at Oxford, the Hague Academy of International Law, and in China, India, Nepal, and Cambodia, and has been a Visiting Professor at Harvard. He has a doctorate in law from Oxford and honours degrees in Arts and Law from Sydney. Ben practises as a barrister in international, regional, and national courts, and was counsel in the largest successful case against Australia before the United Nations Human Rights Committee, *FKAG v Australia* and *MMM v Australia* (2013), involving the illegal indefinite detention of over 50 refugees. Ben has advised or consulted to various international organisations, governments, and NGOs and delivered technical assistance projects in developing countries. He has served on various professional and international bodies, including the International Law Association's International Committee for the Compensation of Victims of War. Ben often appears in the national and international media, including writing opinion in *The New York Times*.

**Dana Cordell** is a Research Principal at the Institute for Sustainable Futures, University of Technology Sydney. Dr Cordell leads and undertakes transdisciplinary research projects on sustainable food and resource futures at the Institute for Sustainable Futures. Many projects involve high-level stakeholder engagement to improve the research relevance, impact, and foster mutual learning. In 2008 Dr Cordell co-founded the Global Phosphorus Research Initiative – the first global platform to undertake research, facilitate networking and debate among policy-makers, industry, scientists, and the public to ensure food systems are resilient to the emerging global challenge of phosphorus scarcity. As a food security expert, Dr Cordell also provides expert advice and commentary to UNEP, the UK Parliament, and Australia's Chief Scientist.

**Andrea Turner** is a Research Director at the Institute for Sustainable Futures, University of Technology Sydney. She is a charted civil engineer with a postgraduate degree in environmental engineering and over 20 years experience in the water industry. She has led numerous water efficiency, drought, and resource planning research projects from city to regional scale for utilities and government agencies in Australia and internationally. She has worked extensively with organisations such as the International Water Association, EU Switch, US based Alliance for Water Efficiency, and Australian based National Water Commission and Water Services Association of Australia to develop resources, guides, training, and tools to aid best practice water management and planning.

**Joanne Chong** is a Research Director at the Institute for Sustainable Futures, University of Technology Sydney. Joanne leads cross-sectoral, multi-disciplinary applied research working in collaboration with governments, civil society, donors industry, enterprise, and community stakeholders to build and enhance policy, governance, and practices for sustainable resource outcomes. Joanne is a water resource sector specialist and has undertaken risk, vulnerability and capacity assessment, scenario analysis, strategic planning and monitoring and evaluation in urban and rural contexts in Australia and in Asia Pacific countries.

**Fadel Kamal,** a Saharawi lawyer, is a senior executive in the Saharawi Republic (SADR) Petroleum and Mines Authority. He currently serves as the Frente Polisario representative in Australia and New Zealand.

**Pedro Pinto Leite** is a Portuguese/Dutch international jurist who lives in Leiden. He studied at the Law Faculty of the University of Lisbon and obtained a masters degree in international law from the Leiden University. Since November 1991 he is the secretary of the International Platform of Jurists for East Timor (IPJET). He is also a member of the International Council of the International Association of Jurists for the Western Sahara (IAJUWS). He is the editor of two collective works, *International Law and the Question of East Timor* (1995) and *The East Timor Problem and the Role of Europe* (1998), co-editor of *International Law and the Question of Western Sahara* (2007), *Le droit international et la question du Sahara occidental* (2009) and *El Derecho Internacional y la Cuestión del Sáhara Occidental* (2012), and wrote many monographs, chapters in other books and articles on self-determination questions.

**Erik Hagen** is board member of Western Sahara Resource Watch and director of the Norwegian Support Committee for Western Sahara. He has followed the issue of the plundering of Western Sahara's resources since 2002, as both an investigative journalist and a civil society activist.

# The role of resources in the resolution of the Western Sahara issue

Damien Kingsbury

*Faculty of Arts and Education, Deakin University, Melbourne, Australia*

The westernmost corner of Algeria, near the border with Morocco, Western Sahara and Mauritania, is a desolate and unforgiving place, where summer temperatures reach and sometimes exceed 50 degrees C. This barren plateau type of desert is known as *hammada* and has historically been referred to as 'the Devil's Garden'. It is an apt name for an environment where sustaining life is impossible without complete reliance on external support.

It is in this area, near the Algerian town of Tindouf, that the Popular Front for the Liberation of Saguia el-Hamra and Rio de Oro (Frente Popular de Liberación de Saguía el Hamra y Rio de Oro, or Polisario Front) administers refugee camps for Saharawi people displaced by Morocco's 1975 invasion of Spanish Sahara (later known as Western Sahara). Between around 100,000 and 165,000 people live in the six camps in the area,[1] surviving on aid from Algeria, South Africa and the wider international community. The Polisario Front also administers the 'liberated' territory of Western Sahara, known as the Saharawi Arab Democratic Republic (SADR).[2]

It is in this all but forgotten place that the four-decades-old claim to Western Saharan independence was again building towards armed conflict. A growing young population, educated but with very few jobs, almost no opportunities and little future, was pushing for its administration to reclaim their land from Moroccan occupation. As the Saharawi refugees wait in these remote and desolate camps, their compatriots in occupied Western Sahara are regularly subjected to abuse and oppression; dissent is not allowed in occupied Western Sahara and is dealt with harshly, often through extra-judicial means.

Meanwhile the relative wealth that the Saharawi people regard as their birthright and which might provide a basis for them to build more complete lives in a future independent state is being sold off to foreign companies, in return for which they receive nothing. Almost all of these resources are finite and such financial legacy as might have been available to the SADR is being depleted by Morocco as a colonial occupier.[3] Faced with being locked into an indefinite and futile future in 'the Devil's Garden' or pressing the issue militarily, with some hope of breaking the current deadlock, the latter was increasingly the preferred option.

The papers in the collection consider aspects of the role of Western Sahara's resources in finding a resolution to the status of Saharawi refugees and Morocco's illegal military occupation of Western Sahara. In part, Western Sahara's natural resources might provide an avenue for finding a way towards a resolution of this issue but, probably more so, the lack of access to

---

1  Population figures are disputed, but the Algerian government claims 165,000, possibly for reasons of greater foreign aid. The camps are named after towns in occupied Western Sahara, including Dakhla, El-Aaiun, Smara and Awserd, as well as Boujdour and the administrative camp of Rabouni.

2  Arabic: al-Jumhūrīyah al-'Arabīyah aṣ-Ṣaḥrāwīyah ad-Dīmuqrāṭīyah, Spanish: República Árabe Saharaui Democrática.

3  WSRW, *P is for Plunder: Morocco's Export of Phosphates from Occupied Western Sahara 2012, 2013* (Melbourne: Western Sahara Resource Watch, 2014).

those resources by the Saharawi people, and their being plundered under Moroccan administration, is an increasing source of conflict. There is, therefore, an increasing likelihood that, should the issue of Morocco's occupation of Western Sahara not be settled, there will be a return to war in north-west Africa.

This potential and increasingly likely return to war will destabilize north-west Africa at a time when much of North Africa is already in turmoil. The costs to the Saharawi, and perhaps to Morocco, Algeria and the region, will be high.

## Background to the conflict

The oasis of Tindouf, in the middle of this otherwise uninhabitable land, had been settled in 1852 by one of the Saharan tribes, the Tajakant, which, along with other regional tribes, was descended from the Arabic Beni Hassan tribe that had conquered the north of Africa in the eleventh century and which blended with local Berber and Tuareg tribes. As a result of tribal conflict, 43 years later, the Tajakant were displaced by the Reguibat tribe, which continues to dominate not just this town but has become the dominant tribe in the region, including in Western Sahara. The colonial French did not reach Tindouf until 1934, when they established it as an outpost of French Algeria.

Although Morocco claims historical ownership of a much greater region than it now occupies, historical maps show that, for example, in 1595 it was divided into two provinces, together being smaller than current Morocco. The following century, an expansionist Morocco seized territory as far south as Senegal, but in 1765 signed a peace treaty with Spain recognizing it did not have authority over Tekna tribes in the border area between Morocco and Western Sahara. While the Tekna continued to acknowledge Moroccan sovereignty, their territory marked the boundary of the Moroccan state.

The Spanish had, since the seventeenth century, used ports in what was to become Western Sahara to facilitate the slave trade from Mauritania. When the French occupied Algeria and imposed a protectorate over Morocco, they set the southern limit at the Draa River (just north of the current southern border). The French did not delineate the southern land border in the desert on the basis that it was uninhabitable. Growing tensions between Spain and France over regional control resulted, in the 1884 Berlin Conference at which the region was divided between colonial powers, with, Spain controlling the north of Morocco and what was to become Spanish Sahara between just south of the Draa River in Morocco and Mauritania. The Reguibat resisted Spanish colonialism, not being subdued in what was Spanish Sahara until 1934, a half a century after Spain's colonial takeover.

Following its independence from France in 1956, Morocco had claimed the oasis of Tindouf, but so had the recently independent Algeria. In the 1963 'Sand War', Algeria ensured that Tindouf remained as part of Algeria and thus set the international boundaries of the new state.[4] However, Tindouf is in an otherwise inhospitable region, and the area to the south of it is perhaps even more so. This is the area of six self-administered Saharawi refugee camps, administered independently by the Polisario Front which claims to be the legitimate representative of the Saharawi people of former Spanish Sahara.

## Morocco's invasion

From the dying days of European colonialism, the position of the United Nations had been that there should be a referendum among the indigenous population of Spanish Sahara in order to

---

4 'Simply – Western Sahara', *New Internationalist*, no. 297; 'A Brief History of the Territory and its People', http://www.arso.org/05-1.htm (accessed August 15, 2015); Janos Besenyo, *Western Sahara* (Budapest: Publikon Publishers, 2009).

settle the status of the Spanish colony. With the growth of a new national consciousness among still colonized peoples, in 1971 a group of Saharawi students formed a political organization that, two years later, would become the Polisario Front. The intention of the Polisario Front was to end Spanish colonialism in what was then Spanish Sahara, to which end the organization initiated a guerrilla campaign against the colonial administration.

The Polisario Front grew quickly, especially with the defection of Saharawi Spanish troops. Spain backed the National Saharawi Union Party (Partido de Union Nacional Saharaui – PUNS), privileging ties with Spain, Morocco moved to claim Spanish Sahara on the basis of claimed historical links between its royal family and the Saharawi people, while Mauritania claimed Spanish Sahara based on a common ethnicity. In June 1975, a visiting UN envoy, Simeon Ake, noted that there was 'overwhelming consensus' in Spanish Sahara for independence.[5]

However, Morocco had claimed the territory since its own independence and had won and lost territory to the colonial Spanish in the late 1950s. In response to this move towards decolonization, the Moroccan army began attacks from early October 1975 and the following month initiated its 'Green March' of about 350,000 militarily supported civilians to occupy Spanish Sahara. Under pressure from Morocco, in mid-November 1975, Spain signed the 'Madrid Accords' which divided the colony between Morocco and Mauritania (not published by the Official State Bulletin and hence not formalized), just four days later ratifying the contradictory 'Law on the Decolonization of Sahara'.

As Morocco and Mauritania invaded, war with the Polisario Front ensued. In February 1976, the Polisario Front declared the Saharawi Arab Democratic Republic. With war raging, Saharawi refugees flooded across the border to what were to become the camps near Tindouf. Though severely outnumbered, the Algerian-backed Polisario Front had initial military successes to the extent that, in 1978, the understaffed and divided Mauritanian army had to withdraw. The following year, Mauritania formally recognized SADR. By August 1979, however, Morocco had annexed that southern part of Western Sahara abandoned by Mauritania. Between 1982 and 1987, Morocco built a series of six walls, each further consolidating its territorial control over Western Sahara, the last partitioning Western Sahara with around 70% of the territory inside the 'useful' zone and the arid and resource-poor outer region ('liberated zones') remaining under SADR control.

Under international law, Morocco's invasion of Spanish Sahara remains illegal.[6] However, the functional military stalemate created by the construction of the 1987 wall meant that, as the Cold War was drawing to an end, the parties agreed to an internationally monitored referendum on self-determination for the Saharawi people in 1988, ratified in 1991.[7] This was to be implemented and monitored by the United Nations Mission for Referendum in Western Sahara (MINURSO), which has continued to have its mandate renewed by the UN Security Council, despite its inability to implement most of its originally stated agenda. Morocco has since refused to allow the ballot. Initial disputes were over who would be eligible to vote, with the Polisario Front arguing in favour of those included in the last Spanish census and their descendants, and Morocco claiming the right to vote by settlers since then.

There have been a number of attempts to find a settlement to the Western Sahara problem but, despite no progress, the 1988 ceasefire between the Polisario Front and Morocco (ratified by the UN in 1991) has held. Morocco's rejection of a vote has led to a stalemate. There have been

---

5  T. Shelley, *Endgame in the Western Sahara: What Future for Africa's Last Colony?* (London: Zed Books, 2004), 171–2.
6  *Western Sahara, Advisory Opinion*, ICJ Reports 1975, 12; Hans Corell, 'Western Sahara: UN Legal Counsel Renders Opinion on Oil Prospecting Contracts', UN News Centre, February 5, 2002; Hans Corell, 'Letter dated 29 January 2002 from the Under-Secretary-General for Legal Affairs, the Legal Counsel, addressed to the President of the Security Council', S/2002/161, United Nations, February 12, 2002.
7  United Nations Security Council Resolution 690: The Situation Concerning Western Sahara, New York, 1991.

further attempts to find a resolution, including the Houston Agreement of 1997 for a referendum in 1998 and the subsequent Moroccan-drafted 'Baker Plan I' of 2001[8] and 'Baker Plan II' of 2003, which was endorsed by the United Nations Security Council (UNSC)[9] but which Morocco refused to accept. The Baker Plans were followed by the Manhasset Negotiations of 2007–8, which similarly failed to find a solution to the deadlock.

This, however, could change. Morocco has put forward an 'autonomy' proposal for Western Sahara, in which the territory could be self-administering within the state of Morocco. However, there is little faith among the Saharawi in that autonomy being genuine, and it does not include an alternative to autonomy. The Polisario Front has, however, said it will accept the autonomy proposal if the Saharawi people are allowed to vote on it. They expect the proposal would be rejected, thereby further establishing grounds for the alternative of independence. Hans Corell, meanwhile, has written that the UNSC should simply declare Western Sahara independent. Corell also noted that companies were entering into illegal contracts with the government of Morocco for exploitation of Western Sahara's natural resources.[10]

Western Sahara continues to be listed by the UN as a non-self-governing territory, with Spain as its *de jure* administering authority, which Spain refuses to accept.[11] For Spain to represent Western Sahara in the UN would raise questions of remaining colonialism at Ceuta, which Spain is reluctant to give up. Ceuta controls the Straits of Gibraltar and provides a control point for African immigration. The UN also acknowledges Morocco as the de facto administering authority for 80% of the territory and SADR as the de facto administering authority for the other 20% of the territory).[12]

## Return to war?

Two generations of Saharawis have grown up either in the refugee camps or under often brutal Moroccan occupation. Based on informal responses from younger Saharawis in the SADR-run camps, there is a strong and growing sense of frustration among them that they are trapped, while the resources of their homeland are being exploited by Morocco. Many seem to believe that returning to war with Morocco to reclaim their land is now the only option.

The Polisario Front has also expressed frustration with Morocco and the failure of an internationally mediated settlement that allows a democratic vote.[13] There is now explicit recognition within the SADR administration that returning to war is possible. The decision about whether SADR will return to war was intended to be made at its four-yearly General Popular Congress in November 2015. There was a growing sense that if SADR does not escalate the situation, the Saharawis will remain doomed to being a people divided by occupation; half repressed, half exiled, with a view increasingly being expressed in conversation with Polisario leaders that the resources upon which they intend to build the economic future of their state are being exploited and depleted by Morocco.

The view that the Polisario Front may return to war followed comments by SADR Foreign Minister Mohammed Salem in 2014 when, in response to a pledge by Morocco's King Moham-

---

8  J. Mundy, 'Seized of the Matter: The UN and the Western Sahara Dispute', *Mediterranean Quarterly* 15, no. 3 (2004): 130–48.
9  United Nations Security Council Resolution 1495, New York, 2003.
10  Hans Corell, 'The Responsibility of the UN Security Council in the Case of Western Sahara', *International Judicial Monitor* (Winter 2015).
11  United Nations General Assembly, Article 73e of the UN Charter; also see: A/5446/Rev.1, annex 1; UN Security Council S/2002/161, 'Letter dated 29 January 2002 from the Under-Secretary-General for Legal Affairs, the Legal Counsel, addressed to the President of the Security Council'.
12  UN Security Council A/RES/68/91 of 11 December 2013, also United Nations Annual Working Paper on Western Sahara, A/AC.109/2014/1.
13  See 'Polisario Urges UN to Press for Western Sahara Referendum', Agence France Presse, February 16, 2016.

mad to maintain its presence in Western Sahara 'until the end of time', he said: 'We will have no other choice but to return to armed struggle'.[14]

Should SADR return to war, it will at least require the tacit agreement of its host country, Algeria. This will then escalate tensions between Algeria and Morocco which, despite recently more normalized relations, have a history of antagonism dating back to the 'Sand War' of 1963, in particular over the territory around Tindouf.[15] The conflict could also spill over into the conflict in neighbouring Mali, where Islamist fighters from North African jihadi groups have descended. Such conflict could also involve Mauritania, which had initially also invaded southern Western Sahara.

With conflict across the Arab world, from Libya to Iraq to Yemen, war between SADR and Morocco, perhaps involving Algeria and other regional states, would very likely further destabilize an already deeply unstable part of the world. There is, then, a desire by many, both within the region and beyond it to avoid such an outcome. But Moroccan intransigence in the face of international law and its continued exploitation of Western Sahara's natural resources appears to be making such an outcome increasingly inevitable. As one Saharawi leader said,[16] it would now take only a small incident for the situation to descend into war.

According to SADR Prime Minister Abd Alkadar Taleb Omar, the Polisario Front did not wish to return to war if that was avoidable. 'We will consider all options for the future at the Congress later this year', he said. 'We have been very patient and waited many years. We have the support of many friends, especially in the African Union. But France and Spain are blocking progress [towards the referendum].' Prime Minister Omar said that diplomacy, politics and war were all along the same spectrum of possibilities, meaning that where one failed it would lead to another along that spectrum. 'There is much conflict in this region', he noted, 'and we wish to avoid adding to that if we are able to do so.'[17]

The Governor of Awserd[18] camp and member of Polisario Front Secretariat, Salek Baba Hasana, was more blunt:

> We prefer a peaceful solution in accordance with international law and UN Security Council resolutions. But there has been a weakness of the UN to impose a solution. Morocco's affiliation with France, as a permanent member [with power of veto] has blocked a resolution through the UN Security Council. But we have not lost hope in an international solution. But if it fails, all other choices are on the table, including armed struggle.[19]

Governor Hasana noted that 'If there is conflict, we have the permission from Algeria, which has stood by us as good friends. The main thing depends on the will of our people and the will of friendly countries, which adopt the principles of freedom and justice'.

Despite a slight thaw in Algerian–Moroccan relations, the bilateral relationship remains tense.[20] However, Algeria faces some threat to its east from Islamist insurgents stemming from the civil war in Libya, and would be unlikely to want to open up a new war on its western front. Having noted that, it is possible that it could remain passive in the face of a Polisario

---

14 'Polisario Threatens War with Morocco after Speech by King', *World Tribune.com*, November 12, 2014, http://www.worldtribune.com/2014/11/12/polisario-threatens-war-morocco-speech-king/ (accessed May 5, 2015).

15 Michael Jacobs, 'Hegemonic Rivalry in the Maghreb: Algeria and Morocco in the Western Sahara Conflict', University of South Florida, January 2012; 'Morocco and Algeria: The Impossible Reconciliation?', *Al Monitor*, July 7, 2013, http://www.al-monitor.com/pulse/politics/2013/07/reconciliation-between-morocco-and-algeria-possible.html# (accessed August 15, 2015).

16 Informal discussion with the author, Rabouni camp, April 10, 2015.

17 Informal Interview with the author, Rabouni camp, April 12, 2015.

18 Also spelled Aousserd.

19 Interview with the author, Awserd camp, April 11, 2015.

20 'Morocco–Algeria Relations Tense Despite Breakthrough Periods', *Middle East Monitor*, 2014, https://www.middleeastmonitor.com/news/africa/15984-morocco-algeria-relations-tense-despite-breakthrough-periods (accessed May 4, 2015).

Front return to war, supporting it by not engaging in the conflict. Morocco would be similarly reluctant to try to punish Algeria for its support for the Polisario Front, given it would be unlikely to achieve any positive outcomes but would draw away from its significant military presence in Western Sahara of about 140,000.

'No-one wants to go to war', Governor Hasana said, 'but we may be forced. It is already 16 years. Our army is better than before and we can certainly defend our people and get back our land. In 1976, we just had militias and Morocco was considered one of the strongest African armies. We have trust in our people [to decide the issue].' Governor Hasana's view of the Saharawi people's options appeared to be less diplomatic than those of the Prime Minister but more in line with those expressed informally by others. 'We have been here [in the camps] for 40 years, but our presence here is only temporary', he said. 'We have in our minds that we came yesterday and will go tomorrow. We continue to resist and are able to continue to resist.'[21]

When asked about the option of Saharawi autonomy within Morocco, he replied:

> There is only the democratic solution in accordance with international law. There are three choices; integration, autonomy or independence. Integration is in contradiction with international law. So we are just talking about autonomy or independence. There cannot be a solution without respect for the right of self-determination. The presence of Morocco [in Western Sahara] is colonial and illegal. This is a decolonization case. There is no state that acknowledges the sovereignty of Morocco over Western Sahara.

While it is technically correct that no country recognizes Morocco's legal sovereignty over Western Sahara, more than 20 countries either support Morocco's territorial claim over Western Sahara or support an autonomy proposal under Moroccan sovereignty. However, SADR is recognized by 84 countries, the African Union (of which it is a member) and the UN Security Council has approved more than 100 resolutions in favour of self-determination for Western Sahara.[22] Of international organizations, only the Organization of Islamic Cooperation recognizes Morocco's sovereignty over Western Sahara.

The SADR Minister Delegate for Asia and former ambassador to the UN and Washington, Mouloud Said, argued that France has primarily been behind the impasse which has led to the Polisario Front again considering returning to war.

> There were several attempts under James Baker to find a resolution to the problem, but the French stopped him [in the UN Security Council]. So the situation depends more on than the Moroccan position, but the French position. The French like to see this part of the world as their back yard.[23]

Minister Mouloud acknowledged that diplomatic pressure had to date not been sufficient and that there might need to be a crisis that paralleled that in relation to Timor-Leste, with which SADR sees itself most closely aligned in terms of the characteristics of its struggle.[24] He noted that the Santa Cruz Massacre of 1991 galvanized world attention on Timor-Leste, after which the EU shifted its position to one of more strongly seeking a final resolution to the territory's status. This was followed, in 1998, by Indonesia's economic crisis, the resignation of President Suharto, the differing approach to occupation by his successor, President Habibie, which led to a referendum and, finally, Australian-led military intervention to quell post-referendum violence by the Indonesia military and its proxy militias.

The view of SADR's Minister for Education, Mariam Salek Hmada, was that the Polisario Front's commitment to education had led to growing frustration and an increasing desire for a

---

21  Interview with the author, Awserd camp, April 11, 2015.
22  44 resolutions since 1991 are listed at MINURSO, United Nations Mission for the Referendum in Western Sahara, http://www.un.org/en/peacekeeping/missions/minurso/resolutions.shtmla (accessed August 15, 2015).
23  Interview with the author, Awserd camp, April 11, 2015.
24  Indonesia invaded what was then Portuguese Timor in late 1975 following moves for its Portuguese colonial masters to withdraw, and the occupation was not recognized by the UN.

final resolution. 'The path to freedom is knowledge. If you don't have education you don't know the meaning of freedom', she said.

> But there are no markets and no jobs for our youth. The UN can't solve the problem of the referendum or of the plundering of resources without any benefit to the indigenous people. This has created frustration among the youth in particular. The youth have been pressing Polisario to go back to war as the talks between the UN and Morocco are just a waste of time.[25]

'The youth are therefore angry. Eventually Polisario will be forced to follow the will of the people', according to Ms Hmada.

> We know what war means. We know the challenges faced by the region, in Libya and Mali. Any movement will take the region to the brink. Yet the last thing to be given by the UN is human rights monitoring and to stop plundering of Saharawi resources. The UN says to the Saharawi people to stay where we are and does not give anything in return, which is not possible.

Ms Hmada also expressed concern that if the Polisario Front leadership did not act, some youth would be attracted away by radical Islamist agendas. 'We are not extremists, but the lack of progress for the youth means we cannot always be an exception [to Islamist extremism].'

In all discussions in the SADR camps, there was recognition that change was only likely to come about through there being an event that acted as a catalyst for growing tensions among the Saharawi population. Such a catalyst, or critical juncture, might involve a radical shift in Morocco's economic or political circumstances, such as an economic embargo or the death, abdication or forced removal of not just the king but also his immediate successors, or the creation of an opportunity cost that becomes too high for Morocco to bear. For this to be the case, the cost would have to be borne by Morocco's elite rather than its citizens, if it is to have any likely impact on perceptions about viability.

However, the Moroccan economy is stable and growing, its political environment is also stable and effectively set (if with a lack of tolerance for dissent). Despite Western Sahara's similarity with Timor-Leste's position under international law, its practical similarities have more in common with West Papua, in that regardless of the moral or legal claims, there is little likelihood of resolution under the current circumstances.

Should Polisario return to war, it will at least require the tacit agreement of its host country, Algeria. This will then escalate tensions between Algeria and Morocco which, despite recently more normalized relations, have a history of antagonism dating back to the 'Sand War' of 1963, over the territory around Tindouf. There could also be spill-over into the conflict in neighbouring Mali, where Islamist fighters from northern jihadi groups have descended. Such conflict could also involve Mauritania, which had initially also invaded southern Western Sahara. The essays presented here each look at what is driving this conflict and what might need to be addressed, including a recognition of the basic rights of the Saharawi people, for it to be avoided.

Jeffrey Smith opens the discussion by looking at the role of natural resources in the continuing issue of Western Sahara's occupation by Morocco. Aspects of the development of the territory's resources have featured in the United Nations and efforts to arrive at self-determination for the Saharawi people. Misconceptions about the effect of resources development continue, however, because of a lack of credible information and analysis of the causal connection of resources to the stalled process of self-determination and the territory's occupation. Smith begins with Spain's colonial establishment of Western Sahara and resource development and then considers how the revenue accruing since 1975 from resource extraction compares to the cost of occupying Western Sahara. He concludes that taking resources from occupied Western Sahara has never been profitable relative to the costs of occupation. He argues that exploitation of natural resources is pursued as a basis for the settlement of Moroccan nationals in the

---

25   Interview with the author, Rabouni camp, April 12, 2015.

territory to help generate acceptance for its territorial acquisition among the international community.

Stephen Zunes follows this discussion by considering the established illegality of facilitating the exploitation of natural resources by an occupying power in a non-self-governing territory. Yet, as he notes, as in the cases as Namibia and East Timor, this illegality has often been overlooked by foreign corporations and governments. The resource-rich territory of Western Sahara is no exception, as European, North American and Australian companies have sought to take advantage of lucrative fishing grounds or mineral deposits. While some have tried to claim that such resource extraction is legal since Morocco reinvests the money it receives into the territory through ambitious development programmes, the benefits of such 'development' have largely gone to Moroccan settlers and occupation authorities, rather than the indigenous population. As with Namibia and East Timor, it has fallen to global civil society to pressure such companies, through boycotts and divestment campaigns, to end their illegal exploitation of Western Sahara's natural resources.

Ben Saul similarly explores international law on occupation and its implications on natural resources in Western Sahara. He argues that much of the international legal analysis of dealings in natural resources in Western Sahara has focused on its status as a non-self-governing territory, as well as the right of self-determination of the Saharawi people. What he says is overlooked in the legal debates is a close examination of the application of the international law of occupation under international humanitarian law (IHL). Saul's paper therefore considers whether and how Western Sahara constitutes an 'occupied territory' under IHL, discussing some of the unique peculiarities that complicate the legal answer. He then considers issues of state and individual criminal responsibility under international law for illegal dealings with natural resources and property in Western Sahara by Moroccan and foreign companies, including under Australian federal criminal law implementing international obligations.

Dana Cordell et al. follow this exposition of international law by identifying the larger social and environmental burden of phosphate mining in Western Sahara. She notes that without phosphorus, many foods would not be produced, as farmers need access to phosphate fertilizers to ensure high crop yields. Yet the world largely relies on non-renewable phosphate rock that is mined in only a few countries. Growing global demand for phosphorus could surpass supply in the coming decades, while Morocco alone controls 75% of the remaining reserves, including those in Western Sahara. The market price of phosphate fertilizers also hides a far deeper burden, with consequences as far-ranging as the exploitation and displacement of the Saharawi people, to nutrient pollution with the result that some aquatic ecosystems have been classified as 'dead zones', along with jeopardizing future generations' ability to produce food. The full cost of phosphate rock might indicate that it should be used more sparingly, to extend the availability of high-quality rock for future generations, to diversify phosphorus sources to include those with lower societal costs, and to share responsibility for these costs and consequences.

Exploitation of Western Sahara's natural resources do, however, have an important role in nation building, according to SADR representative Fadel Kamal. He claims the SADR government believes that its significant natural resources will play an important part in the development of a viable, self-reliant and democratic nation which will contribute to the peace, stability and progress of the entire Maghreb region. His paper examines the SADR's efforts to manage its natural resources through the establishment of the SADR Petroleum and Mines Authority, the launch of licensing rounds, its claim to an exclusive economic zone in the Atlantic Ocean and the recent enactment of a Mining Code. The paper draws on the SADR's efforts to protect its natural resources and examines the SADR oil and gas licensing rounds as an example of SADR's assertion of sovereignty. The SADR natural resources strategy has, Fadel says, two basic goals: to deter Morocco's efforts to exploit the SADR natural resources and to prepare for the recovery of full sovereignty.

It is not enough, of course, to identify a problem; it is also necessary to consider possible ways forward. Pedro Pinto Leite does this by moving beyond the impasse that existed at the time of writing, and which was threatening a dire outcome, to how Western Sahara's independence could be achieved. In doing this, Leite contrasts Western Sahara with the example of East Timor (Timor-Leste), identifying the International Commission of Jurists' common position on the right to self-determination of both Sahrawis and East Timorese.

Leite notes that East Timor is now independent, but that most of Western Sahara remains under foreign occupation, subject to serious human rights violations, with its natural resources pillaged. Morocco refuses to hold a promised referendum, as noted above, while the UN Security Council has been unable to take suitable action due to the use or threat of veto by France and the US. Leite asserts that it is therefore time to recall that the Sahrawi Republic (SADR) was proclaimed and that its government controls the majority of the people and a part of the territory. In that respect, SADR qualifies as a state, and is recognized as such by more than 80 countries. The UN, he argues, should follow the example of the African Union and welcome SADR into its fold. In order to reach that goal, the UN General Assembly should 'consider the matter immediately', recognize SADR and force a breakthrough.

These papers are followed by a 'communication' from Erik Hagen, tracing what he calls the 'Saharawi conflict phosphates' and their link to the Australian dinner table. Hagen notes that companies in Australia and New Zealand have been large importers of phosphate rock from Western Sahara for many years. A report launched by Western Sahara Resource Watch (WSRW), for which Hagen works, showed that companies in New Zealand and Australia accounted for a fifth of the purchases from Western Sahara for the year 2014. WSRW estimates that the total exports from the occupied territory last year was around 2.1 million tonnes, at a value of US$230 million, carried on board 44 bulk vessels. These exports took place, he noted, even though the Saharawi people objected to it, and despite its clear violation of international law. Several international investors have also deemed such trade unethical, while a handful of previously importing companies have ceased importing from the occupied territory due to legal and ethical concerns. Hagen elaborates on the global phosphate trade of the Saharawi phosphate rock, and the research and international campaigning done by Western Sahara Resource Watch in halting the controversial trade.

According to Minister Mouloud:

> The UN has lost all credibility it had with the people. That leaves the leadership up against the wall. There is frustration and disappointment. Some people say we should have not stopped the war in '91. This frustration makes people more upset than they were in 1975. They are more ready for war. The people are more committed to the issue. In the occupied territories, they hate Morocco more than we do, they are more radical than us.

As a result, he said, 'We are in an area of the unknown, where anything can happen at any time. A small incident can restart a war'.[26].

It is important to note, following Leite's suggestion, that there remains time for a resolution to this growing threat of a new Sahara war but, with Morocco appearing to harden its stance on not allowing a popular vote, this is looking increasingly remote. From the perspective of Polisario, if Morocco does not move soon, many Saharawi believe it will be left with little choice but to return to war. With conflict across the Arab world, from Libya to Iraq to Yemen, war between Polisario and Morocco, perhaps involving Algeria and other regional states, can only further destabilize an already deeply unstable part of the world. There is, then, a desire by many, both within the region and beyond it to avoid such an outcome.

---

26  Informal interview, Rabouni camp, April 12, 2015.

## Disclosure statement

No potential conflict of interest was reported by the author.

# The taking of the Sahara: the role of natural resources in the continuing occupation of Western Sahara

Jeffrey J. Smith

*Faculty of Law, McGill University, Canada*

The role of natural resources in the continuing 'question' of Western Sahara is not fully understood. In recent years, the development of the territory's resources has been at issue in efforts to arrive at self-determination for the Saharawi people. Misconceptions about the effect of such development persist, however, because of a lack of credible information and limited analysis of the connection of resources to the stalled process of self-determination and the territory's occupation. The present analysis surveys the history, problems resulting from and consequences of the exploitation of resources in a Western Sahara that has for 40 years been under armed occupation. It begins with Spain's colonizing of Western Sahara and involvement with its resources before turning to the territory's abandonment to Morocco and Mauritania following which Spain retained some resource rights. Revenue from extraction of the two primary resources since 1975 is then assessed and compared to the costs to occupy Western Sahara. The relevant international law is considered, including the right of non-self-governing peoples to sovereignty over natural resources, and the application of international humanitarian law. Rationales for Morocco's extraction of resources are examined, the evidence revealing that the activity is pursued as a basis for the settlement of Moroccan nationals in the territory to better serve an ostensible annexation project, and generate acceptance for territorial acquisition in the organized international community. The prospects for application of the law and the place of natural resources in the resolution of the question of Western Sahara are finally contemplated.

> The restraints which are implicit in the non-recognition of South Africa's presence in Namibia … impose on member States the obligation to abstain from entering into economic and other forms of relationship or dealings with South Africa on behalf of or concerning Namibia which may entrench its authority over the Territory.[1]

In the final months of 2015 the pillage of resources from Western Sahara continued uninterrupted while the people of the territory marked 40 years of occupation. The taking has been constant: fish from the richest coastal area in Africa, the Canary Current Large Marine Ecosystem, along with the large-scale export of phosphate mineral rock. The year had, for a time, brought the start of seabed petroleum drilling on the territory's Atlantic coast. These and other resources continue to be removed despite the protests of the territory's original inhabitants, the Saharawi people, who insist such acts violate their sovereign right of ownership to the resources. For their part, the United Nations and the states most interested in Western Sahara have remained silent.

Only in recent years has the question of resources in Western Sahara received attention. There has been little analysis of how the production and export of resources may contribute to Morocco's annexation of the territory. When it comes to ensuring for the Saharawi people their right to

---

1 International Court of Justice, *Namibia Advisory Opinion*, 1971 ICJ Reports 16, para. 124.

self-determination – the obligation of all states and collectively the organized international community – the implications of exporting resources from the territory have featured infrequently even as the Saharawi have been emphatic in their opposition. As with the right of sovereignty over natural resources for a non-self-governing people, so has the requirement of international humanitarian law (IHL) that prohibits the plunder of natural resources gone unremarked.[2] Under occupation, the exploitation of Western Sahara's resources has been substantial and occasionally revealed as unsustainable, with some fish stocks in the territory's coastal waters near collapse in the late 1990s.[3] Equally serious, the exploitation of fish, phosphate, and production of minor agricultural resources, together with salt and sand, has impeded the prospect of self-determination for the Saharawi people, entrenching the status quo of occupation.

The 'question' of Western Sahara, as the United Nations describes it, is one about the right of the Saharawi people to exercise their choice of self-determination as the inhabitants of the former colony of Spanish Sahara. A long delayed self-determination referendum and the active conflict between the Frente Polisario and Morocco from 1975 until 1991 (which included Mauritania until 1979) have been the principal features of such a question. However, serious human rights abuses (including the maltreatment of the Saharawi population in Moroccan-occupied areas, forced disappearances and the introduction of settlers into the territory) remain significant. That there has been comparatively limited concern about the territory's resources and what the taking of them entails for an occupation and the stalled self-determination of the Saharawi people should not be surprising.

Western Sahara's principal natural resources are phosphate mineral rock from the Bu Craa mine and fish from a highly productive area of the Atlantic Ocean.[4] Possible land and seabed petroleum reserves may yet add to this. In the 30 years after invasion, the fishery was the most highly valued. After 2008 phosphate became the leading resource as a result of its sudden increase and then a sustained historically high market price. It has become apparent that, as with earlier decolonization cases such as Namibia and East Timor, the exploitation of natural resources perpetuates the occupation of Western Sahara and thereby delays its people's self-determination. In light of the territory's increasing potential for mineral resources and petroleum, there is a greater need to understand how the exploitation of resources is part of the 'question' of Western Sahara.

The present analysis surveys the history, problems resulting from, and consequences of the exploitation of resources in a Western Sahara that has for 40 years been under armed occupation. It begins with Spain's colonizing of Western Sahara and involvement with its resources before turning to the territory's abandonment to Morocco and Mauritania, following which Spain retained some resource rights. Revenue from extraction of the two primary resources since 1975 is then assessed and compared to the costs of occupying Western Sahara. The relevant international law is considered, including the right of non-self-governing peoples to sovereignty

---

2  Morocco occupies three-quarters of Western Sahara which has an area of 266,000 km$^2$within colonial frontiers established by France and Spain. Mauritania and Morocco partitioned Western Sahara in April 1976. Mauritania quit the territory in 1979 upon concluding a peace treaty with the Saharawi national liberation movement, the Frente Polisario (the Popular Front for the Liberation of Saguia el-Hamra and Río de Oro). Morocco then occupied the area left by Mauritania.The term 'occupation' is used in its ordinary meaning in international affairs and law, noting the UN General Assembly's declaratory use of it in the case of Western Sahara and the conclusion of the International Court of Justice in 1975, discussed below, that Morocco did not have any legal basis for a claim to the territory.

3  The Canary Current Large Marine Ecosystem on the coast of northwest Africa is the third most globally productive fishery. UNFAO, 'Protection of the Canary Current Large Marine Ecosystem' (undated), http://www.canarycurrent. org/resources/publications (accessed December 1, 2014).

4  Phosphate rock exports from the Bu Craa (Bou Craa; بوكراع) site by the Moroccan state-owned Office Chérifien des Phosphates (OCP SA) through its subsidiary operating entity, PhosBouCraa, are planned to continue at 2.6 million tonnes/year, averaging 2.2 million tonnes in recent years, with a notable peak of 2.78 million tonnes in 2011, OCP SA *Prospectus – 17 April 2014* (a debt-financing prospectus issued on the Irish Stock Exchange), 95 [OCP 2014 *Prospectus*] (unpublished, copy on file with author). The coastal fishery is carried out by Moroccan, European Union member state, Russian and Japanese vessels, the latter joining for a seasonal tuna fishery in October 2014.

over natural resources, and the application of international humanitarian law. Rationales for Morocco's extraction of resources are examined, the evidence revealing that the activity is pursued as a basis for the settlement of Moroccan nationals in the territory to better serve an ostensible annexation project, and generate acceptance for territorial acquisition in the organized international community. Finally, the prospects for application of the law and the place of natural resources in the resolution of the question of Western Sahara are contemplated.

## I.   Natural resources in Africa's last colony

The history of foreign involvement in Western Sahara's resources is one of appropriation by outsiders. From the time the Saharawi were colonized, they never enjoyed the entire benefit of the coastal fishery or the later mining of phosphate rock, even as the two commodities came to be exploited at industrial levels. The year 1885 marked Spain's formal establishment of the colony, ostensibly for a Canary Islands fleet which had fished the coast for centuries. Spain's early concern for a territory it obtained by Europe's division of Africa at the Conference of Berlin was negligible. Only after 1895 did it build settlements, in the north at el Aauin (Laayoune) and mid-coast at Dakhla (Villa Cisneros), and it would not consolidate possession of the territory until the 1930s.[5] Geological surveys in the 1940s revealed promising phosphate deposits at Bu Craa in the northern part of the territory. In 1962 Spain decided they should be developed, enacting the necessary legislation and constructing a 100-kilometer conveyor belt to transport the phosphate to a loading facility at the coast near el Aauin.[6] By the time Spain decided to leave Western Sahara, Bu Craa was producing 2.7 million tonnes per year after it started operation in 1973. Long after it gave up the territory, the Spanish government would retain a 35% share in the enterprise.[7]

To understand why Western Sahara's natural resources have received little attention, the means by which Spain abandoned its colony must be recalled.[8] The formal pretext was the November 1975 Madrid Accords.[9] That treaty allowed Mauritania and Morocco to occupy the territory (something that was by then already underway) and noted that the three states would assure the Saharawi people their right to self-determination. The Accords were meant to give Spain legitimacy in quitting the Sahara, and an acceptance that its colony could be annexed by two neighboring states, whatever provision was made or not for the rights of the Saharawi people. The Accords were contrary to international law, for Spain did not have the right to transfer away the Saharawi people's territory or delegate the conduct of their self-determination to

---

5   The territory's frontiers were established by the *Convention pour la délimitation des possessions françaises et espagnoles dans l'Afrique occidentale*, 1900, 92 BFSP 1014; the *Convention between France and Spain respecting Morocco*, 1904, 102 BFSP 432; and the *Treaty between France and Spain regarding Morocco*, 1912 (1913) AJIL 7 at Supplement 81.

6   'The phosphate mined at Boucraa is sedimentary [i.e. is apatite] and consists of two layers of phosphate ... Mining of the second layer, which is less rich [in phosphoric content] and contains more silica, is expected to commence in 2014, following the completion of the necessary processing infrastructure.' No part of the Bu Craa enterprise appears set for capital improvement or expansion in coming years. See OCP 2014 *Prospectus*, 81–2.

7   The government of Spain divested its ownership in 2002. The entire corporate interest is now held by OCP SA, which became an incorporate entity in 2008, assuming control of all phosphate extraction and export activities in Morocco from the government agency of the same name.

8   Western Sahara is a case of unique dualities in its factual and legal setting. It (its people) are characterized as non-self-governing, and so Western Sahara in law and by UN declaration is a colony. But is also a place under armed occupation, given the absence of a legal claim to the territory by the occupying state. The territory proper has two present de facto sovereigns, a 'government in exile' that is the Saharawi Republic and Morocco. It has a divided original population, one part under occupation, the other self-governing refugees. And, as discussed below, two bodies of law apply to the development and export of its resources.

9   *Declaration of Principles (Tripartite (Madrid) Accords (Mauritania/Spain/Morocco))* (November 14, 1975), 14 ILM 1512.

others.[10] The tragedy of Western Sahara resulted out of Spain's failure to act consistently with international law and what were by then the many successful decolonization cases.

The Madrid Accords accomplished more than simply a territorial cession. The treaty created the basis for exploitation of the territory's resources, if unwittingly, up to the present. With the Accords were protocols revealed only after 2009. The first allowed Spain continued access to the Saharan fishery, an arrangement that continued until Spain joined the European Economic Community (the EEC) in 1986. (Control of member state fishing was and is through the Common Fisheries Policy that began with the 1957 Treaty of Rome.) Morocco agreed that Spain could have 20 years of fishing for as many as 800 vessels in 'Saharan waters' with fine-tuning to be done in specific treaties after 1976.[11] A second protocol ratified Spain's ownership share in the Phosboucraa enterprise and detailed arrangements for Morocco to receive assistance with geological exploration, the building of vessels to transport phosphate (*roca fosfatos*), tourism and agriculture. The third protocol continued arrangements for fishing in Mauritanian waters, which had been open to Spanish vessels after the country's independence in 1964.[12] The division of the territory's ocean resources has been discussed by Driss Dahak, a Moroccan law of the sea advisor and UNCLOS (UN Convention on the Law of the Sea) negotiator. He describes how Spanish–Moroccan fisheries cooperation was made part of the Accords because Morocco considered itself obliged to accept Spain's demands given the 'particular political circumstances' of the time.[13] Subsequent fishery treaties between the two states were short-lived, revisited in June 1979, December 1979, April 1981, December 1982 and August 1983. The last provided for reciprocal commitments, with Spain to continue with access and Morocco to receive 'assistance in the technical domain and the financing of projects'.[14] A similar arrangement continues under the present 2006–07 European–Morocco fisheries treaty.

After Spain joined the EEC, the first Brussels-directed treaty came into operation in 1988.[15] It had a four-year term, during which Morocco was to be paid 282 million European Currency Units (ECU). Subsequent treaties were agreed upon in 1992 (310 million ECU) and 1995 (500 million ECU). The treaties with Morocco ended for a time in 1999 when no agreement for renewal could be reached because of concerns over the sustainability of fish stocks.[16] In retrospect, the amounts paid were remarkable; more than 1 billion ECU for 11 years of access to the Saharan fishery. This is explained in part by the volumes of fish taken, the redistributionist and developmental goals of the EEC/EU common fisheries policy, and perceptions of the importance of the Saharan fishery to the Canary Islands economy.

Morocco and Spain also reportedly considered dividing the continental shelf between the Canary Islands and the Saharan coast. (Mauritania and Morocco did so through their April 1976 treaty, above.) However, the two states did not apparently begin to negotiate maritime

---

10  The *Madrid Accords* arguably lapsed on February 26, 1976 when Spain withdrew its remaining presence in Western Sahara. They were undoubtedly abrogated when Mauritania and Morocco partitioned the territory that April under the *Convention concerning the State Frontier Line established between the Islamic Republic of Mauritania and the Kingdom of Morocco*, April 14, 1976, 1977 UNTS 117 (in force November 10, 1976).

11  *Madrid Accords* first protocol, 1975. The protocol provided for joint oversight with a review five years into its 20-year term and compensation for Spanish government property connected to the fishing industry left in the territory.

12  Respectively, the second and third protocols to the Madrid Accords.

13  D. Dahak, *Les Etats Arabes et le Droit de la Mer*, Tomes I et II (Rabat: Les Editions Maghrébines, 1986), 409. Dahak notes that a 1977 fishing agreement was not ratified by Morocco in response to 'Spain declaring after 1976 that it had only ceded administration of the territory, and not its sovereignty'. Ibid., 410, translation.

14  Ibid., 411 (footnote omitted). The 1983 agreement prescribed a first annual catch limit of 136,602 tonnes, to be reduced for conservation reasons in following years by 5%, 10% and 14%.

15  *Agreement on Relations in the Sea Fisheries Sector between the European Community and the Kingdom of Morocco*, OJ L181 (June 23, 1988).

16  T. Shelley, *Endgame in the Western Sahara: What Future for Africa's Last Colony?* (New York: Zed Books, 2004), 74. During these years, the ECU exchange rate averaged US$0.84. On the 1995 treaty see G. White, 'Too Many Boats, Not Enough Fish: The Political Economy of Morocco's 1995 Fishing Accord with the European Union', *Journal of Developing Areas* 31 (1997): 313.

boundaries in the area. The concept of extended maritime jurisdictional areas was only then emerging, with many states awaiting the result of the UN Law of the Sea Conference in the middle of developmental meetings.[17] The issue is of renewed interest in recent years, with both states authorizing seabed petroleum exploration in waters south and east of the Canary Islands in 2014 and 2015.

Today, the direct involvement of third states in Western Sahara's natural resources remains limited to the fishery. Mauritania has no connection with the territory's resources except indirectly by an extended continental shelf claim that appears to encroach on the Saharan seabed.[18] The government of Spain has relinquished its interest in Phosboucraa, the local operating subsidiary of Morocco's Office Chérifien des Phosphates (OCP SA), the government phosphate mining, marketing and export entity recreated as a corporation in 2008. No other state is involved with production or commercial trade of the territory's phosphate. After 2000, petroleum development in Western Sahara had been limited to exploration, including seismic surveys. This changed in December 2014 with the American firm Kosmos Energy Ltd. starting seabed drilling northwest of Dakhla at the Gargaa (El-Khayr, or CB-1) deepwater site.[19] Commercial involvement with the Saharan fishery is through a 2013 Morocco–Russia treaty (a renewal of earlier ones dating from 2006) and the resumed[20] EU–Morocco Fisheries Partnership Agreement (the FPA) that first operated from 2007 until December 2011.[21]

The Frente Polisario, as the national liberation movement for the Saharawi people and government of the Saharawi Arab Democratic Republic, constantly protests at the taking of the territory's natural resources. It does so in matters large and small. The Frente Polisario condemned the FPA to the European Commission when its first protocol was set to expire in February 2011. A November 2010 letter from Mohamed Sidati, the Frente Polisario's EU delegate, to the then EC Fisheries Commissioner Maria Damanaki is typical:

---

17  '[T]he negotiations for the Madrid Accord ... provided that "The experts of the two countries will meet prior to 31 December 1975 for the purpose of mapping the median line between the coasts of the two countries' and that the government of Spain had expressed reservations about petroleum exploration permits issued by the government of Morocco in 1971 in areas between Morocco and the Canary Islands, considered by Spain as having exceeded an equidistance line between the coasts of the two countries"'. Dahak, *Les Etats Arabes et le Droit de la Mer*, 239 (translation, footnote omitted).

18  The claim to an extended continental shelf (ECS) was first defined in a preliminary submission to the UN Commission on the Limits of the Continental Shelf (CLCS) in May 2009, and further detailed in September 2014. The claim most likely encroaches into Western Sahara's seabed area as there is not yet a territorial sea boundary or an exclusive economic zone (EEZ) boundary between the two states at Cape Blanc. In December of the same year, Spain delivered to the CLCS its ECS claim for the seabed west of the Canary Islands that also appears to overlap with a presumptive Saharan seabed. Morocco has protested at the claim, and the government of the Saharawi Republic has, in turn, protested at Morocco's protest on the basis that it could only be advanced with Morocco in (the illegal) possession of the relevant Saharan coastline. See Letter of Ahmed Boukhari, Frente Polisario representative to the UN at New York to the UN Secretary-General (April 12, 2015) (unpublished, copy on file with the author).

19  Kosmos Energy Ltd. undertook extensive seabed surveys in 2012–14, and has suggested to investors that up to 1 billion equivalent-to-petroleum barrels may be present in its Boujdour Offshore block. In completing test well assessment in March 2015, the company noted petroleum was present but not economically viable for the time being, http://www.kosmosenergy.com (accessed March 20, 2015).

20  In September 2014.

21  See the *Agreement between the Government of Russian Federation and the Government of The Kingdom of Morocco for a Marine Fisheries Partnership*, 2010 (unpublished, copy on file with the author) and *Fisheries Partnership Agreement between the European Communities and the Kingdom of Morocco*, July 28, 2005 (entered into force March 7, 2007) (the FPA), http://eur-lex.europa.eu (accessed December 1, 2014). The operative protocol to the FPA was extended in February 2011 as its four-year term was about to expire. That December, the European Parliament ended the extension. In 2013, a new protocol was reached, entering into force July 2014 with fishing beginning that September. It has a term of four years and will see Morocco annually paid €30 million. EU fishing in Saharan waters – not geographically defined under the FPA's protocols – has been criticized. See J. Smith, 'Fishing for Self-determination: European Fisheries and Western Sahara – The Case of Ocean Resources in Africa's Last Colony', *Ocean Yearbook* 27 (2013): 267.

[We] repeat our previous communications to the Commission that *fishing by European vessels in Western Sahara's waters pursuant to an arrangement with the Kingdom of Morocco is contrary to the interests and wishes of the people of Western Sahara, and is therefore contrary to international law.*[22]

In June 2014 the SADR (Saharawi Arab Democratic Republic) government wrote to the government of New Zealand with a request that it prohibit the import of phosphate rock by two companies.[23] In January 2015, the president of the SADR wrote to UN Secretary-General Ban Ki-moon to protest at seabed oil drilling, calling for intervention by the UN Security Council:

> The Saharawi government concludes that the present petroleum activity is illegal and impedes progress toward the conduct of a 'free and fair referendum' as that has been accepted by the parties. (See report of Secretary-General 18 June 1990, UN document S/21360, paragraph 47(g).) The activity underscores to the Saharawi people that a violation of well settled, universally [accepted] rules of international law is allowed to continue. That suggests the organized international community is unwilling to ensure the paramount obligation of self-determination flowing from Article 73 of the UN Charter.[24]

## II.   The plunder of the Sahara

A starting point to assess what has resulted from 40 years of resource extraction in an occupied Western Sahara is to consider the value of what has been taken, and assess that in light of the economic cost of annexing the territory. To this end, a survey of how the two originally occupying states dealt with resources is useful before turning to the matter of the resources' value. For its part, Mauritania realized virtually no resource income, having garrisoned and fought for its part of the territory at great financial and political cost. Assessing the economic rents taken by Morocco reveals little better result for that country. The kingdom has incurred significant direct cost to maintain an occupation which, even in recent years of high phosphate market prices and assured foreign flag fishing, has been a demand on its state treasury.

The more consequential impact, however, has been that of creating a semblance of normalcy to what is a project of annexation. Resource exports allow Morocco to foster the international community's acceptance that it is legitimately in possession of the territory. That a majority of the population in the occupied part of the territory are now Moroccan settlers who benefit most from the resources is overlooked. In some respects, the issue can only be discounted by states and the UN, because to engage it as the law requires would demand addressing the legality of an occupation itself. The significance of Western Sahara's resources for Morocco has been far-ranging, on a parallel with resource exploitation in South African-occupied Namibia and Indonesian-annexed East Timor.

---

22   Emphasis in original. The 2010 letter added: 'The waters adjacent to the coast of Western Sahara are NOT Morocco's, as confirmed by the declaration by the Saharawi Arab Democratic Republic (SADR) of an Exclusive Economic Zone on 21 January 2009 ... Exploitation by EU vessels of Western Sahara's fisheries resources, without the prior consultation and consent of the representatives of the Saharawi people, is in direct conflict with the non-derogable right of the Saharawi people to exercise sovereignty over their natural resources, and is therefore in violation of international law, including international human rights law and the relevant principles of the Charter of the United Nations' (unpublished, copy on file with the author). On the history of the Frente Polisario and development of the Saharawi state, see S. Zunes and J. Mundy, *Western Sahara: War, Nationalism, and Conflict Irresolution* (Syracuse, NY: Syracuse University Press, 2010).

23   Letter of SADR Minister of Foreign Affairs to the New Zealand Minister of Foreign Affairs, 'The import to New Zealand of phosphate from occupied Western Sahara', June 12, 2014. Morocco responded with a June 16 letter to New Zealand, requesting the SADR's letter be disregarded. Morocco's letter was disclosed through a Twitter account in November 2014 by someone with access to its ministry of foreign affairs diplomatic cables, 'Le Makhzen'. (The correspondence is unpublished, copies on file with the author.)

24   Letter of SADR president Md. Abdelaziz to UN Secretary-General Ban Ki-moon, January 26, 2015, http://www.spsrasd.info (accessed April 1, 2015). The Secretary-General noted the letter in his annual report to the UN Security Council, 'Report of the Secretary-General on the Situation Concerning Western Sahara' (April 10, 2015) UN doc. S/2015/246, para. 62.

The activities to support resource extraction have been manifested in several ways, including a substantial military presence and the construction of civil and military works, such as port facilities at el Aauin and Dakhla. Morocco does not hold the territory by force alone. Rather, it has introduced an ever-larger population of settlers into Western Sahara who partly rely on resource development for employment and to create a local production economy.[25] Morocco's capacity to support its settlers in Western Sahara, to be clear, does not turn only on the exploitation of natural resources. But given the lack of industry, manufacturing, higher education facilities and market services for a largely urbanized population of what is now about 400,000 people (including the Saharawi), resources have a central role in the pursuit of a seemingly viable local economy.

Allowing, if not promoting, the settlement of Moroccan nationals, arguably the most acute 'problem on the ground', does two things to delay Saharawi self-determination. The first has been to confuse the demographic of those properly entitled to vote in a self-determination referendum. The second is to introduce a population, a part of which might prefer or be compelled to be relocated should Saharawi independence result. The result has been paralysis, with the ability of the UN to ensure a proper referendum now seriously doubted. An increasing Moroccan population coupled with a denial of self-determination, founded in part on the exploitation of natural resources, is clearly a valuable result for Morocco.

A calculation of the value of resources taken from Western Sahara since 1975 is possible. Some gaps in the data exist, because they are not available on the public record or because they cannot be sufficiently assessed to be credible. Export volumes of phosphate rock, also checked against the decline in reserves at the Bu Craa mine site, together with known market values for the commodity, allow a ready calculation. The value of the fishery from 1975 through 1988 is more obscure. After 1988, that value can be derived from the payments under the EC/EU–Morocco fisheries treaties and later the Russia–Morocco treaties. Of course, allowance has to be made for fisheries other than those under the EU and Russian treaties, for example by locally operated vessels (with some registered in flag of convenience states) after the first FPA protocol was ended in 2011 and a brief tuna fishery conducted by Japan in late 2014.[26] It should be noted that little European and no recorded Russian fishery since 1975 has taken place in waters immediately adjacent to those of Western Sahara, that is, to the north in the area between Spain's Fuerteventura Island and the mainland of Morocco. Fisheries 'with Morocco' take place in the highly productive waters of the Canary Current area on the mid-coast of Western Sahara and to the south.

Therefore, the following calculation is proposed in order to arrive at a net present value resulting from the exploitation of the Saharan fishery since 1975, as of 1 October 2015. There are four sources (or categories) of revenue to assess, namely: (i) the Spanish fishery until 1988; (ii) payments by the EEC/EU from 1988 until the present; (iii) the Russian fishery, notably the payments under 2010 and 2013 agreements; and (iv) a local commercial fishery based in Dakhla using Moroccan and flag of convenience vessels which increased after the temporary end of EU fisheries in late 2011. Periodic fisheries by other states, such as a 2014 tuna fishery by Japanese

---

25 Even less about natural resources has been the organized international community's response to Morocco introducing its nationals as settlers into Western Sahara. 'The Occupying Power shall not deport or transfer parts of its own civilian population into the territory it occupies.' Article 49, *Fourth Geneva Convention: Convention (IV) relative to the Protection of Civilian Persons in Time of War*, August 12, 1949, 75 UNTS 287 (entered into force October 21, 1950).

26 In October 2014 four or possibly five Japanese flag longliners operated southwest of Dakhla in a seasonal tuna fishery, landing their catch in Las Palmas. It is estimated that the four-week activity resulted in a total catch of 1600 tonnes at a market value of $12 million. The vessels were detected by Saharawi authorities and a protest at their presence was made by the Western Sahara Resource Watch NGO to the government of Japan. (Personal conversations of the author with SADR officials and Western Sahara Resource Watch (WSRW) managers, October 2014). The calculation of the value of the catch is the author's from a variety of stated market prices for yellowfin tuna in October 2014 following an estimate of the capacity and likely catch taken by the four vessels. For fisheries market prices, see the UN Food & Agriculture Organization (UNFAO) seafood pricing website: http://www.globefish.org (accessed April 15, 2015).

flag vessels, together with permit fee revenue realized by Morocco for local (artisanal) fishing, are discounted.[27] Fishing revenues from the period after 1999 until resumption of EU fishing in early 2007, from all states, are also discounted because of the lack of credible figures. A base date of 1 October 2015 for the valuation was chosen to allow for a full 40-year analysis.

To begin with, data for Spain's payments to Morocco from 1975 until 1988 is difficult to obtain. Accurate figures in what few records are publicly available are obscure and not always directly connected to the Saharan fishery. For this analysis the present value of Spain's payment during that period is dismissed. The present value of EEC/EU-era payments from 1988 through 1999 is straightforward; taking the 1.1 billion ECU paid until 1999 and calculating its value on 1 October 2015 results in a Figures of $1.072 billion.[28] Figures for Russia's actual payments from January 2010 through mid-2015 are not publicly available, although from the presence of Russian vessels on the Saharan coast, their patterns of activity, transshipment of catches to freezer ships, and prices stated for various species such as mackerel and sardines an annual catch-of 50,000 tonnes is indicated. Under its 2010 treaty with Morocco, Russia was to pay 17.5% of a stated value of all species caught of $255 per tonne, to an annual maximum of 120,000 tonnes. In the 2013 successor treaty that operated through 2015, Russia was required to pay 17.5% of a stated value of $497 per tonne for up to 100,000 tonnes and a lump sum payment of $5 million annually.[29] A realistic (i.e. one supported by observation) annual catch of 50,000 tonnes, as noted, is applied here. From 2010 through 1 October 2015, therefore, a present value of $27 million results.[30]

Payments by the European Commission under the 2006–07 FPA can next be calculated. Such payments were nominally €36.1 million annually for the first four years of the treaty starting in 2007 with an additional €30 million during the extension of its protocol until December 2011 and then, under a second four-year protocol agreed in 2013, €30 million annually.[31] (European flag vessels returned to Saharan waters in September 2014.) Morocco did not actually seek

---

27  Such occasional and local fisheries are discounted because of the entire lack of credible data about catches and market earnings from them. A crude estimate is that they may be worth $10 million annually. The author's personal observation (and from discussions with expatriate Saharawi fishers from Dakhla) is that there is little third state or otherwise IUU (illegal, unregulated, unreported) fishing in Saharan coastal waters (i.e. a presumptive exclusive economic zone). In July 2015 the SADR government protested to the government of the Faroe Islands about the presence of a vessel suspected of IUU fishing west of Cape Blanc. (Unpublished letter dated July 7, 2015, copy on file with the author.)

28  A conservative approach to calculating the present value of the 1.1 billion ECU is used: an exchange rate figure of $800 million; a benchmark date of December 31, 1999 for the 2015 present value; and inflation compounded at 2.00% per annum. If accurately known, historic inflation in Morocco could be the better determinant of present value, but it is not used in the present analysis.

29  The best figure for comparative purposes is present value; the current value of annual revenues remaining after capital, operation and maintenance costs. Under its 2010 three-year agreement with Morocco, Russia was obligated to pay 17.5% of $255/tonne for most species, with an allowable catch of up to 120,000 tonnes in the first year (and a further 80,000 tonnes shared jointly with Morocco). Russia is now required to annually pay $5 million and 17.5% of the caught value of fish (at $497 per tonne for frozen fish) for up to 10 vessels and a maximum of 100,000 tonnes under its 2013 treaty. Payments under the first three-year 2006 agreement are disregarded in the present analysis because of a lack of accurate catch data. A copy of the 2013 agreement can be found at WSRW's website, http://www.wsrw.org (accessed January 15, 2015).

30  The size (capacity) and fishing patterns of Russian flag vessels in Saharan waters suggests a higher value catch. The trawler *Oleg Naydenov* was one such vessel observed by Saharawi authorities after 2010, which had a capacity of 3372 tonnes. In April 2015 the vessel caught fire in Las Palmas and, after being towed out to sea, sank south of Gran Canaria where it began to release fuel oil. Saharawi authorities monitor fishing using several methods, including at-sea observation, vessel port visit reconciliations, satellite tracking and publicly available records such as catch landing by EU member state fishing vessels. (Personal conversations with SADR officials 2014–15.)

31  The second protocol, 'Protocol between the European Union and the Kingdom of Morocco setting out the fishing opportunities and financial contribution provided for in the Fisheries Partnership Agreement between the European Union and the Kingdom of Morocco', OJ L328/2 (July 12, 2013), was concluded in 2013 and entered into force in 2014. The second protocol and the Fisheries Partnership Agreement are stated to form an integral part of the 1996 EU–Morocco Association Agreement; Article 1 of the second protocol. Article 2 provides that €16 million is payment for the annual catch by EU permitted vessels and €14 million is 'support for the fisheries sector in Morocco'.

payment of a sector resource development component of the €36.1 million first protocol overall annual rent in at least one of its five years. Therefore, the present value (as at 1 October 2015) of annual FPA payments is €190 million, or $240 million. Finally, no value is assigned to the catch payments made by commercial vessels operating locally from Dakhla. This reduces the present value of the overall catch, of course, as such vessels work in relatively rich waters and are capable of week-long voyages to obtain 400 tonnes of fish. Accordingly, a *conservative* present value of the Saharan fishery under 40 years of occupation is $1.34 billion.

The *indirect* economic result of the Saharan fishery during this period has been considerable, although in the absence of accurate data, no attempt is made here to calculate it. But some discussion is useful. The commercial fishery is largely based at Dakhla. The port experiences continual activity associated with vessel provisioning and repair, and catch processing. Employment in primary fisheries and secondary support services in Dakhla may account for more than 10,000 persons. Assigning a *present* annual value of $60 million for direct rent of the Saharan fishery under treaties with other states and the EU, as well as local vessel fees, and a further $60 million from resulting economic activity yields a current total annual return of $120 million.

Calculating the value of extracted phosphate is straightforward, although there is little credible information about the cost of operating the Bu Craa enterprise.[32] Even during the long period from 1975 through 2006 when the market price of phosphate remained stable at $30 per tonne and production averaged 1.1 million tonnes, Phosboucraa may conceivably have been profitable, although that seems unlikely if the capital cost of the infrastructure (including the long conveyor belt and loading dock facilities) is accounted for. In recent years, the relative values of the fishery and phosphate have become reversed, starting with an unexpected price spike for phosphate in 2008. During 2011 the market price for phosphate again increased before stabilizing at $200/tonne, a figure it would hold through 2012 before declining through 2013 and leveling at about $110 per tonne through 2015.[33] The value of phosphate exports in recent years has been as much as six times that of the fishery and much greater than agricultural production, and sand and salt exports.

From an annual 1.1 million tonnes average in each of 31 complete years from 1976 through 2006 at $30 per tonne, there results a net present value of $1.81 billion as at 1 October 2015.[34] figures from 2007 through to 1 October 2015 can be adjusted for value of the latter date, $2.46 billion, and added to the to-2006 present value total, for an overall total of $4.27 billion.[35]

---

32  See *OCP-Bou Craa Production 1975–2006* (unpublished, copy on file with the author). In 1975 production was 2.7 million tonnes. In 1980, 1981 and 1982, there was no production. Annual production did not exceed 1 million tonnes until 1989. It would not return to the 1975 level until 2006. Less than 1 million tonnes per year was produced at Bu Craa during much of the 1980s, exceeding 2 million tonnes only after 1998. In 2011, exports reached a high of 2.78 million tonnes: OCP 2014 *Prospectus*, 95. In 2012, 2013 and 2014, production and exported annually averaged 2.1–2.2 million tonnes. In late 2014 and early 2015 exports were delayed because of reported structural problems at the el Aauin phosphate loading dock.

33  See 'OCP SA Note d'Information: Emission d'un Emprunt Obligatoire', http://www.ocpgroup.ma (accessed January 5, 2015), which details two bond offerings of 2 billion Dirhams each, opened for subscription September 22, 2011, with interest at 4.46\% on a seven-year term. Bo Craa is discussed at pages 104, 126 and 149–50. No data is given in the 2011 prospectus about the volume of reserves or production at the site.

34  Present value is calculated here on the basis of annual production of 1.1. million tonnes (1976–2006, inclusive), $30/tonne (idem), and average annual inflation rate of 2.50% from 1976 until 1986, and 2.00% thereafter, compounded annually, not in advance, and known production, export and market value figures for the years 2007–15 (until October 1, 2015), inclusive. Again, the better rate of inflation may be local figures, that in Morocco perhaps averaging 5% in these years. See also figures available from the US Geological Survey at its website, http://minerals.usgs.gov/minerals (accessed December 1, 2014).

35  This figure does not include phosphate rock exports in 2015, the known value of which, until July 15, 2015, was $80 million from 700,000 tonnes shipped. It is expected that 1.4 to 1.8 million tonnes will be exported in the year, with a total value of $160 to $200 million. (Conversations of the author with SADR officials and WSRW managers, July 2015.)

Table 1.  Value of natural resources exported from Western Sahara, 1976–2015

| Resource | Present value at 1 October 2015 |
| --- | --- |
| Fishery | $1.34 billion |
| Phosphate rock | $4.27 billion |
| Petroleum | $0 (single well production December 2014–March 2015) |
| Other | $40 million(estimated: sand and salt, excluding agricultural products) |
| Total | $5.65 billion |

2250 persons are reported employed in the Bu Craa enterprise, 10% of OCP SA's overall work-force.[36]

These figures can be compared to the sums Morocco claims to have spent in developing the territory. In 2011 and 2015 the figures were made public. The former was a total of $900 million (€600 million) said to have been spent from 2004 through 2009, and 20 billion Dirhams ($2.5 billion at 2011 exchange rates) since 1975.[37] These amounts, ostensibly spent until 2015, were made available by the Kingdom of Morocco through its embassy in Australia in March 2015. They also appear to include the 2011 figures, above. The document notes that:

> Concretely, an important budget has been developed, since 1976, to the development of the region. *This effort that surpasses, by far, the income generated by the exploitation of natural resources,* comes as follows:

> -For the period 2001/2005, an average annual amount of 9.5 billion Dirhams was devoted to the Southern Provinces (Western Sahara) (1 AUD = 8 MAD)
> -Since the creation of the Agency for the Development of the Southern Provinces, the state spent more than 7.7 billion Dirhams for the period of 2006–2009.[38]

The declared investment (i.e. its present value for comparative purposes), whether as stated in 2011 or in 2015, is about 90% of the present value of the two principal resources taken from Western Sahara during the years of occupation. (It should be recalled that, until 2009, less than half the $4.27 billion present value of phosphate rock had by then been realized.) Generally after 2000 and until 2009, therefore, Morocco's stated civil expenditures exceeded the gross market value of the territory's principal resources. Making good an annexation project, however, is a continuing task. What counts is the revenue from resources from year to year, and an overall calculation or estimate of all that has gone before is useful only to illustrate the relative cost of the occupation, something discussed below, and to assess an idealized eventual

---

36   OCP 2014 *Prospectus*, 110. Some 400 Saharawi persons are said to be employed in this workforce, a figure the author arrived at after interviews with persons living in the occupied part of Western Sahara and SADR government officials from October 2012 until February 2015. In an undated document titled 'Allegations regarding exploitation of natural resources' made available in March 2015 by Morocco's embassy in Australia, Morocco notes 'the basis of [OCP's] exploitation is motivated, above all, by social considerations imposed by the necessity to preserve the jobs of the Western Sahara workers who support more than 700 families' (unpublished, copy on file with the author).

37   See e.g. submissions made in October 2011 to the UN General Assembly Special Political and Decolonization Committee at New York, http://www.un.org/en/ga/fourth (accessed February 1, 2015). Morocco did not provide data to support its figures. It is not clear if the figures include costs to construct and maintain public infrastructure in the territory.

38   'Allegations regarding exploitation of natural resources', a document issued by the Embassy of the Kingdom of Morocco in March 2015 (undated) (unpublished, copy on file with the author). (Emphasis in original.) The document notes the expenditures were directed to 'urbanisation', 'basic infrastructure' (964 km of roads, three airports, three sea ports) and 'drinking water supply'.

reparations claim.[39] It is the entire result of exploiting Western Sahara's natural resources that must be considered. How international law applies, to which we turn next, is vital to understanding how Western Sahara's natural resources are allowed to be taken.

## III.  Western Sahara's resources and the law

The international law which applies to the development and export of Western Sahara's natural resources is now mature. It has evolved in the modern era, including by cases in the International Court of Justice, the International Criminal Court and international criminal tribunals.[40] What makes the law remarkable when it comes to Western Sahara is how widely and continually it has been disregarded. The problem is enforceability. The measures available in law are for states to act on, and not the Saharawi people or an incompletely recognized Saharawi Republic. Two bodies of international law prohibit the taking of Saharawi resources. The first is the permanent sovereignty of non-self-governing peoples over their natural resources.[41] The second is international humanitarian law, and it is the more restrictive, prohibiting commercial exploitation of Western Sahara's resources except to meet the immediate needs of the original Saharawi population.[42]

During the 40 years of Western Sahara's occupation, there has been little declared interest in applying international humanitarian law in the territory, and less so in protecting the civil population by safeguarding public and private property including natural resources. The UN and the organized international community have been unwilling to declare that this body of law, IHL, applies. To insist on its application would be to acknowledge that the territory is occupied as defined in the Geneva and Hague Conventions and related customary international law, thereby raising the question of whether international criminal law applies. A declaration confirm-

---

39  The SADR government has presented a reparations claim to a phosphate purchasing company, Potash Corporation, stating: ' Our purpose in writing is to deliver to Potash Corporation notice of a pending or eventual claim for compensation resulting from your company's purchase of phosphate mineral rock from occupied Western Sahara ... The historical record and precedent bear out a claim for reparations, recalling the examples of the United Nations (Iraq–Kuwait) Compensation Commission and the mechanisms in the 1998 *Rome Statute* of the International Criminal Court ... We calculate the claim conservatively to be at least $400 million (in 2014 dollars).' SADR Petroleum and Mines Authority letter of January 10, 2014 (unpublished, copy on file with the author).

40   The leading ICJ decision on the right of non-self-governing peoples to self-determination is the *Kosovo Advisory Opinion* (*Accordance with International Law of the Unilateral Declaration of Independence in Respect of Kosovo*, Advisory Opinion), ICJ Reports 2010, 403. 'During the second half of the twentieth century, the international law of self-determination developed in such a way as to create a right to independence for the peoples of non-self-governing territories and peoples subject to alien subjugation, domination and exploitation.' Ibid., at para. 79 (citations omitted). The ICJ has not pronounced on the legality of resource development in non-self-governing territories or those considered occupied within international humanitarian law.

It is the right of permanent sovereignty to resources, coupled with the right to self-determination, that requires Morocco as an administering state in Western Sahara to ensure the consent of the original inhabitants of the territory is obtained to resource development, and that the benefits of such development accrue to them. This was the basis for the governance of Namibia's resources under occupation, by decree of the UN Council for Namibia, created in the 1960s and discussed below.

The leading international criminal law decisions for the taking of public resources under occupation remain those of the International Military Tribunal after the Second World War, for which see the discussion in James G. Stewart, *Corporate War Crimes: Prosecuting the Pillage of Natural Resources* (New York: Open Society Initiative, 2010).

41  This body of law traces back to the UN's decolonization mission with the UN General Assembly issuing its 1962 declaration, *Permanent Sovereignty over Natural Resources*, GA Res 1803 (XVII) (December 14, 1962), discussed below. Arguably, because Spain could not assign or transfer responsibility for self-determination of the Saharawi people to other states, Spain remains responsible for resource development in Western Sahara, that is, ensuring the consent of and benefit to the Saharawi people from such activity.

42   International humanitarian law and international criminal law is discussed below. As noted above, Spain's courts have accepted the application of international criminal law in recent months. Pillage may result in the setting of an international or a non-international armed conflict, from the taking of public and private resources. The Fourth Geneva Convention, 1949 and the Rome Statute 1998 of the International Criminal Court, discussed below, govern. Because of the stricter obligation to protect an occupied population, Morocco is arguably first bound to comply with international humanitarian and criminal law in its administration of Western Sahara.

ing the occupation was made early on by the General Assembly, but it has not been acted on.[43] Recognizing the annexation of Western Sahara as a continuing occupation would make inescapable the obligation on states to deny support to Morocco in its project. That is something the organized international community has not been prepared to accept. As with East Timor (Timor-Leste) until 1999, the occupation of Western Sahara remains disregarded under this branch of international law. Even as IHL rapidly developed in the first decade of the new millennium, including a creation of the International Criminal Court with a war crimes jurisdiction that includes pillage, there has been no interest in applying its criminal law adjunct to Western Sahara. That changed in the second half of 2014, and there are now two criminal appeals decisions in Spain which have directed investigations to proceed against alleged serious crimes in the occupation of Western Sahara on the basis of international criminal law.[44]

The reluctance of the organized international community to contemplate the application of international law in general to Western Sahara and within that its resources is the result of several factors. To begin with, few states have any interest in the legal protection of the territory's natural resources. This position is understandable when it is recalled that they defer to the United Nations in its oversight role for self-determination. The problem in having states recognize and apply international legal obligations is something that comes from treating the 'question' of Western Sahara exclusively as an incomplete self-determination project. In any event, and apart from Palestine's particular status, the case of Western Sahara is one now largely singular, almost unique. The treatment of Western Sahara therefore remains one of self-determination (that is, of completing decolonization) and not the reality of territorial acquisition through *re-colonization*. Considered this way, and consistent with the history of colonizing nations having particular and apparently non-transferable obligations to complete self-determination for peoples who were once a part of their imperiums, the UN's decolonization project arguably no longer has much useful application. Portugal, it seems, was the last colonizing state to realize its obligations, acting in 1999 to assure for the Timorese people their right to self-determination. (France in New Caledonia must be noted as a contemporary example.) When it is recalled that the Saharawi people have been consistent in expressing their desire for independence should self-determination eventuate (as well as their relatively uncontroversial declaration of independence in 1976), the UN decolonization project is revealed as fading in importance. A better approach might now be to categorize cases as either secessionary (including those of state dissolution) or the occupation of non-self-governing territories by (usually) neighboring states.

Another factor that has restricted the application of international law to Western Sahara (across several subjects, notably that of human rights) is found in the locus of international responsibility for the Saharawi people and their territory. Spain renounced its continuing colonial ('administering power') role despite half-hearted later statements that it did not intend to abandon the territory under the Madrid Accords.[45] Without Spain the Saharawi people have no colonial interlocutor to pursue diplomatic or legal redress for self-determination. But that does not

---

43  Resolution 34/37 'deeply [deplored] the aggravation of the situation resulting from the continued occupation of Western Sahara by Morocco and the extension of that occupation to the territory recently occupied [until August 1979] by Mauritania'. *Question of Western Sahara*, GA Res 34/37 (November 21, 1979).

44  The first was a decision of the *Audiencia Nacional* directing an investigating magistrate to proceed on a criminal complaint about the death of a dual Saharawi/Spanish citizen at Gdeim Izek in November 2010. The court concluded that international criminal law applied in the territory as a result of Spain's adoption of such law into its national legal system. The same court concluded the following April that an investigation for genocide could proceed against 11 Moroccan citizens in the early years of Western Sahara's occupation. See the Decisions of the *Audiencia Nacional*, Auto no. 40/2014 (July 4, 2014), and Sumario 1/2015 (April 9, 2015). The latter decision effectively set aside Spain's November 1975 statute that purported to abrogate the country's colonial responsibility for Western Sahara, Ley 40/ 1975. See Fernando J. Pérez, 'Ruz procesa 11 mandos militares marroquíes por genocidio en el Sáhara', *El País*, April 9, 2015.

45  Spain formally legislated an end to its responsibility. See *Ley* [Law] *40/1975, de 19 de noviembre, sobre descolonización del Sahara*. 'The Government is authorized to perform such acts and adopt measures as may be necessary for

mean the responsibility has become Morocco's. The obligation to ensure decolonization after 1991 has remained with the United Nations. By resolution and precedent, this responsibility in the UN system should fall first to the General Assembly, something that had its apogee in the case of Namibia.[46] The discussion of Western Sahara in the General Assembly and in a Security Council content to annually renew the mandate of the UN self-determination mission in the territory, MINURSO, has not been one in which annexation of territory or an occupation has featured.[47]

The two areas of law concerning natural resources, permanent sovereignty and IHL, are usefully returned to. The first prohibits states and individuals from taking the territory's natural resources without the consent of the Saharawi people and a benefit to them. The obligation to respect a people's sovereignty to resources originates from the United Nations Charter. Articles 73 and 74 of the Charter were intended to ensure the well-being of peoples of non-self-governing territories until they are no longer colonized. The duty for colonizing, administering and occupying states has several aspects. There must be consultation with the people of the colonized territory. They must give free consent, arrived at on an informed basis, to the exploitation of their natural resources. It is they who are to have the benefit of the exploitation. Settlers introduced by a colonizing state or an occupying power do not qualify.

> Members of the United Nations which have or assume responsibilities for the administration of territories whose peoples have not yet attained a full measure of self-government recognize the principle that the interests of the inhabitants of these territories are paramount, and accept as a sacred trust the obligation to promote to the utmost, within the system of international peace and security established by the present Charter, the well-being of the inhabitants of these territories.[48]

The obligation for consent has resulted from the two General Assembly Resolutions on which the UN self-determination process is founded, Resolutions 1514 (XV) and 1541 (XV) of 14 December 1960.[49] Resolution 1514 declares that 'peoples may, for their own ends, freely dispose of their natural wealth and resources … based on the principle of mutual benefit and international law' in order to realize the right to 'freely pursue their economic, social and cultural development'. In the five decades since, the two have uncontroversially entered into international law and are the core of Saharawi sovereignty over the resources of occupied Western Sahara.

In 1962 the General Assembly addressed permanent sovereignty over natural resources, declaring in Resolution 1803 that 'economic and financial agreements between the developed and the developing countries must be based on the principles of equality and of the right of peoples and nations to self-determination'.[50] That sovereignty to natural resources is vested in the

---

the decolonization of the non-autonomous territory of the Sahara, safeguarding Spanish interests.' (Translation by the author.)

46   The UN General Assembly-created Council for Namibia had legislative and executive jurisdiction for the territory after the termination of South Africa's mandate, exercising it including by legal action in the protection of natural resources. See *The Question of Namibia*, GA Res 2248 (S-V) (May 19, 1967). In November 2011, the Frente Polisario first called for UN oversight and possibly a form of trusteeship of natural resources in Western Sahara.

47   UN Security Council Resolution S/2218 (April 28, 2015) is the most recent annual extension of MINURSO's mandate. The UN assumed the obligation to ensure Saharawi self-determination in its referendum agreement with Morocco and the Frente Polisario which took effect in September 1991. The agreement is detailed in two reports of the UN Secretary-General, S/21360 (June 18, 1990) and S/22464 (April 19, 1991). 'The two parties, namely the Kingdom of Morocco and the Frente POLISARIO, recognize in the settlement proposals that the sole and exclusive responsibility for the organization and conduct of the referendum is vested in the United Nations.' S/22464, para. 9.

48   Article 73, *Charter of the United Nations* (June 26, 1945) 1 UNTS 16 (in force October 24, 1945). The UN Secretary-General noted the application of Article 73 in his annual report to the UN Security Council of April 10, 2015, above.

49   *Declaration of the Granting of Independence to Colonial countries and Peoples*, GA Res 1514 (XV) (December 14, 1960) and *Principles which should Guide Members in Determining whether or not an Obligation Exists to Transmit the Information called for under Article 73e of the Charter*, GA Res 1541 (XV) (December 14, 1960). See also *Permanent Sovereignty over Natural Resources*, GA Res 1803 (XVII) (December 14, 1962).

50   Ibid., *Sovereignty over Natural Resources* resolution.

people of a non-self-governing territory – and not an occupying or administering state – is clear by the resolution: 'The right of peoples and nations to permanent sovereignty over their wealth and natural resources must be exercised in the interest of their natural development and of the well-being of the people of the State concerned.' The General Assembly has observed that a '[v]iolation of the rights of peoples and nations to sovereignty over their natural wealth and resources is contrary to the spirit and principles of the Charter of the United Nations'.[51]

The Saharawi people's sovereignty over natural resources could theoretically be enforced by any state. That is because there exists a universal (*erga omnes*) requirement on all states to uphold the law in this respect.[52] The organized international community accepts the protection of non-self-governing peoples' sovereignty to natural resources, as the work of the UN Council for Namibia, and the Nauru and Palestine Wall decisions of the International Court of Justice have shown.[53] Although by 1990 there were only a few remaining self-determination cases, the obligation of administering-occupying states to safeguard the resources of such territories had become a peremptory norm of international law. The most recent UN General Assembly Resolution on the subject emphasizes

> the right of the peoples of the Non-Self-Governing Territories to self-determination in conformity with the Charter of the United Nations and with General Assembly resolution 1514(XV) ... as well as their right to the enjoyment of their natural resources and their right to dispose of those resources in their best interest.[54]

The development of this area of the law was discussed by Judge Christopher Weeramantry in his dissent to the ICJ's 1995 *East Timor (Portugal/Australia)* decision. He concluded that the 1989 Timor Gap Treaty was illegal, noting the obligation *erga omnes* on states to oppose the operation of the treaty:

> At such time as the East Timorese people exercise their right to self-determination, they would become entitled as a component of their sovereign right, to determine how their wealth and natural resources should be disposed of. Any action prior to that date which may in effect deprive them of this right must thus fall clearly within the category of acts which infringe on their right to self-determination, and their future sovereignty, if indeed full and independent sovereignty be their choice. This right is described by the General Assembly, in its resolution [1803] ...
>
> The exploration, development and disposition of the resources of the Timor Gap, for which the Timor Gap Treaty provides a detailed specification, has most certainly not been worked out in accordance with the principle that the people of East Timor should 'freely consider' these matters, in regard to their 'authorization, restriction or prohibition'.

---

51  Ibid., Articles 1 and 7, respectively.

52  *Legal Consequences of the Construction of a Wall in the Occupied Palestinian Territory,* Advisory Opinion, 2004 ICJ Reports 136 [*Palestine Wall,* Advisory Opinion]. Paragraph 159 of the Opinion is worth recalling: 'Given the character and the importance of the rights and obligations involved, the Court is of the view that all States are under an obligation not to recognize the illegal situation resulting from the construction of the wall in the Occupied Palestinian Territory, including in and around East Jerusalem. They are also under an obligation not to render aid or assistance in maintaining the situation created by such construction. It is also for all States, while respecting the United Nations Charter and international law, to see to it that any impediment, resulting from the construction of the wall, to the exercise by the Palestinian people of its right to self-determination is brought to an end. In addition, all the States parties to the Geneva Convention relative to the Protection of Civilian Persons in Time of War of 12 August 1949 are under an obligation, while respecting the United Nations Charter and international law, to ensure compliance by Israel with international humanitarian law as embodied in that Convention.' The Court noted that the taking of resources for construction of the wall was to be remedied, including payment of compensation. Ibid., para. 153.

53  Respectively, *Case concerning Phosphate Lands in Nauru (Nauru v Australia)*, Preliminary Objection, 1992 ICJ Reports 240, *East Timor (Portugal v Australia)*, 1995 ICJ Reports 139 [*East Timor*], and *Palestine Wall*, Advisory Opinion, ibid.

54  *Economic and Other Activities which Affect the Interests of the Peoples of Non-Self-Governing Territories*, GA Res 69/98 (December 16, 2014), paragraph 1.

The Timor Gap Treaty, to the extent that it deals with East Timorese resources prior to the achievement of self-determination by the East Timorese people, is thus in clear violation of this principle.[55]

In 2002, the law of non-self-governing peoples' sovereignty to natural resources was considered by Hans Corell, then the UN Under-Secretary-General for Legal Affairs. The Security Council had requested his opinion on the legality of seabed petroleum exploration on the coast of Western Sahara. Corell was not asked to consider the territory's fishery and phosphate resources.

> The conclusion is, therefore, that, while the specific [petroleum exploration] contracts which are the subject of the Security Council's request are not in themselves illegal, if further exploration and exploitation activities were to proceed in disregard of the interests and wishes of the people of Western Sahara, they would be in violation of the international law principles applicable to mineral resource activities in Non-Self-Governing Territories.[56]

There is an additional source of international law to be recalled when it comes to the Saharan fishery. All EU states, the EU itself and Russia are signatories to the UN Convention on the Law of the Sea; Morocco acceded in 2007.[57] UNCLOS states have an obligation to comply with Resolution III of the Final Act of the Law of the Sea Conference to ensure that for a 'people [who] have not attained full independence ... or a territory under colonial domination, provisions concerning rights and interests under the Convention [are] implemented for the benefit of the people of the territory with a view to promoting their well-being and development'.[58] The phrasing is consistent with General Assembly Resolution 1803. Resolution III has been overlooked in the case of Western Sahara.

The UN and the organized international community could be motivated to apply international law to Western Sahara if the principles of territorial integrity were recalled.[59] It is, after all, in the interest of the international community to promote the norm, as the response to Iraq's attempt to annex Kuwait in 1990 and by Western states to the incorporation of Crimea into Russia in 2014 have demonstrated. Dealing with the territorial integrity of Western Sahara would mean having to accept that international humanitarian law applies. Even if the facts on the ground are compelling – and they include the international nature of the conflict, the parties' 1991 ceasefire referendum arrangement, the presence of a substantial occupying force, the building of the berm and, not least, Morocco's admission that Western Sahara remains 'technically, a war zone' – what has been a deference to the UN to ensure self-determination displaces the suggestion that international humanitarian law can apply, even given the stark circumstances of a separated and refugee Saharawi people.[60]

When it comes to IHL, although 1991 brought an end to active hostilities between the Frente Polisario and Morocco, the occupation of Western Sahara continues. As such, there continues the

---

55 Dissenting Opinion in *East Timor*, 198.

56 'Report of the UN Office of Legal Affairs on the Legality of the Oil-Contracts Signed by Morocco over the Natural Resources of the Western Sahara' (letter dated January 29, 2002), UN doc. S/2002/161 (February 12, 2002), http://www.arso.org/UNlegaladv.htm (accessed December 1, 2014).

57 United Nations *Convention on the Law of the Sea*, 1982, December 10, 1982, 21 ILM 1261 (in force November 16, 1994) [UNCLOS].

58 UNCLOS Resolution III, para. 1. There has been virtually no mention of Resolution III in the context of the 'question' of Western Sahara by any state, the UN, or any commentator.

59 Territorial integrity finds its starting place in the UN Charter, at Article 2. The basis to assert the territorial integrity of Western Sahara has several dimensions, including the necessity of such a circumstances in order to ensure the exercise of the Saharawi people's right to self-determination, the commitments of the parties in the 1990–91 ceasefire and referendum arrangements, the principle of *uti possiditis* in the maintenance of the inviolability of Western Sahara's territory and, notably, the conclusion of the ICJ that Morocco has not basis in law for a territorial claim to the Sahara. The UN General Assembly's declaration of Western Sahara to be occupied and the African Union's position on the nature of Morocco's presence in the territory, discussed above, are a part of this imperative.

60 US diplomatic cable, 'Seven Saharawi activists charged with intelligence cooperation with a foreigner' (US embassy Rabat) (October 16, 2009), http://www.wikileaks.ch (accessed December 1, 2014).

obligation to protect the territory's original population. The Fourth Geneva Convention prohibits pillage after cessation of hostilities for the entire period a state or territory is occupied:

> In the case of occupied territory ... the Occupying Power shall be bound, for the duration of the occupation, to the extent that such Power exercises the functions of government in such territory, by the provisions of [the articles against pillage and introducing settlers into occupied lands, among other provisions] of the present Convention.[61]

No state recognizes Morocco's claim to Western Sahara. As with Namibia, East Timor and Palestine, Morocco's annexation of the territory continues to be universally rejected.[62] That is a useful start to making out the norm of territorial integrity as it applies to Western Sahara and accepting the legal circumstances of the existence of an occupation. The discussion recalls the ICJ's task 'to assist the General Assembly to determine its future decolonization policy and in particular to pronounce on the claims of Morocco and Mauritania to have had legal ties with Western Sahara involving the territorial integrity of their respective countries' by its 1975 *Western Sahara* advisory opinion.[63] The court concluded:

> [T]he materials and information presented to it do not establish any tie of territorial sovereignty between the territory of Western Sahara and the Kingdom of Morocco or the Mauritanian entity. Thus the Court has not found legal ties of such a nature as might affect the application of resolution 1514 (XV) in the decolonization of Western Sahara and, in particular, of the principle of self-determination through the free and genuine expression of the will of the peoples of the Territory.[64]

If the rules of international law are clear enough in the case of Western Sahara's natural resources, we are left with the question of why they have not been applied. The answer should not be complicated, but it has become so. It includes the lack of any single state interested in upholding international law coupled with a leaving of the matter to a United Nations unwilling to act outside of a self-determination referendum approach. The consequence for international law is just as much the inability of any state or the Saharawi people being able to apply it to their circumstances as it is the creation of another precedent for the violation of territorial integrity, denial of self-determination and pillage of occupied lands. The taking of Saharawi resources damages the law in more ways than one. The organized international community has been slow to appreciate that.

## IV. Pillage made good

If the value of Western Sahara's natural resources can be approximated, the consequences of their taking have not been wholly understood. The exploitation of resources is only a part of Morocco's efforts to annex the territory. The historical record strongly suggests that Western Sahara would have been invaded by Mauritania and Morocco whatever resource potential the territory had.[65] However, as we have seen, the two states were quick to divide resources between them, although Mauritania does not seem to have benefited from the fishery. And several years were needed for Morocco to reestablish production at Bu Craa. Resource exploitation certainly acquired greater

---

61  *Fourth Geneva Convention*, Article 6.
62  Consider the statements of United States, Norway and Switzerland that their free trade agreements with Morocco do not apply to Western Sahara.
63  *Western Sahara*, Advisory Opinion, para. 161
64  Ibid., para. 162.A useful fact in applying international humanitarian law is Mauritania's admission of its wrongful occupation of Western Sahara, made in its 1979 treaty with the Frente Polisario. If a court has yet to pronounce definitively on the legal situation resulting from Morocco's occupation, the statement of an occupier asserting a similar historic claim as Morocco (and which agreed with Morocco to partition the territory in 1976) is compelling.
65  The best historical record is that presented in voluminous records to the ICJ by Spain, Mauritania and Morocco in the 1975 advisory opinion proceedings. Mauritania could never hope to share in the phosphate reserves at Bu Craa. The most in-depth discussion of the 'siren call' of resources and the idea sometimes suggested that Morocco hoped to acquire a monopoly of global phosphate production by its annexation is that of Tony Hodges, *Western Sahara: The Roots of a Desert War* (Westport, CT: Lawrence Hill, 1983).

importance because an economy was needed for settlers after 1975 (who entered in increased numbers after the 1991 ceasefire). While revenue from the trade in resources is important, the real benefit to Morocco has been to create the appearance of a viable annexation. Work available for settlers in the resource sector serves as the basis for a labor market, with employment for Moroccan nationals justifying the success of settlement. The purported return of resource revenues back into the local economy as something that benefits the 'local' population – now a majority of Moroccan citizens – helps satisfy international concerns that resource revenues are being properly applied in the territory.

The consequences of taking natural resources from occupied Western Sahara can be categorized as: (i) Morocco's unrealized financial enrichment; (ii) a present and perhaps future denial of natural resources to the Saharawi people; (iii) the consolidation of Morocco's occupation including the settlement of its nationals in the territory (together with the related problem of the delay of a self-determination referendum); and (iv) the promotion of the appearance of legitimacy for the occupation through the 'credibility mechanism' of trade in resources. An additional problem beyond these four, and noted above, is the diminished application and availability to the Saharawi people of international law along with a further incident of state practice which erodes the two basic norms of international law: territorial sovereignty and the protection of peoples under occupation. These consequences are not isolated from each other, being connected in their causes and having a common point of a delayed self-determination.

The consequences are now considered in turn. Over four decades the annexation of Western Sahara has resulted in a financial loss to Morocco. Its hold on the territory is one secured by large expenditures. Just as it is difficult to determine the extent to which the benefits of Western Sahara's resources have been applied in the territory, so it is equally difficult to gauge the cost of an occupation that allows for the taking of resources. It may be reasonable to conclude that recent revenues from resources – annually averaging $300 to $400 million from 2010 through 2014 – if directed back into the occupied territory, would substantially provide for the civil economy, meeting at least the basic cost of sustaining settler and Saharawi populations within existing Moroccan state expenditures (including taxation benefits and commodities subsidies) but not the cost of the military presence in the territory.[66]

The ongoing result for the Saharawi people from the taking of their resources is not something that is easily quantified. The Saharawi have a subordinate (or marginalized) role in the economy of Western Sahara. However, it is not accurate to say that the Saharawi population inside the occupied territory is deprived of all benefits from development of natural resources. Small numbers of Saharawi are employed by Phosboucraa, in the fishery and in related services. Labor figures are not reliable; however, the number of Saharawi employed in the formal sector appears to be between 25,000 and 40,000, less than a majority of the adult population in the occupied territory.[67] But few of these are involved directly or secondarily in resource industries, no more than several thousand. What is known is that preferred employment, housing and amenities overwhelmingly favor Moroccan settlers.[68]

---

66  There are few available figures about the cost of Morocco's military presence in Western Sahara. The CIA's 2014 *World Factbook* notes that the Kingdom's annual military spending in 2012 was 3.55% of a $105 billion GDP (2013 estimated), https://www.cia.gov/library/publications/the-world-factbook/geos/mo.html (accessed March 1, 2015). Morocco's reported state (government) budget for 2013 was estimated at $34.5 billion. (Transparency International states GDP in 2010 at $90.8 billion.) On the basis that one-third of Morocco's armed forces and military support infrastructure, including as many as 100,000 FAR members, is located in Western Sahara, the annual *military cost* of the occupation is approximately $1.2 billion.

67   Personal interviews, Saharawi government officials at the Boujdour and Rabouni refugee camps, October 2010 and December 2012.

68  In late 2010 the Saharawi protest camp at Gdeim Izek near el Aauin and others in the occupied territory were expressions of Saharawi discontent over marginalized economic circumstances. See Association Sahraouie des Victimes des Violations Graves des Droits de l'Homme Commises par l'Etat du Maroc, *Rapport de l'ASVDH sur le campement de Gdeim Izik et les événements qui ont suivi son démantèlement* (Tindouf, Algeria: January 2011).

That half the Saharawi population – those who live in the camps at Tindouf – is denied any benefit of their natural resources is a significant problem, a matter also overlooked during the early conflict. In recent years, the annual direct and indirect donor support including food aid and essential commodities to this population of perhaps 140,000 has been between €40 and 60 million.[69] The amount is small in comparison to the revenue in the same period from phosphate and the fishery. As far as the occupied territory is concerned, there is no reason why resource revenues could not be allocated to both Saharawi and Moroccans, including indirectly through employment schemes. However, Morocco has not been prepared to acknowledge any right of the Saharawi people to their resources and, in any event, the large settler population in the occupied territory, outnumbering the Saharawi population by at least two to one, depends on continued financial support from Rabat.[70]

The long-term value of Western Sahara's natural resources and so their potential loss to the Saharawi people in the future turns on three factors. The first is the uncertainty of the remaining time until the Saharawi people achieve self-determination. Changes in market prices for the two leading resources is another. (East Timor's experience with increases and the late 2014/15 decline in petroleum prices after independence is recalled.) A third factor is petroleum development in a time of unstable world prices for the commodity, which has now tentatively started in the territory.

An optimistic prediction might be made that fish stocks will continue undiminished. A 2011–12 fisheries research program, the Northwest Africa Ecosystem Survey (a joint undertaking of the UN Food and Agriculture Organization and Norway's Institute of Marine Research), will provide data about long-term sustainability in the area including the Saharan fishery.[71] The history of fishing in Saharan waters since 1975 should be recalled, for there have frequently been too many vessels involved. The allowance for more than 100 European vessels under the Fisheries Partnership Agreement has continued the tradition. Concerns persist that some stocks are overexploited.[72]

The extent of phosphate reserves at Bu Craa is uncertain, with present estimates ranging from a low of 100 million tonnes to 1.3 billion tonnes.[73] The latter figure seems too high and may come from outdated survey data. In its 2014 debt financing prospectus issued through the Irish Stock Exchange, OCP claims present reserves at Bu Craa (known also as Oued Eddahab) to be 500 million tonnes.[74] Phosphate extraction will continue to be limited by the capacities of the conveyor belt to el Aauin and facilities at the coast.

Overall, an annual revenue of about $300 million can be forecast to come from Western Sahara's resources over the next few years, until petroleum and mineral resources come to be

---

69    See UN Office for the Coordination of Humanitarian Affairs (Financial Tracking Services), 'Aid to Saharawi Refugee Camps in 2013' (December 12, 2014), http://fts.unocha.org (accessed April 1, 2015). In 2013, a total of $24 million was given by various governments (e.g. Spain) and agencies (WFP, UNHCR, UNICEF) as aid into the Tindouf camps. The SADR government has few sources of revenue, but obtains modest operating funds of perhaps $10 million annually from AU member states. Algeria offers considerable in-kind and material support to the Tindouf camps, including electricity and, through the Algerian Red Crescent, cooking gas. In the author's visits to the camps, discussion with aid agency managers, and interviews of SADR officials, the figure of €40–60 million for 2014 is arrived at.

70    Petrol is taxed less in occupied Western Sahara than in Morocco and is supplied by chartered vessels to El Aauin and Dakhla. See Western Sahara Resource Watch, 'Fuelling the Occupation: The Swedish Transport of Oil to Occupied Western Sahara' (WSRW: Brussels, July 2014).

71    The work is part of the UN Food & Agriculture Organization's Canary Current Large Marine Ecosystem (CCLME) Project. See the UNFAO project website: http://www.canarycurrent.org (visited April 1, 2015).

72    See the 2010 report prepared by the consultancy Oceanic Développement, 'Framework Contract Fish/2006/20 Convention Specifique N°26: Evaluation ex-post du protocole actuel d'accord de partenariat dans la domaine de peche entre l'union europeenne et le royaume du maroc, etude d'impact d'un possible future protocole d'accord – Rapport – Décembre 2010', http://www.fishelsewhere.eu/files/dated/2012-03-05/evaluation-app-maroc-2010.pdf (accessed December 1, 2014).

73    WSRW, *P for Plunder*, 9. Toby Shelley put the 'known exploitable reserves' in 2004 at 132 million tonnes, Shelley, *Endgame in the Western Sahara*, 70.

74    OCP 2014 *Prospectus,* 79. The figure is stated as 1% of 50 billion tonnes under control by OCP SA, i.e. Morocco, from the January 2013 United States Geological Survey published 'Mineral Commodities Summaries'.

exploited in commercial quantities.[75] Of course, the future value of resources should account for how much will remain for the Saharawi people at independence. As with East Timor, the international community has an interest in preserving such resources, the better to make a viable economy for an independent Saharawi Republic after self-determination is resolved. Along the way, the question of Western Sahara's two primary resources should not detract from the preservation of other resources including groundwater, the territory's limited arable land, and environmental protection generally.[76]

Another consequence of the development and export of resources from Western Sahara has been what seems to be a useful domestic political and international gaining of support (or at least a tacit acceptance) of the annexation. In general, development and trade in the resources has created a useful internal legitimacy for the Moroccan monarchy, its armed forces and civil society. The 'national project' to acquire Western Sahara, in other words assuring the success of returning to the Kingdom its lost southern provinces, is made more acceptable by apparent financial gain and economic activity in the territory. Moreover, the presence of a standing army in Western Sahara has been partly justified by the necessity to protect resources. (That there was no phosphate production at Bu Craa for several years before the berm was built bears this out.) The taking of resources also offers a greater stake for Moroccan government agencies, state corporations and individuals in the continued occupation of the territory. Perhaps most importantly, resource development serves as a pretext for economic activity to support Morocco's settlers. This is especially true given the absence of industry and manufacturing in Western Sahara. In other words, the acceptance by Moroccan society of repossessing the Sahara has been more readily perpetuated because of apparent productive activity and financial return.

On the international stage, states have for the most part avoided commenting about the trade in Western Sahara's phosphate. Norway is a rare exception; in late 2011 its government directed the state pension fund to sell off interests in the FMC Corporation and Canada's Potash Corporation.[77] To their credit, Norway, Switzerland and the United States declared that their post-2000 free trade agreements with Morocco do not extend to products from Western Sahara. (However, Saharawi phosphate enters the United States free of import taxes.)

It is the fishery which most secures for Morocco international support for its exploitation of the territory's resources. The European Commission has been satisfied to have the benefit of the FPA be realized by the entire population of Western Sahara, side-stepping the question of Saharawi resource rights.[78] Although not as well known, the same has been true for the recent Russia–Morocco fisheries treaties. The absence of measures to ensure compliance with the law of sovereignty to natural resources has reinforced the willingness of states to tolerate Morocco's presence in Western Sahara. An example is the statement in an internal document from the

---

75 Metalex Resources Ltd. of Canada has conducted aerial surveys in a joint venture with Morocco's state oil and mineral development agency, ONHYM. See the company website at: http://www.metalexventures.com (accessed April 1, 2015) and the 2013 ONHYM annual report at page 32: http://www.onhym.com (accessed April 4, 2015). Exploration for petroleum on land continues, for which see again the ONHYM 2013 annual report. Hanno Resources of Australia has extensively surveyed the liberated zone and found extensive deposits of iron ore and other minerals, under technical cooperation agreements with the SADR government.

76 Groundwater resources and water use in urban areas of occupied Western Sahara is not well understood.

77 See the website of Norway's state pension fund, http://www.regjeringen.no/en/dep/fin/pressesenter/pressemeldinger/2011/statens-pensjonsfond-utland-nye-beslutni/ statens-pensjonsfond-utland-to-selskaper.html?id=665637 (accessed December 15, 2014). The Swedish state pension fund has also more recently divested itself of share ownership in Western Sahara resource-receiving companies.

78 See Smith, 'Fishing for Self-determination' and the observations of the EU Parliament Fisheries Rapporteur Carl Haglund, 'Report to the EU Parliament Fisheries Committee, 2011', http://www.europarl.europa.eu/sides/getDoc. do?type=REPORT&reference=A7-2011-0394&language=EN (accessed December 1, 2014).

Moroccan government published by a whistle-blower on 21 November 2014.[79] Titled 'La Fédération de Russie et la Question du Sahara Marocain', it explains that:

> To this objective, Morocco has to ... implicate Russia in activities in the Sahara, as is already the case in the field of fisheries. Oil exploration, phosphates, energy and touristic development are, among others, the sectors that could be involved in this respect ... In return, Russia could guarantee a freeze on the Sahara file within the UN, the time for the Kingdom to take strong action with irreversible facts with regard to the *marocanité* of the Sahara.[80]

For its part, the United Nations would do well to consider how the two areas of law described above can be used to help achieve Saharawi self-determination. Eliminate a substantial reason for the annexation of Western Sahara – the taking of its resources – and Morocco's capacity and justification to maintain its annexation should be diminished. The reasoning of the International Court of Justice in its *Palestine Wall* advisory opinion is relevant:

> The Court would observe that the obligations violated by Israel include certain obligations erga omnes. As the Court indicated in the Barcelona Traction case, such obligations are by their very nature 'the concern of all States' and, 'In view of the importance of the rights involved, all States can be held to have a legal interest in their protection' ... The obligations erga omnes violated by Israel are the obligation to respect the right of the Palestinian people to self-determination, and certain of its obligations under international humanitarian law. [ ... ]
>
> In addition, all the States parties to the Geneva Convention relative to the Protection of Civilian Persons in Time of War of 12 August 1949 are under an obligation, while respecting the United Nations Charter and international law, to ensure compliance by Israel with international humanitarian law as embodied in that Convention.[81]

It is unfortunate that the well-established rules of international law have been made marginal in the case of Western Sahara. If the law is considered properly, Morocco's annexation of Western Sahara will be again revealed as illegal. For the present, there continues a tacit acceptance of the occupation and so the approval of the taking of resources from the Saharawi people's territory.

## V.  Will the taking of the Sahara continue?

The organized international community meets the 'question' of Western Sahara most directly through trade in the territory's natural resources. The other aspects of Morocco's occupation and the stalled right of self-determination for the Saharawi people are not so much the concern of states, deferring as they have to the United Nations to ensure decolonization. None of the concern for a large Saharawi refugee population at Tindouf, the problem of human rights abuses inside occupied Western Sahara or the partition of the territory by the berm have sufficed to overcome a status quo that has prevailed since 1991. If international law in its various forms can be applied to the question of Western Sahara, it will be over natural resources, as the EU Parliament's rejection in 2011 of the Fisheries Partnership Agreement – if only partly out of concern for the Saharawi people – demonstrated.

A few predictions can be ventured. It is unlikely that the United Nations, whether the General Assembly or the Security Council, will act to apply international law to the taking of Western Sahara's natural resources. Enforcing obligations to ensure for the Saharawi people their right of sover-

---

79   Government of Morocco, 'La Fédération de Russie et la Question du Sahara Marocain' (undated), http://www.arso. org/Coleman/Note_Russie_Saharacorrige.pdf (accessed January 5, 2015). The Moroccan government has not contested the validity of much of the leaked documents. See e.g. TelQuel, 'Chris Coleman: le government dénonce finalement une campagne <enragée>' (December 12, 2014); *Le Monde*, 'L'étrange marocain' (January 4, 2015); *Le Monde*, 'Un hacker ne peut déstabiliser à lui tout seul la monarchie marocaine' (January 6, 2015).

80   The document was made available through a Twitter account: @chris_coleman24 on November 21, 2014. It is undated, but contains information suggesting it was created after 2010. The Twitter account has sometimes been taken offline. See e.g. TelQuel, 'Twitter a supprimé le compte de Chris Colement, sans s'expliquer' (December 17, 2014).

81   *Palestine Wall* Advisory Opinion, paras. 155 and 159 [citation omitted]. *Legal Consequences of the Construction of a Wall in the Occupied Palestinian Territory, Advisory Opinion, I. C. J. Reports 2004, p. 136*

eignty over natural resources, even where the UN has an interest in the future availability of those resources to an independent Saharawi Republic restored to its territory, would mean confronting Morocco. The UN's declared aim of resolving the question of Western Sahara on a 'just, lasting and mutually acceptable basis' suggests that it will not prefer the application of the law to the detriment of one of the parties, no matter how serious the violation. That proved to be the case in the aftermath of self-determination in Timor, and is arguably what prevails in Palestine.[82] And so it appears to be the same over the short term when it comes to the natural resources of Western Sahara. In the short term, the best that might be hoped for from the UN is that it supports initiatives of the Personal Envoy of the Secretary-General to have the Frente Polisario and Morocco engage over natural resources.[83]

Another prediction is that international law will inevitably, if slowly, come to be applied to the case of Western Sahara, including international humanitarian law. Morocco, of course, remains immune to legal action for the occupation and plunder of Western Sahara. The kingdom is not a member of the International Criminal Court; nor can it be expected to join while the occupation of Western Sahara continues. And it will not consent to proceedings against it in any international forum, not when its defeat in the *Western Sahara* advisory case is recalled. If there are to be legal remedies against the taking of Saharawi resources, noting there is no similar recourse to challenge the fact of the occupation or human rights violations in Western Sahara, they will necessarily be against third states trading with Morocco for the resources, and individuals and corporations involved with purchasing those resources. The current docket of the International Criminal Court, together with the precedent of the UN Council for Namibia seeking civil remedies to protect natural resources, suggest the law can be applied in the defence of Saharawi resources.[84]

Ultimately, international law can only work at the margins of the Western Sahara case. The problem of Western Sahara is one of a stalled right of self-determination, impeded by an occupation and displacement of the Saharawi people. No body of law yet exists that is sufficient to force the resolution of such matters. We are left with an ordering norm of clear but unenforceable rules for those involved in the taking of Western Sahara's resources. Recent successes reveal the promise of reminding those involved about such norms, noting the successes in Norway and Sweden to withdraw government pension funds from phosphate trading companies and the EU Parliament in 2011 rejecting the FPA's extended first protocol.

There are good reasons for the organized international community to reject Morocco's annexation of Western Sahara. Self-interest in the preservation of the principle of territorial integrity is one. The general acceptance of the desirability of self-determination of non-self-governing peoples is another. The tragic circumstances of the Saharawi people in occupied Western Sahara and at the Tindouf camps is a third. A fourth is to ensure for a future Saharawi Republic sufficient resources for a functioning national economy. Where the international community concerns itself with Western Sahara's natural resources it will be to end the international trade in them, or least ensure Saharawi consent and benefit to their use, thereby reducing a pretext for an illegal occupation that has been allowed to continue too long.

## Disclosure statement

No potential conflict of interest was reported by the author.

---

82   The United Nations Secretariat had called on the government of an independent Timor-Leste after 2002 to consider pursuing criminal investigations into serious human rights violations during Indonesia's occupation from 1975 until 1999 and notably arising in the months prior to the August 1999 self-determination referendum, without result. See Mohamed C. Othman, *Accountability for International Humanitarian Law Violations: The Case of Rwanda and East Timor* (New York: Springer, 2005).

83   See the 2014 'Report of the Secretary-General on the situation concerning Western Sahara' which noted continuing protests over resources (April 10, 2014), UN doc. S/2014/258.

84   As noted above, Spanish criminal law and therefore Spain's complementary jurisdiction under the Rome Statute of the International Criminal Court now appear to apply in Western Sahara.

# Western Sahara, resources, and international accountability

Stephen Zunes

*University of San Francisco, San Francisco, California, USA*

The illegality of facilitating the exploitation of natural resources by an occupying power in non-self-governing territories is well-established in international law, yet – as in such cases as Namibia and East Timor – the legal principles are often overlooked by foreign corporations and their governments. The resource-rich territory of Western Sahara, under Moroccan occupation since 1975, is no exception, as European, North American, and Australian companies have sought to take advantage of lucrative fishing grounds or mineral deposits. While some have tried to claim that such resource extraction is legal since Morocco reinvests the money it receives into the territory through ambitious development programs, the benefits of such 'development' have largely gone to Moroccan settlers and occupation authorities, not the indigenous population. As with Namibia and East Timor, it may fall to global civil society to pressure such companies, through boycotts and divestment campaigns, to end their illegal exploitation of Western Sahara's natural resources.

## Introduction

The significance of the debate over natural resources in Moroccan-occupied territory in Western Sahara goes beyond the relatively small number of people in that country who are most directly affected, but to broader questions involving decolonization, self-determination, and international law. Ongoing Moroccan control of what is often referred to as 'Africa's last colony' in violation of a series of United Nations Security Council resolutions and a landmark ruling of the International Court of Justice is a direct challenge to the UN Charter and other longstanding international legal principles and has placed the kingdom's continued extraction of non-renewable resources in the territory as a major issue of international contention. The failure of the United Nations to enforce Moroccan compliance with international norms, due large part to the pro-Western monarchy's close economic and strategic ties to veto-wielding members of the Security Council, has given special impetus to global civil society to step in to push for a just resolution to the conflict.

## Background

Western Sahara is a sparsely populated territory about the size of Italy, located on the Atlantic coast in northwestern Africa, just south of Morocco. Traditionally inhabited by nomadic Arab tribes, collectively known as Sahrawis and famous for their long history of resistance to outside domination, the territory was occupied by Spain from the late 1800s through the mid-1970s. With Spain holding onto the territory well over a decade after most African countries had achieved their freedom from European colonialism, the nationalist Polisario Front launched an armed independence struggle against Spain in 1973. This – along with pressure from the United Nations – eventually forced Madrid to promise the people of what was then known as the Spanish Sahara, a referendum on the fate of the territory by the end of 1975. The International Court of Justice (ICJ) heard irredentist claims by Morocco and Mauritania and ruled in October of 1975 that – despite pledges of fealty to the Moroccan sultan back in the nineteenth century by some tribal leaders bordering the territory and close ethnic ties between some Sahrawi and Mauritanian tribes – the right of self-determination was paramount.[1] A special visiting mission from the United Nations engaged in an investigation of the situation in the territory that same year and reported that the vast majority of Sahrawis supported independence under the leadership of the Polisario, not integration with Morocco or Mauritania.[2]

During this same period, Morocco was threatening war with Spain over the territory and assembled over 300,000 Moroccans to march into Western Sahara to claim it as theirs regardless of the wishes of the indigenous population whose dialect, dress, and culture was very different to that of the Moroccan Arabs to their north. Though the Spaniards had a much stronger military, they were preoccupied with the terminal illness of their longtime dictator, General Francisco Franco. At the same time, Spain was facing increasing pressure from the United States, which wanted to back its Moroccan ally, King Hassan II, and did not want to see the leftist Polisario come to power.[3] As a result, Spain reneged on its promise of self-determination and instead agreed in November 1975 to allow for Moroccan administration of the northern two-thirds of the Western Sahara and for Mauritanian administration of the southern third.[4]

Only hours after the ICJ released its opinion affirming Western Sahara's right to self-determination, King Hassan announced a planned march of 350,000 unarmed Moroccans into the Spanish colony to reclaim the territory. The 'Green March' only penetrated a few kilometers into Western Sahara, but armored columns of invading Moroccan forces moved into the territory en masse supported by large-scale aerial bombardment, resulting in nearly half of the population fleeing into neighboring Algeria, where they and their descendants remain in refugee camps to this day. Morocco and Mauritania rejected a series of unanimous United Nations Security Council resolutions calling for the withdrawal of foreign forces and recognition of the Sahrawis' right of self-determination. The United States and France, meanwhile, despite voting in favor of these resolutions, blocked the United Nations from enforcing them. At the same time, the Polisario – which had been driven from the more heavily populated northern and western parts of the country – 'declared' independence as the Sahrawi Arab Democratic Republic (SADR).

Thanks in part to the Algerians providing significant amounts of military equipment and economic support, Polisario guerrillas fought well against both occupying armies and defeated Mauritania by 1979, making them agree to turn their third of Western Sahara over to the Polisario. However, the Moroccans then annexed the remaining southern part of the country.

The Polisario then focused their armed struggle against Morocco and by 1982 had liberated nearly 85% of their country. Over the next four years, however, the tide of the war turned in Morocco's favor thanks to the United States and France dramatically increasing their support for the Moroccan war effort, with US forces providing important training for the Moroccan army in counterinsurgency tactics. In addition, the Americans and French helped Morocco construct a 1200-kilometer 'wall', primarily consisting of two heavily fortified parallel sand berms,

---

1   International Court of Justice, *Advisory Opinion on Western Sahara* (The Hague: International Court of Justice, 1975).
2   United Nations General Assembly, 'Report of the United Nations Visiting Mission to Spanish Sahara', *Official Records: Thirtieth Session*, Supplement no. 23, vol. 3, chap. XIII, A/10023/Add.5 (New York: United Nations, 1977).
3   Jacob Andrew Mundy, 'Neutrality or Complicity? The United States and the 1975 Moroccan Takeover of the Spanish Sahara', *Journal of North African Studies* 11, no. 3 (2006): 275–306.
4   'Declaration of Principles on Western Sahara by Spain, Morocco, and Mauritania', *United Nations Treaty Series, 1975*, November 19, 1975, 988, 1-14450, 259.

which eventually shut off more than three-quarters of Western Sahara – including virtually all of the territory's major towns and natural resources – from the Polisario.

Meanwhile, the Moroccan government, through generous housing subsidies and other benefits, successfully encouraged tens of thousands of Moroccan settlers – some of whom were from southern Morocco and of ethnic Sahrawi background – to immigrate to Western Sahara. By the early 1990s, these Moroccan settlers outnumbered the remaining indigenous Sahrawis by a ratio of more than two to one.

While rarely able to penetrate into Moroccan-controlled territory, the Polisario continued regular assaults against Moroccan occupation forces stationed along the wall until 1991, when the United Nations ordered a ceasefire to be monitored by a United Nations peacekeeping force known as MINURSO (the French acronym for United Nations Mission for the Referendum in Western Sahara).[5] The agreement included provisions for the return of Sahrawi refugees to Western Sahara followed by a United Nations-supervised referendum on the fate of the territory, which would allow Sahrawis native to Western Sahara to vote either for independence or for integration with Morocco.[6] Neither the repatriation nor the referendum took place, however, due to the Moroccan insistence on stacking the voter rolls with Moroccan settlers and other Moroccan citizens whom it claimed had tribal links to the Western Sahara. Secretary General Kofi Annan enlisted former US Secretary of State James Baker as his special representative to help resolve the impasse. Morocco, however, continued to ignore repeated demands from the United Nations that it cooperate with the referendum process, and French and American threats of a veto prevented the Security Council from enforcing its mandate.

## Legal Status

In 1963, the United Nations placed Spanish Sahara on its list of known colonies. In 1965, following deliberations in the Fourth Committee, the General Assembly passed, in a nearly unanimous vote, Resolution 2072, which 'Urgently' requested that 'the Government of Spain ... take immediately all necessary measures for the liberation of the Territory of Ifni and Spanish Sahara from colonial domination'.[7] Morocco, Mauritania and Algeria voted for the resolution; Spain and Portugal were the only two nations to vote against it; the abstainers were the governments of France, South Africa, the United Kingdom and the United States. (Ifni was returned to Morocco in 1968.)

In 1966, the General Assembly passed Resolution 2229,[8] which contained the basic formula for a referendum in Western Sahara that the United Nations would use in the 1990s, although the questionable status of some of the 'exiles' complicated efforts to ensure that only 'indigenous' Western Saharans voted. Morocco, Mauritania and Algeria voted in support of the resolutions; Portugal and Spain continued their lonely dissent.

In 1971 the Fourth Committee and the General Assembly decided to wait a year before addressing Spain's Saharan colony. When it returned to the issue in 1972, the General Assembly's Resolution 2983[9] not only reaffirmed 'the inalienable right of the people of the Sahara to self-determination', but also 'to independence'. The Spanish government convinced several Latin American dictatorships, along with fascist Portugal and apartheid South Africa, to join it in

5 United Nations Security Council Resolution 690, *The Situation Concerning Western Sahara* (April 29, 1991), http://www.un.org/en/sc/repertoire/89-92/Chapter%208/AFRICA/item%2008_Western%20Sahara_.pdf.

6 *Official Records of the Security Council*, Forty-fifth Year, Supplement for April, May, June 1990, S/21360.

7 United Nations General Assembly Resolution 2072, 'Ifni and Spanish Sahara', *United Nations Yearbook 1965* (New York: United Nations Office of Public information, 1967), 585.

8 United Nations General Assembly Resolution 2229, *Question of Ifni and Spanish Sahara* (December 20, 1966), http://daccess-dds-ny.un.org/doc/RESOLUTION/GEN/NR0/005/32/IMG/NR000532.pdf?OpenElement.

9 United Nations General Assembly Resolution 2983, *The Question of Spanish Sahara* (December 14, 1972), http://daccess-ods.un.org/TMP/7801474.33280945.html.

voting against the resolution. The United States government abstained with a number of countries, including Morocco.[10]

The Spanish government announced in July 1974 that it intended to hold a self-determination referendum in early 1975. In response to a Moroccan request, supported by Algeria, the General Assembly passed Resolution 3292 (XXIX) on 14 December 1974, asking the International Court of Justice for an advisory opinion regarding Moroccan and Mauritanian claims to Spain's colony, and whether or not those claims trumped the Western Saharans' right to self-determination. It also called for a special visiting mission to assess the realities on the ground.[11] Spain agreed to postpone the referendum.

The ICJ held hearings on the question of Western Sahara from late June to late July 1975. This came almost a month after the UN visiting mission went to the region in May. The latter's findings, which confirmed broad indigenous support for both independence and Polisario in Western Sahara, were released on 15 October.[12] The ICJ's ruling, which recognized the Saharawis' right to self-determination, was issued the following day.[13]

When it became clear that, rather than abide by the ICJ's ruling, the Moroccans would attempt to seize the territory through the Green March, the Spanish government immediately brought the issue to the attention of the United Nations Security Council while simultaneously beginning urgent discussions with King Hassan. The Security Council opened debate on a draft resolution calling on the Moroccan government to 'desist from the proposed march on Western Sahara'. Instead, on 22 October 1975, the Security Council, under pressure from the United States and France, adopted Resolution 377[14] that appealed for 'restraint' on all sides and requested the Secretary-General to enter into consultations with the parties.[15] With this weak response from the United Nations, Spain was forced to pursue direct negotiations with Morocco simultaneously, which resulted in a postponement of the march until November. As ordered by the Security Council, the Secretary-General toured the region between 25 and 28 October but obtained little cooperation from King Hassan, who favored keeping up the pressure until Spain relented.

The following week, on 2 November, the Security Council answered another Spanish request for a further emergency meeting 'to oblige the Government of Morocco to desist from the march it has announced'[16] by adopting Resolution 379, urging all parties to avoid any actions that might escalate tensions and requesting the Secretary-General to intensify his mediation efforts.[17] As the Moroccan government began ferrying marchers to the border on the evening of 5 November, the Spanish representative to the United Nations again pressed the Security Council for action. The President of the Council quickly sent an 'urgent request to put an end forthwith to the declared march into Western Sahara' to King Hassan, who replied that until the Spanish government agreed to 'undertake urgent bilateral negotiations' the march would continue.[18] The Security

---

10   United Nations Office of Public Information, 'Spanish Sahara', *United Nations Yearbook 1972* (New York: United Nations Office of Public information, 1975), 569–70, 579–80.

11   United Nations General Assembly Resolution 3292, 'Spanish Sahara', *United Nations Yearbook 1974* (New York: United Nations Office of Public information, 1977), 794, 805–6.

12   United Nations General Assembly, 'Report of the United Nations Visiting Mission to Spanish Sahara, *Official Records: Thirtieth Session*, Supplement no. 23, vol. 3, chap. XIII, A/10023/Add.5 (New York: United Nations, 1977).

13   For analysis, see Thomas M. Franck, 'The Stealing of the Sahara', *American Journal of International Law* 70, no. 4 (1976): 694–721; Thomas M. Franck, "Theory and Practice of Decolonization', in *War and Refugees: The Western Sahara Conflict*, ed. Richard Lawless and Laila Monahan (New York: Pinter, 1987).

14   United Nations Security Council Resolution 377, *The Situation Concerning Western Sahara* (October 22, 1975), http://daccess-ods.un.org/TMP/7421183.58612061.html.

15   Karel Wellens, ed., *Resolutions and Statements of the United Nations, 1945–1989* (Leiden: Martinus Nijhoff Publishers, 1990), 49.

16   United Nations Security Council, *Documents Officiels* 30 (1975): 29.

17   Wellens, *Resolutions and Statements of the United Nations, 1945–1989*, 49.

18   United Nations Security Council, *Presidential Appeal*, November 6, 1975.

Council finally passed a more strongly worded resolution (380) late on 6 November, which 'deplored' the Green March, called on the Moroccans to withdraw immediately, to respect the Western Saharans' right to self-determination, and to cooperate with the Secretary-General's mediation efforts.[19]

However, France and the United States made sure that this resolution was not enforced. According to the United States' ambassador to the United Nations, Daniel Patrick Moynihan,

> The United States wished things to turn out as they did, and I worked to bring this about. The Department of State desired that the United Nations prove utterly ineffective in whatever measures it undertook. This task was given to me, and I carried it forward with no inconsiderable success.[20]

Not only was Resolution 380 not enforced, it was the last Security Council action on the Western Sahara issue for 10 years. Unable to obtain any meaningful response from the Security Council to stop Hassan's invasion, Spain decided to cut a secret trilateral deal with Morocco and Mauritania, finalized between 12 and 14 November 1975 in Madrid.[21]

Notwithstanding the trilateral agreement in Madrid, the United Nations Fourth Committee held hearings between 14 November and 4 December, where the Western Sahara was a major focus of the agenda. The Committee forwarded two draft resolutions to the General Assembly. One resolution (3458A), adopted by a vote of 88 to zero on 10 December, with 41 abstentions (including the United States), called on Spain, with the help of the Secretary-General, to hold a popular referendum on self-determination in the Western Sahara.[22] The other resolution (3458B), passed by a vote of 56 to 42, with 34 abstentions, took note of the Madrid Agreement and requested that the parties to the agreement 'ensure' that all persons originating from the territory 'exercise their inalienable right to self-determination'.[23]

Throughout 1976, the United Nations, with attention focused on the guerrilla war and the massive refugee exodus triggered by the Moroccan invasion, failed to address the underlying issue of self-determination. That December, the General Assembly passed resolution 31/45, in which the body decided to hold off further deliberations on the matter until the United Nations could learn the results of a scheduled extraordinary session of the Organization of African Unity on the Western Sahara.[24] Resolutions adopted over the next three years revealed that the United Nations had deferred the matter totally to the Organization of African Unity.[25]

The Security Council again became involved in the conflict in 1990 with a series of resolutions which put in place a ceasefire between Moroccan and Polisario forces, the stationing of United Nations' peacekeeping forces in the country, and an internationally supervised referendum in which the remaining Saharawi population in Western Sahara, combined with repatriated refugees, would take part in a referendum. A series of United Nations Security Council resolutions urged the referendum process to move forward (Resolutions 690, 725, 809, 973, 995, 1002, 1017, 1033 and 1056),[26] but Morocco remained intransigent.

---

19  Wellens, *Resolutions and Statements of the United Nations, 1945–1989*, 49–50.

20  Daniel Patrick Moynihan, *A Dangerous Place* (Boston: Little, Brown, 1980), 247.

21  'Declaration of Principles on Western Sahara by Spain, Morocco, and Mauritania', *United Nations Treaty Series, 1975*, November 19, 1975, 988, 1-14450, 259.

22  United Nations General Assembly Resolution 3248A, *Question of Western Sahara* (December 10, 1975), http://daccess-dds-ny.un.org/doc/RESOLUTION/GEN/NR0/001/71/IMG/NR000171.pdf?OpenElement.

23  United Nations General Assembly Resolution 3248B, *Question of Western Sahara* (December 10, 1975), http://daccess-dds-ny.un.org/doc/RESOLUTION/GEN/NR0/001/71/IMG/NR000171.pdf?OpenElement.

24  United Nations General Assembly Resolution 31/45, *Question of Western Sahara* (December 1, 1976), http://daccess-dds-ny.un.org/doc/RESOLUTION/GEN/NR0/302/28/IMG/NR030228.pdf?OpenElement. The Organization of African Unity (OAU) was the precursor to the African Union (AU).

25  See, for example, United Nations General Assembly, *Question of Western Sahara* (November 21, 1979), http://www.un.org/documents/ga/res/34/a34res37.pdf.

26  See United Nations Security Council Resolutions, http://www.un.org/en/sc/documents/resolutions/.

In 1997, UN Special Envoy Baker oversaw the signing of the Houston Accords which codified the modalities of the referendum process, including identification of voters. However, despite a series of additional United Nations Security Council resolutions),[27] Morocco refused to allow the referendum to go forward and, as they had done since the beginning of United Nations Security Council involvement, French and American threats of a veto prevented the Security Council from enforcing its mandate.

## Subsequent developments

For more than 40 years, the United Nations had been recognizing the question of Western Sahara as that of an incomplete decolonization, a non-self-governing territory which had the right of self-determination, including the option of independence. However, Morocco's major allies – France and the United States – pushed the idea that Western Sahara was not an occupied territory but instead a 'disputed' territory. Were the latter designation to be accepted, the transfer of Moroccan settlers into the territory and the exploitation of its natural resources would no longer be illegal.

In 2000, the Clinton administration successfully convinced Baker and Annan to give up on efforts to proceed with the referendum as originally agreed by the United Nations 10 years earlier and instead to accept Moroccan demands that Moroccan settlers be allowed to vote on the fate of the territory along with the indigenous Saharawi. This proposal was incorporated into the first Baker Plan presented to UN Secretary General in early 2001, which would have held the plebiscite under Moroccan rule after a four- to five-year period of very limited autonomy with no guarantee that independence would be one of the options on the ballot.[28]

Though this first Baker Plan received the enthusiastic backing of the French and US governments, most of the international community rejected the proposal, since it would have effectively abrogated previous United Nations resolutions granting the right of self-determination with the option of independence and would have led to the unprecedented action of the United Nations placing the fate of a non-self-governing territory in the hands of the occupying colonial power.

As a result, Baker then proposed a second plan where, as with his earlier proposal, both the Sahrawis and the Moroccan settlers would be able to vote in the referendum, but the plebiscite would take place only after Western Sahara had enjoyed far more significant autonomy for the four to five years prior to the vote, independence would be an option on the ballot, and the United Nations would oversee the vote and guarantee that advocates of both integration and independence would have the freedom to campaign openly. The United Nations Security Council approved the second Baker plan in the summer of 2003.

Under considerable pressure, Algeria, and eventually the Polisario, reluctantly accepted the new plan, but the Moroccans – unwilling to allow the territory to enjoy even a brief period of autonomy and risk the possibility they would lose the plebiscite – rejected it. Once again, the United States and France blocked the United Nations from enforcing its mandate by pressuring Morocco to comply with its international legal obligations.

In what has been widely interpreted as rewarding Morocco for its intransigence, the Bush administration subsequently designated Morocco as a 'major non-NATO ally' in June of 2004, a coveted status currently granted to only 15 key nations, such as Japan, Israel and Australia. The following month, the Senate ratified a free trade agreement with Morocco by an 85–13 margin, making the kingdom one of only a half dozen countries outside of the Western hemisphere to enjoy such a close economic relationship with the United States. US aid to Morocco grew five-fold under the Bush administration, ostensibly as a reward for the kingdom undertaking

---

27  See United Nations Security Council Resolutions 1182, 1215, and 1359, available at http://www.un.org/en/sc/documents/resolutions/.

28  United Nations Security Council, *Report of the Secretary-General on the Situation Concerning Western Sahara,* S/2001/613 (June 20, 2001).

a series of neoliberal economic reforms and to assist the Moroccan government in 'combating terrorism'. While there has been some political liberalization within most of Morocco in recent years under the young King Mohammed VI, who succeeded to the throne following the death of his father in 1999, gross and systematic human rights violations in the occupied Western Sahara and Saharawi-populated segments of southern Morocco continues unabated, with public expressions of nationalist aspirations and organized protests against the occupation and human rights abuses routinely met with severe repression.

The Obama administration pressed Morocco on its human rights record and briefly joined other nations calling on the Security Council to expand MINURSO's mandate to include monitoring the human rights situation in both the occupied territory and the refugee camps in Algeria.[29] France and Morocco successfully blocked the effort, however, and MINURSO remains the only UN peacekeeping force without such a mandate.

## The illegality of the exploitation of natural resources

UN General Assembly Resolution 1514, passed as part of a series of resolutions addressing the rights of inhabitants of non-self-governing territories, declares that 'peoples may, for their own ends, freely dispose of their natural wealth and resources ... based on the principle of mutual benefit and international law' in order to realize the right to 'freely pursue their economic, social and cultural development'.[30] Resolution 1803, passed two years later, underscores that 'economic and financial agreements between the developed and the developing countries must be based on the principles of equality and of the right of peoples and nations to self-determination'. The resolution makes clear that sovereignty over natural resources belongs to the indigenous inhabitants of a non-self-governing territory rather than the occupying power in noting, 'The right of peoples and nations to permanent sovereignty over their wealth and natural resources must be exercised in the interest of their natural development and of the well-being of the people of the state concerned.' The resolution further put the General Assembly on record emphasizing that 'Violation of the rights of peoples and nations to sovereignty over their natural wealth and resources is contrary to the spirit and principles of the Charter of the United Nations'.[31]

A series of decisions by the International Court of Justice regarding Namibia, Nauru, East Timor and Palestine further codified protection of the peoples of non-self-governing territories to sovereignty over their natural resources.[32] As recently as 2011, the General Assembly reiterated 'the right of the peoples of the Non-Self-Governing Territories to self-determination in conformity with the Charter of the United Nations and with General Assembly resolution 1514(XV) ... as well as their right to the enjoyment of their natural resources and their right to dispose of those resources in their best interest'.[33]

29 Louise Charboneau and Aziz el Yaakoubi, 'U.S. Proposes U.N. Western Sahara Rights Monitor; Morocco Warns of "Missteps"', *Reuters*, April 17, 2013, http://uk.reuters.com/article/2013/04/17/uk-westernsahara-un-idUKBRE93G00Z20130417.

30 United Nations General Assembly Resolution 1514, *Declaration on the Granting of Independence to Colonial Countries and Peoples* (December 14, 1960), http://daccess-dds-ny.un.org/doc/RESOLUTION/GEN/NR0/152/88/IMG/NR015288.pdf?OpenElement.

31 United Nations General Assembly Resolution 1803, *Permanent Sovereignty over Natural Resources* (December 14, 1962), http://www.ohchr.org/Documents/ProfessionalInterest/resources.pdf.

32 See, for example, International Court of Justice, 'Certain Phosphate Lands in Nauru' (Nauru v. Australia), *Application Instituting Proceedings Filed in the Registry of the Court on 19 May 1989* (The Hague: International Court of Justice, 1989); International Court of Justice, 'East Timor' (Portugal v Australia), *Application Instituting Proceedings Filed in the Registry of the Court on 22 February 1991* (The Hague: International Court of Justice, 1991).

33 UN General Assembly Resolution 52/72, *Economic and Other Activities which Affect the Interests of the Peoples of the Non-Self-Governing Territories* (December 10, 1997), http://www.un.org/ga/documents/gares52/res5272.htm.

The application of these legal principles to Western Sahara was examined by UN Under-Secretary for Legal Affairs Hans Corell in regard to a request from the Security Council regarding oil exploration off the Western Sahara coast. He concluded:

> while the specific contracts which are the subject of the Security Council's request are not in themselves illegal, if further exploration and exploitation activities were to proceed in disregard of the interests and wishes of the people of Western Sahara, they would be in violation of the international law principles applicable to mineral resource activities in Non-Self-Governing Territories.[34]

As with other issues regarding the illegality of Morocco's occupation of Western Sahara, however, the United States and France blocked the Security Council from taking further action on this question.

In late 2001, Morocco announced hydrocarbon exploration in Western Sahara and offshore. That September, Morocco's National Office for Petroleum Exploration and Exploitation (Onarep) signed contracts with French-based 'supermajor' TotalFinaElf (now Total) and the United States-based firm Kerr-McGee. As president of the Security Council in November 2001, Jamaica requested an official opinion from the Under-Secretary-General for Legal Affairs, which resulted in Corell's report, released on 5 February 2002. The opinion not only highlighted Morocco's precarious legal position in the territory (i.e. illegally obtaining status as the de facto administering power), it also clearly reiterated that Western Sahara is a non-self-governing territory (i.e. a colony) requiring self-determination. Its conclusion, however, was that resource exploration in itself, what the Moroccan concessions offered, would not be illegal under international law. However, it would be illegal for the Moroccan government, as the de facto colonizing power in a non-self-governing territory, to extract Western Sahara's resources without adequate approval from the population.

The acquisition of Western Sahara adds significant sources of revenue to Moroccan state coffers. Foremost are the phosphate deposits at Boucraa, first developed by Spain in the 1960s and now exploited by Morocco. Even without Western Sahara, Morocco is the world's leading exporter of this fast dwindling resource, which is key to modern industrial agriculture. The reserves in Western Sahara are of an extremely high quality and are close to the surface, though they still only account for a small percentage of Moroccan phosphate exports. Perhaps of more value to Morocco has been the rich fishing grounds found off the coast of Western Sahara, which is of increasing importance in light of the decline of fishing stocks off Morocco itself. In addition to Moroccan fleets, the government has signed lucrative contracts with other countries and, more recently, the European Union. Furthermore, there are numerous other sources of revenue yet to be explored or exploited, whether minerals or hydrocarbons.

Though not explicit on Western Sahara's two main exports, fisheries and phosphates, the opinion clearly implied that profits gained from those industries by the Moroccan government were in contravention of international law. In the Security Council, the opinion provoked a debate on Morocco's ambiguous and illegal status in Western Sahara, though members of the Council and Secretariat dismissed such talk as unproductive.[35]

Petroleum resources remain a particularly significant question. Unlike fisheries, which in most cases can be regenerated, fossil fuels are a finite resource. The burgeoning interest by industrialized countries in offshore oil in West Africa has added a significant geostrategic component. On the one hand, petroleum prospects in the Western Sahara are not a phenomenon unique to the new century. In the late 1950s, the Spanish government made moves towards exploiting known

---

34  United Nations Security Council, *Letter dated 29 January 2002 from the Under-Secretary-General for Legal Affairs, the Legal Counsel, addressed to the President of the Security Council*, S/2002/161 (February 12, 2002).

35  Ibid. See also Carola Hoyos and Toby Shelley, 'UN Throws Doubt on Oil Deals in Western Sahara', *Financial Times*, February 6, 2002, 7; 'Security Council Disagrees Over Oil Prospecting in W Sahara', *Agence France Presse*, February 20, 2002.

and assumed reserves. By the mid-1960s, different contractors had found over 27 different potential inland sites, although none were considered worth the effort. North of the Spanish Sahara, the Moroccan government commissioned an offshore study by the firm Esso, which apparently discovered a 60-mile-long field stretching off the coast of Tarfaya into the Spanish-administered waters. Following the Moroccan–Mauritanian takeover of the Western Sahara, different companies accepted various exploration contracts for the Tarfaya region yet the collapse of global oil prices inhibited interest.[36]

A number of countries, particularly the United States, have shown serious interest in tapping into potential West African sources. Despite the numerous conflicts that plague West Africa, the move towards offshore sources translated into a 'stable' source of oil for the United States, unlike Middle Eastern and Central Asian providers. Vice President Dick Cheney's National Energy Policy report noted that West Africa had become 'one of the fastest-growing sources of oil and gas for the American market'.[37] Some estimates have predicted that West African oil could soon provide up to 25% of US petroleum imports. The Institute for Advanced Strategic and Political Studies, a Jerusalem-based think tank, convened a working group comprised of US business and policy leaders called the African Oil Policy Initiative Group. Among its list of recommendations, it advised the US government to declare the Gulf of Guinea an area of 'Vital Interest'.[38] Just south of Western Sahara, Mauritania signed agreements to begin oil and gas production at 75,000 barrels a day from its offshore wells by the year 2005.[39] However, when production finally began in 2006, output was revised significantly downward several times, eventually below 50% of the original assessment, which had been based on a single test well. Still, the increasing importance of West African oil may make it even more difficult for influential foreign governments to discourage their companies from taking advantage of Western Saharan oil resources.

Parsing the 2002 opinion, Morocco and its supporters seized on the fact that simple exploration was deemed legal. As an oil-importing country, the Moroccan regime had good reason to secure any potential Western Saharan oil reserves. Off the coast of Western Sahara the US 2000 Geological Survey of World Energy thought that reserves could be 'substantial', whereas sources in Morocco proper were 'low and insecure'.[40] The Moroccan regime's moves in late 2001 towards exploration and exploitation specifically targeted the waters off the coast of the Western Sahara. The firm conducting the exploration for Kerr-McGee and Total, TGS-Nopec, however, came under intense grassroots pressure from Norwegian activists, citing the company's activities as complicit with the Moroccan occupation.[41] These efforts led TGS-Nopec to hastily withdraw from the affair, but only after it had completed most of its survey.

With all of this talk of oil in Western Sahara, Baker's own oil interests began to be called into question, especially his connections with Kerr-McGee as well as the Bush–Cheney administration, known for its close ties with Big Oil. Indeed, one US journalist claimed that the Bush administration's first ambassador to Morocco, Margaret Tutwiler, a very close and personal friend of Baker and who had served as State Department spokesperson when he was Secretary

---

36   Tony Hodges and Anthony G. Pazzanita, *Historical Dictionary of Western Sahara*. 3rd ed. (Lanham, MD: Scarecrow Press, 2006), 347–50.

37   Quoted in Simon Robinson, 'Black Gold', *Time*, October 28, 2002, A10.

38   Institute for Advanced Strategic and Political Studies, 'African Oil: A Priority for US National Security and African Development' (Jerusalem: IASPS, 2002).

39   Toby Shelley, 'Premier Oil Acquires Stakes in West Africa', *Financial Times,* May 29, 2003: 25; Toby Shelley, 'Oil Groups Target NW Africa: The Little-Explored Region is Attracting Much International Interest', *Financial Times*, July 12, 2002, 28.

40   Stefan Armbruster, 'Western Sahara's Future Hinges on Oil', *BBC News Online*, March 4, 2003, http://news.bbc.co.uk/1/hi/business/2758829.stm (accessed October 8, 2004).

41   Janos Besenyo, *Western Sahara* (Pecs: Publikon Publishers, 2000), 18.

of State, was specifically placed in Rabat to, among other things, expedite oil deals.[42] With the Total–Kerr-McGee deal unfolding in the context of Baker's pro-Moroccan Framework Agreement, it was difficult for observers not to think that Western Sahara was being sold out to US energy interests. Baker, however, would prove a more honest broker, and supporters of international law in the US Congress made sure that Western Sahara was specifically exempt from provisions of a free trade agreement with Morocco. As US trade representative (and future World Bank president) Robert Zoellick noted, 'The United States and many other countries do not recognize Moroccan sovereignty over Western Sahara'.[43] By then, 2004, Total had dropped out of Western Sahara ostensibly for business reasons. Isolated, Kerr-McGee came under increasing pressure, even from conservative Christian activists in its home state of Oklahoma. In 2005, Norway's Government Pension Fund, the world's largest sovereign-wealth fund, began divesting its $52 million investment in Kerr-McGee stock because their Western Sahara operations constituted an 'unacceptable risk for contributing to other *particularly serious violations of fundamental ethical norms*'.[44] Kerr-McGee finally withdrew in 2006.

The Moroccan government, however, has continued to seek companies interested in exploring and exploiting potential Western Saharan oil and gas. In a counter-move, the SADR signed an exploration contract in 2003 with the Anglo-Australian oil company Fusion to access the entire acreage off the coast of the Western Sahara.[45] Then, in 2005, SADR signed contracts with seven different companies covering areas onshore and offshore, mostly British and Australian companies. Knowing their favorable position under international law, SADR officials hoped these concessions could force some kind of international legal battle regarding sovereignty over Western Sahara, which would be to the advantage of those seeking self-determination. Yet the prospects that there might be significant deposits on- or offshore Western Sahara continue to be treated with significant skepticism, even when global oil prices were at all-time highs in 2006.

Subsequently, the Moroccan state oil company Office National des Hydrocarbures et des Mines (ONHYM) has granted five licenses for oil exploration and production in Western Sahara without the consent of the population. Kosmos Energy Offshore Morocco HC, a subsidiary of the US-based but Bermuda-registered firm Kosmos Energy Ltd, holds the license once held by Kerr-McGee off the shore from Boujdour. Total SA has signed new licenses for an offshore block to the south in 2011, 2012 and 2013. Both companies have signed agreements with ONHYM for future production. The British companies San Leon Morocco Ltd and the PetroMaroc (formerly known as Longreach Oil and Gas Ventures) hold two onshore exploration licenses in conjunction with ONHYM, primarily consisting of oil shale, in the northwestern corner of the territory.

Efforts for self-determination were set back when the European Union, in an apparently illegal move, signed a fisheries agreement with Morocco in early 2006 which included areas off Western Sahara. Organizing efforts by human rights groups in various European countries, particularly the Norwegian-based Western Sahara Resource Watch, led to it not being extended in 2011. However, in December 2013 it was surprisingly renewed, with vague references about benefits to the 'local population', but with no specific mention of the Sahrawis.[46] Former United

---

42  Wayne Madsen, 'Big Oil and James Baker Target the Western Sahara', *Counter Punch*, January 8, 2003, http://www.counterpunch.org/madsen01082003.html (accessed October 8, 2004). See also Frank Bruni, 'A Loyal Lieutenant [i.e. Tutwiler] Re-enlists to Serve the Bush Brigade', *New York Times*, March 26, 2001, A12.

43  Quoted in Jacob Mundy, 'Mixing Occupation and Oil in Western Sahara', *CorpWatch*, July 21, 2005, http://www.corpwatch.org/article.php?id=12506 (accessed September 2006).

44  Ministry of Finance, Norway, 'Recommendation on Exclusion from the Government Petroleum Fund's Investment Universe of the Company Kerr-McGee Corporation', June 6, 2005, http://www.regjeringen.no/nb/dep/fin/tema/statens_pensjonsfond/ansvarlige-investeringer/tilradninger-og-brev-fra-etikkradet/Recommendation-on-Exclusion-from-the-Government-Petroleum-Funds-Investment-Universe-of-the-Company-Kerr-McGee-Corporation.html?id=419582.

45  Petroleum Exploration Society of Australia (PESA), *PESA News*, April–May 2003, 53–8.

46  European Commission, *Proposal for Council Decision on the Conclusion of the Protocol between the European Union and the Kingdom of Morocco Setting out the Fishing Opportunities and Financial Contribution Provided*

Nations legal counsel Corell declared that 'The E.U.'s interpretation of the legal opinion is preposterous. It is utterly embarrassing that the international community has been unable to solve this conflict. Since Morocco is able to capitalize in Western Sahara, there will be no incentive at all to change the situation'.[47]

The Moroccan government and its supporters point to its ambitious large-scale development projects in Western Sahara, particularly in the urban areas. Morocco claims it has invested more than US$2 billion in infrastructure development in the territory, significantly more than Morocco has procured from Western Sahara's natural resources and more than they would be likely to obtain in the foreseeable future.[48] For this reason, the Moroccan government and its supporters argue that they have fulfilled the requirements regarding interests, well-being, and development needs of the indigenous population.[49] However, most of the infrastructure development has involved the elaborate internal security system of military bases, police facilities, prisons, surveillance, and related repressive apparatuses; housing construction, subsidies, and other support for Moroccan settlers; and airport, seaport, and other transportation development designed to accelerate resource extraction, not build up the standard of living for the territory's people. More fundamentally, the decisions on how to use the proceeds from resource extraction are being made by the Moroccan government in the capital of Rabat, not by the indigenous people of Western Sahara.

As a result, international pressure has been increasing. In March of 2015, the Peace and Security Council of the African Union called on the UN Security Council to intervene to stop the illegal exploitation of Western Sahara's natural resources and called for a 'global boycott of products of companies involved in the illegal exploitation of the natural resources of Western Sahara'.[50] International outcry placed former US Senator and Secretary of State Hillary Clinton – a leading contender in the 2016 US presidential race – on the defensive when it was revealed that the Office Cherifien des Phosphates (OCP), a Moroccan government-owned mining company that controls one of the world's largest phosphate mines in the occupied Western Sahara, was the primary donor to the May 2015 Clinton Global Initiative conference in Marrakech.[51]

## The future

Since the 1991 ceasefire, the Sahrawis have fought for their national rights primarily by legal and diplomatic means, not through armed struggle. Unlike a number of other peoples engaged in national liberation struggles, the Saharawi have never committed acts of terrorism. Even during their armed struggle against the occupation, which ended 15 years ago, Polisario forces restricted their attacks exclusively to the Moroccan armed forces, never targeting civilians. The failure of the international community to defend the legal rights of the Sahrawis despite this moderation effectively sends a signal that such moderation will not be rewarded.

*for in the Fisheries Partnership Agreement in Force between the two Parties* (Brussels: European Commission, 2013), http://eur-lex.europa.eu/legal-content/EN/TXT/PDF/?uri=CELEX:52013PC0648&from=EN.

47  Per Liljas, 'There's a New Terrorist Threat Emerging in Western Sahara, and the World Isn't Paying Attention', *Time*, August 8, 2014.

48  Sarah A. Topol, 'Amid Moroccan Investment in Western Sahara, Tensions Simmer', *Bloomberg Business*, May 30, 2013, http://www.bloomberg.com/bw/articles/2013-05-30/amid-moroccan-investment-in-western-sahara-tensions-simmer.

49  Aidan Lewis, 'Morocco's Fish fight: High Stakes over Western Sahara', *BBC News*, December 15, 2011, http://www.bbc.com/news/world-africa-16101666.

50  African Union, *Communiqué of the Peace and Security Council of the African Union (AU), at its 496th meeting held on 27 March 2015, on the situation in Western Sahara*, http://www.peaceau.org/en/article/communique-of-the-peace-and-security-council-of-the-african-union-au-at-its-496th-meeting-held-on-27-march-2015-on-the-situation-in-western-sahara#sthash.TYOHI9YB.dpuf.

51  Stephen Zunes, 'Hillary Clinton, Phosphates, and the Western Sahara', *National Catholic Reporter*, May 12, 2015.

The nonresolution of the Western Sahara conflict has important regional implications. It has encouraged an arms race between Morocco and Algeria and, on several occasions over the past four decades, has brought the two countries close to war. Perhaps even more significantly, it has been the single biggest obstacle to a fuller implementation of the goals of the Arab Maghreb Union – consisting of Morocco, Algeria, Libya, Tunisia, and Mauritania – to pursue economic integration and other initiatives which would increase the standard of living and political stability in the region. The lack of unity and greater coordination among these nations and their struggling economies has contributed to the dramatic upsurge in illegal immigration to Europe and the rise of radical Islamist movements.

Over the past three decades, the Sahrawi Arab Democratic Republic has been recognized as an independent country by more than 80 governments, with Kenya and South Africa becoming the latest to extend full diplomatic relations. The SADR has been a full member state of the African Union (formerly Organization for African Unity) since 1984 and most of the international community recognizes Western Sahara as Africa's last colony. (By contrast, with only a few exceptions, the Arab states – despite their outspoken opposition to the Israeli occupation of Palestinian and Syrian land – have supported Morocco's occupation of Western Sahara.)

With Morocco's rejection of the second Baker Plan and the threat of a French and American veto of any Security Council resolution that would push Morocco to compromise, a diplomatic settlement of the conflict looks highly unlikely. With Morocco's powerful armed forces protected behind the separation wall, and Algeria unwilling to support a resumption of guerrilla war, the Polisario appears to lack a military option as well.

As happened during the 1980s in both South Africa and the Israeli-occupied Palestinian territories, the locus of the Western Sahara freedom struggle has recently shifted from the military and diplomatic initiatives of an exiled armed movement to a largely unarmed popular resistance from within. In recent years, young activists in the occupied territory and even in Saharawi-populated parts of southern Morocco have confronted Moroccan troops in street demonstrations and other forms of non-violent action, despite the risk of shootings, mass arrests, and torture. The construction of a tent city of up to 12,000 Sahrawi human rights activists on the outskirts of Al Aioun in the fall of 2010 was met by severe repression from Moroccan authorities.[52]

The failure of the Kingdom of Morocco and the Polisario Front to agree on the modalities of the long-planned United Nations-sponsored referendum on the fate of Western Sahara, combined with a growing non-violent resistance campaign in the occupied territory against Morocco's 40-year occupation, has led Morocco to propose granting the former Spanish colony special autonomous status within the kingdom. The plan has received the enthusiastic support of the American and French governments as a reasonable compromise to the abiding conflict. As illustrated below, there are serious problems with this proposal. However, the very fact that Morocco has felt obliged to propose a special status for the territory constitutes an admission that its previous insistence that Western Sahara was simply another part of Morocco was false. As visitors to Western Sahara in recent years have noticed, not only has Morocco's 40-year campaign of assimilation failed, but the younger generation of Saharawis are at least as nationalistic as their parents.

It is unfortunate, therefore, that the Moroccan plan for autonomy falls so well short of what is required to bring about a peaceful resolution to the conflict. Moreover, it seeks to set a dangerous precedent which threatens the very foundation of the post-World War II international legal system.

To begin with, the proposal is based on the assumption that Western Sahara is part of Morocco, a contention that has long been rejected by the United Nations, the ICJ, the African Union, and a broad consensus of international legal opinion. To accept Morocco's autonomy

---

52   Stephen Zunes, 'Upsurge in Repression Challenges Nonviolent Resistance in Western Sahara', *Open Democracy*, November 17, 2010.

plan would mean that, for the first time since the founding of the United Nations and the ratification of its Charter more than 60 years ago, the international community would be endorsing the expansion of a country's territory by military force, thereby establishing a very dangerous and destabilizing precedent.

If the people of Western Sahara accepted an autonomy agreement over independence as a result of a free and fair referendum, it would constitute a legitimate act of self-determination. However, Morocco has explicitly stated that its autonomy proposal 'rules out, by definition, the possibility for the independence option to be submitted' to the people of Western Sahara, the vast majority of whom – according to knowledgeable international observers – favor outright independence.

Even if one takes a dismissive attitude toward international law, there are a number of practical concerns regarding the Moroccan proposal as well.

One is that the history of respect for regional autonomy on the part of centralized authoritarian states is quite poor, and has often led to violent conflict. For example, in 1952, the United Nations granted the British protectorate (and former Italian colony) of Eritrea autonomous, federated status within Ethiopia. In 1961, however, the Ethiopian emperor unilaterally revoked Eritrea's autonomous status, annexing it as his empire's fourteenth province, resulting in a bloody 30-year struggle for independence and subsequent border wars between the two countries, which have claimed hundreds of thousands of lives.

Based upon Morocco's habit of breaking its promises to the international community regarding the United Nations-mandated referendum for Western Sahara and related obligations based on the ceasefire agreement 18 years ago, there is little to inspire confidence that Morocco would live up to its promises to provide genuine autonomy for Western Sahara. Indeed, a close reading of the proposal raises questions as to how much autonomy is even being offered. Important matters such as control of Western Sahara's natural resources and law enforcement (beyond local jurisdictions) remain ambiguous.

In addition, the proposal appears to indicate that all powers not specifically vested in the autonomous region would remain with the Kingdom. Indeed, since the king of Morocco is ultimately invested with absolute authority under article 19 of the Moroccan Constitution, the autonomy proposal's insistence that the Moroccan state 'will keep its powers in the royal domains, especially with respect to defence, external relations, and the constitutional and religious prerogatives of His Majesty the King' appears to afford the monarch considerable latitude in interpretation.

While encouraging such compromise, or 'third way' between independence and integration, as a possible win/win situation can often be a successful formula for conflict resolution in some ethnic conflicts and many international disputes, Western Sahara is a clear-cut case of self-determination for a people struggling against foreign military occupation. This is not a matter of 'splitting the difference', given that one party is under an illegal foreign military occupation and the other party is the occupier. This is why the international community rejected Iraq's proposals in 1990–91 for some kind of compromise regarding its occupation of Kuwait. The Polisario Front has already offered guarantees to protect Moroccan strategic and economic interests if allowed full independence.[53] To insist that the people of Western Sahara must give up their moral and legal right to genuine self-determination is therefore not a recipe for conflict resolution, but for far more serious conflict in the future.

Morocco has succeeded in resisting its international legal obligations for more than four decades through support from permanent members of the United Nations Security Council. As a result of the French and US veto threats, the Security Council has failed to place the Western Sahara issue under Chapter VII of the United Nations Charter, which would give the international

---

53    United Nations Security Council, *Letter dated 16 April 2007 from the Permanent Representative of South Africa to the United Nations addressed to the President of the Security Council*, S/2007/210 (April 16, 2007).

community the power to impose sanctions or other appropriate leverage to force the Moroccan regime to abide by the United Nations mandates it has to date disregarded. Polisario's unwillingness to compromise further should not be seen as the major obstacle impeding the resolution of the conflict.

Similar support from Western industrialized nations for Indonesia for many years prevented resolution to the occupation of East Timor. It was only after human rights organizations, church groups and other activists in the United States, Great Britain, and Australia successfully pressured their governments to end their support for Indonesia's occupation that the Jakarta regime was finally willing to offer a referendum which gave the East Timorese their right to self-determination. It may take similar grassroots campaigns in Europe and North America to ensure that Western powers live up to their international legal obligations and pressure Morocco to allow the people of Western Sahara to determine their own destiny.

The growth of the non-violent resistance struggle in the occupied territories offers a unique opportunity to build international awareness of the conflict among civil society organizations that could offer much-needed solidarity with the freedom struggle inside Western Sahara. Such massive non-violent action and other forms of non-cooperation provides an important signal to the Moroccan occupiers and the international community that the people of Western Sahara still demand their freedom and will not accept any less than genuine self-determination. The use of nonviolent methods of resistance also makes it easier to highlight gross and systematic violations of international humanitarian law by Moroccan occupation forces, gain sympathy and support from the international human rights community, and provide greater pressure on the French, American, and other governments which continue to provide security assistance to Morocco and otherwise support the Moroccan occupation.

Human rights groups have increasingly been highlighting the poor human rights situation in Western Sahara, which has contributed to recent diplomatic rows between Morocco and the United States, Spain, and France. Freedom House has ranked Western Sahara as having one of very worst human rights situations in the world.[54] In April 2015, a Spanish court indicted 11 Moroccan former officials for genocide in connection with killings and torture in Western Sahara.[55] The following month, Amnesty International issued another scathing report on the human rights situation, targeting the widespread torture of political prisoners.[56]

There is a small but growing movement in Europe supporting the Saharawi's right to national self-determination, as well as similar civil society efforts in South Africa, other African countries, Australia, Japan, and the United States. More focus on the issue of the illegal exploitation of natural resources in Western Sahara could provide proponents of international law and human rights an issue through which to challenge governments and companies which take advantage of the occupation is such a way through campaigns advocating boycotts, divestment, and sanctions. At this point, however, such movements are too small to have much impact on government policies, particular those of France and the United States, which are the two governments most responsible for the failure of the United Nations to enforce its resolutions dealing with the conflict. This can change, however. Just over 20 years ago, there was relatively little civil society activism regarding East Timor, but a dramatic growth in such activism in the late 1990s contributed to East Timor's eventual independence.

A similar campaign may be the best hope for the people of Western Sahara and the best hope we have to save the vitally important post-World War II principles enshrined in the United Nations Charter.

---

54  Human Rights Watch, *Freedom in the World 2013* (Washington, DC: Human Rights Watch, 2013).
55  Carolotta Gall, 'Spanish Judge Accuses Moroccan Former Officials of Genocide in Western Sahara', *New York Times*, April 10, 2015.
56  Amnesty International, 'Morocco: Endemic Torture Used to Incriminate Suspects, Gag Dissent', *Amnesty International*, May 19, 2015, https://www.amnesty.org/en/latest/news/2015/05/morocco-endemic-torture/.

If the international community cannot fulfill its responsibilities on this issue – where the legal and moral imperatives are so clear – how can it deal with more complex issues? If the international community cannot uphold the fundamental right of self-determination, how can it successfully defend other human rights? If the international community cannot enforce a series of United Nations Security Council resolutions regarding such a blatant violation of the UN Charter as a member state invading, occupying, annexing, and colonizing a neighboring country, how can it enforce other provisions of international law?

The stakes are not simply about the future of one small country, but the question as to which principle will prevail in the twenty-first century: the right of self-determination, or the right of conquest? The answer could determine the fate not just of the Western Sahara, but that of the entire international legal order for many decades to come.

## Disclosure statement

No potential conflict of interest was reported by the author.

# The status of Western Sahara as occupied territory under international humanitarian law and the exploitation of natural resources

Ben Saul

*Professor of International Law and Australian Research Council Future Fellow, University of Sydney, Australia*

Much of the international legal analysis of dealings in natural resources in Western Sahara has focused on its status as a Non-Self-Governing Territory, as well as the right of self-determination of the Sahrawi people. Surprisingly overlooked in the legal debates is a close examination of the application of the international law of occupation under international humanitarian law (IHL). This article considers whether and why Western Sahara is 'occupied territory' under IHL, discussing some of the unique peculiarities that complicate the legal answer. It then considers issues of state responsibility and individual criminal liability under international law for unlawful dealings with natural resources in Western Sahara by Moroccan and foreign companies.

## Introduction

Both the international community and scholars have paid surprisingly little attention to whether Western Sahara is occupied territory under international humanitarian law (IHL), as well to the legal implications of Moroccan occupation for dealings with natural resources there. This article explores these questions and argues that Western Sahara has met the legal criteria for occupation under IHL from early 1976 to the present (2015). It further argues that certain commercial dealings with Western Saharan resources, from phosphates to fisheries, are prohibited by the international law of occupation and may attract individual criminal responsibility as war crimes.

In its resolutions since the Moroccan invasion of Western Sahara in November 1975, the UN Security Council has not characterized Western Sahara as 'occupied' under IHL,[1] including in its extensive documentation on the UN Mission for the Referendum in Western Sahara since 1991.[2] While the General Assembly twice deplored Morocco's 'occupation' of Western Sahara (in resolutions in 1979 and 1980),[3] it has refrained from repeating that characterization in the 35 years since.[4] In its *Western Sahara Advisory Opinion* of 16 October 1975, the International Court of Justice (ICJ) did not consider question of occupation because at that time Morocco had not yet

---

1 Christine Chinkin, 'Laws of Occupation', paper presented at the Conference on Multilateralism and International Law with Western Sahara as a Case Study, South African Department of Foreign Affairs and the University of Pretoria, December 4–5, 2008 (Pretoria Conference), 198, 199–200.
2 MINURSO was created by UNSC resolution 690 (April 29, 1991). See UN Documents on MINURSO, Resolutions of the Security Council, http://www.un.org/en/peacekeeping/missions/minurso/resolutions.shtml.
3 UNGA resolutions 34/37 (November 21, 1979) and 35/19 (November 11, 1980).
4 Chinkin, 'Laws of Occupation', 200. See also Marcel Brus, 'The Legality of Exploring and Exploiting Mineral Resources in Western Sahara', in *International Law and the Question of Western Sahara*, ed. Karin Arts and Pedro Pinto Leite (Leiden: International Platform of Jurists for East Timor, 2007), 201, 206.

invaded Western Sahara. As one author observes, Morocco is 'rarely described as an occupying power',[5] although this may reflect political considerations as much as definitive legal positions or uncertainties. In the scholarly literature too, while it has occasionally been suggested that Western Sahara is occupied under IHL,[6] most sources do not provide detailed legal analyses.

One reason for the relative inattention to IHL in debates over the exploitation of natural resources in Western Sahara is that most of the focus has been on other legal paradigms. It is widely accepted that Western Sahara remains a Non-Self-Governing Territory under Chapter XI of the United Nations Charter.[7] As such, according to the then UN Legal Counsel, resource exploitation 'in disregard of the interests and wishes of the people of Western Sahara would be in violation of the international law principles applicable to mineral resource activities in Non-Self-Governing Territories'.[8] Such law encompasses the principles of self-determination and permanent sovereignty over natural resources.[9] Further, as recognized by the International Court of Justice (ICJ) in the *Western Sahara Advisory Opinion* (1975), Morocco does not possess sovereignty over Western Sahara, whose people enjoy a right of self-determination.[10] Such right encompasses a right of the Sahrawi people to freely pursue their 'economic ... development' and to, 'for their own ends, freely dispose of their natural wealth and resources' and to not 'be deprived of ... [their] own means of subsistence'.[11]

Such legal considerations apply to Morocco's exploitation, or licensing of foreign corporate exploitation, of resources such as oil, minerals and fisheries in Western Sahara. Much scholarly commentary has considered self-determination in Western Sahara,[12] including its political[13] and economic[14] dimensions. Further, as noted by the ICJ in the *Israeli Wall Advisory Opinion* (2004), other states owe an obligation *erga omnes* (that is, to all other states) not to recognize the illegal situation created by the denial of self-determination, not to render aid or assistance in maintaining such illegality, and to remove impediments to the realization of

---

5 Jacob Mundy, 'The Legal Status of Western Sahara and the Laws of War and Occupation', *Collaborations* no. 1790, Strategic Studies Group, June 22, 2007.

6 Chinkin, 'Laws of Occupation', 199–200; Stuart Casey-Maslen, ed., *The War Report 2012* (Oxford: Oxford University Press, 2013), 63–5; Vincent Chapaux, 'The Question of the European Community-Morocco Fisheries Agreement', in *International Law and the Question of Western Sahara* (see note 4), 217, 224–6; Hans-Peter Gasser, 'The Conflict in Western Sahara – An Unresolved Issued from the Decolonization Period', *Yearbook of International Humanitarian Law* (2002): 375, 379; Rule of Law in Armed Conflicts Project (RULAC), 'Morocco: Applicable International Law' (Geneva Academy of International Humanitarian Law and Human Rights), http://www.geneva-academy.ch/rulac-project/profile/pages/140/morocco/8/applicable-international-law.html; Stephanie Koury, 'The European Community and Member States' Duty of Non-Recognition under the EC-Morocco Association Agreement: State Responsibility and Customary International Law', in *International Law and the Question of Western Sahara* (see note 4), 172.

7 On which see Carlos Ruiz Miguel, 'Spain's Legal Obligations as Administering Power of Western Sahara', in Pretoria Conference (see note 1), 222.

8 Letter dated January 29, 2002 from the Under Secretary-General for Legal Affairs, the Legal Counsel, addressed to the President of the Security Council, UN Doc S/2002/161, February 12, 2002 (Corell Opinion), para. 25.

9 Ibid., paras. 9–14. See in particular UNGA resolutions: 1514 (XV) (December 14, 1960): Declaration of the Granting of Independence to Colonial Countries and Peoples; 1541 (XV) (December 14, 1960): Principles which should guide members in determining whether or not an obligation exists to transmit the information called for under Article 73e of the Charter; 1542 (XV) (December 15, 1960): Transmission of information under Article 73(e) of the Charter; 1803 (XVII): Permanent Sovereignty over Natural Resources (December 14, 1962).

10 *Western Sahara (Advisory Opinion)*, ICJ Rep 12, October 16, 1975, para. 70.

11 International Covenant on Economic, Social and Cultural Rights (adopted December 16, 1966, entered into force January 3, 1976, 993 UNTS 3), Article 1(1) and (2). See Ben Saul, David Kinley, and Jacqueline Mowbray, *The International Covenant on Economic, Social and Cultural Rights: Commentary, Cases and Materials* (Oxford: Oxford University Press, 2014), chapter 2.

12 See, e.g., Thomas Franck, 'The Stealing of the Sahara', *American Journal of International Law* 70 (1976): 694; Roger Clark, 'Western Sahara and the Right to Self-Determination', in *International Law and the Question of Western Sahara* (see note 4), 45; Catriona Drew, 'The Meaning of Self-Determination: "The Stealing of the Sahara" Redux?', in ibid., 87; Stephen Zunes, 'East Timor and Western Sahara: A Comparative Analysis of Prospects for Self-Determination', in ibid., 109.

13 See, e.g., Carlos Ruiz Miguel, 'The Self-Determination Referendum and the Role of Spain', in *International Law and the Question of Western Sahara* (see note 4), 305.

14 See, e.g., Koury, 'The European Community', 170–2, 176–8.

self-determination.[15] This has implications, for instance, for foreign states' dealings with Western Saharan resources,[16] including in relation to the licensing of foreign fishing in waters under Moroccan sovereignty or jurisdiction;[17] permitting national corporations to exploit resources; and allowing the import or export of goods related to such exploitation.

In principle, the abovementioned legal frameworks provide considerable normative constraints on Morocco's utilization of Western Saharan resources and substantial protections for the proprietary interests of the Sahrawi people. However, these paradigms – the law on Non-Self-Governing Territories, permanent sovereignty over natural resources, and self-determination – principally operate only on the legal plane of (inter-)state responsibility. That is, the states concerned owe obligations to one another and the breach of an international obligation attracts state responsibility and triggers obligations to make reparation (typically in the form of cessation, restitution and compensation, apology and guarantees of non-repetition). While self-determination is also a human right, the UN human rights treaty bodies have refused to admit individual petitions alleging violations of this collective right.[18]

The application of IHL to Western Sahara, and the classification of the conflict, deserve more detailed consideration, which this article undertakes. Under international law, the existence of an armed conflict or occupation is an objective matter which does not depend on the subjective determination of the political organs of the United Nations or individual states, though such assessments are relevant facts. This chapter explores whether Western Sahara is 'occupied' under IHL, then discusses the provisions of IHL governing natural resources in occupied territory. It finally considers the criminal law consequences of characterizing Western Sahara as occupied territory in the context of natural resource exploitation.

IHL makes a distinctive contribution to regulation of the Western Sahara dispute. Like the other legal frameworks already mentioned, the law of occupation establishes state responsibility for breaches of IHL obligations governing natural resources. Under common article 1 of the Geneva Conventions of 1949, states parties also have a duty to ensure respect for IHL[19] and to take measures to suppress breaches of IHL.[20] In addition, however, there exists individual criminal responsibility for war crimes under international law, whether as 'grave breaches' of certain IHL treaties, other violations of the laws and customs of war, or pursuant to specific international criminal law regimes such as the 1998 Rome Statute of the International Criminal Court (ICC).[21] Specifically, under the Geneva Conventions, states must establish criminal jurisdiction over war crimes (including extraterritorially), search for suspects, and prosecute or extradite them.[22] Further, because of such treaty-based quasi-universal jurisdiction under the Geneva Conventions and the 1998 Rome Statute of the ICC, many states have enacted domestic legislation which enables them to prosecute war criminals in domestic courts. In addition, some national laws

---

15   *Legal Consequences of the Construction of a Wall in the Occupied Palestinian Territory* (2004) ICJ Rep 136 (*Israel Wall Advisory Opinion* (2004)), paras. 154–9 and 163. Cf. *Portugal v Australia* (1995) ICJ Rep 90, paras. 31–2.

16   See generally New York City Bar (Committee on United Nations), Report on Legal Issues Involved in the Western Sahara Dispute: Use of Natural Resources, April 2011; Erik Hagen, 'The Role of Natural Resources in the Western Saharan Conflict, and the Interests Involved', Pretoria Conference (see note 1), 292.

17   See, e.g., Koury, 'The European Community', 180–97.

18   *Chief Bernard Ominayak and Lubicon Lake Band v Canada*, UN Human Rights Committee Communication No. 167/1984, UN Doc. CCPR/C/38/D/167/1984 (March 26, 1990), para. 13.3.

19   See also *Israel Wall Advisory Opinion* (2004), para. 163(D).

20   See, e.g., Geneva Convention IV Relative to the Protection of Civilian Persons in Time of War (adopted August 12, 1949, entered into force October 21, 1950) (Fourth Geneva Convention 1949), Article 146(3).

21   Respectively: see, e.g., Fourth Geneva Convention 1949, ibid., Article 147; ICRC, *Customary International Humanitarian Law* (Cambridge: Cambridge University Press, 2005) (ICRC Customary IHL Study), Rules 151 (individual criminal responsibility) and 156 (war crimes); and Rome Statute of the International Criminal Court (adopted July 17, 1998, entered into force July 1, 2002), 2187 UNTS 3, Article 8 (war crimes). On the technical distinction between 'grave breaches' and war crimes (which is not the subject of the present article), see Marko Öberg, 'The Absorption of Grave Breaches into War Crimes Law', *International Review of the Red Cross* 91 (2009): 163.

22   See, e.g., Fourth Geneva Convention 1949, Article 146(1)–(2).

provide for corporate criminal liability for war crimes. Accordingly, if certain dealings with Western Saharan natural resources are contrary to the international law of occupation under IHL, the individuals and companies involved not only bear direct criminal responsibility under international law, but may be liable to prosecution in national courts. Further, pursuant to international obligations of cooperation, other states may be required to assist in the investigation and extradition of suspects.

## Classification of armed conflict: is Western Sahara 'occupied territory'?

Under common article 2 of the 1949 Geneva Conventions, an international armed conflict can arise in two relevant situations – first, where there are armed hostilities between two or more states, including through the use of irregular forces 'belonging' to a state;[23] and secondly, where one state partially or totally occupies the territory of another state, 'even if the said occupation meets with no armed resistance'.[24] A territory is considered 'occupied' under IHL where the local authority is displaced and 'when it is actually placed under the authority of the hostile army',[25] and regardless of whether underlying sovereign title to the territory is contested.[26]

An international conflict can also arise between national liberation or self-determination movement and a state party under Additional Protocol I of 1977, which alters the pre-existing characterization of such conflicts as non-international.[27] Morocco ratified Protocol I in 2011, long after signing it 1977. In June 2015 Polisario deposited a unilateral declaration of adherence to the Geneva Conventions and Protocol I under the procedure provided for in article 96(3) of Protocol I. The depository state, Switzerland, duly notified the declaration to states parties, formally accepting the first ever article 96(3) declaration. A non-international armed conflict exists under common article 3 of the 1949 Geneva Conventions where there is sufficiently intense armed violence between a state and an organized non-state armed group, or between two or more organized groups.[28]

The violence that engulfed Western Sahara in 1975 was complex because it involved an array of state and non-state armed actors at varying levels of intensity, in a rapidly changing security environment, and affected by legally significant intervening events. This article focuses only on whether Western Sahara is occupied territory as a result of Morocco gaining control of the territory, commencing in late November 1975. It should be mentioned, however, that it is likely that there were a series of parallel armed conflicts of different kinds during this period – a non-international armed conflict between Spain and Polisario in 1974–75; a brief international armed conflict between Spain and Morocco in 1975, constituted by a number of armed engagements between regular forces;[29] a non-international conflict between Polisario and Mauritania from 1975 to 1979, in both Western Saharan and Mauritanian territory;[30] and a brief and low-intensity international conflict between

---

23 Geneva Conventions I–IV 1949, common Article 2(1).
24 Ibid., common Article 2(2).
25 Hague Regulations Respecting the Laws and Customs of War on Land (adopted October 18, 1907, entered into force January 26, 1910) (Hague Regulations 1907), Article 42.
26 *Israel Wall Advisory Opinion* (2004), para. 95.
27 Protocol I Additional to the Geneva Conventions of August 12, 1949 and Relating to the Protection of Victims of International Armed Conflicts (adopted June 8, 1977, entered into force December 7, 1978), 1125 UNTS 3 (Additional Protocol I 1977), Article 1(4).
28 *Prosecutor v Tadic (Interlocutory Appeal on Jurisdiction)*, ICTY, IT-94-1, October 2, 1995, para. 70; *Prosecutor v Limaj et al.*, ICTY, IT-03-66-T, November 30, 2005, para. 83; *Prosecutor v Boskoski*, ICTY, IT-04-82-T, July 10, 2008.
29 *Keesings Contemporary Archives* (1975), vol. XXI, November 3–9, 1975, 27416; ibid., 27418; see also Stephen Zunes and Jacob Mundy, *Western Sahara: War, Nationalism and Conflict Irresolution* (Syracuse, NY: Syracuse University Press, 2010), 4.
30 See Tony Hodges, *Western Sahara: Roots of A Desert War* (Westport, CT: Lawrence Hill, 1983), 230–1; *Keesings Contemporary Archives* (1976), vol. XXII, February 13, 1976, 27579; ibid., May 28, 1976, 27746; Zunes and Mundy, *Western Sahara*, 11–12; John Mercer, *The Sahrawis of Western Sahara*, Minority Rights Group Report

Morocco and Algeria in 1976.[31] The principal active hostilities, between Polisario and Morocco from 1975 to the present, have probably constituted a non-international conflict between a state and a non-state actor, taking place in occupied territory but legally distinct from international conflict.[32] After Morocco's ratification of Protocol I in 2011, those hostilities were transformed from a non-international conflict into an international conflict, alongside the continuing international conflict constituted by the persisting occupation of Spanish Sahara since 1975.

## International armed conflict by occupation: Morocco in Spanish Sahara 1975–present – timeline of legally significant events

After the ICJ delivered its Western Sahara *Advisory Opinion* on 16 October 1975, Morocco announced a peaceful 'Green March' of 350,000 Moroccans into Spanish Sahara to claim the territory for Morocco. Spain told the Security Council on 20 October 1975 that such an 'invasion' would threaten international peace and security, and on 2 November 1975 warned in the Council that Spain would 'repel it with all means at her disposal, including use of armed force'.[33] Algeria also protested. The UN intensified its diplomatic efforts. Spain commenced negotiations with Morocco, Mauritania, Algeria and Polisario.[34]

On 25 October, Spain and Morocco reached a 'tacit agreement' to permit the marchers to enter Spanish Sahara up to a limited distance and for a brief period,[35] seemingly to avert a military confrontation with Moroccan civilians (and their military backers). On 28 October 1975, Spain imposed a curfew on the territory, and then dismissed its Sahrawi soldiers, evacuated European civilians, withdrew its troops to a fortified 'dissuasion line' some miles from the Moroccan border, and mobilized nearby warships, aircraft and reserve troops.[36] Moroccan and Algerian forces also mobilized on their borders.

Spanish concessions to Moroccan demands had, however, gone further than was evident from Spain's public position. By 4 November, the essence of a trilateral agreement between Spain, Morocco and Mauritania had been agreed, to transfer sovereignty and administration to the latter states.[37] On 5 November, Morocco gave an ultimatum to Spain to immediately negotiate to cede Spanish Sahara to Morocco and Mauritania or Morocco's marchers would be ordered to proceed to the dissuasion line, and if Spain attempted to stop them, Morocco would militarily intervene.[38] The marchers entered Spanish Sahara on 6 November 1975 and the Security Council deplored the march that day and called for its withdrawal.[39] The marchers' numbers swelled until 9 November, when Morocco called off the march.[40] Spain's Cabinet had decided on 8 November to cede the territory without a referendum.[41] All of the marchers were consequently withdrawn from Western Sahara by 13 November.[42]

---

no. 40 (1979), 13; Letter dated August 18, 1976 from the Permanent Representative of Mauritania to the United Nations addressed to the Secretary General, UN Doc S/2002/161 (February 12, 2002).

31  *Keesings Contemporary Archives* (1976), vol. XXII, 28 May 1976, 27746; ibid., 27748.
32  See, e.g. *Hamdan v Rumsfeld*, US Supreme Court, 548 US (2006), 126 S Ct 2749 (on the interpretation of common Article 3 of the Geneva Conventions). Cf. the approach taken in *Public Committee against Torture in Israel v Government of Israel*, Supreme Court of Israel, HCJ 769/02, December 11, 2005, paras. 18, 21 (all hostilities in occupied territory are part of the international conflict, even if involving non-state actors).
33  *Keesings Contemporary Archives* (1976), vol. XXII, February 13, 1976, 27575.
34  *Keesings Contemporary Archives* (1975), vol. XXI, November 3–9, 1975, 27413.
35  Hodges, *Western Sahara*, 216–17.
36  *Keesings Contemporary Archives* (1976), vol. XXII, February 13, 1976, 27576.
37  Hodges, *Western Sahara*, 220.
38  Ibid., 222.
39  UNSC resolution 380 (November 6, 1975).
40  *Keesings Contemporary Archives* (1976), vol. XXII, February 13, 1976, 27576.
41  Hodges, *Western Sahara*, 222.
42  Ibid., 223.

Talks in Madrid from 11 November 1975 led to the conclusion, on 14 November 1975, of the tripartite Madrid Agreement between Spain, Morocco and Mauritania. Spain agreed to decolonize Western Sahara and end its responsibilities and powers as administering power; establish a provisional administration involving Morocco and Mauritania, in cooperation with the Spanish Sahara General Assembly of Sahrawi representatives (the *Yemaá*); appoint two assistant governors from Morocco and Mauritania; and end its presence by 28 February 1976. While the Agreement provided that '[t]he views of the inhabitants of the Sahara as expressed through the *Yemaá* shall be respected', and for 'respect for the principles of the UN Charter', there was no provision for a referendum. Side agreements preserved certain Spanish economic interests, including fishing rights, a 35% share in the Bou Craa phosphate mine, and compensation for its citizens.[43] The November talks had involved the Director General of the Office chérifien des phosphates (OCP), the Moroccan state phosphate company.[44] The Madrid Agreement reflected a secret arrangement between Morocco and Mauritania in October 1974 to partition Spanish Sahara and share its economic exploitation.[45] Morocco and Mauritania agreed on the actual partition of the territory on 14 April 1976.

Morocco ordered the marchers to return home from the border on 18 November 1975, after the Spanish Parliament approved a decolonization law giving effect to the Madrid Agreement.[46] On 18 November Spain informed the UN Secretary General of its intention to terminate its presence in Western Sahara by 28 February 1976.[47] On the same day, Polisario described these events to the UN decolonization committee as a 'Moroccan aggression' and 'military invasion'.[48] The Moroccan and Mauritanian assistant governors were appointed on 22–23 November and by 1 December 'military and civilian officials from both countries had taken over most public services and government posts in the territory'.[49] From 1 January 1976, residents ceased to be Spanish citizens and Morocco was already issuing passports and identity cards, and appointing regional administrators.

As Spanish administrative and military personnel withdrew, Moroccan military forces rapidly entered to secure the territory. In fact, Spanish forces had begun withdrawing from outer regions by 30 October 1975, with Polisario taking over many posts.[50] On 31 October, Moroccan forces secretly entered Spanish Sahara to take over three of the outposts (Jdiriya, Haousa and Farsia) evacuated by Spanish troops.[51] By 13 November – the day before the Madrid Agreement – Moroccan forces had reached Tifariti, near the Mauritanian border.[52]

After the Madrid Agreement purported to legalize Morocco's presence, hundreds of advance Moroccan troops entered the administrative capital El Aaiún on 25 November with Moroccan officials.[53] Around 5000 more troops entered El Aaiún on 11 December, with Spanish forces leaving on 20 December, and Moroccan forces assuming control over airfields and military bases by 28 December. Moroccan forces also took over the second largest town, Smara, on 27 November. The Bou Craa phosphate mine was under Moroccan control by late December. Moroccan forces spread throughout the territory and reached Villa Cisneros (now Dakhla) in the south by 11 January 1976, joined by Mauritanian troops; and, in the north-east, reached Tifariti,

---

43    Ibid., 224. By February 7, 1976 Spain had sold 65% of Fosbucraa to Morocco, retaining 35%; the remaining 35% was divested in 2003.
44    *Keesings Contemporary Archives* (1976), vol. XXII, February 13, 1976, 27577.
45    *Keesings Contemporary Archives* (1975), vol. XXI, November 3–9, 1975, 27417.
46    *Keesings Contemporary Archives* (1976), vol. XXII, February 13, 1976, 27577.
47    UN Doc. S/11880 (November 19, 1975).
48    *Keesings Contemporary Archives* (1976), vol. XXII, February 13, 1976, 27577.
49    Ibid., 27577.
50    Hodges, *Western Sahara*, 219.
51    Ibid., 220.
52    Ibid., 223.
53    Ibid., 229.

Bir Lehlou and Mahabes in the first weeks of February.[54] Polisario held on to some smaller settlements for some months, with heavy fighting,[55] but by 19 April 1976 Morocco had taken all of the major former Spanish settlements and outposts.[56] The International Committee of the Red Cross (ICRC) reported 40,000 Sahrawis displaced by early January 1976 and most Sahrawis had fled by mid-1976.[57] Today Morocco controls (with over 100,000 troops)[58] around 80% of Spanish Sahara, but for the so-called 'liberated territories' east of the fortified military sand wall (the 'berm') constructed by Morocco from 1980. It has extended its control through development plans, the sedentarization and 'modernization' of the nomadic population, the exploitation of resources,[59] and mass Moroccan migration.

The last Spanish troops departed around 8–12 January 1976[60] and the remnants of the Spanish administration by 26 February. Spain announced to the UN on 26 February that its participation in the temporary administration established under the Madrid Agreement had immediately ceased and that it 'considers itself henceforth exempt from any responsibility of an international nature in connection with the administration of the said Territory'.[61] It added, however, that '[t]he decolonization of Western Sahara will reach its climax when the views of the Saharan population have been validly expressed'. That caveat was a response to the unanimous vote by the Sahrawi *Yemaá*, originally appointed by the Spanish authorities and identified as expressing the 'views' of Sahrawis under the Madrid Agreement, to ratify the Agreement on 26 February 1976. Only 57 of 102 members of the *Yemaá* attended,[62] the rest having joined Polisario or fled to Algeria.[63] Polisario claimed that the *Yemaá* had dissolved itself on 28 November 1975, at a meeting attended by 67 members,[64] and had regarded the *Yemaá* as elderly, conservative colonial collaborators not representative of all Sahrawis.[65]

The UN similarly did not regard the above process as an exercise of self-determination. UN General Assembly resolution 3458A of 10 December 1975, adopted by 88 votes to none, with 41 abstentions, provided that Spain as administering power was to organize the exercise of self-determination in Spanish Sahara. On the same day, resolution 3458B, supported by Morocco, and with much less support – 56 votes in favour to 42 against, with 34 abstentions – noted the Madrid Agreement and provided that the interim administration was to ensure self-determination through free consultations assisted by a UN representative, including by consulting 'all the Saharan population originating in the territory'. The UN representative who visited Western Sahara in early February 1976 concluded that genuine consultation was impossible because of the military presence, political oppression, displacement and conflict.[66] On 25–26 September 1976, both Spain and UN Secretary General Waldheim stated that self-determination had not been exercised in the required manner.[67]

---

54  Ibid., 232.
55  Ibid., 229.
56  Ibid., 238.
57  Ibid., 229.
58  Eyal Benvenisti, *The International Law of Occupation* (Princeton: Princeton University Press, 2004), 152.
59  David Price, *The Western Sahara*, The Washington Papers, vol. VII (Sage Publications, 1979), 38–41.
60  *Keesings Contemporary Archives* (1976), vol. XXII, February 13, 1976, 27578; Hodges, *Western Sahara*, 230.
61  Letter dated February 26, 1976 from Spain's Permanent Representative to the United Nations addressed to the UN Secretary General, UN Doc. S/11997.
62  Hodges, *Western Sahara*, 237.
63  *Keesings Contemporary Archives* (1976), vol. XXII, May 28, 1976, 27747.
64  Mercer, *The Sahrawis of Western Sahara*, 10.
65  Hodges, *Western Sahara*, 224.
66  Ibid., 236.
67  Ibid., 237.

## *The legal test for belligerent occupation*

In assessing whether Western Sahara is occupied territory under IHL, it is clear that Morocco has actual[68] or effective governmental and administrative control over most of Western Sahara, secured by the presence of its military forces. Having successfully substituted its authority for that of Spain by early 1976, the decisive legal question is whether Morocco *forcibly* displaced the Spanish authorities in the course of the events of 1975–76 described above. As mentioned earlier, IHL envisages that occupation can arise by a classic invasion involving inter-state hostilities, or by 'bloodless occupation' of foreign territory involving no actual hostilities. As noted earlier, there were a handful of minor skirmishes between Spanish and Moroccan forces in 1975, and large-scale civilian penetration of Spanish Saharan borders in the Green March of November 1975, but no active armed hostilities after the Madrid Agreement of November 1975. Western Sahara was accordingly not occupied in this orthodox sense under article 2(1) of the Geneva Conventions.

The situation is arguably more assimilable to a so-called 'bloodless invasion' under article 2(2) of the Geneva Conventions, by which Morocco occupied Spanish Saharan territory without active hostilities against Spain. Technically the lack of *consent* of the legitimate authority to the presence of foreign forces is not an explicit precondition for the existence of an occupation under IHL treaties. It is, however, widely accepted that the absence of consent is 'a central element and a precondition for establishing occupation'.[69] In doctrine and practice, a state that validly consents to the presence of foreign troops is not considered 'occupied'. Consent must be 'genuine, valid and explicit', not 'engineered' (as in the cases of the United States invasion of Panama in 1989 or the Soviet Union's occupation of Czechoslovakia in 1968) or coerced (as in the cases of Haiti in 1994 and the Indonesian invasion of East Timor in 1975).[70] Coercion may be usefully articulated in the IHL context by reference to broader international law,[71] particularly the law on treaties. Article 52 of the Vienna Convention on the Law of Treaties 1969 (VCLT) provides that a treaty is void for 'coercion' 'if its conclusion has been procured by the threat or use of force in violation of' the UN Charter.[72] Article 52 reflects customary international law.[73] In addition, a treaty is void under article 53 of the VCLT 'if, at the time of its conclusion, it conflicts with a peremptory norm [*jus cogens*] of general international law'.[74] The prohibition on the use of force, the related prohibition on the acquisition of title to territory by force, and self-determination are three potentially relevant *jus cogens* principles.[75]

In the light of the factual situation leading up to and including the Madrid Agreement, the critical question is whether Spain validly consented to Morocco and Mauritania's entry, so as to preclude the existence of an occupation under IHL, or whether Spain's consent was invalidated by coercive threats of, or the use of, force, thus resulting in a 'bloodless' occupation. There is a closely related question of whether Spain's apparent consent to the entry of Morocco and

---

68  *Armed Activities on the Territory of the Congo* (*Democratic Republic of the Congo v Uganda*), ICJ Judgment, December 19, 2005 (*Congo v Uganda* (2005)), para. 173.

69  ICRC, 'Occupation and Other Forms of Administration of Foreign Territory', Expert Meeting, March 2012, 21.

70  Ibid. On Portuguese Timor, see Ben Saul, 'Prosecuting War Crimes at Balibo under Australian Law: The Killing of Five Journalists in East Timor by Indonesia', *Sydney Law Review* 31 (2009): 3.

71  ICRC, 'Occupation and Other Forms of Administration of Foreign Territory'.

72  Vienna Convention on the Law of Treaties (adopted May 23, 1969, entered into force January 27, 1980) (VCLT 1969), Article 52.

73  *Dubai–Sharjah Border Arbitration,* Award, October 19, 1981, *International Law Reports* 91 (1981): 543, 569.

74  VCLT 1969, Article 53 defines a peremptory norm as 'a norm accepted and recognized by the international community of States as a whole as a norm from which no derogation is permitted and which can be modified only by a subsequent norm of general international law having the same character'.

75  The ICJ described self-determination as an obligation *erga omnes* (*Israeli Wall Advisory Opinion* (2004), para. 88; *East Timor v Portugal* (1995) ICJ Rep 102, para. 29) but did not characterize it as *jus cogens*.

Mauritania is alternatively or additionally invalid because it conflicts with the peremptory norms on the prohibition on the use of force, the non-acquisition of title to territory by force, and self-determination. The invalidation of Spain's consent on this basis would also mean that Moroccan and Mauritanian forces bloodlessly occupied Spanish territory under IHL, notwithstanding Spain's purported agreement.

## Lack of valid consent: coercion

Spain's exit from Western Sahara in 1975–76 was motivated by a number of considerations. Spain had been on the way out since 1963, having committed to decolonization in principle by listing Western Sahara as a non-self-governing territory in that year.[76] Regularly from 1966 to 1973, the UN General Assembly had called on Spain to hold a referendum under UN auspices to enable the indigenous population to freely exercise self-determination.[77] Pressure from Sahrawi liberation movements grew from 1969, starting with demonstrations and progressing to violent resistance by Polisario and the Front de Libération et de l'Unité (FLU) from 1973.

Such pressures hastened Spain to announce, in August 1974,[78] a procedure for the exercise of Sahrawi self-determination: a referendum in the first half of 1975, postponed because of the request made of the ICJ in December 1974, resulting in the *Advisory Opinion* of 16 October 1975. As mentioned earlier, Moroccan military incursions and threats intensified throughout 1975, culminating in the civilian Green March of November 1975. In the midst of Morocco's provocations, a domestic political crisis threw Spanish policy into disarray, with General Franco becoming suddenly ill on 17 October and dying on 20 November. Spain also faced Basque separatism at home.[79] Spain abandoned its referendum proposal and agreed to the tripartite interim administration under the Madrid Agreement on 14 November 1975, leaving the territory entirely by 26 February 1976.

Under article 52 of the VCLT, a treaty is void due to coercion if it is 'procured' by the unlawful threat or use of force. The plain meaning of 'procure' is '[t]o obtain; to bring about'.[80] In the simplest case, coercion may be the *sole* reason a state consented to a treaty. However, in other cases, as in Spanish Sahara, consent may have been influenced by a combination of factors of varying weight in the decision-making process. The text of article 52, and the International Law Commission (ILC) Commentary on the draft on which it was based,[81] gives little guidance on when a treaty will be considered 'procured' by coercion where multiple motives drive a state's consent. At a minimum the term 'procured' suggests some 'causal link' is required, but the drafting record evidences little attention to this issue.[82] In principle, a spectrum can be envisaged: at one end, coercion might be the *sole* reason for consent; in the upper middle of the spectrum, it could be a dominant influence; at the lower middle, it could be a substantial or significant

---

76 By transmitting information under Article 73e of the UN Charter: see UN Doc. A/5446/Rev.1, annex 1. See also UNGA resolutions 2072 (December 17, 1965); 229 (December 20, 1966); 2354 (December 19, 1967); 2428 (December 27, 1968); 2591 (December 16, 1969); 2711 (December 14, 1970); 2983 (December 14, 1972); 3162 (December 14, 1973); and Miguel, 'Spain's Legal Obligations', 223, 237.

77 UNGA resolutions 2229 (XXI) (December 20, 1966); 2354 (XXII) (December 19, 1967); 2428 (XXIII) (December 18, 1968); 2591 (XXIV) (December 16, 1979); 2711 (XXV) (December 14, 1970); 2938 (XXVII) (December 14, 1972); 3162 (XXVIII) (December 14, 1973).

78 Letter dated August 20, 1974 from the Permanent Representative of Spain to the United Nations to the Secretary-General, UN Doc. A/9714.

79 Hodges, *Western Sahara*, 215.

80 Oxford English Dictionary, 'procure', online.

81 International Law Commission, Draft Articles on the Law of Treaties with Commentaries (1966) II Yearbook of the International Law Commission 187 (ILC Commentary), 247.

82 Olivier Corten, 'Article 52', in *The Vienna Conventions on the Law of Treaties: A Commentary*, vol. II, ed. Olivier Corten and Pierre Klein (Oxford: Oxford University Press, 2011), 1201, 1211.

factor, even if not dominant; and at the bottom end, coercion might simply be one of many factors, and not necessarily especially important. The first three approaches are consistent with the 'but for' test often deployed in various domestic legal contexts, namely, 'but for' the coercion, consent to a treaty, at the time of its conclusion, would not have been given.

Relevant international jurisprudence is sparse. In the *Fisheries Jurisdiction* case, the ICJ held briefly that a treaty 'concluded under' the threat or use of force is void, but on the facts of that case the Court found that the agreements 'were freely negotiated by the interested parties on the basis of perfect equality and freedom of decision on both sides'.[83] After the Second World War a Dutch national court took the view that coercion required that the victim state 'could not escape' the effects of coercion;[84] a similar approach is reflected in the *Aminoil Arbitration* ('the absence of any other possible course')[85] and was favoured by the jurist Hersch Lauterpacht ('unable to resist').[86] However, the manifest nature of coercion in some of these cases arguably accounts for the restrictive approaches adopted.[87] A more liberal view is that a treaty is procured by coercion where it would not have been entered into in the absence of the coercion.[88] On this view, coercion may be 'a decisive influence' but it need not entail a 'total absence of choice', or be the exclusive or essential reason.[89]

The latter approach is also consistent with developments in national laws. Domestic jurisprudence is of qualified utility in that treaties are not assimilable to contracts under domestic law and are governed by international not domestic law. Domestic contract law also varies between civil and common law states on basic matters, including the legal significance and effects of coercion or duress, such as whether a contract thus affected is void or voidable at the election of a party. Further, coercion in those contexts is typically unlike the threat or use of force in international relations, although it may involve threats to the person. It is also inapposite to simply transpose terminology from other legal contexts to interpret what it means to 'procure' a treaty by coercion, such as criminal law concepts of complicity in the procuring of offences (which can entail stricter notions of causation).[90]

Comparable domestic principles may nonetheless be of some assistance, and particularly if they are sufficiently widespread to reflect general principles of (international) law.[91] In the common law of contract, for instance, a contract is affected by duress (including threats to life) where the agreement to contract was induced by an illegitimate threat amounting to compulsion.[92] Duress may be crystallized by a series of threats.[93] Importantly, the case law establishes that the pressure need not be the sole or even principal cause of the decision to contract.[94] It is sufficient for the duress to be *an* inducement to contract,[95] in part because 'any degree' of duress taints the

---

83   *Fisheries Jurisdiction (Federal Republic of Germany v Iceland)*, Judgment of February 2, 1973, *ICJ Reports* (1973) 49, at 59, para. 24.

84   *Amato Narodni Podnik v Julius Keilwerth Musikinstrumentenfabrik*, District Court of The Hague, December 31, 1955–November 11, 1956, *International Law Reports* 24 (1957): 437 (concerning the 1938 Munich Agreements and the German–Czechoslovak Nationality Treaty).

85   *Kuwait v The American Independent Oil Company (Aminoil)*, Arbitral Award, March 24, 1982, para. 43.

86   Cited in Corten, 'Article 52', 1212.

87   Ibid., 1213.

88   Ibid.

89   Ibid.

90   See, e.g., *Attorney-General's Reference (No. 1 of 1975)* [1975] 2 All ER 684 at 686, at 687.

91   Pursuant to Article 38(1)(c) of the Statute of the International Court of Justice, annexed to the Charter of the United Nations 1945.

92   John Carter, 'Chapter 23: Duress', in *Carter on Contract* (LexisNexis, Service 40: February 2015), database.

93   *Ampol Ltd v Caltex Oil (Australia) Pty Ltd* (unreported, NSW SC, Foster J, 82/9033, December 22, 1982).

94   See e.g. *Barton v Armstrong* [1976] AC 104; [1973] 2 NSWLR 598, PC; *Crescendo Management Pty Ltd v Westpac Banking Corp* (1988) 19 NSWLR 40 at 45 per McHugh JA; *Vantage Navigation Corp v Suhail and Saud Bahwan Building Materials LLC (The Alev)* [1989] 1 Lloyd's Rep 138, Hobhouse J; *Hawker Pacific Pty Ltd v Helicopter Charter Pty Ltd* (1991) 22 NSWLR 298, CA.

95   Carter, 'Chapter 23: Duress', [23-030] (citing *Crescendo Management Pty Ltd v Westpac Banking Corp* (1988) 19 NSWLR 40, CA).

contract's foundation.[96] Further, the common law cases establish that the victim need not be so 'overborne' by duress as to deprive him or her of any free will and thereby vitiate consent.[97] Rather, it is recognized that the victim still exercises a choice, from amongst alternatives, to knowingly enter into the contract, even if the alternatives are constrained or costly (and even involve death).[98] Duress thus constitutes an improper pressure rather than one which vitiates consent.[99] The focus is therefore on the quality of consent[100] rather than if it was voluntary, wilful, compelled, coerced and the like.

The domestic principles provide useful analogies in the interpretation of article 52 of the VCLT. They support an interpretation to the effect that a treaty may be 'procured' by coercion where the threat or use of force induces a state to agree to the treaty, even if the coercion is not the sole or even the dominant cause of the state giving its consent. Such an approach is consistent with the language of article 52, which does not provide that coercion must be 'exclusively', 'solely', 'predominantly' or 'substantially' procured by force; rather, coercion is *a* reason the treaty was procured. This approach is also consistent with the object and purpose of the strict prohibition on the threat or use of force under the UN Charter to which article 52 is pegged. A breach of the prohibition on the threat or use of force is recognized as one of the most fundamental wrongs in the international legal order. As such, a treaty tainted by it to *any extent* deserves to be treated as void.

Applying this interpretive approach, it is strongly arguable that Spain would not have entered into the Madrid Agreement – at that time (14 November), and on those terms – but for the coercion arising from a series of Moroccan threats and use of force in the lead-up to it. Morocco had sponsored the FLU attacks on Spanish Sahara since 1973. There was a build-up of 25,000 Moroccan troops on the border by May 1975, with no apparent defensive purpose given Spain's lack of aggressive intent. This was followed by border skirmishes in May 1975. Regular Moroccan forces mounted a number of incursions and attacks inside Spanish Sahara in June, July and August 1975. On 16 October 1975, Morocco announced that it would take over Spanish Sahara through a civilian Green March and later warned Spain that attempts to stop it would provoke a military response. The march took place from 6 to 13 November 1975, rendering Spain's position untenable. Already by 31 October, Moroccan forces were secretly occupying evacuated Spanish outposts.

The subjective intention of the coercive state is an important consideration.[101] Throughout this period Morocco had made it clear to Spain that it regarded Spanish Sahara as its own, and that it was prepared to take it forcibly; and Spain protested such threats of aggression, including to the Security Council. Further, as is required under article 52, Morocco's threats and uses of force were internationally unlawful, being neither in self-defence nor authorized by the Security Council, and being inconsistent with Spanish sovereignty and territorial integrity, and the right of self-determination of the Sahrawi people.

That Spanish forces could have ably resisted a Moroccan invasion if ordered to do so – Spain had superior military forces[102] – is not relevant; Spain, faced with the more harmful alternative of full-scale hostilities against Morocco, chose to de-escalate and not defend its territory. There are other examples of such 'bloodless invasions' procured by coerced agreements,

---

96  *Barton v Armstrong*, citing *Reynell v Sprye* (1852) 1 De GM & G 660 at 708.
97  As suggested in earlier cases: Carter, 'Chapter 23: Duress', [23-020].
98  Ibid. [23-020] (citing, among others, *Crescendo Management Pty Ltd v Westpac Banking Corp* (1988) 19 NSWLR 40, 45 per McHugh JA, CA).
99  Carter, 'Chapter 23: Duress', [23-020].
100  Ibid., [23-001] (citing, among others, *Commercial Bank of Australia Ltd v Amadio* (1983) 151 CLR 447, 474 per Deane J (Wilson J agreeing)).
101  Corten, 'Article 52', 1213.
102  Hodges, *Western Sahara*, 215.

such as Latvia's consent to Soviet occupation in 1940,[103] Czechoslovakian consent to Soviet forces in 1968,[104] or France's consent to a peace treaty with Thailand in 1941 in the face of Japanese threats.[105]

That Spain also secured economic concessions in the Madrid Agreement does not obviate the coercion; Spain still lost most, just not all, of its prior economic possessions, and an imbalance of benefits under a treaty can objectively indicate coercion.[106] Further, whereas the Security Council had authorized force in relation to a treaty imposed on Haiti under the threat of US military force in 1994,[107] there was no Council authorization in relation to Spanish Sahara.[108]

In sum, Morocco's actual and threatened use of force is a critical factor explaining how 'Spanish policy had turned full circle'[109] within a single month in late 1975 – from staunchly supporting Sahrawi self-determination and a referendum, and resolutely opposing Moroccan ambitions (with the Spanish military especially keen to preserve its honour), to transferring its administration to Morocco and Mauritania and rapidly quitting the territory. Other factors were certainly influential, such as the Sahrawi insurgency, Franco's illness and Spain's political transition. The Madrid Agreement also provided Spain with a quick exit from its decolonization responsibilities and the residual economic concessions softened the blow. But the Agreement would not have been concluded on that date, on those terms, but for Moroccan aggression. Moroccan coercion was more than a mere influence on Spain's consent; it was a decisive factor, even if it was not the sole or essential reason, or Spain could have resisted at considerable cost.

## Lack of valid consent: jus cogens

A treaty is also void if, at the time of its conclusion, it conflicts with a peremptory norm. In terms, the Madrid Agreement did not authorize the unlawful use of force by Morocco or Mauritania against Spain contrary to the UN Charter. As discussed above, Morocco used and threatened force against Spain to coerce it into concluding the Agreement, obviating the need for further force, and the Agreement does not make provision for the military enforcement of its terms against Spain in the event of a breach of its obligations. Nor did the Agreement expressly authorize the forcible acquisition of sovereign title to territory; rather, the Agreement created a temporary administration by Morocco and Mauritania, in collaboration with the *Yemaá*, respecting the views of the Saharan population (through the *Yemaá*), and 'with due respect for the principles of the Charter of the United Nations, and as the best possible contribution to the maintenance of international peace and security'. Morocco's annexation of the territory was subsequent to the Agreement, even if Spain must have known that annexation was Morocco's aim, and that Morocco was contracting in bad faith.

103 *Kariņš and Others v Parliament of Latvia and Cabinet of Ministers of Latvia,* Latvian Constitutional Court, Case No. 2007-10-0102, November 29, 2007.

104 Treaty on the Temporary Sojourn of Soviet Forces in the Territory of the Czechoslovak Socialist Republic (adopted 16 October 1968).

105 Peace Convention between France and Thailand (adopted May 9, 1941).

106 Corten, 'Article 52', 1213.

107 Meinhard Schröder, 'Treaties, Validity', *Max Planck Encyclopedia of Public International Law*, online, last updated December 2010 (on the Agreement concerning the restoration of the Government of President Aristide (adopted September 18, 1994)).

108 On whether the UNSC can lawfully ratify post facto an agreement procured by coercion, see Serena Forlati, 'Coercion as a Ground Affecting the Validity of Peace Treaties', in *The Law of Treaties Beyond the Vienna Convention*, ed. Enzo Cannizzaro (Oxford: Oxford University Press, 2011), 320; and Jochen Frowein and Nico Krisch, 'Introduction to Chapter VII', in *The Charter of the United Nations: A Commentary*, ed. Bruno Simma. 2nd ed. (Oxford: Oxford University Press, 2002), 701, 711.

109 Hodges, *Western Sahara*, 223.

The Madrid Agreement is void for the different reasons that it conflicts with the peremptory norm of self-determination. Critically, the Agreement makes no provision for a referendum. Regularly from 1966 to 1973, the UN General Assembly had called on Spain to hold a referendum under UN auspices as the proper procedure to enable the indigenous population to freely exercise self-determination.[110] Self-determination thus required a free expression of the will of all Sahrawis, not only the *Yemaá*; and, in any event, there were serious doubts about both the representativeness, and ongoing capacity to function with all members, of the *Yemaá* during the relevant period.

Further, in the decolonization process Spain had responsibilities as the administering power of a Non-Self-Governing Territory to enable the exercise of Sahrawi self-determination. In the opinion of then UN Legal Counsel Hans Corell, the Madrid Agreement did not affect the international status of Western Sahara as a Non-Self-Governing Territory, or 'confer upon any of the signatories the status of administering Power, a status which Spain alone could not have unilaterally transferred'.[111] As a result, the Agreement conflicts with Sahrawi self-determination because it neither provides for a referendum to enable its full exercise, nor lawfully transfers the powers and responsibilities of the administering power to Morocco so as to enable decolonization through that UN Charter-based mechanism. Subsequent debate about who is now the administering power is immaterial;[112] the issue is whether the treaty was void due to conflict with a peremptory norm at the time of its conclusion.

## Legal consequences of coercion and conflict with jus cogens

Under the law of treaties, a treaty procured by coercion or in conflict with *jus cogens* is 'void' *ab initio* under articles 52 and 53 of the VCLT. An ILC commentary on the draft provisions indicated that this language indicates that such treaties 'must be characterized as void rather than as voidable at the instance of the injured party'.[113] This is because, for instance, the prohibitions on the threat and use of force 'are rules of international law the observance of which is legally a matter of concern to every State'.[114] As such, a treaty procured by coercion is void *ab initio* '[e]ven if it were conceivable that after being liberated from the influence of a threat or of a use of force a State might wish to allow a treaty procured ... by such means'.[115]

Despite the plain textual meaning and drafting intention that such treaties are indeed 'void', articles 52 and 53 are still expressly subject to the procedure for impeaching the validity of a treaty under articles 65–68 of the VCLT, so that such treaties are, curiously, not automatically invalid.[116] Article 69 of the VCLT makes clear that a treaty is void only once its invalidity has

---

110 UNGA resolutions 2229 (XXI) (December 20, 1966); 2354 (XXII) (December 19, 1967); 2428 (XXIII) (December 18, 1968); 2591 (XXIV) (December 16, 1979); 2711 (XXV) (December 14, 1970); 2938 (XXVII) (December 14, 1972); 3162 (XXVIII) (December 14, 1973).

111 Corell Opinion, para. 6.

112 Morocco is not listed as administering power in the UN list of Non-Self-Governing Territories: http://www.un.org/en/decolonization/nonselfgovterritories.shtml. See also Corell Opinion, para. 7. Neither, however, is Spain, although it is listed as such in some UN Secretary General reports: Miguel, 'Spain's Legal Obligations', 243 (citing UN Docs. A61/70 (2006) and A/62/67 (2007)). Spain could be the de jure administering power in absentia; or its role as administering power may have lapsed due to ineffectiveness, the elapse of time, or (more doubtfully) its unilateral renunciation of its responsibilities.

113 ILC Commentary, 247.

114 Ibid.

115 Ibid. Any subsequent agreement between the same parties not tainted by coercion and to the same effect must also comply with other rules of the law on treaties, including conflict with peremptory norms under Article 53.

116 Annalisa Ciampi, 'Invalidity and Termination of Treaties and Rules of Procedure', in *The Law of Treaties* (see note 108), 360; see also Schröder, 'Treaties, Validity', para. 23; Alessandra Gianelli, 'Absolute Invalidity of Treaties and Their Non-Recognition by Third States', in *The Law of Treaties* (see note 108), 333. The procedure requires notification to the other parties; proposed measures of settlement; and a waiting period before implementing said measures. If another state objects, the parties must pursue the peaceful settlement of disputes in accordance with Article 33 of the UN Charter. If there is no solution within 12 months of the objection, in the case of Article 53

been established. One qualification in respect of a treaty that is 'void' is that a state cannot subsequently acquiesce to it (under article 45 of the VCLT) and thereby waive its right to seek to invalidate it.[117]

In relation to Western Sahara, none of Spain, Morocco or Mauritania has sought to impeach the validity of the Madrid Agreement on the basis of coercion or conflict with *jus cogens*. As noted, the subsequent conduct of the parties cannot amount to acquiescence to a treaty tainted by such defects, so as to waive the right to challenge the treaty in future. The fact remains that none of the parties has initiated the VCLT procedure and, on an orthodox view, the Madrid Agreement remains effective between the parties. Notwithstanding the earlier drafting intention signalled by the ILC, the VCLT as adopted enables a state, such as Spain, that is later liberated from the threat or use of force, to allow a treaty procured by coercion, simply by refraining from challenging its validity. As noted earlier, Spain was keen to decolonize Spanish Sahara; coercion hastened its timing and the form it took, but Spain had no interest in resuming its burden as administering power even if the coercion dissipated.

As regards the position of third states, non-parties to such a treaty cannot consider it invalid independently of the parties,[118] because article 42 of the VCLT provides that the validity of a treaty may only be impeached through the application of the VCLT, and the VCLT procedure only recognizes a right of states parties to seek to impeach validity. There is, however, some state practice indicating that third states have sometimes treated as invalid agreements which infringe self-determination. Thus UN General Assembly resolution 34/65 B (1979) described the Camp David Accords of 1978 as having 'no validity in so far as they purport to determine the future of the Palestinian people and of the Palestinian territories occupied by Israel since 1967'.[119] The resolution objected to the exclusion of the Palestinian Liberation Organization, 'the representative of the Palestinian people', from the negotiations, and provisions of the accords which 'ignore, infringe, violate or deny the inalienable rights of the Palestinian people'.

The resolution may indicate subsequent practice or agreement amongst the parties to the VCLT that third states (and international organizations) may claim that a treaty in conflict with a peremptory norm (or, equally, procured by coercion) is void, without depending on the parties to the treaty to impeach its validity pursuant to the VCLT procedures.[120] Alternatively, such an approach by third states could be based on qualifying the conclusion of such treaties as a wrongful act towards the international community as a whole,[121] given the interests at stake. The VCLT procedure for impeaching the validity of treaties has never been invoked in practice and it is unlikely that it reflects general international law rules.

Another example is the ICJ's *Case Concerning East Timor*, where Portugal alleged that Australia had violated the obligation to respect Portugal's powers as administrator of that Non-Self-Governing Territory by concluding the Timor Gap Treaty with Indonesia, to explore continental shelf resources.[122] While the case was found to be inadmissible because of Indonesia's non-participation, it focused the international community's disquiet about dealings in natural resources that conflicted with the right of self-determination.

---

of the VCLT (*jus cogens*), a state may unilaterally initiate proceedings in the ICJ (or pursue arbitration by consent). As regards Article 52 (coercion), a state may invoke the Conciliation Commission under the VCLT.

117  Ciampi, 'Invalidity and Termination of Treaties'.
118  Gianelli, 'Absolute Invalidity of Treaties'.
119  UNGA resolution 34/65 B (November 29, 1979). See also UNGA resolution 33/28 A (1979); Gianelli, 'Absolute Invalidity of Treaties'; Ciampi, 'Invalidity and Termination of Treaties'.
120  Gianelli, 'Absolute Invalidity of Treaties', 336; see also Ciampi, 'Invalidity and Termination of Treaties', 330 (suggesting further that national courts are obliged to impeach the validity of such treaties).
121  Gianelli, 'Absolute Invalidity of Treaties'.
122  Treaty between Australia and the Republic of Indonesia on the Zone of Cooperation in an Area between the Indonesian Province of East Timor and Northern Australia (adopted December 11, 1989, entered into force February 9, 1991, [1991] ATS No. 9); *East Timor (Portugal v Australia)* [1995] ICJ Rep 90.

Regardless of whether the Madrid Agreement is void between the parties, or is considered void by third states, the position under the law of treaties must be carefully distinguished from the situation under IHL. As argued at the outset, a lack of genuine consent to the presence of foreign forces is an indispensable requirement of the existence of an occupation. In the absence of explicit guidance in IHL, reference to the grounds of invalidity under the law of treaties is a useful source of guidance in determining when consent under IHL may be considered free and genuine, or coerced or otherwise contaminated for conflicting with a peremptory norm. Both situations impermissibly taint the consent given under the law of treaties and under IHL.

However, under the law of treaties, the VCLT procedure must then be pursued to technically invalidate a treaty and render it definitively void. Under IHL, however, no such procedure is required to establish whether there exists a lack of genuine consent to foreign forces on either of these substantive grounds. The VCLT establishes a partially subjective regime that depends on a party choosing to impeach validity. In contrast, IHL is an objectively applicable legal regime which does not formally depend on a party electing to plead a lack of consent, or even a third state identifying a lack of consent. Rather, the lack of consent under IHL is an objective fact. The invalidation of a treaty in consequence of the VCLT procedure will certainly provide good evidence of a lack of genuine consent under IHL, but it is not indispensable in cases where a victim of aggression chooses not to impeach the treaty. The way in which treaty law substantively (not procedurally) assesses coercion or conflict with *jus cogens* is instead drawn upon as a source or analogue for the separate IHL assessment; it is a borrowing or transplant of principles, not an application of treaty law as *lex specialis*.

## Final issues concerning Morocco's occupation

To summarize the argument so far, there are strong indications that Morocco's threat and use of force was an important factor in coercively procuring Spain's purported consent to the entry and presence of Moroccan forces under the Madrid Agreement. In addition, the consent given was not otherwise valid in that it conflicted with the peremptory norm of self-determination. The absence of free and valid consent to an Agreement authorizing the entry of foreign forces, the termination of Spanish administrative authority, and the substitution of Moroccan and Mauritanian authority can only be characterized as an occupation of foreign territory by a 'bloodless' invasion. This is so notwithstanding the many peculiarities of the situation, including Spain's mixed motives, which set it apart from orthodox occupations.

An issue remains whether the dispute over legal title to Western Sahara affects the application of IHL and the existence of an occupation there. In the *Israeli Wall Advisory Opinion*, Israel argued that the West Bank was not occupied because it was not sovereign Jordanian territory.[123] As such, despite there having been an armed conflict between Jordan and Israel in 1967, there was not an 'occupation of territory of a High Contracting Party' as required by common article 2(2) of the Geneva Conventions. By analogy, Morocco had contested Spain's title to Spanish Sahara prior to its entry in 1975, so that it might argue there was no occupation of the sovereign territory of another state.

Such an argument must be rejected for the reasons given in the *Israeli Wall Advisory Opinion*. The ICJ found that as long as an armed conflict has arisen between two states, IHL applies under common article 2(1) of the Geneva Conventions, 'in particular, in any territory occupied in the course of the conflict by one of the contracting parties' – and specifically including 'territories not falling under the sovereignty of one of the contracting parties'.[124] It observed that article 2 (2) emphasizes that an occupation can exist even if it meets no armed resistance, and is not

---

123  *Israeli Wall Advisory Opinion* (2004), paras. 91, 93.
124  Ibid., para. 95.

intended to restrict the scope of application of IHL. On this analysis, any dispute over legal title to Spanish Sahara is immaterial; an occupation arose there because of taking of territory held by Spain, even if there was no armed Spanish resistance. Further, as Corell's legal opinion notes, '[t]he Madrid Agreement did not transfer sovereignty over the Territory',[125] and Morocco cannot acquire sovereign title to Western Sahara by force or prolonged occupation.[126]

## Regulation of natural resources under the law of occupation

The law of occupation provides a high level of protection for the proprietary interests of the inhabitants of occupied territory, while recognizing the military and administrative needs of the occupying power. First, it is forbidden to destroy private or public property (real or personal) in occupied territory 'except where ... rendered absolutely necessary by military operations'.[127] Secondly, it is prohibited to pillage (or steal) private or public property in occupied territory,[128] including, for instance, state companies.[129]

Thirdly, it is prohibited to confiscate moveable private property,[130] except military material,[131] or requisitions in kind and services 'for the needs of the army of occupation' and in proportion to the resources of the country.[132] Fourthly, moveable public property (including natural resources which have already been extracted or produced)[133] may only be requisitioned if it comprises military material;[134] or if it is for the needs of the occupying army (proportionate to the country's resources);[135] or if it could be used for military operations.[136] Taxes may also be levied to fund the military and administrative costs of occupation.[137]

Fifthly, the immovable public property of occupied territory (including natural resources *in situ*)[138] must be treated in accordance with the principle of trusteeship, for the benefit of the local inhabitants, and its capital must be safeguarded.[139] The occupant cannot appropriate,

---

125 Corell Opinion, para. 6.
126 Declaration on Principles of International Law Concerning Friendly Relations and Co-operation among States in accordance with the Charter of the United Nations, in UNGA resolution 2625 (October 24, 1970) (reflecting customary law); see also Benvenisti, *The International Law of Occupation*, 151–3.
127 Fourth Geneva Convention 1949, Article 53 and ICRC Commentary 1958 thereto; see also Hague Regulations 1907, Articles 46 and 56.
128 Fourth Geneva Convention 1949, Article 33 and ICRC Commentary; Hague Regulations 1907, Article 47; ICRC Customary IHL Study, rule 52.
129 *The IG Farben Trial: The Trial of Carl Krauch and 22 Others*, US Military Tribunal, Nuremberg, August 14, 1947–July 29, 1948, in UN War Crimes Commission, *Law Reports of Trials of War Criminals*, vol. X (London: HMSO, 1949), 1.
130 Hague Regulations 1907, Article 46. Private owners may, however, lawfully transact with the occupying power where their consent is voluntarily and not obtained by threats, intimidation, pressure, or exploitation: *The IG Farben Trial*, 46–7.
131 Hague Regulations 1907, Articles 46 and 53(2).
132 Ibid., Article 52; ICRC Customary IHL Study, rule 50.
133 See Iain Scobbie, 'Natural Resources and Belligerent Occupation: Perspectives from International Humanitarian and Human Rights Law', in *International Law and the Israeli-Palestinian Conflict: A Rights-based Approach to Middle East Peace*, ed. Susan Akram, Michael Dumper, Michael Lynk and Iain Scobbie (Abingdon: Routledge, 2011), 229, 234.
134 Hague Regulations 1907, Article 53(2). 'Munitions de guerre' includes arms, ammunition, transport, communications equipment, and other things that have a sufficiently close connection with direct military use, and does not include, for instance, crude oil in the ground: *NV de Bataafsche Petroleum Maatschappij v The War Damage Commission*, Singapore Court of Appeal, April 13, 1956 (in violation of Article 53 of the Hague Regulations 1907), *American Journal of International Law* 51 (1957): 802.
135 Hague Regulations 1907, Article 52.
136 Ibid., Article 53.
137 Ibid., Articles 48–9.
138 Scobbie, 'Natural Resources and Belligerent Occupation', 234.
139 Article 55 of the Hague Regulations 1907 provides that: 'The occupying State shall be regarded only as administrator and usufructuary of public buildings, real estate, forests, and agricultural estates belonging to the hostile State, and situated in the occupied country. It must safeguard the capital of these properties, and administer them in accordance with the rules of usufruct'. See also ICRC Customary IHL Study, rule 51.

acquire title to, or sell such public assets,[140] but has the right to utilize the proceeds thereof for the benefit of the inhabitants.[141] Immovable public property may, however, be destroyed or seized where required by imperative military necessity.[142]

It is unlawful to appropriate or utilize foreign public property to benefit the occupying state's own economy or companies,[143] or its own civilian settlers transferred to occupied territory contrary to IHL.[144] The payment of a price does not relieve an appropriation of its unlawful character,[145] nor does the apparently legal form or purported voluntary character of a transaction.[146] Any transfers or dealings with property, rights and interests not justified by IHL are invalid,[147] including where a person or legal entity plans to subsequently acquire the property from those who unlawfully confiscated it.[148]

The principle of usufruct applies more strictly in the case of non-renewable than renewable natural resources,[149] given that the former is prone to exhaustion, particularly in cases of protracted occupation. An administrator should not exercise rights over immovable property in such a wasteful and negligent manner so as to seriously impair its value.[150] As such, an occupying power may continue to extract non-renewable resources at the ordinary pre-occupation rate, but may not abusively increase production of existing assets or permit new resource developments.[151]

Finally, the occupying power must respect, 'unless absolutely prevented', the laws in force at the time of occupying the territory.[152] This includes local property laws, insofar as such laws are consistent with international human rights law[153] and other relevant international laws. In the case of occupation of Non-Self-Governing Territories, this entails respect for the property laws of the legitimate administering power – Spain at the time of Morocco's occupation of Spanish Sahara – insofar as Spanish property laws respected the right of economic self-determination, and permanent sovereignty over natural resources, of the Sahrawi people.[154]

In the case law, numerous decisions have found violations of IHL by the exploitation of the resources of occupied territories without regard for the local economy,[155] including by state officials,[156] corporate actors[157] and individuals. In the Nazi occupation of Europe this included the

---

140   *In re Flick (US Military Tribunal at Nuremberg)*, 14 Ann Dig 266, 271; UK Ministry of Defence, *The Manual of the Law of Armed Conflict* (Oxford: Oxford University Press, 2004), 303. See Scobbie, 'Natural Resources and Belligerent Occupation', 233.

141   Scobbie, 'Natural Resources and Belligerent Occupation', 235.

142   ICRC Customary IHL Study, rules 50–51.

143   Koury, 'The European Community', 174; *The IG Farben Trial*, 50.

144   The transfer of civilian populations into occupied territory itself is unlawful under IHL: Fourth Geneva Convention 1949, Article 49(6); Rome Statute of the International Criminal Court, Article 8; see also *Israeli Wall Advisory Opinion* (2004), para. 120 (Israeli settlements in the West Bank violate international law).

145   *The IG Farben Trial*, 44.

146   Ibid., 45.

147   Ibid.

148   Ibid., 44.

149   Scobbie, 'Natural Resources and Belligerent Occupation', 234–5.

150   US Army Field Manual 27-10: The Law of Land Warfare, July 18, 1956, para. 402.

151   Scobbie, 'Natural Resources and Belligerent Occupation', 234–5; see, e.g., UK Ministry of Defence, *The Manual of the Law of Armed Conflict*, 303; *In re Krupp* (US Military Tribunal at Nuremberg, 1948), 15 Ann Dig 620, 622–5.

152   Hague Regulations 1907, Article 43.

153   Human rights law applies concurrently with IHL in armed conflict, including extraterritorially in occupied territory: *Israeli Wall Advisory Opinion* (2004), paras. 105–7.

154   On which, see Corell Opinion.

155   See, e.g., International Military Tribunal at Nuremberg, Judgment, 22 IMT 481, September 30, 1946; *In re Flick* (1947) US Military Tribunal at Nuremberg; *In re Krupp* (1948) US Military Tribunal at Nuremberg, in UN War Crimes Commission, (1949) 10 *Law Reports of Trials of War Criminals* 69; *In re Krauch* (1948) US Military Tribunal at Nuremberg (illegal transfer of shareholdings in private companies to industrialists of the occupying power).

156   E.g., German Finance Minister Schwerin von Krosigk responsible for the taking of oil, coal, ores and raw materials from Poland: UN War Crimes Commission, (1949) 14 *Law Reports of Trials of War Criminals* 784.

157   See, e.g., *The IG Farben Trial*; *In re Krupp*.

systematic requisitioning and taking to Germany of agricultural products, food, raw materials, tools, transportation, finished products and financial securities resulting in famine, inflation and black marketeering.[158] In the Japanese occupation in Asia it included the exploitation of immoveable oil reserves in existing oil production facilities for civilian and military use at home and abroad by the occupying power.[159] Iraq eventually paid compensation for the pillage of Kuwaiti state resources after the 1991 Gulf War.[160]

In *Congo v Uganda* (2005), the ICJ found Uganda responsible for pillage by failing to prevent its armed forces from looting, plundering and commercially exploiting Congolese resources including diamonds, gold, coffee, wildlife and forest agricultural products.[161] Such exploitation was unlawful because it was not carried out for the benefit of the local population.[162] Its focus on breaches of IHL may be significant for Western Sahara because the ICJ also determined (without explanation) that such exploitation did *not* constitute a violation of permanent sovereignty over natural resources. As mentioned earlier, much of the debate about the illegality of Moroccan dealings with Sahrawi resources has been based on Corell's legal opinion on the law governing Non-Self-Governing Territories, which in turn rests heavily on the principle of permanent sovereignty (in addition to self-determination).

Certain breaches of the above IHL prohibitions attract not only state responsibility but individual criminal liability. Pillage of private or public property is a war crime in international and non-international conflicts.[163] There is also a related war crime (in international conflicts only) of the 'extensive destruction and appropriation of property, not justified by military necessity and carried out unlawfully and wantonly'.[164] Any deprivation of property, including pillage, plunder, theft or requisition, is a form of appropriation.[165] Pillage and unlawful appropriation of property cover individual acts of looting for private gain as well as organized seizure and systematic exploitation of occupied territory.[166] In the case law, pillage has extended to receiving property illegally taken by others[167] (echoing common domestic offences such as receiving stolen goods). There is a further war crime in international and non-international conflict of 'destroying or seizing the enemy's property', where such property is protected by IHL and the destruction or seizure is not justified by military necessity.[168]

The contemporary modes of criminal participation for war crimes generally are reflected in article 25(3) of the Rome Statute of the ICC, namely to (a) commit an offence, (b) order, solicit or induce, (c) facilitate by aiding, abetting or otherwise assisting (including providing the means to commit), and (d) contribute to a crime by a group acting with a common purpose, with the aim of furthering the criminal activity or purpose, and with knowledge of

---

158    International Military Tribunal at Nuremberg, Judgment, 22 IMT 481, September 30, 1946.

159    *NV de Bataafsche Petroleum Maatschappij v The War Damage Commission.*

160    See UN Claims Commission for Kuwait, Report and Recommendations of Commissioners, UN Doc. S/A.22/1999/10 (1999).

161    *Congo v Uganda* (2005), paras. 222–50 (under the Hague Regulations 1907, Article 47; Fourth Geneva Convention, Article 33; and the African Charter on Human and Peoples' Rights, Article 21 (which requires restitution or compensation in the case or spoliation)).

162    *Congo v Uganda* (2005), para. 249.

163    ICC Rome Statute, Article 8(2)(b)(xvi) and (e)(v) (as a serious violation of the laws and customs of war).

164    Fourth Geneva Convention 1949, Article 147. Also ICC Rome Statute, Article 8(2)(a)(iv) (as a grave breach of the Geneva Conventions).

165    *Prosecutor v Blaskic*, ICTY Trial Chamber, ICTY-95-14-T, March 3, 2000), para. 184, and *Prosecutor v Delalic*, ICTY Trial Chamber, IT-96-21-T (November 16, 1998), para. 591, plunder was found to embrace all unlawful appropriation of property, including pillage. See also *Prosecutor v Kunarac*, ICTY Trial Chamber, ICTY-96-23/1-T, February 22, 2001, para. 15 (plunder and pillage are synonymous). 'Spoliation' and 'plunder' are also synonymous: *The IG Farben Trial*, 44.

166    *Prosecutor v Delalic* (1998), para. 590.

167    *Trial of Christian Baus*, Permanent Military Tribunal at Metz, Judgment of August 21, 1947, (1949) IX *War Crimes Reports* 68 (where a German caretaker was convicted for taking property from French farms which had been given to him by another German custodian of the farms).

168    Rome Statute, Article 8(2)(b)(xiii) (international conflict) and 8(2)(e)(xii) (non-international conflict).

the group's intention. There is, however, no state or corporate criminal liability under IHL, although state officials and corporate personnel may be held individually liable, and some national laws implementing war crimes in domestic law provide for corporate criminal liability.[169] Some national laws also apply additional modes of liability to war crimes, such as 'accessory after the fact' (by receiving, or assisting another to dispose of, the proceeds of crime),[170] or receiving stolen goods.

The application of the law of occupation is significant because it provides much greater protection in relation to natural resources than IHL applicable to non-international conflicts. While pillage of private or public property is also prohibited in the latter conflicts, there is no requirement of trusteeship over natural resources for the benefit of the local inhabitants. In ordinary civil wars, this is because the state is sovereign over the territory and has the right to make property laws, appropriate or nationalize natural resources, and exploit natural resources in exercising permanent sovereignty over them. In transnational non-international conflicts where the belligerent state is not the sovereign, powers are more limited (and still structured by the principles of self-determination and permanent sovereignty); but only under the law of occupation applicable in international conflicts are the full and detailed protections of the trusteeship principle applicable.

## Conclusion: legal implications for exploitation of Sahrawi resources

Having established that Western Sahara has been occupied territory since early 1976, a number of general conclusions can be drawn below about the application of the law of occupation to dealings with its natural resources (including phosphate, oil, gas, minerals and fisheries). In sum, certain commercial dealings with Western Saharan natural resources are both prohibited by the international law of occupation and attract individual criminal responsibility as war crimes.

First, under IHL Morocco does not gain proprietary legal title to such resources, or the right to pass title to others, but is required to administer them on trust for the people of Western Sahara. The law of occupation accordingly cannot cure any legal defects in the purported transfer of legal title to phosphate and fishing rights by Spain to Morocco in the side deals to the Madrid Agreement (including a 65% share in Bou Craa mine). As discussed above, those agreements were entered into before the occupation was established but in principle were void by coercion and conflict with self-determination. While neither Spain nor Morocco has invoked the treaty law procedure to render them void, as noted earlier, non-party states must regard such agreements as legally ineffective to transfer property rights.

Secondly, Morocco must administer the natural resources of Western Sahara on trust for the benefit of the Sahrawi people and otherwise only to fulfil imperative military needs. As regards finite phosphate resources, IHL supposes that Morocco is entitled to maintain the pre-existing Spanish levels of production in 1975, with some leeway to account for both the pre-existing intended expansion of production (since the mine was then in its early stages of development) and the sustainable development of the Sahrawi people over the protracted period of the Moroccan occupation (of almost 40 years). Morocco is also not supposed to exploit new finite resources, such as by developing or licensing new mines or other minerals. Insofar as Morocco exploits or permits exploitation of renewable resources such as fisheries, this must be sustainable and not abusive, consistent with the inter-generational dimension of the trusteeship principle and concurrently applicable principles of international environmental law.[171]

---

169   E.g., Australian Criminal Code, s. 12.1.
170   See, e.g., Crimes Act 1914 (Australia), s. 6.
171   Stockholm Declaration of the UN Conference on the Human Environment (1972), principle 13; Rio Declaration on Environment and Development (1992), principle 15.

The critical legal question is whether Morocco's exploitation of resources is reasonably done for the benefit of the local inhabitants or otherwise out of military necessity. This requires a detailed factual assessment of the evidence as to how, to whom and for what purposes the Moroccan exploitation of Sahrawi natural resources accrues. This could include, for instance, evidence as to the profits made from resource exploitation, and whether these are repatriated into Morocco's general state revenues or quarantined for expenditure in Western Sahara; the level of expenditure on public administration, infrastructure and services, and whether this is linked to resources profits; and the costs of military occupation. Accurate information about some of these matters is not readily available on the public record. While a full assessment is therefore outside the scope of this article, some general considerations may be offered which cast grave doubt on the lawfulness of Moroccan resource exploitation.

First, the demographic balance in Western Sahara has been fundamentally altered by both the mass exodus of Sahrawi refugees and Morocco's sponsorship and facilitation of large-scale inward Moroccan migration. On one estimate, 400,000 people live in Moroccan-occupied Western Sahara, of which 250–300,000 are Moroccan civilian settlers and 100–150,000 are Sahrawis; in addition, there are perhaps 160,000 Moroccan military and police personnel.[172] In 1999, MINURSO identified 86,425 eligible Sahrawi voters for the referendum; and estimates of the Algerian refugee camp population vary from 90,000 to 155,000.

The key legal point is that profits from the exploitation of natural resources may only be lawfully directed under IHL to benefiting the indigenous inhabitants of occupied territory. That means the local population at the time the occupation is established, adjusted for subsequent natural growth. As a result, the fruits of natural resources cannot be spent on public administration, services and infrastructure to benefit Moroccan settlers (who comprise the majority of the territory's current population), or the military protection of such settlers. Employment opportunities in resource developments must also exclusively benefit Sahrawis, not settlers. Further, profits must be held on trust to benefit all Sahrawi people, including those in the liberated zone (perhaps 20–30,000 people) and in the Algerian and Mauritanian refugee camps (up to 160,000 people), or, at a minimum, the 86,425 registered by MINURSO. Since most of these Sahrawis are outside Morocco's jurisdiction, their share of the profits from resource exploitation should be held on trust and not expended.

Secondly, while the trusteeship principle does not require the consent of the inhabitants to resource exploitation, consent or lack thereof may be a relevant factual indicator of whether the trustee is discharging its obligation. Polisario, as the internationally recognized representative of the Sahrawi people, has resolutely opposed Moroccan resource exploitation, and even issued resource exploration licences of its own to counter Morocco's; and there does not appear to be any legitimate mechanism within Western Sahara for local consultation.

Thirdly, Morocco denies that it is the occupying power of occupied territory. As such, it necessarily does not, and cannot in good faith, argue that its exploitation of resources is justified by imperative military necessity under IHL. The benefits of the law of occupation run with the burdens, and a state cannot take advantage of the law if it denies that it applies. Further, even if Morocco seeks to rely upon its IHL powers as occupant, any utilization of resources to support its military needs cannot be out of proportion to the capacity of the local economy to bear such imposition. In other words, even if Morocco's military costs exceeded the profits from resource exploitation, Morocco may only utilize an amount in proportion to the capacity of the local economy, precisely so as not to deprive the inhabitants of their means of sustenance and their proprietary rights as beneficiaries. The occupant cannot fund its war effort by decimating

---

172   Norwegian Refugee Council, *Western Sahara: Occupied Countries, Displaced People*, NRC Reports, Issue 2, 2008, 4. The statistics are, however, uncertain. According to the UN, the total population of Western Sahara was 549,000 people in 2012: https://data.un.org/CountryProfile.aspx?crName=Western%20Sahara.

the local economy. Morocco's military needs must also be assessed in light of the existence of a ceasefire since 1991 and the cessation of active hostilities.

Fourthly, there is some historical evidence that Morocco's occupation of Western Sahara was partly motivated by its concerns in the 1970s about the adverse effects of Spanish phosphate mining on the domestic Moroccan phosphate industry. This was at a time when the Moroccan economy relied significantly on phosphate exports and the global commodity price had decreased markedly, undermining the Moroccan economy. The exploitation of resources in occupied territory is not permitted to improve the position of the occupant's economy.

As regards individual criminal liability, there are implications for a range of actors, depending on the nature of particular dealings with Western Saharan resources. Moroccan state and corporate personnel are most likely liable for the ordering and commission of war crimes. The crime of pillage is constituted by the appropriation of property; the intent to deprive the owner of it, and to take it for private or personal use (not out of military necessity); the absence of consent by the owner; and the existence of an armed conflict of which the perpetrator knew.[173] The crime of 'extensive destruction and appropriation of property' requires an appropriation of property that the perpetrator was aware is protected by IHL, that is extensive and deliberate, not justified by military necessity, and where the perpetrator was aware an international conflict existed.[174] The crime of 'destroying or seizing the enemy's property' requires that the property belongs to the enemy and is protected by IHL, the perpetrator was aware of the facts as to the property's status and the existence of a conflict, and the destruction or seizure is not justified by military necessity.[175]

The directors and employees of foreign companies that deal with Morocco and Moroccan companies in relation to the natural resources of Western Sahara may also bear individual criminal liability for war crimes. Contracting with Moroccan companies to buy and import phosphate, for instance, could variously amount to soliciting or inducing the commission of a war crime;[176] facilitating by aiding, abetting or otherwise assisting in a war crime (including providing the means, such as finance or orders to purchase, to commit it);[177] or contributing to a crime by a group acting with a common purpose, with the aim of furthering the criminal purpose, and with knowledge of the group's intention.[178] In general, perpetrators must intend their conduct to assist in the commission of the crime by another and be aware of the elements of the war crime. It is unnecessary, however, to show that such conduct caused another to commit the crime, or that the other person has been convicted of an offence.

The characterization of resource exploitation in Western Sahara as war crimes also has implications for all states. Under the Geneva Conventions of 1949, states parties have a duty to respect IHL and to ensure respect by others.[179] Specifically, states must establish universal criminal jurisdiction over war crimes, search for suspects and prosecute or extradite them.[180] No such obligations exist in relation to the legal principles governing Non-Self-Governing Territories, self-determination, or permanent sovereignty over natural resources. This is why the application of IHL and the law of occupation to Western Sahara matters most: it enables the punishment of those who unlawfully exploit others' natural resources, and in so doing may deter future wrongful conduct by states and corporations alike.

---

173   ICC, Elements of Crimes: Rome Statute, Article 8(2)(b)(xvi) and (e)(v), UN Doc. PCNICC/2000/1/Add.2 (2000).
174   Ibid., Article 8(2)(a)(iv).
175   Ibid., Article 8(2)(b)(xiii) and 8(2)(e)(xii).
176   Rome Statute, Article 25(3)(b).
177   Ibid., Article 25(3)(c).
178   Ibid., Article 25(3)(d).
179   See also *Israel Wall Advisory Opinion* (2004), para. 163(D).
180   See, e.g., Fourth Geneva Convention 1949, Article 146(1)–(2).

The prosecution of war crimes in domestic courts is likely to be the only practical means of bringing to justice those responsible for the illegal exploitation of Western Saharan resources. While such crimes also fall within the substantive criminal jurisdiction of the ICC, as outlined above, the ICC is unlikely to be able to exercise jurisdiction to prosecute. ICC jurisdiction is primarily territorial and largely depends on the consent of state parties to the Rome Statute,[181] but Morocco is not a party to it, and only states can become parties, thus ruling out consent by Polisario. Technically the UN Security Council could still refer the situation to the ICC prosecutor[182] – but that is highly unlikely given the close ties with Morocco by two veto-wielding permanent members, the US and France. Political will is ultimately required to effectively bring to justice the corporate thieves and pillagers who plunder the natural resources belonging to others.

## Disclosure statement

No potential conflict of interest was reported by the author.

---

181   Rome Statute, Articles 12–14.
182   Ibid., Article 13(b).

# The hidden cost of phosphate fertilizers: mapping multi-stakeholder supply chain risks and impacts from mine to fork

Dana Cordell, Andrea Turner and Joanne Chong

*Institute for Sustainable Futures, University of Technology Sydney, Sydney, NSW, Australia*

Without phosphorus, we could not produce food. Farmers need access to phosphate fertilizers to achieve the high crop yields needed to feed the world. Yet growing global demand for phosphorus could surpass supply in the coming decades, and the world currently largely relies on non-renewable phosphate rock that is mined in only a few countries. Morocco alone controls 75% of the remaining reserves, including those in the conflict territory of Western Sahara. While some argue that the market will take care of any scarcity, the market price of phosphate fertilizers fails to account for far-ranging negative impacts. Drawing on multi-stakeholder supply chain risk frameworks, the article identifies a range of negative impacts, including the exploitation and displacement of the Saharawi people, the destruction of aquatic ecosystems by nutrient pollution, and jeopardizing future generations' ability to produce food. This paper fills a crucial gap in understanding phosphorus impacts by mapping and discussing the nature of phosphorus supply chain risks, and the transmission of such risks to different stakeholder groups. It also identifies a range of potential interventions to mitigate and manage those risks. In addition, the paper highlights that while risks are diverse, from geopolitical to ecological, those groups adversely affected are also diverse – including the Saharawi people, farmers, businesses, food consumers and the environment. Potential risk mitigation strategies range from resource sparing (using phosphorus more sparingly to extend the life of high quality rock for ourselves and future generations), to resource diversification (sourcing phosphorus from a range of ethical sources to reduce dependence on imported phosphate, as a buffer against supply disruptions, and preferencing those sources with lower societal costs), and sharing the responsibility for these costs and consequences.

## 1 Introduction

The importance of phosphorus is well established: phosphorus underpins our ability to produce food anywhere in the world.[1] Like water, oxygen and carbon, phosphorus is a fundamental building block of life and there is no substitute for phosphorus in food production. The positive impact of applying phosphate fertilizers is evidenced by high crop yields compared to their unfertilized counterparts (Figure 1).[2] Higher crop yields in general mean greater agricultural productivity, higher returns for the farmer, increased food available to feed populations, and increased food security. Indeed, the use of phosphate fertilizers has contributed to feeding billions of people over the past century.[3]

---

1 A.E. Johnston, *Soil and Plant Phosphate* (Paris: International Fertilizer Industry Association, 2000).

2 K. Syers, A.E. Johnston, and D. Curtin, 'Efficiency of Soil and Fertilizer Phosphorus Use: Reconciling Changing Concepts of Soils Phosphorus Behaviour with Agronomic Information', *FAO Fertilizer and Plant Nutrition Bulletin* 18 (Rome: Food and Agriculture Organization of the United Nations, 2008).

3 IFPRI, *Green Revolution: Curse or Blessing?* (Washington, DC: International Food Policy Research Institute, 2002).

Figure 1. Agricultural test field indicating the results of phosphate fertilizer use on crop cover.
Source: Tennessee Valley Authority, Franklin D. Roosevelt Presidential Library and Museum.

While the importance of phosphorus is well known within the agricultural sector, the negative impacts of the whole phosphorus fertilizer supply chain from production to end use are not fully accounted for, or well understood.[4] The world's agriculture today relies on phosphorus sourced from finite phosphate rock reserves mined in only a few countries. Much of this is inefficiently used and is lost or wasted along the supply chain, largely ending up in rivers and oceans where it causes pollution.[5]

The phosphorus supply chain spans the system of phosphorus use in the global food system, from mine to field to fork. It is highly globalized and includes sectors and processes related to mining, processing and trade of phosphate rock; production and trade of phosphate fertilizers; application of fertilizers in agriculture to crops and pastures; harvesting of phosphorus-containing crops; production, processing and distribution of food; consumption of food; and, finally, the management of phosphorus-containing wastewater, food waste and eutrophied waters (Figure 2).[6]

From a single-stakeholder perspective, each actor in the phosphorus supply chain has a specific objective, such as commercial farmers efficiently converting natural capital (phosphorus)

4   M. Bekunda et al., 'Phosphorus and food production', UN*EP Yearbook: Emerging Issues in Our Global Environment* (Paris: United Nations Environment Programme, 2011); D. Cordell and S. White, 'Life's Bottleneck: Sustaining the World's Phosphorus for a Food Secure Future', *Annual Review of Environment and Resources* 39, no. 1 (2014): 161–88, http://www.annualreviews.org/doi/full/10.1146/annurev-environ-010213-113300.

5   Cordell & White. Life's Bottleneck.

6   D. Cordell, J.-O. Drangert, and S. White, 'The Story of Phosphorus: Global Food Security and Food for Thought', *Global Environmental Change* 19, no. 2 (2009): 292–305, http://linkinghub.elsevier.com/retrieve/pii/S095937800800099X; J.J. Schroder et al., 'Sustainable Use of Phosphorus', Rep.357, European Union Tender ENV.B.1/ETU/2009/0025 (Wageningen, Netherlands: Plant Research International, 2010).

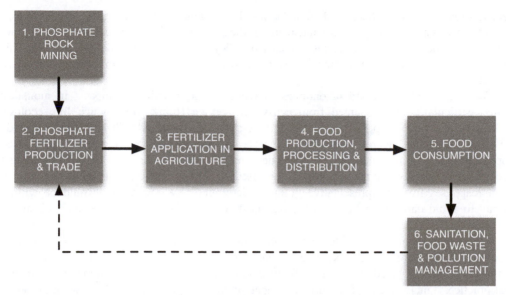

Figure 2. Key sectors directly involved in the phosphorus supply chain, from mining to application in agriculture through to environmental management. Arrows indicate material flows. A minimal amount of phosphorus reuse from organic waste sources is also indicated by the dotted line.

into financial capital (agricultural commodities) through productive farming. However, in this paper we take a multi-stakeholder, sustainable systems and food security perspective, where the fundamental objective of the phosphorus supply chain is to ensure that farmers have sufficient access to phosphorus to efficiently produce food for the global population while ensuring ecosystem integrity and supporting farmer livelihoods.[7] By taking this approach, we reveal a vast and diverse array of negative impacts, the 'sustainability costs', associated with mining and using phosphate rock for food production. Together, these impacts compromise humanity's ability to meet this fundamental objective.

This paper identifies the nature of the associated risks to different stakeholder groups, laying the conceptual foundations for why the sustainability costs associated with phosphate rock, from mine to fertilizer application, through to the dinner table need to be considered. However, it does not attempt to quantify these costs or impacts in monetary terms for reasons explained below.[8] Examples of interventions to mitigate and manage such risks are provided, ranging from market-based to social in nature.

## 2 Valuing the invaluable and the uncertain

In this section we briefly introduce two approaches to valuing impacts – monetizing approaches and risk-based approaches and explain why the latter is more appropriate in the case of the phosphorus supply chain.

### 2.1 *Monetizing approaches*

The need for assessing and quantifying impacts is not unique to phosphorus. Quantifying impacts in monetary terms is a long-established convention for weighing up costs and benefits to inform

---

7   D. Cordell, 'The Story of Phosphorus: Sustainability Implications of Global Phosphorus Scarcity for Food Security' Doctoral thesis, no. 509 (Linköping: Linköping University Press, 2010), http://liu.diva-portal.org/smash/record.jsf?pid=diva2:291760.
8   See section 2.

decision-making. With theoretical foundations in welfare economics,[9] the use of cost–benefit analysis and the net-present-value metric is the standard and in many cases regulated practice[10] for public policy-makers to test whether a policy, law or program should proceed. This approach considers whether the 'monetary sum' of positive impacts outweigh that of the negative impacts.

There are well-established taxonomies of methods for quantifying impacts in monetary terms, particularly those adapted from ecosystem services frameworks which link ecology and economics but are applicable to a wide range of other impacts.[11] These methods include 'revealed preference' approaches, which use price in associated or proxy markets; cost-based approaches, which consider the cost of measures to replace, mitigate or avoid damage; and stated preference approaches, which are based on survey and other methods that aim to elicit responses from a representative group to determine how much they would be willing to pay to avoid damage, or how much payment they would be willing to receive to bear the impact.

Such methods could be used to quantify the monetary impacts of some of the costs and risks associated with global phosphorus production and use. For example, the costs and risks associated with an algal bloom, based on the values frameworks established in the ecosystem services theory and practice,[12] include loss of a source of irrigation water; damage to a fish spawning ground; reductions in tourism; as well as lost 'intrinsic' value of ecosystems and nature. Methods to monetize these impacts include lost production value from agriculture and commercial fisheries; travel cost method for reductions in tourism; and a stated preference method to survey recreational fishers and the community more generally about existence value.

Many of these methods enable quantification of impacts that are 'negative externalities' – that is, those not taken into account in the direct market transactions in the supply chain of the global phosphorus industry. It is well accepted, at least in theory, that inclusion of externalities in decision-making is critical to ensure welfare is maximized. Valuation techniques enable environmental, social and cultural values and impacts to be considered 'on a par' with the more conventional production and consumption values, and have been successfully used to make the case for conservation and wise management of natural resources.[13] However, a drawback of focusing only on the monetization of impacts is the array of complexities and uncertainties in monetizing impacts, particularly those that are not associated with direct production or consumption. Methodological criticisms, particularly of non-market approaches, the cost of conducting robust stated-preference studies, and ethical debates about commodification,[14] can sideline the intent of highlighting these very impacts.

Furthermore, monetizing approaches, in practice, often draw attention to the quantification of a specific level (or range) of cost or impact when, in reality, the amounts and likelihoods are uncertain. Hence despite the wide-ranging application of monetary decision-making frameworks, this paper does not deal with valuation, but rather draws on more appropriate frameworks to identify impacts and risks.

9   N. Kaldor, 'Welfare Proposition of Economics and Interpersonal Comparisons of Utility', *Economic Journal* 49 (1939): 549–52.

10  Australian Government, *The Australian Government Guide to Regulation* (Canberra: Department of the Prime Minister and Cabinet, Commonwealth of Australia, 2014); OECD, *Cost–Benefit Analysis and the Environment: Recent Developments* (Paris: Organisation for Economic Co-operation and Development, 2006).

11  TEEB, 'The Economics of Ecosystems and Biodiversity: Mainstreaming the Economics of Nature: A Synthesis of the Approach, Conclusions and Recommendations of TEEB' (2010).

12  Ibid.

13  Millennium Ecosystem Assessment, 'Ecosystems and Human Well-being: Wetlands and Water Synthesis' (Washington D.C: World Resources Institute, 2005). Available: http://www.millenniumassessment.org/documents/document. 358.aspx.pdf

14  C. Spash, S. Stagl, and M. Getzner, 'Exploring Alternatives for Environmental Valuation', in *Alternatives for Environmental Valuation*, ed. M. Getzner, C. Spash, and S. Stagl (Abingdon: Routledge, 2005).

## 2.2   *Assessing and managing risks*

Risk management approaches are diverse and are applied in a myriad of scales and fields, including assessing and managing organizational risks; epidemiological studies on public health risks; disaster risk management; negotiating risk-sharing in contracts; and management of corporate financial and reputational risks. However, all approaches aim to identify and manage risks to better meet objectives, and many of the underlying principles are the same, including that risk management should be systematic, based on the best available information, inform decision-making, and create and protect value.[15]

Supply chain risk literature typically draws attention to the identification and management of external or internal business risks that can adversely affect a firm's operational, market or financial performance.[16] Internal business risks can include process and control risks, while risks internal to the whole supply chain can include demand and supply-side risks.[17] Environmental risks external to both a firm and a supply chain can also adversely affect a firm's performance. Increasingly long and global supply chains, coupled with growing scarcity of critical resources, means effective management of supply chain risks is becoming increasingly important.[18]

Healthy supply chains are agile and proactive, and can both respond to and pre-empt potential disruptions. Because phosphorus is critical and non-substitutable in food production, it will be essential for supply chain managers to minimize supply disruptions to ensure customers (farmers) have access to fertilizers. However, in their typology of natural resource scarcity, Bell et al. warn that there is little research on mitigation strategies for supply chain managers to deal with the potential impacts of resource scarcity.[19] They also conclude that 'as resources become increasingly scarce ... the value of interorganisational connections may play a significant role in a firm's ability to secure and use scarce resources in a cost- and time-efficient manner'.[20]

While there are numerous supply chain risk management frameworks related to natural resources and/or the agri-food system, few take a multi-stakeholder and systems approach. Matopoulos et al. comprehensively reviewed 96 papers related to resource-efficient supply chains (RESC) in the agri-food sector.[21] The authors identify four key characteristics of effective RESCs: resource awareness, resource sensitivity, resource sparing and resource responsiveness. Further, their framework captures current gaps and future needs, identifying a lack of comprehensive assessment linking all stages of an agri-food supply chain, and a need to better link different actors in the chain and consequently collaboratively identify and manage risks.

In this paper we draw from the World Bank's RapAgRisk Assessment conceptual framework to highlight phosphorus supply chain risks.[22] We choose this framework by way of example because, importantly, it takes a multi-stakeholder and systems approach to supply chain risk management. Taking an inherently systems approach to risk management involves multiple sectors and actors and implies the need for collective action to mitigate and manage risks. Causal links and influences

15  International Organization for Standardization, 'ISO 310000:2009 Risk Management – Principles and Guidelines' (2009).
16  R. Narasimhan and S. Talluri, 'Perspectives on Risk Management in Supply Chains', *Journal of Operations Management* 27, no. 2 (2009): 114–18.
17  M. Christopher et al., 'Approaches to Managing Global Sourcing Risk', *Supply Chain Management: An International Journal* 16, no. 2 (2001): 67–81.
18  J.E. Bell et al., 'A Natural Resource Scarcity Typology: Theoretical Foundations and Strategic Implications for Supply Chain Management', *Journal of Business Logistics* 33, no. 2 (2012): 158–66; Christopher et al., 'Approaches to Managing Global Sourcing Risk'.
19  Bell et al., 'A Natural Resource Scarcity Typology'.
20  Ibid., 163.
21  A. Matopoulos, A. Barros, and J.G.A.J. Van der Vorst, 'Resource-Efficient Supply Chains: A Research Framework', *Literature Review and Research Agenda, Supply Chain Management: An International Journal* 20, no. 2 (2015): 218–36.
22  S. Jaffee, P. Siegel, and C. Andrews, 'Rapid Agricultural Supply Chain Risk Assessment, A Conceptual Framework', *Agriculture and Rural Development Discussion Paper* 47 (Washington D.C: The World Bank, 2010).

between sectors through the supply chain, such as the transfer of risks between stakeholder groups, are also important. Jaffee et al.'s framework provides a systematic approach to identify risks, the severity of impact, and risk management strategies that can be actions by individual or collective stakeholders within the supply chain, or by external stakeholders such as policy-makers. The framework enables the identification and assessment of risks from different stakeholder perspectives. Rather than solely a conceptual academic framework, RapAgRisk aims to provide practical guidance on how to systematically identify key vulnerabilities and priority actions to reduce risks and loss in a given agricultural commodity system.

# 3   Approach

In the remainder of this paper, while taking an interdisciplinary perspective, we use the RapAgRisk framework to identify and typologize a range of phosphorus supply chain risks from different stakeholder perspectives, and different stages in the supply chain. To do this, we draw on a synthesis of our own and others' extensive body of sustainable phosphorus research.[23] This research identifies multiple dimensions of phosphorus scarcity – physical, geopolitical, economic, institutional, managerial[24] – and the context-specific interactions and consequences in a phosphorus vulnerability assessment framework,[25] in addition to integrated sustainable phosphorus measures and governance structures[26] and other work in this new and rapidly growing field related to geopolitics,[27] ecological impacts[28] and fertilizer market dynamics.[29]

We also draw from and adapt a 'sustainability cost framework' that we developed for the water service provision sector.[30] This framework has been developed and applied through extensive work conducted in the water industry to identify and assess the broader sustainability costs of supply- and demand-side options in water service provision decision-making.[31] In this paper we define 'sustainability costs' as negative impacts – that is, loss of social, financial, physical or psychological capital to any stakeholder internal or external to the phosphorus supply chain as a consequence of supply chain activities. 'Risk' is defined as the likelihood and consequence of those negative impacts.

---

23   E.g. Cordell and White, 'Life's Bottleneck'.
24   Cordell et al., 'The Story of Phosphorus'.
25   D. Cordell and T.S.S. Neset, 'Phosphorus Vulnerability: A Qualitative Framework for Assessing the Vulnerability of National and Regional Food Systems to the Multi-dimensional Stressors of Phosphorus Scarcity', *Global Environmental Change* 24 (January 2014): 108–22, http://linkinghub.elsevier.com/retrieve/pii/S0959378013001970; D. Cordell et al., 'Adapting to Future Phosphorus Scarcity: Investigating Potential Sustainable Phosphorus Measures and Strategies', Phase II of the Australian Sustainable Phosphorus Futures project, prepared by Institute for Sustainable Futures, University of Technology Sydney (Canberra: Rural Industries Research and Development Corporation, Australian Government, 2014); P-FUTURES website: Transforming the Way Cities Secure Food & Water through Innovative Phosphorus Governance; 'Transformations to Sustainability' Programme, Future Earth, International Social Science Council, http://www.p-futurescities.net/.
26   E.g. D. Cordell and S. White, 'Sustainable Phosphorus Measures: Strategies and Technologies for Achieving Phosphorus Security', *Agronomy* 3, no. 1 (2013): 86–116; D. Cordell and S. White, 'Phosphorus Security: Global Non-governance of a Critical Resource for Food Security', in *Edward Elgar Encyclopedia of Global Environmental Politics and Governance*, ed. P. Pattberg and F. Fariborz Zelli (Cheltenham, UK & Northampton, MA, USA: Edward Elgar, 2015).
27   E.g. HCSS, *Risks and Opportunities in the Global Phosphate Rock Market: Robust Strategies in Times of Uncertainty* (The Hague: Hague Centre for Strategic Studies, 2012).
28   E.g. W. Dodds et al., 'Eutrophication of U.S. Freshwaters: Analysis of Potential Economic Damages', *Environmental Science & Technology.* 43, no. 1 (2009): 12–19.
29   E.g. IFA, 'Food Prices and Fertilizer Markets: Factors influencing variations in fertilizer market conditions' (Paris: International Fertilizer Industry Association, June 2011); IFDC, 'Fertilizer Supply and Costs in Africa' (Chemonics International Inc. and the International Center for Soil Fertility and Agricultural Development, 2007).
30   S. Fane, A. Turner, and C. Mitchell, 'The Secret Life of Water Systems: Least Cost Planning beyond Demand Management', in *2nd IWA Leading-Edge on Sustainability in Water-Limited Environments*, ed. M.B. Beck and A. Speers (London: IWA Publishing, 2006), 35–41.
31   Ibid.; A. Turner et al., 'Guide to Demand Management and Integrated Resource Planning' (paper prepared for the National Water Commission and the Water Services Association of Australia, Inc., at Institute for Sustainable Futures, University of Technology Sydney, 2010).

Due to the diversity and complexity of risks and impacts identified in section 4, we subsequently highlight key stakeholder groups that are impacted by risks occurring at different stages of the phosphorus supply chain, and the transmission of impacts. Finally, we provide examples of potential risk-mitigating measures to demonstrate a diverse range of interventions. The intention of this paper is not to provide a complete identification and management assessment, but rather to open up the debate and make the case for such a comprehensive and collaborative assessment as a way towards better managing phosphorus for food security.

# 4   Typology of phosphorus supply chain risks and impacts

The international market price of phosphate reflects its economic value as a fertilizer, and, like many other resources, this does not reflect the full sustainability cost of mining and using phosphorus. This section illustrates the spectrum of costs and risks associated with phosphorus fertilizers. These costs and risks are highly diverse, ranging from geopolitical to ecological, global to local, short to long term and with positive to negative impacts, as discussed below.

In Figure 3 we indicate a range of direct costs and externalities to different stakeholders in the phosphorus supply chain, which are described in the subsequent text. Importantly, consistent with Jaffee et al., this takes a whole-of-society approach, as opposed to a narrow single stakeholder perspective.[32]

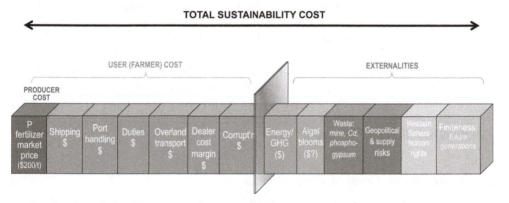

Figure 3. The full sustainability costs associated with phosphate fertilizers, indicating costs to the user (farmer), plus externalities affecting a wider set of stakeholders that are not reflected in transactional prices along the supply chain – environmental and social costs.
Source: Adapted to phosphorus from our sustainability cost framework developed for water (S. Fane, A. Turner, and C. Mitchell, 'The Secret Life of Water Systems: Least Cost Planning beyond Demand Management', in *2nd IWA Leading-Edge on Sustainability in Water-Limited Environments*, ed. M.B. Beck and A. Speers (London: IWA Publishing, 2006).

Externalities are defined as those impacts resulting from transactions that affect third parties not involved in the primary transaction (and those impacts are not themselves traded in markets). Some of these externalities can be costed and internalized, such as life-cycle energy ($/tonne) or algal blooms (as discussed in section 2). For others it may not be appropriate to monetize, but rather require other means of valuing or comparing, such as qualitative risk assessments or multi-criteria assessments that involve deliberative stakeholder engagement, as has been used in the water industry.[33]

---

32   Jaffee et al., 'Rapid Agricultural Supply Chain Risk Assessment'.
33   S. White et al., 'Putting the Economics in its Place: Decision-making in an Uncertain Environment', in *Deliberative Ecological Economics*, ed. C. Zografos and R. Howarth (New Dehli: Oxford University Press, 2008), 80–106.

According to the RapAgRisk framework, major risk categories facing agricultural supply chains include market-related risks, biological and environmental risks, political risks, public policy and institutional risks, weather-related risks and natural disasters, logistical and infrastructural risks, and management and operational risks.[34] In sections 4.1 to 4.4 we use the first four categories to exemplify a range of phosphorus supply chain risks. Overlaps with both logistical and infrastructural risks and management and operational risks are also identified. Implications for specific stakeholders are then highlighted in Table 1 and section 5. Examples are also provided throughout.

## 4.1 *Market-based risks*

Market-based risks related to fertilizers range from price volatility of raw materials, to high fertilizer distribution costs for some farmers. The phosphate price is affected by typical supply–demand market dynamics and future contracts at negotiated prices with producers.[35] In 2008, the price of phosphate spiked 800% (Figure 4). While there were multiple interrelated causes for this spike – ranging from unforecast demand, capacity constraints, increases in input costs, unfavourable exchange rates and possible speculation[36] – it was largely farmers, the end users, who were affected. While the degree of impact depended in part on farmer purchasing power, it resulted in reduced net profit and/or loss of crop yields.

The farm gate price of fertilizers represents the total cost to the farmer, including the raw fertilizer product price (FOB[37]), plus other distribution costs, such as shipping, port handling, duties, inland transport costs and dealer cost margins (Figure 5). These non-product costs can be highly variable across regions due to geography, state of road and rail infrastructure, local market dynamics, logistics inefficiencies and corruption.[38] This therefore also represents a logistics and infrastructure risk. This higher input cost puts land-locked farmers at greater risk and disadvantage. For example, farmers in some land-locked African countries can pay 2–5 times as much for the same fertilizer product as European farmers, or even countries like Thailand that have more efficient distribution and transparency.[39]

## 4.2 *Environmental and biological risks*

Environmental and biological risks occur at local to global scales, such as toxic waste generated during fertilizer mining and production, widespread water pollution from farm nutrient runoff, or the global life cycle energy cost of producing and transporting fertilizers.

As with most supply chains, waste is generated at each stage of the phosphorus supply chain. However, for phosphorus this is relatively high: globally, 80% of phosphorus is lost or wasted from mine to fork.[40] These inefficiencies also arise from management-related risks. During mining, phosphorus losses are variable, though can be as high as 30%.[41] As lower grade and more difficult to reach phosphate reserves are mined, more waste is generated per tonne of

34 Jaffee et al., 'Rapid Agricultural Supply Chain Risk Assessment'.
35 IFA 'Feeding the Earth: Fertilizers and Global Food Security' (Paris: International Fertilizer Industry Association, May 2008).
36 See section 5 and Figure 7.
37 'Free on Board' at port of loading.
38 IFDC, 'Fertilizer Supply and Costs in Africa'.
39 Ibid.; A. Runge-Metzger, 'Closing the Cycle: Obstacles to Efficient P Management for Improved Global Food Security', in *Phosphorus in the Global Environment: Transfers, Cycles and Management*, ed. H. Tiessen, SCOPE 54 (Chichester: Wiley, 1995), 27–42.
40 Cordell et al., 'The Story of Phosphorus'.
41 M. Prud'homme, 'World Phosphate Rock Flows, Losses and Uses' (paper presented at International Fertilizer Industry Association Phosphates International Conference, Brussels, March 22–24, 2010).

Table 1. Phosphorus supply-chain risks and examples of transmission of impacts to stakeholder groups (*indicates indirect stakeholders).

| Location of risk in supply chain (*where risk occurs*) | Risk and consequences | Stakeholders impacted and nature of expected impact | | | | | | |
|---|---|---|---|---|---|---|---|---|
| | | Phosphate industry | Western Sahara* | Farmers | Food consumers | Policy-makers* | Environmental representatives* | Future generations* |
| **1. Phosphate rock mining** | **Political risk:** five countries controlling 85% of world's phosphate. Political instability or deliberate market interventions in a producing country can lead to supply disruptions and price fluctuations | Supply delays in the fertilizer production and distribution chain, leading to monetary losses | Resource curse leading to increased social inequity | Farmers unable to afford or access P fertilizers, leading to reduced productivity; in 2008 there were farmer riots and suicides in some countries | Food prices can increase as a result, leading to increased food insecurity | National security risk for importing countries leading to reduced agricultural productivity, affecting both the economy and domestic food security | | |
| | **Political risk:** Morocco's occupation of Western Sahara and the territory's phosphate rock | Reputation risk for phosphate producers and importers of 'conflict phosphates' | Financial, physical and psychological exploitation of Saharawi people who have legal right to their land and phosphate | Farmers knowingly or unknowingly supporting mining in an illegally occupied territory | Food consumers knowingly or unknowingly supporting mining in an illegally occupied territory | | | |
| | **Environmental risk:** depletion a finite resource, creating an intergenerational risk for future generations. | The quality and accessibility of future reserves are lower than those currently under production, leading to increased production costs in the future | | | | | | Future generations don't have the same access to a critical resource (or a say in how it is managed today), hence their food security is threatened |
| **2. Fertilizer production and trade** | **Environmental risk:** stockpiling radioactive byproduct, phosphogypsum | | | | | | Toxic material can potentially leach from stacked stockpiles and contaminate drinking water or ecologically sensitive water bodies | |

(*Continued*)

Table 1. Continued.

| Location of risk in supply chain *(where risk occurs)* | Risk and consequences | Stakeholders impacted and nature of expected impact | | | | | | |
|---|---|---|---|---|---|---|---|---|
| | | Phosphate industry | Western Sahara* | Farmers | Food consumers | Policy-makers* | Environmental representatives* | Future generations* |
| **3. Fertilizer application in agriculture** | **Market-related risk:** high and/or variable fertilizer distribution costs, especially for land-locked countries | | | Reduced farmer purchasing power (e.g. can't afford fertilizers) resulting in lower yields | High fertilizer prices can in turn increase food prices (where farmers are not price takers) | | | |
| **4. Food production, processing and distribution** | **Environmental and Management risk:** huge amounts of food waste generated between farm-gate and consumption means embodied phosphorus is wasted (up to 40%) | | | | | | | More phosphorus wasted now means higher grade phosphate rock is depleted faster and less will be available for future generations |
| **5. Food consumption** | **Market-related risk:** changing dietary preferences can and have dramatically altered (increase) the demand for phosphorus | A lack of long-term planning and foresight can lead to a lagged supply constraint (as per 2008) | | | | | | (as above) |

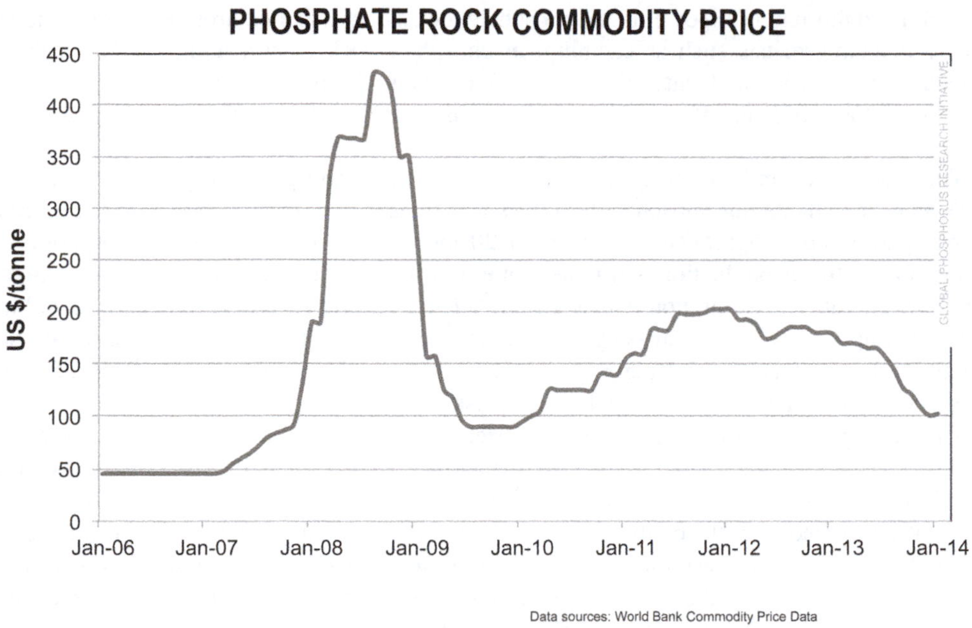

## PHOSPHATE ROCK COMMODITY PRICE

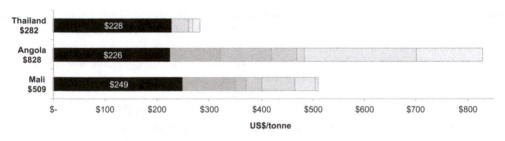

Data sources: World Bank Commodity Price Data

Figure 4. Phosphate rock price 2006–14, indicating a 800% price spike in 2008.
Data source: World Bank Commodity Price data.

### Farm-gate fertilizer costs

| | |
|---|---|
| Thailand $282 | $228 |
| Angola $828 | $226 |
| Mali $509 | $249 |

US$/tonne

■Product cost  ▨Shipping  ▨Port handling  ▢Duties  ▨Inland transport costs  ▢Dealer cost margin  ▢Other costs

Figure 5. Farm-gate fertilizer costs are highly variable, as indicated by Sub-Saharan Angola and Mali compared to Thailand, largely due to local transport and retail costs.
Data source: IFDC, 'Fertilizer Supply and Costs in Africa' (Chemonics International Inc. and the International Center for Soil Fertility and Agricultural Development, 2007).

phosphate extracted. United Nations Environment Programme (UNEP) has documented the extent of local environmental impacts of phosphate rock mining and processing.[42] During the predominant phosphate fertilizer production process, five tonnes of phosphogypsum by-product are generated for every tonne of phosphate fertilizer.[43] Complicating this picture is that phosphogypsum is deemed radioactive by the US Environmental Protection Agency (EPA), due to the transfer

42  UNEP, 'Environmental Aspects of Phosphate and Potash Mining' (Paris: UN Environment Programme & International Fertilizer Industry Association, 2010).
43  Schroder et al., 'Sustainable Use of Phosphorus'.

of radium and thorium isotopes from the phosphate rock stock. Other environmental risks include transfer of heavy metals such as cadmium in phosphate rock to agricultural soils which can be taken up by crops and enter the human food chain.[44] These environmental waste risks can pollute the environment, create expensive management costs, and lead to human health impacts.

The lifecycle energy and greenhouse gas cost of mining and processing lower grade phosphate rock, manufacturing phosphate fertilizers and transporting these commodities from mine to farm gate is not insignificant, estimated at 20 megajoules per kilogram of phosphorus for mining and fertilizer production and trade alone. Phosphate is one of the world's most highly traded commodities at 30 million tonnes a year.[45] The transport fuel used for shipping, rail and road has implications for increasing greenhouse gas emissions that contribute to climate change, and, simultaneously deplete scarce fossil fuels such as oil and gas. This life-cycle energy consumption also represents a logistical risk.

The ecological cost of eutrophication (nutrient pollution) of the world's rivers, lakes and oceans receives relatively more awareness than other environmental impacts of phosphorus use. Globally, this impact is a consequence of the mobilization of thousands of millions of tonnes of phosphate from the earth's upper crust over the past half-century, 8–9 times the background flow,[46] essentially resulting in the one-way flow of phosphorus from mines to oceans, in turn leading to pollution of the world's aquatic ecosystems,[47] from the Gulf of Mexico to China's Shandong Province to Australia's Great Barrier Reef.

Eutrophication can lead to toxic algal blooms, which can kill fish and entire aquatic ecosystems, pollute drinking water and damage fishing and recreation industries. Globally, the World Resources Institute estimates over 400 'dead zones'.[48] In the US alone the annual cost of algal blooms was conservatively estimated at over US$2.2 billion.[49] In the North American summer of 2014, the drinking water of the US town of Toledo (population 400,000) was rendered toxic from phosphorus pollution associated with algal blooms in the Great Lakes,[50] resulting in the city importing bottled water from interstate. In Australia, floodwaters in Queensland during extreme events carry large volumes of phosphorus-rich sediments from the fertile topsoil of farms to the Great Barrier Reef. This can lead to an irrecoverable loss of valuable nutrients in farmland, and loss of aquatic biodiversity and to fishing, recreation and tourism industries.[51]

Ultimately, resource scarcity of phosphate rock is likely to present the most significant long term environmental risk. As with any critical and finite resource, the quantity of high-concentrate, easy to access phosphate resources have been mined first, leaving behind more expensive, lower-quality and more difficult to access resources, physically, socially and economically.[52] This compromises future generations' ability to efficiently utilize phosphorus resources to support affordable food production and food security.

Phosphate rock has taken hundreds of millions of years to form from under the sea bed to mountains through tectonic uplift. However, a number of recent studies suggest that current

---

44 Ibid.
45 Ibid.
46 J. Rockström et al., 'A Safe Operating Space for Humanity', *Nature* 461 (2009): 472–75.
47 E. Bennett, S. Carpenter, and N. Caraco, 'Human Impact on Erodable Phosphorus and Eutrophication: A Global Perspective', *Bioscience* 51 (2001): 227–34.
48 R. Diaz and R. Rosenberg, 'Spreading Dead Zones and Consequences for Marine Ecosystems', *Science* 321, no. 5891 (2008): 926–9.
49 Dodds et al., 'Eutrophication of U.S. Freshwaters'.
50 D. Mitchell, 'Lake Erie's Green Sludge Highlights our Phosphorus Problem', *Fortune* (August 2014). Available at: http://fortune.com/2014/08/06/peak-phosphorus-toledo-water/.
51 Bennett et al., 'Human Impact on Erodable Phosphorus and Eutrophication'.
52 S. Van Kauwenbergh, 'World Phosphate Rock Reserves and Resources' (Washington, DC: International Fertilizer Development Centre, IFDC, 2010).

reserves are likely to peak mid-century, around 2035–75.[53] Others argue there are 'hundreds' of years remaining.[54] The controversy and inherent uncertainty regarding longevity of phosphate reserves results from differing methods and assumptions underpinning estimates of future demand and supply. For example, the more optimistic studies tend to project static demand into the future, ignoring the significant per capita phosphorus demand increases associated with changing dietary preferences towards more animal protein (particularly in China and India), which require substantially more phosphate fertilizer to support.[55] Further, supply estimates are based on self-reporting by individual companies and/or countries to the US Geological Survey, which collates these figures as a public service without validation of the figures or consistency of underlying assumptions between countries.

This uncertainty and a stark lack of transparency regarding one of the most globally critical resources, coupled with the certainty that we have used up the cheap high-quality phosphate, is enough to warrant some caution when considering availability for future generations.

## 4.3  *Political risks*

Geopolitical risks carry perhaps the greatest consequences and result from the supply concentration of phosphate producers in potentially politically unstable regions. Although the topic of far less discussion and monitoring, phosphate resources are more geopolitically concentrated than oil. While all countries and farmers need access to phosphorus, only five countries combined control 88% of remaining phosphate reserves.[56] Exacerbating this situation, just one company in one country alone controls 75% of the world's remaining phosphate reserves: the Moroccan kingdom-controlled phosphate company Office Chérifien des Phosphates (OCP). It is predicted that Morocco's market share could increase to 80–90% by 2030.[57] Other countries in the top five include Syria, Algeria, China and South Africa.[58]

The geopolitical risks are both long term, with respect to remaining reserves, and short term, with respect to production. Producing countries (i.e. those countries where phosphate rock is mined and traded) are also concentrated: China, the US, Morocco, Russia and Jordan together hold an 82% market share.[59] Recent civil and political unrest in the Middle East and North Africa has also raised concerns about potential disruptions to phosphate rock supply and capacity development in associated countries.[60]

The implications are potential supply disruptions and price fluctuations. This supply concentration of both producing countries and countries controlling remaining reserves creates both a short-term business risk and a long-term national security risk for importing countries.[61]

---

53  These studies have used post-2010 phosphate reserve data from IFDC 2010 or USGS 2011–13 to calculate supply in different regions. S. Mohr and G. Evans, 'Projections of Future Phosphorus Production', *Philica.com* (2013), http://www.philica.com/display_article.php?article_id=380; P. Walan, 'Modeling of Peak Phosphorus: A Study of Bottlenecks and Implications' (Master's diss., Uppsala University, Sweden, 2013); Cordell and White, 'Life's Bottleneck'.

54  Van Kauwenbergh, 'World Phosphate Rock Reserves and Resources'; D.P.P. Van Vuuren, A.F. Bouwman, and A.H. W. Beusen, 'Phosphorus Demand for the 1970–2100 Period: A Scenario Analysis of Resource Depletion', *Global Environmental Change* 20, no. 3 (2010): 428–39, http://linkinghub.elsevier.com/retrieve/pii/S0959378010000312 (accessed March 18, 2013); D. Vaccari and N. Strigul, 'Extrapolating Phosphorus Production to Estimate Resource Reserves', *Chemosphere* 84, no. 6 (2011): 792–97, http://www.ncbi.nlm.nih.gov/pubmed/21440285 (accessed March 8, 2013).

55  G. Metson, E. Bennett, and J. Elser, 'The Role of Diet in Phosphorus Demand', *Environmental Research Letters* 7, no. 4 (2012): 1–10, 044043.

56  USGS, 'Phosphate Rock', *Mineral Commodity Summaries*, ed. S.M. Jasinski (US Geological Survey, January 2014).

57  J. Cooper et al., 'The Future Distribution and Production of Global Phosphate Rock Reserves', *Resources Conservation and Recycling* 57 (2011): 78–86; HCSS, 'Risks and Opportunities in the Global Phosphate Rock Market.

58  USGS, 'Phosphate rock'.

59  Ibid.

60  HCSS, 'Risks and Opportunities in the Global Phosphate Rock Market.

61  Ibid.

Figure 6. The world's longest conveyor belt transporting phosphate rock 100 km from the Bou Craa phosphate mine in Western Sahara to the port for global export.
Source: Google Maps 2012; Photo credit: Santiago Cordero.

Figure 6 indicates a 'lifeline' of the global food system: the world's longest conveyor belt transporting phosphate rock from Western Sahara 100 km to the Moroccan-controlled port for shipments to Australia, Canada, Lithuania and other importing countries.[62]

Further exacerbating the geopolitical situation is the occupation of Western Sahara. Moroccan forces took control of the territory in 1975 as Spanish colonial powers withdrew.[63] Resource ownership and the legality of the occupation are vigorously contested by Morocco, which claims rightful ownership of the land and resources. However, no other African nation or the UN acknowledge Morocco's claim.[64]

This classic 'resource curse' has led to a concentration of economic/market power and increased social inequity, where Morocco benefits from the processing and trade of the region's phosphate rock, while the Saharawi people are in a situation of social and economic disadvantage. Morocco's state-run phosphate company owns and operates the phosphate mines in the disputed territory, largely employing Moroccan nationals and with profits directly injected into the Moroccan economy, estimated at $4.27 billion over the current life of the mines.[65] While as many as 165,000 Saharawi people live in exile in refugee camps in neighboring Algeria, those in the disputed territory risk persecution, incarceration and have their rights limited.

---

62  WSRW, 'Morocco's Exports of Phosphates from Occupied Western Sahara, 2012 & 2013' (Melbourne: Western Sahara Resource Watch, 2014).
63  Ibid.
64  J. Smith, 'The Taking of the Sahara: The Role of Natural Resources in the Continuing Occupation of Western Sahara, *Journal of Global Change, Peace & Security* (2015).
65  Ibid.

This trade of 'conflict phosphates' implies that importers, distributors, farmers and food consumers in Australia and other importing countries are knowingly or unknowing supporting mining in a disputed territory and therefore potentially illegal trade. Regardless, the direct social impacts result in 'risk transfer' up and down the supply chain, including significant reputational risks for suppliers and consumers associated with a lack of corporate social responsibility.

## 4.4 *Public policy and institutional risks*

Institutional risks include those that arise from poor governance and can result in a range of consequences, such as increasing the vulnerability of food systems to any unforeseen shock.[66] For example, there are no international bodies responsible for ensuring long-term availability and accessibility of phosphorus for food production.[67] Further, there are no comprehensive, independent, transparent and robust data sets on remaining phosphate rock reserves and trade. Inadequate monitoring, evaluation, forecasting and long-term scenario planning of global phosphate demand can lead to planning errors such as underestimating demand. Further, a lack of policy instruments to stimulate and support effective use of phosphorus means there is little resilience in the system to buffer or mitigate risks.[68]

## 5 Implications for stakeholders

The implications of not assessing the spectrum of costs, impacts and risks to different sectors are significant for all major stakeholders in the supply chain, whether or not these risks are yet to be realized. Current impacts and potential risks adversely affect direct supply chain participants (such as phosphate producers, farmers, food consumers and policy-makers) and other stakeholder groups (indirect participants), such as the environment, future generations and the Saharawi people of Western Sahara.

The social implications of environmental and geopolitical risks range from local community impacts at mine sites through to indirect impacts further down the supply chain such as the health risk associated with consuming food contaminated with cadmium. Globally, perhaps the most significant single social impact associated with phosphate production is upstream – the social injustice due to the ongoing exploitation and displacement of the Saharawi people whose land and phosphate rock is currently occupied by Morocco.

The case of phosphorus also illustrates the inter- and intra-generational inequity that results when those who gain from resource extraction avoid paying the full costs. Here, the depletion of the resource and the adverse impacts through the supply chain tend to affect the poorest and most vulnerable, as well as future generations.

Table 1 indicates at which stage of the supply chain the risks identified in section 4 occur. It then exemplifies the transmission of these phosphorus supply chain risks and impacts to a range of direct and indirect stakeholder groups. These examples are drawn from our prior research,[69] and are by no means exhaustive. In reality, these impacts will be nuanced and varied between the many actors within each stakeholder group. For example, phosphate industry actors in the global market can be further broken down to include mining companies, fertilizer manufacturers, traders, shipping companies, inspection agencies and banks. Domestic phosphate industry actors

---

66  Cordell and White, 'Phosphorus Security.

67  Ibid.

68  For a fuller description of phosphorus global non-governance and associated vulnerabilities, see ibid. and Cordell and Neset, 'Phosphorus Vulnerability'.

69  E.g. Cordell and White, 'Life's Bottleneck; Cordell and Neset, 'Phosphorus Vulnerability'.

include importers, domestic manufacturers, transporters, banks, port authorities, policy-makers, regulators, wholesalers and agro-dealer retailers.[70]

The transmission or 'ripple effect' from the risk location in the supply chain through to different system stakeholders can be demonstrated by the 2008 price spike. A cocktail of events occurred to that led the 800% price spike (Figure 7). Firstly, the increasing food and agricultural commodity prices meant more farmers were willing to risk purchasing fertilizers to maximize their crop yields and take advantage of high agricultural selling prices. At the same time, a new Ethanol Policy in the US triggered a surge in first-generation biofuel production, which in turn led to a burst of demand for fertilizer to grow biofuel crops.[71] A slower but substantial demand growth was gradually brewing in the background, associated with China and India's increasing appetite for meat and dairy products as a result of increasing affluence, which

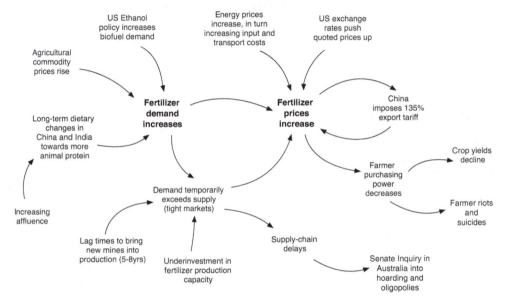

Figure 7: the 2008 phosphate price spike explained, indicating the numerous factors influencing the spike, and examples of negative stakeholder impacts.

results in higher per capita fertilizer demand to support such diets. The few phosphate producers were unable to meet this unexpected demand, in part due to insufficient forecasting, historical underinvestment in fertilizer capacity and lag times in bringing new mines into production.[72]

This temporary supply constraint created tight phosphate markets and led to increasing phosphate prices. Exacerbating these price increases were the spike in energy prices (a key input for phosphate mining, production and transport) and unfavorable US exchange rates pushing up phosphate prices, which are quoted in US dollars.[73] In late 2008, China, one of the major producers of phosphate rock on the market, suddenly imposed a 135% export tariff, further pushing up the price. This unforeseen price spike compounded the food and energy price spikes, leading to farmer riots and suicides in highly vulnerable regions.[74] Even relatively secure countries like Aus-

70  IFDC, 'Fertilizer Supply and Costs in Africa'.
71  Cordell, 'The Story of Phosphorus.
72  IFA, 'Feeding the Earth; Cordell, 'The Story of Phosphorus.
73  IFA, 'Feeding the Earth.
74  Cordell and White, 'Life's Bottleneck'.

tralia were affected, triggering a Senate Inquiry into the potential presence of oligopolies and hoarding behavior.[75]

This crisis, although short term, demonstrated how vulnerable the global food system is to even a short-term perturbation in the supply of phosphate. While many factors were unforeseen, there was and still is no transparent international body monitoring long-term phosphorus demand, supply and risk drivers.[76]

The nature and severity of stakeholder impacts can vary within a sector depending on the local sensitivities and local capacity to adapt.[77] For example, extending the case above, farmers who have phosphorus-deficient soils due to geology or mismanagement may be more sensitive to a price spike, while their counterparts working with phosphorus-rich soils might be able to more easily skip a year of fertilizer application and rely on the buffering capacity of their phosphorus soil reserves.[78] However Doody et al. caution that this perceived buffer provided by 'legacy' soil phosphorus from years or decades of fertilizer over-application can also create a leakage risk resulting in loss of nutrient to water bodies, thereby increasing the eutrophication risk.[79]

These impacts can also differ over time: the impact of a tonne of phosphate in the future is greater than a tonne today. For example, as lower grades are mined (containing less phosphorus and more impurities), to extract the same amount of elemental P from ore requires more energy, generates more waste and is overall more costly.

## 6   Interventions to mitigate and manage risks

Interventions to mitigate or manage risks can enable stakeholders to reduce losses or negative impact by avoiding, coping, transferring, adapting or transforming in response to the risk. The RapAgRisk framework categorizes interventions as technical, market-based, public policy or social in nature.[80] Table 2 provides examples of such interventions to address the different risks identified in Table 1. The text below elaborates on the examples. It is not intended as a complete and systematic analysis of options, but rather to highlight a spectrum of options. In some cases, the same intervention can address multiple risks. In reality, managing risks will need to involve a suite of interventions.

Diversifying input sources is a market-based or public policy strategy that is 'resource responsive' – i.e. responding to external phosphorus supply chain risks.[81] This implies shifting the profile of phosphorus inputs away from dependence on a single or few sources. This can be a public policy decision at the national/regional level – for example the decision of the European Union, a region almost entirely dependent on imported phosphate, to foster markets for domestic recycled phosphate to reduce the region's exposure to geopolitical risks in producing countries.[82] It could also be a business decision for a fertilizer company to source phosphate from diverse phosphate rock producing countries/companies, to reduce the risk of supply disruptions.

75   Commonwealth of Australia, 'Pricing and Supply Arrangements in the Australian and Global Fertiliser Market', *Final Report*, Senate Select Committee on Agricultural and Related Industries (Commonwealth of Australia, 2009).
76   Cordell and White, 'Phosphorus Security'.
77   R. Nelson et al., 'The Vulnerability of Australian Rural Communities to Climate Variability and Change: Part I – Conceptualising and Measuring Vulnerability', *Environmental Science Policy* 13 (2010): 8–17.
78   Cordell and Neset identify 26 risk factors leading to phosphorus vulnerability in a national food system, including exposure, sensitivity and adaptive capacity factors. Cordell and Neset, 'Phosphorus Vulnerability'.
79   D.G. Doody, P.J. Withers, and R.M. Dils, 'Prioritizing Water Bodies to Balance Agricultural Production and Environmental Outcomes', *Environmental Science and Technology* 48, no. 14 (2014): 7697–9, http://www.ncbi.nlm.nih.gov/pubmed/24971468.
80   Jaffee et al., 'Rapid Agricultural Supply Chain Risk Assessment'.
81   Matopoulos et al., 'Resource-Efficient Supply Chains'.
82   HCSS, 'Risks and opportunities in the global phosphate rock market; ESPP, 'Special Issue: European Sustainable Phosphorus Conference', 111 (Brussels: European Sustainable Phosphorus Platform, March 2015), http://phosphorusplatform.eu/images/download/ScopeNewsletter_111_special_ESPC2.pdf.

Table 2. Examples of sustainable phosphorus interventions to mitigate different phosphorus supply chain risks.

| | INTERVENTIONS | | | | | |
|---|---|---|---|---|---|---|
| | MARKET/PUBLIC POLICY: | MARKET/ PUBLIC POLICY: | PUBLIC POLICY: | TECHNICAL: | TECHNICAL: | SOCIAL: |
| RISKS: | e.g. diversifying sources (reduce dependence on imported rock) | e.g. divestments and ethical investments | e.g. future sovereign wealth fund | e.g. increasing efficient phosphorus use by crops | e.g. increasing recycling and reuse of phosphorus | e.g. changing diets towards P-efficient foods |
| Political risk: market concentration | ✪ | | | | ✪ | |
| Political risk: Western Sahara conflict | ✪ | ✪ | | | ✪ | |
| Environmental risk: algal blooms | | | | ✪ | ✪ | ✪ |
| Environmental risk: resource scarcity | | | ✪ | ✪ | ✪ | ✪ |
| Market-related: risk: High/ variable farm-gate distribution costs | ✪ | | | ✪ | ✪ | |

Divestment strategies can discourage investment in 'conflict phosphates', as has been the case for major Scandinavian funds such as the Swedish government pension fund AP-Fonden, Norway's sovereign wealth fund and Denmark's largest bank, Danske Bank, all of which have divested from or excluded Australian companies Incitec Pivot Limited and Westfarmers, and Canada's PotashCorp which are importing/have imported phosphates from Western Sahara via Morocco's OCP. Upon divesting, Dankse Bank noted '[The company] imports natural resources which are extracted in conflict with human rights norms'.[83]

Another potential public policy intervention is future funds (sovereign wealth funds) that could specifically target phosphorus and food security for future generations. While there are no effective examples for phosphorus, Norway's 'Oil Fund'[84] is a good example that uses profits from oil sales to ensure national economic security to buffer against the depletion of oil and fluctuating prices. However it is crucial that such funds are appropriately governed and managed. The mismanagement of funds from the Nauru Phosphate Royalties Trust is a case in point. The Trust was established in the 1960s to provide reliable national income from foreign mining and export of Nauru's guano phosphate deposits (largely destined for Australia), however corruption and misuse of the funds left the Trust – and the Island State – essentially bankrupt.[85]

Increasing the efficiency of crop phosphorus use is another important strategy and can be achieved through a number of biophysical pathways, including improved fertilizer placement and timing, crop breeding, improved soil composition and the use of mycorrhizal fungi.[86] All of these reduce the need for phosphorus inputs while maintaining crop yields – that is, improving productivity. This not only reduces farmers' input costs, it also reduces the ecological risk of phosphorus erosion and runoff from agricultural fields to rivers and lakes, and can reduce global phosphorus demand and thereby increase the longevity of the world's remaining phosphate rock for future generations.

According to Matopoulos et al., resource sparing in response to resource scarcity is also a means to maintain competitive advantage.[87] Increasing recycling and reuse of phosphorus means recovering phosphorus from all potential losses in the phosphorus supply chain (crop and food waste, animal manure, human excreta) and reusing the recovered phosphorus formally or informally as a renewable fertilizer.[88] In the sanitation sector alone, there are 30–50 technologies for the recovery of phosphorus from wastewater and excreta for reuse in agriculture.[89]

Changing diets refers to a deliberate downward shift in the current high-phosphorus diet economies (such as Argentina or Australia) and contracting the upward trajectory of emerging economies such as China and India with increasingly intensive phosphorus diets, where increasing affluence is increasing demand for meat and dairy foods.[90] Meat- and dairy-based diets are known to require 2–3 times more phosphorus fertilizers than more plant-based diets.[91] Hence a shift to nutri-

83  WSRW, 'Morocco's Exports of Phosphates from Occupied Western Sahara, 2012 & 2013'.
84  The Government Pension Fund Global, https://www.regjeringen.no/en/topics/the-economy/the-government-pension-fund/id1441/.
85  J. Garrett, *Island Exiles* (ABC Publishers, 1996).
86  M.J. McLaughlin et al., 'The Chemical Nature of P-accumulation in Agricultural Soils – Implications for Fertiliser Management and Design: An Australian Perspective', *Plant Soil* 349 (2011): 69–87.
87  Matopoulos et al., 'Resource-Efficient Supply Chains.
88  D. Cordell et al., 'Towards Global Phosphorus Security: A Systems Framework for Phosphorus Recovery and Reuse Options', *Chemosphere* 84, no. 6 (2011): 747–58.
89  C. Sartorius, J. Von Horn, and F. Tettenborn, ,Phosphorus Recovery from Wastewater – State-of-the-art and Future Potential (paper presented at the International Conference on 'Nutrient Recovery and Management 2011: Inside and Outside the Fence', Miami, FL, January 9–12, 2011).
90  N. Alexandratos and J. Bruinsma, 'World Agriculture towards 2030/2050: The 2012 Revision', ESAWork. paper no. 12-03, Agricultural Development Economics Division, Food and Agriculture Organization of the United Nations 2012, http://www.fao.org/3/a-ap106e.pdf

tious diets that depend less on animal protein can substantially reduce global phosphorus demand, and reduce manure generation, which is often responsible for nutrient pollution in countries like Denmark, the Netherlands and the US.

# 7   Conclusion

Through the lens of a multi-stakeholder supply chain risk assessment framework, this paper has revealed a vast and diverse array of risks and impacts associated with the phosphorus supply chain from mine to fork that together are compromising the achievement of phosphorus security and hence food security. While many of the risks identified are located at the top end of the supply chain (e.g. political and environmental risks occurring in the mining and fertilizer production and trade stages), the negative impacts are transmitted to other stakeholders further down the supply chain, such as farmers and food consumers, and also to non-supply chain stakeholders, such as policy-makers, future generations and the aquatic environment. However, conversely, risks occurring towards the end of the supply chain, such as the changing dietary preferences of food consumers, can have a significant impact on top-end supply chain participants such as mining and fertilizer companies, as was the case in the 2008 price spike where insufficient demand forecasting contributed to price spikes and supply disruptions.

It is hoped that this paper will open up the debate about phosphorus supply chain risks from mine to fork and make the case for a comprehensive, integrated and collaborative assessment that identifies and assesses risks and impacts to all key stakeholders both within and external to the phosphorus supply chain. The RapAgRisk framework has been suggested by way of example; however, other multi-stakeholder agri-food systems frameworks may also be applicable. Undertaking such a comprehensive assessment should also seek to identify a plausible and desirable suite of risk management options to value, mitigate and/or share risks and impacts. Importantly, the phosphorus supply chain and its stakeholders need to be agile and pro-active to manage both known risks and unforeseen shocks. Such risk management interventions can be market-based, policy-oriented, technical, social or hybrid in nature. This in turn can enable policy-makers, industry, investors and the public to make more informed, and socially and environmentally responsible decisions about sourcing and using phosphorus to ensure the global population is fed, farmers and other livelihoods are secure, and waters are free from pollution.

# Acknowledgments

The authors would like to thank the two blind peer reviewers for their insightful, thoughtful and constructive comments and suggestions in relation to supply chain risks and ethics that have improved this paper.

# Disclosure statement

No potential conflict of interest was reported by the authors.

---

91   Metson et al., 'The Role of Diet in Phosphorus Demand'; Cordell et al., 'The Story of Phosphorus'.

# The role of natural resources in the building of an independent Western Sahara

Fadel Kamal

*Saharawi Republic Petroleum and Mines Authority, Bir Lahlou, Saharawi Arab Democratic Republic*

The Saharawi Arab Democratic Republic (SADR) is a founding member of the African Union (AU) and is the sovereign governing authority in Western Sahara. The SADR government believes that the territory's significant natural resources will play an important part in the development of a viable, self-reliant and democratic nation which will contribute to peace, stability and progress of the Maghreb region. The paper examines the SADR's efforts to manage its natural resources through the establishment of the SADR Petroleum and Mines Authority, the launch of licensing rounds, its claim to an exclusive economic zone in the Atlantic Ocean and the recent enactment of a Mining Code. The paper discusses the SADR's efforts to protect its natural resources in a territory that is under occupation, and examines the SADR oil and gas licensing rounds as an example of SADR's assertion of sovereignty. The SADR natural resources strategy has two basic goals: to deter Morocco's efforts to exploit the country's natural resources and to prepare for the recovery of full sovereignty.

## I. Introduction

The organized international community has been successful in a remarkably brief period at the twin projects of ending colonialism and ensuring that the principle of self-determination has taken root, with one notable exception in Africa. Western Sahara, Africa's last colony, remains locked in conflict, its people unable to achieve self-determination while enduring an illegal occupation after the comparable cases of Namibia and East Timor (Timor-Leste) were successfully resolved. The failure to realize the most basic norms of international law, including application of the UN Charter and international humanitarian law in Western Sahara, reveals the limits of international justice and the ability of the United Nations organization to act. The pillage of natural resources from the occupied area of Western Sahara illustrates the aspects of an ongoing denial of self-determination, due to the manner in which the resources are used and the connection they create between the world and Western Sahara. How the Saharawi people govern natural resources in such circumstances is important for the immediate realization of self-determination and the fashioning of an eventual Saharawi state independent in all dimensions.

This paper considers the policy and history of Saharawi governance of the natural resources of their territory, Western Sahara. The development of constitutional and legislative schemes for resource preservation and development, including their intersection with international law, is reviewed. The principal theme of the paper is the national development of natural resources and the prospects they hold for the Saharawi people upon their achieving self-determination. The basis under international law for sovereignty to resources, both under occupation and at independence, receives only limited discussion here, the goal being to consider policy.[1] The activities of the Saharawi Republic's Petroleum and Mines Authority are reviewed as an example of political commitment and capacity to govern natural resources. Finally, prospects for the near-term development of resources and questions about justice in the pillage of those resources from the occupied area of Western Sahara are considered.

## II.  Pursuing an ideal – Saharawi sovereignty over resources

There are several paradoxes in the Saharawi people's efforts to govern for themselves the natural resources of their country while under occupation and awaiting a UN (and international law) guaranteed right of self-determination. It is useful to understand them in order to acquire a better appreciation of Saharawi government policy. The first is that of the dual roles of the government of the Saharawi Arab Democratic Republic (the SADR) and the Saharawi people's national liberation movement, the Frente Polisario.[2] The mandate and goals of the two entities are complementary when it comes to the natural resources of Western Sahara. A democratically elected government acting through the Saharawi state – that is, the SADR – is responsible for resource development in the liberated area of the territory, including environmental protection, exploration activities and security.[3] The SADR government also assumes a lead role in asserting territorial sovereignty and preservation of natural resources pending the restoration of complete independence through the UN-mandated (and Sahawari agreed) self-determination process. Examples include the engagement of other governments in resource-related matters and the legislation which established the SADR's maritime zones in the Atlantic Ocean.[4] This is governance in the classic sense of mature statehood, not much different from the best current examples in Africa. As a national liberation movement, the Frente Polisario represents the concerns of the Saharawi people about the implications of the pillage of natural resources for self-determination, including externally in their relationship with the United Nations.[5]

---

1 Questions of the sovereignty of the Saharawi people to the natural resources of Western Sahara, while awaiting the exercise of self-determination (as a basic right in international law and specifically assured in their case by the United Nations), have been contentious in recent years. The basis for the Saharawi people to assert resource sovereignty flows from UN General Assembly Resolution 1803 (XVII), 'Permanent sovereignty over natural resources' (December 14, 1962). For a useful discussion of the development of that right in modern decolonization, see Nico Schrijver, *Sovereignty Over Natural Resources: Balancing Rights and Duties* (Cambridge: Cambridge University Press, 1997). The application of international law in this regard to the resources of Western Sahara was the particular concern of the United Nations jurisconsult, Hans Corell, in an opinion to the UN Security Council delivered in 2002, discussed below.

2 *Frente Popular de Liberación de Saguía el Hamra y Río de Oro*; the Popular Front for the Liberation of Saguia el-Hamra and Río de Oro (Frente Polisario). The United Nations deals singularly with the Saharawi people through the Frente Polisario, although it de facto accepts SADR governance in the refugee camps and the liberated zone within Western Sahara proper. Annual reports of the UN Secretary-General to the UN Security Council, read in their entirety, reveal UN policy on Western Sahara. See that for 2015, 'Report of the Secretary-General on the Situation Concerning Western Sahara' (April 10, 2015) UN doc. S/2015/246.

3 Saharawi constitutional norms, the functioning of the state and democratic structures are discussed below. The Frente Polisario and the SADR (its government) may be viewed simply as two entities that for a Saharawi civil society which they represent are concerned with national liberation on the one hand and governance (and the conduct of some international relationships, but not with the UN) on the other. See also the discussion below in footnote 30.

The liberated area east of the separation wall or 'berm' constructed by Morocco in the 1980s extends over a third of Western Sahara's land area of 266,000 square kilometers within territorial frontiers established between 1900 and 1912. The SADR has signed contracts with six oil and mining companies. A mineral company, Hanno Resources, is currently undertaking exploration activities in the liberated area.

4 An example is a letter dated June 12, 2014 from the SADR foreign minister to the foreign minister of New Zealand about the import of Saharawi phosphate rock into the latter country (unpublished, on file with the author). See also Law no. 3 of January 21, 2009 Establishing the Maritime Zones of the Saharawi Arab Democratic Republic, discussed below.

5 The Frente Polisario is the accepted representative organization of the Saharawi people, particularly for those under occupation in Western Sahara, in the refugee camps near Tindouf inside Algeria and among the diaspora. The Sahar-

The second paradox can be appreciated in what is the present program for development of resources, a responsibility of the SADR government, in contrast to the mutual policy position of both the government and the Frente Polisario to preserve the territory's resources until self-determination is achieved and occupation ended. The paradox is resolved geographically. In the liberated area, the SADR government is committed to the present sustainable development of resources, notably minerals. For the occupied area, its position is entirely the opposite, and that is to insist on the complete preservation of resources until self-determination has been realized.[6] While both the government and the national liberation movement accept that the Saharawi people under occupation need access to natural resources and that some activity is necessary to ensure an economy sufficient for their needs, there is great concern that resource activities, especially the fishery and phosphate mining, deepens the occupation and annexation of the territory and therefore delays self-determination. Phosphate rock mining in particular is consistently objected to by the SADR government and the Frente Polisario not only because of the illegality of the act but also due to the fact that the resource is finite (non-sustainable) and less will be available to the Saharawi people in future.[7] Faced with the scale of resource development in recent years, the Frente Polisario has called on the United Nations to administer resources in a manner similar to the two decades of work done by United Nations Council for Namibia, if not directly controlling resource extraction, then possibly accounting for and holding revenues in trust for the Saharawi people.[8]

Two other issues are usefully canvassed. Governments of other states are divided on the status of the Saharawi people and their representative institutions. While on one hand, all member states

awi, who were the exclusive inhabitants of Spanish Sahara and when the process for a UN-delivered self-determination referendum began in September 1991, were definitively identified in the UN's December 1999 census-registration. For a useful discussion of the UN census-registration process, see Erik Jensen, *Western Sahara: Anatomy of a Stalemate* (Boulder, CO: Lynne Rienner, 2005).

The Frente Polisario and the SADR government assert sovereignty over all of Western Sahara on several grounds, including the settled rule (*jus cogens*) of international law which confers the right of self-determination (with a choice of independence) on non-self-governing peoples, the declared position of the colonial power, Spain, for Saharawi self-determination (declared in 1974), the Advisory Opinion of the International Court of Justice 1975 on Western Sahara denying any other state title or legal claim to the territory, and the commitments to ensure self-determination made by the United Nations upon entering into the 1990–91 ceasefire and referendum agreement with the Frente Polisario. It is these factors which ground an overwhelming (i.e. legally exclusive) sovereign right to the territory.

The term 'pillage' (interchangeable with plunder) is used here in its ordinary legal meaning, as defined by the Fourth Geneva Convention 1949 and the Rome Statute 1998 of the International Criminal Court. The SADR government employs the term on the basis that a part of Western Sahara is under armed occupation the International Court of Justice having concluded that the occupying power has no legal claim to the territory. The ICJ's 1975 *Western Sahara Advisory Opinion* is discussed below. The decision of Spanish courts in 2014 and 2015 to apply international humanitarian and criminal law in Western Sahara is also considered below.

6 The SADR government accepts that Saharawi under occupation west of the berm must subsist through some form of a functioning economy. However, the overwhelming participation in the Atlantic fishery, phosphate rock mining and transport, agriculture and aquaculture (at Dakhla) is by a settler population introduced after 1975. For example, in numerous personal conversations with Saharawi from the occupied area and after studying available information, the author concludes that no more than 400 of the 2014 workforce of 2200 persons were Saharawi with some original tie, residency or citizenship in the territory.

7 Phosphate rock mining and exports are controlled through the Office Chérifien des Phosphates SA (OCP SA), a state corporation of the occupying power. In 2014 the company issued a securities financing prospectus which noted that the highest quality top layer of phosphate rock at the Bu Craa mine site would be worked to exhaustion that year. 50 million tonnes of phosphate rock were exported from occupied Western Sahara between 1975 and 2014. Reserves of perhaps 500 million tonnes remain. See OCP SA *Prospectus of 17 April 2014* (debt financing on the Irish Stock Exchange), which may be found with a similar 2015 prospectus at the website of the Irish Stock Exchange, http://www.ise.ie (accessed July 24, 2015)

8 'We call on the United Nations to establish a UN Council for the Natural Resources of Western Sahara. The UN Council for Namibia which, among other things, legislated for and oversaw the development of natural resources in occupied Namibia until 1990 is a good example and precedent. The UN should retain the revenues received from the exploitation of the natural resources of Western Sahara in trust until the Saharawi people exercise their right to self-determination and decide their future.' Statement by Fadel Kamal, Representative of the Frente Polisario-Western Sahara at the Seminar of the UN Special Committee of Decolonization (C-24) Fiji, May 21–23, 2014.

of the African Union (and many other countries) have recognized the Saharawi state, on the other, most Global North and Asian governments are yet to extend recognition while the Frente Polisario continues as the single representative entity to the United Nations. When it comes to natural resources, this issue is resolved by the fact that it is non-recognizing states which deal in resources exported from the occupied area of the territory, including the European Union in the Atlantic seacoast fishery.[9] Minor exceptions can be found, of course, including small-scale import of phosphate rock by a multinational corporation into a recognizing state (Venezuela) and the failure of the UN Food and Agricultural Organization (the UNFAO) to engage the Saharawi people when it carries out fisheries surveys on the Saharan seacoast.[10] The African Union has long accepted both dualities, treating the SADR as the government of a member state like any other while externally insisting on the Saharawi people's right to self-determination.[11]

Then there is the issue of difficulties that arise in relation to enforcement of settled international law on pillage of resources from territories experiencing conflict. In the case of Western Sahara, the rights of the Saharawi people have proven unrealizable during four decades of occupation and reasons for this are straightforward: (i) the lack of recognition of the Saharawi state which excludes it from the jurisdiction of international legal institutions such as the International Court of Justice; (ii) the general absence of a factual and legal nexus between the occupation of the territory (or export of its resources) and the domestic legal systems of most countries; and (iii) the deferral by states of the 'question' of Western Sahara to a United Nations which has pursued self-determination through negotiation and not by legal remedies. There is also Spain's sidestepping of any singular diplomatic or legal initiatives that it could pursue as *de jure* administering power, for example by bringing the issue before the International Court of Justice, similar to Portugal's action in relation to East Timor from 1991 through 1995.[12] Within both international and domestic legal systems, sufficient measures exist to stop the pillage of Western Sahara's resources.[13]

---

9   The SADR government estimates the current (2014) direct rent (revenue) from the coastal fishery at US$60 million. (The author derives this from personal conversations in 2014 and 2015 with government officials and by reconciling estimates with known payments made by the European Union and Russia to Morocco for fishing in the Saharan Atlantic area.) In September 2014 fishing resumed by European vessels under a renewed EU–Morocco Fisheries Partnership Agreement, by which the occupying power is annually paid €30 million, the remainder being from Russia under an agreement renewed in 2013, a local offshore commercial fishery, and in October 2014 a seasonal tuna fishery conducted by Japanese vessels. Academic commentary on the economic and legal aspects of what in recent years has been a controversial EU fishery remains limited. See notably Jeffrey Smith, 'Fishing for Self-Determination: European Fisheries and Western Sahara – The Case of Ocean Resources in Africa's Last Colony', *Ocean Yearbook* 27 (2013): 267.

10  For current details of phosphate rock exports from occupied Western Sahara, see Western Sahara Resource Watch, *P for Plunder* (Brussels: Western Sahara Resource Watch, 2015). The FAO's Canary Current Large Marine Ecosystem Project of fisheries and ecosystem assessment (and the building of governance capacity in participating states) is detailed at http://www.canarycurrent.org (accessed March 15, 2015).

11  See African Union Peace and Security Council Communiqué of March 27, 2015, AU doc. PSC/PR/COMM./1 (CDXCVI). The Council called on 'the UN Security Council to address the issue of the illegal exploitation of the Territory's natural resources, bearing in mind the call made in the UN Secretary-General report of 10 April 2014, for all relevant actors, in the light of the increased interest in the natural resources of Western Sahara, to "recognize the principle that the interests of the inhabitants of these territories are paramount", in accordance with Chapter XI, article 73 of the Charter' and recommended 'consideration of a strategy of global boycott of products of companies involved in the illegal exploitation of the natural resources of Western Sahara as a way of further sustaining the attention of the international community on the situation in Western Sahara'. Ibid., para. 11.

12  See *Case Concerning East Timor (Portugal v Australia)*, ICJ Reports 1995, 90.

13  The SADR government engages the law where it can, asserting permanent sovereignty of the Saharawi people to their resources under the UN Charter and UN General Assembly Resolution 1803 (XVII), December 14, 1962 (most famously applied by Hans Corell in his 2002 legal opinion for the UN Security Council on the subject of petroleum exploration in Western Sahara), as well as international humanitarian law with its prohibition against pillage under the Fourth Geneva Convention 1949. The Saharawi government also pursues the enforcement of national criminal, civil and regulatory law throughout Western Sahara and accepts that the criminal law of Spain as the colonial-administering power may have a protective role, including after a 2014 *Audiencia Nacional* decision concluded that Spanish criminal law has continued in at least the occupied area of the territory. On April 9, 2015, a judge of the same

## III.   From out of the desert – the Saharawi people and their natural resources

For millennia, what is now called Western Sahara sustained settlement and migration. Ancient paintings in overhead rock galleries located in the liberated area west of Tifariti town depict human uses of the land including pasturing and hunting of animals. The territory has never been heavily populated, at least not until the last years of the twentieth century, and the resources of the land were sufficient for a semi-nomadic society to develop in the centuries prior to colonial contact.[14] Much is made about primary natural resources in Western Sahara, especially the phosphate mining industry and the coastal fishery, together valued at about US$300 million in 2014. However, the greatest resource for the Saharawi people has always been land, and within that, available fresh water which is most abundant as groundwater.[15]

While land is symbolic for Saharawi national identity, including the project to recover the entire territory and thereby bring an end to the legacy of colonialism, there are significant practical matters for the SADR government to address. Foremost is the loss of habitat areas for pasturing and environmental degradation in urban areas and along the length of the berm. Secondary effects from the occupation include loss and disruption of private and communally used land areas, and partitioning of the territory with all the implications for environmental conservation, changed social contact and internal migration, and the problem of the land mine corridor created by the occupying power along the length of the berm.[16] A Saharawi people who come to enjoy independence after self-determination will have a decades-long task to redress the environmental damage which has been caused by the berm.[17] However, a greater concern is the possible overuse and declining supplies of groundwater in the occupied area of the territory.[18] The evidence is incomplete, given the lack of recent studies and record-keeping in the occupied area, and uncertain data about consumption patterns. What is known is that more groundwater is being taken near the principal cities of El Aauin and Dakhla for a growing population of foreign settlers who have migrated into the territory. Water, hardly a commercial resource, is insufficiently valued in its development and delivery cost charges in this setting. Its availability and quality, and future reserves (and aquifer replenishment dynamics) are a continuing problem for the SADR government.[19] Few tangible practical or legal measures are available to ensure water conservation.

---

court determined that a criminal prosecution case on the basis of genocide could be pursued against eight Moroccan military and three civilians for acts in Western Sahara from 1976 to 1991. See Fernando J. Pérez, 'Ruz procesa 11 mandos militares marroquíes por genocidio en el Sáhara', *El País*, April 9, 2015.

14   For an historical background, see Tony Hodges, *Western Sahara: The Roots of a Desert War* (Westport, CT: Lawrence Hill, 1983).

15   Western Sahara may be unique among nations in that it routinely has no surficial water courses. Most *wadi* are dry for a majority of the year, and there are no appreciable sized bodies of fresh water.

16   The SADR government considers the construction and continued operation of the berm unlawful, and a criminal act within the relevant provisions of the Geneva and Hague Conventions and the Rome Statute (International Criminal Court). By comparison, the International Criminal Court has concluded that part of Israel's security fence which passes through lands of the State of Palestine to violate international law, concluding that in such places it must be removed. See *Legal Consequences of the Construction of a Wall in the Occupied Palestinian Territory (Advisory Opinion)*, ICJ Reports 2004, 136.

17   Mine action organizations estimate the number of land mines throughout the territory, principally along the inland length of the berm, at more than 7 million. See e.g. http://unrec.org/default/index.php/en/2012-08-14-15-04-20/2013-10-30-09-26-03/conventional-arms-issues (accessed April 7, 2015).

18   The SADR government conducts aquifer studies and regulates groundwater use in the liberated area, which is lightly populated including permanent residents and units of the Saharawi People's Liberation Army as well as, in one location east of the berm, a UN MINURSO site. (Personal conversations and field observations of the author in the presence of Saharawi officials, 2014–15.)

19   The largest use of water in the occupied area is for human consumption, although agriculture applications are considerable, for example in hydroponic farms around Dakhla. Water use for fish processing and phosphate rock washing is comparatively small. In addition to the Saharawi population and around 200,000 Moroccan settlers, there are also over 100,000 occupying troops mostly deployed all along the berm. (Personal conversations of the author with UN officials, Saharawi residents of the occupied part of Western Sahara, and Saharawi officials, 2014–15.)

Western Sahara's secondary (and as yet underdeveloped) resources feature in different ways in the occupation, including as a basis to employ settlers and to ground the pretext of a viable economy. They include ongoing exports of sand (to the Canary Islands for construction and beach development) and salt, as well as hydroponically cultivated vegetables. The exploitation of oil reserves, with no substantial recovery yet achieved, has been the *cause célèbre* in recent years, culminating with test well drilling in 2015. Considerable areas in the occupied zone and the entire continental shelf on the coast of Western Sahara (to an average distance of 100 nautical miles) have been allocated for 'reconnaissance' exploration under petroleum licensing permits from the occupying power's state-owned Office National des Hydrocarbures et Mines (ONHYM). The granting of two of such seabed petroleum permits prompted the UN Security Council in 2001 to seek the advice of the UN's principal jurist, Hans Corell. Mr. Corell evidently concluded that he only needed to consider UN Resolution 1803 before concluding that further petroleum development (exploration or recovery) would violate international law unless done with the consent of the Saharawi people and for their benefit.[20] It was in response to renewed petroleum exploration in 2008 that the SADR government created maritime jurisdiction legislation, bringing it into force in January 2009.[21] Despite this, large-scale and costly seabed exploration has been conducted in two large seabed areas since 2012, with a test well in 2100 meters of water at one site northwest of Boujdour drilled in early 2015.[22] The activity brought a protest from the Frente Polisario Secretary-General to the UN Secretary-General:

> [T]he present petroleum activity is illegal and impedes progress toward the conduct of a 'free and fair referendum' as that has been accepted by the parties. (See report of Secretary-General 18 June 1990, UN document S/21360, paragraph 47(g).) The activity underscores to the Saharawi people that a violation of well-settled, universally [accepted] rules of international law is allowed to continue. That suggests the organised international community is unwilling to ensure the paramount obligation of self-determination flowing from Article 73 of the UN Charter.[23]

The goal of the SADR government is to preserve petroleum, which is a finite resource, until complete independence has been achieved. The making of timely protests to the United Nations and

---

20  Letter dated January 29, 2002 from the Under-Secretary-General for Legal Affairs, the Legal Counsel, addressed to the President of the Security Council, UN doc. S/2002/161. The letter is routinely misquoted by petroleum companies and corporations which purchase phosphate rock. The operative conclusion and therefore legal guidance to the Security Council is at paragraph 25: '[I]f further exploration and exploitation activities were to proceed in disregard of the interests and wishes of the people of Western Sahara, they would be in violation of the principles of international law applicable to mineral resource activities in Non-Self-Governing Territories.' This requirement has its origins in UN General Assembly Resolution 1803 of December 14, 1962 declaring the right of non-self-governing peoples to sovereignty over their natural resources.

21  The Maritime Zones statute, above, was remarked upon by the UN Secretary-General in his 2009 report to the Security Council and appears to have caused the EU Parliament to reconsider the 2007 EU–Morocco Fisheries Partnership Agreement, resulting in its rejection in December 2011. See Johann Schoo, 'Letter – Fisheries Partnership Agreement between the European Community and the Kingdom of Morocco – Declaration by the Saharawi Arab Democratic Republic (SADR) of 21 January 2009 of jurisdiction over an Exclusive Economic Zone of 200 nautical miles off the Western Sahara – Catches taken by EU-flagged vessels fishing in the waters off the Western Sahara' (European Union/Commission Legal Service Opinion), July, 13 2009. The letter was made public in February 2010 and can be found on the website of Western Sahara Resource Watch, http://www.wsrw.org.

22  The two areas are from Dakhla south to the Cape Blanc peninsula (Groupe Total SA) and the Boujdour Offshore Block (Kosmos Energy Ltd.) where the *Gargaa/El Khayr* website was drilled in Q1 2015. The Saharawi government protested to both companies.

23  Letter of January 26, 2015, http://www.spsrasd.info (accessed March 2, 2015). The UN Secretary-General noted the protest in his annual report to the Security Council, 'Report of the Secretary-General on the situation concerning Western Sahara' (April 10, 2015) UN doc. S/20-15/246, para. 62. And see para. 80: 'In the light of increased interest in the natural resources of Western Sahara, it is timely to call upon all relevant actors to "recognize the principle that the interests of the inhabitants of these territories are paramount", in accordance with Chapter XI, Article 73 of the Charter of the United Nations.'

others helps to underscore the political and economic risks faced by the corporations involved.[24] For the present, such risks have joined with depressed market prices for petroleum to make petroleum development unattractive.

Exploration for minerals other than phosphate rock has been pursued in the occupied area of Western Sahara, notably since 2004. Despite seemingly good prospectivity for metal ores in numerous locations, no commercial extraction is in the works. The most valuable resources in Western Sahara remain those when Spain departed in 1975, the Atlantic fishery and phosphate rock, not yet eclipsed by mining and petroleum extraction. With high market values for each, the revenues from them even in recent years of record phosphate prices have been used to offset the costs of the military occupation. The occupation of Western Sahara was costing Morocco during the years of war an estimated $1.9 billion a year.[25]

## IV.    Toward a just future – the role of resources in Saharawi self-determination

Western Sahara's natural resources have important implications for an eventually independent Saharawi nation. The cornerstone of Saharawi government policy is to ensure availability of the resources as one basis for economic development, including through creation of employment, secondary market and services activities, and taxation revenues. A balance of resources (and public transparency in their development) are features of avoiding the 'resource curse' of excessive reliance on a single high-value (and non-renewable) commodity such as petroleum.[26] Finally, with resources comes trade, and that is an important dimension of how the Saharawi state will interact with others in the international community.

The prospects for economic returns from the territory's resources are promising. With a small population and an abundance of natural resources, the future independent SADR will be a viable and a flourishing nation that will be a factor of stability and peace in the Maghreb region and an example of a modern and democratic nation in North Africa, one tolerant and willing to interact with all its neighbors and with the international community. Such a state is keen to attract investment in a transparent and open manner and for the benefit of all.

It is estimated that the annual revenue streams from Saharawi resource commodities is likely to be US$1260 million (2015).[27] The combined taxation and commodity (rent) return to

---

24  In January 2014 the SADR detailed a compensation claim to the largest purchaser of Saharawi phosphate, Potash Corporation of Saskatchewan Inc., noting the claim then to be a minimum of US$400 million. (A copy of the Saharawi Republic's unpublished letter is on file with the author.)

25  'Burden or Benefit? Morocco in the Western Sahara', lecture given at the Middle East Studies Centre, Oxford University, February 18, 2005 by Toby Shelley (author of *Endgame in the Western Sahara: What Future for Africa's Last Colony?* (London: Zed Books, 2004)). The text of the lecture is available at http://www.arso.org/TSh180205.htm (accessed April 8, 2015).

26  Energy security in a future Western Sahara has been studied by the SADR government with a view to alternative energy sources given the cost of petroleum and desired national contributions to reducing greenhouse gases from the use of fossil fuels.

27  This is the author's calculation, arrived at through the following methodology. The net present annual revenue-taxation return from the territory's present four leading resources is calculated over a 25-year period. 250 million barrels of petroleum is assumed to be available at a market price of US$60 per barrel and extracted at 10 million barrels annually, for a revenue stream of $600 million per annum. The second resource, the fishery, is accepted as having a $60 million taxation (rent) revenue, unchanged from 2014 when EU fishing resumed. The amount is then doubled to account for secondary economic production in the sector, notably processing and services to vessels, for a fisheries sector total of $120 million. Third, phosphate mineral rock exports are put at 2.5 million tonnes per year, up slightly from the five-year average (2010–14) of 2.1–2.2 million tonnes, at $120 per tonne for a total market (commodity) payment to government of $300 million annually. (From this amount would be deducted the cost to operate the mine and transport infrastructure, about $100 million per year.)

It is the fourth resource, iron ore, that has the greatest variability in making estimates. Details about the volume and quality of reserves in the occupied area are not available or lack credibility. However, enough is known from the experience of the high value site at *Kedia d'Idjil-Zouerate* nearby in Mauritania and recent prospecting in the liberated

government would be less than half this amount, perhaps $300 million (as a matter of expected royalty and taxation in an independent SADR). The contribution of the primary resources to the Saharawi economy is understood by calculating gross domestic product (GDP) in comparison to other countries.

The SADR government's natural resources policy – applicable throughout all of Western Sahara – has important economic and legal dimensions, together with the engagement of the Saharawi people for a viable future. The Saharawi people will proceed through self-determination with a substantial endowment of resources and, equally importantly, with an increasingly sophisticated and democratically accountable governance of them.

The SADR aims to adopt a prudent, far-sighted strategy with regard to the management of the natural resources.[28] The goal is for resources to be used for the benefit of the Saharawi people while also contributing to the prosperity of the Maghreb region. The intention is also that resources play a role in the peaceful resolution of the conflict and become a factor of peace and stability in the region. Hence, the 2007 Proposal of the Frente Polisario for a mutually acceptable political solution provides that '[t]he guarantees to be negotiated by the two parties would [include] agreement on equitable and mutually advantageous arrangements permitting the development and the joint exploitation of the existing natural resources or those that could be discovered during a determined period of time'.[29]

## V.   Of states and sovereigns – the SADR and its resource governance policies

The Saharawi people govern their natural resources in a manner which is unique in the era of decolonization achieved in the aftermath of General Assembly Resolution 1514. Their leading political institutions, the Frente Polisario and the SADR state, are democratic, they govern themselves in refugee exile, and, through the SADR itself, hold a part of Western Sahara.[30] Moreover, they have the advantage of settled international law when it comes to proposed resource activities in the liberated area and to constrain the pillage of resources in the occupied area west of the berm (even as that law goes unenforced). The Saharawi government is conscious of the imperative to

---

area that estimates can be done with confidence. A future iron ore mine with reserves of 300 million tonnes yielding recoverable ore at 35% and an annual net production of four million tonnes at $60 per tonne results in revenue of $240 million.

The four annual revenue streams total ($600 million + $120 million + $300 million + $240 million) US$1260 million.

28   Examples of this policy stance include legislation and governing mechanisms for resource development in the liberated zone, the general maintenance and improvement of rule of law measures in the SADR government such as initiatives for transparency in decision-making and civil society participation in resource planning, the call for United Nations involvement in current resource exports, and continual protests over the taking of resources (and environmental protection concerns) in the occupied area of Western Sahara.

29   'Proposal of the Frente Polisario for a mutually acceptable political solution that provides for the self-determination of the people of Western Sahara', UN doc. S/2007/210 (April 16, 2007), at para. 9.3.

30   The political economy of the Saharawi state must be considered in the context of the setting of the Saharawi refugee camps and the pursuit of national liberation through the Frente Polisario. The SADR assumes a form closest to a classically Western (i.e. Global North) democratic ideal in the electoral mandate it receives to govern for the maintenance of civil society in the camps. That mandate, when it comes to self-determination, and engaging external entities such as the United Nations, is conferred through the Saharawi parliament (the National Council) upon government for exercise by the Frente Polisario. 'The Sahrawi National Council is the legislative organ of the SADR. Its fifty-three members are elected each eighteen months. The council meets in two annual sessions with commissions functioning between times. It considers the programme put forward by the government and if two-thirds of the members consistently oppose it, the head of state must choose between dissolving the council or choosing a new cabinet. The council can censure the government. Along with the prime minister, deputies of the National Council can propose legislation.' Shelley, *Endgame in the Western Sahara*, 183. For a discussion of governance in Saharawi refugee camps see Stephen Zunes and Jacob Mundy, *Western Sahara: War, Nationalism, and Conflict Resolution* (Syracuse, NY: Syracuse University Press, 2010).

balance such matters, and to put them in proper context given the overarching goal of self-determination and the restoration of independence.

The focal point of government policy for natural resources is the SADR Constitution.[31] Apart from allocating authority to government for the administration of resources, democratic norms are established by the Constitution which require stewardship of resources in the national interest. This includes a high degree of consensus among legislators and, in crucial matters, the whole Saharawi population. The Constitution, last amended in December 2011 by the 13th Saharawi National Congress, draws upon modern liberal concepts and Islam as a source of law, and it is accepted that environmental conservation principles flow from the Qu'ran.[32] Article 17 provides that natural resources ('public goods') are the 'property of the people, consisting of mineral riches, energy resources, the resources of the seabed and territorial waters, and other resources defined by law'.[33] Article 18 requires that resources be defined and managed in accordance with national law. In general, it falls to ministers of the SADR government (and, in a general executive context, the SADR president) to properly manage resources under Articles 64–74. The Saharawi legislature (i.e. parliament, the National Council) has authority in respect of legislation through which government officers act, as detailed in Articles 75–123.[34] Although a state institution, the Saharawi judiciary is formally independent of the two branches of government. Because the courts act in the name of the Saharawi people and government must comply with their decisions, judicial review of government decision-making about natural resources and environmental matters is possible, although no case has yet been pursued.

Similarly, the Constitution guarantees private property rights, at Article 35. The question of such rights and the development of natural resources, for example the state licensing of mineral exploration in areas that include privately owned real property is an ongoing policy topic, although no conflict in practice has yet emerged. The SADR government has considered how private property interests in the occupied area will be accommodated after that area is restored to the state.[35] An example is the allocation of petroleum exploration areas on the Atlantic coast, which extend seaward from the low-water mark; 'public lands' under the Constitution, so designed to ensure a demarcation with upland private holdings (and to be consistent with the practice of states generally). Current policy planning includes how mineral and groundwater access development exercised by the Sahawari state can reconcile private property interests, including through a scheme of expropriation compensation, social and environmental impact assessment, and judicial review. The question of private property has been engaged in the liberated area in limited instances though not much land has been given over to private uses or settlement.[36]

---

31 An Arabic language version of the *Constitution* is available at http://www.20may.org/ar/wp-content/uploads/2014/ 06/دستور-الجمهورية-العربية-الصحراوية-الديمقراطية-الصادر-عن-المؤتمر-13-للجبهة.pdf (accessed March 5, 2015). Accountability of the Saharawi government to its citizens is realized for the most part through the dialogue and review of government programs and decisions by the National Council, as noted above. There is not a tradition of judicial review of executive action or government decision-making, or commentary by third parties including external entities such as the Office of the UN High Commissioner for Refugees. Human rights organizations are routinely invited into the refugee camps for open-access visits, such as a delegation from the Robert F. Kennedy Center in the summer of 2012, but they have not considered governance institutions or the adequacy of democratic norms in Saharawi society.

32 The just allocation of water in a society (*Qu'ran* 16:65) and the conservation of resources from past generations for future ones (*Qu'ran* 89:19) are relevant tenets of Islam.

33 SADR Constitution, Article 17.

34 Ibid., Articles 75–123.

35 The experience of Timor-Leste after 24 years of occupation during which there were significant changes of property ownership (and expropriation by the occupying state) is instructive.

36 The SADR government is sensitive to cultural heritage, and has studied and regulated the protection of historic sites in the liberated zone, for example the rock gallery paintings west of Tifariti. Provisions of the 2014 Mining Code restrict government grants of mining license areas ('Tenements') over certain types of private property and provide for expropriation compensation.

While there are various legislative initiatives for environmental protection and to regulate (including by application of criminal law) the removal of natural resources from Western Sahara, the most recent 'projects of law' have been the 2009 Maritime Zones Act and the 2014 Mining Code. The constitutional basis for resource development in the two statutes is territorial sovereignty: in classical terms, the Saharawi state's assertion of sovereign, original and indivisible title from which rights and obligations for resources may be identified and transferred to others. Article 4 of the Maritime Zones Act continues such sovereignty into the offshore consistent with the 1982 UN Convention on the Law of the Sea, which includes possession and territorial rights seaward to 12 nautical miles and to the resources of the sea within a 200 NM exclusive economic zone and, further seaward, the resources of an extended continental shelf. The dual aspects of the development and preservation of resources until independence is restored through self-determination can be appreciated in the following provisions of Article 8 of the Act, Article 8(3), allowing the Saharawi government the flexibility to permit exploration and development to proceed or to take a preservationist stance in light of the occupation:

Rights and Obligations

1. In the exclusive economic zone, the Saharawi Arab Democratic Republic has sovereign rights for the purpose of exploring, exploiting, conserving and managing the natural resources, whether living or non-living, of the sea-bed and subsoil and the superjacent waters, and with regard to other activities for the economic exploitation and exploration of the zone, such as the production of energy from water, currents and winds. ...

3. There shall be no exploration or economic exploitation of the natural resources of the exclusive economic zone by persons or vessels other than nationals of the Saharawi Arab Democratic Republic ... unless such activity has been authorized by the Government of the Saharawi Arab Democratic Republic.

The Mining Code was several years in the making. There were a number of reasons for this, including the need to consult widely in Saharawi civil society and to ensure a framework that would provide confidence for mining exploration firms that would remain uninterrupted through self-determination and make for seamless application thereafter through all of Western Sahara.[37] The Mining Code governs mineralogical exploration and extraction and is distinct from the petroleum survey-production sharing regime which has been in place since the opening of a first licensing round in May 2005. A useful precursor was the evaluation of a Technical Cooperation Agreement that had operated from 2007 through 2011 for a mining exploration firm to conduct surveys in the liberated area.[38]

The Mining Code defines the terms of exploration permits, mining permits, small-scale mining permits and infrastructure permits. Exploration permits allow for the exclusive exploration of all minerals within a designated area. An exploration permit may comprise an area of up to 2000 km$^2$ with any one person or entity able to be granted up to 10 permits. A permit is valid for an initial period of three years, renewable twice each for further three-year terms. After demonstrating an economically viable mineral deposit, the exploration permit holder can apply to convert their rights in the deposit area by the grant of a mining permit valid for 30 years, renewable twice each for a further 10 years. These provisions are thought by Saharawi officials to make for good governance and to be consistent with best regulatory practice in Africa.

---

37 Law No. 02/2014. The Code was adopted on May 26, 2014 after considerable review by elected legislators and revisions to satisfy their public policy concerns. It had latterly been revised by the Economic Committee of the National Council after consultation with the SADR executive branch. A principal goal was a statute drafted to international standards including with the assistance of legal firms with extensive experience in advising governments on mining law. See http://www.sadrpma.com (accessed March 2, 2015).

38 In July 2011 Hanno Resources Limited (formerly Excalibur Resources Group Limited) presented the results of its work under the Technical Cooperation Agreement (TCA), noting that Western Sahara is highly prospective for iron ore, gold, base metals and uranium. The results of more detailed assessments were provided in March 2015 and are discussed below.

Actual mining activity is to be carried out under establishment and infrastructure licenses. Establishment agreements require feasibility studies of the proposed mining operation by independent third party experts, as well as an acceptable plan to work and eventually decommission (i.e. remediate) a mine site, together with measures to comply with environmental protection controls. An important part of establishment licenses is the implementation of 'community development agreements' which are intended to mitigate the adverse effects of mining operations by sustaining economic and social viability of local population centers, and ensuring the protection of cultural sites. Establishment permits also contain extensive provision for the free import and use of equipment and matériel for mining operations, payment of rent taxation to the SADR government, arbitral dispute resolution, and compliance measures with labor standards, and occupational health and safety regulations. Infrastructure licenses may be thought of as a 'global building permit', within which a mining company may 'construct and maintain buildings, roads, pipelines, powerlines' and 'things incidental' to mining operations. The framework of the Mining Code is designed to balance state and social requirements for sustainable extraction of mineral resources having a high degree of environmental protection and Saharawi civil society 'social license' with commercial efficacy including an acceptable return for mining companies for their initial exploration and capital development costs.[39]

Mining activities, including administration of the Mining Code and the granting of petroleum exploration permits throughout Western Sahara is presently the responsibility of the SADR Petroleum and Mines Authority (the PMA). The Authority is designated as the Mining Department under the Code, and reports to the Saharawi government through a chief executive and a responsible minister. In addition to administrative and technical (e.g. geological survey) work, the PMA also has the dual roles of overseeing environmental protection in the occupied area of Western Sahara, that is, gathering data and providing policy advice to Saharawi leaders about environmental impacts and resource depletion in the area west of the berm, and coordinating responses to the illegal extraction and export of resources under occupation.[40]

## VI. The future arrives – the potential of Saharawi resources

The SADR government, from an initial foray into regulating resource development activity, has for more than a decade issued petroleum exploration permits for the seabed of Western Sahara.[41] With the advent of mining regulation, this is intended to set the stage for resource development, with a diminishing requirement that independence (or the 'restoration of full independence' as the usual employed phrase) must first result. The territory's petroleum and mining areas can be broadly divided into two general geological parts: the 'El Aauin basin' extending inland from the Atlantic coast, and the interior Reguibat Shield, which is highly prospective for iron ore, gold and base metals, part of the regional pre-Cambrian 'West Africa Craton' shield.[42] This is something of a simplification, although a dividing line can be seen on political maps of the territory, namely the berm which through much of its course follows ridge elevations between the two areas, except in the far northeast in

---

39 The Mining Code also establishes the state royalty on extracted, marketable minerals. It was first thought that royalty rates should be governed though a flexible scheme of government regulations and ministerial directions; however, the need for commercial certainty under a National Council (parliament) created statute was eventually preferred.

40 This role extends to the fisheries although shared with the SADR Ministry of Foreign Affairs because of the international relations implications of European and other states' treaty fisheries on the Saharan coast.

41 The SADR government granted a Technical Cooperation Agreement to Fusion Oil and Gas in 2000 which enabled that company to assess the potential of the territory.

42 The El Aauin basin is also known as the Coastal basin. See Nasser Ennih and Jean-Paul Liégeois, *The Boundaries Of The West African Craton, With Special Reference To The Basement Of The Moroccan Metacratonic Anti-Atlas Belt* (London: Geological Society, 2008) and Jean Fabre, *Géologie du Sahara occidental et central* (Tervuren: Musée royal de l'Afrique centrale – Belgique, 2005).

the inland Tindouf Basin, which it traverses. It is in the El Aauin basin that the extensive deposit of phosphate mineral rock at Bu Craa is found. This area consists of sediments, including the seabed offshore, and is accordingly considered to have the best petroleum prospectivity. The area is under the control of the occupying power and therefore access and credible data about the possible presence of minerals is incomplete. Tiris Iron Ore Province extends northwest from the Zouerate Mining Complex in neighboring Mauritania, with multi-billion tonne iron ore potential demonstrated in the SADR. Visible gold in quartz veins and numerous significant gold and base metals anomalies have also been identified in greenstone belts within Western Sahara proper. In recent years a Canadian mineral exploration company has carried out field and aerial surveys in the central south, around Auserd and Tichla, but has not made its findings public.[43] Offshore petroleum prospectivity is similarly obscured by a lack of disclosure from the two leading enterprises involved, both of which conducted extensive seabed seismic surveys during the summers of 2012, 2013 and 2014.[44]

The PMA has divided the offshore and onshore prospective oil and gas basins of Western Sahara into 18 license blocks. The SADR has engaged a number of independent advisors to develop agreements that are competitive and typical of the region. This professional counsel has included independent oil and gas consultants, academic experts and legal professionals, all of whom have a wealth of international oil industry and contractual experience.

In May 2005 the SADR government announced an inaugural oil licensing round in London and agreements are now in place with four international companies in eight permit areas. The exploratory rights are contracted under assurance agreements that will convert to production sharing contracts following any UN resolution which provides for (i.e. assures the immediate realization of) the Saharawi people's right to self-determination. The aim of the assurance agreements is primarily to create a low-cost option over exploration areas ('acreage' in regulatory usage) until such time as the sovereignty issue is resolved. The PMA does not require the assurance agreements to be worked by active exploration given the considerable presence of armed forces throughout the occupied area of Western Sahara.

Mining development in the liberated area of the territory has proceeded only after detailed appraisals under the 2007 Technical Cooperation Agreement.[45] It was only in 2014 that government arrangements were considered satisfactory to begin issuing mineral exploration permits.[46] In October 2014 the SADR government signed seven Exploration Permits with Hanno Resources. The company is now advancing in its exploration of the permit areas.[47]

The SADR PMA continues to assess how to undertake mining operations and extract minerals in the liberated area east of the berm. The SADR PMA and its foreign partners are in discussion on how to overcome logistical hurdles to the extraction and export of minerals, including

---

43  See http://metalexventures.com (accessed March 1, 2015). The company claims possible deposits of gold, zinc, lead and other metals, and diamonds in kimberlite in what is the Mauritanides Thrust Belt of the Reguibat Shield which extends 50–80 km west of the berm.

44  The PMA has assessed data made available to it, and accepts a general statement made in 2014 by Kosmos Energy Ltd. that the Boujdour Offshore permit area may contain up to 1 billion Barrels of Proved Oil Equivalent (BPOE). Following the decline in petroleum prices in the second half of 2014, the PMA assigned a figure of $70 per barrel as the threshold for return of viable deepwater petroleum recovery on the Saharan coast.

45  The SADR entered into a TCA with Hanno Resources in March 2007. Under the terms of the agreement Hanno undertook to provide a technical appraisal of the mineral potential of the SADR. See http://www.hannoresources. com/ (accessed July 24, 2015)

46  Much of the liberated area was surveyed in the seven years of the TCA, including assessments of how extracted ore can be transported for export. A significant challenge was ensuring the safety of prospecting teams working near unmarked, unexploded munitions, particularly land mines deployed by the occupying power east of the berm. Studies to assess mineral deposits in the occupied area continue, including literature surveys, analysis of satellite data, and appraisal of samples.

47  The exploration permits cover the Oum Abana Greenstone Belt, an area highly prospective for gold and base metals, and the Tiris Iron Ore Province noted above as prospective for iron ore.

transportation to the coast or a seaport for export.[48] The commodities most likely to be developed first are gold and iron ore, because they are concentrated in readily accessible deposits. The area of present iron development is the Tiris Iron Ore Province described above, near the semi-circular border with Mauritania in the southeast, with the 2014 prospecting licenses described above within a 100 km radius.[49] The area is relatively distant from population centers in the liberated zone and government support, with prospecting teams (mixed Saharawi and foreign nationals from the contracted company) necessarily operating with a high degree of autonomy but receiving support of the Saharawi military regions situated throughout the SADR's liberated area. Government planning for urban development and the availability of workers for possible mines in this area after self-determination has extended to assessments of infrastructure in nearby towns in the occupied area; Guelta Zemmur, Bir Anzarene and Auserd.

The current mineral prospecting licenses are intended to advance several policy objectives of the SADR government. Foremost is an accessible commercial and regulatory regime for mining companies and investors to begin mineral development. With acceptable environmental protection measures and civil society involvement, it was time for the Saharawi state to pursue resource development, particularly with other resources such as the Atlantic fishery being out of reach. Taxation-rent revenue is an important feature of this development, in part because the Saharawi people in their refugee exile depend greatly on external aid, and to better pursue the development of financial regulation and transparency within the SADR government.

An important secondary objective of present mining policy is the growth of institutional and intellectual capacity in the Saharawi state. This entails the development of a professional cadre of geologists, technicians, economists, planners and policy analysts equipped to deal with the complexities of a new resource regime that is intended to expand for all activities in Western Sahara once self-determination is realized. Advanced graduate education of geologists at leading African and European universities is an example. So, too, is the explicit policy of obtaining advice from third party governments and mining enterprises on regulating mining and measures to ensure social responsiveness of the Saharawi government to its people.

Mining activities and the granting of *in futuro* petroleum prospecting licenses in the Saharan offshore are a part of the expression of Saharawi aspirations to self-determination and the *effectivités* of demonstrating territorial sovereignty.[50] While the objective of such an expression is to couple sovereignty to natural resources to the right of self-determination, and to underscore the fact of an illegal occupation, it has the result of highlighting the ongoing pillage of primary resources from Western Sahara. Overlapping or ostensibly competing seabed petroleum licenses, for example, are useful to illustrate the fact of an occupying state taking resources without a legal basis.[51] The Saharawi government has considered how fishing rights could be exercised, conclud-

---

48  Nouadhibou is a possible industrial harbour for exports, located on the Cape Blanc peninsula, the seaward side of which is the southernmost part of the SADR liberated area, including the town of Laguera.

49  Four of the licenses are in the ore province, and three are 60–80 km to the north.

50  The SADR government and the Frente Polisario have noted for decades that Saharawi territorial integrity is settled, in part by customary international law through the *uti posseditis* principle and the African Union Charter, and by the conclusion of the International Court of Justice in 1975 that neither Mauritania nor Morocco had any tenable claim to the territory of the then Spanish Sahara. See *Western Sahara Advisory Opinion*, ICJ Reports 1975, 12 at para. 162.

While no court of competent jurisdiction has declared Western Sahara to be occupied as such, the combination of the ICJ's 1975 opinion, resolutions of the UN General Assembly which declare the territory to be occupied, the positions of neighbouring states such as Algeria and Mauritania, and, crucially, the facts on the ground (a sustained armed occupation and the military partitioning of the territory by construction of the berm) make clear the legal status of the territory. Moreover, it must be recalled that the occupying power has always committed to relinquishing possession of Western Sahara on the completion of a referendum for self-determination of the Saharawi people, should they choose independence. The commitments made by the occupying power under the 1990–91 UN sponsored ceasefire and referendum agreement remain unchanged.

51  Two sources of law apply to the pillage of resources from Western Sahara: Resolution 1803 permanent sovereignty rights (requiring consent and benefit of resource extraction exclusively to the Saharawi people) much discussed after

ing that a similar approach of offering future access to the fishery is impractical because of the commercial nature of the industry and the possibility to re-engage the European Union after self-determination.[52]

There is, finally, the important project of advancing and demonstrating a viable rule of law in the Saharawi state and its governing institutions. All countries have an interest in the development of their resources as a vehicle or basis to foster the rule of law. This is true of the SADR, for the expected reason of sound democratic governance and for the crucial matter of ensuring the understanding across Saharawi society that government transparency and accountability will successfully transpose into a post-self-determination setting. The present development of Saharawi resources through the SADR PMA offers an opportunity to assess such obligations.

## VI.   Conclusion: resources, sovereignty and statehood

It remains a daunting prospect for the Saharawi people to move to what they call the 'restoration of their independence'. A Saharawi state with sovereignty over all of Western Sahara will have diverse natural resources. The lessons from Namibia and Timor-Leste suggest this will be a good thing, Namibia having diverse natural resources with an economy not bound to rents alone from them, and Timor-Leste conversely with an overwhelming reliance on petroleum revenues into the state. The particular challenge, therefore, will be the effective governance of such resources.[53] This will be crucial to demonstrate to an organized international community that has invested much, including political capital, in support of newly created and emergent states such as South Sudan and Timor-Leste in recent years that a self-determined Saharawi people have the social, institutional and economic capacity to succeed in the project of independence. Establishing a present framework for future resource development is a stark lesson drawn from the successes (and failures) of recent self-determination cases. The careful approach to the creation of a mining regime by the SADR government, coupled with its policy-making while under occupation for the Atlantic fishery and seabed petroleum exploration in recent years augur well for robust governance.

At the same time, the singular pursuit of a resource-dependent or -oriented post-independence economy will not be a panacea. Resource extraction and, where possible, processing, can never entirely assure employment and just social conditions in a post-occupation society. Even if considerable wealth is immediately realized from the Saharawi people's national resources, the policy choice is to avoid an over-reliance on that sector in state building. A Saharawi economy and labor market (and thus the services related to them, including education) must necessarily have a diverse foundation. The present policy of preparing to govern resources for the future is an attempt to realize this.[54]

---

the 2002 Corell–UN Security Council opinion, and international humanitarian law with its criminal law prohibition on pillage except for resources for the needs of a civil population under occupation. The SADR government routinely asserts both sources of law in its protests about resource development and exports. Letters of protest are occasionally made public, such as that of January 26, 2015, referred to above.

52  The Frente Polisario is presently challenging the legality of the EU–Morocco Fisheries Partnership Agreement in the European Court of Justice, in part on the basis that the 2009 Treaty on the Functioning of the European Union prohibits an arrangement contrary to international law. See EJIL Talk (blog of the *European Journal of International Law*) 'Trade Agreements, EU Law, and Occupied Territories – A Report on EU Council' (July 1, 2015) at http://www.ejiltalk.org (accessed July 3, 2015).

53  The challenges to transparent, accountable and democratic control of resources in post-conflict states are manifold, and go to the core of establishing the rule of law. The design of institutions, the reviewing role of courts, and then engagement of civil society in resource planning are a part of this. For extensive useful commentary in the case of Timor-Leste after that country's 2002 independence, see the website of the Timor-Leste Institute for Development Monitoring and Analysis, http://www.laohamutuk.org (accessed April 1, 2015).

54  SADR PMA executives and others in Saharawi civil society, galvanized after 2012 by the prospect of petroleum in the Saharan seabed, have started to consider how a permanent, transparent and well-governed sovereign resource fund can be created along the lines of those in Norway and Timor-Leste. The policy analysis about that has usefully informed appeals for UN oversight or trust administration of resources while under occupation.

In many respects, the natural resources of Western Sahara mirror the circumstances of the Saharawi people themselves. In the 50 years since the organized international community has pursued the self-determination of colonized peoples, the legal principles toward that end together with those for the protection of sovereign rights to natural resources have become increasingly settled. Few can doubt that the Saharawi people will capably manage the transition from self-determination to a fully restored independence. That is now increasingly true when it comes to the governance and accountability in relation to development of natural resources in a liberated Western Sahara.

## Acknowledgments

The author gratefully acknowledges the comments of Jeffrey Smith, barrister, on drafts of this paper.

## Disclosure statement

No potential conflict of interest was reported by the author.

# Independence by *fiat*: a way out of the impasse – the self-determination of Western Sahara, with lessons from Timor-Leste

Pedro Pinto Leite

*Secretary, International Platform of Jurists for East Timor*

Western Sahara and Timor-Leste (East Timor) are twin cases marking an incomplete end to the era of decolonization. The two are remarkably similar: they are former European colonies with peoples who had been promised self-determination only to be invaded within weeks of each other in late 1975 by neighboring states, themselves recently decolonized. Decades would pass while the international community stood by. The people of Timor-Leste eventually achieved freedom against the odds while most of Western Sahara and half the Saharawi people remain under foreign occupation, the scene of established human rights violations and the ongoing export of natural resources. For 25 years, Morocco has refused the Saharawi people a referendum, with the United Nations organization unable to respond as a result of a threatened veto by some permanent members of the Security Council. However, a Saharawi state arguably has come into being, enjoying popular legitimacy, governing institutions and accepted control over a part of Western Sahara. Moreover, regionally and within the African Union, the Saharawi Republic enjoys broad recognition and advocacy for its people. While drawing on lessons from the comparative experience of self-determination in Timor-Leste, this paper contends that the UN should follow the example of the African Union and welcome the Saharawi Republic as a member state. To achieve that result, a wider recognition among states is needed. The UN General Assembly, by employing its 1950 Uniting for Peace resolution, can decide to 'consider the matter immediately' and compel a breakthrough which the Security Council has so far not been able to deliver.

## Introduction

The brave era of decolonization has all but passed. 2015 is a time to recall the successes of humanity's most important modern project: the universal realization of human rights through the emancipation of peoples worldwide under colonial domination. The year marks 55 years since the United Nations under the General Assembly's leadership declared the right to self-determination in Resolutions 1514 and 1541; 45 years since the UN took charge of the difficult case of Namibia;[1] 40 years since the International Court of Justice affirmed for the Saharawi people their right of self-determination in the *Western Sahara* Advisory Opinion,[2] and 20 years since the same result from the Court for the East Timorese people in the *Timor Gap Treaty (Portugal/Australia)* decision.[3] The shared values among states and the nature of international law in this landscape have never been clearer. And yet the Saharawi people – half refugees in exile in desert camps and half under military occupation – are among the last of all peoples awaiting the right to self-determination, the support of which right is the paramount obligation of all

---

1 'Namibia – UNTAG Background', United Nations, New York, http://www.un.org/en/peacekeeping/missions/past/untagFT.htm (accessed August 10, 2015).
2 *Western Sahara, Advisory Opinion*, ICJ Reports 1975, 12.
3 *East Timor (Portugal* v. *Australia), Judgment*, ICJ Reports 1995, 90.

members of the organized international community, including the United Nations.[4] Despite a formal process for their self-determination established nearly a quarter of a century ago, it is a right that continues to be denied to them. The international community has deferred to a United Nations unable to break the impasse over Saharawi self-determination because of a Security Council that is unwilling to act and a General Assembly which has relinquished its successful historical role in decolonization.

Two fundamental obligations of international law, namely the prohibition against aggression and the outlawing of territorial conquest, continue to be violated in Western Sahara. These obligations are the basis for peace and stability in the modern order among nation-states. There are other continuing violations, of course, ones routinely noted by outside commentators, for example human rights abuses and the stripping (pillage) of resources.[5] The norms of international law have apparently been forgotten in the Sahara, the resulting impunity enjoyed by Morocco being an objectionable precedent and a phenomenon that arguably damages international law. The case of Western Sahara could not be more compelling, whatever one's perspective, including as a matter of international relations, law, the social and economic development of northwest Africa, and justice itself. Jacob Mundy, an American scholar who writes about Western Sahara, has expressed the circumstances as follows:

> The [International Court of Justice's 1975] opinion on Western Sahara is most often cited as proof definitive that Western Sahara is owed a referendum on self-determination. However, this claim is based upon a half-reading of the *summary* of the Court's opinion. A full reading of the Court's entire opinion shows that the ICJ was very clear that the sovereign power in Western Sahara was and is the native Western Saharans [the Saharawi people]. The purpose of a self-determination referendum in Western Sahara is not to decide between competing sovereignties, whether Moroccan or Saharawi, but to poll the Saharawis as to whether or not they wish to retain, modify or divest their sovereignty. We need to stop talking about self-determination as an act that constitutes sovereignty in Western Sahara. Sovereignty is already constituted in Western Sahara. As the ICJ said, Western Sahara has never been *terra nullius*.[6]

With such reasoning as a starting point, and given the stalled dynamic of realizing the Saharawi people's rights and resolving their circumstances, this paper examines the issue of self-determination which has been the single demand of the Saharawi people as the path to decide their political and legal status including perhaps as an independent state. The analysis takes regard of the close parallel to the successful realization of self-determination for the people of Timor-Leste in 1999. A proposal to overcome the impasse is then advanced.

## Decolonization's promise and precedent

The historical circumstances that led to the Saharawi people being offered a United Nations administered referendum to resolve their status in the post-colonial world as a non-self-

---

4   'Saharawi' refers to the name of the original people of the territory of Western Sahara which was known as Spanish Sahara until 1975. The Saharawi population as an identifiable ethnic, cultural and linguistic group is about 350,000 people: 160,000 in the refugee camps at Tindouf, 120,000 in occupied Western Sahara and a diaspora concentrated in Mauritania and Spain. On 27 February 1976 the Saharawi Arab Democratic Republic was proclaimed, the act later ratified by the Saharawi electorate in the acceptance of a national constitution.

5   See most recently the annual report of the UN Secretary-General to the UN Security Council, 'Report of the Secretary-General on the situation concerning Western Sahara' (April 10, 2015), UN doc. S/246/2015. The Secretary-General is properly oblique about the application of international law in its various forms to Western Sahara, consistent with the wider UN organization's characterization of the matter not as conflict or territorial occupation or, for the most part, a matter of decolonization, but in anodyne terms as 'the question' of Western Sahara. Annual Secretary-General Reports on Western Sahara can be found online at http://www.un.org/en/peacekeeping/missions/minurso/reports.shtml (accessed July 26, 2015).

6   Jacob Mundy, 'The Question of Sovereignty in the Western Sahara Conflict' (presentation at the IAJUWS conference 'La Cuestión del Sáhara Occidental en El Marco Jurídico Internacional', Las Palmas, Canary Islands, June 27–28, 2008).

governing people have been addressed at length elsewhere.[7] A United Nations administered referendum for the Saharawi people is to be the same in the substance of elective choices as was successfully delivered by the UN in Namibia in 1989 and Timor-Leste (East Timor) a decade later.

The case of Timor-Leste is particularly instructive in relation to Western Sahara. Both Spain and Portugal were in the process of ending their colonial ventures by the mid-1970s and in both Timor-Leste and Western Sahara neighboring powers invaded, in 1975, before the colonization process was completed. In both cases, the United Nations recognized the former colonial power to have maintained continuing legal authority pending formal decolonization and in both cases occupation by the invading neighboring power – Indonesia in the case of Timor-Leste and Morocco in the case of Western Sahara – has not been recognized under international law.

Through a confluence of circumstances, including international pressure on continuing human rights abuses (highlighted by the Santa Cruz Massacre of 1991), the cost of occupation, a change of regime in Indonesia and Portugal's continuing advocacy, the UN brokered a 'popular consultation' among East Timorese people (as defined by the UN) on the question of whether the territory would remain as an autonomous part of Indonesia or whether it would move towards independence. Amid widespread pro-Indonesia violence and destruction, on 30 August 1999 the vote in favor of independence was carried by 78.5% of the voting population.[8] This result then spurred a further wave of pro-Indonesia violence and destruction, leading the UN to mandate the intervention of a peace-keeping force and to apply a UN interim administration ahead of elections and independence on 20 May 2002. Although Spain has not actively represented Western Sahara in the UN and the pressures on Morocco differ, the UN could legally assume advocacy for such a ballot in the occupied territory, applying the same process of transitional administration should the ballot similarly decide in favor of independence.

Having noted that, the majority of decolonization cases, especially in Africa, were accomplished without such a consultative act. But the difficult cases suggest that the organized international community confers the realization of self-determination upon the neutral implementing organization which the UN is perceived to be and it is delivered through a formal democratic, transparent process. These requirements are sufficient and they have been at the heart of the impasse over Western Sahara.

A few observations can be made about a referendum for Saharawi self-determination. An inconvenient legal fact is that a self-determination referendum, which is a consultative electoral choice by the legitimate inhabitants of a colonized territory to settle their political status, is not required generally under international law or as a matter of the UN decolonization resolutions, General Assembly Resolutions 1514 (XV) and 1541 (XV) of 14 December 1960. The requirement for a referendum, regardless of who was to arrange it, has never been UN policy or otherwise compulsory (such as, for example, by operation of customary international law) in decolonization cases. Electoral consultation did not occur in the majority of instances during the era of decolonization in the 1950s and 1960s. Of course, a referendum would confer legitimacy on a United Nations organ-

---

7   See Tony Hodges, *Western Sahara: The Roots of a Desert War* (Westport, CT: Lawrence Hill, 1983); Jeffrey Smith, 'State of Exile: The Saharawi Republic and its Refugees', in *Still Waiting for Tomorrow: The Law and Politics of Unresolved Refugee Crises*, ed. Susan Akram and Tom Syring (Newcastle upon Tyne: Cambridge Scholars, 2014, 25–53); Stephen Zunes and Jacob Mundy, *Western Sahara: War, Nationalism, and Conflict Irresolution* (Syracuse, NY: Syracuse University Press, 2010); Karin Arts and Pedro Pinto Leite, eds., *International Law and the Question of Western Sahara* (Leiden: IPJET, 2007).

8   For useful histories of the invasion of Timor-Leste and the 1999 referendum see James Dunn, *East Timor: A People Betrayed* (Milton, Queensland: Jacaranda Press, 1983); Carmel Budiardjo and Liem Soei Liong, *The War Against East Timor* (London: Zed Books, 1984); Irena Cristalis, *East Timor: A Nation's Bitter Dawn*, 2nd ed. (London: Zed Books, 2009); and Richard Tanter, Mark Selden, and Stephen R. Shalom, eds., *Bitter Flowers, Sweet Flowers: East Timor, Indonesia, and the World Community* (Oxford: Rowman & Littlefield, 2001).

ization which by its current presence in Western Sahara has the self-assumed obligation to ensure orderly and democratic self-determination as it did in Timor-Leste. The form of realizing self-determination – the process of ensuring a colonized people have before them a truly elective choice – is less important than the substantive right to be decided upon, be it continuing colonization (incorporation into the colonizing state), association with the former colonizing state, or independence. The UN has been clear such outcomes are to be always available to non-self-governing peoples, even as the number of cases dwindles. And it has assured the Saharawi people that such a range of elective choices will be available to them. There seems to be little choice for the UN in the matter, after the International Court of Justice (ICJ) confirmed the expansive scope of self-determination in its 2010 *Kosovo* Advisory Opinion:

> During the second half of the twentieth century, the international law of self-determination developed in such a way as to create a right to independence for the peoples of non-self-governing territories and peoples subject to alien subjugation, domination and exploitation ... A great many new States have come into existence as a result of the exercise of this right.[9]

Of course, the UN Security Council has noted Morocco's pursuit of its 2007 autonomy referendum proposal, which would retain the territory within Morocco as its so-called Southern Provinces, to be 'serious and credible'.[10] The conduct of a referendum by the UN as a neutral interlocutor can allow for a more politically acceptable outcome for the occupying state, as with Indonesia in Timor-Leste. (Although hardly a 'just' result, the acquiescence of the occupying state to self-determination can serve to absolve it in part of the wrongful annexation of a territory, extending even to crimes committed during an occupation, as was the result for an *apartheid* South Africa in Namibia.[11]) Moreover, the important factor of political recognition of a new state – if the choice of a self-determining people is for independence – in the organized international community is a useful advantage. The need to promote peace, community order and social development in a newly independent former colony, after a period of annexation, where peoples from the occupying state may choose to remain is helped by a transparent, externally assured and democratic process.[12]

## The roots of a referendum

The issue of independence and the subsequent act of self-determination of a colonized people is the responsibility of the decolonizing power, in this case of Spain as the colonizing state in Spanish Sahara. Then and now, international law did not allow the obligation to be cast aside, even by Spain's agreement in November 1975 with Mauritania and Morocco to jointly administer the territory under a vague promise that the three parties would somehow see to Saharawi self-determination.[13] The UN's intervention would come more than a decade later, drawing on the

---

9   *Accordance with International Law of the Unilateral Declaration of Independence in Respect of Kosovo, Advisory Opinion*, ICJ Reports 2010, 403, para. 79.

10  This began with UN Security Council 1754 (2007) (April 30, 2007) and has continued, for which see now UN Security Council Resolution 2218 (2015) (April 28, 2015). The Security Council resolutions have also reflected the change in the UN organization's position that there be a 'just and lasting' resolution of the question of Western Sahara, to one that is 'just, lasting and mutually acceptable'.

11  See United Nations Security Council Resolution 435 Namibia, July 27, 1978.

12  This might be called *civil society consensus*, a shared values structure that was important in Timor-Leste given the legacy of violence during the occupation of that territory, and the challenges of reconciliation after the August 1999 referendum.

13  For a discussion of the 1975 agreement, the Madrid Accords, see Hodges, *Western Sahara*. The crucial obligation to ensure for the Saharawi people a referendum was assumed by the UN in 1991, in agreement with Morocco and the Saharawi people (acting through their national liberation movement the Frente Polisario), the terms of which are in two reports of the UN Secretary-General to the Security Council in 1990 and 1991.

In November 1975 Spain legislated an end to its colonial responsibility for the Sahara, the position of successive governments since. However, Spanish criminal law (and by incorporation international criminal law under the Rome

work of the Organization of African Unity (OAU, now the African Union – AU) which after 1984 culminated in a 1988 settlement proposal accepted by Morocco and the Frente Polisario in the form of measures adopted by the Security Council in 1990–91. The agreement came at a vital moment.[14] Mauritania had earlier abandoned its claim to the territory and recognized the Saharawi Republic.[15] In the aftermath of Mauritania's 1979 peace treaty, which contained the admission that it had conducted an 'unjust war', the Saharawi people had only a single occupier with which to contend. In this era, the Moroccan army sustained heavy losses and therefore the 'berm', the sand wall that now partitions the territory, was constructed.[16] By the late 1980s an active end to hostilities spurred peacemaking efforts and allowed Morocco to consolidate its occupation, both demographically by the settlement of its nationals and on the world stage.[17]

Arrangements for peoples in territories under occupation to exercise their right of self-determination tend to come with complications. In retrospect, the 1988–91 agreement for an act of self-determination for the Saharawi people was flawed because of the lack of capacity bestowed upon the United Nations Mission for the Referendum in Western Sahara (MINURSO). MINURSO was unable to ensure impartial and accurate registration of Saharawi nationals for the referendum and to effectively ensure public order and the protection of human rights in the occupied part of the territory prior to a referendum.[18] Such shortcomings were also evident in Timor-Leste's referendum for independence in 1999, from which the UN could have applied its lessons to help ensure that a referendum would proceed in Western Sahara. Instead, compromise demanded that Morocco be allowed flexibility to challenge voter identification and add people to the register for the referendum. The result was that the kingdom demanded the acceptance of large numbers of persons with limited or no connection to the Saharawi people and their territory. This pattern of events continued until the referendum registration process ground to a halt in 2004.[19] The result has been that, during the active years of the UN's administration of the referendum process, Morocco boycotted meaningful voter identification and insisted on adding large numbers of its nationals, thereby ensuring postponement of the referendum.[20] It should be recalled, however, that MINURSO did complete voter registration. Nearly a decade after it came into being, MINURSO identified 86,386 Saharawis as eligible. Morocco, perhaps fearful of defeat in a referendum to follow, contested the result.[21]

---

Statute 1998 of the International Criminal Court) applies in Western Sahara as a matter of recent decisions by the appeals court the Audencia Nacional (July 2014 and April 2015).

14  The Settlement Plan, built on the earlier peace proposal of the Organization of African Unity, became effective in September 1991 with a ceasefire and measures to prepare for a referendum. MINURSO, the United Nations Mission for the Referendum in Western Sahara, was established by UN Security Council Resolution 690 (April 29, 1991) with a mandate to monitor the ceasefire and conduct the referendum.

15  Mauritania signed a peace treaty with the Frente Polisario in August 1979 and recognized the SADR in February 1984.

16  This was acknowledged by independent observers and also Morocco. See e.g. 'Desert War Flares Anew', *Chicago Tribune*, October 6, 1988, http://articles.chicagotribune.com/1988-10-06/news/8802050099_1_polisario-front-morocco-moroccan (accessed April 2, 2015).

17  See also Jacob Mundy, 'Morocco Settlers in Western Sahara: Colonists or Fifth Column', *Arab World Geographer* 15 (2012): 95.

18  See the statement of former US Ambassador Frank Ruddy, a former senior official with MINURSO, to the United States Congress on January 25, 1995 at http://www.arso.org/06-3-1.htm (accessed April 2, 2015).

19  The berm in its successively built segments is longer than 2400 kilometres. It remains heavily fortified, the largest minefield in the world, with perhaps 65,000 Moroccan FAR soldiers stationed along it. The berm was reportedly constructed with the assistance of Israel, the USA and Saudi Arabia, although few details are available. Following the ICJ's reasoning in its 2004 *Palestine Wall* Advisory Opinion, it can be safely concluded that construction of the berm violated international law.

20  Ruddy's report, above, denounced the obstacles put by Morocco to MINURSO's work. Francesco Bastagli, who in 2005 was appointed UN Special Representative for Western Sahara, strongly criticized UN inaction on Western Sahara and resigned in protest in 2006.

21  This was the voter registration figure on 30 December 1999. The Identification Commission announced the result on 15 January 2000 and the Secretary-General reported it to the Security Council that 17 February. See UN doc. S/2000/

The former United States Secretary of State, James Baker, appointed in early 1997 as the UN Secretary-General's Personal Envoy for Western Sahara, offered a proposal to overcome these problems. It was labeled the Framework Agreement and informally known as Baker Plan I.[22] The plan for a path out of the impasse did not allow for independence as an option[23] – only autonomy within Morocco[24] – and it was therefore contrary to international law which stipulates that the people of a non-self-governing territory can only be said to have achieved self-government if they have available all options to be an independent state.[25] As has been observed, the norm is the core of the right of peoples to self-determination, with a quality of (sometimes debated) *jus cogens* and one to be supported in principle (if sometimes not in practice) by all states as an obligation *erga omnes*.[26] The Saharawi people had always favored independence, expressing that ambition through the Frente Polisario to the UN and in the work of their social and government institutions, and therefore it surprised no one that they rejected the first Baker Plan.[27]

As a result, Baker pursued a second plan for self-determination. It provided for Saharawi self-rule under a 'Western Sahara Authority' to operate for a transitional five years then followed by an independence referendum. The 'Baker Plan II' guaranteed that Moroccan settlers, who by 2000 began to outnumber Saharawis in the occupied part of the territory, would be permitted to vote. This was, again, contrary to norms of self-determination.[28] By comparison, in Timor-Leste's 1999 referendum, Indonesian settlers were disqualified from voting. Nevertheless the Security Council endorsed Baker Plan II. The Frente Polisario reluctantly – even 'surprisingly' according to some observers – accepted the plan.[29] The Saharawi leadership endorsed it, confident of an outcome where Moroccan settlers would reliably choose independence – a remarkable thing

---

131 (February 17, 2000). 'From Morocco's point of view, the numbers indicated total defeat'. Zunes and Mundy, *Western Sahara*, 215.

22 *Framework Agreement on the Status of Western Sahara*, Annex I of UN Secretary-General Report S/2001/613 of June 20, 2001.

23 UN Secretary-General Kofi Annan may have instructed his personal envoy to go no further than autonomy for Western Sahara within the Moroccan state. Marrack Goulding, a former UN Undersecretary-General, said that Annan asked him 'to go to Houston to persuade James Baker III to accept an appointment as Special Representative and try to negotiate a deal based on enhanced autonomy for Western Sahara within the Kingdom of Morocco'. Marrack Goulding, *Peacemonger* (London: John Murray, 2002), 214–15.

24 Timor-Leste's 1999 referendum had two options: autonomy within the state of Indonesia, and independence. Under the Western Sahara Framework Agreement autonomy would be imposed on the Saharawi people. This is contrary to Principle IX of Resolution 1541 (XV): '[I]ntegration should be the result of the freely expressed wishes of the Territory's peoples acting with full knowledge of the change in their status, their wishes having been expressed through informed and democratic processes impartially conducted and based on universal adult suffrage'.

25 'A Non-Self-Governing Territory can be said to have reached a full measure of self-government by: (a) Emergence as a sovereign independent State; (b) Free association with an independent State; or (c) Integration with an independent State.' Resolution 1541, Principle VI.

26 'The exceptional importance of the principle of the self-determination of peoples in the modern world is such that today the principle has been held to constitute an example of jus cogens, that is, 'a peremptory norm of general international law', to quote the expression used in article 53 of the Vienna Convention on the Law of Treaties'. Hector Gros Espiell, *The Right to Self Determination: Implementation of United Nations Resolutions*, study prepared by the Special Rapporteur of the Sub Commission on Prevention of Discrimination and Protection of Minorities, E/CN.4/Sub.2/405/Rev.1, 1980.

27 During the time of Baker's appointment until his second plan, the people of Timor-Leste completed their self-determination and achieved independence. The Saharawi people were certainly aware of the rapid progress and eventual successful result of independence under UN administration of the self-determination process in Timor. The two states recognize each other, exchange diplomatic representatives and have some social and cultural contacts.

28 Even the New York City Bar Association has noted that 'the right to self-determination under international law pertains to the indigenous inhabitants of a Non-Self-Governing Territory – in this case the Saharawis who inhabited the territory – and cannot be invoked by non-indigenous settlers'. *The Legal Issues Involved in the Western Sahara Dispute – The Principle of Self-Determination and the Legal Claims of Morocco* (New York: New York City Bar Association, Committee on the United Nations, June 2012), 94.

29 Tobey Shelley, 'Behind the Baker Plan for Western Sahara', *Middle East Research and Information Project*, August 1, 2003

given the uncertain prospect of Saharawi rule.[30] Moreover, Morocco feared that democracy during the five years of transitional administration leading to the referendum might 'infect' the kingdom.[31]

Since 2002, Morocco has rejected the idea of a self-determination referendum in Western Sahara – regardless of the population accepted as eligible to participate. Despite the commitments of Morocco's Hassan II to the UN's 1990–91 settlement terms and the 1997 Baker process, his successor Mohammed VI has rejected a referendum except for the narrow option of a circum-scribed regional autonomy, declaring as irrevocable Morocco's claimed sovereignty over the Southern Provinces.[32]

To maintain the perception of a Morocco willing to engage the 'question' of Western Sahara, in April 2007 the kingdom's government transmitted to the new UN Secretary-General Ban Ki-moon a proposal for the territory's autonomy. The 'Moroccan initiative for negotiating an auton-omy statute for the Sahara region' was put forward as 'a basis for dialogue, negotiation and com-promise'.[33] The Frente Polisario had anticipated the move, delivering a day earlier to the Secretary-General its 'Proposal for a Mutually Acceptable Political Solution Assuring the Self-Determination of the People of Western Sahara'.[34] Later that same month the Security Council issued Resolution 1754, urging Morocco and the Frente Polisario to 'enter into direct negotiations without preconditions and in good faith'.[35] Discussions between the two, which have been over-seen by successive personal envoys of the Secretary-General, began that June in Manhasset, New York. Numerous rounds have since been held in various locations. While these negotiations, led in recent years by the well-regarded former US diplomat Christopher Ross, have forced Morocco to deal with the Frente Polisario as an equal, there has been effectively no progress since the two parties' 2007 proposals, referred to above. Discussions during a 2011 session in Geneva on the subject of natural resources in Western Sahara proved fruitless, as have efforts in recent years to create a role for MINURSO to observe and report on human rights conditions, the only UN mission of its kind without such a mandate.[36] This lack of a human rights mandate is indicative of the weakness of the overall mandate of MINURSO in Western Sahara and illustrates the lack of commitment to resolving the impasse. From the standpoint of the involvement of the UN and the organized international community, the impasse following Baker's resignation from the process in 2004 continues and there has been no reconciliation or common negotiating space

---

30  Statement by Emhamed Khadad, member of the National Secretariat of the Frente Polisario and coordinator for MINURSO, at a meeting on Western Sahara at the University of Utrecht, March 25, 2002.

31  On the response of the Saharawi people and Morocco to Baker Plan II see Zunes and Mundy, *Western Sahara*, 234 ff.

32  In March 2006 during a visit to the territory Mohammed VI declared: 'Morocco will not cede a single inch, nor a grain of sand of its dear Sahara'. See the statement at http://www.arso.org/01-e06-1314.htm (accessed July 26, 2015).

33  See http://w-sahara.blogspot.com/2007/04/moroccos-plan-full-text.html (accessed April 4, 2015). Frank Ruddy described the proposal as 'the latest in a long line of illusions that Morocco has created over the years to distract world attention from the real issue', adding 'The Moroccan limited autonomy plan for Western Sahara ... might sound like a step forward, at least until one reads the not-so-fine print. Article 6 of the plan provides that Morocco will keep its powers in the royal domain, especially with regard to defense, external relations and the constitutional and religious prerogatives of his majesty the king. In other words, the Moroccans are offering autonomy, except in everything that counts. It gets even more disingenuous where the Moroccans say their plan will be submitted to a referendum, but fail to provide details'. 'Foreword' in Arts and Pinto Leite, *International Law and the Question of Western Sahara*, 12.

34  The Proposal is at http://www.arso.org/PropositionFP100407.htm#en (accessed April 5, 2015). The Frente Polisario restated its acceptance of Baker Plan II, held out the prospect of citizenship to Moroccan settlers at independence, and waived reparations claims between the two states. The Frente's 2007 Proposal remains its formal position as well as a commitment to a 'genuine referendum'.

35  Resolution 1754 (2007) adopted by the Security Council at its 5669th meeting, April 30, 2007.

36  See e.g. the 2012 annual report of the Secretary-General to the Security Council, 'Report of the Secretary-General on the situation concerning Western Sahara' (April 5, 2012), UN doc. S/20121/197, paras. 72 ff. See also 'Preliminary Observations: Robert F. Kennedy International Delegation Visit to Morocco Occupied Western Sahara and the Refugee Camps in Algeria' (September 3, 2012), http://rfkcenter.org/images/attachments/article/1703/Final091012.pdf (accessed April 1, 2015).

resulting from the parties' 2007 proposals. While such a status quo is regarded as unacceptable, the community of states defers wholesale to the UN's conduct of the matter and that, in part, has perpetuated the stalemate.

## Impasse in the desert

Almost a quarter of a century on, it would appear that the prospect of a legitimate process of self-determination for the Saharawi people is as remote as it ever has been. This is the result of the inability of the parties to transform or step away from closely held positions. For its part, the Frente Polisario is perceived to be intransigent in its demand for a referendum that includes the option of independence, and less the question of who is qualified to vote or how human rights and protection of the territory's natural resources from pillage should be resolved in the run-up to a referendum. Insisting on a Saharawi climb-down is difficult because of the close identification by the Frente Polisario with and understanding of what international law guarantees them. For the Saharawi, the success of the East Timorese people in their 1999 referendum and the ICJ's *Kosovo* Advisory Opinion in favor of independence[37] are sources of inspiration. While it cannot be said that the Saharawi people were deceived when they agreed to a ceasefire and referendum process that was to begin in the second half of 1991, what was promised has since been denied to them. Further, there has been no challenge to that principal foundation of peace and security – territorial integrity – even as the ICJ uniquely concluded among all its decolonization decisions that Morocco had no basis for a territorial claim. None of this should be surprising when it is recalled that the organized international community at large, the UN or Spain as the colonial power responsible have not sought to ensure the protection of the Saharawi civil population, which suffers documented war crimes while under occupation.[38] The parallels with Timor-Leste from 1975 until 1999 are close, given the lack of commitment by the international community to find a solution to Indonesia's occupation of and war crimes in East Timor (until international opinion began to turn after a military massacre of civilians in Dili in 1991 and the collapse of the Indonesian economy and subsequent resignation of authoritarian President Suharto in 1998).

There are two other things about the impasse over Western Sahara that are to be regretted, namely the diminished role of the African Union as a respected interlocutor to the 'question' of Western Sahara and the failure of the Security Council to act to resolve the matter under its 1990–91 agreement commitments and the UN Charter.[39] The second of these is the more ominous in light of the UN, led by the Security Council, being successful in arranging referenda on self-determination for the peoples of Namibia and Timor-Leste. For the Saharawi people who have relied on the assurances of the organized international community acting through the UN, the possibility of their referendum appears to have been deferred indefinitely.

If the delay in resolving the issue of Western Sahara has resulted from a now entirely stalled process to arrive at a self-determination referendum for the Saharawi people, then the means by which the referendum process was arrived at and pursued must be critically questioned. The ICJ confirmed in its *Western Sahara* advisory opinion that 'the application of the right of self-determination requires a free and genuine expression of the will of the peoples concerned'.[40] This is an

---

37 *Accordance with International Law of the Unilateral Declaration of Independence in Respect of Kosovo, Advisory Opinion*, ICJ Reports 2010, 403

38 Ali Lmrabet, 'Un responsable marroquí reconoce crímenes de guerra en el Sahara', *El Mundo*, June 17, 2008, see also 'Morocco', *Country Reports on Human Rights Practices*, Bureau of Democracy, Human Rights, and Labor, US State Department, February 23, 2001.

39 The AU has been a consistent supporter of the Saharawi state. On 27 March 2015 the AU Peace and Security Council issued a *communiqué* to the UN Secretary-General insisting on Saharawi self-determination and calling the export of natural resources from Western Sahara 'illegal exploitation'. See http://www.peaceau.org (accessed April 15, 2015).

40 *Western Sahara, Advisory Opinion*, para. 55.

acknowledgement, even as the practice of the UN in the three cases that followed was for a formal referendum, of the importance of a credibly expressed popular choice. The people of Western Sahara were understood by the UN's visiting mission in May 1975, a group of General Assembly diplomats, to overwhelmingly want independence. The release of the mission's report that October,[41] within a day of the ICJ's advisory opinion, could have been the entire end of the matter. The need to account for the collective will of a colonized people does not necessarily turn on that consensus being expressed through an externally administered plebiscite, meaning that Western Sahara could have, and could still be, recognized as independent by the UN without further discussion. This is where the UN in Western Sahara has by its conduct de facto limited the options for self-determination.[42] Such conduct, of course, is the failure of the UN to see through a referendum on terms it committed to during the process from 1988 to 1991.

It is useful at this point to return to what had become accepted practice in the organized international community in the legitimate cases of decolonization. The majority of them in the busy years of decolonization reveal the acceptability of peoples exercising the right to self-determination and accession to independence without referenda. Among these can be counted all former Portuguese colonies with the exception of Timor-Leste (and perhaps Macao).[43] The risk of carrying out a less than fully credible (or democratic) referendum in Western Sahara should be considered carefully. A sham process, with unforeseen consequences for the creation of the new state, could harm the Saharawi people and damage international law, as the fraudulent consultative exercise in West Papua, the 1969 'Act of Free Choice', has demonstrated.[44] A UN administered referendum conducted in Western Sahara would now most likely include Moroccan nationals although settled illegally by Morocco in the territory.[45] Hence, the UN could and arguably should simply declare Western Sahara to be independent.

## The parallels of Timor and the Sahara

To consider the case against an externally conferred referendum, it must be remembered that the Saharawis exercised for themselves their right of self-determination when they constituted the Saharawi Republic in February 1976. That event and the later ratification of it by the Saharawi in later years seems to have been credible – that is, acceptable in law and by democratic decision.[46] However, when it comes to the close historical and legal parallels between Timor-Leste and Western Sahara, an important difference must be noted. For the Timorese a referendum was arguably necessary because, while there had been a declaration of independence and Timor

41  Dietrich Rauschning, Katja Wiesbrock, and Martin Lailach, *Key Resolutions of the United Nations General Assembly 1946–1996* (Cambridge: Cambridge University Press,1997), 186.

42  'The validity of the principle of self-determination, defined as the need to pay regard to the freely expressed will of peoples, is not affected by the fact that in certain cases the General Assembly has dispensed with the requirement of consulting the inhabitants of a given territory. Those instances were based either on the consideration that a certain population did not constitute a "people" entitled to self-determination or on the conviction that a consultation was totally unnecessary, in view of special circumstances' (*Western Sahara, Advisory Opinion*, para. 59).

43  During the era of decolonization after 1960, Africa saw few formal acts of self-determination. The 1956 referendum in French Togoland was not about self-determination per se, because it did not include the option of independence and would be later rejected by the UN General Assembly. The 1989 and 2011 referenda in Namibia and South Sudan were done with all parties having agreed that a choice for independence would be accepted. The 1993 referendum in Eritrea served to confirm a de facto independence because Eritrea had successfully broken away from Ethiopia, its referendum done to gain UN and OAU recognition.

44  See Esther Heidbüchl, *The West Papua Conflict in Indonesia: Actors, Issues and Approaches* (Berlin: Verlag, 2007).

45  Apart from the positions of the parties, there remains the problem of establishing a current (accurate) voter roll for self-determination. Arguably, the UN remains responsible for that as a matter of its commitments in the 1990–91 referendum and ceasefire agreement. But it is difficult to envision the UN having liberty of action in Western Sahara to conduct an objective registration. The problem is alleviated, of course, if the referendum is on those terms proposed by Morocco in 2007. Completeness of registration matters less where independence is not at stake.

46  Saharawi vote each four years for local government in the 'independent' zones of the territory, and in self-administering camps in Algeria.

briefly met the conditions for statehood under the Montevideo Convention and customary international law, when it was invaded by Indonesia the Timorese people lost governance and territorial control.[47] The short-lived Democratic Republic of East Timor achieved only limited recognition from 11 states. The regional organization, Association of Southeast Asian Nations (ASEAN), sided with Indonesia. In addition, the exiled East Timorese leadership did not attempt to govern from exile, instead adopting the narrative of a non-self-governing and occupied people. This was reinforced by a Portugal that maintained it was the *de jure* colonial administering power. It demonstrated this by challenging the 1989 Australia–Indonesia Timor Gap Treaty for seabed petroleum and through becoming a party to the 1999 agreement with Indonesia for a referendum in the territory.[48] Finally, following the initial referendum of 1999, a UN administered referendum was needed to promote the consensus within East Timor that the UN could legitimately govern the territory and to create institutions of state until independence in May 2002.[49] The utility of a legitimate consultative plebiscite can be seen at present in Kosovo and was an important culminating step in South Sudan's long campaign to secede.

The Saharawi people find themselves in manifestly different circumstances. It seems clear that, however limited in financial resources and suffering the constraints of being operated from a refugee exile inside Algeria, the Saharawi Arab Democratic Republic (SADR) is a state. The criteria for such a legal existence are well established: (i) a people culturally and linguistically different from those of Morocco;[50] (ii) a defined territory within colonially prescribed and universally accepted boundaries, one-fifth of which is under its control;[51] (iii) a government with exclusive jurisdiction over a substantial part of the Saharawi population in the liberated area of Western Sahara and the refugee camps at Tindouf; and (iv) the capacity to enter into relations with other states, the SADR having been recognized by more than 80 states (and conducting diplomatic relations with 40 of them, with embassies in 18 capitals).[52] In addition, the SADR was admitted in 1982 to the regional organization, the OAU (something that resulted in Morocco quitting the organization) and is a founding member of OAU's successor, the African Union.[53] The qualification is that, while it is recognized as having statehood status, at the time of writing, no external power, including the UN, was prepared to use force to expel Morocco from the territory.

While it is true that the larger urban and economic heart of the territory is controlled by Morocco, illegal occupation cannot by itself terminate statehood.[54] Indeed, as Kuwait's 1990 invasion by Iraq demonstrated, there is an obligation under international law expressly to maintain (or restore) territorial integrity in cases of annexation. An additional factor is the absence of an engaged colonial administering state. International law and widespread state practice is clear

---

47 Article 1 of the *Montevideo Convention on the Rights and Duties of States* (December 26, 1933) 165 LNTS 19: a permanent population, a defined territory, a government, and capacity to enter into relations with the other states.

48 Although it did not recognize the Democratic Republic of East Timor after its unilateral declaration of independence in November 1975, Portugal severed diplomatic relations with Indonesia after the invasion.

49 Or, more accurately, the restoration of independence or 'realization of full independence'.

50 The Saharawi speak Hassaniya, a distinct Arab dialect.

51 After Morocco completed the berm in the late 1980s, the Saharawi acquired control to the east of it, confirmed by the 1990–91 UN ceasefire and referendum agreement together with free passage to the area allowed by Mauritania and Algeria.

52 These figures were obtained in interviews with SADR officials at international conferences, including in Algiers in December 2012 and Abuja in May 2015. Algeria's position in international law appears to be unique: it recognizes the SADR and accords it a refugee and government-in-exile presence within its territory. "Security Council Extends Western Sahara Mission until 30 April 2016, Unanimously Adopting Resolution 2218" (2015), April 28, 2015.

53 In July 2002 SADR President Mohamed Abdelaziz was elected vice-president of the African Union at the new organization's inaugural summit. Morocco is the only African state not a member of the organization.

54 Ian Brownlie, *Principles of Public International Law*, 3rd ed. (Oxford: Clarendon Press, 1979), 83. Similarly, Hector Gros Espiell (*The Right to Self-Determination*, para. 45) notes that the 'foreign occupation of a territory – an act condemned by modern international law and incapable of producing valid legal effects or of affecting the right to self-determination of the people whose territory has been occupied – constitutes an absolute violation of the right to self-determination'.

that a colonizing state continues in the obligation to ensure the self-determination of a subject non-self-governing people, however much that state may have attempted to relinquish the responsibility. Spain's abandonment of Western Sahara can be viewed not as any recognition of a Saharawi state but of the reality that all other options for self-determination have been exhausted.[55] The problem with the existence of the Saharawi state is two-fold: the requirement for recognition by all states as a political act whatever the material-factual existence of the Saharawi Republic, and the deference to the UN in resolving the 'question' of Western Sahara exclusively within the construct and norms of self-determination and not – as recently with Kosovo and South Sudan (and, in a somewhat different context, Palestine) – a new state emerging into the organized international community.

The problem with accepting an existing, functional Saharawi state may be the result of confusion over what has come to be a desired single standard of the international community, visible in the recent cases of secession, that peoples who wish to create a new state for themselves must pursue equivalent legitimacy requirements including a credible democratic choice for independence, and obtain the consent of the former colonial or occupying state.[56] However, the better reason for the lack of acceptance of the Saharawi state is the reluctance of the organized international community to disturb the status quo of a claim clearly rejected by the ICJ but which continues to be persisted in by Morocco. Whatever the overarching norms of international law, deferring the matter to the United Nations has contributed to the impasse.

## Occupied with a referendum

It is clear that a referendum for self-determination arranged for the Saharawi people is not a mandatory requirement of international law, state practice or UN norms. If the *right* to self-determination is accepted – and it almost universally is by states in the case of Western Sahara – it can be accomplished by other means. The overwhelming precedent is that of colonized peoples simply being allowed their independence, of moving directly to it (unlike East Timor which underwent a referendum on the question). The Saharawi people have been resolute about their choice for independence. This is why all efforts to negotiate a compromise since 2007 have ended in failure. No serious argument, much less any credible evidence, can be asserted that the Saharawi people favor anything less than outright statehood. That part of their population which has been in self-governed exile and therefore able to express a consensus has demanded it continuously. The problem that confronts the organized international community in accepting Saharawi statehood, in other words recognition of the SADR, is not of tolerating a Saharawi state so much as the reluctance to confront an illegal occupation. There is also the understandable concern about the implications for a Morocco that has constructed a national identity with considerable reliance on its annexation project – what it calls the 'national question'. In any event, a UN administered referendum offered as the sole route to self-determination, whether in a non-self-governing or secessionary context, establishes a norm that may be unworkable in future cases where an occupying state's cooperation and consent is considered necessary to the exercise.

---

55   Hans Corell, the former UN Under-Secretary-General for Legal Affairs, describes the Madrid Accords in these terms: 'The Madrid Agreement did not transfer sovereignty over the territory, nor did it confer upon any of the signatories the status of an administering power; Spain alone could not transfer that authority unilaterally. The transfer of the administration of the territory to Morocco and Mauritania in 1975 did not affect the international status of Western Sahara as a Non-Self-Governing Territory. On 26 February 1976, Spain informed the Secretary-General that as of that date it had terminated its presence in Western Sahara and relinquished its responsibilities over the territory, thus leaving it in fact under the administration of both Morocco and Mauritania in their respective controlled areas.' Hans Corell, 'Western Sahara – Status and Resources', *New Routes* 4 (2010): 10–13.

56   Hector Gros Espiell reasoned that: 'the right of peoples to self-determination has lasting force, [and] does not lapse upon first having been exercised to secure political self-determination … ', *The Right to Self Determination*, 45.

We should ask why if, when it comes to the Saharawi people, a referendum is not required under the law or in practice there remains such insistence on it. After all, there is not much doubt, and seemingly less than in the cases of Namibia and Timor-Leste, that independence would be overwhelmingly chosen. This said, it should be accepted that the Saharawi people would benefit from the perception of an externally administered referendum. Nothing, as the case of Timor-Leste after 1999 has shown, engages the support of the organized international community quite like the perception of legitimate resolution. Even the Saharawi accept this; in the language of the UN in recent years, the 'question' of Western Sahara must be resolved in a manner that is 'just, lasting and mutually acceptable'.[57] A referendum would more readily bring universal recognition by states and the further legitimization of the Saharawi statehood project by the participation of the whole of Saharawi society. As with Timor-Leste, a useful result of a referendum would be to eliminate obstacles in the SADR's new relationship with more powerful states such as France and to a certain extent the United States that have resulted from their support to Morocco.

## Can justice be achieved through the Security Council?

Within the UN the 'question' of Western Sahara has become almost exclusively the preserve of the Security Council. The role of the General Assembly, in its idealized best during the 1960s and 1970s to end the occupation of Namibia – including the creation of a council to govern the territory in absentia – has faded in the decades since. Annual resolutions of the General Assembly received from the Special Political and Decolonization Committee which restate the right of self-determination are of little consequence to the Security Council.[58] The discussion in UN corridors is a wearied acceptance of Morocco as a proper party, to be dealt with as if it had a legitimate claim over Western Sahara or to be present in the territory.

There is also the fact of Western Sahara's continuing inclusion on the UN's list of Non-Self-Governing Territories conferring a degree of protection not so much to the Saharawi people as to the one right they nominally possess.[59] For years there has been a concern among Saharawi leaders that emphasizing an existing statehood would put that fragile consensus of the right to self-determination at risk.[60] This must be the reason the SADR government has not pursued a more active diplomacy beyond Africa and the AU, quietly staying away from UN organizations such as the UN Food & Agriculture Organization which carries out fisheries research in Saharan coastal waters without Saharawi participation.[61]

57 Resolution 1813, 'The Situation Concerning Western Sahara', United Nations Security Council, New York, April 30, 2008.

58 The 2014 resolution of the General Assembly was formulaic, unchanged in its preamble and operative recitals from those of the past decade. See UN General Assembly Resolution, 'Question of Western Sahara', A/Res/69/101 (December 5, 2014) at para. 2: '[The General Assembly] *Supports* the process of negotiations initiated by Security Council resolution 1754 (2007) and further sustained by Council resolutions 1783 (2007), 1813 (2008), 1871 (2009), 1920 (2010), 1979 (2011), 2044 (2012), 2099 (2013) and 2152 (2014), with a view to achieving a just, lasting and mutually acceptable political solution, which will provide for the self-determination of the people of Western Sahara, and commends the efforts undertaken by the Secretary-General and his Personal Envoy for Western Sahara in this respect'.

59 A protection, however, that cannot be taken for granted when the case of West Papua is considered. Although the 'Act of Free Choice' was fraudulent (admitted as such by the then UN Under-Secretary-General Chakravarthy Narasimhan and confirmed recently by the Dutch academic Pieter Drooglever), West Papua was removed from the UN's list of non-self-governing territories and has since been considered part of the Republic of Indonesia. See Pieter Drooglever, *An Act of Free Choice: Decolonisation and the Right to Self-Determination in West Papua* (The Hague: Institute of Netherlands History, 2009).

60 Personal communication with senior Saharawi officials in 2012 and 2015. The present inchoate form of Saharawi statehood appears to have been a successful effort, alongside maintaining the Frente Polisario as the Saharawi people's national liberation movement. Comporting itself as a state has gained the SADR acceptance in AU circles and serves to valuably prepare the state for what is referred to as the 'restoration of full independence'.

61 See the Food and Agriculture Organization of the United Nations (FAO)/ United Nations Environment Programme (UNEP) 'Canary Current Large Marine Ecosystem Project' at http://www.canarycurrent.org/ (accessed April 1, 2015).

We can diagnose the situation as a kind of schizophrenia. The Saharawis conduct their affairs as a state, at least for that part of the population in exile that can do so, while much of the community of states is not willing to accept the legal existence of such a state.[62]

## Out of the impasse – a consideration of options

When it comes to the Saharawi people, the insistence of the UN and those states concerned about a referendum has been a pragmatic choice. But that insistence has allowed the underlying right of the people of Western Sahara – the ability to actually achieve their desired status – to be frustrated. It would be different if a referendum were imposed or could be organized by Saharawi acting collectively on both sides of the berm. Neither is likely. Morocco suppresses all efforts at public dialogue in the matter by both censoring alternative opinions within its own media and arguing strongly against dissenting views in public forums. The UN, for its part, is very unlikely to act unilaterally, especially when it cannot even assure a basic level of human rights protection in a territory for which it is responsible, as reflected in the lack of a human rights mandate for MINURSO. And therefore the long-running demand on some kind of process not only obscures the desired right, it has obstructed its realization.

So how might the present situation be addressed? What innovative approaches are available, especially by those states and organizations concerned and which, through the UN, exercise a power dynamic to determine the fate of the Saharawi people and their territory. To that we turn.

In considering an alternative to a referendum, the UN Charter offers a useful place to start. Several prescriptions are available.[63] In the event of territorial annexation – and for years there has been no clearer case than Morocco in Western Sahara – the Security Council is able, through one or some combination of the rules in Chapters VI and VII of the Charter, to act on and resolve this matter. Despite the unstated conclusion that the impasse over Western Sahara will not soon be resolved (leaving aside the sheer illegality of its initial occupation and annexation) there has been no serious consideration of applying the Charter's compulsory provisions. This is, of course, a reflection of the prevailing status quo.

What clearly engages the UN Charter, assuming the legitimacy of decolonization and the broad recognition of SADR, is the violation of Western Sahara's territorial integrity. The right to self-determination of the Saharawi people having been denied by the invasion of their territory, such an act must be ended by the withdrawal of Moroccan government control from the territory.[64] The Security Council had an accurate understanding of this at the material time when it demanded in Resolution 380 of 6 November 1975 that 'Morocco immediately ... withdraw from the Territory of Western Sahara ... '[65] How can the Security Council be compelled to act?

A coordinated campaign for recognition of the Saharawi Republic by UN member states is now timely. It has been given impetus recently by the AU Council for Peace and Security's

---

62  The status of Saharawi diplomats reflects this. Ubbi Bachir and Ali Mahamud Embarek, formerly Frente Polisario representatives in The Netherlands were later SADR ambassadors in Nigeria and Panama, respectively.

63  The former United Nations juris consult Hans Corell, in his private capacity, has recently suggested alternatives to a UN directed referendum. See 'The Responsibility of the UN Security Council in the Case of Western Sahara', *International Judicial Monitor* (Winter 2015): 1. He posits three options, namely: (i) a mandated governing presence for the UN in Western Sahara, similar to that in Timor-Leste during its post-referendum transition to independence; (ii) Security Council direction to Spain to resume its responsibilities as the colonial administering state; and (iii) recognition of the Saharawi Republic. Corell recognizes the options could be combined. '[Recognizing] Western Sahara as a sovereign state ... should be acceptable from a legal point of view. It would not deprive the people of Western Sahara from seeking a different solution to their self-determination in the future, if they so wish.' Ibid., 2.

64  See Susan Marks, 'Kuwait and East Timor: A Brief Study in Contrast' (in Arts and Pinto Leite, *International Law and the Question of East Timor*, 174–9), comparing the invasion of Kuwait by Iraq with the Indonesian invasion of Timor. For the reasons outlined above, her conclusions apply *a fortiori* to the Moroccan invasion of Western Sahara.

65  At paragraph 2 of the resolution. Article 25 of the UN Charter obligates members of the United Nations to implement decisions of the Security Council.

2015 resolution.[66] An example of the appetite for recognition can be seen in the 2004 letter from the President of the Republic of South Africa, Thabo Mbeki, to Morocco's Mohammed VI, explaining the colonial legacy underpinning South Africa's decision to recognize the Saharawi Republic.[67] Further afield, political parties in Austria, Brazil and Denmark pursued initiatives for governmental recognition of the Saharawi state in 2014. Of course, as a matter of contemporary international law, recognition is not strictly necessary for the existence of statehood because it has a limited declaratory value. But international politics is something else and here the concept matters. So it is worth repeating that the SADR has been recognized widely and participates extensively in the African Union.[68]

In recent years, apart from being recognized by a few states *ex novo* (most recently South Sudan) and establishing diplomatic relations with others sometime after recognition (most recently Guyana), the SADR has managed to reverse the position of eight states that had suspended or 'withdrawn' recognition: Nicaragua, El Salvador, Ecuador, Paraguay, Chad, Uganda, Sierra Leone and Vanuatu. There are also indications that states in the Global North are considering recognition, for example Sweden, where the Parliamentary Committee on Foreign Affairs approved a resolution in November 2012 calling on that country's government to extend recognition.[69]

It is in this endeavor – a campaign for universal recognition of the Saharawi state – that solidarity groups have a vital place. What is needed across transnational civil society is to coordinate action among the many groups concerned. The necessary umbrella organization does not yet exist and the need for it is increasingly obvious.[70] As an example, when it comes to protecting the resources of the territory from ongoing pillage, the Brussels-based Western Sahara Resource Watch pursues campaigns that are coordinated across several countries and languages.[71] External NGO (non-governmental organization) monitoring and action over human rights in occupied Western Sahara is nearly as sophisticated, with the Geneva-based Bureau International des Droits pour le Respect humains au Sahara Occidental (BIRDHSO) created in 2002.[72] A newly created NGO, Western Sahara Human Rights Watch (WSHRW), has the broader self-declared

---

66  See the March 27, 2015 Peace and Security Council of the African Union (AU PSC) *communiqué*.

67  'For us not to recognise SADR in this situation is to become an accessory to the denial of the people of Western Sahara of their right to self-determination. This would constitute a grave and unacceptable betrayal of our own struggle, of the solidarity Morocco extended to us, and our commitment to respect the Charter of the United Nations and the constitutive act of the African Union.' Letter of August 1, 2004 at http://arso.org/MBK.htm (accessed April 1, 2015).

68  Even as the organized international community will not urge the UN to act on the 'question' of Western Sahara, no state publicly supports Morocco's territorial claim to the Sahara. The kingdom's isolation was highlighted in 2011 when South Sudan achieved independence, joined the AU and established diplomatic relations with the SADR. There has been a campaign in recent years by Morocco to promote withdrawal of recognition of the SADR by states in the Global South, with mixed success. Commentators agree that withdrawal of recognition does not signify or hasten the end to a state's formal existence, for which see article 6 of the Montevideo Convention. Such 'withdrawals' have bordered on the absurd, for example Guinea-Bissau's first recognizing the SADR in 1976, withdrawing recognition in 1997, again extending recognition in 2009 and withdrawing it in 2010.

69  See 'Committee on Foreign Affairs at the Swedish Parliament Calls on the Government to Recognize SADR', Sahara Press Service, November 15, 2012, http://www.spsrasd.info/en/content/committee-foreign-affairs-swedish-parliament-calls-government-recognize-sadr (accessed April 11, 2015).

70  Stephen Zunes has compared solidarity movements in the causes of Timor and Western Sahara, and noted this is a 'factor working against Saharawi independence … despite their impressive efforts at building well-functioning democratic institutions in the self-governed refugee camps where the majority of their people live, the Saharawis have never had the degree of international grassroots solidarity that the East Timorese were able to develop, which eventually eroded support of the Indonesian occupation by Western powers'. See http://www.spectrezine.org/resist/wsahara.htm (accessed April 2, 2015). 'Though an international solidarity movement does exist for Western Sahara, primarily in Europe, it pales in comparison with the movement in support of East Timor, which grew dramatically in the 1990s, and helped encourage greater media coverage on the human rights situation.' (East Timor and Western Sahara: a Comparative Analysis on Prospects for Self-Determination, Presentation to the Conference on International Law and the Question of Western Sahara, Institute of Social Studies, The Hague, October 27–28, 2006).

71  See http://www.wsrw.org (accessed April 7, 2015).

72  See http://www.birdhso.org (accessed April 7, 2015).

task 'to promote and support campaigns for the defense of human rights in the Western Sahara, civil and political, as well as economic or cultural'.[73] The space for coordinated action remains open for the vital work of a single competent and respected organization. It would need to have regard for and even work loosely alongside Saharawi public diplomacy.

It is also clear that the Saharawi Republic must increasingly create institutions as if it were a state on the global stage, including the pursuit of deeper (if informal) relationships with Global North states and to prepare governance capacity in anticipation of the restoration of full independence. Timor-Leste offers an example of the steps that might have been taken over 24 years of occupation, given the challenges faced there by the UN and the first government after independence to build civil society organizations and democratic institutions. On the narrow issue of asserting territorial sovereignty, the SADR has from time to time acted with sophistication, for example by its 2009 creation of ocean jurisdiction legislation which would later influence the European debate over the acceptability of fishing arrangements with Morocco on the coast of the occupied territory.[74]

None of this is to suggest that the Saharawi people and their leadership – both in exile at Tindouf and inside occupied Western Sahara – should maintain anything less than an outspoken demand for the exercise of self-determination. Such an option must always necessarily remain available along with, in theory – if only because it is legal within international law – the resumption of armed hostilities.[75] However, the time has come for the most tenable and at least equally acceptable option to be advanced, and that is greater recognition of the Saharawi Republic. What is to result is no more of an uncertain or damaging prospect for international relations, political stability in the states concerned, and the maintenance of the international legal order than has resulted from the present circumstances.

## Determining the future

A campaign for recognition of the Saharawi Arab Democratic Republic will need to articulate the goal of achieving a majority of approving member states in the UN General Assembly. For practical purposes, recognition means acceptance as a UN member state and therefore the support of the Security Council. Hans Corell has explained it as follows:

> In view of the fact that the issue of Western Sahara has been on the agenda of the United Nations for four decades, the solution may be a … more radical option, namely that the Security Council recognises Western Sahara as a sovereign state. Also this option should be acceptable from a legal point of view. It would not deprive the people of Western Sahara from seeking a different solution to their self-determination in the future, if they so wish.[76]

Subject to the specific requirements of the UN Charter for the SADR's membership in the UN, two things would result: (i) the extension of formal relationships by previously uninterested states, and (ii) a putting into perspective for possible action by the UN and the organized international community the problem of the illegal occupation of Western Sahara and continuing aggression of that act revealed in the carrying out of the annexation, including human rights abuses, settler in-migration and the pillage of natural resources.

---

73  See http://www.wshrw.org (accessed April 7, 2015).
74  Law 03/2009 of January 21, 2009 Establishing the Maritime Zones of the Saharawi Arab Democratic Republic. The legislation resulted in the European Parliament reviewing the EU–Morocco 2007 Fisheries Partnership Agreement, which had allowed European fishing in the coastal waters of Western Sahara. The EU Parliament rejected such fishing in December 2011 which resumed in 2014 under revised arrangements with Morocco.
75  The use of force against colonial or otherwise illegal armed occupation is permissible under international law. In its resolution 'Importance of the universal realization of the right of peoples to self-determination' (December 3, 1982), UN doc. A/RES/37/43, the General Assembly affirmed 'the legitimacy of the struggle of peoples for independence, territorial integrity, national unity and liberation from colonial and foreign domination and foreign occupation by all available means, including armed struggle'.
76  Corell, 'The Responsibility of the UN Security Council in the Case of Western Sahara', 1.

The General Assembly has previously assumed the leading role for decolonization and the creation of states, the best example being that of its work for the Namibian people. While the UN Charter and precedent confer sufficient authority, it should be recalled that the General Assembly's 1950 Uniting for Peace resolution can also be invoked, Western Sahara being an instance where the Security Council, because of a

> lack of unanimity of the permanent members, fails to exercise its primary responsibility for the maintenance of international peace and security in any case where there [is a] breach of the peace, or act of aggression, the General Assembly shall consider the matter immediately with a view to making appropriate recommendations to Members for collective measures ... to maintain or restore international peace and security.[77]

There may be no better example of the intended use of the resolution than the long-running and unjust case of Western Sahara.

Even the casual observer must conclude that there is little prospect of the Saharawi people being offered in the years to come a self-determination referendum that has much credibility or acceptability. Only a determinedly new approach by the UN Security Council or fundamental political change in Morocco can apparently change the impasse. Neither seems likely. With an organized international community more concerned with the aftermath and complex problems that have resulted from the 2011 Arab Spring, there is a reluctance to act when it comes to Western Sahara. The status quo may continue to prevail. And therefore the time is right to recall that the Saharawi people are the sovereigns of their territory, and the fact of their state is well established. From such a place there should be little distance to travel to a completed and universally accepted statehood, and that is by the path of recognition.[78] The Saharawi people, their international supporters and the member states of the General Assembly each have a role in the achievement of that goal.

## Acknowledgments

I am grateful to several reviewers who offered comments in the preparation of this paper. All errors remain mine.

## Disclosure statement

No potential conflict of interest was reported by the author.

---

77 UN General Assembly Resolution 377 A (November 3, 1950). See Jean Krasno and Mitushi Das, 'The Uniting for Peace Resolution and Other Ways of Circumventing the Authority of the Security Council', in *The UN Security Council and the Politics of International Authority*, ed. Bruce Cronin and Ian Hurd (London: Routledge, 2008), 173–95.

78 The emergence of a fully independent Saharawi state will engage the question of Morocco's presence in Western Sahara. The case of Timor-Leste suggests acceptance in the face of such a *fait accompli*.

# Saharawi conflict phosphates and the Australian dinner table

Erik Hagen

*Board Member, Western Sahara Resource Watch*

This article describes how the investor community has intervened vis-à-vis the global fertilizer companies sourcing phosphate rock from occupied Western Sahara. The territory holds large phosphates deposits, and the export of such rock constitutes the biggest source of income for the Moroccan government in the territory it has annexed. Due to the particular nature of the conflict in that territory, such practice is associated with concerns of human rights breaches, international law violations and political controversy. A dozen companies purchase these phosphates from the Moroccan government, while their traditional and legal owners are increasingly active in trying to stop the practice. Investor engagement and company improvement are discussed with a particular focus on Australia. By the end of the 1980s, 39% of all phosphate rock in Western Sahara ended up in Australia. After a massive shareholder campaign directed at the Australian importers, the country has basically ended its dependence on such phosphate rock. The article also looks at import cases in North America. The article outlines the different arguments and strategies of investors, based on public statements and on internal dialogues between international investors and the civil society organization Western Sahara Resource Watch over the last decade.

## Introduction

Sourcing phosphate rock from a Moroccan state-owned company operating a mine in occupied Western Sahara is associated with numerous ethical, political and legal concerns. The exports of Western Sahara phosphate is Morocco's biggest source of income in the territory, and the trade is regarded by many as complicating the finding of a solution to the Western Sahara conflict.

This article places a particular focus on Australia, which for decades was one of the leading importers of phosphate rock from Western Sahara. Such rock is crucial to Australia's agricultural industries after being turned into fertilizers in Australian fertilizer plants. It is due to these fertilizers that Australia has become a global producer of meat, wheat and wool, and is able to engage in large-scale farming for domestic and international consumers. After two decades of heavy dependence on this rock, two of the three importing companies in Australia de facto ceased to import, with only one producer remaining today.

This article sets out to describe how the investor community has intervened vis-à-vis the global fertilizer companies sourcing phosphate rock from occupied Western Sahara. Investors, both in Australia and globally, have been a key force in guiding the companies towards behaving better. In fact, the investor community has become an important player in the world community's approach to the conflict.

Investors' concerns can be traced back to a legal opinion prepared for the UN Security Council in 2002.[1] Western Sahara is a territory rich in resources and in 2001 Morocco issued

---

1 United Nations, 'Letter dated 29 January 2002 from the Under-Secretary-General for Legal Affairs, the Legal Counsel, addressed to the President of the Security Council', S/2002/161, 2002.

the first oil licences to foreign companies in Western Sahara. The UN Security Council responded by asking its legal office whether such a move was legal. In his response, the UN Legal Counsel concluded that any further oil exploration or exploitation in Western Sahara would be illegal if the indigenous Saharawis did not consent to it and also if they did not benefit from it. The argument was deduced from the rights of the people of the territory to self-determination, and the legal status of the territory not having completed the process of decolonization.

Yet the oil companies proceeded with further oil exploration, without seeking the consent of the Saharawi people. Large bulk carriers transporting phosphate rock from the occupied territory also kept up the same pace of exporting as they had previously done.

On this basis, in response to the companies' continued activities in Western Sahara, civil society groups, governments and investors responded. The international non-governmental association Western Sahara Resource Watch (WSRW) emerged in part because of these events. WSRW, established in 2004, investigates the companies and governments that choose to enter into deals with the Moroccan government for resources located in Western Sahara. WSRW confronts each of the companies with an essential question: did they check with the owners of the resources, or did they only consult the Moroccan government? Their answers vary, although the WSRW has found they generally avoid responding to the question altogether.

WSRW exposes this corporate behaviour to the media, through which international investors then learn of it. The WSRW also nurtures contact directly with the investors outside of the public realm. Some elements in this article regarding the investors' behaviour are based on general observations that the author and WSRW has made from its decade-long dialogue with investors.

The companies involved in the trade have become increasingly well prepared, notably by having elaborate answers to send to concerned investors. The documents look impressive enough and it takes time to discover the flaws in their presentation. Yet some investors take time to study these replies in detail. These investors make assessments of the international and human rights law and decide on that basis whether they will continue to engage or to divest, with some not accepting the arguments provided by the companies and thus divesting.

## Controversial industry

Only weeks after the 1975 invasion of what was then Spanish Sahara by Morocco, the phosphate rock of the Bou Craa mine in Western Sahara was being exported to fertilizer companies overseas. Now controlling the Bou Craa mine and the exports was the Office Chérifien des Phosphates SA (OCP), Morocco's national phosphate company.

Phosphates de Boucraa SA (Phosboucraa) is a fully owned subsidiary of OCP. Its main activities are the extraction, so-called beneficiation, transportation and marketing of phosphate ore from the Bou Craa mine, as well as operating a treatment plant located on the Atlantic coast, at El Aaiún. OCP puts production capacity in Western Sahara at 2.6 million tonnes annually. Though OCP claims that the Bou Craa mines represent only 1% of all phosphate reserves exploited by Morocco, no less than a quarter of its exported phosphate rock departs from El Aaiún.[2] The exceptionally high quality of Western Sahara's phosphate ore makes it a much-coveted commodity for producers of fertilizers.

However, that export process could be coming to an end. The Bou Craa phosphate deposit consists of two layers. So far, only the first, top layer has been mined. This particular layer contained phosphate rock of the highest quality across all of the reserves controlled by OCP. In 2014, Bou Craa phosphate mining moved on to the second layer, which is of lower quality. Morocco has

---

2   OCP SA, 'Prospectus', April 17, 2014, http://www.ise.ie/debt_documents/Base%20Prospectus_b81be83f-8e8f-43ef-85d9-cc5a4ae0277a.PDF?v=402015.

now sold all of the high-quality phosphate that ought to have been available to the Saharawi people upon realizing their right to self-determination.

OCP claims that Phosboucraa is the largest private employer in the wider Bou Craa area, with around 2200 employees. More than half of those are claimed to be locally recruited. It also claims that Phosboucraa is a major provider of economic viability and well-being for the region's inhabitants. OCP equally boasts of the social impact of Phosboucraa, in terms of providing pensions to retirees, and medical and social advantages to employees, retirees and their families. OCP presents the purported economic and social benefits as a justification for its exploitation of phosphate mines outside of Morocco's internationally recognized borders.

The illegally exploited phosphate rock is the Moroccan government's main source of income from Western Sahara, which it continues to occupy contrary to international law. Representatives of the Saharawi people have been consistently outspoken against the trade, both in the UN, generally, and to specific companies. The refugees from Western Sahara, representing half of the Saharawi people, do not see any benefits from the trade, having been forced to flee as Morocco invaded the territory. Some Saharawis had worked at the phosphate production unit up until the Moroccan invasion.

Morocco uses the Bou Craa phosphates for its political lobbying to gain the informal acceptance of other countries for its illegal occupation. An official Moroccan document leaked in 2014 explicitly states that Western Sahara's resources, including phosphate, should be used 'to implicate Russia in activities in the Sahara'. The document goes on to say that 'in return, Russia could guarantee a freeze on the Sahara file within the UN'.[3] This corresponds to other statements from the Moroccan government. A former fisheries minister once stated that Morocco's fisheries agreement with the EU was more of a political agreement than a financial one.[4] Morocco's current Minister of Communication has been quite outspoken in this regard. He declared that all agreements that do not exclude 'the Moroccan Sahara' from their application prove that the area is Moroccan.[5] With control over not only its own, but also Western Sahara's phosphorous reserves, Morocco has placed itself in a very important position geopolitically. Approximately 75% of global phosphate reserves are now controlled by the Moroccan government. Importantly, phosphate is a mineral containing the element of phosphorous which is fundamental for all living cells.

## Massive trade

WSRW tracks all shipping traffic in the waters of Western Sahara on a daily basis, and routinely publishes reports on Moroccan exports from the occupied territory, identifying all shipments of phosphates taking place. The latest report, *P for Plunder 2014*, was issued in March 2015.[6]

WSRW believes that it has detected, tracked and accounted for all vessels departing from El Aaiún harbour since the second half of 2011. For 2014, the total exported volume from Western Sahara was calculated by WSRW at 2.1 million tonnes, shipped in 44 bulk vessels. That constitutes a slight decline in sales from 2013.

The amount of phosphate loaded into a ship is ordinarily calculated to be 95% of the ship's overall cargo capacity. In cases where ships had a cargo carrying capacity of less than 40,000 tonnes, the 95% factor was reduced to account for a higher relative amount of fuel and provisions. Ships are then tracked and confirmed to have arrived at stated destinations. Where possible,

3 WSRW, 'Morocco Admits to Using Saharawi Resources for Political Gain', November 25, 2014, http://www.wsrw.org/a105x3070.
4 Mohamed Boudarham, 'Accord de pêche: naufrage polisarien', *Aujourd'hui Le Maroc*, May 24, 2006, http://www.aujourdhui.ma/maroc/societe/accord-de-peche-naufrage-polisarien-41767.
5 Al Hayat, وزير الاتصال المغربي لـ«الحياة»: الجزائر و«بوليساريو» يمنعان إحصاء اللاجئين في مخيمات تيندوف January 14, 2013, http://www.alhayat.com/Details/472155.
6 WSRW, *P for Plunder 2014* (2015), http://www.wsrw.org/a105x3185.

estimated loaded amounts were checked against shipping documents, including bills of lading and port arrival receipts.

As has been noted, phosphate rock is the biggest financial engine for Morocco's settlement project in Western Sahara. In recent years, global phosphate prices have increased exponentially. For decades, the price for phosphate remained stable at around $40–50 per tonne. However, in the last decade there have been fluctuations in price. It peaked briefly in 2008, at around $500 a tonne. Since then it has stabilized between $200 and $100 a tonne. In 2014, it averaged at around $110. For our calculations, phosphate prices are obtained from the commercial commodities pricing website 'Index Mundi' and checked against other sources.[7]

The Moroccan state earns massively from the mine it controls in the occupied territories. The volume exported would be an estimated US$230 million for 2014. In comparison, the value of the annual multilateral humanitarian aid to the Saharawi refugee camps is approximately €30 million.

WSRW's *P for Plunder 2014* report attributes the purchased phosphate to nine identified and one unknown importers in nine countries internationally. There is little change from year to year in the customer pattern. Of the nine identified importing companies in 2014, five are listed on international stock exchanges or are majority owned by enterprises which are listed. All of these have been subject to blacklisting by ethically concerned investors due to this trade.

The report reveals that between them, the Canadian company Agrium Inc. and the Lithuanian company Lifosa AB in 2014 accounted for 58% of all purchases from Western Sahara.

## The Australian imports

The Australian farming industry is dependent on phosphate imports to fertilize pastures for live-stock and for agriculture. There has always been a domestic production of phosphates in Australia, but the industry remains heavily reliant on imports. Three companies control the Australian market of so-called 'super phosphates' fertilizers – Wesfarmers Ltd, Incitec Pivot Ltd and Impact Fertilisers Pty Ltd.

Throughout the twentieth century, the major share of Australia's phosphate demand was supplied from large deposits on Christmas Island. From 1981 to 1987, this mine was operated by the Australian Phosphate Corporation (APC), a government-owned entity. By 1987–88, the transports from Christmas Island to Australia had come to a complete stop, except for a limited resumption of trade from the mid-1990s onwards. These Christmas Island phosphates were mostly replaced with imports from Nauru, Western Sahara and a few other sources, Australian import statistics show.

From what WSRW has been able to establish, APC started importing on a massive scale from the occupied territory of Western Sahara in 1987. During that calendar year, APC received 292,000 tonnes of phosphate rock from Boucraa, corresponding to 39% of the total Boucraa production of that year. The following years, the APC imports declined steadily, and from 1992 APC did not itself import phosphates, as other Australian importers took over.[8]

By 2006, Incitec Pivot imported a probable 238,010 tonnes, Wesfarmers 105,200 tonnes and Impact 50,350 tonnes, totalling 424,710 tonnes. These figures, from calculations of shipments from Bou Craa, correspond more or less with the import statistics from Australian official databases. 2006 was a year of particularly high phosphate exports from Bou Craa, and the Australian imports amounted to around 14% of the total production in the occupied territory.[9]

---

7  Index Mundi, http://www.indexmundi.com/.

8  http://www.businessofaustralia.com/c/b/australian-phosphate-corporation-limited/005788072 (accessed August 10, 2015).

9  http://www.iama.org.au/sites/default/files/Australian%20Fertilizer%20Industry%20Value%20and%20Issues%20August%202010.pdf (accessed August 10, 2015).

During the financial year 2005/6, the rock, which according to Australian trade statistics originates from 'Morocco', accounted for 62% of all Australian phosphate imports. At the time, WSRW found that the importers and the investor community had very shallow knowledge about the concerns related to the phosphate exports from Western Sahara.[10]

Around this time, the Australian government also formulated its opinion on the matter of the plundering of the territory. The main approach is to recommend that Australian companies seek independent legal advice.[11] At one point, in 2010, the Australian government was placed in a position where it had to clarify its policy: an Australian company had requested the government to produce a letter of support which it could in turn send to Morocco. The company had been invited by the Moroccan government to take part in a tender for an exploration permit in Western Sahara for a 'potentially world class multi-commodity (uranium, rare earths, tantalum and iron) project'.[12] There was a particular interest in the uranium extraction.

The government concluded that it could not comply with the request. The government stated that '[g]iven the status of Western Sahara, we do not consider it appropriate for the Australian Government to assist [and to] write a letter of support', and 'a letter of support may prejudice Australia's position on the conflict, which strongly recognises the UN-mediated process and advises companies of the international law considerations of operating in the region'.[13]

The Fertilizer Industry Federation of Australia (FIFA) has, for its part, systematically defended the imports of phosphates. Its members cover basically the entire market of fertilizer produced, imported and sold on the Australian market. In a communication, FIFA noted that '[t]he resolution of the long-running dispute between Morocco and the Polisario in relation to the sovereignty of the area known as Western Sahara is, and should be, in the hands of the international community, not individuals or companies'.[14]

Eight years later, in 2015, two of the three importers have de facto stopped purchasing from Western Sahara, and the imported volume to Australia has reduced to a fourth of that of 2006. In the following paragraphs, the involvement of the three companies Incitec Pivot, Wesfarmers and Impact Fertilisers are discussed.

## Incitec Pivot (IPL)

Incitec Pivot Ltd, also referred to as IPL, is an Australian multinational corporation that engages in the manufacturing, trading and distribution of fertilizers. The company's fertilizer segment includes Incitec Pivot Fertilizers (IPF), Southern Cross International (SCI), and Fertilizers Elimination (Elim).

IPL has been importing from Western Sahara for the past 30 years. The company is headquartered in Melbourne, Australia, and is registered on the Australian Securities Exchange. In 2015, Incitec Pivot was the largest supplier of fertilizer products in Australia, but it also markets its products abroad, such as in India, Pakistan and Latin America. IPL manufactures a range of fertilizer products, but uses the Saharawi phosphate for its so-called superphosphate products produced at plants in Geelong and Portland.

---

10  Ibid.
11  Australian Department of Foreign Affairs and Trade, 'Important Information on Western Sahara', http://www.dfat. gov.au/geo/morocco/Pages/important-information-on-western-sahara.aspx.
12  Australian Department of Foreign Affairs and Trade, various declassified files and correspondence, 2007–10: 238–45, http://www.wsrw.org/files/dated/2015-05-04/dfat_australia_docs_2007-2010.pdf.
13  Ibid.
14  FIFA, 'Phosphate Rock imports from the Western Sahara', December 12, 2007, http://www.wsrw.org/files/dated/2015-05-03/fifa_13.12.2007.pdf.

In February 2015, IPL confirmed to WSRW that it received three shipments of phosphate rock from Western Sahara in 2014, a total volume of 94,600 tonnes.[15] This volume corresponds to the cargo capacity of the three bulk carriers received that year.

IPL's sustainability report provides a good summary of the company's arguments and approach to the topic.

> The situation regarding the Kingdom of Morocco and the status of the Non Self Governing Territory of Western Sahara is a complex one, managed under the auspices of the United Nations … We remain satisfied that we are not in breach of either Australian law or International law, as there has been no determination by the UN or any other competent legal authority that the production and use of phosphate from the Non Self Governing Territory of Western Sahara is in violation of any applicable law or the Geneva Convention [sic]. Over many years IPL has engaged in dialogue and enquiry with many parties on this matter. In particular, IPL meets periodically with the Australian Department of Foreign Affairs and Trade, and has had discussions with Office Cherifien des Phosphates, its supplier of phosphate rock from the Non Self Governing Territory of Western Sahara, as well as with Australian ambassadors to the Kingdom of Morocco.[16]

Although IPL fully consulted Australian and Moroccan authorities in this instance, it has never responded to a central question asked by WSRW: 'What steps, if any, has IPL taken to assure itself of the continuing consent of the Saharawi people to such purchases, consistent their right to self-determination, the 2002 UN Legal Opinion (S/2002/161) and international humanitarian law?'[17]

## Impact Fertilisers

Impact Fertilisers (Impact), based in Hobart, Tasmania, imported phosphates from Western Sahara from about 2002 until 2013. It is not possible to accurately conclude what caused Impact Fertilisers' exit from Western Sahara. However, from 2010, a Swiss trading company Ameropa AG became majority owner, and the company was shortly after pressured by Swiss parliamentarians to halt the trade.[18] In 2013, the company announced that it had ended the imports. WSRW observed the last shipment to Impact in August 2012. Before then, the company's response to WSRW's query regarding trading in Western Sahara phosphates was that it had 'a contrary view and advice to that expressed by you regarding the legitimacy of the trade'.[19] In particular, the company had said:

> Whilst we continually review our rock sources based on suitability and cost for our production system, this source remains a key and viable source for our production requirements. In relation to your assertion that if all Australian importers were to act together to cease this trade it would alter the issues or referendum, this is fundamentally flawed. Australia is a relatively small proportion of the trade from Western Sahara and any void left would soon be filled by other purchasers.[20]

## Wesfarmers CSBP

Wesfarmers Limited is one of Australia's largest public companies, headquartered in Perth, Western Australia. The company is listed on the Australian Securities Exchange. Its fertilizer

15  Incitec Pivot to WSRW, February 13, 2015, http://www.wsrw.org/a240x3172.
16  Incitec Pivot, *Sustainability Report 2013* (2014), http://www.incitecpivot.com.au/~/media/Files/IPL/Sustainability/2013%20Sustainability%20Report.pdf.
17  WSRW letter to Incitec Pivot, February 6, 2015, http://www.wsrw.org/a240x3171.
18  WSRW, '8 Swiss Parliamentarians Protest Ethics of Tasmanian Company', September 9, 2010, http://www.wsrw.org/a105x1585.
19  Impact Fertilisers to WSRW, May 12, 2008, http://www.wsrw.org/a128x718.
20  Ibid.

subsidiary, Wesfarmers CSBP, was a major importer of phosphates from Western Sahara for at least two decades.

The earliest known imports of Saharawi phosphates by CSBP date back to 1990. Wesfarmers used to import between 60% and 70% of its phosphates from Western Sahara. The imports to CSBP/Wesfarmers probably amounted to between 63,000 tonnes and 159,000 tonnes during the years 1992–97, corresponding to 4% to 10% of the entire annual production from the Bou Craa mine.

However, it was not concerns over international law that first drew attention to Wesfarmers' involvement in Western Sahara phosphate imports. In November 2005, two stowaways were found dead in the vessel *Furness Karumba* as it arrived in Australia from Western Sahara with phosphates for Wesfarmers. From then on, the media became more interested in the matter, and, on 7 November 2005, Wesfarmers for the first time sought advice from the Australian government:

> The Australian Government has not imposed any trading restrictions with Western Sahara. CSBP is satisfied that it is not in breach of international law and will continue to be guided by the Australian Government's position on trade with the region.[21]

As will be discussed below, Wesfarmers has now de facto halted its purchases, at least temporarily.

## How the investors argue

The reasons why investors engage with the fertilizer companies vary greatly, and the highly diverse ethical policies and guidelines of each investor is a major factor in this variation. The arguments of each investor are mainly founded in human rights, international law or overall ethical principles established in their respective responsible investment guidelines. Some employ a legalistic approach, concluding that the operations in Western Sahara violate the law, and that the investors cannot be the owners of such companies.

Numerous studies seek to address to what extent ethical fund management is less or more profitable than fund management which does not take ethical considerations into account. This article does not seek to explore that discussion. It is worth noting, however, that some shareholders declare that there is a real financial risk in maintaining their ownership in companies associated with this controversial trade. For example, one Canadian investor noted that '[r]eputational and political risks brought on through Agrium's business relationship with the Moroccan government-owned phosphate company (OCP) has the potential to negatively impact shareholder value'.[22]

When analysing corporate behaviour in light of investors' ethical standards, a hierarchy is applied to the issue of responsibility, with certain types of involvement being considered as having more serious implications than others. A company's majority ownership in a controversial licence is considered more serious than in the cases where the company has a minor stake. An operator exploiting the resources is more involved than the client of the plundered goods. A long-term customer with a ten-year supply contract from Bou Craa is seen as much more involved than one purchasing a random shipment from Bou Craa on the spot market. Shipping companies transporting the phosphate rock with a long-term transport agreement with the importer are seen as more involved than shipping companies taking an accidental load on the spot market. Contractors helping with infrastructure, consultancy or seismic studies, for example, are seen as even less involved. Yet companies engaged in all such activity have been approached by ethical investors.

21   Wesfarmers to Norwegian Support Committee for Western Sahara, February 15, 2012, http://www.wsrw.org/files/dated/2012-10-05/wesfarmers-skvs_15.02.2012.pdf.
22   Vancity, *2014 Shareholder Engagement Report* (2015), https://www.vcim.ca/pdfs/2014ShareholderReport.pdf.

However, the level of shareholder engagement, and the probability of exclusion, follows the pyramid: the more involved companies are, the more likely they are to receive concerned calls from their investors.

Active ownership and exclusions are confidential matters for many banks and investors. They often do not want to reveal which companies they are in dialogue with, which companies they have divested from, or the value of the shares they have sold in divestment cases. It is thus not normally known which investors have blacklisted companies involved in Western Sahara, or the value of these divestments. There are exceptions: some investors publish press releases of their divestments as they happen, while others declare these decisions in the annual reports. Others describe their active ownership processes in various company responsibility reports. The largest known single exclusion incident was around US$350 million.[23]

A common argument against excluding a company breaching ethical standards is stated as follows: 'When we blacklist a company, we lose the opportunity to influence them positively'. WSRW considers this an exaggeration because it appears that divestors are well able to maintain a dialogue with the companies even after they have been blacklisted, being clear that they will reinvest once the operation in question has been halted. The threat of exclusion is only a real threat if exclusions are routinely carried out.

A common denominator in the investor–importer relationship is the two criteria established in the UN 2002 legal opinion.[24] This asks whether the Saharawi people wish for the trade to take place and, if so, whether they benefit from it. The investors highlight either one or both of these criteria in their dialogue with the involved companies. Some investors conclude on the compliance with these two principles simply by looking at the political infrastructure of Western Sahara. As long as Morocco does not seek the consent of the Saharawi refugees, and as long as neither Morocco nor the companies seek the consent from any Saharawi group seeking self-determination, it is clear that the exploitation and trade cannot take place in line with the wishes of the people of the territory. Even if Morocco had wanted to seek consent from the Saharawis in Western Sahara, it would be impossible to do so as the political infrastructure imposed by the Moroccan government would not allow it. For instance, groups advocating for self-determination are actively undermined.[25] By concluding the argument already at that stage, these investors do not even start assessing the question of benefits to the Saharawis.

The following arguments are used by investors.

(a) *Violation of international law due to failure to seek consent*

Upon exclusion of PotashCorp and Incitec Pivot from its portfolios, the Swedish government pension fund AP-Fonden stated:

> Western Sahara has been under Moroccan occupation since 1975 and is on the United Nations' list of non-self-governing territories that should be decolonised. The UN's legal counsel stated in January 2002 that exploration of mineral resources in Western Sahara without local consent would be in breach of the International Covenant on Civil and Political Rights and the International Covenant on Economic, Social and Cultural Rights.[26]

---

23    Norwegian Ministry of Finance, 'Government Pension Fund Global: Two Companies Excluded from the Fund's Investment Universe', news release, June 12, 2011, https://www.regjeringen.no/en/aktuelt/government-pension-fund-global-two-compa/id665637/.

24    United Nations, 'Letter dated 29 January 2002 from the Under-Secretary-General for Legal Affairs, the Legal Counsel, addressed to the President of the Security Council', S/2002/161, 2002.

25    Human Rights Watch, *World Report 2015: Morocco/Western Sahara* (2015), http://www.hrw.org/world-report/2015/country-chapters/morocco/western-sahara.

26    WSRW, 'Swedish Government Pension Fund Blacklists Sahara Importers', September 30, 2013, http://www.wsrw.org/a217x2664.

The latest exclusion from this particular investor was announced in the fund's annual report 2014, published in 2015.[27]

(b) Violation of international law due to failure to guarantee local benefit

The Norwegian company KLP stated, regarding its divestments from Wesfarmers, Incitec Pivot, PotashCorp and FMC Corp in 2010:

> The company is thus indirectly funding Morocco's illegal occupation of the territory. In an opinion, issued in 2002, by the UN Under-Secretary General for Legal Affairs, the exploitation of natural resources in colonized territories, Western Sahara in particular, was declared illegal if it is not to the benefit of the people of the territory.[28]

(c) *Violation of human rights norms*

'[The company] imports natural resources which are extracted in conflict with human rights norms', noted the largest bank in Denmark, Danske Bank, upon divesting from PotashCorp, Wesfarmers, FMC Corp and Incitec Pivot.[29]

(d) *Violation of fundamental ethical norms*

Upon the divestment from PotashCorp and FMC Corp, the Ethical Council of the Norwegian sovereign wealth fund stated:

> Since this concerns non-renewable resources, these will be lost to the exiled local population, even if the territory's status at some time in the future should change and the exiled local population is able to return. The view of the Council on Ethics is therefore that OCP's activities in Western Sahara must be considered grossly unethical.[30]

Similarly, Norwegian investor KLP stated that purchase of phosphates from Western Sahara 'via a long-term contract with the state-owned Moroccan company Office Chérifien des Phosphates (OCP), is deemed to represent an unacceptable risk of contributing to violations of basic ethical norms, and therefore contravenes KLP's guidelines for responsible investment'.[31]

(e) *Violation of UN Global Compact principles*

Both Innophos Holdings and PotashCorp have been excluded for being in breach of the Global Compact principles by the American SRI Fund of the BrownAdvisory.[32]

(f) *Illegality*

'Illegal exploitation of natural resources', stated the Luxemburg pension fund Fonds de Compensation commun au régime général de pension upon blacklisting all the involved phosphate companies.[33]

## How the investors act and succeed

Multinational companies on the international stock exchanges are often 'ownerless', in that they are owned by everyone but not necessarily by a single major shareholder. Institutional investors, such as a national pension fund holding 1–2% of the shares in a company, could be among the biggest investors in that company. Those owners often administer the savings of millions of

27 WSRW, 'Swedish Government Fund Excludes Agrium over Western Sahara Imports', April 10, 2013, http://www.wsrw.org/a105x3208.

28 KLP, *Responsible Investments, SRI Report June 2010*, June 1, 2010, https://www.klp.no/polopoly_fs/1.10504.1359544017!/menu/standard/file/sri_report_june_2010.pdf.

29 Danica Pension, 'Ekskluderte selskaper', http://wsrw.org/files/dated/2010-12-18/danica_webpage_17.12.2010.pdf.

30 WSRW, 'European Banks Divest from Unethical Sahara Fertiliser Industry', November 30, 2010, http://www.wsrw.org/a159x1704.

31 KLP, 'Exclusion from Investment Portfolios', news release, December 1, 2014, http://english.klp.no/polopoly_fs/1.29227.1417436404!/menu/standard/file/Agrium%20decision%20to%20exclude%2001122014%20ENGLISH.pdf.

32 BrownAdvisory, 'October 2014 Factsheet', http://www.brownadvisory.com/LinkClick.aspx?fileticket=iobRki8gxSc%3D&tabid=383.

33 WSRW, 'Luxembourg Pension Fund Blacklists Six Firms over Saharan Imports', November 19, 2014, http://www.wsrw.org/a106x3065.

people. The problem is who will call the management and board of the companies to account if they behave irresponsibly when no owner controls more than a small proportion of the shares?

The only way an investor can get any leverage with a company they partly own is if other owners do the same. It is in these joint efforts, coordinated or uncoordinated, that we see the full force of change in corporate behaviour in relation to the Western Sahara phosphate trade. This was noted by one head of responsible investments at Finnish investor Ilmarinen: 'We hope to see more investors join us in urging companies linked to the territory to act responsibly and help Western Sahara get the attention it needs'.[34]

Together with other Nordic investors, Ilmarinen has carried out engagement with companies in Western Sahara over a number of years, assisted by the Swedish screening company GES Investment Services. Among the companies that have been approached are PotashCorp, FMC Corp, Incitec Pivot and Wesfarmers. On this engagement, the Ilmarinen Director said:

> Although Western Sahara has not attracted as much media attention as some other conflict areas, this does not mean that it is not of importance to investors. The latest UN reports strengthen the case for investors to engage with companies operating in this area to improve the situation'.[35]

In other words, the investors have not only a responsibility to act, but also possibilities for action which are very different from the behaviour of states or civil society, which until now have been considered the main actors in the issues relating to basic human rights and self-determination in Western Sahara.

There are limitations, of course. First of all, not all of the companies involved in Western Sahara are appropriate for investors to approach on the international stock markets. In general, and perhaps naturally, the investors are mainly interested in engaging those companies that they have themselves invested in. There are some exceptions to this: for instance, investors who want to keep engaging companies which they have already divested from. Some also seek to engage companies in which they could potentially invest in the future. In terms of the Western Sahara phosphate trade, this automatically excludes some of the importers from the reach of the players on the global stock market.

Another hurdle for the investors is the lack of documentation. The reports coming out of Western Sahara are inherently biased one way or the other. No state in the world functions as the administrative power of Western Sahara vis-à-vis the UN today, meaning that no state takes on the obligation for reporting on the well-being or self-determination process of the people of Western Sahara. As noted in the UN Legal Opinion, Morocco is not the administrative power of the territory, and even refuses to characterize itself as such.[36] Morocco also denies any ability on the part of the UN Mission for Referendum in Western Sahara (MINURSO) to observe and report on the human rights situation. The companies involved are sometimes also not keen to provide detailed reports about their activities. Most importantly, they fail to answer how the trade is carried out with respect for the wishes of the people. Some do not respond at all. The best-known case of a totally silent company is Innophos Holdings, the parent of an importing subsidiary in Mexico. Such silence makes it harder to verify the company's participation in trade. 'A company we invest in should not be rewarded by keeping quiet when we confront them with our concerns', stated one investor regarding Innophos.[37]

---

34  WSRW, 'Investors Calling on Company Responsibility', June 20, 2012, http://www.wsrw.org/a214x2343.

35  Ibid.

36  United Nations, 'Letter dated 29 January 2002 from the Under-Secretary-General for Legal Affairs; Morocco World News, 'Full Text of King Mohammed VI's Speech on 39th Anniversary of Green March', November 6, 2014, http://www.moroccoworldnews.com/2014/11/143369/full-text-of-king-mohammed-vis-speech-on-39th-anniversary-of-green-march/.

37  Interview with investor, 2014. None of the investors that the author and WSRW have been in contact with have ever received an answer from Innophos. WSRW letters remain unanswered. An example of the lack of response can be seen in Council of Ethics for the Norwegian Government Pension Fund Global, 'Recommendation 26 September

In practical terms, it is sometimes complicated to exercise the actual power inherent in the ownership. The owners are not always investing in the companies directly, but via external fund managers. These managers handle the capital of numerous clients. The challenge emerges then if one of the dozens of companies in that particular fund starts dealing with Western Sahara phosphates. The composition of the fund would in such a case no longer comply with the ethical guidelines of the investors. 'Either you remove that company from the fund you are selling us, or we have to find another fund or manager', would be an expected response from the investor. Needless to say, some of the larger investors could have remarkable leverage on the fund managers. A company like the Kempen Capital Management (KCM) from the Netherlands notes that it has both possibilities at the same time: it can influence the importer directly, and it can try to engage the manager.[38] In 2010, the importer FMC Corp was present in one fund which JPMorgan managed for KCM. The Dutch company then engaged JPMorgan to act.[39] On the other hand, some fund managers could decide not to engage in the behaviour of companies represented in the portfolio of a particular fund. The investor would then need to decide whether to abandon the fund or the fund manager altogether. This is normally associated with great administrative and financial costs. Some accept that cost for the sake of an ethically tidy portfolio.

## Making the contact

As the investors make contact with the involved fertilizer producers, they quickly receive a ready-made answer package. The packages typically contain two types of documentation. The first goes into the operations on the ground, detailing what social programmes and employment conditions exist, and the investments which the Moroccan state-owned phosphate company, OCP, has carried out in the territory. The second type of documentation contains legal opinions written for OCP, analysing and supporting the legality of the trade. These documents are all readily distributed by OCP to the importing companies, and the importing companies in turn distribute them under strict confidentiality to their investors. Ideally, what is required at this stage is for investors to engage in their own investigations around related ethical and legal issues before making a decision on the trade. The question is to what extent does the material received contain any substance? Do the reports really answer the concerns of the Saharawi people or the criteria outlined in the UN Legal Opinion? The ethical investors mentioned in this article believe that this is not the case, and that the conclusions drawn by those directly involved in the trade are not well enough proven.

The on-the-ground analysis has been done by OCP itself, helped in recent years by the audit company KPMG. The conclusion of the reports – none publicly disclosed or viewed by the author – is said to be that the local population benefits.[40] But what was really the question which led to that conclusion? As the report is not published, it is impossible to know what terms of reference or research questions the study used. All Saharawi groups which are critical of the Moroccan presence in Western Sahara have confirmed to the author that they were not involved in the study. Indeed, all known Saharawi civil society groups and their government in exile have consistently rejected the benefits of the trade.

---

2014 to Exclude Innophos Holdings Inc', September 26, 2014, http://www.etikkradet.no/en/recommendation-26-september-2014-to-exclude-innophos-holdings-inc/.

38  Kempen Capital Management, *Annual Report 2012, Sustainability Report* (2013), http://www.kempen.nl/uploadedFiles/Kempen/01_Asset_Management/Specialismen/Duurzaam_beleggen/Annual%20report%202012%20sustainability.pdf.

39  Ibid.

40  WSRW contact with all investors confirms this trend. An indication of the content of the analysis is to be found in a statement by the importer PotashCorp: 'Phosphate Rock from Western Sahara', August 2014, http://www.wsrw.org/files/dated/2015-07-26/potashcorp_rock_position_aug2014.pdf.

The legal opinions commissioned by OCP, on the other hand, were prepared by three international law firms: one opinion has been drafted by the US company Covington and Burling LLP, which has been actively representing OCP for a number of years.[41] Another legal opinion was produced by DLA Piper in collaboration with Spanish firm Palacio y Asociados. These documents, all commissioned by the Moroccan operator of the mine, is that its operations are in line with international law, fulfilling the requirements that the UN Legal Office has set forward.

None of these firms, or the importers, want to disclose the opinions, as they are said to be the property of OCP. Based on statements from the importing companies, the legal opinions appear to come to the same conclusion: that the trade in Western Saharan phosphate rock through OCP is acceptable under international law, citing benefits to the 'local population' as validation for the exploitation and subsequent export to take place.[42]

OCP has not replied to questions regarding the trade, whether from WSRW or from concerned Saharawis. One Saharawi has on numerous occasions tried to obtain the opinions from the management of OCP, but without success.[43] When she posted a video on YouTube about how she wanted to get access to the document, an entity called 'OCP Maroc' tried to have her videos removed.[44] If the dialogue between the importers and their investors gets serious, the importing company calls in the lawyers Covington and Burling to pay the investors a visit.[45]

These interactions between the importing companies and their investors take different routes, and the outcomes vary accordingly, influenced by many different factors. On one hand, it depends on the characteristics of the importer, including the company's dependence on the Boucraa rock, whether it purchases the phosphate on the spot-market or through long-term contracts, and the duration of the contract. On the other hand, it also depends on the investor's dispositions – for example, the nature of their investment guidelines, their capacity, their partnerships with other investors, if they have invested themselves or via fund managers. Lastly, the dynamics take different routes depending on the national government policy on Western Sahara and the media or civil society pressure in the home countries of the investor and of the importer.

In the following, three different cases will be presented, where in each case the interaction ended with a different result. Each case illustrates investors willing to go to great lengths to improve the behaviour of the importers.

## CASE A: Mosaic Co., the easy way out

The Swedish bank Nordea in its 2010 annual report accounted for its successful active ownership process with one of the importers. The company was the Florida-based fertilizer producer Mosaic Co. WSRW had during the period from 2001 to 2009 documented 15 shipments from Western Sahara to its plant in Tampa, USA.

> Nordea's engagement with the Mosaic Company (US) was successfully ended in June 2010. Mosaic has now disclosed that they have discontinued their purchase of phosphate from Western Sahara, which also has been independently confirmed. The company has acknowledged the human rights issues involved with importing phosphate from Western Sahara.[46]

Some years later, Mosaic confirmed that the reason behind its decision to halt Western Sahara imports was 'because of widespread international concerns regarding the rights of the Sahrawi

---

41   WSRW, 'US Law Firm Continues Pro-occupation Lobby', December 8, 2013, http://www.wsrw.org/a204x2181.
42   WSRW, *P for Plunder 2014*.
43   WSRW, 'OCP Refuses to Respond to Saharawi Refugee', March 4, 2015, http://www.wsrw.org/a105x3169.
44   WSRW, 'This Video is Too Tough for OCP, Tries to Stop Youtube Stunt', November 16, 2013, http://www.wsrw.org/a217x2704.
45   Norwegian Government Pension Fund, Council on Ethics, 'Recommendation', October 15, 2010, https://www.regjeringen.no/globalassets/upload/fin/etikk/2011/rec_phospahte.pdf.
46   WSRW, 'European Banks Divest from Unethical Sahara Fertiliser Industry'.

people in that region', a Mosaic spokesman stated to Bloomberg.[47] The news service clearly juxtaposed Mosaic's responsible approach to the contrary behaviour of its North American competitors, still involved in the trade. Mosaic also confirmed in a letter to WSRW that in 2009 it had received its last shipment from Western Sahara and that it 'had no plans' to import again.[48]

Luxembourg-based Sparinvest group noted that

> Mosaic was held up as an example of good … practice when (in contrast to its competitors) it immediately terminated involvement with the Non-Self-Governing Territory of Western Sahara once alerted to the fact that it was against international norms to exploit the natural resources of a territory with unresolved sovereignty.[49]

Another successful shareholder engagement was by the Norwegian insurance company Storebrand in 2008, when the latter used its ownership to make Chinese shipping company Jinhui to terminate its transports from Western Sahara to New Zealand. Storebrand stated Jinhui's operations had been 'in conflict with Storebrand's company standards'.[50] Only two weeks after Storebrand made Jinhui aware of the breach, the shipping company stated it would 'quit this business'.[51] Jinhui confirmed to local Chinese media it would not do 'any more business out of there'.[52]

## CASE B – Wesfarmers, the hard way out

What happened in the case of Wesfarmers' imports of Western Sahara's phosphates into Australia was unique. Through an investment in its processing plant in Perth, the company de facto changed its supply chain and started taking in all its phosphates from elsewhere. Although it might not represent a particular response on the global scene of investor engagement and company response, it does stand out among the Western Sahara phosphate importers. A multitude of shareholders pursued engagement with the company, and the outcome can serve as an example for other importers of how to solve the dilemma.

Two years after the media's interest was drawn to Wesfarmers' imports due to the two dead stowaways on the *Furness Karumba*, investors from all over the world were making both coordinated and uncoordinated requests to Wesfarmers. The Australian pension fund Christian Super became aware of Wesfarmers' involvement in the trade in 2009. At the time, Wesfarmers represented the tenth largest holding of Christian Super. The CEO of Christian Super even travelled to Wesfarmers' headquarters to discuss the issue, together with other investors. Christian Super also visited the company's fertilizer production facilities to better understand the nature of the operations.[53] The dialogue lasted for three consecutive years, and Christian Super acted as a representative of several investors. 'Because we were local, we could speak to the company', the CEO Tim Macready stated.[54]

---

47   Christopher Donville, 'Agrium Was No. 1 Buyer of Phosphate From Western Sahara', *Bloomberg*, March 13, 2015, http://www.bloomberg.com/news/articles/2015-03-13/agrium-was-no-1-buyer-of-phosphate-from-western-sahara.

48   WSRW, 'No More Mosaic Phosphate Imports from Western Sahara', August 26, 2010, http://www.wsrw.org/a159x1568.

49   Sparinvest, 'Sparinvest Responsible Investment Review', July 2014, http://www.sparinvest.co.uk/~/media/international/downloads/ri/jul2014_sparinvest%20responsible%20investment%20review.ashx.

50   WSRW., 'The Jinhui Decision to Stop Shipping Western Sahara Phosphate Rock', April 24, 2015, http://www.wsrw.org/a128x3216.

51   Gerald Hayes, 'Conquering the World or Baby Steps? SRI's Puzzling Progress', Global Capital, September 9, 2013, http://www.globalcapital.com/article/jbxq1jtctxz6/conquering-the-world-or-baby-steps-sris-puzzling-progress.

52   Ivan Broadhead, 'A Line in the Sand', *South China Morning Post,* May 11, 2008, http://www.scmp.com/article/637220/line-sand.

53   UNPRI, *Report on Progress 2010* (2011), http://2xjmlj8428u1a2k5o34l1m71.wpengine.netdna-cdn.com/wp-content/uploads/2010_Report-on-Progress.pdf.

54   Rachel Alembakis, 'Christian Super Engaging with Companies on African Assets', *The Sustainability Report*, October 12, 2014, http://www.thesustainabilityreport.com.au/christian-super-engaging-with-companies-on-african-assets/.

This was only one of many engagements with the company whereby shareholders acted more formally together. A partnership of North European investors, the Nordic Engagement Cooperation, was in close dialogue with Wesfarmers from 2008.[55] Another instance of formal cooperation, through the UN-supported Principles for Responsible Investment initiative, outlined that Wesfarmers's involvement may 'unwittingly aggravate the conflict or become complicit to the oppression' occurring in the area; it was signed by many shareholders.[56] One of those joining that initiative, the Australian equities manager Northward Capital, separately met with the company in 2009. 'Trade in phosphates from occupied Western Sahara is a violation against international law', Northward stated.[57]

The main problem for Wesfarmers' subsidiary CSBP[58] was that its plant could smell bad, literally. The local neighbours of the production plant suffered from the smell of the production whenever the phosphate rock was sourced from places other than Bou Craa. Phosphate rock has numerous qualities, and in order to fix the odour issue regarding non-Bou Craa rock, Wesfarmers had to make investments in the plant. In October 2009, Wesfarmers CSBP announced it was willing to accept the financial cost to source the rock from somewhere other than Western Sahara.

'Following several years of research, CSBP announced an investment of almost $5 million in a regenerative thermal oxidiser (RTO) that will oxidise waste gas to address odour issues associated with processing phosphate rock from new sources', Wesfarmers noted.[59]

'The RTO will enable CSBP to broaden supply options … and reduce dependence on phosphate rock from Western Sahara. If CSBP did not invest in the RTO, it would not be able to use alternate product', Wesfarmers said, noting that it had been 'in dialogue with interested parties regarding the importation of phosphate rock from Western Sahara such as ethical investment funds, Wesfarmers shareholders, the Australian Western Saharan Association, and other interested members of the public'.[60]

The news was very well received in the investor community. 'Christian Super congratulates Wesfarmers for its willingness to listen and act upon concerns raised by its stakeholders', said CEO of Christian Super, Tim Macready. 'This course of action is encouraging for the whole ethical investment industry, as it demonstrates that a respectful dialogue with companies can lead to a change of behaviour, which in turn helps companies and its investors mitigate risks', Macready stated.[61] F&C Asset Management and the Swedish bank Folksam both underlined the importance of the joint investor initiatives for the success.[62] Folksam hinted that Wesfarmers might be re-included in the portfolios. 'Imports from Moroccan-occupied Western Sahara led to a decision by Folksam to dispose of its holding in Wesfarmers in 2008. If these imports stop, it will be possible for Folksam to reconsider its decision'.[63] As seen, investors can exert pressure even after they have disposed of shares in a company.

Folksam still keeps Wesfarmers on its list of excluded shares, because Wesfarmers has never committed categorically to halting the imports.[64] The lack of clear promises is particularly visible

---

55  UNPRI, 'PRI Reporting and Assessment Survey 2010, Full Responses', Your Organisation: Folksam, http://unpri. org/report10/2010_PDFs/PRI%202010%20-%20Full%20Responses%20for%20publication%20-%20Folksam% 20%280017000000N7cw1%29.pdf.

56  Northward Capital, 'Environmental Social and Governance News', February 2012, http://www.northwardcapital. com/sites/default/files/ESG%20Update%20Feb%202012%20FINAL_1.pdf.

57  Ibid.

58  This is the formal name of the company, rather than being the company's initials.

59  Wesfarmers to Norwegian Support Committee for Western Sahara, February 15, 2012, http://www.wsrw.org/files/ dated/2012-10-05/wesfarmers-skvs_15.02.2012.pdf.

60  Ibid.

61  Rachel Alembakis, 'Christian Super Engaging with Companies on African Assets'.

62  F&C Investments, 'F&C Portfolios Fund Interim Period ending 31 March 2013', www.fandc.com/documents/ portfolios-fund-reo-report-q1-2013/.

63  UNPRI, 'PRI Reporting and Assessment Survey 2010, Full Responses'.

64  Folksam, 'Företag i vilka vi inte placerar' [Companies in which we do not invest], http://omoss.folksam.se/ varthallbarhetsarbete/varaplaceringskriterier/uteslutnaforetag (accessed July 20, 2015).

in correspondence between the company and a Western Sahara solidarity association in 2011.[65] So far, the company has still only said it would 'reduce its dependence' on the imports, and it seems to leave open the possibility that the imports could continue, albeit to a limited degree, depending on price and availability of alternative sources.[66] From daily observations of the ship traffic in Western Sahara in October 2012 until August 2015, WSRW has not identified a single shipment to Wesfarmers.

## CASE C – PotashCorp, no way out

The Canadian/US company PotashCorp has the longest track record of importing from Western Sahara. The company has imported since 1996 when it acquired another company that had already been sourcing its rock in Bou Craa since the 1980s. Because of its massive imports and long-term strategic contract with OCP, PotashCorp was the first company in the sector to be scrutinized by the investor community. From the early days, the trade was well documented not only through shipment monitoring, but also through the transparent reports issued by the US Customs service. PotashCorp is also represented in very many funds internationally, as a consequence of being the world's biggest fertilizer company.[67] These factors probably explain why this particular company received more and earlier attention than the other companies importing such phosphates.

PotashCorp today appears among the standard 'blacklists' of ethical investors globally. A French study from 2013 looked into 19 ethical investors in Holland, Belgium, Luxembourg and Scandinavia, with a combined investment portfolio of €1500 billion. Of these funds, seven investors had excluded PotashCorp, while many had also excluded other companies involved in the Western Sahara trade.[68] Similarly, a research paper from the Dutch Association of Investors for Sustainable Development in 2011 found that one-fifth of 25 pension funds reviewed in the Netherlands had excluded PotashCorp from their portfolios.[69] There is reason to believe that the number of funds blacklisting PotashCorp internationally has increased considerably since then.[70]

In order to justify its ongoing purchases, PotashCorp has published a number of position statements on Western Sahara imports entitled 'Phosphate Rock from Western Sahara'.[71] Shareholders who have divested from PotashCorp have found these documents offer inadequate explanation.

---

65  WSRW, *P for Plunder. Morocco's Exports of Phosphates from Occupied Western Sahara, 2012 & 2013* (2014), http://www.wsrw.org/a228x2905.

66  Ibid.

67  PotashCorp, 'PotashCorp Confirms Friendly Proposal to K+S', news release, June 25, 2015, http://www.potashcorp.com/news/2034/.

68  Novethic, *Entreprises controversées, Les listes noires d'investisseurs changent-elles la donne?* (2013), http://www.novethic.fr/fileadmin/user_upload/tx_ausynovethicetudes/pdf_complets/Entreprises_controversees_2013_Etude.pdf.

69  Dutch Association of Investors for Sustainable Development (VBDO), 'Responsible Investment, Human Rights and the Extractive Industry', May 2013, http://www.profundo.nl/files/download/VBDO1305.pdf.

70  See for example, Triodos Bank, 'Disputed Territories', April 8, 2014, https://www.triodos.com/en/investment-management/who-we-are/news/newsletter-research/disputed-territories/. See also Armina Ligaya, 'Desert Storm: Why Canadian Fertilizer Firms' Phosphate from Western Sahara is Causing Controversy', *Financial Post Magazine*, February 11, 2014, http://business.financialpost.com/financial-post-magazine/desert-storm-why-canadian-fertilizer-firms-phosphate-from-western-sahara-is-causing-controversy; Meritas, *Shareholder Engagement Activity Report*, Q1/2013, January 1–March 31, 2013, http://www.standardlife.ca/sri/pdf/Engagement_Report-2013Q1.pdf.

71  PotashCorp, 'Phosphate Rock from Western Sahara', August 2014, http://www.wsrw.org/files/dated/2015-07-26/potashcorp_rock_position_aug2014.pdf; PotashCorp, 'Phosphate Rock from Western Sahara', April 2013, http://www.wsrw.org/files/dated/2014-03-25/potashcorp_rock-position_apr2013.pdf; PotashCorp, 'Phosphate Rock from Western Sahara', April 2012, http://www.wsrw.org/files/dated/2013-04-08/potashcorp_rock-position_apr2012.pdf; PotashCorp, 'Phosphate Rock from the Western Sahara', April 2011, http://www.wsrw.org/files/dated/2011-05-15/potashcorp_statement_apr2011.pdf.

Much of the Canadian shareholder engagement vis-à-vis PotashCorp has taken place through the shareholder association SHARE. Canadian investor Desjardins Funds and the SHARE in 2012 expressed concern to PotashCorp vis-à-vis the lack of benefit to the exiled Saharawi population in refugee camps in Algeria.[72] The Canadian investment group NEI, 50% owned by Desjardin Group, is in dialogue with PotashCorp over the matter.[73] Canada's United Church, through SHARE, raised its investment concerns in June 2014.[74]

In 2013, the Swedish government pension fund announced it had blacklisted PotashCorp and the Australian Incitec Pivot:

> The Ethical Council has engaged with both companies since 2010 with the aim of persuading them to cease procurement of phosphate from Western Sahara or to prove that the extractive process complies with the interests and wishes of the Western Saharan people, in accordance with the UN legal counsel's statement of 2002. The Ethical Council has also urged both companies to adopt policies undertaking to refrain from actions that violate international humanitarian law. The Ethical Council concludes that further dialogue with Potash and Incitec Pivot would be to no avail as neither company has indicated an intention to cease procurement of phosphate from Western Sahara in the near future or been able to demonstrate that the extractive process accords with the interests and wishes of the Western Saharan people.[75]

This statement on PotashCorp and Incitec Pivot illustrates a situation where the importer fails to terminate its sourcing from Western Sahara. An exclusion is the last resort for an investor. PotashCorp, Incitec Pivot, Innophos Holdings and Agrium are the main ones in this situation, all of them on new or old long-term purchasing agreements they insist on continuing or renewing.

The most recent of these is Agrium Inc., also from Canada, which entered into a long-term agreement even after the phosphate trade in Western Sahara became a controversial topic for its investors. Agrium signed a large purchase agreement with OCP for Bou Craa rock only recently (2013) and is now under heavy pressure from the same investors, for example being excluded by the government pension fund of Sweden and the bank Folksam.[76]

## Coming to an end?

The investor community has shown a remarkable ability to influence positively the behaviour of Western Sahara phosphate importers. Public and private investors, from all corners of the world, have over the last decade engaged in pressure against half a dozen fertilizer companies. Several of the importers have halted the imports, one way or the other. Through that pressure, the fertilizer-dependent country of Australia has more or less ended its decade-long imports from the occupied territory, sourcing its raw materials elsewhere. The remaining companies that have not shown a will to improve observed that hundreds of millions of dollars' worth of shares were sold, with the reputational risk that implies.

These remaining importers are from agricultural nations in North and Latin America, Australasia and Eastern Europe. Australia was the biggest importer in the past; now it only receives a

72   Desjardins Funds, 'Bulletin', 3, no. 3 (September 2012), http://www.fondsdesjardins.com/information/bulletin-monde-en-action-2012-t3-en.pdf; SHARE, Shareholder Association for Research & Education, *Shareholder Engagement Activity Report*, Q1/2013, January 1–March 31, 2013, http://www.share.ca/files/Q1_2013_Shareholder_Engagement_Activity_Report_PUBLIC_1.pdf.

73   NEI Investments, 'Ethical Investments, Corporate Engagement Focus List, Update, July 2014', http://www.neiinvestments.com/documents/FocusList/Focus%20List%202014%20July%20Update%20EN.pdf.

74   United Church of Canada, Responsible Investment Update: June 2014', http://www.noodls.com/view/B3629ABB578776679E12989AEEDFACD1D2ED8B42?1793xxx1404476090.

75   WSRW, 'Swedish Government Pension Fund Blacklists Sahara Importers', September 30, 2013, http://www.wsrw.org/a217x2664.

76   AP-Fonden, *Annual Report 2014* (2015), http://www.ap2.se/Global/Etikr%C3%A5det/Arsrapport%202014%20Etikr%C3%A5det%20150409%20SE.pdf;Folksam, *Sustainability Report 2013* (2014), http://media.folksam.se/en/files/2014/05/Folksam-Sustainability-report-2013.pdf.

fraction of what it did. Instead, Canada has taken over as a lead importer. The international investment community must now continue the work in North America. A particular responsibility lies in the hands of the main shareholders in Canada.

Later developments seem to give the importers one less argument to continue sourcing the rock from Sahara. Some companies claim that only phosphate rock from Western Sahara is suitable for the production of some of their products, although this is not regarded as necessarily the case. While Incitec Pivot and others are adamant that they can only depend on the phosphates from Bou Craa, the activity level at the loading dock in Western Sahara is low. In mid-November 2014, the phosphate dock south of El Aaiún reportedly experienced structural damage or failure. That problem seems to have continued for several consecutive months. WSRW has observed that vessel departures from El Aaiún are unusually slow and many vessels are kept waiting to load for weeks on end. In fact, during the first four months of 2015, only five vessels loaded phosphate cargo in Western Sahara. If that trend continues, the total exports of 2015 will be less than half those of 2014. The leading importing companies Lifosa (Lithuania) and Agrium (Canada) in 2014, accounting for 58% of the total imports, had only received one vessel altogether during the first four months of 2015. As the northern hemisphere agricultural season starts from middle of the calendar year, it appears nearly all phosphate supplies must come from other sources. Some importers that have always argued that they could not do without phosphate rock from Western Sahara have now done without it for at least half a year – undercutting their assertion of absolute dependency. The investors have a chance, and the means, to push them to look somewhere else.

Since the 1980s, Australia may have imported as much as 4–5 million tonnes of phosphate rock from Western Sahara, although the exact figure is uncertain. This rock belongs to the Saharawi, both those living as refugees and those living under occupation. The rock could have been the foundation of the establishment of a new state. Regrettably, after four decades of exploitation, the Saharawi last year lost the top layer of their phosphate reserve – the most valuable part. A large volume of that national wealth is spread over farmland and pastures all across Australia, to the Moroccan government's and Australian farmers' benefit.

Even though the large-scale import of this valuable rock into Australia has nearly ended, the phosphorus of Bou Craa is still, and will for a long time to come, be found throughout food products made from Australian soil.

## Disclosure statement

No potential conflict of interest was reported by the author.

# Index

CPSIA information can be obtained
at www.ICGtesting.com
Printed in the USA
JSHW011653201219
3107JS00003B/53

# Handbook of School-Family Partnerships

School-family partnerships are increasingly touted as a means of improving both student and school achievement. This recognition has led to an increase in policies and initiatives that offer the following benefits: 1) improved communication between parents and educators, 2) home and school goals that are mutually supportive and shared, 3) better understanding of the complexities impinging on children's development, and 4) pooling of family and school resources to find and implement solutions to shared goals.

This will be the first comprehensive review of what is known about the effects of school-family partnerships on student and school achievement. It provides a brief history of school-family partnerships, presents evidence-based practices for working with families across developmental stages, and provides an agenda for future research and policy. Key features include the following:

- Provides comprehensive, cross-disciplinary coverage of theoretical issues and research concerning school-family partnerships.
- Describes those aspects of school-family partnerships that have been adequately researched and promotes their implementation as evidence-based interventions.
- Charts cutting-edge research agendas and methods for exploring school-family partnerships.
- Charts the implications such research has for training, policy, and practice especially regarding educational disparities.

This book is appropriate for researchers, instructors, and graduate students in the following areas: school counseling, school psychology, educational psychology, school leadership, special education, and school social work. It is also appropriate for the academic libraries serving these audiences.

**Sandra L. Christenson** is Birkmaier Professor of Educational Leadership at the University of Minnesota.

**Amy L. Reschly** is Assistant Professor of Educational Psychology & Instructional Technology at the University of Georgia.

# Handbook of School-Family Partnerships

Edited by

## Sandra L. Christenson
## Amy L. Reschly

Routledge
Taylor & Francis Group

NEW YORK AND LONDON

First published 2010
by Routledge
711 Third Ave, New York, NY 10017

Simultaneously published in the UK
by Routledge
2 Park Square, Milton Park, Abingdon, Oxon OX14 4RN

*Routledge is an imprint of the Taylor & Francis Group, an informa business*

© 2010 Taylor & Francis

Typeset in Minion by EvS Communication Networx, Inc.

*Library of Congress Cataloging in Publication Data*
Handbook of school-family partnerships / Sandra L. Christenson and Amy L. Reschly, editors.
p. cm.
Includes bibliographical references and index.
1. Home and school—United States—Handbooks, manuals, etc. 2. Education—Parent participation—United States—Handbooks, manuals, etc. 3. Community and school—United States—Handbooks, manuals, etc. I. Christenson, Sandra, 1946- II. Reschly, Amy L.
LC225.3.H356 2009
371.19'2—dc22
2008054218

ISBN 10: 0-415-96375-3 (hbk)
ISBN 10: 0-415-96376-1 (pbk)
ISBN 10: 0-203-87604-0 (ebk)

ISBN 13: 978-0-415-96375-6 (hbk)
ISBN 13: 978-0-415-96376-3 (pbk)
ISBN 13: 978-0-203-87604-6 (ebk)

**In recognition of...**

educators and families who work tirelessly to care for and educate our nation's youth.

and,

our hope for children, including our own children and grandchildren (Jonah, Kelsey, Brady, and Courtney), that the contents of this *Handbook* will propel partnership attitudes, behaviors, and practices forward immeasurably, making them common-place and expected in schools and communities.

# CONTENTS

# FIGURES AND TABLES

## FIGURES

## TABLES

# PREFACE

Although schools are the institution formally charged with educating our nation's youth, the role of families and the home environment in students' development and academic, behavioral, social, and emotional competence is undisputed. Together, families and schools are the primarily socialization agents of youth. Too much time has been spent describing the contributions of one *or* the other and interventions have been limited to singular targets rather than maximizing the synergistic influences of home *and* school.

Ecological systems theory provides a compelling theoretical basis for considering home and school contexts in concert (Bronfenbrenner, 1992), and draws attention to *relationships* and *congruence* across these contexts, as well as how students' time is passed not only during the school day, but outside of school (Reschly & Christenson, 2009). Implicit in this theoretical orientation is the notion that well-functioning homes and schools and positive, engaged relationships across these contexts are a protective factor for children and youth. Further, unlike socioeconomic circumstances or other demographic risk conditions, relationships and consistency across these critical contexts for development is an alterable variable related to the promotion of student competence. Of course, the converse is also true: discontinuity between home and school, particularly in terms of expectations, messages and the value placed on learning and effort, and communication patterns, create high-risk circumstances for children and adolescents (Pianta & Walsh, 1996). Many students are being educated in high-risk circumstances due to conditions in their homes and/or schools and a lack of consistency and disengagement across home and school systems.

In terms of understanding risk and student outcomes, much variation is apparent in the affordance value of students' learning environments. There are long-standing differences in educational outcomes for students in the United States as a function of income and ethnicity. In a recent report from the U.S. Department of Education, White and Asian students continued to earn higher scores than Black and Hispanic students on national reading and mathematics assessments—and large disparities remain in performance among students attending low and high poverty schools. Further, these disparities continued in outcomes such as high school dropout and college graduation rates (Planty et al., 2008). This *achievement gap*, as it is commonly referred to, is often attributed to *educational disparities* in students' learning environments (home and/or school). Hundreds of articles and books have been written about the achievement gap (Paik & Walberg, 2007; Rothstein, 2004). At the time of the publication of this volume, the national debate concerning how we face the challenge to address educational disparities or close the achievement-, opportunity- or standards-, gap continues.

Engaged, positive relationships across home and school contexts are a promising avenue for addressing educational disparities and enhancing competence among all youth. Coleman, a sociologist, theorized and demonstrated, in general, the power of home-school interaction for correcting the erosion of social capital in children's lives (i.e., the quality and depth of relationships), noting, in specific, the essential building blocks from homes (i.e., home inputs) as vital to the development of children's positive attitudes about learning, willingness to put forth effort, and conception of self (Coleman, 1987). Four variables beyond the control of schools (parent-student ratio, absenteeism, reading to young children, excessive television watching) predicted with impressive accuracy the results on the federal eighth grade reading test for each state (Barton & Coley, 2007). Particularly sobering was the finding that many students start school behind their peers, and the gap is not closed; a finding that has been replicated by others (Alexander, Entwisle, & Olson, 2001; Hart & Risley, 1995). Barton and Coley stated, "This report clearly establishes that the gaps in critical home experiences mirror the gaps in early school achievement—gaps that persist through the end of high school" (p. 39).

Once children enter school, the instructional, home support, and home-school support correlates of various positive student achievement indicators are well known and articulated (Ysseldyke & Christenson, 2002). In other words, factors related to promotion of competence within and across contexts for youth are not in question, nor is the rationale or need to work across contexts for children and youth. Consistent with Coleman, early interventionists have called for a transactional perspective between home and school, underscoring the necessity of congruence in shared goals and messages across these environments for ensuring a positive trajectory for children's learning and development (Pianta & Walsh, 1996).

More recently, Rothstein (2004) argued and supported the integral role played by the influences beyond either the home or school for closing the achievement gap for low income and ethnically diverse students. Finally, Weiss (2005) argued that without a network of learning supports beyond the school it will be difficult, if not impossible, to educate all children, particularly those who are economically disadvantaged. Referred to as complementary learning, this network of supports includes non-school supports and opportunities that complement learning in schools and together result in better developmental outcomes. Raising overall levels of achievement and closing the achievement gap requires that we attend comprehensively to the starting line for children (as much as we do the finish line). The centrality of partnerships across settings and over time, what Bronfenbrenner (1992) has referred to as the chronosystem, is evident. In short, children must be supported from birth through adolescence (including workforce preparation and college readiness) to close the achievement gap.

There is a compelling rationale for working across families and schools to support student learning and positive outcomes. The most pertinent questions before us at this time are: *How can families and schools work together to enhance student learning and development? How does research inform these efforts? What is needed to advance this field?* The purpose of this *Handbook* was to provide (a) state-of-the art coverage of theoretical and empirical research on school-family partnerships, (b) advance the momentum of evidence-based interventions, and (c) delineate the next steps for research, policy, and practice, with particular attention to addressing educational disparities.

This *Handbook* adds immeasurably to the power and value of connecting to and partnering with families to promote children's competence in academic, behavioral, social, and emotional domains (Christenson & Sheridan, 2001; Henderson & Mapp, 2002). In this volume, we underscored the family-school engagement process to enhance children's learning and development. Often referred to as family-school partnerships, we have selected school-family partnerships for the title. This decision was in recognition of the importance for school personnel to reach out to, be willing to support families to enhance home support for learning programs and constructive use of out of school time, and to co-construct a meaningful pathway for child success. These are necessary, but not sufficient components of the parent-school engagement process (Christenson, 2004). What does it mean to have an engaged family-school relationship? We suggest that an engaged relationship refers to the socializing environments of family and school that support and guide students to develop an identity as learners who, irrespective of student characteristics believe they can and want to learn. Furthermore, this occurs through dialogue, problem solving, and decision making about shared expectations and learning goals, mutual responsibility for supporting students, and shared accountability for student performance outcomes. Hence, an engaged relationship between home and school is oriented to attaining positive, optimal student outcomes—whether in academic, social, behavioral, or emotional domains with the acknowledgement that achievement outcomes vary as a function of student characteristics.

We invited and were honored to have such noted and prominent authors contribute to the *Handbook*. The quality of their contributions adds immeasurably to the knowledge base and future of school-family partnerships for promoting student competence. We did not constrain these authors to a particular chapter structure. As such, an overview of chapter organization and content is provided at the beginning of each chapter, and authors delineated their thoughts on future research in an area and often included implications for practice as well. Further, as editors of this volume, we encouraged authors to use and define their preferred term for these engaged relationships between home and school. Regardless of the term selected, all authors recognized the value and importance of families to children's learning and development and advocated the essential nature of the partnership or relationship to achieve optimal child outcomes. Hence, promoting a systemic orientation in practice, research, training, and policy characterizes the contents of this *Handbook*.

This volume is organized into three sections: the theoretical and empirical base for partnerships, considerations across developmental levels, and setting the research agenda to inform policy and practice. A number of common themes emerged across chapters:

- The importance of understanding culture and the effect culture may have on family support for learning and the formation of engaged relationships between families and educational personnel.
- Irrespective of the referral concern for a child/adolescent, evidence-based family-school interventions and practices exist to address academic, behavioral, mental health, communication, and motivational concerns for youth. They exist to promote competence of youth.
- Constructive, effective school-family partnerships do not perceive families as the problem, but rather as an educational resource—as part of the solution to enhance developmental and learning gains for students.
- The value of relationships whether the student-teacher, peer-peer, family-school, or family-school-community for comprehensive, systemic interventions to address educational disparities.
- The characteristics of constructive relationships or the conditions that allow for a family-school connection or interface between homes and schools are not only clear, but evidence based. If a student is performing well in school, educators less often underscore the role of the partnership between home and school; and yet, undoubtedly, specific characteristics of the engaged relationship are present.
- It is also clear that much research is still needed. Questions remain in terms of process knowledge, but also there is a great need for clear terminology and more sophisticated measurement, designs, and statistical models. In a similar vein, there has been substantial progress in the delineation of promising programs and practices; however, further evaluation is needed as programs are disseminated to other settings and populations.
- The research base is strong enough to move beyond "random acts of parent involvement" (see Weiss, this volume) to a strategy for comprehensive partnerships to promote child competence.

We can and must strive to provide opportunities to learn for all students from birth to preparation for the workforce and for college. Environment matters. Schools and homes are socializing environments for children and adolescents. School personnel cannot—alone—achieve optimal outcomes for youth; however, they can reach out to families and community professionals—developing and integrating systemically-oriented national, state, and local policies—to establish shared goals, contributions, and accountability for educational outcomes (Fantuzzo, Tighe, & Childs, 2000). We underscore optimal outcomes for all students, whether they are described as poor or rich, white or nonwhite, motivated or unmotivated, or engaged or disengaged learners. As illustrated by the contents of the chapters, it is possible to attain a strong, constructive parent-educator connection, to truly engage learners irrespective of demographic characteristics, and to maximize opportunities to learn through the school-family partnership. Engaged relationships between parents and educators is essential integral to desired outcomes for youth. We believe that this is a worthy endeavor to addressing the far too apparent educational disparities reflected in national data. The time has arrived to conceptualize school-family partnerships as "essential not only laudable" (see Tolan and Woo, this volume).

S.L.C.
A.L.R.

## REFERENCES

Alexander, K. L., Entwisle, D. R., & Olson, L. S. (2001). Schools, achievement, and inequality: A seasonal perspective. *Educational Evaluation and Policy Analysis, 23,* 171–191.

Barton, P. E., & Coley, R. J. (2007). *The family: America's smallest school.* Princeton, NJ: Educational Testing Service, Policy Information Report. Retrieved April 24, 2009, from http://www.ets.org/familyreport

Bronfenbrenner, U. (1992). Ecological systems theory. In R. Vasta (Ed.), *Annals of child development. Six theories of child development: Revised formulations and current issues* (pp. 187–249). London: Jessica Kingsley.

Christenson, S. L. (2004). The family-school partnership: An ppportunity to promote the learning competence of *all* students. *School Psychology Review, 33*(1), 83–104.

Christenson, S. L., & Sheridan, S. M. (2001). *School and families: Creating essential connections for learning.* New York: Guilford.

Coleman, J. (1987, August-September). Families and schools. *Educational Researcher,* 32–38.

Fantuzzo, J., Tighe, E., & Childs, S. (2000). Family involvement questionnaire: A multivariate assessment of family participation in early childhood education. *Journal of Educational Psychology, 92*(2), 367–376.

Hart, B., & Risley, T. R. (1995). *Meaningful difference in the everyday experience of young American children.* Baltimore: Paul H. Brookes.

Henderson, A. T., & Mapp, K. L. (2002). *A new wave of evidence: The impact of school, family, and community connections on student achievement.* Austin, TX: Southwest Educational Development Laboratory.

Paik, S. J., & Walberg, H. J. (Eds.). (2007). *Narrowing the achievement gap: Strategies for Latino, Black, and Asian students.* New York: Springer.

Pianta, R., & Walsh, D. B. (1996). *High-risk children in schools: Constructing sustaining relationships.* New York: Routledge.

Planty, M., Hussar, W., Snyder, T., Provasnik, S., Kena, G., Dinkes, R., et al. (2008). *The Condition of Education 2008* (NCES 2008-031). National Center for Education Statistics, Institute of Education Sciences, U. S. Department of Education. Washington, DC.

Reschly, A. L., & Christenson, S. L. (2009). Parents as essential partners for fostering students' learning outcomes. In R. Gilman, E. S. Huebner, & M. Furlong (Eds.), *A handbook of positive psychology in the schools: Promotion of wellness in children and youth* (pp. 257–272). New York: Blackwell.

Rothstein, R. (2004). *Class and schools: Using social, economic, and educational reform to close the black-white achievement gap.* New York: Teachers College Press.

Weiss, H. B. (2005). Beyond the classroom: complementary learning to improve achievement outcomes. *The Evaluation Exchange XI* (1), 2–6, 17.

Ysseldyke, J. E., & Christenson, S. L. (2002). *FAAB: Functional assessment of academic behavior: Creating successful learning environments.* Longmont, CO: Sopris West.

# I

## The Backdrop
*Theoretical and Empirical Bases of Partnerships*

# 1

## APPLICATION OF A DEVELOPMENTAL/ECOLOGICAL MODEL TO FAMILY-SCHOOL PARTNERSHIPS

JASON T. DOWNER AND SONYA S. MYERS

The application of developmental/ecological theory to understanding how multiple layers of context, and in particular the family-school link, play a role in student learning is nothing new to education and developmental science. It is well-established that a student's success in school is multidetermined—by characteristics that reside within the student, experiences in familiar contexts, and more distal influences of culture and society (Pianta & Walsh, 1996). Families provide experiences and set up educational expectations that are consistently and often powerfully linked to students' early and later schooling outcomes (Bornstein & Tamis-LeMonda, 1989; McWayne, Hampton, Fantuzzo, Cohen, & Sekino, 2004; Morrison & Cooney, 2002; National Institute of Child Health and Human Development Early Child Care Research Network [NICHD EC-CRN], 2003; NICHD ECCRN & Duncan, 2003; Sameroff, Seifer, Baldwin, & Baldwin, 1993). Similarly, an entire literature exists to support the notion that experiences with teachers in classrooms make a difference in what and how students learn at school (Hamre & Pianta, 2001, 2005; Mashburn et al., 2008; Rowan, Correnti, & Miller, 2002; Sanders & Rivers, 1996). The primary emphasis of this chapter, however, is an oft-overlooked and underappreciated mesosystem element of the ecological framework, which sits at the intersection of these influential microsystems—family-school partnerships. Moving away from historically static, reductionistic views of family and school roles in the lives of students, these partnerships reflect recognition of the dynamic nature of shared responsibility and collaboration between parents and school practitioners for supporting students' learning across their academic career (Christenson, 2004; Christenson & Sheridan, 2001). As such, family-school partnerships are operationalized as multidimensional, including components that range from communication between parents and teachers to parents' contributions to learning in the home (Epstein, 1996).

In the context of a doggedly persistent achievement gap in the United States (Johnson, 2002; National Center for Education Science [NCES], 2000, 2002), research that indicates a key facilitative role of the family-school link for students' educational success (e.g.,

Fan & Chen, 2001; Hughes & Kwok, 2007; Jeynes, 2005, 2007; Seginer, 2006; Sheldon, 2007; Sheridan, Clarke, Knoche, & Edwards, 2006) has set the stage for the next wave of empirical inquiry into family-school partnerships. In the context of planning for research that will unfold over the next decade, the present chapter makes a case for the continued and expanded application of a developmental/ecological framework to defining and understanding family-school partnerships. The chapter has four specific aims: (a) to provide a brief, updated overview of the assumptions and contextual levels of a developmental/ecological model; (b) to bring the developmental elements of this model into the foreground; (c) to introduce contemporary educational policy and family issues with mesosystemic implications; and (d) to highlight implications of the model for methodology in future studies of family-school partnerships.

## DEVELOPMENTAL/ECOLOGICAL THEORY

Pianta and Walsh (1996) characterized the ecology of schooling as an organized system of interactions and transactions among persons (parents, teachers, students), settings (home, school), and institutions (community, governments) that are oriented to support developmental and educational progress of students during the prek-12 period. More developmentally and ecologically informed models of family-school partnerships attend to the diverse set of inputs to student development and the ways in which such inputs are linked with one another at any given time. A *developmental/ecological* perspective takes into account the key changes in relationships among the student, school, family, and community as the student transfers from one grade to another and the ways in which these relational interactions figure prominently in support of students. Thus, rather than understanding a student's educational progress solely in terms of a student's skills, or contextual influences on those skills at any given time, this perspective emphasizes the organization of assets within a social ecology, how this organization emerges, and how it operates to support (or inhibit) student competence over time (Pianta & Walsh, 1998). In this developmental/ecological framework, efforts to assess and improve student development are likely to be broad-based and focused on the interactions within and across families and classrooms from grade to grade. As such, family-school partnerships arise as a particularly relevant construct in relation to students' educational progress. Developmental/ecological theory rests on a set of fundamental assumptions about systems and how these systems are organized in relation to a developing student, all of which having far-reaching implications for family-school partnerships and related research. These basic assumptions and elements of organization are described in the next two sections and are reflected in Figure 1.1.

### Basic Assumptions of General Systems Theory

Developmental/ecological theory is guided by a set of basic assumptions and principles, emanating from general and contextual systems theory (Ford & Lerner, 1992; Pianta & Walsh, 1996) that are directly relevant to understanding and studying family-school partnerships. As applied to student development, these assumptions are summarized below, while their implications for research on family-school links will be integrated into later sections.

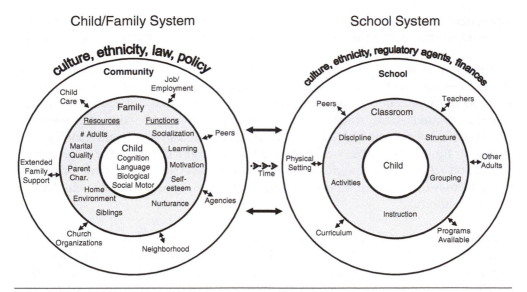

**Figure 1.1** Developmental/ecological model (as adapted from Pianta & Walsh, 1996).

*Students Are an Open System*    Far too often we apply a reductionist, traitlike, and child-centric explanation to students' school adjustment and success (Pianta & Walsh, 1996; Rimm-Kaufman & Pianta, 2000), which overvalues internal maturation and underestimates the influence of developmental context. In contrast, systems theory suggests that internal processes and individual characteristics, such as intelligence, approaches to learning, attention, and self-regulation, do not sufficiently describe a student. Rather, the developing student is an open system that has continual, reciprocal interchanges with all surrounding contexts (e.g., classrooms, families). This dynamic process leads to adaptation, or lack thereof, both on the part of the student and the context itself, and this on-going interchange results in student outcomes that then provide feedback to the system. It is this assumption, and the concept of students being forever "fused" with their environments (Ford & Lerner, 1992), that makes the connection between families and schools such an important contributor to explaining student outcomes.

*Relationships Between Systems Are More Than Just the Sum of Their Parts*    Another principle of systems theory indicates that when two systems interact, such as the developing student and parents or parents and teachers, a relationship is formed (Pianta & Walsh, 1996). Importantly, this relationship then reflects a new system in and of itself, which is superordinate to the interactions that contributed to its formation (Sameroff & Emde, 1989); in other words, the whole is greater than the sum of its parts. Consider this principle in relation to an element of family-school partnerships—parent-teacher relationships. The quantity and quality of interactions between a parent and teacher contribute to the formation of their relationship. However, this relationship becomes more than just the summation of these interactions, such as a teacher's notes sent home in a student's backpack and a parent's phone calls to clarify classroom assignments. Rather, the parent-teacher relationship becomes its own system that is likely to influence subsequent interactions that occur among parents and teachers (Hinde, 1987) and is therefore worthy of attention as an outcome in its own right (Pianta & Walsh, 1996).

*Systems, and Patterns of Interactions Between Systems, Change Over Time* While student development occurs, the environmental systems that surround them are adapting to changes in the student, as well as to other relevant super and subordinate systems. In other words, students are not developing in a static context, but instead are embedded within multiple, developing systems that also may be influencing each other over time. For example, welfare-to-work legislation, a change in the macrosystem (legislation reform) that amounts to a change in an exosystem (incentives for parents to work), may influence the amount of time available to some parents for volunteering in the classroom.

*Multiple Pathways to Student Outcomes Are Not Just Possible, but Probable* Given the premise that student development is the product of multiple, interdependent, and dynamic systems, general systems theory urges us to appreciate and embrace the complexity of this process. One implication is that the same student outcome, such as motivation to learn, could be produced by a diverse range of developmental pathways (Ford & Lerner, 1992). Likewise, the reverse is true; a particular input, such as back-to-school nights that bring parents and teachers together, may have starkly different outcomes on parent-teacher relationships and/or students' attachment to school depending on the particular intersection of the developing student, family, and school systems. This complexity is due in large part to the likelihood that any given student outcome is the result of multiple systems acting together (Sameroff, 1995), and also reflects issues of Person X Environment fit.

*Systems Operate at Many Different Levels, from Proximal to Distal* Students are nested within a set of interlocking, dynamic systems that have been organized by Bronfenbrenner, and others related to family-school partnerships (Epstein, 1987, 2001), into several levels. These levels radiate out from the student in concentric circles of influence, with circles closer to the student reflecting more proximal experiences and those further away denoting distal factors. All levels of the system are interconnected, indicating that a change anywhere is likely to have a ripple effect on other elements of the system that may or may not trickle down to the developing student. Important to note, however, is that proximal experiences of a student are expected to be the true mechanisms of development, with distal parts of the ecology having less direct influences on student outcomes. Details about the organizing framework for these nested systems are now described.

### Nested Levels of Developmental/Ecological Model

The ecology of human development, as posited by Bronfenbrenner (1986), is comprised of multiple environmental systems that provide a context in which student development occurs. This ecology consists of five interrelated, nested systems, which are defined below and discussed in relation to family-school partnerships.

*Microsystem*   Microsystems are the principal contexts in which development occurs and consist of any environment in which a student has direct experiences, whether that is peer groups, after-school care arrangements, or, of course, the two settings in which students spend almost all of their time—home and school. There are extensive literatures on the extent to which family and school/classroom processes independently contribute to positive youth development, but for the purposes of this chapter study of these microsystems is essential to understanding the development and maintenance of family-school partnerships. An endless list of family microsystem elements may contribute, directly or indirectly, to family-school links, such as parent mental health, marital relations, parenting beliefs and styles, cultural values and mores, etc. Likewise, characteristics of schools and classrooms may serve as either barriers or facilitators for partnerships with families, including factors like principal leadership style, sense of community among teaching staff, teacher attitudes toward parents, etc.

*Mesosystem*   The transitions and links between microsystems are referred to as meso-systems, of which family-school partnerships are a perfect example. Although clearly reliant on many microsystem factors, mesosystems are a relational unit unto them-selves, as previously highlighted in the second assumption above. As noted in models that emphasize the multidimensionality of family-school partnerships (Epstein, 2001), this particular mesosystem is reflected in a multitude of independent and interactive activities, all of which are conducted with students in mind. For example, parents and teachers may communicate with each other during a parent-teacher conference about how to build on a student's strengths at home and at school, or teachers may provide guidance to a student about peer relationships in a way that aligns with that student's family values.

*Exosystem*   Exosystems are environments that are not directly experienced by students but affect development nonetheless. Common exosystems that may impact student development and family-school partnerships are parents' workplaces, teachers' college education programs, and sense of community within a neighborhood.

*Macrosystem*   The macrosystem is the sociocultural context in which students and their micro, meso, and exosystems operate, providing influence in the form of gender role stereotypes, unemployment rate, racism, etc. (Bronfenbrenner, 1986). Two aspects of the macrosystem with consistent, far-reaching consequences for subordinate systems are culture and government legislation, each of which will receive more attention jux-taposed with family-school relationships later in the chapter.

*Chronosystem*   As a late-comer to Bronfenbrenner's nested systems theory, the chro-nosystem is an all-important temporal element of the developmental/ecological model. It reflects both changes over time within the student (e.g., physiological changes as part of puberty) as well as changes in each of the other systems that interact with the devel-oping student (e.g., timing of a mother returning to work); important to note is that these changes can be predictable (e.g., school transitions) or unexpected (e.g., death of a parent). The chronosystem is an aspect of the developmental/ecological model that often seems to receive less attention than other levels, with ample room for inclusion in future research on family-school partnerships, as covered in greater detail later.

## Summary

Basic assumptions of general systems theory and the nested levels of a developmental/ ecological model hold great relevance for understanding family-school partnerships and their role in student development. Notably, students' school success does not occur in a vacuum, and the family-school link is an integral part of a set of interconnected systems that contribute to this success. Based on the premise that the multidimensional nature of family-school partnerships are best understood when grounded in a developmental/ecological model, the remainder of this chapter uses this framework and related assumptions to set the stage for future research, policy, and practice on family-school partnerships by emphasizing the developmental nature of systems, bringing attention to contemporary micro, exo, and macrosystem issues, and introducing key methodological implications.

## DEVELOPMENTAL NATURE OF FAMILY-SCHOOL PARTNERSHIPS

As described above, Bronfenbrenner's (1986) concept of the chronosystem takes into account changes within the student and their environment over time, and how these changes may influence other elements of the student's ecology. For one, the chronosystem underscores the relevance of examining how students' social, cognitive, and biological maturation can affect interactions within the family and school microsystems (e.g., parent-child and teacher-child interactions), and how these interactions may then contribute to the developing family-school relationship. In addition, it is equally important to recognize that while the student is adapting and changing over time, so too are the contexts that surround the student. As noted in the fifth assumption above, shifts anywhere in a student's ecology hold implications for other parts of the system, thus making it important to study and understand how, for example, changing philosophies at a school about how students learn may contribute to altered family-school partnerships. As outlined below, this dual chronosystem lens, encompassing development within the student and the contexts within which the student is embedded, provides directions for an understudied element of family-school partnerships.

## The Developing Student

All too often ignored in research on family-school partnerships (Epstein, 1996), it is essential to understand the role of the central figure who connects the family and school microsystems—the developing student. As students mature, developmental changes in their physical and cognitive capabilities not only affect how they relate to individuals and groups in the social world, but contribute to how they interact with parents, teachers, and others within the school context (Thompson, 2006). At the most basic level, all of these relationships naturally incorporate features of individuals. These include biological facts (such as gender), biological processes (such as temperament, genetics, responsivity to stressors), developed features (such as personality, self-concept, or social skills), as well as the perceptions each individual holds of their relational collaborators and the relationship itself (Myers & Pianta, 2008). Important to consider is the fact that maturation in the student may directly contribute to redefining and reorganizing their interactions and relationships within family and school microsystems, while also influencing the connection between the two. Not surprisingly, there are myriad biological and cognitive processes that are developing during a student's schooling experience, from pre-kindergarten into college, any of which could be studied in relation to family-school partnerships. A few examples are now provided to illustrate ways in which developmental changes within the student may directly and indirectly influence how parents and teachers interact with both the student and one another.

As one prime example of indirect transactional processes occurring within the context of family-school partnerships, students make a cognitive shift in elementary school from simply perceiving themselves as objects of attention to understanding how their past experiences with parents, teachers, and peers can influence current and future contexts (Howe & Courage, 1997; Thompson, 2006). While students become more cognizant of the social and behavioral expectations placed upon them within both home and school environments, they also become increasingly motivated to set courses of action that will produce desired outcomes and minimize the undesired ones (Bandura, 1991). Maturation of structures within the brain that facilitate the ability to plan and regulate behaviors allow students to begin utilizing concepts related to strategic planning, compliance, evaluation of behavior, and self-regulation in regard to their thoughts and actions (Rothbart & Bates, 1998); however, it is through interactions with parents and teachers that students gain the tools that they will need in order to navigate their social environment (Denham et al., 2000; Hamre & Pianta, 2001).

Vygotsky's sociocultural perspective emphasized that development is guided by adults interacting with students, with the context determining how, where, and when these interactions take place (Bjorklund, 2004). A student's thinking is challenged within a social context (e.g., home and school environments), which occurs through interactions with people who are more skilled or provide asymmetrical transactions (Vygotsky, 1987). Parents and teachers influence a student's emerging cognitive skills through the social and personal experiences they provide and by encouraging and modeling behaviors for social interaction (Gauvain, 2001). As a result of these exchanges, students are able to take a more active role in their interactions with parents, teachers, and the school environment over time by learning to integrate their own and others' perspectives in order to understand and interact within the social environment (Bronfenbrenner, 1990; Pellegrini & Blatchford, 2000).

Students' perceptions of parents' and teachers' roles are key aspects of their social-cognitive development and can affect how they view their own role within the context of the family-school relationship (Gauvain, 2007). For instance, parents generally define their role in students' education as seeing to socioemotional needs and making sure that they have the materials needed to be actively engaged in their academic environment (Crozier, 1997, 1999; Fine, 1993). In contrast, parents (and many teachers) see teachers' roles in terms of providing students with the tools that they need to succeed academically (e.g., understanding the fundamentals of academic content; Crozier,

1997, 1999). Evidence confirming that teachers are most likely to contact parents when students are having problems such as lack of effort and behavior issues, suggest that parents assume that their children are progressing normally in academic areas and therefore, do not see the need for seeking out their children's teachers, especially in later grades (Dornbush & Glasgow, 1996). If students begin to incorporate these roles into their cognitive schemas in relation to their parents and teachers, they may be less likely to seek out parents when it comes to academic needs or seek teachers in relation to socioemotional support, thus solidifying defined roles in a way that inhibits collaboration and partnership between parents and teachers. Improved understanding of how students' cognitive development can indirectly affect how parents and teachers relate to one another is an area often unexplored, yet may be an important factor in explaining variations in both parent involvement and family-school relationships.

In terms of direct effects, biological and cognitive changes in student's self-regulatory abilities in early childhood provide the impetus for the merging of parents' and teachers' goals, set the foundation for early parent-teacher interactions, and thus highlight one of the ways in which individual differences in student's development can affect developing family-school relationships. Parents and teachers share responsibility for socializing appropriate behaviors in young students, which is often one of the first common tasks across home and school in regard to students' school adjustment (Piotrkowski, Botsko, & Matthews, 2000). The concept of self-regulation involves modulating the initial physiological responses (cardiac and emotional arousal) to situations, and managing these dominant responses in socially appropriate and adaptive ways (Rothbart & Bates, 1998). Within the school environment, both parents and teachers usually agree that students need to regulate their emotions and related behaviors in order to effectively attend to moments in which social, emotional, behavioral, and academic learning takes place (West, Germino-Hausken, & Collins, 1993). When parents and teachers agree and have similar goals related to students' self-regulation, teachers are more likely to contact parents and increase activities in the classroom that involve parents (Epstein & Dauber; 1991; Murdock & Miller, 2003; Walker & Hoover-Dempsey, 2006). Though potentially beneficial throughout the entire prek-12 system, this sharing of socialization goals between parents and teachers in early childhood, as a response to students' developing regulatory skills, offers an explanation as to why more family-school interaction is reported during early years of school than in later grades (Epstein & Dauber, 1991).

Parents of children who have behavioral problems or self-regulatory difficulties are also more likely to have high frequency communication with school staff about their children's difficulties, suggesting that a large proportion of parent-school interactions are in reference to students' difficulties (Deslandes & Bertrand, 2005; Sui-Chu & Willms, 1996). According to Lightfoot (1977), although specificities of teacher and parent roles may differ, both share similar socialization responsibilities, thus problems within parent-teacher relationships come from the fact that their spheres of influence and responsibilities in relation to the student are not clearly delineated. For example, when students have difficulties at school, although both parents and teachers feel that the individual student has responsibility for his own behaviors, parents often attribute these behaviors to factors in the classroom and feel that it is the teacher's responsibility to control these behaviors in the classroom, while teachers assign more responsibility to parenting and home factors (Vernberg & Medway, 1981). Additionally, when parents and teachers meet, they often follow the standard rules of teacher-conference communication, with the teacher being in control yet understanding that misunderstandings or negative perceptions can create conditions in which parents remove themselves from interactions with teachers and administrators (Phtiaka, 1999). When parents and teachers disagree, they are both less likely to interact in positive ways, initiate contact with one another, or be involved in direct classroom activities; however, when parents feel as though their thoughts and opinions are valued, they are likely to become more engaged in school-initiated family-partnership practices (Epstein, 2001; Simon, 2004; Van Voorhis, 2003). Fostering collaboration between families, teachers, and schools may help to avoid these differences in perspectives and promote mutual understanding and corroboration of similar expectations (Bodner-Johnson & Sass-Lehrer, 1999). These findings suggest that focusing on the chronosystem, in this case dynamic relations between students' individual differences in self-regulation, the home, and the school environment, may provide unique insight into family-school relationships.

## Changing Systems

In addition to developmental changes within the student, shifts at other levels of the student's ecology, including family, school, parents' work, teachers' training experiences, legislation, etc., may serve a contributing role to family-school partnerships. The many potential changes in systems cover more ground than can be discussed herein, so a few illustrations from within the family and school microsystems are provided below.

*Parenting Efficacy*   As subject matter intensity and content changes, parents, especially those with less education, may feel less efficacious in their attempts to help their children in school-related matters (Downer & Mendez, 2005; Eccles & Harold, 1993; Hoover-Dempsey & Sandler, 1997), which could be an explanation for reduced parental involvement over time. Efficacy theory holds that when parents feel inadequate about their own academic ability and their efforts to enhance their children's academic capabilities, they are more likely to avoid being involved in their children's schooling because they feel that their involvement will not produce positive outcomes for their children (Bandura, 1997; Hoover-Dempsey & Sandler, 1997). Parents with low levels of education may doubt their academic capabilities; thus, once they fulfill their duty as parent (i.e., provide clothing, be available for emotional support, get children to school), they rely on teachers, who are considered the professionals, to educate and provide their children with the knowledge needed to increase their children's social mobility and economic success (Crozier, 1999; Drummond & Stipek, 2004; Goldenberg & Gallimore, 1995; Lareau, 1987). Less educated parents (often also lower-income parents) are characterized more often as "teacher-supporters" who encourage teachers' decisions in the classroom and feel that their main goal is, given the U.S. school system's emphasis on individual success, to encourage their children to be self-directed in their schoolwork (Drummond & Stipek, 2004; Lareau & Shumar, 1996). These parents feel that they are fulfilling their obligation to support their children's autonomy, while also offering underlying support for the authority of teachers, which suggests that when parents feel that they are satisfying their parental responsibilities and their efforts are benefiting their children, they are more likely to be involved in their children's schooling (Hoover-Dempsey, Walker, & Sandler, 2005). These findings suggest that the developmental trajectory of parenting efficacy and its association with school expectations of students and families ought to be studied in relation to the formation and maintenance of family-school connections over time.

*Beliefs about Parenting Role*    Parents generally believe that they will have more influence over their children's lives, academic or otherwise, during the earlier school years than during the upper grades, which suggests that shifts in family-school relationships could reflect changes in parenting beliefs and practices in response to student development (Freedman-Doan, Arbreton, Harold, & Eccles, 1993). According to McDermott (2008), parents' concerns during early childhood focus on the influence of teacher beliefs and classmate behaviors on their children, while during the middle school years parents are attempting to understand their changing roles and what is expected of them. During early school years, parents feel that it is their duty to focus on their children's socioemotional and socialization needs, such as fostering emerging self-concept, rule compliance, and the basics of how to interact with others, so they are more likely to be involved with these classrooms during the early grades (which are often more family focused) in ways that ensure that these goals are met (Crozier, 1999; Lombardi, 1992). As children enter middle childhood and adolescence, parent-child conflict often increases, while peers become central sources of emotional support and teachers become greater sources of academic support; therefore, children are more likely to communicate with peers and teachers than parents about their socioemotional and academic difficulties (Allen & Land, 1999; Collins & Repinksi, 1994; Nickerson & Nagle, 2005). In this context of diminished parent-child communication, parents may feel as though disengaging from the schooling aspect of their children's lives is a natural developmental progression that serves to foster their children's autonomy and independence (Cooper, Lindsay, & Nye, 2000; Eccles & Harold, 1996).

Other explanations regarding changes in parent-school interaction over time suggest that as children are better able to regulate their social and academic behaviors, parent involvement in their children's academic lives does not diminish, but parental behaviors adapt to meet both their own and their children's changing needs over time. For example, both parents and children indicate that parents engage in home-based learning rituals such as helping children with homework, checking homework, helping with projects, and monitoring their children's school progress, which has been shown to remain relatively steady over time (Eccles & Harold, 1996; Souto-Manning & Swick, 2006). Schools, on the other hand, often evaluate parental involvement based on volunteering or attendance at school council meetings, which do little to accurately describe the degree to which parents are actually involved in their children's academic lives (Fantuzzo, Tighe, & Childs, 2000; Flessa, 2008). Although parental participation of this nature, which is often done of parents' own accord, is related to greater achievement for students, especially those students with difficulties (Bailey, 2004; Hoover-Dempsey et al., 2001), students report that teachers exert little effort to involve their parents in their school work (Eccles & Harold, 1996). Parents often feel that their efforts at home are undervalued and underappreciated, which may be related to parents' lack of communication and involvement with schools (Haynes & Ben-Avie, 1996). These findings suggest that research taking into account the changing needs of both parents and teachers, and how parental behaviors, attitudes, and obligations change in response to the developing child, may offer valuable insight on ways to increase positive parent-school interactions over time.

*Changes in School Personnel Beliefs/Expectations*    As with parents, school personnel beliefs about their role and their expectations of what constitutes appropriate parental involvement changes over time, and, as a result, are likely to influence the nature of family-school interactions. Although parental involvement in issues pertaining to school curricula and policies are encouraged during their children's early school years, as children transition to upper grades, most school programs only promote parental participation to the point of supporting school policies, volunteering, or helping children at home and are likely to resist input with regard to their own teaching practices (Ranson, Martin, & Vincent, 2004; Tett, 2001). As a result, parents interpret these exclusionary norms and behaviors to denote the lack of value schools place on parents' time and effort, thus facilitating the family-school disconnection (Souto-Manning & Swick, 2006). Research indicates that teachers, in general, have positive attitudes toward parental participation when schools have strong programs and utilize more teacher-led parent involvement strategies; however, when school systems are rigid in their assumptions and expectations or lack specific strategies for parental involvement, negative family-school interactions may ensue (Dauber & Epstein, 1989; Ranson et al., 2004). These negative parent involvement situations can create stereotypes of parent interactions for school personnel, which reduce the likelihood of school personnel initiating contact with parents beyond memos, notices, and report cards (Dauber & Epstein, 1989; Swick, 2004). Consequently, these beliefs, expectations, and behaviors can contribute to a continuous cycle of negative family-school interactions, thus offering an explanation as to why family-school communication tends to diminish over time.

## INTERSECTION OF CONTEMPORARY ISSUES AND DEVELOPMENTAL/ECOLOGICAL MODEL

In a search of the literature, one finds that hundreds of articles on parent involvement and family-school relationships use a developmental/ecological model, or systems theory, as the starting point for understanding the family-school link. But, microsystems, exosystems, and macrosystems have changed as we have entered the 21st century, and these shifts are likely to have important implications for how the mesosystem operates. Thus, the purpose of this section is to focus on contemporary issues in school-family partnerships from a systems perspective in order to shed light on new and less explored aspects of the mesosystem. As a result, we consider contemporary educational policy and family issues that deserve attention in upcoming research on family-school relationships.

## Educational Policies

The No Child Left Behind Act (NCLB, 2002) was implemented shortly after the turn of the century in order to improve documentation and performance standards for U.S. schools with the underlying goal to reduce achievement gaps and hold schools accountable for the performance of all students (Elze, 2006). In addition, the latest incarnation of NCLB takes into account the need for multilevel leadership regarding parental involvement, recognizes that parental involvement is integral to children's school success and should be incorporated into school curricula, and highlights the need for schools to increase efforts to facilitate involvement regardless of a parent's current level of involvement (Epstein, 2005). In several ways, NCLB legislation has dramatically changed the context within which family-school partnerships will be initiated, developed, and maintained, as noted in more detail below.

*Evidence-Based Practices and Teacher Quality*    Traditional school communications with parents have been far different from the provisions outlined in NCLB, so the mandate that state education programs must support the collection and dissemination of effective parental involvement practices using the most current research and educational standards brings forth the question—to what extent has current research identified what constitutes effective parent involvement practices? Current research on family-school partnership interventions has placed a heavy emphasis on acknowledging and addressing common barriers, such as culture, beliefs, motivation, and lack of access to resources, to parents' involvement in their children's schooling (Anderson-Butcher, 2006). For example, family support interventions now integrate components such as life-skills training, parent education, cultural events, family resource centers, referral services, occupational opportunities, family counseling, and emergency support into their programs, all of which have been shown to be effective strategies for increasing students' positive socioemotional development, academic achievement, and family-school communication (Anderson-Butcher, 2006; Anderson-Butcher, Khairallah, & Race-Bigelow, 2004; Comer & Fraser, 1998; Kumpfer & Alvarado, 2003). These strategies are effective means of promoting positive family-school relationships, as well as student outcomes, but many of them have yet to be utilized to their fullest potential within the U.S. educational system.

School systems realize that creating high-quality, long-lasting family-school relationships takes time and effort given that no strategy will work for every school system or every set of families (Chavkin, 2006; Hoover-Dempsey, Walker, Jones, & Reed, 2002). However, results of the Chicago Longitudinal Study's parent involvement efforts indicate that not only is continued parental participation related to children's positive outcomes, but every \$1 invested in these types of parental participation programs offers a possible \$7 return to society, highlighting the long-term benefits of investing in family-school partnerships (Reynolds & Clements, 2005). Although the evidence base for parent involvement interventions is considered somewhat mixed (Fishel & Ramirez, 2005), there is growing empirical support for a wide variety of effective intervention models that include focuses on parent consultation, parent education and training, family-school collaborations, and parent educational involvement (Carlson & Christenson,

2005; Sheridan et al., 2007). Application of experimental designs to these intervention approaches is key to substantiating the case that family-school partnerships are crucial to students' success.

Despite the existence of a literature base for some of the family-school interventions above, little about what is known on how to effectively work with parents has made its way into the pre-service training opportunities provided to teachers, principals, and other school personnel, leaving them relatively ill-prepared to work with families. Epstein and Sanders (2006) noted that there is a trend toward this changing, but by and large there are still no systematic, research-based standards for how to prepare teachers to work with parents and many certification and licensing requirements lack an emphasis on family-school partnerships (Radcliffe, Malone, & Nathan, 1994; Shartrand, Weiss, Kreider, & Lopez, 1997). In the context of NCLB requiring teachers to be "highly qualified," there is substantial room for investigating how to translate research on effective practices in working with families and fostering positive school, family, and community partnerships into pre-service and in-service training for teachers and principals.

*Academic Accountability*    One of the most significant changes that NCLB (2002) has made in regard to how schools operate is in terms of academic accountability. Specifically, this federal legislation has regulated the frequency with which students are required to be tested and has implemented guidelines for establishing accountability systems. In addition, students must achieve proficiency by 2014, and all schools must provide yearly progress of subgroups of students via Adequate Yearly Progress reports (Sipple & Banach, 2006). Some scholars argue that schools should be accountable only to parents and students and cite that the new NCLB components promote a reductionist view of education that emphasizes test scores and conformity at the expense of student creativity and individuality (Perry & McWilliam, 2007). These requirements have serious implications for family-school partnerships because in order to meet these federal regulations, schools could make the argument that the time and effort needed to ensure that these requirements are met will impede their abilities to devote time to developing adequate family-school relationships. In contrast, Christensen (2004) suggested that partnering with families to meet the new accountability demands may offer an effective way to improve children's learning outcomes. For example, evidence from previous research on parent involvement found that its effects on student outcomes were strongest for programs that utilized tutoring in the home by parents (i.e., parents assisting children in academic-related skills) and were targeted toward specific academic skills, such as reading or math (Fishel & Ramirez, 2005). These findings suggest that involving parents in the school accountability process not only enhances family-school connections, but improves students' academic outcomes, both of which comply with NCLB requirements. NCLB accountability mandates clearly offer unique opportunities to study different pathways that schools choose to address the new standards, either through hyper-focus on classroom time spent on academic content aligned with standardized tests or by taking greater advantage of partnerships with families.

*Family Right to Transfer*    NCLB now requires that schools classified as "low performing" (i.e., failed to meet progress standards for 2 or more consecutive years) have to provide alternatives to students to ensure that they receive a quality education, such as transferring to higher performing schools and tutoring options. In the past, it has been relatively easy for school systems to conceal discrepancies between subgroups of students, especially low-income and minority students, by only disclosing aggregated scores on various measures of student performance (Sipple & Banach, 2006); thus, parents of these children are likely not adequately informed of their children's academic progress. Additionally, minority families are often not informed of their children's progress due to poor communication, lack of understanding of school policies, and depleted access to resources needed to foster consistent communication between parents and schools (Alexander & Entwisle, 1996; Gamoran, 1996), which adds to the disconnect between families and schools in relation to communication about the services available to students. Parents in high poverty schools, where access to resources are often sparse, place more of an emphasis on teachers' ability to improve their children's academic achievement than student satisfaction; however, these same low-income parents are less likely to contact teachers and make teacher requests regarding their children than parents with higher incomes (Jacob & Lefgren, 2007). When schools make an effort to inform the parents of children at risk for school difficulties and the support services available to them, parents are more likely to access these services and increase their interactions with teachers and school administrators (Violand-Sanchez, Sutton, & Ware, 1991). There is much to be learned about whether a family's right to transfer their child in low performing schools leads to tension between parents and school personnel, as well as how families make decisions about the option of moving their child to a new school versus staying put and accepting extra resources offered by the current school (e.g., tutoring).

*Title I Mandated Family-School Communication*   Although parents state that they would like to receive more communication from schools to help children meet their educational goals regardless of grade level, parents report that school-to-parent communication efforts tend to occur more often in the earlier grades than during middle/ high school grades (Dauber & Epstein, 1989; Eccles & Harold, 1996). In the past, parent-school communication was defined in terms of parents receiving report cards on time, scheduling parent-teacher conferences when children were having difficulties, and offering PTA membership options; however, NCLB has not only changed the level of involvement of the federal government in public education, but has also set a new standard for the quality and quantity of parent-school interactions. The recent inception of the NCLB federal law has attempted to reduce the ambiguity in what constitutes adequate parent-school communication.

NCLB defines this communication in terms of regular, bidirectional, and meaningful interactions between parents and schools that ensure that parents play a central role and are actively encouraged to be involved in their children's academic learning and other aspects of schooling (Igo, 2002). Specifically, any school receiving federal funding (e.g., Title I funds) has to make significant policy and structural changes to meet the federal funding requirements, such as providing understandable written and verbal communication to inform parents of their rights, gaining parental input to inform involvement policies and school improvement plans, allotting 1% of their budget for parent engagement efforts, and distributing report cards on the school's performance. In addition to federally mandated communication efforts on the part of schools, NCLB (2002) also opens the door for parent-initiated communication by giving parents the right to request and be provided information regarding teacher qualifications, especially for cases in which teachers do not meet the requirements of being "highly qualified" (i.e., state certified, bachelor's degree, demonstrated competency in the subject area being taught). At a minimum, these NCLB requirements offer opportunities to track how parents, teachers, and principals perceive family-school partnerships before and after the application of new communication patterns.

## The Changing Face of American Families

Representing one-half of the family-school mesosystem, families are key players in initiating, developing, and maintaining collaborative connections with schools. This crucial role has been readily recognized and closely examined in past research, with foci that range from parent motivations to work-related barriers. As such, it follows that major shifts in family systems across the United States over recent years, in terms of family structure, racial/ethnic diversity, and English Language Learners, offer new avenues of inquiry that are essential to understanding how family-school partnerships will operate in upcoming decades.

*Nontraditional Families as the Norm*    According to the U.S. Census, as of 2007, over 60% of children under the age of 18 lived in what used to be considered an "unconventional" American family (U.S. Census Bureau, 2007a). The idealized concept of the nuclear family (first time married parents, biological children, no other adults in the home) has diminished greatly over the time, making less "traditional" arrangements (i.e., single-parent households, blended families, grandparent-headed families) more commonplace (Allen, Fine, & Demo, 2000; Barbour, Barbour, & Scully, 2008; Reynolds, Wright, & Beale, 2003). Literature on family structure has highlighted that students from single-parent or grandparent-headed households are more likely to be absent, skip school, and exhibit disruptive behaviors than students from two-parent homes, which may contribute to negative perceptions that could affect how school personnel interact with these families (Lee & Grover, 2006; Oman et al., 2002; Rodriguez-Srednicki, 2002). In general, school administrators feel that family participation, especially from these contemporary family structures, is inadequate and reflects the value that these parents place on their children's education (Lareau, 1987). However, in reality, families living in more contemporary household arrangements are often overburdened, lack social support, and live in poverty (Auerbach, 2001; Lareau, 2003; Lareau & Horvat, 1999; Lee & Grover, 2006). For example, compared to much lower rates in two-parent families, single-mother (51.3%) and single-father households (26.5%) are much more likely to live below the Federal Poverty Line and are more likely to experience multiple losses, increased childcare responsibilities, feelings of isolation, and work multiple jobs (Kitson & Morgan, 1990; McLanahan & Booth, 1989). Given the abundance of social, emotional, and economic stressors that these families endure, most single-parent and grandparent-headed households lack the resources and time to devote sustained efforts to certain school-based activities, such as making donations and volunteering in their children's classroom (Lareau, 1987).

Due to a lack of financial resources, nontraditional families often rely on their connections to others (e.g., family, community, friendships) for emotional support related to raising children and tackling diversity (Cochran & Davila, 1992). In other words, what these nontraditional families lack in financial capital, they make up for in social capital, or learning that results from connections and relationships (Barbour et al., 2008). Social capital incorporates many forms, including community norms, intergenerational structures, and parent-child interactions (Coleman, 1988). Although parent-child interactions are the primary means by which parents transmit skills, the intergenerational structure or networks in the community that incorporate others, such as parents of their children's friends, ensure that parents know of their children's activities in both community and school environments (Kao & Rutherford, 2007). With these networks already in place, schools can utilize them when attempting to foster positive family-school partnerships. For example, Terrion (2006) found that frequency of parent involvement is not what is most important for facilitating parent-school interactions in families at risk, but more utilization or formation of social capital (e.g., bonding—spending quality time, bridging—using other families as resources, and linking—providing access to resources) that increase parental involvement and foster positive parent attitudes about schools. These findings indicated that investing in the social capital of families, especially those who are at risk, may not only promote positive family-school relationships, but also foster a sense of connectedness in the communities in which children and families reside. Investigations are needed into how schools invest in community networking to facilitate partnerships with families, and how families stay connected (or not) to schools under conditions of limited social capital.

*Rapid Expansion of Racial/Ethnic Diversity*  The increasing cultural diversity of American families is apparent given that racial/ethnic minorities account for approximately 30% of students across the United States (U.S. Census Bureau, 2007b). This shift in the makeup of the classroom, as well as the fact that certain cultural groups are not flourishing within the current educational system, suggest that the discontinuity between home cultures and school environments may explain cultural variations in student behaviors and academic achievement (Corbett & Wilson, 1990; Darling-Hammond, 1991; Marcias, 1987). Although ethnic background and social class are often interconnected both in U.S. society and in research, the fact that controlling for socioeconomic status is often not enough to explain variations in educational findings highlight why educators should examine the impact of cultural beliefs and practices on both student adjustment and parental participation (Sirin, 2005).

Culture can be defined as "the ever-changing values, traditions, social and political relationships, and worldview created and shared by a group of people bound together by a combination of factors and how these are transformed by those who share them" (Nieto, 1996, p. 390). American schools often propagate the values and expectations of the dominant culture, which values independence, self-reliance, and individual thinking, perhaps making it challenging for minority youth to adjust coming from families with potentially different belief systems and socialization practices (Auerbach, 2001; Jordan,

Orozco, & Averett, 2002; Pigott & Cowen, 2000). According to cultural discontinuity theory, differences in communication and learning styles of minority students, which are initiated and maintained within the context of the family microsystem, may lead to disagreements and misinterpretations within the dominant (i.e., European American) culture of schools (Clarke, 1997). For example, Alexander, Entwisle, and Thompson (1987) posited when students' backgrounds differ from those of the dominant school culture, school practitioners are more likely to place amplified importance on "misleading cues" (e.g., style of dress, language use) and perceive these cues as fundamental weaknesses in students than those teachers for which these cues are familiar. Although parents within ethnic minority groups often instill cultural knowledge that promotes coping when faced with challenges to their cultural beliefs, minority children often cope with the discontinuity between their own values and what is valued within their school environment by assimilating (conforming) to the values of the dominant school culture (Murray & Mandara, 2003; West-Olatunji, 2008). While easier to accommodate for students during early and middle childhood than later developmental periods, cultural assimilation not only places stress on students' developing cultural identity (e.g., self-concept, sense of belonging to a cultural group), but can also foster conflicts between the school systems promoting these practices and parents' own cultural values and expectations for their children.

Discontinuity between ideals, values, and expectations serves to amplify this disconnect between students' familial and school environments (Pigott & Cowen, 2000). However, integration of families' cultural resources into the school climate is an effective means of increasing student engagement and learning (Lucas, Henze, & Donato, 1990; Nieto, 2002), and is related to higher parental involvement with their children's school (Delgado-Gaitan, 2004; Mercado & Moll, 2000). Thus, these findings suggest that schools emphasizing cultural understanding, and integration of these ideals into the school environment, are likely to cultivate positive family-school relationships and may also foster socioemotional and academic competence in students from minority families.

*Proliferation of English Language Learners*   According to Thomas and Collier (2002), by the year 2030, almost half of all school-aged children will be classified as English Language Learners (ELL), the majority of whom will be Latino with a dominant language of Spanish. The increasing rate of students classified as ELL within the U.S. public education system makes it imperative that teachers, school administrators, and researchers recognize and understand the complex processes of bilingual student development and identify the contributions of families, classrooms, and schools to effective promotion of development among this population of students in the United States. Lack of proficiency in the English language is one of the biggest obstacles to Latino parents' participation in the educational context (Tinkler, 2002). For example, Latino parents are more likely to cite lower levels of shared responsibility for their children's education, which is often due to unfamiliarity with American education curricula and low parental efficacy with regard to their children's school work, which is typically in English (Floyd, 1998; Wong & Hughes, 2006). Also, ethnic minority status is often synonymous with reduced access to socioeconomic resources, so Latino parents, particularly those who are not yet proficient in the English language, are at a double disadvantage (Klein, Bugarin, Beltranena, & McArthur, 2004; Nieto, 2002). Unfortunately, in addition to lack of resources such as transportation, childcare, and work restraints, inconsistent school policies/practices and communications from schools that are in English or are not understandable due to poor translation make Latino parents' continued participation in school programs a real challenge (Christenson, 2004; Stritikus & Garcia, 2005). Latino parents, whose cultures often emphasize showing respect to authority, are also not likely to participate in school matters more out of respect for the teacher's authority in that domain rather than due to lack of interest in their children's education (Drummond & Stipek, 2004; Holloway, Rambaud, Fuller, & Eggers-Pierola, 1996; Wong & Hughes, 2006).

Even when taking into account income level, ethnicity, and student ability level, Latino parents place a strong value on their children's educational attainment and report that if they received information on school procedures, such as the grading system, schedules, and homework, they would use this information to help their children academically (Chavkin & Williams, 1993). These findings suggest that lower parent involvement for language minority families does not denote a lack of interest in their child's schooling and education, but reflects a disconnect between cultural understandings of a families' role in education and expectations for parent involvement in the United States educational system (Cassanova, 1996; Gonzalez, 1986). Much is still to be learned about the complicated process of connecting families of ELL students to the educational system, particularly given that almost 22% of children under the age of 5 are Latino and about to enter the education system (Calderon, Gonzalez, & Lazarin, 2004).

## INTERSECTION OF METHODS AND THE DEVELOPMENTAL/ECOLOGICAL MODEL

In the wake of considering contemporary issues that require attention in the study of family-school partnerships, this section briefly outlines a few implications of the developmental/ecological model for research methodology focused on the family-school link.

### *Using Developmental/Ecological Framework to Guide Measurement*

From a bioecological standpoint (Bronfenbrenner, 1986, 1992), the transactional nature of relationships between individuals and their environment means that, to some degree, individuals define their own reality through perceptions of their context. In this sense, the developmental/ecological model underscores the importance of assessing family-school partnerships from the perspective of all those involved, including parents, teachers, and students. The extent to which family-school relationships develop and contribute to students' success may be due to the subjective realities of each contributor to these relationships. By and large, research on family-school partnerships has relied heavily on informant-report measures, whether to assess parent involvement across multiple tasks (e.g., Family Involvement Questionnaire; Fantuzzo et al., 2000), teacher attitudes toward parents (e.g., Pelco & Ries, 1999), or any number of other aspects of family-school links. Increased efforts are needed to triangulate these informant-reports in studies, and given the central role of the developing student, there is an especially noticeable need for more student-report measures of family-school partnerships.

Despite the utility of assessing perceptions, in today's educational environment with an emphasis on hard evidence, the time has come for the field to extend and expand measurement of family-school partnerships, placing a greater emphasis on objectivity. In particular, as noted in the systems theory assumptions above, partnerships between families and schools constitute a mesosystemic level in the social ecology of students, which is a relational unit unto itself. This begs the question of how to most objectively and directly measure this connection, which has been addressed in two recent studies that will serve here as examples of this approach to measurement.

First, Rimm-Kaufman and Zhang (2005) used father-school contact logs completed daily by teachers to study communication patterns between fathers and schools across the preschool-kindergarten transition. These logs covered contacts in which a father and teacher communicated two or more sentences to each other about the father's child, including home visits, school visits, volunteer efforts, phone calls, etc. This diary or time log approach has also been applied in other research on father involvement, with a focus on parenting activities and responsibilities at home (McBride & Mills, 1993). New technologies such as PDAs and Blackberries increase the feasibility of having parents, teachers, or students record daily activities in an efficient, systematic way that can result in objective information about communication patterns and content between families and schools.

A second example applies observation methodology to family-school relationships, with the intention of capturing real-time, objective data about how families and school personnel interact with each other. In Martin and colleagues' (2006) recent study, standardized observations were conducted during a common context for interactions between parents and teachers—Individualized Education Plan (IEP) meetings. Though this study focused primarily on the student's role in the meeting, it offers a window into a novel method for learning about how families, school personnel, and students interact with one another under potentially stressful circumstances. Using time-sampling of short 10-second intervals, trained observers coded who talked, when they talked, and what they talked about. Applicable in situations such as IEP meetings or parent-teacher conferences, an observational approach has the potential to help the field understand what kind of parent-teacher interactions build strong relationships, what a student's role is within these interactions, and what types of parent and teacher characteristics influence interaction styles. In summary, the integration of observations with multiple informant-reports and other objective measurement approaches is recommended for future studies to more deeply and comprehensively understand and synthesize family-school partnership constructs.

### Study Designs that Test Mechanisms

From a developmental/ecological standpoint, student learning is most directly influenced by proximal processes, or those everyday experiences that they have at home and in classrooms with people and available learning materials (Bronfenbrenner & Morris, 2006). Yet, as outlined previously, students do not necessarily experience family-school partnerships in person, nor do they directly experience related aspects of the exo and macrosystems. In fact, these elements of a student's ecology may be most likely to influence learning through indirect routes. Hoover-Dempsey, Walker, and Sandler (2005) provided just such a model to explain why parents become involved in their children's education, but then also how these motivations and related involvement are likely to be related to student learning either under certain conditions (moderators) or by creating certain conditions that then facilitate learning (mediators). For example, a father may first be motivated to become involved somehow in his child's drama class because his child actively requests this involvement. The father then becomes involved by teaching his child some strategies for memorizing lines and staying relaxed during performances. However, rather than having a direct influence on the child's acting skills, the model suggests that this home-based instruction will only serve as a mechanism for learning if the father's efforts are developmentally appropriate and aligned with what the child's drama teacher expects and teaches at school. When using conceptual models such as this one that take into account how nested systems interact to result in student outcomes, it makes sense to design studies that allow investigators to examine one or more aspect of the links and mechanisms by which family-school partnerships come to exist and in the end lead to student learning and school success.

Hoover-Dempsey and Sandler (2005) are systematically working toward testing the indirect and mediational relationships proposed in their model, and are not alone in this endeavor. Looking at early adaptation to school, Hughes and Kwok (2007) recently examined parent-teacher relationships in relation to students' academic achievement in elementary school; however, they hypothesized that students' behavioral engagement in the classroom setting would mediate this association. Results indicated that parent-teacher relationships were indeed associated with student achievement through the proximal process of engagement in the classroom, and therefore offered more information about the mechanisms by which family-school partnerships may contribute to student development. With an emphasis on testing indirect and mediational pathways, these study designs can and will further refine the field's conceptual models, and, in particular, generate new knowledge about how family-school partnerships and other elements of a student's ecology interact and work through one another to result in student learning.

## CONCLUSION

Developmental/ecological theory continues to provide a relevant conceptual framework to guide empirical inquiry into the family-school partnerships that play such an important role in students' educational success (Christenson & Sheridan, 2001). However, at the early part of the 21st century, it is an ideal time to reconsider how to expand and extend the ways that this framework informs research on family-school partnerships. Key features of micro, exo, and macrosystems, all of which are critical ingredients or contributors to the mesosystemic link between families and schools, have changed. These shifts not only broaden the types of research questions that can and should be asked with family-school partnerships in mind, but also necessitate revisiting old questions with greater integration of a developmental lens, more diverse samples of students and families, multi-method assessments that pair objective measures with informant-report, and study designs that examine mechanisms. Perhaps most important in this age of accountability, however, is that researchers focus on developing and empirically validating meso-systemic interventions that recognize the need to alter systems within students' ecology in order to improve school success in measurable and generalizable ways.

## AUTHORS' NOTE

Special appreciation is extended to Sara Rimm-Kaufman and Eliane Stampfer for their invaluable input into the organization and content of this chapter.

## REFERENCES

Alexander, K. L., & Entwisle, D. R. (1996). Schools and children at risk. In A. Booth & J. Dunn (Eds.), *Family-school links: How do they affect educational outcomes?* (pp. 67–88). Mahwah, NJ: Erlbaum.

Alexander, K. L., Entwisle, D. R., & Thompson, M. (1987). School performance, status relations, and the structure of sentiment: Bringing the teacher back. *American Sociological Review, 52*, 665–682.

Allen, K. A., Fine, M. A., & Demo, D. R. (2000). An overview of family diversity: Issues, controversial questions, and future prospects. In D. H. Demo, K. A. Allen, & M. A. Fine (Eds.), *Handbook of family diversity* (pp. 1–14). New York: Oxford University Press.

Allen, J., & Land, D. (1999). Attachment in adolescence. In J. Cassidy & P. Shaver (Eds.), *Handbook of attachment: Theory, research, and clinical applications* (pp. 319–335). New York: Guilford.

Anderson-Butcher, D. (2006). Building effective family support programs and interventions. In C. Franklin, M. B. Harris, & P. Allen-Meares (Eds.), *The school services sourcebook: A guide for school-based professionals* (pp. 651–662). New York: Oxford University Press.

Anderson-Butcher, D., Khairallah, A., & Race-Bigelow, J. (2004). An in-depth examination of a mutual support group for long-term, Temporary Assistance for Needy Families recipients. *Social Work, 49*, 131–140.

Auerbach, S. (2001). *Under co-construction: Parent roles in promoting college access for students of color.* Unpublished doctoral dissertation, University of California, Los Angeles, Graduate School of Education and Information Studies.

Bailey, L. B. (2004). Interactive homework for increasing parent involvement and student learning. *Childhood Education, 81*, 36–40.

Bandura, A. (1991). Social cognitive theory of self-regulation. *Organizational Behavior & Human Decision Processes, 50*, 248–287.

Bandura, A. (1997). *Self-efficacy: The exercise of control.* New York: Freeman.

Barbour, C., Barbour, N., & Scully, P. A. (2008). *Families, schools, and communities.* Upper Saddle River, NJ: Prentice Hall.

Bjorklund, D. (2004). *Children's thinking: Cognitive development and individual differences* (4th ed). Florence, KY: Wadsworth.

Bodner-Johnson, B., & Sass-Lehrer, M. (1999). *Family-school relationships, concepts and premises.* Washington, DC: Gallaudet University, Pre-College Programs.

Bornstein, M. H., & Tamis-LeMonda, C. S. (1989). Maternal responsiveness and cognitive development in children. *New Directions for Child Development, 43*, 49–61.

Bronfenbrenner, U. (1986). Ecology of the family as a context for human development: Research perspectives. *Developmental Psychology, 22*, 723–742.

Bronfenbrenner, U. (1990). Discovering what families do. In D. Blankenhorn, S. Bayme, & J. B. Elshtain (Eds.), *Rebuilding the nest: A new commitment to the American family* (pp. 27–38). Milwaukee, WI: Family Service America.

Bronfenbrenner, U. (1992). Ecological systems theory. In R. Vasta (Ed.), *Annals of child development: Six theories of child development: Revised formulations and current issues* (pp. 187–249). London: Jessica Kingsley.

Bronfenbrenner, U., & Morris, P. A. (2006). The bioecological model of human development. In R. M Lerner (Ed.), *Theoretical models of human development. Handbook of child psychology* (Vol. 1, 6th ed., pp. 793–828) Hoboken, NJ: Wiley.

Calderon, M., Gonzalez, R., & Lazarin, M. (2004). *State of Hispanic America 2004*. Washington, DC: National Council of La Raza.

Carlson, C., & Christenson, S. L. (2005). Evidence-based parent and family interventions in school psychology [Special issue]. *School Psychology Quarterly, 20*, 345–351.

Cassanova, U. (1996). Parental involvement: a call for prudence. *Educational Researcher, 25*, 30–32.

Chavkin, N. F. (2006). Best school-based practices for family intervention and parental involvement. In C. Franklin, M. B. Harris, & P. Allen-Meares (Eds.), *The school services sourcebook: A guide for school-based professionals* (pp. 629–640). New York: Oxford University Press.

Chavkin, N. F., & Williams, D. L. (1993). Minority parents and the elementary school: Attitudes and practices. In N. F. Chavkin (Ed.), *Families and schools in a pluralistic society* (pp. 73–83). Albany: State University of New York Press.

Christenson, S. L. (2004). The family-school partnership: An opportunity to promote the learning competence of all students. *School Psychology Review, 33*, 83–104.

Christenson, S. L., & Sheridan, S. M. (2001). *Schools and families. Creating essential connections for learning.* New York: Guilford.

Clarke, J. J. (1997). *Oriental enlightenment: The encounter between Asian and Western thought.* London: Routledge.

Cochran, M., & Davila, V. (1992). Societal influences on children's peer relationships. In R. D. Parke & G. W. Ladd (Eds.), *Family-peer relationships: Modes of linkage* (pp. 191–212). Hillsdale, NJ: Erlbaum.

Coleman, J. C. (1988). Social capital in the creation of human capital. *American Journal of Sociology, 94*, 95–120.

Collins, W. A., & Repinski, D. J. (1994). Relationships during adolescence: continuity and change in interpersonal perspective. In R. Montemayor, G. R. Adams, & T. P. Gullotta (Eds.), *Personal relationships during adolescence* (pp. 7–36).Thousand Oaks, CA: Sage.

Comer, E. W., & Fraser, M. W. (1998). Evaluation of six family support programs: Are they effective? *Families in Society, 72*, 134–148.

Cooper, H., Lindsay, J. J., & Nye, B. (2000). Homework in the home: How student, family, and parenting-style differences relate to the homework process. *Contemporary Educational Psychology, 25*, 464–487.

Corbett, H. D., & Wilson, B. (1990). *Testing, reform and rebellion.* Norward, NJ: Ablex.

Crozier, G. (1997). Empowering the powerful. *British Journal of Sociology of Education, 18*, 187–200.

Crozier, G. (1999). Is it a case of 'we know when we're not wanted'? The parents' perspective on parent-teacher roles and relationships. *Educational Research, 41*, 315–328.

Darling-Hammond, L. (1991). The implications of testing policy for educational quality and policy. *Phi Delta Kappan, 73*, 220–225.

Dauber, S. L., & Epstein, J. L. (1989). *Parents' attitudes and practices of involvement in innercity elementary and middle schools* (CREMS Report 33). Baltimore: Johns Hopkins University, Center for Research on Elementary and Middle Schools.

Delgado-Gaitan, C. (2004). *Involving Latino families in schools: Raising student achievement through home-school partnerships.* Thousand Oaks, CA: Corwin Press.

Denham, S. A., Workman, E. C., Cole, P. M., Weissbrod, C., Kendzior, K. T., & Zahn-Waxler, C. (2000). Prediction of externalizing behavior problems from early to middle childhood: The role of parental socialization and emotion expression. *Development & Psychopathology, 12*, 23–45.

Deslandes, R., & Bertrand, R. (2005). Motivation of parent involvement in secondary-level schooling. *The Journal of Educational Research, 98*, 164–175.

Dornbush, S. M., & Glasgow, K. L. (1996). The structural context of family school relations. In A. Booth & J. F. Dunn (Eds.), *Family-school links: How do they affect educational outcomes?* (pp. 35–44). Mahwah, NJ: Erlbaum.

Downer, J. T., & Mendez, J. (2005). African American father involvement and preschool children's school readiness. *Early Education and Development, 16*, 317–340.

Drummond, K. V., & Stipek, D. (2004). Low-income parents' beliefs about their role in children's academic learning. *Elementary School Journal, 104*, 107–213.

Eccles, J. S., & Harold, R. D. (1993). Parent–school involvement during the early adolescent years. *Teachers College Record, 94*, 568–587.

Eccles, J. S., & Harold, R. D. (1996). Family involvement in children's and adolescents' schooling. In A. Booth & J. F Dunn (Eds.), *Family-school links: How do they affect educational outcomes?* (pp. 3–34). Hillsdale, NJ: Erlbaum.

Elze, D. (2006). Working with gay, lesbian, bisexual, and transgender students. In C. Franklin, M. B. Harris, & P. Allen-Meares (Eds.), *The school services sourcebook: A guide for school-based professionals* (pp. 851–870). New York: Oxford University Press.

Epstein, J. L. (1987). Toward a theory of family-school connections: Teacher practices and parent involvement. In K. Hurrelmann, F. Kaufmann, & F. Losel (Eds.), *Social interaction: Potential and constraints* (pp. 121–136). New York: deGruyter.

Epstein, J. L. (1996). Perspectives and previews on research and policy for school, family, and community partnerships. In A. Booth & J. F. Dunn (Eds.), *Family-school links: How do they affect educational outcomes?* (pp. 209–246). Mahwah, NJ: Erlbaum.

Epstein, J. L. (2001). *School, family, and community partnerships: Preparing educators and improving schools.* Boulder, CO: Westview Press.

Epstein, J. L. (2005). Attainable goals? The spirit and letter of the No Child Left Behind Act on parental involvement. *Sociology of Education, 78,* 179–182.

Epstein, J. L., & Dauber, S. L. (1991). School programs and teacher practices of parent involvement in inner-city elementary and middle schools. *The Elementary School Journal, 91,* 289–305

Epstein, J. L., & Sanders, M. G. (2006). Prospects for change: Preparing educators for school, family, and community partnerships. *Peabody Journal of Education, 81,* 81–120.

Fan, X., & Chen, M. (2001). Parental involvement and students' academic achievement: A meta-analysis. *Educational Psychology Review, 13,* 1–22.

Fantuzzo, J., Tighe, E., & Childs, S. (2000). Family Involvement Questionnaire: A multivariate assessment of family participation in early childhood education. *Journal of Educational Psychology, 92,* 367–376.

Fine, M. (1993). {Ap}parent involvement: Reflections on parents, power, and urban public schools. *Teachers College Record, 94,* 682–710.

Fishel, M., & Ramirez, L. (2005). Evidence-based parent involvement interventions with school-aged children. *School Psychology Quarterly, 20,* 371–402.

Flessa, J. (2008). Parental involvement: What counts, who counts it, and does it help? *Education Canada, 48,* 18–21.

Floyd, L. (1998). Joining hands: A parental involvement program. *Urban Education, 33,* 123–135.

Ford, D. H., & Lerner, R. M. (1992). *Developmental systems theory: An integrative approach.* London: Sage.

Freedman-Doan, C. R., Arbreton, A. J. A., Harold, R. D., & Eccles, J. S. (1993). Looking forward to adolescence: mothers' and fathers' expectations for affective and behavioral change. *Journal of Early Adolescence 13,* 472–502.

Gamoran, A. (1996). Effects of schooling on children and families. In A. Booth & J. F. Dunn (Eds.), *Family-school links: How do they affect educational outcomes?* (pp. 107–114). Hillsdale, NJ: Erlbaum.

Gauvain, M. (2001). *The social context of cognitive development.* New York: Guilford.

Gauvain, M. (2007). Cognitive development in social context: Implications for early childhood education. In O. N. Saracho & B. Spodek (Eds.), *Contemporary perspectives on socialization and social development in early childhood education* (pp. 79–97). Greenwich, CT: Information Age.

Goldenberg, C., & Gallimore, R. (1995). Immigrant Latino parent's values and beliefs about their children's education: Continuities across cultures and generations. In M. L. Maehr & P. R. Pintrich (Eds.), *Advances in motivation and achievement* (Vol. 9, pp. 183–228). Greenwich, CT: JAI.

Gonzalez, B. (1986). Schools and the language minority parents: The optimum solution. *Catalyst for Change, 16,* 14–17.

Hamre, B. K., & Pianta, R. C. (2001). Early teacher-child relationships and the trajectory of children's school outcomes through eighth grade. *Child Development, 72,* 625–638.

Hamre, B. K., & Pianta, R. C. (2005). Can instructional and emotional support in the first grade classroom make a difference for children at risk of school failure? *Child Development, 76,* 949–967.

Haynes, N. M., & Ben-Avie, M. (1996). Parents as full partners in education. In A. Booth & J. Dunn (Eds.), *Family-school links: How do they affect educational outcomes?* (pp. 45–55). Hillsdale, NJ: Erlbaum.

Hinde, R. (1987). *Individuals, relationships, and culture.* New York: Cambridge University Press.

Holloway, S. D., Rambaud, M. F., Fuller, B., & Eggers-Piérola, C. (1996). What is "appropriate practice" at home and in child care? Low-income mothers' views on preparing their children in school. *Early Childhood Research Quarterly, 10,* 451–473.

Hoover-Dempsey, K. V., Battiato, A. C., Walker, J. M., Reed, R. P., DeJong, J. M., & Jones, K. P. (2001). *The influence of parental involvement in homework: What do we know and how do we know it?* Symposium paper presented at the Annual Meeting of the American Educational Research Association, Seattle, WA.

Hoover-Dempsey, K. V., & Sandler, H. M. (1997). Why do parents become involved in their children's education? *Review of Educational Research, 67,* 3–42.

Hoover-Dempsey, K. V., & Sandler, H. M. (2005). *Final performance report for OERI Grant # R305T010673: The social context of parental involvement: A path to enhanced achievement.* Presented to Project Monitor, Institute of Education Sciences, U.S. Department of Education, March 22, 2005.

Hoover-Dempsey, K. V., Walker, J. M., Jones, K. P., & Reed, R. P. (2002). Teachers Involving Parents (TIP): Results of an in-service teacher education program for enhancing parental involvement. *Teaching and Teacher Education, 18,* 843–867.

Hoover-Dempsey, K. V., Walker, J. M. T., & Sandler, H. M. (2005). Parents' motivations for involvement in their children's education. In E. N. Patrikakou, R. P. Weisberg, S. Redding, & H. J. Walberg (Eds.), *School-family partnerships for children's success* (pp. 40–56). New York: Teachers College Press.

Howe, M. L., & Courage, M. L. (1997). The emergence and early development of autobiographical memory. *Psychological Review, 104,* 499–523.

Hughes, J., & Kwok, O. (2007). Influence of student-teacher and parent-teacher relationships on lower achieving readers' engagement and achievement in the primary grades. *Journal of Educational Psychology, 99,* 39–51.

Igo, S. (2002). Increasing parent involvement. *Principal Leadership, 3,* 10–12.

Jacob, B., & Lefgren, L. (2007). What do parents value in education? An empirical investigation of parents' revealed preferences for teachers. *Quarterly Journal of Economics, 122,* 1603–1637.

Jeynes, W. (2005). A meta-analysis of the relation of parental involvement to urban elementary school student academic achievement. *Urban Education, 40,* 237–269.

Jeynes, W. (2007). The relationship between parental involvement and urban secondary school student academic achievement: A meta-analysis. *Urban Education, 42,* 82–110.

Johnson, R. S. (2002). *Using data to close the achievement gap: How to measure equity in our schools.* Thousand Oaks, CA: Corwin Press.

Jordan, C., Orozco, E., & Averett, A. (2002). *Emerging issues in school, family and community connections: Annual synthesis 2001.* Austin, TX: Southwest Educational Development Laboratory.

Kao, G., & Rutherford, L. T. (2007). Does social capital still matter? Immigrant minority disadvantage in school-specific social capital and its effects on academic achievement. *Sociological Perspectives, 50,* 27–52.

Kitson, G. C., & Morgan, L. A. (1990). The multiple consequences of divorce: A decade in review. *Journal of Marriage and the Family, 52,* 913–924.

Klein, S., Bugarin, R., Beltranena, R., & McArthur, E. (2004). *Language minorities and their educational and labor market indicators—Recent trends* (NCES 2004–009). U.S. Department of Education. Washington, DC: National Center for Education Statistics.

Kumpfer, K. L., & Alvarado, R. (2003). Family strengthening approaches for the prevention of youth problem behaviors. *American Psychologist, 58,* 457–465.

Lareau, A. (1987). Social class differences in family-school relationships: The importance of cultural capital. *Sociology of Education, 60,* 73–85.

Lareau, A. (2003). *Unequal childhoods: Class, race, and family life.* Berkeley: University of California Press.

Lareau, A., & Horvat, E. (1999). Moments of social inclusion: Race, class and cultural capital in family school relationships. *Sociology of Education, 71,* 39–56.

Lareau, A., & Shumar, W. (1996). An excessive emphasis on individualism: Formulation of policy in education. *Sociology of Education* (Special Issue), 24–39.

Lee, M. Y., & Grover, C. L. (2006). Effective intervening with students from single-parent families and their parents. In C. Franklin, M.B. Harris, & P. Allen-Meares (Eds.), *The school services sourcebook: A guide for school-based professionals* (pp. 705–716). New York: Oxford University Press.

Lightfoot, S. L. (1977). Family-school interactions: The cultural image of mothers and teachers. *Signs, 3,* 395–408.

Lombardi, J. (1992). Beyond transition: Ensuring continuity in early childhood services. *ERIC Digest* [Online]. Available: http://ceep.crc.uiuc.edu/eecearchive/digests /1992/lombar92.html

Lucas, T., Henze, R., & Donato, R. (1990). Promoting the success of Latino language-minority students: An exploratory study of six high schools. *Harvard Educational Review, 60,* 315–340.

Marcias, J. (1987). The hidden curriculum of Papago teachers: American Indian strategies for mitigating cultural discontinuity in early schooling. In G. Spindler & L. Spindler (Eds.), *Interpretive ethnography of education: At home and abroad* (pp. 363–380). Hillsdale, NJ: Erlbaum.

Martin, J. E., Van Dycke, J. U., Christensen, W. R., Greene, B. A., Gardner, J. E., & Lovett, D. L. (2006). Increasing student participation in IEP meetings: Establishing the self-directed IEP as an evidenced-based practice. *Exceptional Children, 72,* 299–316.

Mashburn, A. J., Pianta, R. C., Hamre, B. K., Downer, J. T., Barbarin, O., Bryant, D., et al. (2008). Measures of classroom quality in prekindergarten and children's development of academic, language, and social skills. *Child Development, 79,* 732–749.

McBride, B. A., & Mills, G. (1993). A comparison of mother and father involvement with their preschool age children. *Early Childhood Research Quarterly, 8,* 457–477.

McDermott, D. (2008). *Developing caring relationships among parents, children, schools and communities.* Thousand Oaks, CA: Sage.

McLanahan, S., & Booth, K. (1989). Mother-only families: Problems, prospects, and politics. *Journal of Marriage and the Family, 51,* 557–580.

McWayne, C., Hampton, V., Fantuzzo, J., Cohen, H. L., & Sekino, Y. (2004). A multivariate examination of parent involvement and the social and academic competencies of urban kindergarten children. *Psychology in the Schools, 41,* 363–377.

Mercado, C., & Moll, L. (2000). Student agency through collaborative research in puerto Rican communities. In S. Nieto (Ed.), *Puerto Rican students in U.S. schools* (pp. 297–329). Mahwah, NJ: Erlbaum.

Morrison, F., & Cooney, R. (2002). Parenting and academic achievement: Multiple paths to early literacy. In J. Borkowski, S. Ramey Landesman, & M. Bristol-Power (Eds.), *Parenting and the children's world: Influences on academic, intellectual, and social-emotional development* (pp. 141–160). Mahwah, NJ: Erlbaum.

Murdock, T. B., & Miller, A. (2003). Teachers as sources of middle school students' motivational identity: Variable-centered and person-centered analytic approaches. *The Elementary School Journal, 103,* 383–399.

Murray, C. B., & Mandara, J. (2003). An assessment of the relationship between racial socialization, racial identity and self-esteem in African American adolescents. In D. A. Azibo (Ed.), *African-centered psychology* (pp. 293–325). Durham, NC: Carolina Academic Press.

Myers, S. S., & Pianta, R. C. (2008). Developmental commentary: Individual and contextual influences on student-teacher relationships and children's early problem behaviors. *Journal of Clinical Child &Adolescent Psychology, 37,* 600–608.

National Center for Education Statistics. (2000). *The kindergarten year.* Washington, DC: Author.

National Center for Education Statistics. (2002). *Children's reading and mathematics achievement in kindergarten and first grade.* Washington, DC: Author.

National Institute of Child Health and Human Development Early Child Care Research Network. (2003). Social functioning in first grade: Associations with earlier home and child care predictors and with current classroom experiences. *Child Development, 74,* 1639–1662.

National Institute of Child Health and Human Development Early Child Care Research Network & Duncan, G. J. (2003). Modeling the impacts of child care quality on children's preschool cognitive development. *Child Development, 74,* 1454–1475.

Nickerson, A., & Nagle, R. (2005). Parent and peer attachment in late childhood and early adolescence. *Journal of Early Adolescence, 25,* 223–249.

Nieto, S. (1996). *Affirming diversity: The sociopolitical context of multicultural education.* White Plains, NY: Longman.

Nieto, S. (2002). *Language, culture, and teaching: Critical perspectives for a new century.* Mahwah, NJ: Erlbaum.

No Child Left Behind Act of 2001, Pub. L.117-110, 115 Stat. 1425 (2002). Retrieved August 1, 2008, from http://www.ed.gov/policy/elsec/leg/esea02/107-110.pdf

Oman, R. F., McLeroy, K. R., Versely, S., Aspy, C. B., Smith, D. W., & Penn, D. A. (2002). An adolescent age group approach to examining youth risk behaviors. *American Journal of Health Promotion, 16,* 167–176.

Pelco, L. E., & Ries, R. R. (1999). Teachers' attitudes and behaviors towards family-school partnerships: What school psychologists need to know. *School Psychology International, 20,* 265–277.

Pellegrini, A. D., & Blatchford, P. (2000). *The child at school: Interactions with peers and teachers.* London: Arnold.

Perry, L., & McWilliam, E. (2007). Accountability, responsibility, and school leadership. *Journal of Educational Inquiry, 7,* 32–43.

Phtiaka, H. (1999). *Teacher, tutor, parent: The eternal triangle.* Paper presented at the European Research Network About Parents in Education, Amsterdam, October, 1999.

Pianta, R. C., & Walsh, D. J. (1996). *High risk children in the schools: Creating sustaining relationships.* New York: Routledge.

Pianta, R. C., & Walsh, D. J. (1998). Applying the construct of resilience in schools: Cautions from a developmental systems perspective. *School Psychology Review, 27,* 407–417.

Pigott, R. L., & Cowen, E. (2000). Teacher race, child race, racial congruence, and teacher ratings of children's school adjustment. *Journal of School Psychology, 38*, 177–195.

Piotrkowski, C. S., Botsko, M., & Matthews, E. (2000). Parents' and teachers' beliefs about children's school readiness in a high-need community. *Early Childhood Research Quarterly, 15*, 537–558.

Radcliffe, B., Malone, M., & Nathan, J. (1994). *Training for parent partnership: Much more should be done*. Minneapolis: University of Minnesota, Hubert H. Humphrey Institute of Public Affairs, Center for School Change.

Ranson, S., Martin, J., & Vincent, C. (2004). Storming parents, schools and communicative inaction. *British Journal of Sociology of Education, 25*, 259–274.

Reynolds, A., & Clements, M. (2005). Parental involvement and children's school success. In E. N. Patrikakou, R. P. Weissberg, S. Redding, H. J. Walberg, & A. R. Anderson (Eds.), *School-family partnerships: Promoting the social, emotional, and academic growth of children*. New York: Teachers College Press.

Reynolds, G. P., Wright, J. V., & Beale, B. (2003). The roles of grandparents in educating today's children. *Journal of Instructional Psychology, 30*, 316–326.

Rimm-Kaufman, S. E., & Zhang, Y. (2005). Father-school communication in preschool and kindergarten. *School Psychology Review, 34*, 287–308.

Rimm-Kaufman, S. E., & Pianta, R. C. (2000). An ecological perspective on the transition to kindergarten: A theoretical framework to guide empirical research. *Journal of Applied Developmental Psychology, 21*, 491–511.

Rodriguez-Srednicki, O. (2002). The custodial grandparent phenomenon: A challenge to schools and school psychology. *NASP Communique, 3*(1), 41–42.

Rothbart, M. K., & Bates, J. E. (1998). Temperament. In W. Damon (Series Ed.) & N. Eisenberg (Vol. Ed.), *Handbook of child psychology: Vol. 3. Social, emotional, and personality development* (5th ed., pp. 105–176). New York: Wiley.

Rowan, B., Correnti, R., & Miller, R. J. (2002). What large scale, survey research tells us about teacher effects on student achievement: Insights from the Prospects study of elementary schools. *Teachers College Record, 104*, 1525–1567.

Sameroff, A. J. (1995). General systems theories and developmental psychopathology. In D. Cichetti & D. Cohen (Eds.), *Developmental psychopathology: Theory and methods* (pp. 659–695). New York: Wiley.

Sameroff, A. J., & Emde, R. N. (1989). *Relationship disturbances in early childhood: A developmental approach*. New York: Basic Books.

Sameroff, A. J., Seifer, R., Baldwin, A., & Baldwin, C. (1993). Stability of intelligence from preschool to adolescence: The influence of social and family risk factors. *Child Development, 64*, 80–97.

Sanders, W., & Rivers, J. (1996). *Cumulative and residual effects of teachers on future student academic achievement*. Knoxville: University of Tennessee Value-added Research and Assessment Center.

Seginer, R. (2006). Parents' educational involvement: A developmental ecology perspective. *Parenting: Science and Practice, 6*, 1–48.

Shartrand, A. M., Weiss, H. B., Kreider, H. M., & Lopez, M. E. (1997). *New skills for new schools: Preparing teachers in family involvement*. Cambridge, MA: Harvard Family Research Project.

Sheldon, S. B. (2007). Improving student attendance with school, family, and community partnerships. *Journal of Educational Research, 100*, 267–275.

Sheridan, S., Beebe-Frankenberger, M., Greff, K., Lasser, J., Lines, C., Miller, G., et al.. (2007). Back to the future: The Futures Task Force on family-school partnerships. *NASP Communique, 36*, 17–18.

Sheridan, S. M., Clarke, B. L., Knoche, L. L., & Edwards, C. P. (2006). The effects of conjoint behavioral consultation in early childhood settings. *Early Education and Development, 17*, 593–618.

Simon, B. S. (2004). High school outreach and family involvement. *Social Psychology of Education, 7*, 185–209.

Sipple, J., & Banach, L. (2006). Helping schools meet the mandates of federal policies: No Child Left Behind and other cutting edge federal policies. In C. Franklin, M. B. Harris, & P. Allen-Meares (Eds.), *The school services sourcebook: A guide for school-based professionals* (pp. 873–882). New York: Oxford University Press.

Sirin, S. R. (2005). Socioeconomic status and academic achievement: A meta-analytic review of research. *Review of Educational Research, 75*, 417–453.

Souto-Manning, M., & Swick, K. (2006). Teachers' beliefs about parent involvement: Rethinking our family involvement paradigm. *Early Childhood Education Journal, 34*, 187–193.

Stritikus, T. T., & Garcia, E. (2005). Revisiting the bilingual debate from the perspective of parents: Policy, practice, and matches or mismatches. *Education Policy, 19*, 729–744.

Sui-Chu, E. H., & Willms, J. D. (1996). Effects of parental involvement on eighth grade achievement. *Sociology of Education, 69*, 126–141.

Swick, K. (2004). *Empowering parents, families, schools, and communities during the early childhood years.* Champaign, IL: Stipes.

Terrion, J. L. (2006). Building social capital in vulnerable families: Success markers of a school-based intervention program. *Youth and Society, 38,* 155–176.

Tett, L. (2001). Parents as problems or parents as people? Parental involvement programmes, schools and adult educators. *International Journal of Lifelong Education, 20,* 188–198.

Thomas, W. P., & Collier, V. P. (2002). *A national study of school effectiveness for language minority students' long-term academic achievement.* Santa Cruz, CA and Washington, DC: Center for Research on Education, Diversity & Excellence.

Thompson, R. A. (2006). The development of the person: Social understanding, relationships, self, conscience. In W. Damon & R. M. Lerner (Series Eds.), N. Eisenberg (Vol. Ed.), *Handbook of child psychology (6th ed.): Vol. 3. Social, emotional, and personality development* (pp. 24–98). New York: Wiley.

Tinkler, B. (2002). *A review of literature on Hispanic/Latino parent involvement in K-12 education.* Retrieved October 9, 2005, from http://www.coe.uga.edu/clase/Ed_Resources/latinoparentreport.pdf

U.S. Census Bureau (2007a). *Living arrangements of children under 18 years and marital status of parents, by age, gender, race, and Hispanic origin of the child for all children: 2007.* Washington, DC: U.S. Department of Commerce, Economics, and Statistic Administration, U.S. Census Bureau.

U.S. Census Bureau (2007b). *Annual estimates of the Hispanic origin population by sex and age for the United States: April 1, 2000 to July 1, 2007.* [NC-EST2007-04-HISP] Washington, DC: U.S. Department of Commerce, Economics, and Statistic Administration, U.S. Census Bureau.

Van Voorhis, F. L. (2003). Interactive homework in middle school: Effects on family involvement and students' science achievement. *Journal of Educational Research, 9,* 23–39.

Vernberg, E. M., & Medway, F. J. (1981). Teacher and parent causal perceptions of school problems. *American Educational Research Journal, 18,* 29–37.

Violand-Sanchez, E., Sutton, C., & Ware, H. (1991, Summer). *Fostering home-school cooperation: Involving minority families as partners in education.* Washington, DC: The National Clearinghouse for Bilingual Education, Program Information Guide Series.

Vygotsky, L. S. (1987). Thinking and speech. In R. W. Reiber & A. S. Carton (Eds.), *The collected works of L.S.Vygotsky. Vol. 1: Problems of general psychology* (pp. 37–285). New York: Plenum.

Walker, J. M. T., & Hoover-Dempsey, K. V. (2006). Why Research on Parental Involvement Is Important to Classroom Management. In C. Evertson & C. Weinstein (Eds.), *Handbook of classroom management: Research, practice, and contemporary issues* (pp. 665–684). Mahwah, NJ: Erlbaum.

West-Olatunji, C. (2008). Equal Access, Unequal resources: Appreciating cultural, social and economic diversity in families. In E. Amatea (Ed.), *Building culturally responsive family-school partnerships: From theory to practice* (pp. 144–168). Upper Saddle River, NJ: Merrill.

West, J., Germino-Hausken, E., & Collins, M. (1993). *Readiness for kindergarten: Parent and teacher beliefs.* Washington, DC: U.S. Department of Education, NCES.

Wong, S. W., & Hughes, J. N. (2006). Ethnicity and language contributions to dimensions of parent involvement. *School Psychology Review, 35,* 645–662.

# 2

## MOTIVATION AND COMMITMENT TO FAMILY-SCHOOL PARTNERSHIPS

KATHLEEN V. HOOVER-DEMPSEY, MANYA C. WHITAKER,
AND CHRISTA L. ICE

Although parents' and families' motivations for becoming involved in their children's and adolescents' education have often been assumed as schools plan varied family-school events in support of student learning, parents' motivations for involvement have also become the focus of explicit attention as many communities have sought increasingly to develop home-school partnerships that promise on-going, student-specific support for *all* child and adolescent learning. Rooted in understanding that families' hopes for children's educational success are generally quite strong across varied communities, many educators' attention has focused increasingly on tapping the full array of family motivations for becoming actively engaged (at home, at school, and/or in the community) in supporting their students' learning.

Grounded in a theoretical model of the parental involvement process and ecological-systems theory, this chapter examines the interrelated issues of motivation and commitment to effective family engagement in children's learning. Because the development of successful parental involvement and family-school partnerships involves *both* family and school, the discussion focuses on variables that motivate members of both systems to become actively engaged in supporting productive family-school relationships. After a brief review of evidence on parental involvement's influence on students' educational success (*Why* is parental involvement is so important for students' and schools' success?), theoretical and empirical insights into the parental involvement process are examined, especially as related to parents' motivations for becoming involved in their students' school learning (What *motivates parents* to become actively involved in their children's education?). Findings in both areas are then applied to the task of understanding school system members' motivations for actively enabling and supporting productive family involvement (What *motivates school system members* to develop effective family-school partnerships in support of student learning?). Finally, guided by principles from ecological-systems theory, the chapter concludes with consideration of variables underlying family and school systems' development of *commitment* to building and sustaining the interactive family-school partnerships that are often essential to students' school success.

## *WHY* IS PARENTAL INVOLVEMENT IMPORTANT TO STUDENTS' SCHOOL SUCCESS?

An increasingly sophisticated body of research suggests that parental involvement in students' education, pre-kindergarten through secondary school, offers critically important contributions to student learning. Consistent with Bandura's (1986, 1997) observation that individuals and systems tend to invest energy and time in those activities they believe are important in reaching valued personal, group, and community goals, a brief review of relevant research suggests that families' active involvement in their students' education across childhood and adolescence is indeed generally associated with students' development and use of personal attributes and skills that are essential to successful school learning (e.g., Caspe, Lopez, & Wolos, 2006/2007; Fan & Chen, 2001; Gonzalez-DeHass, Willems, & Doan Holbein, 2005; Henderson & Mapp, 2002; Hoover-Dempsey et al., 2005; Jeynes, 2003, 2005, 2007; Kreider, Caspe, Kennedy, & Weiss, 2007; Senechal & LaFevre, 2002; Weiss, Caspe, & Lopez, 2006). Importantly, these findings generally pertain to students across ethnic, cultural, and socioeconomic groups. Families across these demographically defined groups may vary in preferences and opportunities for specific forms of involvement (e.g., home-based, school-based, community-based), and may vary as well in the learning mechanisms they choose to engage in the course of involvement activities (e.g., expressing personal, familial, and cultural expectations for the student's learning; encouraging students' engagement and persistence during work on learning tasks; modeling attitudes, beliefs, skills and behaviors important to successful learning; reinforcing students' learning efforts and accomplishments; offering instructional support, consistent with parents' own knowledge, for students' work on school assignments). Families across demographically defined groups may also vary in the culturally grounded meanings they draw from participation in their children's education. Across such variations, however, this body of research suggests strongly that students' educational success is enhanced when families are actively engaged in offering developmentally appropriate support for student learning (e.g., Caspe et al., 2006/2007; Clark, 1983; Delgado-Gaitan, 1992; Gonzalez, Doan Holbein, & Quilter, 2002; Grolnick, Kurowski, Dunlap, & Hevey, 2000; Henderson & Mapp, 2002; Hoover-Dempsey et al., 2005; Jeynes, 2003; Kreider et al., 2007; Meidel & Reynolds, 1999). This evidence is briefly reviewed below in three major areas: the development of student learning attributes and behaviors that support school success, the enhancement of student learning as reflected in summary measures of school learning and achievement, and the enhancement of longer-term outcomes that depend in part on students' successful school learning.

### *The Development of Student Learning Attributes and Behaviors that Support School Success*

Several student attributes and behaviors that support learning have been identified in the research literature as often critical to students' school success. These include attributes related students' beliefs and attitudes about education, beliefs about oneself as a learner, knowledge and use of self-regulatory strategies for learning, and behaviors engaged in the course of learning tasks at school and at home.

## Student Beliefs and Attitudes about Education

Research on parental involvement across the full range of elementary, middle, and secondary education has suggested that family engagement in students' education—particularly as it focuses on encouragement, praise, and assertion of parents' valuing of education—is consistently linked to positive student attitudes about school and learning as well as attitudes about spending effort on school tasks (e.g., Cooper, Lindsay, Nye, & Greathouse, 1998; Gonzalez-DeHass et al., 2005; Marchant, Paulson, & Rothlisberg, 2001; Sanders, 1998; Trusty, 1999). In particular, parents' active support of student efforts and activities related to school tasks have been positively linked to students' work orientation (e.g., Steinberg, Elmen, & Mounts, 1989), interest in school work (e.g., Koskinen et al., 2000), positive mood while engaged in school work (Leone & Richards, 1989), and intrinsic motivation for school work; the latter is especially true when parental involvement includes encouragement and praise for student effort during learning activities as well as learning outcomes (e.g., Ginsberg & Bronstein, 1993; Gonzalez-DeHass et al., 2005; Marchant et al., 2001). Others have identified positive relationships between parental involvement and students' longer-term educational aspirations, which may be particularly important as internalized goals that support student effort on learning tasks through the elementary and secondary years (e.g., Gonzalez-DeHass et al., 2005, Paulson, 1994; Steinberg, Lamborn, Dornbusch, & Darling, 1992).

## Student Beliefs about Oneself as Learner

Investigators have also identified parent attitudes about education and involvement practices as important contributors to students' beliefs about their own learning abilities. These student beliefs include personal assumptions about one's ability to learn and succeed in school tasks, including a positive sense of efficacy for learning and a sense of personal competence in school tasks (e.g., Bandura, Barbaranelli, Caprara, & Pastorelli, 1996; Fantuzzo, Davis, & Ginsberg, 1995; Frome & Eccles, 1998; Ginsberg & Bronstein, 1993; Hoover-Dempsey et al., 2005; Sanders, 1998; Shumow, 1998), as well as a mastery orientation toward learning (Ginsberg & Bronstein, 1993; Gonzalez et al., 2002; Hoover-Dempsey et al., 2001). Others have reported strong connections between positive parental involvement practices and students' perception of personal control over school and learning outcomes (i.e., students' understanding that their own work and effort is a cause of successful learning: e.g., Glasgow, Dornbusch, Troyer, Steinberg, & Ritter, 1997; Grolnick & Slowiaczek, 1994).

## Student Knowledge and Use of Self-Regulatory Strategies for Successful Learning

Students' knowledge and use of self-regulatory strategies are particularly important to school success because they enable students to: monitor their own progress on learning tasks, identify needs for different learning strategies as appropriate for different tasks, identify points at which learning will be best served by accessing others' help and guidance, and assume personal responsibility for one's own learning (e.g., Martinez-Pons, 1996; Schunk & Zimmerman, 2003; Stipek & Gralinski, 1996). These self-regulatory skills are critical targets of parental involvement because they are subject to parental influence (e.g., Brody, Flor, & Gibson, 1999; Grolnick & Ryan, 1989) and they are important to student's school learning (e.g., Brody et al., 1999; Grolnick & Slowiaczek, 1994; Hoover-Dempsey et al., 2001; Xu & Corno, 2003; Zimmerman, 1986; Zimmerman & Martinez-Pons, 1990).

## Student Behavior during Learning Tasks

Successful school learning generally requires students' active engagement in the work at hand, a skill and attribute well supported by parental involvement. Specific indicators identified and examined in the literature include active participation in school tasks, effective work habits, on-task behavior, focused attention to the requirements of specific learning tasks, adaptation to changing needs and expectations across assignments, and tolerance for frustration in the process of completing assignments (e.g., Fantuzzo et al., 1995; Gonzalez-DeHass et al., 2005; Grolnick et al., 2000; Izzo, Weissberg, Kasprow, & Fendrich, 1999; Sanders, 1998; Sheldon & Epstein, 2005 Shumow, 1998; Steinberg et al., 1992). Students homework behavior and success have also been positively linked to parental involvement in supporting student learning, particularly as parents offer specific support for attending to homework, developing a personal sense of responsibility for homework performance, engaging in effective work habits, enjoyment of homework tasks, completion of homework, and strength of homework performance overall (e.g., Balli, Demo, & Wedman, 1998; Callahan, Rademacher, & Hildreth, 1998; Cooper et al., 1998; Hoover-Dempsey et al., 2001; Hutsinger, Jose, & Larson, 1998; Shumow, 1998; Xu & Corno, 1998). Families' involvement has also been identified as quite important to students' development of several social skills that support learning, such as accessing adult or knowledgeable peer help as needed and engaging appropriately with peers during learning tasks and other school activities (e.g., Conduct Problems Prevention Research Group, 2004; McWayne, Hampton, Fantuzzo, Cohen, & Sekino, 2004; Webster-Stratton, Reid, & Hammond, 2004).

## Summary: Student Learning Attributes and Behaviors

Research suggests that effective parental involvement in student education supports several student beliefs (e.g., about the importance of education, about oneself as a learner) and behaviors (e.g., the use of effective self-regulatory strategies during learning processes, effective engagement in current learning tasks) essential to students' school success. Our work has suggested that parents' and families' most important contributions to their students' educational success may be found precisely in their explicit support of such learning-related beliefs and behaviors (e.g., Hoover-Dempsey et al., 2005; see also Deci & Ryan, 1985; Grolnick, Kurowski, & Gurland, 1999; Grolnick, Ryan, & Deci, 1991). These proximal outcomes of parental involvement (i.e., the development of student learning attributes and skills that are used by students in the course of varied school learning tasks) are particularly important targets for parental involvement and family-school partnerships because they are subject to parental influence and are closely linked to students' performance on distal, summary measures of school achievement.

## The Development of Student Learning and Knowledge as Assessed by Summary Measures of Achievement

Parent and family involvement in supporting child and adolescent school learning has also been related to student performance on several summary measures of school achievement. Such summary measures have included: teacher ratings of overall student performance and competence; grades as assigned over varied periods of time (e.g., progress reports, report cards); grade point averages; and standardized measures of achievement in varied subjects including but not limited to reading, mathematics, science, and writing skills (e.g., Caspe et al., 2006/2007; Deslandes, Royer, Potvin, & Leclerc, 1999; Englund, Luckner, Whaley, & Egeland, 2004; Epstein & Van Voorhis, 2001; Fan & Chen, 2001; Gonzalez-DeHass et al., 2005; Gutman & Midgely, 2000; Henderson & Mapp, 2002; Hill & Craft, 2003; Hoover-Dempsey et al., 2005; Jeynes, 2003, 2005, 2007; Kreider et al., 2007; Meidel & Reynolds, 1999; Senechal & LeFevre, 2002; Sheldon, 2002). Across varied studies and reviews, findings have suggested that students whose parents are more involved in activities that support their learning skills generally record stronger achievement on summary indicators of school learning than is true for peers whose parents are less involved.

These findings for student performance on summary measures of achievement are quite important to contemporary community understanding of students' and schools' success in accomplishing the publicly and politically valued goals of education in this culture. However, it is quite likely that student performance on such summary indicators of achievement are more distally related to family involvement practices than are more proximal student learning attributes, such as those reviewed above, which students *use*—once developed—in support of school learning and performance. Thus, it seems quite likely also that the most direct and proximal links between family involvement and students' school success are to be found in parents' nurturance, support and teaching of positive attitudes toward schooling, positive beliefs about oneself as learner, knowledge and use of self-regulatory strategies during learning activities, and the development and use of varied other behaviors that offer and enable on-going support for students' academic performance and achievement.

## The Enhancement of Education-Related Outcomes across Childhood, Adolescence, and Adulthood

Parental and family involvement in supporting children's school learning has also been related to longer-term indicators of educational and personal accomplishment. Many such findings have emerged in long-term follow-up of students and families enrolled in early intervention efforts designed to enhance the school success of students growing up in very poor communities or neighborhoods. Many of these programs have included a strong emphasis on varied approaches to supporting parents' active involvement supporting their children's learning. The High/Scope Perry Preschool Project, for example, focused in part on empowering parents "by involving them as *partners with teachers* in supporting their children's development" (Schweinhart, 1994, p. 3, emphasis added). Others have focused on parental involvement at varied points in students' school careers and have examined specific long-term markers of students' educational success.

Findings in general have suggested that active parental involvement in and support of students' school learning—even if concentrated primarily in the early years of schooling—is related to varied longer-term indicators of students' school success and adult accomplishment achieved in part through successful school learning. For example, long-term comparisons of students involved in early interventions and their control group counterparts have suggested that students whose parents were actively involved in supporting their learning have generally recorded lower levels of retention in grade, referrals for special education services, and drop-out rates, as well as stronger literacy, more successful transitions from one level of schooling to the next (e.g., elementary to middle school), and higher rates of on-time graduation from high school (e.g., Barnard, 2004; Dearing, Kreider, Simpkins, & Weiss, 2006; Gray, Ramsey, & Klaus, 1983; Meidel & Reynolds, 1999; Schweinhart, 1994; Schweinhart, Barnes, & Weikart, 1993; Trusty, 1999). Other findings have identified even longer term benefits to participation in early intervention programs with an explicit focus on parental involvement, including lower rates of adolescent pregnancy, higher likelihood of attending four-year colleges, stronger cognitive skills in adulthood, higher rates of employment, better paying jobs, higher rates of home ownership, and lower rates of criminal behavior in adulthood (Campbell, Ramey, Pungello, Sparling, & Miller-Johnson, 2002; Schweinhart, 1994; Schweinhart et al., 1993, 2005).

While such long-term benefits to active parental engagement in children's schooling may appear beyond the realm of immediate concern to many schools serving children, the findings underscore the importance of developing and supporting home-school collaboration early in children's education, perhaps especially for children at risk of poor educational outcomes (e.g., Campbell et al., 2004; Dearing et al., 2006; Dearing, McCartney, Weiss, Kreider, & Simpkins, 2004; see also Englund et al., 2004). The findings also underscore the on-going importance of family-school *partnerships* to students' successful learning and subsequent achievements. Many community and societal goals for children's and adolescents' education focus on assumptions that schooling will enable students to gain the personal, cognitive, and social understandings essential to successful individual development and to productive participation in the community across childhood, adolescence and adulthood. Findings that productive family engagement in student learning supports such long-term benefits offers additional context for understanding the importance of effective family-school relationships to students' educational success.

Given the links between effective parental involvement and a wide range of socially valued student learning attributes and outcomes, how might school systems enhance the effectiveness of parental involvement and family-school relationships? Responses are grounded not only in systemic understanding of family involvement's contributions to students' school success, but also in systemic understanding of variables central to parents' motivations for becoming involved in their students' education. Understanding what motivates families to become actively involved in supporting their students' learning is critical to *schools'* success in engaging and supporting parental involvement. It also suggests important insights into school system members' motivations for actively inviting, supporting and engaging family participation in family-school partnerships.

## THE ORIGINS OF MOTIVATION AND COMMITMENT TO EFFECTIVE PARENTAL INVOLVEMENT AND FAMILY-SCHOOL PARTNERSHIPS

As suggested in much of the research reviewed above, varied investigators have offered perspectives on elements of effective family-school partnerships that support students' school success. Several programs of research in recent decades have also offered information important to understanding more fully the origins and consequences of parental involvement and family-school partnerships as essential elements in successful schooling for all students.

Epstein and her colleagues, for example, have offered an influential body of work focused on the teacher, school, and community supports that enable varied forms of family involvement in children's education, from early childhood through adolescence (e.g., Epstein, 1983, 1986; Epstein, Sanders, Simon, Salinas, & Jansorn, 2002; Epstein & Van Voorhis, 2001; Sheldon & Epstein, 2005). The work has pointed repeatedly to the critical role of teacher practices and attitudes in encouraging and motivating parents' active engagement in student learning (e.g., Epstein, 1986; Epstein & Van Voorhis, 2001). The work has also suggested strongly that parent and family contributions to student learning take many different forms (i.e., there is not only one way or one right way to be involved; see also Christenson, 2004).

This principle is well reflected in Epstein's widely used categorical description of involvement (e.g., Epstein et al., 2002; Sheldon & Epstein, 2005). The typology incorporates the basic responsibilities of families and schools for students' educational success. Families, for example, have basic responsibilities to offer parenting practices consistent with student learning and a home environment supportive of student learning; schools should have basic responsibilities for communicating with families about students' school work and engaging in two-way exchanges about student learning.

The four remaining categories of family involvement included in Epstein's typology include: parental help and support at home for student learning; family members' engagement in volunteer work that supports the school and its students' learning; parents' participation as partners in varied domains of school decision-making; and family members' collaboration with varied community organizations in support of schools and student learning (e.g., Epstein et al., 2002; Sheldon & Epstein, 2005). Although schools have basic responsibilities (see above), they also play very important roles in offering and encouraging parents' involvement in the other four categories of involvement, for example: offering specific suggestions for parents' support of student learning at home; offering and inviting varied and accessible opportunities for involvement in the school; offering specific invitations and well-developed opportunities for parental participation in varied domains of school decision-making; offering specific information and requests related to community support of the school). Consistent with this emphasis on schools' responsibilities for inviting and supporting families' access to and successful engagement in all types of involvement, Epstein and her colleagues have also focused strongly on building school systems' capacities for offering diverse and effective approaches to establishing productive family-school relationships (e.g., Epstein et al., 2002; Epstein & Van Voorhis, 2001; Sheldon & Epstein, 2005).

Grolnick and colleagues' program of research has also enriched understanding of parents' roles in students' schooling, particularly as they influence the development of student motivational attributes important to successful learning. Her work, which has defined parental involvement as "the dedication of resources by the parent to the child" (Grolnick & Slowiaczek, 1994, p. 238), has focused on three broad sets of involvement practices: personal involvement (expressing interest in and enjoyment of interactions with one's children about school learning), cognitive involvement (offering intellectually stimulating activities at home), and behavioral involvement (participating in varied school activities that support student learning).

Grounded in part in self-determination theory (Deci & Ryan, 1985; Grolnick et al., 1991), Grolnick and her colleagues have examined the links between parental involvement and students' development of key motivational attributes. These attributes include students' control understanding (i.e., understanding that one's own actions influence personal success and failure in learning tasks), perceptions of personal competence (the student's belief and understanding that she or he can do those things necessary for learning success), and development of self-regulation (broadly defined as a "sense of autonomy … in which action is experienced as choicefully self-initiated:" Grolnick et al., 2000, p. 468). These motivational attributes are powerful, her work has suggested, because they meet students' developmental needs for autonomy, competence, and relatedness, and because they are essential to students' learning across varied school tasks (e.g., Deci & Ryan, 1985; Grolnick et al., 1999, Grolnick et al., 1991). Grolnick and her colleagues have reported positive links between parental involvement and students' development of these motivational outcomes. These student outcomes (or proximal learning attributes) have, in turn, been positively linked to student performance on varied indices of school success (e.g., successful transition from elementary to junior high school; Grolnick et al., 1999; Grolnick & Slowiaczek, 1994) and to successful performance on summary measures of achievement. Taken together, findings from Grolnick's research program have supported the assertion that parental involvement is critical to students' school success because it contributes to students' development of specific motivational resources, which are, in turn, used by students in support of successful learning.

Hoover-Dempsey and Sandler (1995, 1997), grounded in part on findings reviewed above, suggested a theoretical model of the parental involvement process focused on explaining *why* parents become involved in their children's education and *how* their involvement influences student learning; as revised in subsequent work (Green, Walker, Hoover-Dempsey, & Sandler, 2007; Hoover-Dempsey & Sandler, 2005; Walker, Wilkins, Dallaire, Sandler, & Hoover-Dempsey, 2005), the current model is presented in Figure 2.1. The process delineated in the model begins in parents' motivations for becoming involved, moves through parents' choice of varied involvement forms and use of varied learning mechanisms as they actively support their children's and adolescents'

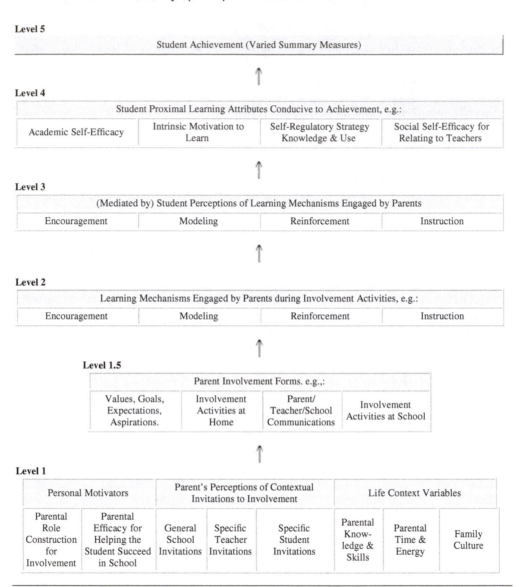

**Figure 2.1** Model of the parental involvement process (adapted from Hoover-Dempsey & Sandler, 1995, 1997, 2005). This figure also appears in Hoover-Dempsey, K. V., Ice, C. L., & Whitaker, M. C. (in press). "We're way past reading together:" Why and how does parental involvement during adolescence make sense? In N. Hill & R. Cha, (Eds.), *Family–school relationships in adolescence: Linking interdisciplinary research*. New York: Teachers College Press.

learning; moves further through a sample of proximal student learning attributes (attitudes, beliefs, skills and behaviors) that are influenced by parents' involvement, and concludes in consideration of the links between student proximal learning outcomes and performance on summary measures of school learning and achievement.

Research findings related to the model's first level, which examines parents' motivations for becoming involved in their students' learning are reviewed briefly below. As noted in Figure 2.1, Level 1, three categories of motivators are included in the model:

*personal motivators* (role construction for involvement; sense of efficacy for helping the student succeed in school); *contextual motivators* (invitations to involvement from three sources: general invitations from the school; specific invitations from the student's teacher(s); specific invitations from the student); and *life context variables*, issues that must be taken into account in order to fully understand and support parents' motivations for becoming involved (parent and family skills, knowledge, time, energy, and family culture).

### Personal Motivators of Parental Involvement

The model suggests that two sets of personal belief systems motivate parents' decisions about becoming actively engaged in supporting their children's education. Parental role construction for involvement includes parents' beliefs about their personal responsibilities for their children's education outcomes, and accompanying ideas about whether, and to what extent, they should be involved the student's school learning. Parental sense of efficacy for helping the child succeed in school includes parents' beliefs about the likelihood that personal involvement in helping their children learn will in fact contribute to students' success in learning and school. Both constructs serve as a primarily personal foundation for parents' answers to these two questions: "Am I supposed to be involved in my child's education?" and "Will my involvement make a difference in my child's learning and school success?" (Hoover-Dempsey & Sandler, 1997; Hoover-Dempsey et al., 2005).

### Parental Role Construction for Involvement in the Student's Education

Role theory (e.g., Biddle, 1979, 1986) suggests that parents' role construction for involvement in their children's schooling is grounded in personal ideas and expectations about one's role as the parent of a student in school, their perceptions of important others' expectations about the role they should play in their children's schooling, and their perceptions of important groups' expectations for parents' behaviors related to children's education. Grounded in these expectations, parents select and enact involvement behaviors they believe are consistent with the expectations. Although considered conceptually to be a personal motivator of involvement, parents' role construction for involvement is also fundamentally socially constructed (i.e., it is created over time from parents' experiences and related understandings of their own and important others' expectations about the roles that parents should play in their children's education: Hoover-Dempsey et al., 2005; see also Auerbach, 2007). Role construction thus is influenced, on an on-going basis, by family, school, and community members important to the parent (e.g., Auerbach, 2007; Chrispeels & Rivero, 2001; Delgado-Gaitan, 1992; Drummond & Stipek, 2004; Scribner, Young, & Pedroza, 1999).

Across varied studies, parental role construction for involvement in children's and adolescents' schooling has been related to or found to predict parents' home-based or school-based involvement across varied levels of schooling (Anderson & Minke, 2007; Deslandes & Bertrand, 2005; Green et al., 2007; Grolnick, Benjet, Kurowski, & Apostoleris, 1997; Sheldon, 2002). Although the part played by role construction in motivating parents' decisions about involvement appears to be somewhat less strong than originally hypothesized by Hoover-Dempsey and Sandler (1995, 1997), research with students and families across varied levels of schooling has suggested that the construct does indeed function as a motivator of parents' involvement practices *and* is subject to social influence from teachers, others in the school, family members and other members of parents' social support systems (Auerbach, 2007; Delgado-Gaitan, 1992; Drummond & Stipek, 2004; Scribner et al., 1999), as well as intervention programs designed to strengthen parents' role beliefs and involvement (Chrispeels & Rivero, 2001).

### Parent's Sense of Efficacy for Helping the Child Succeed in School

Parents' sense of efficacy for helping their children succeed in school is grounded in Bandura's (1997) self-efficacy theory, which suggests that parents guide their choices and actions regarding involvement by considering and evaluating the outcomes they believe will likely follow from their involvement behaviors. These beliefs are focused not so much on parents' skills per se, but on their beliefs about whether engaging these skills will make a difference in students' school outcomes. Parents' sense of self-efficacy for involvement, like role construction, is socially constructed; that is, it is subject to influence by important others, including students, family members, personal social network members, and school system members (e.g., teachers, school staff, principals). In general, it is shaped primarily by personal mastery experiences (e.g., previous successful involvement activity), vicarious mastery experiences (e.g., observing similar others succeed in similar tasks), verbal persuasion from relevant others (e.g., family members, other parents, teachers, other school support staff) and affective arousal regarding the importance of children's school success and parents' potential for contributing to that success (Bandura, 1997).

Bandura's work further suggests that parents with relatively strong self-efficacy for helping the child succeed in school generally set high goals for their own behavior in support of the child's school learning and follow through with those goals; if difficulties arise, they tend to believe that they can—and they most often do—work through those difficulties to achieve success. On the other hand, parents with relatively weak self-efficacy for helping the child succeed tend to doubt their abilities or the usefulness of their involvement, may generally avoid involvement activities, and may give up altogether if challenged by difficulties or failure. Very importantly, sense of efficacy for helping the child succeed in school, like role construction for involvement, is subject to *social construction* or influence by important others, including teachers, family members, social network members, and other members of the school community. As true of role construction, parents' self-efficacy has been positively related to parents' decisions about becoming involved in their children's schooling and learning (Bandura et al., 1996; Eccles & Harold, 1993; Green et al., 2007; Grolnick et al., 1997; Hoover-Dempsey, Bassler, & Brissie, 1992; 2002; Shumow & Lomax, 2002). In some circumstances, efficacy has been related especially to home-based activities, but at times with less strength than predicted by efficacy theory and Bandura's considerable work in the field. Especially given results summarized below for the influence of varied contextual invitations on parents' involvement decisions, it is possible that efficacy's influence is secondary to that of role construction (e.g., "If I believe I'm *supposed* to be involved, I'm likely to make efforts in that direction—especially if encouraged by the child and teacher—even if I have doubts about the potential effectiveness of my efforts"). It may be also be the case that efficacy emerges as a modest contributor when assessed in conjunction with parents' perceptions of child, teacher, and school invitations to involvement. The direct power of those invitations—especially if relatively specific, clear, and accompanied by effective information on *how* to be involved—may outweigh doubts about the likely effectiveness of one's efforts. All in all, the pattern of results to date suggests the importance of supporting efforts that enhance parents' beliefs about their abilities to be specific and important contributors to their children's education simply because efficacy, like role construction, is subject to considerable influence by others and events in the parents' environment.

### Perceptions of Contextual Invitations to Involvement

The fundamental issue within this set of constructs may be summarized in parents' answers to these questions: Does the school want and value my involvement? Does my child's teacher (or do my child's teachers) want and value my involvement? Does my child want or need my involvement? The power of contextual invitations is often quite direct, manifested in explicit expression of requests and specific opportunities for the parent's involvement from the child, the child's teacher(s), and the school in general. They may also be expressed more indirectly, as in the case of well identified and well supported opportunities for the parent's engagement in activities designed to enhance the child's learning (e.g., Chrispeels & Rivero, 2001; Epstein & Dauber, 1991), or as the parent observes the child experiencing difficulty in mastering elements of varied learning tasks (e.g., Pomerantz & Eaton, 2001; Pomerantz, Grolnick & Price, 2005). In many ways, too, contextual invitations contribute to the parent's on-going development of role construction and sense of efficacy for helping the child learn. In short, contextual invitations represent several elements of the environment's contributions to parents' ideas about what they should do in relation to supporting the child's school learning, just as they shape parents' ideas about the importance of their involvement and their beliefs about the likelihood that their involvement will make a positive difference in the student's educational outcomes.

### General Invitations from the School

General invitations for parental involvement from the school are manifested perhaps most importantly in school climate that explicitly welcomes parents' and families' engagement in the school and students' learning. They are manifested also in frequent and specific school invitations to involvement that offer ideas for supporting students' learning at home as well as community-based opportunities for involvement. Such broad school attributes and practices are generally developed through: school management practices and activities that reflect positive regard for families' essential roles in supporting student learning; school-wide practices that offer specific, manageable suggestions for family involvement; and practices that build relationships between schools and families that are grounded in mutual trust and recognition of the roles each plays in ensuring student success (e.g., Adams & Christenson, 2000; Christenson, 2004; Christenson & Sheridan, 2001; Hoover-Dempsey et al., 2005). Comer's work with schools serving predominantly poor and socially marginalized families, for example (e.g., Comer, 1995), has focused strongly on schools' active engagement in developing a welcoming school climate through consistently respectful two-way communication practices, meaningful roles for parents in support of their children's education, and positive feedback on why and how their contributions "make a difference" in student outcomes. Griffith's work, too, has emphasized the importance of school climate for parental involvement. For example, he has reported that schools consistently characterized by parents as welcoming and empowering record more involvement than schools with more limited practices (Griffith, 1998; see also Lopez, Sanchez, & Hamilton, 2000; Scribner et al., 1999). Griffith's work (e.g., 2001) has also underscored the school principal's critical role in creating a positive school climate for parental involvement (e.g., explicit support for the work of teachers, staff and parents, regular visits to classrooms, strong public advocacy for school improvements). While school climate or general invitations to family involvement from the school thus play an important role in supporting parents' active involvement, specific invitations from the teacher and from student appear to play even stronger roles in supporting parental involvement.

### Specific Invitations from the Student's Teacher(s)

Specific invitations from teachers have consistently been identified as important contributors to parents' decisions about involvement in their students' education (e.g., Balli et al., 1998; Dauber & Epstein, 1993; Epstein, 1986; Epstein & Van Voorhis, 2001; Hoover-Dempsey et al., 2001, 2005). Such invitations may be powerful because they respond to many parents' desire for information on how they might be involved, as well as their wish to know of specific activities likely to be most helpful in supporting children's learning (e.g., Epstein & Van Voorhis, 2001; Hoover-Dempsey, Bassler, & Burow, 1995; Hoover-Dempsey et al., 2001). They may draw some of their power, too, from affirmation that parents' participation in school processes is welcome and valued, and from the insights they afford into students' current learning processes and tasks (e.g., Hoover-Dempsey et al., 2005; Patrikakou & Weissberg, 2000; Soodak & Erwin, 2000).

Research on specific teacher invitations has suggested that they play a role in parents' active engagement in student education across the elementary, middle, and secondary school levels (e.g., Anderson & Minke, 2007; Balli et al., 1998 Deslandes & Bertrand, 2005; Green et al., 2007; Simon, 2004), and parents' positive responses to specific invitations from teachers have been linked to increases in student learning and achievement (e.g., Shaver & Walls, 1998; Shumow, 1998; Starkey & Klein, 2000). Specific invitations from the teacher may also contribute to the development of trust within the parent-teacher relationship, an essential component of effective family-school partnerships (Adams & Christenson, 1998, 2000; Christenson, 2004). The fact that some investigators have found teacher invitations more strongly related to parental involvement than either role construction or efficacy (e.g., Anderson & Minke, 2007; Deslandes & Bertrand,

2005; Green et al., 2007) underscores the power of teachers' invitations in engaging parents' active support for their children's learning. To the extent that invitations explicitly reflect teachers' affirmation of the importance of parents' engagement in their children's learning, they likely also offer social-contextual support for the importance of parents' active roles in supporting children's learning. To the extent that they include explicit affirmation of parents' effectiveness in supporting students' learning, explicit teacher invitations may also support the development of parents' beliefs in their own efficacy for helping their children succeed in school.

### Specific Invitations from the Student

Research in developmental psychology suggests that specific child invitations may be powerful in part because parents generally wish to respond well to their children's developmental needs (e.g., Baumrind, 1991) and because they want their children to succeed in school (Hoover-Dempsey et al., 1995; Pomerantz et al., 2005). Other work suggests that children's attributes and characteristics may serve as implicit invitations to parents' engagement in student learning (e.g., Collins, Maccoby, Steinberg, Hetherington, & Bornstein, 2000; Pomerantz et al., 2005). Thus, invitations from their students may be notably effective in encouraging parents' active engagement with their children in support of learning activities. Specific invitations to involvement from the child may emerge in implicit forms, as in parental observations that the child needs help in structuring or engaging in school-related tasks (e.g., Cooper et al., 2000; Pomerantz & Eaton, 2001; Xu & Corno, 1998). They may also emerge, particularly from younger students, in explicit and often specific requests for parental help with schoolwork (e.g., Deslandes & Bertrand, 2005; Hoover-Dempsey et al., 1995). Student invitations may also emerge as a function of teacher planning, prompting, or structuring homework assignments to include parents in specific tasks (e.g., Balli et al., 1998; Gonzalez, Andrade, Civil, & Moll, 2001). Several studies have reported that specific invitations from students play a particularly powerful role in motivating parents' involvement in home-based activities that support learning (Deslandes & Bertrand, 2005; Epstein & Van Voorhis, 2001; Green et al., 2007; Hoover-Dempsey et al., 1995, 2001). Given their power in motivating parents' involvement in students' learning, schools wishing to increase rates and focus of parental home support for learning tasks may do well to examine the effectiveness of school- or teacher-supplied suggestions for support of student homework or increased focus on structuring homework assignments to incorporate specific tasks or points of connection for family response and support.

### Family Life Context Variables

Varied elements of families' lives also influence parents' decisions about becoming involved in their children's education. While personal psychological motivators (role construction, efficacy) and contextual motivators of involvement decisions (general school invitations, specific teacher invitations, and specific student invitations) are often subject to school influence, parents' family life context variables generally lie outside the bounds of direct school influence. They are, however, quite important to parents' involvement decisions, and schools generally must be aware of and responsive to them if they are to succeed in supporting parents' active engagement in their children's school learning.

The model suggests that parents' understanding of their own *skills and knowledge* influences their thinking about the kinds of involvement activities they might reasonably take on. Hoover-Dempsey et al. (1995), for example, reported that parents often referred to their own levels of knowledge and skill in discussing ways in which they help or might help their students with school work. When they believed that students' or teachers' requests for involvement fit their skills, they were generally pleased to help and believed that their responses were likely to contribute to their children's learning. However, if they believed their skills or knowledge were inadequate to the task, they tended to report that their efforts did not succeed or, in some instances, that they sent the student on to another source of possible help (e.g., "Ask Mr. Barber next door; he might know about things like that"; see also Delgado-Gaitan, 1992). The model also suggests that parents' perceptions of the *time and energy* they have available for involvement influence their decisions about involvement. This appears particularly true when parents are constrained by non-negotiable work hours or low levels of alternative support for meeting numerous and varied family obligations (e.g., Garcia Coll et al., 2002; Hoover-Dempsey et al., 1995, 2005; Weiss et al., 2003). In both areas—parents' perceptions of personal skills and knowledge, parents' perceptions of personal time and energy available for involvement—schools' clear and positive responsiveness to varied families' constraints is often critical to parents' decisions about becoming involved. School and teacher efforts to offer clear, specific, and manageable instructions about *how* to be helpful have been successful in supporting parents' direct involvement in varied learning tasks, and school efforts to offer alternative times and locations for important events have been helpful in supporting parents' decisions to participate (e.g., Balli et al., 1998; Comer, 1995; Shumow, 1998).

Similarly, *family culture* may play a significant role in parents' ideas about the ways in which they might and should be involved in supporting their students' learning, as well as the range of responses they might offer when schools request involvement (e.g., Delgado-Gaitan, 1992; Garcia Coll et al., 2002; Hoover-Dempsey et al., 2005; Moll, Amanti, Neff, & Gonzalez, 1992; Murry et al., 2004). For example, families whose cultures have traditionally suggested distal roles for parents in students' formal schooling may experience considerable difficulty initiating involvement practices perceived as inconsistent with familial and cultural expectations. Conversely, families whose cultures expect considerable direct family engagement in initiating and supporting students' formal learning may offer considerably more active engagement than their children's schools expect (or in come cases, prefer).

Taken together, findings for family life context variables suggest strongly that school systems take family life context variables into account as they plan to encourage and offer opportunities for family involvement in students' education (e.g., Epstein et al., 2002; Henderson, Mapp, Johnson, & Davies, 2007; Hoover-Dempsey et al., 2005). For example, offering *specific* information and suggestions for parent support of student work may address some parents' perceived limitations in personal skills or knowledge, as may ensuring that school-family communications are offered in languages appropriate for all families served by the school. Similarly, schools may work quite effectively to create a better fit between parents' work and family obligations, on the one hand, and school-initiated opportunities or events supporting students' learning, on the other (e.g., setting school functions and events at non-standard times; offering events across varied time slots and across school and nearby community settings; offering transportation and care for younger children as needed, incorporating food or potluck meals into family-school events).

Fundamentally, however, the role of family life context variables in shaping families' decisions about their involvement in students' learning underscores the critical importance of school systems' focus on developing effective, communicative, and mutually supportive *relationships* with families served by the system's schools. Often, it is only within the context of such relationships that barriers to many families' active and effective involvement may be understood sufficiently well to enable creation of effective approaches to addressing those barriers. While some barriers (e.g., chronically poor physical or mental health in the family; chronically dangerous conditions in the community) present more challenges than may be effectively addressed by families or schools alone (i.e., in the absence of systemic and other community supports), school responsiveness to families' life circumstances—in the context of active, mutually respectful and trusting family-school relationships—promises important contributions to increased, and increasingly effective, family support for student learning.

### Summary: What Motivates Parents to Become Involved?

Implicit in the model's conceptualization of parents' motivations for involvement is the idea that family members' motivations are in many ways a function of the social systems to which they belong. Thus, the primary personal motivators of involvement (role construction and sense of efficacy for helping the child succeed in school) are influenced by the family and school systems parents experienced during their own school years and they are influenced, probably even more strongly, by their current family systems and by their recent and concurrent experiences in the school systems that their children attend. Parents' experience of major contextual motivators of involvement decisions is grounded in part in the power of current experience to shape parents' beliefs about their ability to be involved and their beliefs about the likely outcomes of their involvement. Schools, as social systems with considerable power to influence parents' involvement decisions, manifest that power in their support for the climate that individual schools create for family involvement and in the support that individual schools receive for generating specific invitations to parental involvement from teachers and, through teachers, from students. Finally, school systems' sensitivity and responsiveness to the influence of parents' life context variables (personal skills, knowledge, time, and energy available for involvement, as well as family culture) on parents' ideas about involvement play a substantial role in shaping parents' current ideas about their ability to engage effectively in supporting their students' learning.

## SCHOOL SYSTEMS' MOTIVATIONS FOR SUPPORTING PARENTAL INVOLVEMENT AND FAMILY-SCHOOL PARTNERSHIPS

Research findings on parents' and families' contributions to students' school success, as well as theory and research on parents' motivations for involvement in their students' education reviewed above, are examined here for their contributions to understanding *school system members' motivations* for supporting parental involvement and family-school partnerships as influential contributors to students' learning success.

### How Does Research on Parental Involvement Inform Understanding of School Members' Motivations for Supporting Family-School Partnerships?

Principles of social-cognitive theory suggest that individuals spend time and energy on goals and activities that they value by evaluating the consequences they believe will follow from their activities (e.g., Bandura, 1997). Thus, members of school systems (teachers, school support staff, principals, district members) are likely to spend time and energy supporting parental involvement and family-school collaboration if they believe their efforts will add value to classroom teaching and further strengthen student learning. This suggests, in turn, that school system members' motivations for supporting parental involvement and family-school partnerships will be strengthened by informed consideration of the evidence that parents' active engagement in student learning supports student attitudes, beliefs, skills, and behaviors that are critical to their learning and school success. Students' development of these proximal student learning attributes (which are directly influenced by families' effective engagement in students' school learning), in turn, offer teachers and schools critical resources for student learning and achievement—for example, students' beliefs that education is important, students' personal belief that "I can do this work," students' development of self-regulatory strategies essential for learning, and students' development of behaviors (e.g., effective work habits) that contribute to learning success.

School members' engagement with such information on a regular basis (e.g., in focused, interactive discussions during school faculty and department meetings) offers several benefits. For one, it gives school members specific information about *why* school-based efforts to support parents' engagement in their students' learning are important, and thus specific reasons to support varied personal and systemic efforts to increase the incidence and effectiveness of parents' active engagement in student learning. Such discussions among school members also offer opportunities to examine the benefits that parent-supported learning attributes bring to students' classroom learning conditions (e.g., increased engagement in classroom instruction, more positive attitudes about school learning, increased skill in seeking help when needed, etc.). They also offer opportunities to focus on benefits to classroom management efforts that may well follow individual students' progress in these areas (e.g., Walker & Hoover-Dempsey, 2006). Such discussions are also likely to be helpful in offering teachers and other school members specific targets toward which family involvement may be directed, a benefit especially helpful when the content of student learning moves beyond family members' expertise.

*How Does Research on Parents' Motivations for Involvement Inform Understanding of School Members' Motivations for Family-School Partnerships?*

Theory and research on parents' motivations for active involvement in student learning offer insight into parallel processes influencing school system members' motivations for actively involving parents and families. In particular, application of this work to understanding the personal and contextual motivators of school system members' support for parental involvement offers useful insight into steps schools might take to improve the development and functioning of family-school collaborations that support student learning.

## Personal Motivators

*Role Construction*   Just as parents' decisions about becoming actively involved in supporting student learning are influenced by their ideas about the roles they are supposed to play in their children's education, so too are school members' ideas about supporting family engagement in student learning influenced by the roles they believe they are expected to enact with students' families. These ideas are shaped by personal experiences of family-school relationships (e.g., Graue, 2005) and perceptions of important others' expectations for the roles one is to play as a member of the school system with reference to family involvement in student learning (e.g., Biddle, 1979, 1986; Hoover-Dempsey & Sandler, 1997). In the context of the generally hierarchical administrative structure that characterizes most workplaces, role theory suggests specifically that system members' ideas about the roles they will or should assume are influenced by the expectations of important others in the system, including those with whom one works most closely in the school and those responsible, at the school and district levels, for supervising and evaluating one's work. If the system's expectations for school member roles and behaviors with students' families are clear and backed by systemic support for those roles and behaviors, system members are more likely to engage in those activities (and seek help as needed) than will be the case if little or no systemic support is forthcoming for members' efforts to develop family-school collaborations in support of student learning.

*Self-Efficacy*   Teachers' sense of self-efficacy for working collaboratively with students' families in support of their learning is strongly influenced by personal beliefs about the likely success of one's efforts in this arena (e.g., Bandura, 1997; Hoover-Dempsey et al., 1992; Hoover-Dempsey, Walker, Jones, & Reed, 2002; Hoover-Dempsey & Sandler, 1997). Consistent with efficacy theory, system members' beliefs about their likely success in working with students' families are influenced most strongly by personal mastery experiences (e.g., preparation for parental involvement followed by successful experiences in the area), vicarious experience (e.g., talking with important and trusted others, observing their successful work with students' families), and, to a lesser degree, verbal persuasion from important others, especially if those others also offer specific support for one's skills and the fit of one's skills with the task of supporting effective parental involvement (e.g., Bandura, 1997; Hoover-Dempsey et al., 2002). Also consistent with self-efficacy theory, system members who believe that they will be successful in family involvement efforts are those most likely to engage in that work, especially if the school and system offer active support for skill development and personal success in the area.

## Contextual Motivators

Just as contextual motivators have been identified as critical to parents' decisions about involvement (e.g., an overtly welcoming school climate, specific invitations from teachers, and specific requests from students), so are contextual motivators important in school system members' decisions to actively invite parents' engagement in supporting their students' learning. Such contextual motivators for system members include system-wide policies, requests, invitations, and resources for members' active engagement in initiating and supporting family involvement; at the school level, they also include the school's clearly stated priorities, practices, requests, and supports for family involvement.

*System-Wide Invitations, Requests, and Support*   Research findings on the influence of school-wide invitations on parents' decisions about involvement suggest the potential power of overt, system-wide support for system members' active engagement in family involvement (e.g., systemic policies and practices that emphasize, expect and support members' active engagement in inviting parental involvement). Such systemic support may include consistent, clear and focused communications regarding the system's commitment to family-school collaboration as a key element of students' learning success (e.g., Goldring, Crowson, Laird, & Berk, 2003; Smrekar, 1996). This may be offered in several different ways, for example, through the system's publications and websites and the system's explicit inclusion of such expectations in hiring policies, evaluation practices, and all public statements of system goals for student learning. Also critical to effective systemic support of schools' and school members' roles in creating effective family-school collaboration is the dedication of systemic resources (e.g., expertise, time, materials) to principals', teachers', and support staff members' development of skills, initiatives and programs pertinent to effective support of family involvement in student learning (see also Epstein et al., 2002; Epstein & Van Voorhis, 2001; Sheldon & Epstein, 2005).

*Specific Invitations from School Leaders*   The systemic parallel for the role of specific teacher invitations in motivating parents' involvement lies in individual schools' efforts to build systemically supported and community-appropriate family involvement practices. Key to implementing such programs at the school level is a committed principal who has consistent support (e.g., knowledge, expertise, time and resources) from the school system for growing family-school collaboration efforts within the school and the community it serves (e.g., Constantino, 2003; Goldring et al., 2003; Ross & Gay, 2006). Similarly, as teacher invitations to involvement draw power from their responsiveness to many families' wish to know *how* they can help their students' learn (e.g., Hoover-Dempsey et al., 1995; see also Frijters, Barron, & Brunello, 2000), so too should specific principal and school-based requests for active teacher and staff engagement in family-school collaborations focus on *how* school members may effectively engage with families. Faculty and staff discussion of family engagement and sharing ideas for effective work in this area are also likely critical components of school-based efforts to support effective family engagement (e.g., Graue, 2005; Hoover-Dempsey et al., 2002).

## The Influence of Life Context Issues

The life context issues that influence parents' motivations for involvement also offer parallel understandings of teachers' and principals' motivations for supporting family-school collaboration. Parents' ideas about ways in which they might be involved in their students' learning are influenced by the fit they perceive between expressed needs, opportunities, and requests for involvement, on the one hand, and their understanding of the knowledge, skills, time and energy they have for involvement, on the other. So too are *school system members'* ideas about how they might support parental involvement often dependent on the fit they perceive between the system's needs and requests for involving families, on the one hand, and their perceptions of the knowledge, skills, time and energy they have to bring to such efforts. Similarly, just as family culture often influences parents' ideas about actively supporting student learning, so too does the culture of a school and the school system influence system members' ideas about whether they should (and can) actively support family engagement in student learning.

*Knowledge, Skills, Time, and Energy*    Consistent with evidence on the role of life context variables in shaping parents' involvement decisions and practices, school system members' beliefs about the adequacy of their knowledge, skills, time, and energy for developing parental involvement are quite likely to influence their thinking about potential personal efforts to support parental involvement and the likely success of those efforts. Thus, observations in the literature suggesting that teachers and principals are often only minimally prepared for engaging effectively in learning-supportive collaborations with students' families (e.g., Constantino, 2003; Graue, 2005; Griffith, 2001; Hoover-Dempsey et al., 2002) suggest that many school system members, on the basis of knowledge and skills alone, are likely to avoid involvement with students' families unless their participation is mandated (e.g., as it generally is for annual parent-teacher conferences). These observations also suggest that the emergence of skilled and productive support from system members for parental involvement is likely to depend in substantial part on system-wide support for effective in-service programming focused on building well-grounded, developmentally appropriate, and community appropriate strategies for effective support of parental involvement and family-school collaboration (see also Epstein et al., 2002; Epstein & Van Voorhis, 2001; Sheldon & Epstein, 2005). Similarly, just as families tend to seek involvement opportunities that fit the time and energy they have or can make available, so too are system members likely to evaluate requests for building and supporting family-school collaborations in light of current and on-going demands for their professional time and energy. System-wide assistance in dealing creatively and effectively with the demands on professional time often associated with effective parental involvement efforts is likely to be required, as is system-wide offering of options and flexibility in regard to specific family-school involvement opportunities.

*Culture*   Finally, just as family culture influences family members' understanding of personal responsibilities for involvement with schools in supporting children's learning, so too is the professional and working culture of a school system quite likely to influence system members' understanding of personal responsibilities for building and sustaining productive family-school relationships. Thus, if school systems are to succeed in enrolling strong support from system members for family-school collaboration, they must make clear—in policies and practices related to hiring, evaluation, community engagement, and, most importantly, **support** for the development of effective family-school relationships—their expectations that system members (particularly principals, teachers, and school staff) will engage actively in developing effective family-school collaborations that offer support for students' learning success.

Grounded in these applications of knowledge about parents' motivations for involvement to understanding school members' motivations for participation in family-school partnerships, discussion turns now to principles of ecological-systems theory that offer perspectives on how family and school *commitment* to family-school partnerships may be developed and sustained.

### How Does Ecological Systems Theory Inform the Development of Commitment to Effective Family-School Partnerships?

Ecological systems theory offers further insight into circumstances that support families and schools in developing partnerships that promise collaborative support—beyond the support available from family or school alone—for students' learning and school success. Several investigators, for example, have suggested that such partnerships are best defined as two (or more) entities or systems holding the shared goal of students' learning success as supported by the interests, perspectives, goals and strengths of each partner (e.g., Christenson, 2004; Epstein et al., 2002). It is with particular focus on family-school partnerships or collaborations that principles of systems theory offer important insights into the development of relationships among participants that are at the core of partnerships' success in offering targeted support for student learning as tailored to the needs of individual students. Selected observations drawn from systems theory are particularly salient in understanding the development of family-school partnerships: relationships within which all participants' observations and goals are respected, where information pertinent to the student's learning success is offered and received, and where plans for each partner's complementary contributions to student learning are made and, following implementation, evaluated and adjusted as needed.

Primary among these principles is the observation that each of the social contexts within which children develop offers unique, and uniquely important, contributions to students' on-going learning and development (e.g., Bronfenbrenner, 1979, 1992; Bronfenbrenner & Morris, 1998; Lawrence-Lightfoot, 2003; Sameroff, 1995). In the United States, as true in many cultures, families generally serve as the primary immediate context for children's development, especially in the early years of life. Indeed, much of young children's success in development is dependent on the knowledge, skills, and sustained nurturance offered by family members. Families' contributions, in turn, are influenced by the wider range of social settings in which their members participate (e.g., neighborhood, work settings, and community institutions, organizations, and programs with which families regularly interact: e.g., Bronfenbrenner, 1992; Ceballo & McLoyd, 2002; Delgado-Gaitan, 1992).

As children develop and move into direct participation in community institutions, particularly schools, their learning and development comes to be influenced directly not only by family members but also by members of other systems in which they participate (e.g., Bronfenbrenner, 1992; Bronfenbrenner & Morris, 1998). Thus, for example, as children enter school, they experience a new context whose purposes focus (as do family purposes) on supporting their development and learning, but from perspectives often unique to schools' specific societal purposes. Schools, for example, typically focus on teaching commonly held elements of knowledge and socialization considered important for all children's learning within the broader society, across variations in family processes, family values and families' cultural identity. School and family thus offer contributions to children's development that have similar purposes (e.g., enhanced student knowledge and competence) and often somewhat unique purposes (e.g., families often focus on developing the child's sense of identity and connection to family, family values, and family culture; schools often focus on developing students' formal knowledge in domains considered by the broader society to be essential not only to individual well-being but to the well-being of the society as a whole).

Ecological systems theory suggests that the full power of each setting's (i.e., family's and school's) contributions to students' development often depends on the development of a collaborative family-school *relationship* that offers support for the shared *and* unique contributions each context offers children's learning and development (e.g., Bronfenbrenner, 1986; Bryk & Schneider, 2002; Caspe & Lopez, 2006; Christenson, 2004; Lawrence-Lightfoot, 2003; Murry et al., 2004). Systems theory thus underscores the importance of both systems' understanding of their complementary contributions to students' learning and development; that is, each setting contributes often unique support for students' learning processes and outcomes, and some of the contributions each offers to students' development are not easily replicated or replaced by the contributions of the other system. Thus, *both* systems' full participation in students' learning processes is often critical to students' learning success (e.g., Caspe & Lopez, 2006; Christenson, 2004; Lawrence-Lightfoot, 2003; Murry et al., 2004; Tseng & Seidman, 2007). This suggests specifically that family-school partnerships are often essential to the full success of each system's efforts to support the learning and development of the children they share for the duration of schooling in this culture. Closely following this principle is the observation that family engagement in students' schooling must offer more than irregular or pro forma contact with school members (contacts that tend to offer few if any opportunities to share information in the context of interactive and ongoing communication between contexts) if students' learning is to be fully supported by family and school.

Systems theory also suggests that the quality of students' experiences within and across family and school contexts (including the complementary contributions of each to student learning and development, as well as their collaborative contributions to students' learning outcomes) will be enhanced to the extent that the family-school relationship is characterized by consistently respectful, informative, and mutually supportive interactions (e.g., Christenson, 2004; Pianta & Walsh, 1998; Tseng & Seidman, 2007). The development of these relational characteristics, in turn, is dependent on a commitment by both members that the interests, purposes, and perspectives of *each* participant are to be heard and seriously considered, a commitment most often supported by building into the relationship ample opportunity for both members' giving *and* receiving information about the student's learning and development (e.g., Bryk & Schneider, 2002; Christenson, 2004; Lawrence-Lightfoot, 2003). Thus, systems theory suggests strongly that positive educational outcomes for children and adolescents' will be enhanced to the extent that family and school members communicate regularly and fully, understand and respect the contributions of each to students' learning and school success, and work toward the goal of mutually supportive interactions that benefit the student's learning and development.

Also critical to the development of effective family-school collaborations is the understanding that both parties experience intimacy and vulnerability as they share information about the student and the student's learning processes, needs, and progress. These qualities are present because both sets of participants are often personally invested in the student's development and learning success (e.g., Bryk & Schneider, 2002). Parents and families are generally so invested because the student's learning success—and the lifetime opportunities and accomplishments it may enable—are often central to families' goals and hopes for their children's lives. School system members are generally so invested because the effectiveness of their professional functioning is often measured and judged by the learning achievements of the students they teach.

The issue of vulnerability within the family-school relationship is often especially salient for parents and families when the home-school relationship is characterized by power differentials (e.g., Bryk & Schneider, 2002; Lawrence-Lightfoot, 2003; Murry et al., 2004; Tseng & Seidman, 2007). This is true to some extent for all families, because student learning success and achievement are so often taken as indicators of families' success in raising their children. It is more likely and more strongly the case, however, for families from groups that are often marginalized by the broader culture: poorly educated families, ethnic minority families, families living in poverty, immigrant and refugee families.

Particularly in such circumstances, a commitment on the part of the school system to initiating and sustaining regular and respectful communications—and to bridging the vulnerability and defensiveness that school and family members may bring to the relationship—is often critical to the development of a mutually supportive family-school collaboration (e.g., Bryk & Schneider, 2002; Christenson, 2004). Epstein's frequent observations that teacher practices and attitudes often play a critical role in encouraging and motivating families' active engagement in student learning are consistent with this principle (e.g., Epstein, 1986; Epstein & Van Voorhis, 2001). Also critically important here is the observation that family-school collaborations are generally most effective in supporting students' learning when they are characterized by mutual trust and mutual understanding that the collaboration of home and school is essential for students' full development and learning (Bryk & Schneider, 2002; Christenson, 2004; Pianta, Kraft-Sayre, Rimm-Kaufmann, Gercke, & Higgins, 2001; see also Dearing et al., 2006). Overt support from both parties for each member's knowledge and participation, in turn, contributes to members' "sense of belonging, mattering, and engagement" in the goals and tasks of student learning (Tseng & Seidman, 2007, p. 220). It is in this combination of interpersonal regard, respect, and personal investment in the goals and outcomes of the family-school relationship that both systems' *commitment* to collaborative support of student learning is developed and nurtured.

## CONCLUSIONS: MOTIVATION AND COMMITMENT TO FAMILY-SCHOOL PARTNERSHIPS

Theory and research reviewed in this chapter suggest that family and school motivations for developing and sustaining productive family-school partnerships are well informed by specific information in the four domains of inquiry considered here. For example, research on student outcomes associated with parental involvement and family-school partnerships suggests that critically important student learning attributes—including personal attitudes about education, beliefs about oneself as learner, development of self-regulatory knowledge and skills, and development of varied learning behaviors—are enhanced by families' and family-school partnerships' involvement activities. The evidence suggests further that student performance on summary measures of school achievement and accomplishment, across childhood, adolescence, and into adulthood, benefits from students' application of these attributes during school learning and from the on-going support of families and family-school partnerships in students' learning.

Theory and research considered here also suggest that parents' and families' motivations for becoming involved in students' education are *socially constructed*; that is, they are influenced by family, school, and community actions. Thus, families' motivations for engagement in student learning are influenced by psychological variables (role construction for involvement; sense of efficacy for helping one's children learn) that are directly susceptible to school and community influence. Family involvement and engagement decisions are also strongly influenced by selected contextual variables (invitations to involvement generated by schools, students' teachers, and students themselves), a set of motivators not only influenced by schools but often controlled by schools. The evidence on parents' motivations also suggests that schools' responsiveness to elements of families' life context is also quite likely to influence families' decisions about involvement; particularly important here is the development of opportunities for family engagement that fit families' knowledge and skills, time, and energy, and varied aspects of family culture.

Application of this theory and research to understanding school system members' motivations for supporting family involvement and family-school partnerships suggests that parallel constructs are quite likely at work. For example, school members' (e.g., teachers, principals, support staff) understanding of their own professional roles as including responsibility for developing family-school collaborations is quite likely to influence those members' thinking and behavior in this domain, as is their sense of efficacy for developing effective family-school collaborations. In similar fashion, school members' perceptions of system- and school-based invitations and requests to support family engagement in student learning are quite likely to influence their efforts and behaviors in this area. Thus, members who understand—from the system's hiring and evaluation criteria *and* from consistent systemic support and mentoring focused on developing the knowledge, skills, time, and resources required for collaborations—are also quite likely to engage seriously with the issues and tasks involved. While empirical tests of these applications are needed, theory and related work underscore the potential usefulness of such work in understanding more clearly the development, role and functioning of family-school partnerships in offering unique and valuable support for student learning. We believe that the principles of ecological-systems theory reviewed—particularly those focusing on the development of relationships characterized by respect, trust, and sharing of information (i.e., partnerships that are grounded in commitment to their work and functioning in supporting student learning)—offer several starting points for the development and examination of well-grounded family-school collaborations' contributions to student learning.

## AUTHORS' NOTES

We gratefully acknowledge support for portions of this work from the Institute for Education Sciences (formerly Office for Educational Research and Improvement), U.S. Department of Education (*Parental Involvement: A Path to Enhanced Achievement*, 2001–2004, No. RR305T01673-02); see Hoover-Dempsey & Sandler, 2005. Many thanks to Joan M. Walker, PhD, and Drew Wilkins for contributions to our early thinking about applying the model of the parental involvement process (Figure 2.1) to understanding teachers' motivations for supporting parental involvement and family-school partnerships.

The terms "family" and "parent" are used interchangeably in discussing family engagement and parental involvement in children's education. We mean by both terms any or all family, extended family, or surrogate family members who play a primary role in supporting children's and adolescents' school learning. Similarly, the terms "involvement" and "engagement" are used interchangeably in this chapter; both refer to parents' or families' behaviors (manifested at home, at school, in communications with school personnel, or in the community) that are intended to support varied aspects of children's and adolescents' school learning and success. The terms "student" and "children" are used throughout the chapter to refer to all students, from the preschool through the secondary school years. While forms of family involvement, engagement, and collaboration with schools are generally subject to change consistent with students' changing developmental needs across childhood and adolescence, families continue to offer substantial and important contributions to their children's school learning and success throughout the adolescent years (e.g., Hoover-Dempsey, Ice, & Whitaker, in press; Simon, 2004). Finally, the terms "parental involvement" and "family-school partnerships" are used in some circumstances interchangeably, but grounded in the understanding that "family-school partnerships" and "family-school collaboration" are generally used to denote a more interactive, mutually supportive and on-going relationship between family and school in support of student learning.

# REFERENCES

Adams, K. S., & Christenson, S. L. (1998). Differences in parent and teacher trust levels: Implications for creating collaborative family-school relationships. *Special Services in the Schools, 14*(1/2), 1–22.

Adams, K. S., & Christenson, S. L. (2000). Trust and the family-school relationship: An examination of parent-teacher differences in elementary and secondary grades. *Journal of School Psychology, 38*, 447–497.

Anderson, K. J. & Minke, K. M. (2007). Parent involvement in education: Toward an understanding of parents' decision making. *Journal of Educational Research, 100*, 311–324.

Auerbach, S. (2007). From moral supporters to struggling advocates: Reconceptualizing parent roles in education through the experience of working-class families of color. *Urban Education, 42*, 250–283.

Balli, S. J., Demo, D. H., & Wedman, J. F. (1998). Family involvement with children's homework: An intervention in the middle grades. *Family Relations, 47*, 149–157.

Bandura, A. (1986). The explanatory and predictive scope of self-efficacy theory. *Journal of Social and Clinical Psychology, 4*, 359–373.

Bandura, A. (1997). *Self-efficacy: The exercise of control.* New York: W. H. Freeman.

Bandura, A., Barbaranelli, C., Caprara, G. V., & Pastorelli, C. (1996). Multifaceted impact of self-efficacy beliefs on academic functioning. *Child Development, 67*, 1206–1222.

Barnard, W. M. (2004). Parent involvement in elementary school and educational attainment. *Child and Youth Services Review, 26*, 39–62.

Baumrind, D. (1991). Parenting styles and adolescent development. In R. M. Lerner, A. C. Petersen, & J. Brooks-Gunn (Eds.), *Encyclopedia of adolescence. Vol. 2* (pp. 746–758). New York: Garland.

Biddle, B. J. (1979). *Role theory: Expectations, identities, and behaviors.* New York: Academic Press.

Biddle, B. J. (1986). Recent developments in role theory. *Annual Review of Sociology, 12*, 67–92.

Brody, G. J., Flor, D. L., & Gibson, N. M. (1999). Linking maternal efficacy beliefs, developmental goals, parenting practices, and child competence in rural single-parent African American families. *Child Development, 70*, 1197–1208.

Bronfenbrenner, U. (1979). *The ecology of human development: Experiments by nature and design.* Cambridge, MA: Harvard University Press.

Bronfenbrenner, U. (1986). Ecology of the family as context for human development: Research perspectives. *Developmental Psychology, 22*(6), 723–742.

Bronfenbrenner, U. (1992). Ecological systems theory. In R Vasta (Ed.), *Annals of child development. Six theories of child development: Revised formulations and current issues* (pp. 187–249). London: Jessica Kingsley.

Bronfenbrenner, U., & Morris, P. A. (1998). The ecology of developmental processes. In W. Damon (Series Ed.) & R. M. Lerner (Vol. Ed.), *Handbook of child psychology. Vol. 1: Theoretical models of human development* (pp. 993–1028). New York: Wiley.

Bryk, A. S., & Schneider, B. (2002). *Trust in schools: A core resource for improvement.* New York: Russell Sage Foundation.

Callahan, K., Rademacher, J. A., & Hildreth, B. L. (1998). The effect of parent participation in strategies to improve the homework performance of students who are at risk. *Remedial and Special Education, 19*(3), 131–141.

Campbell, F. A., Ramey, C. T., Pungello, E., Sparling, J., & Miller-Johnson, S. (2002). Early childhood education: Young adult outcomes from the Abecedarian Project. *Applied Developmental Science, 6*(1), 42–57.

Caspe, M., & Lopez, M. E. (2006). Lessons from family-strengthening interventions: Learning from evidence-based practice. Cambridge, MA: Harvard Family Research Project. Retrieved September 10, 2008, from www.hfrp.org

Caspe, M., Lopez, M. E., & Wolos, C. (2006/2007). *Family involvement makes a difference: Family involvement in elementary school children's education.* Cambridge, MA: Harvard Family Research Projects. Retrieved September 10, 2008, from http://www.gse.harvard.edu/hfrp/content/projects/fine/resources/research/elementay/html

Ceballo, R., & McLoyd, V. C. (2002). Social support and parenting in poor, dangerous neighborhoods. *Child Development, 73*(4), 1310–1321.

Chrispeels, J., & Rivero, E. (2001). Engaging Latino families for student success: How parent education can reshape parents' sense of place in the education of their children. *Peabody Journal of Education, 76*, 119–169.

Christenson, S. L. (2004). The family-school partnership: An opportunity to promote the learning competence of all students. *School Psychology Review, 33*(1), 83–104.

Christenson, S. L., & Sheridan, S. M. (2001). *School and families: Creating essential connections for learning.* New York: Guilford.

Clark, R. (1983). *Family life and school achievement: Why poor black children succeed or fail.* Chicago: University of Chicago Press.

Collins, W. A., Maccoby, E. E., Steinberg, L., Hetherington, E. M., & Bornstein, M. (2000). Contemporary research on parenting: The case for nature and nurture. *American Psychologist, 55,* 218–232.

Comer, J. P. (1995). *School power: Implications of an intervention program.* New York: Simon & Schuster.

Conduct Problems Prevention Research Group (2004). The effects of the Fast Track Program on serious problem outcomes at the end of elementary school. *Journal of Clinical Child and Adolescent Psychology, 334,* 650–661.

Constantino, S. M. (2003). *Engaging all families: Creating a positive school culture by putting research into practice.* Lanham, MD: Scarecrow Education.

Cooper, J. H., Lindsay, J. J., & Nye, B. (2000). Homework in the home: How student, family, and parenting style differences relate to the homework process. *Contemporary Educational Psychology, 25,* 464–487.

Cooper, H., Lindsay, J. J., Nye, B., & Greathouse, S. (1998). Relationships among attitudes about homework, amount of homework assigned and completed, and student achievement. *Journal of Educational Psychology, 90*(1), 70–83.

Dauber, S. L. & Epstein, J. L. (1993). Parents' attitudes and practices of involvement in inner-city elementary and middle schools. In N. F. Chavkin (Ed.), *Families and schools in a pluralistic society* (pp. 53–71). Albany: State University of New York Press.

Dearing, E., Kreider, H., Simpkins, S., & Weiss, H. B. (2006). Family involvement in school and low-income children's literacy performance: Longitudinal associations between and within families. *Journal of Educational Psychology, 98,* 653–664.

Dearing, E., McCartney, K., Weiss, H. B., Kreider, H., & Simpkins, S. (2004). The promotive effects of family educational involvement for low-income children's literacy. *Journal of School Psychology, 42,* 445–460.

Deci, E. L. & Ryan, R. M. (1985). *Intrinsic motivation and self-determination in human behavior.* New York: Plenum.

Delgado-Gaitan, C. (1992). School matters in the Mexican-American home: Socializing children to education. *American Educational Research Journal, 29,* 495–513.

Deslandes, R., & Bertrand, R. (2005). Motivation of parent involvement in secondary-level schooling. *Journal of Educational Research, 98*(3), 164–175.

Deslandes, R., Royer, E., Potvin, P. & Leclerc, D. (1999). Patterns of home and school partnership for general and special education students at the secondary level. *Exceptional Children, 65*(4), 496–506.

Drummond, K. V., & Stipek, D. (2004). Low-income parents' beliefs about their role in children's academic learning. *Elementary School Journal, 104,* 197–213.

Englund, M. M., Luckner, A. E., Gloria, J. L., Whaley, G. J. L., & Egeland, B. (2004). Children's achievement in early elementary school: Longitudinal effects of parental involvement, expectations, and quality of assistance. *Journal of Educational Psychology, 96*(4), 723–730.

Eccles, J. S., & Harold, R. D. (1993). Parent-school involvement during the early adolescent years. *Teachers College Record, 94,* 568–587.

Epstein, J. L. (1983). Longitudinal effects of family-school-person interactions on student outcomes. *Research in Sociology of Education and Socialization, 4,* 101–127.

Epstein, J. L. (1986). Parents' reactions to teacher practices of parent involvement. *Elementary School Journal, 86,* 277–294.

Epstein, J. L., & Dauber, S. L. (1991). School programs and teacher practices of parent involvement in inner-city elementary and middle schools. *Elementary School Journal, 91,* 291–305.

Epstein, J. L., Sanders, M. G., Simon, B. S., Salinas, K. C., & Jansorn, N. R. (2002). *School, family, and community partnerships: Your handbook for action.* Thousand Oaks, CA: Corwin Press.

Epstein, J. L., & Van Voorhis, F. L. (2001). More than minutes: Teachers' roles in designing homework. *Educational Psychologist, 36,* 181–193.

Fan, X., & Chen, M. (2001). Parental involvement and students' academic achievement: A meta-analysis. *Educational Psychology Review, 13,* 1–22.

Fantuzzo, J. W., Davis, G. Y., & Ginsberg, M. D. (1995). Effects of parent involvement in isolation or in combination with peer tutoring on student self-concept and mathematics achievement. *Journal of Educational Psychology, 87*(2), 272–281.

Frijters, J. C., Barron, R. W., & Brunello, M. (2000). Direct and mediated influences of home literacy and literacy interest on prereaders' oral vocabulary and early written language skill. *Journal of Educational Psychology, 92*(3), 466–477.

Frome, P. M. & Eccles, J. S. (1998). Parents' influence on children's achievement-related perceptions. *Journal of Personality and Social Psychology, 74*, 435–452.

Garcia Coll, C., Akiba, D., Palacios, N., Bailey, B., Silver, R., DiMartino, L., et al. (2002). Parental involvement in children's education: Lessons from three immigrant groups. *Parenting: Science and Practice, 2*(3), 303–324.

Ginsburg, G., & Bronstein, P. (1993). Family factors related to children's intrinsic/extrinsic motivational orientation and academic performance. *Child Development, 64*, 1461–1474.

Glasgow, K. L., Dornbusch, S. M., Troyer, L., Steinberg, L., & Ritter, P. L. (1997). Parenting styles, adolescents' attributions, and educational outcomes in nine heterogeneous high schools. *Child Development, 68*, 507–529.

Goldring, E., Crowson, R., Laird, D. & Berk, R. (2003). Transitional leadership in a shifting policy environment. *Educational Evaluation and Policy Analysis, 25*(4), 473–488.

Gonzalez, A., Doan Holbein, M., & Quilter, S. (2002). High school students' goal orientations and their relationship to perceived parenting styles. *Contemporary Educational Psychology, 27*, 450–470.

Gonzalez-DeHass, A. R., Willems, P. P., & Doan Holbein, M. F. (2005). Examining the relationship between parental involvement and student motivation. *Educational Psychology Review, 17*(2), 99–123.

Gonzalez, N., Andrade, R., Civil, M., & Moll, L. (2001). Bridging funds of distributed knowledge: Creating zones of practice in mathematics. *Journal of Education of Students Placed at Risk, 6*, 115–132.

Graue, E. (2005). Theorizing and describing preservice teachers' images of families and schooling. *Teachers College Record, 107*(1), 157–185.

Gray, S. W., Ramsey, B. K., & Klaus, R. A. (1983). The Early Training Project: 1962–1980. In Consortium for Longitudinal Studies (Ed.), *As the twig is bent: Lasting effects of preschool programs* (pp. 33–69). Hillsdale, NJ: Erlbaum.

Green, C. L., Walker, J. M. T., Hoover-Dempsey, K. V., & Sandler, H. M. (2007). Parents' motivations for involvement in children's education: An empirical test of a theoretical model of parental involvement. *Journal of Educational Psychology, 99*, 532–544.

Griffith, J. (1998). The relation of school structure and social environment to parent involvement in elementary schools. *Elementary School Journal, 99*(1), 53–80.

Griffith, J. (2001). Principal leadership of parent involvement. *Journal of Educational Administration, 39*(2), 162–186.

Grolnick, W. S., Benjet, C., Kurowski, C. O., & Apostoleris, N. H. (1997). Predictors of parent involvement in children's schooling. *Journal of Educational Psychology, 89*, 538–548.

Grolnick, W. S., Kurowski, C. O., Dunlap, K. G. & Hevey, C. (2000). Parental resources and the transition to junior high. *Journal of Research on Adolescence, 10*, 465–488.

Grolnick, W. S., Kurowski, C. O., & Gurland, S. T. (1999). Family processes and the development of children's self-regulation. *Educational Psychologist, 34*(1), 3–14.

Grolnick, W. S., & Ryan, R. M. (1989). Parent styles associated with children's self-regulation and competence in school. *Journal of Educational Psychology. 81*, 143–154.

Grolnick, W. S., Ryan, R. M., & Deci, E. L. (1991). Inner resources for school achievement: Motivational mediators of children's perceptions of their parents. *Journal of Educational Psychology, 83*, 508–517.

Grolnick, W. S., & Slowiaczek, M. L. (1994). Parents' involvement in children's schooling: A multidimensional conceptualization and motivational model. *Child Development, 65*, 237–252.

Gutman, L. M., & Midgely, C. (2000). The role of protective factors in supporting the academic achievement of poor African American students during the middle school transition. *Journal of Youth and Adolescence, 29*, 223–248.

Henderson, A. T., & Mapp, K. L. (2002). *A new wave of evidence: The impact of school, family and community connections on student achievement.* Austin, TX: Southwest Educational Development Laboratory.

Henderson, A. T., Mapp, K. L., Johnson, V. R., & Davies, D. (2007). *Beyond the bake sale: The essential guide to family-school partnerships.* New York: The New Press.

Hill, N. E., & Craft, S. A. (2003). Parent-school involvement and school performance: Mediated pathways among socioeconomically comparable African-American and Euro-American families. *Journal of Educational Psychology, 95*(1), 74–83.

Hoover-Dempsey, K. V., Bassler, O. C., & Brissie, J. S. (1992). Explorations in parent-school relations. *Journal of Educational Research, 85*, 287–294.

Hoover-Dempsey, K. V., Bassler, O. C., & Burow, R. (1995). Parents' reported involvement in students' homework: Parameters of reported strategy and practice. *Elementary School Journal, 95*, 435–450.

Hoover-Dempsey, K. V., Battiato, A. C., Walker, J. M. T., Reed, R. P., DeJong, J. M., & Jones, K. P. (2001). Parental involvement in homework. *Educational Psychologist, 36*, 195–210.

Hoover-Dempsey, K. V., Ice, C. L., & Whitaker, M. C. (in press). "We're way past reading together:" Why and how does parental involvement during adolescence make sense? In Hill, N., & Chao, R. (Eds.), *Family–school relationships in adolescence: Linking interdisciplinary research.* New York: Teachers College Press.

Hoover-Dempsey, K. V., & Sandler, H. M. (1995). Parental involvement in children's education: Why does it make a difference? *Teachers College Record, 97,* 310–331.

Hoover-Dempsey, K. V., & Sandler, H. M. (1997). Why do parents become involved in their children's education? *Review of Educational Research, 67,* 3–42.

Hoover-Dempsey, K. V., & Sandler, H. M. (2005, March 22). *Final Performance Report for OERI Grant #R305T010673: The Social Context of Parental Involvement: A Path to Enhanced Achievement.* Presented to Project Monitor, Institute of Education Sciences, U.S. Department of Education Available at http://vanderbilt.edu/Peabody/*family-school*

Hoover-Dempsey, K. V., Walker, J. M. T., Jones, K. P., & Reed, R. P. (2002). Teachers Involving Parents (TIP): Results from an in-service teacher education program for enhancing parental involvement. *Teaching and Teacher Education, 18,* 843–867.

Hoover-Dempsey, K. V., Walker, J. M. T., Sandler, H. M., Whetsel, D., Green, C. L., Wilkins, A. S., et al. (2005). Why do parents become involved? Research findings and implications. *Elementary School Journal, 106,* 105–130.

Hutsinger, C. S., Jose, P. E., & Larson, S. L. (1998). Do parent practices to encourage academic competence influence the social adjustment of young European American and Chinese American children? *Developmental Psychology 34,* 747–756.

Izzo, C. V., Weissberg, R. P., Kasprow, W. J., & Fendrich, M. (1999). A longitudinal assessment of teacher perceptions of parent involvement in children's education and school performance. *American Journal of Community Psychology, 27*(6), 817–839.

Jeynes, W. H. (2003). A meta-analysis: the effects of parental involvement on minority children's academic achievement. *Education and Urban Society, 35*(2), 202–218.

Jeynes, W. H. (2005). The effects of parental involvement on the academic achievement of African-American youth. *Journal of Negro Education, 74,* 260–275.

Jeynes, W. H. (2007). The relationship between parental involvement and urban secondary school student academic achievement: A meta-analysis. *Urban Education, 42,* 82–110.

Koskinen, P. S., Blum, I. H., Bisson, S. A., Phillips, S. M., Creamer, T. S., & Baker, T. K. (2000). Book access, shared reading, and audio models: The effects of supporting the literacy learning of linguistically diverse students in school and at home. *Journal of Educational Psychology, 92*(1), 23–36.

Kreider, H., Caspe, M., Kennedy, S., & Weiss, H. (2007). *Family involvement makes a difference: Family involvement in middle and high school students' education.* Cambridge, MA: Harvard Family Research Project. Available at: http://www.gse.harvard.edu/hfrp/content/projects/find/resources/research/elementary/html

Leone, C. M., & Richards, M. H. (1989). Classwork and homework in early adolescence: The ecology of achievement. *Journal of Youth and Adolescence, 18,* 531–548.

Lawrence-Lightfoot, S. (2003). *The essential conversation: What parents and teachers can learn from each other.* New York: Random House.

Lopez, L. C., Sanchez, V. V., & Hamilton, M. (2000). Immigrant and native-born Mexican-American parents' involvement in a public school: A preliminary study. *Psychological Reports, 86,* 521–525.

Marchant, G. J., Paulson, S. E., & Rothlisberg, B. A. (2001). Relations of middle school students' perceptions of family and school contexts with academic achievement. *Psychology in the Schools, 38*(6), 505–519.

Martinez-Pons, M. (1996). Test of a model of parental inducement of academic self-regulation. *Journal of Experimental Education, 64,* 213–227.

McWayne, C., Hampton, V., Fantuzzo, J., Cohen, H. L., & Sekino, Y. (2004). A multivariate examination of parent involvement and the social and academic competence of urban kindergarten children. *Psychology in the Schools, 41,* 363–377.

Meidel, W. T., & Reynolds, A. J. (1999). Parent involvement in early intervention for disadvantaged children: Does it matter? *Journal of School Psychology, 37*(4), 379–402.

Moll, L., Amanti, C., Neff, D. & Gonzalez, N. (1992). Funds of knowledge for teaching: Using a qualitative approach to connect homes and classrooms. *Theory Into Practice, 31,* 132–141.

Murry, V .M., Kotchick, B. A., Wallace, S., Ketchen, B., Eddings, K., Heller, L., et al. (2004). Race, culture and ethnicity: Implications for a community intervention. *Journal of Child and Family Studies, 13*(1), 81–99.

Patrikakou, E., & Weissberg, R. P. (2000). Parents' perceptions of teacher outreach and parent involvement in children's education. *Journal of Prevention and Intervention in the Community, 20*(1-2), 103–119.

Paulson, S. (1994). Relations of parenting style and parental involvement with ninth-grade students' achievement. *Journal of Early Adolescence, 14*, 250–267.

Pianta, R. C., Kraft-Sayre, M., Rimm-Kaufmann, S., Gercke, N., & Higgins, T. (2001). Collaboration in building partnerships between families and schools: The National Center for Early Development and Learning's Kindergarten Transition Intervention. *Early Childhood Research Quarterly, 16*, 117–132.

Pianta, R. C., & Walsh, D. J. (1998). Applying the construct of resilience in schools: Cautions from a developmental systems perspective. *School Psychology Review, 27*(3), 407–417.

Pomerantz, E. M., & Eaton, M. M. (2001). Maternal intrusive support in the academic context: Transactional socialization processes. *Developmental Psychology, 37*, 174–186.

Pomerantz, E. M., Grolnick, W. S., & Price, C. E. (2005). The role of parents in how children approach achievement. In A. J. Elliott & C. S. Dweck (Eds.), *Handbook of motivation and competence* (pp. 259–278). New York: Oxford University Press.

Ross, J. A., & Gay, P. (2006). School leadership and student achievement: The mediating effects of teacher beliefs. *Canadian Journal of Education, 29*, 798–822.

Sameroff, A. J. (1995). General systems theory and developmental psychopathology. In D. Cicchetti & D. Cohen (Eds.), *Developmental psychopathology: Theory and methods* (pp. 659–695). New York: Wiley.

Sanders, M. (1998). The effects of school, family, and community support on the academic achievement of African-American adolescents. *Urban Education, 33*, 385–409.

Schunk, D. H., & Zimmerman, B. J. (2003). Self-regulation and learning. In W. M. Reynolds & G. E. Miller (Eds.), *Handbook of psychology: Educational psychology* (pp. 59–78). Hoboken, NJ: Wiley.

Schweinhart, L. J. (1994). *Lasting benefits of preschool programs*. ERIC Digest ED365478. Urbana, IL: ERIC Clearinghouse on Elementary and Early Childhood Education. Retrieved from http:/www.ericdigests/1994/lasting/html

Schweinhart, L. J., Barnes, H. V., & Weikart, D. P. (1993). *Significant benefits: The High/Scope Perry Preschool Study through Age 27*. (Monographs of the High/Scope Educational Research Foundation, Vol. 10). Ypsilanti, MI: High/Scope Press.

Schweinhart, L. J., Montie, J., Xiang, Z., Barnett, W. S., Belfield, C. R., & Nores, M. (2005). *Lifetime effects: The High/Scope Perry Preschool Study through Age 40*. (Monographs of the High/Scope Educational Research Foundation No. 14). Ypsilanti, MI: High/Scope Press.

Scribner, J. D., Young, M. D., & Pedroza, A. (1999). Building collaborative relationships with parents. In J. D. Scribner & A. Paredes-Scribner (Eds.), *Lessons from high-performing Hispanic schools: Creating learning communities* (pp. 36–60). New York: Teachers College Press.

Senechal, M., & LeFevre, J. (2002). Parental involvement in the development of children's reading skill: A five-year longitudinal study. *Child Development, 73*(2), 445–460.

Shaver, A. V., & Walls, R. T. (1998). Effect of Title I parent involvement on student reading and mathematics achievement. *Journal of Research and Development in Education, 31*(2), 90–97.

Sheldon, S. B. (2002). Parents' social networks and beliefs as predictors of parent involvement. *Elementary School Journal. 102*, 301–316.

Sheldon, S. B., & Epstein, J. L. (2005). Involvement counts: Family and community partnerships and mathematics achievement. *Journal of Educational Research, 98*(4), 196–206.

Shumow, L. (1998). Promoting parental attunement to children's mathematical reasoning through parent education. *Journal of Applied Developmental Psychology, 19*(1), 109–127.

Shumow, L. & Lomax, R. (2002). Parental efficacy: Predictor of parenting behavior and adolescent outcomes. *Parenting: Science and Practice, 2*, 127–150.

Simon, B. S. (2004). High school outreach and family involvement. *Social Psychology of Education, 7*, 185–209.

Smrekar, C. (1996). *The impact of school choice and community: In the interest of families and schools*. Albany: State University of New York Press.

Soodak, L. C., & Erwin, E. J. (2000). Valued member or tolerated participant: Parents' experiences in inclusive early childhood settings. *Journal of the Association for Persons with Severe Handicaps, 25*(1), 29–41.

Starkey, P., & Klein, A. (2000). Fostering parental support for children's mathematical development: An intervention with Head Start families. *Early Education and Development, 11*(5), 569–580.

Steinberg, L., Elman, J., & Mounts, N. (1989). Authoritative parenting, psychosocial maturity, and academic success among adolescents. *Child Development, 60*, 1424–1436.

Steinberg, L., Lamborn, S. D., Dornbusch, S. M., & Darling, N. (1992). Impact of parenting practices on adolescent achievement: Authoritative parenting, school involvement, and encouragement to succeed. *Child Development, 63*, 1266–1281.

Stipek, D., & Gralinski, J. H. (1996). Children's beliefs about intelligence and school performance. *Journal of Educational Psychology, 88,* 397–407.

Trusty, J. (1999). Effects of eighth-grade parental involvement on late adolescents' educational experiences. *Journal of Research and Development in Education, 32*(4), 224–233.

Tseng, V., & Seidman, E. (2007). A systems framework for understanding social settings. *American Journal of Community Psychology, 39,* 217–228.

Walker, J. M. T., & Hoover-Dempsey, K. V. (2006). Why research on parental involvement is important to classroom management. In C. M. Evertson & C. S. Weinstein (Eds.), *Handbook of classroom Management: research, practice and contemporary ossues* (pp. 665–684). New York: Erlbaum.

Walker, J. M. T., Wilkins, A. S., Dallaire, J. P., Sandler, H. M., & Hoover-Dempsey, K. V. (2005). Parental involvement: Model revision through scale development. *Elementary School Journal, 106,* 85–104.

Webster-Stratton, C., Reid, M. J., & Hammond, M. (2004). Treating children with early onset-conduct problems: Intervention outcomes on parent, child, and teacher training. *Journal of Clinical Child and Adolescent Psychology, 33*(1), 105–124.

Weiss, H., Caspe, M., & Lopez, M. E. (2006). *Family involvement makes a difference: Family involvement in early childhood education.* Cambridge, MA. Harvard Family Research Project. Available at http://www.gse.harvard.edu/hfrp/content/

Weiss, H. B., Mayer, E., Kreider, H., Vaughan, M., Dearing, E., Hencke, R., et al. (2003). Making it work: Low-income working mothers' involvement in their children's education. *American Educational Research Journal, 40*(4), 879–901.

Xu J. & Corno, L. (1998). Case studies of families doing third-grade homework. *Teachers College Record, 100,* 402–436.

Xu, J., & Corno, L. (2003). Family help and homework management reported by middle school students. *Elementary School Journal, 103*(5), 503–536.

Zimmerman, B. J. (1986). Becoming a self-regulated learner: What are the key subprocesses? *Contemporary Educational Psychology, 11,* 307–313.

Zimmerman, B. J., & Martinez-Pons, M. P. (1990). Student differences in self-regulated learning: Relating grade, sex, and giftedness to self-efficacy and strategy use. *Journal of Educational Psychology, 82,* 51–59.

# 3

## ELEMENTS OF HEALTHY FAMILY-SCHOOL RELATIONSHIPS

BRANDY L. CLARKE, SUSAN M. SHERIDAN, AND KATHRYN E. WOODS

What is a relationship? In its most basic sense, "relationship" is defined as "the state of being related or interrelated... the relation connecting or binding participants" (Merriam-Webster on-line, 2008) A relationship is both a personal and interpersonal experience that brings individuals and entities together. Human nature, by default, creates opportunities for the formation of several diverse and unique relationships among individuals. Among those most central to a child's development are the relationships that exist between members within his or her family, and relationships between the support systems in his or her life—namely, the family and school. It is the latter—family-school relationships—that are the foci of the present chapter.

We define *family-school relationships* as a child-centered connection between individuals in the home and school settings who share responsibility for supporting the growth and development of children. Family-school relationships persist and evolve over time. Indeed, a relationship always exists among families and schools (Pianta & Walsh, 1996). The purpose of this chapter is to describe elements that are specific to *healthy* family-school relationships, rather than a continuum of all possible forms of relationships that may exist between families and schools. We differentiate family-school relationships from parental involvement, family participation, family-school partnerships and home-school collaboration. Beyond events that represent "involvement" or "participation" of families in learning-related or school events, the establishment and maintenance of *relationships* reflect a dynamic, interpersonal perspective. Whereas "collaborating" and "partnering" as active verbs often represent actions or structural means for interacting with families, the family-school relationship represents the affective, personal qualities associated with these actions. Thus, we view supportive, interpersonal relationships between families and teachers as the groundwork for intentional, collaborative partnerships to occur (Christenson & Sheridan, 2001; Dinnebeil, Hale, & Rule, 1996, 2000), with the intent of supporting children's education and healthy development.

## OVERVIEW

One of the most crucial relationships to a child's development is the relationship between his or her family members and the school personnel responsible for their formal education. In this chapter we present a framework for healthy relationships between families and schools that optimize educational outcomes for children. Specifically, we provide a rationale for the importance of healthy family-school relationships as a necessary condition for partnerships, outline principles associated with healthy family-school relationships, discuss elements of healthy relationships, and offer strategies for promoting positive relationships among families and schools. Important linkages between principles, elements, and practices (actions) are stressed throughout the chapter. We also propose an agenda for future research that will propel further inquiry and expand the knowledge base regarding healthy family-school relationships.

### Why Consider Relationships in Education?

Schools as a place and schooling as a process are social enterprises. Learning takes place in a highly relational context. The goals and priorities of education (i.e., the preparation of children and youth to achieve cognitively physically, behaviorally, socially, and emotionally, in ways that prepare them to contribute productively in society) are couched in myriad relationships. An extensive amount of research has accumulated corroborating the benefits of quality relationships in a child's educational achievement. First, relationships experienced directly by the child are important. Comer (1984) noted that "attachment and identification with a meaningful adult motivates or reinforces a child's desire to learn" (p. 327), and the importance of positive attachments between students and teachers has been demonstrated empirically (Hamre & Pianta, 2005). Further, the quality of family-school interactions has been shown to be positively related to student achievement and behavior to a greater extent than simply the number or amount of contacts families and teachers have with one another (Patrikakou & Weissberg, 1999). When family-school relationships are framed in a positive and constructive fashion, they can lead to benefits for children, families, teachers, and schools. Alternatively, when framed in negative and destructive ways, they can preclude or deny access to beneficial experiences for children.

Healthy relationships between parents and teachers are essential, prerequisite conditions for the establishment of family-school partnerships (Christenson & Sheridan, 2001) and provide a child access to optimal learning experiences. Particularly in potentially adversarial or challenging situations, the establishment of positive, constructive relationships among partners provides an opportunity for dialogue and problem-solving. This "window of opportunity" is not necessarily present when systems operate in isolation of or counter to one another. Strained, adversarial, or absent relationships between a child's primary caregivers (parents and teachers) create barriers and greatly limits the amount, quality, and scope of services available to assist a child in meeting his or her learning or behavioral goals.

### Ecological Model as a Framework for Family-School Relationships

Among the many types of relationships evident in the education of children are those involving parents and children, teachers and children, parents and teachers, schools and communities, and families and broader social networks. These various types of relationships evident in educational settings mirror the ecological systems characterizing developmental-systems theory. According to Bronfenbrenner (1977), a child's development occurs in the context of multiple and reciprocal systems. Specifically, an individual child is an inseparable, central part of a small social system comprised of four interrelated systems: microsystem, mesosystem, exosystem, and macrosystem. To understand the child, it is necessary to understand the separate ecosystems (e.g., home or school) within which the child lives, the relationship of those separate systems with each other, and the relationship of the ecosystems within a larger, overarching developmental context.

The *microsystem* includes the immediate relationships in settings within which children live, grow, and function. Examples include the parent-child relationship at home, and the support and encouragement that parents provide to their child vis á vis learning, effort, and achievement (Christenson & Sheridan, 2001). It also includes relationships the child experiences with his or her teachers and peers, including the degree to which teachers form affective connections with students (Pianta, 1999) and the resultant attachment the child feels with school and formal learning. The importance of a warm, responsive relationship and secure attachment between a parent and child early on and throughout the child's life is associated with improved cognitive, emotional, and behavioral adjustment (Ainsworth, Bell, & Stayton, 1972; Raver & Knitzer, 2002; Thompson, 2002). Likewise, an increasing empirical literature supports the importance of nurturing teacher-child relationships in the early and sustained learning experiences of children (Pianta & Stuhlman, 2004).

The *mesosystem* is comprised of the various relationships among microsystems within which children reside. This includes relationships between families and teachers as they interact around children's educational, behavior, and developmental experiences and outcomes. At their best, mesosystems represent close relationships established among key individuals in these immediate settings that are characterized by constructive dialogue and communication, trust, and shared commitment to maintaining the relationship in support of the child. Key considerations for achieving a healthy, positive family-school relationship (i.e., the family-school mesosystem) are the focus of this chapter.

The *exosystem* is represented by conditions and events in settings in which the child does not directly participate, but that affect the micro- and mesosytems in important ways. These are influences from other contexts that impinge upon the microsystem and mesosystem, such as the degree to which parental work environments support their involvement in their child's school-day activities (Sheridan & Kratochwill, 2008) or the manner in which school policies, professional development opportunities, and administrative practices influence teachers' efforts to involve families. Indeed, the overarching school culture, and its support and provision of opportunities to involve and access one another (and thereby form relationships), represent an important exosystemic influence. It includes process variables (i.e., the tone, messages, and climate for healthy relationships to develop) and structural components at the school level that must be in place before effective relationships may be created among individual teachers and family members. Among the specific exosystemic influences affecting family-school relationships is the leadership and structures within a school. The presence of an administrative system that supports, invites, and encourages parents and teachers to communicate openly and frequently establishes the context for meaningful family-school relationships to develop. The degree to which parents and teachers embrace and act upon such open structures is dependent upon the specific parent-teacher dyad, and their intentionality related to the formation of a partnership.

Bronfenbrenner defined the *macrosystem* as "consistencies in the form and content of lower-order systems ... that exist at the level of the subculture or the culture as a whole, along with any belief system or ideology underlying such consistencies" (1979, p. 26). All settings and systems within which a child functions exist within a cultural context. The macrosystem represents the overall cultural or subcultural patterns that affect children, families, teachers, decision makers, and other individuals across settings and levels. The passage and reauthorization of federal policy (e.g., No Child Left Behind, IDEA) is an example of a macrosystemic influence that affects school curriculum, organization, priorities, instructional and assessment practices, homework, and home-school practices.

### Core Principles Underlying Healthy Relationships

The notion that healthy family-school relationships are important in supporting children's learning and development is based on several underlying principles. These principles represent core, fundamental tenets that guide the actions and decisions of individuals who are responsible for the relationship. Thus, they serve as both (a) prerequisites for efforts related to the establishment of family-school relationships, and (b) guides for decisions related to what types of relationships will be formed, how they will be established and maintained, by whom, and for what purpose. The principles underlying healthy family-school relationships surround beliefs, commitment, and continuity. The dynamic relationship between the core principles, critical elements, overt actions, and resultant family-school relationship is depicted in Figure 3.1, and stressed throughout the remainder of this chapter. The core principles are presented in Table 3.1 and described below.

*Beliefs* Certain beliefs are essential for creating positive relationships among families and schools. Given the duality of relationships, both families and teachers are expected to espouse this fundamental belief for healthy relationships to form. The first principle posits that families and educators share the same goals concerning children's positive development and achievement. That is, families and teachers desire similar outcomes, and these outcomes are associated with a child's success in school and other life contexts. A second belief principle posits that both in- and out-of-school experiences and their relationship to attaining the goals of education are important to a child's success (Henderson & Mapp, 2002). Third, families and educators each have unique and important roles in educating and socializing children. This principle is played out in

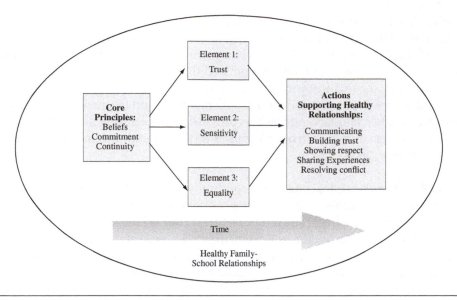

**Figure 3.1** Framework for healthy family-school relationships.

relationships characterized by mutual respect and shared responsibility. Fourth, it is important for both teachers and family members to believe that families are essential to a child's learning and development (Hoover-Dempsey et al., 2005). That is, establishing healthy relationships with families involves both a belief and a practical approach that views families as not only important, but essential to children's success.

*Commitment*  Beyond core beliefs embraced by families and educators, another set of principles is concerned with the commitment necessary for working together and maintaining a family-school relationship. This commitment is manifested in many ways,

**Table 3.1** Principles Underlying Healthy Family-School Relationships

*Belief: There is a shared belief that healthy relationships between families and schools are important.*

    Principle 1: Families and educators share the same goals around promoting positive development and achievement in students.

    Principle 2: Both in- and out-of-school experiences are important to achieve the goal of education.

    Principle 3: Families and educators each have unique and important roles in educating and socializing children.

    Principle 4: Families are essential to a child's learning and development.

*Commitment: Families and schools are committed to establishing and maintaining a positive relationship throughout a child's schooling.*

    Principle 5: Family-school relationships are developed over time and need to be maintained throughout a child's development and education

    Principle 6: Maintaining the family-school relationship is a high priority for families and teachers.

*Continuity: Consistency across systems and settings is important for a child's adaptation.*

    Principle 7: Establishing consistent goals and communicating common messages about the value of learning and education is helpful for and important to children

    Principle 8: Demonstrating a number of practices that exemplify a strong family-school connection on a consistent basis supports consistent, long-term positive outcomes.

including deliberate efforts to uphold personal responsibilities to support a child's learning, and connection to other adults with whom those responsibilities are shared. A fifth principle regarding healthy relationships recognizes that family-school relationships are developed over time and need to be maintained throughout a child's development and education. Sixth, the maintenance of a positive, constructive relationship between the family and school is a high priority for family members and teachers. This principle is demonstrated when families and teachers provide encouragement and remain flexible, accessible, and sensitive to each other's emotions (Blue-Banning, Summers, Frankland, Nelson, & Beegle, 2004).

*Continuity*   The principles concerning continuity represent the importance of consistency in a child's life across time and settings. Attention to transitions that occur across contextual (home and school) and temporal (preschool to kindergarten) bases is clearly important (Mangione & Speth, 1998). Children who experience congruent messages and experiences across socializing contexts such as home and school (i.e., **horizontal** continuity) have smoother and more stable transitions than those who experience incongruent or conflicting messages. Likewise, linkages in supports and relationships during temporal transitions (e.g., from preschool to kindergarten and elementary to middle school; **vertical** continuity) also create seamless experiences. Thus, common and shared approaches across home and school (horizontally) and over time (vertically) promote reliable and consistent learning opportunities. Specifically, the seventh principle indicates that establishing consistent goals and communicating common messages about the value of learning and education across home and school is helpful for and important to children (Henderson & Mapp, 2002). A final principle suggests that strong family-school connections practiced on a regular basis support consistent, long-term positive outcomes.

These core, underlying principles specify assumptions that appear essential to create healthy relationships among families and schools. When these key principles are evident, the establishment of the key elements of healthy relationships is possible. Next, the elements of healthy relationships and connections to core principles are described.

### Elements of Healthy Relationships

Interpersonal relationships are greatly affected by the personal and affective attributes of each party and their interaction with one another. The elements of a healthy relationship are affective and dynamic in nature, and include trust, sensitivity, and equality. These elements and their impact on healthy family-school relationships are discussed in the following section.

*Trust*   Trust in the family-school relationship is defined as confidence that another person will act in a manner to benefit and/or sustain the relationship, or the implicit or explicit goals of the relationship, so as to achieve positive outcomes on behalf of the student (Holmes & Rempel, 1989; Rempel, Holmes, & Zanna, 1985). Trust is often viewed as one of the most critical elements in an interpersonal relationship (Ammeter, Douglas, Ferris, & Goka, 2004; Nugent & Abolafia, 2006), and this is certainly true in family-school relationships (Dunst, Johanson, Rounds, Trivette, & Hamby, 1992). The in loco parentis responsibility conferred on schools requires a high level of trust from families (Goddard, Tschannen-Moran, & Hoy, 2001). Conversely, an increasing demand to actively include families in the educational decision-making process requires that teachers trust families and that families, in turn, trust teachers and take an active role in supporting their child's learning and development.

Trust between parents and teachers has been shown to correlate with students' credits earned, GPA, and attendance (Adams & Christenson, 2000), and to predict student achievement (Bryk & Schneider, 2002; Goddard et al., 2001). Parents with higher versus lower levels of trust in the parent-teacher relationship hold more positive attitudes with regard to the value of their involvement in schools, are more engaged in their child's learning (Dunsmuir, Frederickson, & Lang, 2004), and are less likely to attach undue significance to occasional negative events, demonstrating greater tolerance and a willingness to forgive (Lake & Billingsley, 2000). In a study of the effects of relational trust in schools on student productivity, Bryk and Schneider (2002) found that relational trust fosters a set of organizational conditions (structural and social-psychological) within a school that make it more likely for individuals to initiate and sustain efforts to improve productivity. More specifically, relational trust reduces the sense of vulnerability that educators feel when embarking on reform efforts. Furthermore, relational trust facilitates public problem-solving within an educational system and creates a moral resource for school improvement.

In interpersonal relationships, trust develops over time and is multifaceted, dynamic, and context dependent (Dunsmuir et al., 2004). Trust is built in a developmental progression of stages based on a series of positive interactions (Adams & Christenson, 2000; Christenson & Hirsch, 1998). The basic foundational stage of trust is predictability based on the reliability and stability of interactions. As the relationship progresses toward dependability, trust becomes a personal attribute bestowed on the members of the relationship. In the final stage, trust develops into faith in the other that is an emotional security beyond dispositional attributes and available evidence (Adams & Christenson, 2000).

Several components of trust have been proposed and examined as they relate to interpersonal relationships. Bryk and Schneider (2002) and Minke (2006) suggest that relational trust is built on the dynamic interplay of four components: respect, competence, personal regard for others, and integrity. *Respect* is the recognition that all parties in the relationship play an important role in a child's education and that a mutual dependency upon one another exists. Respect requires a sense of genuineness in which each person's ideas and perspectives are listened to, valued, and taken into account when planning future actions. *Competence* is the fulfillment of one's role obligations. The perception of another's competence may exist even in the presence of considerable variation in how he/she carries out his/her role. A *personal regard for others* refers to the actions taken by one member of the relationship to reduce the other's sense of vulnerability. Relational trust grows with the perception that others care and are willing to extend beyond the formal requirements of their role in a given situation. Finally, *integrity* is the consistency between a person's words and behavior. High integrity implies that one's actions are guided by a moral-ethical perspective.

Another component related to the development of trust in interpersonal relationships is *accountability*. Accountability refers to one's dependability and reliability in meeting role expectations. Common to many definitions of trust is an expectancy that the person in whom trust is given will act in a predetermined manner (Ammeter et al., 2004). The level of clarity regarding expectations has been shown to directly relate to the level of trust and commitment in a relationship (Bushe & Stets, 1999; Goddard et al., 2001) as it demonstrates predictability and dependability (Principle 7; Holmes & Rempel, 1989). Relational trust, as it is developed within a school organization, requires that the expectations held among its members are consistently validated via actions (Bryk & Schneider, 2002). It is reliability and dependability developed through repeated interactions that allows an individual to be optimistic about future expectations and the benevolence of others. Thus, through accountability trust develops and becomes self-reinforcing (Dunsmuir et al., 2004).

*Consideration* has also been proposed to be a key building block in the development of trust in interpersonal relationships (Nugent & Abolafia, 2006). According to Nugent and Abolafia, consideration involves the voluntary giving of a resource with little sacrifice on the part of the giver, implying that he/she perceives the need of another. Consideration is an intentional act that depends on the existence of five specific conditions. These include: (a) *empathy* (role taking to perceive the other's need); (b) *agency* (perception of one's self as an agent who can meet that need); (c) *nonsacrifice* (the effort to meet the need requires little sacrifice on the part of the giver); (d) *choice* (an awareness that the action of consideration is voluntary); and (e) *nonroutine* (the act occurs outside of highly routine or customary behavior). For example, a teacher may show a sign of consideration to a parent by allowing a child to stay after school knowing the child's parent will not be able to pick him or her up right away due to a late meeting. A parent might also show consideration for a teacher by sending an e-mail asking a question about a homework assignment rather than stopping by in the morning because he/she recognizes that it is a very busy time of day. In doing so, the parent allows the teacher to respond at a convenient time.

*Sensitivity*   The second element of healthy relationships is sensitivity, including the sensitivity required when working cross-culturally. With the increasing diversity in American schools and families, sensitivity to the cultural and linguistic experiences of others is essential in building healthy family-school relationships. Minority students made up 42% of the national public school enrollment in prekindergarten through secondary school in 2004 (Kewal Ramani, Gilbertson, Fox, & Provasnik, 2007). Additionally, the number of students in English Language Learner (ELL) programs in public schools increased from approximately two million in 1993–1994 to three million in 1999–2000. Unfortunately, children of minority status continue to experience greater difficulty in school than their non-minority peers (e.g., McKay, Atkins, Hawkins, Brown, & Lynn, 2003; National Center for Education Statistics, 2007; Olivos, 2004). Furthermore, the levels of school achievement for children living below the poverty threshold are lower than achievement levels of children above the threshold (U.S. Department of Education, 2007). Thus, there is a need to bridge the achievement gap for these children, and the formation of constructive family-school relationships may influence positively their educational trajectories.

Many students bring a variety of social, cultural, historical, and linguistic experiences with them as they enter the school system. When entering into relationships with diverse students and their families, it is important for school personnel to develop an *understanding* of the cultural and linguistic backgrounds and create a school environment that is an extension of those cultures (Berger, 2000; Esler, Godber, & Christenson, 2002). Building bridges between the diverse cultures of families and schools is critical for educators to make a difference in the lives of children (Harry, Kalyanpur, & Day, 1999; Haynes & Ben-Avie, 1996). Such bridges allow for the creation of continuities that respect family and school cultures and concomitantly explore opportunities for interacting with understanding (Principle 7).

*Equality*   The third element of healthy relationships is equality. In a study investigating the factors that escalate and deescalate conflict among families and educators, an imbalance of power and authority was found to increase discord in family-school relationships (Lake & Billingsley, 2000). As relationships are being formed, families and teachers have the opportunity to acknowledge and *value* the expertise of the other as being equal to their own. For example, teachers have a wealth of knowledge about learning and development, and parents are the experts on their child and the cultural experiences of the family. Collectively, both parents and teachers have important roles in educating children and the expertise of a parent *and* teacher can be used to more effectively and efficiently meet the learning needs of each student than the expertise of any one individual (parent *or* teacher; Principle 3).

Power struggles can often be avoided when families and teachers focus on the relationship they share with one another. In doing so, each member can be made to feel valued and respected, allowing for conflicts to be addressed more easily while preserving the relationship (Lake & Billingsley, 2000). However, good intentions are often not enough to amicably resolve all conflicts. Necessary conflict resolution skills that help to maintain healthy relationships will be discussed in a later section.

Although co-equality between families and teachers is a desired condition, it cannot be ignored that families often enter into family-school relationships at a disadvantage. In the context of parent-teacher interactions, teachers often possess the power to uphold their values and epistemologies as valid, whereas families tend to lack the social standing, resources, and capital to exert their opinions (Lareau & McNamara-Horvat, 1999). As a result of this asymmetry in power, the duty falls on educators to initiate interactions with families that reduces their sense of vulnerability, provides them with a sense of co-equality in the relationship (Bryk & Schneider, 2002), and communicates an honest and genuine invitation to work together to promote their child's learning (Principle 2).

### Actions Involved in Healthy Relationships Among Families and Schools

Families and teachers engage in many behaviors that may lead to the development of healthy relationships among families and schools. These actions include purposeful, child-centered activities that seek to unite families and teachers, including communicating effectively, building trust, showing respect, sharing learning experiences, and resolving conflict. These practices are described in the section below.

***Communicating Effectively*** Communication is the primary method by which human beings empower one another, develop intimacy, and create interpersonal relationships (Swick, 2003). For families and teachers, establishing effective, bi-directional communication practices allows both parties to understand the needs and goals of one another and may assist in preventing problems before they occur (Whitaker & Fiore, 2001). As families and educators communicate in a coordinated and organized manner, both parties may have access to important information and resources that may improve the child's functioning in both environments (Blue-Banning et al., 2004). Providing families with information on a consistent basis also demonstrates the belief that they are essential in promoting educational success, which may create goodwill and increase families' willingness to enter a fruitful relationship. Consistent communication also empowers families to view themselves as essential players in their child's progress (Sykes, 2001). Similarly, communication from home to school validates the child as an individual who learns and develops across multiple contexts.

To foster effective bi-directional communication among families and teachers, both individuals may focus on increasing the quantity and quality of their communication with one another over time to develop and maintain a strong connection and consistent support network for each other (Principle 8). The frequency of casual conversation has been shown to directly affect the quality of the parent-teacher relationship. Thus, it is important for families and teachers to have time and opportunities to interact with one another and discuss topics pertinent to the child's progress (Gestwicki, 2000). Written communication methods in the form of e-mails, notes, newsletters, and two-way home-school notes are important tools that can be used to increase communication. For example, families can be encouraged to e-mail teachers to check in on their child's progress, or to communicate events in the home that may affect the child's functioning in the classroom (e.g., the need for an extended absence, the death of a family member). Informal communication opportunities, such as those that exist when family members are dropping off or picking up their child from school are particularly helpful in eliminating barriers that may exist for those who have difficulty reading or who do not speak English (Liontos, 1992). Parent-teacher conferences are another common technique in which teachers and family members may share information and begin to establish successful relationships, especially when conferences are arranged in ways that are jointly determined and conducted in a manner that invites mutual goal-setting and the bi-directional sharing of information.

Strategies focused on increasing the quality of effective communication practices recognize that families and teachers may need to change the manner in which they share information with one another. Blue-Banning et al. (2004) examined what parents and teachers believed to be most important for communicating in an open and honest manner. Both parents and teachers stressed the importance of listening carefully to the other person; avoiding the use of jargon; being nonjudgmental, sensitive, and non-blaming; and including positive comments in addition to describing the challenges that a child currently experiences at home and school.

***Building Trust*** Trust is a critical element to healthy relationships in schools and also a significant predictor of school improvement and parent involvement (Bryk &

Schneider, 2002; Mapp, 2002; Payne & Kaba, 2001). Trust may be strengthened among families and teachers as each party demonstrates to the other that they are committed to following through with an action or promise that was made to the other (Principle 6; Swick, 1993). Families may demonstrate trust for their child's educators by supporting decisions made to promote their child's academic development, returning phone calls, and responding to school correspondence as needed. Teachers communicate trust to families by seeking their input and appreciating their involvement. When teachers elicit information directly from families, they communicate that their involvement and knowledge is critical to student success and a teacher's ability to understand and relate to their students. Teachers who share information about their own backgrounds and experiences help to foster a sense of closeness in the relationship. For example, when teachers share with families how their teaching practices have evolved through various opportunities for personal growth and development, families are able to see and appreciate the honesty and integrity with which teachers conduct their daily lives and may report a deeper sense of closeness in their relationship (Swick, 2003).

The atmosphere of a school also fosters trust among members of a school community. By creating a climate in which families are welcome and invited to participate in their child's education, families may begin to perceive their child's school as an environment in which their involvement and participation is valued and crucial to their child's success (Principle 4; Elizalde-Utnick, 2002). Welcoming environments may be created by greeting family members by name, initiating positive contact when they enter the building, maintaining a clean physical appearance, and using bulletin boards with information that is printed in a family's native language that provides information on activities that will allow families and teachers to connect with one another. Trust is also demonstrated when concerns are responded to in a prompt manner and when teachers try to reach out and increase the length of the interaction between both parties. Such features reinforce the idea that families are welcome in schools, their knowledge and input is vital, and that school professionals value them, their concerns and their suggestions (Adams & Christenson, 1998; McNamara, Telzrow, & DeLamatre, 1999; Soodak & Erwin, 2000). Collectively, these trust-building actions hold promise for strengthening relationships between families and schools.

*Showing Respect*    Respect among families and teachers may be displayed as each member demonstrates esteem, nondiscrimination, and value for the other person (Blue-Banning et al., 2004). Respect from school professionals demonstrates to families an understanding of and appreciation for the many aspects of their daily lives and the environments in which they function (Rudney, 2005). Teachers who enter into relationships with families demonstrate respect for their position as the most important people in a child's life (Gestwicki, 2000). These teachers respect the experiences, knowledge, and expertise that each family member has and, in turn, respect their rights to define their own needs in the education and care of their children. Teachers also demonstrate respect when they show interest and openness in understanding the child and their family (Ramsey, 2002).

The amount of respect families feel from school personnel has been found to be more important in the family-school relationship than how much time families spend at school (Grossman, 1999). Demonstrating respect for families involves avoiding educational jargon and using specific, pertinent information when describing a child's educational growth and social development. Teachers who ask families for their opinions and make use of the information they provide along with respecting the confidentiality of all students and families assists in creating healthy relationships among families and teachers (Gestwicki, 2000).

*Sharing Learning Experiences*   Involving families in meaningful ways to enhance the education of their child is an empowering process that serves to strengthen family-school relationships and promote learning opportunities at home and school. By engaging in shared learning activities, teachers maintain the view that families are co-equal educators and essential to promoting child learning and development throughout their educational career (Esler et al., 2002). Through shared learning experiences, families and teachers are able to provide each other with information and strategies to learn from one another and enhance child well-being (Principles 2 and 3; Swick & Graves, 1993).

Several actions have the potential to crate shared learning experiences (Esler et al., 2002). First, asking families what they desire from their child's teachers is a highly useful and important tactic. This may be accomplished by asking families what their goals are for their child or conducting surveys or assessments to determine what types of information and services families would like to facilitate learning at home. This information can be used for presentations on curriculum, school policy, or parent education in specific areas to meet family needs and enhance child skills.

Second, opportunities to extend the learning environment into the home setting are important, and families can be supported in supplementing information that is taught in schools at home. For example, schools may assist families in such activities by providing them with information to complement school activities and learning experiences. Information on school expectations, curricula, teaching strategies, and child development assist families in understanding how schools function and provide information on how they can assist in their child's development (Christenson, Hurley, Sheridan, & Fenstermacher, 1997; Scott-Jones, 1995). Families may be given specific information about what they can do to be involved, the general effects of family involvement on student learning, and information about their child's curriculum and learning goals (Hoover-Dempsey et al., 2005). As families utilize various sources of information and strategies to assist in their child's learning at home and other out-of-school settings, they may also provide teachers with feedback on how these strategies worked for their child and how they may continue to support their child's education. This form of shared learning allows both parties to contribute constructive information that assists in maintaining constructive relationships between families and educators over time (Hess, Fannin, & Pollom, 2007).

Finally, supporting learning initiatives that families are currently practicing at home can enhance child learning. Families often engage in a number of practices at home to support children as learners in the form of reading books, engaging in cultural rituals, setting expectations for their behavior, providing them with a routine, and monitoring their use of time. Extending the usefulness of these practices by complementing them with consistent experiences at school is one way to share learning experiences across home and school. By taking advantage of pre-existing strategies and techniques utilized in a child's natural learning environment, teachers may expand the usefulness of this setting and create additional opportunities for families and teachers to interact with one another and enhance their relationship.

*Resolving Conflict*    As in any relationship, differences in opinions and viewpoints will inevitably occur among families and teachers. Though many individuals avoid conflict by not sharing their concerns with one another, such avoidance may actually undermine relationships between families and teachers and obstruct student develop-ment. The acquisition of conflict resolution skills allows both parties to find solutions and possibilities in challenges that may otherwise persist throughout one's relationship if not handled effectively. Implementing successful conflict resolution techniques may allow an increase in communication and the flow of information for both parties to maintain healthy relationships throughout a child's development and education (Prin-ciples 1 and 5).

Rudney (2005) describes three nonadversarial approaches to managing conflict in interpersonal relationships: the use of consensus, negotiation skills, and strategies for dealing with anger. *Consensus-based strategies* involve the use of structured problem-solving techniques that aim to satisfy the needs of families, teachers, and students through constructive interactions. The first step in this process is to define the problem or source of conflict. In this stage an important goal is to understand the concerns and perspectives of those involved in addition to factors that may impede goal attainment. Next, a plan is made to gather or share information to ensure that both parties have information to assist them in remediating the problem. Once information is shared, goals for both parties are set in concrete, observable terms. Strategies and solutions that are practical and likely to assist in ameliorating the problem then can be developed by both parties and put in place. Expectations for improvement are discussed along with a time in which parties will come together to review progress, make necessary modifica-tions, and determine if each partner is satisfied with the obtained result.

The use of *negotiation skills* such as engaging in perspective taking, viewing the person apart from the concern, using communication that is focused on the best in-terest of the child and his or her family, or identifying strategies in which parties can work together to support student learning and academic success also assist in conflict resolution (Hanhan, 1998). *Strategies to deal with anger* include meeting with families as soon as problems are identified, listening empathically, asking for clarification as needed, acting as a problem-solver, inviting the family to contribute suggestions, focus-ing on the present, and using a mediator if needed to demonstrate mutual concern for the child and an ability to listen and identify cooperative solutions to assist with the problem (Margolis, 1999).

Throughout the conflict resolution process, it is imperative to focus on the needs of the student and engage in open communication to better understand the problem and any additional areas of concern that may exist. By demonstrating patience, understand-ing, and assurance that families and teachers may continue to work together to address problems and resolve conflicts as they arise.

*Challenges to Establishing Healthy Relationships*

As emphasized in this chapter, and in other chapters in this volume, there are a number of benefits of healthy family-school relationships. However, it is also important to recognize that challenges may exist that prevent families and teachers from establishing constructive relationships. Challenges encountered by adults in a child's home and school environments have been grouped into three categories: interpersonal, logistical, and systems-level challenges (Liontos, 1992). If potential issues are recognized and considered at the outset, steps may be taken to overcome these issues and establish a foundation to sustain close, interpersonal relationships among families and teachers for the duration of a child's education.

Interpersonal challenges exist in a number of forms for families and teachers alike. Many challenges concern attitudes and perceptions that run counter to the ability to form positive relationships. For families, resentment over the way in which their child is viewed at school, alienation due to diverse cultural or language backgrounds, and suspicion over schools not treating them equally may cause families to adopt a passive role (Esler et al., 2002; Liontos, 1992). Furthermore, personal challenges such as lack of a clear role construct for supporting their child's learning, or limited efficacy regarding their parenting skills and ability to help teachers, may preclude families' desires to invest in a relationship with educators. As a result, families may underestimate the influence of their involvement in their child's success at school, and as time passes developing healthy relationships with teachers may become increasingly difficult. Similar attitudinal issues or belief systems operate for teachers as well. For teachers, challenges often include: (a) a lack of understanding for the ways in which families support children, (b) failure to see differences as strengths, (c) fear of criticism concerning their teaching skills and ability to work with families, (d) lack of commitment to family involvement, (e) low expectations for families from disadvantaged backgrounds (e.g., low-income), (f) stereotypes about families and their ability to address concerns for their child, and (g) fear of conflict with families (Christenson & Sheridan, 2001; Esler et al., 2002; Liontos, 1992). All of these barriers may keep families at a distance and prevent them from sharing valuable information to assist in their child's educational development.

Logistical issues also influence the ability of families and teachers to form relationships with one another. Time constraints are frequently reported as a challenge for both parties when attempting to engage with one another (Gestwicki, 2000). Families may face logistical challenges when trying to arrange interactions with teachers due to time conflicts that result from job obligations, child care arrangements, transportation schedules, and other needs that must be met on a regular basis in and out of the home (Esler et al., 2002). Teachers face increased responsibilities in their classrooms due to large class sizes and a lack of flexibility in their daily schedules (Shartrand, Weiss, Kreider, & Lopez, 1997). As a result, teachers are often unable to meet with families when parental work schedules do not coincide with those of the typical school day, and these families may be unable to attend school events such as meetings, programs, and other activities held throughout the year. As a result of these constraints, accommodating the needs of one another is often necessary for families and teachers to have the opportunity to enhance their relationship on behalf of the child's learning.

A lack of family-centered system-level administrative policies may also prevent families and teachers from forming and sustaining healthy relationships. In addition to scheduling constraints, teachers often note a lack of coursework, training, and opportunities for professional development when attempting to engage with families (Radcliffe, Malone, & Nathan, 1994). Limited funding for family outreach programs also derails proactive efforts of teachers attempting to foster family-school relationships (Weiss & Edwards, 1992). By providing information, training, and opportunities for teachers to work together, share information, and coordinate services across grade levels and educational teams, teachers may expand their skill base and feel more efficacious in their role as professionals who are able to effectively form relationships with families to meet the needs of their students (Magito-McLaughlin, Spinosa, & Marsalis, 2002).

Developing cultural sensitivity can be challenging for schools with families representing a wide range of cultural and linguistic backgrounds. Family members can be encouraged to educate school staff as to the beliefs, ideologies, and experiences of the family as they impact the child's learning and development. A willingness on the part of families to communicate information regarding their experiences with teachers allows teachers to broaden their understanding of family backgrounds and to sensitively respond to and respect different cultures. Furthermore, in the same way that it is important for schools to be sensitive to the culture of families, families have a responsibility to understand and respect the culture of the school.

Challenges such as these should not be viewed as negative aspects to forming relationships with families as they can provide families and teachers with opportunities to voice their concerns, engage in a deeper level of perspective taking and problem-solving, and result in a change to pre-existing conditions or practices that fail to promote positive relationships between families and schools (Virginia Department of Education, 2002). To meet these challenges, schools and families must both be willing to identify and systematically address barriers that prevent the development of healthy relationships (Principle 7). It is important that opportunities be established early on for family members to share their hopes, expectations, and goals; facilitate healthy relationships; and promote role constructs reinforcing meaningful family involvement.

## Future Research

Despite the theoretical backdrop and practical significance of the literature base in the area of family-school relationships, its empirical base is wanting. There are several issues that require careful scientific scrutiny to uncover key variables related to the construct of healthy relationships between families and schools. It is clear that one approach to engaging families or one solution to resolving family-school conflicts is neither effective nor appropriate in all situations. However, the specific variables that mediate relationship formation, including the key elements of trust, sensitivity and equality, are speculative at this time. Furthermore, factors that interact with or moderate efforts to support family-school relationships, such as presenting child characteristics, family background, or teacher training are not well understood. Thus, continued investigations using empirically validated measures and complex research methods (e.g., structural equation modeling), are needed to identify the causal links between critical elements and the development of healthy family-school relationships.

In addition, specific means to structure actions intended to build and strengthen relationships are becoming more widespread in the literature; however, few have been subjected to rigorous empirical investigation. Indeed, we hypothesize that relationships are prerequisite to family-school partnership and collaboration models; however, the manner and nature by which these constructs are related has not been the subject of research. Contextual, developmental, and cultural differences are likely, and thus, what is determined to be efficacious in one situation will not necessarily generalize across all. Therefore, large-scale examinations of proposed family-school relationship models are needed with diverse samples across a variety of settings. Indeed, conceptual, structural, and empirical questions remain, and lay the groundwork for fruitful inquiry in the immediate future.

## CONCLUSION

Children's learning and development are influenced by a number of factors, some of which are fixed, others are malleable. One of the earliest predictors of a child's academic and social-emotional functioning is found in his or her relationships with primary caregivers. Indeed, relationships that a child experiences with his or her parents from the earliest stages of development set the stage for a host of important interactions as he/she matures. It is therefore not surprising that those relationships a child's parents hold with teachers and other significant adults is also correlated with important child outcomes throughout the school years. Relationships between families and schools provide the context for the formation of partnerships in education, and fortunately, can be shaped and reinforced with positive attitudes, deliberate attention, and sufficient care. Constructive belief systems that recognize and support cross-system continuity and promote commitment to the maintenance of meaningful family-school connections are prerequisite to healthy relationships. The core elements—trust, sensitivity, and equality—are fundamental to positive relationships and set the stage for intentional, child-centered, effective actions. As relationship elements and deliberate actions evolve, the potential to form and maintain healthy relationships persists and grows.

Although the importance of healthy relationships between families and schools has been established, further empirical investigation is needed to determine the processes by which these relationships are developed and factors that influence their development. Advancements in these areas will help to determine the conditions under which different approaches are effective in building healthy relationships and how these relationships foster family-school partnerships.

## AUTHORS' NOTE

Preparation of this chapter was supported in part by research (NIH #1R01H00436135; IES #R305F05284) and training (OSEP #H325D030050) grants awarded to the second author. The opinions expressed herein are those of the authors and do not suggest endorsement or positions of the granting agencies.

# REFERENCES

Adams, K. S., & Christenson, S. L. (1998). Differences in parent and teacher trust levels: Implications for creating collaborative family-school relationships. *Special Services in the Schools, 14,* 1–22.

Adams, K. S., & Christenson, S. L. (2000). Trust and the family-school relationship examination of parent-teacher differences in elementary and secondary grades. *Journal of School Psychology, 38,* 477–497.

Ainsworth, M. D., Bell, S. M., & Stayton, D. J. (1972). Individual differences in the development of some attachment behaviors. *Merrill-Palmer Quarterly, 18,* 123–143.

Ammeter, A. P., Douglas, C. R., Ferris, G. R., & Goka, H. (2004). A social relationship conceptualization of trust and accountability in organizations. *Human Resource Management Review, 14,* 47–65.

Berger, E. H. (2000). *Parents as partners in education: Families and schools working together.* Upper Saddle River, NJ: Prentice-Hall.

Blue-Banning, M., Summers, J. A., Frankland, H. C., Nelson, L. L., & Beegle, G. (2004). Dimensions of family and professional partnerships: Constructive guidelines for collaboration. *Exceptional Children, 70,* 167–184.

Bronfenbrenner, U. (1979). Toward an experimental ecology of human development. *American Psychologist, 32,* 513–531.

Bronfenbrenner, U. (1979). *The ecology of human development: Experimental by nature and design.* Cambridge, MA: Harvard University Press.

Bryk, A. S., & Schneider, B. (2002). *Trust in schools: A core resource for improvement.* New York: Russell Sage Foundation.

Bushe, P. J., & Stets, J. E. (1999). Trust and commitment through self-evaluation. *School Psychology Quarterly, 62,* 347–360.

Christenson, S. L., & Hirsch, J. (1998). Facilitating partnerships and conflict resolution between families and schools. In K. C. Stoiber & T. Kratochwill (Eds.), *Handbook of group interventions for children and families* (pp. 307–344). Boston: Allyn & Bacon.

Christenson, S. L., Hurley, C. M., Sheridan, S. M., & Fenstermacher, K. (1997). Parents' and school psychologists' perspectives on parent involvement activities. *School Psychology Review, 26,* 111–130.

Christenson, S. L., & Sheridan, S. M. (2001). *Schools and families: Creating essential connections for children's learning.* New York: Guilford.

Comer, J. P. (1984). Home-school relationships as they affect the academic success of children. *Education and Urban Society 16,* 323–337.

Dinnebeil, L. A., Hale, L., & Rule, S. (1996). A qualitative analysis of parents' and service coordinators' descriptions of variables that influence collaborative relationships. *Topics in Early Childhood Special Education, 16,* 322–347.

Dinnebeil, L. A., Hale, L. M., & Rule, S. (2000). Early intervention practices that support collaboration between parents and service coordinators. *Topics in Early Childhood Special Education, 19,* 225–235.

Dunsmuir, S., Frederickson, N., & Lang, J. (2004). Building home-school trust. *Educational and Child Psychology, 21,* 110–128.

Dunst, C. J., Johanson, C., Rounds, T., Trivette, C. M., & Hamby, D. (1992). Characteristics of parent-professional partnership. In S. Christenson & J. C. Conoley (Eds.), *Home-school collaboration: Building a fundamental educational resource* (pp. 157–174). Washington, DC: National Association of School Psychologists.

Elizalde-Utnick, G. (2002). Best practices in building partnerships with families. In A. Thomas & J. Grimes (Eds.), *Best practices in school psychology IV* (pp. 413–429). Bethesda, MD: National Association of School Psychologists.

Esler, A. N., Godber, Y., & Christenson, S. L. (2002). Best practices in supporting home-school collaboration. In A. Thomas & J. Grimes (Eds.), *Best practices in school psychology IV* (pp. 389–411). Bethesda, MD: National Association of School Psychologists.

Gestwicki, C. (2000). *Home, school, and community relations: A guide to working with families, 4th edition.* Albany, NY: Thomson Learning.

Goddard, R. D., Tschannen-Moran, M., & Hoy, W. K. (2001). A multilevel examination of the distribution and effects of teacher trust in students and parents in urban elementary schools. *Elementary School Journal, 10,* 3–17.

Grossman, S. (1999). Examining the origins of our beliefs about parents. *Childhood Education, 76,* 24–27.

Hamre, B. K., & Pianta, R. C. (2005). Can instructional and emotional support in the first-grade classroom make a difference for children at risk of school failure? *Child Development, 76,* 949–967.

Hanhan, S. F. (1998). Parent-teacher communication: Who's talking? In M. L. Fuller & G. Olson (Eds.), *Home-school relations* (pp. 106–125). Needham Heights, MA: Allyn & Bacon.

Harry, B., Kalyanpur, M., & Day, M. (1999). *Building cultural reciprocity with families: Case studies in special education*. Baltimore: Paul H. Brookes.

Haynes, N., & Ben-Avie, M. (1996). Parents as full partners in education. In A. Booth & J. Dunn (Eds.), *Family school links* (pp. 45–56). Mahwah, NJ: Erlbaum.

Henderson, A. T. & Mapp, K. L. (2002). *A new wave of evidence; The impact of school, family, and community connections on students achievement*. Austin, TX: National Center of Family & Community Connections with Schools: Southwest Educational Development Laboratory.

Hess, J. A., Fannin, A. D., & Pollom, L. H. (2007). Creating closeness: Discerning and measuring strategies for fostering closer relationships. *Personal Relationships, 14,* 25–44.

Holmes, J. G., & Rempel, J. K. (1989). Trust in close relationships. In C. Hendrick (Ed.), *Close relationships* (pp. 187–220). Newbury Park, CA: Sage.

Hoover-Dempsey, K. V., Walker, J. M., Sandler, H. M., Whetsel, D., Green, C. L., Wilkins, A. S., & Closson, K. (2005). Why do parents become involved? Research findings and implications. *The Elementary School Journal, 106,* 105–130.

Kewal Ramani, A., Gilbertson, L., Fox, M., & Provasnik, S. (2007). *Status and trends in the education of racial and ethnic minorities* (NCES 2007-039). Washington, DC: U.S. Department of Education, National Center for Education Statistics.

Lake, J. F., & Billingsley, B. S. (2000). An analysis of factors that contribute to parent school conflict in special education. *Remedial and Special Education, 21,* 240–251.

Lareau, A., & McNamara-Horvat, E. (1999) Moments of social inclusion and exclusion: Race, class and cultural capital in family-school relationships. *Sociology of Education, 71,* 37–53.

Liontos, L. B. (1992). *At-risk families and schools: Becoming partners* (ERIC Document Reproduction Service No. EA 023 283). Eugene, OR: ERIC.

Magito-McLaughlin, D., Spinosa, T. R., & Marsalis, M. D. (2002). Overcoming the barriers: Moving toward a service model that is conducive to person-centered planning. In S. Holburn & P. M. Vietze (Eds.), *Person-centered planning: Research, practice, and future directions* (pp. 127–150). Baltimore: Paul H. Brookes.

Mangione, P. L., & Speth, T. (1998). The transition to elementary school: A framework for creating early childhood continuity through home, school, and community partnerships. *The Elementary School Journal, 98,* 381–397.

Mapp, K. L. (2002). *Having their say: Parents describe how and why they are involved in their children's education.* Paper presented at the annual meeting at the American Educational Research Association, New Orleans, LA.

Margolis, H. (1999). Mediation for special education conflicts: An opportunity to improve family-school relationships. *Journal of Educational and Psychological Consultation, 10,* 91–100.

McKay, M. M., Atkins, M. S., Hawkins, T., Brown, C., & Lynn, C. J. (2003). Inner-city African-American parental involvement in children's schooling: Racial socialization and social support from the parent community. *American Journal of Community Psychology 32,* 107–114.

McNamara, K., Telzrow, C., & DeLamatre, J. (1999). Parent reactions to implementation of intervention-based assessment. *Journal of Educational and Psychological Consultation, 10,* 343–362.

Merriam-Webster. (2008). Relationship. In *Merriam-Webster Dictionary On-Line*. Retrieved January 9, 2008, from http://www.merriam-webster.com/dictionary

Minke, K. M. (2006). Parent-teacher relationships. In G. G. Bear & K. M. Minke (Eds.), *Children's needs III: Development, prevention, and intervention* (pp. 73–85). Bethesda, MD: National Association of School Psychologists.

National Center for Education Statistics. (2007). *Status and trends in the education of racial and ethnic minorities* (NCES 2007-039). Washington, DC: U.S. Department of Education.

Nugent, P. D., & Abolafia, M. Y. (2006). The creation of trust through interaction and exchange: The role of consideration in organizations. *Group and Organizational Management, 31,* 628–650.

Olivos, E. M. (2004). Tensions, contradictions, and resistance: An activist's reflection on the struggles of Latino parents in the public school system. *The High School Journal, 87,* 25–35.

Patrikakou, E. N., & Weissberg, R. P. (1999). The seven P's of school-family partnerships. *Education Week XVIII, 21,* 36.

Payne, C. M., & Kaba, M. (2001). So much reform, so little change: Building-level obstacles to urban school reform. *Journal of Negro Education, 2,* 1–16.

Pianta, R. C. (1999). *Enhancing relationships between children and teachers.* Washington, DC: American Psychological Association.

Pianta, R. C., & Walsh, D. J. (1996). *High-risk children in schools: Constructing sustaining relationships.* New York: Routledge.

Pianta, R., & Stuhlman, M. (2004). Teacher–child relationships and children's success in the first years of school. *School Psychology Review, 33,* 444–458.

Radcliffe, B., Malone, M., & Nathan, J. (1994). *Training for parent partnership: Much more should be done.* Minneapolis: Center for School Change, Hubert H. Humphrey Institute of Public Affairs, University of Minnesota.

Ramsey, R. D. (2002). *How to say the right thing every time: Communicating well with students, staff, parents, and the public.* Thousand Oaks, CA: Corwin Press.

Raver, C. C., & Knitzer, J. (2002). *Ready to enter: What research tells policymakers about strategies to promote social and emotional school readiness among three- and four-year-old children.* New York: National Center for Children in Poverty.

Rempel, J. K., Holmes, J. G., & Zanna, M. P. (1985). Trust in close relationships. *Journal of Personality and Social Psychology, 49,* 95–112.

Rudney, G. L. (2005). *Every teacher's guide to working with parents.* Thousand Oaks, CA: Corwin.

Scott-Jones, D. (1995). Parent-child interactions and school achievement. In B. A. Ryan, G. R. Adams, T. P. Gullotta, R. P. Weissberg, & R. L. Hampton (Eds.), *The family-school connection: Theory, research, and practice: Vol. 2. Issues in Children's and Families Lives* (pp. 75–107). Thousand Oaks, CA: Sage.

Shartrand, A. M., Weiss, H. B., Kreider, H. M., & Lopez, M. E. (1997). *New skills for new schools: Preparing teachers in family involvement.* Cambridge, MA: Harvard Family Research Project.

Sheridan, S. M., & Kratochwill, T. R. (2008). *Conjoint behavioral consultation: Promoting family-school connections and interventions.* New York: Springer.

Soodak, L. C., & Erwin, E. J. (2000). Valued member or tolerated participant: Parents' experience in inclusive early childhood settings. *Journal of the Association for Persons with Severe Handicaps, 25,* 29–41.

Swick, K. J. (1993). *Strengthening parents and families during the early childhood years.* Champaign, IL: Stipes.

Swick, K. J. (2003). Communication concepts for strengthening family-school-community partnerships. *Early Childhood Education Journal, 30,* 275–280.

Swick, K. J., & Graves, S. (1993). *Empowering at-risk families during the early childhood years.* Washington, DC: National Education Association.

Sykes, G. (2001). Home-school agreements: A tool for parental control or for partnership? *Educational Psychology in Practice, 17,* 273–286.

Thompson, R. A. (2002). The roots of school readiness in social and emotional development. *Kauffman Early Education Exchange, 1,* 8–29.

U.S. Department of Education, National Center for Education Statistics. (2007). *The condition of education 2007* (NCES 2007-064). Washington, DC: U.S. Government Printing Office.

Virginia Department of Education (2002). *Collaborative family-school relationships for children's learning: Beliefs and practices.* Richmond, VA: Author

Weiss, H. M., & Edwards, M. E. (1992). The family-school collaboration project: Systemic interventions for school improvement. In S. L. Christenson & J. C. Conoley (Eds.), *Home-school collaboration: Enhancing children's academic and social competence* (pp. 215–243). Silver Spring, MD: National Association of School Psychologists.

Whitaker, T., & Fiore, D. J., (2001). *Dealing with difficult parents and with parents in difficult situations.* Larchmont, NY: Eye on Education.

# 4

## DIVERSITY IN FAMILIES

*Parental Socialization and Children's Development and Learning*

LYNN OKAGAKI AND GARY E. BINGHAM

Maria walks her twin boys—Rafael and Manual—to their first day of school. The boys are excited and little afraid. What will school be like? Who will be their teacher? But most of all, how can it be that their teacher doesn't speak Spanish like they do? What does that mean? Maria and her husband Miguel moved to California from Mexico a few months before school started. They believe that school is important and want their boys to learn so that one day they can have good jobs and good lives in the United States. Maria and Miguel do not know that much about how school works in California or what their children will be expected to learn and do. They prepare the boys by telling them to behave, to respect their teacher, and to follow what the other children are doing. They believe that if children are well behaved they will be ready to learn in school.

Most parents want their children to do well in school. However, parents have different ideas about (a) what children should learn, (b) how children learn, (c) what it means to do well in school, (d) what children need to do to succeed in school, and (e) what parents and schools should do to support children's education. This constellation of social cognitions—beliefs, values, perceptions, attributions, and expectations—that are related to education and learning contribute to parents' cultural models of education and learning (Gallimore & Goldenberg, 2001; Lareau, 1996). Cultural models are widely shared views within a group about "how the world works, or ought to work" (Gallimore & Goldenberg, 2001, p. 47).

### OVERVIEW

In this chapter, empirical research that attempts to describe and unpack parents' cultural models of education and consider how these cultural models of education may inform parents' involvement in their child's schooling was reviewed. Many parents are directly engaged in their child's schooling in ways that meet the expectations of teachers and school administrators; other parents utilize indirect strategies to support their child's education. A broad definition of parental support for children's schooling and engagement in schooling activities is utilized in order to capture the wide range of approaches that parents utilize to support their children's schooling. The coverage of research in this chapter is not intended to be comprehensive; rather studies were selected that highlight diversity in parental socialization for learning and may thereby contribute to expanding understanding of parent-school relationships. To begin the chapter, a thumbnail overview of the cultural and socioeconomic diversity in U.S. schools is provided.

## CULTURAL AND SOCIOECONOMIC DIVERSITY IN THE UNITED STATES

Across the United States, the public school population is remarkably diverse. According to the U.S. Department of Education (2007), children of color in kindergarten through high school represent about 40% of the public school enrollment. The cultural diversity among U.S. students reflects many aspects of students' backgrounds, including race and ethnicity, ancestry, immigrant or generational status, socioeconomic status, and home language. Typically, however, data are reported using broad racial/ethnic groupings. For example, although the U.S. Department of Education generally reports outcomes for five broad racial/ethnic groupings—non-Hispanic White, non-Hispanic Black, Hispanic, Asian/Pacific Islander, and American Indian/Native Alaskan—these broad categories mask the variation in cultural heritage within groups and may lead to overgeneralizations of differences among ethnic groups (Okagaki & Bingham, 2005). For example, consider the diversity among Hispanic Americans in the United States. As of 2006, the U.S. Census Bureau (2006) estimates that 44.3 million Americans are of Hispanic descent. Within this broad group, however, are those who identify themselves as being Mexican (65.5%), Puerto Rican (8.6%), Cuban (3.7%), Central American (8.2%, with the largest subgroups being Salvadorans, Guatemalans, and Hondurans), South American (6%, with the largest subgroups being Colombians, Ecuadorians, and Peruvians), and other Hispanics (8%, including those who only identified as Hispanic, Latino, or Spanish without indicating specific ancestry or nationality; U.S. Census Bureau, 2006). Across these subgroups, the level of education varies widely; Hispanics of South American origins (e.g., Colombians, Ecuadorians, and Peruvians) have the highest percentage of adults with high school and college educations (82.6% and 31%, respectively; U.S. Census Bureau, 2006), while Hispanic adults of Mexican origins have the lowest levels (53.1% and 8.5%, respectively; U.S. Census Bureau, 2006). Further, the histories, customs, economies, and political contexts of each of the countries of origin contribute to the heterogeneity of the Hispanic population (e.g., Carrasquillo, 1991; Torres, 2004) and have been suggested as important factors to consider when studying Hispanic school achievement (Tapia, 2004).

Another factor related to the experiences of students from non-majority backgrounds is the distribution of students within a particular community. Although American Indian/Alaska Native students are only 1.2% of the total population of U.S. students, they are a sizable minority in Alaska (25.9%), Oklahoma (17.9%), Montana (10.9%), and North and South Dakota (8.1% and 10.6%, respectively; U.S. Department of Education, 2007). Overall, Hispanic students constitute about 20% of U.S. students. However, 90% of Hispanic students live in 16 states (U.S. Census Bureau, 2001). In California and Arizona, Hispanic students represent more than a third of the student population. Students in communities with higher percentages of minority students may have a substantially different educational experience as compared to students in communities with less diversity.

Understanding the cultural diversity of U.S. school children is further complicated by the fact that students' socioeconomic status relates to many school outcomes and in and of itself produces considerable variation within ethnic groups. About 41% of all fourth grade students are eligible to receive free and reduced priced lunch; however the proportion of eligible students varies greatly by racial/ethnic group. In contrast to the 24% of White students who qualify to receive a free or reduced-priced lunch, 73% of Hispanic students, 70% of Black students, and 65% of American Indian students are eligible (U.S. Department of Education, 2007).

Growing up in poverty is associated with students' academic achievement (Sirin, 2005) and with students' general orientation to school. On average, students from low-income backgrounds report missing more days of school relative to children from middle-income or high-income backgrounds (U.S. Department of Education, 2007). Students' socioeconomic backgrounds are also related to their expectations for higher education course taking. About 29% of low-income Grade 12 students anticipate graduating from college; 22% foresee obtaining a graduate or professional degree. In contrast, 36% of students from middle-income backgrounds and 33% of students from higher socioeconomic backgrounds expect to obtain a bachelor's degree; 31% of middle-income students and 53% of higher-income students expect to obtain a graduate or professional degree (U.S. Department of Education, 2007).

Finally, in contrast to the great diversity among students, kindergarten through high school teachers are a relatively homogenous group. Of the three million teachers in public education, the vast majority (83.2%) are White (U.S. Department of Education, 2007). Across minority groups, we find about 7.8% of teachers in U.S. public schools are Black; 6.2% are Hispanic; and 1.4% are Asian. Less than 1% of teachers identify themselves as being in each of the following groups: Pacific Islanders, American Indian/Alaskan Natives, or multiracial. Finally, the majority of teachers are women, particularly in elementary schools (84%), with most teachers above the age of 40 (59%).

The diversity among students in U.S. public schools coupled with the homogeneity of U.S. public school teachers provides the opportunity for schools to be settings in which the participants—school staff, students, and parents—may hold very different expectations for their roles and responsibilities (e.g., Hauser-Cram, Sirin, & Stipek, 2003; Lasky, 2000). In the following sections, research is highlighted to provide insight into the ways in which parents' cultural models of education differ both across and within cultural and socioeconomic groups. It cannot be overemphasized, however, that caution is needed to guard against over generalizing the findings of these studies. Despite observed differences in parental belief systems across cultural and socioeconomic groups, considerable variation in parents' beliefs exists within these groups. As this chapter describes different cultural models of education and learning, significant caution should be taken against stereotyping individuals within these groups.

## DIVERSITY AND PARENTAL SUPPORT FOR LEARNING

In this section, research on parents' conceptions of education, their expectations and aspirations for their children's education, their involvement in schooling, and their beliefs about the development of literacy skills is examined. Some have argued that the variation observed across racial and ethnic groups may be more attributable to socioeconomic differences within a culture than differences across cultural groups (e.g., Hoff, Laursen, & Tardiff, 2002). Research that teases apart the contributions of racial/ethnic background and socioeconomic backgrounds to cultural models of education is relatively limited. Where possible, explicit differences are noted that reflect racial and ethnic cultures versus socioeconomic differences. In the descriptions of individual studies, the terminology for describing particular groups (e.g., Latino, Hispanic) that was chosen by the authors of the studies was used.

### Perspectives on Education

Studies of non-majority families have revealed conceptions of education that intertwine academic knowledge with morality and virtue (e.g., Gibson, 1993; Goldenberg & Gallimore, 1995; Hieshima & Schneider, 1994). In a longitudinal study of immigrant Latino families from Mexico and Central America, parents articulated a conception of education as one that depended on children knowing right from wrong and culminated in a person who is morally upright. Parents thought the most important preparation for their child's education was to give the child a strong moral foundation and socialize the child to respect adults and to behave well (Reese, Balzano, Gallimore, & Goldenberg, 1995).

> It's more necessary to educate children morally than academically. In order to educate, if a teacher is given a child who doesn't have moral principles, or who isn't morally prepared, it will be difficult to teach this child academic things. A child will learn more easily if he already knows how to respect and treat others. (Case #33, Reese et al., 1995, p. 65)

For this group of parents, to be well educated meant that an individual had become a good, morally upright person. A common theme that emerged from the interviews was the interlacing of gaining academic knowledge with becoming a person with good morals who respected others.

> If one is a good person, you are going to be a good student. And if you are not a good person it is not possible to be a good student. These are things that cannot be separated. (Case #64, Goldenberg & Gallimore, 1995, p. 198)

Believing that teaching children to abide by moral and behavioral standards is important to enabling children to succeed in school has also been observed among poor African American families (e.g., Brody & Flor, 1998; Gutman & McLoyd, 2000).

In Asian cultures, the importance of education has been linked to a strong belief in human malleability and an emphasis on the importance of bringing honor to one's family (Chen & Uttal, 1988). These beliefs may provide a context in which motivation for educational achievement is high and a context in which parents and children believe that educational achievement is attainable—it is simply a matter of effort. A number of researchers have suggested that in Asian American families, children are encouraged to do well in school because school achievement brings honor to the family. Schneider and her colleagues (Hieshima & Schneider, 1994; Schneider & Lee, 1990) have argued that the economic rewards for obtaining additional education are lower for Asian American students than for European American students. Therefore, they suggested that the motivation for educational attainment must include the hope for noneconomic rewards such as self-improvement and bringing honor to the family. Moreover, among many Asian American families, educational success reflects not only on the student, but also on the parent (e.g., Caplan, Choy, & Whitmore, 1992; Hieshima & Schneider, 1994; Kibria, 1993). In her work with immigrant Chinese mothers, Chao (1994, 2001) reported that one of the primary goals of the mothers was to help their children succeed in school; to be a good mother was operationalized as having children who do well in school.

As with the Latino immigrant families in the study by Goldenberg and colleagues (Goldenberg & Gallimore, 1995; Reese et al., 1995), in some Asian American cultural groups, to be well-educated is part of what it means to be a good person. Education functions as a pathway to virtue and honor. In an ethnographic study of Punjabi high school students, Gibson (1993) observed that students were "told that those who do well in school can expect to find better marriage partners, that their accomplishments bring credit to their family, and that they set an example for other younger Punjabis to follow" (p. 121).

The importance of moral development as a part of becoming an educated person has the potential to create conflicts with school. Research on both immigrant Latino and Asian parents have uncovered parents' concerns about what are perceived to be negative influences that children are exposed to at school (e.g., Kibria, 1993; Reese et al., 1995). Reese and colleagues (1995) reported that immigrant Mexican and Central American parents were concerned about children being taught content related to moral issues before their children were morally prepared to handle such topics (e.g., sexually transmitted diseases). Parents were also apprehensive about the potential for children being introduced to drugs or gangs in school. Such concerns could lead parents, for example, to remove children from U.S. schools and send them to live with relatives in Mexico. In an ethnographic study of Vietnamese immigrants living in Philadelphia in the early 1980s, Kibria (1993) described similar worries expressed by parents. From parents' perspectives, schools contributed to the "Americanization" of their children and becoming American was not entirely a good quality for their offspring.

> The biggest problem of living here is that it's difficult to teach your children how to be good and to have good behavior. The children learn how to be American from the schools, and then we don't understand them and they don't obey us. The customs here are so different from our culture. (Vietnamese American mother, Kibria, 1993, p. 132)

Parents not only have different global conceptions of education, but also have different ideas about what teachers should be doing in the classroom. For example, Okagaki and Sternberg (1993) examined parents' ideas about primary grade teachers' classroom goals among Cambodian, Filipino, Mexican, and Vietnamese immigrant parents and parents who were born in the United States with European American and Mexican American backgrounds. They found that European American and Mexican American parents believed that it was important for teachers to help their students develop knowledge and problem-solving skills. The immigrant parents reported that teaching children how to do their work neatly was just as important as developing children's knowledge and thinking skills.

Even though parents may perceive negative aspects of schooling, in most studies of minority cultural groups in the United States, researchers have found that parents do value education. Many parents believe that education provides access to opportunities—a means to attaining a better life (e.g., Goldenberg & Gallimore, 1995: Sue & Okazaki, 1990)—and want their children to do well in school. But, what does it mean to do well in school? In the next section, parents' expectations and aspirations for their child's education are examined.

### Parents' Aspirations and Expectations for Their Child

In a meta-analysis including 25 studies, Fan and Chen (2001) examined the relations between parenting and school achievement. Across the studies, they identified five dimensions of parenting: educational expectations, communication with child about school, supervision, parental participation in school activities, and other/general parental involvement. Across the five dimensions, parents' expectation for their child's education was the strongest predictor of children's academic outcomes. A similar finding was obtained in an analysis of data from the National Education Longitudinal Study of 1988 (NELS-88), a nationally representative sample of eighth grade students in 1988 (Trivette & Anderson, 1995). Comparing four aspects of parenting—parental expectations for children's education, parent-child communication about school, parents' participation in school activities, and supervision—Trivette and Anderson found that parental expectations had the strongest relation to student achievement. Parental expectations have also been found to predict specific aspects of educational achievement, such as participation in advanced mathematics courses (e.g., Ma, 2001).

Numerous studies have demonstrated that parents' expectations differ across racial and ethnic groups (e.g., Alexander, Entwisle, & Bedinger, 1994; Hao & Bonstead-Bruns, 1998; Okagaki & Frensch, 1998). Hao and Bonstead-Bruns (1998) examined differences in parents' expectations across immigrant Chinese, Filipino, Korean, and Mexican parents and native Mexican, Black, and White parents using data from NELS:88. Across the sample, parents' expectations were predicted by immigrant status and ethnicity, as well as by indicators of socioeconomic status. In general, they found that the Asian immigrant parents reported higher expectations for their children as compared to native White, Black, and Mexican parents and immigrant Mexican parents. In addition, across groups, parents' expectations were positively related to student achievement. Hao and Bonstead-Bruns (1998) also documented that parents' education, occupation, and income were positively related to their expectations for their child's educational attainment. However, with parents' expectations in the model, these indicators of socioeconomic status were not directly related to student achievement.

Within cultural and socioeconomic groups, parents' expectations have been positively correlated with children's school performance (a) among African American families (e.g., Flowers & Flowers, 2008; Gill & Reynolds, 2000; Halle, Kurtz-Costes, & Mahoney, 1997; Luster & McAdoo, 1996); (b) Asian American families (e.g., Okagaki & Frensch, 1998), and Latino families (e.g., Goldenberg, Gallimore, Reese, & Garnier, 2001; Okagaki & Frensch, 1998). Flowers and Flowers (2008) investigated the relations between a number of child and family variables and urban African American eighth graders' reading achievement using a subsample of students from the Educational Longitudinal Study of 2002, a study following a cohort of over 15,000 eighth grade students in 2002. Parents' expectations for their child's educational attainment were positively correlated with reading achievement. Among indicators of socioeconomic status, family income was positively related to reading achievement; however, parents' education was not.

Current research efforts have sought to determine the causal direction of the relation between parents' expectations and children's achievement and the process by which parents' expectations may affect their child's achievement. A limitation of most research on parental expectations and children's achievement has been that studies have typically captured the relation between the two at a single point in time. A notable exception is a study by Goldenberg and colleagues (2001) examining the aspirations and expectations of Latino immigrant parents from the time their child began kindergarten to sixth grade. Over the course of the child's elementary school years, parents' *aspirations* for school attainment—that is, how much education they wanted their child to have—remained high and were generally not correlated with the child's previous year's school performance. Parents wanted their children to go to college. Parents' *expectations* for their child's school attainment—the amount of formal education parents thought their child would obtain—were lower than parents' aspirations and fluctuated more from year to year. Path analyses were conducted to test whether parents' expectations predicted student achievement or student achievement predicted parents' expectations; among these Latino immigrant families, student performance in the previous year generally predicted parents' expectations with small to moderate correlations between student performance and subsequent expectations. Information garnered from parent interviews supported this model. For instance, when parents observed that their son's or daughter's performance and interest in school had improved, they thought their child would ultimately go further in school. When parents noted that their child was not doing well in school, their expectations were lower.

Scholars have suggested that the causal direction and the strength of relations between parents' expectations and their children's academic achievement may in fact differ across ethnic groups for a number of reasons. First, parents have different ideas about which decisions (e.g., how much schooling, what type of job to pursue) should be determined by the child and which should be decided by the parents (e.g., Azmitia, Cooper, Garcia, & Dunbar, 1996; Goldenberg et al., 2001; Harry, 1992; Joe & Malach, 1992). Second, as Alexander and colleagues (1994) noted, high expectations are not particularly helpful (or in turn, predictive of subsequent child outcomes) if parents do not have an accurate perception of where their child is in terms of knowledge and skills (i.e., what does the child have to learn to achieve the desired goal), do not have an effective plan of action for helping the child achieve the goal, or do not have access to the resources to enact the plan of action. They observed that the relation between parents' expectations and their child's subsequent performance was stronger for parents who more accurately recalled their child's prior grades. Third, when parents say they expect their son or daughter to go to college or to graduate from college, this does not necessarily mean that parents have an accurate conceptualization of what that means. For example, the connection between postsecondary education and careers may not be understood by the parents. In a study of low-income Mexican American families, parents had high aspirations for the types of jobs they hoped their child would have (e.g., doctors, lawyers, scientists), but it was clear from their educational aspirations (e.g., none mentioned graduate education) that they did not have an accurate understanding of the educational pathways that would lead their child toward that goal (Azmitia et al., 1996). Finally, the impact of parents' expectations on children's achievement may also be a function of the transmission of those expectations to the child. Researchers have found that there is greater agreement between parents' expectations and their young adolescent's expectations when parents and students work together on learning activities (Hao & Bonstead-Burns, 1998).

Researchers have explored multiple aspects of parents' expectations. Okagaki and Frensch (1998) asked Asian American, European American, and Latino parents for fourth and fifth graders about their aspirations and expectations for their child's education, and in addition, asked what would be the *very least amount* of schooling they would allow their child to attain. Compared to other parents, Asian American parents had higher educational aspirations and expectations for their children. Asian American parents ideally wanted their children to obtain a graduate or professional degree; they expected their children to graduate from college. The minimum educational attainment they set for their children was college graduation. In contrast, the ideal educational attainment level for Latino and European American parents was for their children to graduate from college. However, Latino and European American parents expected their children to get some college education. For European American parents, the lower boundary was high school graduation; for Latino parents, the lower boundary was some college education. Finally, controlling for the child's grades from the previous year and parents' perceptions of their child's ability to do school work, differences across groups on expected school attainment and minimum school attainment remained. In other words, differences in parents' expectations for their child's educational attainment were *not* solely a function of how well the child actually performed during the previous year or parents' perceptions of their child's abilities. Although this particular study focused on differences across groups, other studies have found that within ethnic groups, parents of high- and low-achievers differ in their aspirations and expectations for their child's education (e.g., Okagaki, Frensch, & Gordon, 1995).

Okagaki and Frensch (1998) also examined parents' expectations for their child's day-to-day school performance. Parents were asked how happy or satisfied they would be if their child received an A, B, C, D, or F for his or her schoolwork. Everyone was happy with As and unhappy with Ds and Fs. The difference came with parents' responses to Bs and Cs. Compared to other parents, Asian American parents were less satisfied with grades of Bs and Cs. Moreover, parents' expectations for their child's school performance obtained at the beginning of the school year were correlated with children's school achievement at the end of the year. For Latino and European American families, parents' responses to Ds predicted student performance; for Asian American families, parents' responses to Bs were correlated with student performance.

Parents have different ideas about how much education they want and expect for their child and how well they expect their child to do in school. In addition, parents have different ideas about their roles and responsibilities in the education process. In the section, we consider various approaches that parents take to their support and engagement in their child's education.

## Parent Engagement in Children's Learning and Schooling

Numerous studies have demonstrated that higher levels of certain types of parental engagement with learning are associated with better child outcomes (e.g., Dearing, Kreider, Simpkins, & Weiss, 2006; Fan, 2001; Fan & Chen, 2001; Hill & Craft, 2003). Although researchers have developed various categorization rubrics for describing parental engagement in learning strategies (e.g., structural versus managerial strategies, Chao, 2000; parent-child communication, home supervision, educational expectations, and school contact, Fan & Chen, 2001), for the sake of this chapter, parental engagement in learning strategies is divided into two global categories: direct strategies (e.g., helping with homework, participating in school activities) and indirect strategies (e.g., setting rules for doing homework and watching television, creating a space within the home for the child to study, providing extra workbooks to give the child more practice). In this section, examples of the diverse ways in which parents are involved in their children's schooling are highlighted. The objective is to provide insight into parents' perspectives on how they view their role in their child's schooling and what they do to support their child's education. Finally, the majority of the research that we describe is descriptive studies of relatively small samples of racial and ethnic minority families and working and lower-class families. Given the great diversity within these groups, the findings should be considered as examples of how parents from a particular group might respond but should not be over-generalized to represent the beliefs and practices of all parents within a group. To underscore this point, research comparing parents of high- and low-achieving students within groups is included.

When racial and ethnic minority parents and parents from low socioeconomic households do not appear to be involved in their child's schooling by participating in school events and communicating with teachers and school staff, this limited involvement does not necessarily reflect parents' lack of interest in their child's education (e.g., Delgado-Gaitan, 1992; Lareau, 1996; Ramirez, 2003). Hoover-Dempsey and colleagues (2001) posited that parental engagement in homework was a function of parents' conceptions of their roles, the belief that helping will make a difference, and their perceptions of the degree to which their child or their child's teacher wants them to help. Similarly, Overstreet, Devine, Bevans, and Efreom (2005) examined predictors of school engagement (defined as visiting the school and participating in school events) in a group of

159 low-income parents and guardians of elementary through high school students from an urban public-housing development. Two key predictors of parents' engagement in school activities were parents' educational aspirations for their child and their perception of the degree to which the school listens to them and provided activities for parents. Qualitative studies provide insight into parents' perceptions of their children's schools. Ramirez (2003) conducted interviews with 43 immigrant Latino parents. Based on these interviews, he identified barriers to parents' participation in school activities, such as lack of interpreters for Spanish speakers at school meetings and failure on the school's part to communicate when meetings would occur. In addition, parents in this study expressed frustration that the school staff assumed that parents had an understanding of the culture of the school—for instance, knowing when traditional events (e.g., Open House) occurred and what to do at such events. Parents also were dismayed that teachers seemed to have limited knowledge about the cultural backgrounds of the families and a lack of awareness that the language, history, and customs of different nationalities (e.g., Guatemalan, El Salvadoran, Mexican) are not the same. Sometimes parents may limit their participation in school activities because they do not perceive the school to be welcoming to them. Such an assertion is supported by Patrikakou & Weisberg (2000) who found that the strongest predictor of parents' involvement with school (conceptualized as both parents' participation in home activities, such as homework and reading to their child, and direct interactions with the school and teacher) was parents' perceptions of teacher outreach practices (i.e., teacher behaviors that encourage parents to be engaged in their child's schooling). Hence, parents are more likely to participate in school activities when they perceive that teachers and schools are welcoming and supportive.

Wanting to help children with their education and knowing what to do to help children are different. Drummond and Stipek (2004) interviewed 234 low-income African American, Caucasian, and Latino parents of second and third grade students to assess their beliefs about their role in children's schooling. In general, parents affirmed the belief that parents should help their child with reading, math, and homework, that parents should be aware of what their child is learning in school, and that they should help their child with other things related to school. However, in response to probes about *what* parents should do, half of the parents provided only vague suggestions, such as "help" or "support" the child. It was not clear from their responses that these parents had specific strategies for helping or supporting their child. In general, parents' ratings of their beliefs about helping children with schoolwork did not vary across ethnic groups; parents of second graders had higher overall ratings on helping children with math and being aware of what children are doing in school relative to parents of third graders. One insight from this study comes from an analysis in which parents were divided into two groups based on whether their child's teacher indicated that he or she had given the parent specific suggestions about helping the child in reading or in math. For reading, parents of second and third graders rated helping their child as being more important when teachers had given them specific ideas about what to do with their child. For math, the same was true for parents of third grade students, but there was no difference for parents of second graders. Drummond and Stipek posited that although most low-income parents believed that parents should help their child with schoolwork that many may not have very clear ideas about how to help their child and that if teachers provide parents with some specific suggestions, this may increase parents' instrumental help with their child's schoolwork.

Lareau and colleagues (Horvat, Weininger, & Lareau, 2003; Lareau, 1996; Lareau & Horvat, 1999) have observed that compared to middle-class parents, working-class and poor parents may enact a different approach of engagement in their child's schooling. For example, middle-class parents are more likely to see themselves as being equal partners with teachers and other school staff in working out their child's education. They are more likely to take initiative to obtain access to special programs for their child (Horvat et al., 2003; Lareau & Horvat, 1999), to request a particular teacher for their child (Horvat et al., 2003), and to contact their child's teacher to monitor the child's progress in school (Lareau & Horvat, 1999). Moreover, the ways in which they intervene for their child and interact with teachers and other school staff are generally more aligned with the expectations and social norms of the school staff and thereby viewed more positively by the school staff (Horvat et al., 2003; Lareau & Horvat, 1999). Working-class and poor parents are more likely to view school staff as experts who have more knowledge and better judgment regarding what is best for their child's education than they do. Lareau (1996) suggested that working-class and poor parents do not necessarily assume that they have the right or responsibility to intervene in their child's schooling. This does not mean that parents are disinterested in their child's education, but that their conception of how the system works and their relationship to the system may be quite different from the ways in which most educators typically view parents' roles and responsibilities. Similar findings have emerged from some studies of immigrant families in which parents with little formal education and lack of familiarity with the U.S. school system view responsibility for children learning and doing well in school as primarily being the school's responsibility (e.g., Okagaki & Sternberg, 1994).

Not all parents from lower socioeconomic classes have difficulty engaging with their child's teachers and other school personnel. Gutman and McLoyd (2000) compared parenting strategies of African American parents of 17 high-achieving and 17 low-achieving students in sixth grade. In this study, all of the families were living at or below the 1995 U.S. poverty threshold. Consistent with Drummond and Stipek's (2004) work, parents of high-achieving students articulated more specific strategies to help their children with school (e.g., establishing homework schedules, giving extra reading and writing assignments) and were more aware of the specific difficulties that their child had. Parents of high achievers provided more examples of giving their child positive feedback and encouraging their child when he or she was struggling in class. They intentionally tried to bolster their child's confidence when the child was having problems in a subject. Compared to parents of low-achieving students, the parents of high-achieving students were more likely to initiate regular contact with teachers and other school personnel.

> I don't like to wait for the report cards to come out; every so often I make periodic checks at my children's school; I ask the teacher for a progress report in private to see how they are doing and just keeping in touch with the teacher, the counselor, and the principal on a monthly basis. (Parent of a high achiever, Gutman & McLoyd, 2000, p. 13)

In contrast, the parents of low achievers reported that they spent time helping their child, but did not identify specific approaches that they utilized to support their child. Typically, their contact with the school came as a result of the teacher or other school staff wanting to discuss a particular problem that had arisen with respect to the child. Gutman and McLoyd (2000) also noted that parents of high achievers appeared to see themselves as working together with teachers, counselors, and principals to help their child. In contrast, parents of low achievers expressed more distrust of school staff, were more likely to report experiencing negative interactions with school staff themselves, and would rather have the school allow parents to handle disciplinary problems with their child themselves without school involvement. For example, one mother explained, "You know, if he is acting up, I want to know about it. I don't want them taking no action; I want them to call me" (p. 14). Finally, Gutman and McLoyd observed that parents of high achievers were more likely to indicate that having their child participate in religious activities was an important way in which they fostered their child's development.

Brody and Flor (1998) posited that religiosity may increase maternal engagement in schooling among poor African American families. In a study of 156 6- to 9-year-old African American children living in rural, single-parent families, they examined a number of potential predictors of child outcomes, including maternal engagement in school activities and religiosity. The majority of these families were poor; over half of the mothers had less than a high school education. Ratings by the child's teacher were used to assess maternal engagement in school activities (e.g., attending parent-teacher conferences, school events, volunteering to help with class field trips). To measure religiosity, mothers were asked to report on how much time they engaged in religious activities (e.g., attending worship services) and how important religion was to them. Both maternal education and religiosity were directly related to maternal involvement in school activities. That maternal education was positively associated with mothers' engagement in school activities is not surprising, but why might religiosity be related to involvement in school? Brody and Flor suggested that religious beliefs and practices may enable families to better cope with financial stressors and thereby leave the parent with the emotional energy to be more involved in her child's education. In addition, religiosity may promote more positive interpersonal relationships. Religiosity, but not maternal education, was positively correlated with quality of the mother-child relationship and parenting practices. Perhaps, religiosity contributed to maternal engagement in school activities by establishing a norm for becoming involved in a community—in this case the school, rather than a religious organization—and reinforcing skills that enabled mothers to more easily interact with school personnel.

Hoover-Dempsey and Sandler (1997) posited that one of the key factors contributing to parents' engagement in their child's schooling is parents' perception of their ability to help their child–parental efficacy. Researchers have observed that parents differ in their sense of efficacy (e.g., Hoover-Dempsey, Bassler, & Brissie, 1992; Okagaki & Frensch, 1998; Okagaki et al., 1995). In a study by Hoover-Dempsey and colleagues (1992), 390 parents of elementary school children reported on their sense of efficacy for helping their child with school (e.g., knowing how to help child do well in school) and their engagement in their child's schooling (e.g., helping with homework, other educational activities with children, volunteering at school, contact with school). The sample, predominantly mothers, represented a wide range of education backgrounds. About one-third of the parents had completed high school; another third had completed some college; one-fourth had a bachelor's degree or higher. A small percentage of the parents either had less than a high school education or did not respond to the question on education. Parental efficacy was positively correlated with parents' report of volunteering at school and engaging in other educational activities with their child, but not significantly correlated with helping with homework. That is, parents who were more confident about their ability to help with schooling reported having more contact with the school. The researchers did find, however, that efficacy was negatively related to telephone calls with the school. They suggested that this negative relation might be a function of lower efficacy parents contacting the school more often because they feel unsure of how to help their child and/or lower efficacy parents having a child who is not doing as well and therefore the school is contacting the parent more frequently about the child.

Even when parents are unable to provide effective instrumental assistance, however, they may still provide indirect help for their children. Parental encouragement and indirect help, coupled with high expectations for their adolescent's school performance has been associated with Latino high school students' success. In an ethnographic study of Central American immigrant adolescents, Suarez-Orozco (1993) noted that indirect help was associated with school success among the older Central American immigrant adolescents in the study. For example, instead of allowing the adolescent to work after-school to contribute to the family finances, the parents would work two or three jobs. The parent's role in the adolescent's schooling was not to help the adolescent with the schoolwork. Rather, the parent's role was to insure that the adolescent had sufficient time to study and to create a climate in which the adolescent's job was to study and do well in school.

The importance of indirect help and encouragement also seems to apply to Asian American families. Several researchers have observed that Asian American parents structure the home environment to facilitate the child's learning rather than directly helping the child with schoolwork (e.g., Caplan et al., 1992; Schneider & Lee, 1990). For example, parents set aside a specific time for the child to do homework and limit the amount of time the child spends watching television or playing with friends. The indirect nature of parents' encouragement is highlighted in this example from an ethnographic study of Japanese American families. Hieshima and Schneider (1994) observed that Japanese American parents did not directly tell their child what to do, instead parents made indirect comments such as, "You sure finished with your homework fast" or "Not much homework tonight?" (p. 322). Along the same dimension, Schneider and Lee (1990) found that Asian American parents were more likely than European American parents to encourage their child to take private classes in music, language, and computer science and that their children spent more time practicing for their lessons than did European American children. In essence, the parents created an overall environment in which discipline, studying, and practice were integral elements of the child's role in multiple contexts.

Parents' approaches to facilitating their child's education vary greatly (e.g., Muller & Kerbow, 1993). As Lareau (1996) observed, some parents support their child and engage teachers and school staff in ways that conform to the expectations of school personnel; others do not. Some parents, however, may not have had sufficient formal education to provide effective instrumental help to their children, particularly as children advance through school. We conclude this section with an example of a parent intervention program designed to help parents better manage their child's education. In 2003–2004 academic year, an experimental evaluation was conducted on the Parent Institute for Quality Education (PIQE) program (Chrispeels, González, & Arellano, 2004). The PIQE program is designed to help parents learn how the school system functions, how parents can effectively partner with schools, and how to interpret the information schools provide parents about their child's performance. Parents are given practical advice about what they and their child need to accomplish for the child to be ready to go to college. The middle school program consists of six instructional sessions. For the evaluation of the program, parents of middle school students were randomly assigned to the treatment or the control group (parents in treatment group attended PIQE classes in the fall semester; parents in the control condition were given the opportunity to attend PIQE classes in the spring semester). After the PIQE program, parents in the treatment group reported significantly higher scores relative to the control group parents on seven of eight domains of school engagement, including home learning activities, college preparation activities, knowledge about the school system, parenting practices, communicating with child, sense of efficacy, and parental role construction. Moreover, teachers reported more overall contact with parents in the treatment group than with parents in the control group and more parent-initiated contact from parents in the treatment group. This and other evaluations of the PIQE program (e.g., Chrispeels & Rivero, 2001) provide evidence that parent interventions can expand parents' knowledge and repertoire of strategies for supporting their child's schooling.

## Cultural Models of Literacy Development

Unpacking the cultural models of learning and education that guide families can shed light on why parents and students do or do not engage in the types of activities that educators believe will support student learning. In this section, cultural models of literacy development from the perspectives of Latino immigrant parents and from parents of different socioeconomic backgrounds are examined. The importance of understanding cultural models of literacy is best understood by highlighting the strong relationship between children's experiences in their home environments, their reading and writing development, and their academic school success. For example, a large body of research documents the important connection between the quality of the home literacy environment (i.e., their access to both literacy materials in the home and parent-child reading and writing activities) and children's subsequent literacy development (Sénéchal, 2006; Snow, Burns, & Griffin, 1998; Storch & Whitehurst, 2001). The early literacy skills that children bring with them to school, in turn, strongly influence their school experiences and success (Alexander & Entwisle, 1988; Juel, 1988; Taylor, & Pearson, 2004).

The first example comes from research on Latino immigrant families from Mexico and Central America (Gallimore & Goldenberg, 2001; Reese, Garnier, Gallimore, & Goldenberg, 2000; Reese & Gallimore, 2000). The parents had relatively little formal education, generally only an elementary school background, and were primarily skilled or unskilled laborers. The parents believed that children fundamentally begin to learn how to read in school and did not view emergent literacy behaviors as meaningful learning activities (e.g., a child pretending to read a book or pretending to write her or his name). As a consequence, parents generally did not read to their child until they thought the child actually understood the meaning of the story, usually not until the child was about five years old or had entered school. Parents expressed the belief that to prepare their children to do well in school they needed to teach their children to know right from wrong. In keeping with this framework, parents read stories to their children as a way to convey moral content, rather than to help children begin to read or develop their language or encourage other aspects of cognitive development. With respect to how children learn to read, the Latino parents described a process that begins with learning the letters and the sounds and putting them together to make words with lots of repetition and practice. It was not the case that the parents were uninterested in their child's education. In fact, they were doing what they believed was most important to help their child succeed in school, which was to teach the child to behave properly and give the child a good moral foundation. Understanding this cultural model of literacy development shed light on how parents made use of short Spanish storybooks that teachers sent home for the parents to read with their child. The teachers intended that parents engage their child in reading and talking about the stories. Instead, parents used to the books in the way that was consistent with their models of literacy development—to have their child practice recognizing words. Unpacking the Latino immigrant parents' cultural model of literacy development provided a way for the researchers and the teachers not only to better understand why parents did what they did, but also to identify likely avenues for intervention that would allow parents to hold on to what was most important to them but modify their behaviors to better support their children's learning.

Recently, a number of researchers have examined cultural models of literacy development across socioeconomic groups. Among other findings, researchers have noted that parents with less education or lower socioeconomic status are more likely to emphasize the importance of providing direct instruction in basic literacy skills (e.g., teaching children the alphabet) to help children learn to read; in contrast parents with more education or middle socioeconomic status typically consider a wide range of language, reading, and writing activities to foster children's literacy development (e.g., reading children a book, modeling reading and writing to children) (e.g., Baker & Scher, 2002; Lynch, Anderson, Anderson, & Shapiro, 2006; Sonnenschein, Baker, Serpell, & Schmidt, 2000; Weigel, Martin, & Bennett, 2006).

In a series of studies, Sonnenschein and colleagues (Baker & Scher, 2002; Sonnenschein et al., 1997; Sonnenschein et al., 2000) compared lower- and middle-class parents' models of literacy development. Using structured interviews to uncover parents' literacy beliefs, parent diaries to document the child's activities during the week, and a literacy inventory to detail the child's participation in specific language experiences and home literacy activities (e.g., parent-child book reading, meal time conversations, writing and drawing activities, engagement in pretend play, teaching of the alphabet, and family outings), this team of researchers identified two fairly distinct orientations to literacy development. Lower-class parents were described as having a skill-based orientation to literacy development. That is, lower-class parents were more likely to believe that parents should help children cultivate a set of skills through direct teaching and that learning to read required hard work. The lower-class parents focused on activities such as completing workbooks or using flashcards. In contrast, middle-class parents were more likely to endorse what the researchers called an entertainment orientation to literacy development. Parents wanted to make learning to read fun; they believed that reading and writing activities should be enjoyable for children, keep their attention, and foster their motivation for reading. The middle-class parents exposed their children to print and writing opportunities in the context of engaging activities (e.g., cooking with a recipe card, joint book reading interactions, or trips to the library or grocery store). Belief in an entertainment orientation to fostering literacy development was found to be positively correlated with children's early literacy skills in kindergarten and first grade and with children's first grade motivation for reading. In contrast, belief in a basic skills orientation to literacy development was not related to children's reading development in kindergarten and was negatively related to children's motivation for reading in first grade (Baker & Scher, 2002; Sonnenschein et al., 2000).

Weigel and colleagues (2006) found that maternal education significantly predicted mothers' endorsement of what they termed "facilitative" and "conventional" literacy beliefs (p. 199). Mothers who held facilitative literacy beliefs (a) perceived their parenting role to be important to children's developing early literacy skills, (b) strongly believed that sharing books with children enhances young children's communication and literacy development, and (c) reported that they enjoyed reading and writing activities, both personally and when sharing them with their child. In contrast, mothers who were identified as having conventional beliefs were more likely to report that teaching children reading was primarily the responsibility of schools rather than of parents and endorse statements about preschool aged children being too young to learn about reading. Similarly, in a study of 551 preschool and kindergarten children and their parents (Stipek, Millburn, Clements, & Daniels, 1992), less-educated parents were more likely to endorse didactic or skills oriented instruction for their children than mothers who were more educated.

Although findings from these literacy studies highlight the variation in parents' cultural models of literacy development, perhaps more important is the relation between parents' belief systems and their parenting practices (Bingham, 2007). At first blush, it may appear that parents with an entertainment or holistic orientation to literacy development are simply making literacy more fun for their child by presenting activities for their child while not focusing on explicitly teaching literacy skills. Rather, these parents have a different model of how to foster young children's literacy skills compared to parents who have a more didactic, skills-based orientation. Parents who have a holistic orientation embed their teaching of language and literacy concepts into family routines by making literacy development an integral part of their child's upbringing. Serpell, Sonnenschein, Baker, and Ganapathy (2002) found that parents' endorsement of an entertainment orientation relates to how frequently parents participate in a variety of literacy activities they engage in with their children and it is these activities which predict their children's subsequent reading development. Weigel and colleagues (2006) found no difference between the conventional and facilitative mothers with respect to how many books they owned or when they began reading to their children; however, compared to mothers with conventional beliefs, mothers with facilitative beliefs reported reading to their children and engaging their children in literacy activities (i.e., such as singing songs, telling stories, or playing games) significantly more often. Finally, Stipek and colleagues (1992) found that although parental education was not related to parents' participation in formal teaching strategies with their child (e.g., practicing writing letters or words, teaching children numbers, teaching children letters), parents with more education reported participating in significantly more informal learning activities (e.g., reading stories, listening to the child read, teaching numbers or reading while doing other activities, such as cooking, and talking more to their children) than less-educated mothers.

In summary, although researchers have found that across cultural and socioeconomic groups parents want their children to learn how to read, there is a range of beliefs about how children develop literacy skills and what adults need to do to foster that development. Parents with less education are more likely to approach and view their children's literacy development as a discrete set of skills that children need to acquire. In contrast, parents with more education are more likely to consider a wider range of language, reading, and writing activities to foster children's literacy development and to embed such activities within regular family routines. Understanding how parents approach their child's learning in the home environment can inform the ways in which teachers engage parents in school-learning activities.

## CONCLUSIONS

This chapter has explored the ways in which parents approach engagement in their child's education. As a final note, this chapter concludes with two general observations from this review of the literature—one directed toward practice and the other toward research.

Across cultural and socioeconomic groups, most parents believe that education is important for their child and want their child to do well in school; how parents act on these beliefs, however, varies greatly. Some parents—particularly those who are less familiar with U.S. schools and those who have had less formal education—have difficulty communicating with teachers and other school personnel, accessing resources for their child, providing instrumental help for their child, and intervening for their child. Along the same lines, teachers and other school personnel often find it easier to work with some parents and not others. Cultural and social class differences between school personnel and parents may contribute to miscommunication and misunderstanding of actions when social norms and expectations do not match. It is easy to sometimes forget that schools are places in which people from different cultures interact over high stakes issues—that is, the education of and future opportunities for children. Practitioners need to be careful not to automatically interpret parents' actions through their own cultural lenses. Although it is important for readers not to overgeneralize the descriptions of the beliefs or practices of a group to all members of a group, this review highlighted some key concepts to consider in understanding parents' perspectives, such as finding out what parents believe their role is and how parents see themselves helping their child. Understanding parents' perspectives should provide practitioners with a beginning point for creating a successful school-parent dialogue.

Currently the field is far from a comprehensive understanding of how parents' cultural models of education and learning influence their beliefs and engagement in their child's schooling. Certainly more research is needed to more fully understand the cultural models of education and learning of the many cultural and socioeconomic groups within our country. This research has the potential to yield practical benefits, especially if researchers would conduct the work with an eye toward identifying possible points for intervention. What issues do parents frequently need clarification or more information in order to better understand their child's educational needs? How can educators build on or extend what parents are already doing in ways that help parents better support their child's schooling?

Given that there is great diversity within groups and, consequently, that practitioners cannot generalize research findings about a group to particular individuals within that group, it would be helpful if researchers also focused attention on developing and testing protocols that would enable practitioners to more easily ascertain parents' perspectives and to work collaboratively with parents in ways that bridge the gap between home and school cultures. Such protocols could provide guidance on how to approach parents in culturally sensitive ways regarding parents' expectations about, for example, their role and their child's teacher's role in helping the child do well in school, and their ideas about how to establish strong parent-school partnerships. Are there basic practices, for instance, that teachers can routinely utilize to reduce miscommunications with parents? Are there ways to make the culture of the school more visible or understandable to parents from different cultural and linguistic backgrounds so that parents can more effectively partner with schools?

Parents interpret information from the school through the filter of their cultural models of education and learning. Some understandings will facilitate children's education and subsequent opportunities in life; some will not. Research needs to go beyond describing differences in parents' beliefs and practices to creating ways that will enable schools to more effectively work with parents so that their children will one day have the knowledge and skills to be able to choose among many opportunities in life rather than being left with few options in our society.

## REFERENCES

Alexander, K. L., & Entwisle, D. R. (1988). Achievement in the first two years of school: Patterns and processes. *Monographs for the Society for Research in Child Development, 53* (Serial No. 218).

Alexander, K. L., Entwisle, D. R., & Bedinger, S. D. (1994). When expectations work: Race and socioeconomic differences in school performance. *Social Psychology Quarterly, 57,* 283–299.

Azmitia, M., Cooper, C. R., Garcia, E. E., & Dunbar, N. D. (1996). The ecology of family guidance in low-income Mexican-American and European-American families. *Social Development, 5,* 1–23.

Baker, L., & Scher, D. (2002). Beginning readers' motivation for reading in relation to parental beliefs and home reading experiences. *Reading Psychology, 23,* 239–269.

Bingham, G. E. (2007). Maternal literacy beliefs and the quality of mother-child book-reading interactions: Associations with children's early literacy development. *Early Education and Development, 18,* 23–50.

Brody, G. H., & Flor, D. L. (1998). Maternal resources, parenting practices, and child competence in rural, single-parent African American families. *Child Development, 69,* 803–816.

Caplan, N., Choy, M. H., & Whitmore, J. K. (1992). Indochinese refugee families and academic achievement. *Scientific American*, 36–42.

Carrasquillo, A. L. (1991). *Hispanic children and youth in the United States: A resource guide*. New York: Garland.

Chao, R. K. (1994). Beyond parental control and authoritarian parenting style: Understanding Chinese parenting through the cultural notion of training. *Child Development, 65*, 1111–1119.

Chao, R. K. (2000). The parenting of immigrant Chinese and European American mothers: Relations between parenting styles, socialization goals, and parental practices. *Journal of Applied Developmental Psychology, 21*, 233–248.

Chao, R. K. (2001). Extending research on the consequences of parenting style for Chinese Americans and European Americans. *Child Development, 72*, 1832–1843.

Chen, C., & Uttal, D. H. (1988). Cultural values, parents' beliefs, and children's achievement in the United States and China. *Human Development, 31*, 351–358.

Chrispeels, J., González, M., & Arellano, B. (2004). Evaluation of the effectiveness of the Parent Institute for Quality Education in Los Angeles Unified School District: September 2003 to May 2004. Retrieved June 18, 2006, from http://www.piqe.org/Assets/Home/chrispeels.pdf

Chrispeels, J. H., & Rivero, E. (2001). Engaging Latino families for student success: How parent education can reshape parents' sense of place in the education of their children. *Peabody Journal of Education, 76*, 119–169.

Dearing, E., Kreider, H., Simpkins, S., & Weiss, H. B. (2006). Family involvement in school and low-income children's literacy: Longitudinal associations between and within families. *Journal of Educational Psychology, 98*, 653–664.

Delgado-Gaitan, C. (1992). School matters in the Mexican-American home: Socializing children to education. *American Educational Research Journal, 29*, 495–513.

Drummond, K. V., & Stipek, D. (2004). Low-income parents' beliefs about their role in children's academic learning. *The Elementary School Journal, 104*, 197–213.

Fan, X. (2001). Parental involvement and students' academic achievement: A growth modeling analysis. *The Journal of Experimental Education, 70*, 27–61.

Fan, X., & Chen, M. (2001). Parental involvement and students' academic achievement: A meta-analysis. *Educational Psychology Review, 13*, 1–22.

Flowers, T. A., & Flowers, L. A. (2008). Factors affecting urban African American high school students' achievement in reading. *Urban Education, 43*, 154–171.

Gallimore, R., & Goldenberg, C. (2001). Analyzing cultural models and settings to connect minority achievement and school improvement research. *Educational Psychologist, 36*, 45–56.

Gibson, M. A. (1993). The school performance of immigrant minorities: A comparative view. In E. Jacob & C. Jordan (Eds.), *Minority education: Anthropological perspectives* (pp. 113–128). Norwood, NJ: Ablex.

Gill, S., & Reynolds, A. J. (2000). Educational expectations and school achievement of urban African American children. *Journal of School Psychology, 37*, 403–424.

Goldenberg, C., & Gallimore, R. (1995). Immigrant Latino parents' values and beliefs about their children's education: Continuities and discontinuities across cultures and generations. *Advances in Motivation and Achievement, 9*, 183–228.

Goldenberg, C., Gallimore, R., Reese, L., & Garnier, H. (2001). Cause or effect? A longitudinal study of immigrant Latino parents' aspirations and expectations, and their children's school performance. *American Educational Research Journal, 38*, 547–582.

Gutman, L. M., & McLoyd, V. C. (2000). Parents' management of their children's education within the home, at school, and in the community: An examination of African-American families living in poverty. *The Urban Review, 32*, 1–24.

Halle, T. G., Kurtz-Costes, B., & Mahoney, J. (1997). Family influences on school achievement in low-income, African American children. *Journal of Educational Psychology, 89*(3), 527–537.

Hao, L., & Bonstead-Bruns, M. (1998). Parent-child differences in educational expectations and the academic achievement of immigrant and native students. *Sociology of Education, 71*, 175–198.

Hauser-Cram, P., Sirin, S. R., & Stipek, D. (2003). When teachers' and parents' values differ: teachers' ratings of academic competence in children from low-income families. *Journal of Educational Psychology, 95*, 813–820.

Harry, B. (1992). *Cultural diversity, families, and the special education system: Communication and empowerment*. New York: Teachers College Press.

Hieshima, J. A., & Schneider, B. (1994). Intergenerational effects on the cultural and cognitive socialization of third- and fourth-generation Japanese Americans. *Journal of Applied Developmental Psychology, 15*, 319–327.

Hill, N. E., & Craft, S. A. (2003). Parent-school involvement and school performance: Mediated pathways among socioeconomically comparable African American and Euro-American families. *Journal of Educational Psychology, 95*, 74–83.

Hoff, E., Laursen, B., & Tardiff, T. (2002). Socioeconomic status and parenting. In P. M. Greenfield & R. R. Cocking (Eds.), *Cross-cultural roots of minority children development* (pp. 285–313). Hillsdale, NJ: Erlbaum.

Hoover-Dempsey, K. V., Bassler, O. C., & Brissie, J. S. (1992). Explorations in parent-school relations. *Journal of Educational Research, 85*, 287–294.

Hoover-Dempsey, K. V., & Sandler, H. M. (1997). Why do parents become involved in their children's education? *Review of Educational Research, 67*(1), 3–42.

Hoover-Dempsey, K. V., Battiato, A. C., Walker, J. M. T., Reed, R. P., DeJong, J. M. (2001). Parental involvement in homework. *Educational Psychologist, 36*, 195–209.

Horvat, E. M., Weininger, E. B., & Lareau, A. (2003). From social ties to social capital: Class differences in the relations between schools and parent networks. *American Educational Research Journal, 40*, 319–351.

Joe, J. R., & Malach, R. S. (1992). Families with Native American roots. In E. W. Lynch & M. J. Hanson (Eds.) *Developing cross-cultural competence: A guide for working with young children and their families* (pp. 89–119). Baltimore: Paul H. Brookes.

Juel, C. (1988). Learning to read and write: A longitudinal study of 54 children from first through fourth grades. *Journal of Educational Psychology, 80*, 437–447.

Kibria, N. (1993). *Family tightrope: The changing lives of Vietnamese Americans*. Princeton, NJ: Princeton University Press.

Lareau, A. (1996). Assessing parent involvement in schooling: A critical analysis. In A. Booth & J. F. Dunn (Eds.) *Family-school links: How do they affect educational outcomes?* (pp. 57–64). Mahwah, NJ: Erlbaum.

Lareau, A., & Horvat, E. M. (1999). Moments of social inclusion and exclusion: Race, class, and cultural capital in family-school relationships. *Sociology of Education, 72*, 37–53.

Lasky, S. (2000). The cultural and emotional politics of teacher-parent interactions. *Teaching and Teacher Education, 16*, 843–860.

Luster, T., & McAdoo, H. (1996). Family and child influences on educational attainment: A secondary analysis of the High/Scope Perry Preschool data. *Developmental Psychology, 32*, 26–39.

Lynch, J., Anderson, J., Anderson, A., & Shapiro, J. (2006). Parents' beliefs about young children's literacy development and parents' literacy behaviors. *Reading Psychology, 27*, 1–20.

Ma, X. (2001). Participation in advanced mathematics: Do expectation and influence of students, peers, teachers, and parents matter? *Contemporary Educational Psychology, 26*, 132–146.

Muller, C., & Kerbow, D. (1993). Parent involvement in the home, school, and community. In B. Schneider & J.S. Coleman (Eds.), *Parents, Their Children, and Schools* (pp. 13–42). Boulder, CO: Westview Press.

Okagaki, L., & Bingham, G. E. (2005). Parents' social cognitions and their parenting behaviors. In T. Luster & L. Okagaki (Eds.), *Ecological perspective on parenting*, 2nd ed. (pp. 3–33). Hillsdale, NJ: Erlbaum.

Okagaki, L., & Frensch, P. A. (1998). Parenting and children's school achievement: A multi-ethnic perspective. *American Educational Research Journal, 35*, 123–144.

Okagaki, L., Frensch, P. A., & Gordon, E. W. (1995). Encouraging school achievement in Mexican-American children. *Hispanic Journal of Behavioral Sciences, 17*, 160–179.

Okagaki, L., & Sternberg, R. J. (1993). Parental beliefs and children's school performance. *Child Development, 64*, 36–56.

Okagaki, L., & Sternberg, R. J. (1994). Perspectives on kindergarten: Rafael, Vanessa, and Jamlien go to school. *Childhood Education, 71*, 14–19.

Overstreet, S., Devine, J., Bevans, K., & Efreom, Y. (2005). Predicting parental involvement in children's schooling within an economically disadvantaged African American sample. *Psychology in the Schools, 42*, 101–111.

Patrikakou, E. N., & Weisberg, R. P. (2000). Parents' perceptions of teacher outreach and parent involvement in children's education. *Journal of Prevention and Intervention in the Community, 20*(1-2), 103–119.

Ramirez, A. Y. F. (2003). Dismay and disappointment: Parental involvement of Latino immigrant parents. *The Urban Review, 35*, 93–110.

Reese, L., Balzano, S., Gallimore, R., & Goldenberg, C. (1995). The concept of education: Latino family values and American schooling. *International Journal of Educational Research, 23*, 57–81.

Reese, L., & Gallimore, R. (2000). Immigrant Latinos' cultural model of literacy development: An evolving perspective on home-school discontinuities. *American Journal of Education, 108*, 103–134.

Reese, L., Garnier, H., Gallimore, R., & Goldenberg, C. (2000). Longitudinal analysis of the antecedents of emergent Spanish literacy and middle-school English reading achievement of Spanish-speaking students. *American Educational Research Journal, 37*, 633–662.

Schneider, B., & Lee, Y. (1990). A model for academic success: The school and home environment of East Asian students. *Anthropology & Education Quarterly, 21*, 358–377.

Sénéchal, M. (2006). Testing the home literacy model: Parent involvement in kindergarten is differentially related to grade 4 reading comprehension, fluency, spelling, and reading for pleasure. *Scientific Studies of Reading, 10*, 59–87.

Serpell, R., Sonnenschein, S., Baker, L., & Ganapathy, H. (2002). Intimate culture of families in the early social-ization of literacy. *Journal of Family Psychology, 16*, 391–405.

Sirin, S. R. (2005). Socioeconomic status and academic achievement: A meta-analytic review of research. *Review of Educational Research, 75*, 417–453.

Snow, C. E., Burns, M. S., & Griffin, P. (1998). *Preventing reading difficulties in young children.* New York: National Academy Press.

Sonnenschein, S., Baker, L., Serpell, R., Scher, D., Goddard Truitt, V., & Munsterman, K. (1997). Parental beliefs about ways to help children learn to read: The impact of an entertainment or a skills perspective. *Early Child Development and Care, 127–128*, 111–118.

Sonnenschein, S., Baker, L., Serpell, R., & Schmidt, D. (2000). Reading is a source of entertainment: The important of the home perspective for children's literacy development. In K. A. Roskos & J. F. Christie (Eds.), *Play and literacy in early childhood: Research from multiple perspectives* (pp. 107–124). Mahwah, NJ: Erlbaum.

Stipek, D., Millburn, S., Clements, D., & Daniels, D. (1992). Parents' beliefs about appropriate education for young children. *Journal of Applied Developmental Psychology, 13*, 293–310.

Storch, S. A., & Whitehurst, G. J. (2001). The role of family and home in the literacy development of children from low income backgrounds. *New Directions for Child and Adolescent Research, 92*, 53–71.

Suarez-Orozco, M.M. (1993). "Becoming somebody": Central American immigrants in U.S. inner-city schools. In E. Jacob & C. Jordan, *Minority education: Anthropological perspectives* (pp. 129–143). Norwood, NJ: Ablex.

Sue, S., & Okazaki, S. (1990). Asian-American educational achievement: A phenomenon in search of an explana-tion. *American Psychologist, 45*(8), 913–920.

Taylor, B. M., & Pearson, P. D., (2004). Research on learning to read—at school, at home, and in the community. *The Elementary School Journal, 105*, 167–181.

Tapia, J. (2004). Latino households and schooling: Economic and sociocultural factors affecting students' learning and academic performance. *International Journal of Qualitative Studies in Education, 17*, 415–436.

Torres, V. (2004). The diversity among us: Puerto Ricans, Cuban Americans, Caribbean Americans, and Central and South Americans. *New Directions for Student Services, 105*, 5–16.

Trivette, P., & Anderson, E. (1995). The effects of four components of parental involvement on eighth grade student achievement: Structural analyses of NELS-88 data. *School Psychology Review, 24*, 299–318.

U.S. Census Bureau. (2001). The Hispanic population in the United States: Population characteristics by Melissa Therrien and Robert R. Ramirez, U.S. Department of Commerce, Economics and Statistics Administration. Washington, DC: U.S. Census Bureau.

U.S. Census Bureau (2006). *Current Population Survey, Annual Social and Economic Supplement 2006.* Wash-ington, DC: U. S. Census Bureau.

U.S. Department of Education (2007). *The Condition of Education 2007* (NCES 2007-064). U.S. Department of Education, Institute of Education Sciences, National Center for Education Statistics. Washington, DC: U.S. Government Printing Office.

Weigel, D. J., Martin, S. S., & Bennett, K. K. (2006). Mothers' literacy beliefs: Connections with the home lit-eracy environment and pre-school children's literacy development. *Journal of Early Childhood Literacy, 6*, 191–211.

# 5

## CULTURALLY-BASED WORLDVIEWS, FAMILY PROCESSES, AND FAMILY-SCHOOL INTERACTIONS

### NANCY E. HILL

Despite appeals from research and policies for families and schools to form partnerships, parents and teachers, alike, are often perplexed by the difficulty in establishing and maintaining productive relationships, especially in middle and high school (N. E. Hill & Chao, 2009; N. E. Hill & Taylor, 2004). As families prepare their children for school and support their cognitive, social, and emotional development, they do so within a worldview that is shaped and informed by their culture and environment. Further, schools function within their own cultural milieu and with their own worldview, at times both explicit and implicit. When the worldviews and beliefs at school and home are consistent or compatible, children's adjustment is enhanced and communication between home and school is more facile and less constrained (Lareau, 1987). However, the scientific and popular press has alluded to the incongruence between the cultures, beliefs, and practices at home and at school, especially for ethnic minority populations. This incongruence has often led to misunderstandings between teachers and parents, competing expectations for children, and undeveloped potential.

## OVERVIEW

This chapter begins with theory and empirical evidence that define and explain variations in beliefs systems as they shape parenting practices and their influence on child outcomes, especially for ethnic minority families. This is followed by an analysis of the explicit and often invisible cultural framework of the American school system. Using these cultural frames and the (in)congruence between the home and school realms, ethnic variations in academic socialization, parental involvement in education, and family-school engagement, and their association with developmental outcomes are examined. This chapter concludes with a call for more nuanced research on culture, families, and achievement and an analysis of mechanisms that challenge the family-school relationship, undermine the effectiveness of programs and policies to strengthen the family-school relationship, and ultimately are the key for understanding culturally grounded parenting in the context of the "invisible" cultural framework of American schools.

## WORLDVIEWS AND PARENT COGNITIONS: WHOSE OBJECTIVITY IS OBJECTIVE?

Despite our best attempts at objectivity, each of us holds a set of assumptions about the nature of the world and the sources of change and stability (i.e., worldviews) that guide and inform our interpretations of the events observed in the world around us, guide interpersonal behaviors and interactions with others; and guide and integrate the information gleaned from the world (Pepper, 1942). Worldviews are embedded in culture and shape parental cognitions including parental beliefs, values, and goals. These worldviews are often not based on an objective analysis of data, but are beliefs that are held without evidence, are resistant to change, and are considered as part of the natural and moral order (Goodnow, 2002).

Beliefs are necessary to organize and make sense of the world, provide certainty about what will happen, and to serve as a regulatory function within the family. They are often used to represent ideas that individuals, in this case parents, accept as true (McGillicuddy-DeLisi & Sigel, 1995). Beliefs define the processes by which human nature unfolds. They determine how one feels about the world, events, and people; and how one perceives and interprets others' actions (Sigel & McGillicuddy-DeLisi, 2002). These ideas and practices are so commonly used and thoroughly integrated into the larger culture that they do not need rationalization and are not necessarily given conscious thought (Super & Harkness, 1996).

These beliefs seem universal. Indeed, perceptions of agreement among people who are like oneself (e.g., same family, community, culture) contribute to the sense that a belief is objectively valid or true (Turner & Oakes, 1986). Although the beliefs themselves are not universal, the presence of parental beliefs about the nature of child development within a culture is universal (N. E. Hill, 2006; Reid & Valsiner, 1986). They are both automatic or unconscious and intentional or deliberate (McGillicuddy-DeLisi & Sigel, 1995). To date, worldviews have been used to explain the linkages among parental beliefs, parental practices, and child outcomes, along with ethnic differences in these relations. However, theories pertaining to beliefs and worldviews have not been applied to understanding the interactions between families and schools as they influence children's development.

Parental beliefs are constructed from ongoing interactions with family members, with members of one's cultural group or society, and with children themselves. These everyday interactions serve to confirm or solidify beliefs, often making them resistant to change. Parenting beliefs pertain not only to the processes of children's development and parents' role in shaping development, but to the parents' understanding of the world for which they are preparing their child (Goodnow, 2002). Among families, these worldviews have been characterized and described as parents' ethnotheories (Super & Harkness, 1996), belief systems (Sigel & McGillicuddy-DeLisi, 2002), cognitions (Bugental & Johnson, 2000; Darling & Steinberg, 1993), and attitudes (Holden & Buck,

2002; Holden & Edwards, 1989). Early theory and research on parenting beliefs deemed them as important because they were believed to transcend behavior, were relatively stable, reflect a broader climate to which children are exposed (Pearson, 1931) and they shape parental goals and socialization strategies.

Related to the concept of parental beliefs is the concept of values. Values refer to longstanding goals parents have for children (Kohn, 1969). They represent the important outcomes for the child and for the relationship between the parent and child (Holden & Buck, 2002). Although often considered singly or in isolation (i.e., a parent's value for academic achievement), values are interrelated and, often, hierarchical. When conflicting, families find themselves making tradeoffs between values (Goodnow, 2002). For example, a family may simultaneously value academic achievement *and* cultural diversity and in an ideal world wish to select the school that has the best academic record and is also ethnically diverse. However, faced with few options, parents may have to choose a school that has a somewhat lower academic record in order to reach the goal of an ethnically diverse environment or choose to forgo the goal of ethnic diversity in favor of an excellent academic record. "To focus only on parents' overt behaviors is to treat parents as unthinking creatures, ignoring the fact that they interpret events, with these interpretations probably influencing their actions and feelings" (Goodnow, 1988, p. 287).

Parents and families are not alone in holding worldviews about child development. Teachers and school personnel hold worldviews that impact their teaching style, interactions with children, and interactions with families. At times, teachers' and schools' worldviews serve to marginalize some and subtly advantage others. Research on the hidden curriculum of schools and the symbolic and implicit interactions at school has documented the process by which children who do not match the dominant social class and culture within the United States are subtly made to feel as though they do not belong and ultimately disengage from schooling (Arce, 2004; Giroux, 1981; Tyson, 2003). Apart from the study of school policies for family-school relationships and teacher-parent relationship quality, school climate/culture has largely been ignored as it relates to family-school relationships. The possible exception is the work that has examined the promotion of school readiness by making *schools* ready, rather than (and in addition to) making children ready (cf. Pianta & Rimm-Kaufman, 2006).

Whereas these worldviews have largely been used to explain and examine parental beliefs about childrearing (e.g., discipline, warmth, developmental timetables) and expectations for children's current and ultimate roles within the family and society, they can also be applied to understand parents' engagement with schools and school personnel. Indeed, a framework of culturally-embedded parental worldviews may be heuristic for understanding often cited incongruence between home and school cultures that impede the development of partnerships between families and schools.

## CULTURALLY-EMBEDDED BELIEFS, VALUES, AND SOCIALIZATION STRATEGIES AT HOME AND SCHOOL

When parental or school-level beliefs and goals intersect, socialization occurs. Socialization is the "process by which people acquire the behaviors and beliefs of the social world—that is the culture—in which they live" (Arnett, 1995, p. 618). Socialization includes the establishment of limits or impulse control; preparation for roles within society, including citizenship, occupational roles, gender roles, and family roles (e.g., marriage, parenthood); and the process of internalizing the values, morals and sources of meaning defined within the culture. Socialization happens through parental or teacher interactions with children, which is shaped by beliefs and worldviews.

Parenting beliefs, goals, and socialization strategies are each shaped by the culture and context in which the family exists. Indeed, culture has been defined as a "system of meanings…beliefs, norms, attitudes, and roles" (Hermans & Kempen, 1998, p. 115), "a set of control mechanisms for the governing of man's behavior" (Geertz, 1973, p. 64), and "total lifestyle of people from a particular social grouping, including all the ideas, symbols, preferences, and material objects they share" (Franzoi, 1996, p. 15). Culture shapes parents' and society's beliefs about the nature of child development and how it occurs; the behaviors and goals that are the focus of socialization; the interpretations and attributions of children's behavior and misbehavior; and beliefs about the appropriateness and effectiveness of particular parenting strategies and behaviors (N. E. Hill, 2006; Palacios, 1990). Indeed, "culture provides the lens through which we view the world…. While this worldview is likely to be modified by our own personalities, experiences, education, and other factors, it is nevertheless the context in which certain values, behaviors, and ideas will be reinforced while others are rejected" (Garcia & Guerra, 2006, p. 115). Further, parenting beliefs and goals are shaped by socioeconomic status of the family (Hoff, Laursen, & Tardif, 2002; Kohn, 1969; Luster, Rhoades, & Haas, 1989; Pinderhughes, Dodge, Bates, Pettit, & Zelli, 2000) and neighborhood of residence (N. E. Hill & Herman-Stahl, 2002; Leventhal & Brooks-Gunn, 2000). In the following sections, the existing literature on worldviews, cultural beliefs, and practices is highlighted for the largest ethnic groups in the United States (i.e., mainstream American—middle class, Euro American; African American; Asian American; and Latino American; Greico & Cassidy, 2001). This is followed by a description of the cultural beliefs and worldview of U.S. schools.

### Cultural and Familial Beliefs, Values, and Practices among Ethnic Groups in the U.S.

Mainstream American worldviews, along with other Western and European cultures, regarding education are largely based on the philosophy and approaches exemplified by Socrates and the Socratic methods (Tweed & Lehman, 2002). Knowledge is generated individually and focuses on public and private questioning of extant knowledge. Expression of one's own hypotheses is valued. Learning and knowledge are used to understand the world and develop skills so that personal goals can be reached (Li, 2005). Education is largely focused on the individual, along with his or her personal goals, intrinsic enjoyment, and curiosity. As much as a focus on knowledge, Americans tend to focus on social skills, general cognitive abilities, and learning skills (Chao, 2000). That is, education focuses on the traits of the mind and mental abilities that are used to inquire about the world. Further, Americans tend to value what is new and are always seeking a better way to do things and, therefore, parents are obligated to be alert to new and better ways of parenting (Brooks, 2004; Goodnow, 2002).

In the United States, there is an explicit and implicit focus on the development of the self as an individual and individuation from parents and family, resulting in an emphasis on self-confidence, self-esteem, and independence (Reese, 2002; Santayana, 1934). Endorsement of such values is evident in the willingness of Americans to move away from family and start over. Because of the focus on the individual and individualism, belief in oneself and one's own initiative are seen as keys to success (Heine et al., 2001). Also because of the central emphasis on the self and self-esteem, education and learning is presented as fun, enjoyable, exciting, and self-directed—following one's interests and dreams. Education is viewed as a necessity to achieving one's own goals. Similarly, because of the focus on the self and self-esteem, feedback from teachers and others emphasizes the positive aspects of achievement and successes and minimizes errors and mistakes. Concomitantly, when asked of their chief concerns and goals for parenting, middle-class Euro American mothers expressed concerns about the self, including building self-esteem, confidence and encouraging self-expression, all of which are part of an individualistic worldview (Chao, 1995; Greenfield, 1994; Markus & Kitayama, 1991).

Despite the commonalities among Americans from diverse cultural backgrounds in a desire to achieve and succeed, ethnic minority and immigrant families often bring with them styles of engagement and commitments among family that differ from mainstream American culture (N. E. Hill, 2006). Further, collectivism and interdependence, which are characteristics of all non-Western culture (Triandis, 1988), are often enhanced because experiences of discrimination and marginalization with the United States promotes and sustains within-group identities (N. E. Hill, 2006). In the following sections, culturally embedded beliefs, goals, and socialization strategies are outlined for African Americans, Asian Americans, and Latinos. The characterizations that follow are not intended to be exhaustive or to paint these ethnic groups as monolithic or homogeneous. However, these are some of the values, beliefs, and practices that shape parents interactions with schools and with their children as they promote academic success.

*African American Families*    African American culture and heritage draws on the traditions and practices of a West African cultural worldview, which has been maintained through socialization processes, active attempts by African Americans to reconnect with their African cultural heritage, and from traditions and practices that have developed as result of centuries living in the United States (Boykin, 1983, 1986; Mitchell, 1975). West African belief systems that are evident in modern African American culture include a positive view of life despite difficult circumstances; belief in the spiritual realm and spirituality, including trusting in a God that will provide for one's needs; communalism, including a sense of unity among family and others; harmony, expressiveness and expressive individualism (also known as verve) and an oral tradition (Boykin, 1983; Sankofa, Hurley, Allen, & Boykin, 2005; Tyler, Boykin, Miller, & Hurley, 2006). Based on the African American cultural values celebrated through Kwanzaa, Grills and Longshore (1996) developed and validated a measure of Africentrism, which included the values of unity, self-determination, collective work and responsibility, cooperative economics, collective purpose, creativity, and faith. Among these cultural values and beliefs, the bulk of the research on African American values and family processes has focused on communalism, verve, and spirituality.

Communalism has been defined as a fundamental interdependence among people, with a focus on sharing and working towards the good of the group (Boykin, 1983), giving priority to family or group goals over one's personal or individual goals, and an emphasis and importance placed on human relationships (Cokley, 2005). It has also been characterized by the African saying, "We are, therefore I am" (Hines & Boyd-Franklin, 1982). Contemporary manifestations of communalism include strong kinship networks, a unity developed as part of a collective struggle, and a sense of an African American community that transcends physical boundaries (N. E. Hill, Murry, & Anderson, 2005). In research in academic contexts, it is often operationalized as working collaboratively, sharing ideas and materials with fellow students, and believing that one can learn by working with others (Sankofa et al., 2005).

Verve, also known as expressiveness and the psychology of movement (Stevenson, Winn, Walker-Barnes, & Coard, 2005), is an appreciation for movement and an orientation to high levels of physical stimuli and sensations (Tyler et al., 2006). Styles of movement are often seen as part of one's personality among African Americans (Stevenson et al., 2005). In studies of achievement and academic settings, it has been operationalized as a preference for (and efficacy of) focusing on many activities at the same time, moving from one activity to the next, and circulating among several activities as a means of learning multiple topics (Sankofa et al., 2005).

Spirituality is a belief in the spiritual realm and that a powerful God is the originator and sustainer of the universe and all that is in it (Mitchell, 1975) and governs all day to day affairs (Woods & Jagers, 2003). Through a relationship with and belief in a powerful God, one can call upon Him for help, clarity of purpose, and inner peace. There is an emphasis on being spiritual, rather than practicing spirituality (Cokley, 2005). It is reflected in a trust in God that all of one's needs will be met and as a source of strength. This is reflected by the fact that African Americans often praise God even in difficult times (Mitchell, 1975). This commitment to spirituality is represented in virtually all West African traditional religions, in African American slaves' striving for freedom and maintaining hope, and in the resilience seen among many African Americans families living in the most challenging neighborhoods (N. E. Hill et al., 2005).

Goals African American parents have for their children include representing their race well by achieving academically, as it is often said that education cannot be taken away; keeping God at the center of one's life; and maintaining a commitment to family. Academic achievement and attaining a good education, including high school and college completion, were endorsed as the top immediate and long-term goals, respectively, in a study that identified the hierarchy of goals among an economically diverse sample of African American families (S. A. Hill & Sprague, 1999). Related to a good education, securing a good job is a top priority for African American parents across socioeconomic levels, as is developing and maintaining a strong and loving family (S. A. Hill & Sprague, 1999). The importance and value African American families have placed on education and the sacrifices that African American families have made for the education of their children from slavery through the 20th century are evident in historical and contemporary records (Cross, 2003; Spencer, Cross, Harpalani, & Goss,

2003). With years of oppression and poverty in the African American community, parents are often well aware of the relations among economic security, family stability, and the role of education.

African American families also focus on developing their children's sense of self, although in a different way than do Euro American families. It is important to African American families that their children feel good about themselves (S. A. Hill & Sprague, 1999). Part of a parental worldview that shapes parenting practice is an understanding about the nature of the world in which children will live. For good reason, African American parents find that they are preparing their children for a hostile world that will not always give them a fair chance and will often misinterpret their behavior and actions in the most unfavorable light. African American parents must prepare their children to cope with and understand discriminatory experiences while maintaining their sense of self and self-concept (Hughes et al., 2006; Stevenson, Davis, & Abdul-Kabir, 2001). Unless African American parents challenge the negative stereotypes about African American children, they run the risk that the negative stereotypes will be internalized by their children and undermine the children's potential.

African American parenting has been characterized as authoritarian and no-nonsense (Brody & Flor, 1998; Steinberg, Dornbusch, & Brown, 1991). American society often views African American misbehavior as more dangerous than the same behaviors exhibited by Euro American children, and teachers and the criminal justice system mete out harsher punishments on African American children, compared to Euro American children for the same misbehaviors (Cross, 2003). Because of this, African American parents are often more exacting about their children's behavior and place high demands for obedience. American society is very willing to label African American children as delinquents and is much less likely to give African American children a second chance (Cross, 2003). Some African American parents justify their no nonsense parenting by adages such as "it is better that I be hard on you now so that the world does not have to be hard on you later," which is a derivative of the African proverb, "He who is not chastised by his parents is chastised by his ill-wisher" (Stevenson et al., 2001, p. 86).

Characterizations of African American parenting as harsh are inaccurate. African American socialization strategies must be interpreted and understood with the frame of African American cultural values and beliefs. For example, the role of parents' tone of voice; body language, movement, and rhythm; and mannerism are evident in parenting practices (i.e., verve). African American parents often use sarcasm or playful aggression to communicate warmth and displeasure/discipline in a playful but culturally sensitive way. If taken out of its cultural context, it can be interpreted as aggressive (Gonzales, Cauce, & Mason, 1996). However, harsher or stricter parenting practices are positively related to perceived warmth, love, and acceptance among African American children (Mason, Walker-Barnes, Tu, Simons, & Martinez-Arrue, 2004). Moreover, the combination of high levels of strict or authoritarian parenting and warmth are associated with lower levels of mental health problems (Deater-Deckard & Dodge, 1997; N. E. Hill & Bush, 2001) and higher levels of achievement (Steinberg et al., 1991).

Although much of the research on African American parenting has been limited to samples that are low-income, single-parent, or urban households, there is a growing body of literature that has examined African American parenting across socioeconomic status (N. E. Hill, 2001; N. E. Hill & Bush, 2001; Smetana & Chuang, 2001). Consistent with work on lower income families, Smetana and Chuang (2001) found that middle-class African American parents endorsed setting firm, and, at times, nonnegotiable limits on adolescents and justified it by appealing to the need for social order and fitting into societal and social customs, consistent with a value of communalism. Further, these middle-class parents endorsed firm limit setting as a means of instilling responsibility. In an examination of parental involvement in education and academic achievement among African American and Euro American samples from similar economic backgrounds, there were few ethnic differences in the amount of parental involvement in education. However, the relation with achievement differed. For African Americans, involvement at school was positively related to math achievement; whereas the relation was negative for Euro Americans (N. E. Hill & Craft, 2003). For African Americans, the positive relation between school involvement and achievement was due to an increase in teachers' perceptions of students' academic skills.

*Asian American Families*   Like African Americans, high values for achievement and strict parenting also characterize Asian American families. Most Asian cultures, especially East Asian cultures such as Chinese, Japanese, and Korean cultures, are based in Confucian thinking, which includes an emphasis on social harmony, social relationships, and moral virtues. People are defined by their relationships, which are structured hierarchically (Chao, 2000). Moreover, the East Asian cultures emphasize filial piety, age stratification, and the veneration of age (Chao, 1994, 1995). Social harmony is maintained by honoring the requirements and responsibilities of one's social position. The subordinate member in a relationship is required to show honor and loyalty to the superordinate member. Self-improvement is sought for the good of the whole and for social harmony. Relatedly, despite material goods and success, one is deemed powerless unless they are virtuous and moral (Li, 2005). To achieve moral virtue, one must demonstrate personal discipline, delay of gratification, respect for authority, and the ability to bring honor to the family through one's accomplishments (cf. family piety). Excelling academically and showing respect in social relationships, especially to elders, are also part of family piety (D. Y. F. Ho, 1994; D. Y. F. Ho & Kang, 1984).

As it relates to academic achievement, learning is not done for knowledge's sake but for self-improvement, the pursuit of perfection in the context of challenges, and ultimately for the good of society (Li, 2005). The primary goal for learning is one's internal transformation and behavioral reform (Tweed & Lehman, 2002). Knowledge and education are holistic, including aspects of character and cognitive knowledge. Learning includes developing virtue, diligence, perseverance, endurance during hardship, and concentration, along with a respect for knowledge and others. Effort, hard work, and humility are esteemed. Whereas some, especially teachers, see the respect for authority that is characteristic of Asian students as a lack of questioning and blind acceptance, a deeper examination shows that the respect is based in the humility of the learner, a valued characteristic (Li, 2005). In order to continue self-improvement, the learner must be humble. Greater importance is placed on effort than accomplishments and there is a distinct focus on errors, as mistakes highlight places for improvement (Heine et al., 2001). A quote from a focus group study illustrates the emphasis on hard work and effort: "Chinese success is not the result of intelligence but the results of diligence, self-discipline, and self-regulation" (Li, 2001, p. 482).

Based on the Confucian worldview, parenting is seen as cultivating and training the next generation, with a greater focus on the younger ages than on older children (Chao, 1994, 1995). East Asian parents often see their children as a blank surface, which they must shape, and schooling is the primary responsibility of parenting (Chao, 2000). The role of schooling is not limited to knowledge of academic subjects, but includes knowledge about morality, about the world, and about how to function in social relationships (Li, 2005). Based on the primacy of social relationships and social hierarchy, obedience and respect for parents is deemed necessary for children to succeed in school, and thereby bring honor to their parents. Parents' role is to govern, teach, and discipline their children. They show their love and affection for their children through involvement and investment, rather than emotional expressiveness (Chao, 2000).

As with other ethnic minority families, most models of parenting and parental involvement in education (Baumrind, 1971; Epstein & Sanders, 2002) do not fully capture the culturally-embedded parenting strategies of Asian American families. Because Asian parents see training and guiding their children as their primary responsibility and show their love and affection through involvement and investment, they are often characterized as having an authoritarian or strict parenting style (Steinberg et al., 1991; Steinberg, Lamborn, Dornbusch, & Darling, 1992). However, others have found that rather than being authoritarian, Asian parents are guided by *chiao shun* or *guan*, which implies training, guiding, and continuous monitoring of behavior, with a goal of continual improving (Chao, 1994, 2000). This training model of parenting has been found to be positively correlated with both authoritarian and authoritative (democratic) parenting practices and is positively related to the parenting goals of familial piety and respect for authority (Chao, 1994).

Among Asian Americans, being a good parent is defined, in large measure, by how well one's children perform academically (Chao, 2000). Therefore, many of their parenting practices focus on the development or training of their children academically. Asian families are often characterized as having the lowest levels of involvement in education, as defined by most frameworks of parental involvement (E. S. C. Ho & Willms, 1996; Kao, 1995; Peng & Wright, 1994). However, they attend to different aspects of achievement and utilize different strategies—strategies that are focused within the home (Chao, 2000; Ran, 2001). Asian parents tend to monitor and structure their children's time outside of school and augment school work with academic activities at home. For example, to accelerate achievement, Asian parents often assign additional homework, arrange for tutors outside of school to accelerate achievement, and assist and monitor their children's preparation for standardized tests and college planning (Hieshima & Schneider, 1994; E. S. C. Ho & Willms, 1996). In addition, because of the Confucian focus on humility and self-improvement, resulting in de-emphasizing achievements and focusing on mistakes and errors as indicators of areas for improvement, Ran (2001) found that Chinese parents emphasized accuracy and perfect scores. In addition, the Chinese parents in Ran's study wanted teachers to help them in identifying the weakest areas in their children, rather than celebrating achievements.

*Latino Families* As with Asian American and African American families, Latino parents place a primacy on social relationships and the dynamics of social interactions. There are several cultural values that shape social relationships for Latinos, especially with those outside the family. These include *obligación, respeto, personalismo*, and *dignidad* (Marin & Marin, 1991; Simoni & Perez, 1995). *Personalismo* reflects a desire to relate to and trust people, rather than institutions, and a genuine interest in people and their welfare, in contrast to a professional distance or indifference. Similarly, *respeto* indicates a desire for empathy, respect, and intimate connection in relationships (Andres-Hyman, Ortiz, Anez, Paris, & Davidson, 2006; Simoni & Perez, 1995). *Dignidad* reflects a sense of honor and worthiness between people and an expectation that people deserve respect and reverence regardless of their status of in life (Andres-Hyman et al., 2006). This sense of honor and respect for others is often contrasted with the respect for social hierarchies and the promotion of deference and respect toward powerful others (Simoni & Perez, 1995). The value of *obligacion* to others in one's role influences their expectations for teachers. Among Latinos, teachers are expected to advocate for all of their students and to know what is best for them as part of their caring role as teachers (L. C. Lopez, Sanchez, & Hamilton, 2000; Padilla, Pedraza, & Rivera, 2005). This is often in stark contrast to what Latino parents find in American schools where teachers may not advocate for and believe in every student. Each of these values make it more difficult and culturally foreign for Latino parents to press for and advocate for their children against teachers and other school personnel.

There are cultural models or worldviews among Latino families that inform the ways of knowing and learning. For example, for EuroAmericans to "know" is positive and absolute—that is, to know a fact; whereas "to know" for Latinos is conceptualized by the Spanish word *saber*—to know a fact, as conceptualized in English—and by *conocer*—to know in a more personalized and interactive type of knowing that is built through a relationship (Padilla et al., 2005) or by learning occurs though observation, supportive, gradual mastery of information through cooperation and collaboration (Carger, 1996). The later type of "knowing" is not conceptualized in American schools. Evidence of additional differences in worldviews is present in beliefs about how children learn to read. Some Latino cultures maintain that reading develops through the repetitive practice of linking the first words or vowels into syllables and then into words (Reese & Gallimore, 2000). Because of this belief and experience, Reese and Gallimore found that Latino parents may pay less attention to American-defined pre-literacy (i.e., imitating reading, scribbling, and noticing letters).

> … when literacy is perceived as beginning to emerge with the child's first attempts to imitate the reading and writing that he sees … then parents are motivated to respond to these early attempts with interest and engagement. However, when reading is viewed as a formal process that begins later and is characterized by rote practice, there is not such motivation to respond to [American-defined] naturally occurring emergent literacy behaviors. (Reese & Gallimore, 2000, p. 114)

In interacting with their children, Latino families stress the value of hard work and a general work ethic, even exposing their children to the harsh realities of manual labor as a means of communicating the value of education (G. R. Lopez, 2001). The high value placed on school is coupled with a high value that is placed on a good day's work. Regardless of one's position, one should work hard. Based in part on this value of hard work, parents conceptualization of a good education is often defined broadly and includes being a good person, having a high moral standard, and being hard working, in addition to being educated academically (Carger, 1996; Hidalgo, Pedraza, & Rivera, 2005; Olmedo, 2003).

In part because of the high regard placed on the family unit (i.e., *familismo*), developing and basing one's identity on the family is important (Blair, Blair, Madamba, Rosier, & Kinney, 2003). In addition to the desire to learn English, Latino parents desire that their children retain their fluency in Spanish for both communicating with relatives and for developing their ethnic identity (Jones, 2003; Marchant, Paulson, & Rothlisberg, 2001; Olmedo, 2003). The socialization of family and cultural values is enmeshed in the semantics of the native language (Buriel, 1993). Most often the second source of information or the experts consulted for advice are grandparents or godparents (i.e., *compadres* or *comadres*; Correa & Tulbert, 1993).

Parenting strategies of families of Mexican descent have been characterized as responsibility oriented, especially for first generation parents in the United States (Buriel, 1993). They expect children to make productive use of their time, take advantage of the opportunities they have, and be more autonomous and responsible at earlier ages, which often results in parenting strategies that are both stricter (e.g., about not wasting time) and more permissive (e.g., expectation that children will handle their responsibilities with little direct assistance; N. E. Hill & Torres, in press). In fact, harsher and more authoritarian parenting strategies were positively correlated with warmth and were associated with better mental health, suggesting that stricter parenting is interpreted as caring and concern (N. E. Hill, Bush, & Roosa, 2003). Based on focus groups with Latino families, mothers reported being consistent, firm, and responsive to children's misbehavior; they valued strictness as a strategy more so than leniency, although strictness must occur in the context of a warm relationship (Guilamo-Ramos et al., 2007).

Grounded in cultural beliefs and practices like these, Latino parents, especially of Mexican descent, strive to help their children succeed. However, their strategies and practices for promoting achievement are not often captured in typical models of parental involvement (N. E. Hill & Torres, in press; Ibenez, Kuperminc, Jurkovic, & Perilla, 2004). They are likely to embrace a split in the responsibilities of home and school in fully educating their children. Home based education should focus on moral development and respect for others as a foundation for the academic development that is the role for the school (Auerbach, 2007). Immigrant Latino families also use stories and narratives to motivate their children (i.e., *consejos*; Auerbach, 2002). These stores reflect cautionary tales based on the life experiences of family members designed to guide children away from pitfalls and onto the right path. Further, as a means of parental involvement in education that is often invisible to schools and frameworks of involvement, many Latino parents make significant sacrifices to support their children's education (Auerbach, 2007). For example, they may limit chores and family responsibilities to provide study time, sacrifice on other family needs to support attendance in the better schools or permit an older child to work along with parents to support the education of a younger sibling (G. R. Lopez, 2001), suggesting that school success should be evaluated in the context of the family as a whole.

All children are raised with worldviews, beliefs, and practices that are guided by their cultural background and experiences and they bring culturally-defined strengths, assumptions, and behavioral tendencies to the school context. However, they do not enter schools that are neutral cultural environments. Schools, themselves, operate with cultural assumptions and worldviews. Even if they believe themselves to be objective, their worldviews and biases are tacit and certainly affect classroom dynamics, teaching, and evaluation styles. Although much of the work outlining the cultural assumptions of American schools is conducted as a point of comparison for examining the culturally based engagement styles of ethnic minority, a consistent picture emerges.

## BELIEFS, VALUES, AND PRACTICES IN U.S. SCHOOLS

In U.S. public schools, there is an emphasis on individual achievement (and individual attention), on promoting self-esteem and self-expression, on competition, and a devaluing of cooperation, interdependence, conformity (Linney & Seidman, 1989). American schools serve the interests of capitalism and social stratification. Schools have the goals of teaching academic skills and knowledge and, implicitly, teaching students to embrace American values, attitudes, and cultural orientation. Because such cultural socialization is implicit, when ethnic minority children do not meet expectations, they are often uncertain about the ways in which they are falling short (Fordham, 1996), which may cause students to internalize that lack of success. U.S. schools tend to present material and teach skills in a linear, sequential, step by step methodology, rather than the holistic learning style of many ethnic minority families. U.S. schools often operate with the implicit and explicit goal of re-socializing ethnic minority and low income children into middle-class, Euro American ways through the emphasis on social skills and through linear methodologies for teaching basic skills (Hollins & Spencer, 1990). Teachers, regardless of their own cultural background, are trained to engage students who ultimately reproduce the American dominant culture and it shows in their curriculum, the structure of the classroom and learning, and explicit and implicit expectations for deportment.

Other dimensions of school culture that differentially impact ethnic minority families include language use and language formality and flexibility in the curriculum. First, whether it is the controversy over the primacy of standard English, relative to dialects of English, or bilingual education, the language of instruction has implications for educating ethnic minority families. The level of formality of language in the classroom makes a difference. Five levels of formality of speech have been identified, ranging from intimate to formal/frozen (Joos, 1972). Whereas many English language learners are skilled at communicating in English at a casual or colloquial level, teachers educate and evaluate students using a formal level of language, which puts students at a disadvantage in terms of understanding the lessons and communicating their knowledge effectively. Second, classrooms and schools can be evaluated on the flexibility of their curriculum and thereby their ability to meet the individual needs, abilities, and interests of students (Kugelmass, 2006). The increased emphasis on standardized testing as a means holding teachers and schools accountable for educating students has created greater inflexibility in curriculum, as curricula are more likely mandated at district and state levels. Because ethnic minority children are more likely to be different from mainstream school culture, they are more likely to benefit from a flexible curriculum that accounts for their learning style and the academic foundation developed at home.

Although ethnic minority and immigrant parents may hold beliefs and goals for raising their children, they do not always know how to achieve them in American society, especially when they aspire for their children to follow a different path than themselves or when the cultural foundation on which their beliefs and goals are based differ from the cultural foundation of the school or larger society. The next section focuses on interactions between home and school as they are influenced by the culturally based worldviews families bring and the implicit culture and worldview of schools.

## CULTURES COLLIDE: SYNERGY, CHAOS, AND CONFUSION

When families and school interact, cultural beliefs and practices are engaged both unconsciously and deliberately. When they are consistent and compatible, communication is efficient and students benefit (i.e., synergy). However, incongruence results in misunderstandings, chaos, and confusion.

### Synergy

Current frameworks call for family-school collaborations and partnerships (e.g., Epstein & Sanders, 2002). Partnerships come with an expectation that families and schools will collaborate and share responsibility for educating children. Partnerships works best when teachers, schools, and families share a similar worldview about the nature of child development, the efficacy of particular types of instruction, and appropriate child behavior. These unspoken rules for engagement are taken for granted and seldom articulated or discussed (Garfinkel, 1967). In this case, when home and school cultures are congruent, synergy is created and students reap the greatest benefit—the impact of the whole of cognitive and intellectual engagement at home and school is greater than the sum of its parts. That is, the cultural experiences in the home facilitate and accelerate students' adjustment to and success in school (Lareau, 1987). Students receive consistent messages across contexts, which results in greater internalization of behavior, cognitive skills, and knowledge (N. E. Hill & Taylor, 2004).

As evidence of this synergy, when describing their interactions with parents, teachers reported that they felt more comfortable talking with college-educated, Euro American parents; they felt like they could be heard and understood better by parents like themselves—college-educated and Euro American; and they felt they had higher quality relationships with them, compared to African American and parents who did not have a college degree (N. E. Hill, Castellino, & Lansford, 2002). This is consistent with other work that has shown that middle-class families feel more welcomed in the school than do other families (Lareau, 1987; Lightfoot, 1978). Lareau found that, for lower socioeconomic families, the amount of contact with the school was not associated with an increase in the amount of knowledge they had about the school curriculum or their child's progress.

In addition, the curriculum is based on a Euro American worldview. There is an emphasis on and tacit belief that Euro American, middle-class culture is the norm and is universal, with all other cultural or economic variations as deviants. Even when the school curriculum focuses on ethnic minority culture, it is done so with interactions between Europeans or Euro Americans as the point of departure (Freng, Freng, & Moore, 2006). For example, instruction on African Americans begins with slavery, rather than African cultural heritage; instruction on Mexican Americans begins with the conquest of the southwestern United States; and instruction on Native Americans begins with their interactions with the early settlers from Europe and colonization. In contrast, American History begins with Euro Americans and their discovery of America, their arrival, and settlement of the North American continent. "[This implicit practice] gives Euro-Americans a sense of continuity in their history" (Hollins & Spencer, 1990, p. 94). The subtle implication for ethnic minorities is that they can only be understood in relation to Euro Americans.

There is substantial evidence that shows that teachers hold higher expectations for middle-class Euro American students, compared to ethnic minority students (Tenenbaum & Ruck, 2007). Further, Tenenbaum and Ruck found that teachers engaged Euro American students with more positive and neutral speech than they did with ethnic minority students. Conversely, teachers use more negative speech with African American and Latino children than with Euro American students, making the school context a more inviting one for Euro American students. When students misbehave, teachers are more likely to interpret such behavior by Euro American children in benign ways, as evidence of boredom and the need for more engaging materials, whereas the same behavior exhibited by African American children is interpreted as disinterest and disengagement (Ferguson, 1998; N. E. Hill & Bromell, 2008). As an apt summary, "parents who agreed with the administrators' and teachers' definition of partnership appeared to offer an educational advantage to their children" (Lareau, 1987, p. 76).

The benefit of common worldviews between families and schools are not always limited to Euro American, middle-class families. Among Native American parents and schools on a reservation, the parents who expressed that they had high quality relationships with their children's teachers also held formal positions in the school district (e.g., school board or employee; Freng et al., 2006). Similarly, Asian American students are believed to be more prepared academically than students from other ethnic backgrounds, including Euro Americans (Wong, Lai, Nagasawa, & Lin, 1998), and they often benefit from a perceived common worldview between families and schools about the importance of education. As evidence, teachers hold the highest expectations for the achievement of Asian American students, compared to Euro American, Latino, and African American students (Tenenbaum & Ruck, 2007). Asian Americans are often described as the "model minorities," because of their academic success (Wong et al., 1998). These findings suggest that it is in the context of perceived common worldviews that partnerships are developed, even if a common worldview exists across differing ethnic backgrounds. But, this benefit of common expectations does not make these parents immune to feelings of disconnection, confusion, and chaos when interacting with the school.

## Chaos and Confusion

Among the ways in which home and school cultures collide and create chaos and confusion are: (a) when home and school cultures result in differing expectations for behavior, (b) when prior experience or discrimination results in a lack of trust, (c) when families and teachers do not feel understood, and (d) when families find that their cultures are not appreciated or valued. There are expected ways of behavior in school that may not map onto children's experiences in their home life. An example is Euro American middle-class ways of turn taking during classroom instruction and individual notions of performance, rather than the more collaborative and spontaneous ways that are more common among ethnic minorities, such as Latinos and African Americans (Hollins & Spencer, 1990). Due to differences between the implicit school culture and home culture for many ethnic minority students, school and society can seem like an unwelcoming or hostile environment in which they must be prepared to defend their cultural identity. Each of these four ways in which cultures collide and create chaos are discussed below.

*Differing Expectations for Behavior*   Teachers may misinterpret some behaviors among ethnic minority children as reflecting a cultural deprivation and a lack of readiness to learn (Hollins & Spencer, 1990). Movement and exuberance exhibited by ethnic minority children was interpreted as evidence of a lack interest in school or lack of value for education and, at times, as evidence of Attention Deficit Hyperactivity Disorder (ADHD), despite that such expressive movement is consistent with the cultural value of verve (Ferguson, 1998; N. E. Hill & Bromell, 2008; Tyler et al., 2006). Quiet or deferential behavior, such as not making eye contact or speaking up in class, exhibited by some ethnic minority students, is sometimes interpreted as a lack of interest or engagement. However, for many Asian cultures, speaking interferes with learning and they believe that one should speak only after they have understood the material—not as a process for understanding new material (Li, 2005). Similarly, Latin American parents often teach their children that direct eye contact with someone in authority is disrespectful, whereas teachers expect eye contact as a signal of attention and engagement (Conchas, 2001; Trumbull, Rothstein-Fisch, & Hernandez, 2003). In addition, Latinos often expect that others will respond to non verbal for assistance that avoid the embarrassment of requesting help, as is consistent with their culture (Correa & Tulbert, 1993).

Consistent with their values for interdependence and cooperation, ethnic minority children performed better academically when they collaborated in small groups than when they worked on projects alone (Boykin, Tyler, Watkins-Lewis, & Kizzie, 2006; La Roche & Shriberg, 2004). For example, peer perceptions of academically successful African American students was dependent on whether they engaged in communal, collaborative and cooperative learning styles or independent and self-focused learning styles. African American students rated high achieving African American students who endorsed communal, collaborative styles of learning more positively than they related high achieving African American students who endorsed independent values (Sankofa et al., 2005). This changes our understanding of the notion of acting White. Rather than deeming the act of academic success as acting White, it is perhaps the endorsement of independent and self-focused behaviors of American schools that is often correlated with academic success, that connotes acting White

Whereas some differences in behavioral expectations can be handled by code-switching, for others, it is more difficult. Many African American and Latino parents find that the school culture of independence and self-focus undermines their authority with their children, resulting in their children's disrespectful behavior. Because of this, some Latino parents grapple with potentially sending their teens back to their home country and must weigh the benefits of the educational advantages in the United States with the costs of creating disrespectful relations between the parents and the children (Olmeda, 2003; Reese, 2002). Similarly, African American students reported being punished more for displaying "vervistic" and communal behaviors than for displaying individualistic behaviors at school, whereas they were punished more at home for showing individualistic behaviors than vervistic and communal behaviors (Tyler et al., 2006), creating dissonance about expected behaviors.

There are also differences in expectations regarding the purpose of homework and parents' roles in helping with homework. For example, many Asian families work closely with their children in their early years and then decline significantly in their involvement when their children are older because they believe that their children should know what to do by the time they are in late elementary school (Chao, 2000). Despite this, many schools continue to assign homework that requires parents to work with their children. Further, in some cultures, homework is assigned when not all materials can be covered during the school day (e.g., in countries where the resources to fund a full day of school are limited). Families from these countries, such as Brazil, come to the United States expecting high quality full day schooling and, thereby, very little homework (deCarvalho, 2001). They are then surprised by the amount of homework and even more so by the expectation that they should be involved. Some see parental involvement in homework as a form of cheating—as children should complete it on their own. Differences in expectations for behavior are created and perpetuated by difficulties in communication.

*Misunderstandings and Not Being Heard*    Teachers will often assume that parents will ask about things they do not know or understand. However, one must consider the culturally embedded aspects of asking and telling and the influence of the quality of the relationships between the parent and teachers on communication (Goodnow, 2002). Some parents may not ask for information if they think asking will cause the teacher to see them as ignorant. In addition, there are times when parents just "do not know what they do not know." This is especially problematic when parents see the school as impenetrable and uncaring. Further, knowledge is, at times, controlled, guarded, and provided only to a few select people (Goodnow, 2002). In a qualitative study of family-school interactions, Latino parents with lower education levels found that their experiences and interactions with school personnel left them feeling inferior, embarrassed, helpless, and shameful (Auerbach, 2002). Latino parents felt uninformed about and uncomfortable with the expectations schools had for them (Ramirez, 2003). This conflicts with the values that promote social harmony and the ***obligacion*** of teachers to advocate on behalf of students.

Whereas the most logical source of miscommunication is due to language differences and a lack resources to provide translators. However, some research shows that communication problems are as much about differences between parents' values and the implicit values of the school as they are about language barriers (Trumbull et al., 2003). For example, Ran (2001) found that because Asian parents place greater emphasis on students' accuracy, perfect scores, and errors that needed correction, they are often frustrated with teachers who focused only on how well their students were doing in school. Rather than focusing on the strengths and accomplishments, which is consistent with the mainstream American worldview, these parents wished to identify the mistakes as indicators of how their child can improve. In addition, many African American students found that despite meeting and talking with teachers, they often left these meetings with unanswered and even unasked questions (Gutman & McLoyd, 2002). Part of the misunderstanding and difficulty with communication is due to the lack of appreciation for and understanding of cultural beliefs.

*Unappreciated Cultures* Ethnic minority children are often made to feel that the skills and language that they bring from home are not valid bases from which to begin formal learning. When parents' cultural background is different from the schools, they often find that their culture and worldview is ignored by the school, thereby undermining partnerships (Spring, 1997; Szaz, 1999). For example, an evaluation of a Native American school on a reservation found that there were no opportunities to learn the indigenous languages of the tribe. In fact, the only foreign language that was offered was Spanish (Freng et al., 2006). There was no realization or concern that the school curriculum required Native American students in the U.S. Southwest to learn the language of their colonizers and oppressors, rather than their native language. When the curriculum included the native culture, it focused on more material culture (e.g., bead and feather work and foods), rather than on the values, meanings, and practices of culture.

Despite a desire for partnerships between parents and teachers, the majority of parents in a study of Native Americans indicated that parent-teacher relationships were superficial or nonexistent (Freng et al., 2006). In addition, many African Americans feel that they are unheard when engaging with teachers (Gutman & McLoyd, 2002). When children's behaviors are misinterpreted, communication is difficult, and families feel unwelcome, it is difficult to build relations and work together. A lack of trust ensues.

*Discrimination and Lack of Trust* Mistreatment, misunderstandings, and misinterpreted behaviors often result in a lack of trust that makes it difficult to build partnerships between families and schools. African Americans have a long and tumultuous history with American schools including a persistent denigration of educational opportunities for African American children (Cross, 2003; Spencer et al., 2003). The "separate, but unequal" schools that resulted in the under-education of African Americans and the discrimination experienced by many African Americans in desegregated schools has developed into a mistrust of schools and teachers by many African American parents (Lareau, 1987; Ogbu, 1978). Similarly, with feelings of helplessness, and frustration, Latino parents feared retribution from teachers toward their children if they intervened on behalf of their children (Ramirez, 2003). These experiences have impacted the family-school relations for ethnic minorities and may influence the nature and influence of parental involvement on achievement. African American parents tend to monitor schools and teachers more so than actively engaging teachers (Lareau, 1987). Rather than working with teachers, parents find that they must defend their children against their teachers and advocate with great difficulty for the basic academic needs for their children. African American and Latino parents indicated that they were involved at school, in part, to demonstrate their commitment and dedication to schooling and education, because they knew that teachers did not hold them (or their children) in high regard (Gutman & McLoyd, 2002; N. E. Hill, Tyson, & Bromell, 2009).

When families and schools come together, cultures and worldviews collide. If there is common and even unspoken understanding, a synergy is created that advantages children. However, when there are cultural misunderstandings, diminished expectations for children, discrimination, and unrecognized cultural strengths, as is the case for many ethnic minority children, the path of reaching their potential becomes an increasingly difficult one to navigate. Further research is needed to understand the processes through which culturally-embedded practices promote achievement.

## IDENTIFYING CULTURALLY INCLUSIVE PATHWAYS TO ACADEMIC ACHIEVEMENT: A CALL FOR RESEARCH

Although considerable research has documented ethnic differences in academic indicators such as grades, test scores, and school completion and documented ethnic differences in parents' levels of engagement in sanctioned parental involvement strategies as they relate to achievement, more nuanced research is needed in three areas. First, empirical research that tests the associations between culturally-embedded parenting and achievement is needed. Much of the research that has identified culturally embedded strategies is qualitative by design. Whereas qualitative research is highly useful for identifying and describing processes, it is much less useful in testing hypotheses about the efficacy of culturally embedded strategies to support achievement. This must begin with the development of assessments for the culturally embedded strategies and then link them empirically to academic success. There are some examples of this work. The Chinese parenting strategy of *Guan* has been studied as it relates to academic achievement among Chinese immigrants and Chinese Americans (Chao, 1994), although more is needed with other aspects of parenting among Chinese and other Asian Americans. Also, the Latino cultural value of *familism* has been examined in relation to achievement among families of Mexican descent (Rodriguez, 2002). However, other aspects of Latino cultural values have not been examined in relation to achievement. Among African Americans, communal and collaborative cultural values have been examined as they related to students' perceptions of academically successful peers (Sankofa et al., 2005), but not in relation to achievement itself. Significantly more research needs to be done to assess and understand the efficacy of culturally embedded strategies for promoting achievement. Finally, in developing a measure and framework for family-school relations among middle school students, Hill et al. (2009) included the perspectives of multiple ethnic groups to assure that the framework is culturally inclusive at its inception.

Second, additional research is needed that clarifies the associations between family worldviews about success and the strategies parents use to promote success. Doing so will identify the ways in which parents are efficacious in developing the goals they have for their children and identify ways in which parents must compromise their goals or tradeoff among a hierarchy of goals. In this chapter, theory and research on parenting beliefs and worldviews were applied to cultural variations in experiences and interactions between families and schools. However, research about parenting beliefs about the nature of learning academic skills, appropriate levels of engagement on a more specific set of academic outcomes are needed to inform theories, research and practice.

Third, culturally inclusive research on parenting and achievement needs to consider developmental changes in effective parenting and appropriate levels of engagement with schools. To date, the vast majority of research on family-school relations and parental involvement in achievement has focused on elementary school aged children and has not focused on the unique needs of adolescents (N. E. Hill & Chao, 2009). Many strategies deemed appropriate for parental involvement during the elementary schools years are more difficult to implement in middle schools (e.g., developing relationships with multiple teachers), are less effective, and are not consistent with the developmental needs of adolescents, which includes increased autonomy, independence, and decision-making skills. This is particularly important because cultures vary in their beliefs about the age in which children become responsible. Whereas for many middle-class Euro American parents, the expectation for dependence and significant parental involvement remains through much of adolescence (N. E. Hill et al., 2009). In contrast, among immigrant families, adolescents have significant roles and responsibilities in the family that support the well-being of the family. Continued high levels of involvement in education may be incongruent with these understood expectations for and evidence of responsibility.

Empirical evidence in each of these areas of research is necessary to develop programs and policies that will reach families from culturally diverse backgrounds and reach ethnic minorities and their families at a time when they are most at risk for disengagement (i.e., middle school). Although some programs and policies are designed to enhance parental involvement and family-school relations, they are often unsuccessful in reaching the very people they wish to engage (i.e., ethnic minorities). Indeed, unless a program is *more* successful in reaching ethnic minorities, than middle-class Euro American families, it is doomed to create even greater gaps in involvement and achievement (Lichter, 1996).

## BEYOND PROGRAMS AND POLICIES: WHAT DO WE REALLY NEED?

Given that all parenting practices, including those that are in the context of schooling and academic development, are embedded in culturally regulated worldviews, is it possible to change the ways that parents from diverse cultural backgrounds engage in school to fit a model of school-family partnerships that is based on a middle-class, Euro American worldview? Maybe. Should this be our goal? Maybe not. Numerous programs have been developed over the decades and policies have been effected to mandate parental involvement—even legislation that mandates policies (e.g., No Child Left Behind). With so many programs and policies, why do we still have problems engaging families? Indeed, even within the same school, partnerships may be established between parents and teachers who believe they share similar goals (i.e., between middle-class, Euro American parents and teachers) and not between other parents and teachers. Ethnic minority parents and teachers find it difficult to establish these relations and, by default, separate realms are maintained between these families and schools and both partners report lower levels of comfort or understanding when engaging each other, with negative repercussions for students.

Rather than expecting that teachers and other school personnel can learn and memorize aspects of different cultures and pull them out when dealing with a parent from that culture, it is more productive to consider one's own cultural biases, assumptions and worldviews so that we can be mindful of them as we engage with any parent, student, or family member. Doing so will assist in treating each student and his/her family like individuals, rather than representatives of their ethnic or cultural background. Understanding that additional time and energy may be needed when engaging families with different cultural backgrounds is also key. In addition, there are several tenets that are not new, but are worth repeating, that teachers and schools can engage in to help parents from diverse backgrounds support their children academic development.

### Give Information Freely, Wholly, and Willingly

Useful knowledge is sometimes treated as a commodity and is not given willingly (Goodnow, 2002). Further, schools should not count on other parents, even parents in the PTA/PTO to be the arbiters of information. Families with low levels of social capital are less likely to know parents who have the most useful and accurate information (Lareau, 2003; Lareau & Horvat, 1999). In addition, parents involved in the PTO/PTA may create a hierarchy of involvement activities and information based on their own social cliques and exclude ethnic minority parents from the very activities that will provide information (Pena, 2000). In Pena's study, the PTO developed teams and all of the Spanish speaking parents were relegated to the playground committee, whereas the English speaking parents were able to participate more completely in the school decision-making processes, resulting in uneven information and differential empowerment.

### Sometimes Parents Can't "Hear" You. Why?

Although teachers and school personnel may believe they are communicating with parents, there are times and situations when parents just cannot hear the teachers or incorporate what they are saying into parenting practices. First, parents are less likely to seek new information when they believe things are going well for their child. This is especially true if the new information is inconsistent with their current parenting beliefs and practices (Goodnow, 2002). Further, middle-class parents are much more avid information seekers than are working-class parents. Therefore, greater effort may be needed to establish the relevance of the information for parents who may not be seeking new information.

Second, the timing of information is important. Parents are most receptive to new information, even if it conflicts with their existing beliefs and worldviews, if they receive it right before or right as they need it—transition periods. For example, if parents believe that one does not have to think about college plans until high school, they will be less likely to hear and integrate information about planning for college in middle school. The relevance of this information is not understood. Increasing understanding of the pathway to college (or other goal) and a families location on that pathway will facilitate communication and benefit children.

Third, parents have a hard time hearing teachers and other school personnel when information is not provided in a form or format that is most useful to the family. This goes beyond the translation of materials into the language the parents speak. For example, if parents work during the day without access to a telephone, they cannot be reached by teachers during their planning period. Similarly, many low income immigrant parents are not literate in English or in their native language. Therefore, fliers and other written material sent home to parents are not easily accessible to parents regardless of their language (Carger, 1996).

Finally, and most importantly, parents cannot hear teachers when they feel that the teachers are not listening to them, do not have their children's best interests as a goal, or do not treat them respectfully. That is, communication happens in the context of a trusting relationship. Programs and policies designed to increase parental involvement will not work if they do not help teachers build trusting relationships with students and parents from diverse backgrounds. Teachers and school personnel sometimes give the impression that they believe that parents lack competence or *need* improvement, which creates a defensiveness in parents that undermines the intended message. This is especially pernicious when the families are from low income or ethnic minority backgrounds. In some cases, teachers will have to build bridges over valleys they did not create and mend wounds that they did not cause in order to reach families.

### Create a Culturally Inclusive Classroom or School

For many ethnic minority students, the American school's notions of self-expression and individualism feel more like self-restraint and conformity. They come to learn that some aspects of who they are "naturally" among their families are not acceptable (Tyson, 2003) outside that group. The most effective means of reaching students and families from diverse backgrounds is helping them feel valued as an individual and feel that their culture is affirmed and included. Cultural inclusion goes beyond simply adding more ethnic minority teachers and books. It entails incorporating the culture of individual students into the school in academic context in ways that provide scaffolding and support for learning and promotes the development of an integrative cultural identity (Hollins & Spencer, 1990) and eliminating the unspoken bias favoring Euro American middle-class values.

The concept of family-school relationships is culturally embedded and culturally defined. Schools have their own cultural worldviews that define and shape styles of teaching, evaluation, and engagement with students and their families, albeit unacknowledged and implicit at times. Meanwhile, parents and families hold their own beliefs about the nature of development, the effectiveness of particular parenting strategies, the role the school has in the development of the whole child, and the nature of the world for which they are preparing their children. On the surface, it would seem that families and schools should naturally work together towards the common goal of children's development. However, more than a generation ago, families and schools were defined as natural enemies (Waller, 1965). In some ways, this still rings true. Parents are supposed to hold schools accountable and exercise choice when schools do not measure up, on the one hand. But, on the other hand, they are to work collaboratively and to have co-responsibility for the child's outcome. It rings most true for ethnic minority families whose cultural worldview is devalued and clashes with the implicit worldview of the school. To remain globally competitive and help all children reach their potential for the good of society, we must make implicit values explicit and repair trust and inclusiveness where it has been broken.

## AUTHOR'S NOTE

This chapter was written while Professor Hill was on leave from the Department of Psychology and Neuroscience at Duke University. She thanks Kathryn Torres, Mary Catherine Seward, and Jonathan Whichard for their assistance with identifying relevant research and editing this chapter.

## REFERENCES

Andres-Hyman, R. C., Ortiz, J., Anez, L. M., Paris, M., & Davidson, L. (2006). Culture and clinical practice: Recommendations for working with Puerto Ricans and other Latinas(os) in the United States. *Professional Psychology: Research and Practice, 37*(6), 694–701.

Arce, J. (2004). Latino bilingual teachers: The struggle to sustain an emancipatory pedagogy in public schools. *International Journal of Qualitative Studies in Education, 17*(2), 227–246.

Arnett, J. J. (1995). Broad and narrow socialization: The family in the context of a cultural theory. *Journal of Marriage and the Family, 57*, 617–628.

Auerbach, S. (2002). 'Why do they give the good classes to some and not to others?' Latino parent narratives of struggle in a college access program. *Teachers College Record, 104*(7), 1369–1392.

Auerbach, S. (2007). From moral supporters to struggling advocates: Reconceptualizing parent roles in education through the experience of working-class families of color. *Urban Education, 42*(3), 250–283.

Baumrind, D. (1971). Current patterns of parental authority. *Developmental Psychology Monographs, 41*(1, part 2).

Blair, S. L., Blair, M. C. L., Madamba, A. B., Rosier, K. B., & Kinney, D. A. (2003). *Race/ethnicity, gender, and adolescents' occupational aspirations: An examination of family context.* New York: Elsevier Science.

Boykin, A. W. (1983). The academic performance of Afro-American children. In J. Spence (Ed.), *Achievement and achievement motives* (pp. 321-371). San Francisco: Freeman.

Boykin, A. W. (1986). The triple quandary and the schooling of Afro-American children. In U. Neisser (Ed.), *The school achievement of minority children* (pp. 57–92). Hillsdale, NJ: Erlbaum.

Boykin, A. W., Tyler, K. M., Watkins-Lewis, K., & Kizzie, K. (2006). Culture in the sanctioned classroom practices of elementary school teachers serving low-income African American students. *Journal of Education for Students Placed at Risk, 11*(2), 161–173.

Brody, G. H., & Flor, D. L. (1998). Maternal resources, parenting practices, and child competence in rural, single parent African American families. *Child Development, 69*, 803–816.

Brooks, D. (2004). *On paradise drive: How we live now (and always have) in the future tense.* New York: Simon & Schuster.

Bugental, D. B., & Johnson, C. (2000). Parental and child cognitions in the context of the family. *Annual review of Psychology, 51*, 315–344.

Buriel, R. (1993). Childrearing orientations in Mexican American families: The influence of generation and sociocultural factors. *Journal of Marriage and the Family, 55*(4), 987–1000.

Carger, C. L. (1996). *Of borders and dreams: A Mexican American experience of urban education.* New York: Teachers College Press.

Chao, R. K. (1994). Beyond parental control and authoritarian parenting style: Understanding Chinese parenting through the cultural notion of training. *Child Development, 65,* 1111–1119.

Chao, R. K. (1995). Chinese and European-American cultural models of the self reflected in mothers' child rearing beliefs. *Ethos, 23,* 328–354.

Chao, R. K. (2000). Cultural explanations for the role of parenting in the school success of Asian American children. In R. W. Taylor & M. C. Wang (Eds.), *Resilience across contexts: Family, work, culture, and community* (pp. 333–363). Mahwah, NJ: Erlbaum.

Cokley, K. O. (2005). Racial(ized) identity, ethnic identity, and afrocentric values: Conceptual and methodological challenges in understanding African American identity. *Journal of Counseling Psychology, 52*(4), 517–526.

Conchas, G. Q. (2001). Structuring failure and success: Understanding the variability in Latino school engagement. *Harvard Educational Review, 71*(3), 475–504.

Correa, V. I., & Tulbert, B. (1993). Collaboration between school personnel in special education and Hispanic families. *Journal of Educational & Psychological Consultation, 4*(3), 253–265.

Cross, W. E. (2003). Tracing the historical origins of youth delinquency & violence: Myths & realities about black culture. *Journal of Social Issues, 59*(1), 67–82.

Darling, N., & Steinberg, L. (1993). Parenting style as context: An integrative model. *Psychological Bulletin, 113*(3), 487–496.

Deater-Deckard, K., & Dodge, K. A. (1997). Externalizing behavior problems and discipline revisted: Nonlinear effects and variations by culture, context, and gender. *Psychological Inquiry, 8,* 161–175.

deCarvalho, M. E. (2001). *Rethinking family-school relations: A critique of parental involvement in schooling.* Mahwah, NJ: Erlbaum.

Epstein, J. L., & Sanders, M. G. (2002). Family, school, and community partnerships. In M. H. Bornstein (Ed.), *Handbook of parenting* (Vol. 5, pp. 507–437). Mahwah, NJ: Erlbaum.

Ferguson, R. F. (1998). Teachers' perceptions and expectations and the Black-White test score gap. In C. Jencks & M. Phillips (Eds.), *The Black-White test score gap* (pp. 273–317). Washington, DC: Brookings Institution Press.

Fordham, S. (1996). *Blacked out: Dilemmas of race, identity, and success at Capital High School.* Chicago: University of Chicago.

Franzoi, S. (1996). *Social psychology.* Madison, WI: Brown & Benchmark.

Freng, A., Freng, S., & Moore, H. A. (2006). Models of American Indian education: Cultural inclusion and the family/community/school linkage. *Sociological Focus, 39*(1), 55–74.

Garcia, S. B., & Guerra, P. L. (2006). Conceptualizing culture in education: Implications for schooling in a culturally diverse society. In J. R. Baldwin, S. L. Faulkner, M. L. Hecht, & S. L. Lindsley (Eds.), *Redefining culture: Perspectives across the disciplines.* Mahwah, NJ: Erlbaum.

Garfinkel, H. (1967). *Studies in ethnomethodology.* New York: Prentice-Hall.

Geertz, C. (1973). *The interpretation of cultures.* New York: Basic.

Giroux, H. A. (1981). *Ideology, culture, and the process of schooling.* Philadelphia: Temple University.

Gonzales, N. A., Cauce, A. M., & Mason, C. A. (1996). Interobserver agreement in the assessment of parental behavior and parent-adolescent conflict: African American mothers, daughters, and independent observers. *Child Development, 67*(4), 1483–1498.

Goodnow, J. J. (1988). Parents' ideas, actions, and feelings: Models and methods from developmental and social psychology. *Child Development, 59,* 286–320.

Goodnow, J. J. (2002). Parents' knowledge and expectations: Using what we know. In M. H. Bornstein (Ed.), *Handbook of parenting* (2nd ed., Vol. 3, pp. 439–460). Mahwah, NH: Erlbaum.

Greenfield, P. (1994). Independence and interdependence as developmental scripts: Implications for theory, research, and practice. In P. Greenfield & R. Cocking (Eds.), *Cross-cultural roots of minority child development* (pp. 1–40). Hillsdale, NJ: Erlbaum.

Greico, E. M., & Cassidy, R. C. (2001). *Overview of race and Hispanic origin. Census brief.* Retrieved June 15, 2008, from www.census.gov/prod/2001pubs/czkbr01-1.pdf

Grills, C., & Longshore, D. (1996). Africentrism: Psychometric analyses of a self-report measure. *Journal of Black Psychology, 22*(1), 86–106.

Guilamo-Ramos, V., Dittus, P., Jaccard, J., Johansson, M., Bouris, A., & Acosta, N. (2007). Parenting practices among Dominican and Puerto Rican mothers. *Social Work, 52*(1), 17–30.

Gutman, L. M., & McLoyd, V. C. (2002). Parents' management of their children's education within the home, at school, and in the community: An examination of African-American families living in poverty. *Urban Review, 32*(1), 1–24.

Heine, S. J., Kitayama, S., Lehman, D. R., Takata, T., Ide, E., & Leung, C. (2001). Divergent consequences of success and failure in Japan and North America: An investigation of self improving motivations and malleable selves. *Journal of Personality and Social Psychology, 81*, 599–615.

Hermans, H. J. M., & Kempen, H. J. G. (1998). Moving cultures: The perilous problems of cultural dichotomies in a globalizing society. *American Psychologist, 53*(10), 1111–1120.

Hidalgo, N. M., Pedraza, P., & Rivera, M. (2005). Latino/a Families' Epistemology. In *Latino education: An agenda for community action research* (pp. 375–402). Mahwah, NJ: Erlbaum.

Hieshima, J., & Schneider, B. (1994). Intergenerational effects on the cultural and cognitive socialization of third and fourth generation Japanese Americans. *Journal of Applied Developmental Psychology, 15*, 319–327.

Hill, N. E. (2001). Parenting and academic socialization as they relate to school readiness: The roles of ethnicity and family income. *Journal of Educational Psychology, 93*, 686–697.

Hill, N. E. (2006). Disentangling ethnicity, socioeconomic status, and parenting: Interactions, influences, and meaning. *Vulnerable Children and Youth Studies, 1*(1), 114–124.

Hill, N. E., & Bromell, L. (2008). *Ethnic and SES differences in the corroboration of teachers' and parents' reports of child behavior across early elementary school.* Unpublished manuscript, Durham, NC.

Hill, N. E., & Bush, K. R. (2001). Relationships between parenting environment and children's mental health among African American mothers and children. *Journal of Marriage and the Family, 63*, 954–966.

Hill, N. E., Bush, K. R., & Roosa, M. W. (2003). Parenting and family socialization strategies and children's mental health: Low-income Mexican American and Euro-American mothers and children. *Child Development, 74*(1), 189–204.

Hill, N. E., Castellino, D. R., & Lansford, J. E. (2002, April 12). *Parental involvement, school achievement, and career aspirations: Mediated pathways of influence.* Paper presented at the Society for Research on Adolescence, New Orleans, LA.

Hill, N. E. & Chao, R. K. (2009). Background in theory, policy, and practice. In N. E. Hill & R. K. Chao (Eds.) *Families, schools and the adolescent: Connecting research, policy, and practice* (pp. 1–15). New York: Teachers College Press.

Hill, N. E., & Craft, S. A. (2003). Parent-school involvement and school performance: Mediated pathways among socioeconomically comparable African American and Euro-American families. *Journal of Educational Psychology, 95*, 74–83.

Hill, N. E., & Herman-Stahl, M. A. (2002). Neighborhood safety and social involvement: Associations with parenting behaviors and depressive symptoms among African American and Euro-American mothers. *Journal of Family Psychology, 16*(2), 209–219.

Hill, N. E., Murry, V. M., & Anderson, V. D. (2005). Sociocultural Contexts of African American Families. In V. C. McLoyd, N. E. Hill, & K. A. Dodge (Eds.), *African American family life: Ecological and cultural diversity* (pp. 21–44). New York, NY: Guilford Press.

Hill, N. E., & Taylor, L. C. (2004). Parental school involvement and children's academic achievement: Pragmatics and issues. *Current Directions in Psychological Science, 13*(4), 161–164.

Hill, N. E., & Torres, K. (in press). Negotiating the American dream: The paradox of Latino students' goals and achievement and engagement between families and schools. *Journal of Social Issues.*

Hill, N. E., Tyson, D. F., Bromell, L., & Flint, R. C. (2009). Parental involvement in middle school: Developmentally appropriate strategies across ethnicity and socioeconomic status. In N. E. Hill & R. K. Chao (Eds.), *Family-school relations during adolescence: Linking interdisciplinary research and practice* (pp. 53–72). New York: Teachers College.

Hill, S. A., & Sprague, J. (1999). Parenting in Black and White families. *Gender and Society, 13*(4), 480–502.

Hines, P. M., & Boyd-Franklin, N. (1982). African American families. In M. McGoldrick, J. Giordano, & J. K. Pearce (Eds.), *Ethnicity and family therapy* (pp. 66–84). New York: Guilford.

Ho, D. Y. F. (1994). Cognitive socialization in Confucius heritage cultures. In P. Greenfield & R. Cocking (Eds.), *Cross cultural roots of minority child development* (pp. 285–314). Hillsdale, NJ: Erlbaum.

Ho, D. Y. F., & Kang, T. K. (1984). Intergenerational comparisons of childrearing attitudes and practices in Hong Kong. *Developmental Psychology, 20*(6), 1004–1016.

Ho, E. S. C., & Willms, J. D. (1996). The effects of parental involvement on eighth grade achievement. *Sociology of Education, 69*, 126–141.

Hoff, E., Laursen, B., & Tardif, T. (2002). Socioeconomic status and parenting. In M. H. Bornstein (Ed.), *Handbook of parenting* (Vol. 2, pp. 231–252). Mahwah, NJ: Erlbaum.

Holden, G. W., & Buck, M. J. (2002). Parental attitudes toward childrearing. In M. H. Bornstein (Ed.), *Handbook of parenting* (2nd ed., Vol. 3, pp. 537–562). Mahwah, NJ: Erlbaum.

Holden, G. W., & Edwards, L. A. (1989). Parental attitudes toward child rearing: Instruments, issues, and implications. *Psychological Bulletin, 106*(1), 29–58.

Hollins, E. R., & Spencer, K. (1990). Restructuring schools for cultural inclusion: changing the schooling process for African American youngsters. *Journal of Education, 172*(2), 89–100.

Hughes, D., Rodriguez, J., Smith, E. P., Johnson, D. J., Stevenson, H. C., & Spicer, P. (2006). Parents' ethnic-racial socialization practices: A review of the research and directions for future study. *Developmental Psychology, 42*, 747–770.

Ibenez, G. E., Kuperminc, G. P., Jurkovic, G., & Perilla, J. (2004). Cultural attributes and adaptations linked to achievement motivation among Latino adolescents. *Journal of Youth and Adolescence, 33*, 559–568.

Jones, T. G. (2003). Contribution of Hispanic parents' perspectives to teacher preparation. *School Community Journal, 13*(2), 73–97.

Joos, M. (1972). The styles of the clocks. In R. D. Abrahams & R. C. Troike (Eds.), *Language and cultural diversity in American education* (pp. 145–149). Englewood Cliffs, NJ: Prentice-Hall.

Kao, G. (1995). Asian Americans as model minorities? A look at their academic performance. *American Journal of Education, 103*(2), 121–159.

Kohn, M. L. (1969). *Class and conformity: A study of values.* Homewood, IL: Dorsey.

Kugelmass, J. W. (2006). Sustaining cultures of inclusion: The values and limitations of cultural analyses. *European Journal of Psychology of Education, 21*(3), 279–292.

La Roche, M. J., & Shriberg, D. (2004). High Stakes Exams and Latino Students: Toward a Culturally Sensitive Education for Latino Children in the United States. *Journal of Educational & Psychological Consultation, 15*(2), 205–223.

Lareau, A. (1987). Social class differences in family-school relationships: The importance of cultural capital. *Sociology of Education, 60*, 73–85.

Lareau, A. (2003). *Unequal childhoods: Class, race and family life.* Berkeley: University of California.

Lareau, A., & Horvat, E. M. (1999). Moments of social inclusion and exclusion: Race, class, and cultural capital in family-school relationships. *Sociology of Education, 72*, 37–53.

Leventhal, T., & Brooks-Gunn, J. (2000). The neighborhoods they live in: The effects of neighborhood residence on child and adolescent outcomes. *Psychological Bulletin, 126*, 309–337.

Li, J. (2001). Expectations of Chinese immigrant parents for their children's education: The interplay of Chinese traditions and the Canadian context. *Canadian Journal of Education, 26*(4), 477–494.

Li, J. (2005). Mind or virtue: Western Chinese beliefs about learning. *Current Directions in Psychological Science, 14*, 190–194.

Lichter, D. T. (1996). Family diversity, intellectual inequality, and academic achievement among American children. In A. Booth & J. F. Dunn (Eds.), *Family-school links: How do they affect educational outcomes* (pp. 265–273). Mahwah, NJ: Erlbaum.

Lightfoot, S. L. (1978). *Worlds apart.* New York: Basic Books.

Linney, J. A., & Seidman, E. (1989). The future of schooling. *American Psychologist, 44*(2), 336–440.

Lopez, G. R. (2001). The value of hard work: Lessons on parent involvement from an (im)migrant household. *Harvard Educational Review, 71*(3), 416–437.

Lopez, L. C., Sanchez, V. V., & Hamilton, M. (2000). Immigrant and native-born Mexican-American parents' involvement in a public school: A preliminary study. *Psychological Reports, 86*(2), 521–525.

Luster, T., Rhoades, K., & Haas, B. (1989). The relation between parenting values and parenting behavior: A test of the Kohn hypothesis. *Journal of Marriage and the Family, 51*, 139–147.

Marchant, G. J., Paulson, S. E., & Rothlisberg, B. A. (2001). Relations of middle school students' perceptions of family and school contexts with academic achievement. *Psychology in the Schools, 38*, 505–519.

Marin, G., & Marin, B. V. (1991). *Research with Hispanic populations* (Vol. 23). Newbury Park, CA: Sage.

Markus, H. R., & Kitayama, S. (1991). Culture and the self: Implications for cognition, emotion, and motivation. *Psychological Review, 98*, 224–253.

Mason, C. A., Walker-Barnes, C. J., Tu, S., Simons, J., & Martinez-Arrue, R. (2004). Ethnic differences in the affective meaning of parental control behaviors. *Journal of Primary Prevention, 25*(1), 59–79.

McGillicuddy-DeLisi, A. V., & Sigel, I. E. (1995). Parent beliefs. In M. H. Bornstein (Ed.), *Handbook of parenting* (Vol. 3, pp. 333–358). Mahwah, NJ: Erlbaum.

Mitchell, H. H. (1975). *Black Belief: Folk beliefs in America and West Africa.* New York: Harper & Row.

Ogbu, J. U. (1978). *Minority education and caste: The American system in cross-cultural perspective.* New York: Academic Press.

Olmeda, I. (2003). Accommodation and resistance: Latinas' struggle for their children's edcuation. *Anthropology of Education Quarterly, 34,* 373–375.

Olmedo, I. M. (2003). Accommodation and resistance: Latinas struggle for their children's education. *Anthropology and Education Quarterly, 34,* 373–395.

Padilla, R. V., Pedraza, P., & Rivera, M. (2005). Latino/a education in the 21st century. In P. Pedraza & M. Rivera (Eds.), *Latino education: An agenda for community action research* (pp. 403–423). Mahwah, NJ: Erlbaum.

Palacios, J. (1990). Parents' ideas about the development and education of their children: Answers to some questions. *International Journal of Behavioral Development, 13,* 137–155.

Pearson, G. H. (1931). Some early factors in the formation of personality. *American Journal of Orthopsychiatry, 1,* 284–291.

Pena, D. C. (2000). Parent involvement: Influencing factors and implications. *Journal of Educational Research, 94*(1), 42–54.

Peng, S. S., & Wright, D. (1994). Explanation of academic achievement of Asian American Students. *Journal of Educational Research, 87*(6), 346–352.

Pepper, S. C. (1942). *World hypotheses: A study in evidence.* Berkeley: University of California.

Pianta, R. C., & Rimm-Kaufman, S. (2006). The social ecology of the transition to school: Classrooms, families, and children. In K. McCartney & D. Phillips (Eds.), *Blackwell handbook of early childhood development* (pp. 490–507). Malden, MA: Blackwell.

Pinderhughes, E. E., Dodge, K. A., Bates, J. A., Pettit, G. S., & Zelli, A. (2000). Discipline responses: Influence of parents' socioeconomic status, ethnicity, and beliefs about parenting, stress, and cognitive-emotional processes. *Journal of Family Psychology, 14*(3), 380–400.

Ramirez, A. Y. F. (2003). Dismay and disappointment: Parental involvement of Latino immigrant parents. *Urban Review, 35*(2), 93–110.

Ran, A. (2001). Traveling on parallel tracks: Chinese parents and English teachers. *Educational Research, 43*(3), 311–328.

Reese, L. (2002). Parental strategies in contrasting cultural settings: Families in Mexican and "El Norte." *Anthropology and Education Quarterly, 33,* 30–59.

Reese, L., & Gallimore, R. (2000). Immigrant Latinos' cultural model of literacy development: An evolving perspective on home-school discontinuities. *American Journal of Education, 108*(2), 103–134.

Reid, B. B., & Valsiner, J. (1986). Consistency, praise, and love: Folk theories of American parents. *Ethnos, 14,* 976–980.

Rodriguez, J. L. (2002). Family environment and achievement among three generations of Mexican American high school students. *Applied Developmental Science, 6,* 88–94.

Sankofa, B. M., Hurley, E. A., Allen, B. A., & Boykin, A. W. (2005). Cultural expression and black students' attitudes toward high achievers. *The Journal of Psychology, 139*(3), 247–259.

Santayana, G. (1934). *Character and opinion of the United States.* New York: Norton.

Sigel, I. E., & McGillicuddy-DeLisi, A. V. (2002). Parent beliefs are cognitions: The dynamic belief systems model. In M. H. Bornstein (Ed.), *Handbook of parenting* (Vol. 3, pp. 485–508). Mahwah, NJ: Erlbaum.

Simoni, J. M., & Perez, L. (1995). Latinos and mutual support groups: A case for considering culture. *American Journal of Orthopsychiatry, 65*(3), 440–445.

Smetana, J., & Chuang, S. (2001). Middle-class African American parents' conceptions of parenting in early adolescence. *Journal of Research on Adolescence, 11*(2), 177–198.

Spencer, M. B., Cross, W. E., Harpalani, V., & Goss, T. N. (2003). Historical and developmental perspectives on Black academic achievement: Debunking the "acting white" myth and posing new directions for research. In C. C. Yeakey & R. D. Henderson (Eds.), *Surmounting all odds: Education, opportunity, and society in the new millennium* (pp. 273–303). Greenwich, CT: Information Age.

Spring, J. (1997). *Deculturalization and the struggle for equity* (2nd ed.). New York: McGraw-Hill.

Steinberg, L., Dornbusch, S., & Brown, B. (1991). Ethnic differences in adolescent achievement: An ecological perspective. *American Psychologist, 47,* 723–729.

Steinberg, L., Lamborn, S. D., Dornbusch, S. M., & Darling, N. (1992). Impact of parenting on adolescent achievement: Authoritative parenting, school involvement, and encouragement to succeed. *Child Development, 63,* 1266–1281.

Stevenson, H. C., Davis, G., & Abdul-Kabir, S. (2001). *Stickin' to, watchin' over, and gettin' with: An African American parent's guide to discipline.* San Francisco: Jossey-Bass.

Stevenson, H. C., Winn, D. M., Walker-Barnes, C., & Coard, S. I. (2005). Style matters: Toward a culturally relevant framework for interventions with African American families. In V. C. McLoyd, N. E. Hill, & K. A. Dodge (Eds.), *African American family life: Ecological and cultural diversity* (pp. 311–334). New York: Guilford.

Super, C. M., & Harkness, S. (1996). The developmental niche: A conceptualization at the interface of child and culture. *International Journal of Behavioral Development, 9*, 545–569.

Szaz, M. C. (1999). *Education and the American Indian.* Albuquerque: University of New Mexico.

Tenenbaum, H. R., & Ruck, M. D. (2007). Are teachers' expectations different for racial minority than for European American students? A meta-analysis. *Journal of Educational Psychology, 99*(2), 253–273.

Triandis, H. C. (1988). Collectivism and individualism: A conceptualization of a basic concept in cross-cultural social psychology. In C. Bagley & G. K. Verma (Eds.), *Personality, cognition, and values* (60–95). London: MacMillan.

Trumbull, E., Rothstein-Fisch, C., & Hernandez, E. (2003). Parent involvement in schooling: According to whose values? *School Community Journal, 13*(2), 45–72.

Turner, J. C., & Oakes, P. J. (1986). The significance of the social identity concept for social psychology with reference to individualism, interactionism and social influence. *British Journal of Social Psychology, 25*, 237–252.

Tweed, R. G., & Lehman, D. R. (2002). Learning considered with a cultural context: Confucius and Socratic approaches. *American Psychologist, 57*(89–99).

Tyler, K. M., Boykin, A. W., Miller, O., & Hurley, E. A. (2006). Cultural values in the home and school experiences of low-income African American students. *Social Psychology of Education, 9*, 363–380.

Tyson, K. (2003). Notes from the back of the room: Problems and paradoxes in the schooling of young Black students. *Sociology of Education, 76*, 326–343.

Waller, W. (1965). *The sociology of teaching.* New York: Science Editions.

Wong, P., Lai, C. F., Nagasawa, R., & Lin, T. (1998). Asian Americans as a model minority: Self-perceptions and perceptions by other racial groups. *Sociological Perspectives, 41*, 95–118.

Woods, L. N., & Jagers, R. J. (2003). Are cultural values predictors of moral reasoning in African American adolescents? *Journal of Black Psychology, 29*(1), 102–118.

# II

## Partnerships Across Development

# 6

# THE HOME LEARNING ENVIRONMENT AND ACHIEVEMENT DURING CHILDHOOD

ERIC DEARING AND SANDRA TANG

The home serves as children's first library, their first laboratory, their first art studio, and their first playground. In their homes, children make initial explorations into literacy, mathematics, science, art, and music. Indeed, it is in the home that children formulate and test some of their first hypotheses about the nature of the world, building and progressively refining their knowledge and skills as well as their learning expectations, beliefs, goals, and strategies. Accordingly, the home environment has long been considered central in shaping children's growth, although most scholars now reject socialization theories that gave little regard to genetics and the ways that children also shape their homes (Bjorklund & Yunger, 2001; Collins, Maccoby, Steinberg, Hetherington, & Bornstein, 2000; Kellaghan, Sloane, Alvarez, & Bloom, 1993; Maccoby, 1984, 1992).

## OVERVIEW

In this chapter, empirical work on home learning environments and their role in children's achievement is reviewed. To organize this work, recent theoretical advances addressing the role of sociocultural contexts in children's development are relied upon (e.g., Chase-Lansdale, D'Angelo, & Palacios, 2007; García Coll et al., 1996; Magnusson & Stattin, 1998; Spencer, 2006). In addition, existing conceptual frameworks of the home learning environment were helpful in organizing the present chapter (e.g., Bornstein, 2006; Bradley & Corwyn, 2004; Brooks-Gunn & Marksman, 2005). Building on these frameworks, the goal of the chapter is to answer the question: What characteristics of children's homes matter for their achievement?

### Developmentally Salient Domains of the Home Environment: What Matters for Children's Achievement?

Compared with the young of other species, children are unusually dependent on their parents. Because of the large amount of child brain growth that occurs postnatal, and because human society is exceptionally complex, parents invest extensive resources and time in child-rearing across several years. As Bjorklund and colleagues point out, Homo sapiens "have taken parenting to new heights" (Bjorklund, Yunger, & Pellegini, 2002, p. 3).

Children's safety and survival are a parenting priority, particularly when resources are scarce or risk is pervasive (Bowlby, 1982; 1988; LeVine & White, 1897). Beyond these basic needs, parents also use the home as a learning environment to educate their children for successful adaptation to the cultural, physical, and social milieu, passing on knowledge and life skills that children use to their advantage (Bjorklund et al., 2002; Bornstein, 2006; Harkness & Super, 2002; Lerner, Rothbaum, Boulos, & Castellino, 2002; LeVine & White, 1987). Parental investment in children within the home learning environment involves processes of socialization toward particular value orientations, but it also involves parents passing along what Swidler (1986, p. 273) referred to as a cultural "toolkit" of habits, skills, and styles" that provide "strategies of action" that children may use to thrive. These value orientations and toolkits are shaped by parents own socialization experiences, biologically-based motivation systems, intuitive parenting skills, the greater sociocultural context, and children themselves (Bowlby, 1988; Fleming & Li, 2002; LeVine & White, 1987; Papoušek & Papoušek, 2002).

In Figure 6.1, a conceptual model is provided that helps structure the discussion of the home learning environment, depicting both physical and psychosocial elements of the home and extended developmental contexts as well as intra-psychic processes relevant for child achievement. The home learning environment is illustrated as one

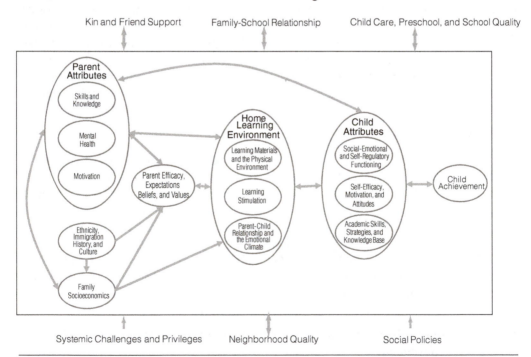

**Figure 6.1** Conceptual model of the home learning environment and its connection to more general family systems, child achievement, and developmental contexts outside the family.

component of a larger child-family system that influences, and is influenced by, child achievement. From left to right, pathways of mediation are noted within this system, moving from relatively distal elements on the left that generally have indirect effects on achievement to relatively proximal elements on the right that generally have direct effects on achievement. Also highlighted in the figure are a few of the many connections between the child-family system and contexts outside the family that have either direct (e.g., child care) or indirect (e.g., social policy) implications for both the home learning environment and child achievement.

An exhaustive list of contextual elements and processes inside and outside of children's homes cannot easily be included in a single figure (nor can all possible connections within the system), and encircling unique elements of the system necessarily oversimplifies what are, in reality, porous boundaries and dynamic subsystems with mutual influences on one another. Moreover, although not explicitly illustrated, three points are critical for understanding the meaningfulness of children's home learning environments. First, children's achievement is generally the net result of child vulnerabilities and competencies combined with contextual risks and protective factors (Bronfenbrenner & Morris, 1998; Sameroff, 1975; Spencer, 2006). Second, the optimal home learning environment for promoting children's achievement is, in part, determined by person-environment fit (Lerner, 1983; Magnusson & Stattin, 1998); for example, the optimal complexity, frequency, and intensity of experiences in the home are dependent on child developmental stage (Eccles et al., 1993). Third, associations between the more general system depicted in the figure, the home learning environment, and children's achievement are often bidirectional, non-linear, non-additive, and changing with maturation (Gottlieb, 1998; Lerner et al., 2002; Sameroff, 2000). Yet, with these complexities in mind, much evidence has accumulated over decades of work on (a) the consequences of home learning environment quality for children's achievement, (b) the mechanisms by which these consequences are transmitted to children, and (c) the determinants of home learning environment quality.

## Organizational Framework of the Home Learning Environment

Several groups of theorists have offered frameworks to help organize families' diverse and complex child-rearing efforts. Some frameworks organize the home environment as it is relevant for child growth broadly construed, including cognitive, language, and social-emotional growth. Notable frameworks of this type include those proposed by Bornstein (e.g., Bornstein, 2006) and Bradley and colleagues (e.g., Bradley & Corwyn, 2004). On the other hand, some frameworks have focused on the relevance of the home environment for narrowly defined domains of achievement. Two notable examples of this latter type include a framework for understanding parenting effects on school readiness provided by Brooks-Gunn and Markman (2005) and a framework for understanding home environment effects on literacy development provided by Hess and Holloway (1984).

Importantly, across these broad and narrow frameworks, there are many points of convergence with regard to home environment characteristics that matter for children's growth. Regarding children's achievement, these points of convergence indicate at least three elements of the home learning environment that are critical for promoting children's achievement: (a) materials that stimulate children's learning within a physical environment that is structurally conducive to learning, (b) parent engagement in activities with their children that stimulate learning, and (c) a parent-child relationship and emotional climate that is supportive of learning. Each of these three elements is considered in greater depth.

### Learning Materials and the Physical Environment of the Home

Children learn about the world and themselves through interaction with the world and objects in it (Piaget, 1950, 1951, 1985). Indeed, both animal and human studies highlight the impact of an enriched environment on brain development. In a classic series of animal studies, for example, Greenough Black, and Wallace (1987) demonstrated that complex environments with access to stimulating toys (e.g., climbing ladders and spinning wheels) are necessary for optimal synaptic growth in young rats. These studies suggest that a basic level of material resources in the environment is likely necessary for typical brain development and, on the other hand, deprivation limits neural growth (Blakemore & Firth, 2005). In fact, consistent with the animal studies, infants raised in extremely deprived orphanages display later cognitive deficits perhaps resulting from neural damage, although some of these children also evidence considerable cognitive recovery when adopted into enriched home environments (Rutter & O'Connor, 2004).

*Learning Materials*  Most studies on the value of home learning materials for achievement do not have the design advantages of animal studies (randomized experiments) or orphanage-adoption studies (natural experiments). Nonetheless, many non-experimental between-family comparisons have indicated a strong correlation between having learning materials in the home and nearly all areas of achievement. Children's access to literacy materials in the home, for example, is an excellent predictor of literacy achievement. The number of children's books and other print materials within the home predict reading outcomes contemporaneously such that children from homes that contain high quantities of print materials have better vocabulary skills, show more interest in book reading, and have higher reading achievement scores than those from homes with fewer print materials (Connor, Son, Hindman, & Morrison, 2005; Morrow, 1983; Sénéchal, LeFevre, Hudson, & Lawson, 1996; Wahlberg & Tsai, 1985).

Bradley, Caldwell, and colleagues noted the developmental value of material resources in their series of studies on the home learning environment and achievement (e.g., Bradley & Caldwell, 1984; Bradley, Caldwell, & Rock, 1988). Their work pointed toward a heightened importance of access to home learning materials during infancy and toddlerhood, findings consistent with Piaget's emphasis on physical exploration of the environment during the sensory-motor stage of early development. The presence of play materials and toys in children's homes at age 2, in fact, was a robust predictor of achievement through age 10, even controlling for contemporaneous levels of learning materials in the home (Bradley et al., 1988). Yet, researchers have also noted the importance of materials in middle-childhood and beyond. Simpkins and colleagues (Simpkins, Davis-Kean, & Eccles, 2005), for example, documented associations between parents' provision of math and science toys and games in the home during the elementary-school years and children's involvement in math and science activities outside of school.

For learning materials, variety and match with developmental stage also matter. Children's reading comprehension, for example, is promoted by having access to many different kinds of reading materials (Snow, Burns, & Griffin, 1998). It is not clear, however, that diversity of experience is always explicitly designed by parents. Although some families provide a range of materials and products purchased solely for the purposes of enriching the learning of children (e.g., educational games, children's books), other families provide variety by giving children access to materials not originally intended for learning stimulation per se (e.g., magazines, coupons, religious reading materials such as the Bible), but are stimulating nonetheless (Purcell-Gates, 1996).

In addition, materials in the home are effective only to the extent that they provide challenge that is aligned with children's cognitive maturity, skill levels, and interests (Bradley, 2006; Eccles et al., 1993; Eccles & Midgley, 1989). During infancy, access to brightly colored concept books that have very large pictures accompanied with a few words of print is important (Morrow, 2001). Toddlers and children in kindergarten should have a wider variety of print materials: alphabet and number books, poetry, nursery rhymes, and books with limited vocabulary that have pictures matching the text (Morrow, 2001). Once children develop foundational reading skills, more challenging materials (e.g., chapter books) are appropriate, and considerations for topics of interest and child-specific curiosities become relevant through middle-childhood and adolescence (Baker & Wigfield, 1999; Morrow, 2001).

***Organization and Physical Quality of the Home***   Beyond material resources, the organization and structural quality of the physical home environment are also relevant for children's growth, albeit areas that have received less study by child development scholars (e.g., Bradley & Corwyn, 2004; Evans, Kliewer, & Martin, 1991; Evans, Wells, & Moch, 2003). In one interesting set of studies on the organization of the home, Dunifon and colleagues (e.g., Dunifon, Duncan, & Brooks-Gunn, 2001, 2004) have found that home cleanliness is predictive of children's years of educational attainment and, in turn, later earnings as an adult. The proclivity towards cleanliness and organization may be determined, in part, by personality traits that parents pass on to children, and these personality traits may also have achievement benefits. Dunifon and colleagues noted, however, that the cleanliness of children's homes during childhood is more strongly predictive of later outcomes such as earnings during adulthood than is the cleanliness of their homes during adulthood. This finding appears most consistent with environmental, rather than heritable, explanations of the impact of home cleanliness on children's achievement.

Home cleanliness findings may also provide insight into the importance of household efficiency. Because Dunifon and colleagues statistically controlled for the amount of time that parents spent cleaning the house, cleanliness may have been an indicator of efficient investment in their children and the household. Based on historical and cross-cultural evidence, LeVine and White (1987, p. 289) argued that "there is probably an optimal strategy of parental investment, i.e., a most efficient way of maximizing culture-specific parental goals" in every society. On the other hand, there is accumulating evidence that the physical home environment per se (i.e., the organization, physical integrity, and safety of the home) has implications for children's achievement (Evans, 2004, 2006).

In comprehensive reviews, Evans (2004, 2006) has documented the implications of physical environments for children's growth, integrating evidence of both direct and indirect effects of home organization and physical structure on children's achievement. As a function of housing quality and location, for example, some children are exposed to higher concentrations of toxins linked with cognitive impairment such as lead, mercury, and PCBs (e.g., Needleman et al., 1979). Noise levels in the home matter as well; children whose homes have high noise levels (e.g., from transportation) are at risk for reading, memory, and attention problems. This is likely due to both the direct negative impact that noisy environments have on children's efforts to learn and through the negative impact that noise can have on parents' levels of stress and patience (e.g., Evans & Maxwell, 1997). Furthermore, home size, crowding, and access to outside play areas are relevant for learning in the home (Evans, Lepore, Shejwal, & Palsane, 1998). More densely crowded homes with little access to natural play settings limit exploration and learning opportunities and, in turn, are associated with poor cognitive, literacy, and achievement outcomes. In addition, the effects of crowding can be indirect, mediated by the extent to which parents engage in learning stimulation. In densely crowded homes, for example, parents may read less often with their children.

### Learning Stimulation

Several theoretical perspectives on children's development have emphasized the important role of parent stimulation of children's learning through parent-child interaction, including ecological systems theory (Bronfenbrenner & Morris, 1998), sociocultural theory (Vygotsky, 1978), and social cognitive theory (Bandura, 1997). In particular, sociocultural theory emphasizes the central importance of parent-child interactions for stimulating the development of culturally-relevant skills and strategies (Vygotsky, 1978). Further, empirical work disentangling the roles of material resources in the home from the transmission of skills via parent-child interaction has indicated that the "human resources" in the home are more valuable to children's achievement than material resources, even after accounting for likely genetic transmission of skills (e.g., Murnane, Maynard, & Ohls, 1981). Three domains of learning stimulation in the home have received considerable empirical attention: parent-child talk, joint reading and problem-solving activities, and parent teaching. Across these three domains, both the quantity and quality of parent stimulation have proven to be consequential for children's achievement.

*Parent-Child Talk*   According to Vygotsky's sociocultural theory of development (Vygotsky, 1978), parent-child language interactions are a fundamental mechanism through which children develop cognitive and language skills. That is, the agent of developmental change is language; parents scaffold their children linguistically, helping co-construct skills and knowledge that children may internalize (Fivush, Haden, & Reese, 2006). Even in infancy, children are active participants in these interactions (e.g., directing gaze, attention, and pre-verbal gestures and sounds). With age, children increasingly become conversational partners.

In their classic study on parent-child talk during infancy and toddlerhood, Hart and Risley (1995) observed and recorded 1,200 hours of parent-child interaction in the homes of 42 children living in families representing a range of socioeconomic statuses. One of the most striking findings from this intensive study was the tremendous variability in the amount of talk parents directed toward their infants and toddlers. In a given hour, some parents spent as much as two-thirds of their time interacting with their children and expressed encouragement or approval more than 40 times during that hour. Other parents, on the other hand, spent less than one-quarter of an hour of their time in interaction with their infants and expressed encouragement or approval as little as 4 or fewer times.

Equally dramatic were the large differences in total amount of talk with children that Hart and Risley (1995) observed between parents. Based on their observations, they estimated that some parents spoke more than 33 million words to their children by the age of 3; yet, other parents spoke less than one-third of this amount by the time their children were 3. Although more and less talkative parents engaged in similar amounts of what Hart and Risley referred to as "business talk" (e.g., "come here," "stop that," "put that down"), the more talkative parents spent more time using talk that was descriptive and conversational in nature. These variations in parent talk were correlated with family socioeconomics such that children in the poorest families generally received the least stimulation and those in the more affluent families with parents who had professional occupations received the most.

In turn, the enormous differences in amount of talk during infancy and toddlerhood were strongly predictive of children's later developmental outcomes, and explained socioeconomic differences in achievement. Across early childhood, for example, high levels of parent talk were associated with children speaking more and practicing their verbal skills more often. Children's rate of vocabulary growth was also correlated with amount of parent talk such that more talk predicted a faster rate of growth. Moreover, amount of parent talk during infancy and toddlerhood was positively associated with children's intelligence scores at age 3 and 9.

Beyond quantity, qualities of parent speech also have implications for children's achievement. Vocabulary development, for example, is more rapid among children that hear a broader range of words and more sophisticated words compared with children who are exposed to a more restricted range and simpler words (for a review, see Hoff, 2006). In early childhood, parent use of multi-clause sentences in their speech positively predicts children's understanding and proficient use of complex sentences (Huttonlocher, Vasilyeva, Cymerman, & Levine, 2002). Furthermore, there is increasing evidence that what parents say during conversations with their children is important for developing metacognitive abilities (e.g., Astington & Jenkins, 1999; Fivush et al., 2006; Lohman & Tomasello, 2003; Peterson & Siegal, 1999, 2000).

Parents' discussion of mental states, perspective-shifting discourse, and elaborations of children's ideas have consequences for children's understandings of their own and other's viewpoints (Lohmann & Tomasello, 2003; Rudek & Haden, 2005). Consider, for example, work on the value of conversations that Peterson and Siegal have conducted using false-belief tasks with deaf children who vary in their exposure to parent-child conversations in the home environment due to variations in their parents' fluency with sign language (for a review, see Peterson & Siegal, 2000). In the classic false-belief procedure, children are shown the true location of an object and then asked to guess where another person will look for that object if told an incorrect location; children who fail the task, predict that the other person will look in the correct location. Profoundly deaf children with "native signing" parents (parents who are also deaf and fluent in sign language at child birth) perform similarly on false-belief tasks as do hearing children, but deaf children growing up with hearing parents perform worse on these tasks, even into adolescence.

Considerable empirical work has also demonstrated the developmental value of parents elaborating while reminiscing about past events with their children (for a review, see Fivush et al., 2006). Parents' use of a highly elaborative style of reminiscing—using many questions and statements to focus the child's attention on additional aspects of a recalled event (e.g., "What animals did you see at the zoo?")—is positively associated with children's use of productive memory strategies and later recall abilities, both contemporaneously and longitudinally. Moreover, highly elaborative styles of parent talk while reminiscing predict better child literacy skills longitudinally in both observational and experimental parent-training studies. These findings are consistent with the theoretical perspective that decontextualized parent-child talk in which the focal object of discussion is an internal representation is particularly valuable for promoting children's language growth (Snow, 1983).

*Shared Book Reading and Other Parent-Child Activities*  Shared book reading and joint problem-solving activities provide exceptional opportunities for parents to interact and talk with their children. Indeed, in the context of shared book reading parents can label objects, introduce vocabulary, refer to elements of print, ask open-ended questions, and elaborate on child responses (Bus, van IJzendoorn, & Pellegrini, 1995; Deckner, Adamson, & Bakeman, 2006; Karrass & Braungart-Rieker, 2005; Ninio & Bruner, 1978; Snow et al., 1998; Whitehurst et al., 1988). Although frequency of shared reading, as early as infancy, has been positively associated with children's expressive language outcomes through middle childhood (e.g., Karrass & Braungart-Rieker, 2005), these associations are generally modest in magnitude (Scarborough & Dobrich, 1994; Sénéchal, LeFevre, Thomas, & Daley, 1998).

However, estimates of the average association between shared reading experiences and achievement may obscure individual differences in: (a) the richness of parent-child interactions, (b) the quality of parent guidance, and (c) the social-emotional climate when reading together (De Jong & Leseman, 2001; Leseman & De Jong, 1998; Sénéchal et al., 1998). That is, the consequences of shared reading for children's achievement may depend on what happens during these parent-child interactions. In fact, parents' use of cognitively demanding comments during reading predict better language outcomes during early and middle childhood (e.g., Deckner et al., 2006; De Jong & Leseman, 2001). Moreover, when embedded within a positive affective relationship, shared reading may impact achievement indirectly by promoting children's interests in reading. Positive affective relationships during shared reading in early elementary school, for example, predict reading of challenging materials later in school, which in turn is associated with better literacy achievement (Baker, Mackler, Sonnenschein, & Serpell, 2001).

Although much less research has been conducted on mathematics stimulation in the home learning environment than on literacy stimulation, a handful of studies indicate that parents do spontaneously initiate discussions related to numeracy in play and other interactions with their children (Anderson, 1997; Anderson, Anderson, & Shapiro, 2005; Vandermaas-Peeler, Nelson, & Bumpass, 2007). In fact, shared book reading may be one context in which discussion of mathematical concepts like size and number occur (Anderson et al., 2005). In addition, as Bjorklund and colleagues (Bjorklund, Hubertz, & Reubens, 2004, p. 348) noted in their work on parent-child interactions and math strategy development, playing board games are "ideal venues for informal instruction and opportunities for parents to teach children important technological skills in a highly motivating context." In a microgenetic study of parent-child interactions during a game of *Chutes and Ladders*, these authors found that parents alternated between the roles of playmate and scaffolding instructor, focusing often times on mathematical strategies. Children who demonstrated the most sophisticated arithmetic strategies during play had parents who initially supported game efforts using more cognitive directives than other parents. Then, over time, these parents gradually provided less direction.

Parents can also engage their children in scientific reasoning by helping them to generate and interpret evidence (Crowley, Callahan, Tenenbaum, & Allen, 2001; Tenenbaum & Leaper, 2003). In turn, children consider evidence for longer durations and with greater depth and focus when doing so with their parents than when considering evidence alone (Crowley et al., 2001). Similar to home literacy environments, however, there may be salient individual differences in how much parents encourage math and science in the home. Although too few studies have addressed this topic directly, one notable exception was conducted by Simpkins and colleagues (Simpkins et al., 2005). These authors found that more frequent parent-child joint participation in math and science activities (beyond homework) during elementary school predicted higher levels of children's involvement in math and science activities outside of school.

*Parent Teaching* Throughout childhood and adolescence, parents also engage their children using teaching and instruction with the explicit goal of promoting their children's skills and strategies for achievement (Bradley & Corwyn, 2004). Across a large, ethnically and economically diverse sample of families, for example, Bradley and colleagues (Bradley, Corwyn, McAdoo, & García Coll, 2001a) found that over 90% of parents, regardless of ethnicity or economic status, reported either usually or always taking responsibility for teaching their toddlers new skills. Moreover, this emphasis on parent teaching continued into middle childhood, with between 75% and 97% of parents reporting that they (or someone else in the home) taught their children numbers, the alphabet, colors, shapes, and sizes (Bradley et al., 2001a). During the school years, approximately 75% of parents report that they help at least sometimes with their children's homework assignments (National Center for Educational Statistics, 2002). Yet, there are also substantial between-family differences in quantity and quality of instruction that takes place in the home, with implications for between-child differences in achievement (Brooks-Gunn & Markman, 2005).

For children's literacy achievement, there is some evidence that although oral language skills are predicted by parent-child shared reading experiences, written language skills are best predicted by parents' explicit attempts to teach their children reading and writing skills (Sénéchal & LeFevre, 2001; Sénéchal et al., 1998). In addition, parents teaching their children letters and words has been linked with children's alphabet and print knowledge contemporaneously and reading fluency up to four years later (e.g., Ebey, Marchand-Martella, Martella, & Nelson, 1999; Kraft, Findlay, Major, Gilberts, & Hofmeister, 2001; Lopez & Cole, 1999; Sénéchal, 2006). Nonetheless, children's literacy achievement appears to benefit most when high levels of teaching literacy skills are combined with shared book reading. With only high levels of teaching, children's emergent literacy skills begin to decline by third grade relative to their peers who receive high levels of teaching and shared book reading (Sénéchal & LeFevre, 2001).

Furthermore, when Bradley and colleagues (Bradley, Corwyn, Burchinal, McAdoo, & García Coll, 2001b) statistically isolated the achievement impacts of parent teaching, controlling for correlated forms of learning stimulation in the home, effect sizes were generally modest in magnitude. As these authors acknowledge, counts of the frequency with which parents engage in teaching academic skills do not capture variability in the quality of instruction. Just as developmental appropriateness helps determine whether material resources are likely to affect child achievement, so too does parents' ability to match instruction style to children's developmental level (Bornstein, 2006).

To stimulate growth, parents must gauge children's understanding of learning stimuli, their knowledge of the wider environment, and their learning progress. Then, parents must adjust their teaching and interaction style accordingly to best scaffold their children's evolving learning needs (Vygotsky, 1978). During didactic interactions, for example, this process may include regulating the difficulty of tasks or guiding children through more or less challenging aspects of a task (Bradley, 2006). Individual differences in parents' abilities to do this (e.g., by offering an appropriate amount of support, rather than too little or too much support) have, in fact, been linked with children's achievement during the elementary school years (Mulvaney, McCartney, Bub, & Marshall, 2006). Yet, researchers and theorists have also called attention to children's roles in both establishing and maintaining these effective teaching interactions with their parents (e.g., Fagot & Gauvain, 1997; Mulvaney et al., 2006). Moreover, it is increasingly clear that efficacy of parent teaching is dependent on parent teaching style and the social-emotional climate in which teaching is embedded (Cooper, Lindsay, & Nye, 2000; Pomerantz, Wang, & Ng, 2005).

During the school years, parent teaching may often be centered on homework (Hoover-Dempsey et al., 2001). Schools and teachers generally encourage parent involvement with homework, with the goals of creating home-school learning links and, in turn, promoting children's achievement. Empirical work on whether the amount of parent help with homework promotes children's achievement has produced inconsistent results, however (Cooper, 1989; Hoover-Dempsey et al., 2001). Positive associations between homework help and children's achievement have been reported in some studies (e.g., Pomerantz & Eaton, 2001), but no association or even negative associations have been reported in other studies (Epstein, 1988; Levin et al., 1997). The inconsistency in findings may be due, at least in part, to the fact that children who evidence academic problems are often more likely than those who evidence academic success to receive high levels of homework help from parents (Epstein, 1988; Hoover-Dempsey et al., 2001;

Levin et al., 1997; Pomerantz & Eaton, 2001). Yet, even accounting for this reciprocal relationship between homework and achievement, it is apparent that the efficacy of parent teaching during homework does not only depend on how often or how much parents help.

In their review and theoretical extension of the empirical literature on parent help with homework, Hoover-Dempsey and colleagues (Hoover-Dempsey et al., 2001) identified three qualitative elements of parents' help with homework that have implications for students attitudes and perceptions of competence. First, when parents have positive attitudes towards homework, children are likely to develop positive attitudes towards homework and learning in general. Second, when parents use help with homework to communicate positive beliefs in their children's competence and ability to perform, children are likely to internalize these beliefs and see themselves as competent. Third, when parents are knowledgeable about the homework task, children are likely to have positive perceptions of task difficulty as well as develop effective problem-solving strategies and work habits.

Particularly in late childhood and adolescence, encouragement of child autonomy may also increase the likelihood that parents' help with homework will, in fact, be helpful. Compared with children whose parents are more directive during homework interactions, children whose parents encourage child autonomy display higher rates of homework completion, higher class grades, and higher standardized test scores (Cooper et al., 2000). Furthermore, parents' use of mastery-oriented practices in their help with homework predicts positive achievement outcomes. Mastery-oriented practices combine direct teaching with encouragement for children to complete their homework on their own as well as emphasize effort in response to challenge rather than focus on performance and ability (Dweck & Leggett, 1988; Grant & Dweck, 2003; Pomerantz, Ng, & Wang, 2006). When parents use this orientation to help with homework, children whose perceptions of academic competence are low begin to display a greater mastery orientation in their academic work (Pomerantz et al., 2006). In turn, developing a mastery orientation and mastery goals have proven to be robust predictors of children's cognitive self-regulation and future achievement, even when controlling for past achievement levels (e.g., Dweck & Sorich, 1999; Elliot, McGregor, & Gable, 1999; Kaplan & Maehr, 1999; Meece & Holt, 1993).

Parent-child interactions around homework are not always positive experiences, however, from either the parent or child point of view. In fact, children often report increased negative affect when working on homework, and parents often report increased negative affect when helping with homework (e.g., Fuligni, Yip, & Tseng, 2002; Leone & Richards, 1989; Pomerantz et al., 2005). Yet, parents can buffer their children from feelings of frustration and irritation using positive affect during homework interactions. Children display better motivation orientations towards academic work as well as greater emotional well-being when their parents use positive affect to buffer the negative emotions they feel about helping their children with homework (Pomerantz et al., 2005). These results are consistent with theoretical and empirical work calling attention to the achievement consequences of the emotional climate within the home learning environment.

## Parent-Child Relationships and the Emotional Climate of the Home Learning Environment

Theorists from multiple scholarly traditions have argued that parent affection has long-term implications for the development of children's cognitive self-regulation (e.g., Ainsworth, Blehar, Waters, & Wall, 1978; Bowlby, 1989; Piaget, 1981). In general, the success of parents' socialization strategies appear to be dependent on the extent to which parents are sensitive and responsive to children's needs and, in turn, parents and children develop mutually responsive orientations (Kochanska, 1991,1997). In the context of mutually responsive parent-child orientations, children are more likely to internalize parent goals and values, rather than ignore or rebel against them (Kochanska, 1991, 1997).

More specific to children's cognitive development and achievement, a positive affective relationship between parents and children may support children's efforts to explore their worlds and engage in stimulating interactions with others (Jacobsen, Edelstein, & Hofmann, 1994). As such, the developmental consequences of children's access to learning materials and stimulation in the home may depend on affective qualities of the parent-child relationship and, more generally, the emotional climate of the home (Belsky & MacKinnon, 1994). In addition, developing school readiness skills and then achieving in school may depend, at least in part, on children's social-emotional competence—regulating negative emotions (e.g., anger), paying attention and following directions, and getting along with parents, peers, and teachers—a developmental domain for which there is overwhelming evidence supporting the value of sensitive and responsive caregiving (Raver, 2002, 2004).

Moreover, there is some evidence that both mothers' and fathers' positive affective relationships with their children matter for children's achievement (Forehand, Long, Brody, & Fauber, 1986). More affectionate parent-child relationships and secure parent-child attachment relationships have been associated with a variety of positive cognitive, language, and achievement outcomes. Positive affective relationships, for example, are predictive of higher school readiness scores, better teacher ratings of competence, and higher math and reading achievement scores (Bradley & Caldwell, 1981; Estrada, Arsenio, Hess, & Holloway, 1987; Pianta, Smith, & Reeve, 1991; Singer & Weinstein, 2000).

Children with secure attachment relationships with their parents also display better cognitive self-regulation and better performance on cognitive tasks and achievement indicators through childhood and adolescence. A secure attachment relationship, for example, is predictive of high cognitive engagement and mastery motivation (Moss & St. Laurent, 2001). In addition, compared with children who display insecure attachment relationships with their parents, children who display secure attachment relationships have better school grades, higher scores on achievement tests, and better adjustment to school (Granot & Mayseless, 2001; Jacobsen et al., 1994). Moreover, children with secure attachment relationships with their parents perform better on a variety of Piagetian tasks from middle childhood through adolescence (Jacobsen et al., 1994).

When considering this literature, however, it is worth noting that the effects of the affective nature of parent-child relationships and attachment may be difficult to disentangle from other aspects of the home learning context, because parents who are responsive may also provide more material resources and more learning stimulation than parents who are not responsive. This possibility has been addressed directly in the extensive work on the home environment conducted by Bradley and colleagues (e.g., Bradley & Caldwell, 1984; Bradley et al., 1988; Bradley et al., 2001b). These researchers have demonstrated that parental responsiveness is predictive of children's reading and math achievement, even after controlling for multiple other aspects of the home context such as learning materials and parents' provision of learning stimulation. Thus, the emotional climate of the home has unique implications for children's achievement. Yet, partitioning unique portions of variance may not fully address the ways in which multiple aspects of parenting, and the home environment more generally, function together to impact achievement (Baumrind, 1978; Maccoby & Martin, 1983). That is, individual parenting practices are nested within a more global parent-child relationship context (Steinberg, 2001). One way researchers have tried to address this global relationship context is to examine parenting styles.

*Parenting Style*    A key determinant of the emotional climate in the home is parenting style (Steinberg, 2001). In a series of classic studies, Steinberg, Dornbush, and colleagues (Glasgow, Dornbush, Troy, Steinberg, & Ritter, 1997; Dornbush, Ritter, Leiderman, Roberts, & Fraleigh, 1987; Steinberg, Lamborn, Dornbusch, & Darling, 1992) demonstrated that authoritative parenting styles are associated with high levels of school achievement during adolescence. Authoritative parents match parental warmth and responsiveness with consistent rules as well as high expectations with support for autonomy. In turn, this style of parenting is hypothesized to promote positive attitudes towards work, responsibility, internal attributions (effort and ability) for academic success, and a better sense of academic competence and self-efficacy (Glasgow et al., 1997; Grolnick, Ryan, & Deci, 1991; Steinberg, Elmen, & Mounts, 1989; Steinberg, 2001). In essence, children and adolescents are thought to internalize more positive attitudes and attributions, both about achievement and self, in the context of parenting that balances support and structure. The optimal balance of parent support and structure likely varies with child age and perhaps ethnicity and community context, however (Baldwin, Baldwin, & Cole, 1990; Dearing, 2004; Furstenberg, Cook, Eccles, Elder, & Sameroff, 1999; Gonzales, Cauce, Friedman, & Mason, 1996; Gutman, Friedel, & Hitt, 2003).

As children transition from childhood into adolescence, physical and cognitive maturation coalesce around a developing sense of identity (Erikson, 1963). Parents can support identity development by providing adolescents with increasing autonomy and decision-making responsibilities (Eccles, 1999; Eccles et al., 1993). Parenting that is over-controlling and restrictive during adolescence may stifle achievement motivation and achievement per se (Steinberg, 2001). Consistent with stage-environment fit theory, the effectiveness of parent management style is dependent on its match with children's developing needs (Eccles et al., 1993).

There is also evidence that the effectiveness of parent management style is dependent on ethnicity and community context. More restrictive parent management strategies, in fact, may promote academic achievement for some youths, most notably African American and Latino American youths living in neighborhoods characterized by poverty and high crime (Baldwin et al., 1990; Dearing, 2004; Gonzales et al., 1996). This positive association between restrictive parent management and child achievement may be due to cultural (e.g., a strong value for family connectedness) and contextual (e.g., protection against danger in the community) reasons (Dearing, 2004). Nonetheless, across ethnicities and community contexts, parents' increasing their support for autonomy as children transition into adolescence appears beneficial for achievement outcomes (Dearing, 2004; Gutman et al., 2003).

### The Home Learning Environment in Psychosocial and Socioeconomic Context

As a proximal context of development, home learning environments are part of a more complex system in which children grow. As depicted in Figure 6.1, the attributes of children, parents, families, and contexts outside the family all help determine the quality of home learning environments. Children with better language and reading skills, for example, evoke more language and reading stimulation from their parents (Maccoby, 2002; Patterson & Fisher, 2002; Scarr & McCartney, 1983; Stanovich, 1986). Higher levels of learning stimulation in the home can also be promoted by contexts outside of the family; higher quality neighborhoods, school, and child care contexts, for example, all have positive effects on parent well-being and, in turn, home learning stimulation (e.g., Leventhal & Brooks-Gunn, 2000; McCartney, Dearing, Taylor, & Bub, 2007; Parker, Boak, Griffen, Ripple, & Peay, 1999). Moreover, variations in family culture associated ethnicity and immigration are critical for determining valued developmental skills as well as the type of home learning contexts that families build to foster those skills (Chase-Lansdale et al., 2007; García Coll et al., 1996; Spencer, 2006). In considering this more complex system in which home learning occurs, two factors are discussed that have received particularly large amounts of empirical attention as influences on the stimulation that children receive in their homes and, in turn, children's achievement: (a) parents learning beliefs, expectations, and values; and (b) family socioeconomics.

*Parental Learning Beliefs, Expectations, and Values*   Parents' behaviors, practices, and styles of investment in their children are determined, at least in part, by their parenting beliefs, attitudes, and attributions (Benasich & Brooks-Gunn, 1996; Gerdes & Hoza, 2006; Luster & Kain, 1987; Luster, Rhoades, & Haas, 1989; Okagaki & Divecha, 1993; Pinderhughes, Dodge, Bates, Pettit, Zelli, 2000; Wentzel, 1998). The character of the home learning environment and, in turn, children's achievement are a function of what parents expect of their children in school and life, their beliefs about the value of education and learning, and their sense of efficacy for affecting their children's achievement and life chances. Indeed, a number of studies have underscored the importance of parents' holding high expectations for their children's academic attainment and strongly valuing education (Alexander, Entwisle, & Bedinger, 1994; Davis-Kean, 2005; Englund, Luckner, Whaley, & Egeland, 2004; Halle, Kirtz-Costes, & Mahoney, 1997; Okagaki & Frensch, 1998). For instance, high expectations for academic achievement and educational attainment as well as positive perceptions of children's abilities predict better reading and math outcomes, even when children's prior academic performance is statistically controlled (Englund et al., 2004; Halle et al., 1997; Neuenschwander, Vida, Garrett, & Eccles, 2007).

Parental expectations and ability beliefs are also strongly predictive of children's academic self-concept and self-efficacy, sometimes more so than previous academic performance or self-perceptions of ability (Bandura, 1997; Hoover-Dempsey & Sandler, 1995; Jacobs, 1991; Marsh, Koeller, Trautwein, Luedtke, & Baumert, 2005; Parsons, Adler, & Kaczala, 1982). In turn, children's academic attitudes, beliefs, and self-efficacy are powerful predictors of their contemporaneous and future academic aspirations and success (Bandura, 1997; Grolnick & Slowiaczek, 1994; Lynch, 2002; Valeski & Stipek, 2001; Zimmerman, Bandura, & Martinez-Pons, 1992). Several studies on gender socialization, for example, have emphasized the role that parents' beliefs (e.g., how interesting and easy is science for a child?) and attributions (e.g., is child math performance a function of effort or talent?) have in predicting children's self-efficacy and achievement in science and math from early childhood through late adolescence and emerging adulthood (e.g., Bleeker & Jacobs, 2004; Jacobs & Eccles, 1992; Tenenbaum & Leaper, 2003). Furthermore, parents' beliefs about their ability to improve their child's academic progress (i.e., parenting self-efficacy) are associated with students' perceived academic efficacy and aspirations. Thus, a chain of processes promoting achievement may unfold whereby parenting self-efficacy and positive perceptions of children's abilities promotes children's self-efficacy and, in turn, improves their academic achievement (e.g., Bandura, Barbaranelli, Caprara, & Pastorelli, 1996).

Interestingly, however, there may be differential student outcomes depending on the gender of the parent high in self-efficacy such that high maternal self-efficacy may be more likely to promote achievement than high paternal self-efficacy (Lynch, 2002). Furthermore, some researchers have suggested that it is developmentally optimal if parents have academic expectations that are congruent with their children's abilities (Alexander et al., 1994; Scott-Jones, 1984). This line of argument suggests that children are likely to perform their best when parents' high expectations match children's current abilities, whereas mismatched beliefs and actual academic performance may lead parents to provide a home environment that does not adequately address their children's current learning needs (Alexander et al., 1994; Scott-Jones, 1984).

Yet, parental expectations, beliefs, and efficacy often do not influence children directly; rather, in many cases, it appears that beliefs and attitudes are psychological mechanisms that impact practices in the home learning context thereby affecting achievement. Mothers who believe strongly that infants are capable of learning, for example, are more likely than other mothers to introduce cognitively enriching activities, such as constructive play, at an earlier time point (Ninio, 1979). Parenting efficacy is also positively associated with parental involvement in the home, hours spent in educational activities with the child, a warm home learning environment, and more positive parent-child interactions (e.g., Hoover-Dempsey et al., 1992; Sheldon, 2002). Moreover, parents high in efficacy give more helpful suggestions and strategies and appear more sensitive to children's skills and ability during joint problem solving tasks compared with parents low in efficacy (Mondell & Tyler, 1981). Indeed, parental efficacy may be a stronger predictor of parental involvement in children's academic progress than parents' own level of education (Hoover-Dempsey et al., 1992).

Parents' attitudes, beliefs, and efficacy are also conveyed through the ways that they structure the environment and establish daily routines (Weisner, 2002). Some researchers have argued that the effect of the home on children's achievement may rely less on how instrumental the help is or the specific academic skills taught, and more on whether the overall climate of the home emphasizes the importance of learning, studying, and education (Okagaki & Frensch, 1998). This may help explain why parents' attitudes, beliefs, and efficacy have demonstrated stronger associations with children's academic performance than specific parenting behaviors directed towards children's learning (Fan & Chen, 2001; Halle et al., 1997). On the other hand, the reciprocal relation between children's achievement and parents' attitudes, beliefs, and expectations may also help explain the strength of this association.

Englund and colleagues (2004) provided an elegant empirical analysis of the bidirectional relationship between parent expectations and children's achievement through early and middle childhood. These authors found that the quality of instruction that parents provided in the home during early childhood positively predicted child IQ at age 5. In turn, higher IQ at age 5 predicted higher child achievement at first grade as well as both higher parent expectations for achievement and more parent involvement in school at first grade. Moreover, children's achievement at first grade positively predicted parents' expectations at third grade, which predicted higher involvement in school and, in turn, higher achievement at third grade. In other words, they documented a chain of associations summarized by the following pathway: early learning stimulation→early child achievement→parent expectations→parent involvement in school→later child achievement.

Considering the roles of parents' academic beliefs, attitudes, and expectations, it is also worth noting that parents' socialization goals may not always be complete parent-child agreement over values, ideals, and standards. Instead, parents may often feel satisfied with partial acceptance of their socialization goals (Grusec, Goodnow, & Kuczynski, 2000). Thus, parents may view their children's achievement related behaviors and outcomes on a continuum, from ideal to acceptable to unacceptable (Grusec et al., 2000; Hastings & Grusec, 1998).

*Family Socioeconomics and the Home Learning Environment*   On nearly every dimension of the home learning environment covered in this review, children living in families with low income and little education are disadvantaged compared with children living in families of higher socioeconomic status. With regard to learning materials, for example, children in lower socioeconomic status families have limited access to books, art materials, puzzles, toys, games, and musical instruments, to name a few (e.g., Bradley et al., 2001a; Davis-Kean, 2005; Hoff-Ginsberg & Tardif, 1995). This material deprivation also extends to the physical structure of the home. On average, children in lower socioeconomic families are at exceptional risk to live in homes characterized by unsound and unsafe structure, poor lighting, exposure to toxins such as lead, and limited access to play areas and adequate space for learning (Evans, 2004). Their homes are also, on average, likely to be noisy, crowded, and disorganized/unkempt (Bradley et al., 2001a; Evans, 2004; Dunifon et al., 2004).

In addition, children in lower SES homes, on average, receive dramatically less learning stimulation compared with children in higher SES homes. As Hart and Risley (1995) found, children in lower SES families can hear as little as one-third as much talk from their parents during infancy and early childhood. This discrepancy affects the total frequency with which parents talk to their children, the length of their conversations, the range of word types that children hear, and whether or not parents respond to their children's attempts to start conversations (e.g., Bradley et al., 2001a; Hart & Risley, 1995; Hoff, 2003). Children in lower SES families are also encouraged to speak less often themselves (Bradley et al., 2001a).

Compared with parents in higher SES families, parents in lower SES families, on average, read less often with their children, make fewer attempts to interest them in activities or play with toys, are less likely to discuss television programs they have watched together, and are less likely to encourage them to engage in a hobby (Bradley et al., 2001a). In early childhood, lower SES families also spend less time teaching school readiness concepts (e.g., alphabet, numbers, colors, shapes) to their children. During the school years, parents in lower SES families are, on average, more likely to be intrusive and are less likely to support autonomous work when helping with homework (Cooper et al., 2000).

The consequences of low SES for the home learning environment also extend to the affective quality of the parent-child relationship and parents' beliefs, attitudes, and expectations. Parents living in poverty are, on average, less likely than other parents to be highly responsive to their children's emotional needs and are more likely to be punitive with their children than are other parents (Bradley et al., 2001a; Conger et al., 2002; McLeod & Shanahan, 1996). Parents with relatively low levels of education and income are also, on average, less likely than other parents to have confidence in their ability to help their children succeed in school, and they often have lower academic expectations for their children (e.g., Bandura et al., 1996; Davis-Kean, 2005). Moreover, lower SES parents' academic expectations of their children may be less closely matched with their children's actual abilities compared with the expectations of parents in more advantaged families (Alexander et al., 1994).

Why is socioeconomic status so strongly and pervasively associated with home learning environment quality? Most social scientists agree that at least three interacting factors are at work: human capital, financial resources, and family stress. Relative to parents that are well educated and economically secure, parents who are less educated and economically insecure have limited skills and financial resources to invest in the home learning environment (Heckman, 2000; Becker & Tomes, 1986; Dearing & Taylor, 2007; Magnuson, 2007; Mayer, 1997; Votruba-Drzal, 2003; Yeung, Linver, & Brooks-Gunn, 2002). In addition, the economic stress of living in poverty undermines parent mental health, which hinders parents' abilities to invest in the home learning environment, primarily by hindering effective parenting practices such as warmth, responsiveness, and consistency (Conger & Donnellan, 2007; Dearing, Taylor, & McCartney, 2004; Dearing & Taylor, 2007; Elder & Caspi, 1988; Yeung et al., 2002).

Importantly, the underachievement of children from families of lower socioeconomic status can be explained, in large part, by their deprived home learning contexts (Bandura et al., 1996; Dearing, McCartney, & Taylor, 2001; Gershoff, Aber, Raver, & Lennon, 2007; Magnuson, 2007; Yeung et al., 2002). Stated differently, the developmental consequences of low parent education and family income appear to be relayed to children, in large part, through their home learning environment. One implication of these findings is that improving the home learning environments of children growing up in low SES families may be crucial to improving their achievement.

### From Research to Policy and Practice: Home (Learning Environment) Improvements

Considered as a whole, the immense body of evidence on home learning environments converges on the fundamental premise that the quality of these learning environments is an excellent predictor of children's long-term achievement. Furthermore, home learning environments function as one of the primary proximal mechanisms through which more distal characteristics of developmental context (e.g., family SES) impact achievement. As such, there is interest among researchers, policy makers, and practitioners in whether deprived home learning environments can be improved, and whether any such improvements would benefit child achievement. In answering these questions, at least three lines of research are particularly noteworthy: (a) evaluations of parenting interventions, (b) studies of within-family changes in home environments, and (c) evaluations of early childhood education interventions.

Training parents to manage children's behavior and provide sensitive care, is a proven method for changing parenting behaviors (e.g., increased sensitivity) and, in some cases, the general quality of the home environment (for reviews, see Bakersmans-Kranenburg, van IJzendoorn, & Juffer, 2003; Brooks-Gunn, Berlin, & Fuligni, 2000; Magnuson & Duncan, 2004). There is also some evidence supporting the value of parenting interventions that target specific aspects of the home learning environment, most notably the home literacy environment (Kellaghan et al., 1993). Yet, evidence on whether such parenting intervention programs promote the achievement of low SES children is mixed (Brooks-Gunn et al., 2000; Magnuson & Duncan, 2004). Although initial reviews (e.g., Kellaghan et al., 1993) indicated that parenting intervention programs designed to increase learning stimulation in the home resulted in improved child achievement, more recent summaries of empirical work on the topic (e.g., Magnuson & Duncan, 2004) have indicated that the achievement impacts are rather modest and often statistically insignificant.

Studies of naturally occurring changes in children's homes are also relevant here, however. There is, for example, emerging evidence that improvements in family socioeconomic conditions—due to parents increasing their level of education or family income—predict improvements in the home learning environment. During infancy and early childhood, for example, increases in family income are associated with improvements in nearly every dimension of the home learning environment, including the presence of learning materials, quality of the physical structure of the home, level of cognitive and language stimulation, and parental warmth and responsiveness during interactions with their children (Dearing & Taylor, 2007; Votruba-Drzal, 2003). These home improvements are particularly dramatic for families who are initially very poor with exceptionally deprived home learning contexts. Similar improvements in the quality of the home environment have also been demonstrated recently for increased maternal education during middle childhood, with the largest effects on the home evident for the youngest and least-educated mothers (Magnuson, 2007). Moreover, within-family studies indicate that increased income and education are associated with improved achievement for children in poor and less-educated families, and these effects may be largely explained by improvements in the home environment (Dearing et al., 2001; Magnuson, 2007).

Two sets of findings from evaluations of early childhood education interventions point to the promise of improving the home learning environments of children in low SES families as well. First, consider that early childhood education interventions appear most likely to promote children's achievement when they include components focused on home-school connections and family supports that improve the home learning environment (Reynolds, Ou, & Topitzes, 2004; Magnuson & Duncan, 2004). Second, the long-term achievement benefits of early education interventions are explained, in part, by their benefits for parenting, including parent attitudes, expectations, and involvement in education (e.g., Reynolds et al., 2004). Taken together, the results of within-family and early education intervention studies imply that practices aimed at improving the quality of home learning environments for children in low SES families can benefit their achievement. Yet, how can these findings be reconciled with those from studies of interventions focused on parenting?

One answer to this question may be that improved home learning environments are most likely to benefit child achievement when such improvements occur within a broader context of security and support for children and their families. In the context of family economic stress, in fact, interventions that target only parenting may be counterproductive, placing time and energy demands on families whose financial and employment concerns are overwhelming (Magnuson & Duncan, 2004). Furthermore, the developmental effectiveness of improvements in the home learning context may depend on: (a) children experiencing high-quality education outside of the home and, in turn, (b) the establishment of positive home-school connections. Education scholars have begun to recognize that expectations for achievement gains resulting from school improvement policies and practices are likely to be unreasonably high if family poverty and deprived home learning environments are not also addressed (e.g., Berliner, 2006). Similarly, expectations for achievement gains resulting from home improvement policies and practices are likely to be unreasonably high if family poverty, school quality, and home-school disconnections are not addressed.

## CONCLUSION

Children's growth is dependent on extensive resource and time investments from parents, and it is within the home that many of these investments are made. There is, in fact, now decades of empirical work demonstrating the critical role that home learning environments play in children's long-term achievement outcomes, with studies highlighting the importance of both the physical and psychosocial context in which children grow up. It is also clear that children vary widely in the level and quality of physical and psychosocial resources that they encounter in the home. Often linked with social-contextual factors such as family socioeconomic circumstances, these differences between families in the quality of the home are often strong predictors of whether children will succeed or fail in school and later life. Yet, the potential for home improvement has also been observed within families, especially among families most disadvantaged. Thus, rather than stable characteristics of families, home learning environments appear to be dynamic and malleable contexts that can change to better children's achievement and life chances.

## REFERENCES

Alexander, K. L., Entwisle, D. R., & Bedinger, S. D. (1994). When expectations work: Race and socioeconomic differences in school performance. *Social Psychology Quarterly, 57*(4), 283–299.

Anderson, A. (1997). Families and mathematics: A study of parent-child interactions. *Journal for Research in Mathematics Education, 28*(4), 484–511.

Anderson, A., Anderson, J., & Shapiro, J. (2005). Supporting multiple literacies: Parents' and children's mathematical talk within storybook reading. *Mathematics Education Research Journal, 16*, 5–26.

Ainsworth, M. S., Blehar, M. C., Waters, E., & Wall, S. (1978). *Patterns of attachment: A psychological study of the strange situation.* Oxford: Erlbaum.

Astington, J. W., & Jenkins, J. M. (1999). A longitudinal study of the relation between language and theory of mind development. *Developmental Psychology, 35*, 1311–1320.

Baker, L., Mackler, K., Sonnenschein, S. & Serpell, R. (2001). Parents' interactions with their first-grade children during storybook reading and relations with subsequent home reading activity and reading achievement. *Journal of School Psychology, 39*(5), 415–438.

Baker, L., & Wigfield, A. (1999). Dimensions of children's motivation for reading and their relations to reading activity and reading achievement. *Reading Research Quarterly, 34*, 452–477.

Bakersmans-Kranenburg, van IJzendoorn, M. H., & Juffer, F. (2003). Less is more: Meta-analyses of sensitivity and attachment interventions in early childhood. *Psychological Bulletin, 129*(2), 195–215.

Baldwin, A. L., Baldwin, C., & Cole, R. E. (1990). Stress-resistant families and stress-resistant children. In J. Rolf, A. S. Masten, D. Ciccihetti, K. H. Nuechterlein, & S. Weintraub (Eds.), *Risk and protective factors in the development of psychopathology* (pp. 257–280). New York: Cambridge University Press.

Bandura, A. (1997). *Self-efficacy: The exercise of control.* New York: Freeman.

Bandura, A., Barbaranelli, C., Caprara, G. V., & Pastorelli, C. (1996). Multifaceted impact of self-efficacy beliefs on academic functioning. *Child Development, 67*(3), 1206–1222.

Baumrind, D. (1978). Reciprocal rights and responsibilities in parent-child relations. *Journal of Social Issues, 34*(2), 179–196.

Becker, G. S., & Tomes, N. (1986). Human capital and the rise and fall of families. *Journal of Labor Economics, 4*, S1–39.

Belsky, J., & MacKinnon, C. (1994). Transition to school: Developmental trajectories and school experiences. *Early Education and Development. Special Issue: School Readiness: Scientific Perspectives, 5*(2), 106–119.

Benasich, A. A., & Brooks-Gunn, J. (1996). Maternal attitudes and knowledge of child-rearing: Associations with family and child outcomes. *Child Development, 67*(3), 1186–1205.

Berliner, D. C. (2006). Our impoverished view of educational reform. *Teachers College Record, 108*, 949–995.

Bjorklund, D. F., Hubertz, M. J., Reubens, A. C. (2004). Young children's arithmetic strategies in social context: how parents contribute to children's strategy development while playing games. *International Journal of Behavioral Development, 28*(4), 347–357.

Bjorklund, D. F., & Yunger, J. L. (2001). Evolutionary developmental psychology: A useful framework for evaluating the evolution of parenting. *Parenting: Science and Practice, 1*(1–2), 63–66.

Bjorklund, D. F., Yunger, J. L., & Pellegrini, A. D. (2002). The evolution of parenting and evolutionary approaches to childrearing. In M. H. Bornstein (Ed.), *Handbook of parenting: Vol. 2: Biology and ecology of parenting* (pp. 3–30). Mahwah, NJ: Erlbaum.

Blakemore, S. J., & Firth, U. (2005). *The Learning Brain: lessons for education.* Oxford: Blackwell.

Bleeker, M. M., & Jacobs, J. E. (2004). Achievement in math and science: Do mothers' beliefs matter 12 years later. *Journal of Educational Psychology, 96*, 97–109.

Bornstein, M. H. (2006). Parenting science and practice. In W. Damon & R. M. Lerner (Series Eds.) & I. E. Sigel & K. A. Renninger (Vol. Eds.), *Handbook of child psychology, Vol. 4. Child psychology and practice* (6th ed., pp. 893–949). New York: Wiley.

Bowlby, J. (1982). Attachment and loss: Retrospect and prospect. *American Journal of Orthopsychiatry, 52*(4), 664–678.

Bowlby, J. (1988). *A secure base: Parent-child attachment and healthy human development.* New York: Basic Books.

Bowlby, J. (1989). The role of attachment in personality development and psychopathology. In S. I. Greenspan & G. H. Pollock (Eds.), *The course of life, Vol. 1: Infancy* (pp. 229–270). Madison, CT: International Universities Press.

Bradley, R. H. (2006). The home environment. In N. F. Watt, C. Ayoub, R. H. Bradley, J. E. Puma, & W. A. LeBoeuf (Eds.), *The crisis in youth mental health: Critical issues and effective programs, Vol. 4: Early intervention programs and policies. Child psychology and mental health* (pp. 89–120). Westport, CT: Praeger Publishers/Greenwood.

Bradley, R. H., & Caldwell, B. (1981). The HOME Inventory: A validation of the preschool scale for Black children. *Child Development, 52*(2), 708–710.

Bradley, R. H., & Caldwell, B. (1984). The relation of infants' home environments to achievement test performance in first grade: A follow-up study. *Child Development, 55*, 803–809.

Bradley, R. H., Caldwell, B. M., & Rock, S. L. (1988). Home environment and school performance: A ten-year follow-up and examination of three models of environmental action. *Child Development, 59*(4), 852–867.

Bradley, R. H., & Corwyn, R. F. (2004). "Family Process" investments that matter for child well-being. In A. Kalil & T. DeLeire (Eds.), *Family investments in children's potential: Resources and parenting behaviors that promote success. Monographs in parenting* (pp. 1–32). Mahwah, NJ: Erlbaum.

Bradley, R. H., Corwyn, R. F., McAdoo, H. P., & García Coll, C. (2001a). The home environments of children in the United States part I: Variations by age, ethnicity, and poverty status. *Child Development, 72*(6), 1844–1867.

Bradley, R. H., Corwyn, R. F., Burchinal, M., McAdoo, H. P., & García Coll, C. (2001b), The home environments of children in the United States part II: Relations with behavioral development through age thirteen. *Child Development, 72*(6), 1868–1886.

Bronfenbrenner, U., & Morris, P. A. (1998). The ecology of developmental processes. In W. Damon & R. M. Lerner (Eds.), *Handbook of child psychology: Volume 1: Theoretical models of human development (5th ed.)* (pp. 993–1028). Hoboken, NJ: Wiley.

Brooks-Gunn, J., Berlin, L. J., & Fuligni, A. S. (2000). Early childhood intervention programs: What about the family? In J. P. Shonkoff, & S. J. Meisels (Eds.), *Handbook of early childhood intervention* (2nd ed; pp. 549–588). New York: Cambridge University Press.

Brooks-Gunn, J., & Markman, L. B. (2005). The contribution of parenting to ethnic and racial gaps in school readiness. *The Future of Children, 15*(1), 139–168.

Bus, A. G., van IJzendoorn, M. H., & Pellegrini, A. D. (1995). Joint book reading makes for success in learning to read: A meta-analysis on intergenerational transmission of literacy. *Review of Educational Research, 65*(1), 1–21.

Chase-Lansdale, P. C., D'Angelo, A. V., & Palacios, N. (2007). A multidisciplinary perspective on the development of young children in immigrant families. In J. E. Lansford, K. Deater-Deckard, & M. H. Borstein (Eds.), *Immigrant families in contemporary society* (pp. 137–156). New York: Guildford.

Collins, W. A., Maccoby, E. E., Steinberg, L., Hetherington, E. M., & Bornstein, M. H. (2000). Contemporary research on parenting: The case for nature and nurture. *American Psychologist, 55*(2), 218–232.

Conger, R. D., & Donnellan, M. B. (2007). An interactionist perspective on the socioeconomic context of human development. *Annual Review of Psychology, 58*, 175–199.

Conger, R. D., Wallace, L. E., Sun, Y., Simons, R. L., McLoyd, V. C., & Brody, G. H. (2002). Economic pressure in African American families: A replication and extension of the family stress model. *Developmental Psychology, 38*, 179–193.

Connor, C. M., Son, S. H., Hindman, A. H., & Morrison, F. (2005). Teacher qualifications, classroom practices, family characteristics, and preschool experiences: Complex effects on first graders' vocabulary and early reading outcomes. *Journal of School Psychology, 43*, 343–375.

Cooper, H. (1989). *Homework*. New York: Longman.

Cooper, H., Lindsay, J. J., & Nye, B. (2000). Homework in the home: How student, family, and parenting-style differences related to the homework process. *Contemporary Educational Psychology, 25*(4), 464–487.

Crowley, K., Callanan, M. A., Tenenbaum, H. R., & Allen, E. (2001). Parents explain more often to boys than to girls during shared scientific thinking. *Psychological Science, 12*(3), 258–261.

Davis-Kean, P. E. (2005). The influence of parent education and family income on child achievement: The indirect role of parental expectations and the home environment. *Journal of Family Psychology, 19*(2), 294–304.

Dearing, E. (2004). The developmental implications of restrictive and supportive parenting across neighborhoods and ethnicities: Exceptions are the rule. *Journal of Applied Developmental Psychology, 25*(5), 555–575.

Dearing, E., McCartney, K., & Taylor, B. A. (2001). Change in family income-to-needs matters more for children with less. *Child Development, 72*(6), 1779–1793.

Dearing, E., & Taylor, B. A. (2007). Home improvements: Within-family associations between income and the quality of children's home environments. *Journal of Applied Developmental Psychology, 28,* 427–444.

Dearing, E., Taylor, B. A., & McCartney, K. (2004). The implications of family income dynamics for women's depressive symptoms during the first three years following childbirth. *American Journal of Public Health, 94,* 1372–1377.

Deckner, D. F., Adamson, L. B., & Bakeman, R. (2006). Child and maternal contributions to shared reading: Effects on language and literacy development. *Journal of Applied Developmental Psychology, 27*(1), 31–41.

De Jong, P. F., & Leseman, P. P. M. (2001). Lasting effects on home literacy on reading achievement in school *Journal of School Psychology, 39*(5), 389–414.

Dornbusch, S. M., Ritter, P. L., Leiderman, P. H., Roberts, D. F., & Fraleigh, M. J. (1987). The relation of parenting style to adolescent school performance. *Child Development, 58*(5), 1244–1257.

Dunifon, R., Duncan, G. J. & Brooks-Gunn, J. (2001). As ye sweep, so shall ye reap. *American Economic Review: Papers and Proceedings, 91*(2), 150–154.

Dunifon, R., Duncan, G. J., & Brooks-Gunn, J. (2004). The long-term impact of parental organization and efficiency. In A. Kalil & T. DeLeire (Eds.), *Family investments in children's potential: Resources and parenting behaviors that promote success. Monographs in parenting* (pp. 85–118). Mahwah, NJ: Erlbaum.

Dweck, C. S., & Leggett, E. L. (1988). A social-cognitive approach to motivation and personality. *Psychological Review, 95*(2), 256–273.

Dweck, C. S., & Sorich, L. A. (1999). Mastery-oriented thinking. In C. R. Snyder (Ed.), *Coping: The psychology of what works* (pp. 232–251). New York: Oxford University Press.

Ebey, T. L., Marchand-Martella, N., Martella, R., & Nelson, J. R. (1999). Using parents as early reading instructors: A preliminary investigation. *Effective School Practices, 17,* 65–71.

Eccles, J. S. (1999). The development of children ages 6 to 14. *The Future of Children, 9*(2), 30–44.

Eccles, J. S., & Midgley, C. (1989). Stage-environment fit: Developmentally appropriate classrooms for young adolescents. In C. Ames & R. Ames (Eds.), *Research on motivation in education: Vol. 3. Goals and cognitions* (pp. 13–44). New York: Academic Press.

Eccles, J. S., Midgley, C., Wigfield, A., Buchanan, C. M., Reuman, D., Flanagan, C., et al. (1993). Development during adolescence: The impact of stage environment fit on young adolescents' experiences in schools and in families. *American Psychologist. Special Issue: Adolescence, 48*(1), 90–101.

Elder, G. H., & Caspi, A. (1988). Economic stress in lives: Developmental perspectives. *Journal of Social Issues, 44,* 25–45.

Elliot, A. J., McGregor, H. A., & Gable, S. (1999). Achievement goals, study strategies, and exam performance: A mediational analysis. *Journal of Educational Psychology, 91*(3), 549–563.

Englund, M. M., Luckner, A. E., Whaley, G. J. L., & Egeland, B. (2004). Children's achievement in early elementary school: Longitudinal effects of parental involvement, expectations, and quality of assistance. *Journal of Educational Psychology, 96*(4), 723–730.

Epstein, J. L. (1988). *Homework practices, achievements, and behaviors of elementary school children.* Baltimore: John Hopkins University. (ERIC Document Reproduction Service No. ED250351)

Erikson, E. H. (1963). *Childhood and society.* New York: Norton.

Estrada, P., Arsenio, W. F., Hess, R. D., & Holloway, S. D. (1987). Affective quality of the mother-child relationship: Longitudinal consequences for children's school-relevant cognitive functioning. *Developmental Psychology, 23*(2), 210–215.

Evans, G. W. (2004). The environment of childhood poverty. *American Psychologist, 59*(2), 77–92.

Evans, G.W. (2006). Child development and the physical environment. *Annual Review of Psychology, 57,* 423–451.

Evans, G. W., Kliewer, W., & Martin, J. (1991). The role of the physical environment in the health and well-being of children. In H. E. Schroeder (Ed.), *New directions in health psychology assessment. Series in applied psychology: Social issues and questions* (pp. 127–157). Washington, DC: Hemisphere.

Evans, G. W., Lepore, S. J., Shejwal, B. R., & Palsane, M. N. (1998). Chronic residential crowding and children's well-being: An ecological perspective. *Child Development 69*(6), 1514–1523.

Evans, G. W., & Maxwell, L. (1997). Chronic noise exposure and reading deficits: The mediating effects of language acquisition. *Environment and Behavior 29*(5), 638–656.

Evans, G. W., Wells, N. M., & Moch, A. (2003). Housing and mental health: A review of the evidence and a methodological and conceptual critique. *Journal of Social Issues, 59*(3), 475–500.

Fagot, B. I., & Gauvain, M. (1997). Mother-child problem solving: Continuity through the early childhood years. *Developmental Psychology, 33*(3), 480–488.

Fan, X. & Chen, M. (2001). Parental involvement and students' academic achievement: A meta-analysis. *Educational Psychology Review, 1*, 1–22.

Fivush, R., Haden, C. A., & Reese, E. (2006). Elaborating on elaborations: Role of maternal reminiscing style in cognitive and socioemotional development. *Child Development, 77*(6), 1568–1588.

Fleming, A. S., & Li, M. (2002). Psychobiology of maternal behavior and its early determinants in nonhuman mammals. In M. H. Bornstein (Ed.), *Handbook of parenting: Volume 2: Biology and ecology of parenting* (pp. 61–97). Mahwah, NJ: Erlbaum.

Forehand, R., Long, N., Brody, G. H., & Fauber, R. (1986). Home predictors of young adolescents' school behavior and performance. *Child Development, 27*, 1528–1533.

Fuligni, A. J., Yip, T., & Tseng, V. (2002). The impact of family obligation on the daily activities and psychological well-being of Chinese American adolescents. *Child Development, 73*(1), 302–314.

Furstenberg, F. F., Cook, T. D., Eccles, J., Elder, G. H., & Sameroff, A. (1999). *Managing to make it: Urban families and adolescent success.* Chicago: University Chicago Press.

García Coll, C. T., Lamberty, G., Jenkins, R., McAdoo, H. P., Crnic, K., Wasik, B. H., et al. (1996). An integrative model for the study of developmental competencies in minority children. *Child Development, 67*(5), 1891–1914.

Gerdes, A. C., & Hoza, B. (2006). Maternal attributions, affect, and parenting in attention deficit hyperactivity disorder and comparison families. *Journal of Clinical Child and Adolescent Psychology, 35*(3), 346–355.

Gershoff, E. T., Aber, J. L., Raver, C. C., & Lennon, M. C. (2007). Income is not enough: Incorporating material hardship into models of income associations with parenting and child development. *Child Development, 78*, 70–95.

Glasgow, K. L., Dornbusch, S. M., Troy, L., Steinberg, L., & Ritter, P. L. (1997). Parenting styles, adolescents' attributions, and educational outcomes in nine heterogenous high schools. *Child Development, 68*(3), 507–529.

Gonzales, N. A., Cauce, A. M., Friedman, R. J., & Mason, C. A. (1996). Family, peer, and neighborhood influences on academic achievement among African-American adolescents: One-year prospective effects. *American Journal of Community Psychology, 24*, 365–387.

Gottlieb, G. (1998). Normally occurring environmental and behavioral influences on gene activity: From central dogma to probabilistic epigenesis. *Psychological Review, 105*(4), 792–802.

Granot, D., & Mayseless, O. (2001). Attachment security and adjustment to school in middle childhood. *International Journal of Behavioral Development, 25*(6), 530–541.

Grant, H., & Dweck, C. S. (2003). Clarifying achievement goals and their impact. *Journal of Personality and Social Psychology, 85*(3), 541–553.

Greenough, W. T., Black, J. E., & Wallace, C. S. (1987). Experience and brain development. *Child Development, 58*(3), 539–559.

Grolnick, W. S., Ryan, R. M., & Deci, E. L. (1991). Inner resources for school achievement: Motivational mediators of children's perceptions of their parents. *Journal of Educational Psychology, 83*(4), 508–517.

Grolnick, W. S., & Slowiaczek, M. (1994). Parents' involvement in children's schooling: A multidimensional conceptualization and motivational model. *Child Development, 64*, 237–252.

Grusec, J. E., Goodnow, J. J., & Kuczynski, L. (2000). New directions in analyses of parenting contributions to children's acquisition of values. *Child Development, 71*(1), 205–211.

Gutman, L. M., Friedel, J. N., & Hitt, R. (2003). Keeping adolescents safe from harm: Management strategies of African-American families in a high-risk community. *Journal of School Psychology, 41*(3), 167–184.

Halle, T., Kirtz-Costes, B., & Mahoney, J. (1997). Family influences on school achievement in low-income, African American children. *Journal of Educational Psychology, 89*, 527–537.

Harkness, S., & Super, C. M. (2002). Culture and parenting. In M. H. Bornstein (Ed.), *Handbook of parenting: Volume 2: Biology and ecology of parenting* (pp. 253–280). Mahwah, NJ: Erlbaum.

Hart, B., & Risley, T. R. (1995). *Meaningful differences in the everyday experience of young American children.* Baltimore: Paul H. Brookes.

Hastings, P. D., & Grusec, J. E. (1998). Parenting goals as organizers of response to parent-child disagreement. *Developmental Psychology, 34*(3), 465–479.

Heckman, J. J. (2000). Policies to foster human capital. *Research in Economics, 54*, 3–56.

Hess, R. D., & Holloway, S. D. (1984). Family and school as educational institutions. In R. D. Parke (Ed.), *Review of Child Development Research* (Vol. 7). Chicago: University of Chicago Press.

Hoff, E. (2003). The specificity of environmental influence: Socioeconomic status affects early vocabulary development via maternal speech. *Child Development, 74*, 1368–1378.

Hoff, E. (2006). How social contexts support and shape language development. *Developmental Review, 26*, 55–88.

Hoff-Ginsberg, E., & Tardif, T. (1995). Socioeconomic status and parenting. In M. H. Bornstein (Ed.), *Handbook of parenting, Vol. 2: Biology and ecology of parenting* (pp.161–188). Hillsdale, NJ: Erlbaum.

Hoover-Dempsey, K. V., Battiato, A. C., Walker, J. M. T., Reed, R. P., De Jong, J. M., & Jones, K. P. (2001). Parental involvement in homework. *Educational Psychologist, 36*(3), 195–209.

Hoover-Dempsey, K. V., Bassler, O. C., & Brissie, J. S. (1992). Explorations in parent school relations. *Journal of Educational Research, 85*, 287–294.

Hoover-Dempsey, K. V. & Sandler, H. M. (1995). Parental involvement in children's education: Why does it make a difference? *Teachers College Record, 97*, 310–332.

Jacobs, J. E. (1991). Influence of gender stereotypes on parent and child mathematics attitudes. *Journal of Educational Psychology, 83*, 518–527.

Jacobs, J. E., & Eccles, J. S. (1992). The impact of mothers' gender-role stereotypic beliefs on mothers' and children's ability perceptions. *Journal of Personality and Social Psychology, 63*, 932–944.

Jacobsen, T., Edelstein, W., & Hofmann, V. (1994). A longitudinal study of the relation between representations of attachment in childhood and cognitive functioning in childhood and adolescence. *Developmental Psychology, 30*(1), 112–124.

Kaplan, A., & Maehr, M. L. (1999). Achievement goals and student well-being. *Contemporary Educational Psychology, 24*(4), 330–358.

Karrass, J., & Braungart-Rieker, J. M. (2005). Effects of shared parent-infant book reading on early language acquisition. *Journal of Applied Developmental Psychology, 26*(2), 133–148.

Kellaghan, T., Sloane, K., Alvarez, B., & Bloom, B. S. (1993). *The home environment and school learning: Promoting parental involvement in the education of children*. San Francisco: Jossey-Bass.

Kochanska, G. (1991). Socialization and temperament in the development of guilt and conscience. *Child Development, 62*(6), 1379–1392.

Kochanska, G. (1997). Mutually responsive orientation between mothers and their young children: Implications for early socialization. *Developmental Psychology, 33*(2), 228–240.

Kraft, B. L., Findlay, P., Major, J., Gilberts, G., & Hofmeister, A. (2001). The association between a home reading program and young children's early reading skill. *Journal of Direct Instruction, 1*, 117–136.

Leone, C. M., & Richards, M. H. (1989). Classwork and homework in early adolescence: The ecology of achievement. *Journal of Youth and Adolescence. Special Issue: The changing life space of early adolescence, 18*(6), 531–548.

Lerner, R. M. (1983). A "goodness of fit" model of person-context interaction. In D. Agnusson & V. L. Allen (Eds.), *Human development: An interactional perspective* (pp. 279–294). New York: Academic Press.

Lerner, R. M., Rothbaum, F., Boulos, S., & Castellino, D. R. (2002). Developmental systems perspective on parenting. In M. H. Bornstein (Ed.), *Handbook of parenting: Vol. 2: Biology and ecology of parenting* (2nd ed., pp. 315–344). Mahwah, NJ: Erlbaum.

Leseman, P. P. M., & de Jong, P. F. (1998). Home literacy: Opportunity, instruction, cooperation and social-emotional quality predicting early reading achievement. *Reading Research Quarterly, 33*(3), 294–318.

Leventhal, T., & Brooks-Gunn, J. (2000). The neighborhoods they live in: The effects of neighborhood residence on child and adolescent outcomes. *Psychological Bulletin, 126*, 309–337.

Levin, I., Levy-Shiff, R., Appelbaum-Peled, T., Katz, I., Komar, M., & Meiran, N. (1997). Antecedents and consequences of maternal involvement in children's homework: A longitudinal analysis. *Journal of Applied Developmental Psychology, 18*(2), 207–227.

LeVine. R. A. & White, M. (1987). Parenthood in social transformation. In J. B. Lancaster, J. Altmann, A. S. Rossi, & L. R. Sherrod (Eds.), *Parenting across the lifespan: Biosocial dimensions* (pp. 271–294). Piscataway, NJ: Transaction.

Lohman, H., & Tomasello, M. (2003). The role of language in the development of false belief understanding: A training study. *Child Development, 74*, 1130–1144.

Lopez, A., & Cole, C. L. (1999). Effects of a parent-implemented intervention on the academic readiness skills of five Puerto Rican kindergarten students in an urban school. *School Psychology Review. Special Issues: Beginning school ready to learn: Parental involvement and effective educational programs, 28*(3), 439–447.

Luster, T. & Kain, E. L. (1987). The relation between family context and perceptions of parental efficacy. *Early Child Development and Care, 29*, 301–311.

Luster, T., Rhoades, K., & Haas, B. (1989). The relation between parental values and parenting behavior: A test of the Kohn hypothesis. *Journal of Marriage and the Family, 51*(1), 139–147.

Lynch, J. (2002). Parents' self-efficacy beliefs, parents' gender, children's reader self-perceptions, reading achievement and gender. *Journal of Research in Reading, 25*(1), 54–67.

Maccoby, E. E. (1984). Socialization and developmental change. *Child Development, 55*(2), 317–328.

Maccoby, E. E. (1992). The role of parents in the socialization of children: An historical overview. *Developmental Psychology, 28*(6), 1006–1017.

Maccoby, E. E. (2002). Parenting effects: Issues and controversies. In J. G. Borkowski, S. L. Ramey, & M. Bristol-Power (Eds.), *Parenting and the child's world: Influences on academic, intellectual, and social-emotional development. Monographs in parenting* (pp. 35–46). Mahwah, NJ: Erlbaum.

Maccoby, E. E., & Martin, J. A. (1983). Socialization in the context of the family: Parent–child interaction. In P. H. Mussen (Ed.) & E. M. Hetherington (Vol. Ed.), *Handbook of child psychology: Vol. 4. Socialization, personality, and social development* (4th ed., pp. 1–101). New York: Wiley.

Magnuson, K. (2007). Maternal education and children's academic achievement during middle childhood. *Developmental Psychology, 43*, 1497–1512.

Magnuson, K. & Duncan, G. J. (2004). Parent- versus child-based intervention strategies for promoting children's well-being. In A. Kalil & T. DeLeire (Eds.), *Family investments in children's potential: Resources and parenting behaviors that promote success. onographs in parenting* (pp. 209–236). Mahwah, NJ: Erlbaum.

Magnusson, D. & Stattin, H. (1998). Person-context interaction theories. In W. Damon (Series Ed.) & N. Eisenberg (Volume Ed.), *Handbook of child psychology: Vol. 3. social, emotional, and personality development* (5th ed., pp. 685–750). New York: Wiley.

Marsh, H. W., Koeller, O., Trautwein, U., Luedtke, O., & Baumert, J. (2005). Academic self-concept, interest, grades, and standardized test scores: Reciprocal effects model of causal ordering. *Child Development, 76*, 397–416

Mayer, S. E. (1997). Trends in the economic well-being and life chances of America's children. In G. J. Duncan & J. Brooks-Gunn (Eds.), *Consequences of growing up poor* (pp. 49–69). New York: Russell Sage Foundation.

McCartney, K., Dearing, E., Taylor, B. A., & Bub, K. L. (2007). Quality child care supports the achievement of low-income children: Direct and indirect pathways through caregiving and the home environment. *Journal of Applied Developmental Psychology, 28*(5-6), 411–426.

McLeod, J. D., & Shanahan, M. J. (1996). Trajectories of poverty and children's mental health. *Journal of Health and Social Behavior, 37*, 207–220.

Meece, J. L., & Holt, K. (1993). A pattern analysis of students' achievement goals. *Journal of Educational Psychology, 85*(4), 582–590.

Mondell, S., & Tyler, F. (1981). Parental competence and styles of problem-solving/play behavior with children. *Developmental Psychology, 17*, 73–78.

Morrow, L. M. (1983). Home and school correlates of early interest in literature. *Journal of Educational Research, 76*, 221–230.

Morrow, L. M. (2001). *Literacy development in the early years: Helping children read and write* (4th ed.). Needham Heights, MA: Allyn and Bacon.

Moss, E., & St. Laurent, D. (2001). Attachment at school age and academic performance. *Developmental Psychology, 37*(6), 863–874.

Mulvaney, M. K., McCartney, K., Bub, K. L., & Marshall, N. L. (2006). Determinants of dyadic scaffolding and cognitive outcomes in first graders. *Parenting: Science and Practice, 6*(4), 297–320.

Murnane, R. J., Maynard, R. A., & Ohls, J. C. (1981). Home resources and children's achievement. *The Review of Economics and Statistics, 63*(3), 369–377.

National Center for Educational Statistics. (2002). *The Digest of Education Statistics, 2001* (NCES Publication 2002-130). Washington, DC.

Needleman, H. L., Gunnoe, C., Leviton, A., Reed, R., Peresie, H., Maher, C., et al. (1979). Deficits in psychological and classroom performance of children with elevated dentine lead levels. *New England Journal of Medicine, 300*–695.

Neuenschwander, M. P., Vida, M., Garrett, J. L., & Eccles, J. S. (2007). Parents' expectations and students' achievement in two western nations. *International Journal of Behavioral Development, 31*(6), 594–602.

Ninio, A. (1979). The naïve theory of the infant and other maternal attitudes in two subgroups in Israel. *Child Development, 50*, 976–980.

Ninio, A., & Bruner, J. (1978). The achievement and antecedents of labeling. *Journal of Child Language, 5*(1), 1–15.

Okagaki, L., & Divecha, D. J. (1993). Development of parental beliefs. In T. Luster & L. Okagaki (Eds.), *Parenting: An ecological perspective* (pp. 35–67). Hillsdale, NJ: Erlbaum.

Okagaki, L. & Frensch., P. A. (1998). Parenting and children's school achievement: A multiethnic perspective. *American Educational Research Journal, 35*, 123–144.

Papoušek, H., & Papoušek, M. (2002). Intuitive parenting. In M. H. Bornstein (Ed.), *Handbook of parenting: Volume 2: Biology and ecology of parenting* (pp. 183–203). Mahwah, NJ: Erlbaum.

Parker, F. L., Boak, A. Y., Griffen, K. W., Ripple, C., & Peay, L. (1999). Parent-child relationship, home learning environment, and school readiness. *School Psychology Review, 28*, 413–425.

Parsons, J. E., Adler, T., & Kaczala, C. (1982). Socialization of achievement attitudes and perceptions: Parental influences. *Child Development, 53*, 310–321.

Patterson, G. R., & Fisher, P. A. (2002). Recent developments in our understanding of parenting: Bidirectional effects, causal models, and the search for parsimony. In M. H. Bornstein (Ed.), *Handbook of parenting: Vol. 5: Practical issues in parenting* (2nd ed., pp. 59–88). Mahwah, NJ: Erlbaum.

Peterson, C. C., & Siegal, M. (1999). Representing inner worlds: Theory of mind in autistic, deaf, and normal hearing children. *Psychological Science, 10*, 126–129.

Peterson, C. C., & Siegal, M. (2000). Insights into theory of mind from deafness and autism. *Mind and Language, 15*, 123–145.

Piaget, J. (1950). *The psychology of intelligence* (M. Piercy & D. E. Berlyne, Trans.). London: Routledge.

Piaget, J. (1951). *Play, dreams and imitation in childhood*. London: Heinemann.

Piaget, J. (1981). *Intelligence and affectivity: Their relationship during child development*. (T. A. Brown & C. E. Kaegi, Eds. & Trans.). Oxford, England: Annual Reviews.

Piaget, J. (1985). *The equilibration of cognitive structures: The central problem of intellectual development*. Chicago: University of Chicago Press.

Pianta, R. C., Smith, N., & Reeve, R. E. (1991). Observing mother and child behavior in a problem-solving situation at school entry: Relations with classroom adjustment. *School Psychology Quarterly, 6*(1), 1–15.

Pinderhughes, E. E., Dodge, K. A., Bates, J. E., Pettit, G. S., & Zelli, A. (2000). Discipline responses: Influences of parents' socioeconomic status, ethnicity, beliefs about parenting, stress, and cognitive-emotional processes. *Journal of Family Psychology. Special Issues: Cultural Variation in Families, 14*(3), 380–400.

Pomerantz, E. M., & Eaton, M. M. (2001). Maternal intrusive support in the academic context: Transactional socialization processes. *Developmental Psychology, 37*(2), 174–186.

Pomerantz, E. M., Ng, F. F., & Wang, Q. (2006). Mothers' mastery-oriented involvement in children's homework: Implications for the well-being of children with negative perceptions of competence. *Journal of Educational Psychology, 98*(1), 99–111.

Pomerantz, E. M., Wang, Q., & Ng, F. F. (2005). Mothers' affect in the homework context: The importance of staying positive. *Developmental Psychology, 41*(2), 414–427.

Purcell-Gates, V. (1996). Stories, coupons, and the *TV Guide*: Relationships between home literacy experiences and emergent literacy knowledge. *Reading Research Quarterly, 31*(4), 406–428.

Raver, C. C. (2002). Emotions matter: Making the case for the role of young children's emotional development for early school readiness. *Social Policy Report, 16*, 3–18.

Raver, C. C. (2004). *Childcare as a work support, a child-focused intervention, and a job*. Mahwah, NJ: Erlbaum.

Reynolds, A. J., Ou, S. & Topitzes, J. W. (2004) Paths of effects of early childhood ntervention on educational attainment and delinquency: A confirmatory analysis of the Chicago Child-Parent Centers. *Child Development, 75*, 1299–1338.

Rudek, D., & Haden, C. A. (2005). Mothers' and preschoolers' mental state language during reminiscing over time. *Merrill-Palmer Quarterly, 51*, 557–583.

Rutter, M., & O'Connor, T. G. (2004). Are there biological programming effects for psychological development? Findings from a study of Romanian adoptees. *evelopmental Psychology, 40*(1), 81–94.

Sameroff, A. (1975). Transactional models in early social relations. *Human Development, 18* (1-2), 65–79.

Sameroff, A. (2000). Developmental systems and psychopathology. *Development and Psychopathology. Special Issue: Reflecting on the past and planning for the future of developmental psychopathology, 12*(3), 297–312.

Scarborough, H. S., & Dobrich, W. (1994). On the efficacy of reading to preschoolers. *Developmental Review, 14*(3), 245–302.

Scarr, S. & McCartney, K. (1983). How people make their own environments: A theory of genotype -> environment effects. *Child Development, 54*(2), 424–435.

Scott-Jones, D. (1984). Family influences on cognitive development and school achievement. *Review of Research in Education, 11*, 259–304.

Sénéchal, M. (2006). Testing the home literacy model: Parent involvement in the kindergarten is differentially related to grade 4 reading comprehension, fluency, spelling, and reading for pleasure. *Scientific Studies of Reading, 10*(1), 59–87.

Sénéchal, M., & LeFevre, J. (2001). Storybook reading and parent teaching: Links to language and literacy development. In P. R. Britto & J. Brooks-Gunn (Eds.), *The role of family literacy environments in promoting young children's emerging literacy skills. New directions for child and adolescent development* (pp. 39–52). San Francisco: Jossey-Bass.

Sénéchal, M. LeFevre, J., Hudson, E., & Lawson, E. P. (1996). Knowledge of storybooks as a predictor of young children's vocabulary. *Journal of Educational Psychology, 88*(3), 520–536.

Sénéchal, M., LeFevre, J., Thomas, E. M., & Daley K. E. (1998). Differential effects of home literacy experiences on the development of oral and written language. *Reading Research Quarterly, 33*(1), 96–116.

Sheldon, S. B. (2002). Parents' social networks and beliefs as predictors of parent involvement. *The Elementary School Journal, 102*(4), 301–316.

Simpkins, S. D., Davis-Kean, P. E., & Eccles, J. S. (2005). Parents' socializing behavior and children's participation in math, science, and computer out-of-school activities. *Applied Developmental Science, 9*(1), 14–30.

Singer, A. T. B., & Weinstein, R. S. (2000). Differential parental treatment predicts achievement and self-perceptions in two cultural contexts. *Journal of Family Psychology. Special Issues: Cultural Variation in Families, 14*(3), 491–509.

Snow, C. E. (1983). Literacy and language: Relationships during the preschool years. *Harvard Educational Review, 53*(2), 165–189.

Snow, C. E., Burns, M. S., & Griffin, P. (1998). *Preventing reading difficulties in young children*. Washington, DC: National Academy Press.

Spencer, M. B. (2006). Phenomenology and ecological systems theory: Development in diverse groups. In W. Damon & R. Lerner (Eds.), *Handbook of child psychology, vol. 15, theory* (pp. 829–893). New York: Wiley.

Stanovich, K. E. (1986). Matthew effects in reading: Some consequences of individual differences in the acquisition of literacy. *Reading Research Quarterly, 21*(4), 360–406.

Steinberg, L. (2001). A fresh perspective on nature and nuture. *PsycCRITICQUES, 46*(4), 333–335.

Steinberg, L., Elmen, J. D., & Mounts, N. S. (1989). Authoritative parenting, sychosocial maturity, and academic success among adolescents. *Child Development, 60*(6), 1424–1436.

Steinberg, L., Lamborn, S. D., Dornbusch, S. M., & Darling, N. (1992). Impact of parenting practices on adolescent achievement: Authoritative parenting, school involvement, and encouragement to succeed. *Child Development, 63*(5), 1266–1281.

Swidler, A. (1986). Culture in action: Symbols and strategies. *American Sociological Review, 51*, 273.

Tenenbaum, H. R., & Leaper, C. (2003). Parent-child conversations about science: The socialization of gender inequities? *Developmental Psychology, 39*(1), 34–47.

Valeski, T. N. & Stipek, D. J. (2001). Young children's feelings about school. *Child Development, 72*, 1198–1213.

Vandermaas-Peeler, M., Nelson, J., & Bumpass, C. (2007). "Quarters are what you put into the bubble gum machine": Numeracy interactions during parent-child play. *Early Childhood Research & Practice, 9*(1). Retrieved May 12, 2007, from http://ecrp.uiuc.edu/v9n1/vandermaas.html

Votruba-Drzal, E. (2003). Income changes and cognitive stimulation in young children's home learning environments. *Journal of Marriage and Family, 65*, 341–355.

Vygotsky, L. S. (1978). *Mind in society: The development of higher mental processes*. Cambridge, MA: Harvard University Press.

Wahlberg, H. J., & Tsai, S. (1985). Correlates of reading achievement and attitude: A national assessment study. *Journal of Educational Research, 78*(3), 159–167.

Weisner, T. S. (2002). Ecocultural understanding of children's developmental pathways. *Human Development, 45*, 275–281.

Wentzel, K. R. (1998). Parents' aspirations for children's educational attainments: Relations to parental beliefs and social address variables. *Merrill-Palmer Quarterly, 44*(1), 20–37.

Whitehurst, G. J., Falco, F. L., Lonigan, C. J., Fischel, J. E., DeBaryshe, B. D., Valdez-Menchaca, et al. (1988). Accelerating language development through picture book reading. *Developmental Psychology, 24*, 552–559.

Yeung, W. J., Linver, M. R., & Brooks-Gunn, J. (2002). How money matters for young children's development: Parental investment and family processes. *Child Development, 73*, 1861–1879.

Zimmerman, B., Bandura, A., & Martinez-Pons, M. (1992). Self-motivation for academic attainment: The role of self-efficacy beliefs and personal goal-setting. *American Educational Research Journal, 29*, 663–676.

# 7

## PARENT INVOLVEMENT IN EARLY EDUCATION

### ARTHUR J. REYNOLDS AND REBECCA J. SHLAFER

Parental involvement is widely regarded as a fundamental contributor to children's school success and long-term educational achievement. Although psychological theory and conventional wisdom have always regarded the family as essential in shaping children's development, empirical validation regarding the impact of specific types of parent involvement in children's education has emerged only recently. Furthermore, few studies have examined the long-term impact of parent involvement on children's outcomes. However, enhancing parental involvement is integral to many educational programs and policies as illustrated by the following trends:

- Parental involvement is a major element of school-wide reforms such as *Schools of the 21st Century* (Finn-Stevenson & Zigler, 1999), the School Development Program (Comer, Haynes, Joyner, & Ben-Avie, 1996) and the charter school movement, as well as new governance arrangements that give parents greater input in decision making.
- Since the beginning of Head Start in 1965, parental involvement has been an essential component of early childhood programs for disadvantaged children. The emphasis on providing comprehensive family services and strengthening family-community partnerships has expanded to Title I, IDEA, and state-run early childhood programs, which now total more than $20 billion in government funding annually (see Zigler, Gilliam, & Jones, 2006).
- Stand-alone family support interventions have increased in popularity in schools and communities. These include Even Start (U.S. Department of Education, 1993), Early Head Start (Love et al., 2005), Family Resource Centers (Waddell, Shannon, & Durr, 2001), Parents as Teachers (Wagner & Clayton, 1999), and home visitation and parenting education programs (Sweet & Appelbaum, 2004).

Why is parental involvement a focus of so many programs and policies to promote child and youth outcomes? First, children spend more time with parents and family members, especially in the first decade of life, than in any other social context. During most of the formative years, about one-quarter of children's time is spent in school and three-quarters is spent at home. Thus, changing parental involvement by just a small amount can have a larger cumulative effect than behaviors that occur less frequently. A second reason why parent involvement is a target of program and policy formulation is that it is open to influence by educators. Teachers and parents have a common interest in educating and socializing children effectively. Furthermore, because parental involvement is multidimensional, many avenues exist through which parents' attitudes and behaviors can be encouraged, for example reading to children at home or participating in school. Third, encouraging parent participation and engagement in children's education may provide parents with sources of social support and personal empowerment, thus promoting positive school and community climate that are important for children's learning. Therefore, family involvement sets the conditions upon which other educational and personal experiences impact children's outcomes (Bronfenbrenner, 1975; Comer, 1993; Reynolds, 2000).

## OVERVIEW

In this chapter, findings for three categories of evidence about how parent involvement impacts children's school achievement and success are summarized. First, interventions with a family support component positively affect children's outcomes. Second, parent involvement is a mechanism through which the long-term effects of intervention are achieved. And finally, indicators of parental involvement are associated with significantly higher levels of school performance and success.

Evidence in these three domains is based primarily on a longitudinal study of urban children and is supplemented by findings from other empirical studies. Throughout this chapter, parent involvement is defined within the context of school-family partnerships to include behavior with, or on behalf of, children at home or in school, attitudes and beliefs about parenting or education, and expectations for children's future. Further, it is recognized that parent involvement can take many forms. Common indicators include home support for learning (e.g., helping the child with homework), parenting practices, child-parent interactions (e.g., cooking with the child), participation in school activities (e.g., volunteering in the child's classroom), involvement in school associations, involvement in school governance or in community activities, and expectations for children's success or educational attainment (see Table 7.1). This multidimensional definition reflects the complexity and breadth of parental influence and is consistent with human capital perspectives of involvement as investments in children (Haveman & Wolfe, 1994).

From the outset, it is important to note that although the accumulated evidence strongly suggests that parental involvement is associated with better school performance and is a key ingredient in the success of early childhood programs (Patrikakou, Weissberg, Redding, & Walberg, 2005), our current understanding of these processes is limited in a number of important ways. For example, definitions of parent involvement are inconsistent across studies and findings vary in methodological rigor. Often, the direction of influence from involvement to child outcomes is difficult to establish. In

Table 7.1 Common Types of Parent Involvement and Relevant Indicators

| Common Types of Parent Involvement | Indicators |
|---|---|
| *Parent participation at school* | Parent participation in school activities |
| | Parent helps in child's classroom |
| *Parent involvement at home* | Parent reads to child |
| | Parent cooks with child |
| | Parent goes on outings with child |
| | Parent and child take trips to other cities |
| | Parent takes trips to the zoo |
| *Parent involvement in school and learning* | Parent helps child with homework |
| | Parent makes sure child does homework |
| | Parent provides learning experiences for the child |
| | Parent communicates with the school regularly |
| | Parent talks to child's teacher |
| | Parent communicates with the school |
| | Parent discusses school progress with child |
| | Parent and child discuss school at home |
| | Parent picks up child's report cards |
| *Parent participation in community activities* | Parent attends local school council meetings |
| | Parent votes in school elections |
| | Parent is a member of a community organization |
| | Parent is a member of PTA or other school group |

addition, children of involved parents may experience greater school success for reasons other than involvement per se, such that these children may have higher cognitive abilities than children with less involved parents. The growth of longitudinal studies of children's learning in the past decade has helped advance the field in understanding the predictive value and independent contribution of parent involvement. Some of this evidence comes from the Chicago Longitudinal Study. After describing findings from this and other studies, some limits to the knowledge base and several implications for strengthening parent involvement will be discussed. Over the past decade, measures of parent involvement have shown long-term effects on children's learning and development. These findings continue to advance our current knowledge base about the effects of parent involvement on children's development.

## Chicago Longitudinal Study

This chapter illustrates how parent involvement contributes to children's school success primarily using data from the Chicago Longitudinal Study (Reynolds, 1999). This on-going investigation follows the progress of a cohort of 1,539 low-income children (93% African American) who participated in the Child-Parent Center (CPC) Program beginning in 1983–84 and a matched comparison group that enrolled in an alternative intervention in kindergarten. Three major goals of the Chicago study were to (a) evaluate the effects of the Child-Parent Center Program over time, (b) identify the mechanisms through which the effects of participation are manifested, and (c) investigate the contribution of a variety of family and school factors on children's adjustment. Over the two decades of the study, extensive information on parent involvement as measured by teachers and parents has been collected along with other child and family experiences, and children's school success. This information provides a unique opportunity to investigate the links between parent involvement and children's outcomes. The contribution to children's long-term outcomes of an established intervention with intensive parent involvement also can be determined.

*Chicago Child-Parent Centers*  The Chicago Child-Parent Center Program (CPC; Sullivan, 1971) is a center-based early intervention that provides comprehensive educational and family support services to economically disadvantaged children and their parents from preschool to early elementary school. The CPC program began in 1967 through funding from the Elementary and Secondary Education Act of 1965. Title I of the Act provided grants to local public school districts serving high concentrations of low-income children. As the nation's second oldest federally funded preschool program, the CPCs operate in 23 centers across the city.

As shown in Figure 7.1, the centers provide comprehensive services under the direction of a Head Teacher and in collaboration with the elementary school principal. Each center also staffs a parent resource teacher, the school-community representative, classroom teachers and aides, nurses, speech therapists, and school psychologists. The major rationale of the program is that the foundation for school success is facilitated by the presence of a stable and enriched learning environment during the entire early childhood period (ages 3 to 9) and when parents are active participants in their children's education. Five program features are emphasized: early intervention, parent involvement, a structured language and basic skills learning approach, health and social services, and program continuity between the preschool and early school-age years.

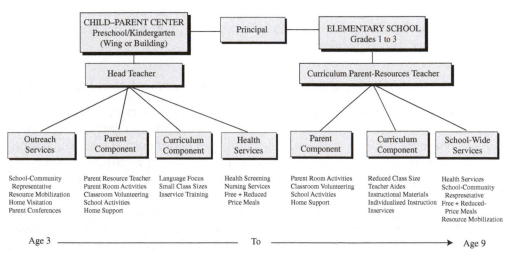

**Child–Parent Center Program**

Figure 7.1 Chicago child-parent center program.

Sullivan (1971) described the philosophy of the Child-Parent Centers as a way to enhance the family-school relationship:

> In a success-oriented environment in which young children can see themselves as important, they are 'turned on' for learning. Attitudes toward themselves and others, interest in learning, increased activity, conversation, and enthusiasm are all evidences of the change. Parents are increasingly aware of the role of the home in preparing children for school and have renewed hope that education will develop the full potential of their children. (p. 70)

To accomplish this, the centers offer a structured program of parent involvement and language enrichment.

*Parent Involvement Component*   As the program's title indicates, direct parent involvement in the program is expected to enhance parent-child interactions, parent and child attachment to school, social support among parents, and consequently promote children's school readiness and social adjustment. Unlike most other programs, the centers make substantial efforts to involve parents in the education of their children. The program requires at least one-half day, per week of parent involvement activity, though this can take a variety of forms. The unique feature of the parent program is the parent resource room that is physically located in the center adjacent to the classrooms. A full-time parent-resource teacher organizes the parent room in order to implement parent educational activities, initiate interactions among parents, and foster parent-child interactions. With funds for materials, supplies, and speakers, areas of training include consumer education, nutrition, personal development, health and safety, and homemaking arts. Parents may also attend GED classes at the centers as well as serve on the School Advisory Council. A wide range of activities are encouraged in the program including parent room activities (e.g., arts & craft projects), classroom volunteering, participation in school activities, class field trips, help preparing meals, and engaging in education and training activities. The diversity of activities is designed to accommodate parents' daily schedules.

### Evidence for Early Childhood Interventions with a Parent Involvement Component

Given the extensive family support services offered in the program, the impact of the intervention on children's outcomes is considered as the first category of evidence on parent involvement. CPC participation beginning in preschool has been consistently associated with better educational performance and social adjustment (Reynolds, Temple, Robertson, & Mann, 2001). Table 7.2 summarizes major findings in the Chicago Longitudinal Study, the largest study ever of the CPC program. Preschool participation at ages 3 or 4 is associated with educational and social outcomes spanning ages 5 to 24, up to 20 years after the end of intervention. As expected, the program had the largest impact immediately; about one half the program group scored at or above national norms on the Iowa Test of Basic Skills (ITBS; Hieronymus, Lindquist, & Hoover, 1982) scholastic readiness composite at school entry compared to only one quarter of the

**Table 7.2** Proportion of the Chicago Child-Parent Center Program Preschool and Comparison-Group Children Achieving School and Social Competence

| Child Outcome | Age | Program Group | Comparison Group | Difference | Change (%) |
|---|---|---|---|---|---|
| At/above national norm on scholastic readiness | 5 | 46.7 | 25.1 | 21.6 | 86 |
| Child maltreatment | 4-17 | 5.0 | 10.3 | 5.3 | 51 |
| Socioemotional adjustment | 6-8 | 19.6 | 18.3 | 1.3 | 7 |
| Repeated a grade | 6-15 | 23.0 | 38.4 | 15.4 | 40 |
| Special education | 6-18 | 14.4 | 24.6 | 10.2 | 41 |
| Juvenile arrest | 10-18 | 16.9 | 25.1 | 8.2 | 33 |
| Arrest for violent offense | 10-18 | 9.0 | 15.3 | 6.3 | 41 |
| Acting out | 12-13 | 12.1 | 12.9 | 0.8 | 6 |
| At/above grade level on reading achievement | 13-14 | 34.2 | 25.2 | 9.0 | 36 |
| Completed high school | 18-24 | 63.1 | 53.3 | 9.8 | 18 |
| Adult felony arrest | 18-24 | 15.3 | 21.6 | 6.3 | 29 |
| Adult incarceration | 18-24 | 18.4 | 24.9 | 6.5 | 26 |
| Adult depression | 18-24 | 13.7 | 18.5 | 4.8 | 26 |
| Average income equal to or higher than nat'l average | 22-24 | 37.7 | 33.5 | 4.2 | 13 |
| College attendance or stable employment | 22-24 | 49.5 | 42.4 | 7.1 | 17 |
| Attended a 4 year college | 22-24 | 13.2 | 7.9 | 5.3 | 67 |

comparison group. This represented an 86% improvement over the comparison group; this is a large and significant impact.

Substantial differences were detected through the school age years, as program participation was associated with improvements ranging from 6% to 51% over the comparison group. The large reduction in child abuse and neglect is particularly important given that other early childhood programs have not reported these effects. Major reasons the CPC program reduces child maltreatment may be the focus of the parent program in increasing social support, increasing parent education and improving parenting skills. Furthermore, parent involvement may also reduce social isolation among families, potentially reducing family conflict and punitive parenting practices (Reynolds & Robertson, 2003).

Reductions in special education placement and grade retention are consistent with many of the findings from other programs (Barnett, 1995; Reynolds, 2000). The significant program impacts on delinquency and high school completion are rare for a large-scale program and are particularly notable given their economic and social impact. High school completion is a basic requirement for nearly all career endeavors and for access to college. Besides contributing to a more productive life, reduction in criminal activity results in major government savings within the justice system.

In addition to the positive impact on children's outcomes during the school years, the program has impacts lasting into adulthood. For example, participation in the CPC program had an impact on participants' attendance at a four-year college. This represented a 67% improvement over the comparison group. Additionally, children who participated in the program were less likely to be arrested (15% vs. 22%) or incarcerated (18% vs. 25%) and they were less likely to exhibit depressive symptoms (14% vs. 19%) in adulthood. Although these are small to moderate impacts, they are impressive considering they were measured decades after the intervention.

These findings indicate that interventions with strong family support components can influence many domains of performance, with impacts lasting into adulthood. CPC intervention that continues into the elementary grades also contributes significantly to children's later success. The primary features are reduced class sizes, increased instructional support, and parent room activities. Compared to children who participated for 1 to 4 years, children with 4 to 6 years of intervention had higher reading and math achievement in the elementary grades, lower rates of special education (13.5% vs. 20.7%) and grade retention (21.9% vs. 32.3%), and lower rates of child maltreatment (3.6% vs. 6.9%).

On the basis of other program evaluations and intervention research, early childhood programs with family support components are more likely to provide long-term benefits for children than programs that do not have such components (Olds et al., 1997; Schweinhart, Barnes, & Weikart, 1993). One exception is the Carolina Abecedarian Project (Campbell & Ramey, 1995) that has shown long-term program impacts, but does not include a family support component. Providing intensive child education and family support, the High/Scope Perry Preschool Project and the CPC program have shown the broadest impact on child and family outcomes. In the High/Scope Perry Preschool Project (Barnett, Young, & Schweinhart, 1998), mother's participation in their child's education significantly influenced school success, although the preschool program did not significantly enhance mother's participation. Other frequently-cited effective early childhood programs with family support components include the Syracuse Family Development Program, Early Training Project, Houston Parent-Child Development Center, and the Yale Child Welfare Research Program (see Consortium for Longitudinal Studies, 1983). Moreover, in a study of Head Start children, long-term effects on cognitive, social and personal abilities were enhanced when a stronger and longer lasting parental involvement component was included (Zeece & Wang, 1998).

In their review of early interventions, Clarke and Clarke (1989) found that a variety of programs had enduring effects only when parents continued to be involved with the program after it had officially ended. Also, Fantuzzo, Davis, and Ginsburg (1995) examined the effects of an intervention partly designed to enhance parental involvement with the child's education and found that the parental involvement component led to higher childhood scholastic and behavioral adjustment.

Other studies suggest that the contribution of parent involvement in early childhood intervention is limited. In a meta-analysis of over 300 early childhood interventions, White (1986) did not find strong support for a parental involvement component even when only high-quality programs were examined and when the type and extent of parent involvement was taken into account. Studies of programs including parental involvement were effective in improving children's outcomes, but no more than programs without a parental involvement component. However, the outcome measure for most of the studies was child intellectual development, and White conceded that parent involvement may have stronger effects on other child outcomes.

*Parental Involvement is a Mechanism of Long-Term Effects of Intervention*

What is the specific contribution of the family component of the CPC program to children's outcomes? Although it is difficult to separate the effects of parent involvement from child education and other services, one approach is to investigate the extent to which the main effects of program participation are explained by parent involvement and other factors. Parent involvement as a mechanism of effects of intervention indicates that it is an intervening or indirect influence on children's outcomes. Because indirect effects are more subtle than direct effects, they are largely unrecognized in the intervention literature. Very few studies have investigated parent involvement as a mechanism of intervention effects.

Figure 7.2 shows five hypotheses as identified in the accumulated literature that explain the link between early intervention and competence outcomes. In addition to the family support hypothesis, intervention effects may be explained by cognitive advantage, social adjustment, motivational advantage, and school support hypotheses. Family support behavior may include several components, including support for learning at home, parent involvement at school, and improved parenting skills. To identify the contribution of family support on the long-term effects of program participation, measures of parent involvement and participation must be considered together with alternative hypotheses, thus yielding its unique contribution or "value added."

Here, parent involvement and its unique contribution to children's long-term developmental outcomes, is considered as one aspect of the family support hypothesis.

## Common Paths from Early Childhood to Adult Well-Being

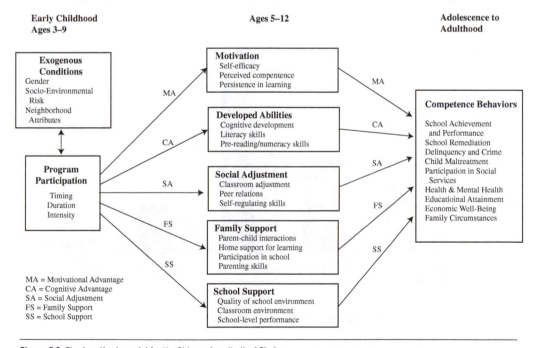

Figure 7.2 Five hypothesis model for the Chicago Longitudinal Study.

Figure 7.3 summarizes the major contributing pathways to the long-term effects of CPC participation on two major outcomes as a proportion of the total indirect effect. The total indirect effect is the sum of all paths of influence starting with preschool participation and leading to high school completion and juvenile arrest. Thus, it denotes the extent to which the influence of CPC participation depends on or is mediated by the hypotheses. The indirect effects were categorized by mediator, with the primary emphasis on the mediators that initiated the indirect effect and that were directly and significantly associated with program participation. Values for each hypothesis are above and beyond the influence of other hypotheses.

The family support hypothesis was measured in two ways. The first was the frequency of teacher and parent ratings from ages 8 to 12 on the item "parents' participation in school." Teacher and parent ratings were used to minimize possible reporter bias. The second measure used was substantiated reports of child abuse and neglect between ages 4 and 12. The family support hypothesis accounted for 28% of the total contribution of the effect of preschool on high school completion and 21% of the total contribution on juvenile arrest. In other words, controlling for other hypotheses, program participation was directly associated with higher levels of parent involvement and these higher levels of involvement were significantly linked to school completion and juvenile arrest.

The school support hypothesis, measured by school mobility and attendance in magnet schools, accounted for 31% of the link between CPC preschool participation and high school completion and 48% of the link between participation and juvenile arrest. The cognitive advantage hypothesis, measured by word analysis test scores at age 6, accounted for 23% of the total indirect effect of preschool participation on high school completion and 19% of the total indirect effect on juvenile arrest. The social ad-

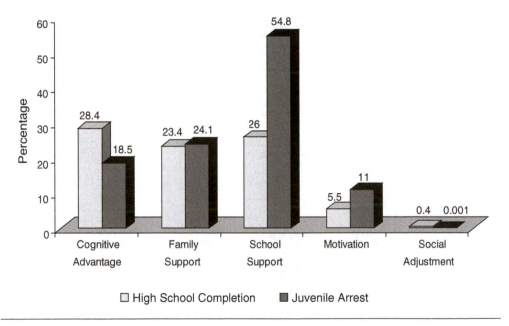

**Figure 7.3** Percentage of total indirect effect of preschool as accounted for by hypothesized mediators.

justment and motivational advantage hypotheses made smaller contributions. Overall, these findings indicate the substantial contributions of parent involvement and other intervening factors on long-term outcomes. The extent to which other measures of parent involvement, from expectations to parenting practices, yield the same findings needs further investigation.

To illustrate the potential economic implications of these findings, a cost-benefit analysis of the CPC program showed that for every dollar invested in the preschool component seven dollars was returned to society at large through government savings on remedial education and justice system treatment, and increases in economic well-being (Reynolds, Temple, Robertson, & Mann, 2002). Extrapolating from Figure 7.3, about $2 of these economic benefits can be attributed to the family support program or about $14,000 per participant (in discounted 1998 dollars). This estimate is conservative to the extent that parental involvement has synergistic effects with other components of the program. Nevertheless, the cognitive benefits of participation and school support experiences in the elementary grades contribute significantly to the total effect of preschool participation.

Through an intensive parent program in the centers, CPC intervention encourages parent involvement in school and in children's education so that when the intervention ends parents are more likely to continue to provide the nurturance and support necessary to maintain benefits, which makes later school attainment more likely and antisocial behavior less likely. The finding that parent involvement directly predicted the rate of juvenile arrest is especially significant since this has not been documented previously. In the High/Scope Perry Preschool Study (Barnett et al., 1998), parent involvement was an independent predictor of later educational attainment but did not mediate the effects of preschool. Nevertheless, family support was a major component of the program through biweekly home visits. Indeed, the only early childhood programs that have shown effectiveness in preventing delinquency are interventions that have significant family support components (Zigler, Taussig, & Black, 1992). Our findings indicate that school-based parent involvement provides another avenue to enhance family support behaviors.

### *Indicators of Parent Involvement Predict Children's Learning and Development*

In most of the research on parent involvement, natural variation in parental attitudes and behaviors is associated with children's outcomes including school performance, achievement test scores, and educational attainment. Overall, higher parental involvement is positively associated with academic performance for young children and adolescents (Graue, Weinstein, & Walberg, 1983; Reynolds, & Berzuczko, 1993; Reynolds, & Gill, 1994; Seefeldt, Denton, Galper, & Younoszai, 1998). These predictive relations usually remain after controlling for background variables such as socioeconomic status (SES). Furthermore, variables such as maternal education, socioeconomic status, child gender, and child motivation level have all been found to work through parental involvement to influence child academic performance (Reynolds, 1989; Stevenson, & Baker, 1987), further supporting the importance of the parental influence. Parent involvement has also been related to such factors as school completion, self-regulation, and self-concept (e.g., Grolnick & Slowiaczek, 1994).

**Table 7.3** Select Youth and Adult Outcomes by Parent Involvement Ratings

| Parent Involvement | Grade 8 Reading Achievement at or Above Nat'l Norms | Juvenile Delinquency | High School Completion | 4-Year College Attendance | Adult Depression | Adult Felony Arrest |
|---|---|---|---|---|---|---|
| 0 | 19.1 | 30.2 | 46.1 | 3.6 | 19.3 | 28.5 |
| 1 | 34.4 | 24.0 | 60.1 | 6.2 | 20.4 | 23.7 |
| 2 | 47.3 | 16.8 | 74.0 | 12.8 | 13.9 | 15.5 |
| 3 | 54.7 | 12.9 | 76.4 | 13.6 | 12.6 | 14.9 |
| 4 | 65.6 | 14.0 | 79.1 | 19.5 | 8.5 | 9.2 |
| 5 or 6 | 59.4 | 10.0 | 91.6 | 33.2 | 10.1 | 6.5 |

One measure developed in the Chicago Longitudinal Study is the number of years between first and sixth grades that teachers rate parent participation in school as average or better. This provides a cumulative index of involvement over many years. As shown in Table 7.3, a functional relation exists between the number of positive ratings of parental school involvement and participant outcomes in childhood and adulthood. Rates of high school completion increase as ratings of parent involvement increase. Children with 5 or 6 years of positive parent ratings had a high school completion rate of 92% by age 21. These same children had a juvenile delinquency rate of only 10%, compared to 30% of children whose parents were not at all involved. High school completion and delinquency rates are substantially better than those of other inner-city children. Further, children with the most involved parents were more likely to attend college, less likely to exhibit depression and less likely to be arrested when compared to children whose parents were less involved. Findings were unaffected after controlling for family demographic factors such as the child's race, gender, and socioeconomic status.

In further support of the predictive value of this measure and others, the independent influence on high school completion at age 20 for 1,286 youth (after controlling for many other predictors of school completion including school performance, family socioeconomic status, school commitment, and school quality) was examined. This analysis revealed that a 1-year change in parental school involvement was associated with a 16% increase in the odds of high school completion. A change in involvement from 1 to 4 years, for example, increased the odds of high school completion by 48%. Parent expectations for children's educational attainment were also associated with significantly higher levels of completion. A change of 1 year in expected years of education was associated with a 9% increase in the odds of high school completion. A change of 4 years (expecting college vs. high school completion) increased the odds of high school completion by 36%. These findings are suggestive of the long-term benefits. Notably, parent educational attainment also significantly predicted high school completion above and beyond parent involvement and expectations; this impact was similar to parent expectations.

In other research conducted by the Chicago Longitudinal Study, parent involvement predicted academic success and socio-emotional adjustment in first grade (Reynolds,

1989) as well as increased reading achievement, lower grade retention, and fewer years in special education by age 14 (Miedel & Reynolds, 1999). Parent involvement also significantly predicted school achievement across two successive school years and predicted academic growth from year 1 to year 2, after controlling for demographic variables. Parental school involvement also predicts growth in reading achievement from kindergarten through ninth grade, such that higher parental involvement predicts greater acceleration in reading achievement over time.

In investigating differences by source of report, Reynolds (1992) found that teacher, parent, and child ratings of parent involvement were only weakly correlated with each other. Teacher ratings of school involvement had the strongest association with achievement outcomes; parent-reported measures had significant but weaker associations with achievement. Child-reported measures of parent involvement at home also had positive effects on achievement but parent ratings of home involvement did not significantly influence achievement.

Moreover, while CPC parent involvement at the site-level was found to be the only program factor (i.e., instructional approach, size of site) associated with early academic outcomes in kindergarten, parent involvement at the individual or child level was significantly related to early and later academic achievement as well as high school completion and juvenile delinquency (Clements, Reynolds, & Hickey, 2004). The most powerful site-level finding was that lower income levels within a school district were linked with poorer school and social outcomes. This finding suggests that children's early school success can be enhanced by providing opportunities for parents to be involved in school and in children's education. In addition to the positive effects of parental school involvement on children's educational outcomes, Niles, Reynolds, Clements, and Robertson (2002) found that both a phonics and child-centered instructional approach in preschool independently contributed to children's success over time.

Many other studies support the positive and significant link between measures of parental involvement and children's school success. A meta-analysis of 25 studies by Fan and Chen (2001) found that parent expectations or aspirations had the largest effect size ($ES = .40$) in relation to measures of academic achievement with parental supervision at home ($ES = .09$) having the smallest effect size. Effect sizes between parent involvement and academic achievement were also larger for global (i.e., GPA) as compared to subject-specific academic achievement measures. Parental commitment and volunteer behavior have smaller positive influences (Fan & Chen, 2001). Parental contact and supervision tend to have small but negative influences on achievement outcomes. It is likely that children receiving more supervision and contact with the school were more in need of such supervision and contact possibly because of prior problematic behavior or academic achievement.

Parent involvement also has been found to positively influence motivational outcomes such as academic self-concept, attributions for academic achievements, and self-regulation as well as high school dropout and truancy behaviors (Gonzalez-Pienda et al., 2002). In reports from National Educational Longitudinal Study (NELS; Keith, Keith, Troutman, & Bickley, 1993; Trivette & Anderson, 1995), parent expectations or aspirations for children's education were most consistently associated with eighth grade achievement even after controlling for the influence of SES and ethnicity. Moreover, the association between parental expectations and achievement was strongest for higher SES students. Relatively few studies have examined the relation between involvement and children's social and emotional learning, and even fewer have investigated differential effects over time by SES and ethnicity.

### Limitations of the Overall Knowledge Base

Despite the overall positive evidence described in this chapter, three limitations remain in the knowledge base on parent involvement. First, while parental involvement is associated with higher school success and can predict school performance, its link to children's outcomes should not be regarded as causal. Indeed, some studies show no relation between parent involvement and outcomes (for reviews, see Barnard, 2004 and Fan and Chen, 2001). The quality and amount of parent involvement, for example, may be key ingredients rather than involvement per se. In addition, parent involvement may be an effect of children's performance as much as a cause and few studies have investigated this and other possibilities. The field needs a better understanding of *why* parent involvement works, for *whom* it works best, and *how* schools and families can improve this component of children's educational experiences (Bouffard & Weiss, 2008; Caspe, 2008). Moreover, understanding of specific mechanisms linking parental involvement to different children's outcomes is just beginning, which is a key element for establishing cause.

Second, the definition and measurement of parent involvement varies greatly from study to study. Findings vary as a function of children's age and circumstances, whether the source of report is parents or teachers, and whether the behaviors and attitudes concern home or school support for children's learning. The reliability and validity of these different operationalizations can be variable, and the correspondence between parent and teacher ratings relatively low. Although it is recognized that parent involvement can take many forms and that it includes activities both at home and at school, the overall lack of consensus about the definition and measurement of parent involvement has hindered integration of knowledge for policy decisions.

Third, there is a presumption among researchers and educators that parent involvement is necessarily positively associated with children's adjustment. This is not the case. Involvement in response to child problems is not generally associated with positive outcomes. The conditions under which parent involvement yields the most and least positive links with children's outcomes need further investigation.

Finally, researchers need to broaden the indicators that are used, moving beyond children's early achievement with test scores and grades (Caspe, 2008). Parent involvement has consistently been linked to children's achievement and success in elementary school. In order to understand the full impact of parent involvement, scientists must expand their research and begin to routinely include questions about the long-term impacts of early involvement on children's outcomes over time.

### Summary

Enhancing parental involvement is a goal of many educational policies and practices. Our review indicates that parental involvement, in all its forms, can contribute substantially to children's school success and their long-term adult well-being. In the past decade, two of the greatest advances in knowledge are that parent involvement in the education of low-income children helps explain the long-term effects of early childhood intervention and that parent involvement in the elementary grades is associated with significantly higher rates of later educational attainment. These findings have not been reported before. Within the CPC program, there was stronger evidence for some indicators of parental involvement than others. Parent expectations for children's educational attainment and participation in school activities had the most consistent influence on children's outcomes. Parental supervision had smaller impacts. This pattern of findings is consistent across studies, from the Chicago Longitudinal Study to meta-analyses of the whole field.

### Implications for Policy and Practice

The policy implications of the findings presented in this chapter are directed to early childhood programs and to schools and families more generally. In regard to early childhood intervention, greater investments in programs that provide child education and intensive resources for parent involvement are needed. Findings from the Child-Parent Centers and other similar programs demonstrate their positive long-term effects on a wide range of outcomes that span the ages of 5 to 24. Compare this evidence to programs that take up the largest share of public spending. Small class sizes in the early grades are associated with increased school achievement, but impacts are not large or enduring. The benefits of remedial education such as tutoring, after-school programs, and summer school are, at best, inconsistent and short-lived. The track record of delinquency and dropout prevention programs is weak. Finally, rather than benefiting children, the school practice of grade retention is associated with lower levels of achievement and higher rates of dropout. To expand effective programs such as the CPCs, one recommendation is to increase the proportion of expenditures on Title I programs beyond the 5% that currently goes to preschool programs.

Are large payoffs from early childhood education inevitable? Not if the programs are low in quality or poorly coordinated. Judging from the accumulated evidence, four elements are critical to the success of early education programs. First, a coordinated system of early care and education should be in place that spans at least the first five years of a child's life. Public schools, where over 90% of children end up, are in the best position to take a leadership role in partnership with the community. Second, preschool teachers should be trained and compensated well. It is no coincidence that the Perry and Chicago programs were run by staff with at least bachelor's degrees and certification in their specialties. Third, educational content should be responsive to all of children's learning needs but special emphasis on literacy skills is needed. Finally, family services and parent involvement activities should be available that are intensive and comprehensive in scope, especially for children who have special needs or reside in low-income families. One advantage of the school-based model of the Child-Parent Centers is that they help forge school-family partnerships.

With regard to enhancing parent involvement more generally, three recommendations are offered. First, schools and communities must actively provide a variety of ways for parents to get involved. School-family partnership must recognize that parent involvement takes many forms, often takes place in a variety of settings, and may look different depending on families' culture, family practices, and parenting attitudes (Caspe, 2008) More than "lip service" is required—both physical and human resources are needed. Instead of reacting to children's difficulties, proactive strategies are required, often with appropriate resources. To increase involvement, the Child-Parent Centers have a staffed parent room in each preschool and elementary school site to provide a comprehensive set of activities tailored to the needs of families. The provision of physical and staff resources for a parent program is a primary reason that the centers maintained an 80% rate of regular participation, compared to less than 50% in many other programs. This approach warrants expansion in other settings.

Second, teachers would benefit from greater opportunities for training and professional development in working with families. Existing teacher training usually de-emphasizes or ignores parent-teacher collaboration. Among the areas needing greater attention are: overcoming barriers to involving parents, alternative ways of involving parents in children's education and schooling, promoting effective communication with families, and resolving and reducing conflicts with parents and other family members.

Finally, based on the accumulated evidence that parent expectations for children's education is a key factor in school success, greater emphasis on promoting high expectations, values toward education, and shared expectations between parents and youth is needed. In order to promote academic achievement, it is vital that children have similar expectations for learning at home and school and that both environments support these expectations (Pianta & Walsh, 2002; Ysseldyke & Christenson, 2002). Combined with our current findings from the CPC, this research indicates that strategies to increase behavioral involvement are not the only approaches for enhancing children's school success. We believe school-family partnerships that provide many ways to strengthen involvement and shared expectations can contribute substantially to children's school success and long-term well-being into adulthood.

## REFERENCES

Barnard, W. M. (2004). Parent involvement in elementary school and educational attainment. *Children and Youth Services Review, 26*(1), 39–62.

Barnett, W. S. (1995). Long-term effects of early childhood programs on cognitive and school outcomes. *The Future of Children, 5*(3), 25–50.

Barnett, W. S., Young, J. W., & Schweinhart, L. J. (1998). How preschool education influences long-term cognitive development and school success: A causal model. In W. S. Barnett & S. S. Boocock (Eds.), *Early care and education for children in poverty: promises, programs, and long-term results* (pp. 167–184). Albany: State University of New York Press.

Bronfenbrenner, U. (1975). Is early intervention effective? In M. Guttentag & E. Struening (Eds.), *Handbook of evaluation research* (Vol. 2, pp. 519–603). Beverly Hills, CA: Sage.

Bouffard, S., & Weiss, H. (2008). Thinking big: A new framework for family involvement policy practice and research. *The Evaluation Exchange, XIV*, 2–5.

Campbell, F. A., & Ramey, C. T. (1995). Cognitive and school outcomes for high risk African-American students at middle adolescence: Positive effects of early intervention. *American Educational Research Journal, 32*(4), 743–772.

Caspe, M. (2008). Building the field. *The Evaluation Exchange, XIV*, 6–30.

Clarke, A. M., & Clarke, A. D. B. (1989). The later cognitive effects of early intervention. *Intelligence, 13*(4), 289–297.

Clements, M., Reynolds, A. J., & Hickey, E. J. (2004). Site-level predictors of children's school and social competence in the Chicago Child-Parent Centers. *Early Childhood Research Quarterly, 19*(2), 273–296.

Comer, J. P. (1993). School *power: Implications of an intervention project.* New York: Free Press.

Comer, J. P., Haynes, N. M., Joyner, E. T., & Ben-Avie, M. (1996). *Rallying the whole village: The Comer process for reforming education.* New York: Teachers College Press.

Consortium for Longitudinal Studies. (1983). *As the twig is bent...lasting effects of preschool programs.* Hillsdale, NJ: Erlbaum.

Fan, X. T., & Chen, M. (2001). Parental involvement and students' academic achievement: A meta-analysis. *Educational Psychology Review, 13*(1), 1–22.

Fantuzzo, J. W., Davis, G. Y., & Ginsburg, M. D. (1995). Effects of parent involvement in isolation or in combination with peer tutoring on student self-concept and mathematics achievement. *Journal of Educational Psychology, 57*(2), 272–281.

Finn-Stevenson, M., & Zigler, E. F. (1999). *Schools of the 21st century: Linking child care and education.* Boulder, CO: Westview Press.

Gonzalez-Pienda, J. A., Nunez, J. C., Gonzalez-Pumariega, S., Alvarez, L., Roces, C., & Garcia, M. (2002). A structural equation model of parental involvement, motivational and aptitudinal characteristics and academic achievement. *Journal of Experimental Education, 70*(3), 257–287.

Graue, M. E., Weinstein, T., & Walberg, H. J. (1983). School-based home instruction and learning: A quantitative synthesis. *Journal of Educational Research, 76*(6), 251–260.

Grolnick, W. S., & Slowiaczek, M. L. (1994). Parents' involvement in children's schooling: A multidimensional conceptualization and motivational model. *Child Development, 65*(1), 237–252.

Haveman, R., & Wolfe, B. (1994). *On the effects of investments in children.* New York: Russell Sage Foundation.

Hieronymus, A. N., Lindquist, E. F., & Hoover, H. D. (1982). *Iowa Tests of Basic Skills: Manual for school administrators.* Chicago: Riverside Publishing

Keith, T. Z., Keith, P. B., Troutman, G. C., & Bickley, P. G. (1993). Does parental involvement affect eighth-grade achievement? Structural analysis of national data. *School Psychology Review, 22*(3), 474–496.

Love, J. M., Kisker, E. M., Ross, C., Raikes, H., Constantine, J., Boller, K., et al. (2005). The effectiveness of Early Head Start for 3-year-old children and their parents: Lessons for policies and programs. *Developmental Psychology, 41*(6), 885–901.

Miedel, W. T., & Reynolds, A. J. (1999). Parent involvement in early intervention for disadvantaged children: Does it matter? *Journal of School Psychology, 37*(4), 379–402.

Niles, M. D., Reynolds, A. J., Clements, M., & Robertson, D. L. (2002). Origins of the cognitive and scholastic effects of early childhood intervention: Findings from the Chicago Longitudinal Study. In A. J. Reynolds (Chair), *The Chicago Child Parent Centers: Prevention and cost-effectiveness.* Symposia conducted at Head Start's Sixth National Research Conference, Washington, DC.

Olds, D. L., Eckenrode, J., Henderson, C. R., Cole, R. Eckenrode, J., Kitzman, H., et al. (1997). Long-term effects of home visitation on maternal life course and child abuse and neglect. Fifteen-year follow-up of a randomized trial. *Journal of the American Medical Association, 278*, 637–643.

Patrikakou, E. N., Weissberg, R. P., Redding, S., & Walberg, H. J. (2005). School-family partnerships: Enhancing the academic, social, and emotional learning of children. In E. N. Patrikakou, R. P. Weissberg, S. Redding, & H. J. Walberg (Eds.) *School-family partnerships for children's success.* New York: Teachers College Press.

Pianta, R., & Walsh, D. B. (1996). *High-risk children in schools: Constructing sustaining relationships.* New York: Routledge.

Reynolds, A. J. (1989). A structural model of first-grade outcomes for an urban, low socioeconomic status, minority population. *Journal of Educational Psychology, 81*(4), 594–603.

Reynolds, A. J. (1992). Comparing measures of parental involvement and their effects on academic achievement. *Early Childhood Research Quarterly, 7*(3), 441–462.

Reynolds, A. J. (1999). Educational success in high-risk settings: Contributions of the Chicago Longitudinal Study. *Journal of School Psychology, 37*(4), 345–354.

Reynolds, A. J. (2000). *Success in early intervention: The Chicago Child-Parent Centers.* Lincoln: University of Nebraska Press.

Reynolds, A. J., & Bezruczko, N. (1993). School adjustment of children at risk through fourth grade. *Merrill-Palmer Quarterly, 39*(4), 457–480.

Reynolds, A. J., & Gill, S. (1994). The role of parental perspectives in the school adjustment of children at risk. *Journal of Youth and Adolescence, 23*(6), 671–694.

Reynolds, A. J., & Robertson, D. L. (2003). School-based early children intervention and later maltreatment in the Chicago Longitudinal Study. *Child Development, 74*(1), 3–26.

Reynolds, A. J., Temple, J. A., Robertson, D. L., & Mann, E. A. (2001). Long-term effects of an early childhood intervention on educational achievement and juvenile arrest: A 15-year follow-up of low-income children in public schools. *Journal of American Medical Association, 285*(18), 2339–2346.

Reynolds, A. J., Temple, J. A., Robertson, D. L., & Mann, E. A. (2002). Age 21 cost-benefit analysis of the Title I Chicago Child-Parent Centers. *Educational Evaluation and Policy Analysis, 24*(4), 267–303.

Schweinhart, L. J., Barnes, H.V., & Weikart, D. P. (1993). *Significant benefits: The High-Scope Perry Preschool study through age 27.* Ypsilanti, MI: High/Scope Press.

Seefeldt, C., Denton, K., Galper, A., & Younoszai, T. (1998). Former Head Start parents characteristics, perceptions of school climate, and involvement in their children's education. *Elementary School Journal, 98*(4), 339–349.

Stevenson, D. L., Baker, D. P. (1987). The family-school relation and the child's school performance. *Child Development, 58*(5), 1348–1357.

Sullivan, L. M. (1971). *Let us not underestimate the children.* Glenview, IL: Scott, Foreman.

Sweet, M. A., & Appelbaum, M. I. (2004). Is home visiting an effective strategy? A meta-analytic review of home visiting programs for families with young children. *Child Development, 75*(5), 1435–1456.

Trivette, P., & Anderson, E. (1995). The effects of four components of parental involvement on eighth grade student achievement: structural analysis of NELS-88 data. *School Psychology Review, 24*(2), 299–318.

U.S. Department of Education. (1993). *National evaluation of the Even Start Family Literacy Program: Report on effectiveness.* Washington, DC: U.S. Department of Education, Office of Policy and Planning.

Wagner, M. M., & Clayton, S. L. (1999). The Parents as Teachers Program: Results from two demonstrations. *The Future of Children, 9*(1), 91–115.

Waddell, B., Shannon, M., & Durr, R. (2001, August). *Using Family Resource Centers to support California's young children and their families.* Los Angeles: UCLA Center for Healthier, Children, Families, and Communities.

White, K. R. (1986). Efficacy of early intervention. *Journal of Special Education, 19*(4) 401–416.

Ysseldyke, J. E., & Christenson, S. L. (2002). *FAAB: Functional assessment of academic behavior: Creating successful learning environments.* Longmont, CO: Sopris West.

Zeece, P. D., & Wang, A. (1998). Effects of the family empowerment and transitioning program on child and family outcomes. *Child Study Journal, 28*(3), 161–177.

Zigler, E., Gilliam, W. S., & Jones, S. M. (Eds.). (2006). *A vision for universal preschool education.* New York: Cambridge University Press.

Zigler, E., Taussig, C., & Black, K. (1992). Early childhood intervention: A promising preventive for juvenile delinquency. *American Psychologist, 47*(8), 997–1006.

# 8

## PARTNERING TO FOSTER ACHIEVEMENT IN READING AND MATHEMATICS

MARIKA GINSBURG-BLOCK, PATRICIA H. MANZ, AND CHRISTINE MCWAYNE

Family involvement in children's educational experiences is recognized as a vital component of their achievement (Zigler & Muenchow, 1992). The apparent importance of family involvement across the school years has been supported by numerous correlational studies and, to a far lesser extent, experimental studies, which demonstrate relationships between parent involvement and children's school-related outcomes. Much of this research has emphasized the relationship between specific parent involvement behaviors and children's achievement. For example, parental involvement at school (e.g., with school activities, direct communication with teachers and administrators) has been associated with greater achievement in reading and mathematics (Griffith, 1996; Reynolds, Weissberg, & Kasprow, 1992; Sui-Chu & Willms, 1996). Higher levels of parent involvement in their children's educational experiences at home (e.g., supervision and monitoring, daily conversations about school) have been associated with children's higher achievement scores in reading, writing, and mathematics, as well as higher report card grades (Epstein, 1991; Griffith, 1996; Sui-Chu & Willms, 1996; Keith et al., 1998; Prelow & Loukas, 2003; Steinberg, Lamborn, Dornbusch, & Darling, 1992). Still other research has shown that parental beliefs and expectations about their children's learning are strongly related to children's beliefs about their own competencies, as well as their achievement (Galper, Wigfield, & Seefeldt, 1997; Goldenberg, Gallimore, Reese, & Garnier, 2001).

Furthermore, family involvement has been identified as a potential protective factor for ethnic minority children and youth. In his meta-analysis of studies conducted with ethnic minority youth, Jeynes (2003) reported small to moderate effect sizes for various family involvement dimensions across standardized achievement tests, overall GPA, and teacher ratings concerning a variety of learning behaviors and outcomes. Furthermore, the effect sizes were strongest for the relationships between school outcomes and parent attendance at school functions for African American youth. Thus, understanding and promoting positive connections between families and schools may be one way of narrowing the achievement gap between White and ethnic minority students (Wong & Hughes, 2006).

## OVERVIEW

The purpose of this chapter is to provide a critical analysis and summary of the current research literature which examines the links between family involvement and academic achievement outcomes in reading and mathematics for preschool through elementary-aged children. Conceptual, methodological, and cross-cultural considerations will be explored in order to provide a context for the research findings presented later in this chapter. Implications for current educational practices and future research will also be examined.

## ANALYSIS OF THE FAMILY INVOLVEMENT LITERATURE

### Conceptual Considerations

Typically, family involvement has been conceptualized solely as their contributions to school activities, such as volunteering in the classroom, attending parent meetings, and organizing fund-raisers. However, current thinking is evolving from viewing family involvement as a uni-dimensional, uni-directional construct to recognizing that involvement is both multidimensional and bidirectional (Christenson, 2004; Fantuzzo, Tighe, & Childs, 2000). More recent conceptualizations of this construct acknowledge that family involvement encompasses more than school-based activities and includes what parents do at home and in the community to encourage children's learning, as well as activities that reflect transactional experiences between home and school and between school and community. Epstein's (1995) framework of family involvement, perhaps the best known available to date, outlined six main types of activities that connect families, schools, and communities. According to her typology, family involvement was operationalized to include basic obligations of parenting, obligations of schools (communicating), parental and community involvement at school (volunteering), parents' provision of learning activities at home, parents' participation in school decision making, and their advocacy within the community. This understanding recognizes that multiple contexts and their interactions are critical influences on children's educational success (Bronfenbrenner & Morris, 1998).

For several decades the empirical literature has moved towards validating family involvement as a multidimensional construct (e.g., Becker & Epstein, 1982). Guided by Epstein's typology of parent involvement, Fantuzzo and colleagues (2000) developed the first multidimensional parent rating scale of family involvement—the *Family Involvement Questionnaire* (FIQ)—with a predominantly African-American, low-income, early childhood population. Research on the FIQ has revealed three robust dimensions of parent-reported involvement: Home-Based Involvement, School-Based Involvement, and Home-School Communication, which have been shown to be differentially associated with student learning and classroom behavioral adjustment outcomes among low-income African American samples (Fantuzzo, McWayne, Perry, & Childs, 2004).

To date, the FIQ has been developed and statistically-validated for low-income, and ethnic-minority families representing a range of populations, who vary in age (FIQ-Early Childhood, Fantuzzo et al., 2000; FIQ-Elementary School Age; Manz, Fantuzzo, & Power, 2004) and native language (e.g., FIQ-Early Childhood English and Spanish versions, McWayne, Manz, & Ginsburg-Block, 2007). A unique feature of the FIQ instruments is that they were developed through an integration of qualitative and quantitative scale development methods. The content for the early childhood and elementary versions of the FIQ was derived through two independent series of focus groups with families of preschool or elementary school aged children (and teachers in the case of the elementary version). Across the development studies for the early childhood and elementary FIQ versions, psychometric investigations have consistently yielded a three-factor model which reflects the dimensions of Epstein's model. The Home-Based Involvement factor is a representative sampling of caregiver behaviors occurring in the home or community that engage children in learning activities with the caregiver, expose children' to learning opportunities, create space and provide materials for learning, and provide routines or structure for important daily activities. The School-Based Involvement factor includes caregiver involvement behaviors that take place in early childhood centers or school settings, like volunteering, participating in decision-making committees, and fostering fundraising activities. The third dimension, Home-School Communication, entails various forms of contact between family members and school personnel, such as calling or writing notes, and caregivers' informing school staff of relevant family information.

Several investigations demonstrating the stability of the FIQ factor structure across populations varying in age, ethnicity, and linguistic backgrounds supported a multidimensional conceptualization of family involvement behavior. Manz, Fantuzzo, and Power (2004) demonstrated the congruence of the three FIQ dimensions across families of children who were preschool and elementary school aged. The factor structure derived for preschool-aged children was tested on the elementary age sample, using confirmatory factor analysis. The adequacy of the goodness-of-fit statistics provided evidence for the generalizability of the three major FIQ dimensions across these important age groups.

A multisite examination of the applicability of the FIQ dimensions, which were initially derived on a primarily African American sample, to diverse Latino samples drawn from various geographical locations in the Unites States, supported the generalizability of the FIQ dimensions across ethnic groups (McWayne et al., 2007). Independent exploratory factor analytical studies of the FIQ-EC, administered with three predominantly Latino samples in the northeast and southwest regions of the United States, replicated the three FIQ dimensions. Of note, the Latino samples included families whose primary language was either English or Spanish. Factorial congruence was statistically examined across the independently derived three-factor structures for these distinct samples. Appropriate patterns of high congruence coefficients among similar factors and low congruence coefficients among dissimilar factors emerged, supporting the generalization of the FIQ dimensions across African American and Latino populations and English- and Spanish-speaking Latinos. Similarly, Ginsburg-Block and Manz (2005) demonstrated the generalizability of the FIQ dimensions for elementary-age children across samples varying in ethnicity and geographical region.

Thus, recent empirical studies provide evidence that (a) family involvement is indeed a multidimensional construct including both home and school-based family activities as well as communication between home and school, and (b) there is limited, but growing evidence that these multiple family involvement constructs may hold across some age (e.g., pre-K–elementary) and ethnic (e.g., African American and Latino) groups.

### Cross-Cultural Considerations

Although more recent empirical research has begun to investigate family involvement across diverse demographic groups (e.g., McWayne, Campos, & Owsianik, 2008; McWayne, Manz, & Ginsburg-Block, 2008; Parke et al., 2004; Steinberg et al., 1992), the vast majority of research with ethnic minority and culturally diverse families has been qualitative in nature. These studies have illuminated numerous ways that mainstream ideas about family involvement may inadequately tap this construct for diverse groups. Based on this evidence, it appears that, in general, a lack of cross-cultural awareness, understanding, and communication pervades educational practice and policy decisions that present structural and institutional barriers to culturally diverse families' involvement in their children's education (Fuller, Eggers-Pierola, Holloway, Liang, & Rambaud, 1996; Gándara, 2001; Goldenberg, 1987; Orfield, 2001; Suárez-Orozco & Paéz, 2002).

For some parents, incongruence often extends beyond the linguistic differences between school and home. For example, in many Mexican societies, it is common for parents to defer to teachers who are viewed as educational experts. Questioning a teacher may be seen as disrespectful and an infringement on the teacher's expertise (Suárez-Orozco & Suárez-Orozco, 2001; Valenzuela, 1999). When Mexican families immigrate to the United States, they may not be comfortable with some types of school involvement, such as serving on a policy council or participating in a parent-teacher organization. Many immigrant parents who fear deportation or other government interventions are reluctant to be involved in the school if they do not trust educators or administrators. Moreover, long work hours of many low-income families often preclude parent participation in school activities scheduled during school hours (Aspiazu, Bauer, & Spillett, 1998; Sosa, 1997). These families are likely to be considered "uninvolved" when quite the opposite may be true. These discontinuities in expectations between home and school contexts can manifest as early as when a child enters preschool (Slaughter-Defoe, 1995; U.S. Department of Health and Human Services [DHHS], 2001).

Thus, an examination of the qualitative literature describing family involvement practices for marginalized groups suggests that traditional indicators of family involvement may not adequately capture salient family involvement behaviors for these families. This raises the possibility that although multiple dimensions of family involvement may be measured within diverse families, the relative importance of these practices for student achievement may vary.

It cannot be assumed that the relationships between family involvement practices and child outcomes will remain constant across diverse cultural groups. An example from the growing empirical literature supports this point. Fantuzzo, McWayne, Perry, and Childs (2004) found the strongest relationships were between home-based involvement and child outcomes for preschoolers from predominantly low-income African American families. In two independent studies of Latino children, however, only school-based family involvement and home-school conferencing were related to children's school readiness outcomes (Manz & Lehtinen, 2005; McWayne, 2006). Therefore, advancing our knowledge of family involvement must go beyond validating its multiple dimensions across cultures to discerning the differential relationships of involvement dimensions to salient child outcomes as well as child and family characteristics.

### Methodological Considerations

Numerous studies have employed variations of Epstein's typology to investigate relationships between family involvement and child outcomes. These studies, however, have yielded inconsistent results; some studies have linked parental involvement to child outcomes (e.g., Heller & Fantuzzo, 1993), while other studies have failed to uncover significant relationships between these variables (e.g., Powell-Smith, Shinn, Stoner & Good, 2000). A more careful look at this literature has surfaced a number of methodological issues that help explain these mixed findings (Fantuzzo, McWayne, Perry, & Childs, 2004; Kratochwill & Hoagwood, 2005).

First, many studies use surveys or solitary items from surveys to assess parent involvement (e.g., Griffith, 1996; Reynolds, Mavrogenes, Bezruckzko, & Hagemann, 1996; Watkins, 1997). These isolated items are not representative of the broader, more comprehensive conceptualizations of parent involvement as identified in this chapter. Second, as noted previously, many studies have included children of various ages, cultural groups and SES in their samples, and have not specifically tried to understand findings given these differences (e.g., Binford & Robertson, 1996; Hall & Schaverien, 2001; McBride, Bae, & Wright, 2002; Seefeldt, Denton, Galper, & Younoszai, 1999; Sheldon, 2002). Third, the overwhelming majority of studies are correlational rather than experimental in design (Carlson & Christenson, 2005). While correlational studies may be helpful in describing the strength and direction of the relationship between family involvement and child outcomes, they tell us nothing about intervening variables that may do more to explain student achievement (e.g., poverty status) than family involvement. Few randomized experimental studies of family involvement exist with the majority of group comparison studies being quasi-experimental in nature. While experimental studies as opposed to correlational studies of family involvement may reveal more about causality, given the threats to internal validity associated with quasi-experimental designs, it has been documented (e.g., Graue, Weinstein, & Walberg, 1983; Nye, Turner, & Schwartz, 2007) that different conclusions about the effectiveness of family involvement may be drawn from quasi-experiments as compared to true-experiments (i.e., randomized control trials). Thus, the precise nature of the relationship between family involvement and student achievement, including underlying processes, remains hard to neatly define.

Many of these methodological shortcomings of the research literature on family involvement have been noted by others who have taken on the task of summarizing this literature (e.g., Carlson & Christenson, 2005; Christenson, Rounds, & Gorney, 1992; Mattingly, Prislin, McKenzie, Ridriguez, & Kayzar, 2002; Nye et al., 2007). An examination of these and other research syntheses demonstrates a variety of approaches to dealing with these shortcomings and drawing conclusions about the existing literature, including both qualitative and quantitative research synthesis methods. As noted with primary studies of family involvement, research syntheses vary in the degree to which they endorse family involvement as a strategy for enhancing student achievement. For example, two well-known qualitative reviews of the family involvement literature have drawn very different conclusions. In their review of 125 data-based studies linking family factors and student achievement, Christenson et al. (1992) concluded that there is a positive relationship between family involvement and student achievement, while in a more recent review by Mattingly et al. (2002), the authors analyzed 41 studies of parent involvement programs and reported that little empirical support exists for this widely held conclusion. Thus, the nature and strength of the relationship between family involvement and student achievement appear to be elusive. Given these methodological considerations and discrepant conclusions, how are we to interpret the research literature?

In recent years, meta-analysis has been used increasingly as a quantitative approach to conducting literature reviews. Notably, meta-analytic studies examining the effects of family involvement on student achievement have universally reported positive effects (i.e., Fan & Chen, 2001; Graue et al., 1983; Jeynes, 2003, 2005; Nye et al., 2007; Sénéchal, 2006). While meta-analytic approaches are limited by the quality of the existing research base, causal relationships including salient moderator variables may be explored more objectively through this technique than through narrative literature reviews (Shadish, Cook, & Campbell, 2002). Thus, our review will draw upon experimental studies and meta-analytic syntheses of the family involvement literature where they are available (See Table 8.1 for a synopsis of published meta-analytic reviews of the effectiveness of family involvement on student achievement outcomes.)

## FAMILY INVOLVEMENT AND READING

Empirical research dating back to the 1960s supports the positive effects of family involvement practices on elementary student achievement in reading. A meta-analytic review of the correlational literature reported a small average effect of $r = 0.18$ (Fan & Chen, 2001) for family involvement on student reading outcomes obtained from eight correlation coefficients. Fan and Chen (2001) defined family involvement broadly including parental expectations, along with home and school-based activities. Student grade range was not reported. Reviews of the experimental literature produced somewhat larger effects including overall mean effect sizes of $d = 0.42$ (Nye et al., 2007), $ES = 0.55$ (Graue et al., 1983), and $ES = 0.68$ (Sénéchal, 2006). Nye and colleagues (2007) limited their review to available (i.e., $N = 12$) randomized control trials (excluding quasi-experimental designs) which operationally defined family involvement as home-based activities such as collaborative reading, education and training programs directed at the home environment, educational games, rewards and incentives. Graue et al. (1983) also focused their review on the effects of programs for enhancing the home environment; however, they included both experimental and quasi-experimental designs for a total of 29 studies and 60 relevant effect sizes. Sénéchal (2006) examined home based reading interventions including reading to children, having children read to parents, and parents teaching specific literacy skills at home. Similar to Graue and colleagues (1983), Sénéchal (2006) included both experimental and quasi-experimental studies

Table 8.1 Summary of Meta-Analyses of the Effectiveness of Family Involvement on Elementary Student Achievement in Reading and Mathematics

| Study | Research Design | Sample | Independent Variables | Dependent Variables | Reading ES(N) | Mathematics ES(N) | Overall ES(N) |
|---|---|---|---|---|---|---|---|
| Nye, Turner & Schwartz (2007) | Experimental (randomized control trials only) | Elementary students | Collaborative reading, education and training, games, rewards and incentives | Norm referenced tests, criterion referenced tests, academic performance rating scales | $d$=.41 (12) | $d$=.34 (5) | .45 (18) |
| Sénéchal (2006) | Experimental and quasi-experimental | K-3 students | Parents read to child, parents listen to child read, Parents teach specific literacy skills | Standardized and non-standardized measures of early literacy, word reading, reading comprehension, and composite measures of reading | .68 (14) | Not applicable | Not applicable |
| Jeynes (2005) | Quantitative (e.g. experimental, quasi-experimental, correlational) | Urban elementary students | Parent-child communication, homework, parental expectations, reading, attendance & participation, parental style | Grades, standardized tests of achievement, other measures (teacher rating scales, indices of academic behaviors and attitudes) | .42 (41)[a] | Not reported | .27 (41)[a] |
| Jeynes (2003) | Quantitative (e.g. experimental, quasi-experimental, correlational) | Minority K-12 students | parental style, parental attendance, reading, expectations, parent-child communication, homework, rules | Grades, standardized tests of achievement, other measures (teacher rating scales, indices of academic behaviors and attitudes) | .39[b] (41) | Not reported | .30 (21)[b] |
| Fan & Chen (1999) | Correlation & Regression | Students | Parental aspirations/expectation, communication with children about school, home supervision, participation in school activities, general | School GPA, tests, other (teacher ratings, educational attainment, grade retention, etc.) | $r$ = .18 (8) | $r$ = .18 (7) | .25 (92)[c] |
| Graue, Weinstein, & Walberg (1983) | Controlled studies (e.g., pre-post experiment, quasi-experiment, true experiment) | Elementary students, K-12+ | Parent training programs for increasing the educationally-stimulating qualities of the home environment | Standardized achievement and cognitive tests, curriculum-based assessments, measures of attitude | Mean weighted ES = .55 (60) | Mean weighted ES = 1.37 (23) | Mean weighted ES = .50 (121)[d] |

[a] As reported for parent involvement programs. The number of studies reported is the total number of studies used to calculate this specific effect size was not reported but is presumed to be lower. Outcomes for reading were based on the effects of shared reading only.
[b] As reported for studies with mostly or all African-Americans. The number of studies reported is the total number of studies found in the meta-analysis. The precise number of studies used to calculate this specific effect size was not reported but is presumed to be lower. Outcomes for reading were based on the effects of shared reading only.
[c] Reflects number of correlation coefficients obtained from 25 studies.
[d] Reflects number of learning outcomes obtained from 29 studies.

($N = 14$), limiting her subject pool to children in grades K through 3. For studies of urban elementary (2005) and minority K through 12 (2003) students exclusively, Jeynes reported achievement effect sizes of $ES = 0.42$ and $ES = 0.39$, respectively, as a result of correlational and experimental studies of parent-child shared reading.

Overall, meta-analytic reviews of the correlational and experimental literature have shown positive small ($r = 0.18$; Fan & Chen, 2001) to large ($ES = 0.68$; Sénéchal, 2006) effects for family involvement on reading achievement in elementary school children. To provide a context for these effect sizes, an effect size of .18 would bring an average student performing at the 50th percentile to the 56th percentile, while an effect size of $ES = 0.68$ would bring that student to the 73rd percentile. A number of factors contribute to variation in the reported effect sizes, including wide ranging conceptualizations of family involvement, methodological differences in the literature examined, and characteristics of the subject pools. In addition, the results of Nye and colleagues (2007) were based on standardized outcome measures whereas the other meta-analyses also included non-standardized indicators of reading achievement such as grades in school and homework completion (Fan & Chen, 2001; Jeynes, 2003; 2005; Sénéchal, 2006) or affective outcomes (Graue et al., 1983). Home-based family involvement methods from the experimental literature that have specifically shown evidence for promoting reading achievement include positive parenting skills (e.g., Nye et al., 2007; Sweet & Appelbaum, 2004), an enriched home literacy environment (e.g., Nye et al., 2007), shared reading (e.g., Hewison, 1988; Leach & Siddall, 1990; Tizard, Schofield, & Hewison, 1982), and parent teaching focused on specific literacy skills such as letter-sound correspondence (e.g., Kraft, Findlay, Major, Gilberts, & Hofmeister, 2001) or word reading (e.g., Vinograd-Bausell & Bausell, 1987). While experimental studies are needed, home visiting seems to be a promising approach for supporting home-based involvement strategies that have been shown to enhance reading outcomes (Sweet & Appelbaum, 2004). Home-school communication and school-based involvement have also been linked to reading outcomes, however, these findings were exclusively based on the correlational literature, including a handful of longitudinal studies of family involvement and child outcomes (e.g., Dearing, Kreider, Simpkins, & Weiss, 2006; Englund, Luckner, Whaley, & Egeland, 2004). These evidence-based family involvement strategies for promoting reading outcomes are described below.

### Home-Based Family Involvement and Reading

Both empirical and theoretical support exists for the use of home-based activities to promote child outcomes in reading and other areas of development. Given that positive parenting practices in early childhood seem to have lasting effects on later educational outcomes including reading (e.g., Hart & Risley, 1995), and controlled studies of interventions to promote positive parenting practices have demonstrated positive reading outcomes for elementary children (Nye et al., 2007), an emphasis on early intervention appears warranted. Theoretical considerations, such as the multidimensional conceptualization of family involvement have also illuminated the particular salience of home-based involvement activities for caregivers of young children. Although in its infancy, research suggests that the home is an important and may be a preferable context for ethnic minority families' involvement with their children's learning. Nye et al. (2007) reported the effects of four unpublished experimental studies of parent education and training programs that reported effects on elementary student reading. The effects sizes obtained from these studies represented moderate (i.e., $d = 0.35$) to large (i.e., $d = 1.1$) effects.

Findings from Fantuzzo, Tighe, and Childs (2000) suggested that low-income families may be more freely involved in their children's learning at home than in school contexts. For example, this study showed that caregivers' educational background was not related to their level of involvement in home-based activities with their preschool children, although it did significantly relate to their involvement in center-based activities and home-school communication. In other words, caregivers of varying levels of education were equally involved with their children's learning at home, yet those with a high school education or greater were more likely to be involved at school and interface with teachers than those who did not attain a high school education. Corresponding with the implication that home-based involvement is more readily embraced by low-income families than other forms of involvement, Fantuzzo, McWayne, Perry, and Childs (2004) demonstrated that it is strongly associated with preschool children's acquisition of school readiness competencies. Home-based involvement independently predicted school readiness competencies in preschool children; although school-based and home-school communication were significantly connected to school readiness skills in the bivariate sense, when coupled with home-based involvement in multivariate analyses, their associations attenuated.

Consistent with this research, national trends in enrollment in early childhood educational programs also suggests that certain ethnic minority caregivers have preferences for their young children to remain at home, rather than attend center-based programs. For instance, Latino children are more likely to be in maternal care at the age of 3 year than their same-age peers of other ethnicities. Whereas 49% of Black children and 43% of White children attend preschool, only 23% of Latino children are enrolled (Magnuson & Waldfogel, 2005).

*Home Visiting*   Home visiting is a particularly promising venue for providing early childhood services to ethnic minority families, given that it may be preferred by some ethnic minority groups (e.g., families with less formal education or Latino caregivers) and its salience for important child outcomes. Home visiting offers many unique benefits. It is accessible; families do not have to arrange transportation, child care, or time off from work to participate (Sweet & Appelbaum, 2004). By meeting with families in their homes, home visitors have an opportunity to gain a holistic view of families and their children, which can help them tailor services to meet their particular needs (Wagner & Clayton, 1999) and engage all family members in child-focused activities and interventions (Sweet & Appelbaum, 2004).

Unfortunately, recognition of the promise of home visiting programs for bolstering children's development through increased caregiver involvement has been diminished by research which has not distinguished sufficiently the wide range of goals, foci and strategies inherited in this broad method of service delivery to low-income families. In their meta-analysis of home visiting programs, Sweet and Appelbaum (2004) found that cognitive and socioemotional outcomes were more favorable among home-visited children than for control group children. Similarly, a review prepared for the First 5 California Children and Families Commission (Gomby, 2003) found that home visiting programs produced benefits associated with school readiness for children, but the benefits were modest in magnitude. As noted in the research, these large scale evaluations of home visiting were impeded by the enormous variation in program targets and goals. Some essential differences among programs included a focus on either adult or child goals, targets for improvements specific to caregivers, children or their interaction, and employment of paraprofessionals or professionals to conduct home visiting.

In contrast, evaluations specifically targeting the home visiting services provided through Head Start and Early Head Start programs have yielded consistent and favorable views of their effectiveness. Several studies focused on Head Start's home visiting services have demonstrated gains in preschool children's cognitive and social emotional development, parental participation rates, and supportive parenting skills (Love et al., 2005; Raikes et al., 2006).

Recently, a large scale and comprehensive evaluation of Early Head Start home visiting services (Raikes et al., 2006) illustrated connections between program characteristics and child and family gains. Although these home visiting services have the dual focus of supporting the caregiver as well as the development of the child, Raikes and colleagues showed that when home visits concentrated on involving the caregiver in the child's development and learning, greater gains in the children's language skills emerged. In addition, this large-scale study showed that the quality of engaging caregivers' in the home visiting sessions in addition to the quantity of visits was a powerful predictor of outcome. Congruent with indicated preferences for home based involvement among Latino caregivers (Magnuson & Waldfogel, 2005), this evaluation study found that non-English speaking Latino families were more responsive to the home visiting services than caregivers of other ethnic backgrounds.

Like Early Head Start, the Parent-Child Home Program (PCHP) provides home visiting to families with children between 2 and 3 years of age. However, this program is distinguished in that its sole focus is on strengthening caregiver involvement in language-based activities and interactions with their children. The effectiveness of PCHP has been insufficiently examined, with only a couple of nonexperimental, retroactive studies published to date (Levenstein, Levenstein, & Oliver, 2002; Madden, Levenstein, & Levenstein, 1976). Currently underway is an experimental evaluation of this program's effectiveness with low-income, predominantly Latino caregivers in urban communities (Manz, Barnabas, Bracaliello, Williams, & Zuniga, 2008). Findings from the first year of this longitudinal study showed that PCHP's home visiting services had an immediate impact on 2-year-old children's expressive vocabulary skills, and gradually improved children's receptive language skills. In addition, younger children at the time of enrollment in PCHP showed significantly greater growth in their receptive language skills than older children. While additional research is required, given the positive relationship that has been established in the literature between early language skills and later literacy skills (e.g., Storch & Whitehurst, 2002), PCPH may show promise for promoting early literacy skills.

*Home Literacy Environments*    The home context established by caregivers plays a crucial role in fostering young children's emergent literacy development. Many facets of the home context are relevant, including caregivers' responsiveness to their children's expressions of early literacy abilities, involvement with their children in language and literacy-based activities and routines, and the provision of literacy materials (Hart & Risley, 1995; Roberts, Jurgens, & Burchinal, 2005; Sénéchal, LeFevre, Thomas, & Daley, 1998). Other common aspects of home literacy environments, including the number of books in the home, library visits, time spent reading with the child and the child's age at which shared reading began, have also been shown to predict children's immediate and long-term literacy outcomes (Roberts et al., 2005; Rush, 1999).

Variation in the richness of home literacy environments can often be attributed to socioeconomic status or culturally-rooted perspectives of young children's readiness for literacy skill acquisition. Families who live in socioeconomic disadvantage often experience a diminished capacity to nurture their young children's early literacy development. The financial stress and social complexities associated with poverty (e.g., unemployment, community violence, single-parent status) impact caregivers' mental health and their emotional capacity for effective parenting (Linver, Brooks-Gunn, & Kohen, 2002). Rush (1999) showed that among ethnically diverse Head Start children, minimal caregiver supervision and involvement with children was associated with their underdeveloped vocabulary and phonemic awareness skills in addition to free play which was characterized by passive activity such as television watching, was non-interactive, and was not sustained on a certain activity for a reasonable amount of time. More recently, Roberts and colleagues (Roberts et al., 2005) demonstrated the longitudinal impact of similar aspects of the home environment during infancy on children's literacy skills at the age of four and at kindergarten entry for low-income, African American children.

Shared book reading is perhaps one of the most widely recognized and studied aspects of the home literacy environment for young children. Reviews of the literature have attributed significant variance in reading outcomes to child participation in reading with an adult at home (Bus, van IJzendoorn, & Pellegrini, 1995). Both correlational (e.g., Scarborough & Dobrich, 1994) and experimental studies (e.g., Hewison, 1988; Tizard et al., 1982) have yielded similar positive results. A growing body of research has indicated that the benefits of shared book reading are associated not only with its frequency, but also the nature of the caregiver-child interactions. Several researchers have demonstrated that the particular ways in which preschoolers are read to are related to the language benefits they obtain from shared book reading (Arnold, Lonigan, Whitehurst, & Epstein, 1994; Crain-Thorenson & Dale, 1999; Dickinson & Smith, 1994; Haden, Reese, & Fivush, 1996; Hargrave & Sénéchal, 2000; Reese & Cox, 1999; Whitehurst et al., 1994; Whitehurst et al., 1988). Children show greater language gains when adults create opportunities for children to become active participants in the reading process by using evocative strategies (e.g., asking the child questions about the pictures or the story, or encouraging the child to tell the story along with the adult) than when adults simply read the book to them. This finding has been demonstrated for middle-class (Haden et al., 1996; Hargrave & Sénéchal, 2000; Whitehurst et al., 1988), low-income (Whitehurst et al., 1994; Lonigan & Whitehurst, 1998; Whitehurst et al., 1999), and language delayed children (Crain-Thorenson & Dale, 1999).

Along these lines, dialogic reading has become a widely-known and effective approach for caregiver-child interactive reading. The aim of dialogic reading is to actively engage the child in telling the story in conjunction with the adult (Zevenbergen & Whitehurst, 2003). Adults question children in a variety of ways, expand upon their verbalizations and offer praise for their active participation. Dialogic reading strategies are specified for very young children, ages 2 to 3 years, as well as preschool children between the ages of 4 and 5 years. Dialogic reading has been applied in home settings, with caregiver-child reading, as well as in early childhood education centers, involving teachers reading with small groups of children.

Several experimental studies have demonstrated the benefits of parents' use of dialogic reading strategies with their young children. To begin, parents can easily learn dialogic reading techniques through cost-effective and simple training. Both didactic instruction and training videos, which explain and model dialogic techniques, have been experimentally shown to be effective in preparing parents for dialogic reading with their young child (Arnold, Lonigan, Whitehurst & Epstein, 1994; Huebner & Meltzoff, 2005). In addition to being easily learned, dialogic reading has repeatedly been demonstrated to improve young children's oral language (Zevenbergen & Whitehurst, 2005). Consistently across studies, children have shown improvement in expressive language skills after typically a brief period of intervention (e.g., 4 to 6 weeks; Arnold et al., 1994; Huebner, 2000; Lonigan & Whitehurst, 1998). On the other hand, findings from the examination of caregiver dialogic reading on receptive language abilities have been mixed, with some studies demonstrating significant effects and others not.

Although the evidence supports the effectiveness of Dialogic Reading, contemporary research indicating natural variation in parental reading styles across and within cultural groups and subsequent connections between book reading style and specific emergent literacy outcomes, implies that a deeper understanding of natural styles may enhance the application of Dialogic Reading across children varying in cultural background and literacy abilities. In line with previous research dating back to the 1980's, Reese and colleagues (Reese & Cox, 1999; Reese, Cox, Harte, & McAnally, 2003) have identified a continuum of reading styles which vary in the extent to which caregivers demand a child's active participation. The lowest demand style, the describer, refers to caregivers who focus on describing and labeling pictures in the book. Haden et al. (1996) noted that the describer style is similar to the experimental style, dialogic reading. At the other end of the continuum is the comprehender style of shared reading wherein the caregiver focuses on the story content, engaging the child in formulating inferences and predictions.

Both the describer and comprehender styles involve caregiver interruptions while reading the story. However, a third natural reading style has emerged, the performance-oriented style, which is a lively and uninterrupted read of the story, reserving discussion about the book at the start and end. Although initially the performance-oriented style was associated with early childhood educators in classroom contexts (Dickinson & Smith, 1994), a recent study found that it was a preferred, naturally occurring shared reading approach among Peruvian mothers (Melzi & Caspe, 2005). Moreover, Melzi and Caspe showed the connection of culture and natural reading styles. In contrast to the

Peruvian mothers' natural inclination for performance-oriented reading, U.S. mothers naturally adopted styles similar to the describer style.

These three naturally occurring styles of shared reading are distinguished by whether or not caregiver-child dialogic exchanges occur during reading, and the level of cognitive demand in the verbal exchanges between caregivers and children (e.g., labeling pictures or making inferences). Reese and Cox (1999) were interested in how these distinct styles related to various emergent literacy outcomes and interfaced with preschool children's pre-intervention skill levels. Overall, the describer style, that which is similar to dialogic reading procedures, showed the greatest benefits to children's receptive language abilities and print awareness; this finding is consistent with the empirical evidence for dialogic reading. Unique to this study, Reese and Cox demonstrated that children's initial literacy skills affected the outcomes of the reading styles. For instance, children with higher vocabulary abilities, showed the greatest growth in vocabulary when engaged in performance-oriented reading. Children who initially had higher developed comprehension skills benefited the most from the describer style in their acquisition of print awareness. This important study highlights the value of tailoring interventions to children's ability level. However, of note, investigators read to the children, not caregivers. An important future direction will be to test the relative benefits of these styles among caregivers and children.

Group comparison studies at the kindergarten and elementary levels, although limited, have shown similar results to those conducted in early childhood (Sénéchal, 2006). Modest effects have been reported for studies in which parent reading to children was targeted (Foster & Bitner, 1998; Jordan, Snow, & Porche, 2000). In comparison, Sénéchal (2006) reported a large effect size of .51 for studies in which having children read to their parents was the focus of intervention (i.e., Hannon, 1987; Leach & Siddall, 1990; Miller, Robson, & Bushell, 1986; Tizard et al., 1982; Wilks & Clarke, 1988). Experimental studies of the short- and long-term effectiveness of paired reading (Topping, 1992), a strategy employed mainly in the U.K. for shared reading, which involves the parent and child reading together coupled with corrective feedback and praise by the parent, have shown promising results. Studies of paired reading between children and family members have not pinpointed the operational mechanisms as the intervention seems to promote both increases in the quantity of shared reading as well as the quality of the parent-child reading context (Topping, 1992).

Clearly, family involvement is a key component in young children's emergent literacy development and later reading skills. The home literacy environment established by families fosters children's early acquisition of language and literacy skills. Of significant importance is the extent to which shared reading among caregivers and children occurs in home. Current research underscores the importance of quality as well as quantity, highlighting the advantages of reading in a manner that is rich in verbal exchanges between caregivers and their children. For more advanced readers, research suggests that reading to children should also be supplemented with children reading to their parents. More recent research has illuminated important directions for continued study, pointing to the connections between culture and natural, parental reading styles as well as to the interface of children's emergent literacy skills and the relative benefits of various reading styles.

*Parent Teaching*   Parent teaching of specific literacy skills has been shown to result in positive literacy outcomes for children (Sénéchal, 2006). In fact, Sénéchal's (2006) meta-analysis demonstrated that teaching skills may produce greater literacy outcomes for children in grades K to 3 than either reading to children or having children read to parents. For seven group design studies in which parents were trained to teach their children skills either through scripted exercises (i.e., Kraft et al., 2001; Niedermeyer, 1970; Searls, Lewis, & Morrow, 1982; Vinograd-Bausell & Bausell, 1987) or training programs that included both exercises and print materials (i.e., *Reading Recovery*, Faires, Nichols, & Rickelman, 2000; *Teach Your Child to Read in 100 Easy Lessons*, Leach & Siddall, 1990; *Reading Made Easy*, Mehran & White, 1988), a large mean weighted effect size (i.e., weighted for sample size) of $ES = 1.15$ was obtained.

The effectiveness of programs for training parents to teach specific literacy skills to their children has been demonstrated through several experimental studies. In an experimental study of first grade children in Australia, Leach and Siddall (1990) trained parents to administer the *Teach Your Child to Read in 100 Easy Lessons* (Engelmann, Haddox, & Bruner, 1983) curriculum. Children in the treatment group performed significantly higher (i.e. more than one standard deviation) than control children across four indices of early literacy. In another study of first grade children, Vinograd-Bausell and Bausell (1987) also employed an experimental design to evaluate the effectiveness of a short-term program in which parents were taught to use word cards to teach their children new sight words and identify them in sentences. Similarly, the authors found significant effects for children who participated in the intervention versus control conditions. Importantly, these experimental studies, along with additional quasi-experimental studies (e.g., Faires et al., 2000; Kraft et al., 2001) have demonstrated that parents can be trained to successfully instruct their children in learning specific literacy skills, which may be used to supplement instruction at school. In addition, these programs have produced robust effects with both low (e.g., Faires et al., 2000; Mehran & White, 1988) and middle to high SES families (e.g., Kraft et al., 2001; Niedermeyer, 1970).

### Home-School and School-Based Activities

Family involvement activities indirectly related to reading, such as home-school communication and participation in school functions have been correlated with achievement outcomes (e.g., Stevenson & Baker, 1987). It is hypothesized that through participation in schooling in this manner, families socialize their children to value achievement through modeling and reinforcing pro-academic behaviors (e.g., participation in a school play or book fair). A second pathway may involve promoting positive affect and self-efficacy for achievement, which, in turn, leads to higher reading performance among children whose families engage in school-based activities and communication with greater frequency (Dearing et al., 2006; Simkins, Weiss, McCartney, Kreider, & Dearing, 2006). Although not specific to reading outcomes, Jeynes (2005) found for urban elementary students that parental attendance and participation at school events produced relatively smaller (but still significant) effects (i.e., $ES = 0.21$) as compared to other forms of family involvement, such as parental expectations for student achievement (i.e., $ES = 0.58$). It may be that parental expression of high achievement expectations is a more explicit and direct method for promoting achievement than modeling pro-academic behaviors through participation in school-based activities. The relationship between these two facets of involvement, school participation and values expressed in the home, was not studied in the Jeynes (2005) meta-analysis, yet it is likely that they are closely related. Fantuzzo et al. (2004) in a study of primarily African American preschoolers found significant effects for home-school communication and school-based involvement on school readiness indicators, yet these were secondary to the greater effects found for home-based participation. Further exploring the relationships among various forms of family involvement and student achievement, Simkins et al. (2006) found that for low-income kindergarteners, maternal warmth, an aspect of home-based parenting practices served to moderate the effects of school attendance activities on reading and mathematics achievement.

While an indirect relationship between school-based activities and student achievement seems plausible, some studies suggest a more direct relationship. An earlier meta-analytic study by Jeynes (2003) showed that parental attendance yielded a more robust effect ($ES = 0.51$) for African American elementary students than for other minority students (i.e., Latino & Asian) and as compared to other forms of family involvement such as story book reading ($ES = 0.39$). Yet in another study, as stated previously, McWayne, Campos, and Owisanik (2008) found that for Latino pre-schoolers only school-based and home-school communication levels were related to school readiness outcomes as opposed to home-based family involvement activities. Similarly supporting the robust effects of school-based family participation, in their longitudinal study of school-based family involvement for low-income ethnically diverse children from kindergarten through fifth grade, Dearing et al. (2006) demonstrated that increased levels of school involvement actually eliminated the gap in literacy levels observed between children of mothers with low levels of educational attainment and those with higher levels. Likewise, Englund et al. (2004) found a direct relationship between parental involvement with school in grade three and concurrent child overall achievement, in a longitudinal study of the effects of parental involvement on achievement in low-income children. These authors found that parental expectations led to school participation, which, in turn, were related to child achievement outcomes.

Thus, while the precise mechanisms and magnitude of effects linking home-school and school-based family involvement to achievement and reading achievement in particular are unclear, it is clear that a positive relationship, whether direct or indirect, exists between these forms of family involvement and reading outcomes for children. There is also evidence that for low-income and minority children, these forms of family participation in schooling may be critically important. It may be that the effects of home-school communication and school-based involvement are both mediated by and serve to mediate home-based support for learning on child outcomes, forming reciprocal relationships among these variables; however, additional research is needed to sort out these relationships across diverse groups of learners.

## FAMILY INVOLVEMENT AND MATHEMATICS

While the effects of family involvement on mathematics achievement have been studied to a lesser degree than reading achievement, research supports a positive relationship between these two variables. Drawing upon the same set of meta-analyses from the family involvement literature used to highlight reading outcomes for elementary children, effect sizes for mathematics outcomes also range from small ($r = 0.18$; Fan & Chen, 2001) to large ($ES = 1.37$; Graue et al., 1983) effects. Fan and Chen (2001) based their summary statistic on seven correlation coefficients representing the relationship between family involvement and mathematics outcomes, both broadly defined. Nye et al. (2007) reported an average effect size of $d = 0.34$ across five experimental studies of home-based family involvement programs for which standardized mathematics outcomes were reported. Graue et al. (1983) based their findings on 23 standardized and nonstandardized outcomes of experimental and quasi-experimental studies of parent training programs also targeting improvements to the home learning environment.

Overall, meta-analytic reviews of the literature show a significant positive relationship between home-based family involvement and mathematics achievement for elementary students. As with findings for reading outcomes, the experimental literature supports the effectiveness of home-based strategies on mathematics achievement (e.g., Fantuzzo, King, & Heller, 1992), while the correlational literature lends additional support for school-based involvement (e.g., Shaver & Walls, 1998). Parent involvement strategies with potential for improving mathematics achievement include home-based support for learning, increased home-school communication, and school-based involvement and are described below. Conceptually similar mechanisms as suggested for family influences on reading achievement are believed to apply to mathematics, while there may be barriers specific to involvement in mathematics that may be important to consider (e.g., Jackson & Remillard, 2005), such as parent and school perceptions of the family role in mathematics education and parents' familiarity with current mathematics curricula and instructional techniques.

Although limited in number, experimental studies have begun to demonstrate the effectiveness of family involvement in producing significant mathematics outcomes for elementary students. In a series of experimental studies exploring the effects of increasing home-school communication and home-based support for learning on elementary mathematics achievement for low-income predominantly African American children, Fantuzzo and colleagues demonstrated the effectiveness of these parent involvement strategies on student curriculum-based achievement in mathematics computation and teacher reports of student work habits and motivation (Heller & Fantuzzo, 1993), as well as student reports of academic and behavioral self-concept (Fantuzzo, Davis, & Ginsburg, 1995). The parent involvement intervention implemented in these studies involved increasing positive communication between school and home and encouraging families to institute home-based celebrations for student effort in mathematics. In addition, Nye et al. (2007) included in their meta-analysis several un-published experimental studies of home-based activities to support mathematics achievement which reportedly produced small to moderate effects.

Family involvement strategies supporting early mathematics at the preschool level have been studied to a far lesser degree. In a correlational study involving Title 1 students in grades two through eight, Shaver and Walls (1998) demonstrated that school involvement by families regardless of their child's grade level or family socioeconomic status was positively related to academic achievement in mathematics, both in overall measures of mathematics achievement and the application of mathematical concepts. Similarly, although the results were obtained with older students, parental expectations were found to produce positive effects on 12th grade mathematics achievement in an analysis of the 1988 National Education Longitudinal Study (Yan & Lin, 2005).

In addition to correlational studies, group comparison studies also link family involvement to mathematics outcomes for young children. A quasi-experimental study of the *Natural Math* project conducted with Native American preschool children ages 3 and 4 and their families showed significant effects for program participants as compared to a group of non-participants on readiness skills measured prior to kindergarten entry, including counting (Sears & Medearis, 1992). The *Natural Math* program involved parent training and materials for home-based numeracy activities over the summer months, as well as a school-based math fair for children. Additional documentation supports the overall effectiveness of family involvement programs administered at the preschool level and geared towards mathematics (e.g., Landerholm, Rubenstein, & Losch, 1994). Currently, a large scale development and evaluation study of the Evidence-Based Program for the Integration of Curricula (EPIC) led by J. W. Fantuzzo (personal communication, May 23, 2008) at the University of Pennsylvania is being implemented in the Prekindergarten Head Start Program. Results of this study are expected to advance the family involvement literature by examining the contribution of a family involvement component on child readiness outcomes, including numeracy.

Importantly, together, this body of empirical research demonstrates that a variety of family involvement strategies are linked to student achievement in mathematics, including school-based activities, home-school communication, and home-based support for learning. In addition, controlled intervention studies demonstrate that home-school communication and home-based family involvement can be enhanced yielding overwhelmingly positive outcomes for low-income elementary children through readily available low-cost interventions. While school-based family involvement may be difficult to manipulate experimentally, correlational studies suggest that this form of involvement has ties to mathematics outcomes and should be addressed programmatically when considering family involvement.

## WHAT WORKS BEST: FAMILY INVOLVEMENT MODES, CHARACTERISTICS, AND INTERVENING VARIABLES

While it is important to understand the magnitude of the effects of various family involvement strategies on student achievement outcomes in reading and mathematics, it is equally important, for implementation, to understand the conditions under which family involvement strategies work best. Although not exhaustive, several attempts to conduct moderator analyses comparing groups of family involvement studies with and without the presence of a certain program mode or characteristic have been published in meta-analyses of the family involvement literature. The findings of these studies are summarized here.

The relative effectiveness of family involvement modes such as home-based versus school-based involvement for promoting student achievement varies across research syntheses. Fan and Chen (2001) reported, in their synthesis of 25 correlational studies, that the greatest effects on overall achievement were found for parental aspirations for their children ($r = 0.40$, $N = 10$ studies) as compared to: (a) more tangible home-based supports for learning, such as assistance with homework ($r = 0.19$, $N = 10$) or supervision of the home environment ($r = 0.09$, $N = 12$), or (b) parent contact or participation in school ($r = 0.32$, $N = 7$).

Based on 21 correlational and experimental studies, Jeynes (2003) reported moderate to large effects on achievement for African American students in grades K-12 for both home-based (i.e., expectations, $ES = 0.57$; parent-child communication, $ES = 0.53$; supportive parenting style, $ES = 0.44$, parent-child reading, $ES = 0.39$; enforcing rules, $ES = 0.35$) and school-based family involvement activities ($ES = 0.51$), with the largest effects for parental assistance with homework ($ES = 0.72$). In a similar synthesis methodologically, of 41 studies of urban elementary students, Jeynes (2005) reported nonsignificant to large effects for home-based strategies (expectations, $ES = 0.58$; parent-child reading, $ES = 0.42$; parenting style, $ES = 0.31$; parent-child communication, $ES = 0.24$) and only small effects for school-based family involvement ($ES = 0.21$). In contrast to the 2003 study, checking homework produced non-significant effects for urban elementary students (Jeynes, 2005) as opposed to producing the largest effects for K-12 African American students (Jeynes, 2003).

Nye and colleagues (2007) in their synthesis of 18 experimental studies of home-based practices, found the greatest achievement effects for studies involving home-based encouragement for learning in mathematics ($d = 1.18$, $N = 2$), followed by general parent education and training programs to improve academic performance ($d = 0.61$, $N = 4$). Finally, Sénéchal (2006) found support for active family involvement strategies (e.g., having children read to parents) versus more passive strategies (i.e., being read to by an adult). Overall, consistent support exists for the positive effects of both home and school-based varieties of family involvement, while the magnitude and relative importance of these effects may vary according to research methodology or student characteristics. Given the extremely divergent effects reported for family involvement in homework (i.e., non-significant to highly positive effects), further exploration of this type of family participation may be warranted. One explanation may be that in correlational studies of homework participation, increased involvement in homework may actually indicate school problems rather than success, particularly in the upper grades. Further investigation of this hypothesis as well as other plausible explanations would be helpful in clarifying the relationship between parental involvement in homework and student achievement.

In addition to examining the relative effectiveness of various modes of family involvement, meta-analytic reviews of the literature have also examined the effectiveness of interventions according to their duration and characteristics of program participants. No relationship between the length of the family involvement intervention and its' effectiveness was reported across meta-analyses (Graue et al., 1983; Nye et al., 2007;

Sénéchal, 2006). Similarly, Sénéchal (2006) was unable to determine an optimal amount of time for parent training sessions.

Mixed findings have been reported, however, regarding demographic groups for which family involvement is most effective. Graue et al. (1983) reported larger effects for first- and fifth-grade students than for other elementary students, concluding that a linear relationship between grade level and the effectiveness of family involvement does not exist, but rather, the effectiveness of family involvement interventions seems to remain constant despite children's grade level. While Graue and colleagues (1983) showed the greatest effects for minority versus Caucasian students, Jeynes (2005) found effects to be constant across these groups when instituting sophisticated controls. Although Graue et al. (1983) reported large effects across all communities, effects were reportedly greater for children residing in urban and rural versus suburban communities. Thus, based on meta-analyses of the family involvement literature it is unclear how student characteristics are related to intervention effectiveness. Taking the literature as a whole though, family involvement appears to be largely effective across grade level, racial group, and community type.

## IMPLICATIONS FOR FUTURE RESEARCH

### Next Steps in Measuring Family Involvement

Valid measurement tools are essential to educational decision making. For example, these tools are used to conduct needs assessments, target areas for intervention, and evaluate program effectiveness and modify programs appropriately. Currently, there is a great need for valid measurement of family involvement for diverse groups, if we are to better understand its influence on children's achievement outcomes and develop and evaluate family involvement programs. In a recent report, the Federal Interagency Forum on Child and Family Statistics (2008) indicated that children increasingly will have: (a) diverse racial and ethnic backgrounds, (b) diverse households with respect to the nationality of parents and family structure, and (c) exposure to poverty. A decade ago, one-tenth of the U.S. population was comprised of immigrants (Portés & Rumbaut, 2001), and recent figures show that 1 in 5 youth in the United States are either foreign-born or children of immigrants (Suárez-Orozco & Suárez-Orozco, 2001). Despite these trends, by and large, quantitative measurement continues to be developed using mainstream ideals about family involvement and fails to acknowledge the unique ways that culturally and economically diverse families support their children's education. For instance, while home-based involvement provides a promising context for intervention, more precise measurement tools are needed to assess the supports and needs within diverse families and to evaluate program effectiveness. Questionnaires developed to assess home-based literacy and/or numeracy practices would be important, as well as those that can capture reliably parental beliefs specific to these academic areas.

Researchers have delineated several challenges inherent in measurement with culturally diverse families. Lopez (2004) raised the following questions to consider: Does the measurement development process take into consideration variations in languages (including level of language proficiency, as well as general literacy levels)? How were different forms of the same measure developed (e.g., different translation approaches, adaptations, simultaneous item development, etc.)? Within specific language groups, did item development take into consideration major dialectical and sociocultural/sociopolitical differences across subgroups within a language?

In addition to the typically employed methods based on true score theory (e.g., exploratory and confirmatory factor analysis), item response theory (IRT) and Rasch modeling provide for promising means to develop culturally relevant measurement. An advantage of these techniques over true score theory methods (such as EFA) includes the use of fit statistics for identifying aberrant or unusual response patterns that violate model expectations (Smith, 1991). For example, in Rasch analysis, item fit statistics (as per Smith, Schumacker, & Bush, 1998) can be used to detect items not contributing to the definition of the construct shared by the majority of items. Person fit statistics can likewise be examined to identify aberrant participant responses. Examination of item hierarchy maps can help one to determine if the constructs are truly representative with various groups and can guide researchers in any further item addition or revision deemed necessary. Finally, Rasch analysis has been cited as particularly useful when one is interested in examining the issue of cross-cultural equivalence (Choi, Mericle, & Harachi, 2006). In addition to item and person diagnostics, researchers using this method can conduct differential item functioning (DIF) analyses to assess item equivalence across subgroups of interest (Choi et al., 2006).

The authors recently proposed a multistrategy approach to initial measurement development using Rasch models in conjunction with various other qualitative and quantitative techniques (see McWayne et al., 2008). Based on this work, a mixed-methods approach was deemed superior to the use of one analytic method (e.g., factor analysis solely) in that it allows for the examination of convergent evidence with respect to item representativeness and reliability.

## Next Steps in Prevention and Intervention Research

The family involvement literature has documented strong connections between family involvement and student achievement outcomes. As mentioned previously in this chapter, according to Nye and colleagues (2007) we have known that family involvement produces significant effects on student achievement for over 30 years, yet controlled studies of family involvement intervention strategies are sparse. For example, as stated previously, only a few experimental studies of the effects of family involvement on elementary mathematics have been published (i.e., Fantuzzo et al., 1995; Heller & Fantuzzo, 1993). These studies were limited to examining the combined effects of home-based involvement and home-school communication on mathematics outcomes for low-income African American elementary students. Based on the current family involvement literature, as this example illustrates, it is not possible to determine what type of family involvement strategy works best for whom. Studies of school change initiatives such as the *Comer School Development Program* (Haynes, 2007) and *Success for All* (Slavin & Madden, 2006), which include family involvement components among other intervention strategies, have shown positive effects and may work to reduce the observed achievement gap between African American and Caucasian students, yet the independent contributions of the family components are unknown (Carlson & Christenson, 2005). Controlled studies of family involvement and component studies evaluating the relative contributions of family involvement to student achievement, particularly in mathematics, are needed to advance the literature and inform educational practices.

Another facet of experimental research which is conspicuously absent from the family involvement literature is the longitudinal study of children and their families over time. Research has documented the decline of family involvement across educational transitions such as moving from preschool to kindergarten (Rimm-Kaufman & Pianta, 2005). Although declines in family involvement have been documented, existing longitudinal research demonstrates the positive cumulative effects of family involvement on student achievement outcomes (e.g., Englund et al., 2004). The identification and evaluation of strategies that effectively span transitions and promote family involvement over time is needed. While longitudinal studies are costly and difficult to implement, the addition of follow-up data would be an improvement to short-term post-test only research designs.

Finally, the conditions under which family involvement interventions are most effective have undergone much speculation, but limited empirical study. The meta-analyses presented in this chapter initiated exploration of moderators such as program and participant characteristics, while aspects of program development such as the program's theoretical basis and the extent to which the program was developed collaboratively were absent (e.g., Kratochwill & Hoagwood, 2005). Comprehensive experimental and meta-analytic research of this nature would help to fill in the gaps of the current literature and help to inform stakeholders interested in advancing family involvement initiatives in their schools and communities.

## IMPLICATIONS FOR CURRENT EDUCATIONAL PRACTICES

### Family Involvement Works

Family involvement in education appears to improve reading and mathematics outcomes, and, therefore, schools need to partner with families and communities to promote it. Nye et al. (2007) demonstrated through a cumulative analysis of studies of parent involvement over the last 40 years, that solely on the basis of randomized control trials conducted between 1964 and 1971, a well founded conclusion that the effect of parent involvement is positive and statistically significant could have been drawn. In essence, in spite of conflicting qualitative syntheses of the literature, we have known definitively that family involvement is an effective strategy for promoting achievement for over thirty years. Since that time, research targeted overwhelmingly at reading outcomes has documented the numerous ways that families support reading achievement and to a far lesser extent mathematics. Few research studies have developed and evaluated programs to enhance family involvement strategies that have been associated with achievement in these areas. Thus, it is not difficult to explain why it has taken so long for research findings to translate into educational practices. Schools, families, researchers, and policy makers must partner to change this.

Models exist for approaching program development and evaluation research in a way that readily informs practice by addressing shared goals and barriers to program implementation (e.g., Fantuzzo, Bulotsky-Shearer, & McWayne, 2006; Power, 2003). By employing a partnership approach that bridges research and practice, it is likely that family involvement programs will demonstrate greater feasibility, sustainability, and ultimately effectiveness (Kratochwill & Hoagwood, 2005). Consistent with these sentiments, school-wide intervention programs such as *Success for All* actually require an 80% endorsement rate among school faculty in order to institute the program (Cooper, Slavin, & Madden, 1998).

### Family Involvement is Multidimensional

There is a strong theoretical and empirical basis for conceptualizing family involvement as a multidimensional construct (e.g., Epstein, 1995; Fantuzzo et al., 2000). No longer can the definition of family involvement be limited to school-based contributions to education. While school-based participation has been highly correlated with student achievement (e.g., Fan & Chen, 2001), the contributions to student achievement that families provide to their children in the home are significant and undeniable (e.g., Jeynes, 2003, 2005; Nye et al., 2006). In some instances home-based efforts may be more culturally relevant and even more closely related to student achievement outcomes (e.g., Fantuzzo et al., 2004). Efforts to engage families in the educational process need to reflect the multidimensional nature of family involvement, directing efforts to both school and home settings while taking into account families cultural values and routines.

### A Variety of Family Involvement Strategies Work to Promote Reading and Mathematics

We know that family involvement works to promote achievement and that it comes in many forms, yet given the paucity of experimental studies, it isn't possible to specify with much authority which modes of family involvement are more or less salient for a particular content area such as reading or mathematics. The task becomes even more difficult when trying to consider the demographic characteristics of program recipients. The fact of the matter is that component studies of family involvement across demographic groups are unavailable. Thus, it is necessary to carefully examine the work that has been done to evaluate which practices demonstrate effectiveness for some content areas, outcome measures, and groups. Future research may bring us to a more sophisticated level of understanding that would allow for valid comparisons across home, home-school, and school-based venues for family involvement. Theoretically, though, connections among these venues are highly likely, with growing evidence supporting this premise (e.g., Dearing et al., 2006). Here, a summary of findings from the empirical literature is provided.

While the experimental literature is by no means complete, it can be said that a variety of home-based family involvement strategies for promoting reading and mathematics have been supported through experimental research. These home-based strategies have been conducted across a variety of demographic groups including predominantly low-income and minority children and families. For improving early literacy outcomes, experimentally proven home-based family involvement strategies include home visits for families of preschoolers to improve parenting skills (e.g., Manz et al., 2008) and dialogic reading to improve the quality and quantity of shared reading experiences between young children and their caregivers (e.g., Zevenbergen & Whitehurst, 2005). At the elementary level, experimentally supported strategies for promoting reading skills include: (a) shared reading strategies such as having children read to their parents (e.g., Tizard et al., 1982) and paired reading, a specific form of shared reading which includes parents and children reading together along with error correction and positive reinforcement (Topping, 1992), and (b) parent teaching of specific literacy skills both with (i.e., *Reading Recovery*, Faires et al., 2000; *Teach Your Child to Read in 100 Easy Lessons*, Leach & Siddall, 1990; *Reading Made Easy*, Mehran & White, 1988) and without specified print materials (e.g., Kraft et al., 2001). In mathematics, in conjunction with increased positive home-school communication, home-based support for learning in the form of parental encouragement rather than teaching has been linked to both mathematics achievement and behavioral and affective outcomes for low-income elementary students (e.g., Fantuzzo et al., 1995).

Often the home-based strategies employed in these family involvement programs involve elements of home-school communication (e.g., Fantuzzo et al., 1995) as they are generally conducted through the schools which incidentally or intentionally promote home-school contact in the process of providing support to families for their home-based educational involvement. Thus, it is difficult to sort out the unique effects of improved home-school relations outside of home-based support for learning and visa-versa. Finally, correlational research clearly demonstrates positive relationships between school-based family involvement (i.e., participation in school events, conferences, etc.) and both reading and mathematics outcomes for children. Thus, efforts in schools to promote reading and mathematics achievement must consider both home and school-based mechanisms for involving families through increased collaboration and communication with families.

### *Family Involvement Works to Promote Achievement for Vulnerable Student Groups*

The empirical literature shows that family involvement promotes reading and mathematics outcomes in early childhood through elementary school aged children across demographic groups. Two meta-analyses of the family involvement literature specifically validated family involvement as a strategy for supporting achievement in vulnerable groups of students including urban elementary (Jeynes, 2005) and minority students (Jeynes, 2003). On average, across different modalities, family involvement was shown to produce moderate effects on reading and overall achievement (including mathematics). While reading outcomes have been studied more in the literature, the few published controlled studies of family involvement on elementary mathematics outcomes were conducted exclusively with low-income, predominantly African American students and produced quite large effects (i.e., Fantuzzo et al., 1992, 1995). Thus, family involvement, broadly conceptualized, should be considered in addressing individual student achievement as well as systems-level strategies for school improvement.

Family involvement is an evidence-based strategy for promoting reading and mathematics achievement across demographic groups including low-income and minority children. As educational legislation (e.g., No Child Left Behind), initiatives (e.g., Reading

First), and professional practice organizations (e.g., American Psychological Association Division 16, What Works Clearing House) increasingly recognize the importance of instituting educational practices for which sufficient evidence of effectiveness exists, family involvement must be considered as a strategy specifically for children with identified risk factors such as minority or poverty status.

## REFERENCES

Arnold, D. H., Lonigan, C. J., Whitehurst, G. J., & Epstein, J. N. (1994). Accelerating language development through picture book reading: Replication and extensions to a videotape training format. *Journal of Educational Psychology, 24*(4), 552–559.

Aspiazu, G. G., Bauer, S. C., & Spillett, M. (1998). Improving the academic performance of hispanic youth: A community education model. *Bilingual Research Journal, 22*(2–4), 127–147.

Becker, H. J., & Epstein, J. L. (1982). Parent involvement: A survey of teacher practices. *The Elementary School Journal, 83*(2), 85–102.

Binford, V., & Robertson, R. (1996). Fairfield Court Elementary: Teamwork through home, school, and community. *Journal of Education for Students Placed at Risk, 1,* 219–232.

Bronfenbrenner, U., & Morris, P. A. (1998). *The ecology of developmental processes.* Hoboken, NJ: Wiley.

Bus, A. G., van IJzendoorn, M. H., & Pellegrini, A. D. (1995). Joint book reading makes for success in learning to read: A meta-analysis on intergenerational transmission of literacy. *Review of Educational Research, 65*(1), 1–21.

Carlson, C., & Christenson, S. L. (2005). Evidence-based parent and family interventions in school psychology: State of scientifically based practice. *School Psychology Quarterly, 20,* 525–528.

Choi, Y., Mericle, A., & Harachi, T. W. (2006). Using Rasch analysis to test the cross-culturalitem equivalence of the Harvard Trauma Questionnaire and the Hopkins Symptom Checklist across Vietnamese and Cambodian immigrant mothers. *Journal of Applied Measurement, 7,* 16–38.

Christenson, S., Rounds, T., & Gorney, D. (1992). Family factors and student achievement: An avenue to increase students' success. *School Psychology Quarterly, 7,* 178–206.

Christenson, S. L. (2004). The family-school partnership: An opportunity to promote the learning competence of all students. *School Psychology Review, 33*(1), 83–104.

Cooper, R., Slavin, R. E., & Madden, N. A. (1998). Success for All: Improving the quality of implementation of whole-school change through the use of a national reform network. *Education and Urban Society, 30*(3), 385–408.

Crain-Thorenson, C., & Dale, P. S. (1999). Enhancing linguistic performance: Parents and teachers as book reading partners for children with language delays. *Topics in Early Childhood Special Education, 19*(1), 28–39.

Dearing, E., Kreider, H., Simpkins, S., & Weiss, H. B. (2006). Family involvement in school and low-income children's literacy: Longitudinal associations between and within families. *Journal of Educational Psychology, 98,* 653–664.

Dickinson, D. K., & Smith, M. (1994). Long-term effects of preschool teachers' book readings on low-income children's vocabulary and story comprehension. *Reading Research Quarterly, 29,* 104–122.

Engelmann, S., Haddox, P., & Bruner, E. (1983). *Teach your child to read in 100 easy lessons.* New York: Simon & Schuster.

Englund, M. M., Luckner, A. E., Whaley, G. J. L., & Egeland, B. (2004). Children's achievement in early elementary school: Longitudinal effects of parental involvement, expectations, and quality of assistance. *Journal of Educational Psychology, 96,* 723–730.

Epstein, J. (1991). Effects of achievement of teachers' practices of family involvement. *Advances in Reading/Language Research, 5,* 261–276.

Epstein, J. L. (1995). School/family/community partnerships: caring for the children we share. *Phi Delta Kappan, 76,* 701–712.

Faires, J., Nichols, W. D., & Rickelman, R. J. (2000). Effects of parental involvement in developing competent readers in first grade. *Reading Psychology, 21,* 195–215.

Fan, X., & Chen, M. (2001). *Parental involvement and students' academic achievement: A meta-analysis. Educational Psychology Review, 13*(1), 1–22.

Fantuzzo, J. W., Bulotsky-Shearer, R. J., & McWayne, C. M. (2006). *The pursuit of wellness for victims of child maltreatment: A model for targeting relevant competencies, contexts, and contributors*. Washington, DC: American Psychological Association.

Fantuzzo, J., Davis, G., & Ginsburg, M. (1995). Effects of collaborative learning and parent involvement on mathematics achievement and perceived competencies. *Journal of Educational Psychology, 87*, 272–281.

Fantuzzo, J. W., King, J. A., & Heller, L. R. (1992). Effects of reciprocal peer tutoring on mathematics and school adjustment: A component analysis. *Journal of Educational Psychology, 84*(3), 331–339.

Fantuzzo, J., McWayne, C., Perry, M. A., & Childs, S. (2004). Multiple dimensions of family involvement and their relations to behavioral and learning competencies for urban, low-income children. *School Psychology Review, 33*, 467–480.

Fantuzzo, J. W., Tighe, E., & Childs, S. (2000). Family involvement questionnaire: A multivariate assessment of family participation in early childhood education. *Journal of Educational Psychology, 92*(2), 367–376.

Federal Interagency Forum on Child and Family Statistics. (2008). *America's Children in Brief: Key National Indicators of Well-Being, 2008*. Federal Interagency Forum on Child and Family Statistics, Washington, DC: U.S. Government Printing Office.

Foster, S. M., & Bitner, T. R. (1998). A read-aloud project for at-risk kindergarten children and their parents. *The Indiana Reading Journal, 30*, 50–55.

Fuller, B., Eggers-Piérola, C., Holloway, S. D., & Liang, X. (1996). Rich culture, poor markets:Why do latino parents forgo preschooling? *Teachers College Record, 97*(3), 400–418.

Galper, A., Wigfield, A., & Seefeldt, C. (1997). Head start parents' beliefs about their children's abilities, task values, and performances on different activities. *Child Development, 68*(5), 897–907.

Gándara, P. (2001). *Paving the way to postsecondary education: K-12 intervention programs for underrepresented youth. Report of the national postsecondary education cooperative working group on access to postsecondary education* (Report No. NCES-2001-205). Jessup, MD: ED Pubs.

Ginsburg-Block, M., & Manz, P. H. (March, 2005). *Examining Elementary Family School Collaboration Practices Among Diverse Midwestern Families*. Paper presented at the Annual Meeting of the National Association of School Psychologists, Atlanta, GA.

Goldenberg, C. N. (1987). Low-income hispanic parents' contributions to their first-grade children's word-recognition skills. *Anthropology and Education Quarterly, 18*(3), 149–179.

Goldenberg, C., Gallimore, R., Reese, L., & Garnier, H. (2001). Cause or effect? A longitudinal study of immigrant latino parents' aspirations and expectations, and their children's school performance. *American Educational Research Journal, 38*(3), 547–582.

Gomby, D. (2003). Building school readiness through home visitation: A review prepared for the First 5 California Children and Families Commission. Sunnyvale, CA: Deanna Gomby Consulting. Retrieved July 14, 2008, from http://www.ccfc.ca.gov/pdf/help/executivesummaryfinal.pdf

Graue, M. E., Weinstein, T., & Walberg, H. J. (1983). School-based home instruction and learning: A quantitative synthesis. *Journal of Educational Research, 76*, 351–360.

Griffith, J. (1996). Relation of parental involvement, empowerment, and school traits tostudent academic performance. *Journal of Educational Research, 90*, 33–41.

Haden, C. A., Reese, E., & Fivush. R. (1996). Mothers extratextual comments during storybook reading: Stylistic differences over time and across texts. *Discourse Processes, 21*, 135–169.

Hall, R. L., & Schaverien, L. (2001). Families' engagement with young children's cience and technology learning at home. *Science & Education, 85*, 454–481.

Hannon, P. (1987). A study of the effects of parental involvement in the teaching of reading on children's reading test performance. *British Journal of Educational Psychology, 57*, 56–72.

Hargrave, A. C., & Sénéchal, M. (2000). A book reading intervention with preschool children who have limited vocabularies: The benefits of regular reading and dialogic reading. *Early Childhood Research Quarterly, 15*(1), 75–90.

Hart, B., & Risley, T. R. (1995). *Meaningful differences in the everyday experience of young American children*. Baltimore: Paul H. Brookes.

Haynes, N. M. (2007). *The comer school development program: A pioneering approach to improving social, emotional and academic competence*. Westport, CT: Praeger Publishers/Greenwood.

Heller, L. R., & Fantuzzo, J. W. (1993). Reciprocal peer tutoring and parent partnership: Does parent involvement make a difference? *School Psychology Review, 22*(3), 517–535.

Hewison, J. (1988). The longterm effectiveness of parental involvement in reading: A follow-up to the Haringey Reading Project. *British Journal of Educational Psychology, 58*, 184–190.

Huebner, C. E. (2000). Promoting toddlers' language development through community-based intervention. *Journal of Applied Developmental Psychology, 21*(5), 513–535.

Huebner, C. E., & Meltzoff, A. N. (2005). Intervention to change parent-child reading style: A comparison of instructional methods. *Applied Developmental Psychology, 26,* 276–313.

Jackson, K., & Remillard, J. T. (2005). Rethinking parent involvement: African American mothers construct their roles in the mathematics education of their children. *School Community Journal, 15*(1), 51–73.

Jeynes, W. H. (2003). A meta-analysis: The effects of parental involvement on minority children's academic achievement education and urban society. *Education and Urban Society, 35*(2), 202–218.

Jeynes, W. H. (2005). A meta-analysis of the relation of parental involvement to urban elementary school student academic achievements. *Urban Education, 40* (3), 237–269.

Jordan, G. E., Snow, C. E., & Porche, M. V. (2000). Project EASE: The effect of a family literacy project on kindergarten students' early literacy skills. *Reading Research Quarterly, 35,* 524–546.

Keith, T. Z., Keith, P. B., Quirk, K. J., Sperduto, J., Santillo, S., & Killings, S. (1998). Longitudinal effects of parent involvement on high school grades: Similarities and differences across gender and ethnic groups. *Journal of School Psychology, 36*(3), 335–363.

Kraft, B. L., Findlay, P., Major, J., Gilberts, G., & Hofmeister, A. (2001). The association between a home reading program and young children's early reading skill. *Journal of Direct Instruction, 1,* 117–136.

Kratochwill, T. R., & Hoagwood, K. E. (2005). Evidence-based parent and family interventions in school psychology: Conceptual and methodological considerations in advancing best practices. *School Psychology Quarterly, 20,* 504–511.

Landerholm, E., Rubenstein, D., & Losch, M. (1994). *Involving parents of young children in science, math and literacy activities.* Unpublished manuscript, Northeastern Illinois University, Chicago, IL.

Leach, D. J., & Siddall, S. W. (1990). Parental involvement in the teaching of reading: A comparison of hearing reading, paired reading, pause, prompt, praise, and direct instruction methods. *British Journal of Educational Psychology, 60*(3), 349–355.

Levenstein, P., Levenstein, S., & Oliver, D (2002). First grade school readiness of former participants in a South Carolina replication of the Parent-Child Home Program. *Journal of Applied Developmental Psychology, 23*(3), 331–353.

Linver, M. R., Brooks-Gunn, J., & Kohen, D. E. (2002). Family processes as pathways from income to young children's development. *Developmental Psychology, 38*(5), 719–734.

Lonigan, C. J., & Whitehurst, G. J. (1998). Relative efficacy of parent and teacher involvement in a shared-reading intervention for preschool children from low-income backgrounds. *Early Childhood Research Quarterly, 13*(2), 263–290.

Lopez, M. L. (2004). *Multidimensional perspectives on readiness: The evolution of "readiness" within a rapidly changing cultural & ecological context.* Invited address for the 4th Annual Cross-University Collaborative Mentoring Conference. New York University. New York, NY.

Love, J. M., Kisker, E., Ross, C., Raikes, H., Constantine, J., Boller, K., et al. (2005). The effectiveness of Early Head Start for three-year old children and their parents: Lessons for policy and programs. *Developmental Psychology, 41*(6), 885–901.

Madden, J., Levenstein, P, & Levenstein, S. (1976). Longitudinal IQ outcomes of the Mother Child Home Program. *Child Development, 47*(4), 1015–1025.

Magnuson, K. A., & Waldfogel, J. (2005). Early childcare and education: Effects on ethnic and racial gaps in school readiness. *The Future of Children, 15*(1), 15–34.

Manz, P. H., Barnabas, E. R., Bracaliello, C., Williams, P., Zuniga, C. (2008, June). *Project CARES: A case illustration of conducting culturally-valid, early childhood research in partnership with stakeholders.* Poster presentation at Head Start's Ninth National Research Conference, Washington, DC.

Manz, P. H., Fantuzzo, J. W., & Power, T. J., (2004). Multidimensional assessment of family involvement among urban, elementary students. *Journal of School Psychology, 42*(6), 461–475.

Manz, P. H., & Lehtinen, J. (2005, August). The interrelationship of Head Start's home visiting and family involvement. Poster presented at the APA Annual Convention, Washington, DC.

Mattingly, D. J., Prislin, R., McKenzie, T. L., Rodriguez, J. L., & Kayzar, B. (2002). Evaluating evaluations: The case of parent involvement programs. *Review of Educational Research, 72*(4), 549–576.

McBride, B., Bae, J., & Wright, M. S. (2002). An examination of family-school partnership initiatives in rural prekindergarten programs. *Early Education & Development, 13,* 107–127.

McWayne, C. M. (2006, April). *Mothers' and fathers' involvement in low-income preschool children's education.* Symposium presentation, Chaired by Weiss, H. & Hoover-Dempsey, K., New research on family involvement and academic achievement, presented at the American Educational Research Association Annual Meeting, San Francisco, CA.

McWayne, C. M., Manz, P. H., & Ginsburg-Block, G. (2007). *Enhancing the cultural validity of the Family Involvement Questionnaire for low-income, Latino families of preschool children.* Report submitted to the Society for the Study of School Psychology.

McWayne, C., Manz, P. H., & Ginsburg-Block, M. (2008). A multistrategy approach for investigating the cultural relevance of behavioral rating scales: A "Goldilocks and the Three Factors" story. Unpublished manuscript.

McWayne, C., Campos, R., & Owisanik, M. (2008). Family involvement in preschool: A multidimensional, multi-level examination of mother and father involvement among low-income, culturally diverse families. *Journal of School Psychology, 46,* 551–573.

Mehran, M., & White, K. R. (1988). Parent tutoring as a supplement to compensatory education for first-grade children. *Remedial and Special Education (RASE), 9,* 35–41.

Melzi, G. & Caspe, M. (2005). Variations in maternal narrative styles during book reading interactions. *Narrative Inquiry, 15*(1), 101–125.

Miller, A., Robson, D., & Bushell, R. (1986). Parental participation in paired reading: A controlled study. *Educational Psychology, 6,* 277–284.

Niedermeyer, F. C. (1970). Parents teach kindergarten reading at home. *The Elementary School Journal, 70,* 438–445.

Nye, C. Turner, H., & Schwartz, J. (2007). *Approaches to parent involvement for improving the academic performance of elementary school age children.* Retrieved July 14, 2008, from http://www.sfi.dk/sw43574.asp

Orfield, G. (2001). *Schools more separate: Consequences of a decade of resegregation.* Cambridge, MA: Civil Rights Project, Harvard University.

Parke, R. D., Coltrane, Borthwick-Duffy, S., Powers, S., Adams, J., Fabricius, M., et al. (2004). *Assessing father involvement in Mexican-American families.* Mahwah, NJ: Erlbaum.

Portes, A., & Rumbaut, R. G. (2001). *Legacies: The story of the immigrant second generation.* Berkeley and Los Angeles, CA: University of California Press.

Powell-Smith, K. A., Shinn, M. R., Stoner, G., & Good, R. H. (2000). Parent tutoring in reading using literature and curriculum materials: Impact on student reading achievement. *School Psychology Review, 29*(1), 5–27.

Power, T. J. (2003). Promoting children's mental health: Reform through interdisciplinary and community partnerships. *School Psychology Review, 32,* 3–16.

Prelow, H. M. & Loukas, A. (2003). The role of resource, protective, and risk factors on academic achievement-related outcomes of economically disadvantaged Latino youth. *Journal of Community Psychology, 31*(5), 513–529.

Raikes, H., Green, B., Atwater, J., Kisker, E., Constantine, J., & Chazan-Cohen, R. (2006). Involvement in Early Head Start home visiting services: Demographic predictions and relations to child and parent outcomes. *Early Childhood Research Quarterly, 21,* 2–24.

Reese, E. & Cox, A. (1999). Quality of adult book reading affects children's emergent literacy. *Developmental Psychology, 35*(1), 20–28.

Reese, E., Cox, A., Harte, D., & McAnally, H. (2003). *Diversity in adults' styles of reading books to children.* Mahwah, NJ: Erlbaum.

Reynolds, A. J., Mavrogenes, N. A., Bezruckzko, N., & Hagemann, M. (1996). Cognitive and family-support mediators of preschool effectiveness: A confirmatory analysis. *Child Development, 67,* 1119–1140.

Reynolds, A. J., Weissberg, R. P., & Kasprow, W. J. (1992). Prediction of early social and academic adjustment of children from the inner city. *American Journal of Community Psychology, 20,* 599–624.

Rimm-Kaufman, S. E., & Pianta, R. C. (2005). Family-school communication in preschool and kindergarten in the context of a relationship-enhancing intervention. *Early Education and Development, 16*(3), 287–316.

Roberts, J., Jurgens, J., & Burchinal, M. (2005). The role of home literacy practices in preschool children's language and emergent literacy skills. *Journal of Speech, Language, and Hearing Research, 48*(2), 345–359.

Rush, K. (1999). Caregiver-child interactions and early literacy development of preschool children from low-income environments. *Topics in Early Childhood Special Education, 19*(1), 3–14.

Scarborough, H. S., & Dobrich, W. (1994). On the efficacy of reading to preschoolers. *Developmental Review, 14,* 245–302.

Searls, E., Lewis, M. B., & Morrow, Y. B. (1982). Parents as tutors—it works! *Reading Psychology, 3,* 117–129.

Sears, N., & Medearis, L. (1992, October). *Natural math: A progress report on implementation of a family involvement project for early childhood mathematics among children of the Oklahoma Seminole Head Start and Boley Head Start.* Paper presented at the meeting of the Rocky Mountain Research Association, Stillwater, OK.

Seefeldt, C., Denton, K., Galper, A., & Younoszai, T. (1999). The relation between Head Start parents' participation in a transition demonstration, education, efficacy and their children's academic abilities. *Early Childhood Research Quarterly, 14,* 99–109.

Sénéchal. M. (2006). *The effect of family literacy interventions on children's acquisition of reading from kindergarten to grade 3: A meta-analytic review.* Portsmouth, NH: RMC Research Corporation.

Sénéchal, M., LeFevre, J.-A., Thomas, E., & Daley, K. (1998). Differential effects of home literacy experiences on the development of oral and written language. *Reading Research Quarterly, 32,* 96–116.

Shadish, W. R., Cook, T. D., & Campbell, D. T. (2002). *Experimental and quasi-experimental designs for generalized causal inference.* Boston, MA: Houghton Mifflin.

Shaver, A. V. & Walls, R. T. (1998). Effect of title 1 parent involvement on student reading and mathematics achievement. *Journal of Research and Development in Education, 31,* 90–97.

Sheldon, S. B. (2002). Parents' social networks and beliefs as predictors of parent involvement. *The Elementary School Journal, 102,* 301–316.

Slaughter-Defoe, D. T. (1995). Revisiting the concept of socialization: Caregiving and teaching in the 90's—A personal perspective. *American Psychologist, 50*(4), 276–286.

Slavin, R. E., & Madden, N. A. (2006). Reducing the gap: Success for all and the achievement of African American students. *Journal of Negro Education. Special Issue: Research and its Impact on Educational Policy and Practice, 75*(3), 389–400.

Smith, R. M. (1991). The Distributional Properties of Rasch Item Fit Statistics. *Educational and Psychological Measurement, 51,* 541–565.

Smith, R. M., Schumaker, R. E., & Bush, M. J. (1998). Using item mean squares to evaluate fit to the Rasch model. *Journal of Outcome Measurement, 2*(1), 66–78.

Sosa, A. S. (1997). Involving Hispanic parents in educational activities through collaborative relationships. *Bilingual Research Journal, 21* (2/3) 285–293.

Steinberg, L., Lamborn, S. D., Dornbusch, S. M., & Darling, N. (1992). Impact of parenting practices on adolescent achievement: Authoritative parenting, school involvement, and encouragement to succeed. *Child Development, 63*(5), 1266–1281.

Stevenson, D. L. & Baker, D. P. (1987). The family-school relation and the child's school performance. *Child Development, 58,* 1348–1357.

Storch, S. A., & Whitehurst, G. J. (2002). Oral language and code-related precursors to reading: Evidence from a longitudinal structural model. *Developmental Psychology, 38,* 934–947.

Suárez-Orozco, M. M., & Paez, M. M. (Eds.). (2002). *Latinos: Remaking America.* Berkeley: University of California Press.

Suárez-Orozco, C., & Suárez-Orozco, M. M. (2001). *Children of immigration. the developing child series.* Cambridge, MA: Harvard University Press.

Sui-Chu, E. H., & Willms, J. D. (1996). Effects of parental involvement on eighth-grade achievement. *Sociological Quarterly, 69*(2), 126–141.

Sweet, M. A., & Appelbaum, M. I. (2004). Is home visiting an effective strategy? A meta-analytic review of home visiting programs for families with young children. *Child Development, 75*(5), 1435–1456.

Tizard, J., Schofield, W. N. & Hewison, J. (1982). Collaboration between teachers and parents in assisting children's reading. *British Journal of Educational Psychology, 52,* 1–15.

Topping, K. J. (1992). Short- and long-term follow-up of parental involvement in reading projects. *British Educational Research Journal, 18,* 369–379.

U.S. Department of Health and Human Services. (2001). *Head Start FACES: Longitudinal findings on program performance. Third progress report.* Washington, DC: Author.

Valenzuela, A. (1999). *Subtractive schooling: U.S.-Mexican youth and the politics of caring. SUNY series, the social context of education.* Ithaca: State University of New York Press.

Vinograd-Bausell, C. R., & Bausell, R. B. (1987). Home teaching of word recognition skills. *Journal of Research and Development in Education, 20,* 57–65.

Wagner, M., & Clayton, S. (1999). The parents as teachers program: Results from two demonstrations. *The Future of Children, 9,* 91–115.

Watkins, T. J. (1997). Teacher communications, child achievement, and parent traits in parent involvement models. *The Journal of Educational Research, 91,* 3–14.

Whitehurst, G. J., Epstein, J. N., Angell, A. L., Payne, A. C., Crone, D. A., & Fischel, J. E. (1994). Outcomes of an emergent literacy intervention in Head Start. *Journal of Educational Psychology, 86,* 542–555.

Whitehurst, G. J., Falco, F. L., Lonigan, C. J., Fischel, J. E., DeBaryshe, B. D., Valdez-Menchaca, & Caulfield, M. (1988). Accelerating language development through picture book reading. *Developmental Psychology, 24*(4), 552–559.

Whitehurst, G. J., Zevenbergen, A. A., Crone, D. A., Schultz, M. D., Velting, O. N., & Fischel, J. E. (1999). Outcomes of an emergent literacy intervention from Head Start through second grade. *Journal of Educational Psychology, 91*(2), 261–272.

Wilks, R. T. J., & Clarke, V. A. (1988). Training versus nontraining of mothers as home reading tutors. *Perceptual and Motor Skills, 67,* 135–142.

Wong, S. W., & Hughes, J. N. (2006). Ethnicity and language contributions to dimensions of parent involvement. *School Psychology Review, 35*(4), 645–662.

Yan, W., & Lin, Q. (2005). Parent involvement and mathematics achievement: Contrast across racial and ethnic groups. *Journal of Educational Research, 99*(2), 116–127.

Zevenbergen, A. A., & Whitehurst, G. J. (2003). Dialogic reading: A shared picture book reading intervention for preschoolers. In A. van Kleeck, A. S. Stahl, & E. B. Bauer (Eds.), *On reading books to children: Parents and teachers* (pp. 177–200). Mahwah, NJ: Erlbaum.

Zigler, E. F., & Muenchow, S. (1992). *Head start: The inside story of America's most successful educational experiment.* New York: Basic Books.

# 9

## A SCHOOL–FAMILY PARTNERSHIP

### Addressing Multiple Risk Factors to Improve School Readiness and Prevent Conduct Problems in Young Children

#### CAROLYN WEBSTER-STRATTON AND M. JAMILA REID

While researchers have long considered intelligence to be a key predictor of success in school, recent studies indicate that the social and emotional adjustment of young children are strong predictors of early academic achievement even after controlling for variations in children's cognitive abilities and family resources (Grolnick & Slowiaczek, 1994; Raver & Zigler, 1997). Children with emotional difficulties such as Oppositional Defiant Disorder (ODD), Attention Deficit Hyperactivity Disorder (ADHD) and "early onset" conduct problems (CPs) (defined as high rates of aggression, noncompliance, and oppositional behaviors) are at high risk for underachievement, school absences, and eventual school drop out (Moffitt, 1993; Tremblay, Mass, Pagani, & Vitaro, 1996). Data from the National Center for Education Statistics survey of kindergarten teachers indicate that teachers' predominant concern is for regulatory and emotional aspects of children's behavior (West, Denton, & Reaney, 2001). In particular, 84% of teachers endorsed that children need to be able to communicate wants, needs, and thoughts verbally and 60% endorsed that children need to be able to follow directions, not be disruptive in class, and be sensitive to other children's feelings in order to succeed in school. In contrast, only 21% endorsed the idea that children need to be able to use a pencil, and only 7% endorsed knowing several letters of the alphabet and being able to count to 20 as very important to being ready for kindergarten. This survey suggests that teachers are most concerned that children have the prerequisite emotional self-regulation (engagement, ability to stay on task, feelings vocabulary, ability to manage anger) and social skills (cooperation, sharing, helping) that will allow for manageable classrooms, and children's effective academic learning.

Unfortunately, prevalence studies suggest that aggressive and oppositional behaviors in children are starting earlier and escalating in intensity (Patterson, Capaldi, & Bank, 1991; Snyder, 2001). Studies indicate that 7–20% of young children exhibit "early-onset" conduct problems and meet diagnostic criteria for ODD, and these rates may be as high as 35% for low-income families (Rimm-Kaufman, Pianta, & Cox, 2000; Webster-Stratton & Hammond, 1998; Webster-Stratton & Lindsay, 1999). In a survey conducted by the National Center for Early Development and Learning, 46% of a nationally representative sample of kindergarten teachers indicated that over half of the children in their classrooms lacked the kinds of self-regulatory skills that would enable them to function productively in kindergarten (West et al., 2001). Thus, it is clear that there is an urgent need for preventative and early intervention efforts designed to promote school readiness and reduce conduct problems so that children are able to achieve the desired academic outcomes.

## OVERVIEW

In this chapter we will review the Incredible Years (IY) Parent, Teacher and Child Training Curricula and summarize research on the effectiveness of these three programs for reducing risk factors and strengthening protective factors associated with children's social emotional development and school success. The chapter will include a focus on the role of home-school partnerships in preventing and treating children's behavior problems and improving their school readiness as well as practical tips for engaging schools in the prevention and intervention process.

## RISK FACTORS FOR POOR SOCIAL-EMOTIONAL DEVELOPMENT AND CONDUCT PROBLEMS

Children's social-emotional development occurs in a number of important areas: (a) emotional self-regulation (e.g., ability to identify and manage strong emotions such as anger, excitement, and frustration); (b) social competence (e.g., sharing, helping, cooperation, positive peer interactions, prosocial problem solving); and (c) compliance and cooperation to school rules and adults' requests. There is no single risk factor that leads to poor social development and conduct problems, rather it is the cumulative effect of multiple risk factors that intertwine and cascade to increase risk for poor outcomes (Coie et al., 1993; Hawkins, Catalano, & Miller, 1992). Risk factors are grouped into four categories: (a) parent and family risk factors, (b) poverty, (c) school and classroom risk factors, and (d) child biological risk factors.

### Parent and Family Risk Factors

Research has consistently identified a set of family "risk factors" that increase the odds that children will struggle with emotional, behavioral, and cognitive difficulties. Family risk factors indicate that children from low education, highly stressed or isolated families, single-parent families, and families with low proficiency in English are at higher risk for developing social and emotional problems. Children from families where there is marital discord or abuse, maternal depression, or drug abuse are also at risk (Hawkins et al., 1992). Parenting practices associated with the development of behavior problems include inconsistent and harsh discipline, low monitoring, low school involvement, and poor cognitive stimulation at home (Snyder, Schrepferman, & St. Peter, 1997).

*Poverty*

The Early Child Longitudinal Survey (ECLS), a nationally representative sample of over 22,000 kindergarten children, suggests that exposure to multiple poverty-related risks increases the odds that children will demonstrate more behavioral problems and less academic, social, and emotional competence. Offord and colleagues found that low income is a significant risk factor for the early onset of conduct problems and social and academic deficits (Offord, Alder, & Boyle, 1986). A study of low-income preschool classrooms highlights the high need of economically disadvantaged children indicating that, on average, these children exhibited 32 negative behaviors in 10 minutes (Goldstein, Arnold, Rosenberg, Stowe, & Ortiz, 2001).

## School and Classroom Risk Factors

Negative academic and social experiences contribute to poor school performance (Coie & Dodge, 1998). Aggressive, disruptive children quickly become socially excluded (Dodge, Coie, Pettit, & Price, 1990; Ladd, 1990) and so have fewer opportunities to interact socially and to learn friendship skills. Over time, peers become mistrustful and respond to aggressive children in ways that increase the likelihood of reactive aggression (Dodge et al., 1990; Dodge & Somberg, 1987). Evidence suggests that peer rejection eventually leads to association with deviant peers (Patterson, Reid, & Dishion, 1992), which increases the risk for academic underachievement, school drop out, and drug abuse.

Research highlights the role that teachers can play in preventing this negative school cycle by using good classroom management techniques, developing clear classroom rules about bullying and social isolation, and conducting direct instruction in friendship skills and conflict management skills (e.g., Brophy, 1996). Longitudinal research demonstrates that low-income children in high-quality child care settings with positive teacher-student relationships, effective management, and opportunities for positive social interaction are significantly better off, both cognitively and emotionally, than similar children in low quality settings (Burchinal, Roberts, Hooper, & Zeisel, 2000).

Unfortunately, however, the highest-risk children are often placed in school situations that do not provide them with the support they need. A troubling 1994 survey found that teachers serving predominantly low-income children used significantly more harsh, detached, and insensitive teaching strategies than teachers serving middle-income children (Phillips, Voran, Kisker, Howes, & Whitebrook, 1994; Stage & Quiroz, 1997). Other research shows that children with behavior problems are less likely to be accepted by teachers, and receive less academic instruction, support, and positive feedback for appropriate behavior (Arnold, Griffith, Ortiz, & Stowe, 1998; Arnold et al., 1999; Carr, Taylor, & Robinson, 1991). Moreover, teachers are less likely to recognize cognitive competencies in young children whose behaviors they perceive as negative (Espinosa, 1995). In summary, children with behavior problems are more likely to be the recipients of poor classroom management and are often disliked by teachers and peers (Birch & Ladd, 1997).

A preventive model also requires supportive networks between parents and schools, children and schools, and parents and teachers (Hawkins & Weiss, 1985). While most teachers want to be active partners with parents, teacher education programs devote little attention to helping them learn ways to build partnerships with parents (Chavkin, 1991), and many teachers lack the skills or training to work collaboratively with families (Burton, 1992; Epstein, 1992). This can lead to a spiraling pattern of child negative behavior, teacher reactivity, and parent demoralization and withdrawal, which results in a lack of connection and consistency between the school and home (Webster-Stratton, 1996).

Clearly, providing teachers with training in effective classroom management and methods to support children's social development is crucial to providing a school environment where children can learn and excel. A focus on home-school connections and communication will also benefit from parents' increased expectations, interest in, and support for their children's social and academic performance (Hawkins & Weiss, 1985) and a consistent socialization process across home and school settings.

### Child Risk Factors

Child-specific developmental or temperament risk factors such as negative emotionality, attention deficit/hyperactivity disorder, impulsivity, language delays, and deficits in social-cognitive skills contribute to poor emotional regulation (Underwood, 1997), compliance problems and aggressive peer interactions (Dodge & Price, 1994). Children with these self-regulation problems frequently define social interactions in hostile ways, seek less information, generate fewer alternative solutions to social problems, and anticipate fewer consequences for aggression (Richard & Dodge, 1982; Rubin & Krasnor, 1986). These children distort social cues during peer interactions (Milich & Dodge, 1984) and make attributions of hostile intent to neutral interactions, causing them to react aggressively (Dodge, 1993). Aggressive behavior in children is correlated with low empathy (Feshbach, 1989), which may contribute to lack of social competencies and antisocial behavior. Finally, studies indicate that children with conduct problems have significant delays in their peer play skills; in particular, difficulty with reciprocal play, cooperation, turn taking, waiting, and giving suggestions (Webster-Stratton & Lindsay, 1999). These poor play skills result in them being rejected or isolated by other children, which further perpetuates their social problems.

Poor social-emotional development often exists in combination with academic delays (Webster-Stratton & Lindsay, 1999) and learning problems (Moffitt & Lynam, 1994). This relationship between academic performance and social and emotional competence is bi-directional. Academic difficulties may cause disengagement, increased frustration, and lower self-esteem, which may trigger the emergence or escalation of children's behavior problems. At the same time, noncompliance, aggression, elevated activity levels, and poor attention limit a child's ability to engage in learning, and result in less teacher encouragement and instruction. Thus, a cycle is created whereby one problem exacerbates the other (Schonfeld, Shaffer, O'Connor, & Portnoy, 1988). The combination of academic delays and behavior problems eventually leads to more severe behavior problems and school failure.

## A COMPREHENSIVE PREVENTION/INTERVENTION APPROACH

In summary, risk factors for children's conduct problems operate across settings. Comprehensive interventions are needed that address parent/family, teacher/classroom, and child risk factors as well as the interplay between these risk factors in the home and school settings. Interventions delivered in one setting (e.g., home or school) are less effective than interventions that cross settings and foster communication between the important caregivers in a child's life, that is, both parents *and* teachers (Beauchaine, Webster-Stratton, & Reid, 2005). Such coordinated interventions should be delivered as early as possible in children's school experience and should include direct instruction for children in social skills and emotion regulation as well as strategies for parents and teachers that help to effectively manage behavior, increase home-school communication, and create a positive and safe learning environment. Lastly, since children living in poverty are at increased risk, targeting interventions in day care setting and schools that serve socioeconomically disadvantaged families may be a strategic way to reach more children in need.

## INCREDIBLE YEARS PARENT, TEACHER AND CHILD PROGRAMS

The Incredible Years (IY) Parent, Teacher, and Child Training Series is a set of three comprehensive, multifaceted, developmentally based and interlocking programs designed to target the more malleable risk factors for parents, teachers, and children. Although the programs are designed so that they can be delivered in isolation (e.g., a family could participate in the parent program without also receiving the child or teacher intervention), our research shows that the combination of the parent with the teacher or child programs produces the most change in children (Beauchaine et al., 2005). The programs are designed to train parents and teachers to promote children's emotional, social, and academic competence and to prevent, reduce, and treat aggression and emotional problems in young children 2- to 8-years-old. The IY programs target preschool and early school-age children for several reasons. First, school entry is an important transition when children are exposed to a new setting and additional risk factors that begin to intertwine and cascade. Longitudinal research highlights the poor prognosis for children with early-onset conduct and social-emotional problems, suggesting that early intervention is crucial (Coie, 1990). There is evidence that the earlier intervention is offered, the more positive the child's behavioral adjustment at home and at school and the greater chance of preventing later academic and social problems (Taylor & Biglan, 1998).

In addition, preschool, day care, or kindergarten may be the first opportunity to provide services to large groups of high-risk children in a comprehensive but cost effective manner. This is often the first school experience that children have, and thus, is the first chance for intervention delivered in a classroom setting. Intervention during this first school experience can help to start children and their parents out on a positive school trajectory, smoothing the transition from home (or day care) to preschool and then from preschool to elementary school.

## Collaborative Partnerships Between Parents and Teachers

All of the Incredible Years programs are based on a collaborative model with some underlying assumptions that guide the interventions' focus on parent-teacher partnerships.

> *Assumption 1) That all parties involved in a child's care have valuable information to share about the child.* In this model, there is no "expert," rather parents and teachers are both recognized for the information they have to share about the child and his or her behavior in certain circumstances. The therapist helps to highlight this information and to guide discussions and practice around using the information to plan for intervention for the child.
>
> *Assumption 2) That each person involved in the child's care cares for the child and wants the child to be successful.* Frequently parents and teachers both feel overwhelmed and isolated. Each may blame the other for not trying hard enough or not having the answers to a child's problems. Therapists highlight the hard work and caring that both parents and teachers (and other school personnel) are putting in to help a child. They also spend time with parents and teachers separately; discussing ways that each can talk with the other about their concerns in nonconfrontive and supportive ways. As the common goals that parents and teachers have for a child are better defined, each can begin to recognize and provide recognition for the important role that the other plays.
>
> *Assumption 3) That consistency across settings is extremely important in order to provide lasting change in children's behavior.* When parents and teachers communicate about behavior plans, use the same language and strategies, and show the child that they each support the other, intervention effects will be stronger and will generalize from one setting to another. Therapists facilitate parent and teacher meetings and provide scaffolding for jointly developing behavior plans that address targeted behaviors.

### The IY Parent Program

The IY Parent Program objectives focus on strengthening parenting competencies and fostering parents' involvement with school. The goals of the program include improving parent-child relationships, decreasing behavior problems, increasing home-school communication, building supportive family networks, and helping parents to teach children social skills and emotion regulation. The method of delivering the program includes a group format in which a trained group leader facilitates discussions among parents about parenting, child development, and family issues. The program is not a didactic, one-size-fits all approach but rather is based on a collaborative model, which has been described in some detail in a book entitled, Troubled Families—Problem Children: Working With Parents: A Collaborative Process (Webster-Stratton & Herbert, 1994). Collaboration implies a reciprocal relationship based on utilizing equally the group leader's knowledge and the parents' unique strengths and cultural perspectives. Collaboration also implies respect for each person's contributions, a non-blaming relationship built on trust and open communication. For example parents are shown video vignettes of parents in a variety of common parenting situations and settings, and these serve as "triggers" to start discussions among parents. This collaborative process assures interactive learning and self-management. Parents and children shown on the vignettes represent multiple cultural backgrounds.

There are two versions of the "basic" parent curriculum: one series for parents of preschoolers (ages 3–6 years) and another set of programs for parents of early school-age children (ages 6–8 years). Recently a baby (0–12 months) and toddler series (1–3 years) were developed, and the school-age basic program was revised and expanded to include 9- to 13-year-olds. These new programs are currently undergoing evaluation. In addition to the basic parenting programs, there is also an advanced parenting program that focuses on adult interpersonal issues such as anger management, effective communication, and problem solving skills. Finally, there are two supplemental programs designed for helping parents know how to help their children succeed in school. The School Readiness Series designed for 3- to 5-year-olds and the Supporting Your Child's Education Program for 6- to 10-year-olds focus on such as topics as doing homework with children, monitoring children after school, building children's self-confidence and promoting reading skills. There are comprehensive leader's manuals (Webster-Stratton, 1984, 2001, 2007) that provide recommended protocols for offering the programs. These protocols are considered the *minimal* number of core sessions, vignettes, and content to be covered in order to achieve results similar to those in the published literature. The program topics for the basic parent programs are listed in Table 9.1. In addition to learning cognitive, behavioral and social learning principles and management skills, parents are helped to understand and accept individual differences in children's temperaments, attention spans, play skills, and abilities to regulate emotions. Parents are helped to understand how these individual developmental differences will need differing parental responses and to have developmentally appropriate expectations. Each week parents are given chapters to read from a book called *The Incredible Years: A Trouble Shooting Guide for Parents* (Webster-Stratton, 2006a) as well as behavioral practice assignments to complete at home.

**Table 9.1** Parent Program Topics

- Child-directed play
- Academic, persistence, social and emotion coaching to promote school readiness
- Interactive reading with children
- Supporting children's education (predictable homework routines and homework coaching and support)
- Effective praise and encouragement
- Using incentives to help motivate children
- Positive Disciplines: Rules, routines, and responsibilities
- Positive Disciplines: Effective limit setting
- Handling Misbehavior: Ignoring, Time Out to calm down, and logical consequences
- Teaching children to problem-solve
- Anger management
- Problem solving for adults
- Giving and getting support
- How to collaborate with teachers

## *The IY Teacher Program: Classroom Management Training*

The IY teacher classroom management curriculum (IYT) is delivered over 6 days. Like the parent program, the training is delivered in groups with trained leaders who use a collaborative training style. Similarly, video vignettes are used as catalysts for teacher group discussion and problem solving. IYT is designed to be sequenced throughout the academic year and provides time for teachers to practice skills between sessions, maximizing the opportunities for practice and transfer of training into the classroom. Teachers are given "hands on" classroom assignments and are asked to read from the book, How to Promote Children's Social and Emotional Competence (Webster-Stratton, 1999). The program topics are listed in Table 9.2. Promotion of positive teacher relationships with challenging students and developing supportive behavior plans for children who are exhibiting high levels of problem behaviors are other foci of the intervention. Teachers are taught instructional techniques to engage inattentive children in learning, encourage language and reading development by using interactive (dialogic) reading, and to coach and strengthen social skills and emotion language. Teachers work to prevent peer rejection by helping the aggressive child to use appropriate problem-solving strategies and helping his/her peers respond appropriately to aggression. As with parents, training focuses on helping teachers understand individual developmental and temperament differences (i.e., variation in attention span) and how to make adjustments for children with biological deficits (e.g., child with ADHD who is impulsive, hyperactive, and with a short attention span or child with learning delays) and the relevance of these differences for instructional teaching strategies that are positive, consistent, and developmentally appropriate. Physical aggression in unstructured settings (e.g. playground, during choice times) is targeted for close monitoring, teaching, and incentive programs. Another theme throughout this training process is to strengthen the teachers' collaboration with parents through positive phone calls home or emails and regular meetings with parents to coordinate school-home behavior plans. More details about this curriculum can be found in (Webster-Stratton & Reid (2001).

**Table 9.2** Teacher Training Workshops

- Proactive Teaching Strategies: redirection, handling transitions, warnings, clear and positive classroom rules, schedules, predictable routines, specific instructions
- Promoting Academic and Social Competence: "coaching" persistence, social and self-regulatory behavior, on-task behavior, following directions, checking work
- Effective Praise and Encouragement
- Using Individual and Group Incentives to Motivate Students
- Managing Disruptive Behavior: limit setting, ignoring, Time Out and consequences, and self-management instruction
- Building Positive Relationships With Challenging Students
- Working with Parents: teacher-parent partnerships, developing positive home-school bonds, communicating about problems
- Managing Teacher Stress
- Functional Assessment and Development of Behavior Plans

## The Child Program: Dinosaur Curriculum

There are two versions of the Child Program curriculum, each with its own manual. The small group *treatment* model is designed to be offered to small groups of 4 to 6 children in weekly 2-hour sessions. Ideally, this program is offered in combination with the parent group program and lasts 20 to 22 weeks. The small group treatment model has also been used in schools as a "pull out" model whereby small groups of children are pulled out several times a week for extra tutoring with this curriculum. These sessions are usually offered by school psychologists or counselors in 1-hour sessions twice a week. More details regarding this small group intervention can be found in Webster-Stratton and Reid (2003).

The second version is a classroom curriculum that is delivered by teachers (often in partnership with school counselors or school psychologists) and includes up to 90 lessons covering three grade levels, which can be delivered 2 to 3 times a week. The delivery of this curriculum involves 15- to 25-minute large group circle time lesson discussions followed by 20 minutes of small group practice activities. There are over 200 small group activities for teachers to choose from that focus on social emotional skills as well as other school readiness activities, such as pre-reading and pre-writing activities, math and science concepts, fine and gross motor skills and creative art projects. The program topics are listed in the Table 9.3. As with the parent and teacher programs, this content is illustrated through video vignettes that children watch and discuss. In addition, teachers use child-size puppets to discuss and role-play content with the children. Learning is enhanced by activities, games, songs, colorful cue cards illustrating key concepts, and Dinosaur homework activity books. In the classroom, multiple opportunities for problem-solving practice and reinforcement from teachers take place in less structured settings, such as during choice time, in the lunchroom, or on the playground. More details about this curriculum can be found in Webster-Stratton and Reid (2004).

**Table 9.3** Dinosaur Curriculum

- Apatosaurus Unit: Wally and Dina Teach School Rules
  Making new friends; learning classroom rules; understanding what will happen if rules are broken
- Iguanodon Unit: Dina Teaches About Doing Your Best in School
  Learning how to put up a quiet hand; listening and waiting skills; learning how to stop, think and check; practicing cooperation skills
- Triceratops Unit: Wally Teaches About Understanding and Detecting Feelings
  Learning words for different feelings; understanding why different feelings occur; practicing talking about feelings; identifying other feelings; learning relaxation skills
- Stegosaurus Unit: Wally Teaches How to Problem Solve
  Learning to identify a problem; thinking of solutions to hypothetical problems; learning to handle common problems such as being teased, left out, hit; thinking of consequences and evaluating solutions
- Tyrannosaurus Rex Unit: Tiny Turtle Teaches Anger Management
  Recognizing anger; using self-talk, visualization and relaxation methods to control anger and calm down; practicing alternative responses to anger producing situations
- Allosaurus Unit: Molly Teaches How to Be Friendly
  Learning the concept of sharing, helping, and teamwork
- Brachiosaurus Unit
  Learning how to listen; speak up; give compliments, apologies and suggestions; and enter into groups of children already playing

# RESEARCH OUTCOMES

## Treatment Studies With Diagnosed Children

*Parent Training* Extensive research evaluating the Incredible Years Parenting Programs in numerous randomized control group trials (RCTs) indicates that the program is an effective treatment approach for reducing early onset-conduct problems (Brestan & Eyberg, 1998; Taylor & Biglan, 1998). Successful short-term outcomes have been verified by the developer (Webster-Stratton, 1982, 1984, 1989, 1994; Webster-Stratton & Hammond, 1997; Webster-Stratton, Reid, & Hammond, 2004) and by independent investigators, who found significant changes in parents' behavior and reductions in children's levels of aggression (Scott, Spender, Doolan, Jacobs, & Aspland, 2001; Taylor, Schmidt, Pepler, & Hodgins, 1998). The treatment was also effective for children who were comorbid for attention problems as well as conduct problems (Hartman, Stage, & Webster-Stratton, 2003). Generalization of the positive effects of parent training from the clinic setting to the home over reasonable follow-up periods (1 to 3 years) and to untreated child behaviors has also been demonstrated (Webster-Stratton, 1990a). However, while training parents improves children's behaviors at home, it does not necessarily result in improvements in children's behavior at school unless teachers are involved in the intervention.

In our own studies, approximately one third of children with conduct problems whose parents received parent training continued to have peer relationship problems and academic and social difficulties at school 2 to 3 years later, according to parent and teacher reports (Webster-Stratton, 1990a). These data pointed to the need for school-based intervention to help teachers manage children's aggressive behavior, support their education socially and academically, and work collaboratively with parents. A second problem with parent training is that some parents cannot, or will not, participate in parent training because of work conflicts, life stress, personal psychopathology, language barriers, or lack of motivation. Third, some parents have difficulty implementing or maintaining the strategies taught in parent training programs due to their own interpersonal and family issues (Webster-Stratton, 1990b). Furthermore, data from teachers revealed their need for training in classroom management skills, classroom social skills content, and information on home-school collaboration (Webster-Stratton, 1990a; Webster-Stratton & Hammond, 1990; Webster-Stratton, Hollinsworth, & Kolpacoff, 1989) to manage the increasing numbers of children in their classrooms with behavior problems. Since children frequently spend more time in school with teachers than with their parents, it is important to partner with teachers in providing consistent strategies for managing behavior in the classroom setting.

*Teacher Training* The IY Teacher Classroom Management Training program was first evaluated in a randomized study with children diagnosed with ODD/CD (Webster-Stratton et al., 1989). In this study children were randomly assigned to six treatment conditions including parent only training, child only training, parent + teacher training, child + teacher training, or a combination of parent + child + teacher training, and control condition. Results showed that teachers who received training used fewer inappropriate and critical discipline strategies and were more nurturing than control teachers. Ninety-four percent of teachers evaluated the training as very helpful. All of the 72 teachers in the intervention conditions that included teacher training attended or made up all of the training sessions and no teachers dropped out of the study. Immediately after treatment children in all five intervention conditions engaged in fewer aggressive and noncompliant behaviors in the classroom, and exhibited higher levels of school readiness (on-task, cooperative, attentive) than control children. However, by the 2-year follow up there was evidence that the addition of teacher training to either the parent or child treatment conditions enhanced school outcomes for children.

*Child Training*   The Incredible Years Dinosaur curriculum, a social skills, emotion, and problem-solving skills training program was first evaluated as a small group treatment program in two RCTs with 4- to 7-year-old children with conduct problems (ODD/CD). Results for children who participated in the 20 to 22 weekly treatment programs showed reductions in observed aggressive behaviors and increases in observed pro-social behavior compared with an untreated control group (Webster-Stratton & Hammond, 1997; Webster-Stratton et al., 2004). These improvements were maintained 1 and 2 years later. Moreover, treatment was also effective for children with comorbid hyperactivity, impulsivity, and attentional difficulties (Webster-Stratton, Reid, & Hammond, 2001b). Additionally, in an RCT study comparing the IY child training program with child training plus parent training results showed that adding the child program to the IY parent program enhanced long-term outcomes for children who exhibited pervasive behavior problems across settings (home and school). The combined child and parent program reduced behavior problems in both settings and improved children's social interactions and conflict management skills with peers (Webster-Stratton & Hammond, 1997).

### Prevention Studies With Higher Risk Children

Each of the three IY treatment programs, Parent, Child, and Teacher have been adapted and evaluated as selective prevention programs in schools with high numbers of socio-economically disadvantaged families.

*Parent Training*   There have been three RCTs with the parent program in schools. In the first of these studies (Webster-Stratton, 1998), the parent program was delivered to families enrolled in Head Start. Classrooms were randomly assigned to receive the IY parent group in the intervention condition or a control group of the usual Head Start services. Results with 394 parents and their 4-year-old children showed that 85% of the intervention families completed greater than 50% of the program. Following the program, mothers in the intervention condition were observed to be significantly less critical and more positive than control mothers. Teachers reported intervention mothers were more involved in their children's education. Children whose mothers were in the intervention program were observed to exhibit fewer conduct problems, less negative affect, and more positive affect than children in the control group. Teachers reported the children whose mothers were in the intervention condition to be more socially competent than control children. One year later most of the improvements noted in intervention condition mothers and children were maintained. Clinical significance analyses indicated that 71% of children were categorized as responders (i.e., moving into the normal range on standardized measures or showing > 30% improvement). Consumer satisfaction was high in all groups (including Spanish and Vietnamese participants) with 88.7% positive to very positive ratings and 95.8% saying they would recommend it to others.

The parent program has also been evaluated for parents of high-risk kindergarten and first grade students (Reid, Webster-Stratton, & Hammond, 2007). In this study a subset of children who were identified as having high-risk behaviors by parents and teachers on standardized measures were randomly assigned to receive the parent training program plus classroom training in Dinosaur Curriculum (PT+CR) or the classroom training only (CR) intervention. Parents in the combined intervention condition reported that their children showed fewer externalizing problems and more emotional regulation than parents in the classroom only condition or control conditions. Mothers were more supportive, less critical, and more bonded with their children in the condition that included parent training compared to classroom only and control mothers. Teachers reported that mothers in the intervention condition that included parent training were more involved in school than mothers in CR or control conditions. This study shows the added benefit of including a parent program alongside a classroom intervention, for higher risk students exhibiting higher rates of aggressive behavior.

*Teacher and Child Training*   The IY Teacher Classroom Management Training program has also been evaluated as a prevention program (Webster-Stratton & Reid, 2007; Webster-Stratton, Reid, & Hammond, 2001a). Head Start classrooms were randomly assigned to two conditions: an IY teacher + parent training condition or usual Head Start services. At the end of the year, observations in the classroom revealed that trained teachers showed significantly improved classroom management skills and their children showed significantly fewer conduct problems compared with control teachers and children. Results also showed that in the teacher + parent training condition there was significantly higher parent-teacher bonding than in the control condition. Teacher-parent bonding was measured by teacher report on the INVOLVE-T which includes items such as: teacher called or wrote note to parent, invited parent to visit school, attend a conference, or a school meeting, and teacher felt comfortable with parent. This study validates the use of the teacher-training program as a preventive intervention in high-risk classrooms.

Lastly, the child Dinosaur Program has been evaluated as a prevention program delivered to all children in a classroom setting in combination with the teacher-training program. In a recent RCT (Webster-Stratton, Reid, & Stoolmiller, 2008), teachers were trained in the classroom management program as well as the child dinosaur program. They delivered the curriculum in twice weekly lessons throughout the school year to students enrolled in Head Start, kindergarten, and first grade classrooms. Results from 153 teachers and 1,768 students indicated that trained teachers were significantly different from control teachers on four of five variables: harsh/critical, warm/affectionate, inconsistent/permissive, and social/emotional. Intervention teachers used more specific teaching strategies that addressed social and emotional skills than teachers in control classrooms. The effect sizes were moderate to high, indicating that the curriculum had robust effects on changing teachers' classroom management approaches. Students' behavior also changed, and observations showed significant improvement in emotional self-regulation, social competence and conduct problems compared with control students' behaviors. Here the effect sizes were strongest for those students from classrooms with the worst initial scores for school readiness and conduct problems. Teachers in the intervention group reported feeling more bonded or involved with parents of children in their classes, with the strongest effects occurring with teachers who reported initial low bonding with parents. Finally, teacher evaluations indicated that teachers were very satisfied with their training and their ability to implement the curriculum in conjunction with their academic curriculum. This study points to the added impact of a classroom-based child social and emotional training program in terms of strengthening students' overall school readiness and reducing conduct problems.

## SCHOOLS AS AN OPTIMAL SETTING FOR DELIVERING INTERVENTION PROGRAMS FOR PARENTS, TEACHERS, AND CHILDREN

Our original mission was to implement and evaluate these intervention programs in a clinic setting for children referred with the diagnoses of ODD and/or CD and/or ADHD over 25 years ago. We have come to believe there are important reasons for delivering evidence-based programs in daycare centers, Head Start, preschool, and primary schools. From a practical point of view, offering well-validated intervention programs in schools is a strategic way to provide more accessible interventions to families and children. A school-based delivery system is likely to reach many more families, particularly those of different cultural and socioeconomic backgrounds who may be reluctant to seek help in mental health centers or unable to pay for such services. Moreover, there is evidence that parent programs offered in non-stigmatizing locations, such as schools, are more likely to attract multicultural groups than programs offered in mental health clinics (Cunningham, Bremner, & Boyle, 1995). Another related advantage to delivering programs in schools is the sheer number of high-risk children that can be identified early and offered services *before* their problems have escalated, or resulted in a diagnosis, or a negative school reputation. Schools hold the potential for providing one of the most efficient and effective service delivery methods for providing preventive interventions. Schools are ideally positioned to provide parent programs as well as direct services for the children. Providing better access to such services for families is important because currently statistics show that less than 10% of children with emotion-regulation/conduct problems ever receive any mental health services (Kazdin, 1995), and even fewer ever receive an evidence-based intervention (Brestan & Eyberg, 1998). An added advantage of offering parent interventions in schools is that collaboration between teachers and parents can be promoted more easily (than in clinic settings) and offer a greater chance of increasing consistency of approaches for children across settings (from home to school and vice versa) leading to the possibility of sustained effects (Webster-Stratton et al., 2004).

Next, we see tremendous advantages for training daycare providers, teachers, and other school personnel (e.g., school psychologists, nurses) in classroom management strategies and in ways to collaborate with parents. Many caregivers and teachers have had little formal training in ways of counseling parents or working with them to develop behavior plans. Classroom teachers often have had little comprehensive training in evidence-based classroom management strategies. The importance of teacher training is emphasized by the clear consensus among child development experts that the essence of successful early school years resides in the quality of the child-teacher-parent relationship and the ability of teachers to provide a positive, consistent, and responsive classroom environment. Training teachers in effective classroom management skills will enhance the quality of teaching and instruction that teachers deliver. National studies have indicated that the number one concern of teachers is how to manage behavior problems in the classroom (West et al., 2001) and that unless they can do this they are unable to successfully teach academic skills.

Good classroom management is a necessary pre-requisite to delivering a social skills or problem-solving curriculum. While teachers skilled in good classroom management strategies will have classrooms with more cooperative children and fewer problems with aggressive behavior, there is still a need for classroom-wide social skills and problem-solving curriculum to be delivered to all students. Classroom-wide intervention (teacher and child training) is preferable to "pull out" programs for high-risk students because there are increased opportunities for more prosocial children to model appropriate skills and to provide the entire classroom with a common vocabulary and problem-solving steps to use in every day conflicts. Thus, social competence is strengthened for the lower-risk as well as the aggressive children, and the classroom environment generally fosters appropriate social skills for all children on an ongoing basis. Additionally, with a classroom-based model, while formal social skills training may consist of two to three sessions a week, teachers can provide informal reinforcement of the key concepts throughout the day as children encounter real problems. Thus, the dosage of intervention is greatly magnified. Unfortunately, few teachers have been trained to deliver evidence-based social skills curricula or are given the time in their schedule to offer such programs in the ways they were designed to be delivered. Even with the classroom-based social and problem-solving curriculum, it can still be helpful for some children with greater social and emotional needs to have "pull out" tutoring in addition, to give them added practice in social interactions and problem solving. The advantage of this is that when they return to the classroom, their teacher and other students will be reinforcing the concepts they have learned in small group pullout sessions.

In summary, children in their first years of preschool and elementary school are developing social and emotional skills at a pace exceeding any other later stage of life. Their behavior is still flexible and their cognitive processes are malleable and receptive to adult socialization processes. Teaching and learning that happens in this age range is crucial because it either sets a firm or fragile foundation for later relationships and socialization, learning, and attitudes toward school. School-based interventions offer an opportunity for more accessible child, teacher, and parent interventions that coordinate the efforts of families and school personnel to give children the best possible start, perhaps leading to a cycle of lasting improvements in school achievement and mental health.

## PRACTICAL TIPS FOR RECRUITMENT OF SCHOOLS, TEACHERS, AND FAMILIES

### Targeting Intervention Delivery

While we believe that in an ideal world all schools would deliver evidence-based parent, teacher, and child interventions, a practical allocation of resources requires a selection process for service delivery. We began by targeting schools for intervention that served high numbers of socio-economically disadvantaged families and children. As we noted earlier, children living in poverty situations are at greater risk for poor school readiness and conduct problems because of the increased number of family and child risk factors to which they are exposed. Our choice to offer the programs in Head Start and elementary schools that served high percentages of children receiving free lunch reflects the increased needs of children and families in these settings. For example, our data suggest that 28% of families served by the Puget Sound Head Start program were referred to mental health centers for child adjustment problems but very few of them ever sought out services (Webster-Stratton, 1998). When offered our parent program in the Head Start center, 85% of families attended at least half of the parenting sessions. Head Start administrators reported there were fewer referrals for outside mental health programs because teachers felt they could manage the children in the classroom.

### School Engagement

Preparing schools about what it takes to learn and successfully deliver an empirically validated intervention is an important process for administrators and teachers to understand before they purchase curriculum or send teachers for training. Success depends on extensive groundwork to determine whether the intervention's goals, methods, and training requirements are compatible with the school's needs and philosophy.

**Step One: Administrative Support**　The approach we used when recruiting schools was to meet the principals and to present the IY programs' goals, curriculum, and research results. Administrative buy-in is crucial because the effective delivery of the programs depends on adherence to the intervention model, including allowing teachers and other school personnel time to attend trainings and prepare to deliver the parent and child curriculums. While teachers will be delivering the child program and very few will have the time to deliver the parent program, other school personnel such as school counselors, school psychologists, or nurses may be in a position to offer the parent program. Or, partnerships with mental health agencies may be developed to provide the parent programs. In addition, the most effective delivery of the school programs requires a consistent school-wide approach to behavior management and is more likely to be sustained if there is administrative support. To facilitate administrative support for the program, we also recommend that that at least one administrative person attend the training. This will lead to greater understanding of the program as well as indicate support for the teacher's efforts to learn the new curriculum.

**Step Two: Teacher Buy-In**　Once administrative level support is obtained, then the front-line teaching staff and school counselors, school psychologists, or family advocates need to be involved in the decision about whether to use the curriculum. Support and "buy in" for the program by teachers and school personnel is crucial because, ultimately, these people will be participating in the training and doing the work to deliver the programs. For this to happen with high quality and fidelity, teachers and other school personnel need to be enthusiastic and committed to deliver the program. Ideally, the IY programs are delivered to all teachers, parents, and children in the early grades so that there is a consistent intervention model throughout the school. It is important that a school reach consensus that this program fits with their needs and goals. Our approach was to meet with the teachers and the principal to provide an over view of the programs and to tell them what was involved in the training and delivery of the curriculum. We also encouraged schools to include parent advocates or representatives in these meetings so that their opinions, needs, and goals were incorporated into the decision-making process. If teachers do not feel consulted about their views on whether to adopt the curriculum and have a chance to work out how it will fit into other programs they are offering, they will be resistant to the training and to the delivery of the program.

***Step Three: Schools Determine Their Needs and Philosophy***    After this initial introduction to the program, administrators, teaching staff, and parent representatives are encouraged to complete a school-readiness process to assess their perceived needs for intervention and to determine whether the IY program's goals and philosophy match their own needs and goals. This readiness assessment is done with support from the IY staff, but ideally, the final decision and impetus to adopt the IY curricula rests with the school. It is the role of the IY staff to provide realistic information about the training goals, time commitment, cost, and anticipated outcomes so that the school can make an informed decision. Initial investment in an empirically validated intervention is somewhat costly and time consuming, and schools must be willing to make this investment in order to reap the longer-term benefits. In addition, schools may also be offering other social and emotional curriculum so it will be important for them to have a very specific plan for how these programs will work together or how the IY program will replace what they are already doing. It is important that this be worked out before teachers attend training so that their fears are reduced.

***Step Four: Practical and Funding Considerations***    Schools must understand that to deliver the programs with fidelity, the full program must be offered. Therefore, schools must decide whether they have the staff available to deliver the different program components (e.g., school counselors, school psychologists, family advocates, or other interested staff to deliver the parent program). Support staff to assist teachers in material preparation is essential, especially the first time they deliver the curriculum.

Some of the program costs are direct and obvious (e.g., the cost of the curriculum, cost of training). Other costs involve staff time to attend training and the cost of substitute teachers for these training days. Staff also need extra time to prepare and deliver the programs and to receive on-going supervision and consultation. Even family recruitment can be costly in terms of the time that staff will need to spend to ensure that families are informed about the groups. This is especially important with the high-risk families whose parents do not attend school functions. Also, to reach families for the parent component of the program, groups will need to be offered at times of day that families can attend (usually evenings), child care and snacks or meals will need to be provided, and interpreters for non-English-speaking parents will also need to be provided. Ideally transportation would be very helpful for those families who do not have a car or a way of getting to the school. It is of note that those schools with Title 1 funding have mandates to provide parent education so that they can write in the Incredible Years Parent program as their parent education component for improving their children's educational success. This funding will ensure that funding is not a barrier to program delivery.

***Step Five: Attention to Ongoing Monitoring and Program Fidelity***   Schools that make a commitment to use these programs should set up a system for on-going program fidelity and on-going consultation. It is helpful to have a staff person who is responsible for on-going monitoring as part of their job. Administrative attention to program fidelity, evaluation, and certification of leaders is very important so that the program takes hold and produces the expected results. It is also important that administrators and teachers understand the concept of fidelity—and why it is necessary that the program be delivered using the recommended dosage and methods. The fidelity of the Dinosaur curriculum is reduced by offering it once a month instead of twice a week, or only doing the circle times and not the small group practices, or failing to show the videotape modeling or practice exercises, or not involving parents or sending home the Dinosaur homework. When this happens, schools will fail to get the results obtained in research studies. As part of the certification process for teachers, they are encouraged to videotape their lessons and circle times and to meet with other teachers regularly to share their lesson tapes with each other. In addition, they may send DVDs to the Incredible Years for review and feedback.

### Factors to Consider When Selecting Teachers for Training

Whenever one is introducing change to a system, there are those individuals who are early adopters and are eager and motivated to try out new programs and ideas. There are also those who are "late adopters," who will wait to see how a program works with others before wanting to try it. Although we believe that, ultimately, it is best if all teachers in a school adopt the same intervention strategies, sometimes the best method of introducing change is a gradual one. We believe it most effective to let a group of skilled and enthusiastic early adopters begin the program first. These will be the natural leaders in a school, and if they like the program, once they have learned it, they will be in a position to help support others learning the program. We do not recommend mandating teachers to take the program, even if they are the less effective teachers. This sense of being forced to take a program creates resistance and is usually counterproductive. We also have been able to offer teachers CE or credits, which can be motivating for some teachers. One example of the success of starting with volunteer teachers to be trained first to implement the program is that of the work of Hutchings and colleagues (Hutchings, Daley, Jones, Martin, & Gwyn, 2007) in Wales. After only 3 years they now are in over 100 schools with successful results.

### Factors to Consider When Selecting Group Leaders for Training in Parent Program

In addition to selecting the best teachers to begin to pilot and introduce the new curriculum to a school, it is also important to identify those who will be in the best position to deliver the parent groups. Usually, teachers do not have the time to add this to their workload so school counselors or school psychologists are in a better position to offer this program. Again, finding those early adopters or champions who are motivated and interested in delivering parent groups is key to the ultimate success of a program's delivery. Selection criteria include group leaders who have a master's level education and have had courses in child development and social learning theory. If schools do not have these individuals, they may contract with mental health agencies to coordinate delivery of the parent programs. However, even if schools contract with mental health professionals to deliver the parent groups, it is essential that schools be actively involved in recruiting parents for the program—this cannot be left up to the group leaders. This raises the issue of the school's philosophy about the importance of family involvement in the school culture. For example, do schools pay lip service to parent involvement or do they truly value their input? For parent groups to be successful, administrators and teachers will need to set up a plan for recruiting parents and for promoting them. In Head Start, this recruitment process began the very first time a parent showed interest in that Head Start center. Parents were told that part of the services that they offered were not only for the children but also programs for the parents so they could learn how to help their children be successful in school. Brochures were given out explaining the parent program, and teachers recommended it at orientation nights, in parent meetings, and newsletters home.

### Factors to Consider When Selecting Families for Parent Program

Since schools may not be financially able to provide parent programs to all parents in a school, decisions have to be made about who will be eligible for participating in the parent training program. Each school will need to make these decisions based on their funding, philosophies, and needs. For example, in Head Start this program is most often offered to all parents who have children enrolled in Head Start. Head Start's program philosophy, which includes parent education, and staffing with family service workers, made it possible to achieve this goal. The advantage of this universal model is that it presents the program as something that can benefit all parents and takes away the possible stigma that parents might feel if they think they are being singled out because of their child's behavior or their own parenting skills. Public schools that serve many more families are unlikely to be able to offer the program to everyone. In this case, schools may make the decision to offer programs first to parents of children with the highest risk behaviors. It is very important in this case to advertise the program as a program to help children be successful in school not as a program for behavior-problem children. If possible, including some families in the group who do not have children in the high-risk range provides a more balanced group and helps to make the program even more accepted in the school. Another strategy is to offer the parent program universally but have the teachers target and encourage the parents of the higher risk students for personal invitations. As with the teacher programs, initial buy-in to a new program can be difficult. It is our experience that recruitment for a school's first few groups can be very challenging. Once parents begin attending the sessions, they usually become very invested in completing the program. After the first few cycles of groups, other parents hear about the program through word of mouth and it is often the case that the later groups have waiting lists of parents who want to attend the classes. As with the teacher programs, beginning by offering the parent program to some early adopters or parents who are community leaders may be helpful in establishing the groups. Some of these early adopters can become parent volunteers or mentors in subsequent parenting groups.

### Delivering Parent Programs to Diverse Cultures

In our most recent study, 73% of the families enrolled represented diverse cultures and 31% spoke English as a second language. Since many parent groups are multicultural, it is important to train leaders to deliver the parent programs using culturally sensitive principles that are generalizable across cultures. Group leaders who have a multicultural perspective acknowledge, respect, and affirm cultural differences. All parents in the group determine their own goals for themselves and their children in the first session, and the leaders help them learn and apply the behavior management skills to achieve these goals. More information about affirming diversity when leading groups can be found in Webster-Stratton (in press). For many parents these basic behavior management principles are completely unfamiliar, foreign, and difficult to grasp at first. Therefore, group leaders may need to expand the number of sessions on the topic, show more video examples than in the standard protocol, and provide more opportunities for practice and feedback. Sometimes parents will opt to attend the program a second time to get a more secure grasp of the principles.

Partnering with carefully selected interpreters who are well-respected leaders from the same communities and cultural backgrounds as parents can provide another avenue of understanding between the group leaders and the families who do not speak the same language as the leaders. By collaborating closely with these interpreters, group leaders have further opportunities to learn more about a particular culture, values, and parenting beliefs. In preparation for leading groups, group leaders and interpreters can have thoughtful and sensitive discussions about how to translate particular parenting strategies across cultures, so that parents understand how the concepts are relevant for achieving their goals for their children (For additional information see focus group interviews with interpreters in Webster-Stratton, 2006b).

*Training Interpreters*   Before working with the parent groups, interpreters themselves need comprehensive training to understand the rationale, child development principles, and social learning theories underlying the parenting socialization concepts that underpin the Incredible Years program. Initially, interpreters may find the parenting concepts to be foreign to their own experiences and may be unsure of the translations for particular concepts and the value of the skills for their families. Therefore, it is important to take the time to explore these issues with interpreters before starting the group, so that interpreters will be confident and convincing in their translations to parents. To help interpreters understand the behavior management concepts underpinning the program, they are encouraged to participate "as a parent" in a parent group first and then practice the strategies they have learned with their own children or with children in a preschool setting. The interpreters' role is not only to translate words, but to help bridge the gap between the different cultures so that parents understand the *meaning* of the concepts and relevance for their families. It is our belief that multicultural groups lead to greater understanding among parents of differing cultural backgrounds and experiences leading to more respectful and tolerant communities.

## RECOMMENDATIONS

### Planning for Sustainability

Since initial program and training costs are often a significant investment for a school, it is important for a school to build a plan for sustainability of these programs. The IY program has a long-term goal of training those who adopt the program to become self-sufficient so that they eventually have in-house staff who can offer on-going training and support to their schools. This process involves having group leaders or teachers progress through a certification process that ensures program fidelity and then to enter a training process to become a school mentor. This mentor training process may take between 3 to 4 years, but is well worth the time and energy for any school that wants to use IY as a sustainable intervention. The first year of the program is the most expensive in terms of program and training costs. In subsequent years, most program materials will already be purchased and training needs will be less.

### Building a Supportive Infrastructure and Providing Ongoing Consultation

Ideally, a supportive infrastructure will be set up that allows teachers and parent group leaders to participate in on-going peer supervision, to have time and support for materials preparation, and to receive ongoing consultation. When working with a new program with challenging children and families, there is likely to be a steep learning curve. Teachers and parent group leaders will need opportunities to share experiences with each other and also to receive supervision from more experienced leaders. In the first years of implementation, supervision and consultation will need to come from the IY program developers. As schools continue with the program and build up their reservoir of certified teachers and parent group leaders with experience, the need for outside consultation will diminish.

## SUMMARY

Surveys indicate that teachers are very concerned about the number of children who arrive in their classrooms lacking the emotional regulation and social skills to be able to function productively and learn in the classroom. They report that they are unable to teach academic skills because of the behavior management issues in the classroom. Moreover, these issues are even more prevalent in classrooms with high percentages of students from poverty situations and where there is a poor connection or involvement between the parents and teacher. Research with the IY program has shown in multiple RCTs that by working collaboratively with parents, teachers, and children, it is possible to significantly improve children's social competence and emotion regulation, reduce conduct problems, and involve parents in their children's learning. In particular, the highest risk children make the most significant gains. However, in order to implement these programs with success, it is important first for schools and agencies to carefully assess their needs, determine that the program meets their goals, and obtain both administrative and teacher commitment. Schools must also plan carefully to provide adequate training, support, and consultation to those delivering the programs. If they do so, the programs will be delivered with a high degree of fidelity. In addition, planning for future sustainability will be achieved by supporting leaders' certification/accreditation process and identifying mentors for ongoing training who can provide subsequent training and technical support within the agency/school on an ongoing basis.

## REFERENCES

Arnold, D. H., Griffith, J. R., Ortiz, C., & Stowe, R. M. (1998). Day care interactions and teacher perceptions as a function of teacher and child ethnic group. *Journal of Research in Childhood Education, 12*(2), 143–154.

Arnold, D. H., Ortiz, C., Curry, J. C., Stowe, R. M., Goldstein, N. E., Fisher, P. H., et al. (1999). Promoting academic success and preventing disruptive behavior disorders through community partnership. *Journal of Community Psychology, 27*, 589–598.

Beauchaine, T. P., Webster-Stratton, C., & Reid, M. J. (2005). Mediators, moderators, and predictors of one-year outcomes among children treated for early-onset conduct problems: A latent growth curve analysis. *Journal of Consulting and Clinical Psychology, 73*(3), 371–388.

Birch, S. H., & Ladd, G. W. (1997). The teacher-child relationship and children's early school adjustment. *Journal of School Psychology, 35*, 61–79.

Brestan, E. V., & Eyberg, S. M. (1998). Effective psychosocial treatments of conduct-disordered children and adolescents: 29 years, 82 studies, and 5,272 kids. *Journal of Clinical Child Psychology, 27*, 180–189.

Brophy, J. E. (1996). *Teaching problem students*. New York: Guilford.

Burchinal, M. R., Roberts, J. E., Hooper, S., & Zeisel, S. A. (2000). Cumulative risk and early cognitive development: A comparison of statistical risk models. *Developmental Psychology, 36*, 793–807.

Burton, C. B. (1992). Defining family-centered early education: Beliefs of public school, child care, and Head Start teachers. *Early education and development, 3*(1), 45–59.

Carr, E. G., Taylor, J. G., & Robinson, S. (1991). The effects of severe behavior problems in children on the teaching behavior of adults. *Journal of Applied Behavior Analysis, 24*, 523–535.

Chavkin, N. F. (1991). Uniting families and schools: Social workers helping teachers through inservice training. *School Social Work Journal, 15*, 1–10.

Coie, J. D. (1990). Adapting intervention to the problems of aggressive and disruptive rejected children. In S. R. Asher & J. D. Coie (Eds.), *Peer Rejection in Childhood* (pp. 309–337). Cambridge, UK: Cambridge University Press.

Coie, J. D., & Dodge, K. A. (1998). Aggression and antisocial behavior. In W. Damon & N. Eisenberg (Eds.), *Handbook of child psychology, Fifth Edition: Social, emotional and personality development* (Vol. 3, pp. 779–862). New York: Wiley.

Coie, J. D., Watt, N. F., West, S. G., Hawkins, D., Asarnow, J. R., Markman, H. J., et al. (1993). The science of prevention: A conceptual framework and some directions for a national research program. *American Psychologist, 48*, 1013–1022.

Cunningham, C. E., Bremner, R., & Boyle, M. (1995). Large group community-based parenting programs for families of preschoolers at risk for disruptive behaviour disorders: Utilization, cost effectiveness, and outcome. *Journal of Child Psychology and Psychiatry, 36*, 1141–1159.

Dodge, K. A. (1993). Social-cognitive mechanisms in the development of conduct disorder and depression. *Annual Review of Psychology, 44*, 559–584.

Dodge, K. A., Coie, J. D., Pettit, G. S., & Price, J. M. (1990). Peer status and aggression in boys' groups: Developmental and contextual analyses. *Child Development, 61*(5), 1289–1309.

Dodge, K. A., & Price, J. M. (1994). On the relation between social information processing and socially competent behavior in early school-aged children. *Child Development, 65,* 1385–1397.

Dodge, K. A., & Somberg, D. R. (1987). Hostile attributional biases among aggressive boys are exacerbated under conditions of threats to the self. *Child Development, 58*(1), 213–224.

Epstein, A. (1992). School and family partnerships. In M. Alkin (Ed.), *Encyclopedia of Educational Research* (pp. 1139–1151). New York: MacMillan.

Espinosa, L. M. (1995). Hispanic involvement in early childhood programs. ERIC Digest. Urbana, IL: ERIC Clearinghouse on Elementary and Early Childhood Education. Available: http://www.ed.gov/databases/ERIC_Digests/ed382412.html

Feshbach, N. (1989). The construct of empathy and the phenomenon of physical maltreatment of children. In D. Cicchetti & V. Carlson (Eds.), *Child maltreatment: Theory and research on the causes and consequences of child abuse and neglect* (pp. 349–373). Cambridge, MA: Cambridge University Press.

Goldstein, N. E., Arnold, D. H., Rosenberg, J. L., Stowe, R. M., & Ortiz, C. (2001). Contagion of aggression in day care classrooms as a function of peer and teacher response. *Journal of Educational Psychology, 93,* 708–719.

Grolnick, W. S., & Slowiaczek, M. L. (1994). Parents' involvement in children's schooling: A multidimensional conceptualization and motivational model. *Child Development, 65,* 237–252.

Hartman, R. R., Stage, S., & Webster-Stratton, C. (2003). A growth curve analysis of parent training outcomes: Examining the influence of child factors (inattention, impulsivity, and hyperactivity problems), parental and family risk factors. *The Child Psychology and Psychiatry Journal, 44*(3), 388–398.

Hawkins, J. D., Catalano, R. F., & Miller, Y. (1992). Risk and protective factors for alcohol and other drug problems in adolescence and early adulthood: Implications for substance abuse prevention. *Psychological Bulletin, 112,* 64–105.

Hawkins, J. D., & Weiss, J. G. (1985). The social developmental model: An integrated approach to delinquency prevention. *Journal of Primary Prevention, 6,* 73–95.

Hutchings, J., Daley, D., Jones, E. E., Martin, P., & Gwyn, R. (2007). Early results from developing and researching the Webster-Stratton Incredible Years Teacher Classroom Management Training Programme in North West Wales. *British Educational Research journal, 2*(3), 15–26.

Kazdin, A. E. (1995). *Conduct disorders in childhood and adolescence.* Thousand Oaks, CA: Sage.

Ladd, G. W. (1990). Having friends, keeping friends, making friends, and being liked by peers in the classroom: Predictors of children's early school adjustment? *Child Development, 61*(4), 1081–1100.

Milich, R., & Dodge, K. A. (1984). Social information processing in child psychiatric populations. *Journal of Abnormal Child Psychology, 12*(3), 471–489.

Moffitt, T. E. (1993). Adolescence-limited and life-course-persistent antisocial behavior: A developmental taxonomy. *Psychological Review, 100,* 674–701.

Moffitt, T. E., & Lynam, D. (1994). The neuropsychology of conduct disorder and delinquency: Implications for understanding antisocial behavior. In D. C. Fowles, P. Sutker, & S. H. Goodman (Eds.), *Progress in experimental personality and psychopathology research* (pp. 233–262). New York: Springer.

Offord, D. R., Alder, R. J., & Boyle, M. H. (1986). Prevalence and sociodemographic correlates of conduct disorder. *The American Journal of Social Psychiatry, 6,* 272–278.

Patterson, G., Reid, J., & Dishion, T. (1992). *Antisocial boys: A social interactional approach* (Vol. 4). Eugene, OR: Castalia Publishing.

Patterson, G. R., Capaldi, D., & Bank, L. (1991). An early starter model for predicting delinquency. In D. J. Pepler & K. H. Rubin (Eds.), *The development and treatment of childhood aggression* (pp. 139–168). Hillsdale, NJ: Erlbaum.

Phillips, D., Voran, M., Kisker, E., Howes, C., & Whitebrook, M. (1994). Child care for children in poverty: Opportunity or inequity? *Child Development, 65,* 472–492.

Raver, C. C., & Zigler, E. F. (1997). Social competence: An untapped dimension in evaluating Head Start's success. *Early Childhood Research Quarterly, 12,* 363–385.

Reid, M. J., Webster-Stratton, C., & Hammond, M. (2007). Enhancing a classroom social competence and problem-solving curriculum by offering parent training to families of moderate-to-high-risk elementary school children. *Journal of Clinical Child and Adolescent Psychology, 36*(5), 605–620.

Richard, B. A., & Dodge, K. A. (1982). Social maladjustment and problem solving in school-aged children. *Journal of Consulting and Clinical Psychology, 50*(2), 226–233.

Rimm-Kaufman, S. E., Pianta, R. C., & Cox, M. J. (2000). Teachers' judgments of problems in the transition to kindergarten. *Early Childhood Research Quarterly, 15*, 147–166.

Rubin, K. H., & Krasnor, L. R. (1986). Social-cognitive and social behavioral perspectives on problem-solving. In M. Perlmutter (Ed.), *Cognitive perspectives on children's social and behavioral development. The Minnesota Symposia on Child Psychology* (Vol. 18, pp. 1–68). Hillsdale, NJ: Erlbaum.

Schonfeld, I. S., Shaffer, D., O'Connor, P., & Portnoy, S. (1988). Conduct disorder and cognitive functioning: Testing three causal hypotheses. *Child Development, 59*(4), 993–1007.

Scott, S., Spender, Q., Doolan, M., Jacobs, B., & Aspland, H. (2001). Multicentre controlled trial of parenting groups for child antisocial behaviour in clinical practice. *British Medical Journal, 323*(28), 1–5.

Snyder, H. (2001). Child delinquents. In R. Loeber & D. P. Farrington (Eds.), *Risk factors and successful interventions*. Thousand Oaks, CA: Sage.

Snyder, J., Schrepferman, L., & St. Peter, C. (1997). Origins of antisocial behavior: Negative reinforcement and affect dysregulation of behavior as socialization mechanisms in family interaction. *Behavior Modification, 21*(2), 187–215.

Stage, S. A., & Quiroz, D. R. (1997). A meta-analysis of interventions to decrease disruptive classroom behavior in public education settings. *School Psychology Review, 26*, 333–368.

Taylor, T. K., & Biglan, A. (1998). Behavioral family interventions for improving child-rearing: A review for clinicians and policy makers. *Clinical Child and Family Psychology Review, 1*(1), 41–60.

Taylor, T. K., Schmidt, F., Pepler, D., & Hodgins, H. (1998). A comparison of eclectic treatment with Webster-Stratton's Parents and Children Series in a children's mental health center: A randomized controlled trial. *Behavior Therapy, 29*, 221–240.

Tremblay, R. E., Mass, L. C., Pagani, L., & Vitaro, F. (1996). From childhood physical aggression to adolescent maladjustment: The Montreal Prevention Experiment. In R. D. Peters & R. J. MacMahon (Eds.), *Preventing childhood disorders, substance abuse and delinquency* (pp. 268–298). Thousand Oaks: Sage.

Underwood, M. K. (1997). Peer social status and children's understanding of the expression and control of positive and negative emotions. *Merrill-Palmer Quarterly, 43*, 610–634.

Webster-Stratton, C. (1982). The long term effects of a videotape modeling parent training program: Comparison of immediate and 1-year followup results. *Behavior Therapy, 13*, 702–714.

Webster-Stratton, C. (1984). Randomized trial of two parent-training programs for families with conduct-disordered children. *Journal of Consulting and Clinical Psychology, 52*(4), 666–678.

Webster-Stratton, C. (1984). *The Incredible Years Parent Training Manual: BASIC Program*. Seattle, WA: Author.

Webster-Stratton, C. (1989). Systematic comparison of consumer satisfaction of three cost-effective parent training programs for conduct problem children. *Behavior Therapy, 20*, 103–115.

Webster-Stratton, C. (1990a). Long-term follow-up of families with young conduct problem children: From preschool to grade school. *Journal of Clinical Child Psychology, 19*(2), 144–149.

Webster-Stratton, C. (1990b). Stress: A potential disruptor of parent perceptions and family interactions. *Journal of Clinical Child Psychology, 19*, 302–312.

Webster-Stratton, C. (1994). Advancing videotape parent training: A comparison study. *Journal of Consulting and Clinical Psychology, 62*(3), 583–593.

Webster-Stratton, C. (1996). Parenting a young child with conduct problems: New insights using grounded theory methods. In T. H. Ollendick & R. S. Prinz (Eds.), *Advances in clinical child psychology* (pp. 333–355). Hillsdale, NJ: Erlbaum.

Webster-Stratton, C. (1998). Preventing conduct problems in Head Start children: Strengthening parenting competencies. *Journal of Consulting and Clinical Psychology, 66*(5), 715–730.

Webster-Stratton, C. (1999). *How to promote children's social and emotional competence*. London: Sage.

Webster-Stratton, C. (1984; 2001; 2007). *The Incredible Years Parent Training Manual: BASIC Program*. Seattle, WA: Author.

Webster-Stratton, C. (2006a). *The Incredible Years: A trouble-shooting guide for parents of children ages 3–8 years*. Seattle, WA: Incredible Years Press.

Webster-Stratton, C. (2006b). *Training interpreters to deliver the Incredible Years Parent Program: A cross cultural collaboration*. Unpublished manuscript.

Webster-Stratton, C. (1984; 2001; 2007). *The Incredible Years Parent Training Manual: BASIC Program*. Seattle, WA: Author.

Webster-Stratton, C. (in press). Affirming diversity: Multi-cultural collaboration to deliver the Incredible Years Parent Programs *The International Journal of Child Health and Human Development*.

Webster-Stratton, C., & Hammond, M. (1990). Predictors of treatment outcome in parent training for families with conduct problem children. *Behavior Therapy, 21*, 319–337.

Webster-Stratton, C., & Hammond, M. (1997). Treating children with early-onset conduct problems: A comparison of child and parent training interventions. *Journal of Consulting and Clinical Psychology, 65*(1), 93–109.

Webster-Stratton, C., & Hammond, M. (1998). Conduct problems and level of social competence in Head Start children: Prevalence, pervasiveness and associated risk factors. *Clinical Child Psychology and Family Psychology Review, 1*(2), 101–124.

Webster-Stratton, C., & Herbert, M. (1994). *Troubled families—problem children: Working with parents: A collaborative process*. Chichester, UK: Wiley.

Webster-Stratton, C., Hollinsworth, T., & Kolpacoff, M. (1989). The long-term effectiveness and clinical significance of three cost-effective training programs for families with conduct-problem children. *Journal of Consulting and Clinical Psychology, 57*(4), 550–553.

Webster-Stratton, C., & Lindsay, D. W. (1999). Social competence and early-onset conduct problems: Issues in assessment. *Journal of Child Clinical Psychology, 28*, 25–93.

Webster-Stratton, C., & Reid, M. J. (2001). *Incredible Years Teacher Training Program: Content, Methods and Processes*. Unpublished manuscript.

Webster-Stratton, C., & Reid, M. J. (2003). Treating conduct problems and strengthening social emotional competence in young children (ages 4–8 years): The Dina Dinosaur treatment program. *Journal of Emotional and Behavioral Disorders, 11*(3), 130–143.

Webster-Stratton, C., & Reid, M. J. (2004). Strengthening social and emotional competence in young children—The foundation for early school readiness and success: Incredible Years Classroom Social Skills and Problem-Solving Curriculum. *Journal of Infants and Young Children, 17*(2), 185–203.

Webster-Stratton, C., & Reid, M. J. (2007). Incredible Years Parents and Teachers Training Series: A Head Start partnership to promote social competence and prevent conduct problems In P. Tolin, J. Szapocznick, & S. Sambrano (Eds.), *Preventing youth substance abuse* (pp. 67–88). Washington D. C.: American Psychological Association

Webster-Stratton, C., Reid, M. J., & Hammond, M. (2001a). Preventing conduct problems, promoting social competence: A parent and teacher training partnership in Head Start. *Journal of Clinical Child Psychology, 30*(3), 283–302.

Webster-Stratton, C., Reid, M. J., & Hammond, M. (2001b). Social skills and problem solving training for children with early-onset conduct problems: Who benefits? *Journal of Child Psychology and Psychiatry, 42*(7), 943–952.

Webster-Stratton, C., Reid, M. J., & Hammond, M. (2004). Treating children with early-onset conduct problems: Intervention outcomes for parent, child, and teacher training. *Journal of Clinical Child and Adolescent Psychology, 33*(1), 105–124.

Webster-Stratton, C., Reid, M. J., & Stoolmiller, M. (2008). Preventing conduct problems and improving school readiness: Evaluation of the Incredible Years Teacher and Child Training Programs in high-risk schools. *Journal of Child Psychology and Psychiatry 49*(5), 471–488.

West, J., Denton, K., & Reaney, L. M. (2001). *The kindergarten year: Findings from the Early Childhood Longitudinal Study, kindergarten class of 1998–1999* (Publication No. NCES2001-023). Washington, DC: Department of Education, National Center for Education Statistics.

# 10

## FAMILY-CENTERED, SCHOOL-BASED MENTAL HEALTH STRATEGIES TO REDUCE STUDENT BEHAVIORAL, EMOTIONAL, AND ACADEMIC RISK

ELIZABETH STORMSHAK, THOMAS DISHION, AND CORRINA FALKENSTEIN

A growing body of literature suggests that family-centered intervention reduces the risk of problem behavior among youth who are most vulnerable for a variety of later adjustment problems. This chapter provides an overview of an ecological approach to treatment that has emerged from a series of intervention trials that we have conducted during the past 10 years with young adolescents and preschoolers on a trajectory for future problem behavior (Dishion & Kavanagh, 2003; Dishion & Stormshak, 2007; Stormshak, Dishion, Light, & Yasui, 2005). Inspired by the research suggesting an integrative intervention that coordinates services across multiple domains (e.g., home, family–peer, school) for children and families is most successful, we developed an ecological approach to family interventions and treatment called EcoFit.

## OVERVIEW

In this chapter we highlight three research programs that support the effectiveness of the EcoFIT model for reducing problem behavior with at-risk youth. In the first project, Project Alliance, we found that youth and families engaged in a multilevel treatment model including a school-level intervention, a family-level intervention, and selected interventions for at-risk youth resulted in high-risk youth reporting less substance use from Grades 6 through 9 (Dishion, Kavanagh, Schneiger, Nelson, & Kaufman, 2002) and increased academic performance through Grade 11 (Stormshak, Connell, & Dishion, 2009). In addition, strong effects were found on reducing adolescent problem behavior and arrest rates through age 17 (Connell, Dishion, Yasui, & Kavanagh, 2007). In the Next Generation Project a multilevel treatment model was used with middle school–age children, and results included increased parent involvement in the schools and decreased risk behavior during a 3-year period (Stormshak, Dishion, Light, & Yasui, 2005). In the Early Steps Project, the family-centered intervention approach was tested with children age 2 to 4 years. Family-centered services resulted in reduced growth of problem behavior over time, improvements in children's language skills, and maternal reports of inhibitory control from ages 2 to 4 (Lunkenheimer et al., 2008; Dishion et al., 2008). This chapter details the EcoFIT family-centered intervention model and elaborates on the intervention trials that support the use of this model.

The number of children who have mental health problems has been increasing in the past decade. Some reports suggest that the rate is as high as 1 in 5 children, yet only 20% of these children receive the services they need (Biglan, Mrazek, Carnine, & Flay, 2003; Katoaka, Zhang, & Wells, 2002). Clearly, this is a significant concern for schools, whose goals involve helping all children reach their academic potential. It is abundantly clear that academic, emotional, and behavioral risks are closely linked, especially in secondary school. Nationwide policies such as the No Child Left Behind Act, which holds schools accountable for academic progress, also mandate the need to address the concomitant mental health issues that interfere with academic progress and to support programs that meet the needs of low-achieving children.

Developmental science has developed an accumulating knowledge base about the etiology of student problem behavior and associated consequences such as later school failure (Conduct Problems Prevention Research Group, 1999; Dishion & Patterson, 2006). Longitudinal studies on the development of problems in children and adolescents reveal a cascade of difficulties that often emerge from the family and the community contexts and evolve to the school setting, including the academic and peer arenas. This body of research on the ecology of problem behavior has been practical in nature, identifying factors that can be targeted in future prevention trials. For example, we have known for decades that unsafe neighborhoods, poverty, adult mental health problems, and the like are correlated with student problem behavior and academic failure. However, research has also identified a set of parenting practices that can reduce problem behavior and improve outcomes, such as family management practices (Patterson, Reid, & Dishion, 1992).

Historically, schools have typically dealt with these problems by identifying students who need assistance in the form of individualized education plans (IEPs) or other mandated educational planning, and then providing a child-focused, school-based intervention to support achievement and success. Educational planning usually has been provided only for the highest risk youth. We now realize that these child-focused interventions, although successful at one level, do not address all the problems and can be strengthened by including parents and families (Christenson, 2003).

### The School–Family Connection

Family-centered approaches to intervention and school-based interventions have in practice remained separate. Schools are comfortable adopting curricula that focus on providing services to groups of children and more globally targeting problem behaviors such as aggression and social skills (e.g., Second Steps, PATHS). These curricula, which are typically cognitive–behavioral and structured, provide children with many of the skills needed to succeed in the school context. However, the clinical outcome literature clearly suggests that effective approaches to child mental health involve both a child and a family target (Weisz, Jensen-Doss, & Hawley, 2006). In fact, some studies now suggest that excluding parents from treatment approaches can actually worsen child behavior problems (Szapocznik & Prado, 2007). The majority of successful school-based cognitive–behavioral approaches to social skills training are enhanced when the parenting component is included in the curriculum (Lochman & Wells, 2004; Spoth, Redmond, & Shin, 1998).

### Family Management in Schools

It is increasingly clear that parenting practices form both the core of risk for the onset and progression of problem behavior and the potential solution in terms of defining a target for intervention and prevention (Dishion & Stormshak, 2007; Spoth, Kavanagh, & Dishion, 2002). Additional risk factors must also be considered, particularly for low-income children who face numerous barriers to achievement and success that directly affect school achievement. As shown in Figure 10.1, school success indicators such as self-regulation, social competence, and literacy skills shape both problem behavior and achievement and are the key targets of school-based interventions. Developmental research suggests that this model and variations of this model are relatively robust and significant across ages and various cultural groups (Ackerman, Brown, & Izard, 2004; Raver, Gershoff, & Aber, 2007). Contextual stress such as poverty, hardship, and adult mental health problems all directly limit parents' ability to use effective parenting strategies at home and to increase involvement in their child's learning. The implication of the model shown in Figure 10.1 is that motivation and support to improve family management skills can reduce the negative impact of contextual stress on children and increase school competence.

Schools have been reluctant to include families in interventions for a variety of reasons. Many of these reasons have been framed as barriers to family–school partnerships (Christenson, 2003). First, most school personnel are hesitant to become involved with parents about issues such as parenting and family problems. These problems are seen as separate from the school and therefore should be dealt with in another context such as a mental health agency. Second, many schools face budget cuts and demands on staff

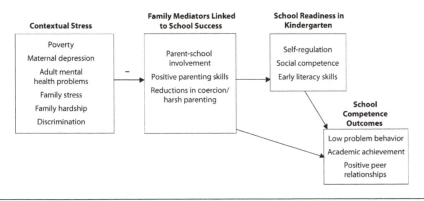

**Figure 10.1** A developmental model for intervening in problem behavior to promote school competence.

time that prohibit involvement with parents or parenting interventions. These interventions are simply too costly and complicated for school personnel to use. Finally, many of the professionals who work in schools—school counselors, behavioral support staff, and psychologists—are trained in an individual child-centered approach to problem reduction. They do not have the background or orientation to work with parents or families, nor do they feel comfortable interacting with families about mental health issues. The result is that schools and families have remained separate when it comes to the treatment of child mental health.

## THE ECOFIT MODEL

Family intervention research is undergoing a critical shift from a purely intervention model to one in which interventions are redesigned to be brief, cost effective, tailored and adaptive, and applied in service delivery settings that affect a large number of children and families, such as in schools (Lochman & van den Steenhoven, 2002; Spoth et al., 2002). If effective, family-centered intervention reduces the risk among youth who are most vulnerable for a variety of later adjustment problems.

The ecological approach to family intervention and treatment model (EcoFIT) emerged from a series of intervention trials with young adolescents and preschoolers at high risk for escalation in problem behavior (Dishion & Kavanagh, 2003; Dishion & Stormshak, 2007; Stormshak et al., 2005). The EcoFIT intervention model comprises three major components: (a) a family resource center (FRC) housed in the school, which provides information on schoolwide discipline, rules, parenting skills, and behavioral support; (b) the Family Check-Up (FCU); and (c) a menu of intervention and/or treatment options. Intervention options for families are based on the family management curriculum from the Adolescent Transitions Program (ATP) and our early childhood parenting materials (Dishion & Patterson, 1996). Key to EcoFIT is that it is assessment driven and tailored to the needs of youth and families (Dishion & Stormshak, 2007; Stormshak & Dishion, 2002). The FCU, the core of the EcoFIT approach, specifically targets parental monitoring, involvement in the parenting process, and positive behavior support to reduce problem behavior and to encourage child and adolescent development of skills and competence. EcoFIT is designed to be "contextualized" in that it is implemented in services settings that have a great deal of contact with children and families, such as the public schools.

Empirically based school interventions are most successful when they include a multilevel intervention model and a tiered service delivery system that is adaptive to the needs of children and families (Hoagwood et al., 2007). Our multilevel model for engaging and intervening with families explicitly integrates intervention targets (e.g., family management, self-regulation) with principles of behavior change (Dishion & Kavanagh, 2003; Dishion & Stormshak, 2007). The intervention approach described in this chapter has three additional emphases that are unique in comparison with traditional approaches to family intervention (Stormshak & Dishion, 2002). First, in the EcoFIT model we tailor our interventions with children and families to fit their current family circumstances revealed in the assessment results of the FCU. The family assessment may indicate a need for interventions that target only encouragement of skills (e.g., positive reinforcement), especially if limit setting, parental monitoring, and communication are found through the assessment to be parenting strengths. Or, if limit-setting skills need to be supported, for example, we may tailor our approach depending on the number of parents in the family, the physical context of the living situation, and the sociocultural background of the family. In this sense, the EcoFIT approach proposes a menu of empirically supported interventions with diverse venues of service delivery. Offering an intervention menu and diverse, flexible service delivery options promotes parent engagement and motivation (Dishion & Kavanagh, 2003; Miller & Rollnick, 2002).

A second unique component of this approach is to offer periodic and sometimes brief interventions during times of developmental and contextual transition (Sameroff & Fiese, 1987). For example, the move from middle school to high school during adolescence is a time of transition. The risk of drug use, problem behavior, and academic failure increases during this period, especially for culturally diverse youth (Nelson & Dishion, 2004; Yasui, Dorham, & Dishion, 2004). Similarly, the transition to elementary school poses a risk for many children, with low early literacy, poor self-regulation, and behavior problems predicting school failure at this age (Blair, 2001; Moffitt, 1990). The optimal service settings for the delivery of EcoFIT are those that provide continual contact with a child and family throughout a specific period of development. Knowing this led us to develop a school-based, family-centered model for intervention that includes the establishment of FRCs in schools. Our approach is similar to that of a health maintenance model of mental health service delivery, and least like a medical disease model of intervention. Specifically, we propose that six to eight intervention contacts provided in contexts that are easily accessible to families can lead to relatively large effect sizes if they are delivered skillfully and strategically during the course of 2 to 3 years.

A third difference is that we actively address motivation to change at all stages of the intervention process. The FCU provides an assessment and addresses parents' motivation to change (see Miller & Rollnick, 2002). During the intervention, we address motivation at several stages of the change process and focus specifically on resistance to change. Resistance is a common obstacle in family intervention and is associated with low family management skills, adult depression, and poor treatment outcomes (Stoolmiller, Duncan, Bank, & Patterson, 1993). Interventions that target resistance directly and help parents work through resistance are more likely to be successful at changing both parenting and child outcomes. In addition, we provide brief, motivational support for families to support persistence and maintenance of change.

Our approach to child and family intervention is ecologically sensitive in that we emphasize the importance of considering the family's needs with respect to a variety of social and community resources. For example, in middle childhood and adolescence, it is critical to focus assessments and interventions with youth in terms of peer relationships and social interactions that may either be protective or serve as a context for risk (Gifford-Smith, Dodge, Dishion, & McCord, 2005). Neighborhood and community resources may be useful in terms of promoting change in family management skills, or they may exacerbate the problems within the family. Attention to these risk factors is critical for a successful intervention model.

### Components of the EcoFIT Model

*The Family Resource Center*   The idea behind providing an FRC in schools is not a new one. In fact, many FRCs were developed in the 1970s and 1980s to bridge the gap between schools and families with students identified as having a disability or being on an IEP. However, these centers rarely focused their attention on parenting issues that may have been exacerbating the child's problems, or on mental health issues in the family. The goal of the FRC is to provide a universal level of intervention in the schools that focuses on parents and family management skills, with particular attention given to those skills that enhance school achievement and success.

The process of forming the FRC in a school involves several different components (see Figure 10.2). First, it is important to develop a team of key school personnel who will work within the FRC framework. For example, in our research projects we staff each FRC with a half-time support person called a *parent consultant.* This person acts as a liaison between the school and home by developing school-to-home behavior plans, coordinating with teachers, communicating with parents, and forming a bridge between parents and school staff. The parent consultant is also responsible for working directly within the school system and attending relevant school meetings such as behavior support meetings and meetings with parents about their child. Many schools use a systemic means of identifying problem behavior and discipline referrals, such as School-Wide Positive Behavior Support (SWPBS; Sprague & Golly, 2005; Sugai, Sprague, Horner, & Walker, 2000, 2001). The FRC is compatible with the SWPBS approach in that school–parent communication is the central goal. By alerting parents to child misbehaviors

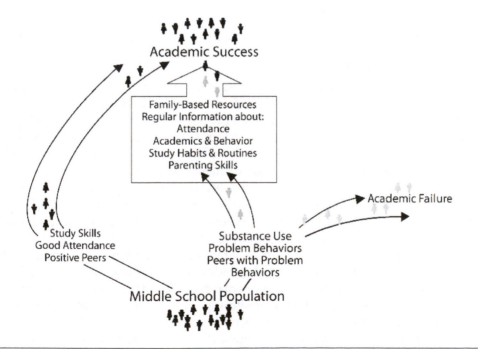

**Figure 10.2** Family resource center: process and outcomes.

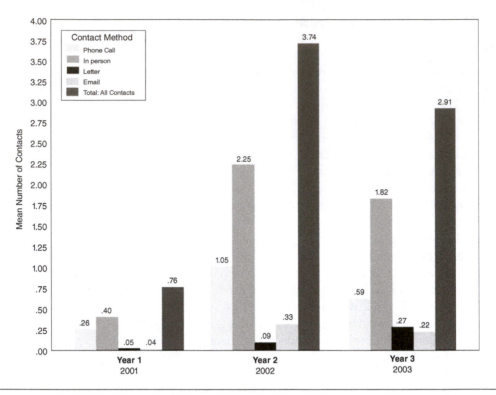

**Figure 10.3** Family resource center contacts by type, 6th through 8th grades.

at school, parents are encouraged to become involved in the behavior management process and to work with school personnel and parent consultants to develop a plan for reducing negative behaviors at school.

As the FRC becomes established in schools, parents will begin to use it as a resource for information about parenting and other life stressors. In our work in middle schools, we have found that once parents understand the purpose of the FRC, they readily use the service. In our randomized trial called the Next Generation (funded by the National Institute on Drug Abuse [NIDA]), we randomly assigned middle schools to receive either the FRC and related services or no treatment except parent support groups. We found that parents increased their use of the FRC during the 3 years of the study. We also found that in-person meetings were not the only way to work with parents. Parents communicated with FRC staff using multiple forms of contact such as email and phone calls in addition to in-person meetings (see Figure 10.3).

The FRC facilitates the dissemination of parenting information and resources in the community. In the three Portland, Oregon, middle schools where we have established FRCs, we offer brochures about many aspects of family life and behavior such as completing homework, limit setting, parental monitoring, and parent involvement in schools. These brochures are based on the content of our empirically validated ATP and are easy for parents to read and understand (see Figure 10.4 for sample brochure content). We track each caregiver contact with our FRC staff by using an online system we call the

**A strong home/school connection** promotes children's school success and feelings of self-worth. School success helps adolescents prepare for life success.

## For School Success . . .

**Teens need to:**
- Be prepared
- Pay attention
- Ask questions
- Respect others
- Be involved in learning
- Follow school rules

**Parents can help by:**
- Setting up routines at home and at school
- Building relationships with teachers
- Following a daily checklist

### Setting up for SUCCESS

### At Home
- Establish a weekly routine.
- Have a daily study time.
- Have a quiet place with good lighting and study materials.
- Check homework log.
- Talk about the importance of education.

### At School
- Know your child's schedule.
- Meet all of your child's teachers each term.
- Know teachers' expectations for classroom behavior.
- Know teachers' expectations for homework.

### Making a Daily Checklist

Have I . . . . .
- Checked on what my child has for homework?
- Talked with my child about classes, experiences, and friends?
- Encouraged efforts and successes?
- Asked if my child needs help with anything?
- Looked at completed assignments?

**Figure 10. 4** Sample informational brochure based on Adolescent Transitions Program content.

Parent Consultant Contact Form. Using this system, we can measure the quantity and type of service that each parent receives. As we track the content of parent meetings with FRC staff (see Table 10.1), we note that the majority focuses on information about parenting skills and family management such as monitoring and supervision, providing incentives, or limit setting (41%). School problems—with teachers, attendance, or homework completion—were second in frequency (25%), followed closely by family problems such as a parent's depression, marital distress, or concerns about housing (16%), or child problems such as substance use, depression, and safety (18%). Clearly, the FRC provides a wide range of services to youth and families in addition to a focus on contextual risk factors that impact youth success.

*The Family Check-Up* A critical feature of any mental health intervention is to explicitly address motivation to change on the part of the participants. The centerpiece of services available for families receiving the EcoFIT intervention is the FCU, which is based on Miller and Rollnick's (2002) motivation-based Drinker's Check-Up. The FCU is an empirically validated intervention that has been used to effectively reduce the growth of substance use, problem behavior at school, and academic problems in middle school and high school, as well as to enhance parenting skills in early childhood

**Table 10.1** Content of Parent Meetings through the Family Resource Center

| Topic | % time spent |
| --- | --- |
| Parenting skills and family management | 41 |
| School problems (homework, attendance) | 25 |
| Family problems (housing, parent depression) | 16 |
| Child problems (substance use, depression, safety) | 18 |

(Dishion et al., 2002; Dishion & Stormshak, 2007). The typical family who presents for mental health services varies in each member's ability to make changes and in their motivation to change their behavior. Guided by Prochaska and DiClemente's stages of change model (1986), the Family Check-Up uses an ecological assessment designed to motivate families to make changes in their parenting and to target the family's stage of change.

The Family Check-Up comprises three steps: an initial interview, ecological assessment, and feedback with motivational interviewing (see Figure 10.5). During the initial interview the parent consultant facilitates discussion with parents about goals and concerns, as well as their personal motivation for change. This meeting establishes a collaborative base for future meetings and can serve to build relationships between the school and the home. The second session involves a brief assessment packet to be completed by the parent, child, and teacher and a videotaped family interaction assessment that is intended to be held in the family's home but could also be conducted in the school. At the third meeting, the feedback session, results of the assessment are discussed in terms of (a) providing motivation to change, (b) providing parents with information about areas of growth (e.g., the need to increase parental monitoring) and areas of parent and child strength (e.g., family cohesion), and (c) identifying the appropriate resources with respect to a menu of family-centered intervention options. This menu might include working with parents to build a home-to-school plan concerning homework, providing incentives for good behavior, or helping the family identify housing resources.

Motivational interviewing includes developing a set of skills that helps promote readiness to change. Drawing from a broad base of research, Miller and colleagues (Brown & Miller 1993; Miller, 1987, 1989; Miller & Sovereign, 1989) designed a set of procedures that provides clients with a basis for better decision making regarding the need for change. Motivational intervention incorporates a set of five behavior-change principles encapsulated in the FRAMES model: F = feedback; R = responsibility; A =

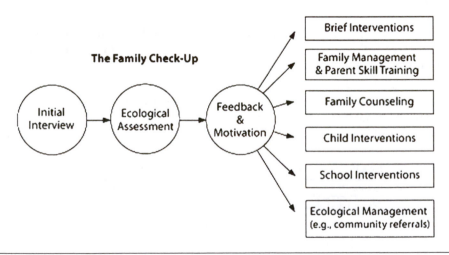

Figure 10.5 Overview of the EcoFIT strategy.

advice; M = menu; E = empathy; S = self-efficacy. The FRAMES model is based on the notion that giving feedback to families that is norm referenced can enhance motivation to change as well as motivate the self-efficacy of caretakers to make the desired changes in behavior.

Consider the following example of the successful implementation of this model in schools. "David" is a 13-year-old boy in the eighth grade. He has problems with aggression and inattention when he attends school, which is infrequent. His mother is sick and he has two younger siblings, so he often stays home to care for her and skips school. Although his mother supports his achievement, she gets lonely during the day and enjoys having her son at home. The child was identified by the school staff as someone who would potentially benefit from the FCU and related services. Our parent consultant visited the family at home and learned of the mother's illness and the context behind the child's truancy. Feedback to the family supported the strengths of the family (e.g., very positive mother–son relationship) as well as the challenges (maternal depression, illness, son's truancy and misbehavior). The consultant problem-solved with the mother to find ways to get her son to school, even when she was not feeling well. David was provided incentives for school attendance, both at home and at school, such as TV time at home and "bonus bucks" at school that could be used in the school store. After working with the family over the course of five meetings, David's school attendance improved.

From the school's perspective, David was a truant, aggressive teen who needed some mental health support. Additional information about the family provided a context for the truancy, which in this case was responsive to a home-to-school behavior plan that was coordinated with the mother and the school. The service was relatively brief, cost effective, and, most important, focused the intervention on the problem, which was related to parenting and family stress.

In its current version, the FCU reduces the amount of intervention time needed to effect change in both problem behavior and parenting practices that exacerbate school problems. Its tailored, adaptive design (see Collins, Murphy, & Bierman, 2004) emphasizes the principles of supporting effective family management and the regulation of negative affect. It can be administered by a variety of school personnel such as school counselors, school psychologists, and behavioral support specialists. On the whole, the FCU can be used as a stand-alone, brief intervention or as a framework for building a relationship and continuing intervention with a family. Most families will continue to seek services, which will be guided by the assessment conducted during the FCU.

## Outcomes Associated with the EcoFIT Model

The Child and Family Center research team has successfully applied the family-centered EcoFIT model to multiple cultural groups to prevent problem behavior and improve parenting practices (Boyd-Ball & Dishion, 2006; Connell & Dishion, 2008; Dishion et al., 2002; Shaw, Dishion, Supplee, Gardner, & Arnds, 2006). We have worked with early childhood, school-age, early adolescence, and late adolescence populations, and we have found that this intervention reduces problem behavior and risk factors for problem behavior across all these age groups.

*Project Alliance 1*   In this first large-scale effectiveness trial, we randomly assigned 998 individual Grade 6 students to the FCU or to public middle school as usual. The NIDA-funded study (DA 07031; Dishion, 1996) was conducted in three middle schools in an ethnically diverse, high-risk metropolitan neighborhood. The treatment used a multilevel intervention model and included a school-level intervention (the FRC), a family-level intervention for at-risk youth and families (the FCU), and selected interventions for high-risk youth and families that draw from the ATP parenting curriculum.

The FCU was offered to at-risk families who scored in the top one third on teacher ratings of behavior problems at school. Of the intervention group, 41% of at-risk families engaged in the FCU and an additional 20% of the at-risk sample received either in-person or phone services with support. Notably, we found that families most in need of family intervention services (e.g., single parents, those from high-conflict homes, those with deviant peer involvement) engaged more consistently in the FCU. This study, which involved a culturally diverse set of youth and families, also revealed that ethnicity (African American and European American) and gender were not related to engagement in or responsiveness to the intervention (Connell et al., 2007). One potential explanation is that the flexible delivery format and the assessment-driven, collaborative, and tailored nature of the family-centered intervention optimized the engagement of culturally diverse families.

We initially analyzed and reported the outcomes of the patterns of substance use from age 11 through age 14 for typically developing and for high-risk students. Students assigned to the FCU were less likely to be using substances in Grade 9, and youth at high risk reduced their reported substance use from Grades 6 through 9 (Dishion et al., 2002). Dishion, Nelson, and Kavanagh (2003) examined the changes in family management that accounted for reduction in risk in the first year of high school. These analyses suggest that the randomly assigned family-centered intervention reduced the downward slope in observations of parental monitoring, which in turn accounted for reductions in risk for deviant peer substance use in the first year of high school (Dishion et al., 2002).

We recently updated our findings to incorporate the role of parent engagement in the intervention for producing outcomes, as well as to follow the youth through high school. To incorporate parent engagement in the overall analysis of effects, we used a statistical procedure referred to as complier average causal effect (CACE) modeling (Jo, 2002). CACE modeling builds on the mixture modeling framework developed by Muthén and Muthén (2004). This procedure retains the strengths of random assignment at the individual level, while also allowing the estimation of a control subgroup who strongly resembles those families who engaged in the FCU and linked interventions. In these analyses, strong effects were found on reducing adolescent problem behavior and arrest rates through age 17 (Connell et al., 2007).

Students who have shown both problem behavior and emotional distress are generally those who are at higher risk in terms of multiple long-term outcomes, including school success (Capaldi, 1992; Dishion, 2000). We suspect that for these students, depression is an indicator of difficulties in multiple domains, including acrimonious relationships with adults and peers and cascading failure in the school context. Thus, it is important to design interventions for high-risk students that address both the behavioral and emotional domains. We recently examined the effects of the EcoFIT approach on adolescent reports of depression among our highest risk students. Using an intention to treat analysis, we found that random assignment to EcoFIT prevented high-risk students from becoming depressed by the first year of high school, whereas high-risk students in the control group increased their levels of depression. When we used CACE modeling to compare those who engaged with the intervention with those who did not, it was clear that the effects on depression for high-risk students were more pronounced (Connell & Dishion, in press).

A primary target of our intervention is academic success in the middle and high school years. We examined the impact of our family-centered model on academic achievement, including grades and attendance. Using data we collected from the school district, we found that random assignment to the intervention group was associated with increases in both GPA and attendance into the 11th grade (Stormshak et al., 2009). Youth in the control group ended high school with failing grades, whereas the intervention group graduated with an average GPA. Similarly, youth in the control group missed an average of 32 days of school per year compared with the intervention group, who missed only 13 days (see Figures 10.6 and 10.7). These results suggest that family-centered, school-based intervention services can impact long-term academic achievement. Our successful work with this age group segued into another randomized trial in the Portland, Oregon, schools, this time to examine the impact of our family-centered model on the transition to high school. This research (Project Alliance 2, Stormshak) is focusing on improving outcomes such as academic achievement, school retention, and reduction of substance use.

The usual assumption is that intervention models that target parenting practices are unwieldy and expensive. However, our intervention model is minimally intrusive and is not costly: effects were obtained with an average of 6 hours of contact with parents during the course of 3 years. The extent of parent engagement in the intervention was predicted by teacher reports of youth risk, youth reports of elevated family conflict, and

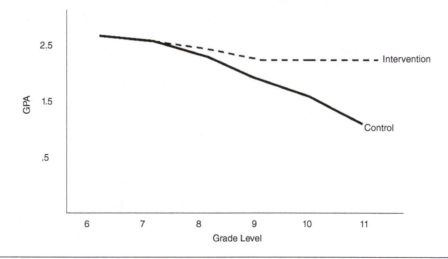

**Figure 10.6** Effects on GPA through high school.

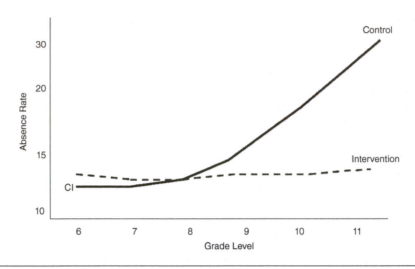

**Figure 10.7** Effects on school absence through high school.

the absence of biological fathers from the youth's home. That is, parent engagement was greatest for our highest risk families (Connell et al., 2007).

*Next Generation Project*   Starting in fall 2000, we were funded by NIDA to implement a prevention program in the middle schools (DA13773, The Next Generation, Dishion & Stormshak). We randomly assigned eight middle schools to intervention or control conditions, and we embedded FRCs and our FCU model successfully into four of them. Parent groups were a central focus of the research design. Control schools, which implemented only parent groups, were compared with intervention schools, which implemented parenting groups and an FRC that included a half-time staff person to deliver the FCU. We hypothesized that in the experimental schools there would be more family involvement and parent group attendance, and subsequent reductions in substance use.

In the Next Generation intervention trial, we collected data about the kind and level of contacts with parents in the experimental schools. Our findings suggest that we were successful in enhancing parent involvement in the schools. We collected FRC contact data about each family who received any intervention in the FRC or support from our staff. Analyses of these data showed that a variety of types of contact seems to be useful to families. We also found that any type of parent contact (e.g., calls, e-mails, in-person contact) was related to decreases in risk behavior over 3 years (Stormshak et al., 2005). The findings suggest the efficacy of many different modes of family intervention that do not necessarily include parenting groups and intensive family therapy. Brief support on the phone, homework monitoring, or brief problem-focused interventions also may be useful to families and lead to positive changes in youth behavior. Results highlight the importance of parent involvement as an intervention target that is amenable to changes over time.

*Intervention Effects: Early Childhood*   The Early Steps Project was funded by NIDA (DA 16110; Dishion, 2002 ) to target children age 2 to 4 whose families we registered through the Women, Infants, and Children Nutrition Program (WIC). The first goal of this project was to investigate whether the FCU intervention was effective for reducing child problem behavior from ages 2 to 4 (Dishion et al., in press). Using latent growth modeling, we found a consistent pattern of intervention effects relevant to reduced problem behavior, as indicated by both the Eyberg Child Behavior Inventory and the Externalizing factor from the CBCL. In addition, we examined the extent to which intervention effects on conduct problems were mediated by changes in observed positive behavior support (PBS), a critical dimension of family management in early childhood. PBS was defined by four observation measures: (a)ratings of parental involvement at the home assessments, (b) videotaped observations of positive reinforcement, (c) joint parent–child socialization time, and (d) ratings of proactive parenting in the videotaped interactions. Notably, the effect of the intervention on children's growth in problem behavior was mediated by increases in the parents' use of PBS strategies (Dishion et al., in press).

Additional outcomes from our work in early childhood (Lunkenheimer et al., 2008) explore the intervention's efficacy for promoting school readiness vis-à-vis improvements in language development and inhibitory control, and whether changes in positive parenting mediate these skills. Similar to the findings described earlier, random assignment to the EcoFIT intervention was associated with improvements in children's language skills (assessed using the Fluharty test; Simmons, 1988) and maternal reports of inhibitory control (Rothbart scale) from ages 2 to 4, and improvements associated with intervention status were mediated by changes in PBS from ages 2 to 3.

### Future Plans

In summary, the EcoFIT intervention model comprises three major phases: (a) the FRC, which provides information about schoolwide discipline, rules, parenting skills, and behavioral support; (b) the FCU; and (c) a menu of intervention and treatment options. All intervention options for families are based on the family management curriculum from the ATP program and our Early Childhood Parenting materials (Dishion & Patterson, 1996). The basic model as described earlier has been tested across three randomized prevention trials to date: Project Alliance 1, the Next Generation Project, and the Early Steps Project. In each separate trial, we have found support for the model for reducing problem behavior, increasing PBS at home, and decreasing long-term adjustment problems for youth.

Project Alliance 2, our current test of this intervention model, involves a diverse population of middle school youth in an urban setting. The project goal is to support successful school adaptation during the transition to high school. We have recruited 593 families in three middle schools, and their students have been randomly assigned to receive the intervention or school as usual. We adapted the current version of the FCU to be sensitive to the demands on families from diverse backgrounds, such as discrimination at school, racial identity, and acculturation. We are measuring each of these issues in this sample and are giving parents feedback during the FCU. For example, we ask youth how much they experience racism and discrimination at school, from peers, and from teachers. The results have been varied; at one school 50% of youth reported feeling discrimination from teachers. As predicted, ethnically diverse youth are the most likely to endorse these items, which lead to disengagement of both youth and families from the school. Analysis of data collected during sixth and seventh grades reveals a significant and positive relationship between students' perceived discriminatory experiences at school and affiliation with deviant peers, depression, and antisocial behavior, and is negatively and significantly correlated with effortful control, one measure of self-regulatory abilities (Falkenstein, Stormshak, Dishion, & Hill, 2008).

Positive ethnic identity, on the other hand, has been shown to be significantly and positively related to constructive family relationships, parental monitoring, the total number of prosocial peers students report spending time with, positive perceptions of teachers, enjoyment of learning, and effortful control. Our parent consultants, who are matched with families' ethnicity, work directly with parents and teachers to support each child's school achievement while being sensitive to parents' negative experiences in the school context in terms of racial issues. Recent study results demonstrate the importance of including feedback to parents and school staff about both the potentially detrimental effects of discriminatory experiences children face at school, and the positive buffering impact ethnic identity may provide for students of color.

### Disseminating the EcoFIT Model to Schools: Goals and Challenges

The ultimate goal of any program of intervention research should be to disseminate and train school personnel to implement a program successfully. Recently, successful dissemination and adoption of empirically validated programming has become even more crucial because of increasing demands for accountability in schools. Dissemination of the EcoFIT model requires several steps that are consistent with those outlined by Flay et al. (2005) in their discussion of the successful dissemination of evidence-based programs. First, schools that are interested in the program and have resources that would enable the successful uptake of the program could be identified. Needed resources may include an available room for an FRC and a school staff person who is willing to take on the delivery of this intervention. Second, clear manuals and a training protocol must be developed. The training should include support for implementation across the school year, monitoring of school staff, and consultation with school leaders to evaluate the program's successful uptake.

Next, fidelity of implementation should be assessed. This includes providing descriptive information about how many students are served. Fidelity measurement tools that can be administered quickly are critical to successful uptake of a program; in the EcoFIT model this step involves coding of feedback session videotapes to examine the delivery fidelity during feedback to parents. At the Child and Family Center (CFC), we are using the Fidelity of Implementation Rating System (FIMP; Forgatch, Patterson, & DeGarmo , 2005). Ideally, parent consultants in each school would send CFC a segment of videotape recorded during a feedback session to parents. Coders at our center would code the tapes and provide feedback about implementation fidelity to school staff. This system could be accomplished online through an interactive website or in person with a consultant to the schools.

We are currently working with two middle schools in Oregon as "model schools" to implement the EcoFIT model and integrate it into existing school structures. In each school, we have set up the program to reflect the school environment. For example, in one school the model is implemented by the school counselor, who contacts parents and provides feedback and information about parenting to families. This model is quite different from the typical role of the school counselor, and the implementation of this program has changed the nature of this person's role in the school. We are also working on research to fund large-scale evaluation and dissemination of the EcoFIT model so that we may examine variables associated with successful uptake of the model, such as school environment, school behavioral management practices, and staff support for the model.

## CONCLUSION

The EcoFIT model is a viable, school-based, family-centered approach to the reduction of problem behavior in schools and at home. The model focuses on encouraging parental involvement in the reduction of child problem behaviors and addresses parents' resistance to change. This model has been tested or is currently in progress across five individual randomized trials with a diverse population of families. In each case, the EcoFIT model successfully reduced risk factors for problem behavior and substance use. Ideally, future research will focus on considerations related to large-scale dissemination of the EcoFIT model and factors that increase its successful uptake in schools.

## AUTHORS' NOTE

This research was supported by National Institutes of Health grants DA 018374 and DA 018760 to the first author and DA 016110 to the second author.

## REFERENCES

Ackerman, B. P., Brown, E. D., & Izard, C. E. (2004). The relations between contextual risk, earned income, and the school adjustment of children from economically disadvantaged families. *Developmental Psychology, 40*, 204–216.

Biglan, A., Mrazek, P. J., Carnine, D., & Flay, B. R. (2003). The integration of research and practice in the prevention of youth problem behaviors. *American Psychologist, 58*, 433–440.

Blair, C. (2001). The early identification of risk for grade retention among African American children at risk for school difficulty. *Applied Developmental Science, 5*, 37–50.

Boyd-Ball, A. J., & Dishion, T. J. (2006). Family-centered treatment for American Indian adolescent substance abuse: Toward a culturally and historically informed strategy. In H. A. Liddle & C. L. Rowe (Eds.), *Adolescent substance abuse: Research and clinical advances* (pp. 423–448). New York: Cambridge University Press.

Brown, J. M., & Miller, W. R. (1993). Impact of motivational interviewing on participation and outcome in residential alcoholism treatment. *Addictive Behaviors, 7*, 211–218.

Capaldi, D. M. (1992). Co-occurrence of conduct problems and depressive symptoms in early adolescent boys: II. A 2-year follow-up at Grade 8. *Development and Psychopathology, 4*, 125–144.

Christenson, S. L. (2003). The family–school partnership: An opportunity to promote the learning competence of all students. *School Psychology Quarterly, 18*, 454–482.

Collins, L., Murphy, S., & Bierman, K. (2004). A conceptual framework for adaptive preventive interventions. *Prevention Science, 5*, 185–196.

Conduct Problems Prevention Research Group. (1999). Initial impact of the FAST Track Prevention trial for conduct problems: I. The high-risk sample. *Journal of Consulting and Clinical Psychology, 67*, 631–647.

Connell, A., & Dishion, T. (2008). Reducing depression among at-risk early adolescents: Three-year effects of a family-centered intervention embedded in schools. *Journal of Family Psychology, 22*(4), 574–585.

Connell, A., Dishion, T. J., Yasui, M., & Kavanagh, K. (2007). An adaptive approach to family intervention: Linking engagement in family-centered intervention to reductions in adolescent problem behavior. *Journal of Consulting and Clinical Psychology, 75*, 568–579.

Dishion, T. J. (2000). Cross-setting consistency in early adolescent psychopathology: Deviant friendships and problem behavior sequelae. *Journal of Personality, 68*, 1109–1126.

Dishion, T. J., & Kavanagh, K. (2003). *Intervening in adolescent problem behavior: A family-centered approach.* New York: Guilford.

Dishion, T. J., Kavanagh, K., Schneiger, A., Nelson, S. E., & Kaufman, N. (2002). Preventing early adolescent substance use: A family-centered strategy for the public middle-school ecology. In R. L. Spoth, K. Kavanagh, & T. J. Dishion (Eds.), Universal family-centered prevention strategies: Current findings and critical issues for public health impact [Special Issue]. *Prevention Science, 3*, 191–201.

Dishion, T. J., Nelson, S. E., & Kavanagh, K. (2003). The Family Check-Up for high-risk adolescents: Preventing early-onset substance use by parent monitoring. In J. E. Lochman & R. Salekin (Eds.), Behavior-oriented interventions for children with aggressive behavior and/or conduct problems [Special Issue]. *Behavior Therapy.*

Dishion, T. J., & Patterson, S. G. (1996). *Preventive parenting with love, encouragement, and limits: The preschool years.* Eugene, OR: Castalia.

Dishion, T. J., & Patterson, G. R. (2006). The development and ecology of antisocial behavior in children and adolescents. In D. Cicchetti & D. J. Cohen (Eds.), *Developmental psychopathology: Vol. 3. Risk, disorder, and adaptation* (pp. 503–541). New York: Wiley.

Dishion, T. J., Shaw, D. S., Connell, A., Wilson, M. N., Gardner, F., & Weaver, C. M. (2008). The Family Check-Up with high-risk indigent families: Preventing problem behavior by increasing parents' positive behavior support in early childhood. *Child Development, 79*(5), 1395–1414.

Dishion, T. J., & Stormshak, E. (2007). *Intervening in children's lives: An ecological, family-centered approach to mental health care.* Washington, DC: APA Books.

Falkenstein, C. A., Stormshak, E. A., Dishion, T. J., & Hill, L. (2008, March). *Perceived discrimination and the development of problem behaviors in adolescence.* Poster presented at the annual meeting of the Society for Research in Adolescence, Chicago, IL.

Flay, B. R., Biglan, A., Boruch, R. F., Castro, F. G., Gottfredson, D., Kellam, S., et al. (2005). Standards of evidence: Criteria for efficacy, effectiveness and dissemination. *Prevention Science, 6*, 151–175.

Forgatch, M. S., Patterson, G. R., & DeGarmo, D. S. (2005). Evaluating fidelity: Predictive validity for a measure of competent adherence to the Oregon Model of Parent Management Training. *Behavior Therapy, 36*, 3–13.

Gifford-Smith, M., Dodge, K. A., Dishion, T. J., & McCord, J. (2005). Peer influence in children and adolescents: Crossing the bridge from developmental to intervention science. *Journal of Abnormal Child Psychology, 33*(3), 255–265.

Hoagwood, K. E., Olin, S. S., Kerker, B. D., Kratochwill, T. R., Crowe, M., & Saka, N. (2007). Empirically based school interventions targeted at academic and mental health functioning. *Journal of Emotional and Behavioral Disorders, 15*, 66–92.

Jo, B. (2002). Statistical power in randomized intervention studies with noncompliance. *Psychological Methods, 7*, 178–193.

Katoaka, S. H., Zhang, L., & Wells, K. B. (2002). Unmet need for mental health care among U.S. children: Variation by ethnicity and insurance status. *American Journal of Psychiatry, 159*, 1548–1555.

Lochman, J. E., & van den Steenhoven, A. (2002). Family-based approaches to substance abuse prevention. *Journal of Primary Prevention, 23*(1), 49–114.

Lochman, J. E., & Wells, K. C. (2004). The Coping Power Program for preadolescent aggressive boys and their parents: Outcome effects at the one-year follow-up. *Journal of Consulting and Clinical Psychology, 72*, 571–578.

Lunkenheimer, E. S., Dishion, T. J., Shaw, D. S., Connell, A. M., Gardner, F., Wilson, M. N., et al. (2008). Collateral benefits of the Family Check-Up on early childhood school readiness: Indirect effects of parents' positive behavior support. *Developmental Psychology, 44*(6), 1737–1752.

Miller, W. R. (1987). Motivation and treatment goals. *Drugs and Society, 1*, 133–151.

Miller, W. R. (1989). Increasing motivation for change. In R. K. Hester & W. R. Miller (Eds.), *Handbook of alcoholism treatment approaches: Effective alternatives* (pp. 67–80). Elmsford, NY: Pergamon Press.

Miller, W. R., & Rollnick, S. (2002). *Motivational interviewing: Preparing people for change* (2nd ed.). New York: Guilford.

Miller, W. R., & Sovereign, R. G. (1989). The checkup: A model for early intervention in addictive behaviors. In T. Loberg, W. R. Miller, P. E. Nathan, & G. A. Marlatt (Eds.), *Addictive behaviors: Prevention and early intervention* (pp. 219–231). Amsterdam: Sweta and Zeitlinger.

Moffitt, T. E. (1990). Juvenile delinquency in attention deficit disorder: Boys' developmental trajectories from age 3 to age 15. *Child Development, 61*, 893–910.

Muthén, L. K., & Muthén, B. O. (2004). *Mplus user's guide, third edition*. Los Angeles: Muthén & Muthén.

Nelson, S. E., & Dishion, T. J. (2004). From boys to men: Predicting adult adaptation from middle childhood sociometric status. *Development & Psychopathology, 16*, 441–459.

Patterson, G. R., Reid, J. B., & Dishion, T. J. (1992). *Antisocial boys*. Eugene, OR: Castalia.

Prochaska, J. O., & DiClemente, C. (1986). Toward a comprehensive model of change. In W. Miller & N. Heather (Eds.), *Treating addictive behaviors: Processes of change* (pp. 3–27). New York: Plenum.

Raver, C. C., Gershoff, E. T., & Aber, J. L. (2007). Testing equivalence of mediating models of income, parenting, and school readiness for White, Black, and Hispanic children in a national sample. *Child Development, 78*(1), 96–115.

Sameroff, A. J., & Fiese, B. H. (1987). *Conceptual issues in prevention*. Unpublished manuscript.

Shaw, D. S., Dishion, T. J., Supplee, L., Gardner, F., & Arnds, K. (2006). Randomized trial of a family-centered approach to the prevention of early conduct problems: Two-year effects of the Family Check-Up in early childhood. *Journal of Consulting and Clinical Psychology, 74*(1), 1–9.

Simmons, J. O. (1988). Fluharty Preschool Speech and Language Screening Test: Analysis of construct validity. *Journal of Speech & Hearing Disorders, 53*, 168–174.

Spoth, R. L., Kavanagh, K., & Dishion, T. J. (2002). Family-centered preventive intervention science: Toward benefits to larger populations of children, youth, and families. [Special Issue]. *Prevention Science, 3*, 145–152.

Spoth, R. L., Redmond, C., & Shin, C. (1998). Direct and indirect latent-variable parenting outcomes of two universal family-focused preventative interactions: Extending a public health oriented research base. *Journal of Consulting and Clinical Psychology, 66*(2), 385–399.

Sprague, J. R., & Golly, A. (2005). *Best behavior: Building positive behavior supports in schools*. Longmont, CO: Sopris West.

Stoolmiller, M. Duncan, T., Bank, L., & Patterson, G. (1993). Some problems and solutions in the study of change: Significant patterns of client resistance. *Journal of Consulting and Clinical Psychology, 61*, 920–928.

Stormshak, E. A., Connell, A. M., & Dishion, T. J. (2009). An adaptive approach to family-centered intervention in schools: Linking intervention engagement to academic outcomes in middle and high school. *Prevention Science*. http://www.springerlink.com/content/2826u6356137k723/fultext.pdf; retrieved 6/26/09.

Stormshak, E. A., & Dishion, T. J. (2002). An ecological approach to child and family clinical and counseling psychology. *Clinical Child and Family Psychology Review, 5*(3), 197–215.

Stormshak, E. A., Dishion, T. J., Light, J., & Yasui, M. (2005). Implementing family-centered interventions within the public middle school: Linking service delivery change to change in problem behavior. *Journal of Abnormal Child Psychology, 33*(6), 723–733.

Sugai, G., Sprague, J. R., Horner, R. H., & Walker, H. M. (2000). Preventing school violence: The use of office discipline referrals to assess and monitor school-wide discipline interventions. *Journal of Emotional & Behavioral Disorders, 8*(2), 94–101.

Sugai, G., Sprague, J. R., Horner, R. H., & Walker, H. M. (2001). Preventing school violence: The use of office discipline referrals to assess and monitor school-wide discipline interventions. In H. M. Walker & M. H. Epstein (Eds.), *Making schools safer and violence free: Critical issues, solutions, and recommended practices*. (pp. 50–57). Austin, TX: PRO-ED.

Szapocznik, J., & Prado, G. (2007). Negative effects on family functioning from psychosocial treatments: A recommendation for expanded safety monitoring. *Journal of Family Psychology, 21*, 468–478.

Weisz, J. R., Jensen-Doss, A., & Hawley, K. M. (2006). Evidence-based youth psychotherapies versus usual clinical care: A meta-analysis of direct comparisons. *American Psychologist, 61*, 671–689.

Yasui, M., Dorham, C. L., & Dishion, T. J. (2004). Ethnic identity and psychological adjustment: A validity analysis for European American and African American adolescents. *Journal of Adolescent Research, 19*(6), 807–825.

# 11

## SCHOOL-FAMILY PARTNERSHIPS TO PROMOTE SOCIAL AND EMOTIONAL LEARNING

MICHELLE I. ALBRIGHT AND ROGER P. WEISSBERG

Key adult figures within home, school, and community shape children's social, emotional, and cognitive development (Bronfenbrenner, 1979; Patrikakou, Weissberg, Redding, & Walberg, 2005a). Home has traditionally been viewed as the primary context for social and emotional learning, and school as the primary context for academic learning. Although families are integral to children's social-emotional development, school is also a critical context for social and emotional growth (Greenberg et al., 2003). Likewise, home is a crucial context that fosters academic achievement (Henderson & Mapp, 2002). Moreover, academic, social, and emotional skills serve children across contexts, and can only be successfully fostered and maintained when mutually supported and reinforced by families[1] and educators[2] (Christenson & Sheridan, 2001; Zins, Weissberg, Wang, & Walberg, 2004).

## OVERVIEW

It is our contention that the conceptualization of the roles parents and teachers play in educating and socializing children need to be broadened and, likewise, notions regarding the educational mission of schools need to be expanded. Schools need to extend the definition of achievement to encompass mastery of a range of competencies and behaviors—not just subjects (Patrikakou et al., 2005a). In order to cultivate successful students and citizens, schools need to educate children to use critical thinking skills, make responsible and ethical decisions, and engage in healthy and pro-social behaviors (Greenberg et al., 2003). When families and educators collaborate—particularly with a social-emotional learning focus—they extend opportunities for learning across contexts, and model the very communication, behavior, and relationship skills they aim to teach to children.

Social and emotional learning (SEL) is the process of developing fundamental social and emotional competencies or skills in children (Elias et al., 1997; Zins & Elias, 2006).

Such skills enable children to recognize and manage emotions, experience empathy, develop positive relationships, make good decisions, behave ethically and responsibly, and avoid negative behaviors (Collaborative for Academic, Social, and Emotional Learning (CASEL), 2003; Payton et al., 2000). SEL also impacts the creation of an engaging and supportive school climate, and the formation of personal and educational goals. Hence, SEL is intrinsic to children's academic learning and performance, motivation to achieve, psychological development and well-being, and social relationships (CASEL, 2003; Elias et al., 1997). In this chapter essential elements of school-family partnerships (SFP) and SEL are described. Next, several exemplary SEL programs that utilize a SFP framework are reviewed. Finally, guidelines for promoting SFP with an SEL focus are offered, and critical considerations for the implementation process are highlighted.

## School-Family Partnership: Defining Features and Focus

Recognition that benefits accrue when parents and teachers collaborate to support children's achievement has brought school-family partnerships to the forefront of the national education agenda. School-family partnerships are associated with a range of positive outcomes for children including improved attendance, higher rates of homework completion, higher grades and test scores, and higher rates of school completion (Barnard, 2004; Henderson & Berla, 1987; Henderson & Mapp, 2002; Jeynes, 2005). However, the beneficial impact of family involvement extends beyond academic outcomes and includes increased self-esteem, improved behavior at home and school, more positive attitudes toward school, and improved interpersonal and decision making skills (Christenson & Havsy, 2004; Patrikakou et al., 2005a). Moreover, research demonstrates that engagement in high-risk behavior is less likely when adolescents perceive a strong affiliation between home and school (Resnick et al., 1997).

School-family partnerships can be characterized in a variety of ways and there is no universal definition of, nor prescription for, creating successful home-school collaboration. Early models and frameworks were used to describe the various kinds of parent-teacher relationships, and resulted in the creation of typologies to differentiate the nature and impact of involvement (see, for example, Swap, 1993; Epstein, 1990, 1995). In recent years, the focus has shifted to examining the nature of the relationship between educators and families; particularly the role of perceptions, rather than practices of involvement (Eccles & Harold, 1993, 1996; Hoover-Dempsey & Sandler, 1997). Our working definition of SFP emphasizes the process of families and educators working collaboratively to enhance children's social, emotional, and educational development via home-, school-, and community-based interaction and involvement. Productive partnerships are intrinsically malleable and need to incorporate the needs and characteristics of the particular school-family-community in which they are based (Christenson, Weissberg, & Klein, 2007). Moreover, practices of involvement that are not supported by perceptions of partnership are unlikely to lead to valuable collaboration.

In framing our work, we expand upon several conceptualizations (i.e., Christenson & Sheridan, 2001; Patrikakou & Weissberg, 1999; Rubenstein, 1998; Rubenstein, Patrikakou, Weissberg, & Armstrong, 1999) to illustrate the A-B-C's of successful SFP. Our A-B-C framework illustrates the essential Approach, Broad Domains, and Core

Characteristics of successful SFP and has utility for implementing and evaluating efforts to enhance home-school communication and family involvement in SEL at home and school. Moreover, the framework allows for flexibility so specific initiatives can be tailored to meet school-community needs while still adhering to key principles and program components.

## Approach

The first component is derived from the work of Christenson and Sheridan (2001) who presented a framework depicting the pathway to partnership that reflects four A's: Approach, Attitude, Atmosphere, and Actions. Approach, Attitudes, and Atmosphere are considered prerequisites for effective implementation of Actions, and are all important for establishing home-school collaboration. As presented in the original conceptualization, creating and sustaining a home-school collaboration that prizes and promotes SEL requires the adoption of an approach that acknowledges academic, social, and emotional learning as the shared responsibility of families and educators. Attitudes refer to perceptions, beliefs, and values about family-school relationships; meaningful collaboration implies the need for perceptions of equality and value, and shared responsibility among partners. Atmosphere refers to the climate in schools. The school community needs to evolve into a school-family community in order to be perceived as a welcoming and receptive environment for all students and their families. Actions refer to the strategies and practices for creating shared responsibility for academic, social, and emotional outcomes.

We have consolidated these dimensions into a focus on *Approach* that encompasses the need to make partnership a priority, and recognize families and educators as essential to the educational process. Accordingly, *Approach* includes the adoption of positive partnership-supporting attitudes, an allegiance to shared developmental and educational goals, and the creation of an atmosphere that values home-school collaboration as essential for academic, social, and emotional learning (Christenson, Rounds, & Franklin, 1992; Seeley, 1989; Weiss & Edwards, 1992). Such an approach leads to practices that enhance the complementary roles of families and educators by promoting consistency and continuity in the messages about, and methods used, to promote academic, social, and emotional learning (Christenson & Sheridan, 2001; Fantuzzo, Tighe, & Childs, 2000; Patrikakou & Weissberg, 2007).

## Broad Domains

In our previous work (see, for example, Patrikakou & Weissberg, 2007; Rubenstein et. al., 1999), we identified three broad dimensions of SFP that include two-way home-school communication, family involvement at home, and family involvement at school. We continue to highlight these domains in the current framework; categorizing programming initiatives according to specific focus areas has utility for implementing and evaluating efforts, and serves as a continual reminder of the range of actions and activities that comprise successful SFP.

*Back-and-Forth: Two-Way Home-School Communication*    Two-way home-school communication is a crucial feature of any effort designed to enhance children's social-emotional and educational development (see, for example Epstein, 1990, 1995; Swap, 1993). Our conceptualization of two-way communication reflects the reciprocal nature of home-school communication, rather than the number of parties involved. An open and dynamic communication channel serves several purposes; first and foremost, it allows schools and educators to share information about program content and implementation. For families to actively and effectively reinforce children's learning at home, they need to know what educators are doing at school and in the classroom (Hoover-Dempsey, Bassler, & Burrow, 1995). Home-school communication also provides an avenue to inform families about children's progress, skills, and strengths, and share specific strategies on how to promote learning and pro-social behavior (Caspe, Lopez, & Wolos, 2007). Finally, open and dynamic communication channels enable parents to share questions, comments, and feedback with teachers; this preserves the "back-and-forth" and ensures that families inform educators, in addition to being informed by them (Christenson et al., 2007; Eccles & Harold, 1993, 1996; Grolnick & Slowiaczek, 1994). Communication is also a mode to share information about other arenas in which to learn more (such as workshops or seminars) and can serve as the conduit to other forms of family involvement.

*Backyard: Family Involvement at Home*    When families support learning outside of the classroom, it reinforces the complementary roles of parents and teachers as co-educators in fostering children's academic, social, and emotional development (Eccles & Harold, 1993; 1996; Hoover-Dempsey & Sandler, 1997). Establishing a home environment that is conducive to learning can include communicating positive attitudes about education, engaging in conversations about school and education, and ensuring that adequate reading, writing, and other educational supplies are present. Actively participating in children's learning is also a hallmark of family involvement at home, and may include monitoring or assisting with homework, reading with children, or engaging in interactive learning activities (Cooper, Lindsay, & Nye, 2000; Epstein, 1988; Hoover-Dempsey et al., 2001). Moreover, daily experiences with siblings and parents provide continuous opportunities to apply, model, and reinforce social skills and pro-social behaviors (Hawkins, Smith, & Catalano, 2004). Parent-teacher communication plays a vital role in efforts to involve families at home; families need invitations, information, tools, and resources to effectively complement and reinforce school-based learning (Balli, Wedman, & Demo, 1997; Hoover-Dempsey & Sandler, 1997).

*Back-to-School: Family Involvement at School*    Schools can influence participation in school-based activities and events by creating a school and classroom climate that values families as active and recognizable partners. Teachers are key facilitators in creating a classroom environment that supports family participation; families who feel welcome and wanted at school are more likely to be actively and effectively involved in their children's education (Christenson et al., 2007; Dauber & Epstein, 1993; Eccles & Harold, 1993, 1996; Hoover-Dempsey & Sandler, 1997). Schools can create a variety of opportunities for family involvement, within both the school and the classroom; parents can play a role in determining school policy and overseeing decisions about curriculum by participating in advisory councils or school governing boards, serving as a classroom volunteer, attending parent-teacher conferences, meetings, or workshops, or observing and participating in lessons or curriculum units as they are being implemented (Center for Mental Health in Schools at UCLA, 2007). In addition, classroom participation can be a first step toward greater school-based involvement.

We advise promoting involvement across the three domains; however, it is imperative to respect the diversity among parent styles and preferences, and facilitate participation at any and all levels. Parents may prefer involvement in a particular domain due to personal or practical issues. For example, some families may be less aware of, and less comfortable with, opportunities for school-based involvement; they may have difficultly participating in school or classroom events due to scheduling conflicts and/ or the competing demands of work and family. Language and literacy issues may also interfere with parent's capability to communicate with educators and participate in children's learning at home. Moreover, the academic socialization practices of families from particular backgrounds may be more likely to complement school and teacher expectations, leading to variation in communication and participation practices (Becker & Epstein, 1982; Epstein & Dauber, 1991, Ginsburg, Bempechat, & Chung, 1992). Likewise, educators have multiple perspectives regarding what constitutes optimal family participation and facilitate involvement in diverse ways (Christenson, Rounds, & Gorney, 1992; Epstein, 1990; Swap, 1993). Hence, providing a range of participation options can encourage and accommodate families and educators with varying needs, schedules, and strengths.

### Core Characteristics

In previous conceptualizations, we identified a set of characteristics of effective SFP delineated by seven P's; these include making the partnership with families a *priority*; engaging in a *planned effort*; being *proactive and persistent* in reaching out to families; using *positive* communication strategies; *personalizing* the way families can be involved; implementing *practical,* specific strategies; and ensuring *program monitoring* and modification based on mutual input (Patrikakou, Weissberg, & Rubenstein, 1998; Patrikakou & Weissberg, 1999). Although all of these features contribute to successful SFP, in the current iteration of the framework, we highlight the four most fundamental: Child-Centered, Constructive, Clear and Concrete, and Continuous.

*Child-Centered*   Although it is important to share information about classroom curriculum and school activities, families are often most interested in specific information about their child (Patrikakou & Weissberg, 1999, 2007). Learning about children's developing skills and strengths will help parents recognize and support progress. Furthermore, asking parents to share their views about children's abilities, styles, and development is a valuable way to engage families. Personalized child-centered communication enhances parental responsiveness, and demonstrates the desire to connect individually with students and their families (Rubenstein et al., 1999). Focusing on the child may also reduce parental concerns about being personally judged or evaluated by educators. Communication regarding children may not always be positive; however, acknowledging strengths as well as weaknesses conveys a balanced, holistic view of the child. Child-centered communication may involve a variety of techniques including phone calls, in-person meetings, progress journals, and written notes.

*Constructive*   Parents are most interested in information that is meaningful, useful, and has practical application. Moreover, parents cannot effectively reward or remedy children's success or failure if they do not understand the cause or consequence, and do not have adequate strategies and tools to promote learning. Constructive communication and information is, by definition, helpful and aims to promote further development or improvement. Positive, solution-oriented language helps parents remain optimistic about children's learning and behavior (subsequently enhancing parental efficacy beliefs) and invites parents' input regarding effective solutions (Christenson et al., 2007). This tone maintains an open dialogue and reduces the likelihood of interpreting comments as judgmental or blaming. In addition, the dissemination of constructive information fosters more valuable discussion not only between parents and educators, but between parents and children as well.

*Clear and Concrete*   Clear guidelines and concrete strategies regarding how to promote learning and pro-social behavior will be most beneficial to families in supporting children's learning. Both teachers and parents are busy with the demands of work and family; streamlining communication and highlighting practical tools and resources will better enable families to put information to use. Using simple language, minimal text, and specific guidelines—whether in written or verbal communication—will maximize responsiveness and impact. Likewise, such techniques will diminish some of the obstacles that arise from varying language and literacy levels.

*Continuous*   Families need ongoing communication and information to maintain meaningful involvement in children's learning and development. Proactive communication efforts by educators at the start (or even prior) to the beginning of the school year help establish a cooperative atmosphere and convey the importance of collaboration (Rubenstein et al., 1999). Structured and persistent communication routines help to synchronize perceptions and practices of children, families, and educators.

### Social and Emotional Learning: Defining Features and Focus

The Collaborative for Academic, Social, and Emotional Learning (CASEL, 2003) described five SEL skill clusters that can be systematically cultivated both at home and at school. *Self-Awareness* includes having an accurate, realistic perception about one's abilities and recognizing emotions as they occur. *Self-Management* includes the ability to manage and modulate emotions and stress, control impulses, exercise discipline, and establish and achieve goals. *Social Awareness* reflects the ability to experience empathy and respect towards others, engage in perspective taking, and appreciate diversity. *Relationship Skills* include the ability to engage in healthy, cooperative, and caring relationships, resist harmful social pressure, and resolve conflicts effectively. *Responsible*

*Decision Making* involves making decisions based upon careful consideration of all relevant factors, evaluating possible consequences of actions, and taking responsibility for one's decisions (CASEL, 2003; Zins et al., 2004).

A growing body of research evidence suggests that SEL programming promotes children's skills, attitudes, social behavior, and academic performance (Durlak, Weissberg, Dymnicki, Taylor, & Schellinger, 2008). Moreover, research demonstrates that children competent in these skill domains are more happy, confident, and capable across contexts and relationships—as students, friends, family members, and employees (Greenberg et al., 2003). SEL skills can benefit parent-child and parent-teacher relationships; social-emotional competencies enable individuals to manage stress more effectively, engage in more skillful problem-solving, and employ more adept communication skills (Patrikakou & Weissberg, 2007). Finally, SEL skills support learning and academic achievement via self-management and decision making.

Social-emotional skill development and success is cultivated within relationships and the interactions between children and the key adults (whether parents, teachers, or figures in the community) in their lives function as cause and consequence. Accordingly, attempting to teach SEL in isolation is both impractical and ineffective; skills and behaviors related to SEL need to be observed, applied, and reinforced across contexts of home, school, and community (Christenson & Havsy, 2004; Zins, Bloodworth, Weissberg, & Walberg, 2004). Embedding SEL programs within a SFP framework represent an avenue to achieve this goal; strengthening the connection between home and school underscores the complementary roles of families and educators, and extends opportunities for learning and skill development across contexts.

SEL skills have the capacity to enhance children's preparedness for learning across the educational spectrum from preschool through high school (CASEL, 2003; Kress & Elias, 2006). SEL impacts academic performance, social relationships, and academic and occupational functioning; accordingly SEL programming has been introduced across developmental levels, including in preschool, elementary, middle, and high school curricula (Weissberg & Greenberg, 1998; Zins & Elias, 2006). Although, historically the best developed SFP and SEL programs focused on younger students, in recent years, innovative approaches have been introduced with secondary school students (Elias, Bryan, Patrikakou, & Weissberg, 2003). SEL skills are intrinsically related to critical thinking, analytical thinking, and problem-solving which take on added significance as students enter secondary (and post-secondary) education and must navigate increasingly complex and ambiguous learning tasks (Conley, 2007).

### SEL Programs That Incorporate A SFP Framework

CASEL (2003) examined 242 nationally-available prevention and positive youth programs and systematically evaluated the quality of 80 multi-year programs; 22 programs were identified as CASEL Select Programs and met standards for excellence in SEL instruction, evidence of effectiveness, and professional development. Programs designated as CASEL Select incorporate instructional practices to promote learning and SEL skills beyond the classroom, demonstrate an impact on student behavior as documented by rigorous research, and use professional development and technical assistance in program implementation. Given the importance of strengthening the link between home and school and involving families in using complementary strategies to promote and sustain SEL skills and competencies, CASEL also evaluated the extent and quality of program efforts to integrate family involvement practices into program content and implementation. Several CASEL Select Programs were identified as utilizing comprehensive outreach and coordinated instruction to promote school-wide community and family involvement.

Durlak et al. (2008) conducted a meta-analysis of 207 school-based SEL programs; programs were categorized according to several criteria including whether SEL curricula were implemented by a classroom teacher or non-school personnel, whether single (e.g., classroom-based core curriculum) or multicomponent strategies (e.g., family component or school-wide initiative) were utilized, and quality of implementation. A range of student outcomes (rated via teacher- and parent-report, as well as child self-report) were used as dependent variables including social and emotional skills, attitudes toward self and others, positive social behaviors, conduct problems, emotional distress, and academic performance. Considerable variation in the ways schools attempted to involve families in SEL programming efforts was evident; hence, four categories were created to distinguish among types of involvement: Parent Training, School-Parent Involvement, Parent-Child Involvement, and School-Parent Contact. *Parent Training* included any attempt to increase parental skills or alter the home environment through parent education. *School-Parent Involvement* comprised efforts to facilitate involvement with the school (such as increased parent-teacher communication and active involvement in decision-making). *Parent-Child Involvement* reflected efforts to facilitate family involvement with children through interactive learning activities or tutoring. *School-Parent Contact* included communication efforts such as flyers or information dissemination via school assemblies. Twenty-seven percent (n = 56) of the 207 programs included in the meta-analysis had at least one of the four family components. Preliminary analyses on the subset of programs that included a family component yielded positive outcomes on children's social skills, attitudes, and school performance. Unfortunately, there were not a sufficient number of studies comparing the differential effectiveness of school-based SEL programming versus school-based plus parent SEL training to determine the extent to which combined school-family programming for SEL adds value to school-only or parent-only training.

Table 11.1 spotlights several exemplary SEL programs that utilize a SFP framework. A brief overview of each program is included, as well as a description of how the program typifies our conceptualization of *Approach*; specifically, how the program contributes to a school-community atmosphere that values home-school collaboration and incorporates SFP practices that support SEL. Although these programs employ a range of strategies to involve families and integrate SEL across contexts of home and school, we use the three *Broad domains* depicted in our A-B-C framework to illustrate how programming efforts may be conceptualized and targeted. Moreover, the three broad domains of our A-B-C framework encompass the four categories used in the meta-analysis: Back-and-Forth: Two-Way Home-School Communication coincides with School-Parent Contact, Backyard: Family Involvement at Home with Parent-Child Involvement, and Back-to-School: Family Involvement at School with School-Parent

**Table 11.1** Exemplary SEL Programs that Utilize a SFP Framework

| Program Name Contact Information | Program Overview | Approach | Back-and-Forth: Two-Way Home-School Communication | Backyard & Back-to-school: Family Involvement at Home and School |
|---|---|---|---|---|
| Caring School Community Developmental Studies Ctr 2000 Embarcadero, Suite 305 Oakland, CA 94606-5300 Phone: 800/666-7270 E-mail: pubs@devstu.org Web site: www.devstu.org | The Caring School Community program focuses on building a school community based on caring relationships among students, between students and teachers, and between schools and families. It stresses good citizenship and provides broad multiyear coverage of this content area. Such caring is expected to increase student attachment to school and mediate positive student social, emotional, and academic outcomes. | • Guidelines for establishing a school-wide coordination team that includes parents, teachers, and other school staff <br> • Book containing "inclusive school-wide activities" with many opportunities to support caring, non-competitive relationships <br> • Teachers pair up to plan, facilitate, and evaluate the buddies program | • Eighteen interactive homework assignments per year for children and adults <br> • Students frequently involved in service-learning projects, including classroom preparation and follow-up reflection | • Parent involvement strategies including a back-to-school night <br> • Family math workshops, science nights, and movie nights |
| Project Achieve 49 Woodberry Road Little Rock, AR 72212 Phone: 501-312-1484 Website: http://www.projectachieve.info/ | Project ACHIEVE helps schools, communities, and families to develop, strengthen, reinforce, and solidify children's resilience, protective, and effective self-management skills to enhance learning and pro-social behavior. Project ACHIEVE also seeks to improve educational staff's professional development and effective instruction interactions, and increase the quality of parent (and community) involvement and engagement. | • Utilizes initial needs assessments to examine the current and desired state of parent involvement and home-school-community collaboration <br> • School improvement process and plan aims to organize staff around collaboration and family outreach and involvement | • Range of communication and materials to inform parents about the school's academic program and how to support students at home | • Directly trains parents to transfer critical school academic and behavioral interventions into the home <br> • Creates Parent Drop-In Centers to encourage parent participation in school activities and parent access to training and learning materials |

| | | | |
|---|---|---|---|
| Reach Out to Schools: Social Competency Program<br>The Stone Center<br>Wellesley College 106 Central St. Wellesley, MA 02481<br>Phone: 781/283-2861<br>Web site: www.open-circle.org | This comprehensive, year-long, grade-differentiated social competency curriculum aims to help children become ethical people, contributing citizens and successful learners, and to help schools foster the development of relationships that support safe, caring, and respectful learning communities. The program has three major content areas: creating a cooperative classroom environment, solving interpersonal problems, and building positive relationships. | • In addition to classroom teachers, other school staff can get training to reinforce program concepts from within their respective roles and support school-wide implementation | • Curriculum includes frequent newsletters to keep parents apprised of program content and vocabulary | • Several homework activities involve family members<br>• Separate parent workshop led by school mental health staff helps parents apply program concepts at home |
| Responsive Classroom® Northeast Foundation for Children<br>39 Montague City Road Greenfield, MA 01301<br>Phone: 800/360-6332, Ext. 150<br>Website: *www.responsive-classroom.org* | The Responsive Classroom® approach to teaching, learning, and living aims to create a strong and safe school community that is responsive to children's physical, emotional, social, and intellectual needs. Rather than structured lessons, the approach consists of 10 classroom and 5 schoolwide practices for deliberately helping children build academic and social-emotional competencies. Classroom practices include classroom organization; morning meeting; rule creation; interactive modeling; positive teacher language; logical consequences; guided discovery; academic choice; collaborative problem-solving; and working with families. | • Extensive commitment to school-wide coordination via all-school meetings and games, all-school council, and inter-school collaborative of Responsive Classroom® schools | • Frequent family letters to keep parents apprised, and occasional student presentations to parents | • Invites parents and others to visit and volunteer, and offers family activities |

*(continued)*

**Table 11.1** Continued

| Program Name Contact Information | Program Overview | Approach | Back-and-Forth: Two-Way Home-School Communication | Backyard & Back-to-school: Family Involvement at Home and School |
|---|---|---|---|---|
| Seattle Social Development Project (SSDP) aka Skills, Opportunities, and Recognition (SOAR) aka Raising Healthy Children 9725 3rd Avenue NE, Suite 401 Seattle, WA 98115-2024 Phone: 206-685-1997 Website: http://depts. washington.edu/ssdp/intervention.shtml | SSDP is a three-part intervention for teachers, students and parents in grades 1 to 6. Teachers receive training in proactive classroom management, interactive teaching and cooperative learning. SSDP also offers training to parents in child behavior management, academic support, and skills to reduce risks for drug use. SSDP also targets children's interpersonal problem solving and refusal skills. | • Creates a community of learners through a school-wide program designed to strengthen instructional practices and increase family involvement. | • Principal plays key leadership role in implementation efforts <br> • Program involves teachers, administrators, and other school staff in school-wide implementation of program components <br> • Educators and parents learn to consistently communicate healthy beliefs and clear standards for behavior | • Extensive family involvement, with parent workshops, newsletters, and activities at school for families <br> • Academic support curriculum |
| Second Step Committee for Children 568 First Ave. S., Suite 600 Seattle, WA 98104-2804 Phone: 800/634-4449 Website: www.cfchildren.org | The Second Step curriculum is designed to develop students' social and emotional skills, while teaching them to change behaviors and attitudes that contribute to violence. The program focuses on teaching empathy, anger management, and impulse control, and provides broad, multiyear coverage of violence prevention. | • School-wide coordination promoted through establishment of interdisciplinary support team comprised of teachers, administrators, social worker/counselor, parents, and youth representative who oversee implementation | • The SECOND STEP Family Guide familiarizes parents and caregivers with the problem-solving, empathy, and emotion-management skills their children are learning in elementary school, so they can reinforce the concepts at home | • Six-session parent workshop in which parents practice the skills children acquire in Second Step and learn how to reinforce them with their children at home |

Involvement. Depending on the focus and venue, Parent Training may be included within any of the three domains.

*Approach*    Exemplary programs share an explicit focus on creating an atmosphere that values collaboration and promoting activities that validate educators and families as essential partners in implementing program initiatives. Many of the highlighted programs mandate the creation of a school-wide team to facilitate school-wide coordination and implementation of SFP and SEL initiatives. Caring School Community employs a team to guide staff and program coordination (Developmental Studies Center, Oakland, California; available on-line at: http://www.devstu.org/). Responsive Classroom (Elliot, 1995, 1999; Rimm-Kaufman, 2006) and Second Step (Cooke et al., 2007; Frey, Nolen, Edstrom, & Hirschstein, 2005; Larsen & Samdal, 2007) utilize teams to enhance interdisciplinary support. Project Achieve makes use of a school improvement process and plan (Knoff, 2004, 2006; Knoff & Batsche, 1995). Project Achieve uses an initial needs assessment to explore the current and desired state of family involvement and home-school collaboration. Relationship building and staff development are also hallmarks of exemplary programs; Caring School Community incorporates guidelines and activities to cultivate collaborative relationships and Seattle Social Skills Development Program (Hawkins, Smith, & Catalano, 2004; Hawkins, Von Cleve, & Catalano, 1991) includes ongoing professional development for educators.

*Back-and-Forth: Two-Way home-School Communication*    Efforts to enhance home-school communication are integrated into all highlighted programs. At the most basic level, all programs utilize communication strategies to introduce the SEL curriculum, and inform parents about program goals and lessons. The majority of programs use written communication (such as newsletters, homework assignments with interactive components, or informational letters that correspond to particular lessons) or workshops as a way to inform parents about program content and assist parents in teaching children SEL skills by familiarizing them with the skills and strategies children are learning in classrooms. Across programs information is shared in multiple ways, including written notes, group meetings or workshops, and individual conferences.

Reach Out to Schools (Krasnow, Seigle, & Kelly, 1992; Taylor, Liang, Tracy, Williams, & Seigle, 2002) and Responsive Classroom are typical of programs that use letters or newsletters to keep parents apprised of program content. Responsive Classroom also utilizes student presentations as a way to share information about lessons and skills learned. Several other programs including Caring School Community, Reach Out to Schools, and Second Step use workshops to keep parents actively informed about SEL curriculum and content; an additional aim of these workshops is to provide parents with skills and strategies to reinforce skill development at home. Accordingly, such workshops can be viewed as means to promote family involvement at home and school since attendance involves school-based participation.

*Backyard: Family Involvement at Home*    Strategies, activities, and materials that extend and reinforce classroom learning at home are typically included in exemplary SEL programs; these materials prompt parent-child discussion and interactive learning as a way to promote the application of new skills to the home environment. For example, Caring School Community incorporates a series of interactive homework assignments and activities to familiarize parents with concepts being taught within the classroom, and prompt parent-child dialogue and interaction. Likewise, Project Achieve and Second Step, include separate family components with corresponding guides designed to train parents in SEL skills and strategies and how to reinforce concepts at home.

*Back-to-School: Family Involvement at School*  Exemplary programs provide a range of opportunities for classroom-, school-, and community-based involvement. To encourage participation at a school governing level, Caring School Community includes guidelines for establishing a school-wide coordination team that consists of parents, teachers, and other school staff. Similarly, Project Achieve provides a structure for creating a school-wide improvement process and plan, and Second Step invites parents to participate on an interdisciplinary support team. Responsive Classroom invites families to visit and volunteer within the classroom to observe how lessons are taught, and Project Achieve features Parent Drop-In Centers within the school.

Workshops are also a common form of increasing involvement at school; workshops achieve multiple aims and simultaneously promote two-way communication and family involvement at home. Reach Out to Schools sponsors a parent workshop led by school mental health staff to teach key program concepts and how to apply these at home, and Second Step includes a multiple session workshop series to learn and practice skills children acquire as part of the program. Caring School Community also includes guidelines for back-to-school nights, family movie nights, and family workshops.

*Core Characteristics*  Using a SFP framework can aid in creating and sustaining home and school learning environments that promote SEL. However, research demonstrates that families look to schools for guidance on becoming involved in children's learning and are more likely to participate when they perceive invitations, demands, and opportunities (Christenson & Sheridan, 2001; Hoover-Dempsey & Sandler, 1997). The C, Core Characteristics, of our A-B-C framework describes critical features of efforts to promote home-school communication, and family involvement at home and school. Table 11.2 provides an overview of initiatives educators can use throughout the year to cultivate communication and involvement around SEL.

### Critical Considerations for the Implementation Process

Establishing meaningful SFP is inherently challenging. True collaboration requires a level of trust and commitment that can often be difficult for educators and families to attain. Moreover, a hallmark of effective partnerships is the creation of a trusting relationship and the ability to recognize and respect the diverse styles, skills, and strengths among participants. This tenet is also a guiding principle of SEL and reflects competencies related to self-awareness, social awareness, and relationship management. The following issues may pose challenges as schools and families attempt to partner to support children's SEL.

**Table 11.2** Guidelines for Promoting SEL Using a SFP Framework

| | Back-and-Forth: Two-Way Home School Communication | Backyard: Family Involvement at Home | Back-to-School: Family Involvement at School |
|---|---|---|---|
| Child-Centered | • Students, families and teachers establish joint SEL goals for the year<br>• Individual meetings with teacher to discuss developing skill sets and accomplishments<br>• Home-school journal or back-and-forth-book to chronicle lessons and skills learned | • Skill chart to record how SEL skills are being incorporated at home<br>• Tip sheets for strategies, tools, or resources that match child's style and skills | • Side-by-side learning opportunities and activities so parents can observe how and what children are learning<br>• Parent SEL group where parents can express experiences and concerns with facilitator a/o other families |
| Constructive | • Good news notes or phone calls acknowledging skill development and how parents can support<br>• "Strategy Spotlight" highlighting lessons learned and accompanying strategies to reinforce at home<br>• Surveys (conducted via mail, email, phone) inquiring whether shared information and strategies are helpful | • Awards for families who utilize strategies at home (students can help create or nominate family members to receive) *This can also serve other B's if distributed at a school ceremony or if sent home with note from teacher*<br>• Activity workbooks for families and children to practice SEL skills | • Family event at school (i.e., fun night, side-by-side day, SEL skits) where parents learn specific strategies and have opportunities to practice with their children<br>• SEL center or corner at school that contains SEL-related resources and materials |
| Clear and Concrete | • Weekly classroom newsletters include a page of practical tips and easy to access resources for families<br>• Worksheets that accompany homework assignments with simple translation of lesson goals and activities | • SEL home toolkit that includes an overview of curriculum, lesson highlights, key strategies, and accessible resources<br>• Magnet or poster with SEL catchphrases | • SEL bulletin board with skill of the week or month and corresponding activities to practice and master<br>• Focus on SEL at parent-teacher conferences that highlights specific skills and strengths of child |
| Continuous | • Welcome note prior to the start of the school year conveying partnership as a priority and focus on SEL<br>• Monthly newsletters or updates sharing information about completed lessons and upcoming events<br>• Bi-monthly check-in (via phone, email, computer) | • SEL Calendars with skill of the month and daily activities to promote learning<br>• Home journals to record activities and skill development | • Monthly community meetings to discuss how SEL impacts home, school, and in the community and status of programming<br>• SEL bulletin board highlighting skills, lessons, and achievements |

***Training and Support*** Lack of training regarding how to effectively engage families via proactive outreach, communication, and involvement strategies has been identified as one of the greatest barriers to attaining collaboration (Epstein, 1986). Just as families may need assistance and support to effectively foster children's learning, educators need professional development training, support, and resources to meaningfully connect with families. Principal and administrator support is often a substantial asset in conveying messages about program priorities and commitment, as well as in garnering resources to implement initiatives. Likewise, the hiring of staff with a primary role related to SFP and/or SEL demonstrates the importance of such a program within the school, and further validates initiatives. A SFP coordinator, or SFP team can assist in providing consultation and technical assistance in implementing SEL or SFP program components and also serve as a liaison between educators and families.

*Varying Levels of Engagement and Diverse Families*    To establish effective partnerships, educators need a more thorough understanding of the families within their school-community; this reflects ethnic, cultural, socioeconomic, and linguistic identities and history, as well as characteristics of family composition, employment, and housing. Variations in parents' cultural repertoires of behavior likely contribute to differences in patterns and types of involvement. The practices of particular cultural groups may complement teacher expectations and school demands more so than others, thereby prompting teachers to feel more comfortable with, and subsequently more likely to involve, parents of a similar social class and ethnic group (Henderson & Berla, 1987; Wong-Fillmore, 1990). Variation in the amount and type of involvement exhibited by parents is often attributed to parents' own skill-sets; however, differences may more accurately reflect teacher perceptions and practices to involve families (Epstein & Dauber, 1991). Thus, schools and educators may need to use more personalized outreach to learn about, communicate with, and ultimately engage families. Shared responsibility reflects the underlying belief that families and educators are essential to the educational process; all parents have strengths and skills, and have valuable perspectives and information regarding their children that contribute to educators' knowledge base and ability to effectively teach. Furthermore, all parents are capable of learning new ways to assist children if provided with information, opportunities, and corresponding support.

*Program Monitoring and Evaluation*    Although many exemplary programs described within this chapter are comprehensive and skillfully designed, few evaluations have examined the impact of a classroom-based SEL intervention in comparison to the same intervention combined with a family component. Thus, it is difficult to empirically validate program components and link these to particular outcomes. Findings from research on school and family interventions targeting high risk behaviors and substance abuse suggest that comprehensive programs that address multiple behaviors and involve families are more effective and yield larger intervention effects (Flay, Graumlich, Segawa, Burns, & Holliday, 2004; Kumfer, Alvarado, Tait, & Turner, 2002). Future research should include direct comparisons of participants in a SEL intervention with a family component, and the same intervention without a family component to examine the "value-added" benefit of SEL programs that utilize family involvement. Such evaluation findings would assist schools in prioritizing programming efforts and coordinating initiatives that are most beneficial and effective in promoting both SEL and SFP. The focus of future evaluation efforts should extend beyond traditional measures of individual social and academic functioning to examine behavior across contexts (e.g., school, home, and community) and relationships with peers, siblings, parents, and other adults.

### Implications for Practice and Policy

Going forward, we need to ensure that SFP and SEL efforts are comprehensive and coordinated; embedding SEL within an SFP framework illustrates that such skills are relevant and reinforced across contexts (Bouffard & Weiss, 2008). Rather than viewing SEL curricula as supplemental programming, initiatives should be framed as an integral part of school- or district-wide educational policy and practice. However, the creation of a continuum of programming from preschool through secondary school requires the substantial commitment and investment of resources including adequate funding, staff, professional development, and classroom materials.

The nature of SFP complicates systematic evaluation because programs are intentionally designed to vary in order to incorporate school-community needs and characteristics. Yet, this intrinsic feature is why we need to more thoroughly examine how the quality of implementation effects outcomes, and how and why variation occurs as programs are disseminated across sites, sociocultural groups, and developmental levels. Likewise, evaluation efforts should employ a broader range of indicators to assess program impact—and include examination of both short- and long-term outcomes—as well as mediators, moderators, and mechanisms (Caspe, 2008). In addition, despite initial evidence that SFP and SEL impact parents and teachers, as well as children, this remains a secondary focus of evaluation efforts. Finally, we need to enhance our capacity to disseminate research findings to practitioners, parents, and politicians, and in this translation ensure that findings have utility for practice (Caspe, 2008; Patrikakou, Weissberg, Redding, & Walberg, 2005b).

### Concluding Remarks

Recognition that benefits are maximized when educators and families collaborate to support children's social and educational development has brought SFP to the forefront of the national educational agenda. Effective SFP are prevention-oriented and represent an agreement between families and schools to provide a quality education for all students. Given the current social and political milieu, the conceptualization of education needs to be broadened to encompass social and emotional learning and skill development, in addition to traditional academic outcomes. Moreover, as SEL programs gain prominence and are increasingly integrated into school-wide curriculum, corresponding efforts to integrate programs within the curriculum of the home are needed. Successful SEL interventions should be embedded within broader school curricula and integrated across other learning environments; hence SFP and the corresponding use of complementary strategies to promote learning yield optimal conditions for fostering children's academic, social, and emotional skill development. We believe that when schools and families effectively partner to promote achievement across contexts of development and domains of learning, our children will truly be on a path to academic, social, and emotional success.

## AUTHOR NOTE

1. The terms "parent" and "family" are used interchangeably throughout this chapter and refer to any adult caregiver (or grouping of caregivers) who plays a supportive role in a child's cognitive, social, and emotional development, including grandparents, foster parents, extended family members, and family friends.
2. We use the term "educator" in the broadest sense to refer to any school staff member involved in children's education; this includes principals, teachers, administrators, school psychologists, social workers, counselors, nurses, and paraprofessional staff.

## REFERENCES

Balli, S. J., Wedman, J. F., & Demo, D. H. (1997). Family involvement with middle-grades homework: Effects of differential prompting. *The Journal of Experimental Education, 66*(1), 31–48.

Barnard, W. M. (2004). Parent involvement in elementary school and educational attainment. *Children and Youth Services Review, 26*(1), 39–62.

Becker, H. J., & Epstein, J. L. (1982). Parent involvement: A survey of teacher practices. *Elementary School Journal, 83*(2), 85–102.

Bouffard, S., & Weiss, H. (2008). Thinking big: A new framework for family involvement policy, practice, and research. *The Evaluation Exchange, 14*(1 & 2), 2–5.

Bronfenbrenner, U. (1979). Contexts of child rearing: Problems and prospects. *American Psychologist, 34*(10), 844–850.

Caspe, M. (2008). Building the field. *The Evaluation Exchange, 14*(1 & 2), 6–7.

Caspe, M., Lopez, M. E., & Wolos, C. (2007). Family involvement makes a difference: *Family involvement in elementary school children's education.* Cambridge, MA: Harvard Family Research Project.

Center for Mental Health in Schools at UCLA. (2007). *Parent and home involvement in schools.* Los Angeles: Author.

Christenson, S. L., & Havsy, L. H. (2004). Family-school-peer relationships: Significance for social, emotional, and academic learning. In J. E. Zins, R. P. Weissberg, M. C. Wang, & H. J. Walberg (Eds.), *Building academic success on social and emotional learning: What does the research say?* (pp. 59–75). New York: Teachers College Press.

Christenson, S. L., Rounds, T., & Franklin, M. J. (1992). Home-school collaboration: Effects, issues, and opportunities. In S. L. Christenson & J. C. Conoley, (Eds.), *Home-school collaboration: Enhancing children's academic and social competence* (pp. 19–52). Bethesda, MD: The National Association of School Psychologists.

Christenson, S. L., Rounds, T., & Gorney, D. (1992). Family factors and student achievement: An avenue to increase student's success. *School Psychology Quarterly, 7*(3), 178–206.

Christenson, S. L., & Sheridan, S. (2001). *Schools and families: Creating essential connections for learning.* New York: Guilford.

Christenson, S. L., Weissberg, R. P., & Klein, J. A. (2007). *Establishing school-family partnerships.* Unpublished manuscript.

Collaborative for Academic, Social, and Emotional Learning. (2003). *Safe and sound: An educational leader's guide to evidence-based social and emotional learning programs.* Chicago: Author.

Conley, D. T. (2007). The challenge of college readiness. *Educational Leadership, 64*(7), 23–29.

Cooke, M. B., Ford, J., Levine, J., Bourke, C., Newell, L., & Lapidus, G. (2007). The effects of city-wide implementation of "SECOND STEP" on elementary school students' prosocial and aggressive behaviors. *The Journal of Primary Prevention, 28*(2), 93–115.

Cooper, H., Lindsay, J. J., & Nye, B. (2000). Homework in the home: How student, family, and parenting-style differences relate to the homework process. *Contemporary Educational Psychology, 25*(4), 464–487.

Dauber, S. L., & Epstein, J. L. (1993). Parents' attitudes and practices of involvement in inner-city elementary and middle schools. In N. F. Chavkin, (Ed.), *Families and schools in a pluralistic society* (pp. 53–71). Albany: State University of New York Press.

Durlak, J. A., Weissberg, R. P., Dymnicki, A. B., Taylor, R. D., & Schellinger, K. B. (2008). *Enhancing students' social and emotional learning promotes success in school: A meta-analysis.* Manuscript submitted for publication.

Eccles, J. S., & Harold, R. D. (1993). Parent-school involvement during the early adolescent years. *Teachers College Record, 94*(3), 568–587.

Eccles, J. S., & Harold, R. D. (1996). Family involvement in children's and adolescents' schooling. In A. Booth & J. F. Dunn (Eds.), *Family school links* (pp. 3–34). Mahwah, NJ: Erlbaum.

Elias, M. J., Bryan, K., Patrikakou, E. N., & Weissberg, R. P. (2003). Challenges in creating effective home-school partnerships in adolescence: Promising pathways for collaboration. *The School-Community Journal, 13*(1)133–153.

Elias, M. J., Zins, J. E., Weissberg, R. P., Frey, K. S., Greenberg, M. T., Haynes, N. M., et al. (1997). *Promoting social and emotional learning: Guidelines for educators*. Alexandria, VA: Association for Supervision and Curriculum Development.

Elliot, S. N. (1995). *The Responsive Classroom approach: Its effectiveness and acceptability*. Washington, DC: The Center for Systemic Educational Change.

Elliot, S. N. (1999). *A multi-year evaluation of the Responsive Classroom approach: Its effectiveness and acceptability in promoting social and academic competence*. Turners Falls, MA: Northeast Foundation for Children.

Epstein, J. L. (1986). Parents' reactions to teacher practices of parent involvement. *Elementary School Journal, 86*(3), 277–294.

Epstein, J. L. (1988). *Homework practices, achievements, and behaviors of elementary school students*. Baltimore: The John Hopkins University, Center for Research on Elementary & Middle Schools.

Epstein, J. L. (1990). School and family connections: Theory, research, and implications for integrating sociologies of education and family. *Marriage and Family Review, 12*, 99–126.

Epstein, J. L. (1995). School/family/community partnerships Caring for the children we share. *Phi Delta Kappan, 76*(9), 701–712.

Epstein, J. L., & Dauber, S. L. (1991). School programs and teacher practices of parent involvement in inner-city elementary and middle schools. *Elementary School Journal, 91*(3), 288–304.

Fantuzzo, J., Tighe, E., & Childs, S. (2000). Family involvement questionnaire: A multivariate assessment of family participation in early childhood education. *Journal of Educational Psychology, 92*(2), 367–376.

Flay, B. R., Graumlich, S., Segawa, E., Burns, J. L., & Holliday, M. Y. (2004). Effects of 2 prevention programs on high-risk behaviors among African-American youth. *Archives of Pediatric Adolescent Medicine, 158*, 377–384.

Frey, K. S., Nolen, S. B., Van Schoiack Edstrom, L., & Hirschstein, M. K. (2005). Effects of a school-based social-emotional competence program: Linking children's goals, attributions, and behavior. *Journal of Applied Developmental Psychology, 26*(2), 171–200.

Ginsburg, H. P., Bempechat, J., & Chung, Y. E. (1992). Parent influences on children's mathematics. In T. G. Sticht, B. A. McDonald, & M. J. Beeler (Eds.), *The intergenerational transfer of cognitive skills* (pp. 91–121). Norwood, NJ: Ablex.

Greenberg, M. T., Weissberg, R. P., O'Brien, M. U., Zins, J. E., Fredericks, L., Resnik, H., et al. (2003). Enhancing school-based prevention and youth development through coordinated social, emotional, and academic learning. *American Psychologist, 58*(6–7), 466–474.

Grolnick, W. S., & Slowiaczek, M. L. (1994). Parents' involvement in children's schooling: A multidimensional conceptualization and motivation model. *Child Development, 65*(1), 237–252.

Hawkins, J. D., Smith, B. H., & Catalano, R. F. (2004). Social development and social and emotional learning. In J. E. Zins, R. P. Weissberg, M. C. Wang, & H. J. Walberg (Eds.), *Building academic success on social and emotional learning: What does the research say* (pp. 135–150). New York: Teachers College Press

Hawkins, J. D., von Cleve, E., & Catalano, R. F. (1991). Reducing early childhood aggression: Results of a primary prevention program. *Journal of the American Academy of Child and Adolescent Psychiatry, 30*(2), 208–217.

Henderson, A., & Berla, N. (1987). *The evidence continues to grow: Parent involvement improves student achievement*. Columbia, MD: National Committee for Citizens in Education.

Henderson, A. T., & Mapp, K. L. (2002). *A new wave of evidence: The impact of school, family, and community connections on student achievement*. Austin, TX: Southwest Educational Development Laboratory.

Hoover-Dempsey, K. V., Bassler, O. C., & Burrow, R. (1995). Parents' reported involvement in students homework: Strategies and practices. *The Elementary School Journal, 95*(5), 436–449.

Hoover-Dempsey, K. V., Battiato, A. C., Walker, J. M., Reed, R. P., DeJong, J. .M., & Jones, K. P. (2001). Parental involvement in homework. *Educational Psychologist, 36*(3), 195–209.

Hoover-Dempsey, K. V., & Sandler, H. M. (1997). Why do parents become involved in their children's education? *Review of Educational Research, 67*(1), 3–42.

Jeynes, W. H. (2005). A meta-analysis of the relation of parent involvement to urban elementary school student academic achievement. *Urban Education, 40*(3), 237–269.

Knoff, H. M. (2004). Inside Project ACHIEVE: A comprehensive, research-proven whole school improvement process focused on student academic and behavioral outcomes. In K. Robinson (Ed.), *Advances in school-based mental health: Best practices and program models* (pp. 19–28). Kingston, NJ: Civic Research Institute.

Knoff, H. M. (2006). Teasing, taunting, bullying, harassment, and aggression: A school-wide approach to prevention, strategic intervention, and crisis management. In M. J. Elias, J. E. Zins, & C. A. Maher (Eds.), *Handbook of prevention and intervention in peer harassment, victimization, and bullying*. Hillsdale, NJ: Haworth Press.

Knoff, H. M. & Batsche, G. M. (1995). Project ACHIEVE: Analyzing a school reform process for at-risk and underachieving students. *School Psychology Review, 24*(4), 579–603.

Krasnow, J., Seigle, P. J., & Kelly, R. (1992). *The Social Competency Program of the Reach Out to Schools project: Project report 1990–1991*. Wellsey, MA: The Stone Center for Developmental Services and Studies.

Kress, J. S. & Elias, M. J. (2006). Building learning communities through social and emotional learning: Navigating the rough seas of implementation. *Professional School Counseling 10*(1), 102–107.

Kumfer, K. L., Alvarado, R., Tait, C., & Turner, C. (2002). Effectiveness of school-based family and children's skills training for substance abuse prevention among 6–8 year-old rural children. *Psychology of Addictive Behaviors, 16*, S65–S71.

Larsen, T., & Samdal, O. (2007). Implementing SECOND STEP: Balancing fidelity and program adaptation. *Journal of Educational and Psychological Consultation, 17*(1), 1–29.

Patrikakou, E. N., & Weissberg, R. P. (1999, February). The seven P's of school-family partnerships. *Education Week, XVIII* (21), 34, 36.

Patrikakou, E. N., & Weissberg, R. P. (2007). School-family partnerships and children's social, emotional, and academic learning. In R. Bar-on, J. G. Maree, & M. J. Elias (Eds.), *Educating people to be emotionally intelligent* (pp. 49–61). Oxford, UK: Heinemann Educational Publishers.

Patrikakou, E. N., Weissberg, R. P., Redding, S., & Walberg, H. J. (2005a). School-family partnerships: Enhancing the academic, social, and emotional learning of children. In E. N. Patrikakou, R. P. Weissberg, S. Redding, & H. J. Walberg (Eds.), *School-family partnerships for children's success* (pp. 1–17). New York: Teachers College Press.

Patrikakou, E. N., Weissberg, R. P., Redding, S., & Walberg, H. J. (Eds.). (2005b). *School-family partnerships for children's success*. New York: Teachers College Press.

Patrikakou, E. N., Weissberg, R. P., & Rubenstein, M. (1998). Five "P's" to promote school-family partnership efforts. *Spotlight on Student Success, 304*. Philadelphia: Mid-Atlantic Regional Educational Laboratory for Student Success.

Payton, J. W., Wardlaw, D. W., Graczyk, P. A., Bloodworth, C. J., Tompsett, C. J., & Weissberg, R. P. (2000). Social and emotional learning: A framework for promoting mental health and reducing risk behaviors in children and youth. *Journal of School Health, 70*(5), 179–185.

Resnick, M. D., Bearman, P. S., Blum, R. W., Bauman, K. E., Harris, K. M., Jones, J., et al. (1997). Protecting adolescents from harm: Findings from the National Longitudinal Study on Adolescent Health. *Journal of the American Medical Association, 278*(10), 823–832.

Rimm-Kaufman, S. (2006). *Social and academic learning study on the contribution of the Responsive Classroom approach*. Turners Falls: MA: Northeast Foundation for Children.

Rubenstein, M. I. (1998). *School-family partnership programs: Theory, research, and practice*. Unpublished manuscript.

Rubenstein, M. I., Patrikakou, E. N., Weissberg, R. P., & Armstrong, M. (1999). *Enhancing school-family partnerships: A teacher's guide*. Philadelphia: Temple University Center for Research in Human Development and Education.

Seeley, D. (1989). A new paradigm for parent involvement. *Educational Leadership, 47*(2), 46–58.

Swap, S. M. (1993). *Developing home-school partnerships: From concepts to practice*. New York: Teachers College Press.

Taylor, C. A., Liang, B., Tracy, A. J., Williams, L. M., & Seigle, P. (2002). Gender differences in middle school adjustment, physical fighting, and social skills: Evaluation of a social competency program. *The Journal of Primary Prevention, 23*(2), 259–272.

Weiss, H. M. & Edwards, M. E. (1992). The family-school collaboration project: Systematic interventions for school improvement. In S. L. Christenson & J. C. Conoley, (Eds.), *Home-school collaboration: Enhancing children's academic and social competence.* (pp. 215–243). Bethesda, MD: The National Association of School Psychologists.

Weissberg, R. P., & Greenberg, M. T. (1998). School and community competence-enhancement and prevention programs. In W. Damon (Series Ed.) & I. E. Sigel & K. A. Renninger (Vol. Eds.), *Handbook of child psychology: Vol 4. Child psychology in practice* (5th ed., pp. 877–954). New York: Wiley.

Wong-Fillmore, L. (1990). Now or later? Issues related to the early education of minority-group children. *Early childhood and family education: Analysis and recommendations of the Council of Chief State School Officers* (pp. 122–145). New York: Harcourt Brace Jovanovich.

Zins, J. E., Bloodworth, M. R., Weissberg, R. P., & Walberg, H. J. (2004). The scientific base linking social and emotional learning to school success. In J. E. Zins, R. P. Weissberg, M. C. Wang, & H. J. Walberg (Eds.), *Building academic success on social and emotional learning: What does the research say?* (pp. 3–22). New York: Teachers College Press

Zins, J. E., & Elias, M. J. (2006). Social and emotional learning. In G. Bear & K. Minke (Eds.), *Children's needs III*. Bethesda, MD: National Association of School Psychologists.

Zins, J. E., Weissberg, R. P., Wang, M. C., & Walberg, H. J. (Eds.). (2004). *Building academic success on social and emotional learning: What does the research say?* New York: Teachers College Press.

# 12

## SCHOOL CONNECTEDNESS AND ADOLESCENT WELL-BEING

CLEA MCNEELY, JANIS WHITLOCK, AND HEATHER LIBBEY

There remains no doubt that positive connections to adults have profound implications for child and adolescent outcomes (Barber, Stolz, & Olsen, 2005; Garmezy, 1985; Hawkins & Weis, 1985; Masten, Best, & Garmezy, 1990; Werner & Smith, 1992). Contemporary notions of school connectedness extend this axiom by emphasizing that reciprocal attachment between youth and individual adults, although essential, is not enough. Connectedness to school and the concomitant positive results it fosters depend on positive exchange both with individual adults *and* with collections of adults, adult institutions, and the values embodied by them (Lerner, 1991; Whitlock, 2006). Families are critical partners in school endeavors to cultivate connectedness for they are part of a social ecology capable of supporting development by rewarding competence and fostering coherence (Werner & Smith, 1992).

The youth development approach embraces the idea that connectedness to key socializing domains, not just key adults, is pivotal to positive adolescent development (National Research Council and Institute of Medicine, 2002). Within the youth development literature, school connectedness is a prominent but rarely unpacked concept, encompassing a diverse array of related constructs including but not limited to: social belonging, group solidarity, teacher support, school attachment, school bonding, perceived school safety, student satisfaction, and positive orientation toward school (Libbey, 2004). Although the study of school connectedness is in its infancy, empirical research is beginning to demonstrate that these concepts, although related, are not interchangeable. Some constructs appear to be strongly related to a wide range of adolescent health and educational outcomes whereas others appear to be less influential or to promote specific outcomes (Libbey, 2007; McNeely & Falci, 2004). The tendency to conflate what are emerging as distinct constructs with differential potency in predicting youth outcomes renders it particularly important to articulate a clear definition that can be easily communicated and assessed by youth development practitioners and educators.

## OVERVIEW

This chapter has two goals. First, it proposes a definition of school connectedness that is clearly distinguishable from other positive socializing experiences at school. Second, it proposes a two-pronged research agenda to better understand (a) the relationship between school connectedness and school-family partnerships and (b) how, when, and why school connectedness fosters positive developmental outcomes.

The first section of the chapter provides a formal definition of school connectedness and presents the theoretical motivation and conceptual framework for understanding school connectedness. The second section presents empirical evidence on school connectedness and how it is related to school-family partnerships. This section presents evidence suggesting that the effect on adolescent well-being of constructs typically grouped under the umbrella school connectedness vary considerably depending on the nature and content of the connection—whether to peers, teachers or school as an institution—and on the definition of the substance of the connection. The third section revisits the proposed definition in more detail, drawing on the theoretical and empirical evidence to provide more clarity. The final section proposes a set of research priorities to clarify for both researchers and practitioners how to measure school connectedness; how school connectedness can be supported by and, in turn, support school-family partnerships; how to foster school connectedness in adolescents; and, finally, to better understand the positive effects that flow from school connectedness.

## DEFINITION OF SCHOOL CONNECTEDNESS

In this chapter the terms *school connectedness* and *connection to school* are used interchangeably. Some researchers (Barber & Schluterman, 2008) have argued that the term "school connectedness" is problematic because it has been broadened too far beyond its original conceptualization as mutuality and responsiveness within a dyadic relationship (Grotevant & Cooper, 1986) and is used instead to describe all social experience at school. Nonetheless, the term resonates with policy makers, educators, and youth development practitioners (Blum & Libbey, 2004). In light of the widespread vernacular use of the term and the many on-the-ground efforts to enhance school connectedness, this chapter endeavors to offer a theoretically robust and empirically testable definition of school connectedness.

Toward this end, the authors propose that school connectedness be defined as a psychological state in which individual youth perceive that they and other youth are cared for, trusted, and respected by adults with authority in the school. This definition was first articulated by Whitlock (2003) and is grounded in multiple theoretical perspectives, including attachment theory (Bowlby, 1969), eco-developmental theory (Bronfenbrenner & Morris, 1998; Lerner, 1991), social capital theories (Coleman, 1990; Lin, 2001) and grounded theory from qualitative research with secondary school youth (Whitlock, 2003). This definition implies the following:

- School connectedness is best conceptualized as the intersection of the individual and the collective. It is neither an individual's private experience nor a more global assessment of the whole school (i.e., school climate). Rather, it is the individual student's perception of the relationship that they *and* other students have with adults in the school.

- Adult-youth relationships in the school are the foundation of school connectedness.
- School connectedness is fundamentally *dynamic* and is thus reciprocal—it is the perception of the quality of the giving and the receiving of care, trust and respect.
- Connectedness is conceptually and empirically distinct from the developmental supports that produce it, such as dyadic exchange between individual youth and individual adults.

This definition of connection to school clearly differentiates school connectedness from liking or having fun at school as well as from one's relationship with peers. This definition also distinguishes school connectedness from investment and engagement in learning itself, thereby allowing researchers and educators to explore health and educational consequences for students who report feeling connected to school but are not invested in learning and vice versa. This chapter returns to each of these points later after presenting the theoretical underpinnings of the construct and the evidence base for the positive outcomes school connectedness engenders.

## SCHOOL CONNECTEDNESS: THEORETICAL UNDERPINNINGS

### Previous Definition and Measurement of School Connectedness

Research on school connectedness has not coalesced around a dominant theoretical perspective or common definition, and measurement strategies reflect this. Measures of school connectedness and similarly-named constructs such as school bonding, school attachment, and student satisfaction are plentiful (see Libbey, 2004, for a catalog of measures). Some of these measures are grounded in a single theoretical perspective whereas others draw from multiple perspectives. Measures of school connectedness tend to fall into two categories described by Barber and Schluterman (2008): the quality of performance in an environment or relationship, and a combination of perceptions about the relationship and the antecedent behaviors that produce those perceptions.

Some school connectedness measures focus on the quality of performance in an environment or relationship. These measures of school connectedness tend to overlap somewhat with measures of school or student engagement (Libbey, 2004) and define connectedness by behaviors such as participation in extracurricular activities and engagement in learning. For example, Finn's (1993) measure combined attendance, disruptive behavior, teacher report of student compliance, and the quality of student-teacher relationships. Although these measures are useful in identifying students who are displaying the positive behaviors associated with connection, by focusing on the behavioral consequences of connectedness, they overlook the fact that connectedness is inherently relational. School connectedness is intrinsic to the relationship between an individual and the school context—including people and institutional policies and practices.

Other school connectedness measures combine perceptions about relationships at school (or to school) and the antecedent behaviors that produce those perceptions. These measures of school connectedness combine items that assess student's affective experiences (e.g., "I like my teachers," "I like being at school," "I feel safe at school," and "I feel like I am part of my school") with items that assess antecedent behaviors that produce those perceptions (e.g., "adults at this school listen to students' concerns," "my teachers care about me," "teachers praise my efforts"); Brown & Evans, 2002; McNeely, Nonnemaker, & Blum, 2002; Resnick et al., 1997). Jenkins (1997) subdivided his measure of school bond into four categories: commitment, attachment, involvement, and belief in school rules. Attachment included items that measure the student's affective experience of their relationships with teachers ("do you like most of your teachers") along with items that measure the experiences that facilitate those relationships ("most teachers are interested in anything I say or do"). Voelkl's (1996) student identification with school also subdivided into two categories: belonging and valuing. Within belonging, similar to Jenkins "attachment," are items assessing whether students felt treated with respect (antecedent experiences) and the extent to which they felt their teachers cared about them (affective bond). Whitlock (2003) demonstrated that the behavioral interactions between adults and young people in school are a separate construct from students' perceptions of their experience. Conflating in a single measure students' perceptions of their connection to school with their perceptions of the conditions in the school that create it precludes empirical clarification of both the definition of connectedness and the practices that produce it.

Central to development of a construct likely to appeal across disciplines is consideration of the theoretical underpinnings on which extant definitions are based. Foundational to the school connectedness construct are theories focused on attachment, group membership, social capital, and the ecological context of development. While each theoretical framework offers a unique perspective on how school connectedness might be best conceptualized and how it might foster positive developmental outcomes, all share areas of overlap useful in illuminating core elements of a "school connectedness" construct. The definition of school connectedness proposed in this chapter—*a psychological state in which individual youth perceive that they* and *other youth are cared for, trusted, and respected by adults with authority in the school*—is grounded squarely in each of these theoretical perspectives.

### Connection as an Extension of Attachment Theory

Connection is frequently articulated as an extension of attachment theory (Barber et al., 2005; Barber & Schluterman, 2008). Attachment theory (Bowlby, 1969) posits that when parents express affection and caring, their children are more likely to fulfill core developmental needs related to security and confidence and to seek help from reliable and trusted sources when needed. The behaviors and self-perceptions established as a result of healthy parental attachments are available as an internal model to children as they later develop and nurture relationships with others and as they encounter opportunities to practice pro-social decisions (Allen & Land, 1999). In contrast, children and adolescents with poor attachment are more likely than their positively attached peers to develop poorer self-concepts and fewer skills in accessing supportive relationships. Attachment to adults in schools is thought to function similarly by building off of and extending early parental attachments (Barber & Olsen, 1997). In this way, schools ideally provide developmental spaces for young people to enhance and extend early positive attachments into other key social and socializing arenas or, alternatively, to compensate for poor parental attachments through connection with positive adult and peer role models.

A second theoretical perspective relevant to understanding how school connection fosters positive developmental outcomes in children and adolescents is symbolic interaction theory. Cooley (1902) coined the term "the looking-glass self" to describe how children formulate ideas about how other people view them, internalize that view, and use it in construction of a self-view. This theory posits that when children believe that their teachers and peers care about them and about their educational and social success, they are more likely to believe they are competent, trustworthy and likable. In contrast, young people who perceive and come to believe that they are negatively evaluated are more likely to create negative self-images which they then project back out into the world through negative behaviors or expectations (Stryker & Stratham, 1985). Symbolic interaction theory suggests that school connectedness is dynamic—students' past experiences affect current perceptions of how they are treated by important adults in the school as well as their choices regarding actions to elicit care and respect at school (e.g., they may act to alienate themselves to adults; Karcher, 2002).

### Development of Group Membership

The next two perspectives presented—social development theory and social learning theory—draw from social theory on group membership and social control. These perspectives are particularly germane to school settings because as Baumeister and Leary (1995) argued, the need for belongingness, defined by as "a pervasive drive to form and maintain at least a minimum quantity of lasting, positive, and significant interpersonal relationships" (p. 497) is a fundamental human motivation. The deprivation of belonging, such as the perceived experience of being rejected, excluded or ignored, leads to intense distress and feelings such as loneliness, grief, jealousy, and anger (Baumeister & Leary, 1995; Osterman, 2001). Schools are particularly important spheres for perceptions of belonging to be formed, positively or negatively, because they are one of the first spheres in which children encounter large groups of peers over sustained periods of time.

Social development theory (Catalano, Haggerty, Oesterle, Fleming, & Hawkins, 2004) is founded on the premise that strong bonds to social institutions raise the costs of problem behavior, thereby promoting conventional behavior (Hirschi, 1969). Bonding within the school, in particular, consists of four elements: (a) involvement (e.g., attendance), (b) attachment or affective relationships with adults and peers, (c) investment or commitment to the school as a place (e.g., school pride), and (d) belief in the perceived values of the school (Catalano et al., 2004). Once each of these elements has been adopted and internalized, individuals are more likely to exhibit behaviors consistent with behaviors perceived to be desirable within the school and less likely to participate in behaviors perceived by the group as undesirable.

Similarly, Bandura's (1977) social learning theory stipulates that children observe and adopt the behaviors and attitudes of the people they value. Bandura's theory is similar to dyadic theories of attachment, but it is slightly broader, including attachment to group. If children have a warm and caring relationship with peers, teachers, and others at school and they feel like they belong, they are more likely to imitate the normative behaviors in the school and to act in accordance with the values they perceive referent others hold in esteem. To the extent that role models in school—be they teachers or peers—practice healthful behaviors, social learning theory suggests that supportive relationships will promote healthy development and learning (Andrews, Hops, & Duncan, 1997).

Of note, most social learning frameworks postulate that specific behavioral outcomes, such as student educational attainment, are not the *direct* result of positive connections between students and staff but, rather, of the level of student engagement that results, in part, as a product of these attachments. Appleton, Christenson, Kim, and Reschly (2006) described how attachments to role models in school influence four types of student engagement: cognitive, behavioral, psychological and academic, which then impact academic outcomes such as school completion and grades. Similarly, Fredricks, Blumenfield, and Paris (2004) illustrated that connections within schools can build emotional, behavioral, and cognitive engagement that leads to better educational and developmental outcomes.

### Eco-Developmental Theories: Stage-Environment Fit

Unlike theories of attachment and group membership, eco-developmental theories incorporate development stage. They seek to explicate the internal and external conditions most likely to foster accomplishment of core developmental tasks at each stage of development. Although varied, most are founded on the work of prominent developmental theorists Erik Erikson (1968) and Abraham Maslow (1968), whose frameworks have proven exceptionally useful for understanding the nature of the relationship between larger social contexts, such as schools, and adolescent development. Erickson delineated eight stages of development and corresponding psychosocial tasks. Adolescence, as currently defined in the United States, falls squarely within Erickson's fifth stage and is associated with successful achievement of ego identity. Ego identity, it turns out, is dependent on an individual's capacity to create a positive story about who he or she is and how he or she fits in to the larger society; it requires that an individual synthesize everything they know about themselves into a unified image that they and their immediate communities—schools in this case—find meaningful.

The bio-ecological model of development, first articulated by Urie Bronfenbrenner (1979), builds on the developmental frameworks of early theorists by postulating and explicating the means through which human development occurs within integrated levels of organization—biological, individual-psychological, social-interpersonal, institutional, and historical systems (Lerner, 1995). Bio-ecological models of development are concerned with the dynamic interplay between and within these levels of organization (Lerner, 1991). They recognize that youth, families, peers, neighborhoods, schools, communities, programs, organizations, and larger cultural values and tensions are inextricably bound and simultaneously influential in shaping the threats to and opportunities for optimum development (Bronfenbrenner & Morris, 1998). Scores of studies seeking to discern reliable patterns within and among the complex interweave of context and personality have been conducted since the introduction of Bronfenbrenner's (1979) theory on the ecology of human development. A number of studies conclude that child and youth development are extremely time and context sensitive in ways that are not always predictable; and that externally generated developmental opportunities (introduction of a school mentor, for example) must coincide with developmental needs at a particularly receptive developmental juncture to be effective (Lerner, 1991).

Building further on this category of theory, stage-environment fit frameworks contain the implicit assumption that the contexts human beings interact with contain "latent potential" or "developmental affordances" that, when capitalized on by the individual, can result in beneficial outcomes for development. What stimulates an individual to seek out and make use of this latent developmental potential is most likely a result of biological and psychological predispositions and previous experiences in combination with the accessibility of the developmental supports offered by each setting (Lerner, 1991; National Research Council and Institute of Medicine, 2002). Schools serve as a powerful example of this dynamic since they house youth of so many different ages; however, they often fail to take into account individual and group-level variation in developmental need and capacity when planning and implementing contextual opportunities. Recognizing and accommodating stage-environment fit is one of the most important elements of effective interventions for enhancing connectedness to schools.

### Social Capital Theory

The final framework of interest here, social capital theory, posits that positive relationships with individuals in the position to facilitate access to desired resources, such as emotional support or job opportunities, allows for individual accomplishments otherwise unattainable (Coleman, 1990). More formally put, social capital is the resources embedded in social relations rather than individuals (Lin, 2001). These resources include flow of information, social credentials or status, identity and recognition (e.g., belonging to a group), and influence. Individuals at school who have positive relationships with teachers and peers are better able to access social capital (Lin, 2001). Affective connections with adults or peers at school with access to resources effectively augments an individual's capacity to meet core developmental needs and, as a byproduct of this, heightens the individual's connection with the setting in which these core relationships are found—schools in this case. Like eco-developmental theory and the broader youth development theories it has spawned, social capital theorists view trust, norms, and exchange as critical resources upon which schools and communities are dependent for healthy civic functioning. Coleman (1990) stressed the role played by what Erickson terms "intergenerational closure"—interrelatedness and exchange between youth and adults and their affiliated networks—in establishing the trust and reciprocity needed for individuals and communities to function healthfully.

*Summary of Theoretical Frameworks*

When considered together, these theoretical models point to several core features of a school connectedness construct likely to withstand the rigors of theoretical and empirical testing (Whitlock, 2006). First, all theories include caring from and for others as well as respect for individuality as fundamental needs for development. Second, most of the theories recognize that individuals receive messages about their value not solely from individuals but also from subtle exchanges with institutions, policies, and practice. Third, all theories recognize that adolescents are active actors in eliciting care and respect for their individuality (or the lack of it) from others. Fourth, the eco-developmental and social capital theories recognize that not all individuals experience an environment similarly. Rather, their experience at school depends on the fit between *multiple* environmental affordances and their developmental needs. Thus the creation of school connectedness and its potential for positive influence will depend on the developmental supports in other contexts. School-family partnerships, which can help link developmental supports across contexts, potentially play a critical role in making the social capital inherent in student-adult relationships accessible to adolescents.

The next section presents the empirical evidence regarding the value of connection to school in fostering healthy development. The findings from this research point to the need for more clarity in definition and measurement so that scientific evidence can maximally guide policies and programs.

## SCHOOL CONNECTEDNESS: EMPIRICAL EVIDENCE

School connectedness is associated with a multitude of positive outcomes, including health, educational performance, and social competence. The positive association between school connectedness and adolescent development holds true across multiple definitions and measures of school connectedness (Libbey, 2004). However, this general conclusion is a macro view, similar to what one could conclude from reading an aerial photo. Closer examination reveals a number of inconsistencies across measures, samples, and outcomes, enough inconsistencies to merit clarification of school connectedness. This review of the literature draws from the multiple definitions and measures, although it focuses on those most consistent with the definition proposed in this chapter.

*Sociodemographic Patterns of School Connectedness*

Sociodemographic disparities in health and educational outcomes are due in large part to disparities in the resources that produce those outcomes. Surprisingly, sociodemographic differences in school connectedness are neither large nor consistent across studies. Because school connectedness is not correlated with sociodemographic characteristics, it cannot explain the large differences in academic success across socioeconomic and racial/ethnic groups.

Although mean differences in school connectedness across racial/ethnic groups are found in the nationally representative sample of students in the National Longitudinal Study of Adolescent Health (Add Health), the differences are not substantively large, typically no more than a fraction of a standard deviation (Crosnoe, Johnson, & Elder, 2004; Libbey, 2007; McNeely, 2004). Moreover, racial/ethnic differences are not consistent across studies or measures of school connectedness. Some studies have shown lower levels of school connection for African American and Latino students compared to White students (Libbey, 2007; McNeely, 2004), whereas others report higher levels of connection to school among minority students. Crosnoe et al. (2004) reported a race-by- gender interaction such that Hispanic and White females reported the highest rates of teacher bonding but African American females the lowest. The few studies that have examined American Indian youth demonstrate they have the lowest level of connection to school (Libbey, 2007; McNeely, 2004).

The evidence also is inconsistent regarding developmental trends in connection to school, with some researchers documenting declines in feelings of school connectedness as students advanced from 8th to 12th grade (Benson, Scales, Leffert, & Roehlkpartain, 1999; Whitlock 2003) and others documenting increases in school connectedness with age (Crosnoe et al., 2004). Although it is not entirely clear whether these discrepant findings are due to differences in samples or differences in measures, it is likely that measurement is at least partially responsible. Whitlock uses a school connectedness construct consonant with that proposed here whereas Crosnoe et al. (2004) use a teacher bonding measure (what Whitlock identifies as a contributor to school connectedness).

There are theoretical reasons to predict developmental trends in both directions. It is possible that as students' social world expands and they form new attachments to work life and peers outside of school, their perceived connection to school as a socializing institution associated with childhood naturally declines. Whitlock (2003, 2006) found that, unlike 8th- and 10th-grade students, seniors exhibited far more attention to the systematic ways in which adults at school shared power, solicited input, and arbitrated conflicts. This recognition of the systematic denial of power to students due to institutionalized policies and procedures may explain the senior slump in connectedness. Alternatively, some argue that high schools are more developmentally appropriate for adolescents than are middle schools (Eccles et al., 1993) and thus do a better job than middle schools of meeting the core developmental needs of students. These competing hypotheses are not mutually exclusive, and they both underscore the role stage-environment fit plays in creating optimal environments for development.

One sociodemographic pattern in school connection is consistent: girls, in general, reported slightly more connection to school than boys (Goodenow, 1993; McNeely, 2004). This consistent finding may be due to the higher salience of connection to peers at school for girls during adolescence.

### School Connectedness and Adolescent Development

This section presents evidence regarding the association between adolescent development and the diverse array of measures that has been labeled school connectedness, school bonding, school attachment, teacher support, or other related terms. Despite this variation in measures, extant studies illuminate important trends and constitute a first step in articulating expectations about antecedents and outcomes of connectedness.

Results of longitudinal research and multi-year interventions suggest that school connectedness can improve academic performance and prevent involvement in health risk behaviors such as substance use and delinquency (Battistitch, Solomon, Watson, & Schaps, 1997; Bond et al., 2004; Catalano et al., 2004). School connectedness appears to be related to higher school completion rates, attendance, motivation, and classroom engagement and lower levels of truancy and bullying (Blum & Libbey, 2004; Osterman, 2001). Students who feel connected to school also are less likely to exhibit disruptive behavior and violence, substance and tobacco use, and emotional distress, and are more likely to delay first sexual intercourse (Battistitch et al., 1997; Catalano, et al. 2004; Crosnoe et al., 2004; Falci & McNeely, 2009; Lonczak, Abbott, Hawkins, Kosterman, & Catalano, 2002; National Research Council and Institute of Medicine, 2002).

In general, the associations between school connectedness and health and educational outcomes are modest. For example, McNeely and Falci (2004) found that a one standard deviation change in teacher support was associated with an increase of approximately two percentage points one year later in the percentage of students who initiated experimental smoking, heterosexual intercourse, experimental marijuana use, and violence. What makes connection to school stand out as a powerful protective factor is the breadth of the outcomes with which it is associated. The ability of relationships built within the confines of school to reach beyond the schoolyard and impact the general health and well-being of its temporary populace speaks volumes about its impact.

The remainder of this section explores some of the nuances of the macro finding that connection to school promotes health and educational performance. Specifically, does school connectedness simply delay initiation of risky behaviors or can it also reduce involvement once it has begun? Does the protective effect of school connectedness hold for all young people in all families and schools, including all levels of school-family partnerships? And, does this association hold across different measures of school connectedness?

### Prevention vs. Risk Reduction

An essential distinction is whether school connectedness primarily prevents (or delays) negative behaviors or whether it can also reduce a student's involvement in those behaviors once initiated. Although most research assesses the association between connection to school and mean levels of health risk behaviors or academic achievement, at least two studies have examined these important distinctions (Dornbusch, Erickson, Laird, & Wong, 2001; McNeely & Falci, 2004). Both studies found that connection to school had a clearer association with starting to engage in deviant behavior than with the intensity of deviance among those who deviated.

Adolescents who are dabbling with delinquency as well as those who are staunchly embedded in antisocial behaviors want teachers to care for them in empathic, supportive, and consistent ways, even as they engage in behaviors that evoke negative reactions (Dance, 2002; Karcher, 2002). The challenge of fostering connection with students who, from the perspective of the teachers, seem bent on provoking a negative reaction must be addressed if school connectedness is to be a route back to school engagement for students on trajectories of problem behaviors. Researchers have found that consistent attempts to create individual bonds with students, despite student ambivalence, are effective tools for facilitating school completion (Sinclair, Christenson, Lehr, & Reschly, 2003). Staff persistence with students, regardless of student motivation levels, was a critical factor in the effectiveness of the Check & Connect drop-out prevention program.

### Additive and Multiplicative Effects of School Connectedness

Is school connectedness associated with positive outcomes for all young people? Does its effectiveness depend on the nature and quality of school-family partnerships? According to the concept of functional substitution (Mirowsky & Ross, 2003), any given resource is more important to those who have fewer resources overall. This would suggest that students with fewer economic resources and social capital outside of school would benefit most from connection to school. Similarly, school connectedness may be more essential in schools with fragile or weak school-family partnerships. For students from neighborhoods or families where behaviors valued by school are neither modeled nor reinforced, a positive connection to adults at school may be essential for their academic and behavioral success at school (Dance, 2002; Furstenberg & Hughes, 1995). School connectedness may also bolster students when they experience difficulties elsewhere in their lives (Luthar & Zigler, 1991; Wehlage, 1989). In contrast, more advantaged students may adopt the school's social norms regardless of their connection to school because these norms are reinforced at home or in their jobs and activities outside of school. Connection to school may not be essential for more advantaged students' success.

An equally plausible argument is that only students with high social capital in multiple contexts have the wherewithal to successfully use connection to school as a developmental resource (Jencks & Meyer, 1989). Under this scenario, advantages accrue to the already advantaged, and social inequalities are reinforced. Development occurs in nested, interdependent systems (Bronfenbrenner, 1979; Jessor, 1991). If a student does not develop connection or social capital in the primary system of the family, and, moreover, their family does not partner effectively with their school, that student might benefit less from school connectedness. Although they may perceive that their teachers and other students care about them and respect them, they may not be able to translate this resource into achieving academic success and avoiding risky behaviors (Stanton-Salazar, 2001). Stanton-Salazar (2001) found that Mexican and Mexican American immigrants were not able to capitalize on interactions with guidance counselors and other adults in the school in positions to give them access to resources because the students did not have the personal and family resources to maximize those interactions.

Quantitative research on school connection and health risk behaviors tends to support neither of these alternatives, but rather suggests that being highly connected to school benefits most students equally. Several researchers have examined the joint effects of connection in multiple contexts (Cook, Herman, Phillips, & Settersten, 2002; Dornbusch et al., 2001; Gerard & Buehler, 2004). All found an additive relationship such that connection to school appears to be equally promotive of health and academic outcomes regardless of a student's connection to their family or community. In short, the quantitative research suggests that students who feel highly connected to school are less likely to participate in health risk behaviors regardless of the quality of their home environment. By extension, one might speculate that these benefits of school connectedness accrue regardless of the nature and quality of school-family partnership, although to the authors' knowledge this hypothesis has not been explicitly examined.

The finding that the effects of connection in multiple contexts on health behaviors are additive (rather than multiplicative) appears to belie the findings of qualitative research (Dance, 2002; Stanton-Salazar, 2001) as well as the accrued wisdom of teachers throughout the United States who identify specific children who were "saved" by a connection to teachers or adults in the school. That is perhaps because the macro overview provided by the quantitative research cannot, by definition, account for variations within group in the complex interactions between context, developmental stage and personality. It may also be because much of the qualitative work, and certainly much of the concern of teachers, tends to focus on students at risk of failing and excludes advantaged students, thereby missing the equal importance of connection to school to their success.

There is stronger evidence for a functional substitution effect for academic outcomes. Croninger and Lee (1991) found that connection to teachers, which they term social capital and assess as the extent to which students perceive that teachers respect them and care about their success, has a stronger protective effect on dropping out of school for students who are academically struggling. They concluded that by gaining students' trust, teachers may be better able to encourage students academically (Croninger & Lee, 2001). Whitlock (2003) concluded this as well. She found that students on the brink of dropping out of traditional school settings reported significant reversals in academic interest and achievement when placed in environments they perceived as high in characteristics which contribute to school connectedness. As a result, their school connectedness scores were significantly higher than those of their more academically accomplished peers.

Other studies have explored whether school connectedness is more promotive of positive outcomes for students in less advantaged demographic groups. Three separate studies using Add Health found no gender or ethnic differences in the association between school connectedness and the initiation or prevalence of cigarette use, alcohol use, marijuana use, delinquency, or violent behavior (Dornbusch et al., 2001), disruptive behavior (Crosnoe et al., 2004), or emotional distress (Libbey, 2007). However, Crosnoe et al. (2004) reported that although teacher support predicted lower levels of disruptive behavior for all students, this relationship was magnified for White girls. This relationship may also be moderated by income levels and welfare status (Croninger & Lee, 2001; DuBois, Felner, Brand, Adan, & Evans, 1992). Demographic categories are heterogeneous categories and poor proxies for whether students are at-risk, a construct of greater interest to educators and youth development professionals.

An under-investigated area of research is whether the relationship between connection to school and health and academic outcomes differs based on features of the school context, including school-family partnerships.

### Measurement Influences on School Connection Effects

Does the effect of school connection depend on the definition and measurement of connection? The answer to this question is a definitive yes. Several researchers have demonstrated that social belonging at school is associated with *increased* participation in some health risk behaviors (Karcher, 2002; Libbey, 2007; McNeely & Falci, 2004). An oft-used measure of social belonging is the measure of social solidarity developed by Bollen and Hoyle (1990), which assesses the extent to which students feel like they are part of school, belong at school, and are happy to be at school. In zero-order associations, this measure is positively correlated with health and academic outcomes. However, once measures of supportive relationships with teachers are included in the model, social belonging becomes a risk factor for experimentation with tobacco, alcohol, and marijuana (Karcher & Finn, 2005; McNeely & Falci, 2004) and is unrelated to violence involvement, the timing of first sexual intercourse, or emotional distress. The reason, the authors hypothesized, is that measures of social belonging tap into students' relationships with peers, and supportive relationships with peers tend to reinforce the norms of the peer group. For most adolescents, experimentation with alcohol is normative.

Clearly, supportive relationships with peers at school is a separate construct from connection to adults with authority at school. Not known is whether adults in certain roles at school are more important than adults in other roles for creating connection to school. Undeniably, it is helpful to feel supported and cared for by at least one adult in a school, but some adults have more power and authority to grant resources than do others. The school clinic staff, community schools coordinator, and guidance counselor—often the adults most committed to fostering connectedness—cannot grant students, as a group, access to respect, decision-making opportunities, or autonomy within the system, as they themselves do not control those resources. Yet these are precisely the personnel typically placed in charge of efforts to promote school connectedness. Students identify administrators as having a key role in making them feel respected and cared for by giving them access to the resources they desire for their development (Whitlock, 2003). An important policy question is whether, when efforts to foster school connectedness are managed by support services personnel rather than by the school leadership, students will feel more connected to school.

## DEFINITION OF SCHOOL CONNECTEDNESS REVISITED

Although the research shows that positive socialization experiences at school promote positive student outcomes, the lack of specificity about those socializing experiences and the overlapping definitions and measures have resulted in a lack of clarity about which socializing experiences are most important, for whom they are most effective, and how to produce them. This chapter addresses this confusion in the research literature by proposing a theoretically-grounded definition of school connectedness. As stated previously, school connectedness is *a psychological state in which individual youth perceive that they and other youth are cared for, trusted, and respected by adults with authority in the school* (Whitlock, 2003). This definition certainly needs to be held up to the scrutiny of research and evaluations of interventions before it is adopted unquestioningly, but there are several features that recommend it.

First, the proposed definition conceptualizes school connectedness at the intersection of the individual and the collective. This definition clarifies that school connectedness is not simply students' perceptions of their own individual relationships with adults at school. Adolescence is a life stage in which peers are particularly powerful in opinion formation. Concurrent with this heightened attention to peers comes a heightened awareness of how adults use age as a criterion for determining social rights and responsibilities and for summarily evaluating youth capacity, need, and motivation. Individual young people are sensitive to the status, treatment, rights, and responsibilities accorded their age-mates in general and other subgroups with which they identify in particular. Consequently, adolescents incorporate the observed or reported experiences of other students into their personal perceptions of care, trust and respect at school. Evidence of this comes out most clearly in qualitative research (Dance, 2002; Morrow, 2001; Whitlock, 2003), in which adolescents report experiences of others as highly salient to their individual perception of the extent to which adults with authority are caring, respectful and trusting of young people.

Second, the proposed definition of school connectedness focuses on relationships between youth and adults with authority. Empirical research suggests that school connectedness and connection to peers are not similarly associated with health, educational attainment, and social development (Karcher & Finn, 2005; McNeely & Falci, 2004). Moreover, confirmatory factor analysis suggests that connectedness to peers and adults are separate constructs (McNeely, 2004). Consequently, the definition proposes explicitly that measures assessing school connectedness specifically assess relationships with adults and not general questions about belonging and liking school or questions about relationships with peers.

Student perceptions of life at school are shaped by the perceived distribution and availability of adult attention and respect at school. Adult love, appreciation, and approval are coveted resources, and trends in distribution of these resources are highly visible and analyzed by students. Additionally, because adults are perceived to hold resources of high value to students, political extensions of this power through school-based policies and practices are included in student (particularly older student) mental evaluations of adult equity and availability. Because of this, small actions and routine policies and practices, many of which would go unnoticed by adults, may assume salience for students often overlooked in measures of school connectedness.

Third, the proposed definition emphasizes the reciprocal nature of connectedness. A definitional and measurement challenge comes in the assumed directionality of the experience. Should connection be conceptualized and measured as something not merely received (e.g., "To what extent do you feel cared for") but reciprocated as well (e.g., "To what extent do you care about your school") (Barber & Schluterman, 2008; Karcher, 2002; Whitlock, 2006)? Eco-developmental and social capital theories posit an agentic role for young people, who actively dissipate or reinforce connection to their school by the way they engage in relationships at school. Although most youth development researchers acknowledge the agentic role of youth, very few employ measures to quantify how much students care about and respect the adults with authority in their school. Efforts to create bidirectional measures of connection are underway (Barber et al., 2007), but these measurement efforts have rarely extended to connection to school.

Fourth, the proposed definition distinguishes school connectedness from the developmental supports that produce it. We propose that school connectedness be defined as a perception of relationships between students and the adults in their school. Although this perception is surely the product of behaviors of the actors in the relationships, it is not one and the same thing. This distinction is crucial because the same actions or policies do not universally produce the same feelings of connectedness in all students. Yet the notion of connectedness is often conflated with the conditions in school that create it. Similarly, consequences of connection, such as engagement in learning or extracurricular activities, are often included in measures of school connection. Although these conglomerate measures of school connection robustly predict developmental outcomes, they do not elucidate the causal pathways or identify specific points of intervention to guide practitioners. Specifically, they do not allow researchers to answer key questions such as: Which factors are most critical for producing school connectedness? Do they work similarly across cultural settings and institutional contexts, such as private vs. public schools? And, very importantly, is the perception of being trusted, cared for, and respected by adults with authority as powerful in promoting adolescent development as current research suggests it is? Once the antecedents are measured distinctly, it is possible that school connectedness may not play a causal role as a mediating variable. The proposed definition allows research to empirically investigate all of these questions.

Fifth, the proposed definition clearly situates school connectedness as distinct from school-family partnerships, thereby allowing for clarification of the relationship between the two constructs. School connectedness and school-family partnerships both emanate from the giving and the receiving of care, trust and respect. However, relationships between students and adults with authority in school are the foundation of school connectedness whereas school-family partnerships encompass a broader set of relationships (e.g., parents-staff, parents-children, and parent-parent).

### School Connectedness and School-Family Partnerships

How do school connectedness and school-family partnerships interact to produce positive developmental outcomes? It has been contended that it is the number rather than the nature of risks that matter for development (Sameroff & Fiese, 2000). This argument readily lends itself to positive developmental supports as well as risks: experiencing connectedness in multiple contexts is cumulatively protective. The empirical evidence reviewed above suggests that the effects of school connectedness and school-family partnership are cumulative. School connectedness can positively influence adolescent outcomes, regardless of family-level factors, but the more settings in which adolescents feel connectedness, the greater the odds of achieving positive outcomes.

Although this research suggests that schools can promote school connectedness without including or reforming school-family partnerships, school-family partnerships can augment and strengthen school-based school connectedness strategies. For example, Comer's School Development Program works to develop collaborative relationships among school, family, students, and the community so that children experience supportive relationships with caring adults in each of these settings. It particularly focuses developing strong school-family collaboration in which parents are directly involved in decision making and implementation. Evaluation of the Comer model determined that when the program is implemented fully and, specifically, when the critical element of parent involvement is present, the program demonstrates success in terms of higher academic achievement, attendance, and connection to school (defined as perceptions of caring and respectful relationships with teachers; Cook, Murphy, & Hunt, 2000). In short, working on school-family partnerships can strengthen school connectedness.

It also has been suggested anecdotally by school personnel in inner-city schools that school connectedness can foster school-family partnerships (personal communication with teachers and after-school staff in Houston and Baltimore, January–May, 2008). When adolescents report positive experiences at school, it may encourage parents to support their education. Although this is an attractive proposition, it does place the least powerful actor in the child-parent-school professional triad in the leadership role for fostering positive relationships. Bryk and Schneider (2002) noted that owing to the substantial power asymmetry in professional-family relationships, the responsibility should fall on the school staff to initiate trust in the relationship. Nonetheless, the possibility that school connectedness can facilitate school-family partnerships is an attractive proposition that merits investigation.

## PROPOSED RESEARCH AGENDA

This chapter had two goals. The first goal was to propose a definition of school connectedness that is clearly distinguishable from other positive socializing experiences at school. The second goal was to propose a two-pronged research agenda to better understand (a) the relationship between school connectedness and school-family partnerships and (b) how, when, and why school connectedness fosters positive developmental outcomes.

As made clear in this chapter, research on school connectedness is in its infancy and, as a result, cannot provide unambiguous guidance as to what school connectedness is, what an investment in strengthening it would buy schools (and students and families), or what, exactly, schools should do to strengthen school connectedness. Although many school reform efforts have proven successful, it is not clear what role school connectedness (vs. school-family partnerships, academic motivation, a sense of belonging, or other related constructs) played in their success.

This chapter proffered a definition of school connectedness to encourage increased conceptual clarity of the construct and a better understanding of how, when, and why it fosters positive adolescent development. The definition does not answer outstanding questions, but it can serve as a vehicle to foster research on this topic. A research agenda should consist of three tasks: (a) develop and test measures of school connectedness consistent with the definition proposed; (b) empirically identify antecedents and developmental consequences of school connectedness for adolescents, their families, and their schools; and (c) empirically test how school connectedness operates in conjunction with other socializing processes in school, particularly school-family partnerships, which emanate from the same mechanisms of trust, care, and respect.

These three aims are best achieved in concert through a research program that does not overly reduce the complexity of socialization in schools. Most quantitative research that explores the relationship between connectedness and adolescent outcomes produce biased estimates of the protective capacity of school connectedness. When statistical models do not include measures of theoretically relevant constructs correlated with connectedness (e.g., the nature and quality of school-family partnership or academic engagement), associations due to shared variance with other constructs are too often interpreted as due to school connectedness alone, no matter the definition used, resulting in overestimations of the importance of connectedness. Conversely, the tendency in the research literature to look at average effects may underestimate the capacity of school connectedness to foster development among certain groups of students, such as those most at risk of dropping out.

Two research programs serve as examples for developing valid measures of school connectedness and estimating its contribution to development. Barber and colleagues (2005) used a mixed-method approach. They constructed a conceptual map placing school connectedness within a theoretical framework containing other socializing experiences. This conceptual map served both to define the constructs (and how to measure them) and to establish hypotheses for how they are theoretically related to each other and to a broad set of developmental outcomes. Specifically, Barber and colleagues (2005) proposed a theoretical framework for how specific dimensions of parenting might be uniquely related to different adolescent outcomes. They focused on three parenting dimensions—connection, psychological control, and parental monitoring—and hypothesized that connection and psychological control would be more strongly associated with social initiative and depressive symptoms whereas parental monitoring would be more strongly associated with so-called antisocial behaviors. They found evidence of these uniquely patterned associations in samples of adolescents from 12 cultural groups in 9 countries. What is salient from this study for the present chapter is that measures of parental connection, *examined alone* without the presence of psychological control and parental monitoring, predicted all three outcomes—social initiative, depressive symptoms, and antisocial behavior. Studying the three constructs jointly showed that connection was not associated with all outcomes.

A similar approach was taken to study the antecedents of school connectedness. Whitlock (2006) set forth a theoretical model of developmental supports of school connectedness and explored them jointly using a mixed-method approach. Consistent with previous research on youth development (Benson et al., 1999; Sameroff & Fiese, 2000), she found that developmental supports operate cumulatively: students who reported more developmental supports in school and in their community reported higher levels of school connectedness. However, Whitlock (2003) also found that not all developmental supports are created equal; some are more important than others for fostering school connectedness. In her study of urban youth in Upstate New York, she found the following developmental supports to be most crucial: adult and institutional willingness to "see" young people, acknowledge the multifaceted dimensions of their lives, provide assistance even when not mandated, and sparingly wield the staff of authority granted by their age and status (Whitlock, 2006). She did not include school-family partnership in her theoretical model, and this is an important next step for research.

The proposed research agenda, as these examples show, must contain the voices of young people. In both the examples, theoretical models were validated both empirically and through eliciting the voices of young people themselves to describe their experiences of connection. The voices of young people provided context and meaning to the a priori developed quantitative measures, as well as provided more valid measures that improved model fit in subsequent tests of the theoretical relationships (Barber et al., 2007).

Carrying out a research agenda to identify how school connectedness works alone and in conjunction with school-family partnership and other socializing experiences will be well worth the effort. Ultimately, it will simplify the translation of research findings into practical application in schools (Barber & Schluterman, 2008). Rather than the current flurry of overlapping definitions and findings, which leave the research community unable to make specific recommendations of where and how to invest scarce educational dollars, researchers will be able to provide straightforward answers to the basic questions of what is school connectedness, how important is it for the adolescents in my school, and, if it is a potent protective factor, how do I foster it?

## CONCLUSION

Schools are being inundated with recommendations for school improvement. If even a fraction of these recommendations were responded to, it would stretch school resources—both financial and human—to the breaking point. In this chapter we endeavored to address the responsibility of researchers in helping to clarify which aspects of child-school-family relationships are most worthy of investment. Our focus was school connectedness.

We offered a theoretically robust and empirically testable definition of school connectedness to distinguish it from other positive socializing experiences in school such as school engagement, academic motivation, and school-family partnership. Once there is a clear and agreed upon definition, the field can tackle the essential questions of how the construct matters for adolescent development, for whom it matters most, and how to create it for all students. To that end, we proposed a research agenda containing two essential elements: (a) the study of school connectedness as part of a theoretical model that contains the other fundamental socializing experiences at school, including school-family partnership, family-child relationships, and peer relationships, and (b) the inclusion of youth voices in the research. We contend that once research, informed by the voices of those it is intending to help, can clarify how school-family partnerships and school connectedness jointly contribute to adolescent outcomes, schools will be able to justifiably and more efficiently invest their scarce capital in building trusting, caring, and respectful relationships.

## REFERENCES

Allen, J. P., & Land, D. (1999). Attachment in adolescence. In J. Cassidy, & P. R. Shaver (Eds.), *Handbook of attachment theory and research* (pp. 319–335). New York: Guilford.

Andrews, J. A., Hops, H., & Duncan, S. C. (1997). Adolescent modeling of parent substance use: The moderating effect of the relationship with the parent. *Journal of Family Psychology, 11*(3), 259–270.

Appleton, J. J., Christenson, S. L., Kim, D., & Reschly, A. L. (2006). Measuring cognitive and psychological engagement: Validation of the student engagement instrument. *Journal of School Psychology, 44*(5), 427–445.

Bandura, A. (1977). *Social learning theory.* New York: General Learning Press.

Barber, B. K., & Olsen, J. A. (1997). Socialization in context: Connection, regulation, and autonomy in the family, school, and neighborhood, and with peers. *Journal of Adolescent Research, 12*(2), 287–315.

Barber, B. K., Olsen, J. A., Higgins, W. B., Kritiyapichatkul, C., Krauskopf, D., & Ward, C (2007). *Report to the World Health Organization of final quantitative analyses. Connection/Regulation tool project—stage 3: Field test.* Unpublished manuscript.

Barber, B. K., & Schluterman, J. M. (2008). Connectedness in the lives of children and adolescents: A call for greater conceptual clarity. *Journal of Adolescent Health, 43*(3), 209–216.

Barber, B. K., Stolz, H. E., & Olsen, J. A. (2005). Parental support, psychological control, and behavioral control: Assessing relevance across time, method, and culture. *Monographs of the Society for Research in Child Development, 70*(4).

Battistitch, V., Solomon, D., Watson, M., & Schaps, E. (1997). Caring school communities. *Educational Psychologist, 32*(3), 137–151.

Baumeister, R. F., & Leary, M. (1995). The need to belong: Desire for interpersonal attachments as a fundamental human motivation. *Psychological Bulletin, 117*(3), 497–529.

Benson, P. L., Scales, P. C., Leffert, N., & Roehlkpartain, E. C. (1999). *A fragile foundation: The state of developmental assets among American youth.* Minneapolis, MN: Search Institute.

Blum, R. W., & Libbey, H. (2004). School connectedness: Strengthening health and educational outcomes for teens: Executive summary. *Journal of School Health, 74*(7), 231–232.

Bollen, K., & Hoyle, R.H. (1990). Perceived cohesion: A conceptual and empirical examination. *Social Forces, 69*(2), 479–504.

Bond, L., Patton, G., Glover, S., Carlin, J. B., Butler, H., Thomas, L., et al. (2004). The Gatehouse Project: Can a multilevel school intervention affect emotional wellbeing and health risk behaviours? *Journal of Epidemiology and Community Health, 58*(12), 997–1003.

Bowlby, J. (1969). *Attachment: Vol 1. Attachment and loss.* New York: Basic Books.

Bronfenbrenner, U. (1979). *The ecology of human development: Experiments by nature and design.* Cambridge, MA: Harvard University Press.

Bronfenbrenner, U., & Morris, P. (1998). The ecology of developmental processes. In R. M. Lerner (Ed.), *Theoretical models of human development. Vol. 1 of the handbook of child psychology* (5th ed., pp. 993–1028). New York: Wiley.

Brown, R., & Evans, W. P. (2002). Extracurricular activity and ethnicity: Creating greater school connection among diverse student populations. *Urban Education, 37*(1), 41–58.

Byrk, A. S., & Schneider, B. (2002). *Trust in schools: A core resource for improvement.* New York: Russell Sage Foundation.

Catalano, R. F., Haggerty, K. P., Oesterle, S., Fleming, C. B., & Hawkins, J. D. (2004). The importance of bonding to school for healthy development: Findings from the social development research group. *Journal of School Health, 74*(4), 252–261.

Coleman, J. S. (1990). *Foundations of social theory.* Cambridge, MA: Harvard University Press.

Cook, T., Murphy, R. F., & Hunt, H. D. (2000). Comer's school development program in Chicago: A theory-based evaluation. *American Educational Research Journal, 37*(2), 535–597.

Cook, T. D., Herman, M. R., Phillips, M., & Settersten, R. A., Jr. (2002). Some ways in which neighborhoods, nuclear families, friendship groups, and schools jointly affect changes in early adolescent development. *Child Development, 73*(4), 1283–1309.

Cooley, C. H. (1902). *Human nature and the social order.* New York: Scribner's.

Croninger, R. G., & Lee, V. E. (2001). Social capital and dropping out of high school: Benefits to at-risk students of teachers' support and guidance. *The Teachers College Record, 103*(4), 548–581.

Crosnoe, R., Johnson, M. K., Elder, & Glen M., Jr. (2004). Intergenerational bonding in school: The behavioral and contextual student-teacher relationships. *Sociology of Education, 77*(1), 60–81.

Dance, L. J. (2002). *Tough fronts: The impact of street culture on schooling.* New York: Routledge.

Dornbusch, S. M., Erickson, K. G., Laird, J., & Wong, C. A. (2001). The relation of family and school attachment to adolescent deviance in diverse groups and communities. *Journal of Adolescent Research, 16*(4), 396–422.

DuBois, D. L., Felner, R. D., Brand, S., Adan, A. M., & Evans, E. G. (1992). A prospective study of life stress, social support, and adaptation in early adolescence. *Child Development, 63*(3), 542–557.

Eccles, J. S., Midgely, C., Wigfield, A., Buchanan, C. M., Flanagan, C., & Mac Iver, D. (1993). Development during adolescence: The impact of stage-environment fit on young adolescents' experiences in schools and in families. *American Psychologist, 48*(2), 90–101.

Erikson, E. (1968) *Identity: Youth and crisis.* New York: W. W. Norton.

Falci, C., & McNeely, C. A. (2009). Too many friends: Social integration, network cohesion and adolescent depressive symptoms. *Social Forces, 87*(4), 2031-2062.

Finn, J. D. (1993) School engagement and students at risk. (Report No. NCES-93-470). Washington, DC: National Center for Education Statistics.

Fredricks, J. A., Blumenfield, P. C., & Paris, A. H. (2004). Student engagement: Potential of the concept, state of the evidence. *Review of Educational Research, 74*(1), 59–109.

Furstenberg, F., & Hughes, M. E. (1995). Social capital and successful development among at-risk youth. *Journal of Marriage and the Family, 57*(3), 580–592.

Garmezy, N. (1985). Stress-resistent children: The search for protective factors. In J. E. Stevenson (Ed.), *Recent research in developmental psychopathology. Journal of Child Psychology and Psychiatry Book Supplement No. 4* (pp. 213–233). Oxford, England: Pergamon Press.

Gerard, J. M., & Buehler, C. (2004). Cumulative environmental risk and youth maladjustment: The role of youth attributes. *Child Development, 75*(6), 1832–1849.

Goodenow, C. (1993). The Psychological Sense of School Membership among adolescents: Scale development and educational correlates. *Psychology in the Schools, 30*(1), 79–89.

Grotevant, H. D., & Cooper, C. R. (1986). Individuation in family relationships: A perspective on individual differences in the development of identity and role-taking skill in adolescence. *Human Development, 29*(2), 82–100.

Hawkins, J. D., & Weis J. G. (1985). The social development model: An integrated approach to delinquency prevention. *Journal of Primary Prevention, 6*(2), 72–97.

Hirschi, T. (1969). *Causes of delinquency*. Berkeley: University of California Press.

Jencks, C., & Meyer, S. E. (1989). Growing up in poor neighborhoods: How much does it matter? *Science, 243*(4897), 1441–1445.

Jenkins, P. H. (1997). School delinquency and the school social bond. *Journal of Research in Crime and Delinquency, 34*(3), 337–367.

Jessor, R. (1991). Risk behavior in adolescence: A psychosocial framework for understanding and action. *Journal of Adolescent Health, 12*(8), 597–605.

Karcher, M. J. (2002). The cycle of violence and disconnection among rural middle school students: Teacher disconnection as a consequence of violence. *Journal of School Violence, 1*(1), 35–51.

Karcher, M. J., & Finn, L. (2005). How connectedness contributes to experimental smoking among rural youth: Developmental and ecological analyses. *The Journal of Primary Prevention, 26*(1), 25–36.

Lerner, R. M. (1991). Changing organism-context relations as the basic process of development: A developmental contextual perspective. *Developmental Psychology, 24*(1), 27–32.

Lerner, R., M. (1995). Developing individuals within changing contexts: Implications of developmental contextualism for human developmental research, policy, and programs. In T. Kindermann & J. Valsiner (Eds.), *Development of person-context relations* (pp. 13–38). Mahwah, NJ: Erlbaum.

Libbey, H. (2004). Measuring student relationships to school: Attachment, bonding, connectedness and engagement. *Journal of School Health, 74*(4), 274–283.

Libbey, H. (2007). *School connectedness: Influence on educational attainment and emotional distress*. Unpublished doctoral dissertation, University of Minnesota, Minneapolis.

Lin, N. (2001). *Social capital: A theory of social structure and action*. London: Cambridge University Press.

Lonczak, H. S., Abbott, R. D., Hawkins, J. D., Kosterman, R., & Catalano, R. F. (2002). Effects of the Seattle Social Development Project on sexual behavior, pregnancy, birth, and sexually transmitted disease outcomes by age 21 years. *Archives of Pediatrics and Adolescent Medicine, 156*(5), 438–447.

Luthar, S. S. & Zigler, E. (1991). Vulnerability and competence: A review of research on resilience in childhood. *American Journal of Orthopsychiatry, 61*(1), 6–22.

Maslow, A. H. (1968) *Toward a psycholog of being* (2nd ed.). Princton, NJ: Van Nostrand Co.

Masten, A. S., Best, K. M., & Garmezy, N. (1990). Resilience and development: Contributions from the study of children who overcome adversity. *Development and Psychopathology, 2*(4), 425–444.

McNeely, C. A. (2004). Connection to school as an indicator of positive youth development. In L. Lippman & K. Moore (Eds.), *Indicators of positive youth development. search institute series on developmentally attentive community and society* (pp. 289–304). Norwell, MA: Kluwer Academic/Plenum Press.

McNeely, C. A., & Falci, C. (2004). School connectedness and the transition into and out of health risk behaviors among adolescents: A comparison of social belonging and teacher support. *Journal of School Health, 74*(7), 284–292.

McNeely, C. A., Nonnemaker, J. M., & Blum, R. W. (2002). Promoting student connectedness to school: Evidence from the national longitudinal study of adolescent health. *Journal of School Health, 72*(4), 138–146.

Mirowsky, J., & Ross, C. E. (2003). *Education, social status, and health*. Piscataway, NJ: Aldine Transaction.

Morrow, V. (2001). Young people's explanations and experiences of social exclusion: Retrieving Bourdieu's concept of social capital. *International Journal of Sociology and Social Policy, 21*(4), 37–63.

National Research Council and Institute of Medicine. (2002). *Community Programs to Promote Youth Development*. Committee on Community-Level Programs for Youth. Jacquelynne Eccles and Jennifer A.Gootman

(Eds.), Board on Children, Youth, and Families, Division of Behavioral and Social Sciences and Education. Washington, DC: National Academy Press.

Osterman, K. F. (2001). Students' need for belonging in the school community. *Review of Educational Research, 70*(3), 323–367.

Resnick, M. D., Bearman, P. S., Blum, R. W., Bauman, K. M., Harris, K. M., Jones, J., et al. (1997). Protecting adolescents from harm: Findings from the national longitudinal study on adolescent health. *JAMA, 278*(10), 823–832.

Sameroff, A. J., & Fiese, B. H. (2000). Models of development and developmental risk. In C. H. Zeanah (Ed.), *Handbook of infant mental health* (2nd ed. pp. 3–19). New York: Guilford.

Sinclair, M. F., Christenson, S. L., Lehr, C. A., & Reschly, A. (2003). Facilitating student engagement: Lessons learned from Check & Connect longitudinal studies. *The California School Psychologist, 8*, 29–41.

Stanton-Salazar, R. D. (2001). *Manufacturing hope and despair: The school and kin support networks of U.S. Mexican youth.* New York: Teachers College Press.

Stryker, S., & Stratham, A. (1985). Symbolic interaction and role theory. In G. Lindzey & E. Aronson (Eds.), *Handbook of social psychology: Vol 1. Theory and method* (pp. 311–378). New York: Random House.

Voelkl, K. E. (1996). Measuring students' identification with school. *Educational and Psychological Measurement, 56*(5), 760–770.

Wehlage, R. (1989). *Reducing the risk: Schools as communities of support.* Philadelphia: The Falmer Press, Taylor & Francis.

Werner, E. E., & Smith, R. S. (1992). *Overcoming the odds: High risk children from birth to adulthood.* Ithaca, NY: Cornell University Press.

Whitlock, J. L. (2003). *Voice, visibility, place and power: Correlates of school and community connectedness among 8th, 10th, and 12th grade youth.* Unpublished doctoral dissertation, Cornell University, Ithaca, NY.

Whitlock, J. L. (2006). Youth perceptions of life at school: Contextual correlates of school connectedness in adolescence. *Applied Developmental Science, 10*(1), 13–29.

# 13

## FAMILY-SCHOOL PARTNERSHIPS AND COMMUNICATION INTERVENTIONS FOR YOUNG CHILDREN WITH DISABILITIES

ANN P. KAISER AND ALACIA TRENT STAINBROOK

Learning to communicate is a significant developmental task for young children. Communication has its foundation in primary social interactions, but effective communication requires the coordinated use of cognitive, social, motor, and linguistic skills. The complexity of the social linguistic communication system, and its interdependence with development in other domains, makes it relatively vulnerable to disruption. If a significant delay occurs in any domain of development, it is likely to affect communication development. Thus, most children with cognitive, motor, or social delays resulting from genetic or environmental causes are at risk for delays in the development of language and communication skills.

## OVERVIEW

The purpose of this chapter is to discuss a contemporary model for family-school partnerships to facilitate young children's language development. We will refer to this model as the Collaborative Communication Model (CCM). The goal of the model is to ensure generalization of newly learned communication skills in young children with language related disabilities by promoting continuity and increasing the incidence of intervention across home and school. In this chapter, we present CCM as a conceptual model in the process of development. The principles underlying the model are grounded in ecological theory (Bronfenbrenner, 1992) as well as best practices in early communication intervention and family-centered practice (Dunst, 2002). Specific components of the model are supported by empirical research and an experimental demonstration of this model is currently underway (Kaiser, Woods, & Hancock, 2008). The emphasis in this chapter is on young children with special needs related to language learning; however, the principles guiding the model are applicable to children with emergent behavior disorders (Webster-Stratton, 1993), children from low income families

(Fantuzzo, McWayne, Perry, & Childs, 2004), and typically developing young children acquiring literacy skills (Snow, Barnes, Chandler, Goodman, & Hemphill, 1991) and older children (Dunst, 2002).

Young children with communication related disabilities who have other developmental delays are served under Part C of the Individuals with Education Improvement Act of 2004 (IDEA, 2004). From its inception, Part C has contained a specific mandate for family-centered services, including the Individualized Family Service Plan (IFSP) as the guiding document for child interventions. Family-service provider partnerships are essential for ensuring positive family and child outcomes, while a strong orientation toward families provides the context of early intervention. Together these two ideas lay the groundwork for the CCM. Thus, for children under the age of 3, the CCM is a systematic extension of the principles and values embedded in the existing service delivery system. While Part B of IDEA does not contain the same specific language about family-centered services, it does emphasize services in the least restrictive, natural, and most developmentally appropriate environment and monitoring of children's response to intervention as the basis for individualized and effective services. For children with disabilities who are learning language and communication throughout the school years, the home environment and family interactions are essential learning contexts. Collaboration across settings continues to be essential for children who are learning to communicate at any age and family-school partnerships as outlined in the CCM continue to be appropriate and valuable for supporting communication development (see Kaiser and Grim, 2005, for an extended example of family-school collaboration to teach communication skills to older students).

In the following sections, family-school partnership is defined as the context for the proposed model. Then, the critical issues related to effective language intervention are reviewed. A model that involves family members and professionals as collaborators in supporting children's language development through naturalistic intervention is presented. Next, the empirical evidence supporting key roles for parents, teachers, and peers in language intervention with children who have disabilities is described. Several key questions related to maximizing child communication development are addressed: (a) Can family-school partnerships in communication intervention maximize child communication development? (b) What are the effective strategies for training individuals and teams to implement communication intervention strategies? (c) How can we promote peer communication partnerships? (d) How can we best develop collaborations among partners to promote communication? The concluding sections contain recommendations for research and practice.

## FAMILY-SCHOOL PARTNERSHIPS DEFINED

We define family-school partnerships following principles outlined by Blue-Banning, Summers, Frankland, Nelson, and Beegle (2004) and following Dunst (2002). Partnerships are mutually supportive interactions between families and professionals that focus on meeting the needs of children and families with competence, commitment, positive communication, and trust. The quality of the relationship between parents and professionals, the opportunities professionals provide to families for participation, and the quality of the services provided to child and family are key factors in an effective partnership. Family-professional partnerships focus on achieving the developmental outcomes families' value for their children. Family-centered practice that is individualized and responsive to family concerns and needs is the hallmark of best practice intervention during the preschool years (Dunst & Trivette, 1996). Although many of the same challenges face families and professionals during preschool years as during the school years, the relatively young age of the child, the obvious need for family involvement, and the strong history of family-centered practice provide a different and potentially more supportive context for family-professional partnerships. Further, because early intervention (birth to age 3) may be provided outside the structure of a school, partnerships are built among individual service providers and family members even when services are structured through agencies. During the preschool years, family-professional partnerships more closely resemble a school age model. While these differences in partnership context are not trivial, they do not change the foundation of partnership. We believe that both the principles for promoting communication outlined in this chapter and the specific strategies for collaboration are applicable to families of school age children as well as to families of young children.

## CRITICAL ISSUES IN EARLY COMMUNICATION INTERVENTION

Early intervention for language and communication is the single most frequently recommended therapy for young children with developmental disabilities. Progress in social communication and language skills is an important indicator of general development and provides the foundation for later cognitive, social, and literacy related skills (Kaiser, Hester, & McDuffie, 1991). Interventions to promote language and communication often begin relatively early, before 36 months, and may continue throughout childhood. Although children with significant disabilities may require continuing intervention to support their communication development, early intervention is nonetheless essential. The continuity and increasing severity of language delays in older preschool children suggests a need for proactive and effective treatment of language delays throughout the preschool years (Paul, 2006).

### Empirical Support for Early Communication Intervention

Nearly four decades of research on interventions to promote early language and social communication have provided a substantive empirical foundation. Beginning in the late 1960s, a series of studies demonstrated that children with significant cognitive disabilities could acquire spoken language when taught using direct instruction strategies (Guess, Sailor, Rutherford, & Baer, 1968; Waryas & Stremel, 1974). These studies were followed by studies examining and promoting generalization and maintenance of newly learned language skills from direct instruction settings to everyday social interactions (Warren & Kaiser, 1986). Evidence of limited generalization from direct teaching to functional use in natural environments, together with data from studies using incidental teaching strategies to promote language in low-income preschoolers (Hart & Risley, 1968), was key to the emergence of naturalistic interventions in everyday environments

(Kaiser, Yoder, & Keetz, 1992). Naturalistic interventions use many of the basic teaching strategies from direct instruction (prompting, reinforcement, fading, shaping) during everyday adult-child interactions to teach communication forms that were immediately functional in the conversational setting.

Just after naturalistic interventions began to appear in the empirical literature in the early to mid-1980s, the federal mandate for early intervention for young children with disabilities was passed (PL 99-457; U.S. Congress, 1986). This mandate for services in the least restrictive and most typical environments to children with disabilities from birth was a further impetus for developing effective strategies to teach functional communication skills to children during interactions in homes, childcare, and preschool settings. Since 1986, research in early communication intervention has expanded to include children at the prelinguistic stage of development as well as children with a range of developmental disabilities, including autism spectrum disorders, who are learning spoken language (Rogers et al., 2006; Yoder & Warren, 2002).

In an attempt to further extend communication intervention into children's typical environments, teachers and parents have been taught and encouraged to implement naturalistic language intervention strategies (Girolametto, 1988; Hancock & Kaiser, 2007; Woods, Kashinath, & Goldstein, 2004). Strategies for promoting social communication with peers have also been developed to extend the naturalistic teaching approach to a wider range of communication partners and contexts in which young children participate and develop (Goldstein & Cisar, 1992; Goldstein, English, Shafer, & Kaczmarek, 1997; McGee, Aimeda, Sulzer-Azaroff, & Feldman, 1992).

## Optimizing Learning Opportunities

While there is convincing evidence that young children with significant language delays can learn new skills during naturalistic language intervention, improving the generalized, functional language outcomes for these children remains a challenge for researchers and practitioners (Goldstein, 1993; Warren, Fey, & Yoder, 2007). The goal of language interventions is not only to teach children to use new language across settings, but also to facilitate continuing language development. To do so requires innovative strategies for changing everyday environments so that children have sufficient opportunities and adequate support for learning new language. Three important issues warrant consideration in developing optimal language interventions: promoting generalization across contexts, providing sufficient dosage of intervention and increasing continuity of intervention over time.

*Promoting Generalization*    To optimize language development, young children with disabilities must have opportunities to learn language that is relevant to their everyday communication settings. Both initial acquisition and appropriately generalized use of new language pose challenges for children with disabilities (Abbeduto & Rosenberg, 1992; Kaiser et al., 2001). Language is based on concepts and has a categorical and rule-based structure. Both the scope and the complexity of the language system pose challenges for children with disabilities. Learning language requires repeated opportunities for learning aspects of the communication system and exposure to multiple exemplars in the specific contexts in which these examples apply. Conceptual and empirical analyses of generalization resulting from language intervention strongly suggested that effective interventions for language learning include multiple exemplars of new forms across multiple settings and partners (Campbell & Stremel-Campbell, 1982; Goldstein, 1993; Stokes & Baer, 1977).

While the need for teaching across settings and persons, with attention to multiple exemplars of the target language, has been recognized for well over a decade (Warren & Kaiser, 1986), language intervention models that include comprehensive strategies for promoting generalization have been relatively limited. Our proposed model follows closely the logic of general-case programming (Halle, Chadsey-Rusch, & Collet-Klingenberg, 1993) and incorporates the ecological premise that child development results from interactions across settings and contexts as a means of promoting generalization of newly learned language skills. General-case programming focuses on the analysis, selection, and presentation of stimulus conditions to teach appropriate responses so that students respond across a range of persons, settings, and situations (Engelmann & Carnine, 1982). The first step in general-case programming is the selection and definition of the instructional universe. The instructional universe consists of the range of settings and situations in which it is desirable for students to produce that targeted behavior (O'Neill, Faulkner, & Horner, 2000). For example, if the instructional objective is requesting, the instructional universe should include settings that provide opportunities for the child to request verbally and in which requesting is important for the child's participation in the event.

Once a representative instructional universe has been determined, the range of relevant stimulus and response variations of that universe are defined. The interventionist considers people who are likely to be present, materials and activities that are likely to be available, and specific communicative responses that will facilitate the child's participation in that universe. Then, the identified communicative responses are taught in an environment similar to one in which they will be used. For example, if the goal is for a child to increase social interactions with peers, intervention should be conducted during classroom center-based activities in which peers are available for interaction. To promote a child's expression of needs to family members, intervention should be conducted in the home, where family members are available to respond to requests. In sum, it is not sufficient to teach a child targeted language skills in an isolated setting and expect that communication will generalize in the broad range of settings in which the child lives. A systematic teaching plan is needed, ideally following general-case programming principles, to optimize development and performance.

The optimal application of general-case programming strategies in this model requires collaboration and partnering between family members and school staff. Involving both family members and professionals (early interventionists, special educators, speech language pathologists) across settings (home, early intervention programs, schools) addresses two of the critical elements of case programming—selection of persons and settings that are part of the child's instructional universe. The third element, selecting target behaviors (language forms) that are used across settings and people requires both typical child assessment of known and unknown skills and systematic information collected from communication partners who are familiar with the activity domains and the communication demands of the settings in which the child participates. Ideally, family members and school personnel would partner in assessing the child's needs and selecting target behaviors to be addressed across settings; shared information is likely to facilitate both parties.

*Dosage of Intervention*    A second major concern in planning intervention is dosage, the amount of instruction and guided practice provided for the child (McCauley & Fey, 2006; Warren et al., 2007). Limited amounts of language intervention, such as two 30-minute sessions of speech therapy per week or speech therapy that is embedded in a single daily classroom activity, may not be sufficient for promoting language development for many young children with special needs. There must be sufficient instruction to achieve learning, mastery, and retention of new forms and functions for language intervention to be effective. Repetition and practice with feedback, as well as exposure to developmentally appropriate models of language, are critical for children with special needs (Kaiser, Hancock, & Nietfeld, 2000). The exact amount of intervention may vary based on the child's abilities. There is little empirical information to guide the planning of dosage of language intervention (Borkowski, Smith, & Akai, 2007; Law & Conti-Ramsden, 2000; Warren et al., 2007), and this is an area where research is needed.

Naturalistic language interventions are more likely to promote generalized use of new language than direct instruction outside the functional contexts for communication (Kaiser et al., 2001) because children learn new forms in their meaningful context. Although teaching in natural environments in response to children's interests and targeting functional forms increases the likelihood of generalization, it makes providing sufficient dosage of interventions challenging in natural settings (Hancock & Kaiser, 2007). Teaching in natural environments and targeting functional forms with an increased level of dosage requires family members and school personnel to partner and share teaching responsibilities. If it is desirable for learning opportunities to carry over into the home, it is necessary for teachers and therapists to communicate instructional strategies, goals, and child progress with the family members. Furthermore, it is important for family members to share information regarding learning opportunities, goals, and child progress in the home with the school personnel. This sharing of responsibility and information may ease the load for each member of the child's intervention team while increasing dosage of treatment.

*Continuity of Intervention*    Many young children with significant communication delays require intervention continuously during toddler, preschool, and early school years (Paul, 2006). Continuity of intervention is essential to have sufficient dosage, intensity, and scope of targets to promote adequate language development (Warren et al., 2007). When children have significant disabilities, their contexts for language learning extend beyond parent-child interactions. For these children, language must be learned in many settings with many partners. Continuity and shared focus in language intervention across partners and settings, without major interruptions due to service and setting transitions, directly affects child outcomes. As children transition from one setting to another, become more socially engaged with peers, and enter community activities, new opportunities for teaching and learning, and new needs for functional language arise. Transitions introduce new professionals, peers, and community members. Addressing children's changing communication ecologies requires consistent allocation of resources to language intervention and planning to insure continuity to prepare children for these new opportunities for communication. Family-school partnerships in which family members and school personnel communicate openly and frequently facilitate such continuity.

## MODEL FOR FAMILY-SCHOOL PARTNERSHIPS

The goal of the proposed Collaborative Communication Model (CCM) is to maximize child communication learning continuously from early identification through age 5. To implement such a model requires a collaborative team approach (Childress, 2004). The purpose of the team is to coordinate and enhance the child's naturalistic language intervention across settings, intervention agents, and time. The members of the team, in addition to the family, define the services the child receives and the specific settings in which services are provided to the child. An ideal intervention team consists of parents, the child's current Early Intervention (EI) or Early Childhood Special Education (ECSE) teacher, assistant teacher, Speech Language Pathologist (SLP), and other therapists and service providers. Ideally, within this model, one person would be appointed to facilitate coordination of intervention strategies, child goals, and training to parents and professionals. In addition, the coordinator provides leadership for the team, ensures that the process is responsive to child and family's needs, and guides the use of a case programming approach to the communication intervention.

The model is organized around principles of language development and effective language intervention. The communication team implements these principles: (a) language intervention for young children with disabilities should be evidence-informed and have meaningful and measurable outcomes (Odom & McLean, 1996), (b) family members should provide continuity and context for their children's communication development (Campbell & Sawyer, 2007; Kaiser, Hancock, & Trent, 2007), and (c) intervention in the child's evolving ecology should take advantage of current, emerging, and future communication opportunities (Cole, Maddox & Lim, 2006). By following three principles, the team directly addresses the critical issues in effective early communication intervention: generalization, dosage, and continuity. Figure 13.1 illustrates this model.

*Ensuring Treatment Integrity*    High levels of integrity in treatment implementation are essential to the effectiveness of any intervention model (Borkowski et al., 2007). In a complex model such as CCM, several levels of treatment integrity must be considered. First, each interventionist or team member must be skilled in the delivery of naturalistic language intervention in the context in which he or she interacts with the child. Naturalistic interventions are challenging and require both strong instructional strategies (e.g., use of the components of Milieu Teaching) and skill at embedding in ongoing activities. Kaiser et al. (2007) provided a detailed examination of the skills and strategies required for effective communication intervention. Previous studies of Milieu Teaching (MT) provide criteria for implementation (see Hancock & Kaiser, 2006). In

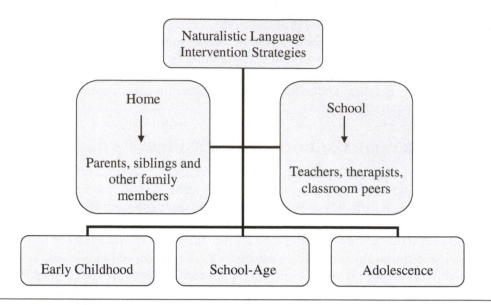

**Figure 13.1** Critical issues in early communication intervention.

the CCM model, a second level of treatment integrity corresponds to the development and implementation of a process for selecting child goals across settings, partners and activities consistent with the general case programming approach. The standards of general-case programming provide a template for evaluation of the implementation at this level. Finally, a third level of treatment integrity relates to the team process by which family members and professionals collaborate to support children's communication intervention and evaluate outcomes.

In the ongoing implementation of the CCM, we have developed brief treatment integrity assessment forms that are used in a formative fashion to monitor treatment fidelity. For example, both the procedures for training parents, therapists, and teachers to use MT are assessed in each training session. The frequency and accuracy of use of the intervention procedures in context (home across activities, therapy sessions in the classroom, across classroom activities) are assessed during probe observations and through self report. Goal selection and planning for MT is evaluated using a checklist of critical features and evaluating the intervention plan. Collaboration among team members is evaluated using forms developed specially for the project during quarterly evaluations of progress. (Examples of these evaluation forms may be obtained from the authors). Assessment of the collaborative process might be accomplished using an instrument similar to the Family-Professional Partnership Scale (Summers et al., 2005).

*Naturalistic Language Interventions*  Language intervention for young children with disabilities should be evidence-informed, and have meaningful and measurable outcomes. Research on naturalistic language interventions including milieu language teaching (Kaiser et al., 1992), prelinguistic milieu teaching (Yoder & Warren, 2001), responsive interaction (Kaiser & Hester, 1994), and pivotal response training (PRT; Koegel, Koegel, & Carter, 1999) support the effectiveness of such interventions. Young children who receive these interventions typically demonstrate improved communication skills, including increased total turns and spontaneous turns taken during interactions, complexity and mean length of utterance, diversity of vocabulary, and improvements on standardized measures of language production and comprehension (see Kaiser & Trent, 2007, for a comprehensive review). In general, naturalistic teaching occurs in children's everyday environments and during activities that have a primary focus that is not language teaching. Instruction occurs when the child is interested and, often, when the child makes an attempt to communicate. An adult's responsiveness to a child's topic and activity are central because language modeling and prompting occur during child-provided opportunities for teaching. The core instructional strategies in naturalistic teaching are often identical to those used in direct teaching (e.g., prompting, reinforcement, time delay, shaping, fading) but naturalistic teaching also includes strategies derived from a social interactionist perspective (e.g., modeling new language without prompting imitation, expansions of child utterances to provide models, recasting child utterance to provide corrected models of language or phonological forms, and a responsive communication style).

Implementing language teaching strategies in children's everyday natural settings increases opportunities for child learning (Daughterty, Grisham-Brown, & Hemmeter, 2001). Dosage is increased when intervention takes place across the day and activities. The functional value of the instruction as well as the efficiency of instruction for learning may be increased with embedding in ongoing activities (VanDerHeyden, Snyder, Smith, Sevin, & Longwell, 2005). Consistent with the case programming approach to language intervention, opportunities to promote generalization and continuity of intervention are increased when intervention is implemented across settings, by multiple partners, focusing skills functional to the context and over time. When family-school partnerships are in place, the opportunities for naturalistic instruction across settings, partners, and skills are increased.

### Parents as Interventionists

Family members provide continuity and social context for their children's communication development. Involving family members as interventionists is consistent with a family-centered approach to early intervention (Campbell & Sawyer, 2007). This approach posits that parents and caregivers are knowledgeable sources of information about the child, and ideally will be active partners in the assessment, intervention, and transition processes. Respecting family members' perspectives, their priorities for intervention, and their preferences for their child's and their own participation are the foundation of family-centered practice and the CCM. In addition, active participation of family members, shared decision-making, and building unity in relation to the intervention are key components of an effective family-centered program. Professionals who take a family-centered approach build family knowledge and skills in communication intervention and empower the family with strategies for supporting their children over time and across contexts. Ideal early communication interventions enhance family members' competence and confidence in their ability to communicate effectively with their children as well as improve child outcomes (Roper & Dunst, 2003).

When parents are empowered with the skills to use language teaching strategies in the home, language learning opportunities are extended across school and home. The variety of settings and situations in which the child has support to learn and practice language is also increased, therefore promoting generalization. Furthermore, because parents are a constant in the child's life, teaching language intervention strategies to parents promotes continuity over time and provides a foundation for teaching more advanced skills as the child's development proceeds. An effective family-school partnership would provide parents and other family members with the support and knowledge base they need to support child communication development at home.

*Evidence to Support Parent Involvement*   Parent-implemented communication intervention is not new (McCollum & Hemmeter, 1997); it is just not consistently used, despite the recent emphasis on natural environment service delivery. Beginning in the 1970s, researchers demonstrated that parents can be taught specific strategies to support their children's language learning (Alpert & Kaiser, 1992; Fey, Cleave, Long, & Hughes, 1993; Hemmeter & Kaiser, 1994; Kaiser et al., 2000; Mahoney & Powell, 1986). While early analysis of the effectiveness of parents as interventionists yielded somewhat mixed results (McCollum & Hemmeter, 1997; Tannock & Girolametto, 1992), recent studies show evidence that changes in children's communication are associated with specific changes in parent behavior (Alpert & Kaiser, 1992; Fey et al., 1993; Hancock, Kaiser, & Delaney, 2002; Kaiser & Delaney, 2001; Kaiser, Hancock, & Hester, 1998; Kaiser et al., 2000; Law, Garret, & Nye, 2004). Positive child outcomes in parent-implemented interventions appear to be accounted for by three factors: (a) specificity of intervention taught to parents, (b) effectiveness of strategies for training parents, and (c) resulting parent generalization and maintenance over time and activity settings. In general, parent-training interventions that teach parents to target specific child language skills have shown the most consistent effects on child language. The reported effects of interactive interventions on child language vary widely, and in part, the variation in outcomes appears to be the result of the broad based nature of the intervention itself (Tannock & Giralametto, 1992). When use of interactive procedures has been modified to include modeling child-specific targets, changes in specific linguistic forms are achieved (Hancock & Kaiser, 2002; Kaiser, Hemmeter, & Hester, 1996).

In two studies, Kaiser and Hancock (2000) and Hancock and Kaiser (2006) found that children learned new language skills equally well when taught by parents or therapists. Children taught by parents who were trained to use naturalistic teaching strategies, however, showed better generalization to home and greater improvement on standardized measures of language development and in clinic observations of language complexity at the 6-month follow-up. Recent studies of Enhanced Milieu Teaching (EMT) have examined the systematic combination of parent plus trainer interventions with some training occurring in the home (Hancock & Kaiser, 2007; Kaiser, Hancock & Vijay, 2007). For children with intellectual disabilities, the combined parent and therapist training is effective in producing both generalized changes in communication at home and changes in developmental outcomes. Two studies of Prelinguistic Milieu Teaching (PMT) have taught parents responsive interaction strategies without prompting (Fey et al., 2006; Yoder & Warren, 2002). In both studies, communication outcomes for children were improved when less responsive parents increased their responsive interactions with their children.

Parents also have been taught to embed communication intervention in their preferred daily routines and activities using naturalistic strategies such as time delay or expansions to increase communication (Kashinath, Woods, & Goldstein, 2006; Woods et al., 2004). When parents used these strategies as part of everyday routines, increased frequency and complexity of child communication usage were observed at home. Typically, parents generalized their strategy use across multiple types of routines (e.g., care giving activities, play, community outings) when they received feedback on their performance in more than one routine type (Kashinath et al., 2006; Woods et al., 2004). The children in these studies were under the age of 3, with emerging vocal, intentional communication. These findings suggest that parent support for early communication development can help children transition into early language.

*Parent Consultation and Training Strategies*  Although there is systematic research demonstrating that parents can learn and use naturalistic teaching strategies to support their children's communication development, there is relatively little research on *how* to teach new communication skills using effective collaboration and training strategies (Kaiser et al., 2007). For example, Hester, Kaiser, Alpert and Whiteman (1996) demonstrated that parents learned and used EMT strategies most efficiently when taught using positive examples, in vivo coaching, and specific feedback about their performance. In the CCM, content for parent consultation and training is derived from the principles of effective early language intervention and particularly, from strategies for use of EMT across routines and settings. In addition to strategies for teaching parents EMT, it is critical that CCM incorporates strategies for working together with parents as team member to address child communication goals. Use of systematic strategies for consultation, such as those described by Sheridan and colleagues (Sheridan, Eagle, Cowan & Mickelson, 2001; Sheridan & Kratochwill, 1992) can insure effective co-consulting between parent and professional. While working together as a communication team, parents and other team members ideally will establish their collaborative intentions, identified roles and responsibilities for each member and develop shared ownership in achieving the child's communication goals. Using a strategy such as Conjoint Behavioral Consultation (CBC; Sheridan & Kratochwill, 2008) provides systematic steps for achieving and evaluating progress toward shared goals. Together, parents and professionals can (a) identify specific communication goals, (b) collect and analyze data related to these goals, including analyses of specific communication contexts, and (c) develop a specific intervention plan to address these goals.

### Learning Opportunities in the Classroom

Intervention in the child's evolving ecology takes advantage of new communication opportunities as children move into classroom and group care settings. For most children, who begin communication intervention under Part C of IDEA (2004), parents may be the primary communication interventionists. Early interventionists and therapists working with children and parents at home have the opportunity to embed language and communication learning opportunities in their interactions with the child. When Part C children attend center-based programs, teachers, teacher assistants, and therapists can implement naturalistic language intervention within classroom activities and embed them into other therapies. As children transition from one classroom to another, become more socially engaged with peers, and enter community activities, new opportunities for teaching and learning and new needs for functional language become part of the child's ecology. Throughout these transitions it is important for family members and school personnel to partner in sharing information regarding the child's communication skills, communication targets, and effective teaching strategies for the child with new teachers and therapists.

*Teachers*    Classroom teachers may spend as much as 30 to 40 hours with the children in their care. Teachers communicate with children across activities and routines and are responsible for adapting classroom activities to meet individual needs and communication abilities of each child. Special education teachers provide direct instruction for a broad range of functional and academic skills, including language and communication. They teach individual, small group, and whole class activities. They are responsible for planning and implementing environmental modifications to promote learning and generalization and for evaluating and monitoring student progress and program effectiveness (McCormick, 2003a, 2003b, 2003c). Given the wide range of opportunities for language instruction, newly taught skills and concepts are more likely to generalize when language interactions are supported by teachers. There are numerous opportunities to practice and use new communication skills in both social and academic interactions. Classroom activities such as playing in centers, playing outdoors, experimenting with water and paint, reading books, and signing songs provide numerous opportunities for teachers to teach students functional skills while experiencing the world around them (O'Brien, 1997).

Research on training teachers suggests that teachers can learn to use a number of language intervention strategies. Teachers have been taught to use environmental arrangement strategies (Kaiser, Ostrosky, & Alpert, 1993), milieu teaching strategies (Kaiser et al., 1993; Yoder et al., 1995), and responsive interaction strategies in preschool classrooms (Yoder et al., 1995). Research focusing on effective teacher training strategies is limited; however, many studies use strategies similar to those used with parent training (i.e., modeling, practice, feedback). In a recent study on the effects of e-mail feedback with written verbatim examples, pre-service classroom teachers increased their use of expansions in the preschool classroom (Barton & Wolery, 2007).

*Peers*    Teachers also may facilitate children's language and communication development by promoting interactions with typically developing classroom peers. When teachers facilitate interventions between typically developing peers and children with special needs, language learning opportunities are extended from teacher-child interactions to peer-child ones. The variety of settings and situations in which the target language learning child can learn and practice language are also increased, therefore promoting generalization. Furthermore, because children will continue to have contact with peers over time and across school and community settings, strengthening the child's ability to interact with peers, and potentially learning new socially appropriate language from peer interaction, continuity of intervention over time is promoted.

Peers have served as interventionists who promoted social communication in children with developmental disabilities in natural environments. In these studies, typically developing peers have been taught strategies to promote social communicative interaction and then paired with targeted children during play activities. Peer-directed interventions can be classified into two broad types: (a) interventions in which the peer uses naturalistic language teaching strategies to teach the target child specific responses (e.g., waiting for a request, asking for a label, providing the target child with the labeled object, and praising appropriate responses; McGee et al., 1992), and (b) interventions that teach the peers strategies and content for communicating with the target child. Peer-directed communication intervention strategies have included script training (Goldstein & Cisar, 1992), sensitivity training (Goldstein et al., 1997), and training in more specific strategies such as maintaining proximity, establishing mutual attention, commenting about ongoing activities, and general acknowledgement of the target partner's communication acts.

*Empirical Basis for Involving Peers*    Results of the peer-directed intervention literature are encouraging. Target children have demonstrated increases in initiations and responses during interactions, with some indication of improved performance of target utterances or specific language forms. Peers have demonstrated the ability to implement intervention strategies and have demonstrated increases in initiations to target children. Teachers have rated the social competence of both peers and target children as higher following intervention (Goldstein & Cisar, 1992; Goldstein et al., 1997; McGee et al., 1992).

Goldstein and Cisar (1992) investigated the effects of three teaching scripts to typically developing preschool peers and classmates with disabilities. Following intervention, target children and peers increased theme-related behavior, with specific verbalizations related to the play themes increasing while unrelated behavior decreased. The effects of the intervention were replicated across all three scripts and were maintained when dyads were re-grouped to assess generalization.

Peers have also been taught communication strategies to facilitate interactions with children with disabilities (Goldstein et al., 1997). Strategy use training consisted of three direct instruction sessions focusing on a sequential behavior chain including behavior such as maintaining proximity, establishing mutual attention, maintaining talking, and playing with the target child (i.e., stay, talk, play). Following training, peers increased their frequencies of social communicative behavior directed towards the target children. Similarly, target children increased their frequencies of social communication directed toward peers.

Stanton-Chapman and Kaiser (2008) taught children to use vocabulary and specific social interaction strategies using story books in a plan-play-report protocol. Both children with low language skills and children with more typical language skills increased their social communicative interactions. Findings from this type of intervention suggest that classroom activities designed to benefit low language children may be structured in a manner that both less- and more-skilled peers learn new strategies. Such activities may promote peer interaction outside the training setting as well.

### Training Parents and Teachers

Involving parents and teachers as interventionists promotes language development for the young child. Both parents and teachers may require specific training in naturalistic teaching strategies to maximize their contributions to children's language development. Preparing teachers and parents to use naturalistic language intervention strategies is challenging because of the range of skills required for fluent use of the strategies (Hancock & Kaiser, 2007) and because few professionals are prepared to train other adults in the use of instructional techniques (Kaiser, Hester, Alpert, & Whiteman, 1995).

*What to Teach*   Naturalistic language intervention is composed of four major components: (a) arranging the environment to promote engagement and communication, (b) responsive interaction with the child, (c) language modeling strategies including expansions and recasting, and (d) language production prompting strategies. In addition, intervention includes a focus on specific communication and language targets that will be modeled and prompted. Implementation of a complex naturalistic intervention model, such as EMT, may be beyond the scope of some adult communication partners because of the wide range of teaching strategies and the precise focus on child targets for learning. One important advantage of a team approach to early communication intervention may be that members of the team, with different levels of instructional skills, may contribute to the child's cumulative opportunities to learn.

Table 13.1 illustrates the range of adult partner strategies that may be taught to parents, teachers, and therapists to support child communication across settings. All of these strategies derive from empirically based naturalistic teaching strategies. In general, strategies at the top of the table (e.g., environmental arrangements, general nonverbal and verbal responsiveness) are easier to implement and require less training than strategies at the bottom of the table (e.g., modeling specific targets, prompting child production of targeted language). When resources for training are limited or when communication partners have limited time or resources for learning specific skills, teaching these general strategies is recommended. For example, parents and childcare teachers can be taught to take nonverbal and verbal turns with children more consistently and to be verbally responsive when children communicate verbally and nonverbally. Increasing adult responsiveness to child communication may be sufficient to promote generalization of communication skills learned in other contexts, as suggested by Yoder and Warren (1998).

*How to Teach Adults*   While significant research has documented that parent-implemented communication interventions are effective, little research has examined the best strategies for "teaching" or "coaching" parents to learn and use these techniques. Currently, there is more evidence about strategies that do not work (e.g., modeling without feedback, general information, isolated workshops or training modules) than about strategies that do (Buysse & Wesley, 2006; McBride & Peterson, 1997). Recom-

**Table 13.1** Adult Strategies for Supporting Children's Communication

| Component | Adult Strategy | Child communication goal | Purpose of strategy |
|---|---|---|---|
| *Environmental Arrangement* | Select routines and materials of interest | Extended engagement with activities | Sets up opportunities for requests and comments; sets up use of prompting procedures |
| | Make physical contact (proximity, eye contact) | Extended social engagement | Maintains social connection |
| | Establish joint activity | Activity and social engagement | Increases joint engagement |
| | Positive affect | Social engagement | Maintains social connection and joint engagement |
| *Nonverbal Responsiveness* | Nonverbal turntaking | Nonverbal turntaking and extended engagement in activity | Sets up opportunities for language modeling |
| | Nonverbal imitation (mirroring) | Nonverbal turntaking | Increases nonverbal turntaking |
| | Follow child's lead in play | Provides opportunity to explore interests | Makes language modeling immediately relevant to child activity |
| *Verbal Responsiveness* | Verbal responding | Verbal responding, continued social engagement | Models verbal responding; increases child verbal responding |
| | Follow child's topic | Verbal responding | Makes modeling immediately relevant to child's topic |
| *Model Language* | Talk at child's target level | Verbalizations at target level | Provides models |
| | Use specific vocabulary | Use specific vocabulary | Models specific vocabulary |
| | Expand child utterances | Verbalizations at target level | Makes target level model immediately relevant to child's topic |
| | Re-cast child utterances | Corrected verbal form | Provides correct forms in context |
| *Prompt Communication or Language* | Provide nonverbal choice opportunities | Nonverbal choice making | Sets up use of other prompting strategies |
| | Elicitive Model "say MORE" | Imitation of specific targets | Correction procedure following other prompting strategies |
| | Mand (instruction to verbalize or question) "Tell me what you want." "What do want"? | Verbal response | Can vary in complexity; correction procedure following other prompting strategies |
| | Time Delay (Pause that provides anticipatory cue) | Initiated verbal response | Useful to help generalize to commenting, initiating |
| | Incidental Teaching in response to requests | Imitated or initiated verbal request | Increases specific verbal requests |

mendations from the National Research Council's *How People Learn* (National Research Council, 2000) based on principles from Knowles (Knowles, 1978; Knowles, Holton, & Swanson, 1998), suggested important principles for adult learning. These are: (a) acknowledge learners' pre-existing knowledge, values, beliefs, and experiences; (b) provide multiple, in-depth examples of targeted practices; and (c) integrate reflective learning opportunities by encouraging ongoing reflection about new practices using these principles as homework. Individualized adult instruction to address the unique strengths and challenges of the parent, teacher, or other adult who will be communicating with a specific child can be informed by considering both the adult's language teaching skills and the child's targeted communication forms, as suggested in Table 13.1.

Research does support use of instructional strategies that incorporate the adult's experiences and interests, sequential instruction, demonstration, and specific feedback (National Research Council, 2000). Problem-solving strategies increase independent decision making and generalized use of information (Buysse & Wesley, 2006; McGee & Morrier, 2005). Teaching adults in the settings in which they will use the new skills via modeling, coaching, and specific feedback facilitates rapid acquisition of the skills and allows adults to immediately begin supporting children's communication (Hanft, Rush, & Shelden, 2004; Zaslow & Martinez-Beck, 2006). In several studies of parent implemented EMT, parents have been taught using modeling, practice with feedback, and written materials (Hancock & Kaiser, 2006).

Research on training teachers to implement specific language intervention strategies in the classroom suggests that teachers can learn and implement such intervention strategies successfully. Teachers have been taught to use a number of strategies to support language, including environmental arrangement strategies (Kaiser et al., 1993), MT strategies (Kaiser et al., 1993), and responsive interaction strategies (Yoder et al., 1995). Teachers also have been trained using strategies similar to those used with parents. By asking teachers to focus on one child or a small number of children, feedback was individualized to support the teachers' application of EMT in a specific context. In contrast, Walker et al. (1997) have taken a class-wide focus in training childcare teachers to use incidental teaching. Walker et al. used modeling, practice, and data-based feedback to individualize their training to fit each teacher's skills, and they established strategies for interacting with children. In sum, there is a need for research to expand evidence-based procedures for teaching parents, teachers, and other team members. There are sufficient studies and principles to guide initial implementation of the proposed model.

## Collaboration across Team Members

The collaborative component of the proposed model provides support for the child across communication partners and aspects of the child's communication universe. Collaboration begins with forming a communication team to support the child, the family, and the professionals who will be providing early communication intervention. Formation of a team with the specific focus on communication and language development insures increased frequency and specificity of communication and language learning opportunities across a variety of settings. As each member of the team identifies the child's opportunities for communication, the skills needed for functional interaction, and natural consequences that can support increased communication, a matrix of contexts and specific communication skills or forms can be developed (Goldstein,1993). When team members identify opportunities for naturalistic or embedded instruction, they can increase the dosage of intervention, as well as insure continuity of intervention settings, and create new opportunities for promoting generalization. When partnerships are sustained over time, the possibility of continuous intervention to support communication development emerges. Outcomes for the family include not only enhanced communication with their child but also competence in selected language intervention strategies and skills by embedding intervention into diverse routines, generating new routines in play, and identifying new communication goals that fit the child's increasing skill in everyday routines. Outcomes for professionals include knowledge of the child's current language skills, goals, and strategies for integrating communication intervention throughout the day, contexts, and settings; and increased accountability for communicating progress and problem-solving strategies across team members. An additional important professional outcome may be improved skills for communicating with family members and the implicit development of strategies that will be used across families and time to collaborate in communication interventions.

For the collaboration to be effective, all members of the communication team need knowledge of the child and of the proposed naturalistic intervention approaches, as well as skills in adult-adult communication. Shared knowledge and skills support team implementation of a comprehensive communication intervention and specific instructional strategies for each child. Shared access to child progress information and communication targets promotes planning and well-specified targets and procedures for intervention implementation by all team members. Systematic support for team members must be consistent and include specific feedback for implementation. Team meetings increase consistent implementation of the interventions across settings and promote opportunities for joint planning and problem solving.

Beginning a communication team presents several challenges. Four strategies are recommended:

1. *Conduct an initial collaboration planning meeting and invite the key members of the child's early intervention team.* At that meeting, a facilitator (parent, case manager, SLP) leads the interactive process of determining the child's continuing communication support needs, a short-term working plan for the team is proposed, need for training and support are identified, and an interim team leader is identified. Each team member selects one to three specific contexts in which he or she will become more effective communication partners for the target child and indicates what supports are needed to meet that objective. Because the focus is on sharing knowledge and accessing resources for training from the EI system, the community, and the schools, the interim leader does not have to be expert in early communication, but the leader does assume responsibility for keeping the group members in communication and for scheduling working meetings.

2. *A follow-up meeting is held to review progress and identify immediate needs for support and training within three months.* At this meeting, child progress notes are compared and synthesized by the group into a working document with two sections: (a) what we have done as communication partners, and (b) what progress we have observed in the child's communication. The emphasis in this meeting is on team building, sharing strategies, and planning for the next three months. At this meeting, a continuing team leader is identified and the group members set

goals for communication support, collaboration, and follow up. The continuing team leader can be the parent, a family member, or a professional.

3. *Develop an ongoing strategy for sharing information about child progress and communication support.* Outside of team meetings, there is need for ongoing communication among the team members as the child's communication universe and opportunities for learning change. E-mail, child-based websites (Zaidman-Zait & Jamieson, 2007), or other informal, accessible communication strategies are extremely useful; information on child progress, teaching strategies, and solutions to everyday implementation issues can be shared. Informal team planning prior to IFSP or IEP meetings can provide functional input to guide the formal plan for the child's early intervention.

4. *Maintenance of continuity on the communication team.* Team members will change as the child's educational and community settings change. Ideally, at least two people (one family member and one professional) will remain with the team from identification through kindergarten. The continuity that is essential to effective early intervention to promote language development can be increased with continuity on the communication team. Planning for transition across settings implies restructuring the communication team to include new members, such as teachers, therapists, and aides. The presence of an established team may smooth the child's transition as well as set expectation for collaboration with new service providers.

## RECOMMENDATIONS FOR PRACTICE

A number of recommendations for practice stem from the collaborative model presented in this chapter. First, parents and professionals should include naturalistic teaching strategies in their therapies and interventions. There are a number of evidence-based naturalistic teaching strategies that have been proven effective with young children with disabilities (Hart & Risley, 1968; Kaiser et al., 1992; Kaiser & Hester, 1994; Koegel et al., 1999; Yoder & Warren, 2001). Naturalistic teaching strategies support the child's functional use of communication skills in natural environments.

Second, practitioners should make it a goal to increase continuity and dosage of the language interventions provided. One way to do this would be to involve parents in a range of intervention roles. As discussed above, parents provide continuity and social context for their children's communication development. Furthermore, when naturalistic teaching strategies are the key intervention approach, the home setting is at the center of functional communication interventions. Parents participate in a variety of routines with their children throughout each day, and these routines present numerous opportunities for language learning. Thus, practitioners should consider at the very least sharing simple, easily implemented naturalistic teaching strategies that they can use in the home (e.g., put preferred items in sight but out of reach so that the child has to request them).

Another important strategy for increasing continuity and dosage of early language intervention is establishing an ongoing communication system between parents and practitioners. A daily note, weekly group e-mail, posting to a child-based website, or a monthly conference call all can facilitate communication about child goals and progress. Such a communication system would also allow practitioners to share timely information about successful intervention strategies and make adjustments to fit the child, changing communication profiles and problem solving when performance goals aren't being met or new challenging behaviors arise. Effective communication intervention results in relatively rapid acquisition of new forms and functions. Thus, an active communication system allows an intervention team to quickly make changes in an ongoing cross-setting intervention as the child learns and makes generalizations.

Finally, practitioners need informal strategies for evaluating child progress so that intervention can be tailored to the child's changing skills. Simple data collection strategies should be developed that can be used to measure performance across the day and week, as well as across settings and interventionists. Furthermore, when expected progress is not observed, practitioners need to quickly adjust intervention procedures so that time is not lost due to ineffective teaching strategies. Data should be shared with team members to enable team members to assist in the modification of intervention procedures.

When team members share the common intervention philosophy of naturalistic intervention to teach functional skills in the contexts in which they are needed, and when they have strategies and tools that allow ongoing assessment and sharing of information, it is highly likely that the goal of effective, continuous early intervention can be met. Early childhood is a brief period, characterized by rapid development and ecological variability. To optimize development of a critical skill such as language, practitioners must coordinate their efforts.

## RECOMMENDATIONS FOR RESEARCH

### Maximizing Child Communication Development

The proposed model presents numerous opportunities for research. While it seems intuitive that developing strong family-school partnerships would maximize child communication development, there is limited empirical support for this assumption. Future research should consider the effects of such family-school partnerships and the components of that partnership on rate of acquisition, degree of generalization, and maintenance of language and communication skills. For example, the proposed model would provide increased dosage of intervention. However, as such a model is put into place, we need to investigate the effects of dosage on child language outcomes. Other studies of interventions for children with Autism Spectrum Disorder (ASD; Reichow & Wolery, in press), there is very little experimental evidence to indicate that higher dosages of intervention produce better developmental outcomes. Further research is needed to determine adequate intensity of intervention across settings and partners to produce dependable positive trajectories of learning.

Research also is needed on how to facilitate continuity of intervention, how to adequately measure this construct, and how to determine the effects of continuity on child communication goals. Continuity is related to dosage and intensity but also includes the pattern or distribution of intervention over time. Because transitions are inevitable for young children with special needs, it is important to determine how practitioners can increase the stability of communication intervention and minimize intervention interruption during transitions.

Finally, future research should investigate the secondary effects of family-school partnerships on younger children with disabilities. Future research may consider investigating the effects of family-school partnerships related to language intervention on student outcome in other academic areas such as literacy (Dickinson, McCabe, Anastasopolous, Peisner-Feinberg, & Poe, 2003). Partner interventions may also affect child behavior across settings; when children have difficulty communicating, problem behaviors tend to increase. In addition, generalization of language and communication skills across people and settings should be improved when language intervention occurs across multiple settings and people, but further evidence is needed to support this argument.

### Teaching Adults to Support Generalization

In many studies involving adult training, a combination of strategies is used to teach adults new skills. These often include strategies such as discussion, modeling, role-play, coaching, and feedback. Further research is needed on how to efficiently and effectively teach adults to implement early language intervention strategies with young children. Clearly, adults have different learning styles, and varying combinations of teaching strategies may work better for some adults than others. The ability to identify effective teaching strategies for each individual would increase the efficiency and effectiveness of adult training.

Research also is needed to determine what components of the team as proposed in this chapter are essential. For example, can either a parent or a professional (teacher, speech pathologist, early interventionist, or special educator) effectively facilitate these early communication home-school teams? To be effective, a team of parents and professionals may need a designated individual whose role is to facilitate collaboration and to lead the team over time. The team may need a point person to schedule regular meetings and conference calls, facilitate sharing of information on child goals and performance, and assist in maintaining the child's website. Ideally, this person would be a consistent individual in the child's life who continues in this role for several years. Some parents choose this role, but not every parent could or would be able to assume these responsibilities. Parents who do choose this role would require some additional training and support in the early years of navigating early intervention and school services. The discontinuity between Part C of IDEA early intervention services and Part B of IDEA preschool services is a serious concern for family-school partnerships that span 0- to 5-year-olds. Identifying, training, and evaluating the effectiveness of professionals and parents who can lead home-school teams and reduce the discontinuity in early intervention will be a challenging research proposition.

### Partnerships in Early Communication Intervention

Additional research is also needed to identify strategies for facilitating team coordination and collaboration. Parents of children with special needs often have busy schedules, and professionals working with children with special needs often have heavy caseloads. For a family-school partnership to be effective, it is necessary to identify the most feasible strategies for supporting coordination and collaboration among communication team members. Coordination may be facilitated by scheduling regular face-to-face meetings, participating in conference calls, or developing a website to share information regarding child goals and performance.

Not only is research needed on how to develop family-school partnerships, but research is also needed on the effects of these partnerships on issues that are broader than the child. Future research should consider the effects of family-school partnerships on parent and teacher satisfaction, formulating and implementing IFSP/IEP, and transition processes from Part C to Part B services; from pre-K to school-age services. If teachers, parents, and therapists are communicating about goals, teaching strategies, progress, and so forth on a regular basis, one might hypothesize that transition and IFSP/IEP meetings would run more smoothly. Due process and litigation are familiar terms in most school systems. When there is disagreement among professionals, parents, and the system, due process is often the result. A collaborative model such as the one proposed may reduce the frequency of these occurrences.

Parent and teacher satisfaction may increase through family-school partnerships. When parents are more involved in the goals that are being addressed in school and therapies, and the progress that is being made, they are likely to be more satisfied with the school experience. Similarly, when teachers are more involved in the goals that are being addressed in therapies, and the progress that is being made, they are likely to be more satisfied with the goals that are selected and more capable of working on these goals in the classroom. Parents are experts on their children and the teachers and therapists are experts in their fields. When the group comes together to share their expertise in setting goals and developing treatment plans for an individual child, the outcome is likely to be a more effective intervention approach (Childress, 2004; DesJardin, Eisenberg, & Hodapp, 2006).

## CONCLUSION

It is imperative that we develop new strategies for promoting collaboration between schools and families in order to achieve optimal outcomes from early communication intervention. Learning to communicate is one of the most challenging long-term tasks for children with disabilities. Addressing this challenging domain of development requires coordinating early intervention efforts by sharing teaching strategies, developing shared goals, and communicating about child progress across home and school service providers. Partnership implies that leadership, responsibility, and, ultimately, credit for child progress will be shared among team members who have contributed to the child's acquisition and use of new communication skills. While existing formal mechanisms for planning and evaluating child progress, the IFSP, the IEP, and the annual review of progress, are necessary, we believe they are often not sufficient to insure the intensity, dosage, and continuity of early communication intervention. The proposed model suggests that informal, collaborative teams in which parents are empowered as interventionists and encouraged as key team members may offer an alternative or ancillary strategy for improving the outcomes of early intervention and laying the foundation for school success.

## AUTHORS' NOTE

Preparation of this chapter was supported in part by NIH grant R01 HD045745-02 and Department of Education grant 4-26-234-2011 to the first author. We gratefully acknowledge the contributions of Dr. Juliann Woods and Dr. Terry Hancock to the model presented in this chapter.

## REFERENCES

Abbeduto, L., & Rosenberg, S. (1992). The development of linguistic communication in persons with mental retardation. In S. Warren & J. Reichle (Eds.), *Causes and effects in communication and language intervention* (pp. 331–359). Baltimore: Brookes.

Alpert, C. L., & Kaiser, A. P. (1992). Training parents as milieu language teachers. *Journal of Early Intervention, 16,* 31–52.

Barton, E. E., & Wolery, M. (2007). Evaluation of e-mail feedback on the verbal behaviors of pre-service teachers. *Journal of Early Intervention, 20*(1), 55–72.

Blue-Banning, M., Summers, J. A., Frankland, C., Nelson, L. G., & Beegle, G. (2004). Dimensions of family and professional partnerships: Constructive guidelines for collaboration. *Exceptional Children, 70*(2), 167–184.

Borkowski, J. G., Smith, L. E., Akai, C. E. (2007). Designing effective prevention programs: How good science makes good art. *Infants & Young Children, 20*(3), 229–241.

Bronfenbrenner, U. (1992). Ecological systems theory. In R. Vasta (Ed.), *Six theories of child development: Revised formulations and current issues* (pp. 187–248). Philadelphia: Jessica Kingsley.

Buysse, V., & Wesley, P. W. (Eds.). (2006). *Evidence-based practice in the early childhood field.* Washington, DC: Zero to Three Press.

Campbell, P. H., & Sawyer, L. B. (2007). *Journal of Early Intervention, 29*(4) 287–305.

Campbell, C. R., & Stremel-Campbell, K. (1982). Programming "loose training" as a strategy to facilitate language generalization. *Journal of Applied behavior Analysis, 15*(2), 295–301.

Childress, D. C. (2004). Special instruction and natural environments: Best practices in early intervention. *Infants and Young Children, 17*(2), 162–170.

Cole, K. N., Maddox, M., & Lim, Y. S. (2006). Language is the key: Constructive interactions around books and play. In M. E. Fey & R. J. McCauley (Eds.), *Treatment of language disorders in children* (pp. 149–173). Baltimore: Brookes.

Daugherty, S., Grisham-Brown, J., & Hemmeter, M. L. (2001). The effects of embedded skill instruction on the acquisition of target and nontarget skills in preschoolers with developmental delays. *Topics in Early Childhood Special Education, 21*(4), 213–221.

DesJardin, J. L., Eisenberg, L. S., & Hodapp, R. M. (2006). Sound beginnings: Supporting families of young deaf children with cochlear implants. *Infants and Young Children 19*(3), 179–189.

Dickinson, D., McCabe, A., Anastasopolous, L., Peisner-Feinberg, E., & Poe, M. (2003). The comprehensive language approach to early literacy: The interrelationships among vocabulary, phonological sensitivity, and print knowledge among pre-school aged children. *Journal of Educational Psychology, 95*(3), 465–481.

Dunst, C. J. (2002). Family-centered practices: Birth through high school. *The Journal of Special Education, 36*(3), 141–149.

Dunst, C., & Trivette, C. (1996). Empowerment, effective help-giving practices, and family-centered care. *Pediatric Nursing, 22*(4), 334–343.

Engelmann, S., & Carnine, D. (1982). *Theory of instruction: Principles and applications.* New York: Irvington.

Fantuzzo, J., McWayne, C., Perry, M., & Childs, S. (2004). Multiple dimensions of family involvement and their relations to behavioral and learning competencies for urban, low-income children. *School Psychology Review, 33*(4), 467–480.

Fey, M. E., Cleave, P. L., Long, S. H., & Hughes, D. L. (1993). Two approaches to the facilitation of grammar in children with language impairment: An experimental evaluation. *Journal of Speech and Hearing Research, 36*(1), 141–157.

Fey, M., Warren, S., Brady, N., Finestack, L., Bredin-Oja, S., Fairchild, M., Sokol, S., & Yoder, P. (2006). Early effects of Prelinguistic Milieu Teaching and Responsive Education for children with developmental delays and their parents. *Journal of Speech, Language, and Hearing Research, 49*(3), 526–547.

Girolametto, L. (1988). Improving the social-conversational skills of developmentally delayed children: An intervention study. *Journal of Speech and Hearing Disorders, 53*(2), 156–167.

Goldstein, H. (1993). Use of peers as communication intervention agents. *Teaching Exceptional Children, 25,* 37–40.

Goldstein, H., & Cisar, C. (1992). Promoting interaction during sociodramatic play: Teaching scripts to typical preschoolers and classmates with disabilities. *Journal of Applied Behavioral Analysis, 25*(2), 265–280.

Goldstein, H., English, K., Shafer, K., & Kaczmarek, L. (1997). Interaction among preschoolers with and without disabilities: Effects of across-the-day peer intervention. *Journal of Speech, Language, and Hearing Research, 40*(1), 33–48

Guess, D., Sailor, W., Rutherford, D., & Baer, D. M. (1968). An experimental analysis of linguistic development: The productive use of the plural morpheme. *Journal of Applied Behavioral Analysis, 1*(4), 297–306.

Halle, J. W., Chadsey-Rusch, J., & Collet-Klingenberg, L. (1993). Applying contextual features of general case instruction and interactive routines to enhance communication skills. In R. A. Gable & S. F. Warren (Eds.), *Strategies for teaching students with mild to severe mental retardation* (pp. 231–267). Baltimore: Brookes.

Hancock, T. B., & Kaiser, A. P. (2002). The effects of trainer-implemented Enhanced Milieu Teaching on the social communication of children with autism. *Topics in Early Childhood Special Education, 22*(1), 39–54.

Hancock, T. B., & Kaiser, A. P. (2006). Enhanced Milieu Teaching. In R. McCauley & M. Fey (Eds.), *Treatment of language disorders in children* (pp. 203–236). Baltimore: Brookes.

Hancock, T. B., & Kaiser, A. P. (2007, March). *An ecological model for facilitating parent-generalization of newly-learned naturalistic teaching strategies.* Presented at the Society for Research in Child Development Biennial Meeting, *SRCD*, Boston.

Hancock, T. B., Kaiser, A. P., & Delaney, E. M. (2002). Teaching parents of preschoolers at high risk strategies to support language and positive behavior. *Topics in Early Childhood Special Education, 22*(4), 191–222.

Hanft, B. E., Rush, D. D., & Shelden, M. L. (2004). *Coaching families and colleagues in early childhood.* Baltimore: Brookes.

Hart, B. M., & Risley, T. R. (1968). Establishing use of descriptive adjectives in the spontaneous speech of disadvantaged preschool children. *Journal of Applied Behavior Analysis, 1*(2), 109–120.

Hemmeter, M. L., & Kaiser, A. P. (1994). Enhanced MT: Effects of parent-implemented language intervention. *Journal of Early Intervention, 18*(3), 269–289.

Hester, P. P., Kaiser, A. P., Alpert, C. L., & Whiteman, B. (1996). The generalized effects of training trainers to teach parents to implement Milieu Teaching. *Journal of Early Intervention, 20,* 30–51.

Individuals with Disabilities Education Improvement Act of 2004 (IDEA). (2004). Pub. L. No. 108-446, § 632, 118 Stat. 2744 (2004).

Kaiser, A. P., & Delaney, E. M. (2001). Responsive conversations: Creating opportunities for naturalistic language teaching. *Young Exceptional Children Monograph Series No. 3,* 13–23.

Kaiser, A. P., & Grim, J. C. (2005). Teaching functional communication skills. In M. Snell & F. Brown (Eds.), *Instruction of students with severe disabilities* (pp. 447–488). Upper Saddle River, NJ: Pearson.

Kaiser, A. P., & Hancock, T. B. (2000, April). *Supporting children's communication development through parent-implemented naturalistic interventions.* Presented at the 2nd Annual Conference on Research Innovations in Early Intervention (CRIEI), San Diego, CA.

Kaiser, A. P., Hancock, T. B., & Hester, P. P. (1998). Parents as co-interventionists: Research on applications of naturalistic language teaching procedures. *Infants and Young Children, 10*(4), 46–55.

Kaiser, A. P., Hancock, T. B., & Nietfield, J. P. (2000). The effects of parent-implemented enhanced MT on the social communication of children who have autism. *Early Education and Development, 11*(4), 423–446.

Kaiser, A. P., Hancock, T. B., & Trent, J. A. (2007). Teaching parents communication strategies. *Early Childhood Services: An Interdisciplinary Journal of Effectiveness, 1*(2), 107–136.

Kaiser, A. P., Hancock, T. B., & Vijay, P. (2007, March). *Parent-child communication at home in preschool children with Down syndrome and Autism spectrum disorders.* Presented at the 40th Annual Gatlinburg Conference on Research and Theory in Intellectual and Developmental Disabilities, Annapolis, MD.

Kaiser, A. P., Hemmeter, M. L., & Hester, P. P. (1996). The facilitative effects of input on children's language development: Contributions from studies of enhanced milieu teaching. In L. B. Adamson & M. A. Romski (Eds.), *Research on communication and language disorders: Contributions to theories of language development* (pp. 267–294). Baltimore: Brookes.

Kaiser, A. P., & Hester, P. P. (1994). Generalized effects of Enhanced Milieu Teaching. *Journal of Speech and Hearing Research, 37*(6), 1320–1340.

Kaiser, A. P., Hester, P. P., Alpert, C. L., & Whiteman, B. C. (1995). Preparing parent trainers: An experimental analysis of effects on trainers, parents, and children. *Topics in Early Childhood Special Education, 15*(4), 385–414.

Kaiser, A. P., Hester, P. P., & McDuffie, A. S. (2001). Supporting communication in young children with developmental disabilities. *Mental Retardation and Developmental Disabilities Research Reviews, 7*(2), 143–150.

Kaiser, A. P., Ostrosky, M. M., & Alpert, C. L. (1993). Training teachers to use environmental arrangement and Milieu Teaching with nonvocal preschool children. *Journal of the Association for Persons with Severe Handicaps, 18*(3), 188–199.

Kaiser, A. P., & Trent, J. A. (2007). Communication intervention for young children with disabilities: Naturalistic approaches to promoting development. In S. Odom, R. Horner, M. Snell, & J. Blacher (Eds.), *Handbook of developmental disabilities* (pp. 224–246). New York: Guilford.

Kaiser, A. P., Yoder, P. J., & Keetz, A. (1992). Evaluating milieu teaching. In S. F. Warren & J. Reichle (Eds.), *Causes and effects in communication and language intervention* (Vol. 1, pp. 9–47). Baltimore: Brookes.

Kashinath, S., Woods, J., & Goldstein, H. (2006). Enhancing generalized teaching strategy use in daily routines by parents of children with autism. *Journal of Speech, Language, and Hearing Research, 49*(3), 466–485.

Knowles, M. S. (1978). *The adult learner: A neglected species.* Houston, TX: Gulf.

Knowles, M. S., Holton, E. F. III, & Swanson, R. A. (1998). *The adult learner* (5th ed.). Woburn, MA: Butterworth-Heinemann.

Koegel, R. L., Koegel, L. K., & Carter, C. M. (1999). Pivotal teaching interactions for children with autism. *School Psychology Review, 28*(4), 576–594.

Law, J., & Conti-Ramsden, G. (2000). Treating children with speech and language impairments. *BMJ, 321*(7266), 908–909.

Law, J., Garret, Z., & Nye, C. (2004). The efficacy of treatment for children with developmental speech and language delay/disorder: A meta-analysis. *Journal of Speech, Language, and Hearing Research. 47*(4), 924–943.

Mahoney, G., & Powell, A. (1986). *The transactional intervention program teacher's guide.* Farmington, CT: Pediatric Research and Training Center.

McBride, S. L., & Peterson, C. (1997). Home-based early intervention with families of children with disabilities: Who is doing what? *Topics in Early Childhood Special Education, 17*, 209–233.

McCauley, R. J. & Fey, M. E. (2006). *Treatment of Language Disorders in Children.* Baltimore: Brookes

McCollum, J. A., & Hemmeter, M. L. (1997). Parent-child interaction when children have disabilities. In M. J. Guralnick (Ed.), *The effectiveness of early intervention* (pp. 549–576). Baltimore: Brookes.

McCormick, L. (2003a). Ecological assessment and planning. In L. McCormick, D. F. Loeb, & R. L. Schiefelbusch (Eds.), *Supporting children with communication difficulties in inclusive settings: School-based language intervention* (pp. 223–256). Boston: Allyn & Bacon.

McCormick, L. (2003b). Language intervention and support. In L. McCormick, D. F. Loeb, & R. L. Schiefelbusch (Eds.), *Supporting children with communication difficulties in inclusive settings: School-based language intervention* (pp. 259–295). Boston: Allyn & Bacon.

McCormick, L. (2003c). Language intervention in the inclusive preschool. In L. McCormick, D. F. Loeb, & R. L. Schiefelbusch (Eds.), *Supporting children with communication difficulties in inclusive settings: School-based language intervention* (pp. 335–368). Boston: Allyn & Bacon.

McGee, G. G., Aimeda, M. C., Sulzer-Azaroff, B., & Feldman, R. S. (1992). Promoting reciprocal interactions via peer incidental teaching. *Journal of Applied Behavioral Analysis, 25*(1), 117–126.

McGee, G. G., & Morrier, M. J. (2005). Preparation of autism specialists. In F. R. Volkmar, R. Paul, A. Klin, & D. Cohen (Eds.), *Handbook of autism and pervasive developmental disorders: Vol. 2. Assessment, interventions, and policy* (pp. 1123–1160). Hoboken, NJ: Wiley.

National Research Council. (2000). *How people learn.* Washington, DC: National Academy Press.

O'Brien, M. (1997). *Inclusive child care for infants and toddlers.* Baltimore: Brookes.

O'Neill, R. E., Faulkner, C., & Horner, R. H. (2000). The effects of general case training of manding responses on children with severe disabilities. *Journal of Developmental and Physical Disabilities, 12*(1), 43–60.

Odom, S. L. & McLean M. E. (Eds.). (1996). *Early intervention/early childhood special education: Recommended practices.* Austin, TX: Pro-ed.

Paul, R. (2006). *Language disorders from infancy through adolescence.* Philadelphia: Mosby.

Reichow, B., & Wolery, M. (in press). Comprehensive synthesis of early intensive behavioral interventions for young children with autism based on the UCLA Young Autism Project Model. *Journal of Autism and Developmental Disorders.*

Rogers, S. J., Hayden, D., Hepburn, S., Charlifue-Smith, R., Hall, T., & Hayes, A. (2006). Teaching young nonverbal children with autism useful speech: A pilot study of the Denver model and PROMPT interventions. *Journal of Autism and Developmental Disorders, 36*(8), 1007–1024.

Roper, N., Dunst, C. J. (2003). Communication intervention in natural learning environments: Guidelines for practice. *Infants and Young Children, 16*(3), 215–226.

Sheridan, S. M., Eagle, J. W., Cowan, R. J., & Mickelson, W. (2001). The effects of conjoint behavioral consultation results of a 4-year investigation. *Journal of School Psychology, 39*(5), 361–385.

Sheridan, S. M., & Kratochwill, R. R. (1992). Behavioral parent-teacher consultation: Conceptual and research considerations. *Journal of School Psychology, 30*(2), 117–139.

Sheridan, S. M., & Kratochwill, T. R. (2008). *Conjoint behavioral consultation: Promoting family-school connections and interventions.* New York: Springer.

Snow, C., Barnes, W., Chandler, J., Goodman, L., & Hemphill, L. (1991). *Unfulfilled expectations: Home and school influences on literacy.* Cambridge, MA: Harvard University Press.

Stanton-Chapman, T. L., & Kaiser, A. P. (2008). *A multi-component intervention to increase peer-directed communication in Head Start children.* Manuscript submitted for publication.

Stokes, T. F., & Baer, D. M. (1977). An implicit technology of generalization. *Journal of Applied Behavior Analysis, 10*(2), 349–367.

Summers, J. A., Hoffman, L., Marquis, J., Turnbull, A. P., Poston, D., & Nelson, L. L. (2005). Measuring the quality of family-professional partnerships in special education services. *Exceptional Children, 72*(1), 65.

Tannock, R., & Girolametto, L. (1992). Reassessing parent-focused language intervention programs. In S. F. Warren, & J. E. Reichle (Eds.), *Causes and effects in communication and language intervention: Vol 1. Communication and language intervention series* (pp. 49–79). Baltimore, MD: Brookes.

U.S. Congress, House of Representatives. (1986). *House Report 99-457.* Education of the Handicapped Act Amendments of 1986, Committee on Education and Labor. Washington, DC: U.S. Government Printing Office.

VanDerHeyden, A. M., Snyder, P., Smith, A., Sevin, B., & Longwell, J. (2005). Effects of complete learning trials on child engagement. *Topics in Early Childhood Special Education, 25*(2), 81–94.

Walker, H. H., Kavanagh, K., Stiller, B., Golly, A., Severson, H. H., & Feil, E. G. (1997). *First step to success: An early intervention program for antisocial kindergartners.* Longmont, CO: Sopris West.

Warren, S. F., Fey, M. E., & Yoder, P. J. (2007). Differential treatment intensity research: A missing link to creating optimally effective communication interventions. *Mental Retardation and Developmental Disabilities Research Reviews, 13*(1), 70–77.

Warren, S. F., & Kaiser, A. P. (1986). Generalization of treatment effects by young language-delayed children: A longitudinal analysis. *Journal of Speech and Hearing Disorders, 51*(3), 239–251.

Waryas, C., & Stremel, K. (1974). On the preferred form of the double object construction. *Journal of Psycholinguistic Research, 3*(3), 271–280.

Webster-Stratton, C. (1993). Strategies for helping families with young oppositional defiant or conduct-disordered children: The importance of home and school collaboration. *School Psychology Review, 22*(3), 437–457.

Woods, J., Kashinath, S., Goldstein, H. (2004). Effects of embedding caregiver-implemented teaching strategies in daily routines on children's communication outcomes. *Journal of Early Intervention, 26*(3), 175–193.

Yoder, P. J., Kaiser, A. P., Goldstein, H., Alpert, C., Mousetis, L., Kaczmarek, L., & Fischer, R. (1995). An exploratory comparison of Milieu teaching and Responsive Interaction in the classroom. *Journal of Early Intervention, 19,* 218–242.

Yoder, P. J., & Warren, S. F. (1998). Maternal responsivity predicts the prelinguistic communication intervention that facilitates generalized intentional communication. *Journal of Speech, Language, and Hearing Research, 41*(5), 1207–1219.

Yoder, P. J., & Warren, S. F. (2001). Relative treatment effects of two prelinguistic communication interventions on language development in toddlers with developmental delays vary by maternal characteristics. *Journal of Speech, Language, and Hearing Research, 44*(1), 224–257.

Yoder, P. J., & Warren, S. F. (2002). Effects of prelinguistic milieu teaching and parent responsivity education on dyads involving children with intellectual disabilities. *Journal of Speech, Language, and Hearing Research, 45*(6), 1158–1175

Zaidman-Zait., & Jamieson, J. R. (2007). Providing web-based support for families of infants and young children with established disabilities. *Infants & Young Children, 20*(1), 11–25.

Zaslow, M., & Martinez-Beck, I. (2006). *Critical issues in early childhood professional development.* Baltimore: Brookes.

# 14

## CREATING SCHOOL-FAMILY PARTNERSHIPS IN ADOLESCENCE

### *Challenges and Opportunities*

BRENDA J. LOHMAN AND JENNIFER L. MATJASKO

Adolescence is a time of rapid change. These changes present challenges and opportunities for developing youth including physical changes, significant cognitive advancements, emotional maturation, and new peer and romantic relationships. For most adolescents, these changes are also accompanied by changes in their environments including more demanding expectations for independence, more challenging academic tasks, and new expectations for social participation from parents and peers. At the same time, adolescents are becoming more independent from their families while also maintaining a sense of connection to them and to their schools.

## OVERVIEW

The aim of this chapter is to understand how maintaining a healthy sense of connectedness and autonomy from both the family and school mutually interact during the rapidly changing time of adolescence, and overall help improve student competence. In addition, the promising avenues for schools and families to partner in order to enhance student competence are highlighted. First, the adolescent well-being and student competence literature associated with autonomy granting and connectedness from the family followed by a similar discussion for the school context is detailed. The overarching theoretical framework described stresses the importance of family-school partnerships during adolescence in order to enhance student competence. The bulk of the chapter then addresses how these constructs are embedded in the key physical, psychosocial, and behavioral opportunities and challenges of adolescence. For each of these opportunities and challenges, how family-school partnerships can either enhance or deter these behaviors for the developing youth is detailed. The chapter ends with brief remarks summarizing the importance of family-school partnerships during adolescence.

## FRAMING THE DEVELOPMENTAL TASKS OF ADOLESCENCE

Adolescence is a time of rapid development. These changes can present challenges and opportunities for the developing youth and typically include a preparation for learning adult roles, responsibilities, and behaviors. To prepare for these roles, one of the key developmental tasks of adolescence is to become more autonomous from authority figures such as parents, while remaining connected to them. According to systems theorists, for an adolescent to achieve healthy adjustment, he or she must individuate successfully from the family of origin. Individuation refers to a process in adolescence when individuals begin to separate themselves from their parents, develop their own identity, and take on new responsibilities (Garber & Little, 2001). Systems theorists argue that a sense of individuation is best fostered in a family climate that balances autonomy granting with connectedness (Perosa, Perosa, & Tam, 1996). The concept of autonomy refers to the ability of an individual to make personal decisions and to gain freedom from parents and other influences (Collins, Laurson, Mortensen, Luebker, & Ferreira, 1997), whereas connectedness refers to the level of attachment or closeness one feels toward the family. In short, for adolescents to individuate successfully and form their own identities, families must be able to balance their need to protect their children with their ability to allow them to make some mistakes.

### Autonomy Granting and Connectedness from Family

Achieving a psychological sense of autonomy from one's parents is a multidimensional task that is accomplished gradually over the course of adolescence. Autonomy is the ability to regulate one's own behaviors, decisions, and actions without undue control from or dependence on one's parents (Steinberg, 1990). Autonomy does not reflect complete independence or alienation from one's family. Rather, it is a mutual process in which parents and children accept the adolescents' growing individuality. Adolescents who achieve a healthy sense of autonomy remain connected to their families and feel a sense of love and understanding. In addition, autonomy-supportive parents spend time with their adolescents, monitoring their daily lives, and providing them with opportunities to explore and master their environments (Grolnick, Benjet, Kurowski, & Apostoleris, 1997). Relatedness, or the need to feel securely connected to others, enables individuals to feel safe to explore their environment (Ryan, Deci, & Grolnick, 1995).

Research suggests that this sense of connection is fostered by an authoritative parenting style, which is marked by responsiveness, warmth, firmness and democracy, and ultimately associated with more positive educational outcomes than an authoritarian style, which is marked by strictness and unilateral parental decision making (Steinberg, Bradford, & Dornbusch, 1996). Monitoring is a specific aspect of parenting that represents a parent's attempts to know about an adolescent's life. This includes physical as well as cognitive and emotional monitoring. For example, when parents are aware of an adolescent's whereabouts, school problems, substance use and delinquency decrease, while social competence and good grades increase (Rodriguez, 2002). In addition, monitoring can foster identity achievement and prosocial behaviors as well as academic growth including school adjustment and engagement (Catsambis, 2001; Rankin & Quane, 2002).

Parenting styles and monitoring and their impact may, however, differ among boys and girls and ethnic groups (Jeynes, 2003). These variations may be due to developmental niches or person-environment fit. For low-income inner-city boys, school engagement was greater when parental monitoring was high; but for girls, school engagement depended on both high parental monitoring and high family cohesion (Annunziata, Hogue, Faw, & Liddell, 2006). In addition, strict limit-setting and monitoring might be more adaptive for families living in high-crime neighborhoods and facing racial discrimination (Leventhal & Brooks-Gunn, 2003). Thus, future work needs to take better account of the geographic, economic, gender, and ethnic differences within these relationships by explicitly considering family socioeconomic (SES) level and adolescent gender in research addressing the links between families and student competence.

This mutual interplay of family connectedness and individual autonomy is reflected in the concept of differentiation, which emerged from family systems theory (Bomar & Sabatelli, 1996). Adolescents must have opportunities to express their separateness within the boundaries of the family (Best, Hauser, & Allen, 1997). Adolescents who experience high levels of parental control and frequent exposure to parental conflict often lack a healthy sense of autonomy (Taylor & Oskay, 1995). On the other hand, connectedness to parents is associated with greater internalization of school-related regulations (Ryan, Stiller, & Lynch, 1994), can promote intrinsic motivation (Ryan & Deci, 2000a, 2000b), and positively affect the academic motivation of girls more than boys. The development of autonomy has also been linked to student competence. Students who are high in autonomy from the family tend to be more engaged in school, in extra-curricular activities, have higher academic performance, and stay in school until graduation (Hardre & Reeve, 2003; Lohman, Kaura, & Newman, 2007). However, it can also be the case that those adolescents who have more autonomy from the family are granted that independence because they are more competent. Future work should address this selection issue through longitudinal investigations of the link between family autonomy and student competence. In one longitudinal study of low-income students, the degree to which mothers encourage autonomous decision making in their 11-year-old children predicted whether children dropped out or completed high school and enrolled in college 7 years later (Tenenbaum, Porche, Snow, Tabors, & Ross, 2007). Students low in autonomy use more defensive styles of coping with failure, such as blaming others and minimizing the significance of failure (Connell & Wellborn, 1991).

Support for autonomy may be especially important during adolescence when students are experiencing several important changes such as puberty, establishing their independence and identity, and transitioning to middle school and high school. This establishment of autonomy requires independence of thoughts, emotions, and actions (Steinberg, 2005) that lead to becoming a self-sufficient adult. A strong sense of autonomy, independence, and self-determination promote healthy socio-cognitive development in early adolescence (Eccles et al., 1993). Autonomy also involves a psychological sense of confidence about one's unique point of view and an ability to express opinions and beliefs that may differ from those of one's parents (Herman, Dornbusch, Herron, & Herting, 1997). Families that are warm, supportive, and responsive tend to have adolescents with better school success and positive psychosocial outcomes including self-reliance, identity formation, higher grade point averages, and positive career-planning aspirations, as well as better physical health and lower rates of depression and delinquency (Pong, Hao, & Gardner, 2005).

### Autonomy Granting and Connectedness from School

Similar to a family system, a school system must establish boundaries for the development of the individual within the school environment. Thus, just as a family strives to balance separateness and connectedness, a school system must also manage levels of separateness and connectedness for its maturing adolescent students. Undeniably, there is a rich literature on the social dimensions of the school environment and the impact these domains have on adolescents' psychosocial and academic adjustment. Autonomy-granting on the part of teachers, social support from classmates as well as school personnel, students' engagement in school activities, and students' perceptions of school climate have all been shown to be significantly related to adolescents' academic and psychosocial well-being (Lohman et al., 2007; Roeser & Eccles, 1998). Specifically, adolescent problem behavior has been related to the level of autonomy that students feel they have in the classroom. In this chapter, we refer to *autonomy* at school as the ability of a student to make personal decisions as well as gain independence from teachers and school administrators.

On the other hand, substantial literature establishes the importance of being connected to one's school system. Students' feelings of belongingness or connectedness to their school have been shown to be positively associated with their motivation toward school, effort, level of participation, and eventual achievement, as well as the delay of their initial encounter with cigarettes, alcohol, marijuana, and sexual intercourse (Blum, McNeely, & Rinehart, 2002; Crosnoe, Erickson, & Dornbusch, 2002). Additional studies find that for some students, difficulties adjusting to a new school may be associated with feelings of alienation and lack of social acceptance or connectedness (Resnick, Harris, & Blum, 1993).

One opportunity in which students may become connected to schools is through their participation in extracurricular activities (for a comprehensive review see Feldman & Matjasko, 2005). The settings of extracurricular activities serve as a place to act out the developmental tasks of adolescence. It is believed that extracurricular activities offer a means to express and explore one's identity, generate social and human capital, and offer a challenging setting outside of academics. Adolescents form their identity by developing skills, discovering preferences, and associating themselves with others (Eccles & Barber, 1999; Youniss et al., 2002). Currently, the literature generally supports that there is a positive relationship between extracurricular activity participation and academic achievement (Eccles & Barber, 1999; Mahoney, Cairns, & Farmer, 2003; McNeal, 1998). While a considerable amount of research has considered the relationship between family or school characteristics and student competence, relatively few studies have brought the two together in order to understand how the family and school can work together to bolster student competence. Below, we define the nature of student competence and how schools and families can partner to enhance student success.

### Bringing the Two Together: School-Family Partnerships during Adolescence

Considerable attention has addressed the role of achievement and academic functioning during adolescence and its' links to lifelong challenges and opportunities during adulthood. A large portion of this literature has focused on academic problems including truancy, academic failure, and dropout rates. Alternatively, in this chapter, we address three areas of student academic competence, by addressing research related to students who: (a) are high achieving, (b) complete high school, and (c) plan for education or vocational work beyond high school. Throughout this review, we collectively refer to these three constructs as adolescent student competence. Family-school partnerships, or the extent to which families and schools are involved in the student's educational endeavors, are viewed as important contributors to student competence. Christenson (2004) defined family-school partnerships as shared goals and monitoring, constructive and collaborative relationships between families and schools, and a range of home- and school-based activities that engaged families in the educational life of their children. Fostering productive family-school partnerships during adolescence may be challenging given the emphasis on autonomy and individuation that characterizes this developmental period.

A major task of this chapter, therefore, is to understand the reciprocal influences of the school-family connection. The overlapping roles of the family and the school have not been clearly delineated in the past. In some cases, adolescents may be experiencing a developmental mismatch between separateness and connectedness in the family and school, and their developing needs. This lack of environmental congruence may create a state of tension for the developing adolescent. Indeed, the person-environment fit perspective (outlined below) emphasizes the need for the fit between the family's balance of separateness and connectedness and the developing adolescent's need for autonomy and connection at school (Eccles et al., 1993).

Similar to this person-environment fit theory, Bronfenbrenner (1979) introduced the concept of dynamic stability to convey the reciprocal relationship between persons and their environment. Links between one sector (i.e., the family) and another (i.e., school) need to be explored for the dynamic stability of ecological niches. In 1983, Epstein (1983) found that adolescents who experienced high decision-making opportunities in the family and the school system had the highest independence and achievement scores. Adolescents who had mismatched levels of decision-making opportunities in the family and school had lower achievement scores. Thus, adolescents who had more optimal development were experiencing communality or dynamic stability of ecological niches. More than a decade ago, Goodenow (1995) pointed out that future research needs to explore ways in which ecological systems support, reinforce, or undermine one another.

In sum, schools offer adolescents the opportunity to both explore their individuality and feel connected. While the literature is not clear about the precise nature of an autonomous school environment, participation in extracurricular activities presents one opportunity for adolescents to exercise choice and feel connected to schools. It may be this process that explains the link between participation and student competence. Future research should include other measures of autonomy and connection in schools such as the extent to which students can make choices in terms of their course schedules, precise course-taking sequences, and the ability to leave campus during lunch breaks. Additional aspects of the school environments should also be tapped, for example if they are responsive, warm, firm, and take into account the developing needs of students for autonomy or if they are strict, nonaccommodating, authoritarian (e.g., zero tolerance laws) environments which can negate student competence. Furthermore, school connectedness should be conceptualized as a multidimensional construct that captures connectedness to teachers as well as a feeling of overall school spirit and pride. Below, we set the stage for our discussion of school-family considerations during adolescence by presenting our theoretical framework that considers the complex nature of adolescent development in context. As mentioned above, they include constructs from ecological systems theory, the risk and resiliency perspective, and person-environment fit.

## SETTING THE THEORETICAL FRAMEWORK

Ecological systems theory, used in concert with a risk and resiliency perspective as well as the person-environment fit perspective, serves as a valuable overall framework for integrating the sociological, biological, and psychological literatures on adolescent student competence. Utilizing a combination of these three frameworks, we address both the direct and indirect effects of adolescent development and well-being on student competence and how family-school partnerships may foster these links.

The macro bioecological theory, characterized by Urie Bronfenbrenner (1979; Bronfenbrenner & Morris, 1998) details the development of adolescents within a set of overlapping multifaceted environmental systems that influence their development, including student competence. Ecological systems theory holds that both immediate and distal aspects of a child's surrounding environment interact and transact to mold development and that the child influences his or her experience of these settings as well. During adolescence, the family and the school environments are central developmental contexts and both have been shown to be significantly related to student competence (Lohman et al., 2007; Roeser & Eccles, 1998). Furthermore, adolescents' characteristics (e.g., pubertal status, autonomy, academic motivation) may interact with their environment in determining student competence. Thus, we address the developmental opportunities and challenges faced by adolescents as well as characteristics of two microsytems: the family and the school.

To frame characteristics of these two systems, a resiliency perspective (Luster & Small, 1994) is used to define system characteristics as protective or risk factors that are associated with adolescents' student competence. A resiliency approach suggests that there are several paths to which student competence can develop, and it is imperative to investigate multiple pathways because it is not likely that only one reason is contributing to academic functioning (i.e., equifinality). Moreover, integrating concepts from the person-environment fit perspective (Eccles et al., 1993), allows us to discuss the important relationship among adolescents, families, and schools and that one size does *not* fit all in terms of the optimal organization of the family and school ecologies that promote student competence. Rather, adolescent characteristics interact with the family and school contexts in determining student competence. Thus, ecological systems theory is an ideal theoretical framework from which to guide this work because it not only includes the contextual levels surrounding a developing individual, but emphasizes the bidirectional processes by which the individual and particular contexts affect each other, such as the case with family-school partnerships.

Bronfenbrenner originally suggested that contextual levels or microsystems overlap each other and that, within a society, systems tend to be consistent (Epstein, 1983; Miller, 2002). Researchers, however, have noted that this is not always the case as systems may also vary in their degree of embeddedness with one another and are sometimes even at odds with each other (Sternberg & Grigorenko, 2001). Thus, an adolescent's developmental course may be dependent on whether systems are in synchrony or in dissynchrony (Mahoney & Bergman, 2002). We contend that the perspective of person-environment fit (Eccles et al., 1993) should also be used in studying synchrony across microsystems, including the congruence and overlap of families and schools on adolescents' student competence. Congruence or synchrony across environments may help foster student competence, while dissynchrony, incongruence or a mismatch in environments may hinder student competence (Goodenow, 1995; Lohman et al., 2007). For example, exploring this overlap rather than assuming that all contexts are in synchrony, such as the degree to which any risk or protective factor from either the family or school can compensate for a suboptimal fit in another context, better captures the idea of a holistic approach to studying adolescent student competence. Researchers can explore this overlap by taking an ecological approach (i.e., including multiple contexts) in inquiries regarding student competence during adolescence.

While research has addressed the unique impact both the family and school microsystems have on student competence, little work has addressed the interactions between the family and school contexts. Mahoney and colleagues (Mahoney & Bergman, 2002) have attempted to tackle such issues, proposing a holistic-interactionistic framework to studying individual adaptation. A more comprehensive and integrative approach such as this is needed; furthermore, it can be extended to assessing factors related to student competence. Below we consider several developmental opportunities and challenges of adolescence as well as key characteristics of the family and school environments that promote student competence. Based on this research, we will make recommendations for some promising avenues for school-family partnerships for each aspect of adolescent development. The majority of the work assessing student competence and its relationship to aspects of adolescent development draws from literature that is non-experimental in nature. As a result, causal statements about the link between families, schools, and student competence cannot be made. Where appropriate, findings from experimental research and those that are nationally representative or longitudinal in nature have been noted. A discussion of the importance of understanding the school-family partnership and how it may foster student growth and development follows.

## DEVELOPMENTAL OPPORTUNITIES AND CHALLENGES OF ADOLESCENCE LINKED TO STUDENT COMPETENCE

Below, a brief overview of the primary developmental opportunities and challenges during adolescence, how each is linked to student competency, the relationship between schools and families and the developmental outcomes, and how schools and families might partner to promote student competence is provided. The developmental opportunities (or tasks) reviewed include: puberty and physical maturation; the development of abstract thinking abilities; peer group membership, and romantic relationships. Beyond these opportunities, there are also many behaviors and experiences that youth must limit or avoid that may have negative consequences for student competence. These may include but are not limited to alcohol and drug use, mental health problems, and externalizing problems. A final aspect that is tied to adolescents' academic competence is their personal motivation and their abilities to set goals and plan for their future beyond high school. We detail each of these as well.

## Puberty and Physical Maturation

Middle childhood is marked by steady physical development. In contrast, adolescence is marked by rapid physical changes including a height spurt and increased muscle mass, maturation of the reproductive system, appearance of secondary sex characteristics, and the redistribution of body weight (Susman & Rogol, 2004). On average, puberty can last 1 to 6 years for girls and 2 to 5 years for boys. Once again, these rapid physical changes can present opportunities or challenges for the developing youth. Adapting to the physical, psychological, and social aspects of puberty requires an integration of biological, psychological, and social changes. In addition, how family members, teachers, and peers respond to these changes effects an adolescent's well being. Finally, depending on if these changes are perceived to be early, on time, or late in relation to their peers by the aforementioned groups can lead to challenges or opportunities for the developing youth.

The majority of the literature linking puberty and physical maturation to student competence has focused on the psychosocial manifestations of puberty. This relationship received attention in the 1960s and 1970s and has received sparse attention since then. The literature concerning the timing of puberty and its relationship to student competence has varied over the years with more recent work opposing past research findings. Indeed, early pubertal maturation has been viewed as a challenge or risk factor for both girls and boys' student competence. Early-maturing boys were shown to have experienced more positive psychosocial consequences (Richards & Larson, 1993) and were more likely to be involved in school activities by the 10th grade (Blyth et al., 1981). In addition, late maturers had the highest grades in comparison to early- and on-time maturers (Dubas, Graber, & Petersen, 1991). In contrast, boys who matured later had negative psychosocial outcomes. More recent work has shown the opposite; with early-maturing boys having more internalizing and externalizing behaviors as well as more problems in school (Ge, Conger, & Elder, 2001; Wichstrom, 2001). Additional work has shown that early-maturing girls experience higher levels of conflict at home and more internalizing behaviors (Williams & Currie, 2000), as well as have lower grades and lower scores on academic achievement tests. (Blyth et al., 1981). Longitudinal work from nationally representative research shows that early maturation for girls predicted lower grade point averages and a higher probability of course failure at the start of high school. Because of this initial failure during the high school transition, it also predicted their probability of dropping out of high school, and among those who graduated, their grade point average at the end of high school (Cavanagh, Riegle-Crumb, & Crosnoe, 2007).

Relatively few studies have provided insights on the extent to which the family and school environments can offset the risks that early or late maturation have on student competence. Off-time maturation may result in feelings of asynchrony and alienation with one's peers in the school context. Those experiencing this asynchrony may, then, feel less connected with the school environment. Thus, opportunities for positive engagement with the school environment may be especially critical for early or late maturing adolescents. Research investigating the relationship between off-time maturation, various aspects of school engagement (e.g., activity participation, opportunities for autonomy, student-teacher relationships), and student competence would reveal how individual differences in maturational status and school characteristics promote or hinder success. Furthermore, in taking an ecological approach, positive and supportive family relationships may offset any deficits within the school environment to promote student competence. Families that are sensitive to the needs of their early or late-maturing adolescents while supporting their engagement with their academic work may promote their academic success.

*Obesity*    Interest in the relationship between physical maturation and academic achievement has recently intensified in the face of increasing rates of obesity during adolescence in the United States. Evidence for the epidemic of childhood obesity in the United States is clearly shown by the three-fold increase in the prevalence of overweight for children over the last three decades (Anderson & Butcher, 2006) and current prevalence rates (17.1% overweight and another 16.5% at risk of overweight; Ogden et al., 2006). These high prevalence rates, along with the adverse physical, psychological, and social consequences of being overweight on children that extend into adulthood (Gunnell, Frankel, Nanchahal, Peters, & Davey Smith, 1998) which, in turn, may lead to a reduced life expectancy (Fontaine, Redden, Wang, Westfall, & Allison, 2003), make childhood obesity one of the most important medical issues among youth today (Hedley et al., 2004). Most of this research has linked adolescent obesity to psychological and physical health outcomes, but recent studies have shown indirect as well as direct relationships between obesity and student competence. Falkner et al. (2001) found that 12% of obese adolescent girls believe that they are below average students; 27% reported being held back a grade; and, 35% expected not to finish college. For boys, being obese or underweight posed academic challenges. Twenty-seven percent of underweight boys and 27% of obese boys reported being held back a grade. In addition, 37% of underweight boys and 33% of obese boys expected not to finish college. Furthermore, obesity during adolescence carries long-term consequences for academic and economic success. Using the National Longitudinal Survey of Youth (NLSY), Gortmaker, Must, Perrin, Sobol, and Dietz (1993) found that women who were obese during late adolescence and young adulthood completed fewer years of education, had lower family income, and had lower marriage rates during adulthood compared to those women who were not obese at the same ages.

Utilizing data from the National Study of Adolescent Health (Addhealth), Crosnoe and Muller (2004) showed that being overweight or obese were linked to poor academic achievement over time. In addition, this relationship was stronger in schools with more romantic involvement among adolescents and in schools with lower average body size among the students than in schools where the opposite was true. This argues for the understanding of a student's person-environment fit when assessing these links. Other research has considered the important mediators of the link between obesity and low achievement. Specifically, Taras and Potts-Datema (2005) found that obesity is linked to anxiety and low self-esteem and that this explained the link between obesity and low student competence. Therefore, it is important to consider other mediators of obesity and student competence so that the families and schools can better respond to the needs of obese adolescents. For example, literature has shown that eating breakfast increases attention in the classroom and ultimately student competence (Berkey, Rockett, Gillman, Field, & Colditz, 2003). However, if an adolescent is too large to sit comfortably in a chair, their anxiety may be heightened, their attention decreased, and, ultimately, may experience lower student competence. Research suggests that it is important to attend to these mediating processes associated with these relationships, including adolescents' emotions. Indeed, positive interpersonal relationships have been found to decrease adolescent anxiety (Graber, 2004).

As outlined above, multiple opportunities exist for positive relationships in both the school and family contexts. Positive interpersonal relationships in the school or family context may be enough to offset the academic risks associated with adolescent obesity to increase short-term and long-term academic and economic success. However, mental health issues may also need to be addressed in order to bolster the academic competence of obese adolescents.

*Sleep Loss*  In addition to the physical maturation and pubertal changes discussed above, adolescence also brings changes in sleep patterns. Adolescents would prefer to sleep about 9 hours a day (Petta, Carskadon, & Dement, 1984). However, this sleep varies in depth and duration compared to childhood, with less time spent in deep sleep (Dahl & Carskadon, 1995). In addition, adolescents are more likely to go to bed later in the evening due to work, homework, entertainment, or socialization with friends and romantic partners. Thus, adolescents get less sleep at the same time when more demands are being placed on them; they are expected to be at school earlier; and changes in their natural biorhythms make them want to sleep in more. These shifts are tied to pubertal status: those teens that are in a more advanced pubertal status show a greater tendency toward this delay and a greater difference between weekend and weekday sleep (Laberge et al., 2001). Two recent reviews of this research (Yan & Slagle, 2007; Wolkfson & Carskadon, 2003) show that American adolescents do not get enough sleep and that this lack of sleep impairs adolescents' learning and development including their academic performance from middle school through the college years. While researchers propose that this relationship could be countered by delaying school start time, it is not clear whether student academic achievement will improve along with a shift in school scheduling.

As in the research on obesity, several studies have investigated the mediators between sleep loss and academic achievement (Allgoewer, Wardle, & Steptoe, 2001; Carskadon,

1999). Carskadon (1999) found that sleep loss was related to depressive symptoms and it may be the depressed mood that is related to lowered achievement. It can also be the case that lowered achievement can lead to depressive symptoms and sleep loss as well. Fredriksen, Rhodes, Reddy, and Way (2004) investigated sleep loss during the transition from middle childhood to adolescence. In their longitudinal study, they found that sleep loss was related to decreasing self-esteem and achievement over time. Furthermore, the decrease in self-esteem explained the link between lack of sleep and low grades.

This literature suggests ways that families and schools can partner in order to increase student competence. First, families can promote consistency between weekday and weekend sleep schedules, which may help to decrease the amount of sleep loss that some adolescents can experience during the week. However, this may be a challenging task for families in the face of adolescents' increasing autonomy from parental control. Because of this, schools may want to experiment with altering start times so that adolescents can get more rest during the week. When adolescents experience inadequate sleep, both families and schools can address the psychological impact of sleep loss by addressing adolescent depressive symptoms. Maintaining synchronous supportive relationships, while providing opportunities for autonomy in both the family and school contexts, may help to diminish the negative consequences of sleep loss on student competence during adolescence.

## Cognitive and Brain Development

Accompanied by the rapid physical maturation of puberty during adolescence is the rapid development of cognitive activity. Youth begin to have greater self-reflection, become more planful and focused, and are able to hypothesize and think about several strategies or outcomes for these hypotheses simultaneously rather than focusing on just one domain or issue at a time (Keating, 2004). Increases in speed, efficiency, and capacity of information storage and retrieval also occurs (Kwon & Lawson, 2000). The most widely known construct related to these rapid cognitive changes is formal operational thought or the ability to raise hypotheses to explain an event, and then to follow the logic that a particular hypothesis implies (Piaget, 1972).

During adolescence, new and more intricate thoughts become possible. These transformations are accompanied by neurological changes in the brain—prefrontal cortex developments, the continuation of myelination of nerve fibers, and the selective reduction of neurological pathways or "synaptic pruning" (Diamond, 2002; Johnson, 2001). These changes present new opportunities for adolescent cognition including the ability to reject irrelevant information, formulate complex hypothetical arguments, organize an approach to a complex task, and follow a sequence of steps to task completion (Davies & Rose, 1999).

However, the development of formal operational thought has been criticized. In general, according to Piaget, formal operational reasoning is viewed as the final stage in the development of logical thought. Recent work claims that formal operational thought is not the end point for cognitive development during the lifespan and that post-formal reasoning in adulthood often occurs, marked by cognitions that are fluid and based on the context or situation at hand (Torbert, 1994). In addition, many adolescents and adults never reach formal operational thinking or at least use it inconsistently (Bradmetz, 1999). Regardless, most cognitive scientists agree that adolescents do become more self-reflective in their thought processes and are able to organize, hypothesize, and evaluate propositions better than in middle childhood (Keating, 2004).

These changes in cognitive thought processes and neurological development have implications for student competence during adolescence. Surprisingly, little work has directly assessed the link between the development of abstract reasoning and student competence (see Chapell & Overton, 2002, for an exception). Chapell and Overton (2002) investigated the development of reasoning for African Americans during adolescence. Reasoning "involves inference, the process where propositions known as premises that have been accepted provide the evidence for arriving at and accepting further propositions known as conclusions" (Chapell & Overton, 2002, p. 296). They found an increase in reasoning and that low-SES students scored lower on reasoning compared to high-SES adolescents. Moreover, research has found that aspects of the school and family contexts are related to cognition. Parenting styles and test anxiety are related to adolescent cognitive performance (Chapell & Overton, 1998).

Furthermore, work has pointed to the need for schools to provide a stimulating context that encourages advanced cognitive thinking characteristic of abstract reasoning (Lee & Freire, 2003). However, not all schools promote advanced cognitive development. This is where person-environment fit theory becomes important. To take full advantage of these cognitive opportunities in adolescence, schools must create environments that fit with the adolescent's development at the time, such as that described by Keating (1990):

> Students need to be engaged with meaningful material; training of thinking skills must be embedded in a knowledge of subject matter, for acquisition of isolated content knowledge is likely to be unproductive; serious engagement with real problems has to occur in depth and over time; students need experiences that lead to placing a high value on critical thinking, to acquiring it as a disposition, not just as a skill; and many of these factors occur most readily, and perhaps exclusively, when students have the opportunity for real, ongoing discourse with teachers who have reasonably expert command of the material to be taught. (p. 77)

The process that Keating described may encourage the development of cognition by increasing self-esteem in the adolescent's ability to handle complex academic tasks. Meaningful engagement with academic material may also decrease test-taking anxiety, which may increase student achievement. Future research should investigate the links between student engagement with academic material, reasoning ability, anxiety, and achievement. Is it the case that anxiety lessens student engagement with academic material or vice versa? What instructional strategies work when this occurs? Understanding those links will provide a solid foundation for unveiling some promising avenues for school-family partnerships to enhance cognitive ability and student competence. Chapell and Overton's (1998) work suggested that families play an important role in the development of reasoning. Hence, parents can enhance school and teacher efforts by also supporting a meaningful engagement with their schoolwork and encouraging critical thinking skills by having ongoing discourse about matters inside and outside of their academic work. Furthermore, schools can make efforts to reduce test-taking anxiety among students by encouraging consistent discourse with high quality teachers.

## Peer Relations

During adolescence, peer relationships change in composition and importance. Belonging to a group and developing a sense of group identity with peers becomes particularly salient. Beginning in early adolescence, the peer group becomes more structured and organized than it was previously (Newman & Newman, 2001). The development of cliques (e.g., small groups of 5 to 10 friends that are often transient) and crowds (e.g., large groups characterized by specific behaviors or identity such as involvement in sports; Brown, 2004) occurs. Crowd labels typically have distinct profiles with respect to the youths' academic achievement levels, educational goals, use of alcohol and drugs, involvement in delinquent acts including violence, and involvement in school activities. While in racially diverse schools, it is not uncommon for students to identify crowds based on ethnic categories. For example, in a racially diverse sample of over 700 middle-school and high-school students, some of the most common crowds mentioned were floaters (belonging to more than one group), nice or regulars, populars, middles (related to income), jocks, nerds/unpopulars, preps, skate-boarders, and misfits/alternatives (Lohman, 2000). However, roughly 20% of the students in that same study said they did not belong to any group. In an additional study of over 3,000 high school students, nine crowd types were identified: jocks, populars, popular nice, average-normal, brains, partiers, druggies, loners, and nerds (Durbin, Darling, Steinberg, & Brown, 1993).

Belonging to one of these peer groups may foster a healthy sense of self as well as the skills necessary to become an active participant in adulthood. Peer group membership allows adolescents to self-reflect about, "Who am I, and with whom do I belong?" (Newman, Lohman, Newman, 2007). During this self-reflective process, the person-environment fit perspective becomes salient as youth must identify the fit or lack of fit between their personal beliefs and interests and those of their peer group. Resolving these challenges can lead to a healthy sense of group membership that has been linked to positive academic and psychosocial outcomes.

A healthy sense of peer group membership has been linked to adolescent student competence, depending on who the peers are. Several studies suggest that peers are particularly influential on adolescents' day-to-day school activities such as doing homework and the effort put forth during class (Midgely & Urdan, 1995; Steinberg et al., 1996). In addition, peer group membership provides the opportunity for accelerating academic competence, when peers earn higher grades and have higher educational aspirations such as continuing their education beyond high school (Steinberg et al., 1996). For African Americans, peer support was related to higher math achievement test scores among adolescents facing multiple risks over time (Gutman, Sameroff, & Eccles, 2002). Also, friendships of higher quality exhibit better psychosocial adjustment and academic achievement in younger children (Berndt, Hawkins, & Jiao, 1999). However, societal expectations and many research studies emphasize that peer group membership may be a challenge or a risk factor for adolescent student competence. For example, students who focus solely on peers or belong to peer groups that do not focus on academic competence often perform worse in school (Bishop, Bishop, Gelbwasser, Green, & Zuckerman, 2003).

The risk and resiliency perspective lends some insight into how schools and families can partner in the face of peers to promote student competence. Peer group membership is often a way for adolescents to exercise their autonomy and express their identity (Newman et al., 2007). Because peer groups are often drawn from shared interests, schools can promote prosocial peer affiliations by providing multiple opportunities for positive activity involvement with adult supervision/monitoring, particularly for adolescents who are at-risk for school failure who are more likely to affiliate with antisocial peers (Feldman & Matjasko, 2005). In turn, parents can encourage participation in such activities. For example, if adolescents enjoy music over sports, families and schools could offer space for youth to participate in these interests. Moreover, when adolescents are affiliated with antisocial or low-achieving peer groups, parents and schools may target their efforts at decreasing the amount of unsupervised time that such peers have together. After-school programs have been found to decrease this unsupervised time and increase achievement among at-risk adolescents (Granger, 2008). However, this may be difficult for families and schools with limited economic resources given that extracurriculars are often cut due to lack of sufficient funds. Families and schools should understand that participation in these events is not just for the adolescent's enjoyment, but these tasks serve as a key protective factor and stimulus for the adolescent's developing autonomy. Indeed, more research is needed on the ways that families and schools can offset the risks of negative peer associations on student competence and foster healthy ones.

### Romantic and Sexual Relationships

Accompanied by the rapid changes of physical development and the surge of importance in peer relationships, interest and participation in romantic relationships also increases during adolescence. Most youth become involved in dating, emotional relationships, and initiate sexual experiences during this time period (Levesque, 1993). In addition, these relationships become increasingly intimate and meet four needs of the developing youth: affiliation, attachment, care giving, and sexual gratification (Furman & Wehner, 1997). A large majority of the work addressing romantic relationships in adolescence has focused on the transition into sexual debut. By the end of high school, over 1 in every 2 teens has had intercourse, one-quarter to one-third of adolescents report having multiple partners, and over one-third of adolescents report having sexual intercourse without condoms (Snyder, 2006).

There has been a recent surge in research on understanding romantic relationships during adolescence beyond sexual relations. It has been shown that adolescent romantic relationships tend to be short in duration (Furman & Shaffer, 2003). Research has also highlighted adolescent's romantic relationships association with psychological functioning (Maccoby, 1990) and intimate relationships in adulthood (Bryant, 2006). Gender and race differences in the quality of these relationships have been shown (Murry, Hurt, Kogan, & Luo, 2006). For example, Maccoby (1990) found that adolescent romantic relationships put some adolescent girls at-risk for depression while Murry et al. (2006) found that boys reported more negative experiences in romantic relationships compared to girls. Furthermore, healthy family relationships and monitoring were positive predictors of romantic relationship quality for girls. For both boys and girls, self-esteem significantly predicted romantic relationship quality. Therefore, families may be particularly important in buffering any of the negative experiences that girls have in romantic relationships.

Very little work has directly linked the associations between romantic relationships and student competence. Several studies have investigated the link between same-sex attraction, stigmatization, and student achievement (e.g., Pearson, Muller, & Wilkinson, 2007). In this line of work, adolescents with same-sex attractions report feeling stigmatized by their peers within the school context. This stigmatization acts as a psychological stressor resulting in a detachment from schools and lower student achievement. Another line of work has focused on the challenge or risk of bearing a child during the teen years, especially for girls. Teen pregnancy has been linked to subsequent poverty (Snyder & McLaughlin, 2004). In addition, many youth who grow up in high poverty neighborhoods are at greater risk for teenage pregnancy and dropping out of school, both of which contribute to continuing to live in poverty during adulthood (Hao & Cherlin, 2004). However, there is large variation regarding the consequences of teenage pregnancy for the developing youth and child.

School and family support for academics and school completion can be key factors in the success of teen mothers (Coley & Chase-Lansdale, 1998; Manlove, 1998). When schools offer an environment that reduces the stigma of teen parenthood through alternative programs that provide the availability of child care, then teen mothers are more likely to re-engage with their academics and complete high school (Allen, Philliber, Herrling, & Kuperminc, 1997). Families and parents also play a key role in this process by providing child care assistance so that teen mothers can complete the necessary school tasks and homework in order to be successful.

Apart from the work on teenage parenthood, little research has been conducted on ways that families and schools can support adolescents when they are navigating the world of romantic relationships. Studies have suggested that adolescents have varied experiences with romance and that the family and school contexts can either exacerbate or mitigate these experiences. While girls have more positive experiences with romantic relationships, they are particularly vulnerable to the intersection between the quality of their relational experiences in the family and with their romantic partners. Families who can foster and maintain a supportive relationship with adolescent girls will reduce the likelihood that they will experience depressive symptoms that are associated with romantic relationships. On the other hand, the school context can be particularly difficult for adolescents with same-sex attractions. This suggests that schools can be instrumental to the academic success of these adolescents by sending messages about inclusivity by not tolerating student discrimination based on sexual preference. The schools efforts may further be enhanced by acceptance and support in the family context. Future research should investigate the interplay between support and acceptance in both contexts and their relationship to student competence for adolescents of all sexual orientations. Does support in one context offset stress in another? Is the family support particularly important in offsetting any relational stressors? Questions such as these should be addressed in future work on the relationship between romantic relationships, families, schools, and student competence.

## Alcohol and Drug Use

During adolescence, youth begin to experiment with alcohol and drugs. The numbers of youth who have tried alcohol or drugs increases during adolescence. For example, slightly over one-third (37%) of teens have tried alcohol in eighth grade, while 14% have been drunk at least once. By the 12th grade, those numbers have double and tripled, respectively; 70% of high school seniors had tried alcohol and 48% have gotten drunk (Johnston, O'Malley, Bachman, & Schllenberg, 2004). By the end of high school, one-half of all adolescents have tried an illegal drug (Johnston et al., 2004). Some experimentation with drugs and alcohol is seen as a normative part of adolescence, yet regular or excessive use can be a risk factor for poor psychosocial and academic functioning, especially when it begins at young ages (Iannotti & Bush, 1992).

Regular substance use during adolescence has been associated with a false sense of autonomy that may impair the adolescents' ability to navigate their key developmental tasks and undermine the establishment of mature relationships that extends into young adulthood (Baumrind & Moselle, 1985). Furthermore, Chassin, Pitts, and De-Lucia (1999) found that adolescents who used illegal drugs were less autonomous and report less involvement in positive activities during young adulthood. Heavy drinking during adolescence was particularly detrimental to autonomy and positive activity involvement during young adulthood. Individual characteristics such as impulsivity and sensation-seeking have also been linked to substance use during adolescence (Leigh & Stall, 1993).

Adolescent alcohol and drug use are also related to lower student competence. Newcomb and Bentler (1988) outlined several pathways through which drug and alcohol use affects adolescent academics. First, adolescent substance use may impair the adolescent's ability to focus. This lack of focus may affect their ability to complete homework, study for tests, and retain material. Given the temporary nature of impairment due to substances, adolescent use may only affect student competence if it is regular and persists over time. Jessor, Donovan, and Costa (1991) found that adolescent substance use was detrimental only if it persisted into young adulthood.

Research has demonstrated that the school and family context is linked to adolescent substance use. For example, extracurricular activity participation has been associated with lower rates of substance use among adolescents (e.g., Eccles & Barber, 1999). However, there are key gender differences in the link between activity participation and substance use. Eccles and Barber (1999) found that boys involved in performing arts were less likely to drink alcohol and that male athletes reported the highest rates of substance use. Research on the family context and adolescent substance use have highlighted the importance of parent characteristics and parent-adolescent relationships (Brook, Brook, Gordon, Whiteman, & Cohen, 1990; Chassin et al., 1999). Parental alcoholism is a strong predictor of adolescent substance use patterns. Furthermore, parental alcoholism is also strongly related to the quality of the parent-adolescent relationship. Adolescents with alcoholic parents are more likely to have conflicted and strained relationships with them (Brook et al., 1990). These conflictual relationships are linked to adolescent depression and poor school performance.

Thus, when adolescents are facing difficult family circumstances in the form of parental alcoholism and family conflict, the school has an opportunity to provide positive experiences for adolescents—either through positive student-teacher relationships or activity involvement. However, both schools and families should be aware that activity participation does not necessarily diminish the likelihood that adolescents will use substances. In actuality, it may be necessary to monitor the behaviors of male athletes more closely given the higher rate of substance use among that population. Furthermore, families and schools should recognize that experimentation with substances can be a normative part of adolescence but regular or excessive use is not. When adults in both contexts are connected to the adolescents, then they may be more likely to recognize when changes in mood or behavior occur—a signal that the adolescent may be using substances—and intervene before substance use becomes a regular feature in the adolescent's life. Consistent and clear communication between families and schools is necessary in order to prevent the transition from experimentation to routine substance use.

### Internalizing Problems

Adolescence is often seen as a period of emotional upheaval including moodiness, outbursts, and emotional rollercoaster rides. However, research has shown that this emotional variability was not found to increase with age (Larson & Lampman-Petraitis, 1989). During this time frame, adolescents must be able to self-reflect and acknowledge these shifts in emotions, as well as learn how to manage these emotional expressions (Hoeksma, Oosterlaan, & Schipper, 2004). However, approximately 5% to 10% of youth may be unable to manage these emotions and internalizing or mental health problems may occur.

One internalizing problem that has received considerable attention is depression (Graber, 2004). Genetic dispositions in combination with environments that may be stressful or rejecting may place adolescent girls and boys at risk for depression (Tomarken, Dichter, Garber, & Simien, 2004). Depression may range from depressed mood to major depressive orders. These internalizing behaviors increase during adolescence with a peak at about ages 17 or 18 (Petersen et al., 1993). While these behaviors increase over time for both boys and girls, no gender differences in depression are generally noted until postpuberty with females having more mental health problems (Crawford, Cohen, Midlarsky, & Brook, 2001).

Feelings of depression are a major challenge. Depression and depressive symptoms have been linked to adolescent drug and alcohol use as well as suicide or suicidal ideations (Brook, Cohen, & Brook, 1998). In addition, depression may lead to lower student competence (and vice versa). Research has demonstrated that lower student competence is related to changes in anxiety and depression for adolescents. Increases in student competence have also been linked to increases in emotional well-being over time (Maughan, Rowe, Loeber, & Stouthamer-Loeber, 2003). Furthermore, adolescents who meet the diagnostic criteria for depressive and anxiety disorders are especially at-risk for academic difficulties (Kovacs & Devlin, 1998). It is hypothesized that depression and anxiety interferes with the ability to sustain one's attention for a long enough period of time in order to retain the material that is integral for academic success. In sum, research has demonstrated a bidirectional relationship between student competence and adolescent depression and that those individuals with diagnosable depressive disorders are particularly at-risk for school failure.

In accord with the person-environment fit perspective, this research suggests that when academic material is aimed at the student's competency, the student can experience boosts in affective functioning that can increase with continuing positive experiences over time (Masten et al., 2005). The structure of the family and school environments is crucial in this process. First, for schools, differentiated instruction is a way to tailor the educational program in order to meet the adolescent's learning needs. By gauging the curriculum to student strengths and deficits, differentiated instruction has been shown to be effective at increasing student achievement (Fuchs, Fuchs, Hamlett, Phillips, & Bentz, 1994). As discussed above, this success can serve to boost self esteem and confidence in one's academic abilities. Furthermore, schools can target psychosocial support to those who meet the diagnostic criteria for depressive disorders in order to increase student competence. Second, for families, it has been shown that coercive and conflictual parent-adolescent interactions is linked to adolescent depressive symptoms (Zahn-Waxler, Klimes-Dougan, & Slattery, 2000). Thus, it is critical that families devise strategies to diminish the level of conflict and coercion in their day-to-day interactions. Furthermore, families can partner with schools in creating a positive learning environment within the home so that adolescents can complete schoolwork in a place free of interruption and outside distractions. In the case of adolescents who are diagnosed with a depressive disorder, families can advocate for additional school resources (in the form of any counseling or intervention) to alleviate internalizing symptoms so that students can succeed in their academic endeavors.

### Externalizing Problems

While internalizing problems deal with the adolescent's difficulty in regulating their emotions, externalizing behaviors deal with adolescent's difficulty regulating one's impulses. Delinquency is an example of externalizing problems that has received considerable attention during adolescence. Delinquent offenses are actions for which an adult could be prosecuted as well as such acts as truancy, or running away. Delinquent activity has been shown to increase during adolescence and has been linked with a variety of other problem behaviors including substance use, truancy, and relationship problems (Ellickson, Saner, & McGuigan, 1997). However, adolescents who engage in antisocial activity are not homogeneous. Two distinct groups of adolescent offenders have been identified in the literature: life course persistent and adolescent-limited offenders.

These two groups are differentiated by the age of first offense, the nature of their crimes, violent or non-violent, whether there offending is chronic or transient, and their long-term developmental trajectories. Life course persistent offenders (LCPOs), also known as early starters, chronic offenders, career criminals, or early onset-persistent offenders are characterized by the violent and drug related crimes they commit, including violence against women and children (Moffitt, Caspi, Harrington, & Milne, 2002).

LCPOs begin offending in childhood and their antisocial behavior is stable across age and situation (Moffitt & Caspi, 2001). They are characteristically male, with the ratio of male to female life course persistent offenders being 10 to 1 (Moffitt & Caspi, 2001). Typically, LCPOs also display neurophsysiological deficits such as impulsivity and inattentiveness (i.e., a symptom of Attention Deficit Disorder), and these deficits remain throughout their life. Later in life, substance dependence, financial and work problems are exhibited (Donnellan, Ge, & Wenk, 2000; Moffitt & Caspi, 2001; Moffitt et al., 2002). Moffitt (1997) theorized these neuropsychological deficits interact with individuals' environments to reinforce and worsen anti-social behavior. For example, LCPOs with little parental supervision and guidance have even more opportunities to offend than those with more supervision. They continue offending into adulthood because they fail to learn prosocial alternatives to antisocial behavior, have reputations as criminals, and because the decisions they made earlier have closed positive life pathways. Similarly, LCPOs in restrictive school environments may never have the socialization experiences necessary to learn alternative behaviors.

On the other hand, adolescent limited offenders (ALOs), also known as late starters and transitory delinquents, are likely to commit nonviolent offenses, such as property offenses and substance abuse (Moffitt et al., 2002). Adolescent limited offending is discontinuous across time and situations, typically increasing as the adolescent approaches puberty and decreasing in late adolescence and early adulthood (Moffitt 1997). In contrast to LCPO's (who have a male to female ratio of 10 to 1), the ratio of male to female adolescent-limited offenders is much smaller—1.5 to 1 (Moffitt & Caspi, 2001). ALOs tend to engage in delinquent behaviors with their peers (Jeglum-Bartusch, Lynam, Moffitt, & Silva, 1997), but, at the same time, may obey school and family rules (Moffitt, 1997). Therefore, effective parenting does little to alter the behavior of ALOs. When these adolescents reach adulthood, they cease offending because the costs of continued offending, such as arrests, fines, and disapproval of family, outweigh the benefits, which were to prove maturity and gain autonomy (Moffitt, 1997). In general, by age 26 the ALOs have completed high school, but not post-secondary education, and are exhibiting both mental health and financial problems (Moffitt & Caspi, 2001; Moffitt et al., 2002).

According to the person-environment fit perspective, school policies can help to diminish adolescent offending trajectories when they work to fit these students' needs. Because there are two different types of adolescent offenders, each with different developmental histories, the student needs of offenders are probably not uniform. For example, disciplinary policies may prevent adolescent-limited offenders from committing delinquent acts in school by threatening them with punishment because this group typically obeys school and family rules and offends with peers. But these same policies that are restrictive and punitive may not help the more troubled life-course persistent offenders because even if the policies create a safer environment, the policies do not help change the aggressive cognitive and behavioral patterns of these youth. Instead, these policies may threaten aggressive youth and increase their aggressive behavior. Schools and families must understand that these behaviors may be a reaction to their developing needs for autonomy in an over controlling environment. This is not to say that rules do not have their place in deterring externalizing behaviors, it is to say that schools and families should note the possibility that these offenses are manifestations in developmental asynchrony for the youth either within or across both the family and school environments.

### Adolescence and Beyond: Identity Development via Goal Planning, Career Choice, and Academic Motivation

Although the theme of identity development is often conceptualized within the framework of the college experience and the transition to the workforce, or for those youth who are 18- to 24-years old, identity begins at much younger ages. For example, societal expectations of parents, teachers, and peers play in to an adolescent's decisions to attend college or go directly to work following high school graduations. Today, in the United States, nearly 2 in every 3 youth attend college following high school graduation (U.S. Census Bureau, 2003). Unfortunately, a college education is not attained easily by all youth: 1 in 3 youth go directly to work, join the military, or enter technical training programs. These adolescents are often low-income, ethnic minority, and immigrant youth who fall behind their more economically advantaged peers when it comes to enrolling in college courses (Fox, Connolly, & Snyder, 2006). Ten years after high school graduation, 25% of these young adults make less than $16,000 per year (Halperin, 1998).

Regardless if adolescents go to college or begin to work, youth must begin to formulate a sense of their own identities as well as goals that must be set and met to achieve that identity. Indeed, many adolescents begin to work during the teenage years. The majority of this work is marked by minimally skilled jobs with high turnover, low pay, little decision-making responsibility, and little stimulation of skill development. In 2002, 47% of 16- to 19-year-olds were in the labor force, and 16% were unemployed, meaning that they were recently fired or were unsuccessful in looking for work during the preceding four weeks (U.S. Census Bureau, 2003). The literature has revealed contradictory findings regarding adolescent work and its impaction on adolescent functioning. Some find that adolescents who work long hours in stressful jobs are more likely to evidence increased cigarette smoking, marijuana and alcohol use, truancy, and poor academic performance in school (Steinberg & Dornbusch, 1991). However, not all work during high school leads to these negative outcomes. When adolescents work under 20 hours a week and their job involves skill improvement related to career development, they have higher levels of well-being, academic achievement, and less involvement in problem behaviors (Mortimer & Johnson, 1999).

Career choice reflects a central component of the youth's emerging identity. There is ample evidence that familial, societal and socioeconomic conditions are major factors influencing adolescent career making decisions. High schools, colleges, and families urge young people to make career decisions as early as possible. Parents' encouragement and discussions about school and higher education promote adolescents' college aspirations and preparation (Catsambis, 2001). Parent discussions with youth about educational issues are associated with greater likelihood of enrolling in college, although the degree of benefit differs by ethnic/racial group as well as by immigration generational status (McCarron & Inkelas, 2006). When parents encourage college enrollment and youth perceive parents' interest in their school success, youth sign up for academic tracks in high school associated with college access, participate in out-of-school time programs that may prepare students for college environments and develop aspirations to attend college (Swail, Cabrera, & Lee, 2004). However, adolescents report that individual factors—such as abilities, attitudes, and expectations—most strongly affect their career decision making and downplay the impact of familial, societal, and socioeconomic factors (O'Neil et al., 1980).

We address the specific individual or self-selection factor of academic motivation which plays a particularly crucial role in goal planning and career choice during the adolescent years. Unfortunately, motivation changes drastically from elementary school to high school, and, many times, it is not in a direction that is optimal for preparation for young adult roles. In general, both competency beliefs and academic values decline from elementary school through high school (Wigfield & Eccles, 2000; Wigfield et al., 1997). Specifically, during the preschool and early elementary years, students have an optimistic view of their ability and define it broadly in terms of characteristics such as social behavior, conduct, work habits, and effort (Eccles, Roeser, Wigfield, & Freedman-Doan, 1999; Wigfield, Eccles, & Pintrich, 1996). The largest changes regarding these views are seen during the transition to middle school when students begin to use normative criteria to judge their ability (Feldlaufer, Midgley, & Eccles, 1988) and tend to view ability more as a stable, internal trait and less related to effort (Dweck, 2002). They also believe that ability is a stable trait that is task specific. For example, if students put in a great deal of effort to accomplish a task and others complete a task with less effort, the implication is that they have lower ability (Dweck & Sorich, 1999). In addition, as students move from elementary to middle school, their desire for easy work increases. This suggests that students may be adopting a work-avoidance goal orientation (Eccles, Wigfield, & Schiefele, 1998). Thus during high school, adolescents have more negative attributions, and beliefs about their competency and academic values.

Furthermore, as students progress from elementary through high school, their self-worth increasingly depends more on their ability to achieve competitively (Harari & Covington, 1981). Extrinsic rewards for learning, such as good grades and performance on standardized tests, are symbols of success that maintain one's self-worth. However, because success is defined by comparing one's performance to others, the self-worth of some students may be threatened (Stipek, 2002). The No Child Left Behind (NCLB) Act of 2001 has implications for students' self-worth and their resulting motivation. NCLB mandates that states set proficiency goals in reading and mathematics and to assess progress toward meeting proficiency goals by testing students in grades three through eight annually and testing students in high school once. To ensure that no group is "left behind," states must document proficiency levels of students from various groups: socioeconomic status, race, ethnicity, disability, and limited English proficiency. Low-achieving students who face standards that are too high for them will risk losing their self-worth (Stipek, 2002). Students with disabilities are possibly most at risk. Even high-achieving students who define their self-worth by their performance success are not immune to the effects of accountability testing. The increased emphasis on competition and evaluation of student performance from elementary through high school (Gottfried, Fleming, & Gottfried, 2001) may, in part, contribute to the documented decline in students' intrinsic motivation from elementary through middle school (Lepper,

Corpus, & Iyengar, 2005), and preference for challenge, curiosity, interest, and mastery from elementary school to high school (Harter & Jackson, 1992).

*Gender and Ethnic Differences in Motivation*    Gender and cultural expectations about student competence, academic expectations, and developmental norms are apparent when assessing academic motivation. Indeed, girls begin to form negative perceptions of ability in elementary school when boys and girls are about equal in achievement (Dweck, 2002). Girls also more often attribute failure to lack of ability (Eccles, Barber, Jozefowicz, Malenchuk, & Vida, 2000). Gender differences in perceived ability are more prominent in male-stereotyped domains such as math and science (Eccles et al., 2000). However, girls' higher values for English and music and their lower ability perceptions in math and science may be due to a greater reported interest and enjoyment in reading and writing activities than boys (Eccles et al., 2000; Jacobs, Lanza, Osgood, Eccles, & Wigfield, 2002). Even girls who are gifted and high-achieving hold an entity view of ability more often than boys (Dweck, 1999; Eccles et al., 2000), despite performance being equally good or better than boys (Cole, Martin, Peeke, Seroczynski, & Fier, 1999). By adolescence, this gap widens with males making internal attributions for success, leading to higher self-esteem and more subsequent effort in comparison to females that tend to be more discouraged after failure, which reduces their confidence to succeed (Oakes, 1990). Parental and teacher beliefs about male and female competences and goals also encourage these gender differences (Meece, Glienke, & Burg, 2006). However, as noted by Meece and colleagues, the literature on these differences is sparse and the gender differences that have been found are small in students' achievement goal orientations.

Ethnic differences in motivation also occur. During adolescence, African American and Hispanic boys are more likely than other groups to reject achievement-related values (Graham, Taylor, & Hudley, 1998). In college, African American students tend to have an incremental view of ability (Aronson, Fried, & Good, 2002) because they attribute their poorer academic performance to causes outside their control such as poor school systems and discrimination (van Laar, 2000). The tendency of minority students to de-value academic achievement and make external attributions may be due to their skepticism regarding the usefulness of education for long-term social and economic success (Ogbu, 2003). However, students from diverse ethnic backgrounds tend to have a positive overall academic self-efficacy (Graham, 1994), but lower self-efficacy on specific tasks or in certain subjects, such as standardized test performance (Mayo & Christenfeld, 1999), math in African American students (Pajares & Kranzler, 1995), and writing in Hispanic students (Pajares & Johnson, 1996). Once again, these ethnic differences in motivation should be interpreted with caution. Even though research cites average differences among ethnic groups in motivational orientations, we should be careful not to make stereotypical assumptions about a student's motivation based on ethnicity. Students' motivation is more likely due to their achievement experiences, the beliefs and values of their family, and the classroom climate than their ethnic or racial identification. A plethora of research needs to be conducted in order to understand ethnic and gender differences in adolescent academic motivation and its' implications for goal planning and career choice in adulthood.

Goal planning, career choice, and academic motivation are key contributors to student competence in which the family and school can partner to foster positive identity and optimal choices in these arenas. Once again, recognizing the one size does *not* fit all philosophy is important to note here. Not all youth desire to attend college. Children who are in noncollege preparatory programs tend to get a general education that does not foster competencies in work skills. In other words, many schools fail to support alternative career trajectories for these adolescents. In addition, maintaining supportive relationships while providing opportunities from both the family and school contexts, could enhance student competence. For example, schools and families could work together to find internships and part-time work for adolescents who would like to work in skilled trades. In addition, families and schools could begin to work together earlier to help those youth who would like to attend college through offering information and financial counseling about saving for college (savings, 529, and state-appropriated accounts) and scholarships. Furthermore, gearing instruction to the needs of the students should help to stem the decline in academic motivation that typically occurs during adolescence by increasing confidence in one's skills and abilities. When that occurs in the context of connectiveness in both the family and school contexts, then adolescents may choose more challenging educational and career paths.

## CONCLUSIONS: THE IMPORTANCE OF INTEGRATING SCHOOL-FAMILY PARTNERSHIPS IN ADOLESCENCE

A person-environment-fit perspective emphasizes the need for the fit between the family's balance of separateness and connectedness and the developing adolescent's need for autonomy and connectedness in the school context. Links between one sector (i.e., the family) and another (i.e., school) need to be explored for the congruence between ecological niches and how it may enhance student competence. Not only is it important for parents to foster connectedness and autonomy-granting at home, but to encourage this balance at school as well. Research needs to further explore ways in which ecological niches differ from one another and how they are linked to adolescents' academic student competence, physical well-being, and psychosocial outcomes by taking an ecological approach and investigating how transactions between contexts serves to strengthen or diminish student competence. As detailed above, school-family partnerships can help youth deter challenges while simultaneously enhancing opportunities for learning adult roles, responsibilities, and behaviors. School-family partnerships that provide stability for adolescents, can address both the direct and indirect effects of an adolescent's environment and development on student competence. We call for more work to test this hypothesis while recognizing the developmental need for separateness and connectedness in both the family and school environments to help bolster adolescents' student competence.

## REFERENCES

Allen, J. P., Philliber, S., Herrling, S., & Kuperminc, G. P. (1997). Preventing teen pregnancy and academic failure: Experimental evaluation of a developmentally based approach, *Child Development, 68*, 729–742.

Allgoewer, A., Wardle, J., & Steptoe, A. (2001). Depressive symptoms, social support, and personal health behaviors in young men and women. *Health Psychology, 20*, 223–227.

Anderson, P., & Butcher, K. (2006). Childhood obesity: Trends and potential causes. *Future Child, 16*, 19–45.

Annunziata, D., Hogue, A., Faw, L., & Liddell, H. A. (2006). Family functioning and school success in at-risk inner-city adolescents. *Journal of Youth and Adolescence, 35*, 105–113.

Aronson, J., Fried, C. B., & Good, C. (2002). Reducing the effects of stereotype threat on African American college students by shaping theories of intelligence. *Journal of Experimental Social Psychology, 38*, 113–125.

Baumrind, D., & Moselle, K. (1985). A developmental perspective on adolescent drug abuse. *Advances in Alcohol and Substance Abuse, 4*, 41–67.

Berkey, C. S., Rockett, H. R. H., Gillman, M. W., Field, A. E., & Colditz, G. A. (2003). Longitudinal study of skipping breakfast and weight change in adolescents, *International Journal of Obesity, 27*, 1258–1266.

Berndt, T., Hawkins, J., & Jiao, Z. (1999). Influences of friends and friendships on adjustment to junior high school. *Merrill-Palmer Quarterly, 45*, 13–41.

Best, K. M., Hauser, S. T., & Allen, J. P. (1997). Predicting young adult competencies: Adolescent era parent and individual influences. *Journal of Adolescent Research, 12*, 90–112.

Bishop, J. H., Bishop, M., Gelbwasser, L., Green, S., & Zuckerman, A. (2003). Nerds and freaks: A theory of student culture and norms. *Brookings Papers on Education Policy*, 141–199.

Blum, R. W., McNeely, C. A., & Rinehart, P. M. (2002). *Improving the odds: The untapped power of schools to improve the health of teens*. Minneapolis: Center for Adolescent Health and Development, University of Minnesota.

Blyth, D. A., Simmons, R. G., Bulcroft, R., Felt, D., Van Cleave, E. F., & Bush, D. M. (1981). The effects of physical development in self-image and satisfaction with body image for early adolescent males. *Research in the Community and Mental Health, 2*, 43–73.

Bomar, J. A., & Sabatelli, R. M. (1996). Family system dynamics, gender, and psychosocial maturity in late adolescence. *Journal of Adolescent Research, 1*, 421–439.

Bradmetz, J. (1999). Precursors of formal thought: A longitudinal study. *British Journal of Developmental Psychology, 17*, 61–81.

Bronfenbrenner, U. (1979). *The ecology of human development*. Cambridge, MA: Harvard.

Bronfenbrenner, U., & Morris, P. A. (1998). The ecology of developmental processes. In W. Damon (Series Ed.) & R. Lerner (Vol. Ed.), *Handbook of child psychology: Vol. 1. Theory* (5th ed., pp. 993–1028). New York: Wiley.

Brook, J., Brook, D., Gordon, A., Whiteman, M., & Cohen, P. (1990). The psychosocial etiology of adolescent drug use: A family interactional approach. *Genetic, Social, and General Psychology Monographs, 116*.

Brook, J., Cohen, P., & Brook, D. (1998). Longitudinal study of co-occurring psychiatric disorders and substance use. *Journal of the American Academy of Child and Adolescent Psychiatry, 37*, 322–330.

Brown, B. B. (2004). Adolescents' relationships with peers. In R. M. Lerner & L. Steinberg (Eds.), *Handbook of adolescent psychology* (2nd ed., pp. 363–394). New York: Wiley.

Bryant, C. M. (2006). Pathways linking early experiences and later relationship functioning. In A. C. Crouter & A. Booth (Eds.), *Romance and sex in adolescence and emerging adulthood* (pp.103–112). Mahwah, NJ: Erlbaum.

Carskadon, M. A. (1999). When worlds collide: Adolescent need for sleep versus societal demands. *Phi Delta Kappan, 80*, 348–353.

Catsambis, S. (2001). Expanding knowledge of parental involvement in children's secondary education: Connections with high school seniors' academic success. *Social Psychology of Education, 5*, 149–177.

Cavanagh, S. E., Riegle-Crumb, C., Crosnoe, R. (2007). Puberty and the education of girls. *Social Psychology Quarterly, 70*, 186–198.

Chapell, M. S., & Overton, W. F. (1998). Development of logical reasoning in the context of parental style and test anxiety. *Merrill-Palmer Quarterly, 44*, 141–156.

Chapell, M. S., & Overton, W. F. (2002). Development of logical reasoning and the school performance of African American adolescent in relation to socioeconomic status, ethnic identity, and self-esteem. *Journal of Black Psychology, 28*, 295–317.

Chassin, L., Pitts, S. C., & DeLucia, C. (1999). The relation of adolescent substance use to young adult autonomy, positive activity involvement, and perceived competence. *Development and Psychopathology, 11*, 915–932.

Christenson, S. (2004). The school-family partnership: An opportunity to promote the learning competence of all students. *School Psychology Review, 33*, 83–104.

Cole, D., Martin, J., Peeke, L., Seroczynski, A., & Fier, J. (1999). Children's over- and underestimation of academic competence: A longitudinal study of gender differences, depression, and anxiety. *Child Development, 70*, 459–473.

Coley, R. L., & Chase-Lansdale, P. L. (1998). Adolescent pregnancy and parenthood: Recent evidence and future directions. *American Psychologist, 53,* 152–166.

Collins, W. A., Laurson, B., Mortensen, N., Luebker, C., & Ferreira, M. (1997). Conflict processes and transitions in parent and peer relationships: Implications for autonomy and regulation. *Journal of Adolescent Research, 12,* 178–198.

Connell, J. P., & Wellborn, J. G. (1991). Competence, autonomy, and relatedness: A motivational analysis of self-esteem processes. In M. R. Gunnar, & L. A. Sroufe (Eds.), *Self processes and development. The Minnesota symposia on child psychology* (Vol. 23, pp. 43–77). Hillsdale, NJ: Erlbaum.

Crawford, T. N., Cohen, P., Midlarsky, E., & Brook, J. (2001). Internalizing symptoms in adolescents: Gender differences in vulnerability to parental distress and discord. *Journal of Research on Adolescence, 11,* 95–118.

Crosnoe, R., Erickson, K. G., & Dornbusch, S. M. (2002). Protective functions of family relationships and school factors on the deviant behavior of adolescent boys and girls: Reducing the impact of risky relationships. *Youth & Society, 33,* 515–544.

Crosnoe, R., & Muller, C. (2004). Body mass index, academic achievement, and school context: Examining the educational experiences of adolescents at risk of obesity. *Journal of Health and Social Behavior, 45,* 393–407.

Dahl, R. E., & Carskadon, M. A. (1995). Sleep and its disorders in adolescence. In R. Ferber & M. H. Kryger (Eds.), *Principles and practice of sleep medicine in the child* (pp. 19–27). Philadelphia: Saunders.

Davies, P. L., & Rose, J. D. (1999). Assessment of cognitive development in adolescents by means of neuropsychological tasks. *Developmental Neuropsychology, 15,* 227–248.

Diamond, A. (2002). Normal development of the prefrontal cortex from birth to young adulthood: Cognitive functions, anatomy and biochemistry. In D. T. Stuss & R. T. Knight (Eds.), *Principles of frontal lobe function* (pp. 466–503). London: Oxford University Press.

Donnellan, M. B., Ge, X., & Wenk, E. (2000). Cognitive abilities in adolescence-limited and life-course-persistent offenders. *Journal of Abnormal Psychology, 109,* 396–402.

Dubas, J. S., Graber, J. A., & Petersen, A. C. (1991). The effects of pubertal development on achievement during adolescence. *American Journal of Education, 99,* 444–460.

Durbin, D. L., Darling, N., Steinberg, L., & Brown, B. B. (1993). Parenting style and peer group membership among European-American adolescents. *Journal of Research on Adolescence, 3,* 87–100.

Dweck, C. S. (1999). *Self-theories: Their role in motivation, personality, and development.* Philadelphia: Psychology Press.

Dweck, C. S. (2002). The development of ability conceptions. In A. Wigfield & J. S. Eccles (Eds.), *Development of achievement motivation* (pp. 57–88). New York: Academic Press.

Dweck, C. S., & Sorich, L. (1999). Mastery-oriented thinking. In C. R. Snyder (Ed.), *Coping* (pp. 232–251). New York: Oxford University Press.

Eccles, J. S., & Barber, B. L. (1999). Student council, volunteering, basketball, or marching band: What kind of extracurricular involvement matters? *Journal of Adolescent Research, 14,* 10–43.

Eccles, J., Barber, B., Jozefowicz, D., Malenchuk, O., & Vida, M. (2000). Self-evaluations of competence, task values, and self-esteem. In N. Johnson, M. Roberts, & J. Worrell (Eds.), *Girls and adolescence* (pp. 53–84). Washington, DC: American Psychological Association.Press.

Eccles, J. S., Midgley, C., Wigfield, A., Buchanan, C. M., Reuman, D., Ranagan, C., & Maclver, D. (1993). Development during adolescence: The impact of stage-environment fit on young adolescents' experiences in schools and in families. *American Psychologist, 48,* 90–101.

Eccles, J., Roeser, R., Wigfield, A., & Freedman-Doan, C. (1999). Academic and motivational pathways through middle childhood. In L. Balter & C. Tamis-LeMonda (Eds.), *Child psychology: A handbook of contemporary issues* (pp. 287–317). Philadelphia: Psychology Press.

Eccles, J. S., Wigfield, A., & Schiefele, U. (1998). Motivation to succeed. In N. Eisenberg (Ed.), *Handbook of child psychology: Vol. 3. Social, emotional, and personality development* (5th ed., pp. 1017–1095). New York: Wiley.

Ellickson, P., Saner, H., & McGuigan, K. A., (1997). Profiles of violent youth: Substance use and other concurrent problems. *American Journal of Public Health, 87,* 985–991.

Epstein, J. L. (1983). Longitudinal effects of person-school-family-interactions on student outcomes. In A. Kerckhoff (Ed.), *Research in sociology of education and socialization: Vol. 4* (pp. 101–128). Greenwich, CT: JAI Press.

Falkner, N. H., Neumark-Sztainer, D., Story, M., Jeffery, R. W., Beuhring, T., & Resnick, M. D. (2001). Social, educational, and psychological correlates of weight status in adolescents. *Obesity Research, 9,* 32–42.

Feldlaufer, H., Midgley, C., & Eccles, J. S. (1988). Student, teacher, and observer perceptions of the classroom environment before and after the transition to junior high school. *Journal of Early Adolescence, 8,* 133–156.

Feldman, A. F., & Matjasko, J. L. (2005). The role of school-based extracurricular activities in adolescent development: A comprehensive review and future directions. *Review of Educational Research, 75*, 159–210.

Fontaine, K., Redden, D., Wang, C., Westfall, A., & Allison, D. (2003). Years of life lost due to obesity. *Journal of the American Medical Association, 289*, 187–193.

Fox, M. A., Connolly, B. A., & Snyder, T. D. (2006). *Youth indicators, 2005: Trends in the well-being of American youth* (NCES Publication No. 2005-050). Washington, DC: National Center for Education Statistics, U.S. Department of Education, Institute of Education Sciences. Available at http://nces.ed.gov/pubsearch/pubsinfo.asp?pubid=2005050

Fredriksen, K., Rhodes, J., Reddy, R., & Way, N. (2004). Sleepless in Chicago: Tracking the effects of adolescent sleep loss during the middle school years. *Child Development, 75*, 84–95.

Fuchs, L. S., Fuchs, D., Hamlett, C. L., Phillips, N. B., & Bentz, J. (1994). Classwide curriculum-based measurement: Helping general educators meet the challenge of student diversity. *Exceptional Children, 60*, 518–537.

Furman, W., & Shaffer, L. (2003). The role of romantic relationships in adolescent development. In P. Florsheim (Ed.), *Adolescent romantic relationships and sexual behavior* (pp. 3–22). Mahwah, NJ: Erlbaum.

Furman, W., & Wehner, E. A. (1997). Adolescent romantic relationships: A developmental perspective. In S. Shulman & W. A. Collins (Eds.), *Romantic relationships in adolescence: Developmental perspectives* (pp. 21–36). San Francisco: Jossey-Bass.

Garber, J., & Little, S. A. (2001). Emotional autonomy and adolescent adjustment. *Journal of Adolescent Research, 16*, 355–371.

Ge, X., Conger, R. D., & Elder, G. H., Jr. (2001). The relation between puberty and psychological distress in boys. *Journal of Research on Adolescence, 11*, 49–70.

Goodenow, J. (1995). Differentiating among social contexts: By spatial features, forms of participation, and social contracts. In P. Moen, G. H. Elder Jr., & K. Luschner (Eds.), *Examining lives in context: Perspective on the ecology of human development* (pp. 269–302). Washington, DC: American Psychological Association.

Gortmaker, S. L., Must, A., Perrin, J. M., Sobol, A., & Dietz, W. H. (1993). Social and economic consequences of overweight in adolescence and young adulthood. *New England Journal of Medicine, 329*, 1008–1012.

Gottfried, A. E., Fleming, J. S., & Gottfried, A. W. (2001). Continuity of academic intrinsic motivation from childhood through late adolescence: A longitudinal study. *Journal of Educational Psychology, 93*, 3–13.

Graber, J. A. (2004). Internalizing problems during adolescence. In R. M. Lerner & L. Steinberg (Eds.), *Handbook of adolescent psychology* (2nd ed., pp. 587–626). New York: Wiley.

Graham, S. (1994). Motivation in African Americans. *Review of Educational Research, 64*(1), 55–117.

Graham, S., Taylor, A., & Hudley, C. (1998). Exploring achievement values among ethnic minority early adolescents. *Journal of Educational Psychology, 90*, 606–620.

Granger, R. C. (2008). After-school programs and academics: Implications for policy, practice, and research. *Society for Research on Child Development Social Policy Report: Giving Child and Youth Development Knowledge Away, XXII*(2),1–20.

Grolnick, W. S., Benjet, C., Kurowski, C. O., & Apostoleris, N. H. (1997). Predictors of parent involvement in children's schooling. *Journal of Educational Psychology, 89*, 538–548.

Gunnell, D., Frankel, S., Nanchahal, K., Peters, T., & Davey Smith, G. (1998). Childhood obesity and adult cardiovascular mortality: A 57-year follow-up study based on the Boyd Orr cohort. *American Journal of Clinical Nutrition, 67*, 1111–1118.

Gutman, L. M., Sameroff, A. J., & Eccles, J. S. (2002). The academic achievement of African American students during early adolescence: An examination of multiple risk, promotive, and protective factors. *American Journal of Community Psychology, 30*, 367–400.

Halperin, S. (1998). *The forgotten half revisited: American youth and young families: 1988–2008.* Washington, DC: American Youth Policy Forum.

Hao, L., & Cherlin, A. J. (2004). Welfare reform and teenage pregnancy, childbirth, and school dropout. *Journal of Marriage and Family, 66*, 179–194.

Harari, O., & Covington, M. V. (1981). Reactions to achievement behavior from a teacher and student perspective: A developmental analysis. *American Educational Research Journal, 18*, 15–28.

Hardre, P. L., & Reeve, J. (2003). A motivational model of rural students' intentions to persist in, versus drop out of, high school. *Journal of Educational Psychology, 95*, 347–356.

Harter, S., & Jackson, B. K. (1992). Trait vs. nontrait conceptualizations of intrinsic/extrinsic motivational orientation. *Motivation and Emotion, 16*, 209–230.

Hedley, A., Ogden, C., Johnson, C., Carroll, M., Curtin, L., & Flegal, K. (2004). Prevalence of overweight and obesity among US children, adolescents, and adults, 1999–2002. *Journal of the American Medical Association, 291*, 2847–2850.

Herman, M. R., Dornbusch, S. M., Herron, M. C., & Herting, J. R. (1997). The influence of family regulation, connection, and psychological autonomy on six measures of adolescent functioning. *Journal of Adolescent Research, 12*, 34–67.

Hoeksma, J. B., Oosterlaan, J., & Schipper, E. M. (2004). Emotion regulation and the dynamics of feelings: A conceptual and methodological framework. *Child Development, 75*, 354–360.

Iannotti, R. J., & Bush, P. J. (1992). Perceived versus actual friends' use of alcohol, cigarettes, marijuana, and cocaine: Which has the most influence? *Journal of Youth and Adolescence, 21*, 375–389.

Jacobs, J. E., Lanza, S., Osgood, D. W., Eccles, J. S., & Wigfield, A. (2002). Changes in children's self-competence and values: Gender and domain differences across grades one through twelve. *Child Development, 73*, 509–527.

Jeglum-Bartusch, D., Lynam, D., Moffitt, T. E., & Silva, P. A. (1997). Is age important: Testing general versus developmental theories of antisocial behavior. *Criminology, 35*, 13–47.

Jessor, R., Donovan, J., & Costa, F. (1991). *Beyond adolescence: Problem behavior and young adult development.* Cambridge: Cambridge University Press.

Jeynes, W. H. (2003). A meta-analysis: The effects of parental involvement on minority children's academic achievement. *Education and Urban Society, 35*, 202–218.

Johnson, M. H. (2001). Functional brain development in humans. *Nature Reviews Neuroscience, 2*, 475–483.

Johnston, L. D., O'Malley, P. M., Bachman, J. G., & Schllenberg, J. E. (2004). *Monitoring the Future: National results on adolescent drug use: Overview of key findings, 2003* (NIH Publications No. 04-5506). Bethesda, MD: National Institute on Drug Abuse.

Keating , D. P. (1990). Adolescent thinking. In S. S. Feldman & G. R. Elliot (Eds.), *At the threshold: The developing adolescent* (pp. 54–90). Cambridge, MA: Harvard University Press.

Keating, D. P. (2004). Cognitive and brain development. In R. M. Lerner & L. Steinberg (Eds.), *Handbook of adolescent psychology* (2nd ed., pp. 45–84). New York: Wiley.

Kovacs, M., & Devlin, B. (1998). Internalizing disorders in childhood. *Journal of Child Psychology and Psychiatry, 39*, 47–63.

Kwon, Y. J., & Lawson, A. E. (2000). Linking brain growth with the development of scientific reasoning ability and conceptual change during adolescence. *Journal of Research in Science and Teaching, 37*, 44–62.

Laberge, L., Petit, D., Simard, C., Vitaro, F., Tremblay, R. E., & Montplaisir, J. (2001). Development of sleep patterns in early adolescence. *Journal of Sleep Research, 10*, 59–67.

Larson, R., & Lampman-Petraitis, C. (1989). Daily emotional states as reported by children and adolescents. *Child Development, 60*, 1250–1260.

Lee, K., & Freire, A. (2003). Cognitive development. In A. Slater & G. Bremner (Eds.), *An introduction to developmental psychology* (pp. 359–387). Malden, MA: Blackwell.

Leigh, B. C., & Stall, R. (1993). Substance use and risky sexual behavior for exposure to HIV: Issues in methodology, interpretation, and prevention. *American Psychologist, 48*, 1035–1045.

Lepper, M. R., Corpus, J. H., & Iyengar, S. S. (2005). Intrinsic and extrinsic motivational orientations in the classroom: Age differences and academic correlates. *Journal of Educational Psychology, 97*, 184–196.

Leventhal, T., & Brooks-Gunn, J. (2003). Children and youth in neighborhood contexts. *Current Directions in Psychological Science, 12*, 27–31.

Levesque, R. J. (1993). The romantic experience of adolescents in satisfying love relationships. *Journal of Youth and Adolescence, 22*, 219–251.

Lohman, B. J. (2000). *School and family contexts: Relationship to coping with conflict during the individuation process.* Doctoral dissertation, The Ohio State University.

Lohman, B. J., Kaura, S. A., & Newman, B. (2007). Matched or mismatched environments? The relationship of family and school differentiation to adolescents' psychosocial adjustment. *Youth & Society, 39*, 3–32.

Luster, S. A., & Small, T. (1994). Factors associated with sexual risk-taking behaviors among adolescents. *Journal of Marriage and the Family, 56*, 622–632.

Maccoby, E. (1990). Gender and relationships: A developmental account. *American Psychologist, 45*, 513–520.

Mahoney, J., & Bergman, L. (2002). Conceptual and methodological considerations in a developmental approach to the study of positive adaptation. *Applied Developmental Psychology, 23*, 195–217.

Mahoney, J. L., Cairns, B. D., & Farmer, T. W. (2003). Promoting interpersonal competence and educational success through extracurricular activity participation. *Journal of Educational Psychology, 95*, 409–418.

Manlove, J. (1998). The influence of high school dropout and school disengagement on the risk of school-age pregnancy. *Journal of Research on Adolescence, 8*, 187–220.

Masten, A. S., Roisman, G. I., Long, J. D., Burt, K. B., Obradovic, J., Riley, J. R., et al. (2005). Developmental cascades: Linking academic achievement and externalizing and internalizing symptoms over 20 years. *Developmental Psychology, 41*, 733–746.

Maughan, B., Rowe, R., Loeber, R., & Stouthamer-Loeber, M. (2003). Reading problems and depressed mood. *Journal of Abnormal Child Psychology, 31*, 50–59.

Mayo, M. W., & Christenfeld, N. (1999). Gender, race, and performance expectations of college students. *Journal of Multicultural Counseling & Development, 27*, 93–104.

McCarron, G. P., & Inkelas, K. K. (2006). The gap between educational aspirations and attainment for first-generation college students and the role of parental involvement. *Journal of College Student Development, 47*, 534–549.

McNeal, R. B., Jr. (1998). High school extracurricular activities: Closed structures and stratifying patterns of participation. *Journal of Education Research, 91*, 183–191.

Meece, J. L., Glienke, B. B., & Burg, S. (2006). Gender and motivation. *Journal of School Psychology, 44*, 351–373.

Midgely, C., & Urdan, T. (1995). Predictors of middle school students' use of self-handicapping strategies. *Journal of Early Adolescence, 15*, 389–411.

Miller, P. H. (2002). *Theories of developmental psychology* (4th ed.). New York: Worth.

Moffitt, T. E. (1997). Adolescence-limited and life-course-persistent offending: A complementary pair of developmental theories. In T. Thornberry (Ed.), *Advances in criminological theory: Developmental theories of crime and delinquency* (pp. 11–54). London: Transaction Press.

Moffitt, T. E., & Caspi, A. (2001). Childhood predictors differentiate life-course persistent and adolescence-limited antisocial pathways among males and females. *Development & Psychopathology, 13*, 355–375.

Moffitt, T. E., Caspi, A., Harrington, H., & Milne, B. J. (2002). Males on the life-course-persistent and adolescence-limited antisocial pathways: Follow-up at age 26 years. *Development & Psychopathology, 14*, 179–207.

Mortimer, J. T., & Johnson, M. K. (1999). Adolescent part-time work and postsecondary transition pathways in the United States. In W. R. Heinz (Ed.), *From education to work: Cross-national perspectives* (pp. 111–148). New York: Cambridge University Press.

Murry, V. M., Hurt, T. R., Kogan, S. M., & Luo, Z. (2006). Contextual processes of romantic relationships: Plausible explanations for gender and race effects. In A. C. Crouter & A. Booth (Eds), *Romance and sex in adolescence and emerging adulthood* (pp. 151–160). Mahwah, NJ: Erlbaum.

Newcomb, M., & Bentler, P. (1988). *Consequences of adolescent drug use: Impact on the lives of young adults.* Newbury Park, CA: Sage.

Newman, B. M., Lohman, B. J., & Newman, P. R. (2007). Peer group membership and a sense of belonging: Their relationship to adolescent behavior problems. *Adolescence, 42*, 241–263.

Newman, B. M., & Newman, P. R. (2001). Group identity and alienation: Giving the WE its due. *Journal of Youth and Adolescence, 30*, 515–538.

Oakes, J. (1990). Opportunities, achievement, and choice: Women and minority students in science and math. *Review of Research in Education, 16*, 153–222.

Ogbu, J. U. (2003). *Black American students in an affluent suburb: A study of academic disengagement.* Mahwah, NJ: Erlbaum.

Ogden, C., Carroll, M., Curtin, L., McDowell, M., Tabak, C., & Flegal, K. (2006). Prevalence of overweight and obesity in the United States, 1999–2004. *Journal of the American Medical Association, 29*, 1549–1555.

O'Neil, J. M., Ohlde, C., Tollefson, N., Barke, C., Piggott, T., & Watts, D. (1980). Factors, correlates, and problem areas affecting career decision making of a cross-sectional sample of students. *Journal of Counseling Psychology, 27*, 571–580.

Pajares, F., & Johnson, M. J. (1996). Self-efficacy beliefs in the writing of high school students: A path analysis. *Psychology in the Schools, 33*, 163–175.

Pajares, F., & Kranzler, J. (1995). Self-efficacy beliefs and general mental ability in mathematical problem solving. *Contemporary Educational Psychology, 20*, 426–443.

Pearson, J., Muller, C., & Wilkinson, L. (2007). Adolescent same-sex attraction and academic outcomes: The role of school attachment and engagement. *Social Problems, 54*, 523–542.

Perosa, L. M., Persoa, S. L., & Tam, H. P. (1996). The contribution of family structure and differentiation to identity development in females. *Journal of Youth and Adolescence, 25*(6), 817–837.

Perosa, L. M., Perosa, S. L., & Tam, H. P. (2002). Intergenerational systems theory and identity development in young adult women. *Journal of Adolescent Research, 17*, 235–259.

Petersen, A. C., Compas, B. E., Brooks-Gunn, J., Stemmler, M., Ey, S., & Grant K. E. (1993). Depression in adolescence. *American Psychologist, 48*, 155–168.

Petta, D., Carskadon, M., & Dement, W. (1984). Sleep habits in children aged 7–13. *Sleep Research, 13,* 86.

Piaget, J. (1972). Intellectual evolution from adolescence to adulthood. *Human Development, 15,* 1–12.

Pong, S., Hao, L., & Gardner, E. (2005). The roles of parenting styles and social capital in the school performance of immigrant Asian and Hispanic adolescents. *Social Science Quarterly, 86,* 928–950.

Rankin, B., & Quane, J. M. (2002). Social contexts and urban adolescent outcomes: The interrelated effects of neighborhoods, families, and peers on African-American youth. *Social Problems, 49,* 79–100.

Resnick, M., Harris, J., & Blum, R. W. (1993). *The impact of caring and connectedness on adolescent health and well-being.* Children Youth and Family Consortium Electronic Clearinghouse.

Richards, M. H., & Larson, R. (1993). Pubertal development and the daily subjective states of young adolescents. *Journal of Research on Adolescence, 3,* 145–169.

Rodriguez, J. L. (2002). Family environment and achievement among three generations of Mexican American high school students. *Applied Developmental Science, 6,* 88–94.

Roeser, R. W., & Eccles, J. S. (1998). Adolescents' perceptions of middle school: Relation to longitudinal changes in academic and psychological adjustment. *Journal of Research on Adolescence, 8,* 123–158.

Ryan, R. M., & Deci, E. L. (2000a). Intrinsic and extrinsic motivation: Classic definitions and new directions. *Contemporary Educational Psychology, 25,* 54–67.

Ryan, R. M., & Deci, E. L. (2000b). Self-determination theory and the facilitation of intrinsic motivation, social development, and well-being. *American Psychologist, 55,* 68–78.

Ryan, R. M., Deci, E. L., & Grolnick, W. S. (1995). Autonomy, relatedness, and the self: Their relation to development and psychopathology. In D. Cicchetti, & D. J. Cohen (Eds.), *Developmental psychopathology, Vol. 1: Theory and methods* (pp. 618–655). Oxford, England: Wiley.

Ryan, R. M., Stiller, J. D., & Lynch, J. H. (1994). Representations of relationships to teachers, parents, and friends as predictors of academic motivation and self-esteem. *Journal of Early Adolescence, 14,* 226–249.

Snyder, A. R. (2006). Risky and casual sexual relationships among teens. In A. C. Crouter & A. Booth (Eds.), *Romance and sex in adolescence and emerging adulthood* (pp. 161–169). Mahwah, NJ: Erlbaum.

Snyder, A. R., & McLaughlin, D. K. (2004). Female headed families and poverty in rural American. *Rural Sociology, 69,* 127–149.

Steinberg, L. (1990). Autonomy, conflict, and harmony in the family relationship. In S. S. Feldman & G. R. Elliott (Eds.), *At the threshold: The developing adolescent* (pp. 255–276). Cambridge, MA: Harvard University Press.

Steinberg, L. (2005). Cognitive and affective development in adolescence. *Trends in Cognitive Sciences, 9,* 69–74.

Steinberg, L., Bradford, B., & Dornbusch, S. (1996). *Beyond the classroom: Why school reform has failed and what parents need to do.* New York: Simon & Schuster.

Steinberg, L., & Dornbusch, S. M. (1991). Negative correlates of part-time employment during adolescence: Replication and elaboration. *Developmental Psychology, 27,* 304–313.

Sternberg, R. J., & Grigorenko, E. L. (2001). Degree of embeddedness of ecological systems as a measure of ease of adaptation to the environment. In E. L. Grigorenko & R. J. Sternberg (Eds.), *Family environment and intellectual functioning: A lifespan perspective* (pp. 243–262). Mahwah, NJ: Erlbaum.

Stipek, D. (2002). *Motivation to learn: Integrating theory and practice* (4th ed.). Boston: Allyn & Bacon.

Susman, E. J., & Rogol, A. (2004). Puberty and psychological development. In R. M. Lerner & L. Steinberg (Eds.), *Handbook of adolescent psychology* (2nd ed., pp. 15–44). New York: Wiley.

Swail, W. S., Cabrera, A. F., & Lee, C. (2004). *Latino youth and the pathway to college.* Washington, DC: Educational Policy Institutes, Inc. Available at http://www.educationalpolicy.org/pdf/Latino_Youth.pdf.

Taras, H., & Potts-Datema, W. (2005). Obesity and student performance and school. *Journal of School Health, 75,* 291–295.

Taylor, R. D., & Oskay, G. (1995). Identity formation in Turkish and American late adolescents. *Journal of Cross-Cultural Psychology, 26,* 8–22.

Tenenbaum, H. R., Porche, M. V., Snow, C. E., Tabors, P., & Ross, S. (2007). Maternal and child predictors of low-income children's educational attainment. *Journal of Applied Developmental Psychology, 28,* 227–238.

Tomarken, A. J., Dichter, G. S., Garber, J., & Simien, C. (2004). Resisting frontal brain activity: Linkages to maternal depression and socio-economic status among adolescents. *Biological Psychology, 67,* 77–102.

Torbert, W. R. (1994). Cultivating postformal adult development: Higher stages and contrasting interventions. In M.E. Miller & S. R. Cook-Greuter (Eds.), *Transcendence and mature thought in adulthood: The further reaches of adult development* (pp. 181–203). Lanham, MD: Rowman & Littlefield.

U.S. Census Bureau (2003). *Statistical Abstract of the United States, 2003.* Washington DC: U.S. Government Printing Office.

van Laar, C. (2000). The paradox of low academic achievement but high self-esteem in African American students: An attributional account. *Educational Psychology Review, 12,* 33–61.

Wichstrom, L. (2001). The impact of pubertal timing on adolescents' alcohol use. *Journal of Research on Adolescence, 11,* 131–150.

Wigfield, A., & Eccles, J. S. (2000). Expectancy-value theory of achievement motivation. *Contemporary Educational Psychology, 25,* 68–81.

Wigfield, A., Eccles, J., & Pintrich, P. (1996). Development between the ages of 11 and 25. In D. Berliner & R. Calfee (Eds.), *Handbook of educational psychology* (pp. 148–185). New York: MacMillan.

Wigfield, A., Eccles, J., Yoon, K., Harold, R., Arbreton, A., Freedman-Doan, C., & Blumenfeld, P. (1997). Changes in children's competence beliefs and subjective task values across the elementary school years: A three-year study. *Journal of Educational Psychology, 89,* 451–469.

Williams, J. M., & Currie, C. (2000). Self-esteem and physical development in early adolescence: Pubertal timing and body image. *Journal of Early Adolescence, 20,* 129–149.

Wolkfson, A. R., & Carskadon, M. (2003). Understanding adolescent's sleep patterns and school performance: A critical appraisal. *Sleep Medicine Reviews, 7,* 491–506.

Yan, B., & Slagle, M. (2007). What has research told us about school schedule, sleep time, and student achievement? [Electronic version] *Teachers College Record.* Retrieved from http://www.tcrecord.org ID number: 14030

Youniss, J., Bales, S., Christmas-Best, V., Diversi, M., McLaughlin, M., & Silbereisen, R. (2002). Youth civic engagement in the twenty-first century. *Journal of Research on Adolescence, 12,* 121–148.

Zahn-Waxler, C., Klimes-Dougan, B., & Slattery, M. J. (2000). Internalizing problems of childhood and adolescence: Prospects, pitfalls, and progress in understanding the development of anxiety and depression. *Development and Psychopathology, 12,* 443–466.

# III

## Driving the Research Agenda to Inform Policy and Practice

# 15

## DEBUNKING THE MYTH
## OF THE HARD-TO-REACH PARENT

### KAREN L. MAPP AND SOO HONG

Over the past 10 years, I (first author) have been fortunate to have the opportunity to travel around the country conducting professional development workshops for district leadership teams, principals, teachers, and other school staff on how to cultivate and sustain meaningful partnerships with the families of the students in their schools and districts. I often begin my workshops by asking, "What would you most like to learn about home-school partnerships? What would be the most important 'take-aways' for you?"

Invariably, participants state, "We hope that you will help us learn how to reach our 'hard-to-reach' families: those that never seem to get involved in their children's education. We have a number of parents [in this article, the term "parent" refers to any adult caretaker] who just don't seem to care about their children's education, and they are impossible to reach. We'd like a list of things we can do to get these families to respond." I probe this response by asking, "Whom do you mean when you say 'hard to reach'? How would you describe the families that fit into this category?" Participants' answers usually fall into one or more of the following categories:

- Poor families
- Families with limited levels of formal education
- Families of color
- Families whose first language is not English
- Recent immigrants

Many of the educators who come to my workshops have indeed tried various strategies to engage families. They are frustrated that their efforts have failed to attract the very families that they are most often trying to reach. Some state that they have "tried everything" to connect with families, and after numerous failed attempts they conclude that these families "just don't care." Pen and paper at the ready, participants are hopeful that

I will tick off a laundry list of easy-to-implement steps to solve this "technical problem" of hard-to-reach parents. Technical problems, according to Heifetz and Linsky (2002), are those that can be solved with current know-how, strategies, and procedures.

What I propose to participants falls outside the realm of easy or quick fixes. Instead, we begin to address this problem as an adaptive and systemic challenge, one that will require experimentation, discovery, and changes in their attitudes and beliefs when working to cultivate partnerships with families (Heifetz & Linsky, 2002). We explore how school culture—the values, norms, expectations, and beliefs about families and their engagement—is usually what stands in the way of our ability to connect with all families and to develop systemic, sustaining family engagement initiatives (Henderson, Johnson, Mapp, & Davies, 2007; Schlechty, 2000).

## OVERVIEW

In this chapter, we challenge the notion that families are hard to reach and uncaring about their children's education. It is critical to acknowledge that for reasons such as mental, physical, and economic distress, some families are indeed overwhelmed and hard-pressed to support the educational well-being of their children. This hard-to-reach net, however, is cast over large groups of families, especially those who are of color, poor, economically distressed, limited English speakers, and/or immigrants. Many of the current parent involvement practices, programs, and policies employed by schools, districts, and other educational entities are based on outdated and inappropriate definitions of family engagement. This results in a fundamental disconnect between what is designed and offered and what families want or need (Jackson & Remillard, 2005; Valdés, 1996). In other words, it is our institutions and the programs, practices, and policies that school personnel design that are "hard to reach," not the families. This chapter offers reasons schools are hard to reach for families and describes a partnership paradigm represented by a parent mentor program. The chapter ends with recommendations drawn from implementation of the parent mentor program that explains how schools can reach out to all families.

## REASONS INSTITUTIONS ARE HARD TO REACH FOR FAMILIES

### Reason One: Incompatible Core Beliefs for Engaging Families

Most educators agree that home-school partnerships are important. The reality is, however, that educators harbor many beliefs, attitudes, and fears about parents that hinder their ability to cultivate partnerships with families (Diamond & Gomez, 2004). From their conversations with district leaders, principals, teachers, school staff, and parents, Henderson and colleagues (2007) identified four core beliefs that are vital for cultivating and sustaining partnerships with families and for breaking down the hard-to-reach institutional dynamic. In schools that embrace partnership with families, these four beliefs infuse every aspect of the school culture and environment:

- Core Belief One: All parents have dreams for their children and want the best for them. It is vital for educators to believe that the families who send their children to them each day want their children to succeed in school and in life. Some parents, because of stressful life circumstances, may act in ways that lead school staff to wonder if they truly value education. We know from the research on family engagement that irrespective of racial, ethnic, socioeconomic, or educational status, all families are concerned about their children's education and value the role education plays in increasing the chances that their children will lead productive and fulfilling lives (Berla, Henderson, & National Committee for Citizens in Education, 1994; Henderson & Mapp, 2002). Sara Lawrence-Lightfoot, in her book *The Essential Conversation*, stated that *all* parents "harbor a large wish list of dreams and aspirations for their youngsters. All families care deeply about their children's education and hope that their progeny will be happier, more productive, and more successful than they have been in their lives" (2003, p. 109). To make authentic connections with families and to maintain and cultivate partnerships, school staff must embrace the core belief that families do have positive dreams and aspirations for their children. This core belief serves as the foundation for building partnerships with families, and it is therefore the most important of the four (Henderson et al., 2007).

- Core Belief Two: All families have the capacity to support their children's learning. Regardless of a family's income status, level of formal education, or racial or ethnic background, all parents can contribute to and support their children's learning (Delgado-Gaitan, 2001). Parents' knowledge, histories, talents, and work and life experiences give them the tools and capacity to support and encourage their children in school (Moll, Amanti, & Neff, 1992). The level and nature of this support will vary from family to family, and school staff can respectfully enhance families' capacity to support children's learning. When approached in a respectful manner that acknowledges and honors what families are already doing, families will partner with school staff to support children's learning (Valdés, 1996). Too often, our educational institutions assume that families have nothing to offer or contribute to children's learning and this ignore families' "intellectual funds of knowledge" (Moll et al., 1992). When families' pick up cues from staff that their ways of contributing to their children's education are being ignored, disrespected, and not valued, they understandably disconnect.

- Core Belief Three: Parents and school staff should be equal partners. Relationships between educational institutions and families are often built on a lopsided power base, where educators are seen as the degreed "professionals" who have all of the power to make decisions about the educational trajectory of children (Bryk & Schneider, 2002). Sometimes families from lower socioeconomic circumstances, who speak little English or who themselves had negative experiences in school, are intimidated or suspicious of school personnel. School cultures often exacerbate these feelings of intimidation and distrust by maintaining asymmetrical power relationships between parents and staff. Rather than supporting and encouraging parental voice and advocacy, educators often balk at families' attempts to learn about school protocols, policies, and procedures, fearful that parents' acquisition of this knowledge will lead to school and district staff losing power (Davies, 2001).

Rudy Crew (2007), in his book *Only Connect*, discussed the need for partnerships between school and home, where both groups share power and responsibility for children's learning:

> Good principals and teachers find it easier to work with strong, organized parents who know what they want and who operate with a sense of their power both as individuals and as a group ... Most high-functioning schools have high-functioning parent leadership integrated into the workings of the school that go well beyond bake sales and helping out on field trips. And underneath it all will be a structured yet open communication between parents and administration—in short, a partnership, challenging but not adversarial ... with the four qualities of mature and conscious contributors to society. (p. 155)

Crew went on to say:

> In many ways, schools and homes have to operate as one unit. They don't have to agree that the same things are important, but they have to respect and support each other's values and clearly communicate that to the kids. (p. 157)

Crew (2007) also discussed the need for educators to cultivate more "demand parents"—those who can serve as equal partners with school staff to support education while also advocating for the best educational opportunities for their and other's children. In the Miami-Dade (Fla.) Public School District, Crew has initiated the Parent Academy program, which offers various courses on education topics identified by parents. In the past two years, nearly 100,000 parents, many of whom fit the hard-to-reach description discussed at the beginning of this chapter, have attended Parent Academy workshops.

- Core Belief Four: The responsibility for building partnerships between school and home rests primarily with school staff, especially school leaders. Because of the aforementioned asymmetrical power dynamic that exists between families and school staff, it is necessary for school personnel to take the first step to build partnership with families (Crew, 2007; Henderson et al., 2007; Mapp, 2003). It is important that school leaders purposefully create opportunities to reach out and build relationships with families, especially if families already feel intimidated by staff. Many parents need school staff to extend a welcoming hand and offer support to steady the relationship and bridge the gap between home and school. If school staff take the position that families should know enough to come to them and initiate the relationship with the school, they create a culture that appears disinterested in and unwelcoming to family engagement.

### Reason Two: Emphasis on Head Count and Information Dissemination versus Relationship-Building

Schools across the country go through the paces of holding two or three obligatory, often compliance-driven events for families. These include traditional open houses, during which parents are herded from the auditorium to classrooms, where they are presented with course schedules, teacher and school expectations, discipline policies—in other words, the rules and regulations of the school and its expectations. The success or failure of school open houses, parent-teacher conferences, and parent "math and literacy nights" often hinges on the number of parents in attendance and the amount of information disseminated, rather than on whether or not the event helped to cultivate trusting relationships between school staff and families and build partnerships between school and home that support children's learning. Most parents find these events intimidating (Lawrence-Lightfoot, 2003), but for families who do not speak English, are from different racial, ethnic, socioeconomic, or educational backgrounds from that of school staff, or who have had their own negative school experiences, these events can be unwelcoming and downright frightening (Valdés, 1996).

We know from the research literature that the development of trusting and respectful parent-to-parent and parent-to-staff relationships is key in creating and sustaining meaningful education partnerships that support children's learning (Bryk & Schneider, 2002; Henderson et al., 2007). Mapp (2003) explored why and how hard-to-reach families—in this case, families of color and those who qualified for free and reduced-price lunch—were engaged in their children's education. Families revealed that the staff's consistent efforts to welcome them into the school community, to honor any type of involvement or contribution that the families made, to listen and respond to their concerns or ideas, and to connect the parents to their children's learning, helped to build strong relationships between families and school personnel. This purposeful process allowed staff to build relationships with *all* families and created a school culture that enabled partnerships to form between home and school, rather than preventing them.

### Reason Three: Narrow Definitions of Parent Involvement

In recent years, researchers have attempted to change the language used to label the role of parents in their children's education. Many have argued for a shift from parent involvement to family engagement for two reasons: (a) to recognize and honor the various family members (aunts, uncles, foster parents, grandparents, etc.) who support children; and (b) to suggest a more active, participatory relationship with others (other parents, school staff, community organizations, afterschool providers, etc.) to support student achievement. Involvement suggests individual participation, whereas engagement connotes more of a joining together, a connection and partnership with others (Shirley, 1997; Warren, Hong, Rubin, & Uy, in press).

Despite the adoption of the family engagement and partnership language by districts and schools, many still operate within a paradigm that limits and narrowly defines the roles of families (Weiss & Edwards, 1992). Limiting families to narrow activities, often defined by the school and district, such as volunteering at school, participating in fundraising events, joining the PTA or PTO, and helping children at home with school work, unwittingly pushes away families who have limited means, time, or capacity to engage in these specific activities.

In 1979, Urie Bronfenbrenner published *The Ecology of Human Development: Experiments by Nature and Design,* in which he presented his seminal work, the Ecological

Systems Theory. Bronfenbrenner's theory identified four nested systems (he later developed a fifth system, the *chronosystem*) that shape a child's development, and he emphasized the interaction between and among these systems. The *microsystem* is the layer closest to the child and contains the structures and systems with which the child has direct contact. The microsystem encompasses the relationships and interactions the child has with his/her immediate surroundings. This system includes the one-on-one relationships the child has with individuals such as his/her parents, as well as teachers, child-care providers, and peers. In contrast, the *mesosytem* is focused on the connections between and among the structures in the child's microsystem. For example, the strength and type of relationship teachers and parents share falls within this layer of the system. The *exosystem* encompasses the external environments that indirectly influence child development and exerts influence on the child via its impact on individuals and institutions in the microsystem (Lopez, Weiss, Kreider, & Harvard Family Research Project, 2005). The parent workplace and schedules rest in the exosystem. The *macrosystem* operates at the broadest level of influence and is comprised of the larger sociocultural context. The effects of cultural values, laws, customs, and policies have a cascading influence throughout the interactions of the other layers of the system. Finally, the *chronosystem* encompasses the dimension of time as it relates to a child's environments.

We contend that most parent involvement policies, programs, and practices operate solely from a microsystem paradigm; specifically, these initiatives focus primarily on changing or improving the one-on-one interaction between child and parent. Well-intentioned and well-meaning parent programs that operate within a microsystem paradigm unwittingly take on a "fix-the-parent" framework (Valdés, 2006). This framework focuses on improving the interaction between parent and child, but not on enhancing the adult-to-adult (mesosystem) relationships between and among parents, teachers, and other staff, or on enhancing parents' social and political capital (exosystem).

## A PARTNERSHIP PARADIGM FOR FAMILY ENGAGEMENT

Based on the argument that it is our educational institutions that are hard for parents to reach, what solutions can be offered to remedy this problem? We must first acknowledge that the issue of engaging parents effectively is a complex and multifaceted one that requires an understanding of the importance of context—the multiple system layers and environments that shape the dynamics between schools and families. This belies the desire for quick and easy solutions: the task of engaging parents effectively takes time, resources, mutual understanding, and radically different visions of schools and families—a paradigm shift of sorts.

The following case is presented as an example of this paradigm shift and of what can happen when educators move away from technical solutions to adaptive, creative strategies. This case features the relational work between schools and families that is facilitated by an outside institution—a community-based organization. The organization—the Logan Square Neighborhood Association (LSNA)—offers expertise on the local families as well as new, creative possibilities for connections between home and school that might previously have been challenging or even impossible. The LSNA approach reflects a focus on inclusion that sees parents as assets and realizes that an initiative must purposefully join with families to engage them effectively. This case illustrates a school-family-community partnership that eliminate the barriers between home and school and cultivated and sustained new institutional cultures that were accessible and easy to reach for families.

### Parents as Assets and Leaders: The Development of LSNA's Parent Mentor Program

In the spring of 1995, the LSNA, in partnership with a local school and another community organization, Community Organizing and Family Issues, developed the Parent Mentor program to encourage new ways to involve parents in schools and address the apparent distance between local schools and the families they served. At the time, Sally Acker, the principal of the Funston Elementary School in Chicago's community of Logan Square, initiated the idea of a parent program based on her observations of the many Latino immigrant parents (primarily mothers) who were staying at home and were often socially isolated from the broader community, in particular from their children's school. Acker and LSNA organizers noticed that many parents arrived at the school entrance only to drop their children off for the day, and then returned to their homes where they would spend the remainder of the day until they returned to pick up their children. These mothers were often not fluent in English and, as immigrants, were socially and culturally isolated from the community, spending much of the school day attending to the duties of the home or working in low-skill jobs.

At the same time, schools were overcrowded and teachers were overwhelmed with the day-to-day management of large classrooms. As a result, LSNA's Parent Mentor program sought to bring parents into those classrooms as teaching assistants to relieve some of the pressures the teachers felt and to foster the development of relationships between parents and teachers. Recognizing parents as assets and potential school leaders, LSNA designed the year-long Parent Mentor training program to support parents' development as leaders and classroom mentors. Each parent participated in a week-long training course at the start of the year and then spent two hours each day in the school—four days a week in the classroom and the fifth day in a training workshop. Parents received a small stipend for their work as parent mentors, but many volunteered extra hours in the classroom because they enjoyed the classroom experience and developed close relationships with students and teachers.

Since 1995, the Parent Mentor program has trained over 1,000 parents in eight local schools. Many of these parents remain involved in their children's school and have also moved on to work in the schools in various capacities—to lead one of LSNA's education programs, enroll in a teacher-training program, or become an elected member of the Local School Council (LSC; a local school governing body instituted in all Chicago public schools in 1988). Amanda Rivera, a Chicago Public Schools administrator in the Office of Professional Development and a former teacher who worked closely with LSNA to develop the Parent Mentor program, explained:

> Some of the benefits that we found—we were developing leadership capacity. I mean, not only were parents actually able to help many students in the classroom, but relationships between teachers and parents changed. Teachers began to develop

a greater respect for parents and viewed them as an asset or a resource, and parents began to understand the complexity of the work of teaching, the challenges that a teacher has with 30–35 students, the challenges that they have with students bringing their personal issues to school, and issues that have nothing to do with the classroom and how that impacted the classroom.

By building parents as leaders and giving them opportunities to play active roles in the schools, the Parent Mentor program offered schools spaces where teachers and parents could work together and where change—on the part of parents and school staff—can be facilitated. Rather than inviting parents to participate in ways that were wholly determined by school needs, the program designed parent participation in a way that was mindful of parents' needs and experiences.

### Branching Out: Expanding Definitions of Parent Engagement

When parents view themselves as assets, leaders, and active participants in the schools, they begin to expand their definitions of parent engagement. Rather than waiting for invitations to participate in schools, LSNA's parent mentors carved out their own agenda for school change. Having parents remain involved in the community and develop as leaders are central and intentional goals of the program, given its roots in community organizing. Through an emphasis on leadership development, the program encouraged participants to set personal goals that they would achieve over the course of the year. According to Monica Garreton, an LSNA organizer, this was "based on the fact that everyone is a leader and that everyone has these capabilities—building self-esteem and setting goals for yourself are pathways to building confidence, realizing your leadership, and inspiring your children." For many parents, these goals were to learn English, obtain their GED, find a job, enroll in a professional training program, or learn to drive a car. Over the course of the year, they took concrete steps to achieve their goals, received support from the broader community of parent mentors, and inevitably built their confidence as individuals. Garreton noted, "All these little steps help them to recognize that they're independent people and leaders who have these strengths in them."

However, in the first year of the Parent Mentor program, parents had great difficulties in reaching their goals—most parents wanted to learn English or obtain their GED, but places that offered these courses were too far away, required complicated routes by public transportation, and did not offer child care or did so at an additional charge (Blanc, Brown, Nevarez-La Torre, & Brown, 2002). A group of parent mentors began envisioning a community center that was based in the school and offered adult education classes, provided child care, and was free of charge. With the support of LSNA, these parent mentors walked the streets and conducted a community survey to get a sense of what the needs were in the community for this type of center. They found that residents wanted GED classes in English and Spanish, English as a second language classes, and affordable child care.

In time, through the perseverance and organizing efforts of this small group of parent mentors and the support of LSNA, the first school-based community-learning center (CLC) was built at the Funston School. LSNA has since expanded CLCs to five of their Parent Mentor program schools, and most parent mentors who want to improve their English or obtain a GED can do so easily through the classes offered at the CLCs. Through an emphasis on leadership development and community organizing, LSNA has provided parents with the necessary skills to become active decision-makers in creating a school community that is important and meaningful to them. Not only do these activities go beyond the traditional forms of parent engagement, they encourage parents to become the authors and leaders of school-wide parent participation.

Admittedly, the realization of one's leadership potential does not always come easily to parents, and organizers must do their best to support and encourage them. Leticia Barrerra, who leads the week-long training sessions at Funston, is a Parent Mentor program graduate herself. She served on Monroe Elementary School's LSC as an elected parent leader and is currently an education organizer at LSNA, overseeing the Parent Mentor program in four schools. Leadership development is central to the program's goals, but many parents are uncomfortable thinking about themselves as leaders and may feel daunted by the prospect of becoming a leader in the school. Because of this, Barrerra makes a point of consistently relating to the parents' experiences in the training:

> Always in the start of the training, I let parents know, now I'm here doing this training in front of you but before, I was like you. I was sitting in those chairs, very quiet, but now I'm not a quiet person. When my son was in pre-K and I first started the Parent Mentor program, I was very shy too. I was a mom, most of the time I was spending at home cleaning and doing different things that moms are supposed to do. But I had an opportunity to be part of a program and discover some new skills that everyone has. We just need an opportunity to know those skills and know that this is what I can do.

For many Latino immigrant parents, not only are schools a new locus of involvement, but public leadership and engagement are often unfamiliar practices. To promote a paradigm shift in parent engagement, LSNA underscores the importance of training and leadership development that is rooted in the experiences of these particular parents.

### Identifying a Cultural Broker: The Role of Community Institutions

A cultural broker is an essential participant in any school's effort to build meaningful relationships between a school and community (Delgado-Gaitan, 2001). But what we found through this case and in our work with schools and communities is that how schools define parent engagement and how they view parents (as assets vs. as deficits) can often determine the kind of cultural broker with whom schools work.

If, as we recommend, parents are viewed as potential leaders and assets within a school community and schools are more flexible about the forms of parent engagement they allow, school personnel will choose to work with cultural brokers who encourage new roles and reconceptualizations promoting—in effect, a more meaningful shift in culture and practice within a school. In many cases, a cultural broker is an individual working within the school (e.g., a family-community outreach coordinator) to facilitate the relationships between a school and the families it serves. In this case, the cultural broker was a community organization. We contend that intermediary organizations like LSNA can play a powerful role in bridging the radically different worlds of school and home.

*LSNA as Cultural Broker*   During the late 1980s, as LSNA began organizing around educational issues, most public schools in Logan Square were over 95% low income and 90% Latino (Blanc et al., 2002). Given the neighborhood demographics and the organization's history of working with the local community, organizers wanted to develop a model of engagement that would reflect the particular needs of the community. In many Latino families, mothers often stayed at home to take care of children while their husbands worked; they spent little time in the school and even less time in the broader community. For many parent mentors, participation in the program was their first meaningful experience outside of the home. For most of these Latina mothers, many of them immigrants, linguistic and cultural differences often kept them in the more comfortable and familiar sphere of home. As Garreton explained, "The culture of Latino families generally is that the women stay home and they cook and clean while the husband goes out to work. Our Parent Mentor program is bringing those women out of the home, feeling like they are contributing something." Barrera added that while it often can be true that, "the man is the strong decision-maker in the family," families also "come to America and see that there is another way to construct family dynamics." In some cases, female parent mentors come to the realization, with their husbands, that "I have my own choices, I have to let [my husband] know what I think to raise our boys and to be part of those decisions." These changes in family dynamics can also have positive effects on the children, who begin to see their parents as more equal players in the household.

With its more than 40-year history of community organizing in Logan Square, LSNA has built a base of experience and knowledge of the local community—understanding residents lives as immigrants, the socioeconomic conditions that shape their lives, the language and culture of an increasingly Latino immigrant population, as well as their struggles and needs as a community. At the same time, as a community organization, LSNA has a base of skills and knowledge that allows them to position themselves comfortably with other mainstream institutions, such as schools. Through this role as "insider" to both the community and its mainstream institutions, LSNA is able to build a model of parent engagement that is culturally conscious of the two radically different worlds of school and community. This model is built with explicit knowledge and recognition of the immigrant mothers who participate as parent mentors.

While the experience as a parent mentor may be their first meaningful experience outside of the home, many of these immigrant women also need supports since they are experiencing a system of schooling that is unfamiliar and even alien to them. In Barrera's native country of Mexico, where she was also a teacher, the school system she described was at sharp odds with what is often common practice in U.S. schools, and she believes this difference is common among many Latino cultures:

> In Mexico, it is totally different than here in United States. Parents are not very involved—they are part of committees, but those committees do not run the same way as here where they make decisions. The teachers say you have to do this, and we would just do the things that the teachers said.

LSNA tries to show parents that being a mentor was an opportunity to get involved in the school system and to inform them of the practices of parent engagement in the United States. Once parents understand the way American schools operate and receive the support they need through the Parent Mentor program, their ways of thinking about schools changes and they enthusiastically accept the new responsibilities. As Barrera explained, "The programs and the organizing in general provide parents access to basic information about the community—who the alderman is, the police commander—basic information that they don't know. It is a process of introducing them to community knowledge, resources, and information."

Once these mothers enter the classroom, they also begin to understand the school environment more clearly. According to Garreton, because "teachers in Mexico and other countries are so respected and parents see them sometimes as a higher being, that can impede parents from getting involved." Throughout their participation in the Parent Mentor program, parents become more comfortable in the school environment and they begin to see teachers in more realistic terms:

> When [parents] go into the classroom, they're learning a lot of things—they're walking into a school that they may have never walked inside before, they're seeing teachers as human beings instead of revering them as these gods that they would see before, learning how the system works, being more comfortable in English-speaking environments and more familiar with a system in this new country—when our school system is completely different than other country's school systems.

For many parents who are not fluent in English or who may not have high levels of education in their home country or here in the United States, their work in classrooms helps them see what ability they *do* have to work with children in support of their learning. The effects of this realization can be profound for the family, as Garreton described:

> Then [parents] get in the classroom and start helping out kids and realizing that it doesn't matter if they don't know how to read or write or if they only graduated from third grade, they have something valuable to offer. Then they also take that home to their kids, and they are able to help their kids with their homework and realize the importance of supporting their kids in school.

For many of these Latina mothers, working in the school is their first public engagement in the community. In many ways "it makes total sense," according to lead education organizer Joanna Brown, that the school is the site where LSNA connects with the community. She noted, "By coming into the [Parent Mentor] program, people actually get pulled into the community, they get pulled out of their private houses [and] into the first public space that they've entered." For many immigrant communities, the school is where, according to Brown, "they have their children, and for most women it's the place they're most interested in and concerned with."

While schools do not often have the time or resources to understand the lives of families or to develop more meaningful forms of parent engagement (Lopez, Kreider, & Coffman, 2005), community institutions such as LSNA often do, with their connections to local residents, families, and extended family members. LSNA's staff is virtually all Spanish-speaking and many Latino/immigrant backgrounds themselves. They often are residents of Logan Square. As a cultural broker between families and schools, LSNA has created programs that have effectively bridged the radically different worlds of immigrant families and schools.

### The Fundamental Nature of Relationships: Building Trust between Schools and Families

While traditional notions of community organizing form the framework for LSNA's work with parents, the organization has also decided to take a more cooperative approach in its education organizing. While organizing is typically seen as confrontational work where conflict is identified and campaigns can be aggressive in nature—and this can certainly be the case in some of LSNA's education campaigns or their other issue, such as housing—in its education work, LSNA has generally opted to be more relational and cooperative in its interactions with the public school system. LSNA executive director Nancy Aardema explained that from the beginning, LSNA identified needs in the community that were in line with the needs of principals, such as overcrowding, and realized that "it was far better for all of us to all be at the table together. Right then and there, we began building those relationships. So 90% of the time we're not confrontational. It doesn't mean we're not clear about what's wanted and needed. But we recognize this is a partnership—we're sharing space." In addition, when parents organize in their children's schools, confrontational approaches can threaten the children's education. Aardema added:

> We do want the kids to get a good education. And this is the issue for us. If an issue couldn't be resolved without a confrontation, what would we do? We'd try to figure out every angle we could to not be confrontational as an organization.

The fundamental nature of LSNA's work in schools is relational, and the goal is to develop trust and understanding between schools and families. Through the Parent Mentor program, parents get an opportunity to see schools as they are and understand the work of teachers. This approach encourages collaboration and fosters relationships built on common experience and trust, which can only benefit children's experiences in a school. Brown explained:

> I think most parents want to be cooperative because they want their children to get educated. And they don't want their children going into a hostile environment. They want their children to be happy and they want their children to be treated well, so they tend to be naturally collaborative. And the more they're inside, the more they see, the more they can be critical, but also, the more they understand the problems—how complex the problems are. Like, the teacher with 32 kids—it's not her fault if she doesn't have an hour to spend individually with my child. Or they understand their role in terms of a parent, as a partner in educating their child.

Through these experiences, parents begin to build relationships with teachers, understanding their struggles and recognizing their success and innovation in the classroom. These relationships begin the process where assumptions are broken down and pathways are cleared for better, more effective communication. As Julia,* a parent mentor at Funston, admitted:

> I see how sometimes they can stress out with so many kids that sometimes you have to ask questions before you just assume and jump down their throat, you know, some people they do that. I try to get the whole information before I start jumping down the teacher's throat. So I learned, you know, talking to them and seeing exactly what they deal with because it can be stressful sometimes with so many kids in a class.

Not only do parents build relationships with teachers as parent mentors, they also develop and sustain relationships with other parents. Under more traditional forms of parent involvement (e.g., volunteering in a child's classroom), parents rarely come in contact with other parents or have opportunities to develop meaningful connections with other families. But through the weekly training sessions, which are geared toward leadership development and community-building, parent mentors build relationships with other parents in the school. This relational aspect of the program is most evident during the week-long training at the start of the school year, as organizers draw parents into a new and unfamiliar community. The training group is a mix of new parents who have never participated in the program and returning parent mentors who share their experiences and reach out to newer parents to support them and answer their questions. During the sessions, parents talk about their children, their fears and anxieties about the classroom, and their expectations for the year ahead. This connection with other parents, as well as with the students and families of the classrooms within which they work as parent mentors, helps to build a sense of collective community. Ofelia Sanchez, an LSNA organizer and former parent mentor, explained this collective sense of responsibility:

> It's not just my kids, but it's everyone's kids. When I walk to the school and I see the kids that I've tutored or even the kids who are in preschool with my daughter, they see me and say, "Hi Ms. Sanchez!" To me, it's this big commitment—I'm the only one there that can actually make a difference for them. If I'm not there, who's going to support them?

A collective sense of responsibility comes not only when parents see themselves as being connected to the life of the school through relationships with students and families, but when the school staff also feels connected to families. When parents become a regular presence in schools and trusted resources in classrooms, they are less likely to be viewed with suspicion or skepticism by school staff and more likely to be viewed in earnest as school partners. Margaret McIntosh, a teacher at the Funston School, described this process as an "opening for those of us who work in the school to begin to see parents in a different light—that they are capable of supporting their children as well as other students in the school." When schools begin to see these parents as assets, they are more likely to dispel rumors or stereotypes about parents.

Liliana Evers, previously a principal of the Funston School, described the changes she witnessed in the school atmosphere from the beginning of the Parent Mentor program. In the early years of the program, LSNA organizers struggled to find enough teachers who were willing to work with parent mentors in their classrooms, due to a pattern of antagonism between parents and teachers. Teachers were skeptical that parents would work in their classrooms without leveling criticism at their practices, and a history of antagonism between parents and teachers eroded trust between them. But Evers witnessed a complete change in the school atmosphere: parents became a regular presence in the school, and now they find they do not have enough parent mentors to fill teachers' requests. Indeed, some teachers realize that their ideas about parents and families were unfounded and have experienced a personal transformation. One teacher, who has worked with parent mentors in the past, admitted her transformation:

> I'm not sure why I had this idea that parents weren't interested or were just disengaged—I guess I was kind of blaming them without really knowing them or their situation. But when I got to know my parent mentor, I realized these parents do care, but we teachers don't often speak in their terms.

By making the development of trust and relationships central to their work in schools, LSNA created school communities where parents could feel part of a larger collective community with shared interests and goals. In this environment, parents and teachers were encouraged to make connections and feel less threatened or intimidated by the other's presence.

### Addressing Institutional Power: Equalizing Relationships between Parents and Schools

Schools and families often have traditional interactions that are steeped in unequal power dynamics. School personnel often decide the terms and conditions of how parents participate in schools and the kinds of relationships they foster with families. Parents may feel accustomed to relationships with schools where they submit to the wishes of school authorities and participate in ways that are openly encouraged and supported.

LSNA organizers believe that addressing power is inherent to building meaningful change in schools. The relationships between parents and schools must be seen more as partnerships where decision-making and power are shared and parents become active participants in the life and culture of a school. The experience of being in classrooms as parent mentors and becoming acute observers of classroom dynamics and the work inside schools gives parents insight and perspective into what needs to be changed within a school. As Aardema explained, the very nature of the relationship between the families and schools is "unusual in that we have hundreds of parents in our community who've spent two hours a day in the school and graduated as parent mentors." This opportunity sets LSNA parents apart in their experience in and knowledge of the school environment. She added:

> So parents here really understand in a deeper way what it's like to be in the school all day—what it's like for the kids, what it's like for the teachers. And that then opens doors for both the kids and the teachers, because if parents see things that

they think aren't fair for the kids, they're the first to speak up. If they see things that they think are unfair to the teachers, they're also speaking up.

LSNA parent mentors have a window into the broader school environment—across classrooms and across families. This broader perspective often led parents to feel more confident in their abilities to raise concerns and speak up on behalf of their children, other children in the school, or for the teachers they had come to know.

## RECOMMENDATIONS FOR PRACTICE

What can we learn from the Parent Mentor program, about how to make our schools and other educational institutions easier to reach and more family friendly? We offer four recommendations:

1.  Adopt a relational paradigm for working with families.
    Educational institutions must focus on building relationships with families as the first step in cultivating meaningful partnerships and establishing family-friendly cultures. The relational piece is the foundation of the Parent Mentor program. By creating an atmosphere where families feel welcome and where staff invite their engagement, parents feel at home and a part of the school community (Henderson & Mapp, 2002). Educational institutions that embrace a relational paradigm make building relationships with families an intentional and systemic part of their work. These opportunities must encourage parent-to-staff and parent-to-parent networking and relationship-building. The building of trusting and respectful relationships between families and school personnel is the first and most important step in breaking down barriers between home and school. These relationships of trust provide the "lubricant" (Bryk & Schneider, 2002) for the developing partnership between families and school staff. In addition, Christenson and Sheridan (2001) underscored the essential nature of family-school relationships for positive child outcomes, and they have articulated a process for building relationships across home and school (see also Christenson, 2004).

2.  Shift the culture from school-centric to parent-centric.
    A major reason for the success of the Parent Mentor and the Community Learning Centers programs is that school and LSNA staff listened to and co-constructed initiatives with parents. Through frequent communication with families and the collection of data through surveys and focus groups, programs were designed to respond to the needs of families, and they were parent-centric rather than school-centric (serving staff needs) in intent, form, content, and structure.

3.  Share power—treat parents as equal partners.
    Through the Parent Mentor program, school staff and families broke down the barriers between them and dissolved stereotypical beliefs and perceptions. As parents and teachers worked to support each other and had opportunities through joint projects to share power, teachers began to see parents in a different light, and both parents and teachers came to view the other as equal partners in the educational enterprise. The Parent Mentor initiative also focused on developing

parents as leaders, enabling them not only to advocate for their own children but for the entire school community. As a result of the Parent Mentor program, the Funston School staff described a change in the culture of the school whereby the antagonistic relations between families and school staff were eliminated, and the school adopted a more collaborative, caring, and family-friendly culture. Increasing opportunities for parents and school staff to work together as equal partners on co-constructed projects that place children at the center encourages the transformation of beliefs, values, and institutional culture.

4. Establish partnerships with cultural brokers.

Outside agencies and organizations often have the credibility and trust of families that educational institutions have yet to earn (Davies, 2001; Delgado-Gaitan, 2001). LSNA served as a cultural broker between home and school, enabling the schools, over time and with LSNA's assistance, to develop relationships of trust and respect with families. By establishing respectful partnerships with community organizations, educational institutions can gain much needed credibility with families. This credibility is an essential component of creating a family-friendly and accessible school culture and climate.

By focusing on relationships, moving to a parent-centric paradigm, building shared power between staff and families, and collaborating with community partners who can serve as cultural brokers, educational institutions will move from a limited microsystem position, which only focuses on the interaction between the parent and child, to an integrated approach that spans Brofenbrenner's ecological systems. The Parent Mentor/Logan Square case offers an example of a family engagement approach that spans the ecological systems model and integrates the multiple spheres of influence (Epstein, 1987). As illustrated in this example, parents and school staff developed relationships of trust and mutual respect, allowing them to work as partners to support the learning of children (mesosystem). Families were empowered and became leaders both at school and in their communities, and the overall culture of the school was shifted from school-centric to parent-centric (exosystem). For our educational institutions to become family friendly and less hard to reach for parents, we believe and have learned that they must engage in the adaptive work required to reject standard parent involvement practices and embrace a relational, inclusive, and collaborative family engagement approach.

## AUTHORS' NOTE

Data cited in this chapter is part of a larger research project that was conducted by Soo Hong from May 2006 to April 2008. Data collection consisted of individual interviews, observations, focus groups, and document analysis. All individuals named fully in this study have given permission to be cited in this and other written reports. During the course of data collection, parents participating in the Parent Mentor program for the first time who were interviewed and observed for this study are given a pseudonym, referred to by a first name only, and marked by an asterisk (*).

# REFERENCES

Berla, N., Henderson, A. T., & National Committee for Citizens in Education. (1994). *A new generation of evidence: The family is critical to student achievement.* Washington, DC: National Committee for Citizens in Education.

Blanc, S., Brown, J., Nevarez-La Torre, S., & Brown, C. (2002). *Case study: Logan Square Neighborhood Association.* Chicago: Cross City Campaign for Urban School Reform.

Bronfenbrenner, U. (1979). *The ecology of human development: Experiments by nature and design.* Cambridge, MA: Harvard University Press.

Bryk, A. S., & Schneider, B. L. (2002). *Trust in schools.* New York: Russell Sage.

Christenson, S. L. (2004). The family-school partnership: An opportunity to promote the learning competence of *all* students. *School Psychology Review, 33*(1), 83–104.

Christenson, S. L., & Sheridan, S. M. (2001). *School and families: Creating essential connections for learning.* New York: Guilford.

Crew, R. (2007). *Only connect: The way to save our schools.* New York: Farrar, Straus and Giroux.

Davies, D. (2001). Family participation in decision-making and advocacy. In D. B. Hiatt-Michael (Ed.), *Promising practices for family involvement in schools* (pp. 107–151). Greenwich, CT: Information Age.

Delgado-Gaitan, C. (2001). *The power of community: Mobilizing for family and schooling.* Lanham, MD: Rowman & Littlefield.

Diamond, J. B., & Gomez, K. (2004). African-American parents' orientations toward schools: The implications of social class and parents' perceptions of schools. *Education and Urban Society, 36*(4), 383–427.

Epstein, J. L. (1987). Toward a theory of family-school connections: Teacher practices and parent involvement. In K. Hurrelmann, F. Kaufmann, & F. Losel (Eds.), *Social interaction: Potential and constraints* (pp. 121–136). New York: deGruyter.

Heifetz, R. A., & Linsky, M. (2002). *Leadership on the line: Staying alive through the dangers of leading.* Boston: Harvard Business School Press.

Henderson, A. T., Johnson, V., Mapp, K. L., & Davies, D. (2007). *Beyond the bake sale: The essential guide to family-school partnerships.* New York: New Press.

Henderson, A. T., & Mapp, K. L. (2002). *A new wave of evidence: The impact of school, family, and community connections on student achievement.* Austin, TX: National Center for Family & Community Connections with Schools, Southwest Educational Development Laboratory.

Jackson, K., & Remillard, J. T. (2005). Rethinking parent involvement: African-American mothers construct their roles in the mathematics education of their children. *School Community Journal, 15*(1), 51–73.

Lawrence-Lightfoot, S. (2003). *The essential conversation: What parents and teachers can learn from each other* (1st ed.). New York: Random House.

Lopez, M. E., Kreider, H., & Coffman, J. (2005). Intermediary organizations as capacity builders in family educational involvement. *Urban Education, 40,* 78–105.

Lopez, M. E., Weiss, H. B., Kreider, H. M., & Harvard Family Research Project. (2005). *Preparing educators to involve families: From theory to practice.* Thousand Oaks, CA: Sage.

Mapp, K. L. (2003). Having their say: Parents describe why and how they are engaged in their children's learning. *School Community Journal, 13*(1), 35–64.

Moll, L. C., Amanti, C., & Neff, D. (1992). Funds of knowledge for teaching: Using a qualitative approach to connect homes and classrooms. *Theory into Practice, 31,* 132–141.

Schlechty, P. C. (2000). *Shaking up the schoolhouse: How to support and sustain educational innovation* (1st ed.). San Francisco: Jossey-Bass.

Shirley, D. (1997). *Community organizing for urban school reform.* Austin: University of Texas Press.

Valdés, G. (1996). *Con respeto: Bridging the distances between culturally diverse families and schools: An ethnographic portrait.* New York: Teachers College Press.

Warren, M. R., Hong, S., Rubin, C., & Uy, P. (in press). Beyond the bake sale: A community-based relational approach to parent engagement in schools. *Teachers College Record, 111*(9).

Weiss, H. M., & Edwards, M. E. (1992). The family-school collaboration project: Systemic interventions for school improvement. In S. L. Christenson & J. C. Conoley (Eds.), *Home-school collaboration: Enhancing children's academic and social competence* (pp. 215–243). Silver Spring, MD: National Association of School Psychologists.

# 16

## FAMILY-CENTERED HELPGIVING PRACTICES, PARENT–PROFESSIONAL PARTNERSHIPS, AND PARENT, FAMILY, AND CHILD OUTCOMES

### CARL J. DUNST AND CAROL M. TRIVETTE

Parent and professional relationships in general (Beckman, 1996; Christenson & Conoley, 1992; Walker, 1989), and parent–professional partnerships in particular (Keen, 2007; Roberts, Rule, & Innocenti, 1998; Turnbull & Turnbull, 1986), are generally recognized as important for optimally affecting child learning and development. Collaboration between parents and professionals is now seen as a crucial component of early childhood intervention, family support, education, and other health and human services programs (e.g., Alexander & Dore, 1999; Bruns & Steeples, 2001; Devore & Bowers, 2006; Jakobsen & Severinsson, 2006; Roberts et al., 1998).

## OVERVIEW

The purposes of this chapter are to describe how parent–professional partnerships are a key element of family-centered helpgiving practices, and how variations in the use of this approach to helpgiving are related to variations in parent and other family member outcomes. The chapter begins where our last discussion of parent–professional partnerships ended (Dunst, Trivette, & Snyder, 2000). In our previous discussion of partnerships, we critically reviewed the literature on parent and professional collaboration and concluded that "the operational characteristics of the [partnership] construct have not been clearly articulated, and available research does not substantiate claims about those elements that define the phenomenon" (Dunst et al., 2000, p. 37). We went on to say that partnerships are best described as a component of "effective helpgiving practices that emphasize [parents and professionals] working together to identify desired goals and courses of action to achieve those goals, bidirectional information sharing so that informed choices and decisions can be made, and joint problem solving and actions by both parties [that] promote a sense of competence and capability" (Dunst et al., 2000, p. 41). Stated differently, partnerships were defined as a collaborative helping style where the focus of intervention is the use of existing family strengths and the acquisition of new capabilities to achieve desired outcomes in ways having empowering and capacity-building consequences. The manner in which parent–professional partnerships conceptualized in this way are related to parent, family, and child behavior and functioning is the main focus of this chapter.

The belief that parent–professional relationships have value-added benefits to parents and their families beyond those associated with traditional professional practices, however, has been mostly assumed and rarely tested. This has been especially the case for parent—professional partnerships where little empirical research has been conducted to assess the consequences and benefits, if any, of these kinds of relationships (see e.g., Reich, Bickman, & Heflinger, 2004; Summers et al., 2007, for exceptions). Additionally, the challenges and difficulties in making parent—professional partnerships a reality have increasingly been noted by both researchers and practitioners (e.g., Crozier, 1999; Galinsky, 1990; Pinkus, 2003; Todd & Higgins, 1998). Pinkus (2003) and Todd and Higgins (1998) have gone so far as to say that parent–professional partnerships are especially difficult to establish in programs and organizations where the locus of power rest primarily with professionals. Notwithstanding these conditions and contentions, the pursuit of information about what makes a parent–professional relationship a partnership continue to be a focus of attention of both researchers and practitioners (Devore & Bowers, 2006; Harry, 2008; Keen, 2007; Shields, Pratt, & Hunter, 2006; Summers et al., 2005).

Many attempts have been made to identify the characteristics that parents and professionals believe are the most important elements of partnerships (see e.g., Dunst et al., 2000). These attempts have generally resulted in lists of characteristics that are subsequently categorized and labeled as "dimensions of partnerships" (Blue-Banning, Summers, Frankland, Nelson, & Beegle, 2004; Dunst, Johanson, Rounds, Trivette, & Hamby, 1992; Dunst, Trivette, & Johanson, 1994). The lists include such things as honesty, respect, trust, open communication, flexibility, active listening, information sharing, and being nonjudgmental. The categorization of those characteristics has led to groupings such as *equality*, *respect*, and *communication style*.

At least four observations can be made about attempts to identify and categorize the characteristics of parent–professional relationships. First, there is generally no agreement about the number of characteristics that operationally define a partnership. Those who have compared lists of characteristics note that the numbers range from as few as 3 to more than 30 (see DeChillo, Koren, & Schultze, 1994; Dunst et al., 2000). Second, no single characteristic is generally identified by a majority of parents or professionals as an important indicator of partnerships. The percentages of persons who list any one characteristic have most often been only 25% to 40% of study participants (DeGangi, Royeen, & Wietlisbach, 1992; Dinnebeil, Hale, & Rule, 1996; Dunst, Johanson et al., 1992). Third, no relative importance is given to any particular characteristic or set of characteristics. Rather, different writers tend to emphasize the importance of different characteristics where the particular features and elements that are claimed to be indicators of parent—professional partnerships appear to be idiosyncratic rather than conceptual or evidence-based (see Dunst et al., 2000). Fourth, the particular characteristics that are listed as partnership characteristics are not very different from other kinds of parent and professional relationships considered important for improving family functioning (e.g., Beckman, Frank, & Newcomb, 1996; Riessman, 1990; Sokoly & Dokecki, 1992; Swanson, 1991). The characteristics that parent–professional partnership enthusiasts claim are the defining characteristics of these kinds of relationships are nearly identical to the key features of caring relationships, effective interpersonal communication, codes of ethics, effective helpgiving, and other relationships (see especially Dunst et al., 2000, p. 36).

## SOME KEY ELEMENTS OF PARENT–PROFESSIONAL RELATIONSHIPS

Our research and practice with young children and their families has included a focus on the key characteristics of parent empowerment (Dunst, Trivette, & LaPointe, 1992), effective helpgiving practices (Trivette, Dunst, & Hamby, 1996a), family strengths-based interventions (Trivette, Dunst, Deal, Hamby, & Sexton, 1994), and social support interventions (Dunst, Trivette, & Jodry, 1997) as ways of understanding how to best support and strengthen parent, family, and child behavior and functioning (Dunst, 1999; Dunst, Hamby, & Brookfield, 2007). Parent–professional partnerships have had a central role in our research and practice in early childhood intervention and family support intervention (Dunst, 1985; Dunst, Johanson et al., 1992; Dunst & Paget, 1991; Dunst, Trivette, & Deal, 1988, 1994; Dunst, Trivette, & Johanson, 1994; Dunst et al., 2000). The main goal of this research and practice has been the identification and use of evidence-based practices that have parent, family, and child capacity-building characteristics and consequences.

The model that has guided our work includes the belief that all people have existing strengths and the capacity to become more capable and competent, and the belief that by supporting and strengthening family capacity, parents and other caregivers are in a better position to provide children development-instigating and development-enhancing learning opportunities and experiences (Bronfenbrenner, 1992). This is accomplished using family-centered capacity-building helpgiving practices (Trivette & Dunst, 2007). As described next, these kinds of helpgiving practices include specific behaviors that have been found to be associated with a host of positive parent, family, and child behavioral consequences.

### Family-Centered Helpgiving Practices

Family-centered practices are now generally recognized as practices that treat families with dignity and respect; that are individualized, flexible, and responsive to family concerns and situations; that include information sharing so families can make informed decisions; involve family choice regarding any number of aspects of program practices and intervention options; use parent and professional collaboration as the context for family–program relations; and actively involve family members in the mobilization and procurement of resources and supports necessary for rearing children in ways having value-added benefits (Allen & Petr, 1996; Dunst, 1997, 2002; Law et al., 2005; Shelton & Stepanek, 1994). Our research on family-centered helpgiving practices has identified two clusters of helpgiving behaviors: Relational practices and participatory practices (Trivette & Dunst, 2007). Relational practices include behavior typically associated with good clinical practice (e.g., active listening, compassion, empathy, respect) and helpgiver positive beliefs about family member strengths and capabilities. Listening to a family's concerns and asking for clarification or elaboration about what was said is an example of a relational helpgiving practice. Participatory helpgiving practices include behaviors that are individualized, flexible, and responsive to family concerns and priorities, and involve information sharing so that family members can make informed choices and act on those choices to achieve desired goals or outcomes having capacity-building consequences. Engaging a family member in a process of comparing options for obtaining desired resources, making a choice between options, and taking action to obtain the resources is an example of a participatory helpgiving practice.

Relational and participatory helpgiving practices are viewed as two separate but interrelated elements of a particular approach to working with families that explicitly focuses on family member capacity building. Family-centered helpgiving practices, as we define them (Dunst, 1997, 2002; Trivette & Dunst, 2007), include the kinds of behavior that Maple (1977) described as the essential components of *shared decision making* and that Rappaport (1981) described as the kind of *enabling experiences* that are likely to have capacity-building and empowering consequences. It is of interest to note that most lists of the characteristics of parent–professional partnerships include predominantly relational indicators and very few participatory indicators (Blue-Banning et al., 2004; Dunst, Johanson, et al., 1992). For example, of the 26 characteristics listed by Dunst et al. (1992), only four or 15% of the indicators, have participatory elements. Of the 39 characteristics identified by Blue-Banning et al. (2004), the largest majority are relational indicators. Therefore, parent–professional partnerships as currently conceptualized appear to emphasize one dimension of family-centered helpgiving practices to the exclusion of the dimension (participatory helpgiving) that is most likely to have capacity-building elements (e.g., Trivette, Dunst, Boyd, & Hamby, 1995; Trivette, Dunst, & Hamby, 1996b).

The fact that partnerships, as most commonly conceptualized, may not include indicators that "matter most" in terms of expected benefits is illustrated with data from a recently completed study (Dunst & Dempsey, 2007). The study participants were 150 parents involved in an early childhood intervention and family support program. A subset of items on the *Enabling Practices Scale* (Dempsey, 1995) were used as indicators of parent—professional partnerships (Table 16.1). The items represent indicators of parent and professional collaboration, cooperative planning, and joint problem solving. A principal components factor analysis of the study participants' scale scores produced a single factor solution accounting for 60% of the variance and an alpha coefficient of .89. The outcome measures in the study were parenting confidence, competence, and enjoyment (Dunst & Masiello, 2002). Hierarchical multiple regression analysis found that the partnership measure accounted for less than 3% of the variance in each of the three parenting measures after the effects of parent age and education, and child age and disability, were first entered in the analyses. Even before the covariates were entered into the analyses, the partnership measure accounted for 4% or less of the variance in each of the three parenting measures. Dunst and Dempsey (2007) concluded that the

**Table 16.1** Parent and Professional Partnership Scale Items

It is easy to work together with staff when planning for my son/daughter
Staff and I agree on what is most important for my son/daughter
I am an equal partner in the relationship I have with staff
With the support of the staff, I am able to solve problems quickly
Working with the staff has made me feel more capable
The staff offer help in response to our family's needs
I feel comfortable giving advice to the staff if asked

Source: Dunst and Dempsey (2007).

findings showed that parents and professionals working together as *equal partners* do not appear to be the characteristics that matter most in terms of affecting parenting confidence, competence, and enjoyment.

The extent and manner in which family-centered practices are related to and influence parent, family and child behavior and functioning has been the focus of investigation for nearly two decades (see Dempsey & Keen, 2008; Dunst, Trivette, & Hamby, 2007; Irlam & Bruce, 2002; Rosenbaum, King, Law, King, & Evans, 1998; Shields et al., 2006; for reviews of these studies). There are now almost 100 quantitative and qualitative studies investigating the relationships between family-centered practices and many different child and family outcomes. The meta-analyses and research syntheses of findings from these studies have been the focus of our recent work (Dunst, Trivette, & Hamby, 2006a; Dunst, Trivette, et al., 2007; Dunst, Trivette, & Hamby, 2008). Selected results from these reviews are described next to illustrate how family-centered helpgiving practices are both directly and indirectly related to the different outcomes constituting the focus of investigative interest.

## META-ANALYSES OF FAMILY-CENTERED HELPGIVING PRACTICES

Two meta-analyses have been conducted that specifically focused on the relationships between family-centered relational and participatory helpgiving practices and different dimensions of parent, family, and child behavior and functioning. One research synthesis included 18 studies, all conducted in the same early childhood intervention and family support program (Dunst et al., 2006a). The other research synthesis included 52 studies conducted by 23 researchers or research teams in seven different countries (Dunst, Trivette, et al., 2007; Dunst et al., 2008). The total number of participants in the two syntheses was 1,100 and 12,211, respectively. The two syntheses are referred to as Meta-Analysis 1 and Meta-Analysis 2 in the following discussion.

The largest majority (more than 90%) of the study participants were the mothers of children with identified disabilities, developmental delays, or other conditions placing the children at-risk for poor outcomes. The participants were involved in early intervention, early childhood education, early childhood special education, elementary schools, rehabilitation centers, mental health programs, public health clinics, neonatal intensive care units, hospitals, specialty clinics, or physician practices. The helpgivers who were the focus of study participant helpgiving practices judgments included early childhood practitioners, educators, nurses, physicians, occupational and physical therapists, rehabilitation specialists, and service coordinators.

### Conceptual Framework

The conduct of both meta-analyses was guided by a conceptual framework that models the direct effects of family-centered helpgiving practices on parent, family, and child behavior and functioning, and the indirect effects of family-centered helpgiving practices on the same outcomes mediated by self-efficacy beliefs and personal control appraisals. According to Bandura (1997), "Perceived self-efficacy refers to beliefs in one's capabilities to organize and execute the courses of actions required to produce given attainments" (p. 3). Skinner (1995) defined perceived control as "naïve causal models individuals hold about how the world works; about the likely courses of desired and undesired events, [and] about their own role in success or failure" (pp. xvi–xvii). Both kinds of personal attributions are indicators of a personal or psychological sense of empowerment (Zimmerman, 2000), and are considered a consequence of capacity-building family-centered practices and a determinant of behavior functioning.

The model used to guide the conduct of the meta-analyses is shown in Figure 16.1. Relational and participatory helpgiving practices are both considered *enabling* (in the good sense of the word) experiences and opportunities to the extent the practices engage people in *decisions and actions* that result in the use of existing capabilities and the development of new competencies. Both types of family-centered helpgiving were expected to be directly related to self-efficacy beliefs, and both directly and indirectly related to parent, family, and child behavior and functioning mediated by self-efficacy beliefs. The strength of the relationships between family-centered helpgiving practices and parent, family, and child behavior and functioning was expected to be strongest where the outcome measures were *proximal* and *contextual* to the focus of the parent-professional relationship. Outcomes are considered proximal and contextual where the targets of outcome assessments are parent appraisals of benefits directly related to the focus of a parent and professional relationship. In contrast, the strength of the

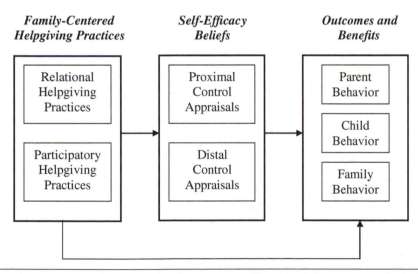

**Figure 16.1** A conceptual model for depicting the effects of family-centered practices, self-efficacy beliefs, and the direct effects of family-centered helpgiving on parent, family and child behavior and functioning.

relationships between measures was not expected to be as strong where the outcomes were *distal* to the focus of the parent–professional relationship. Outcomes are considered distal where the targets of parent appraisals are not directly related to the focus of a parent and professional relationship.

## Measures

The scales used to measure family-centered helpgiving practices included, but were not limited to, one or more versions of the Helpgiving Practices Scale (Trivette & Dunst, 1994), Measure of Process of Care (King, Rosenbaum, & King, 1996), Family-Centered Practices Scale (Dunst & Trivette, 2003b), Enabling Practices Scale (Dempsey, 1995), Family Centered Behavior Scale (Allen, Petr, & Brown, 1995), and the Family/Provider Relationship Instrument (van Riper, 1999) as well as other instruments (e.g., DeChillo et al., 1994; Thompson et al., 1997). The subscales on the different instruments were coded on an a priori basis as either relational or participatory helpgiving practices based on either the factor analyses of the scale items or inspection of the item content of the subscales using the Trivette and Dunst (2007) categorization of indicators of the two types of helpgiving practices.

The dependent measures in the two syntheses were organized into six categories: self-efficacy beliefs, program satisfaction, social supports and resources, parenting, parent and family well-being, and child behavior and functioning. The self-efficacy measures included perceived control over the help provided by a helpgiver, perceived control over the help provided by the program for which a helpgiver worked, and perceived control over life events not the focus of the parent and professional relationship (e.g., Boyd & Dunst, 1996; Koren, DeChillo, & Friesen, 1992). The participant satisfaction measures included satisfaction with the helpgiving staff and satisfaction with the helpgiving program (e.g., Dunst & Trivette, 2004; Larsen, Attkisson, Hargreaves, & Nguyen, 1979). The program and social support measures included program participant judgments of childrearing, parenting, and other kinds of supports provided by a helpgiver or a parent's social support network members (e.g., Dunst, Jenkins, & Trivette, 1984; Dunst & Trivette, 1994). The parenting behavior measures included parenting competence, parenting confidence, and parenting enjoyment (e.g., Dunst & Masiello, 2002; Guidubaldi & Cleminshaw, 1994). The parent and family well-being measures included different measures of personal and family psychological functioning (e.g., Bradburn, 1969; Radloff, 1977). The child behavior measures included parent judgments of child positive and negative functioning, child learning, and child development and competence (e.g., Conners, 1997; Dunst & Trivette, 2003a). The reader is referred to Dunst et al. (2006a), Dunst, Trivette, and Hamby (2006b) and Dunst et al. (2008) for the complete lists and descriptions of the scales and outcome measures in both meta-analyses.

Each outcome measure in each study was coded on an a priori basis as either a proximal or distal dependent variable. An outcome was coded as proximal if the target of study participant appraisals was a benefit related to or associated with a helpgiver or his or her program (e.g., judgments of the helpfulness of support or advice in response to a parent request). An outcome measure was coded as distal if the targets of appraisal included no reference to the helpgiver or his or her program (e.g., judgments of personal well-being and family quality of life). The majority of the six outcome categories had both proximal and distal outcome measures.

### Methods of Analysis

The standardized path coefficients between the independent, mediating, and outcome measures were used as the size of effects between measures, and for ascertaining the direct and indirect effects of family-centered helpgiving practices on parent, family, and child behavior and functioning (Cohen, Cohen, West, & Aiken, 2003; Rosenthal, 1994). Procedures described by Shadish and Haddock (1994) were used to combine effect sizes giving more weight to studies with larger sample sizes. The average weighted effect sizes were used as the best estimate of the strength of the relationship between measures. Data interpretation was further aided by calculating the 95% confidence intervals of the average weighted effect sizes, where an interval not including zero indicates that the average size of effect is statistically different from zero at the .05 level (Hedges, 1994).

The indirect effects of family-centered helpgiving on parent, family, and child behavior and functioning mediated by self-efficacy beliefs were calculated as the product of the direct effect of family-centered helpgiving on self-efficacy beliefs, and the direct effect of self-efficacy beliefs on the outcome measures, using procedures described by Cohen et al. (2003). The extent to which the influences of family-centered helpgiving on parent, family, and child behavior was entirely direct, partially mediated by self-efficacy beliefs, or completely mediated by self-efficacy beliefs, was discerned by examining the patterns of direct and indirect effects. In those cases where the direct effects of the family-centered helpgiving are significantly greater than zero and the indirect effects are nonsignificant, the influences of family-centered helpgiving are *entirely direct*.

In those cases where the average sizes of effect of the indirect influences of family-centered helpgiving on the outcome measures are significantly greater than zero and those for the direct effects of family centered helpgiving are zero (or nonsignificantly different from zero), the influences of family-centered helpgiving on parent, family, and child behavior and functioning are *completely mediated* by self efficacy beliefs. In those cases where the average sizes of effect of both the direct and indirect influences of family-centered helpgiving on parent, family, and child behavior and functioning are significantly differ from zero, the influences of family-centered helpgiving on the study outcomes are *partially mediated* by self-efficacy beliefs.

### Results

Four sets of results are summarized in this section of the chapter. The first are the results of the analyses of the relationships between relational and participatory helpgiving practices and the measures in the six outcome categories. The second are the results for the relationships between family-centered helpgiving practices and the proximal vs. distal outcome measure. The third are the results of the relationships between the proximal self-efficacy belief measures and the five categories of parent, family, and child outcome measures. The fourth are the results of the analyses of the indirect effects of family-centered helpgiving practices on parent, family, and child behavior and functioning mediated by self-efficacy beliefs.

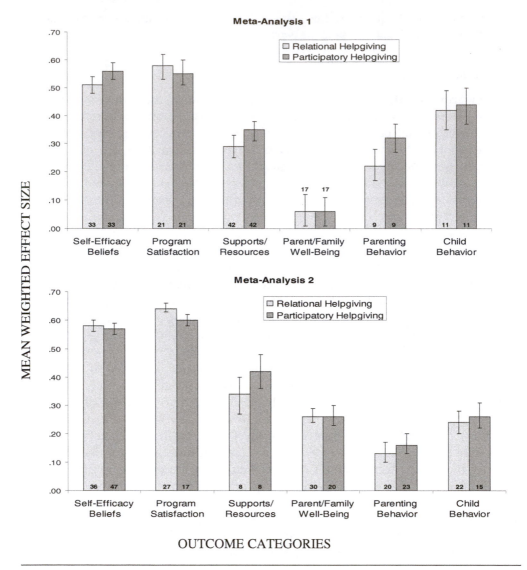

**Figure 16.2** Direct effects of family-centered relational and participatory helpgiving practices in six categories of study outcomes. (The numbers on the bars are the number of effect sizes included in the analyses.)

Figure 16.2 shows the sizes of effect for the relationships between family-centered relational and participatory helpgiving practices and the measures in the six outcome categories. The patterns of relationships between the independent and dependent measures in both meta-analyses were very much alike with one exception (parent and family well-being). Both types of family-centered helpgiving were significantly related to all of the outcome measures, where the strength of the relationships differed as a function of outcome category and type of helpgiving practice.

The strength of the relationships between both types of family-centered helpgiving practices and the outcomes were, in descending order, program satisfaction, self-efficacy beliefs, social support and resources, child behavior and functioning, parenting behavior, and parent and family well-being. Relational (compared to participatory) helpgiving practices were more strongly related to program satisfaction, whereas participatory (compared to relational) helpgiving practices tended to be more strongly related to the social support and resources, parenting behavior, and child behavior and functioning. The strength of the relationships between both relational and participatory helpgiving practices and parent and family well-being were the same in each of the meta-analyses.

The relationships between family-centered helpgiving practices and the proximal vs. distal outcomes are shown in Figure 16.3. The independent measures in both meta-

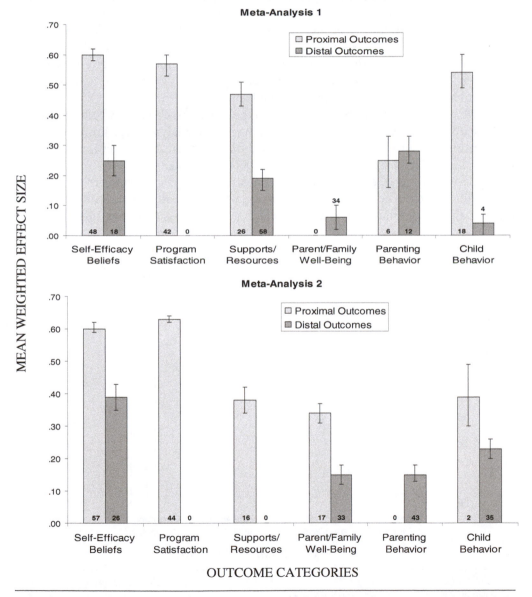

**Figure 16.3** Direct effects of family-centered helpgiving practices on the proximal and distal outcome measures. (The numbers on the bars are the number of effect sizes included in the analyses.)

analyses were the family-centered relational and participatory helpgiving practices measures taken together. The dependent measures were the different measures in each outcome category organized by the targets of study participants' judgments. There were six sets of analyses that included average effect sizes for the relationships between family-centered helpgiving practices and the proximal vs. distal outcome measures. In all the analyses except one (child behavior in Meta-Analysis 1), family-centered helpgiving practices were significantly related to the outcome measures albeit differentially as a function of outcome category and type of outcome measure (proximal vs. distal).

The strength of the relationships between family-centered helpgiving and the outcome measures, with a single exception (parenting behavior in Meta-Analysis 1), were stronger for the proximal compared to the distal outcomes. In most analyses, the size of effects for the relationships between helpgiving practices and the proximal outcomes were twice as large as those for the distal outcome measures. Moreover, the patterns of relationships between the independent and dependent measures were very much alike in both meta-analyses in terms of the average effect sizes for the same outcome measures and the differences in the size of effects.

Figure 16.4 shows the relationship between the proximal self-efficacy belief measures and the outcome measures in both meta-analyses. The analyses were limited to these relationships because so few studies included distal self-efficacy belief measures and proximal and distal parent, family, and child outcome measures.

In all five analyses, the self-efficacy belief measures were significantly related to parent, family, and child behavior and functioning, where the patterns of results in the two meta-analyses were much alike. The self-efficacy belief measures were most related to

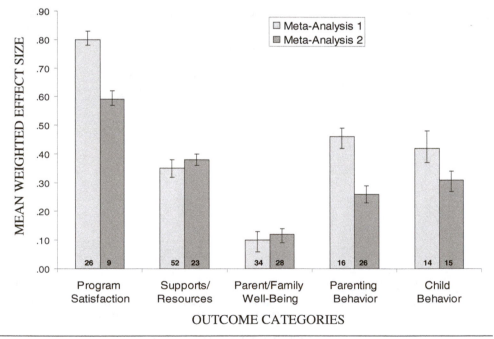

**Figure 16.4** Direct effects of the proximal self-efficacy belief measures on the proximal and distal outcome measures. (The numbers on the bars are the number of effect sizes included in the analyses.)

program satisfaction, followed by parenting behavior, child behavior, and supports and resources, and the least strongly related to parent and family well-being.

The final set of analyses is for the direct and indirect effects of family-centered helpgiving practices on the outcomes mediated by the proximal self-efficacy belief measure. The results are shown in Figure 16.5. Results show for program satisfaction, supports

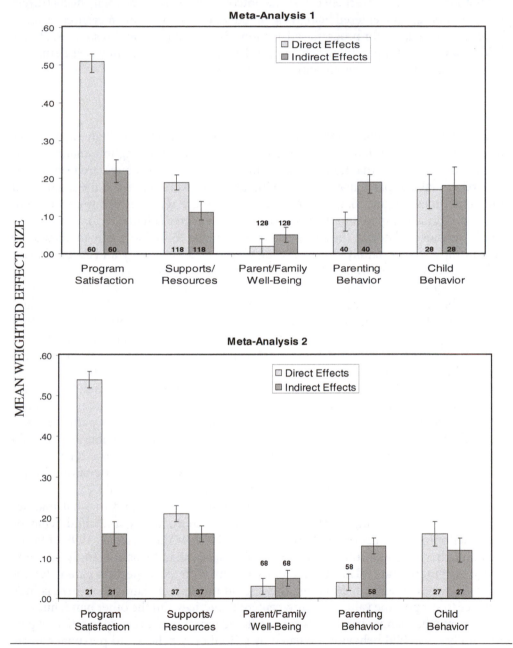

**Figure 16.5** Direct and indirect effects of family-centered helpgiving on parent, family, and child behavior and functioning mediated by self-efficacy beliefs. (The numbers on the bars are the number of effect sizes included in the analyses.)

and resources, parenting, and child behavior and functioning, the influences of family-centered helpgiving on the outcomes are partially mediated by self-efficacy beliefs. In each meta-analysis, family-centered helpgiving practices had indirect effects on all the measures of parent, family, and child behavior and functioning. In all the analyses except one (parent and family well-being in Meta-Analysis 1), family-centered helpgiving had both direct and indirect effects on the outcome measures. The total effects (direct + indirect) of family-centered helpgiving practices on the outcome measures were, in descending order, .71 for program satisfaction, .34 for supports and resources, .32 for child behavior, .22 for parenting behavior, and .07 for parent and family well-being. All the total effect sizes were significantly different from zero.

### Discussion

Findings from both meta-analyses indicated that family-centered helpgiving practices were related to parent, family, and child behavior and functioning in a manner consistent with the conceptual framework guiding the conduct of the research syntheses. Both relational and participatory helpgiving practices were related to the majority of study outcomes (Figure 16.2) where the strength of the relationships were strongest for the proximal compared to the distal outcome measures (Figure 16.3). Self-efficacy beliefs were also related to the study outcomes (Figure 16.4) and partly mediated the relationships between family-centered helpgiving and parent, family, and child behavior and functioning (Figure 16.5). The next step in this line of research is the meta-analytic structural equation modeling (Cheung & Chan, 2005; Shadish, 1996) of the relationships not only between family-centered helpgiving practices and parent, family, and child behavior and functioning, but the relationships between, for example, family-centered helpgiving practices, self-efficacy beliefs, parenting competence and confidence, and child behavior and functioning. These more complex relationships have been the focus of a number of investigations (e.g., Dunst, 1999; Dunst, Hamby, et al., 2007; King, King, Rosenbaum, & Goffin, 1999; Thompson et al., 1997), and the findings from these kinds of studies will be combined by pooling the correlation matrices for the relationships among multiple measures and by building and testing models of multi-pathway influences of family-centered helpgiving and self-efficacy beliefs on parent, family, and child behavior and functioning (Beretvas & Furlow, 2006; Furlow & Beretvas, 2005).

The findings summarized in this chapter, and discussed more extensively in our meta-analytic reports (Dunst et al., 2006a; Dunst, Trivette, et al., 2007; Dunst et al., 2008), should quell criticisms and misunderstandings of how and in what manner family-centered helpgiving practices are related to parent, family, and child behavior and functioning (e.g., Feldman, Ploof, & Cohen, 1999; Mahoney et al., 1999). On the one hand, there is now a considerable body of evidence that the use of family-centered helpgiving practices are related to variations in many different aspects of parent, family, and child behavior and functioning. This should put to rest claims that there is little evidence to support the value of family-centered practices. On the other hand, findings demonstrate the manner in which family-centered practices are related to different parent, family, and child behavior mediated by self-efficacy beliefs and personal control appraisals (Bandura, 1997; Skinner, 1995). This helps place family-centered practices in both theoretical and empirical context by showing the manner in which helpgiving practices are both directly and indirectly related to different domains of parent, family, and child behavior and functioning.

It is also worth noting how and in what manner family-centered helpgiving practices are related to other kinds of interventions. Family-centered practices are *how* other kinds of practices are implemented. Family-centered practices are complementary to any other type of intervention to the extent the intervention is intended to support and strengthen parent and family functioning so as to have capacity-building consequences.

As part of the development, optimization, and evaluation of a family-systems early intervention and family support model (Dunst et al., 1988; Dunst, Trivette, & Deal, 1994), and as part of research examining the characteristics and consequences of social support on families of young children (Dunst, 1985; Dunst & Trivette, 1988; Dunst et al., 1997), we found that effort to be helpful did not always have positive consequences. In some cases, helpgiving was effective; in other cases, it had no discernible positive or negative effects; and in some instances, it actually had negative effects on help receivers. These mixed findings led us to conclude that "It may not just be (a matter) of whether needs are met but rather the manner in which mobilization of resources and support occurs that is a major determinant of…empowering families" (Dunst et al., 1988, p. 44). Karuza, Rabinowitz, and Zevon (1986) as well noted that the "effects of help not only depends on *what* is done but also *how* it's done" (p. 380, emphasis added). What is now clear is the fact that both relational and participatory helpgiving practices both individually and in combination have elements and features that contribute to positive parent, family, and child benefits.

## CONCLUSIONS

The findings presented in this chapter show the manner in which family-centered helpgiving practices are related to parent, family, and child behavior and functioning. We conclude by both describing the findings in terms of parent–professional partnerships and by placing family-centered practices in the context of a broad-based family systems approach to intervention.

As noted early in the chapter and reiterated here, the characteristics that partnership enthusiasts claim define these kinds of relationships overlap considerably with the behavioral indicators of relational and participatory helpgiving practices. We therefore suggest that parent–professional partnerships are best conceptualized as a component of effective helpgiving practices, and are a necessary but not sufficient condition for having value-added benefits. Moreover, and contrary to those who tend to emphasize relational practices as the defining characteristics of partnerships, we would argue, based on the findings described in this chapter, that more equal attention be given to participatory practices as part of parent and professional helpgiving practices.

We also note that family-centered helpgiving practices are but one family and systems variable that would be expected to influence parent, family, and child behavior and functioning. For example, we have always considered family-centered practices as just one practice that would be expected to contribute to positive consequences. It is "part of the equation" of a broader-based approach to early childhood intervention and family support (Dunst, 2004; Dunst et al., 1988; Dunst, Trivette, & Deal, 1994; Trivette, Deal, & Dunst, 1986). In statistical terms, family-centered practices would be expected to account for some but not all the outcomes considered important benefits of program practices.

The purpose of this *Handbook* included a better understanding of the conditions under which parent–professional partnerships are mostly likely to contribute to young children's and older student's education and development (see preface of this volume). Many of the other chapters in the *Handbook* describe those conditions in detail. Our chapter adds to the knowledge base by describing how and in what manner family-centered helpgiving practices have positive influences and are indicated as a practice-of-choice for working with families.

## REFERENCES

Alexander, L. B., & Dore, M. M. (1999). Making the Parents as Partners principle a reality: The role of the alliance. *Journal of Child and Family Studies, 8*, 255–270.

Allen, R. I., & Petr, C. G. (1996). Toward developing standards and measurements for family-centered practice in family support programs. In G. H. S. Singer, A. P. Turnbull, H. R. Turnbull, III, L. K. Irvin, & L. E. Powers (Eds.), *Family, community, and disability: Redefining family support. Innovations in public-private partnerships* (pp. 57–85). Baltimore: Brookes.

Allen, R. I., Petr, C. G., & Brown, B. F. C. (1995). *Family-Centered Behavior Scale and user's manual.* Lawrence: University of Kansas, Beach Center on Families and Disability.

Bandura, A. (1997). *Self-efficacy: The exercise of control.* New York: Freeman.

Beckman, P. J. (Ed.). (1996). *Strategies for working with families of young children with disabilities.* Baltimore: Brookes.

Beckman, P. J., Frank, N., & Newcomb, S. (1996). Qualities and skills for communicating with families. In P. J. Beckman (Ed.), *Strategies for working with families of young children with disabilities* (pp. 31–46). Baltimore: Brookes.

Beretvas, S. N., & Furlow, C. F. (2006). Evaluation of an approximate method for synthesizing covariance matrices for use in meta-analytic SEM. *Structural Equation Modeling, 13*, 153–185.

Blue-Banning, M., Summers, J. A., Frankland, I. C., Nelson, L. L., & Beegle, G. (2004). Dimensions of family and professional partnerships: Constructive guidelines for collaboration. *Exceptional Children, 70*, 167–184.

Boyd, K., & Dunst, C. J. (1996). *Personal assessment of control scale.* Asheville, NC: Winterberry Press.

Bradburn, N. M. (1969). *The structure of psychological well-being.* Chicago: Aldine.

Bronfenbrenner, U. (1992). Ecological systems theory. In R. Vasta (Ed.), *Six theories of child development: Revised formulations and current issues* (pp. 187–248). Philadelphia: Jessica Kingsley.

Bruns, D. A., & Steeples, T. (2001). Partners from the beginning: Guidelines for encouraging partnerships between parents and NICU and EI professionals. *Infant-Toddler Intervention, 11*, 237–247.

Cheung, M. W., & Chan, W. (2005). Meta-analytic structural equation modeling: A two-stage approach. *Psychological Methods, 10*(1), 40–64.

Christenson, S. L., & Conoley, J. C. (Eds.). (1992). *Home-school collaboration: Enhancing children's academic and social competence.* Silver Springs, MD: National Association of School Psychologists.

Cohen, J., Cohen, P., West, S. G., & Aiken, L. S. (2003). *Applied multiple regression/correlation analysis for the behavioral sciences* (3rd ed.). Mahwah, NJ: Erlbaum.

Conners, C. K. (1997). *Conners' rating scales—revised: Technical manual.* North Tonawanda, NY: Multi-Health Systems.

Crozier, G. (1999). Is it a case of 'We know when we're not wanted'? The parents' perspective on parent-teacher roles and relationships. *Educational Research, 41*, 315–325.

DeChillo, N., Koren, P. E., & Schultze, K. H. (1994). From paternalism to partnership: Family and professional collaboration in children's mental health. *American Journal of Orthopsychiatry, 64*, 564–576.

DeGangi, G., Royeen, C. B., & Wietlisbach, S. (1992). How to examine the individualized family service plan process: Preliminary findings and a procedural guide. *Infants and Young Children, 5*(2), 42–56.

Dempsey, I. (1995). The Enabling Practices Scale: The development of an assessment instrument for disability services. *Australia and New Zealand Journal of Developmental Disabilities, 20*, 67–73.

Dempsey, I., & Keen, D. (2008). A review of processes and outcomes in family-centered services for children with a disability. *Topics in Early Childhood Special Education, 28*, 42–52.

Devore, S., & Bowers, B. (2006). Childcare for children with disabilities: Families search for specialized care and cooperative childcare partnerships. *Infants and Young Children, 19*, 203–212.

Dinnebeil, L. A., Hale, L. M., & Rule, S. (1996). A qualitative analysis of parents' and service coordinators' descriptions of variables that influence collaborative relationships. *Topics in Early Childhood Special Education, 16*, 322–347.

Dunst, C. J. (1985). Rethinking early intervention. *Analysis and Intervention in Developmental Disabilities, 5*, 165–201.

Dunst, C. J. (1997). Conceptual and empirical foundations of family-centered practice. In R. Illback, C. Cobb, & H. Joseph, Jr. (Eds.), *Integrated services for children and families: Opportunities for psychological practice* (pp. 75–91). Washington, DC: American Psychological Association.

Dunst, C. J. (1999). Placing parent education in conceptual and empirical context. *Topics in Early Childhood Special Education, 19*, 141–147.

Dunst, C. J. (2002). Family-centered practices: Birth through high school. *Journal of Special Education, 36*, 139–147.

Dunst, C. J. (2004). An integrated framework for practicing early childhood intervention and family support. *Perspectives in Education, 22*(2), 1–16.

Dunst, C. J., & Dempsey, I. (2007). Family-professional partnerships and parenting competence, confidence, and enjoyment. *International Journal of Disability, Development, and Education, 54*, 305–318.

Dunst, C. J., Hamby, D. W., & Brookfield, J. (2007). Modeling the effects of early childhood intervention variables on parent and family well-being. *Journal of Applied Quantitative Methods, 2*, 268–288.

Dunst, C. J., Jenkins, V., & Trivette, C. (1984). *Family Support Scale*. Asheville, NC: Winterberry Press.

Dunst, C. J., Johanson, C., Rounds, T., Trivette, C. M., & Hamby, D. (1992). Characteristics of parent-professional partnerships. In S. Christenson & J. C. Conoley (Eds.), *Home-school collaboration: Building a fundamental educational resource* (pp. 157–174). Washington, DC: National Association of School Psychologists.

Dunst, C. J., & Masiello, T. L. (2002). *Everyday parenting scale*. Asheville, NC: Winterberry Press.

Dunst, C. J., & Paget, K. (1991). Parent-professional partnerships and family empowerment. In M. Fine (Ed.), *Collaboration with parents of exceptional children* (pp. 25–44). Brandon, VT: Clinical Psychology.

Dunst, C. J., & Trivette, C. M. (1988). A family systems model of early intervention with handicapped and developmentally at-risk children. In D. R. Powell (Ed.), *Parent education as early childhood intervention: Emerging directions in theory, research, and practice* (pp. 131–179). Norwood, NJ: Ablex.

Dunst, C. J., & Trivette, C. M. (1994). *Family support availability scale*. Unpublished scale, Orelena Hawks Puckett Institute, Asheville, NC.

Dunst, C. J., & Trivette, C. M. (2003a). *Child learning opportunities scale*. Asheville, NC: Winterberry Press.

Dunst, C. J., & Trivette, C. M. (2003b). *Family-centered practices scale: Long form*. Asheville, NC: Winterberry Press.

Dunst, C. J., & Trivette, C. M. (2004). *Early intervention program satisfaction scale*. Asheville, NC: Winterberry Press.

Dunst, C. J., Trivette, C. M., & Deal, A. (1988). *Enabling and empowering families: Principles and guidelines for practice*. Cambridge, MA: Brookline Books.

Dunst, C. J., Trivette, C. M., & Deal, A. G. (Eds.). (1994). *Supporting and strengthening families: Methods, strategies and practices*. Cambridge, MA: Brookline Books.

Dunst, C. J., Trivette, C. M., & Hamby, D. W. (2006a). *Family support program quality and parent, family and child benefits* (Winterberry Monograph Series). Asheville, NC: Winterberry Press.

Dunst, C. J., Trivette, C. M., & Hamby, D. W. (2006b). *Technical manual for measuring and evaluating family support program quality and benefits* (Winterberry Monograph Series). Asheville, NC: Winterberry Press.

Dunst, C. J., Trivette, C. M., & Hamby, D. W. (2007). Meta-analysis of family-centered helpgiving practices research. *Mental Retardation and Developmental Disabilities Research Reviews, 13*, 370–378.

Dunst, C. J., Trivette, C. M., & Hamby, D. W. (2008). *Research synthesis and meta-analysis of studies of family-centered practices* (Winterberry Monograph Series). Asheville, NC: Winterberry Press.

Dunst, C. J., Trivette, C. M., & Jodry, W. (1997). Influences of social support on children with disabilities and their families. In M. Guralnick (Ed.), *The effectiveness of early intervention* (pp. 499–522). Baltimore: Brookes.

Dunst, C. J., Trivette, C. M., & Johanson, C. (1994). Parent-professional collaboration and partnerships. In C. J.

Dunst, C. M. Trivette, & A. G. Deal (Eds.), *Supporting and strengthening families: Methods, strategies and practices* (pp. 197–211). Cambridge, MA: Brookline Books.

Dunst, C. J., Trivette, C. M., & LaPointe, N. (1992). Toward clarification of the meaning and key elements of empowerment. *Family Science Review, 5,* 111–130.

Dunst, C. J., Trivette, C. M., & Snyder, D. M. (2000). Family-professional partnerships: A behavioral science perspective. In M. J. Fine & R. L. Simpson (Eds.), *Collaboration with parents and families of children and youth with exceptionalities* (2nd ed., pp. 27–48). Austin, TX: PRO-ED.

Feldman, H. M., Ploof, D., & Cohen, W. I. (1999). Physician-family partnerships: The adaptive practice model. *Journal of Developmental and Behavioral Pediatrics, 20,* 111–116.

Furlow, C. F., & Beretvas, S. N. (2005). Meta-analytic methods of pooling correlation matrices for structural equation modeling under different patterns of missing data. *Psychological Methods, 10,* 227–254.

Galinsky, E. (1990). Why are some parent/teacher partnerships clouded with difficulties? *Young Children, 45*(5), 2–3, 38-39.

Guidubaldi, J., & Cleminshaw, H. K. (1994). *Parenting satisfaction scale.* San Antonio, TX: Psychological Corporation.

Harry, B. (2008). Collaboration with culturally and linguistically diverse families: Ideal versus reality. *Exceptional Children, 74,* 372–388.

Hedges, L. V. (1994). Fixed effects models. In H. Cooper & L. V. Hedges (Eds.), *The handbook of research synthesis* (pp. 285–299). New York: Russell Sage Foundation.

Irlam, L. K., & Bruce, J. C. (2002). Family-centred care in paediatric and neonatal nursing: A literature review. *Curationis, 25*(3), 28–34.

Jakobsen, E. S., & Severinsson, E. (2006). Parents' experiences of collaboration with community healthcare professionals. *Journal of Psychiatric and Mental Health Nursing, 13,* 498–505.

Karuza, J., Jr., Rabinowitz, V. C., & Zevon, M. A. (1986). Implications of control and responsibility on helping the aged. In M. M. Baltes & P. B. Baltes (Eds.), *The psychology of control and aging* (pp. 373–396). Hillsdale, NJ: Erlbaum.

Keen, D. (2007). Parents, families, and partnerships: Issues and considerations. *International Journal of Disability, Development and Education, 54,* 339–349.

King, G., King, S., Rosenbaum, P., & Goffin, R. (1999). Family-centered caregiving and well-being of parents of children with disabilities: Linking process with outcome. *Journal of Pediatric Psychology, 24,* 41–53.

King, S. M., Rosenbaum, P. L., & King, G. A. (1996). Parents' perceptions of caregiving: Development and validation of a measure of processes. *Developmental Medicine and Child Neurology, 38,* 757–772.

Koren, P. E., DeChillo, N., & Friesen, B. J. (1992). Measuring empowerment in families whose children have emotional disabilities: A brief questionnaire. *Rehabilitation Psychology, 37,* 305–321.

Larsen, D. L., Attkisson, C. C., Hargreaves, W. A., & Nguyen, T. D. (1979). Assessment of client/patient satisfaction: Development of a general scale. *Evaluation and Program Planning, 2,* 197–207.

Law, M., Teplicky, R., King, S., King, G., Kertoy, M., Moning, T., et al. (2005). Family-centered service: Moving ideas into practice. *Child: Care, Health and Development, 31,* 633–642.

Mahoney, G., Kaiser, A. P., Girolametto, L., MacDonald, J., Robinson, C., Safford, P., et al. (1999). Parent education in early intervention: A call for a renewed focus. *Topics in Early Childhood Special Education, 19,* 131–140.

Maple, F. F. (1977). *Shared decision making.* Beverly Hills, CA: Sage.

Pinkus, S. (2003). All talk and no action: Transforming the rhetoric of parent-professional partnership into practice. *Journal of Research in Special Educational Needs, 3,* 115–121.

Radloff, L. S. (1977). The CES-D scale: A self-report depression scale for research in the general population. *Applied Psychological Measurement, 1,* 385–401.

Rappaport, J. (1981). In praise of paradox: A social policy of empowerment over prevention. *American Journal of Community Psychology, 9,* 1–25.

Reich, S., Bickman, L., & Heflinger, C. A. (2004). Covariates of self-efficacy: Caregiver characteristics related to mental health services self-efficacy. *Journal of Emotional and Behavioral Disorders, 12,* 99–108.

Riessman, F. (1990). Restructuring help: A human services paradigm for the 1990s. *American Journal of Community Psychology, 18,* 221–230.

Roberts, R., Rule, S., & Innocenti, M. (1998). *Strengthening the family-professional partnership in services for young children.* Baltimore: Brookes.

Rosenbaum, P., King, S., Law, M., King, G., & Evans, J. (1998). Family-centred service: A conceptual framework and research review. *Physical and Occupational Therapy in Pediatrics, 18*(1), 1–20.

Rosenthal, R. (1994). Parametric measures of effect size. In H. Cooper & L. V. Hedges (Eds.), *The handbook of research synthesis* (pp. 231–244). New York: Russell Sage Foundation.

Shadish, W. R. (1996). Meta-analysis and the exploration of causal mediating processes: A primer of examples, methods, and issues. *Psychological Methods, 1,* 47–65.

Shadish, W. R., & Haddock, C. K. (1994). Combining estimates of effect size. In H. Cooper & L. V. Hedges (Eds.), *The handbook of research synthesis* (pp. 261–281). New York: Russell Sage Foundation.

Shelton, T. L., & Stepanek, J. S. (1994). *Family-centered care for children needing specialized health and developmental services* (3rd ed.). Bethesda, MD: Association for the Care of Children's Health.

Shields, L., Pratt, J., & Hunter, J. (2006). Family centred care: A review of qualitative studies. *Journal of Clinical Nursing, 15,* 1317–1323.

Skinner, E. A. (1995). *Perceived control, motivation, and coping.* Thousand Oaks, CA: Sage.

Sokoly, M., & Dokecki, P. (1992). Ethical perspectives on family-centered early intervention. *Infants and Young Children, 4*(4), 23–32.

Summers, J. A., Hoffman, L., Marquis, J., Turnbull, A., Poston, D., & Nelson, L. L. (2005). Measuring the quality of family: Professional partnerships in special education services. *Exceptional Children, 72,* 65–81.

Summers, J. A., Marquis, J., Mannan, H., Turnbull, A. P., Fleming, K., Poston, D. J., et al. (2007). Relationship of perceived adequacy of services, family-professional partnerships, and family quality of life in early childhood service programmes. *International Journal of Disability, Development and Education, 54,* 319–338.

Swanson, K. (1991). Empirical development of a middle range theory of caring. *Nursing Research, 40,* 161–166.

Thompson, L., Lobb, C., Elling, R., Herman, S., Jurkiewicz, T., & Hulleza, C. (1997). Pathways to family empowerment: Effects of family-centered delivery of early intervention services. *Exceptional Children, 64,* 99–113.

Todd, E. S., & Higgins, S. (1998). Powerlessness in professional and parent partnerships. *British Journal of Sociology of Education, 19,* 227–236.

Trivette, C. M., Deal, A., & Dunst, C. J. (1986). Family needs, sources of support, and professional roles: Critical elements of family systems assessment and intervention. *Diagnostique, 11,* 246–267.

Trivette, C. M., & Dunst, C. J. (1994). *Helpgiving practices scale.* Asheville, NC: Winterberry Press.

Trivette, C. M., & Dunst, C. J. (2007). *Capacity-building family-centered helpgiving practices* (Winterberry Research Reports Vol. 1, No. 10). Asheville, NC: Winterberry Press.

Trivette, C. M., Dunst, C. J., Boyd, K., & Hamby, D. W. (1995). Family-oriented program models, helpgiving practices, and parental control appraisals. *Exceptional Children, 62,* 237–248.

Trivette, C. M., Dunst, C. J., Deal, A. G., Hamby, D. W., & Sexton, D. (1994). Assessing family strengths and capabilities. In C. J. Dunst, C. M. Trivette, & A. G. Deal (Eds.), *Supporting and strengthening families: Methods, strategies and practices.* (pp. 132–139). Cambridge, MA: Brookline Books.

Trivette, C. M., Dunst, C. J., & Hamby, D. W. (1996a). Characteristics and consequences of help-giving practices in contrasting human services programs. *American Journal of Community Psychology, 24,* 273–293.

Trivette, C. M., Dunst, C. J., & Hamby, D. W. (1996b). Factors associated with perceived control appraisals in a family-centered early intervention program. *Journal of Early Intervention, 20,* 165–178.

Turnbull, A. P., & Turnbull, H. R., III. (1986). *Families, professionals, and exceptionality: A special partnership.* Columbus, OH: Merrill.

van Riper, M. (1999). Maternal perceptions of family-provider relationships and well-being in families of children with Down syndrome. *Research in Nursing and Health, 22,* 357–368.

Walker, B. (1989). Strategies for improving parent-professional cooperation. In G. H. S. Singer & L. K. Irvin (Eds.), *Support for caregiving families: Enabling positive adaptation to disability* (pp. 103–119). Baltimore: Brookes.

Zimmerman, M. A. (2000). Empowerment theory: Psychological, organizational and community levels of analysis. In J. Rappaport & E. Seidman (Eds.), *Handbook of community psychology* (pp. 43–63). New York: Kluwer Academic/Plenum.

# 17

## MAPPING FAMILY-SCHOOL RELATIONS IN COMPREHENSIVE SCHOOL REFORM MODELS AND CHARTER SCHOOL DESIGNS

### *A Call for a New Research Agenda*

**CLAIRE SMREKAR, LORA COHEN-VOGEL, AND JIE-EUN LEE**

A cornerstone of comprehensive school reforms and charter school designs focuses on increasing school community and the involvement of parents in the lives of school children (Schneider & Teske, 2001; U.S. Department of Education, 1994). It is our contention that clarity in the practical as well as policy implications for family-school relations of comprehensive school reform and charter school models is a critically important scholarly endeavor that holds the potential value of considering strong family-school relationships as a foundation of educational excellence.

## OVERVIEW

This chapter examines selected comprehensive school reform and charter school models that situate enhanced family-school relations at the center of the school change effort. It is necessary to identify gaps in the research base in order to fully understand the linkages between comprehensive school reform and robust family-school-community relations. Family-school relations are construed as an inclusive and broad concept that includes notions of school community, family engagement, and parental involvement (Crowson, 1992). Several questions are posed: What are the components for building school community envisioned in each school reform/choice model? How do these components map against a typology of family-school relations adapted from the extant literature in the field? Next, the research and evaluation literature for evidence of community-building practices across each model is reviewed to describe what is known (and what must be known) about the fidelity between the design and implementation of the school community-building elements in comprehensive reform and charter school models. After identifying a significant gap in the research base, a research plan that explicates the nature, quality, and intensity of family-school relations in these reform and charter school models is proposed.

## TYPOLOGY OF FAMILY-SCHOOL RELATIONS

An assumption of our work is that building strong family-school relationships is beneficial to schools, teachers, and the students they serve. Overall, research supports the assumption. Empirical evidence indicates that when families are involved in schools, parents' attitudes about themselves, the school their child attends, and the school staff are enhanced; stronger family-school relationships lead to deeper understanding among both parents and educators about the role each plays in the development of the child (Ames, Khoju, & Watkins, 1993; Becher, 1984; Clark, 1983; Comer, 1980; Dornbusch & Ritter, 1988; Epstein & Dauber, 1991; Henderson, 1981; Scott-Jones, 1987). This increased understanding is thought to promote greater cooperation, commitment, and trust between parents and teachers. More recent research suggests that parents' patterns of participation may be an important factor in mediating the negative impact of neighborhood risk factors on the academic performance of elementary school students (Shumow, Vandell, & Posner, 1999). Additionally, there are indications of the connection between teachers' expectations for student performance and parental behavior (Epstein, 1987). Decisions regarding retention/promotion and ability grouping may well hinge on teachers' perceptions of parental interest and commitment.

Four distinctive models of family-school relationships in schools were derived from case studies of public and private schools, including magnet schools (Smrekar & Goldring, 1999), Catholic schools (Smrekar, 1996), workplace schools (Smrekar, 2001), and neighborhood schools (Smrekar & Cohen-Vogel, 2001)—located in urban and suburban contexts in the United States. These models include: Cooptation; Management; Engagement; and Coalition (Smrekar, 2009). Each model is comprised of four elements that define the nature, quality, and intensity of association between schools and their communities. As illustrated in Table 17.1, these four elements are reflected in the organizational practices and priorities of schools that specify the *goal, function, relationship*, and *outcome* related to school-community connections.

### Cooptation Model

The Cooptation model is derived from studies of public schools located in urban contexts characterized by high poverty and social isolation. In these settings, schools often establish control as a goal in their association with families and community members, preempting other more collaborative two-way approaches. The relationship is defined by a provider-receiver arrangement in which a school assumes the role of provider (of educational services); families, in turn, are assigned the role of receiver (Smrekar & Cohen-Vogel, 2001). The essential outcome of the family-school relationship in this context resembles a contract. The contract may take the form of a school-wide, codified discipline policy and other formal parental agreements including Individualized Educational Plans (IEPs) required for the (often) high percentage of students in these contexts who receive services under the U.S. special education law. This outcome tends

**Table 17.1** Characteristics of Family-School Relationship Types

| Elements | Family-School Relationship Typologies | | | |
| --- | --- | --- | --- | --- |
| | Cooptation | Management | Engagement | Coalition |
| *Goal* | Control | Certainty & Structure | Consensus | Collaboration |
| *Relationship* | Producer-Receiver | Professional-Constituent | Co-Producers | Partners |
| *Function* | Legal – Instrumental | Institutional | Social | Familial |
| *Outcome* | Contracts | Categories | Compacts | *Gemeinschaft* (Community) |
| **Examples** | High poverty urban public schools | Traditional public schools | Public choice & private schools | Workplace schools |

to delimit the nature of family-school relations to the legal-instrumental function specified in a set of requirements and obligations that exist between parents and school officials (see Table 17.1).

In case studies of urban elementary schools characterized by high poverty and high minority enrollment, researchers in the United States have found a persistent pattern of school communities suggestive of a Cooptation model (see Delgado-Gaitan, 1992; Goldenberg, 1996; Harry, 1992; Henry, 1996; Mapp, 2003). Harvard researcher Sarah Lightfoot (1978) argued that the lives of families and schools are "worlds apart." This pattern, it appears, has endured for decades. Willard Waller, author of the classic work, *The Sociology of Teaching*, published in 1932, called parents and teachers "natural enemies."

These studies underscore the formal, often legalistic conditions established by schools through the set of parental agreements created by the school, including school-wide discipline policies, school visiting policies, homework policies, and special education programs. These policies tend to imply an asymmetry of power, knowledge, and control—elements appropriated by school officials. Rather than foster a sense of community grounded in mutual respect, shared commitment, and sustained cooperation (Bryk & Driscoll, 1988), these one-way binding agreements—much like a contract—establish an oppositional and litigious culture that pits parents against school officials.

How do classic or contemporary conceptions of community inform the Cooptation model? The historical distinctions made by Tonnies (1963) between *Gemeinschaft* (community) and *Gesellschaft* (society) provide point and direction to this discussion. These differences relate to the nature of relationships within communities versus societies, which range from more natural and organic in communities to more mechanical and rational in societies. Thus, relationships within an authentic community (*Gemeinschaft*) are rooted in familiarity and interdependence whereas societal relationships (*Gesellschaft*) reflect formal, contractual relations found in legal and commercial institutions and bureaucratic organizations (Tonnies, 1963). *Gesellschaft* provides the conceptual scaffolding for the Cooptation model. The Cooptation model persists in particular school community contexts—characterized by high minority and high poverty status—and stands bolted to the formal, bureaucratic, and contractual relations found in broader societal relations. In these school contexts, the social relations between families and schools are codified in the legalistic relationships and prescribed functions outlined in student discipline codes and Individualized Education Plans (IEPs). These relations fall far from the notion of a school as a community, embracing neither the communal associations and personal relationships described by Bryk and Driscoll (1988) in their study of Catholic communities, nor the familiarity or continuity that characterize Coleman and Hoffer's (1987) value and functional communities.

In general, Cooptation-modeled school communities persist because of enduring instrumental-legal arrangements established to maintain control and to distance families from schools. Emerging evidence suggests that new district policies linked to new organizational priorities may deepen these cleavages. In a growing number of urban districts characterized by high poverty and high minority enrollments (including Chicago, Illinois, one of the largest U.S. school districts), school administrators have instituted "Parental Involvement Report Cards" along with a checklist of daily tasks designed to increase pressures for greater accountability of parents (Schemo, 2000). Designed as a blueprint for establishing the nature, scope, and quality of school communities, parent report cards embody the elements of the Cooptation model in a preemptive, codified set of expectations. Johns Hopkins University researcher Joyce Epstein observed that the parent report cards dismiss elements of a "partnership" model in favor of a "dictatorial" approach; parent groups in Chicago have called the report cards "insulting" (Schemo, 2000, p. A23). Concurrently, some parent groups are moving to enact more collaborative school communities that suggest shared governance and mutual cooperation. In Los Angeles, California, for example, a group of African American and Latino parents have formed CADRE—Community Asset Development Re-defining Education—to call for regular parent-led forums that provide "structured opportunities for parents to give input, receive information, and help make decisions in matters affecting the quality of their children's education" (Mangino, 2005).

## Management Model

The extant research on school-community relations suggested the predominant role of a Management model across U.S. public schools. Schools in this domain emphasize certainty and structure as an essential *goal* in their associations with families and external community members. The *relationship* is defined by a co-production orientation. Schools produce particular educational services; parents produce parallel but distinguishable services in predictable and reliable ways. This institutionalized *function* is both taken for granted and explicated in a set of *outcomes*—categories of family participation that describe (and to some degree, prescribe) a set of community-school interactions (see Table 17.1).

Although the nature of family-school relations could be construed as both broad and complex, the Management model reflects efforts by advocates and policy makers—and even some education researchers—to provide specific categories of parent involvement. In training manuals assembled by school districts for teachers and parents, the charts describe parents acting in roles ranging from "advisers" and "advocates" to "home-based tutors" and "traditional audience" (see Burch, 1993; Chrispeels, 1996; Comer, 1980; Davies, 1993; National Education Goals Panel, 1995; Swap, 1993; U.S. Department of

Education, 1994). Other researchers map the location of potential parent input and action to include the home and the school; within those broad categories, activities are identified as either advisory or collaborative (McLaughlin & Shields, 1987). Perhaps no other model has emerged to dominate the fields of research, policy, and practice more than the "partnership" model developed by Johns Hopkins University researcher Joyce Epstein. The Epstein (2002) framework is designed as a template for school administrators; in effect, the types of interactions and involvement identified by Epstein become the predictable categories of interactions with families and external community members that are (or should be) managed by school officials. The model includes six distinct strands or types of involvement: (a) *parenting*, which includes basic obligations of families to create healthy and nurturing home conditions; (b) *communicating*, which includes basic obligations of schools to communicate with families about school practices and programs; (c) *volunteering*, which involves roles for parents that assist teachers and administrators in supporting academic, sports, and other activities; (d) *learning at home*, which involves family involvement in skill-building and educational enrichment activities at home that support classroom learning; (e) *decision-making*, which involves parent participation in school decision-making and governance through school site councils and other organized policy-making and advocacy groups; and (f) *collaborating with community*, which includes the obligation of schools to identify and integrate community resources and services in order to enhance school and family practices and promote student achievement. Epstein (1992) argued that "the term 'school, family and community partnerships' is a better, broader term than 'parent involvement' to express the shared interests, responsibilities, investments, and the overlapping influences of family, school and community for the education and development of the children they share across the school years" (p. 114). Unlike the Cooptation model, the Management model—with the Epstein template embedded as a blueprint for family-school relations— presumes two-way communication across a more robust array of differentiated tasks— scripted well beyond the legal and formal arrangements prescribed in the former, more asymmetrical model. At the same time, this "partnership" emphasizes the separable and identifiable activities that comprise school, community, and parent activities.

Over time, these distinct categories or roles have become institutionalized in many U.S. public schools, producing common understandings about what is appropriate and fundamentally meaningful behavior for parents, teachers, and external school communities to display. Manuals and reports issued by the U.S. Department of Education embrace these categories as appropriate, research-based activities for parents, teachers, and community members that lead to highly effective, high performing schools (see National Education Goals Panel, 1995; U.S. Department of Education, 1994). Institutional theory (Meyer & Rowan, 1977) helps explain how school-based activities such as fundraising functions and parent-teacher meetings and home-based activities such as helping with homework become ritualized events, further legitimating the roles defined for school community members. The institutional environment then sanctions similar organizations—schools—on the basis of these established norms (Meyer & Rowan, 1977). Parents learn over time the circumscribed roles that they are expected to assume. They learn to think of themselves as supporters, helpers, and fundraisers. Beyond those functions, our studies of elementary schools—both public and private—suggest that parents' zone of involvement in schools as decision makers and partners may be compromised by the press of other obligations, including work and family responsibilities (Smrekar, 1996). The extant research suggests that patterns and degree of involvement are heavily influenced by parents' social class and cultural capital (Lareau, 2000), role construction and the nature of invitations from teachers (Hoover-Dempsey & Sandler, 1997; Mapp, 2003).

## Engagement Model

Evidence suggests that public choice schools and many private (religious) schools, including Catholic schools, develop an Engagement model with parents and external community members (Bryk & Driscoll, 1988; Smrekar, 1996; Smrekar & Goldring, 1999). The *relationship* between families and schools embedded in this model portrays parents as constituents or clients and school officials as professionals, suggesting distinctive roles coupled with mutual respect and shared values. In *functional* relationships defined more as social than legal/instrumental or institutional, public choice and private schools often seek a product-oriented *goal* of consensus. The material *outcome* of this association resembles a co-constructed compact, rather than a restrictive contract (see Table 17.1). The process of consensus-building rests on relationships built upon shared commitment and sustained cooperation—across school families and between families and school officials. Thus, the elements of the Engagement model are mutually reinforcing. The compact is co-constructed between families and schools and may reflect a set of vision statements related to the educational goals for children. These statements establish a set of strategies for achieving these goals—ideas that can evolve only through meaningful and sustained interactions between each student/family and the school. The compact reflects parallel convictions, intentions, and obligations of parents and school officials. Since parents have voluntarily selected the choice school or private school, there is little sense of institutional control or power play.

In a study of magnet and non-magnet schools in two large urban districts in the United States—St. Louis, Missouri and Cincinnati, Ohio—Smrekar and Goldring (1999) found in both survey data and qualitative case studies that parents who selected a magnet school attended more school activities, volunteered more frequently, and visited the school more often than parents whose children were enrolled in a traditional (zoned) public school. This heightened level of commitment among magnet school families reflect the constituent elements of value communities described by Coleman and Hoffer (1987). These families live in neighborhoods scattered across geographical spaces; their social spaces differ from the geographical or functional communities outlined by Coleman and Hoffer, which exhibit a high degree of uniformity and cohesion *within* geographical, social, economic and ideological boundaries.

Under these conditions of geographical dispersion, parents' beliefs regarding common values and shared beliefs are tethered to rather brief, abbreviated, and anonymous parent-to-parent interactions. Paradoxically, these parents reported that they "do not know many other parents" in their choice school, but most maintained an unwavering belief that other magnet parents (Smrekar & Goldring, 1999) or Catholic school parents (Smrekar, 1996) were like-minded in terms of educational values and commitment. To be sure, these are communities formed around commitment to an organization, not grafted to an elevated sense of familiarity (or functional community) with other members.

To the extent that school community is viewed as a crucial aspect of a school's capacity to promote student learning, these findings are important. Schools organized as communities that support robust, reliable, and sustained family engagement, also create conditions for increased collegiality, improved problem-solving, and enhanced capacity-building (Bryk & Driscoll, 1988). Driscoll (1995) observed that "the concept of school community reflects the needs that are derived from shared activities and territory but also embodies the culture of sentiments, traditions, and practices that link its members and from which they take meaning" (p. 220). The need for schools to address these elements simultaneously—shared space and shared meaning—forces educators to take account of the distractions triggered by work lives and family lives that render actual patterns of family engagement in comprehensive school reform models and charter schools—far short of promised (and optimal) levels in terms of magnitude and quality.

### Coalition Model

Coalition models—while rare—may be found in the *relationship* defined as partnerships between public choice schools and their corporate sponsors (Smrekar, 2001). Embedded in a school culture framed by focused instructional designs and sustained by a *goal* of collaboration with members of their corporate community, workplace schools highlight the orientation to a familial *function* among public school teachers, private corporate employers, and their employees. These schools produce an *outcome* closely approximating *Gemeinschaft* community (see Table 17.1).

In the early 1990s, corporate-sponsored elementary schools were established in dozens of workplaces across the United States, including the corporate headquarters of Target Stores, Bank of America, Hewlett-Packard, and Mt. Sinai Medical Center. These arrangements typically require corporate sponsors to provide the facility and assume full responsibility for maintaining it; school districts provide the staff and assume full responsibility for instruction. These public "schools of choice" give parents who are employed by the corporate sponsor the option of selecting the workplace for their "neighborhood" school. By bridging the geographical barrier between work and school, the concept of workplace schools confronts the tension between a socially sanctioned pattern of increased time spent at work—the culture called to work—and the increased demand for parental involvement in the educational lives of schoolchildren.

Almost half of the American work force is comprised of two-parent working families (U. S. Bureau of Labor Statistics, 2000; Galinsky, Bond, & Friedman, 1993). These parent-employees are part of a work force that is spending more and more hours each month at work, taking fewer unpaid leaves, and enjoying shorter vacations each year (U. S. Bureau of Labor Statistics, 2000; Schor, 1991). In an American culture called to work, married couples today spend 185 hours more per year at work than couples spent just 10 years ago. These trends have triggered increased attention to the growing phenomenon that University of California sociologist Arlie Russell Hochschild (1997) called "the time bind," the temporal squeeze between work demands and family obligations during which the workplace becomes a primary place of residence and the essential object of adults' emotional and intellectual commitment.

Among the multi-case studies of family-school-work integration (Smrekar, 2001), the Midwestern Downtown School (pseudonym) provides one of the most illustrative examples of the value of locating a school close to where parents *work* rather than where they *live*. The Downtown School reflects a partnership among a group of businesses that share a physical (downtown or business park) address and a school with whom all partners share an educational philosophy anchored to the value of *Gemeinschaft* communities.

The Downtown School embraces its urban geography. The teachers and students incorporate the city neighborhood as their school without walls. This sense of place (Driscoll, 2001) pays rich dividends to teachers, parents, and community members who nurture the notion that the school's location is much more than an address. Nearby, the highly regarded Midwestern City Art Museum, where a handful of parents of Downtown School children work, provides a free and readily accessible material lesson in art history, architecture, and sculpture. The City Library is the school's library—and the collection is impressive. The students' artwork is regularly displayed on the walls of the skywalk, the corridors of American Equities Group, and in the windows of the Convention Center. Each year, students from the Downtown School make the five-minute skywalk trip to the Bank of America where bank officials (some of whom are parents of Downtown students) relate the concepts of mathematics, currency, and investment strategies to the children. For teachers, these events are considered field work (not an isolated trip) and are wrapped around the curriculum in fundamental ways that are designed to capture the downtown neighborhood as canvas for students' learning and expression.

The case study findings (Smrekar, 2001) suggested that robust and reliable parent involvement naturally occurs under these conditions of convenience, bringing teachers and parents together in the morning rituals of dropping off children at the school located within a minute's walk to one's nearby downtown office door. Parents were welcome any time to stop by and observe class instruction, take their child to lunch (or eat with them at the school), or read to a small group of students. As the Downtown School principal observed: "We've changed what parent involvement means. We're re-connecting with families, making it easier for parents to stop by for 10 minutes in a day. It's perfect for teachers, employees, and employers" (Smrekar, 2001, p. 182).

When the workplace and the neighborhood are fused, as in the Midwestern Downtown School, the coalition is fully formed, and the concepts of functional and value communities (and new geographical communities) merge into something new. The Coalition model explicated in the workplace school community creates new collaborative agreements between schools and employers/employees in terms of more fluid communication, more natural and organic interaction, and greater financial and cultural interdependence between schools and workplaces. The social scaffolding rooted in conceptions of *Gemeinschaft* community helps form relationships intentionally more familial and interdependent than the social fabric interwoven in the Engagement model. These relationships among parents and between the workplace partners and school officials promote the shared expectations that form the uniformity and interconnectedness of functional communities.

The family-school relationship models explicated in this chapter (Cooptation, Management, Engagement, Coalition) are examined against the backdrop of contemporary definitions, including communal associations (Bryk & Driscoll, 1988), communities of shared meaning and space (Driscoll, 1995), geographical communities (Newman & Oliver, 1968), and value communities (Coleman & Hoffer, 1987). Some of the components of the typology described here resemble particular elements embedded in Swap's (1993) model of home-school relationships: protective (*cooptation*); school-to-home transmission (*management*); curriculum enrichment (*engagement*); and partnership (*coalition*). The models unpacked in this chapter are linked to specific school types and particular school contexts—all anchored to the field-based research on parent involvement, family engagement, school communities, and family-school relations. The typology is descriptive, not prescriptive. The findings provide a framework—a typology—for considering how these comparative contexts and conceptual definitions increase our understanding of family-school relationships in comprehensive school reform designs and selected charter school models. Where are these reform models placed along the continuum of social integration—Management? Engagement? Coalition? A hybrid? In the next section, each reform model with an explicit emphasis on the family-school relationship component is described and critiqued.

### Comprehensive School Reforms and Charter School Models

Comprehensive School Reform (CSR) programs refer to a group of whole-school models developed in the 1990s to improve entire schools (Borman, Hewes, Overman, & Brown, 2003). A nonprofit corporation called New American Schools (NAS) conducted a 5-year research and development competition that eventually offered 11 organizations funding and technical assistance to develop comprehensive school designs (Berends, Bodilly, & Kirby, 2002). In 1998, the federal government created the Comprehensive School Reform Program to provide grants that would enable schools to adopt these designs (Borman et al., 2003).

CSR programs focus on raising student achievement using scientifically-based research and effective practices. CSRs are designed to provide schools with support and training for all stakeholders, including teachers, administrators, parents, and school staff (Southwest Educational Development Laboratory [SEDL], 2007).

Charter schools represent a significant plank in recent educational policy developments. Charter schools are designed to give parents and students greater choice among public schools (Mintrom & Vergari, 1997). Minnesota and California passed the first charter school laws in 1991. Today, 40 states and the District of Columbia have a charter school law; more than 4,000 charter schools operate across the United States, serving approximately 1.2 million children (Center for Education Reform [CER], 2007). Charter schools operate autonomously within the public school system under charters or contracts, negotiated between organizers and sponsors (Mintrom & Vergari). Organizers may be parents, teachers, or others from the public or private sector; sponsors may be local school boards, state education boards, or other public authorities. Two broad themes drive the charter schools concept (Bierlein & Bateman, 1995; Bierlein & Mulholland, 1994; Kolderie, 1992, 1994; Nathan, 1994). First, charter schools provide greater responsiveness to the demands of parents and students. Proponents of charter schools claim that a market-based approach in public education can produce better-performing schools. Second, in theory, more opportunities are created for innovation in school organization and pedagogy by attracting new students and recognizing the threats associated with losing students to competition (Mintrom & Vergari).

The comprehensive school reform and charter school models examined in this chapter emphasize enhanced parental and community involvement as a centerpiece of their designs and are amongst the most widely implemented school models. The programs include: Accelerated Schools; Comer's School Development Program (SDP); CoZi (A combined program of Comer's SDP and Zigler's School of the 21st Century); Success for All; Green Dot charter schools; and KIPP charter schools.

## Accelerated Schools

***Model Description***    The Accelerated Schools Project was founded by Henry Levin at Stanford University and began its work with two schools in California during the 1986–1987 school year (Rowan & Miller, 2007). During the next 15 years, Accelerated Schools experienced rapid growth, eventually working with 561 schools across the United States and in Hong Kong (Lee, Levin, & Soler, 2005) and Israel (Gaziel, 2001). Levin's vision in founding Accelerated Schools was to provide students in high-poverty schools with the same quality of instruction found in America's best schools, a vision the program termed "powerful learning."

The process of establishing Accelerated Schools is comprised of six steps (Brunner & Hopfenberg, 1996). First, the school *takes stock* of the entire school community. The school gathers quantitative and qualitative information on the history of the school; data on students, staff, and school facilities; a description of curricular and instructional practices; information on the community and cultures of students and their parents; particular strengths of the school; data on attendance and test scores, and other measures of student performance. Based on these school and community profiles, the entire school community—including students, teachers, parents, support staff, principal, vice principals, central office administrators, and the community—then engages in *forging a vision* for the school that will become the focus of change. Next, the community members compare the *taking stock information* with the vision in order to *set priorities* for change. After setting priorities, the school *establishes its governance structures* that focus on participatory decision-making. All staff and representative students and parents select one of the priority areas on which to work and begin *engaging in the inquiry process.* The inquiry process involves all members of the school community in identifying and defining educational challenges, looking for alternative solutions, and implementing and evaluating those solutions. As the school efficiently takes the five steps, *developing powerful learning strategies throughout the school* finally becomes feasible.

***Family-School Relationship Component***    The family-school relationship component in Accelerated Schools primarily emphasizes using "cultural controls" to promote participation. Under this model, the classroom should form an inviting culture for natural involvement of parents and other community members. Parents are expected to take an active role by setting high expectations, encouraging reading, and supporting the success of their children (Levin, 1987). King (1994) explained that Accelerated Schools are facilitative in creating a culture that provides opportunities for parents to interact with the educational program and actively assist their children. For example, in one Accelerated School, officials created a Parents Room that included comfortable chairs, a pot of coffee, play-pens for toddlers, and a wide array of materials and equipment, including a sewing machine and a typewriter (Levin, 1991). The structure of Accelerated Schools adopts Finnan and Swanson's (2000) claim that it is through involvement *at* the school that parents move from supporting the learning of their own children to supporting the learning of all students.

*Typology Mapping*   By design, the Accelerated School model is suggestive of an Engagement model (Smrekar, 2009) that involves parents in processes of vision-setting and inquiry. The model emphasizes sharing ideas and reaching a consensus among parents, community members, and school officials around new learning strategies, and engages parents in a structured process to achieve those aims. The cultural control aspects, however, and the rather traditional roles outlined for parents pushes the Accelerated School plan toward a hybrid that invokes the properties of the Management model in terms of the explicit outcomes. Parents are assumed to play traditional roles of volunteer, helper, homework assistant, and attendee (see Table 17.2).

*Research and Limitations*   Although a number of research studies show that the Accelerated Schools model improves student achievement on standardized tests, no studies to date have focused upon the family-school relationship component beyond a descriptive notice. A meta-analysis of 29 comprehensive school reform models found the Accelerated Schools to have "promising evidence of effectiveness" in terms of student achievement (Borman, Hewes, Overman, & Brown, 2004). However, this study did not contain any information about family-school relations in the model. Another study of eight elementary schools found that the model improved standardized test scores in reading and mathematics once the schools in the study turned to changing curriculum and instruction in their third or fourth year of implementation (Bloom, Ham, Melton,

**Table 17.2** Classifying the Models' Family-School Components by Typologies

| Reform Models | Family-School Relationship Typologies | | | |
| --- | --- | --- | --- | --- |
| | Cooptation | Management | Engagement | Coalition |
| *Accelerated Schools* | X | X | | |
| *Comer SDP* | | X | X | |
| *CoZi* | | | X | |
| *Success for All* | | X | x | |
| *Green Dot* | X | X | | |
| *KIPP* | X | X | | |

Note: A capitalized X means that the reform model displays characteristics of the school community typology; a lowercase x means that the model displays only limited characteristics

& O'Brien, 2001). Bloom and colleagues observed that schools generally focused on changing school governance and culture in the first 3 years of implementation and turned to curriculum and instruction only in the third or fourth year; there is no mention of the emergence of new forms of family-school relations in this evaluation.

### Comer School Development Program (SDP)

*Model Description*    Comer School Development Program (SDP) was founded and developed by James Comer, MD, at the Yale Child Study Center and was piloted in two New Haven, Connecticut, schools in 1968 (Haynes, 1998). It is now implemented in over 700 schools in the United States and abroad. Comer's SDP maintains a child developmental approach, which focuses on holistic child development along six interlocking pathways—physical, language, ethical, social, psychological, and cognitive. The program's approach is different from other comprehensive school reforms, but its underlying assumption is similar in that all children have the potential to succeed in school and in life and that their realization of this potential depends on how well educators, families, and communities work together to create learning environments that support children's development. Comer SDP's developmental approach has some important implications for creating a positive school climate (Cook, Murphy, & Hunt, 2000). First, promoting children's welfare in just one or two domains will rarely achieve anything of lasting value. Second, evaluating the program requires testing children across many or all of the developmental outcome domains. Third, teacher knowledge of students' backgrounds influences how they treat students.

The basic structure of Comer's SDP is composed of three teams (Cook et al., 2000). The primary part of the structure is the School Planning and Management Team (SPMT), which consists of school administrators, teachers, staff, and parents. The SPMT members are charged with developing a school improvement plan, obtaining support across the school community, monitoring progress, and suggesting corrections throughout the course of development. There are three operations for which the SPMT is primarily responsible—the Comprehensive School Plan (CSP), staff development, and assessment and modification. Comer's SDP also specifies a Social Support Team, which consists of the school professionals most concerned with students' psychological and social welfare—counselors, nurses, social workers, special education teachers, and psychologists. Team members are responsible to address concerns for students with special needs and to help prevent social problems from arising on the school campus. The model specifies that this team disseminates information about child development and its links to the social and racial attributes of local families. The third component of SDP, the Parent Team, is comprised of what is designed to encourage parents to support the school in various ways—in governance, by supervising fieldtrips or fund raising, and through service in classrooms, hallways, and libraries—in the hope that this team will foster close community bonds in schools.

*Family-School Relationship Component*    King (1994) explained that the School Development Program (SDP) advocates the highest level of parent involvement through both facilitative and prescriptive approaches. Parents are involved at three levels in SDP: (a) shaping policy through their representatives on the governance and management team, (b) participating in school activities and supporting academic program, and (c) attending school events. Comer argued that promoting psychological development in students is essential for academic achievement because it encourages bonding to the school. This requires fostering positive interaction between parents and school staff, but most school staff is not trained in building positive relationships with parents (Comer, 1988). Comer stressed that teachers and administrators consequently should be taught how to work with parents and use them as allies in promoting the growth and development of the students.

*Typology Mapping* By design and the extant descriptive evidence, the Comer model reflects the core characteristics of a hybrid Management-Engagement model (see Table 17.2). The Parent Team component of the SDP outlines a range of parent roles associated with traditional categories of parent involvement, including helper, volunteer, and attendee. The model moves conceptually toward processes that define parents and teachers as co-producers in the governance and management team, although the institutionalized boundaries of professional (teacher)-constituent (parent) are maintained.

*Research and Limitations* Only two experimental studies of Comer's SDP are available to date, and only one of these addresses the nature and quality of parent involvement. The first study was conducted in Prince George's County in Maryland (Cook et al., 1999) and the other in Chicago (Cook et al., 2000). The Maryland study found no clear effects of student membership in the SDP during middle school on either student/staff perceptions of the school climate or students' academic achievement. Additionally, the Maryland study contained an empirical component about parental involvement in Comer's SDP. According to the Maryland study, telephone interviews with a random sample of parents of students revealed that the county program was largely successful in stimulating parent involvement in school-based events (Cook et al., 1999). Specifically, analyses of variance indicated that Comer schools invited parents more frequently. Parents in Comer schools also found the staff more caring and sensitive and were more satisfied with the quality of their involvement with the school compared to parents from non-Comer schools. Parents in Comer schools participated in more school events overall, including school-based social events, volunteer activities, and administrative meetings. Although the study concluded that the Comer program in Maryland created schools that were more receptive to parents, researchers found that the program did little to stimulate more or different *home-based* activities relevant to school life (Cook et al., 1999).

The study conducted in Chicago did not contain a family-school relationship component, but it showed a different result from the Maryland study in terms of school climate and student achievement. The Chicago study found that students' ratings of the school's social climate improved soon after the program began. Both the students' and teachers' perceptions of the school's academic climate had also improved compared to non-Comer schools (Cook et al., 2000).

## CoZi (Comer's SDP + Zigler's 21C)

*Model Description*   CoZi is a whole school reform model that combines Comer's SDP with Zigler's School of the 21st Century (21C). The 21C model was conceptualized in 1987 by Edward Zigler to include on-site, day-long, and year-round preschool, after-school care, and family support services based in public schools (Finn-Stevenson & Stern, 1997). A typical 21C school offers before- and after-school care, all-day year-round preschool care, and a home visitation program for parents of children ages zero to three, such as the Parents as Teachers program (PAT, 1995). There are currently more than 500 Zigler's 21C schools operating in 14 states across the country (Desimone, Finn-Stevenson, & Henrich, 2000).

*Family-School Relationship Component*   The major components of CoZi are (a) parent and teacher participation in school-based decision making that is grounded in child development principles, (b) parent outreach and education beginning at the birth of the child, (c) child care for preschoolers and before- and after-school care for kindergarten through sixth graders, and (d) parent involvement programs (Desimone et al., 2000). CoZi incorporates 21C's main goal, which is the optimal development of children through the provision of a comprehensive program of child care, early education, and family support for children from birth to 12 years old. CoZi emphasizes early involvement for parents for continued involvement throughout the child's school career, a key indicator of later academic success (Epstein, 1984).

*Typology Mapping*   The CoZi model reflects the consensus-building and shared decision-making properties embedded in an Engagement model, and emphasizes a long term relationship between parents and school officials more suggestive of socially-oriented functions than institutional ones (see Table 17.2).

*Research and Limitations*   Program effectiveness had been evaluated separately for 21C and SDP until Desimone and colleagues (2000) evaluated the impact of the full CoZi model in a low-income African American community during the 1996–1997 school year. The 1-year evaluation of the CoZi model found its strongest effects on parent involvement and school climate. The study found higher parent and community participation rates at the CoZi school than the comparison school. Both survey and interview data showed that the parent program, outreach, and shared decision making that is a fundamental part of CoZi were largely responsible for the high levels of parent and community involvement in the school. The evaluation study also found a significantly higher school climate in the CoZi school than the comparison school. Some dimensions of school climate related to parent involvement included collaborative decision making, parent involvement, and school-community relationship. The study also tested a hypothesis that CoZi would significantly increase parent social capital and found that CoZi parents did have significantly larger social networks (Desimone et al., 2000).

## Success for All

*Model Description*   Success for All was developed by Robert Slavin, Nancy Madden, and colleagues at Johns Hopkins University at the request of the Baltimore City Public School System, and was piloted in one Baltimore elementary school during the 1987–1988 school year. The model is currently implemented in approximately 2,000 schools throughout the United States. Success for All emphasizes prevention and early/intensive intervention designed to detect and resolve learning problems as early as possible, before they become serious. Students spend most of their day in traditional, age-grouped classes, but are regrouped across grades for reading lessons targeted to specific performance levels. Teachers assess each student's reading performance at eight-week intervals and make regrouping changes based on the results (Borman & Hewes, 2002).

The main conceptual framework supporting Success for All is termed "biosocial developmental contextualism" (Ramey & Ramey, 1998), which emphasizes that fragmented, weak efforts in early intervention are not likely to succeed, whereas intensive, high-quality, ecologically pervasive interventions can and do succeed. This framework highlights six principles: (a) developmental timing, (b) program intensity, (c) direct provision of learning experiences, (d) program breath and flexibility, (e) individual differences in program benefits, (f) and environmental maintenance of development. In contrast to the use of cultural controls as implementation strategy in Accelerated Schools, Success for All uses procedural control" to promote instructional change (Rowan & Miller, 2007). It means that Success for All resides largely in the detailed instructional guidance given to teachers rather than promoting change in school climate as a whole.

*Family-School Relationship Component*   Slavin and Madden (2001), in their book *One Million Children*, described the three ideal family-school relationship components in Success for All schools. In the school governance area, parents are involved through a Building Advisory Team that consists of parents, teachers, and administrators. The team evaluates the entire school climate and advises the principal on school-wide goals. A second set of activities in Success for All involves in-school volunteer support in which parents can physically engage in a wide range of school activities. In one notable volunteer program, parents act as listeners during lunch or free time for those children whose parents work at night or are unavailable for after-school reading time. Alternatively, children can join a Breakfast Reading Club in which parent volunteers are available in the morning to listen to students read and to sign off on Read and Respond forms for students who are unable to read at home. Some schools have established a homework room in which parents and teachers assist children after school.

The third notable area of parent involvement in Success for All is the curriculum (Slavin & Madden, 2001). Most Success for All schools have a Kick-Off Demonstration Night in the fall to keep parents informed of the program of instruction that their child is receiving for reading and to give them tips on how to support the program at home. Another part of parent involvement in curriculum is the Raising Readers program. It consists of a series of workshops in pre-kindergarten through second grade designed to familiarize families with the reading curriculum and to provide parents with both the skills and materials needed to promote parent-child interaction around literacy.

All three areas of parent involvement are realized mainly through a Family Support Team composed of two social workers and one full-time parent liaison (Madden, Slavin, Karweit, Dolan, & Wasik, 1991). This team also conducts home visits, provides referrals to social agencies when necessary, and recruits parents to volunteer at schools. King (1994) explained that Success for All presents a more highly structured, prescriptive model of parental involvement in contrast to the loosely structured, facilitative approach of Accelerated Schools.

*Typology Mapping*   Success for All promotes primarily a Management model with a limited Engagement model overlay that supports parent-school staff consensus building while maintaining institutionalized relations and categorical roles/outcomes for parents (see Table 17.2). From the Volunteer Listener program and the Breakfast Reading Club, to the information-heavy Kick-off Demonstration Night, the model strives to structure programmatic guides for parents that will support literacy development for students.

*Research and Limitations*   A meta-analysis of 29 comprehensive school reform models ranked Success for All as having "strongest evidence of effectiveness" on student achievement (Borman et al., 2004). Several studies indicated that students enrolled in Success for All programs produced higher scores in reading, were less likely to be placed in special education programs, and were less likely to be retained than other matched students (Borman & Hewes, 2002; Madden, Slavin, Karweit, Dolan, & Wasik, 1993; Slavin, Madden, Karweit, Livermon, & Dolan, 1990). Another study suggested that Success for All produced particularly positive student achievement gains in reading for English language learners (Slavin, Madden, Dolan, & Wasik, 1996). In another study, teachers in Success for All programs indicated that the highly detailed and structured nature of the reading curriculum constrained their autonomy and creativity (Datnow & Castellano, 2000). To date, no evaluation or empirical work has focused on parent involvement within the program.

### Green Dot

*Model Description*   Steve Barr founded Green Dot Public Schools in 1999 with the vision of transforming secondary education in California by creating a number of high-performing charter high schools using available public dollars (Green Dot Public Schools, 2007). Under Barr's leadership, Green Dot built one of the first comprehensive public high schools in the Los Angeles area in 30 years in 2000 and a second high school in 2002. Green Dot now operates 12 public charter high schools—all in Los Angeles. Green Dot is focused on leading "School Transformation" projects in which it claims to transform large, failing schools into clusters of small, successful schools that follow these six tenets (Green Dot Public Schools/Bain & Company, 2006): (a) small, safe, personalized schools, (b) high expectations, (c) local control, (d) parent participation, (e) more dollars directed into the classroom, and (f) schools kept open later (Green Dot Public Schools, 2007).

*Family-School Relationship Component*   Under the tenet of parent participation, parents are required to volunteer at least 35 hours of service annually at all Green Dot schools. This requirement is made explicit in a parent contract with the school. Participating activities can range from volunteering in the office on campus to reading at home with one's child. Additional education programs are also provided to new parents to help them learn the best ways to support their children's educations.

*Research and Limitations*   No research has been published on the nature and quality of family-school relations or parent involvement in Green Dot schools. However, published reports are available regarding student achievement in Green Dot schools. The most recent statistics available from state education officials in California indicated a Green Dot student graduation rate of 81%, compared to the Los Angeles Unified School District rate of 47% (California Department of Education, 2007). In 2006, Green Dot schools produced an average API (Academic Performance Index) score of 704—far higher than the average API score of 593 for all high schools in Los Angles Unified School District (California Department of Education, 2007). The API measures student performance and growth on a scale from 200 to 1,000. A school's annual API is based upon a formula that calculates the weighted average of students' scores across content areas on criterion- and norm-referenced tests. The statewide target is an API score of 800 (California Department of Education, 2007).

A recent study conducted by Just For The Kids-California (JFTK-CA; n.d.), an affiliate of the National Center for Educational Accountability, reported that Latino students in Green Dot schools were among the highest performing Algebra I students among schools in California with 50% or more minority students.

## KIPP

*Model Description*   Another widely implemented charter school model is KIPP (Knowledge Is Power Program) middle schools. KIPP began in 1994 when two teachers, Mike Feinberg and Dave Levin, launched a fifth-grade public school program in inner-city Houston, Texas, after completing their commitment to Teach For America (2007). In 1995, Feinberg remained in Houston to lead KIPP Academy Middle School, and Levin returned home to New York City to establish KIPP Academy in the South Bronx. There are currently 57 KIPP charter schools in operation across 17 states and the District of Columbia, enrolling more than 14,000 students. KIPP Foundation seeks to establish schools in historically underserved urban and rural areas across the United States. More than 90% of KIPP students are African American or Latino and more than 80% qualify for free or reduced lunch. KIPP schools are built based on five main operating principles: more time, choice and commitment, power to lead, high expectations, and focus on results (KIPP, 2007).

*Family-School Relationship Component*   KIPP schools require parents to sign a contract similar to those used in many other charter schools. Parents and students in KIPP schools sign a "KIPP Commitment to Excellence Form" in which they promise commitment to the key principles of the charter program. The pledge includes the following three sections and reads:

1. Parents will make sure their child arrives at KIPP every day by 7:25 a.m. (Monday-Friday) or boards a KIPP bus at the scheduled time.
2. Parents will always help their child in the best way they know how and they will do whatever it takes for him/her to learn. This also means that parents will check their child's homework every night, let him/her call the teacher if there is a problem with the homework, and try to read with him/her every night.
3. Parents will always make themselves available to their children and the school, and address any concerns they might have. This also means that if a child is going to miss school, parents will notify the teacher as soon as possible, and they will carefully read any and all papers that the school sends home to them. (KIPP, 2007).

Schools also encourage parents to volunteer in classrooms, accompany students on end-of-the-year school trips, oversee Saturday school, coach sports, work in the office, and serve on the school's board of directors (KIPP, 2007).

*Research and Limitations*    Although no research has been published on family-school relationships in KIPP schools, a few independent reports and mainly descriptive studies are available regarding student academic achievement, climate, and instructional practices. One of the first studies of KIPP student performance identified statistically significant gains in test scores among students in three KIPP schools (Doran & Drury, 2002).

A quasi-experimental study compared achievement data on standardized tests for students at KIPP Diamond Academy in Memphis, Tennessee, with similar students of the same ethnicity, socioeconomic status (SES), gender, and ability in neighboring district-operated schools. Statistically significant differences were found in reading/language arts and mathematics, with the first-year, fifth-grade KIPP students outperforming the comparison group (Gallagher & Ross, 2005). The parent survey results in this study indicated that the overwhelming majority of respondents were satisfied with the academic climate (Ross, McDonald, Alberg, & McSparrin-Gallagher, 2007). The Education Policy Institute (EPI) conducted an analysis of student-level academic data collected from 24 KIPP schools located in different states (EPI, 2005). The analysis showed that fifth grade cohorts at KIPP schools demonstrated greater academic gains on the Stanford Achievement Test (SAT) than predicted, a finding consistent with prior research on KIPP schools (Doran & Drury, 2002). According to the Education Policy Institute data, the KIPP fifth grade cohorts experienced average gains of 9 to 17 points across all tests (EPI, 2005).

*Typology Mapping*    Given the similarity in approach to family-school relations among charter schools generally, and KIPP and Green Dot more specifically, we mapped the two models described here collectively. Green Dot and KIPP reflect the characteristics of a Cooptation-Management model, as exemplified by the emphasis upon a school-designed contract that categorizes parents into tightly scripted, highly prescribed roles and responsibilities. Although elements of control and certainty and structure are evidenced in mission statements and contract language, these charter school models reflect the ideals of market choice and consumer values juxtaposed around the aims of greater accountability for results. These outcome goals frame rather legalistic-instrumental processes adapted to ensure categorical roles (volunteers, homework helpers, meeting attendees) for parents (see Table 17.2).

## RESEARCH ON FAMILY-SCHOOL RELATIONS IN CHARTER SCHOOLS: A FINAL NOTE

Most of the research on charter schools and parent involvement focuses upon the general climate of these choice schools and the unique character and application of parent contracts (Bifulco & Ladd, 2005; Bulkley & Wohlstetter, 2004; Reynolds, 2000; U.S. Department of Education, 2004). Using national data from the Schools and Staffing Survey (SASS), researchers found that charter school parents were, on average, more involved than parents in traditional public schools in the categories of parent participation measured by SASS, including attendance at open house or Back-to-School nights, parent conferences, and parent workshops (Bifulco & Ladd, 2005). Higher levels of school autonomy, parent contracts, a specified role for parents in school governance, and the ability to attract parents to charter schools who are more likely to volunteer for school-based events and assist with homework, accounted for these differences in parent involvement across charter and traditional schools (Bifulco & Ladd, 2005).

According to a study of charter schools in California (Becker, Nakagawa, & Corwin, 1997) and in Michigan (Reynolds, 2000), charter schools engage in a range of outreach activities and invitations designed to encourage parent involvement in learning activities at home and at school. These studies found that charter school parents were more involved in the daily life of the school, including governance issues, than were parents at district-managed public schools nearby with demographically similar student and family populations.

The key component of family-school relationships made explicit in these charter school designs asks parents to sign contracts promising a certain level and type of involvement in the educational process. Contracts can include items such as volunteering at school for a designated number of events or a specific number of times, or agreeing to monitor homework on a daily basis. For instance, a survey of 34 of the first 44 schools chartered by the state of California found that more than half of all charter schools required parents to sign contracts and to participate in certain activities (Dianda & Corwin, 1994).

However, Becker and colleagues' (1997) analysis of the parent contracts used in charter schools suggests that contracts were viewed as a means of obtaining compliance rather than as a positive vehicle for encouraging the growth of a more inclusive school community. The authors concluded that parents were viewed as a consumer rather than a partner. The analysis also revealed that charter schools may have higher levels of parent involvement due to the fact that more school-participation-oriented families self-select into charter schools, while parents who lack the initial interest or circumstances that would enable more participation reject the opportunity to join such a school. Thus, Becker and colleagues (1997) cautioned that parent contracts should not be mechanisms for social control.

## A RESEARCH AGENDA FOR STUDYING FAMILY-SCHOOL RELATIONS

### Lesson Drawing: A Roadmap for Future Research

Three conclusions from our extensive review of the extant research literature on the six selected CSR and charter school design models can be drawn. First, in terms of the way each model is designed, the family-school relationship component of these reform models suggests a Management approach. Five of the six reform models reviewed display relatively strong and explicit characteristics of the Management relationship, wherein school officials are professionals who manage school-community interactions. In this model frame, parents are expected to assume one or more distinct roles, from creating healthy and nurturing home conditions to providing opportunities for educational enrichment, in reliable and predictable ways.

Second, there are qualitative differences in the ways that CSR and charter school models have designed their family-school relationship components. Whereas the CSR models favor an approach that blends elements of Management with Engagement, the charter school models seem to have adopted an approach that combines elements of Management and Cooptation. The degree to which these contrasts reflect larger differences between CSR and charter school models in terms of their philosophies of reform and the ways parents and the greater school community play a role in school change, are topics for future study.

The third key lesson is that the published, scholarly research on family-school relationships in these school types is scant. In contrast to the extensive attention given to student achievement, curriculum, instructional practices, and other outcome measures of the reform models, there is a dearth of empirical research evaluating the implementation and effectiveness of the models on any dimensions of family-school relations. In the remainder of the chapter, a research agenda for studying family-school relations broadly in CSR and charter school designs is provided.

### What is the Nature and Extent of Design Implementation?

To begin, researchers might develop studies to examine the fidelity between the reform models' family-school design components and their implementation. Specifically, such studies, would seek to answer, to what extent are specified community components in the design of whole school reform and charter school models implemented? Do the different reform models rely on similar strategies to carry out their family-school design components? What are the ways family-school relationships are developed and sustained, and do they differ substantively among sites implementing the same reform model? Where there is variation in the implementation of the design components among sites, to what can the variation be attributed?

To answer the questions, researchers must assemble data principally from primary sources. For information on the community design components of individual reform models, providers' brochures, handbooks, and on-line descriptions should be collected. Interviews with key developers could also be conducted. Data on the outcome variable(s) —the level/type of implementation—should be collected from case studies of the individual school sites that might include surveys, interviews, and observations.

In analyzing the data, the elements of Smrekar's (2009) Family-School Relationship Typology might serve as the primary dimensions by which the data are interpreted. By paying attention to the *goal, relationship, function,* and *outcome* of family-school relationships, scholars will enhance understanding about the roles of community members and school officials in the school reform process. For example, the framework could help guide the identification of individuals and groups responsible for establishing the goal of a models' family-school relationship components and the ways the goal and function of those components are communicated to members of the school community. Smrekar's formulation represents the school and the greater school community as singular units that function, for example, as receivers, constituents, or partners. Future studies might explore an augmented or hybrid-formulated framework, wherein individual school communities are recognized as multidimensional and comprised of various members (e.g., PTA, business partners, research partners, politicians) each with differing priorities and interests, conditioning complex relationships between families, communities, and schools. Other studies might address additional ways that members of the school community influence family-school relationships, beyond converting goals to outcomes.

Testing possible explanations for variations in the implementation of a model's design components among schools requires information—both qualitative and quantitative— about the school sites themselves and the communities that surround them. Research suggests that the racial and socioeconomic compositions of the student body in a school (as a proxy for parent race and income), parents' education level, and whether parents speak English at home, for example, can influence the interaction patterns they have with schools and teachers (Smrekar & Cohen-Vogel, 2001). Much of this information is now publicly available on-line. A national source for school level data is the Common Core of Data, a project by the U.S. Department of Education's National Center for Education Statistics. Updated yearly, the database provides information to calculate the percentage of students enrolled by race, gender, and free and reduced priced lunch eligibility in every public school in the country (see http://nces.ed.gov/ccd/). Many states have also developed on-line searchable databases. In Florida, for example, the Florida Schools Indicators Report, presents detailed, longitudinal information about the state's public schools, including, for example, the mobility rate, crime rate, absentee rates, and the percentage of students identified as Limited English Proficient. Moreover, similar information is often easily found on the websites of individual schools and districts.

In considering explanations for observed variations in implementation, scholars might also collect data at the community level as research has demonstrated that community factors can also influence the nature and quality of family-school relationships. Cohen-Vogel, Goldring, & Smrekar (n.d.), for example, looked at the effects of neighborhood conditions on the relationships between families and educators in regular pubic schools and the strategies that principals and teachers used to partner with social service organizations, encourage parental involvement, and build community networks.

Principals of schools in what they term "high liability zones"—zones with higher than average incidences of crime and teen births per capita—reported spending more time attempting to activate assets and build community capacity than their counterparts whose schools are located in low liability zones. The programs they developed and the partnerships they forged with parents and other community members focused largely on providing for children's basic needs (e.g., care, clothing, food, health). Principals of schools in low liability zones, however, rarely needed to leave the building to find resources; instead, they reported that parents and community members come to them with offers of funds and assistance. The funds procured and programs developed in these schools often provided not for children's basic care, but for enrichment activities and capital projects (e.g., technology, new fields).

Collecting data on school communities is made easier by the widespread availability and use of geographic information system software. If schools draw from attendance zones (less likely in charter schools), scholars can build community-level datasets with data from the United States Bureau of the Census (e.g., unemployment rates; single family households) and any databases that contain street addresses for sites (e.g., food banks) or events (e.g., homicides) of interest. Local police and health departments keep information that might be central to researchers' interests in school communities (e.g., specific locations of drug arrests; homicides; teen births; hospitals; food banks; universities; social service organizations; libraries). Because the Census Bureau does not collect information at the school zone level, data at the census block group levels can be used. The block groups are the smallest geographic area for which much of the information the agency collects are available (e.g., economic data, for example, are estimated from data from respondents to the bureau's long form). The block groups can be fit together like a puzzle, and laid over maps of school zones. Census block groups and school zone boundaries are not equivalent; consequently, some block groups will extend beyond the boundaries of a school zone. Decision rules need to be applied uniformly to cope with the incongruency. For example, scholars can choose between decision rules that incorporate into a school zone all block groups that have any portion laying inside the zone or all block groups with their geographic centers located inside the zone.

## What are the Effects of the Design Components?

Apart from issues of implementation, a second generation of studies might examine the impact of the models' design components on the nature and quality of family-school relationships. Such studies might consider whether and to what extent family-school relationships have shifted in schools where the design components are implemented with fidelity, and to what effect. Specifically, randomized control trials could be designed to test the effectiveness of the family-school relations component of a selected reform model on a set of outcome indicators, including parental involvement, teachers' job satisfaction, even student achievement. Researchers might select two schools preparing to adopt one of the reform models (e.g., Accelerated Schools), assigning one school to the treatment condition and the other to the control condition. The same kind of design could also be used with a treatment and control group within the same school. The treatment might consist of initial and ongoing trainings for school staff, parents, and other community members on the family-school relations component of the selected reform model and a full-time staff member dedicated to its implementation. Where it is deemed socially or ethically undesirable to engage in randomized trials in which some students/families/ educators are purposefully denied the potentially-valuable treatment, researchers might use observable characteristics of schools and students to match the treatment school to a comparison school that is implementing the selected reform model without attention to the family-school design component or having implemented an alternative approach (e.g., cooptation; coalition) that does not conform to the design itself. In interviews beginning in the first year of the program's implementation, parents might be asked to describe their role(s) in their children's education and their relationships with teachers and school administrators. Climate surveys might be administered to teachers, a random sample of parents, and members of the school advisory councils, and meetings between parents/community members and school representatives might be observed. Standardized tests might also be administered by outside proctors in order to compare the performance of students enrolled in schools with and without full implementation of the reform model's family-school relationship component.

The questions raised in this chapter, along with methodologies suggested for answering them, address gaps in our understanding of how family-school relationship components embedded in popular school reform models may explain changes to the culture, practices, and outcomes of schooling. In this chapter, we outlined the possibilities and promises of a research agenda focused on unpacking the fidelity of comprehensive school reform and charter school models in an effort to understand the practical and policy implications of each models' family-school concept. We believe the benefit of this scholarly endeavor rests with the potential value of considering strong family-school relationships as a foundation of educational excellence.

## REFERENCES

Ames, C., Khoju, M., & Watkins, T. (1993). *Parents and schools: The impact of school-to-home communications on parents' beliefs and perceptions* (Center Rep. No. 15). Baltimore: Center on Families, Communities, Schools and Children's Learning, Johns Hopkins University.

Becher, R. M. (1984). *Parent involvement: A review of research and principles of successful practice*. Washington, DC: National Institute of Education.

Becker, H. J., Nakagawa, K., & Corwin, R. G. (1997). Parent involvement contracts in California's charter schools: Strategy for educational improvement or method of exclusion? *Teachers College Record, 98*, 511–536.

Berends, M., Bodilly, S., & Kirby, S. (Eds.). (2002). *Facing the challenges of school reform: New American schools after a decade*. Santa Monica, CA: RAND.

Bierlein, L. A., & Bateman, M. (1995, November). Opposition forces and educational reform: Will charter schools succeed? *Network News & Views 14*, 48–58.

Bierlein, L. A., & Mulholland, L. A. (1994). *Comparing charter school laws: The issue of autonomy*. Policy Brief. The Morrison Institute for Public Policy, Arizona State University.

Bifulco, R., & Ladd, H. (2005). Institutional change and co-production of public services: The effect of charter schools on parent involvement. *Journal of Public Administration Research and Theory, 16*(4), 553–576.

Bloom, H. S., Ham, S., Melton, L., & O'Brien, J. (2001). *Evaluating the Accelerated Schools approach: A look at early implementation and impacts on student achievement in eight elementary schools*. New York: Manpower Demonstration Research Corp.

Borman, G. D., & Hewes, G. M. (2002). The long-term effects and cost-effectiveness of Success for All. *Educational Evaluation and Policy Analysis, 24*(4), 243–266.

Borman, G. D., Hewes, G. M., Overman, L. T., & Brown, S. (2003). Comprehensive school reform and achievement: A meta-analysis. *Review of Educational Research, 73*(2), 125–230.

Borman, G. D., Hewes, G. M., Overman, L. T., & Brown, S. (2004). Comprehensive school reform and achievement: A meta-analysis. In C. T. Cross (Ed.), *Putting the pieces together: Lessons from comprehensive school reform research* (pp. 53–108). Washington, DC: The National Clearinghouse for Comprehensive School Reform.

Brunner, I., & Hopfenberg, W. (1996). Growth and learning: Big wheels and little wheels interacting. In C. Finnan, E. P. St. John, J. McCarthy, & S. P. Slovacek (Eds.), *Accelerated schools in action: Lessons from the field* (pp. 24–46). Thousand Oaks, CA: Corwin.

Bryk, A., & Driscoll, M. (1988). *The high school as community: Contextual influences and consequences for students and teachers.* Madison, WI: National Center on Effective Secondary Schools.

Bulkley, K., & Wohlstetter, P. (2004). *Taking account of charter schools: What's happened and what's next?* New York: Teachers College Press.

Burch, P. (1993). Circles of change: Action research on family-school-community partnerships. *Equity and Choice, 10*(1), 11–16.

California Department of Education. (2007). API description: Overview of the Academic Performance Index (API). Retrieved November 3, 2007, from http://www.cde.ca.gov/ta/ac/ap/apidescription.asp

Center for Education Reform (CER). (2007). Retrieved October 30, 2007, from http://www.edreform.com

Chrispeels, J. H. (1996). Effective schools and home-school-community partnership roles: A framework for parent involvement. *School Effectiveness and School Improvement, 7*(3), 7–33.

Clark, R. M. (1983). *Family life and school achievement: Why poor black children succeed or fail.* Chicago: University of Chicago Press.

Cohen-Vogel, L., Goldring, E., & Smrekar, C. (n.d.). *The end of busing and the equity (com)promise: Social service partnerships, parent involvement and community building in neighborhood schools.* Unpublished manuscript.

Coleman, J., & Hoffer, T. (1987). *Public and private high schools: The impact of communities.* New York: Basic Books.

Comer, J. P. (1980). *School power.* New York: University Press.

Comer, J. P. (1988). Educating poor minority children. *Scientific American, 259*(5), 42–48.

Cook, T. D., Habib, F., Phillips, M., Settersten, R. A., Shagle, S. C., & Degirmencioglu, S. M. (1999). Comer's School Development Program in Prince George's County, Maryland: A theory-based evaluation. *American Educational Research Journal, 36*(3), 543–597.

Cook, T. D., Murphy, R. F., & Hunt, H. D. (2000). Comer's School Development Program in Chicago: A theory-based evaluation. *American Educational Research Journal, 37*(2), 535–597.

Crowson, R. L. (1992). *School-community relations, under reform.* Berkeley, CA: McCutchan.

Datnow, A., & Castellano, M. (2000). Teachers' responses to Success for All: How beliefs, experiences, and adaptations shape implementation. *American Educational Research Journal, 37*(3), 775–799.

Davies, D. (1993). Schools reaching out: Family, school and community partnerships for student success. *Phi Delta Kappan, 72*, 376–382.

Delgado-Gaitan, C. (1992). School matters in the Mexican-American home: Socializing children to education, *American Educational Research Journal, 29*(3), 495–513.

Desimone, L., Finn-Stevenson, M., & Henrich, C. (2000). Whole school reform in a low-income African American community: The effects of the CoZi models on teachers, parents, and students. *Urban Education, 35*(3), 269–323.

Dianda, M. R., & Corwin, R. G. (1994). *Vision and reality: A first-year look at California's charter schools.* Los Alamitos, CA: Southwest Regional Laboratory.

Doran, H. C., & Drury, D. W. (2002). *Evaluating success: KIPP educational program evaluation.* Alexandria, VA: New American Schools Education Performance Network.

Dornbusch, S. M., & Ritter, P. L. (1988). Parents of high school students: A neglected resource. *Educational Horizons, 66*, 75–77.

Driscoll, M. (1995). Thinking like a fish: The implications of the image of school community for connections between parents and schools. In P. Cookson & B. Schneider (Eds.), *Transforming schools* (pp. 209–236). New York: Garland.

Driscoll, M. (2001). The sense of place and the neighborhood school: Implications for building social capital and for community development. In R. Crowson (Ed.), *Community development and school development, Vol. 5* (pp. 19–41). Greenwich, CT: JAI Press.

Education Policy Institute (EPI). (2005). *Focus on results: An academic impact analysis of the Knowledge is Power Program (KIPP).* Virginia Beach, VA: Education Policy Institute.

Epstein, J. (1984). School policy and parent involvement: Research results. *Educational Horizons, 62*, 70–72.

Epstein, J. L. (1987). What principals should know about parent involvement. *Principal, 66*(3), 6–9.

Epstein, J. (1992). School and family partnerships. In M. Alkin (Ed), *Encyclopedia of educational research, 6th edition* (pp. 1139–1151). New York: MacMillan.

Epstein, J. (2002). *School, family, and community partnerships: Your handbook for action (2nd ed.).* Thousand Oaks, CA: Corwin.

Epstein, J. L., & Dauber, S. L. (1991). School programs and teacher practices of parent involvement in inner-city elementary and middle schools. *The Elementary School Journal, 91,* 289–305.

Finnan, C., & Swanson, J. D. (2000). *Accelerating the learning of all students: Cultivating culture, change in schools, classrooms, and individuals.* Boulder, CO: Westview Press.

Finn-Stevenson, M. & Stern, B. M. (1997). Integrating early-childhood and family support services with a school improvement process: The Comer-Zigler initiative. *The Elementary School Journal, 98*(1), 51–66.

Galinsky, E., Bond, J., & Friedman, D. (1993). *The changing workforce: Highlights of the national study.* New York: Families and Work Institute.

Gallagher, B. M., & Ross, S. M. (2005). *Analysis of year 2 (2003–2004) student achievement outcomes for the Memphis KIPP DIAMOND Academy.* Tennessee: Center for Research in Educational Policy, The University of Memphis.

Gaziel, H. (2001). Accelerated Schools programmes: Assessing their effectiveness. *International Review of Education. 47*(1), 7–29.

Goldenberg, C. (1996). Accommodating cultural differences and commonalities in educational practice. *Multicultural Education, 4*(1), 16–19.

Green Dot Public Schools. (2007). Retrieved November 10, 2007, from http://www.GreenDot.org

Green Dot Public Schools/Bain & Company. (2006). *The school transformation plan: A strategy to create small, high-performing college-preparatory schools in every neighborhood of Los Angeles.* Los Angeles: Los Angeles Unified School District.

Harry, B. (1992). An ethnographic study of cross-cultural communication with Puerto Rican-American families in the special education system, *American Educational Research Journal, 29*(3), 471–494.

Haynes, N. M. (1998). Guest editor's introduction: Overview of the Comer School Development Program. *Journal of Education for Students Placed At Risk, 3*(1), 3–9.

Henderson, A. (1981). *Parent participation-student achievement: The evidence grows.* Columbia, MD: National Committee for Citizens in Education.

Henry, M. (1996). *Parent-school collaboration: Feminist organizational structures and school leadership.* Albany: State University of New York Press.

Hochschild, A. R. (1997). *The time bind.* New York: Metropolitan Books.

Hoover-Dempsey, K. V., & Sandler, H. M. (1997). Why do parents become involved in their children's education? *Review of Educational Research, 67,* 3–42.

Just For The Kids-California (n.d.). Retrieved February 3, 2008, from http://jftk-ca.org/star/

King, J. A. (1994). Meeting the educational needs of at-risk students: A cost analysis of three models. *Education Evaluation and Policy Analysis, 16*(1), 1–19.

KIPP: Knowledge Is Power Program. (2007). Retrieved December 5, 2007, from http://www.KIPP.org

Kolderie, T. (1992). Chartering diversity. *Equity and Choice, 9,* 28–31.

Kolderie, T. (1994). *The essentials of the "charter school" strategy.* St. Paul, MN: Center for Policy Studies.

Lareau, A. (2000). *Home advantage: Social class and parental interventions in elementary education.* London: Falmer Press.

Lee, J. C., Levin, H., & Soler, P. (2005). Accelerated Schools for quality education: A Hong Kong perspective. *The Urban Review. 37*(1), 63–81.

Levin, H. M. (1987). Accelerated Schools for disadvantaged students. *Educational Leadership, 44*(6), 19–21.

Levin, H. M. (1991). Accelerated visions. *Accelerated Schools, 1*(3), 2–3.

Lightfoot, S. L. (1978). *Worlds apart.* New York: Basic Books.

Madden, N. A., Slavin, R. E., Karweit, N. L., Dolan, L., & Wasik, B. A. (1991). Success for All. *Phi Delta Kappan, 72,* 593–599.

Madden, N. A., Slavin, R. E., Karweit, N. L., Dolan, L., & Wasik, B. A.. (1993). Success for All: Longitudinal effects of a restructuring program for inner-city elementary schools. *American Educational Research Journal, 30*(1), 123–148.

Mangino, M. (2005). Retrieved March 2, 2005, from http://www.access.org

Mapp, K. L. (2003). Having their say: Parents describe why and how they are engaged in their children's learning. *The School Community Journal, 13,* 35–64.

McLaughlin, M. W., & Shields, P. (1987). Involving low income parents in the schools: A role for policy. *Phi Delta Kappan, 69*(2), 156–160.

Meyer, J. W., & Rowan, B. (1977). Institutionalized organizations: Formal structure as myth and ceremony. *American Journal of Sociology, 83*, 340–368.

Mintrom, M., & Vergari, S. (1997). Charter schools as a state policy innovation: Assessing recent developments. *State and Local Government Review, 29*(1), 43–49.

Nathan, J. (1994). *Charter public schools: A brief history and preliminary lessons*. Minneapolis, MN: Center for School Change, Hurbert H. Humphrey Institute of Public Affairs.

National Education Goals Panel. (1995). *Improving education through family-school-community partnerships. Executive Summary to the 1995 National Education Goals Report* (Technical Report 96-03). Washington, DC: U.S. Government Printing Office.

Newman, F., & Oliver, D. (1968). Education and community. *Harvard Educational Review, 37*, 61–106.

Parents as Teachers (PAT). (1995). *Parents as teachers: Investing in good beginnings for children*. St. Louis, MO: Author.

Ramey, C. T., & Ramey, S. L. (1998). Early intervention and early experience. *American Psychologist, 53*, 109–120.

Reynolds, K. (2000). *Innovations in charter schools: A summary of innovative or unique aspects of Michigan charter schools*. Kalamazoo: The Evaluation Center, Western Michigan University.

Ross, S. M., McDonald, A. J., Alberg, M., & McSparrin-Gallagher, B. (2007). Achievement and climate outcomes for the Knowledge is Power Program in an inner-city middle school. *Journal of Education for Students Placed At Risk, 12*(2), 137–165.

Rowan, B., & Miller, R. J. (2007). Organizational strategies for promoting instructional change: Implementation dynamics in schools working with comprehensive school reform providers. *American Educational Research Journal, 44*(2), 252–297.

Schemo, D. J. ( 2000, November 24). Report cards are due, only this time for parents. *New York Times*, National Report, A23.

Schneider, M., & Teske, P. (2001). What research can tell policy makers about school choice. *Journal of Policy Analysis and Management, 20*(4), 609–631.

Schor, J. (1991). *The overworked American: The unexpected decline of leisure*. New York: Basic Books.

Scott-Jones, D. (1987). Mother-as-teacher in the families of high- and low-achieving low-income black first-graders. *Journal of Negro Education, 56*, 21–34.

Shumow, L., Vandell, D. L., & Posner, J. (1999). Risk and resilience in the urban neighborhood: Predictors of academic performance among low-income elementary school children. *Merrill-Palmer Quarterly, 45*, 309–331.

Slavin, R. E.. & Madden, N. A. (2001). *One million children: Success for All*. Thousand Oaks, CA: Corwin.

Slavin, R. E., Madden, N. A., Dolan, L. J., & Wasik, B. A.. (1996). Success for All: A summary of research. *Journal of Education for Students Placed At Risk, 1*(1), 41–76.

Slavin, R. E., Madden, N. A., Karweit, N. L., Livermon, B. J., & Dolan, L. (1990). Success for All: First-year outcomes of a comprehensive plan for reforming urban education. *American Educational Research Journal, 27*(2), 255–278.

Smrekar, C. E. (1996). *The impact of school choice and community: In the interest of families and schools*. Albany: State University of New York Press.

Smrekar, C. E. (2001). Lessons (and questions) from workplace schools on the interdependence of family, school and work. In R. Crowson (Ed.), *School-community relations, under reform, Vol. 5* (pp. 171–192). Greenwich, CT: JAI Press.

Smrekar, C. E. (2009). From control to collaboration: Mapping school communities across diverse contexts. In A. Pomson (Ed.), *The challenges and prospects of community in Jewish day schools*. London: Littman Library.

Smrekar, C. E., & Cohen-Vogel, L. (2001). The voices of parents: Rethinking the intersection of family and school. *Peabody Journal of Education, 76*(2), 75–101.

Smrekar, C. E., & Goldring, E. B. (1999). *School choice in urban America: Magnet schools and the pursuit of equity*. New York: Teachers College Press.

Southwest Educational Development Laboratory (SEDL). (2007). Comprehensive School Reform Program. Retrieved on November 15, 2007, from http://www.sedl.org/csr/welcome.html

Swap, S. (1993). *Developing home-school partnerships: From concepts to practice*. New York: Teachers College Press.

Tonnies, F. (1963). *Community and society* (Ed. & trans., C. P. Loomis). New York: Harper & Row.

U.S. Bureau of Labor Statistics (2000). *Handbook on labor statistics*. Washington, DC: U.S Government Printing Office.

U.S. Department of Education (2004). *Innovations in education: Successful charter schools*. Washington, DC: Office of Innovation and Improvement.

U.S. Department of Education (1994). *Strong families, strong schools*. Washington, DC: U.S. Government Printing Office.

# 18

## FUTURE DIRECTIONS IN FAMILY-SCHOOL PARTNERSHIPS

### CINDY CARLSON

There is remarkable consensus across the chapters in this volume about several important themes relevant to family-school partnerships in the present and the future: (a) Family-school partnership is critically important to the optimization of children's educational experience; (b) An ecological developmental systems theoretical perspective is a useful framework for conceptualizing the complexity and importance of relationships between home and school; (c) Diversity characterizes the changing demographics of the nation, the public school population of students, and is salient to every aspect of the educational enterprise including family-school-community partnerships; (d) Evidence-based practice is valued, and we continue to have important limitations to our knowledge base regarding effective family-school partnerships. The shared voice and vision of the authors is compelling and lends credence to the prediction of Weiss and Stephen (this volume) that we are poised as a nation to take advantage of a critical window of opportunity in educational and social policy, "to realize a vision for a strategic, comprehensive, and continuous system of family, school, and community partnerships that demonstrably contribute to children's development and school success" (p. 449).

Although the consensus that is evident in this volume among the authors is hopeful regarding the improved family-school partnerships that may emerge in the subsequent decade, there are also barriers to this vision. Weiss and Stephen caution wisely that realizing this vision will require major policy and practice changes as well as new ways of conducting, using, and communicating research and evaluation. Furthermore, there are psychological, structural, and historical barriers to home-school collaboration (Christenson & Sheridan, 2001).

### OVERVIEW

Historians argue that if we are to avoid repeating mistakes from the past, we must learn from it. In this chapter the four consensual themes noted at the onset will be examined from the perspectives of their origination in the past, their blossoming in the consensus of the present, and possible considerations for the growth of these themes in the postmodern future. Thus, a goal of this chapter is to situate the discussion of future directions in a larger socio-historical context. Toward this end attention will be given to the economic forces that prompt educational and social change, the organizational structures and processes that develop to fit with economic forces, the impact of these on the teaching and learning of children in schools and on our beliefs and practices of psychological and educational intervention.

### The Past: The Rise and Decline of the Modern Era

School-based psychological and social services to children emerged in the early 19th century, a time that bears some resemblance to our current era; therefore, it is important to begin here. Although the shifts between historical eras are multifaceted (i.e. social, political, and philosophical), the driver largely is economic change that is spurred by scientific or technological advances. The onset of the modern era is linked with the shift from an agrarian to an industrial economy. The factory, with its centralized control, top down hierarchical focus, mass production, and worker as a replaceable part, epitomized the organizational structure of the modern, industrial era. With a primary purpose of education being the preparation of a workforce, the factory also became the model for education in the modern era.[1]

Concomitant with the shift from an agrarian-based economy to an industrialized economy were dramatic philosophical and social changes. Philosophically, the dominant discourse changed from a world organized by spirituality and faith to a world organized by reason, empiricism, mechanism, and materialism. The world became viewed as a place where lawful cause-and-effect reality could be understood through careful study and once understood, the nature could ultimately be controlled. Industrialization demanded a large, semi-skilled, centralized workforce; thus, there was large-scale immigration from rural to urban areas where factories were situated and from the less industrialized to the more industrialized nations. Immigration and urbanization engendered social concerns and problems that demanded solutions. Solutions to these concerns were evident in legislation (e.g. child labor laws, mandated school attendance), school curriculum (e.g. civics lessons, standard curriculum), and the birth of social services in schools.

The helping professions of social work, school nursing, and school psychology, as well as the seeds of family-centered practice, were all rooted in the soil of social concern that accompanied the widespread changes related to industrialization and immigration at the onset of the 20th century. The deplorable and crowded conditions of urban living, the presumed breakdown of the family as multigenerational ties were broken with migration and immigration, and the clashing of cultures as significant numbers of particular ethnic groups immigrated, all engendered grave anxiety and concern for the welfare of children and families. In this social context social workers anticipated family-centered ecological treatment long before ecological psychology, systems theory, or family therapy was introduced. As described by Nichols (2008):

> Turn of the century caseworkers were well aware of something it took psychiatry fifty more years to discover—that families must be considered as units. Mary

Richmond, (1917), in her classic text, *Social Diagnosis*, prescribed treatment of the whole family and warned against isolating family members from their natural context. (p. 19)

Quoting Bardhill and Saunders (1988), Nichols continues:

She graphically depicted this situation [families within the social context] using a set of concentric circles to represent various systemic levels from the individual to the cultural. Her approach to practice was to consider the potential effect of all interventions on every systemic level, and to understand and use the reciprocal interaction of the systemic hierarchy for therapeutic purposes. (p. 19)

Fifty years later, the seeds of ecological practice that were planted at the turn of the century blossomed. Systems theory and ecological theory, later integrated into ecological developmental systems theory, the theoretical foundation of family-school partnerships espoused throughout this volume, emerged in the post-World War II era. The following discussion of these theories is drawn from Nichols (2008). Systems theory had its origins in the models of the structure and functioning of mechanical and biological units developed in the 1940s by mathematicians, physicists, and engineers. Ecological psychology had its roots in Kurt Lewin's 1940's study of group dynamics that resulted in field theory, which drew from Gestalt psychology attention to the larger field or whole of the group (Lewin, 1951). Lewin proposed, for example, that a change in the group behavior requires unfreezing—something that shakes up the group's beliefs and prepares them for change. Ecological psychology and systems theory were elegantly integrated and applied to the development of children by Urie Bronfenbrenner (1979). Although family-school partnership models largely build on Bronfenbrenner's ecological developmental model, the roots of family-centered school treatment are embedded in family systems therapy. Although there were many scattered seeds to contemporary models of family therapy, the father is generally viewed to be Nathan Ackerman, a child psychiatrist who went on record as early as 1938 suggesting that studying the family as a unit was the key to understanding disturbance in any of its members. The golden age of family therapy was the 1970s and 80s, with the flowering of many therapeutic models (see Nichols, 2008) and their application to children's school problems (e.g. Fine & Carlson, 1992). The focus of family-centered treatment has continually expanded toward ever-wider levels of context (Nichols, 2008). Family therapists initially shifted their view of disorder from the individual to the family, first focusing on the behavioral interaction sequences surrounding problems. Next, it was recognized that repeated sequences of behavior were metaphors for the family's structure; therefore, structure became the target of change. Structure came to be viewed to be influenced by a multi-generational process governed by belief systems. Current models of family therapy, therefore, emphasize belief systems, which are viewed to be embedded in culture.

The seeds of contemporary school-based family-centered models of treatment, such as EcoFIT (Dishion & Stormshak, this volume), not surprisingly, were also planted in the past as family therapists generalized their models of treatment to schools. Aponte (1976) pioneered the eco-structural family-school interview, an experiment in conducting a joint initial interview at the school with the family and school staff present in school-referred clinic cases. In the 1980s, the Ackerman Family Institute, in partnership with the New York City schools, initiated the Family-School Collaboration Project (directed by Howard Weiss) with the goal of enhancing collaborative problem-solving partnerships between families and schools (Weiss & Edwards, 1992). Teachers were taught a restructured version of the perennial parent-teacher conference, termed the family-school conference, which included the student in the conference with parents and teachers. Also implemented was a family-school problem solving meeting for children experiencing school problems that brought the family (parents, child, and siblings) together with the school (teacher(s) and other relevant school personnel) to mutually discuss and determine solutions to the child's problem. The program was reported in 1990 to be in more than 50 schools (Weiss & Edwards, 1992); however, data on its current status or effectiveness could not be located.

In summary, ecological-developmental approaches to family-school intervention emerged, but did not firmly take root, in the modern era. Largely the enthusiasm and dreams of the pioneers of family therapy and the proponent's family-school systemic intervention went unfulfilled. Throughout the modern era, home and school remained autonomous functioning systems with clear, and possibly rigid boundaries in roles and responsibilities (Christenson & Sheridan, 2001). Perhaps the educational and social problems of children continued to be adequately managed by schools; perhaps these ecological systems approaches were not viewed to be a practical solution to children's problems; perhaps the climate was not yet right for such a change in the customary way of doing business. Or perhaps, as noted by Nichols (2008), "Looking back, we can see how the early emphasis on homeostasis, as well as the cybernetic metaphor of the family as a machine, led to a view of the therapist as more of a mechanic than healer" (p. 20). Reworded to reflect family-school partnership, we might say, "Looking back, we can see how the modern organizational structure and processes of the school with its emphasis on specialized training and division of labor led to a view of the teacher as more of an education expert and advice-giver than a genuine collaborator with parents."

### The Present: The Early Postmodern Era

We have entered a new historical era, the postmodern world, and this is evident in changes in business, art, architecture, philosophy, literature, religion, politics, psychology, and education. Literally, the postmodern era is defined as "after modernism." This lack of reference to a more clear and certain paradigm is intriguing. Largely postmodernism currently constitutes an attack on modernist beliefs, values, and organizational structures rather than the widespread adoption of a new paradigm. Whereas the scientific and technological advances of the 20th century gave society a sense that truth and scientific laws could be discovered through objective observation and measurement, postmodernism not only questions the validity of existing scientific, political, and religious truths, but also views reality to be extraordinarily complex, filtered through a subjective lens, and questions whether absolute truth can ever be known.

The economic driver of the postmodern era, of course, is technological advances in information processing and communication such that entire national economies are shifting from the production of goods to the production of knowledge, and the concept of a business has expanded from local or national to global in scope and market. Concomitant with a change in our economic base, is a change in the organizational structure of business that, similar to our entrance into the modern era, is placing pressure upon the existing modern organizational structures and processes of education. Features of the postmodern organization appear on Table 18.1. The postmodern era calls for the following: flexible production; decentralized authority and control; the open sharing of information; multi-skilled and empowered work teams with intrinsic individual rewards, team incentives, and control of production; a valuing of diversity and multiple voices; a focus on customer satisfaction both internally and externally; and a focus on process measurement criteria. Evidence of the infusion of some of these ideas within the structure of education may be seen with the development of multiple educational options such as alternative or specialized schools, schools within schools, charter schools, home schooling, and the development of alternative teacher training and certification routes.

Dominant discourses in the postmodern era include social constructionism, chaos theory, feminist philosophy, environmental philosophy, and applied ethics (Carpenter,

**Table 18.1** Comparison of the Modern and Postmodern World

| Economic Base | Modern | Postmodern |
|---|---|---|
| | Industry | Knowledge |
| Organizational Structure | Hierarchical; Bureaucratic; Centralized control; Efficiency increases with specialization & division of labor; Homogeneity is strength; Diversity tolerated; Authority, training, & information are vested in the top; | Flat, horizontal with few layers; Teams of multi-skilled workers; Efficiency decreases with specialization; Diversity and many voices an asset; Authority & control are decentralized; Internal & external customer focus. |
| Organizational Processes | Mass production; vertical planning; Training, authority, & information vested at the top; Extrinsic rewards & punishments; Lots of procedures & rules; Individual incentives; End-of-line inspection; Measure result criteria. | Flexible production; horizontal planning; Authority delegated to leaders by teams; Information given to all; Intrinsic, empowered, ownership over work; Team incentives. Measure process criteria. |
| Dominant Discourse/ Philosophy | Mechanism & materialism: experience, reason, & truth, & empiricism valued; subject/ object duality, mechanical cause/ effect; Western European | Dynamism; co-evolution of system & environment; chaos & complexity theory; social construction; integration of science & ethics; multicultural |
| Education | Factory model-one size fits all. | Choice - individualized |
| Social Forces | Immigration; urbanization; assimilation | Immigration; globalization; multiculturalism |
| Intervention | Problem-focused. Observed patterns of behavior and rigid, unproductive patterns. Expert role; Information hidden; Adherence to a particular treatment model | Strengths focused. Co-constructing meaning and small change; Collaboration; Information shared; Treatment tailored to populations and problems. |

Note: The inspiration for a table comparing the modern and postmodern world, and selected aspects of the organizational structure and processes that appear in the table were based on Boje and Prieto (2000).

2008). Social constructionists embed objectivity or truth within its social, historical, economic, and linguistic contexts arguing broadly that there is no certain truth, but rather the perception of truth through contextual eyes. Feminist and cultural minority scholars across multiple disciplines illuminate how basic principles of traditional Western philosophy or science would change if it incorporated non-dominant perspectives. Environmental philosophy is concerned with how society is challenged to transform in interaction with the environment. The moral and ethical issues that arise with advances in technology have spawned growth in the field of applied ethics. Chaos theory and the sciences of complexity are branches of systems theory that have been developed to help understand highly complex systems (Reigeluth, 2008). "They recognize that beneath the apparently chaotic or unpredictable behavior of a complex system lie certain patterns that can help one to both understand, and…influence the behavior of the system" (Reigeluth, 2008, p. 14). Key features of chaos theory include co-evolution, disequilibrium, positive feedback, perturbation, transformation, fractals, strange attractors, self-organization, and dynamic complexity.

Postmodernism also has given birth to new models of psychological and family-centered treatment. The positive psychology movement and the Solution-oriented and Narrative family therapy models are reflective of postmodernism. Positive psychology at the subjective level is about valued subjective experience, at the individual level it is about positive individual traits, and at the group level it is about the civic virtues and the institutions that move individuals toward better citizenship (Seligman & Csikszentmihalyi, 2000). Consistent with chaos theory, solution-oriented brief therapy focuses assessment and intervention on positive feedback loops. The processes that were viewed by modern systems theorists to reflect a system out of control are now seen as reflecting an ever-changing, resilient system. Solution-oriented therapists search for the exceptions to the problem, as well as existing competencies and strengths that may have been overlooked. Narrative therapists, consistent with social constructionism, focus on the client's story, searching for times when they were strong and resourceful, and using questions in a cautious and respectful way to suggest a new story. The narrative approach further emphasizes that each family is unique, with unique stories and histories, and helps families separate from the dominant cultural narratives they have internalized that may be unhelpful.

The postmodern world is a multicultural world. Social change in the postmodern era is evident in the numerous variations of family organization that have emerged as normative within our nation, the changing demographics of the nations of the world related to immigration, and the shifting balance of global power as new dominant economies emerge. In contrast with the modern era where Western civilization shaped the dominant discourse, non-Western cultures will largely dominate the postmodern world (Zakaria, 2008). In the next few decades, three of the world's four largest economies (Japan, China, and India) will be non-Western, and the fourth, the United States, will be increasingly shaped by its growing non-European population. Zakaria calls this shift in economic and political power, "the rise of the rest." The unipolarity of the 20th century in which Westernization, industrialization, modernization, power and prestige went hand-in-hand is gradually being replaced with multipolarity of power and culture.

## The Postmodern Era and Family-School Partnership

At the beginning of this chapter, four areas of consensus regarding family-school partnerships were identified. This section explores how the shift to the postmodern world impacts each of these domains in the present and speculates on future directions. It is important to note that the change from one historical era to another is a gradual process. Elements of the past persist into the present, and paradigms that will come to be dominant in the future often emerge much earlier as ideas that did not find fertile soil. The period of transition between established paradigms may be neither smooth nor rapid. Thus, we can expect the consensus of the present to reflect a hybrid of the late modern and early postmodern eras with a clearly emergent dominant paradigm for family-school partnerships to be just that—emergent. Proposed future directions, therefore, are more likely proximal than distal.

***Consensus #1: Family-School Partnership Is Critically Important to the Optimization of Children's Educational Experience*** It is hard to imagine in the present context of transition wherein dramatic social, economic, educational, and political upheaval appears more probable than stability that strengthening the partnership between family and school should not remain a priority in the next several decades. However, the nature of the partnership must change. Schools will continue to be challenged by economic forces and technological advances to accommodate postmodern organizational structures and processes. Structurally, the postmodern organization is a networked set of diverse, self-managed, self-controlled teams with many centers of coordination that fold and unfold according to the requirements of the task, with employees highly empowered and involved in the job, information fluid and widely shared, with continuous improvement and customer satisfaction emphasized throughout (Boje & Dennehy, 2000).

How might the family-school partnership change in the postmodern school? I imagine that education teams will become responsible for the learning and development of each child through a developmental period of time, e.g., K–third grade. Team composition may vary depending on the needs of the child, but would always include at a minimum the various teachers of the child, the primary caretakers of the child and the child. Optimally the team would include other school, community, and family members, such as siblings, who play important roles in the development of the child. The team may expand to include other relevant expertise as needed. The team would decide on the priorities and needs of the child. The needs and priorities of the family for their child would be as relevant as the school's curriculum goals. Moreover, the school would be as responsible to the family in helping the child attain the family's goals for their child as the family is currently viewed by the school to be responsible in helping their child attain the school's educational goals. This may seem similar to the current school structure and process; however, I argue there are important differences. First, such teams are seldom convened unless a child is experiencing a learning or behavior problem, or such a meeting is legally mandated. Second, if meetings are convened, they infrequently include the caretakers or child as part of the 'team', nor are they postponed if caretakers cannot attend. Third, the child's education team would meet frequently, at least once per grading period, to assess the child's progress at home and at school.

Fourth, the team would not only be responsible for monitoring the progress of the child but also would be the beneficiary of incentives. Teams responsible for similar products, i.e., children with similar levels of educational needs, or that have successfully met a challenge, might network with other teams facing a similar challenge.

The postmodern family-school partnership demands different processes than are customary in the current partnership. Numerous chapters in this volume have argued this and also highlight the unintentional, but real, bias that may accompany communication and limit collaboration between home and school. Parent-teacher conferences, when examined, are comprised of unidirectional information flow from the teacher to the parent (Minke & Anderson 2003). Moreover, a key variable predicting parent involvement among minority, economically disadvantaged parents is their perception of invitation from the teacher (Anderson & Minke, 2007). Family-school partnership and collaboration requires the development of a relationship that is characterized by interpersonal regard, respect, and personal investment (Hoover-Dempsey, Whitaker, & Ice, this volume). The role of the teacher, or other school personnel who might be heading a team in such a relationship, is similar to the new role that Zakaria (2008) outlines for our nation in the post-American world. Power is derived not by demanding support for the school's agenda, but rather by setting a mutually reciprocal agenda, defining together the issues, and mobilizing and gently guiding the group to coordinated action. From a process perspective, the postmodern world, with its' valuing of diversity, demands processes of consultation, cooperation, and even compromise.

*Consensus #2: An Ecological Developmental Systems Theoretical Perspective Is a Useful Theoretical Framework for Conceptualizing the Complexity and Importance of Relationships between Home and School* This theoretical perspective has broad acceptance among developmental psychologists and provides strong justification for family-school partnership. Particularly noteworthy in the ecological developmental systems approach is the emphasis on relationships and development. The changing nature of the family-school partnership across the development of the child in school, and its implications over time for the achievement of children, deserves greater attention in future research (see Tolan and Woo this volume). Gaining a better understanding of the processes that enhance the development of effective family-school partnerships, and how these might vary for diverse populations, is another critical area of inquiry. The establishment of mutually satisfying and trusting relationships is a process that occurs over time; critical incidents may strengthen or attenuate it.

Missing from the ecological developmental systems theoretical model are elements of the postmodern discourse such as chaos theory or complexity theory that may be useful for understanding family-school partnerships and their development. For example, in applying complexity theory to education, Reigeluth (2008) noted that educational transformation is strongly influenced by strange attractors, which are a kind of fractal in chaos theory. Fractals are patterns, either behavioral or structural, that recur at all levels of a system (self-similarity). In education, they can be considered core ideas and values or beliefs that guide the design of the system. Examples of fractals in education today include top-down, autocratic control, and uniformity or standardization. Both of these fractals guide behavior and processes at every level of the school organization. A strange attractor is a kind of fractal or core idea that once it becomes a fairly widespread cultural norm among the stakeholders most involved with making changes, has a powerful influence over the processes and structures that emerge in a system undergoing transformation. In sum, given that complexity theory represents the further evolution of systems theory, its inclusion into conceptualizations of family-school partnership seems relevant.

As noted earlier, it is difficult, if not impossible, to anticipate the dominant paradigms that may emerge in the future. As the frontiers of science continue to expand, paradigms that are unheard of today are likely to be developed. Given some of today's domains of rapid change, I conjecture that these may reflect the following: our expanding knowledge of the brain and how it interrelates with learning, behavior, and disorder; how our rapidly expanding information technology transforms our interpersonal communication processes; or the incorporation of non-Western ideas or research findings into our education, parenting, and intervention with children.

***Consensus #3: Diversity Characterizes the Changing Demographics of the Nation's Public School Population of Students, and Is Salient to Every Aspect of the Educational Enterprise including Family-School-Community Partnerships*** Forty percent of the public school population is non-White (Swick, Head-Reeves, & Barbarin, 2006). Twelve percent of the nation's population is foreign born and, on average, of lower socioeconomic status with children who perform at lower educational levels compared with peers (NCES, 2007). The vast majority (83%) of the nation's public school teachers are European-American and middle class (NCES, 2004). The challenge such different culturally based worldviews presents to optimal parent-teacher communication or family-school partnerships cannot be overemphasized. Research consistently finds that teachers underestimate the parent involvement of the parents of ethnically diverse children in their classrooms because these parents do not participate in ways that are perceived to be the "right" ways by the teachers. In this volume, several chapters (e.g., Hill; Ogakaki, & Bingham) highlight the educational disadvantage that is created for children when the cultural worldviews of the home and school do not coincide. Throughout this volume are recommendations: research on the ecological diversity of family-school partnerships; practices that are sensitive, respectful, and encouraging to culturally diverse families; required teacher and school staff training on how to engage in effective and culturally competent communication and collaboration with parents and families. It is clear that tailoring the family-school partnership to meet the needs of a diverse student population will remain a dominant discourse within family-school partnership for the next several decades.

***Consensus #4: Evidence-Based Practice Is Valued, and We Continue to have Important Limitations to Our Knowledge Base Regarding Effective Family-School Partnerships*** The need for additional research on the family-school partnership is a theme that echoes throughout this volume. Highlighted is the need for research that helps us understand what works best for whom given the increasing diversity of our nation, and research that focuses on relationship processes over time. Critical to an understanding of the family-school partnership over time is recognition and measurement of the phenomena as a multi-level system. The family system, for example, is comprised of individual members, dyadic relationships, whole units (e.g., residents of a household), extended related units (e.g., a parent, grandparent, aunt, or uncle), and extended non-related units (e.g., non-biological adult who has played a primary caretaker role, but is no longer the member of a household). Further complexity is added because families vary greatly in the composition of their systems. At the most basic organizational level, families may be considered single parent or two parent households, as defined by the 2000 census; however, any family scholar knows this is a far too simplistic a picture to be useful. The school system similarly is comprised of individual teachers, classrooms that may contain more than one teacher, teams of teachers that may coordinate the teaching of a group of students, the school principal, other administrative and non-administrative staff, special service professionals who may or may not be a component of a single school, etc. Hinde and Stevenson-Hinde (1988) argued that each level of a system, and each dyadic or triadic relationship within systems levels or across distinct systems, such as the home and school, requires careful consideration of the variables that are relevant to that particular relationship. This level of careful conceptualization is largely absent from discussion of and research on family-school partnership or home-school collaboration.

Evidence-based intervention is a current focus of many disciplines, including education and psychology, and a related concern of both disciplines is the split between research and practice. Kazdin (2008) addressed this issue in psychology and offered a rapprochement. I take the liberty here to adapt his discussion of psychological clinical practice to family-school partnership. Broadly speaking, the central concern about evidence-based treatment (EBT) involves the generalizability of controlled research to practice given the variability of the individual clients (students). Evidence-based practice (EBP), in contrast, is a broader term that refers to decision making that incorporates evidence about intervention, the expertise of the decision maker, child and family needs, as well as parent values and preferences. Research on EBP is clearly complex, and as Kazdin noted, EBP is not what researchers, at least in psychology, have studied.

Researchers and practitioners, however, in both education and psychology are concerned about identifying and providing the most effective and cost-effective curriculum and interventions. Kazdin suggested three shifts in research emphasis to advance the knowledge base, improve intervention, and reduce the research-practice gulf. These include giving greater priority to (a) the mechanisms of change, (b) the study of moderators of change in ways that can be better translated into practice, and (c) qualitative research. Applied to research on family-school partnerships, this would suggest the following: (a) research on the processes that explain why family-school collaboration works or how it produces change, not that it does produce change; (b) when significant moderators are detected in research, reporting whether the moderator eliminates the intervention effect, predicts (moderates) responsiveness, and what facet of the moderator is relevant; and (c) qualitative research because it meets the criteria of science while permitting the type of intensive and systematic study of experience that will generate hypotheses directly applicable to practice that could subsequently be tested in quantitative and qualitative studies. Kazdin proposed parallel changes in practice to enhance our knowledge of EBP. These include: (a) use of systematic measurement or evaluation of the family-school collaboration or partnership on a regular (e.g., weekly in traditional psychotherapy) basis, (b) codifying the experience of practitioners (teachers) in engaging parents, and (c) genuine collaborations between researchers and practitioners. Many of the suggestions proposed by Kazdin are relevant to the study of family-school partnership and consistent with the postmodern discourse.

*Notable Omissions from the Discourse*    Consensus has been evident throughout much of this volume regarding what is needed to expand the knowledge base and improve family-school partnership practice. In my view two omissions from the discourse are notable. The first reflects the absence of family in the family-school partnership. The second is the lack of attention to the role of technology.

Notable in discussions family-school partnerships is lack of clarity about the terms that are used and their interchangeability. Specifically who or what constitutes "family," and whom or what constitutes "school"? Is family-school partnership the same as home-school collaboration? Is home-school communication the same as parent-teacher communication? Does it matter who is the parent in parent? Is mother involvement the same as father involvement or grandparent involvement or older sibling involvement? Family has multiple definitions, but largely as used in family-school partnership discussion, it refers to the people living together or related to the child who attends public school. In discourse and research about family-school partnerships or family-centered treatment, however, the term "family" is used largely interchangeably with the term "parent," and neither is clearly defined. Peeled back another layer, we find that commonly we have an intervention science in parent training, for example, that is in fact, "mother" training. The same ambiguity of terms applies to the school side of the partnership. Teacher is used largely interchangeably with the term "school" and the fact that most children have multiple teachers is largely ignored.

It does not seem possible to expand our knowledge base on family-school partnership without greater attention to precise definitions about the phenomena we are studying and clearly defining at which level of the multi-level system is the relationship that is the focus of inquiry. The assumption of the interchangeability of terms can also be viewed as reflecting a Western cultural bias that overemphasizes the role of the biological mother and reduces the complexity of family roles that may be characteristic of the socialization of children in non-Western cultures and the reality of complex living arrangements today. Of course, it is challenging to acknowledge such complexity in quantitative studies due to inadequate sample sizes. These variations in roles, however, may represent important moderators of the developmental family-school partnership that deserve measurement and analysis.

Also largely absent from the discussion of family-school partnership is the use of technology in the service of enhanced partnership. A brief search of the literature (via the Web, of course), yielded no citations that suggested the use of technology for home-school communication. Rather the primary focus of the discourse is the use of technology for instructional purposes, i.e., to enhance student learning and motivation in the classroom, and the barriers to its widespread use. It may seem far-fetched to consider the role of technology in family-school partnership when education is continually challenged by inadequate budgets and there is evidence of a technology divide between the economically advantaged and disadvantaged. However, this would appear to be shortsighted. Recently it was reported in the news that over 95% of Americans own mobile phones. Clearly, technology that solves a perceived need for the right price quickly dissolves the technology divide related to socioeconomic status.

A promising direction of evidence regarding the potential of technology in family-school partnership is the use of Virtual Learning Environments (VLEs). Currently, higher educational institutions are using VLEs to manage and enhance teaching, learning, and research related to complex group projects (Cleary & Marcus-Quinn, 2008). VLE software provides group discussion, chat, scheduling, and collaboration tools, all of which are relevant relational processes to family-school partnership that could reduce the structural barrier imposed by varying work schedules of teachers and parents. Online education is another direction to scan for inspiration regarding family-school partnership. Whether the education is reflected by home-schooling at an elementary level (Opsahl, June 18, 2008) or obtaining a doctoral degree (e.g., Waldon University), the availability of educational curriculum online is becoming pervasive in our culture. This reflects the degree to which educational information that would enhance the collaborative teaching roles of the parents and teacher could easily be shared. Finally, Cuban and Cuban (2008) proposed the *coordinated* use of technology in public schools and libraries to create stronger literacy *communities*. This extends the potential use of technology to the family-school-community partnership. Common to advancing technology is the ability to network people and resources in space, which vastly expands the potential for information exchange. It would appear that it is essential to consider how technology may facilitate the family-school partnership in the future.

## Summary

This chapter has explored consensual themes regarding family-school partnership including its importance to children's education and the value of the ecological developmental paradigm to its conceptualization, as well as the need in the future to expand our knowledge base and practices to better reflect the diversity of families and school populations. Future directions for research and practice in the postmodern world were first situated in the organizational processes, structures, and belief systems of the past modern era because these largely represent barriers to transformation of the family-school partnership in the proximal future. As chaos theory proposes, however, strange attractors are powerful movers of transformation. Thus, I believe a change in the core beliefs of educators that regulate family-school partnership at every level of education in the present could dramatically shift, and shift relatively rapidly, in the future. Technology would appear to be assistive in this process; however, technology alone is unlikely to transform family-school partnerships without widespread adoption of not only its added value, but also the core belief that collaboration and coordination of the diverse voices who are concerned about the child's social and educational progress is necessary and essential.

## AUTHOR'S NOTE

1. This discussion of the organization of the school as a reflection of the predominant organization of the economic base is largely based on *Schools for the 21st century: Leadership imperatives for educational reform* by Phillip Schlechty.

## REFERENCES

Anderson, K. J., & Minke, K. M. (2007). Parent involvement in education: Toward an understanding of parents' decision making. *The Journal of Educational Research, 100*(5), 311–323.

Aponte (1976). The family-school interview: An eco-structural approach. *Family Process, 15*, 303–312.

Boje, D., & Dennehy, R. (2000). [Electronic version] *Postmodern management: America's revolution against exploitation.* Available from http://cbae.nmsu.edu/~dboje/mpw.html

Bronfenbrenner, U. (1979). *The ecology of human development.* Cambridge, MA: Harvard University Press.

Carpenter, A. N. (n.d). Western philosophy. Retrieved August 4, 2008, from http://encarta.msn.com/text_761574677_0/Philosophy.html

Cleary, Y., & Marcus-Quinn, A. (2008). Using a virtual learning environment to manage group projects: A case study. *International Journal on E-Learning, 7*(4), 603–621. ERIC #: EJ810074. Retrieved October 28, 2008, from http://eric.ed.gov/ERICWebPortal/custom/portlets/recordDetails

Christenson, S. L., & Sheridan, S. M. (2001). *Schools and families: Creating essential connections for learning.* New York: Guilford.

Cuban, S., & Cuban, L. (2007). *Partners in literacy: Schools and libraries building communities through technology.* ERIC #: ED497822. Retrieved October 28, 2008, from http://eric.ed.gov/ERICWebPortal/custom/portlets/recordDetails

Fine, M. J., & Carlson, C. (1992). *Family-school intervention: A systems approach.* Boston: Allyn & Bacon.

Hinde, R. A., & Stevenson-Hinde, J. (1988). Epilogue. In R. A. Hinde & J. Stevenson-Hinde (Eds.), *Relationships within families: Mutual influences* (pp. 366–385). New York: Oxford University Press.

Kazdin, A. (2008). Evidence-based treatment and practice: New opportunities to bridge clinical research and practice, enhance the knowledge base, and improve patient care. *American Psychologist, 63*(3), 146–159.

Lewin, K. (1951). *Field theory in social science.* New York: Harper & Brothers.

Minke, K. M., & Anderson, K. J. (2003). Restructuring routine parent-teacher conferences: The family-school conference model. *The Elementary School Journal, 104*(1), 49–69.

National Center for Educational Statistics (2004). *Schools and staffing survey.* Available from http://nces.ed.gov/surveys/sass/tables/state_2004

National Center for Educational Statistics (2007). *Status and trends in the education of racial and ethnic minorities.* NCES Publication # 2007039. Available from http://nces.ed.gov

Nichols, M. P. (2008). *Family therapy concepts and methods (8th ed.).* Boston: Pearson

Opsahl, A. (2008). *Public education comes online to Texas homeschoolers.* Retrieved October 28, 2008, from http://www.govtech.com/gt/print_article.php?id=032361

Reigeluth, C. M. (2008). Chaos theory and the sciences of complexity: Foundations for transforming education. In B. Despres (Ed.), *Systems thinkers in action* (pp. 24–38). Lanham, MD: Rowman & Littlefield.

Seligman, M.E.P., & Csikszentmihalyi, M. (2000). Positive psychology: An introduction. *American Psychologist, 55*, 5–14.

Swick, D., Head-Reeves, D., & Barbarin, O. (2006). Building relationships between diverse families and school personnel. In C. Franklin, M. Harris, & P. Allen-Meares (Eds.), *The school services sourcebook: A guide for school-based professional* (pp. 793–802). New York: Oxford University Press.

Weiss, H. M., & Edwards, M. E. (1992). The family-school collaboration project: Systemic interventions for school improvement. In S. L. Christenson & J. C. Conoley (Eds.), *Home-school collaboration: Enhancing children's academic and social competence* (pp. 215–244). Silver Spring, MD: National Association of School Psychologists.

Zakaria, F. (2008). *The post-American world.* New York: Norton & Company.

# 19

## METHODOLOGICAL ISSUES IN FAMILY-SCHOOL PARTNERSHIP RESEARCH

S. NATASHA BERETVAS, TIMOTHY Z. KEITH, AND CINDY CARLSON

For many years, social science researchers have been facing the same methodological dilemmas resulting from the imperfect measurement of latent psychological constructs, from the data dependencies that result from group contexts, and from the complex dynamic interactions that occur in real-world data. Fortunately, over the last couple of decades, a plethora of statistical and psychometric models have been introduced. In addition, software designed to estimate these models is becoming increasingly accessible. The sophistication of these tools enhances the validity of the resulting statistical inferences. However, the complexity of these sophistications prohibits their common use. This chapter is designed to describe some statistical models that are essential for the appropriate modeling of data structures and relationships of relevance to family-school partnership research. This description is designed to help researchers who are interested in investigating family-school partnerships better understand the need for these models and their estimation, thereby encouraging the models' increased appropriate use.

## OVERVIEW

The purpose of this chapter is to link conceptual perspectives on family-school partnerships with associated methodological challenges and solutions. Broadly speaking, research on family-school partnerships addresses three general questions: the testing of theory, description of processes, and program evaluation. Viewed from the scientist practitioner framework commonly accepted in psychology, these three questions are frequently overlapping. Prior to the proposal of statistical model solutions to common methodological problems, we will briefly review the theoretical foundations of family-school partnership research, the contemporary demand for evidence-based practice, and the methodological implications of theory and practice. Several methodological solutions are then proposed, including the use of the structural equation modeling (SEM) and multilevel modeling frameworks.

## Theoretical and Contemporary Basis for Family-School Partnership Research

*Ecological Developmental Systems Model*   As noted by Downer and Myers (this volume), literally hundreds of articles and studies use a developmental ecological systems model as the starting point for understanding family-school relationships. The authors' thoughtful articulation of the model serves as an appropriate framework with which to consider the methodological considerations and challenges facing researchers who seek to understand the processes or to evaluate programs designed to relate family-school linkages with student outcomes. Key aspects of the developmental ecological model, which is rooted in general systems theory, include the following:

- The ecology of schooling reflects an organized system of interactions among persons (parents, teachers, students), settings (home, school), and institutions (community, governments). (Note that the term "interactions" is used here in its more common usage, not in the statistical sense of the word.)
- Student development occurs within the context of these organized and hierarchically nested social systems, which exert proximal and distal influence on student outcomes.
- Organized systems, and the interactions between them, are dynamic, reciprocally influential, and change over time.
- Interactions between elements within systems (i.e., persons, settings, institutions) create a relationship that is distinct from the characteristics of the elements.
- Because each student reflects a unique intersection of system elements, diverse inputs and multiple pathways from inputs to student outcomes are probable.

*Evidence-Based Practice*   The importance of establishing a strong evidence base for educational interventions, as well as the importance of parent involvement in education, is clear in all federal initiatives within the recent decade. Evidence-based interventions are those that have been proven efficacious in well-designed, preferably randomized and controlled, trials. In short, the level of evidence garnered to support a particular educational intervention or strategy is related to the quality of research methods or designs used to test its effectiveness (Carlson & Christenson, 2005).

A recent review of the evidence found that the strongest evidence base could be built for focused home-school collaboration interventions in which either parents and teachers had a two-way exchange of communication, and worked together as co-equals, to implement an intervention on behalf of the child or the school engaged in consistent and focused one-way communication to the home about the child's progress (Cox, 2005). In contrast with the effectiveness of narrowly focused family-school partnership interventions, the evidence supporting broad, school-wide, multiple component interventions was weakened by two problems. One problem entailed the failure to consider the multiple contextual factors that are key in the design and implementation of such interventions. The second problem was the failure to disentangle the individual effects of multiple components in predicting student outcomes.

*Implications of Theory and Contemporary Issues for Research Design and Analyses*

Ecological systems developmental theory, as well as contemporary pressures for evidence based educational intervention, have implications for family-school partnership research. In their discussion of the theory, Downer and Myers (this volume) also highlighted some of the implications of a systems ecological developmental theoretical framework for research:

- The relevance of examining how maturation (i.e., the students' social, cognitive, and biological maturation, as well as the parents' and the teacher's maturation), can affect interactions within and between the family and school microsystems.
- The importance of the relationship of one's social construction of reality. This implication includes two points: what we perceive influences what we do, and family-school partnership research rarely includes the child's perspective.
- The need for better measurement of the family-school partnership.
- The need for research designs that permit testing proposed indirect and mediational relations among proximal inputs.

We argue that several additional considerations are relevant to research in this area. These include the importance of the following:

- Viewing relationship as a separate phenomena from the perceptions or behavior of the involved individuals or entities,
- Focusing on reciprocal processes over time, and
- Being clear about what and who is being measured.

Briefly elaborated, systems theory argues that the relationship between two entities is different from the sum of the parts. Moreover, relationships develop on the basis of reciprocal interactions over time. Use of structural equation modeling (SEM) for testing the pattern of evolving family-school or parent-teacher relationships and their effects on child outcomes will be discussed in the current chapter. The benefits of the flexibility and appropriateness SEM for modeling school-family partnership research will be emphasized.

The family and the school, as well and the environmental contexts in which they are nested, reflect multi-member, multilevel systems. The usefulness of multilevel modeling will also be illustrated as a solution to the complexities commonly encountered when modeling family-school partnerships.

## STRUCTURAL EQUATION MODELING

Structural equation modeling offers much promise for addressing many of the challenges of research on school-family connections. SEM provides a very general framework that allows the testing of the effects of multiple possible causes on multiple possible effects closely matching the complexity of scenarios encountered in family-school research. SEM is commonly used with non-experimental research design results, although it can also be used (and indeed has advantages) in experimental research. One truism of family-school research is that researchers need to consider multiple variables, and a *system* of such variables. SEM is consistent with, and in fact encourages, such systems thinking, where it is possible to consider both the effects of variables on outcomes in addition to the possible effects of those variables on each other. SEM, with its ability to assess direct, indirect, and total effects, is ideal for testing for possible mediation. Multi-group SEM is useful for testing for similarities and differences in patterns of relations among variables across groups (i.e., moderation) and for assessing the factor structure equivalence (i.e., measurement invariance) of scores across groups.

In its simplest form, often referred to as path analysis, SEM focuses on a system of measured variables. When multiple measures are available for each construct, latent variable SEM is possible, allowing the researchers to control for measurement error in both influences and outcomes. In this chapter, the term "SEM" will be used to refer to all types of structural equation models, including those with measured variables and those with latent variables. The first few sections on SEM will focus on modeling relations among measured variables (path analysis). Later sections will extend the discussion of SEM to include latent variable SEM models.

Estimation of structural equation models generally requires specialized statistical software, and there are numerous programs available; each has its own advantages. LISREL (Jöreskog, Sörbom, du Toit, & du Toit, 2000) was the first fully fledged SEM program. Mplus (Muthén & Muthén, 1998–2007) can be used to estimate the most extensive range of models. EQS (Bentler, 1995) and Amos (Arbuckle, 2007) are both somewhat easier to use although more restricted in the models that they can be used to estimate. Amos is available as an add-on to SPSS statistical software and is probably the easiest SEM program to use for a novice, allowing either graphic or syntax input and producing high-quality graphic output. Mx software (Neale, Boker, Xie, & Maes, 1999) offers advanced modeling options and is free for download. The general statistical software SAS (SAS Institute Inc., 1999) also includes some procedures that permit estimation of SEM models. The reader is encouraged to explore use of these software programs for estimating their SEM models. Several textbooks provide details about how to use software programs to estimate SEM models (e.g., Brown, 2006; Byrne, 1994, 1998, 2001; Keith, 2006; Kline, 2005). However, the current chapter is designed to discuss the merits of SEM. It is not intended to teach the reader how to estimate structural equation models

### SEM with Measured Variables

As already noted, the simplest form of SEM uses only measured (not latent) variables, and is often referred to as path analysis. An example will be used to illustrate the technique and its benefits over and above more commonly used multiple regression models. Figure 19.1 shows a model designed to evaluate the effects of parent involvement on High School grade point average. The model is similar to one used in Keith (2006).

*Parent involvement* in this model could be a composite score of parent and students' responses to questions that likely measure two components of parent involvement: parents' involvement in school activities and their involvement in home-related educational activities. This is measured when students were in eighth grade. *Grades* is another

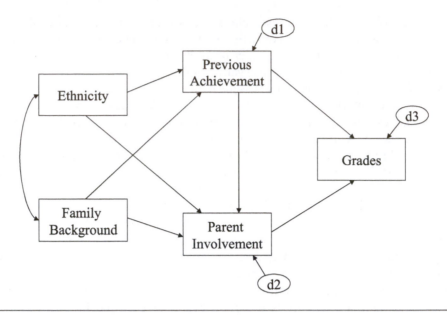

**Figure 19.1** Path model designed to explain students' grades in 12th grade.

composite measure consisting of the students' 12th grade GPA in English, math, science, and social studies. The model also includes several possible background variables of interest: *Ethnicity* (majority/minority), *Family Background* (or socioeconomic status, a combination of parent education and occupational status, and family income), and *Previous Achievement* (students eighth grade test score composites in English, math, science, and social studies).

The paths in the model (represented with one-headed arrows) model the presumed effect of one variable (at the start of the arrow) on another (pointed to by the arrow), given the adequacy of the model. These paths assume what is known as a weak causal ordering. The drawing of a path does not mean that, say, *Parent Involvement* directly affects *Grades*, but rather that if the two variables are related, the direction of influence is from *Involvement* to *Grades*, rather than the reverse.

The small ovals pointing to the endogenous (dependent) variables (e.g. *d3* pointing to *Grades*) are generally referred to as disturbances, or sometimes simply as errors. They represent the unexplained variance in the variable at which they are pointing. Disturbances represent *all other* unmeasured and un-modeled influences on the variable of interest. For example, there is a disturbance term pointing to *Previous Achievement*. Part of the variance in *Previous Achievement* might be explained by *Family Background* and *Ethnicity*. The disturbance represents the unexplained variance in *Previous Achievement*, or the variance explained by variables not included in the model. The disturbances are enclosed in ovals to signify that they are unmeasured, or latent, variables.

The curved double headed arrow between *Ethnicity* and *Family Background* represents a correlation between these independent (or exogenous) variables with no associated assumptions about which of these variables influences the other. Note that not all possible paths are drawn in the model. There is no path, for example, from *Family*

*Background* to *Grades*. This omission means that the researchers assume that *Family Background* does not influence *Grades* over and above the modeled indirect relations between the two variables. As with any kind of modeling, a balance is essential between depicting (and estimating) an exact model of the truth and in using a parsimonious, easy-to-interpret approximation of reality. The more parameters that are estimated in a model, the more complex it is to estimate. But the more parameters included in a model, the better the model will fit the data. At some point, however, there can be more parameters in a model than are estimable (i.e., with an under-identified model). The reader is encouraged to read Kline (2005) and other SEM textbooks for fuller discussions of model identification.

As many readers are likely aware, the prediction of *Grades* using *Ethnicity, Previous Achievement, Family Background*, and *Parent Involvement could* be modeled and analyzed via multiple regression. This regression model is depicted in Figure 19.2. There are several advantages, however, to using a path-analytic model over a multiple regression model. First, multiple regression models are a form of path-analytic models. However, under a multiple regression model, all of the correlations between pairs of predictors are modeled. In addition, there are only two "layers" of variables in a multiple regression model. There is the outcome, here, *Grades*, and then the set of four predictors. In a path-analytic model, there can be additional layers. For example, in the path-analytic model in Figure 19.1, *Previous Achievement* and *Parent Involvement* are modeled as influences on *Grades*, however these two influences are also outcomes in that they are modeled as being influenced by *Ethnicity* and *Family Background*. Thus path-analytic models allow researchers to explore more complex relations among variables. One additional benefit of path-analytic (and more generally, SEM) models is that if they are over-identified (as is the model in Figure 19.1), then measures of model fit can be used to assist with best model selection.

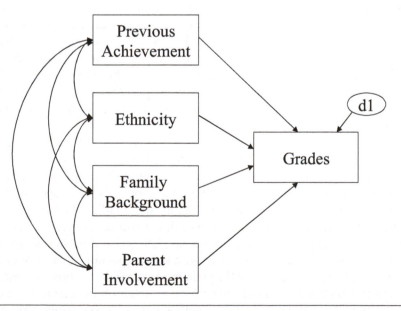

**Figure 19.2** Multiple regression model depicting prediction of grades.

Identification refers to the number of parameters that *could* be estimated in a model versus those that *are* estimated (this is a slight oversimplification). Specifically, when there are fewer parameters estimated than there are known pieces of information (namely, unique elements in the associated covariance matrix and possibly sample means), then the model is over-identified. For the model shown in Figure 19.1, 13 parameters are estimated (7 paths, 5 variances, and 1 covariance), whereas the covariance matrix includes 15 elements. The model is thus over-identified, with two degrees of freedom. When the model is sufficiently parsimonious that it is over-identified (and therefore has positive *df*), it will not perfectly recover the original, observed data (e.g., covariance matrix). The extent of the difference between the observed covariance matrix and that implied by the model indicates the fit of the model. If a model is just-identified, then as many parameters are used as there are known pieces of information and thus the model-implied covariance matrix should exactly equal the observed matrix. With no differences between these two matrices, there is then perfect model fit. While "perfect" fit sounds ideal, a just-identified model is not parsimonious. Last, it will be problematic to estimate an under-identified model because there will be insufficient information to estimate the specified parameters.

All SEM software programs provide fit indices based on the difference between the actual and the model-implied matrices. There are a multitude of such fit indices and the choice of fit indices to use as well as their associated criteria for acceptable versus unacceptable fit is a continuing source of research and debate in the methodological SEM literature (e.g., Hu & Bentler, 1999; Zhonglin, Hau, & Marsh, 2004).

### Causal Assumptions[1]

As noted earlier, the paths in SEM models represent a weak causal ordering, and the results suggest the extent of the influence of one variable on another, given the adequacy of the model. What makes a model adequate? This question is a point of continued confusion among both users and critics of SEM. To be more specific, under what conditions can we interpret, say, a path from Parent Involvement to Grades as representing the effect of parental involvement on student grades? If the standardized path value's estimate is 0.20, under what conditions can we interpret this as meaning that for each one standard deviation (SD) increase in Parent Involvement, Grades will increase by 0.20 SD units?

First, and obviously, the causal direction must be correctly specified. If the model specifies that *Parent Involvement* affects *Grades* when, in fact, *Grades* affect *Parent Involvement*, then any conclusions we make concerning the effect of *Involvement* on *Grades* will be erroneous. Second, the variables (and especially the exogenous variables, or presumed causes) need to be measured reliably and validly. Measurement error in variables affects the estimates of effects, often leading to underestimates of those effects. One of the primary advantages of latent variable SEM is that it takes into account and controls for such measurement error. Third, and very importantly, the model must include all important common causes of the presumed cause (*Parent Involvement*) and the presumed effect (*Grades*). If an important common cause is omitted from the model and neglected in the analysis, then the resulting path will provide a spurious estimate of the effects of one variable on another. In contrast, however, if all important and substantial common causes of *Parent Involvement* and *Grades* are modeled, then the resulting path indeed provides a valid estimate of the effect of *Parent Involvement* on *Grades*.

Note that *common* causes, not all causes, must be included in the model. In other words, if a variable that affects, say, *Parent Involvement* but not *Grades* is excluded from the model, this exclusion will not affect the estimate of the path between *Grades* and *Parent Involvement*. How do researchers know which variables are the important common causes that must be included in the model? They need a solid grounding in relevant theory, an understanding of previous research, and thoughtful consideration and study of the likely causal process (in essence, the same requirements for creating the model in the first place). The reader is encouraged to refer to additional resources to find out more information about the conditions needed to make valid inferences concerning causality (e.g., Keith, 2006; Kenny, 1979; Pearl, 2000).

The careful specification of *nonequivalent* SEM models may also be useful for sorting out questions of causal predominance. Equivalent models are those that cannot be separated based on model fit. In Figure 19.1, for example, the correlation between *Ethnicity* and *Family Background* could be replaced with a directional path. The resulting two models would have exactly the same model fit and thus are technically equivalent. Likewise, the path from *Family Background* to *Previous Achievement* could be reversed without changing model fit. In contrast, reversing the path from *Parent Involvement* to *Grades* would likely result in a change in fit. If the initial model fit better than the model with the *Involvement* to *Grade* path reversed, that finding would provide some evidence that the first model was "better" than the second. The rules for generating equivalent versus nonequivalent models are discussed in detail elsewhere (Keith, 2006; Kline, 2005; Lee & Hershberger, 1990; Stelzl, 1986). The important point is that the careful a priori specification and estimation of nonequivalent models may provide information about which variables are influences and which are effects.

### Longitudinal Models

One of the threats to causal conclusions discussed previously occurs when a model confuses cause and effect: when a variable assumed to be an influence is, in fact, an effect. Obviously, causal inferences made from such results will be mistaken. One reason that researchers value longitudinal data is that such data can bolster causal inferences. If a researcher is not certain whether time spent doing homework is more likely to affect time spent watching TV or the reverse, one way to bolster the model shown in Figure 19.3 would be to measure *Homework* in, say, Grade 10 and *TV Time* in Grade 11. One obvious logical requirement to permit causal inferences is that the effect happens after the cause. Thus, it is much more likely that *Homework* in 10th grade would affect *TV Time* in 11th grade rather than the reverse.

Another advantage of longitudinal data is also embodied in Figures 19.1 and 19.3. Both Figures include the variable *Previous Achievement* as one of the influences on high school *Grades*. Obviously these two variables are highly related, and as a result, it makes sense to think that any effect that background variables (*Ethnicity* and *Family Background*) have on *Grades* is through *Previous Achievement*. If SES influences

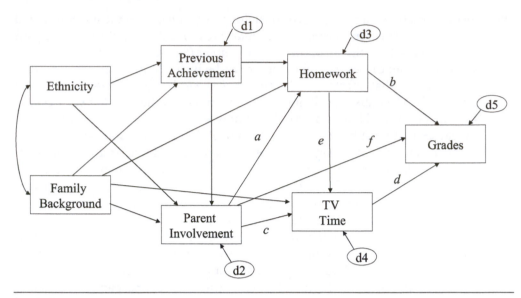

**Figure 19.3** Path analytic model depicting the mediation of the effect of parent involvement on grades through homework and TV times.

*Previous Achievement*, then students who achieve at a high level in eighth grade are also likely to have higher grades by the end of high school. The use of longitudinal data, with repeated measures of the same or related constructs, can thus help deal with the other major threat to valid causal conclusions in nonexperimental research: neglected common causes.

Longitudinal modeling is no panacea, however. One could, for example, measure self-esteem in Grade 8 and gender in Grade 10, but despite the longitudinal nature of the data collection, if these two variables are causally related, the cause must be from gender to self-esteem, not the reverse. Later sections of this chapter discuss longitudinal data analysis further.

### Reciprocal Effects

Another challenge in family-school partnership research is the possibility that variables have reciprocal effects. If the things that happen at school influence the child's and thus the family's reaction, it makes sense that the things the family does should likewise affect the things that happen at school. If a child's educational aspirations affect the parents' aspirations for the child, the reverse could also be true. There are several ways to incorporate and test such reciprocal effects in SEM models.

One method for analysis of possible reciprocal effects is the use of non-recursive SEM models. Figure 19.4 illustrates an example in which the reciprocal effects of a student's and their best friend's educational aspirations are modeled. This reciprocal effect is depicted in the model with one arrow pointing from *Student Aspiration* to *Peer Aspiration* and another arrow simultaneously pointing in the opposite direction. Researchers are often interested in the effects of students' peers on students' behavior.

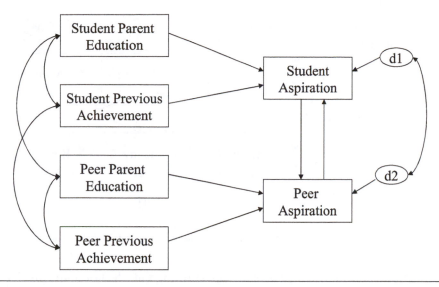

**Figure 19.4** Model of non-recursive simultaneous time reciprocal effects.

The example focuses on the influence of a students' best friend on his or her own level of educational aspiration. Clearly, if a friend influences a student's aspirations, it makes sense that the student's aspirations should similarly influence their friend's. Multiple regression models cannot be used to estimate non-recursive relations. Non-recursive versions can be modeled in the SEM framework.

Non-recursive models are more complex to estimate than are normal (recursive) models. In particular, it is easy for such models to be under-identified, meaning parameters are inestimable unless additional constraints are added to the model. As already noted, the topic of identification is beyond the scope of this chapter, but one key to identification in non-recursive models is to include "instrumental" variables, variables that (in the current example) likely affect a students' aspiration without directly affecting their friend's, and variables that affect the friend's aspiration without directly affecting the student's. For more information about non-recursive SEM models, see Loehlin (2004) or Rigdon (1995).

Longitudinal data and models are another way to incorporate and test reciprocal effects; Figure 19.5 shows an example of a "panel" model. Previous models have assumed that *Parent Involvement* affects subsequent achievement (*Grades*), but also that *Previous Achievement* may affect *Involvement* (see Figure 19.1). The model in Figure 19.5 is designed to test these assumptions more explicitly. It makes sense that the amount of involvement that parents invest in their children at home should depend, in part, on their child's performance in school. So, for example, if children begin to experience problems in their school performance, many parents will respond by spending more time working with their children at home on school-related tasks. Likewise, it makes sense that such home involvement should pay off in learning, which would show up as increased school achievement. The panel model shown could be used to test such effects, with both *Home Involvement* and *Achievement* measured at an initial time point (e.g., the first grading period), at the second grading period (time point 2), and so on.

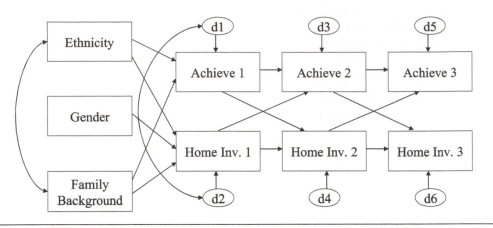

**Figure 19.5** Longitudinal (panel) model of reciprocal effects of student achievement and home involvement over time.

The panel model would thus be useful for determining the effect of home involvement on subsequent achievement, and achievement on subsequent involvement. Researchers also often use panel models to help settle questions of causal predominance. If the results of this analysis showed that *Home Involvement* affected *Achievement*, but that, controlling for this pattern, *Achievement* had no effect on subsequent *Involvement*, this finding would have implications for future research on the effects of and from *Parent Involvement*.

Obviously, detailed examination of reciprocal effects is beyond the scope of this short chapter. Several points are worth considering, however. First, note that the two models (Figures 19.4 and 19.5) address two different types of possible reciprocal effects. The reciprocal effects in Figure 19.4 should be fairly immediate; that is, a child would presumably affect his or her friend at the same time the friend is affecting the child. In contrast, the reciprocal effects in Figure 19.5 would seem to be more time-mediated. Presumably, *Home Involvement* should take some time to affect *Achievement*, and *Achievement* should affect subsequent *Involvement*, and affect it over time. It is likely that the reciprocal effects of the type shown in Figure 19.4 are relatively rare. Time-mediated effects are likely more common. Careful thought about how reciprocal effects likely work will help guard against making too easy assumptions about reciprocal effects when researchers are unsure about causal predominance. A researcher may be unsure, for example, whether *Homework Time* affects *TV Time* or the reverse, and thus simply specify that their effects are reciprocal. Reciprocal effects are not a valid substitute for ignorance, or a lack of theoretical justification, or a lack of careful data gathering. Researchers are urged to consider carefully the sources of reciprocal effects and to specify models and gather data accordingly.

### Modeling Proximal and Distal Causality and Mediating Variables

It should be obvious that SEM models are capable of including both proximal and distal influences and of partitioning their relative effects. In the path-analytic model shown in Figure 19.1, Ethnicity and Family Background are distal variables describing students' families. Ethnic background is determined at the moment of conception, and socioeconomic status (SES), for most children, is likely in place before the child's birth. Both variables clearly take place long before middle or high school. In contrast, Parent Involvement in middle school is much more proximal to high school Grades, and even more contemporaneous effects could be easily included (e.g., in the panel model).

Which proximal and distal influences should be included in a model? Obviously, researchers should include in their models the variables they are interested in testing, but what other effects are needed? The issue of distal effects is often related to that of common causes. That is, concerns with distal causes often reflect a desire to control important "confounding" variables; alternatively researchers may be concerned that if they were to include a different set of distal causes, then perhaps their estimates of effects would change. Again, the rule of common causes addresses this concern: for a model to provide valid estimates of the influence of one variable on another, all important common causes of the presumed cause and the presumed effect must be included in the model.

Questions of proximal and distal effects are also often related to the issue of mediation. Suppose a large effect was found for *Parent Involvement* on student *Grades* (in Figure 19.1). A natural follow-up question might ask *how* this effect comes about. In other words: through what mechanism does higher *Parent Involvement* increase student *Grades*? The model shown in Figure 19.3 is one attempt to answer this question. A researcher might reason, based on school learning theory (e.g., Carroll, 1989), that *Parent Involvement* is likely to affect the time that students spend on various activities that may improve (time spent on homework) or detract from (time spent watching TV) students' *Grades* (e.g., Keith et al., 1993). Assuming the researcher had measures reflecting time spent on homework and TV, then the indirect effect on *Grades* of *Parent Involvement* through *Homework* and *TV Time* could be estimated.

Another term for indirect effect is mediation.[2] In other words, the model contained in Figure 19.3 tests the extent to which *Homework* and *TV Time* mediate the effect of *Parent Involvement* on *Grades*. It is possible to test simple mediation models using multiple regression models, however, SEM provides a more flexible and direct framework for doing so. In the model shown in Figure 19.3, the indirect effect of *Parent Involvement* on *Grades* through *Homework* could be calculated by summing together the product of path *a* times path *b* and the product of paths *a*, *e*, and *d*. And similarly, values of the relevant paths connecting *Parent Involvement* with *Grades* through *TV Time* can be used to calculate the corresponding indirect effect. These tests of indirect effects would indicate whether *Homework* (and *TV Time*) each mediate the effect of *Parent Involvement* on *Grades*. Full (versus partial) mediation can be inferred based on whether the direct effect path *f* (connecting *Parent Involvement* with *Grades*) drops to a trivial value. A test of partial versus total mediation could also be conducted by estimating a model with path *f* constrained to zero and comparing the fit of that model with the one depicted in Figure 19.3. If the model's fit does not drop substantially when *f* is not included in the model, then this provides support for full mediation. The reader is encouraged to refer to several resources containing more information on using SEM models to test for mediation (e.g., MacKinnon, 2008; MacKinnon, Lockwood, Hoffman, West, & Sheets, 2002; Shrout & Bolger (2002).

## Moderation in Path-Analytic Models

SEM is also useful for assessing possible moderating effects. Many research questions in the family-school partnership context refer to moderation in a variety of ways. Referring back to the simple path-analytic model in Figure 19.1, a researcher might wonder whether Parent Involvement (and other variables in the model) has the same effect on Grades for boys versus girls. It may be the case, for example, that Involvement has a strong effect on the Grades of boys, but a smaller effect on the Grades of girls. This question is one of moderation: does Gender moderate the effect of Involvement on Grades? This could also be phrased as a question about an interaction effect (a statistical interaction), specifically: Do Gender and Parent Involvement interact in their effect on Grades?

Interactions between a categorical (e.g., *Gender*) and continuous variable (e.g., *Parent Involvement*) can be easily modeled and estimated via multi-group SEM models. An example of a multi-group version of the initial path model is shown in Figure 19.6. The model that is depicted is designed to test whether the effect of *Parent Involvement* on *Grades* in the model in Figure 19.1 is moderated by *Gender*. In Figure 19.6, the shaded ellipse surrounding the path-analytic model (from Figure 19.1) and pointed to by the grouping variable (*Gender* in Figure 19.6) represents the multi-group nature of the model within the shaded ellipse. Specifically, the model in Figure 19.1 is estimated for both genders. The hatched line between *Gender* and the ellipse and the "@" symbol over the path between *Parent Involvement* and *Grades* specify the multi-group model's parameters' constraints. Specifically, together they indicate that all of the parameters in the path-analytic model are constrained equal across the genders (identified by the

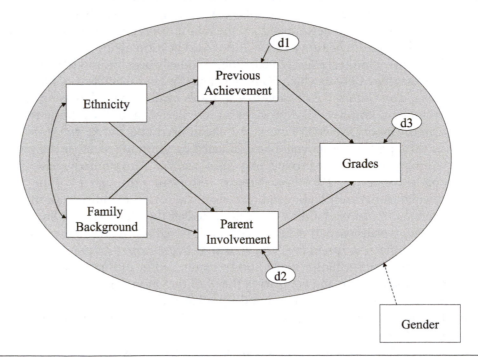

**Figure 19.6** Multi-group path-analytic model with gender distinguishing the two groups.

hatched arrow from *Gender* to the shaded ellipse) except for the path (identified by the "@") between *Parent Involvement* and *Grades*.

The fit of this model with the one path estimated uniquely for boys and for girls can be compared with the fit of a model in which all parameters are constrained equal across genders. If model fit decreases too much by setting that path equal, then this supports that the path differs across the genders; that *Gender* moderates the effect of *Parent Involvement* on *Grades* in the model. Different patterns of parameter constraints can be tested in the SEM framework. Use of SEM for testing moderation allows simultaneous modeling of other complex inter-relations among variables. For example, it would be possible to test whether a variable like *Gender* moderates a mediation effect. Interaction effects among continuous variables can also be modeled using SEM (see Marsh, Wen, & Hau, 2006).

Discussion of the benefits of using SEM and the associated considerations are equally applicable to observed variable (i.e., path-analytic) models and to those using latent variables. The next set of sections describes one of the major contributions of SEM; namely the modeling of latent variables or factors and their inter-relations.

### Latent Variable SEM

One hurdle to social science research, including family-school research, is that measures of important constructs are often measured with imperfect reliability and validity. Measures of cognitive skills—arguably some of the best measures in such research—rarely have reliability estimates higher than the .90s, and validity estimates may be considerably lower. Scores on measures of other important constructs may need to rely on rating scales and Likert scaling, and are often considerably less reliable and valid. Also well known is the fact that the reliability and validity of scores can affect estimates of the effects of one construct on another. Unreliability, for example, places an upper limit on the correlation between two variables; the less reliable the scores, the lower the maximum correlation estimate.

Researchers know that the reliability of a set of scores can be enhanced by using multiple items designed to assess the construct of interest. However, even the total score on a set of items will typically not be perfectly reliable. In family-school partnership research, reliability and validity of scores are further complicated by the fact that different respondents likely have different perceptions of the status of the constructs being assessed. Parents, for example, are likely to have different perceptions of their degree of involvement in their child's education than are their children, or their children's teachers. In addition, even among parents, distinctions can be found between mother's and father's perceptions of a construct such as parent involvement. One solution to this problem is to use a total score from single-respondent's indicators of involvement providing, for example, mother's perception of involvement. This solution works well for research questions involving specific respondents. Alternatively, a researcher could average respondents' responses together and use a composite representing a more general construct of educational involvement. This conceptualization works well when the research is intended to focus on a more general conceptualization of involvement. However, the problem with using a total score in a model is that unless the scores are each perfectly reliable, then the composite (total or mean) score includes measurement error. Use of latent variable SEM overcomes this problem. Latent variable modeling permits modeling the part of each response that is attributable to imperfect measurement and the part that is in common with the other measures of the construct (also known as the true score).

Figure 19.7 contains a simple latent variable model of measures of the child's *Home Involvement* and of *School Involvement* using different raters (specifically, the child's teacher, mother, father, and self). This confirmatory factor analytic (CFA) model is a simple SEM "measurement" model because it depicts a factor structure without modeling any structural relations among the factors of interest. The factors or constructs of interest are *Home* and *School Involvement* and they are simply modeled, here, as correlated (connected by a double-headed arrow). As the figure depicts, scores on each observed variable (contained within rectangles) are partly a function of the relevant factor (either *Home* or *School Involvement*) and partly a function of their respective measurement error. The latent, unexplained error in each variable is represented by the "*e*"s in ovals. Measurement error subsumes error due to both imperfect reliability and validity of test scores. Another way of thinking about each error is that it represents all other influences, other than the specified factor, on the measured variable.

Unlike in exploratory factor analysis (EFA) models, the fit of a CFA model can be assessed for final model selection. In addition, with CFA, unlike EFA, it is possible to specify some indicators' factor loadings to zero. For example, the *Home Involvement* measure is modeled as having a zero loading on the *School Involvement* factor. In addition, in a single CFA model, a subset of factors can be modeled as inter-correlated with other pairs of factors modeled as uncorrelated. While not demonstrated here, it is also possible with CFA (although not EFA) to model correlated measurement errors. The reader is encouraged to see Brown (2006) for more details about CFA models.

CFA is a subset of SEM that provides a useful framework for finding support for the hypothesized dimensionality of a set of measures. SEM, however, allows a researcher to explore patterns of effects among constructs (factors) while partitioning out the effect

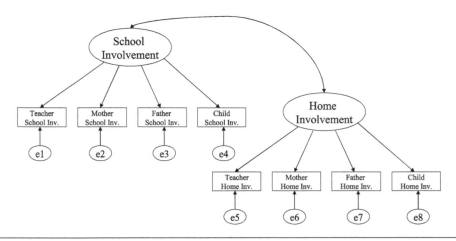

**Figure 19.7** Confirmatory factor analytic model of home and school involvement factors.

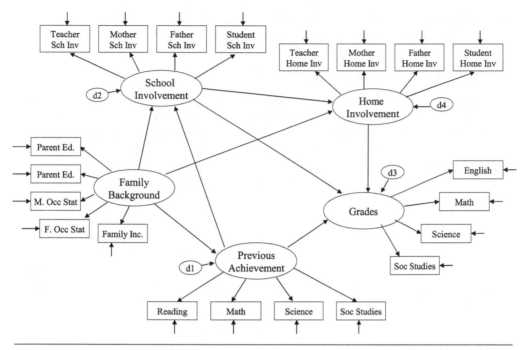

**Figure 19.8** Structural equation model of the effects of school and home involvement on students' grades in 12th grade.

of measurement error on respondents' scores. In the earlier measured variable (path-analytic) models, *Previous Achievement* was a composite variable, namely, the average (or total) of scores on measures of English, math, science, and social studies achievement. *Parent Involvement* and *Grades* were also composite variables. When composite scores are used in multiple regression or path-analytic models, they do not distinguish true scores from (measurement) error. This is not the case with latent variables. In the model in Figure 19.8, *Previous Achievement, Grades,* and *Parent Involvement* are no longer composite scores, but are instead factors estimated using associated directly observed variables.

As in previous models, the small ovals labeled with "*d*"s (e.g., *d*1 through *d*4) represent the disturbances which are the unexplained variances for each endogenous factor. To simplify the model's depiction, the measurement errors for each observed variable are not included in the figure. Only the one-headed arrows from the errors to each variable are presented. As noted, a chief advantage of latent variable SEM over simple path analyses is that these errors of measurement are removed from the estimation of the effects of one construct on another. The structural model thus examines the effects of one *latent* variable on another, with the effects of unreliability and invalidity removed from the estimation of these effects. As a result, latent variable analysis more closely approximates the true effects of one construct on another.

Figure 19.8 uses general latent variables (such as *Parent Involvement*) indicated by multiple raters (teacher, parents, and child). It is clearly also possible to model factors indicated by the same respondent. For example, a researcher might be interested in mothers' perceptions of their involvement as distinct from fathers' perceptions of their involvement. Theory should drive selection of the factor of interest and its indicators.

## Moderation in Latent Variable Models

The earlier discussion of testing for moderation in path-analytic models is equally applicable to latent variables models. In latent variable models it is advisable to test whether measurement models can be assumed equivalent across groups (i.e., whether the factor structure depends on the categorical grouping variable). Given the dependence of social science researchers on measuring unobserved constructs, assessment of measurement invariance of measures across groups of interest (e.g., gender, ethnicity, etc.) is of fundamental importance (Meredith, 1993; Meredith & Horn, 2001). Without support for the measurement invariance of scores on a test across groups, the test scores cannot be assumed to measure equivalent constructs for the two groups. If scores can be assumed to have equivalent factor structures across groups, then groups' test scores can be compared. For example, to compare parent involvement scores of an intervention and a control group, first the measurement of parent and home involvement should be assumed equivalent across the control and intervention groups.[3] Support for measurement equivalence also permits comparison of latent variable (factor) means rather than observed composite means across groups. This enables comparing differences in the estimated true means after removing measurement error (Hancock, 1997).

Measurement invariance is also an important pre-requisite before comparing the equivalence of paths across groups in latent variable models. Just as it is not meaningful to compare factor means for constructs measured differently across groups, so it is not meaningful to test the equivalence of an individual path or sets of paths in a SEM model if the factors cannot be assumed to be invariant. While it is relatively simple to test categorical variables as moderators in SEM, the process of testing for interactions between latent continuous variables is more complex, and beyond the scope of this chapter (Marsh, Wen, & Hau, 2004, 2006).

## Latent Growth Modeling

Longitudinal modeling using SEM can include assessment of reciprocal effects as demonstrated in Figure 19.5. Clearly, this panel model could be further improved if latent factors were used instead of composite scores to represent *Achievement* and *Home Involvement* at each time point. SEM can also be used to describe the growth in some construct and assess factors and variables that affect the average trajectory. The simplest latent growth model assumes linear growth and includes no additional covariates (generally referred to as an unconditional model). Latent factors representing the intercept (typically the value at the first time point) or "level" and linear slope of the trajectory can be estimated using a minimum of three time points. Figure 19.9 depicts the simplest unconditional latent growth (linear growth) model for three measures of *Achievement*.[4] The resulting latent means of the level and slope factors provide the predicted intercept and linear growth values for the *Achievement* trajectory.

This simple longitudinal model can be further expanded to include additional time

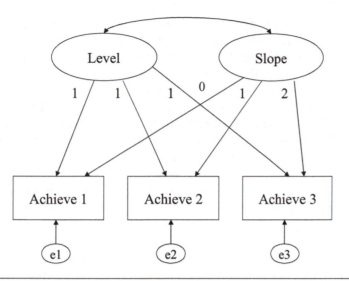

**Figure 19.9** Unconditional latent growth model of linear growth in achievement.

points. If more time points are available, and if theory supports this assumption, non-linear growth can also be explored. Single time-point or time-varying covariates can also be added to the model to explain possible variability in students' initial *Achievement* levels and in their growth in *Achievement* over time. For example, a researcher might hypothesize that there are gender differences in the initial level and patterns of growth on *Achievement*. Also, a growth model for *Home Involvement* could be modeled simultaneously with one for *Achievement* and the relations between *Achievement's* and *Home Involvement's* intercepts and slopes could be explored. This would permit investigation of how the trajectories for *Achievement* and *Home Involvement* are inter-related or even reciprocally influential. More sophisticated latent growth models that model growth in factors (rather than in composites as in Figure 19.9) can also be explored (for further details on second-order latent growth models or curve-of-factors models see, for example, Hancock, Kuo, & Lawrence, 2001; McArdle, 1988).

This SEM section has only provided a review and demonstration of some of the benefits to using basic SEM models. The reader is strongly encouraged to reference more detailed pedagogical texts and chapters to learn more about these powerful modeling techniques (e.g., Bollen, 1989; Keith, 2006; Kline, 2005). While the SEM framework provides a flexible modeling technique for managing the complexities encountered in family-school partnership research, it cannot handle all of them.

One of the primary benefits of using SEM in the context of family-school partnership, and for social science research in general, is the ability to model the dependency amongst indicators of latent variables. Specifically, inter-correlations among observed measures can be explained using factors and the relations among the resulting factors can be modeled with SEM. There are additional sources of dependency in datasets that necessitate the use of multilevel modeling. For example, researchers frequently obtain scores on measures of interest for classrooms of students. Scores (e.g., on an *Achievement* measure) of students in each classroom will be more similar than scores of students sampled from different classrooms. This kind of dependency in a dataset violates assumptions made when using analyses designed for independent data (such as multiple regression and basic SEM). Violating the independence assumption leads to biased statistical inferences. Thus, ignoring this violation is not a viable solution. Some researchers will instead aggregate results to the highest level of clustering (i.e., analyze data at the classroom level in the current example). Aggregation, however, results in a loss of power and in a loss of information at the lower level of measurement (here, at the student level). This means that, in the current example, inferences can only be made about classrooms, not about individual students. In addition, there might be a relation between a student descriptor and the outcome (*Achievement*) that depends on a classroom descriptor. However, aggregation would prohibit investigation of such a "cross-level interaction." Fortunately, it is not necessary to ignore these kinds of dependencies. Instead of using aggregation or disaggregation (i.e., ignoring the dependency) tactics to handle dependencies, multilevel modeling can instead be used. The multilevel modeling framework solves additional dilemmas. The next section will provide an overview of the kinds of research questions that multilevel modeling can address.

## MULTILEVEL MODELING

There are several specialized multilevel modeling software programs. Both HLM (Raudenbush, Bryk, Cheong, Congdon, & du Toit, 2004) and MLwiN (Goldstein et al., 1998) have easy-to-use GUI interfaces. HLM is a little easier to master. MLwiN permits estimation of the most complex multilevel models and thus requires more technical expertise than the other software programs. Mplus software is better known for its estimation of SEM models, but it (as well as LISREL and EQS) can be used to estimate some basic multilevel models. SAS, SPSS, S-PLUS (and its freeware version R) can also be used to estimate many of the basic multilevel models. Several textbooks and chapters (e.g., Beretvas, 2007; Hox, 2002; Kreft & de Leeuw, 1998; Snijders & Bosker, 1999) provide clear introductions to multilevel modeling as well as datasets and directions for estimating the models using different multilevel modeling software. The reader is encouraged to use these resources to help understand the details of estimating these models.

The next few sections describe very basic examples of datasets and research questions that should be addressed using multilevel modeling. The reader is encouraged to consider how alternative examples from their own more specific family-school partnership research might fit within the same scenarios described here.

### Two-Level Models

The hierarchical structure of dependent data is most simply represented as "levels." In fact, while not presented in this general overview, parameterization of multilevel models is frequently presented with equations at each "level" (e.g., Raudenbush & Bryk, 2002). Multiple regression models assume a single "level" of analysis. Thus, a researcher might be interested in the prediction of students' *Achievement* scores using students' *Parent Involvement* scores. The *Achievement* and *Parent Involvement* scores for students in the same classroom will likely have less variability than if the students had been randomly sampled from different classrooms. Thus, if a multiple regression model is used to predict *Achievement* using *Parent Involvement*, ignoring the dependency of students within classrooms, then the test of the effect of *Involvement* on *Achievement* will be biased.

The researcher might also be interested in testing whether a school involvement *Program* implemented to a random sample of classrooms (i.e., all students in a classroom either participate or do not participate in the program) influences *Achievement*. In this scenario, the dichotomous *Program* variable (dummy coded to represent whether the student was involved in the program) is really a classroom level descriptor. However, if the researcher used multiple regression and included *Program* as another predictor of *Achievement*, the statistical test results would again be inaccurate.

Instead, the researcher should recognize that students (level one) are clustered within classrooms (level two) and so multilevel modeling should be used. One way to depict clustering diagrammatically is through the use of network graphs (Rasbash & Browne, 2001) for a small subset of the dataset of interest. Figure 19.10 contains a "network graph" clarifying the clustering of students within classrooms.

Use of multilevel modeling partitions the variability in the outcome (*Achievement*) into the levels of clustering (here, two). Thus, some of the variability is attributable to individual differences among students (level one variability) and the rest is due to differences among classrooms (level two variability). The proportion of the total variability (level one plus level two variability) that is attributable to the level two classification (here, classrooms) represents the degree of dependency found in the dataset. The larger this proportion, the more important it is to model this dependency appropriately.

The modeling allows specification of the level of each predictor. Thus, in the current example, *Parent Involvement* would be recognized as a level one predictor and *Program* as a level two predictor. The researcher might also think that the effect of *Parent Involvement* on *Achievement* might depend on whether the student and their family have been exposed to the treatment *Program*. This is an example of a cross-level interaction. Specifically, the relation between two level one variables (the outcome, *Achievement*, and the predictor, *Parent Involvement*) is assumed to be moderated by a higher level (level two) predictor (namely, *Program*).

Only the simplest two-level scenario has been described here. Additional level one and level two descriptors could be added to the model. Models with multivariate outcomes are also estimable but will not be mentioned further here. In addition, only multilevel models for interval-scaled outcomes are described. It is also possible to estimate models with nominal- and ordinal-scaled outcomes. The reader should refer to multilevel modeling texts (e.g., Goldstein, 2003; Hox, 2002; Raudenbush & Bryk, 2002) for additional information.

**Figure 19.10** Network graph of two-level dataset consisting of students within classrooms.

## Three-Level Models

The reality of real-world datasets is rarely as simple as two levels. For example, while dependency originates for a dataset in which students are clustered within classrooms, the dataset might also consist of data from multiple middle schools (MSs) with multiple classrooms per MS. In this kind of scenario, students (level one) are clustered within classrooms (level two) within middle schools (level three). Figure 19.11 depicts the three levels in the dataset. Just as is the case with two levels of data, the validity of statistical inferences is compromised if the dependency originating in the nesting of students within classrooms and the clustering of classrooms within middle schools is not modeled appropriately. Use of a three-level multilevel model permits appropriate partitioning of the variability in the outcome (e.g., student *Achievement*) into the three components (in the current example, among students, classrooms and MSs). It is also possible to explore more complex cross-level interactions.

For example, the researcher might still be interested in predicting *Achievement* using *Parent Involvement* measures and in whether that effect is moderated by *Program*. This hypothesis can be explored further given the addition of the school level to the model. Now, possible variability across schools in the effect of *Parent Involvement* on *Achievement* can be assessed. If substantial variability is found, then a school characteristic, such as a measure of *School Resources*, could be explored as a possible moderating variable such that the higher the degree of *School Resources*, the less strong the relationship between student *Achievement* and *Parent Involvement*. An even more complex, although useful, three-way interaction could also be explored. The effectiveness of the classroom-based *Program* for reducing the effect of *Parent Involvement* on *Achievement* might depend on (be moderated by) the amount of *School Resources*. For example, the *Program* might be less effective at decreasing the effect in more impoverished schools. This kind of three-way interaction between level one (*Parent Involvement*), level two (*Program*) and level three (*School Resources*) predictors and the outcome (*Achievement*) can be appropriately modeled and estimated using multilevel modeling.

It was noted that SEM provides one way of dealing with the challenge of dependent responses encountered in family-school research in scenarios with multiple respondents' ratings of important constructs. One may, for example, have mothers', fathers', siblings' and child's ratings of the degree of home involvement. The dependency resulting from the clustering of respondents (level one) within families (level two) can also be modeled using a two-level multilevel model.

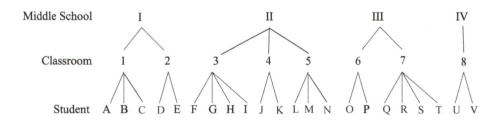

**Figure 19.11** Network graph of three-level dataset consisting of students within classrooms within middle schools.

## Longitudinal Models

There is currently a strong focus on holding schools and teachers accountable for students' learning. Part of this focus requires the use of longitudinal data to track the adequate yearly progress in terms of students' and teachers' performance. This need motivates the importance of understanding how best to model patterns found in longitudinal data. Multilevel modeling can be used to handle the clustering of repeated measures (over time) within students. In the simplest example, a dataset might contain achievement scores for a student at three time points. The dependency of each set of three scores within a student can be modeled with measure at level one and student at level two. It was mentioned above that SEM can be used to estimate latent growth models. Equivalent models are possible with two-level multilevel models. With both, it is possible to obtain estimates of the level and linear growth in an outcome. Conditional multilevel models can be explored that model the relationship between time-invariant and time-varying descriptors and growth in the outcome of interest. SEM provides an easier framework for modeling simultaneous growth trajectories for distinct outcomes and for modeling growth in factors. However, frequently dependencies arise because the level two unit (e.g., student) is clustered within some higher classification unit. For example, sets of students in the dataset come from the same middle school with multiple middle schools sampled. Basic SEM models cannot handle this added level of clustering, however, multilevel modeling can model this added level of dependency.

The example might consist of *Achievement* measures (level one) of students (level two) clustered within schools (level three). With this three-level longitudinal model, it is possible to estimate average level and growth (linear and non-linear) parameters for *Achievement*. It is also possible to explore the relationship between student and school characteristics and the growth parameters. For example, girls' initial *Achievement* scores might be lower than boys', and boys' linear growth in *Achievement* scores might be greater. However, some characteristic of schools might moderate the gender difference in linear growth. Single-sex schools might be associated with no difference in linear growth in *Achievement*. Use of multilevel modeling allows appropriate modeling of the dependency in the data as well as exploration of cross-level interactions.

## Cross-Classified Models

Mastery of two- and three-level models seems complex enough. Unfortunately, real-world datasets can introduce further complexity. It is not always the case that the data's structure is a pure hierarchy. For example, the simple two-level example in which students are clustered within classrooms might not be that simple. The original example was designed to assess the effectiveness of a school involvement program that was implemented in specific classrooms. Instead, the program could have been a program designed to improve parents' involvement in the child's academic learning. This program might have been implemented with groups of participants fitting the structure depicted in Figures 19.12a and 19.12b. Figure 19.12a contains the subset of the sample lined up in order of Classroom. Figure 19.12b contains the same subset lined up by intervention program. The crossed lines between student and the program in which

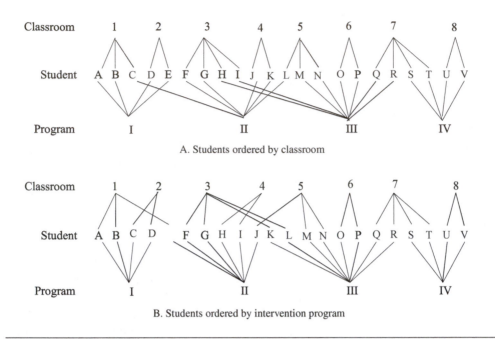

**Figure 19.12** Alternative network graphs of cross-classification of students by classroom and intervention program.

they were enrolled (in Figure 19.12a) and between students and their classroom (in Figure 19.12b) indicates that the hierarchy is not pure. As is evident in the figures, program membership does not correspond with classroom membership. For example, members of program I are associated with students from classrooms 1 and 2. Members of program II are associated with classrooms 1, 3, 4 and 5. While students are clustered within classrooms and students are clustered within programs, classrooms are not purely clustered within programs, nor vice-versa. Instead, students are cross-classified by classroom and by program.

Cross-classified random effects modeling (CCREM) should be used to handle multilevel data where the hierarchies are not pure. Researchers commonly avoid modeling cross-classified data structures by either deleting the subset of cases that lead to the cross-classifications or by ignoring one of the cross-classification factors (here, either program or classroom). Deletion will obviously reduce the power of the resulting analyses and reduce the generalizability of the results. Ignoring one of the cross-classifications results in a mis-specified model and will lead to biased statistical tests of the coefficients and of the variance component estimates (Beretvas, 2008; Goldstein, 2003; Meyers & Beretvas, 2006; Raudenbush & Bryk, 2002).

Cross-classified random effects modeling partitions the variability in the outcome into the component attributable to each classification. Thus, in the current example, the variability will be partitioned into the following three components: variability among individual students, variability among classrooms, and variability among program groups. Descriptors of each classification (student, classroom and program) could be used to explain variability in the outcome and in relationships between the outcome and other descriptors in the model (i.e., a form of cross-level interactions). For example, *gender* differences in the outcome (e.g., *Achievement*) might be partly a function of the classroom teacher's *Experience* and partly a function of the *Fidelity* of implementation of the program in which the student is enrolled.

Estimation of the simplest CCREM models is more complex than for regular multilevel models; it can be accomplished using MLwin, HLM, and SAS software. It is, of course, possible to encounter and model more than a pair of cross-classified factors at a single level, to have multiple levels of cross-classifications, and models with pure hierarchies mixed with cross-classifications. It becomes increasingly harder to estimate these more complex models and it also becomes increasingly harder to understand and interpret the results. Researchers should try to find a balance between modeling every intricacy and nuance of real data and representing and estimating more parsimonious models.

## Multiple Membership Models

There is one final, under-used extension to multilevel modeling that deserves mentioning given its appropriateness for data structures commonly encountered in family-school partnership research. Longitudinal designs introduce further complexities to data structures. For example, a researcher might be interested in high school effects on students' grades (measured using Achievement) in 12th grade. At first glance, it would seem that an associated data structure would be a simple two-level model with student (level one) clustered within high school (level two). However, the reality is that students do not always attend just a single high school. A subset of students might attend multiple high schools by the end of 12th grade. In other words, students are members of multiple high schools. When a lower level unit (here, student) is a member of multiple higher level units (here, high schools), multiple membership random effects modeling (MMREM) should be used.

MMREM fits within the multilevel modeling framework. Figure 19.13 contains a network graph depicting this example. In the graph, the hatched lines connect level one units (students) who are multiple members of level 2 units (middle schools). For example, student A attended high schools I and II and student Q attended high schools VI, VII, and VIII. Given the researcher's interest in modeling the effect of high school on student *Achievement*, it is important to model *Achievement* as a function of every high school that the student attended. When specifying a MMREM, the user must choose the weight to assign each unit of the multiple membership classification (here, high school) associated with the lower level unit (student). Most typically, equal weight is assigned to the set of multiple membership classifications associated with the level one unit (Goldstein, 2003; Rasbash & Browne, 2001) although theory-based weighting can be used instead. The model can be used to partition the variability in the outcome (e.g., *Achievement*) into the lower level classification (student) and the component associated with the multiple membership classification. As with any multilevel modeling, descriptors of each level and interactions between the descriptors can be incorporated into the model to explain relevant variability.

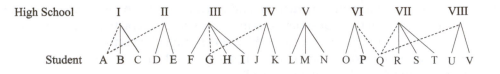

**Figure 19.13** Network graph of students as multiple members of high schools.

Only the simplest two-level MMREM has been briefly described here. More complex models can include additional multiple membership classification variables in a model, additional layers of clustering, as well as cross-classified multiple membership structures. These complex models can only be estimated using MLwiN software. Many datasets commonly encountered in education (especially longitudinal data) require that MMREM be used to explore patterns of relations. Despite the technical sophistication of these models, researchers should consider using this type of model when the data structure requires it.

### Additional Models of Use in Family-School Partnership Research

Multilevel models of moderating relations have been described here. Multilevel models can also be used to assess potential mediating effects. Mediating variables can occur (and be modeled) at any of the levels of the model. However, the issues involved are more complex than can be described here. The reader is referred to a recent textbook by MacKinnon (2008) for in-depth details about both SEM and multilevel models of mediation, moderation, as well as models for moderators of mediation effects and models of mediating variables for moderator effects.

No mention has been made of how to handle dependencies originating in dyadic data structures. Dyadic data are also commonly encountered in family-school partnership datasets (e.g., parent-child dyads, teacher-child dyads, best friend-child dyad, etc.). An example of how to handle dyadic data using SEM is demonstrated in the path model in Figure 19.4. This model could be extended such that latent rather than observed variables are modeled. Multilevel modeling can also be used to model dependencies resulting from dyadic data (Barnett, Brennan, Raudenbush, & Marshall, 1994; Raudenbush, Brennan, & Barnett, 1995). However, SEM seems to offer more flexible parameterizations for dyadic models (e.g., Newsom, 2002).

While not discussed in any detail here, family-school partnership researchers should also consider using mixture modeling and multilevel structural equation modeling (MLSEM). Growth mixture modeling and factor mixture modeling permit investigations of latent classes of growth trajectories and of factor models, respectively. Both kinds of SEM-based mixture modeling should provide useful ways for researchers to explore heterogeneity in their datasets (Allua, Stapleton, & Beretvas, 2008). Recent innovations in estimation procedures have facilitated estimation of MLSEMs using specialized SEM software (Stapleton, 2006). MLSEM merges the benefits of SEM with those of multilevel modeling. Use of MLSEM allows simultaneous modeling of inter-relationships among latent variables while appropriately partitioning variability among clustering units. MLSEM holds a lot of promise for modeling in educational research, however, estimation of MLSEMs is still very complicated and the models that can be estimated are still quite restricted. Estimation of MLSEMs provides a fertile ground for future methodological research and use of these models with real-world datasets should increase.

## CONCLUSIONS

This chapter has only provided a preliminary discussion about how research designs can affect the validity of associated causal inferences. If a study is focused on demonstrating the promising effects of family-school partnerships on youths' outcomes, then the study's design must incorporate sufficient controls for potentially confounding factors. Imprudently designed correlational studies will only provide description of relations among variables with no support for the direction of influence amongst the variables. Random selection and random assignment are optimal, but not always feasible. Measurement and modeling of common causes (of both independent and dependent variables) is essential to reduce identification of spurious relations among variables. Identification, measurement and even manipulation of each component in a multi-component intervention helps validate the contribution of each component to an intervention's effectiveness. Longitudinal measurement of relevant outcomes will assist with detection of crucial patterns of change and development as well as provide stronger support for causal relations. Measuring outcomes using multiple sources (e.g., parent, teacher, child, etc.) can provide more reliable assessment of constructs of interest, or provide important information about discrepancies in respondents' perceptions about the constructs. Researchers are encouraged to reference design textbooks such as that by Shadish, Cook, and Campbell (2002) to remind them of some of the essential components of a well-designed study. Use of sophisticated modeling techniques including multilevel and structural equation modeling does not compensate for unconsidered research designs.

Given that a researcher designs a study that optimally incorporates the relevant design elements, the models described in this chapter can prove particularly useful. This chapter has provided examples of some of the fundamental modeling dilemmas that are commonly encountered in family-school partnership research. It has also demonstrated how SEM and multilevel models can be used to address these challenges. Some of these models are relatively new and their estimation requires specialized software and sophisticated understanding of statistical modeling. Nevertheless, we hope that researchers will carefully consider how their studies are designed and use these more sophisticated modeling techniques to better address the challenges and issues encountered with real datasets and research questions in the family-school partnership research area.

## AUTHOR NOTES

1. The topics that follow apply equally to path-analytic and latent variable SEM.
2. Some researcher make a distinction between indirect effects and mediation (see Holmbeck, 1997), however, we do not.
3. There is no consensus about the minimal degree of measurement invariance that must be met and thus this remains an area of future methodological research. Most typically, a minimum degree of invariance is assumed when each indicator's factor loading can be assumed equal across groups.

4. The design matrix necessary to set up latent growth models, including selection of the loading constraints, is beyond the scope of the current chapter. The reader can refer to longitudinal modeling references (e.g., Singer & Willett, 2003; McArdle & Hamagami, 1991, etc.) for more information.

## REFERENCES

Allua, S., Stapleton, L. M., & Beretvas, S. N. (2008). Testing latent mean differences between observed and unobserved groups using multilevel factor mixture models. *Educational and Psychological Measurement, 68*, 357–378.

Arbuckle, J. L. (2007). *Amos 16.0 user's guide*. Chicago: SPSS.

Barnett, R. C., Brennan, R. T., Raudenbush, S. W., & Marshall, N. L. (1994). Gender and the relationship between marital role quality and psychological distress. *Psychology of Women Quarterly, 18*, 105–127.

Bentler, P. M.(1995). *EQS structural equations program manual*. Los Angeles: Multivariate software.

Beretvas, S. N. (2007). An introduction to hierarchical linear modeling. In J. P. Stevens (Ed.), *Applied multivariate statistics for the social sciences* (5th ed., pp. 321–359). Mahwah, NJ: Erlbaum.

Beretvas, S. N. (2008). Cross-classified random effects models. In A. A. O'Connell & D. B. McCoach (Eds.), *Multilevel modeling of educational data* (pp. 161–198). Charlotte, NC: Information Age.

Bollen, K. A. (1989). *Structural equations with latent variables*. New York: Wiley.

Brown, T. A. (2006) *Confirmatory factor analysis for applied research*. New York: Guilford.

Byrne, B. M. (1994). *Structural equation modeling with EQS and EQS/Windows: Basic concepts, applications and programming*. Thousand Oaks, CA: Sage.

Byrne, B. M. (1998). *Structural equation modeling with LISREL, PRELIS, and SIMPLIS: Basic concepts, applications and programming*. Mahwah, NJ: Erlbaum.

Byrne, B. M. (2001). *Structural equation modeling with Amos: Basic concepts, applications, and programming*. Mahwah, NJ: Erlbaum.

Carlson, C., & Christenson, S. L. (2005). Evidence-based parent and family interventions in school psychology: Overview and procedures. *School Psychology Quarterly, 20*, 345–351.

Carroll, J. B. (1989). The Carroll Model: A 25-year retrospective and prospective view. *Educational Researcher, 18*(1), 26–31.

Cox, D. D. (2005). Evidence-based interventions using home-school collaboration. *School Psychology Quarterly, 20*, 473–497.

Goldstein, H. (2003). *Multilevel statistical models* (3rd ed.). New York: Hodder Arnold.

Goldstein, H., Rasbash, J., Plewis, I., Draper, D., Browne, W., Yang, M., et al. (1998). *A user's guide to MLwiN*. London: University of London, Multilevel Models Project.

Hancock, G. R. (1997). Structural equation modeling methods of hypothesis testing of latent variable means. *Measurement and Evaluation in Counseling and Development, 30*, 91–105.

Hancock, G. R., Kuo, W., & Lawrence, F. R. (2001). An illustration of second-order latent growth models. *Structural Equation Modeling, 8*, 470–489.

Holmbeck, G. N. (1997). Toward terminological, conceptual, and statistical clarity in the study of mediators and moderators: Examples from the child-clinical and pediatric psychology literatures. *Journal of Consulting and Clinical Psychology, 65*, 599–610.

Hox, J. J. (2002). *Multilevel analysis: Techniques and applications*. Mahwah, NJ: Erlbaum.

Hu, L., & Bentler, P. M. (1999). Cutoff criteria for fit indexes in covariance structure analysis: Conventional criteria versus new alternatives. *Structural Equation Modeling, 6*, 1–55.

Jöreskog, K. G., Sörbom, D., du Toit, S., & du Toit, M. (2000). *LISREL 8: New Statistical Features*. Chicago: Scientific Software.

Keith, T. Z. (2006). *Multiple regression and beyond*. Boston: Allyn and Bacon.

Keith, T. Z., Keith, P. B., Troutman, G. C., Bickley, P. G., Trivette, P. S., & Singh, K. (1993). Does parental involvement affect eighth-grade student achievement? Structural analysis of national data. *School Psychology Review, 22*, 474–496.

Kenny, D. A. (1979). *Correlation and causality*. New York: Wiley.

Kline, R. B. (2005). *Principles and practice of structural equation modeling* (2nd ed.). New York: Guilford.

Kreft, I., & de Leeuw, J. (1998). *Introducing Multilevel Modeling*. Thousand Oaks, CA: Sage.

Lee, S., & Hershberger, S. (1990). A simple rule for generating equivalent models in covariance structure modeling. *Multivariate Behavioral Research, 25*, 313–334.

Loehlin, J. C. (2004). *Latent variable models: An introduction to factor, path, and structural analysis* (4th ed.). Hillsdale, NJ: Erlbaum.

MacKinnon, D. P. (2008). *Introduction to statistical mediation analysis*. Hillsdale, NJ: Erlbaum.

MacKinnon, D. P., Lockwood, C. M., Hoffman, J. M., West, S. G., & Sheets, V. (2002). A comparison of methods to test mediation and other intervening variable effects. *Psychological Methods, 7*, 83–104.

Marsh, H. W., Wen, Z., & Hau, K. T. (2004). Structural equation models of latent interactions: Evaluation of alternative estimation strategies and indicator construction. *Psychological Methods, 9*, 275–300.

Marsh, H. W., Wen, Z., & Hau, K. T. (2006). Structural equation models of latent interaction and quadratic effects. In G. R. Hancock & R. D. Mueller (Eds.), *Structural equation modeling: A second course* (pp. 225–265). Greenwich, CT: Information Age.

McArdle, J. J. (1988). Dynamic but structural equation modeling of repeated measures data. In J. R. Nesselroade & R. B. Cattell (Eds.), *Handbook of multivariate experimental psychology* (2nd ed., pp. 561–614). New York: Plenum.

McArdle, J. J., & Hamagami, F. (1991). Modeling incomplete longitudinal and cross-sectional data using latent growth structural models. In L. M. Collins & J. L. Horn (Eds.), *Best methods for the analysis of change: Recent advances, unanswered questions, future directions*. Washington, DC: American Psychological Association.

Meredith, W. (1993). Measurement invariance, factor analysis, and factorial invariance. *Psychometrika, 58*, 525–543.

Meredith, W., & Horn, J. (2001). The role of factorial invariance in modeling growth and change. In L. M. Collins & A. G. Sayer (Eds.), *New methods for the analysis of change* (pp. 203–240). Washington, DC: American Psychological Association.

Meyers, J. L., & Beretvas, S. N. (2006). The impact of inappropriate modeling of cross-classified data structures. *Multivariate Behavioral Research, 41*, 473–497.

Muthén, L. K., & Muthén, B. O. (1998–2007). *Mplus User's Guide* (5th ed.). Los Angeles: Muthén & Muthén.

Neale, M. C., Boker, S. M., Xie, G., & Maes, H. H. (1999). *Mx: Statistical modeling* (5th ed.). Richmond, VA: Department of Psychiatry. Downloadable from www.vcu.edu/mx/executables.html

Newsom, J. T. (2002). A multilevel structural equation model for dyadic data. *Structural Equation Modeling, 9*, 431–447.

Pearl, J. (2000). *Causality: Models, reasoning, and inference*. New York: Cambridge University Press.

Rasbash, J., & Browne, W. J. (2001). Modeling non-hierarchical structures. In A. H. Leyland & H. Goldstein (Eds.), *Multilevel modeling of health statistics* (pp. 93–105). Chichester, UK: Wiley.

Raudenbush, S., Brennan, R. T., & Barnett, R. C. (1995). A multivariate hierarchical model for studying psychological change within married couples. *Journal of Family Psychology, 9*, 161–174.

Raudenbush, S., & Bryk, A. S. (2002). *Hierarchical linear models: Applications and data analysis methods* (2nd Ed.). Thousand Oaks, CA: Sage.

Raudenbush, S., Bryk, A. S., Cheong, Y. F., Congdon, R., & du Toit, M. (2004). *HLM6: Hierarchical linear and non-linear modeling*. Lincolnwood, IL: Scientific Software International.

Rigdon, E. E. (1995). A necessary and sufficient identification rule for structural models estimated in practice. *Multivariate Behavioral Research, 30*, 359–383.

SAS Institute Inc. (1999). *The SAS system for Windows Release 8.02* [Computer software]. Cary, NC: SAS Institute Inc.

Shadish, W. R., Cook, T. D., & Campbell, D. T. (2002). *Experimental and quasi-experimental designs for generalized causal inference*. Boston: Houghton-Mifflin.

Shrout, P. E., & Bolger, N. (2002). Mediation in experimental and nonexperimental studies: New procedures and recommendations. *Psychological Methods, 7*, 442–445.

Singer, J. D., & Willett, J. B. (2003). *Applied longitudinal data analysis*. New York: Oxford University Press.

Snijders, T., & Bosker, R. (1999). *Multilevel Analysis*. Thousand Oaks, CA: Sage.

Stapleton, L. M. (2006). Using multilevel structural equation modeling techniques with complex sample data. In G. R. Hancock & R. D. Mueller (Eds.), *Structural equation modeling: A second course* (pp. 345–383). Greenwich, CT: Information Age.

Stelzl, I. (1986). Changing the causal hypothesis without changing the fit: Some rules for generating equivalent path models. *Multivariate Behavioral Research, 21*, 309–331.

Zhonglin, W., Hau, K., & Marsh, H. W. (2004). Structural equation model testing: Cutoff criteria for goodness of fit indices and chi-square tests. *Acta Psychologica Sinica, 36*, 186–194.

# 20

## FROM PERIPHERY TO CENTER

*A New Vision and Strategy for Family, School, and Community Partnerships*

HEATHER B. WEISS AND NAOMI C. STEPHEN

Research about the determinants of children's school success has pointed to the importance of the family in children's development and academic achievement for over 40 years. The Equality of Educational Opportunity report, more commonly known as the Coleman report (Coleman et al., 1966), and subsequent reanalysis of the Coleman data (Jencks et al., 1972), both found that family factors matter more than school characteristics in predicting the educational outcomes of economically disadvantaged children. Recent results for fifth graders from the national longitudinal NICHD Study of Early Care and Youth Development (Belsky et al., 2007) showed that parenting practices are more significant predictors of cognitive and socioemotional outcomes than a range of other factors, including participation in early care and education. Yet efforts to include family involvement in children's learning and development at home and at school have always been, at best, on the distant margins of educational policy and reform efforts.

## OVERVIEW

Political scientist John Kingdon suggested three elements that are critical in getting issues onto the public policy agenda so that government officials pay serious attention to them: "A problem is recognized, a solution is available, the political climate makes the time right for change" (Kingdon, 2003, p. 88). When these strands converge, as is now the case in the ongoing debate about the reauthorization of the federal No Child Left Behind legislation, there is a real possibility of significant policy change: "The separate streams of problems, policies, and politics come together at certain critical times. Solutions become joined to problems, and both of them are joined to favorable political forces. This coupling is most likely when a policy window—an opportunity to push pet proposals or one's conceptions of problems—is open" (Kingdon, 2003, p. 194). Family, school, and community partnerships focused on children's development and school success are poised to take advantage of just such a policy window, given the increasing recognition that NCLB-shaped education reform confined to schools alone is not sufficient. Family, school, and community partnerships are about to move closer to the center of national school reform efforts, and will be seen as increasingly important in reducing socioeconomic achievement gaps.

There is growing consensus about the problem: the NCLB strategy—with its emphasis on K-12 within-school reform driven by standards and assessment, aligned instructional improvement, high-stakes accountability requirements and consequences, and school choice—has not led to improved educational outcomes for many children, especially poor, minority, and otherwise disadvantaged children. Yet the large socioeconomic achievement gap, as well as concerns about college and workforce preparation, have been brought to the forefront of education reform discussion by NCLB's requirement of disaggregated socioeconomic data on the numbers of students who fail to reach proficiency. As a result, many influential organizations and individuals are calling not just for tinkering with NCLB, but for fundamentally rethinking what it will take to insure that all children can learn, realize their potential, and succeed as workers, citizens and parents (Blank & Berg, 2006; Economic Policy Institute, 2008; Forum for Education and Democracy, 2008; Rothman, 2007; Rothstein, 2004). Many, including some of the staunchest previous advocates of within-school reform strategies, are joining a growing chorus of voices singing that K-12 schools, even good schools, cannot do it alone. So, the big emerging policy question is: If schools cannot do it alone, what can?

Many of the specific proposed solutions to reformulating NCLB, as well as current thinking about education reform more broadly, emphasize that the solution includes opening school doors to welcome the broader family and community partnerships that, research and experience increasingly indicate, are major contributors to children's academic achievement (Blank, Melaville, & Shah, 2003; Caspe, Lopez, & Wolos, 2006/07; Forum for Youth investment, n.d; Gordon, Bridglall, & Meroe, 2005; Henderson & Mapp, 2002; Kreider, Caspe, Kennedy, & Weiss, 2007; Weiss, Caspe, & Lopez, 2006). So, the problem is recognized, family and community partnerships are widely advocated as part of the solution, and the political climate is right for change. The policy window is open: It is likely that the result will be steadily increased attention to and resources for family, school, and community partnerships.

If this prediction proves right, there is now an unprecedented opportunity to use collective knowledge and experience over the next few years to move from what one of the field's leaders called "random acts of parent involvement" (Gil Kressley, 2008) to realize a vision for a strategic, comprehensive, and continuous system of family, school, and community partnerships that demonstrably contribute to children's development and school success. Developing and implementing such a vision is necessary to support the learning and development of all children, but it is especially important for economically and otherwise disadvantaged and immigrant children. These community-based partnerships have the potential to level the playing field for these children by insuring that they have access to the same non-school learning supports that their more-advantaged peers do.

Realizing this vision is going to require major policy and practice changes as well as new ways of conducting, using, and communicating research and evaluation. It will also require and benefit from ongoing discussion and debate among stakeholders about the vision itself, about strategies to accomplish it, and about how to acquire and use information to track and share progress and make the inevitable necessary course corrections along the way. This chapter is an effort to contribute to this needed broader discussion and debate.

The chapter begins with a brief description of past and present policy, starting with the provocative proposition that it has been quite possible to implement this vision, or at least make progress toward it, in the past, but that by and large this has not happened. Following are some answers to the inescapable question of why there hasn't been more progress. Barriers are described, and also progress toward addressing them that can inform future efforts. Next is an analysis of developmental research on how families contribute to children's education, as well as evidence from evaluations of intervention efforts. Both are presented in order to make a strong research-based case for intervention, and to assert that the research can inform the development of a framework to guide the design of demonstrably effective family, school, and community partnerships. The chapter's final section draws on the previous analyses to lay out suggestions for the key elements of a national strategy to make real the vision for a comprehensive, continuous, and demonstrably effective system of family, school, and community partnerships in communities around the country.

### A Note on Terms

The term "family, school, and community partnerships," subsequently shortened to "partnerships," is used in this chapter for several reasons. Research confirms that not only parents, but family members including grandparents, aunts and uncles, siblings, and other kith and kin, are involved in children's learning. Community is included because not only schools, but an array of community learning and support services, need to partner with families and schools in order to insure school success, especially for economically and otherwise disadvantaged children. One name for this set of supports is a complementary learning system (Harvard Family Research Project, 2005); family, school, and community partnerships are leverage for and components of such complementary learning systems. Community is included also because these partnerships should both help build and be accountable to the broader civic community of which they are a part (see the PEN Civic Index http://civicindex4education.org/main/index.cfm). In some instances the term "family involvement" appears alone in reference to the results of studies examining involvement without intentional partnerships.

## A BRIEF OVERVIEW OF PAST AND CURRENT POLICY

Federal leadership and policy are very important drivers of family involvement and partnerships, and the federal government plays a major role in defining, focusing, and positioning the concept of family involvement in school reform efforts. Much of the money for family involvement programs comes from the federal government: legislation, regulations, and monitoring define what involvement is and how high a priority it will be, and legislative funding and earmarks determine what will be available for federal, state, and local capacity-building, monitoring, and infrastructure development. The passage of the landmark 1965 Elementary and Secondary Education Act (ESEA)—bringing the federal government into state and local educational policy for the first time to address the educational achievement of disadvantaged children—initiated the modern era of family involvement and partnerships, calling attention to the importance of family and community involvement. As D'Agostino, Hedges, Wong, and Borman (2001) noted in their legislative history of Title 1 parent involvement, the role of parents, at least in educational policy, has changed many times since 1965.

Title 1 of ESEA, where the family involvement provisions are laid out, initially had no parent involvement regulations, but it did specify a place for families in parental advisory councils (PACs) and it included guidelines suggesting that schools encourage parents to volunteer in classrooms as parent aides. The emphasis shifted in 1988 to a broader home- and school-based learning collaboration model that emphasized parental support for learning activities in the home as well as involvement at school.

By the mid-1990s and Chapter 1 (Title 1) reauthorization, the definition of partnerships had evolved to an even more comprehensive model, in which schools were required to develop school-parent compacts laying out how schools, parents, and students would partner to help children achieve state standards. Schools were required to spend no less than 1% of their Title 1 budget on this more comprehensive model of parent involvement. Evaluations of these Title 1 efforts showed that the more comprehensive model, with parent-school compacts and multiple forms of home and school involvement, including school support for learning at home, were associated with higher student achievement (D'Agostino et al., 2001).

Title 1 and then the 2002 NCLB legislation specify a broad definition of family, school, and community partnerships, but NCLB also has a particular focus on parents in the role of consumers, centering its accountability provisions on the parental option to transfer a child from a failing school, as well as on access to tutoring in the form of Supplemental Education Services (SES). The most recent report from the U.S. Department of Education on the effects of NCLB, which examines data from a sample of nine large urban school districts, found no evidence that the school choice provisions are effective, but students who participated in SES experienced statistically significant gains in achievement (U.S. Department of Education, 2007). Evaluations of the effects of this consumer model of parent involvement model suggest its limits and the consequent need to emphasize a broader, more comprehensive partnership model of family involvement in the next round of NCLB reauthorization.

While different federal administrations have emphasized different models of involvement since the 1990s, including NCLB, legislation has permitted and sometimes encouraged schools and districts to employ a more comprehensive definition of family involvement and partnerships if they so choose. The comprehensive definition specifies: (a) Parents play an integral role in assisting their child's learning; (b) Parents should be encouraged to be actively involved in their child's education at home and at school; (c) Parents are full partners in their child's education and should be included, as appropriate, in decision making and on advisory committees to assist in the education of their child; and (d) A series of institutional and infrastructure supports should be available at the state education agency (SEA), local education authority or district (LEA), and school levels to enable the above. This includes SEA, LEA, and school parent involvement plans, reports to parents on their child's performance, collection and dissemination of effective parent involvement practices, use of Title 1 funds to support involvement, school-parent compacts, provisions for capacity-building and professional development, evaluation, monitoring of compliance with the legislative mandates, and even coordination with other federal programs such as Head Start, Even Start, and Reading First.

So, arguably, for many years districts and schools have had considerable opportunity to define comprehensive family involvement plans and strategies, and at least some resources that would allow them to do so in Title 1 schools, if not in all schools. However, the reality in many states and communities is very different: Much of the legislation is not being implemented, or when it is, the effort is spotty and not sustained, and often fails to achieve the goal of actively involving families, especially disadvantaged ones, in ways that would benefit their children's development, learning, and school success. Given resources and legislative latitude, why haven't we made more progress? What are the barriers to more family involvement and to comprehensive family, school, and community partnerships—and is there any progress in addressing them?

## THE BARRIERS AND LESSONS FOR THE FUTURE

### Barrier 1: Legislative and Governmental Fragmentation

First, the structural separation of parent involvement efforts within and across education and other legislation, and within and across federal departments, has siloed funding streams, programs, and advocacy efforts, making it difficult to develop coordinated, comprehensive, and continuous—never mind sustained—family involvement efforts. NCLB uses the word "parent" or some variation over 650 times (U.S. Department of Education, 2002) and it includes many scattered provisions for parent involvement. (Limited English Proficient and Immigrant Student programs, Title 1, and 21st Century Community Learning Centers are but three of several such provisions, all listed in separate sections of the Act.) The key word here is not "parent," but "scattered." As many recent analyses of efforts to develop more coordinated education and family policies and programs point out, fragmentation is a function of the way the House of Representatives and the Senate develop legislation and of the ways in which the Executive Branch and various federal departments, including the U.S. Department of Education, divide the resulting responsibilities. Family involvement mandates, programs, and funding streams run across NCLB, and across many federal departments: the Department of Education, Health and Human Services, the Justice Department's Office of Juvenile Justice and Delinquency Prevention, etc. This patchwork process results in many small and poorly resourced programs, and raises serious difficulties with respect to monitoring and accountability (Cross, 2004; Dunkle, 1997; Lovell, 2008; Palanki & Burch, 1992).

Siloed funding (e.g., for Head Start, IDEA, and Title 1) has often led to siloed parent groups, and then siloed—and often competing—parent advocacy efforts, rather than advocacy for broader systems of family involvement as part of a collective agenda (Fege, 2006, 2008). Not only does this make it difficult to employ a united national voice on behalf of family involvement and partnerships, it also has local consequences. When local school leaders do want to build an overarching and comprehensive family involvement partnership strategy, they sometimes find it difficult to do so due to competition amongst parent advocacy groups (Weiss & Westmoreland, 2006).

While there have been periodic federal efforts to integrate various funding streams and programs, most of these efforts have been small, have not been sustained, or do not get beyond the pilot stage to any scale (Dunkle, 1997). In his recent analysis of the history of federal involvement in education, Christopher Cross, a former Assistant Secretary of Education, pointed out the problems this fragmentation creates within education and called for a congressional task force to recommend changes to Congress and the president—but he was not optimistic about the prospects for change (Cross, 2004).

The result of the fragmentation in our area of concern is that it creates incentives to silo rather than integrate partnership efforts. Many schools, driven by siloed federal compliance and reporting requirements, then silo family involvement programs by funding stream: one program for Title 1 parents, one for special education parents, one for all parents, etc. It is easier to do this than to make the extraordinary efforts necessary to create a comprehensive school or district plan, including the necessary blending of funding streams and enlisting the collaboration and budgetary support of diverse groups within the school as well as the broader community. Schools, districts, and communities may make these efforts, but they are very difficult to sustain due to changes in leadership or funding, or in other areas. How to adjust federal policy, funding, regulations, and related state and local policies so as to create incentives rather than disincentives to the creation of comprehensive family, school, and community partnerships is a question that must be addressed.

### Barrier 2: Limited Investments in and Use of Monitoring and Capacity-Building

The second barrier also requires rethinking the federal role and allocation of resources in the areas of family involvement and partnerships. Tools of compliance monitoring and evaluation, or of capacity-building and technical assistance, have been little used over the past several decades by the federal government to support the development of family involvement and family, school, and community partnerships. While Title 1 and NCLB mandate a range of types of family-school partnerships, and increasingly focus them directly on specific things that families can do to support children's learning (D'Agostino et al., 2001), there has been relatively little effort to monitor states and districts for accountability and compliance with these parent involvement mandates, signaling that family involvement and partnerships are not a high priority. Many districts are out of compliance or narrowly comply with the letter but not the intent of the legislation. In compliance mode, many adopt boilerplate parent involvement policies with little parent input, which do not require the types of higher-maintenance family involvement activities and partnerships that, research suggests, enhance students' academic achievement. However, even if there were more federal monitoring, decades of research on school reform implementation suggest that the stick of compliance is unlikely to result in effective local family involvement efforts (McLaughlin, 2006; McLaughlin & Shields, 1987).

Also lacking is substantial investment in the carrots of capacity-building, training, technical assistance, and other resources that may enable families, schools, and communities to build more comprehensive partnerships on behalf of better student outcomes. The Parental Information and Resource Centers (PIRCs)—created by federal legislation in the 1990s and maintained in NCLB to provide training, technical assistance, and capacity-building at the state and local levels—are a promising but underfunded effort to support states' and districts' efforts to build systemic and comprehensive family involvement strategies. The low level of investment is a serious barrier because, as McLaughlin and Shields (1987) noted over 20 years ago, systemic, comprehensive, and sustained involvement is dependent on educators' and families' core beliefs, attitudes, and behaviors (Sheldon, 2002). Changing those beliefs will require substantial and long-running capacity-building, training, and technical assistance, as well practitioners' access to the latest research and evaluation results, at each of the layers responsible for policy implementation, from the federal level down through the state, the community, the district, and the school.

### Barrier 3: Lack of Prioritization of Investments in Pre- and In-Service Professional Development

This third barrier grows out of a related capacity-building issue: helping educators to recognize the importance of partnering with families and communities, and providing them the necessary skills and means. There has been and continues to be little leadership from any source demanding or providing pre- or in-service training of teachers and administrators in this area (Chavkin & Williams, 1988; Epstein & Sanders, 2000, 2002; Shartrand, Weiss, Kreider, & Lopez, 1997). Surveys indicate that teachers feel working with families is their biggest challenge, and they feel at a disadvantage because they do not have the necessary training (Markow & Martin, 2005).[1] There are some exemplary pre-service training programs (Shartrand et al., 1997; for more recent examples, see www.hfrp.org/FINE or www.hfrp.org/family-involvement/publications-resources?topic=3) and in many states, standards and requirements for teacher certification specify preparation in family involvement, especially at the early childhood and elementary levels. However, none of this has moved many colleges of education, or teacher or administrator training programs, to offer or require courses related to working with families and communities. As a result, most new teachers and administrators have had little if any preparation for creating family-school partnerships. Such in-service training as exists often is simply a one-shot workshop for individuals, rather than the intensive, continuing, and organization-wide professional development experience that evaluations suggest are necessary to change practice in ways that contribute to better student outcomes (HFRP, 2007; Killion, 2005/06).

While it is clear that pre- and in-service training are crucial to building educators' interest in and capacity to partner with families and communities, it is unclear what mandates or incentives or other means will move trainers to provide it. It is noteworthy in this regard that teachers' unions and school administrators are beginning to call for change. The National Education Association (NEA) is recommending required parental involvement training for teachers (NEA, 2006) and some superintendents, by including progress on family, school, and community partnerships in their performance reviews for principals and teachers, may stimulate colleges, universities and others to provide the necessary training (Crew & Dyja, 2007). These changes may help redefine professional competency to include demonstrated ability to partner with families and communities in order to increase children's school learning and development.

## Barrier 4: Definitions of learning and Expectations of Schools Do Not Address the Ways Poverty Limits Learning

The fourth barrier—which may ultimately become an incentive to support partner-ships—is a curious interaction of expectations about the role of schools in reducing inequality, and assumptions about their means to do so. On one hand is the complex set of issues and limitations that stem from American attitudes about education as a dominant force in efforts to reduce social and economic inequality. On the other hand are the until-recently dominant assumptions about where, how, when, and what it takes for children to learn. These attitudes and assumptions have always been deeply embedded in educational policy and reform efforts. In her paper tracing the history of the federal role in education, entitled "'Our Children's Burden': A History of Federal Policies that Ask (now Require) Our Public Schools to Solve Societal Inequity," Wells (2006) pointed out that in contrast to other industrialized countries, which have built comprehensive social welfare systems to promote socioeconomic equality, the United States regards education as the dominant anti-poverty measure. The question before us going into NCLB reauthorization, Wells argued, is "how much we can continue to require the public schools to accomplish absent broader efforts to make children's overall lives more equal" (p. 2).

Educational policy as written now creates what Ladson-Billings (2006) has called the "educational debt." The debt is compounding because current educational policy nar-rowly defines K-12 schools as the setting where learning occurs and fails to recognize how the capacity of poor children to learn is constricted by circumstances external to the school building. The educational debt compounds because not only do poor and minority children often attend poorer schools with fewer resources, they also have no complementary learning network that their more-advantaged peers can take for granted. They have less access to enriching learning experiences outside of school, less access to health and other social and human services, and other financial, logistical, and social barriers to extra-school activities that promote learning (Ladson-Billings, 2006).

A growing body of research confirms poor children's lack of access to complemen-tary learning supports and indicates how this lack then predicts and contributes to an achievement gap across a child's school career (Alexander, Entwisle, & Olson, 2001; Hart & Risley, 1995; Murnane, Willett, Bub, & McCartney, 2006; Phillips, Brooks-Gunn, Duncan, Klebanov, & Crane, 1998). Families with lower incomes and less education are, on average, less likely to be involved in learning at home and at school (Baker & Stevenson, 1987; Grolnick & Slowiaczek, 1994; Keith et al., 1998; Kohl, Lengua, McMa-hon, & The Conduct Problems Prevention Research Group, 2000). A recent report from the National Center for Education Statistics (Enyeart, Diehl, Hampden-Thompson, & Scotchmer, 2006) found less involvement of poor families; further, while educators report equal outreach to all families, disadvantaged families report receiving less outreach from schools than more-advantaged ones do (Marschall, 2006; Vaden-Kiernan & McManus, 2005). Studies also suggest that disadvantaged children are less likely to participate in out-of-school and youth programs and activities, or to have enriching summer learning opportunities (Bouffard et al., 2006; Kreider, 2005; Pedersen & Seidman, 2005; Wimer et al., 2005). Despite evidence about the ways in which the lack of basic safety net services affects children's development and school success, education policy and reform strategies have rarely included access to health, mental health, or social services in their formulations of elements necessary to improve the academic achievement of poor and immigrant children (Rebell & Wolff, in press; Rothstein, 2004).

But, as argued at the start of this chapter, there are indications that educational policy may be changing in favor of a broader definition of where and how children learn, and that opportunities and resources for a more strategic, comprehensive and continuous system of family, school, and community partnerships are being created as a result. More policy makers and educators understand—as evidenced by new state and federal legislation—that learning begins at birth and occurs in many contexts, and that disadvantaged children lack and need access to the range of complementary learning non-school supports and services that their middle-class peers have. Promising new state and national legislation indicates that more policy makers see the value of family involvement and of partnerships (variously labeled) to leverage and connect families to school and non-school supports, and these supports to each other, in ways that improve children's learning in school.

The inclusion of Family Resource Centers as part of the historic 1990 Kentucky Education Reform Act is one example of a statewide partnership policy effort to increase family involvement in learning at home and at school, and to link families to safety-net services (Kalafat, 2008). Many other states have similar efforts in a pilot program status. The Full Service Community Schools Act passed by Congress in 2007 is an example of a new national pilot partnership effort. It provides funding for districts and states to create full-service community schools, which integrate educational, family, out-of-school time, health, and other services through partnerships with families and community-based organizations. If the response to the first U.S. Department of Education competition for full service school resources in 2008 is an indication, interest in partnerships is growing, as is demand for resources to create them. The competition drew nearly 500 applications for about 12 pilot grants.

There are other examples of proposed legislation that will fund partnership efforts to get children the complementary learning supports they need, and to link those supports with schools. The Keeping Pace Act, a proposed amendment to NCLB introduced in the U.S. Senate in 2007, mandates that schools use Title 1 funds to hire Parent and Community Outreach Coordinators to improve family and community involvement in failing schools. The Education Begins At Home Act (EBAH), reintroduced in 2008 and in 2009, provides funding to states for community-based home visiting programs providing information and support to parents, reinforcing their roles as the child's first and most important teacher, connecting them to other early childhood and to safety net services, and reinforcing the importance of continued family involvement when the child enters school.

This kind of new legislation will provide resources and opportunities that serve as incentives for schools and communities to build partnerships. It will also raise the challenges of siloed funding, discussed earlier, that hamper efforts to create more comprehensive and continuous partnerships that create supportive developmental pathways for children from birth through high school. As just one example, EBAH would enable states to create birth-through-pre-kindergarten home visitation services—but, as proposed, EBAH provides no policy- or program-level incentives or mandates for home visit programs to work with other early childhood providers or schools to make sure that both child and parent transition successfully to kindergarten and thereby increase the chances of continued parent involvement (Weiss, 2008). As the chapter's next section suggests, in policy settings such as EBAH, frameworks to guide the development of strategic, comprehensive, and continuous family, school, and community partnerships may aid state and community planning.

### Barrier 5: The Challenge of Power Sharing

Policy makers' understanding of what disadvantaged children need to increase their academic achievement may be changing, as reflected in new and pending legislation. However, policy change enables but does not automatically create changes in practice. The changes necessary for partnerships are often blocked by beliefs and attitudes about responsibilities as well as by issues of power and control. Many educators do not think that low-income and otherwise disadvantaged parents want to be, or can be, involved in ways that support their children's education and feel that parents' failure to do their jobs makes it difficult for them to do theirs (Langdon & Vesper, 2000; Rose & Gallup, 2006). Many parents do not understand that their involvement matters or do not know how to get involved, or their children attend schools that do not value involvement sufficiently to do the outreach necessary to engage families in meaningful ways. As a result, many communities are stuck in finger-pointing—"parents don't want to be involved" and "schools don't want us involved"—and do not have a sense of shared responsibility for children's education (Henderson, Mapp, Johnson, & Davies, 2007).

Long-time urban superintendent Rudy Crew offered a powerful way to describe this sense of shared responsibility (Crew & Dyja, 2007). Convinced that family and community partnerships are crucial to both school and student success, he argued that partnerships are a two-way street and that that schools must take the first step. In Crew's formulation, the many parents, especially poor ones, who may desire but do not know how to be effectively involved, are "Supply Parents" who "often feel like outsiders in the very schools that are supposed to be serving them." Crew urged schools themselves to create instead "Demand Parents" who "demand things from their schools because they understand that they are indeed owed something and it is their responsibility to get it for their children" (p. 155). As superintendent, Crew attempted to create and respond to "Demand Parents" to improve student outcomes with Parent Academies designed in response to parents' requests for information on how to help their children succeed in school, partnership agreements with private and non-profit organizations, and inclusion of family involvement in principal and teacher performance reviews.

Crew and a number of other superintendents around the country are exceptional in their willingness to share power with family and community partners. Research on school change, interviews with educators and those who train them, and discussions with innovative practitioners, all suggest that issues of power, control, and accountability form a major barrier to partnerships (HFRP, 2008; Lightfoot, 1978, 2003). In their typology of family, school, and community relationships, Henderson et al. (2007) described "fortress schools," which exemplify this control, and contrasted them with "partnership schools" where parents and community organizations are seen individually and collectively as partners who share responsibility in the effort to help children succeed in school. Arguably, the fortress mentality has been exacerbated by the high-stakes accountability provisions of NCLB, which have resulted in narrowing schools' missions and the services they provide, as well as an unwillingness to be accountable for things schools cannot directly control. Moving from a fortress to a partnership school entails risks and costs—relinquishing some control and making the effort to sustain partnerships—and it requires a belief that increased student and school success will make the change worth while. There is a strong research-based case supporting partnerships as a risk worth taking to improve the educational achievement of disadvantaged children.

## THE EMPIRICAL BASIS FOR FAMILY, SCHOOL AND COMMUNITY PARTNERSHIPS

Since the passage of the 1993 Government Performance Results Act (GPRA) underscoring the importance of setting and being accountable for outcomes, and the Education Sciences Reform Act (ESRA) of 2002 emphasizing research-based policy and programs, it has been necessary to make an evidence-based case for new public—and, increasingly, private—investments, or to sustain existing ones. Those who advocate for family involvement and partnerships are in a good position to do so vis à vis GPRA and ESRA, for several reasons.

First, as other chapters in this volume indicate, there is a strong case based in developmental research: Many studies on the determinants of children's social, emotional, and cognitive development, and of the factors influencing children's school trajectories, point to the importance of the family in children's development and academic success. The research makes it clear that parents' or caregivers' behaviors, practices, and attitudes at home—as well as their involvement with school and other institutions—strongly influence children's learning.

Second, this research base provides an increasingly nuanced understanding of how specific types of parenting practices and aspects of partnerships, as well as economic and other disadvantages, influence development. Such detailed data can inform and strengthen specific policy and practice. There are many ways to categorize aspects of parenting that are associated with higher levels of motivation, skills, effort, and achievement in children from birth through high school; for the purposes of this chapter, the following are most useful: (a) parental responsiveness and emotional support; (b) cognitive stimulation in the home; (c) academic socialization; (d) provision of structure, reinforcement, and support for learning; and (e) home-school communication and connections.[2]

As research moves from a deficit-based to a strengths-based approach, the ways in which economic disadvantage, class, and the socioeconomic and policy context (e.g., racism, segregation, poverty) affect these five aspects of parenting and partnerships are becoming clearer, as are ways the ways in which families adapt, manage stress, and engage with schools and other organizations on behalf of their children's education (Baca-Zinn & Wells, 2000; Crosnoe, Mistry, & Elder, 2002; Ishii-Kuntz, 2000; Jackson, Brooks-Gunn, Huang, & Glassman, 2000; Jarret, 1995, 1997; Taylor, 2000). Economically disadvantaged and immigrant families often do not have the financial, social, or cultural capital necessary to navigate educational institutions (Bourdieu, 1987; Gordon et al., 2005). These are Crew and Dyja's (2007) "Supply Parents," who often have less experience with and access to information about school policies, structures, and staff, and are therefore less likely to communicate with teachers, to volunteer, or to act collectively in the face of problems. They are also less likely to know how to make education decisions and support their children's learning at home (Gordon et al., 2005; Horvat, Weininger, & Lareau, 2003; Lareau, 1987; Valenzuela & Dornbusch, 1994).

Accumulating evaluation evidence provides the third reason for investment: it shows that partnerships can effectively engage families, schools, and communities in ways that demonstrably increase children's academic achievement. While investments in the rigorous evaluation of family involvement and partnerships have been limited, and many programs and partnerships are developed at the community level where evaluation funding is scarce, the number of high quality evaluations is increasing. A number of programs that are designed to support families and promote family involvement at home and at school have demonstrated small but significant effects on children's development in early childhood and in elementary and middle school. Parenting interventions are most common in early childhood; one of the most common is home visitation. Meta-analyses of home visit evaluations have found small but statistically significant effects on family processes and child outcomes, including cognitive and academic development (Layzer, Goodson, Bernstein, & Price 2001; Sweet & Appelbaum, 2004; Weiss & Klein, 2007). The overall effect sizes of these studies are similar in magnitude (approximately .20) to effect sizes for class size reduction and other interventions widely considered to be successful (Lipsey & Wilson, 1993; McCartney & Dearing, 2002).

Recent evaluations of more comprehensive interventions employing complex research designs and methods, such as the evaluation of Early Head Start, are beginning to tease out how parent involvement adds value above and beyond other program components, and mediates or explains the effect size of the program on children's outcomes. The evaluations indicate, for example, that home visit programs in conjunction with early childhood programs can increase school readiness, parents' understanding of their role in child development, and children's language and literacy skills (Administration for Children and Families, 2002; Love et al., 2005). There are few longitudinal evaluations of early childhood family involvement programs, but the longitudinal assessment of the Chicago Parent-Child Centers demonstrated long-term effects in terms of higher achievement, less need for remedial and special education, lower rates of grade retention, and increased high school completion rates (Temple & Reynolds, 2007). Underscoring the importance of continuous family involvement, there is also increasing evidence that family involvement across key developmental transitions has academic benefits for children. Efforts to prepare families as well as children during the preschool-to-kindergarten transition can build long-term patterns of parent involvement (Kraft-Sayre & Pianta, 2000) and kindergarten transition practices emphasizing family involvement are associated with higher academic achievement at the end of the kindergarten year (Schulting, Malone, & Dodge, 2005).

Interventions that have been evaluated for families with elementary and middle school-aged children have focused on family involvement in education, particularly learning at home and the prevention of behavioral problems. While recent reviews have pointed out the methodological problems with many evaluations (Mattingly, Prislin, McKenzie, Rodriguez, & Kayzar, 2002), several meta-analyses and narrative reviews of methodologically rigorous evaluations find that a range of programs have small but significant effects on both parent involvement and student achievement (Caspe & Lopez, 2006; Erion, 2006; Henderson & Mapp, 2002; Jeynes, 2005, 2007; Nye, Turner, & Schwartz, 2006; Walker-James & Partee, 2003). Programs that teach parents how to help children with learning activities at home (e.g., shared reading, supplemental math activities, parental academic instruction) have significant effects on achievement as high as .60 (D'Agostino et al., 2001; Erion, 2006; Nye et al., 2006). Programs that train parents in how to be appropriately and effectively involved in their children's homework have found positive effects on parents' supportive involvement, increases in the time children spend on homework, higher homework accuracy, and higher grades (Bailey, 2006; Balli, Demo, & Wedman, 1998; Sheldon & Epstein, 2005; Van Voorhis, 2003).

While the evaluations mirror the current fragmented state of programming, they also suggest the substantial added value of well-designed interventions for children and families, for schools, and for communities. They clearly indicate the benefits that might be achieved, particularly for disadvantaged children, if families are seen not as the problem, but as a crucial part of the solution to the complex issue of children's school learning. They also hint at the many developmental and learning benefits that could accrue if family, school, and community partnerships were more systemic and comprehensive. The developmental research and the promising evaluation evidence together make a strong case for investing in partnerships, and they indicate important aspects of partnerships to guide future interventions.

### A Research-Informed Framework to Guide Community Planning and Investments

Analysis of the challenges facing efforts to build more strategic, comprehensive, and continuous partnerships, as well as of the research and evaluation base, together lead to the development of a research-informed framework to guide future planning of partnerships. The framework emphasizes key elements that increase the likelihood that these partnerships will contribute to children's readiness to enter and graduate from school with the skills needed for success. To be effective, the framework must be individualized to accord with local needs and resources; it is a work in progress that will constantly be modified based on new research, community experience, and evaluation results, and new needs and opportunities.

The framework underscores the importance of provisions for continuous family involvement and support across the developmental span from birth through high school, and it includes support for involvement and partnerships across an array of complementary learning contexts, including early childhood and home visitation programs, pre-kindergarten, school, afterschool, summer learning and youth programs, libraries, arts, recreation and cultural organizations, and faith-based institutions. The argument that partnerships should begin at birth and continue through high school grows out of evidence of the continuous importance of family involvement and of partnerships that enable it. Therefore, the framework emphasizes the importance of support for nurturant parenting, defined in age-appropriate ways; of family-school partnerships focused on the child's education; and of linkages to community services, particularly for low-income and otherwise disadvantaged families. Some evidence suggests that attention to family involvement at one stage in a child's education can set involvement up for the next stage; involvement in one context can leverage it in others. For example, as children enter school, families scaffold and support out of school learning experiences (Gordon et al., 2005) by helping children and youth make choices about how to use their time. Recent cross-context research on afterschool and summer learning programs suggests that family involvement both predicts children's participation in these learning opportunities and is stimulated by them (Little, Wimer, & Weiss, 2008), and a national multi-site evaluation of afterschool programs found that they increased family involvement in school (James-Burdumy et al., 2005). The framework also underscores the importance of attention to key transition points such as pre-kindergarten to school entry and middle school to high school.

The framework is firmly grounded in the importance of shared responsibility for learning outcomes and of co-constructed policy and interventions. Developmental research makes it clear that parents who share responsibility for their children's education, who are involved and stay involved with support from schools and other community institutions and organizations, have children who are more likely to enter school ready to succeed and graduate with the skills they need to succeed as citizens, as workers, and as family members. Intervention research and practice experience make it clear that schools and other organizations that practice shared responsibility are more likely to engage families and other partners. As Crew's formulation of "Supply Parents" and "Demand Parents" noted, one of the most important elements of partnerships is to articulate this message and practice this shared responsibility. Real shared responsibility is more likely if the partnership stakeholders co-construct their plans and activities.

Co-constructing means building relationships among multiple stakeholders that are characterized by trust (Bryk & Schneider, 2002), shared values (Dauber & Epstein, 1993), ongoing bi-directional communication (Hill, 2001; Henderson et al., 2007; Lopez, Kreider, & Caspe, 2004/05), and opportunities for both input and feedback on programs and policies. Without shared responsibility and co-constructed plans and activities embedded at all levels, from the family relationship with teachers to governance of the larger family, school, and community partnerships, these efforts are unlikely to succeed in engaging diverse families, or in demonstrably benefiting children. Nor are such efforts likely to be sustained. Shared responsibility and co-construction extends from parent, school, and student compacts to meaningful participation of all stakeholders on school councils and other governance and advisory boards. Communities implementing the research-informed framework would co-construct a strategic, comprehensive, and continuous system of partnerships that begin at birth, provide comprehensive and linked complementary learning opportunities, and share responsibility for children's education.

While the work of developing family, school and community partnerships must be done at the community level in accord with local needs and resources, there are common design principles that increase a partnership's chances for success and sustainability. These include shared leadership and governance; a commitment to access and equity across the board from the leadership level to the service level; transparent accountability; attention to service continuity; linkages across contexts and transitions; commitment and capacity for evaluation to support learning, continuous improvement, and accountability; and ongoing professional development and organizational capacity-building. Moving from "random acts of parent involvement" to the more strategic, comprehensive, and continuous systems of partnerships envisioned here will also require the development of a national strategy. Key elements for such a strategy are outlined below.

## MOVING AHEAD ON A NATIONAL STRATEGY

As suggested by assessment of the barriers and challenges that have prevented progress in the past, as well as by examples of successful field-building in other service areas, an effective national strategy would include a combination of governmental and nongovernmental pressures to develop more comprehensive and continuous family, school, and community partnership efforts. Also necessary are supports and incentives for doing so. As McLaughlin and Shields (1987) argued and subsequent experience has shown, federal legislative mandates rarely change local educators' and parents' attitudes and behavior. However, national bully pulpit leadership, legislation, and regulations can set the priorities, fund the key infrastructure supports and incentives, and offer the specific guidance (rules and regulations) that do enable change.

### Strategic and Coherent Advocacy

Research about "policy entrepreneurs" who successfully get new ideas onto the public policy agenda for legislative funding underscores the importance of communication and advocacy in getting policy makers' attention and support, as well as successful demonstration efforts and evidence of effectiveness (Mintrom, 2000). The various elements of the family involvement and partnership arena are at best loosely coupled; they do not have national strategic planning, communication, and advocacy capacity. Philanthropic support for the creation of a broad national leadership coalition of organizations and individuals would increase the likelihood of the sustained legislative and public support that will be necessary to enable widespread local change. Such broad leadership would advocate more effectively for family involvement and partnerships, and continue to communicate their demonstrated contributions to learning and school success to policy makers.

*Integrated Infrastructure Supports*

The continued development of national and state legislation, policies, and funding with earmarks for key infrastructure supports is another critical element in a national strategy. An integrated set of infrastructure supports includes training, technical assistance, organizational capacity-building, performance monitoring and evaluation, materials and tools development, and knowledge dissemination. The federally supported national network of state-based PIRCs—in cooperation with Title 1, state departments of education, the National PTA, and others—are emerging as leaders in building these supports in service of more integrated, comprehensive, and continuous family involvement and partnerships. Many PIRCs are working with states, districts, and schools to build continuous family involvement from birth through high school and to link across key transitions and contexts, including afterschool and summer learning. The PIRCs have developed a quality framework (see Figure 20.1; see also www.hfrp.org/PIRC) to guide their leadership and technical assistance to local communities. Undergirded by a commitment to conducting research and evaluation in support of learning and continuous improvement, the framework emphasizes capacity-building for continuous and systemic services for families that are aligned with Title 1 parent involvement requirements. While the PIRCs need more funding for this leadership and capacity-

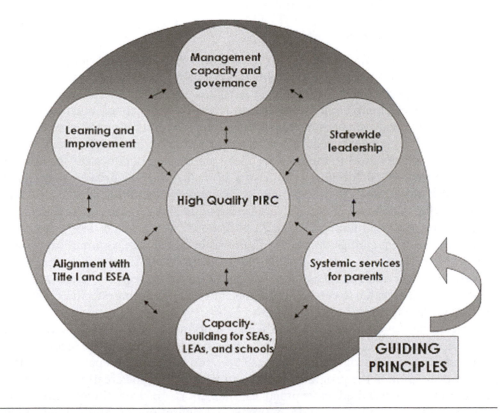

**Figure 20.1** Framework for quality PIRC technical assistance and leadership centers.

building work, many are partnering with researchers and evaluators as well as private funders to support local communities in implementing the vision for more strategic, comprehensive, and continuous partnerships (Caspe, 2008; Cassady & Garvey, 2008; Kirner & Storeygard, 2008; Westmoreland & Bouffard, 2008).

### Practitioner–Private Sector Partnerships

Practitioner partnerships with private sector organizations are another important new resource for training, innovative tool development, and other infrastructure supports. For-profit companies, seeing a new market in family and community involvement, are providing training and testing some innovative and research-informed tools that support comprehensive home-school partnerships. Some companies that provide NCLB student assessments—for example, McGraw Hill's GROW Network—are working with school districts to make regular individual student assessment information available not only to teachers but to parents. Teachers are also provided with materials, keyed to a student's assessment results, to give to families so they can support learning at home. Importantly, evaluating whether or not such processes contribute to greater family involvement, and, ultimately, to children's school success, is built into GROW Network's work with schools and families.

### Professional Development

Training frameworks and other supports for effective pre- and in-service professional development so that, ultimately, the ability to work with families and communities is a core professional competency for both teachers and administrators is another key element in the development of a national strategy. There is little such training now but this is changing rapidly, driven partly by the inclusion of family and community involvement standards and assessments in educators' yearly performance reviews. A national report designed to call attention to the need for more preparation of educators for involvement proposed one such training framework in accord with the broader partnership vision (Shartrand et al., 1997). Experiential and interactive training approaches, such as role playing, school and community internships and field experiences, research with families, and the case method (Weiss, Kreider, Lopez, & Chatman, 1997), would be most effective in equipping educators with the problem-solving, communication, and collaboration skills necessary to enable the interactions with families, that research suggests, improve academic outcomes. Again, evaluation for learning and continuous improvement is essential to determine the specific types of training effective in improving teacher-family involvement practices.

Professional development, like all other elements in a strategic family involvement policy vision, must be conceived broadly, comprising federal legislative incentives for demonstration grant programs to increase pre- and in-service preparation; on-the-ground evaluation of the programs to find out what works; the creation of networks to share innovative and effective practices; state efforts to strengthen teacher certification guidelines with clear and comprehensive definitions of family involvement and partnerships; and course content in training institutions that aligns with those guidelines.

### Research and Evaluation

A national strategy must also include discussion and planning of new approaches to knowledge development and use at a time when conceptions of the role of research and evaluation are shifting in major ways. Often viewed fearfully as an axe with which to chop down programs, evaluation, especially in the policy arena, is actually a far more constructive tool. There should be little argument about the fact that we simply need more evaluations, including some random control trials when possible, to determine what works to guide policy and practice and to test the value-added of partnerships for children's learning and development. The family involvement and partnership field has relatively few rigorous evaluations and they are mostly of discrete and time-limited programs. There are very few longitudinal evaluations or evaluations to assess systemic changes or examine how family involvement in one context leverages involvement in others; also few evaluations of the benefits of involvement at key transition points in a child's school career. The few that exist do illuminate the benefits of involvement (James-Burdumy et al., 2005; Reynolds et al., 2007; Schulting, Malone, & Dodge, 2005). While there is a strong developmental research case for partnerships, there is much less evidence that practical interventions are effective and that they return on investment. This relative lack of evaluation makes it difficult for policy makers and practitioners to prioritize partnerships over other resource claimants, particularly when resources are scarce and other claimants can make a strong case for the effectiveness of other interventions such as pre-kindergarten programs (Heckman, 2008). So independent external evaluation—and funding for it—should be a high priority.

### Knowledge Development and Innovation

At the same time, recent discussions about the success of federal efforts to use research and evaluation to inform educational policy and practice are causing many to rethink the relationships amongst innovation, knowledge development, and use. This has implications for the family involvement and partnership field as well. In a recent work, Bryk and Gomez argued that the research and development infrastructure for school improvement is weak and constitutes a case of "market failure for educational innovation" (Bryk & Gomez, 2008, p. 182). Congressional hearings on the federal role in educational research reached a similar conclusion: randomized control trials will never address every important question teachers and administrators face. It is necessary to support ongoing innovation and learning by enabling practitioners to get and use data to improve their own practices in a process of continuous improvement and accountability (Joftus, 2008). Bryk and Gomez also argued that productive innovations should be co-developed by researchers and practitioners and tried out and refined in a continuous improvement process (see also Garvin, Edmondson, & Gino, 2008; Patton, 2006). They proposed a new R&D model based in partnerships amongst school practitioners, interdisciplinary university researchers, and social entrepreneurs.

## CONCLUSION AND NEXT STEPS

NCLB, as implemented, has proved that schools cannot, indeed, do it alone—that they require additional thrust from complementary learning supports to close achievement gaps. There is a strong case that partnerships are a promising investment and indications that past barriers to more strategic, comprehensive, and continuous approaches can be minimized or overcome. New models for R&D and evaluation offer chances to test partnerships as a core innovation for education reform together with practitioners, families, researchers, and social entrepreneurs. Strategic partnerships can be—will have to be—as complex and multiform as the communities they serve. Above all, any partnership framework must stay open to new information, discussion, debate, implementation, and evaluation in the spirit of continuous improvement. We expect that much from our children throughout their years of education. We can expect no less from ourselves.

The next few years present an unprecedented opportunity to expand family, school, and community partnerships. So, it is time to think strategically and think big. While the fortunes of family involvement policy and practice in k-12 education have waxed and waned over the past 40 years, the policy success of early childhood programs, particularly the prekindergarten movement, holds some important lessons for the family involvement field as it moves forward, especially with respect to the need for coherent leadership and champions for family, school, and community partnerships, as well as for research, evaluation, and advocacy.

First, the early childhood and then the prekindergarten movement have had the benefit of a sustained core of leaders who met in various groups over time and built an evolving national strategy to scale early childhood programs. This strategy included many of the components we have noted previously, plus a deliberate and ongoing advocacy and strategic communications effort, and the recruitment of a series of champions from the corporate as well as the political and research arenas. Second, the field's leaders publicized the results of growing number of high quality studies, including longitudinal studies, showing short-term school readiness benefits as well as longer-term, policy-relevant benefits of early childhood programs through and beyond a child's school career. Third, leaders could draw on well-executed cost-benefit studies that clearly indicated substantial return on investments in early childhood. This strong evaluation research base then attracted large philanthropic investments because foundations saw that the necessary elements for scaling up prekindergarten programs were in place. The research base also brought in an influential new set of champions, including Nobel Prize-winning economist James Heckman (2008).

These lessons from early childhood programs and the prekindergarten movement demonstrate the importance of building strong, sustained, and cross-organizational national leadership for family and community involvement in order to move the field forward. This fluid but sustained leadership group should include representatives from parent groups; national policy and professional organizations; philanthropy; training and technical assistance groups; higher education and other research organizations; and private sector groups developing involvement tools. The group should actively recruit upcoming leaders and champions; develop a comprehensive 10-year strategy for the field; and seek public, private, and philanthropic support for the strategy. The participation of higher education and other research representatives is particularly important, not only to support pre- and in-service professional development, but also to help shape a research and evaluation agenda, including new R&D efforts to test partnerships as a core element of education reform strategies, and conduct longitudinal evaluations and cost-benefit analyses. Researchers will also be important in addressing the arguments against investments in family involvement and partnerships by those who maintain that it is not possible or not cost-effective to try to work with families so that they more effectively support children's learning and development (Jencks & Phillips, 1998). Finally, the group should recruit champions from diverse domains, so that more and more high-profile opinion leaders such as Heckman beat the drum for the importance of family involvement in children's education. We believe coherent, strategic leadership, which brings high visibility and strong supporting data to the construction of family, school, and community partnerships, is crucial to opening our current policy window wide enough to offer all children an equal chance at success.

## AUTHORS' NOTES

1. "Communicating with and engaging parents is the most frequently cited challenge among new teachers and the area they feel least prepared to take on in their first teaching position. One-quarter of secondary school students reports that their parents are not very or at all involved in their education. Students with involved parents are more likely than others to … go to their parents for advice about what classes to take at school. They are also more likely to report being interested in their classes, to value higher education and to feel safe at school" (Markow & Martin, 2005, p. 4).
2. Much of the research on the ways in which specific parenting practices affect children's development and learning has been covered in other chapters in this volume. For detailed reviews of the research, please see the following: Bouffard, Bridglall, Gordon, & Weiss, in press; Caspe, Lopez, & Wolos, 2006/07; Henderson & Mapp, 2002; Kreider, Caspe, Kennedy, & Weiss, 2007; Weiss, Caspe, & Lopez, 2006.

## REFERENCES

Administration for Children and Families. (2002). *Making a difference in the lives of infants and toddlers and their families: The impacts of Early Head Start*. Washington, DC: U.S. Department of Health and Human Services.

Alexander, K. L., Entwisle, D. R., & Olson, L. S. (2001). Schools, achievement, and inequality: A seasonal perspective. *Educational Evaluation and Policy Analysis, 23*, 171–191.

Baca-Zinn, M., & Wells, B. (2000). Diversity within Latino families: new lessons for family social science. In D. Demo, K. Allen, & M. Fine (Eds.), *Handbook of family diversity* (pp. 253–272). New York: Oxford University Press.

Bailey, L. (2006). Interactive homework: A tool for fostering parent-child interactions and improving learning outcomes for at-risk young children. *Early Childhood Education Journal, 34*, 155–167.

Baker, D., & Stevenson, D. (1987). Mothers' strategies for children's achievement: Managing the transition to high school. *Sociology of Education, 59*, 156–166

Balli, S. J., Demo, D. H., & Wedman, J. F. (1998). Family involvement with children's homework: An intervention in the middle grades. *Family Relations, 47*, 149–157.

Belsky, J., Vandell, D. L., Burchinal, M., Clarke-Stewart, K. A., McCartney, K., Owen, M. T., et al. (2007). Are there long-term effects of early child care? *Child Development, 78*, 681–701.

Blank, M. J., Melaville, A., & Shah, B. P. (2003). *Making the difference: Research and practice in community schools.* Washington, DC: Coalition for Community Schools.

Blank, M., & Berg, A. (2006). *All together now: Sharing responsibility for the whole child.* Washington, DC: Institute for Educational Leadership, Coalition for Community Schools.

Bouffard, S. M., Bridglall, B. L., Gordon, E. W., & Weiss, H. B. (in press). *Reframing family involvement in education: Supporting families to support educational equity.* New York: Teachers College Press.

Bouffard, S. M., Wimer, C., Caronongan, P., Little, P. M. D., Dearing, E., & Simpkins, S. D. (2006). Demographic differences in patterns of youth out-of-school time activity participation. *Journal of Youth Development, 1*(1). Retrieved fromwww.nae4ha.org

Bourdieu P. (1987). The form of capital. In J. G. Richardson (Ed.), *Handbook of theory and research for sociology of education* (pp. 241–258). New York: Greenwood Press.

Bryk, A. S., & Gomez, L. (2008). Reinventing a Research and Development Capacity. In F. Hess (Ed.), *The Future of Educational Entrepreneurship: Possibilities for School Reform* (pp. 181–206). Cambridge, MA: Harvard Education Press.

Bryk, A. S., & Schneider, B. (2002). *Trust in schools: A core resource for improvement.* New York Russell Sage Foundation.

Caspe, M. (2008). Building the field. *The Evaluation Exchange: Building the Future of Family Involvement, 14*(1&2), 6–7, 30 Cambridge, MA: Harvard Family Research Project.

Caspe, M., & Lopez, M. E. (2006). *Lessons from family-strengthening interventions: Learning from evidence-based practice.* Cambridge, MA: Harvard Family Research Project.

Caspe, M., Lopez, M. E., & Wolos, C. (Winter 2006/2007). *Family involvement in elementary school children's education.* (Family Involvement Makes a Difference Research Brief No. 2). Cambridge, MA: Harvard Family Research Project.

Cassady, J. C., & Garvey, J. (2008). The Indiana state PIRC's collaborative evaluation process. *The Evaluation Exchange: Building the Future of Family Involvement, 14*(1&2), 24. Cambridge, MA: Harvard Family Research Project.

Chavkin, N. F., & Williams, D. L. (1988). Critical issues in teacher training for parent involvement. *Educational Horizons, 66,* 87–89.

Coleman, J. S. et al. (1966). *Equality of educational opportunity.* Washington DC: U.S. Government Printing Office.

Crew, R., & Dyja, T. (2007). *Only connect: The way to save our schools.* New York: Farrar, Straus and Giroux.

Crosnoe, R., Mistry, R. S., & Elder, G. H. (2002). Economic disadvantage, family dynamics, and adolescent enrollment in higher education. *Journal of Marriage and the Family, 64,* 690–702.

Cross, T. C. (2004) *Political education: National policy comes of age.* New York: Teachers College Press.

D'Agostino, J. V., Hedges, L. V., Wong, K. K., & Borman, G. D. (2001). Title I parent-involvement programs: Effects on parenting practices and student achievement. In G. Borman, S. Stringfield, & R. Slavin (Eds.), *Title I: Compensatory education at the crossroads* (pp. 117–136). Mahwah, NJ: Erlbaum.

Dauber, S. L., & Epstein, J. L. (1993). Parents' attitudes and practices of involvement in inner-city elementary and middle schools. In N. F. Chavkin (Ed.), *Families and schools in a pluralistic society* (pp. 53–72). Albany: State University of New York Press.

Dunkle, M. (1997). Steer, row or abandon ship: Rethinking the federal role for children, youth and families. *The Policy Exchange, Special Report #8,* 4. Washington, DC: Institute for Educational Leadership.

Economic Policy Institute. (2008). *A broader, bolder approach to education.* Washington, DC: Author.

Enyeart, C., Diehl, J., Hampden-Thompson, G., & Scotchmer, M. (2006). *School and parent interaction by household language and poverty status: 2002-03.* (NCES 2006-086) U.S. Department of Education. Washington, DC: National Center for Education Statistics.

Epstein, J. L., & Sanders, M. G. (2000). Connecting home, school, and community: New directions for social research. In M. T. Hallinan (Ed.), *Handbook of the sociology of education* (pp. 285–306). New York: Kluwer Academic/Plenum.

Epstein, J. L., & Sanders, M. G. (2002). Family, school, and community partnerships. In M. Borenstein (Ed.), *Handbook of parenting, Vol.5: Practical issues in parenting* (pp. 407–437). Mahwah, NJ: Erlbaum.

Erion, J. (2006). Parent tutoring: A meta-analysis. *Education & Treatment of Children, 29,* 79–106.

Fege, A. F. (2006). Getting Ruby a quality public education: Forty-two years of building the demand for quality public schools through parental and public involvement. *Harvard Educational Review, 76,* 570–586.

Fege, A. F. (2008). Family Involvement Policy: Past, Present, and Future. *The Evaluation Exchange: Building the Future of Family Involvement 14*(1&2), 16–17. Cambridge, MA: Harvard Family Research Project.

Forum for Education and Democracy. (2008). *Democracy at risk: The need for a new federal policy in education.* Amesville, OH: Author.

Forum for Youth Investment. (n.d.) *Ready by 21: Taking aim on the big picture.* Washington, DC: Author.

Garvin, D. A., Edmondson, A. C., & Gino, F. (2008). Is yours a learning organization? *Harvard Business Review, 86*(3), 109–116.

Gil Kressley, K. (2008, August). *Breaking new ground: Seeding proven practices into proven programs.* Session description from the National PIRC Conference, Baltimore, MD.

Gordon, E. W., Bridglall, B. L., & Meroe, A. S. (2005). *Supplementary education: The hidden curriculum of high academic achievement.* New York: Rowman & Littlefield.

Grolnick, W. S., & Slowiaczek, M. L. (1994). Parents' involvement in children's schooling: A multidimensional conceptualization and motivational model. *Child Development, 64,* 237–252.

Hart, B., & Risley. T. R. (1995). *Meaningful differences in the everyday experience of young American children.* Baltimore: Brookes.

Harvard Family Research Project (HFRP). (2005). [Special issue] *The Evaluation Exchange: Complementary Learning, 11*(1). Cambridge, MA: Author.

Harvard Family Research Project (HFRP). (2007). *Changing the conversation about workforce development: Getting from inputs to outcomes. A report submitted to Cornerstones for Kids.* Unpublished paper. Cambridge, MA: Author.

Harvard Family Research Project (HFRP). (2008). [Special issue] *The Evaluation Exchange: Building the Future of Family Involvement, 14*(1&2). Cambridge, MA: Author.

Heckman, J. J. (2008). Schools, Skills and Synapses. Working Paper 14064. Cambridge, MA: National Bureau of Economic Research. Retrieved September 10, 2008, from http://www.nber.org/papers/w14064

Henderson, A. T., & Mapp, K. (2002). *A new wave of evidence: The impact of school, family, and community connections on student achievement.* Austin, TX: Southwest Educational Development Laboratory.

Henderson, A. T., Mapp, K. L., Johnson, V. R., & Davies, D. (2007). *Beyond the bake sale: The essential guide to family-school partnerships.* New York: New Press.

Hill, N. E. (2001). Parenting and academic socialization as they relate to school readiness: The roles of ethnicity and family income. *Journal of Educational Psychology, 93,* 686–697.

Horvat, E., Weininger, E., & Lareau, A. (2003). From social ties to social capital: Class differences in the relations between schools and parent networks. *American Educational Research Journal, 40,* 319–351.

Ishii-Kuntz, M. (2000). Diversity within Asian American families. In D. Demo, K. Allen, & M. Fine (Eds.), *Handbook of family diversity* (pp. 274–292). New York: Oxford University Press.

Jackson, A., Brooks-Gunn, J., Huang, C-C., & Glassman, M. (2000). Single Mothers in low-wage jobs: Financial strain, parenting, and preschoolers' outcomes. *Child Development, 71,* 1409–1423.

James-Burdumy, S., Dynarski, M., Moore, M., Deke, J., Mansfield, W., & Pistorino, C. (2005). *When schools stay open late: The National Evaluation of the 21st Century Community Learning Centers Program: Final report.* Washington, DC: U.S. Department of Education, Institute of Education Sciences, National Center for Education Evaluation and Regional Assistance.

Jarret, R. L. (1995). Growing up poor: The family experiences of socially mobile youth in low-income African-American neighborhoods. *Journal of Adolescent Research, 10,* 111–135.

Jarret, R. L. (1997) African American family and parenting strategies in impoverished neighborhoods. *Qualitative Sociology, 20,* 275–288.

Jencks, C., & Phillips, M. (1998). The black-white test score gap: An introduction. In C. Jencks & M. Phillips (Eds.), *The Black-White test score gap* (pp. 1–54). Washington, DC: Brookings Institution.

Jencks, C., Smith, M., Akland, H., Bane, M. J., Cohen, D., Gintis, H., et al. (1972). *Inequality: A reassessment of the effect of family and schooling in America.* New York: Basic Books.

Jeynes, W. H. (2005). Parental involvement and secondary school student educational outcomes: A meta-analysis. *The Evaluation Exchange: Evaluating Family Involvement Programs, 10*(4), 6.

Jeynes, W. H. (2007) The relationship between parental involvement and urban secondary school student academic achievement: A meta-analysis. *Urban Education, 42,* 82–110.

Joftus, S. (2008). Innovate, regulate, or conjugate? The federal role in education. Commentary on Policy Forum "Using evidence for a change, the federal role in education: Innovator or regulator?" Retrieved August 14, 2008, from http://www.nekia.org/Forums.html

Kalafat, J. (2008). Measuring the implementation and impact of the Kentucky Family Resource Centers. *The Evaluation Exchange: Building the Future of Family Involvement 14*(1&2), 31. Cambridge, MA: Harvard Family Research Project.

Keith, T. Z., Keith, P. B., Quirk, K. J., Sperduto, J., Santillo, S., & Killings, S. (1998). Longitudinal effects of parental involvement on high school grades: Similarities and differences across gender and ethnic groups. *Journal of School Psychology, 36*, 335–363.

Killion, J. (2005/06). Evaluating the impact of professional development in eight steps. *The Evaluation Exchange: Professional Development, 11*(4), 5, 11.

Kingdon, J. W. (2003). *Agendas, alternatives, and public policies* (2nd ed.). New York: Longman.

Kirner, M., & Storeygard, M. (2008). Building family involvement through a targeted district approach. *The Evaluation Exchange: Building the Future of Family Involvement, 14*(1&2), 25. Cambridge, MA: Harvard Family Research Project.

Kohl, G. O., Lengua, L. J., McMahon, R. J., & the Conduct Problems Prevention Research Group. (2000). Parent involvement in school: Conceptualizing multiple dimensions and their relations with family and demographic risk factors. *Journal of School Psychology, 38*, 501–523.

Kraft-Sayre, M. E., & Pianta, R. C. (2000). *Enhancing the transition to kindergarten: Linking children, families and schools.* Charlottesville: University of Virginia, National Center for Early Development & Learning.

Kreider, H. (2005). Studying contextual predictors of participation in out-of-school time activities. *The Evaluation Exchange: Complementary Learning, 11*(1), 14.

Kreider, H., Caspe, M., Kennedy, S., & Weiss, H. B. (Spring 2007). *Family involvement in middle and high school students' education* (Family Involvement Makes a Difference Research Brief No. 3). Cambridge, MA: Harvard Family Research Project.

Ladson-Billings, G. (2006). *From the achievement gap to the education debt: Understanding achievement in U.S. schools.* Paper presented at the American Educational Research Association Annual Meeting, San Francisco, CA.

Langdon, C. A., & Vesper, N. (2000). The sixth Phi Delta Kappa poll of teachers' attitudes toward the public schools. *Phi Delta Kappan, 81*(8), 607–611.

Lareau, A. (1987). Social class differences in family-school relationships: The importance of cultural capital. *Sociology of Education, 60*, 73–85.

Layzer, J. I., Goodson, B. D., Bernstein, L., & Price, C. (2001). *National evaluation of Family Support Programs, Final Report Volume A: The meta-analysis.* Cambridge, MA: Abt Associates.

Lightfoot, S. L. (1978). *Worlds apart: Relationships between families and schools.* New York: Basic Books.

Lightfoot, S. L. (2003). *The essential conversation: What parents and teachers can learn from each other.* New York: Random House.

Lipsey, M. W., & Wilson, D. B. (1993). The efficacy of psychological, educational, and behavioral treatment: Confirmation from meta-analysis. *American Psychologist, 48*, 1181–1209.

Little, P., Wimer, C., & Weiss, H. B. (2008). *After school programs in the 21st century: Their potential and what it takes to achieve it.* (Issues and Opportunities in Out-of-School Time Evaluation Brief 10.) Cambridge, MA: Harvard Family Research Project.

Lopez, M. E., Kreider, H., & Caspe, M. (2004/05). Co-constructing family involvement. *The Evaluation Exchange: Evaluating family involvement programs, 10*(4), 2–3, 22. Cambridge, MA: Harvard Family Research Project.

Love, J. M., Kisker, E. E., Ross, C., Constantine, J., Boller, K., Chazan-Cohen, R., et al. (2005). The effectiveness of Early Head Start for 3-year old children and their parents: Lessons for policy and programs. *Developmental Psychology, 41*, 885–901.

Lovell, P. (2008). Strengthening family involvement policy. *The Evaluation Exchange: Building the Future of Family Involvement, 14*(1&2), 17. Cambridge, MA: Harvard Family Research Project.

Markow, D., & Martin, S. (2005). The Metlife survey of the American teacher: Transitions and the role of supportive relationships. Harris Interactive. Retrieved April 11, 2008, from http://www.metlife.com/teachersurvey/

Marschall, M. (2006). Parent involvement and educational outcomes for Latino students. *Review of Policy Research, 23*, 1053–1076.

Mattingly, D. J., Prislin, R., McKenzie, T. L., Rodriguez, J. L., & Kayzar, B. (2002). Evaluating evaluations: The case of parent involvement programs. *Review of Educational Research, 72*, 549–576.

McCartney, K., & Dearing, E. (2002). Evaluating effect sizes in the policy arena. *The Evaluation Exchange: Family Support, 8*(1), 4, 7. Cambridge, MA: Harvard Family Research Project.

McLaughlin, M. (2006). Implementation research in education: Lessons learned, lingering questions and new opportunities. In M. I. Honig (Ed.), *New directions in education policy implementation* (pp. 209–228). Albany: State University of New York Press.

McLaughlin, M., & Shields, P.M. (1987). Involving low-income parents in the schools: A role for policy? *Phi Delta Kappan, 69*, 156–160.

Mintrom, M. (2000). *Policy entrepreneurs* and *school choice*. Washington, DC: Georgetown University Press, 2000.

Murnane, R. J., Willett, J. B., Bub, K. L., & McCartney, K. (2006). *Understanding trends in the black-white achievement gaps during the first years of school*. Brookings-Wharton Papers on Urban Affairs. Washington, DC: Brookings Institution.

National Education Association (NEA). (2006). ESEA: It's time for a change!: NEA's positive agenda for the ESEA reauthorization. Retrieved August 15, 2008, from http://www.nea.org/lac/esea/images/posagenda.pdf

Nye, C., Turner, H., & Schwartz, J. (2006). *Approaches to parent involvement for improving the academic performance of elementary school age children*. London: Campbell Collaboration. Retrieved July 22, 2008, from http://www.campbellcollaboration.org/doc-pdf/Nye_PI_Review.pdf

Palanki, A., & Burch, P. (1992). *Mapping the policy landscape: What federal and state governments are doing to promote family-school partnerships*. Washington: U.S. Department of Health and Human Services, Office of Educational Research and Improvement.

Patton, M. Q. (2006). Evaluation for the way we work. *NonProfit Quarterly, 13*(1), 28–33.

Pedersen, S., & Seidman, E. (2005). Contexts and correlates of out-of-school activity participation among low-income urban adolescents. In J. Mahoney, R. Larson, & J. Eccles (Eds.), *Organized activities as contexts of development: Extracurricular activities, after-school and community programs* (pp. 85–109). Mahwah: Erlbaum.

Phillips, M., Brooks-Gunn, J., Duncan, G. J., Klebanov, P., & Crane, J. (1998). Family background, parenting practices, and the Black-White test score gap. In C. Jencks & M. Phillips (Eds.), *The Black-White test score gap* (pp. 103–145). Washington, D.C. Brookings Institution.

Rebell, M. A., & Wolff, J. R. (Eds.). (in press). *NCLB at the crossroads: Examining America's commitment to closing achievement gaps*. New York: Teachers College Press.

Reynolds, A., Temple, J., Ou, S., Robertson, D., Mersky, J., Topitzes, J., & Niles, M. (2007). Effects of a school-based, early childhood intervention on adult health and well-being: A 19-Year Follow-up of low-income families. *Archives of Pediatric Adolescent Medicine, 161*, 730–739.

Rose, L. C., & Gallup, A. M. (2006). *The 38th Annual Phi Delta Kappa/Gallup Poll Of the Public's Attitudes Toward the Public Schools*. Phi Delta Kappa International. Retrieved on April 11, 2008, from http://www.pdkintl.org/kappan/kpollpdf.htm

Rothman, R. (Ed.). (2007). *City schools: How districts and communities can create smart education systems*. Cambridge, MA: Harvard Education Press.

Rothstein, R. (2004). *Class and schools: Using social, economic, and educational reform to close the Black–White achievement gap*. New York: Teachers College.

Schulting, A. B., Malone, P. S., Dodge, K. A. (2005). The effect of school-based kindergarten transition policies and practices on child academic outcomes. *Developmental Psychology 41*(6), 860–871.

Shartrand, A., Weiss, H., Kreider, H., & Lopez, M. (1997). *New skills for new schools: Preparing teachers in family involvement*. Washington, DC: U.S. Department of Education and Cambridge, MA: Harvard Family Research Project. Retrieved September 2, 2008, from http://www.gse.harvard.edu/hfrp//FI_NewSkillsForNewSchools

Sheldon, S. B. (2002). Parents' social networks and beliefs as predictors of parent involvement. *The Elementary School Journal, 102*(4), 301–316.

Sheldon, S. B., & Epstein, J. L. (2005). Involvement counts: Family and community partnerships and mathematics achievement. *Journal of Educational Research, 98*(4), 196–206.

Sweet, M., & Appelbaum, M. (2004). Is home visiting an effective strategy? A meta-analytic review of home visiting programs for families with young children. *Child Development, 75*, 1435–1456.

Taylor, R. D. (2000). An examination of the association of African American mothers' perception of their neighborhoods with their parenting and adolescent adjustment. *Journal of Black Psychology, 26*(3), 267–289.

Temple, J. A., & Reynolds, A. J. (2007). Benefits and costs of investments in preschool education: Evidence from the Child-Parent Centers and related programs. *Economics of Education Review, 26*(1), 126–144.

United States Department of Education. (2007). *State and local implementation of the No Child Left Behind act: Volume I — Title I school choice, Supplemental Educational Services, and student achievement*. U.S. Department of Education Office of Planning, Evaluation and Policy Development, Policy and Program Studies Service. Retrieved September 5, 2008, from http://www.ed.gov/rschstat/eval/choice/implementation/

United States Department of Education. (2002). Public Law print of PL 107-110, the No Child Left Behind Act of 2001. Retrieved August 21, 2008, from http://www.ed.gov/print/policy/elsec/leg/esea02/index.html

Vaden-Kiernan, N., & McManus, J. (2005). *Parent and family involvement in education: 2002–03* (NCES Report No. 2005-043). Washington, DC: National Center for Education Statistics.

Valenzuela, A., & Dornbusch, S. (1994). Familism and social capital in the academic achievement of Mexican origin and Anglo adolescents. *Social Science Quarterly, 75*, 18–36.

Van Voorhis, F. L. (2003). Interactive homework in middle school: Effects on family involvement and science achievement. *Journal of Educational Research, 96*, 323–338.

Walker-James, D., & Partee, G. (2003). *No more islands: Family involvement in 27 school and youth programs.* Washington, DC: American Youth Policy Forum.

Weiss, A. R., & Westmoreland, H. (2006). Family and community engagement in Boston Public Schools: 1995–2006. In S. Reville & C. Coggins (Eds.), *A decade of urban school reform: Persistence and progress in the Boston Public Schools* (pp. 219–242). Cambridge, MA: Harvard Education Press.

Weiss, H. B. (2008, June 11,). Testimony before the United States House of Representatives Committee on Education and Labor Hearing on "H.R. 2343, Education Begins at Home Act (EBAH)." Retrieved September 2, 2008, from http://www.hfrp.org/FI_EBAHWeissTestimony2008

Weiss, H. B., Caspe, M., & Lopez, M. E. (2006). *Family involvement in early childhood education* (Family Involvement Makes a Difference Research Brief No. 1). Cambridge, MA; Harvard Family Research Project.

Weiss, H. B., Kreider, H., Lopez, M. E., & Chatman, C. (Eds.). (1997). *Preparing educators to involve families: From theory to practice.* Thousand Oaks, CA: Sage.

Weiss., H. B., & Klein, L. (2007). *Changing the Conversation About Home Visiting: Scaling Up With Quality.* Cambridge, MA: Harvard Family Research Project. Retrieved August 12, 2008, from http://www.hfrp.org/FI_ChangingTheConversationAboutHomeVisiting

Wells, A. (2006, November). *"Our children's burden": A history of federal education policies that ask (now require) our public schools to solve societal inequality.* Paper presented at The Campaign for Educational Equity Second Annual Symposium on Educational Equity, Columbia University, New York, NY.

Westmoreland H. D., & Bouffard, S. M. (2008). A strategic evaluation approach for the Parental Information and Resource Centers. *The Evaluation Exchange: Building the Future of Family Involvement, 14*(1&2), 22–23. Cambridge, MA: Harvard Family Research Project.

Wimer, C., Bouffard, S. M., & Caronongan, P., Dearing, E., Simpkins, S. D., Little, P. M. D., et al. (2005). *What are kids getting into these days? Demographic differences in youth out-of-school time participation.* Cambridge, MA: Harvard Family Research Project.

# 21

# MOVING FORWARD IN SCHOOL-FAMILY PARTNERSHIPS IN PROMOTING STUDENT COMPETENCE

## *From Potential to Full Impact*

### PATRICK H. TOLAN AND SAMANTHA C. WOO

As the prior chapters in this volume illustrate in many ways, the power of promoting partnership between schools and families is an important basis for the developmental and educational success of children. However, it is also evident here and in other reports that much of the power in these partnerships and the myriad ways in which they can enrich child achievement and mental health, teacher performance and satisfaction, and parental functioning and support for schools remains unrealized, existing merely as great potential. Unfortunately there is limited attention to this partnership as a central aspect of education, and when mentioned in legislation or other calls for reform the framing is often of parental rights against educational system control or of teacher's employment rules pitted against reaching out to parents and innovative partnering. Almost absent and usually misrepresented in such discourse are knowledge and reliance on empirical information about effective models of parental involvement, opportunity to address qualms and presumptions about school-family partnerships, and underestimation of the value of such partnerships in supporting achievement and school success on multiple levels. The focus of this chapter is on some key issues for moving forward so that this underutilized potential can become action and advance from promise to actual benefits for children, families, schools, and the community at-large.

## OVERVIEW

First, a summary of some foundational themes from the research, information presented in this volume, and information from other sources will be provided. These themes are intended to guide larger scale emphasis on school-family partnerships and more appropriate use of what can work. A developmental-ecologically based understanding and organization for school-family partnerships forms the foundation of this discussion, a view which provides not only needed differentiation of promising efforts but also the connections across these areas of utility (Bronfenbrenner, 1992; Christenson, 2003). Central in this perspective is to view child involvement in school to inevitably mean family involvement, even when the involvement is notable for the absence of actual parental engagement or limitations in potential engagement that constrain and impede partnering. Thus, the issue is how parents and schools should partner, not whether or not they might. Perhaps stated more specifically, the more useful question is what relationship should parents and schools have in education, not is this relationship possibly valuable.

From a developmental-ecological perspective, the type and extent of engagement of parents and school personnel in partnership needs to vary depending on age, context, and specific purpose. How partnerships can help, why they are needed, and what are the respective components and roles of families and different school personnel and offices should be guided by and incorporate the developmental issues of most pertinence and the ecological level of expected impact. For example, parental engagement in regard to governance and overall organizational orientation is quite different than how parents of poorly performing students are engaged to help those children get needed educational help and these are both different from engagement to help children transition into school attendance and behavioral expectations (Christenson, 2003). As with child mental health in general, effective use of educational resources rests on recognizing that efforts are needed that promote healthy development, provide incidental aid and education as issues arise, allow for early identification and appropriate preventive efforts for high-risk students, and provide appropriate and accessible directed interventions for those evidencing substantial problems in performance and functioning (Tolan & Dodge, 2005). This framework is applied to suggest not only that there are multiple opportunities and needs that school-family partnerships can meet, but that deriving potential benefits requires due attention to fit of the partnership to the need. Whether fit to the developmental issues related to school involvement, the child's level of functioning compared to others, or the reason for parental involvement, moving forward is not just a matter of more involvement of parents, training of teachers in social skills for parent meetings, or a general lauding of parental influence on child educational direction. Rather, moving forward requires careful and appropriate consideration of the reason, need, and empirical evidence for the specific type and form of school-family partnership.

## SOME BASIC PRINCIPLES FOR SCHOOL-FAMILY PARTNERSHIPS

Although the primary mark of effective education remains academic achievement and particularly that achievement as measured through a child's performance in school, it is increasingly recognized that achievement and motivation to learn and perform are affected by much more than what occurs in the school day and in the classroom (Patrikakou, Weissberg, Manning, Redding, & Walberg, 2003). Whether the emphasis is on how prepared a child is to learn what is typically taught in school, the influence of the motivational level the child has for achievement, or the extent to which basic needs of safety and care are provided so a child can concentrate on learning while at school, the child's home environment and the community in which schooling occurs and that home environment exists, have an ongoing and profound impact on school performance.

Home life and how schooling is a part of it can set the stage for in-class behavior. In addition, the family/home environment provides ample opportunities to practice and reinforce those skills and concepts learned within the classroom. Classrooms and schools as a developmental setting also become additional influences on children's values and behavior. As such, the values and competencies learned in and reinforced at home do not exist in isolation from the school setting where substantial ongoing interactions with peers and educators carry influence on a child's social-emotional development. Studies have shown that close cooperation between schools and families effectively promote a child's school success (Davis-Kean & Eccles, 2003), including direct positive effects on classroom behavior and academic performance and reciprocal benefits for overall family functioning (Comer & Haynes, 1991; Coote, 2000). The recognition of this inextricable link between a child's school and home argues for a more careful consideration of how best to make use of and promote school-family partnerships (Patrikakou et al., 2003).

Parental involvement is one type of school-family partnership and is often the central interest in partnership promotion for good reason. For example, parental involvement, defined as more frequent visits to school and more attention to school activities while at home, has been linked to improvements in a child's attendance, participation, ability beliefs, and a decreased likelihood of engaging in high-risk behaviors (Christenson, Godber, & Anderson, 2005; Hoover-Dempsey, Walker, & Sandler, 2003). However, what is labeled as parental involvement may vary among the reasons parents are at school or in contact. For example, while teachers may more typically label parental engagement for aid or because of child achievement as involvement, there may be less recognition of this when the engagement is around problem behavior of the child or discordant views on the needs of the child (Henry, Miller-Johnson, Simon, Schoeny, & the Multi-site Violence Prevention Project, 2006). Thus, while more parental involvement is valuable and may have many benefits, it is important to delve into the basis for these correlations. It is likely that the *quality* of these linkages is important and may be important in addition to any relations derived from measuring simple frequency (Eccles & Harold, 1993).

Another principle that seems firmly supported by now is that it is not enough simply for families to passively support the programs initiated by schools or for schools to view parents as recipients of unidirectional pre-formed materials and expert determination by others of their child's needs (Eccles & Harold, 1993). Similarly, there may be inherent limitations in a view that parental involvement means primarily soliciting parental assistance in dealing with their child's behavioral and academic problems or engaging a few exemplary parents as volunteers to help in the school or lead parent organizations. Further, while it is clear that increasing the extent of parental involvement for basic organizational activities such as report card pick-up or parent-teacher periodic reports is important, this may constrain the benefits that could be derived for the school, the parents, and the students. Inherent in these basic levels of engagement models of school-family partnership is that parents' roles are primarily as consumers of education, ensuring that their children do not fail to meet standards of motivation and behavioral decorum (Cowan, Napolitano, & Sheridan, 2004). Moreover, such a view carries an underlying assumption that parents must be "trained" in the ways of the school when there are student problems, in order to resolve some kind of deficiency in the home. The relationship is one of parents acting as adjuncts to the school management of this problem student (Baker et al., 1995).

Advocacy for a more engaged and mutually developed relationship between parents and schools may be seen as abdicating responsibility for education by those charged with school administration. Or it may be interpreted as an objection to the complex and extensive imposition on normal and efficient operations that comes from non-professional involvement that is accompanied by limited sophistication and knowledge about the multiple mandates, issues, and demands faced by schools (Cowan et al., 2004). It might be argued that while parent-school partnership is a laudable sentiment, it is unrealistic or impractical and too vague in what it should be and how it would work to be undertaken seriously (to command limited time and resources schools and parents have). However, one lesson of the research to date is that emphasis on a partnership with well-defined purpose and complimentary roles of family and school and coordination of resources and responsibilities will increase student performance, teacher, administrator, and parent satisfaction, overall school functioning, and support for school resources (Cowan et al., 2004). While perhaps sounding like a good idea that is not very practical or plausible, there are, in fact, models with sophisticated implementation considerations included and the effects are substantial enough and broad enough to justify any actual extra effort school-family partnership may require.

By focusing on the interaction between schools and families the intent is to consider developmentally shifting learning, supervision, and motivational needs. Most critically, this view shifts from assigning primary responsibility for learning support to either entity, so that passive support or acquiescence to the requirements of the other are replaced by respect for the capabilities and plausible role of the others and one's self. There is also recognition that neither entity is expected to understand their responsibilities and roles apart from involvement of the other or that there should be independent activity except if there is failure in academic performance (Hoover-Dempsey et al., 2003). Unlike a "school-centric" orientation in which parents passively assist educators in attaining goals defined by the school, a partnership-focused orientation emphasizes the empowerment of families, not only to define their own needs and priorities, but also to become advocates for their children (Minke & Anderson, 2005). In this way, parents are recognized as experts on their own children's experiences and needs, thereby becoming an indispensable member of the partnership. Combined with the educational expertise that schools bring to the relationship, integrated school-family partnerships allow both educators and parents to gain a better understanding of the child's experiences across settings. This provides schools and families with a more complete picture of the child's overall development (Cowan et al., 2004). It provides more than an admirable extension from the necessary requirements for good education to a framework that can provide a more accurate and full understanding of what can make a difference for a given community or student and what are the full set of resources that can be helpful. With this fuller information and perspective, more effective and efficient use of resources will occur. Thus, while perhaps at first glance seeming an elaboration that is of marginal value, active school-family partnerships based in empirical knowledge, when given more than superficial consideration, probably carry many of the very features of organization that are feared lost if such partnerships are undertaken.

One valid concern about undertaking more involved partnerships is that partnerships of this complexity and quality require cultivation through multiple interactions and frequent communication between schools and families. The interest has to be beyond immediate patching up of a rift or crisis management, instead seeking to form the foundation for a long-term collaboration (Christenson, 2003; Cowan et al., 2004). Thus, another principle is that school-family partnerships are best organized for intended ongoing operational aid. For example, efforts to enhance and ease the transitions of school entry and to capitalize on parental enthusiasm as their child starts school are more likely to show substantial benefits than transiently formulated school administrator meetings that consist of statements of policies and procedures prompted by some recent incident.

Another important principle emerging from the field of research on school-family partnerships is the need for developmental sensitivity and appropriateness in the form and intent of these partnerships. Preschool and early elementary school partnerships, for example, are most useful when they include focus on the unique demands of school readiness, helping to ease the child's transition into school, and address the challenges that families and students may experience as they form new relationships, face new expectations, and gain new competencies (Pianta, Kraft-Sayre, Rimm-Kaufman, Gercke, & Higgins, 2001). As children progress in the elementary years the partnership should focus on helping support mastery of basic skills and internalization of motivation to achieve, while considering the special needs of those children facing exceptional challenges, whether environmental or due to personal limitations.

As children enter middle school, partnerships work best when they are based in acknowledging the importance of this transitional period that coincides with multiple other developmental transitions as children enter adolescence. Therefore, focusing on helping children maintain a healthy developmental trajectory is particularly important in light of mounting threats including greater academic pressures, changing peer relationships, increasing exposure to substances and risk behaviors, and decreased parental monitoring (Elias, Patrikakou, & Weissberg, 2007).

Parent-school partnerships during high school may be focused less on direct action by those representing either system. However, this does not mean the partnership and its nature are less critical. Instead, this means these two systems are focused on increasingly supporting student direction and motivation in preparation for post-high school autonomy. Thus, though study of and consideration of partnerships during this developmental period are less common, they are just as important for a child's development and academic success. As students are faced with more openly and directly competitive learning environments, increased choices about classes and extracurricular activities, and an indeterminate course following graduation, cooperation between schools and families to help guide students, while promoting opportunity for choice and the consequences of those choices in developmentally appropriate doses, becomes particularly valuable (Mizelle & Irvin, 2000). Because this is a time when students are presented with and expected to manage choices and increased freedom both at school and at home, it is also a time when risks due to bad choices increase and consequences can be longer lasting (Simon, 2004). For example, it is during this developmental period when problems such as delinquency, drug use, unwanted pregnancy, and school dropout or drop-off in performance become part of the ecology of student life (Mizelle & Irvin, 2000). Thus, this can be a time when what is typically thought of as parent-school partnerships may not seem applicable. However, active parental involvement and developmentally-attuned school-family partnerships are crucial influences on school success at all grade levels (Eccles & Harold, 1993). Therefore, attention is needed at each developmental stage, requiring that linkages between schools and families are established as children enter the educational system and continue to be cultivated through the last years of high school.

Another principle is that partnership between parents and educators is particularly challenging, yet may be especially valuable, within high-risk, low resource settings, such as inner city communities (Tolan, Sherrod, Gorman-Smith, & Henry, 2003). Forced to confront exceptional ecological stressors along with exceptional frequency of other stressors, families living within these neighborhoods are often more isolated from family and community networks and other resources available to families elsewhere (Tolan & Grant, in press). This means they must act on their own devices and with uncertainty of impact, resulting in protection of their children from the negative influences of the neighborhood overshadowing hope for success and support for achievement (Dishion & Kavanagh, 2000; Lareau, 1987). Parental involvement in school frequently takes the backseat to more urgent needs and attempts to minimize exposure to dangers affecting children on a daily basis (Davis-Kean & Eccles, 2003; Eccles & Harold, 1993). In addition, while schools may be viewed as resources and centers of neighborhood life in many communities in inner city communities and other stressful environments, mistrust and alienation from the school is common, whether attributed to vestiges of racism and other felt discrimination or because of limited connection of the school administration and organization to community concerns. At the same time, there may be more reason for families in higher risk communities to impart responsibility for their child's education to the school and its teachers (Lareau, 1987). It is, however, within these most disrupted communities that parent-school partnerships can provide a basis for connections with other parents, opportunity for protective and nurturing parenting practices, and opportunity for stronger school functioning (Dishion & Kavanagh, 2000).

Finally, it is important to note that in addition to the positive potential of school-family partnerships and the importance of developmental and setting characteristics, there is a need to recognize that schools and in particular, the family-school relationship, are at the center of many society contentions. Schools are increasingly expected to provide more community functions and, at the same time, to do so with a greater eye on limited resources and greater documentation of compliance to a growing list of expectations and standards (many times without any additional aid to do so and sometimes contradictory expectations across the standards; Weist, 2003). The breadth and extent of need across the diverse student body and the decreasing access to other public systems of care such as healthcare, mental health services, and childcare have otherwise put schools in this fulcrum of expectations that are quite complex.

Families today are confronted with mounting demands on their time and energy, many lacking the resources and the education necessary to successfully navigate the educational system. Parents who have had negative interactions with the school or had poor experiences as students are likely to be more reluctant to cooperate with the school (Comer & Haynes, 1991). Other parents may simply be unsure of their role or feel incompetent when it comes to helping their children with schoolwork or becoming involved in school activities (Eccles & Harold, 1993). These challenges are only further complicated when language barriers or cultural differences come into play (Cowan et al., 2004). Schools, on the other hand, may lack proper training on how to effectively collaborate with parents (Davis-Kean & Eccles, 2003). Frustration with low parental involvement may produce hostility on the part of educators, leading to reduced interest in involving parents at all (Eccles & Harold, 1993). School policy or administrative barriers, along with the size and organizational structure of the school, may also preclude active partnership between educators and parents (Davis-Kean & Eccles, 2003). Thus, it is important that as actions are put into place to realize the potential of parent-school partnerships, there is due recognition of the multiplicity of and level of strain on schools and families that may lead to skepticism that the "additional" requirements of these partnerships is worth the effort.

These principles (see Table 21.1) provide a strong foundation for moving forward at the individual school, school system, and state and national levels, for promotion of school-family partnerships as valuable and essential components of quality education. In moving forward, work should be guided by three interrelated but distinct considerations. First is that efforts be organized around developmental need, contextual conditions, and differential purpose for general versus high-risk students. Second, these efforts should be grounded as much as possible in empirically tested approaches. Third, whether well-tested or in initial efforts, evaluation of effects should be an integral and ongoing part of the efforts. This is not only to improve the fund of knowledge of what works for whom, but also to provide management information that might be used to refine that specific effort. In the next section, some of the key issues for each of four stages of school involvement are summarized and examples of empirically evaluated programs that have at least shown promise for benefits are identified. It should be noted that the list of such programs to draw from is limited and along with preference for prior-tested programs moving from potential to impact will necessitate enriching the pool of potentially useful approaches and programs as well as better understanding of what works best for which purposes with which population (Tolan & Dodge, 2005).

**Table 21.1** Principles for School-Family Partnerships

- Recognize the inextricable link between a child's school and home.
- Quality of linkages between schools and families is at least as important as frequency.
- Greater engagement of families improves student and school functioning.
- Mutual or shared goal development improves collaboration and benefits for parents, students, and school personnel.
- School-family partnerships are most beneficial when organized as sources of ongoing operational aid.
- Partnerships need to be developmentally sensitive and appropriate.
- Partnerships for specific issues may need different organization than those for general parental involvement.
- School-family partnerships are particularly valuable within high-risk, low resources settings, such as inner city communities.
- Recognize the ongoing multiple forms of strain on schools and families that can impede and undermine partnerships.

## DEVELOPMENTAL OPPORTUNITIES FOR SCHOOL-FAMILY PARTNERSHIPS

### Transition to School

A collaborative relationship between schools and families becomes particularly essential as children enter school. A child's adjustment during this important transitional period depends on the interaction of a wide array of individuals and contexts, including the child, family, teachers, school, peers, and community as a whole (Pianta et al., 2001). Parental involvement early on has also been shown to predict lower grade retention, increased reading achievement, and school success in the first grade (Reynolds & Clements, 2003). According to the continuity framework, a child's development is fostered through a firm grounding in the present stage of development and appropriate challenges presented by the subsequent stage of development. Sudden or drastic changes and inappropriate expectations may impede this progress (Mangione & Speth, 1998; U.S. Department of Education & U.S. Department of Health and Human Services, 1995). To establish the stable foundation required by this framework for children to transition from one stage to the next, continuity should be maintained between the child's environments at school and at home (Miedel & Reynolds, 1999). Responsibility for creating this stability and easing the transition for young children is shared between the family and school, within a community orientation toward promoting this relationship (Mangione & Speth, 1998).

As children enter school, numerous factors affect the creation of successful school-family partnerships. For many children, school entry signifies the transition from the nurturing and supportive environment of their families to school environments with unfamiliar people and expectations (Mangione & Speth, 1998). When left to adapt to these changes on their own, children are placed at increased risk for low school achievement and developmental problems. Parents are often unaware or skeptical of their role within the school setting or feel that they are incapable of contributing in an effective way (Davis-Kean & Eccles, 2003; Eccles & Harold, 1993). The adjustment for parents to their new relationship with their child's school can be particularly challenging, especially for first-time parents (Cowan et al., 2004). Inactivity on the part of parents is often misinterpreted as disinterest by schools, serving only to perpetuate the pattern of poor collaboration between families and schools (Simon, 2004).

*Two Examples* Various programs have demonstrated success in confronting these challenges as children transition into school. The focus, here, is on two examples, one being perhaps the largest and most extensive effort to date for parent-school partnership at school entry or preschool entry and another representing a small scale test of an approach for parents raising children in high-risk communities to facilitate the actual transition into elementary school.

Head Start, an early intervention program for public preschoolers from low income neighborhoods, is aimed at improving the social and educational competence of disadvantaged children so that they may enter school at the same level of their more advantaged peers (Garces, Thomas, & Currie, 2002). This program is organized to accomplish its goals by promoting parental involvement in every aspect of the child's early educational experiences, from the day-to-day activities in the classroom to the development and management of program components (Fantuzzo, McWayne, & Perry, 2004). However, a major limitation to date has been the adherence to these design qualities and related federal guidelines (Garces et al., 2002). Provision of services integral to those versions showing significant positive effects is a considerable challenge given that Head Start programming receives only enough funding to serve about two-thirds of eligible children and to do so in a stripped-down version. Despite these obstacles, however, Head Start has shown significant effects among non-minority populations, including increasing their likelihood of completing high school, attending college, and having higher earnings in their early twenties. Head Start has demonstrated additional benefits for minority ethnicity populations by lowering their probability of later delinquency. However, many of the gains shown seem to be short-term and more evident in improved test scores than observed classroom behavior. The fade out, apparent for most children by the third grade, seems to occur faster in minority populations (Garces et al., 2002).

Important exceptions to these overall findings can be identified (Campbell, Ramey, Pungello, Sparling, & Miller-Johnson, 2002; Reynolds, Temple, Robertson, & Mann, 2001). These exceptions show lasting effects that include academic and behavioral outcomes. For example, Reynolds and colleagues have shown that the academic gains translate to considerable economic benefits (estimated to be $25,000 net benefit per child served with $6,700 per child investment), including saved costs of services that might be needed otherwise and increased productivity and tax contributions of those affected (Reynolds, Ou, & Topitzes, 2004; Reynolds & Temple, in press). Notably, each has a strong core of sustained and defined parental involvement and focus on translating and continuing school-based efforts at home. This suggests that there is great benefit to be gained from preschool programming and programming that helps facilitate readiness for school and productive parental roles (Foster, Prinz, Sanders, & Shapiro, 2008; Greenberg et al., 2003).

Schools and Families Educating Children (SAFEChildren) represents a second type of transition support program through school-family partnership. SAFEChildren was developed as a preventive intervention targeted toward first grade students and their families living in high crime/low income communities, those within Chicago's inner city (Gorman-Smith et al., 2007). The primary goal of this program is to help families and their children make a good transition into academic schooling and to help manage that transition including supporting parental involvement in schooling. By addressing risk and protective factors identified within a developmental-ecological perspective that lead to behavioral and academic problems, the program aims to help parents utilize existing resources, build support and skills, and to retain parental efficacy and related involvement in school. This two part program includes a phonics-based reading tutoring component aimed at promoting educational success in school, as well as a multiple family group intervention focused on aspects of parenting, family relationship characteristics, parental involvement in school, and child development. The tutoring component was developed as part of the Fast Track intervention and found to relate to academic improvement among high-risk children during the first grade (Conduct Disorders Prevention Research Group, 1999). The multiple family group component allows participants to practice parenting and problem solving skills, obtain information, and apply session material at home (see Gorman-Smith et al., 2007, for a detailed description). The tutoring and multiple family group components, in combination, are expected to lead to more positive attitudes about achievement and school involvement for parents and children, and greater self-control, lower aggression, and higher social competence for the children. The tutoring component is administered by undergraduate students, and the family groups are facilitated by mental health professionals.

In a random assignment trial longitudinal study, SAFEChildren has shown effects in decreasing child aggression, improving reading scores and academic functioning, maintaining parental involvement in their child's schooling, and improving or maintaining the child's concentration and prosocial behavior (Tolan, Gorman-Smith, & Henry, 2004). Perhaps most pertinent to the present focus was the finding that the program had a benefit of *maintaining initial level* of parental involvement, which were relatively strong at kindergarten level, through the second grade follow-up, while the controls (same classrooms, families randomly assigned) dropped off quickly in extent of involvement. In addition, there was additional benefit for high-risk families, suggesting the impact on this outcome was greater for families most likely to benefit from sustained involvement in school. Long-term follow-up of this study is currently being conducted with the children from the original study, now in their early high school years. In addition, an effectiveness trial of this original study is being conducted in which seventh and eighth grade students administer the tutoring component and staff from community mental health agencies facilitate the family groups. The data from this effectiveness trial is currently being analyzed.

### Elementary School Years

School-family partnerships that continue throughout elementary school contribute significantly to a child's school success and development. For example, studies have shown that when elementary school teachers integrate parental involvement into their regular teaching practices, parents feel more confident in their abilities to help their children with their schoolwork and tend to interact more with their children at home (Patrikakou & Weissberg, 2000). Students have also shown improvement in their attitudes and achievement (Epstein & Dauber, 1991). Despite the benefits of this close collaboration during elementary school, however, there is relatively little attention to helping parents engage during the elementary years, to differentiate that from the engagement helpful at the start of schooling, or information for teachers and administrators about the derivable benefits of proper partnering with parents. This becomes particularly important as homework and use of basic skills emerge as key curricula foci or engagement with groups is supported in class work and in social aspects of schooling.

Communication between teachers and families rarely occurs unless specific academic or behavior problems arise (Davis-Kean & Eccles, 2003). Communication with parents of children achieving at the expected level or lacking behavioral problems may be actively discouraged to permit more time for focus on troubled students. Parents often hear only about their child's poor performance or bad behavior increasing their reluctance to approach the school for help or to maintain a close relationship. Parent-teacher conferences, though the most common method of communication, are limited and occur even less frequently in schools within high-risk communities (Comer & Haynes, 1991).

Another key developmental consideration of this stage of parent-school partnerships is that a history of these parents with this school or schooling about this child now exists. Parents experience in adjusting to their new relationship with their child's school will often continue through primary school, easily moving into a compounding set of negative experiences that can resonate with their own experiences during their elementary school years (Comer & Haynes, 1991). This emotional aspect of parent-school partnerships can often be overlooked or dismissed as a personal problem of the parents involved, yet it is likely to be a key part of parental motivation that can be utilized to help achieve intended partnership (McGuire, Manghi, & Tolan, 1989). Effort during elementary school, however, serves to target social-emotional problems as they are arising and before they become resistant to change (Davis-Kean & Eccles, 2003; Greenberg et al., 2003). It is also a time when the parent-school partnership can set a frame for industriousness and achievement orientation that will serve protective functions in the ensuing risk-laden entry into adolescence and further beyond into adulthood.

*Two Examples*  The "Parent Assistant in the Classroom" program, developed as part of the School Development Program, provides an approach to defining and maintaining elementary school partnerships between schools and families by focusing on increasing parental involvement in the classroom (Comer & Haynes, 1991). First implemented in two low income schools in New Haven, Connecticut, the approach is part of a whole-school organization plan that had at its core greater involvement of the community in the school and greater involvement of all involved in schools in defining and reaching achievement goals. As initially undertaken in this program, parental assistants were hired for minimum wage to work approximately ten hours per week in the classroom assisting teachers as directed by that teacher. Program developers reported that parents often volunteered 20 to 30 more hours of their time each week. Also, while it was expected that teachers would be reluctant to give over much responsibility for education to the assistants, instead of being assigned to classroom cleanup or busy work tasks, parents were given and managed considerable responsibility for instruction, child management in the classroom and out on field trips, and were engaged as partners by many teachers (Comer & Haynes, 1991). Through their daily school involvement, parents became particularly knowledgeable about their school's particular needs, problems, and opportunities. As such they became useful resources in engaging the community about issues the schools faced and in creating workshops to help other parents to work well with schools. Evaluation of the program suggested improved academic functioning in most of the schools where the program was implemented well, also noting that more emphasis on academic achievement was related and was perhaps as important as general implementation (Cook et al., 1999).

Linking the Interests of Families and Teachers (LIFT) was designed as an intervention program to lessen levels of aggression among students during the elementary schools years by providing teachers with in-class and on the playground behavior management methods (Reid, Eddy, Fetrow, & Stoolmiller, 1999). It also was intended to link the classroom activities and educational goals to parents and to boost parental engagement and support for achievement and good behavior within school. Thus, while originally conceived as a delinquency and youth violence prevention effort, LIFT aims to promote better behavior in school classrooms and in recreational/recess times and to boost parental involvement in the enterprise of learning. Thus, it is a good example of how school-family partnerships might be promoted during the elementary school years (Eddy, Reid, & Fetrow, 2000). The first component of LIFT consists of child problem and social skills training based in the classroom. During twice weekly one hour sessions, students role play specific social and problem solving skills, work as a group to practice these skills, and receive rewards for positive behavior. A modified version of the Good Behavior Game is used during the playground component to teach students positive peer interactions. Students earn rewards for themselves, their group, and their entire class through the demonstration of prosocial behaviors and skills and the avoidance of negative behaviors (Barrish, Saunders, & Wolfe, 1969; Dolan et al., 1993). A third component is to install a phone in each classroom with an answering machine (this was before the ubiquity of cell phones and computer access). Each day the teacher leaves a recorded message about the major focus of the class that day and any homework assignments. This also permits parents to leave messages for the teacher about their child or their child's homework. The final component of LIFT involves weekly group-delivered parent training sessions during which time parents role play and discuss specific discipline and family management skills to be used at home. The specific content of the program curriculum was modified to address the challenges most prevalent to parents with children in each respective age group.

While technology has superseded some of the communication features that stood out at the time of LIFT's implementation, the key issues of linking schools and families that the technology facilitated remains important as one part of a classroom and social behavior management schema. Tested through random assignment and growth modeling of impact over time, LIFT showed increases in academic achievement and aggressive behavior for the whole population included (Reid et al., 1999). Moreover, there were large effects on aggression among the highest risk segment of the student population and long-term effects on the time children became involved with alcohol and marijuana, crime, and antisocial peers during middle school (Eddy et al., 2000).

## Middle School Years

A child's middle school years brings a new set of challenges for both families and schools. Entry into middle school has been defined as a "trajectory-changing event" during which time children are forced to adapt to tremendous change within their personal, social, familial, and cultural environments. Children's capacity for learning and healthy development depends largely on the nature of their coping experiences during this critical time (Elias et al., 2007; Rutter, 1987). Children with poor social skills and low self-esteem are particularly vulnerable as they transition from primary to secondary school, making early intervention and close partnership between schools and families especially important (Davis-Kean & Eccles, 2003). Referrals for mental health services, substance use, incidence of sexually transmitted disease, and predecessors of school failure such as poorer attendance, lesser motivation to learn, and poorer academic performance tend to increase during the middle school years (Elias et al., 2007). Effective parent-teacher communication can help mitigate the effects of the increasing academic workloads and changing peer relationships that characterize middle school (Elias et al., 2007). Partnerships between teachers, parents, and communities can also serve a protective role in the initiation and maintenance of healthy developmental trajectories for these middle school children (Eccles & Harold, 1993).

Despite the apparent benefits of school and family collaboration during middle school and expressed interest in more involvement from teachers and parents, parental involvement and teacher outreach decrease dramatically as children enter secondary school (Beyer, Patrikakou, & Weissberg, 2003; Eccles & Harold, 1993). Difficulties cited as contributors to this undesirable and undesired change are misconceptions about parental influences and teacher interest and how to communicate at this stage of development (Clark & Clark, 1996). If, as the research suggests quite consistently, there is a general decrease in performance by students and satisfaction of children and parents with family relationships, school may become an area of particular sensitivity and even avoidance within the family (Hill & Taylor, 2004). There also may be greater uncertainty, inconsistency across students, and misfit for students to parental and teacher expectations than at any other point. Social interests may also shift and vary considerably among students of the same age and academic capability. As this mismatch of perception, expectations, and need occurs in multiple ways between parents and students, students and teachers, and teachers and parents, failing to communicate effectively is quite likely (Eccles & Harold, 1993). In addition, the increased complexity of the middle school organizational structure with greater emphasis on application of skills, more intensive scholarship expectations, and multiple teachers each with responsibility for a specific subject, may be intimidating for parents who would otherwise like to communicate regularly with their child's school (Beyer et al., 2003). Depending on the parent-child relationship, parents may feel that their children need or want more independence or that they would be embarrassed by their involvement at school. Finally, parents may feel less able to help their children with schoolwork and in influencing behaviors, which may have the effect of increasing their reluctance to be involved at school and at home (Eccles & Harold, 1993). Thus, this is a very challenging time for school-family partnerships, but also a time when that protective link may be critically important, even if acting to minimize problems rather than promote exceptional achievement.

*Examples*   While much has been written about the troubling trends of achievement and behavior that coincide with entry to the middle school years, there has been a notable lack of programmatic efforts to change that effect. In particular, there are few studies that focus on this as a developmental effect; one that is perhaps best understood and addressed at the level of schooling organization. Fewer examples that focus on schools and families as determinants of healthy development in children can be found at the middle school level. One early example to attempt to address the issue of developmental mismatch was the School Transitional Environments Program (Felner et al., 1993). That project emphasized within school organization of teacher teams and limited extent of classroom change. Parental involvement, however, was limited to more and quicker notification of absences and of school activities. While showing some initial benefits in a quasi-experimental test, the longer-term effects of the project and replications have not been as positive or well-documented. However, like this project there is evidence in the literature that school-family partnership strategies which show particular promise at the middle school level, like at the elementary level, emphasize positive communication between teachers and parents, encouraging parental involvement both at school and at home. Techniques that simplify and increase the extent of communication and optimize monitoring of student progress and adjustment seem particularly critical. Through regular phone calls, notes home, formal conferences, and more informal interactions, parents and teachers are able to maintain a shared and fuller understanding of the child's challenges and achievements, creating continuity between the school and the home environments (Beyer et al., 2003; Miedel & Reynolds, 1999). Sustained school-to-home communication such as this has been shown to increase parental involvement (Simon, 2004). It appears that a key effect is to help build a shared and full understanding among parents and those within a school, who each have a specific part of helping children at this educational level.

The development of partnership committees may present a promising approach, in which parents, educators, and community members work together to initiate activities such as school visits and student-led panel discussions, to help students and parents transition into a new school environment or a new grade level. Parents are then encouraged to support the development of social and academic competencies in the home, emphasizing the importance of good study habits and volunteer work in the community. Teachers who integrate into their curriculum homework assignments that encourage family participation may also help to increase parental involvement (Beyer et al., 2003). Programs that help with social skills and other support of social competence and communication skills for students that help improve parent-child and student-teacher relationships may also aid school-family partnering for appropriate developmental supports (Tolan, Szapocznik, & Sambrano, 2007). Communication is of central importance, whether in the form of regular conversations about the child's school day or discussions about the academic, emotional, or social struggles that may be facing the child (Elias et al., 2007).

One example of a program aimed at middle school age children and emphasizing parental involvement at varying levels depending on need is the Adolescent Transitions Program (ATP). The ATP utilizes a family-centered approach to prevent or delay the emergence of antisocial behavior in childhood to lessen the effects of the accumulative risk that results from poor academic skills, peer rejection, and association with a deviant peer group (Dishion & Stormshak, 2006).

ATP includes a universal or whole-school component, a selective or high-risk student component, and an indicated or clearly evident problem student component as part of a service system meant to influence a broad network of contextual factors which affect the social and emotional development in children (Dishion & Stormshak, 2006). The universal strategy consists of a Family Resource Room created to promote collaboration between parents and school staff, support positive parenting norms, and distribute information promoting school success and family management. Home visiting is undertaken by staff to encourage participation in the Family Resource Room. Videotape self-assessment is used at the universal level to help parents identify risk behaviors and effective family management skills from examples of parent-child inter-actions, allowing them to evaluate their own and their child's level of risk (Dishion & Kavanagh, 2000). A six-week health curriculum is also implemented at the universal level which includes parent-child homework assignments focused on reducing sub-stance use and conflict and promoting school success. The selected level component includes the Family Check-Up, which consists of an initial interview, a comprehensive assessment, and a family feedback session. This method is meant to provide parents with a more extensive evaluation of their child's level of risk and resources for reducing risk factors and specific consultation and aid to encourage maintenance of any positive practices. At the indicated level of intervention, families are offered a menu of empiri-cally tested services aimed at providing direct professional intervention and support to families. Over the past decade, Dishion and colleague have refined the delivery and implementation system for ATP, such that it can be provided to family groups or to individual families. The Family Management Curriculum provides a detailed frame-work for conducting family management-focused family groups. Families involved in this indicated intervention learn the skills necessary to bring about behavior change through the use of incentives, set limits and monitor their children, and communicate and problem solve as a family (Dishion & Stormshak, 2006). Empirical tests of the pro-gram show the selected level intervention as measured by teacher ratings to be related to decreased antisocial behavior for high-risk youth related to their use of the Family Resource Center and Family Check-Up. In addition, there were significant reductions in observed parent-child conflict from videotaped problem-solving tasks (Dishion & Kavanagh, 2000). For those involved in the indicated intervention, lower rates of tobacco use and behavior problems were reported (Dishion & Connell, 2008). Pertinent to the present focus, there was a significant correlation between change in mothers' and child's negative engagement and reductions in externalizing behavior at school as reported by teachers (Dishion & Kavanagh, 2000).

## High School

As children enter high school, discussions between parents and their children about school and homework occur less frequently and parents often attend fewer school meet-ings and events (Simon, 2004). For many students, the transition to high school means a much larger, more competitive, impersonal, and grade-oriented environment than they experienced as middle school students (Eccles, Midgley, & Adler, 1984; Mizelle & Irvin, 2000). Upon entry into high school, students are confronted with an increased range of class options and extracurricular activities along with more evident distinc-tion of the academic and related career track ahead of them. In addition, there is an expansion in the number of teachers and diversity among their peer groups. Schools often directly emphasize independence of responsibility for academic performance and completion of required work, including the noted need to see the consequences of failing to self-direct on academic work. At home, parents often implement less directly restrictive rules about scheduling responsibilities and leisure time or in managing competing interests. Thus, many students who are not ready for such self-management, particularly high-risk students, often show a drop-off in performance on entering the high school years (Simon, 2004).

The challenges are not just academic as high school students are often faced with a substantially shifting and diverging set of friends, if not a new set of social groups within the school. The emergence of many risk behaviors as not uncommon, particularly among older peers, can also undercut family norms while being more likely due to limited monitoring across home and school. Increased dropout rates, late graduation, poor performance, delinquent behavior, and low attendance are all effects of these unique challenges (Mizelle & Irvin, 2000). Parental involvement may be impeded by greater involvement with peers and more focus on peers as normative influences.

There are also structural characteristics that challenge adequate communication between schools and families. Parents may hold a view that children need less guidance and more autonomy as high school students or they may be unsure of how to be involved within the complicated environment and curricula of high school. Families may also live farther from their child's high school which makes regular involvement more difficult. Teachers, in turn, may interpret the parents' lack of involvement as disinterest or acceptance that the child's behavior represents a set level of performance (Simon, 2004). That each teacher has more limited involvement with more students may promote superficial focus on performance within that class rather than differentiating a given student or seeing that class as part of an overall educational experience (Epstein, 1986; Mizelle & Irvin, 2000).

However, despite these challenges and discouraging trends, it is evident that parental involvement in their child's academic and social experiences during high school relates to better achievement, more student satisfaction with school, and greater likelihood of graduation/completion (Mizelle & Irvin, 2000). Thus, it is important to focus on how partnerships can be developmentally appropriate and ecologically sustainable at this time of multi-faceted relationships within schools and between students, parents, and schools. It is also important to note that features that characterize this developmental stage and school-family relationship complicate empirical testing of program and approach effects. It can be difficult to create the level of control and maintain randomness of assignment or control over other factors except for condition assignment that is crucial for strong inference about intervention effects. Thus, it is not surprising that there are few studies of parental involvement in high school or school-family partnerships during this time period. In fact, a thorough search produced only programs that are focused on preventing high-risk behavior that included parent education or parent groups when seeking such programs with adequate evaluation. Notably, few of these programs showed much success with parental involvement or sustained effects (Tolan et al., 2007).

*Examples of What Could Work*   School-family partnerships in high school are often less formal and programmatic and more situation specific than in previous years, which may lead to less recognition of their critical role and level of occurrence than is actual. Results from surveys of 11,000 high school students and 1,000 high school principals conducted as part of the National Education Longitudinal Study reported a wide range of partnership activities occurring within high schools across the country (Simon, 2001). Among the common strategies used are workshops and administration-parent meetings about key issues such as homework completion, drug and alcohol issues, college preparation, and driving privileges. Many schools reported formal and informal volunteer programs in which parents may participate as teachers' aids, field trip chaperones, and cafeteria monitors at school. Only one-third of high schools reported an active parent volunteer recruitment and training program and of those only one in eight parents actually chose to volunteer. Presumably this was much higher than the other two-thirds of schools in which no such program was undertaken (Simon, 2001).

There is also a divergence of what is often meant by parental involvement. Many parents in the survey reported involvement directly in their child's academic work and extracurricular activities. Yet, this involvement seemed limited to helping the child rather than engaging with the school in the educational enterprise. In addition, there is limited direct involvement through parent-teacher associations and support groups such as booster clubs (Simon, 2001). Thus, there is substantial parental involvement in high schools but limited school-family partnership of the type research says should make a difference.

There are several areas of key opportunity during this schooling period. Research has shown that when parents are involved in their children's transition from middle school to high school, that they tend to stay involved in their school experiences for a longer period of time (Mizelle & Irvin, 2000). Therefore, a focus on this critical transitional period would increase the likelihood that a close collaboration between schools and families is maintained throughout the years of high school. For example, schools can make efforts to provide families with information about their child's new high school and the process of picking classes. Social support for students is also an essential part of ensuring a healthy transition (Simon, 2004). This may occur in the form of meetings between parents, children, and their high school counselors to discuss course selection and extracurricular activities or high school visits to give students and parents a feel for what the transition will be like. Parents may even be called on to help create and facilitate some of the transition activities for the students (Mizelle & Irvin, 2000).

As children are adjusting to their new high school environments, schools can provide opportunities for regular parent participation in activities and school organization, beyond volunteering for event organization and fundraising. Invitations sent home to parents informing them of specific opportunities have been shown to be effective in increasing parental involvement in school (Simon, 2004). Schools should also reach out to families concerning their child's academic program and specific ways to provide homework help at home. Workshops that provide parents with information and training on how to help their children with math, reading, and other subjects can be particularly useful (Epstein, 1986). The provision of specific and practical skills is especially effective. For example, schools should not simply inform parents about attendance or behavior problems, but rather, should also provide information on ways to reduce these problems. The establishment of a systematic process for parents to contact their child's teacher in order to ask questions or to share information about positive and negative behaviors and progress would facilitate regular communication between families and schools (Epstein, 1986; Simon, 2004). Finally, the creation of an action team, comprised of parents, students, educators, and community members, has also been shown to be an effective way to connect schools and families. The work of these teams focuses on devising and implementing strategies to increase communication and collaboration between schools and families by drawing on the skills and expertise of a child's most significant influences. The inclusion of high school students in this process allows them to contribute a unique perspective, while also helping them to gain a sense of belonging within their communities and within their schools (Beyer et al., 2003).

### Ecological Considerations for School-Family Partnerships

School-family partnerships are best implemented with consideration of important ecological features of the communities and the school system influences. As noted above, these can be related to community resources and risk or to diversity in the needs schools are expected to meet or historical, economic, and political forces that shift, constrain, and direct school priorities. While cataloguing the aspects of these and other ecological influences could easily take all of this chapter's length, the focus here is on two aspects that are perhaps most immediate for on-the-ground advancement of school-family partnerships.

*High-Risk Communities*   Schools serving high-risk communities often face unique challenges for partnership between families and schools. As noted earlier, these include strain on resources due to elevated levels of need, yet these same schools are often the least able to obtain needed resources. These high-risk communities are disproportionately influenced by problems affecting schools overall across the nation such as test driving curricula and perhaps perverting teaching and rapid change in school administration and structure due to not meeting standards.

Across ethnic groups, but with greater concentration in high-risk communities, is the diversifying of family structures, with less stability over time in family makeup (Christenson et al., 2005). Single-parent households are increasingly common and are associated with higher rates of poverty and lower monitoring of children. In addition, schools have limited ability and practices for dealing with divorced parent involvement, multi-generation families, and other non-traditional structures (Taylor, 2003). For example, it is not uncommon for parent work schedules to conflict with school involvement, which is more likely to affect single and divorced parents (Eccles & Harold, 1993). Formulating school activities to consider these needs is often viewed as a special accommodation, rather than a need affecting many if not the majority of families (Christenson et al., 2005; Cowan et al., 2004).

These communities may also be burdened with preconceptions that are misperceptions of parental interest in involvement in school (Miedel & Reynolds, 1999). There can be a tendency to see parents as incapable and as an integral part of the cause of the challenges of educating children rather than as a potentially valuable resource (Eccles & Harold, 1993). These assumptions may feed in or confirm feelings of racial injustice on the part of some minority families that furthers distrust in the school and confounding conflicts that may arise (Lareau & Horvat, 1999).

*Ethnic and Cultural Diversity*    One of the strongest demographic trends in today's society is the increasing diversity of the cultures and languages within schools, with many schools having many cultures and primary languages as well as a shifting makeup. In the context of high-stakes testing for performance, the unique needs of these changing school environments can be more difficult to meet. Moreover, there may be complex cultural relations that vary substantially among ethnic and cultural groups within a given school. Also, school personnel and school system administrators and boards can differ in their attitude about cultural and linguistic diversity, in some cases embracing the value of diversity and in others seeing it as a burden that impedes learning of others within the school. The increasing rate of at least one parent born in a foreign country is disproportionately affecting these schools (Christenson et al., 2005). The increase in immigration in recent years makes language and cultural barriers a particularly important consideration in collaboration and communication between families and schools. Families may have emigrated from countries in which parental involvement is not emphasized within their child's educational system. Some cultural mores adhere to the belief that parents should not question teachers, resulting in families leaving most of the educational decisions to teachers and administrators (Cowan et al., 2004; WestEd, 2007). As a result, partnership with these families may require different approaches or more extensive outreach if they are to be engaged as needed in the current academic environment. Moreover, there may be more complexity in what is culturally appropriate and likely to be effective outreach and methods for school-family partnership.

Within this context, school-family partnership is a challenging, but particularly necessary, endeavor. Most critically, it may be important to undertake extensive engagement with the community not only to promote appropriate involvement but because challenges are so great and resources are so limited in comparison (Comer & Haynes, 1991). Partnerships that connect home and school and community and school system interests may be more vital in these communities than in any others. Community-based organizations, such as local Head Start programs, homeless shelters, and faith-based organizations, are also a particularly valuable resource since they have direct contact with some of the most high-risk populations (WestEd, 2007).

*Some Examples of Ecological Approaches/Programs*    The need for community engagement as a foundation for school-family partnerships is not a new idea. However, systematic approaches and detailed recognition of the needs for close partnership between schools and families have not gained traction in application. Thus, presented here are some tested approaches that emphasize and promote these collaborative relationships and provide potential blueprints or guidelines for such efforts.

The National Network of Partnership Schools (NNPS) is an ongoing project initiated in 1996 by researchers at the Johns Hopkins University. NNPS works with schools, districts, states, and organizations to develop and maintain research-based programs involving communities and families in order to improve student success in school (Michael, Dittus, & Epstein, 2007). The partnership model developed by NNPS functions within a framework of three overlapping spheres of influence: school, family, and community. The theory posits that schools, families, and communities are most effective when they identify and pursue overlapping, or shared, missions, goals, and responsibilities for their children (Epstein & Hollifield, 2003). Teachers and administers are encouraged to create more "family-like schools," thereby fostering an educational environment that acknowledges each student's individuality, recognizing the importance of making every child feel special and included. In the same way, families involved in this partnership are encouraged to create more "school-like families," promoting a home environment that recognizes each child's responsibilities as a student, emphasizing the importance of homework, school, and skill building activities. Communities within which these families and schools interact are encouraged to create both school-like and family-like opportunities, programs, and events that acknowledge and reward students for creativity, good progress, and excellence, and help families to create better support structures for their children (Epstein, 1995).

Teachers and administrators at the elementary, middle, and high school levels work within a framework of six types of involvement operating within the three overlapping spheres of influence. According to extensive research conducted by NNPS, these six types of involvement form the foundation of successful partnerships. This framework includes parenting (helping families create a supportive home environment for children as students and helping schools better understand families), communicating (establishing effective communication between the school and home about student progress and school activities), volunteering (provision of volunteer opportunities to support schools and students), learning at home (create opportunities at home for families to be involved in homework and other school-related decisions and activities), decision making (create opportunities for families to participate in school decisions and develop parents as leaders and representatives), and collaborating with the community (partner with the community to provide resources and services for schools, families, and students) (National Network of Partnership Schools). The implementation of these six types of involvement is facilitated through the establishment of an Action Team for Partnerships within each NNPS school. These Action Teams may be newly formed or develop from an existing school council. Between 6 and 12 members participate in each action team including teachers, administrators, parents, community members, students (in high school action teams), and any others involved in interactions between the school and its families. Through the assessment of present practices, creation of opportunities for new partnerships, and implementation of specific school, family, and community involvement activities, the members of the action teams work together to improve communication and collaboration between families, schools, and communities (Network of Partnership Schools).

The NNPS program has demonstrated success in facilitating the development and strengthening of partnerships between schools and families at the elementary, middle, and high school levels. Implementation of the NNPS model in elementary and middle schools in the Baltimore City Public School system reported improved communication with parents of high-risk children, improved parental participation in school programs and activities, and increased participation by parents on homework at home, which showed positive effects on student learning and attitudes. Implementation of the NNPS model at the high school level also demonstrated the necessity and effectiveness of extending school-family partnerships beyond the elementary and middle school years.

Successful components of this model included goal-setting discussions between students and parents about their goals for attendance, achievement, and self-confidence, interactive homework assignments across various subject areas, and the development of "survival packets" for parents and students comprised of important meeting dates, school policies, and school telephone numbers. Studies conducted in six Baltimore City high schools showed beneficial effects on students' goal-setting abilities, morale, and attendance, along with creating stronger linkages with community services (Epstein & Hollifield, 2003).

Despite the success of the NNPS partnership model in improving collaboration between schools, families, and communities, some families have difficulty meeting those expectations that schools consider to be basic (Minke & Anderson, 2005). Although the model emphasizes the need to target each of the six types of involvement in a variety of ways, parents who have little control over their schedules or limited knowledge of particular school subjects find it challenging to become involved in their child's education to the extent that the model demands. Rather than expecting families to participate equally at all levels of involvement, critics of this model have suggested that school-family partnership be conceptualized along a continuum in which fewer families would be involved as requirements for time and expertise increase (Minke & Anderson, 2005). For example, almost all families and educators would communicate actively and frequently regarding their children's social-emotional development and academic progress. A smaller, but still large, number of families and educators would be involved in support activities at school and at home. Some would participate actively in teaching or learning activities such as workshops. Finally, relatively few educators and families would be involved in the decision-making activities at the district or school level. Through this nuanced version of the partnership model, families and educators would be offered various means for participation, and all would be welcome and encouraged to participate at each level (Minke & Anderson, 2005).

Principles guiding the development and maintenance of school-family partnerships are increasingly applied to a wide range of issues related to a child's social and academic well-being. For example, programs focused on collaboration between schools and families have been shown to improve adolescent self-regulation and reduce behavior problems (Minke & Anderson, 2005), ease the transition to school (Minke & Anderson, 2005; Pianta et al., 2001), and improve school safety (Minke & Anderson, 2005; Smith et al., 2004). The School Development Program (SDP), initiated at Yale University, is one of the strongest examples of the benefits of collaborative principles in bringing about positive social change, and the potential for these principles to vary along a continuum of differing levels of parental involvement (Comer & Haynes, 1991; Minke & Anderson, 2005). The SDP provides both a structure and a process to promote the participation of adults in supporting student learning and development (Comer School Development Program, n.d.).

The basic framework of the SDP is comprised of three structures. The School Planning and Management Team is the main governing mechanism, charged with developing a comprehensive school plan that focuses on both the academic program and the school climate, setting and monitoring this plan as needed, and coordinating staff development and other school activities based on this plan. This team is representative of important stakeholders in the school, including teachers, administrators, support staff, and parents. The second structure is the Student and Staff Support Team, which is meant to create a positive social environment and relationships between parents and school staff, students and staff, and among staff themselves. Through the alliance of student services, sharing of advice and information, and accessing of resources outside the school, this team focuses on addressing the behavioral and developmental needs of students (Comer School Development Program, n.d.). The school principal and staff members, such as social workers, psychologists, and counselors, serve on this team, contributing their knowledge and expertise around issues related to mental health and child development (Comer & Haynes, 1991). The final structure is the Parent Program, which provides opportunities for parents to actively support the school's social and academic programs by focusing on healthy development in both areas. This team is composed entirely of parents and sends representatives to serve on the School Planning and Management Team (Comer School Development Program, n.d.).

The work of the SDP structures is guided by three program guidelines. These guiding principles include "no-fault," which establishes the program's focus on solving problems rather than placing blame, consensus decision making, which promotes communication toward decisions best for child development, and collaboration, which encourages all participants to work respectfully and cooperatively toward common goals (Comer & Haynes, 1991). The SDP focuses on building relationships at all levels of the system (e.g., teacher to parent, student to teacher) and empowering both families and teachers throughout the process (Minke & Anderson, 2005).

The SDP has demonstrated success in affecting positive change on both social and academic outcomes. In high-risk schools, specifically, the program has shown beneficial effects on school climate and student achievement (Minke & Anderson, 2005). One of the key strengths of the SDP is its focus on parental involvement at three different levels, recognizing the differing goals of parents in participating in their child's education, along with the unique challenges they face. The first and most critical level of involvement includes those parents who are selected as representatives on the School Planning and Management Team. Parents involved at this level wish to participate actively in their child's school, serving as a key link between the school and the community and helping to carry out the comprehensive school plan (Comer & Haynes, 1991). The second level of involvement involves participating in day-to-day school and classroom activities and parent organizations. Parents involved at this level are more interested in volunteering in their child's school and participating in school programs. The third level of involvement, or general participation, includes activities such as student performances and positive communication with parents regarding their child's progress. Parents involved at this level are often primarily interested in participating in activities that involve their children. Through its recognition of the broad range of families' interests and capacities to collaborate with schools, the SDP can be effectively applied to a variety of different issues and settings.

One example of an effective program targeted towards high-risk communities is the Families and Schools Together (FAST) intervention, which targets children 5 to 14 years old at risk for school dropout, substance abuse, and violence and delinquency (McDonald & Sayger, 1998). The FAST program focuses on reducing aggression and anxiety while increasing attention spans and social skills through a family-based approach, strengthening protective factors at several levels of the child's ecology (McDonald & Sayger, 1998; SAMHSA Model Programs). Parents are identified as the primary prevention and protective agents for their children. The first component of the FAST program involves parent outreach by a collaborative team of school personnel, trained professionals, and parents. Parent outreach may involve a universal recruitment strategy or a more selected approach, initiated in every instance by a home visit to begin fostering the school-parent relationship. Families attend multifamily groups focused on strengthening parent-child interactions, developing family management and community skills, and building one's social network through interactive activities with other families. Following the 8-week program, multifamily meetings are held every month in order to help maintain social networks and develop or identify common goals (SAMHSA Model Programs, n.d.).

The FAST program has been implemented across many different settings and among many different populations and includes five different developmentally focused programs (i.e., Baby FAST, Pre-K FAST, Kids FAST, Middle School FAST, and Teen FAST). Evaluation studies of the FAST program have demonstrated significant decreases in behavior problems (i.e., stealing, hitting, bullying, lying), withdrawal and anxiety (i.e., social isolation, insecurity), and attention span problems (i.e., distraction, lack of focus), and increases in reading scores (McDonald & Frey, 1999). Longitudinal studies have also demonstrated sustained improvements in child functioning, family cohesiveness, and parental involvement in the school and in the community (McDonald & Frey, 1999). This suggests that a particular focus on the developmental stages of a child's life, along with active outreach to parents and post-program maintenance of skills, may help to bring about the positive outcomes for the child and the family.

Involving Minority Parents of At-risk Children (IMPAC) was a program designed for the expressed purpose of fostering partnership between the school and parents in a high-risk community in Durham County, North Carolina. The program was implemented in Carrington Middle School which served one of the county's largest public housing projects. Ninety-nine percent of the residents were African American, and 75% percent of parents of school-aged children dropped out of either eighth or ninth grade. IMPAC is comprised of a parent involvement component which includes a series of school-parent meetings within the community and at the school focused on helping parents become more comfortable and knowledgeable about their child's education. In response to the specific needs of the community, transportation is provided to and from the meetings and childcare is provided when necessary. The second component of the program is the availability of a learning resource center, which offers tutoring by college students as a supplement to regular class time. To reduce absenteeism among the student population, an incentive program is implemented to reward students for perfect or improved school attendance, improved grades, or placement on the honor roll. A parent- and student-directed monthly newsletter is also created with students serving as reporters, editors, and writers. Although not evaluated as an experimental trial, during the year that IMPAC was implemented, the number of parents who participated in school activities increased dramatically. Students also showed a 13% increase in standardized test scores compared to the year before and a 20% decrease in absenteeism from school (McDaniel & Mack, 1992). IMPAC, specifically created to address the interests of Durham County, suggests the benefits of tailoring interventions to the unique needs of high-risk communities.

There are very few examples of school-family partnership programs for immigrant parents. One rare example is the Alum Rock Even Start Program, implemented in San Jose, California, to provide immigrant Latino families with the tools and strategies to support their children's education. To address the unique cultural and language needs of this population, staff from Even Start who share a common background with the families work with the children and parents in their homes and teachers at school to demonstrate activities meant to increase a child's school success. In this way, teachers gain a better understanding of their students' families and families gain a better understanding of their children's experiences at school. Mothers who participate in the program are also offered English classes at their children's school and are provided with information meant to ease their transition to U.S. society. This includes information on the public transportation system and medical services. Even Start staff reported that parents who participated in the program increased their participation in PTA activities and attendance at parent-teacher conferences. In addition, many parents volunteered in their child's classrooms and some even worked for the school system following completion of the program (Adger & Locke, 2000).

## MOVING FORWARD

There are many opportunities for school-family partnership promotion and the importance of developmentally and ecologically-based approaches, including examples, have been identified. While much of the action in moving forward is probably at the front-line level of local programming and direction of efforts, there are also many opportunities for policy level improvement in support of this partnership. For example, the Collaborative for Academic, Social, and Emotional Learning (CASEL, n.d.) has worked to create standards for promoting social competence and emotional understanding, with heavy emphasis on school-family partnerships in that endeavor (CASEL, n.d.; Patrikakou et al., 2003). Recently, CASEL has succeeded in establishing social-emotional learning as part of the standards for adequate school progress in Illinois, directly leading to each school now being required to indicate how this need will be met. While the standards do not require parental involvement, the guidebook prepared to help with meeting these needs and the actions of many schools have been to increase parental engagement in planning and implementing actions to meet these standards (Patrikakou et al., 2003; Tolan & Dodge, 2005). The growing expectation that schools serve educational and social-developmental needs in an increasingly complex society is an opportunity to help families to be fully engaged in community schools. This can mean gaining additional resources through parental involvement and clearer formulation of expectations and relative roles as well as better attuning of the school to the local community needs. There may be pressing needs that lead to clear joint enterprises between families and schools that can establish a tone of open communication and continuity between the home and the school life and shift toward an assumption of shared decision making and responsibility (Hoover-Dempsey et al., 2003).

Various federal educational initiatives have been funded that ostensibly bring more parental involvement into education. The most far-reaching and powerful in impact of these has been the No Child Left Behind Act of 2001 (NCLB), which serves as an amendment to the Title I program. NCLB defines parental involvement as "regular, two-way, and meaningful communication" meant to ensure that parents play an "integral role" in their child's education, emphasizing parental choice even in public schools (Moles, 2003). In practice, however, the impact of NCLB has been to create requirements that overwhelm many schools' educational capabilities and may counteract parent-school partnership by playing up a presumed conflict about primacy of decision making in the guise of educational choice. Evidence to date is that parents and teacher participation has not been along the lines envisioned and ancillary effects such as undesirable and perhaps unethical efforts to boost test scores recorded for a given school have occurred (Moles, 2003). As these unintended effects are more evident, there are efforts being undertaken to shift focus from test scores to school-community engagement that increases investment in making that school work with and for families in that community, as well as a more sophisticated understanding of markers of a good education. To the extent that policy and financial support for parent involvement and educator-family relationships as integral to a good education are fostered, revisions to this and other federal policy could reverse the problems to date to promote not just stronger accounting but stronger education and greater student competence.

However, NCLB does provide one needed characteristic, which is more emphasis on evaluation of effects of educational practices and approaches. With the development of the Institute for Educational Sciences, which supports randomized trials and other strong methodological tests of basic educational theories and approaches, commonly used but untested programs, and promising innovations, there is also now an important change toward empirically driven practices. Regular evaluation and sound evaluation as the most reliable guides for good practice and improvement of performance are well-established (Sheldon & Van Voorhis, 2004). Thus, funding is increasingly and appropriately directed toward programs that are based in the best scientific knowledge of education, management, child development, and social welfare. However, this general thrust is only now including school-family partnerships as an essential (rather than laudable) component of such efforts. Increasing attention to funding formulations that rest on use of programs with research efforts and ongoing application (whether to test innovations or to evaluate impact in a given setting of programs with prior evidence) are likely to provide a substantial boost in the extent of reliance on such programs, the appreciation of and use of sound evaluation for management decisions, and the prominence of school-family partnerships in education of children (see http://www. promisingpractices.net/ for examples of evidenced-based programs).

Of course, as is illustrated here, there is much that is not yet known about the best methods for school-family partnerships, the system and setting characteristics that are most pertinent for developing, implementing, and sustaining these, and the key supports that are needed to manage various forms of partnerships for optimal benefit. Of particular priority seem to be studies of systems of partnerships to help address general, high-risk, and indicated level problems, partnerships for use within high-risk neighborhoods and with minority and immigrant families, and methods to aid parental involvement appropriately at each stage of education. Guidelines and implementation support and sustaining systems also need to be developed and made available. As is true for children's mental health in general, there is great value in looking toward university expertise, community providers and organizations, and government funding and standards as an interdependent system to push toward empirically based practice, ongoing incorporation of innovation, and pursuit of practical and useful research that can quickly and directly feed back for improving practice (Tolan & Dodge, 2005). While school-family partnerships occur within exceptionally complex ecologies of shifting forces, they have a vitality and ability to organize ongoing as well as shifting influences to maximize educational effectiveness and well-being.

## REFERENCES

Adger, C. T. & Locke, J. (2000). Broadening the base: School/Community partnerships serving language minority students at risk. *Center for Research on Education, Diversity & Excellence. Educational Practice Reports.* Paper epr06. Retrieved May 22m 2009, from http://repositories.cdlib.org/crede/edupractrpts/epr06

Baker, L., Allen, J., Shockley, B., Pellegrini, A. D., Galda, L., Stahl, S. (1995). Connecting school and home: Constructing partnerships to foster reading development. In L. Baker, P. Afflerbach, & D. Reinking (Eds.), *Developing Engaged Readers in School and Home Communities* (pp. 21–41). Mahwah, NJ: Erlbaum.

Barrish, H. H., Saunders, M., & Wolfe, M. D. (1969). Good Behavior Game: Effects of individual contingencies for group consequences and disruptive behavior in a classroom. *Journal of Applied Behavior Analysis, 2,* 119–124.

Beyer, R. D., Patrikakou, E. N., & Weissberg, R. P. (2003). School-family partnerships for adolescents. *The LSS Review, 2*(1), 12–13.

Bronfenbrenner, U. (1992). Ecological systems theory. In R. Vasta (Ed.), *Annals of child development. Six theories of child development: Revised formulations and current issues* (pp. 187–249). London: Jessica Kingsley.

Campbell, F. A., Ramey, C. T., Pungello, E., Sparling, J., & Miller-Johnson, S. (2002). Early childhood education: Young adult outcomes from the Abecedarian Project. *Applied Developmental Science, 6,* 42–57.

Christenson, S. L. (2003). The family-school partnership: An opportunity to promote the learning competence of all students. *School Psychology Quarterly 18*(4), 454–482.

Christenson, S. L., Godber, Y., & Anderson, A. R. (2005). Critical issues facing families and educators. In E. Patrikakaou, R. Weissberg, S. Redding, & H. J. Wahlberg (Eds.), *School-family partnerships for children's learning* (pp. 21–39). New York: Teachers College Press.

Clark, D. C. & Clark, S. N. (1996). Building collaborative environments for successful middle level school restructuring. *NASSP Bulletin, 80, No. 578*, 1–16.

Collaborative for Academic, Social, and Emotional Learning. (n.d.). http://www.casel.org/

Comer, J. P., & Haynes, N. M., (1991). Parent involvement in schools: An ecological approach. *The Elementary School Journal, 91*(3), 271–277.

Comer School Development Program. (n.d.). Overview of the School Development Program. http://www.med.yale.edu/comer/about/overview.html

Conduct Disorders Prevention Research Group (1999). Initial impact of the Fast Track prevention trial for conduct problems: II. Classroom effects. *Journal of Consulting and Clinical Psychology, 67,* 648–657.

Cook, T. D., Habib, F., Phillips, M., Settersten, R. A., Shagle, S. C., & Degirmencioglu, S. M. (1999). Comer's School Development Program in Prince George's County, Maryland: A theory-based evaluation. *American Educational Research Journal, 36,* 543–597.

Coote, S. (2000). Families and Schools Together (FAST). Paper presented at the Conference Reducing Criminality: Partnerships and Best Practice. Perth, Australia.

Cowan, R. J., Napolitano, S. M. S., & Sheridan, S. M. (2004). Home-school collaboration. In *Encyclopedia of Applied Psychology* (Vol. 2, pp. 201–208). Oxford, UK: Elsevier/Academic Press.

Davis-Kean, P. E., & Eccles, J. S. (2003). Influences and barriers to better parent-school collaborations. *The LSS Review, 2*(1), 4–5.

Dishion, T. J., & Connell, A. M. (2008). An ecological approach to family intervention to prevent adolescent drug use: Linking parent engagement to long-term reductions of tobacco, alcohol and marijuana use. In N.

Heinrichs, K. Hahlweg, & M. Doepfner (Eds.), *Strengthening families: Evidence-based approaches to support child mental health* (pp. 403–433). Münster: Verlag für Psychotherapie.

Dishion, T. J., & Kavanagh, K. (2000). A multilevel approach to family-centered prevention in schools: Process and outcome. *Addictive Behaviors, 25*(6), 899–911.

Dishion, T., & Stormshak, E. (2006). *Intervening in children's lives: An ecological, family-centered approach to mental health care.* Washington, DC: American Psychological Association.

Dolan, L. J., Kellam, S. G., Brown, C. H., Werthamer-Larsson, L., Rebok, G. W., Mayer, L. S., et al. (1993). The short-term impact of two classroom-based preventive interventions on aggressive and shy behaviors and poor achievement. *Journal of Applied Developmental Psychology, 14,* 317–345.

Eccles, J. S., & Harold, R. D. (1993). Parent-school involvement during the early adolescent years. *Teachers College Record, 94*(3), 568–586.

Eccles J., Midgley, C., & Adler, T. F. (1984). Grade-related changes in school environment: Effects on achievement motivation. In J. G. Nicholls (Ed.), *Advances in motivation and achievement, 3* (pp. 283–331). Greenwich, CT: JAI Press.

Eddy, J. M., & Reid, J. B., & Fetrow, R. A. (2000). An elementary school-based prevention program targeting modifiable antecedents of youth delinquency and violence: Linking the Interests of Families and Teachers (LIFT). *Journal of Emotional and Behavioral Disorders, 8*(3), 165–176.

Elias, M. J., Patrikakou, E. N., & Weissberg, R. P. (2007). A competence-based framework for parent school community partnerships in secondary schools. *School Psychology International, 28,* 540–554.

Epstein, J. L. (1986). Parents' reactions to teacher practices of parent involvement. *The Elementary School Journal, 86*(3), 277–294.

Epstein, J. L. (1995). School/family/community partnerships: Caring for the children we share. *Phi Delta Kappan, 76*(9), 701–712.

Epstein, J. L., & Dauber, S. L. (1991). School programs and teacher practices of parent involvement in inner-city elementary and middle schools. *The Elementary School Journal, 91*(3), 289–305.

Epstein, J. L., & Hollifield, J. H. (2003). Title I and school-family-community partnerships: Using research to realize the potential. *Journal of Education for Students Placed At Risk, 1*(3), 263–278.

Fantuzzo, J., McWayne, C., & Perry, M. A. (2004). Multiple dimensions of family involvement and their relations to behavioral and learning competencies for urban, low-income children. *School Psychology Review, 33*(4), 467–480.

Felner, R. D., Brand, S. Adan, A. M., Mulhall, P. F., Flowers, N., Sartain, B., et al.. (1993). Restructuring the ecology of the school as an approach to prevention during school transitions: Longitudinal follow-ups and extensions of the School Transitional Environment Project. *Prevention in Human Services, 10,* 103–36.

Foster, E. M., Prinz, R. J., Sanders, M. R., & Shapiro, C. J. (2008). The costs of a public health infrastructure for delivering parenting and family support. *Children and Youth Services Review, 30,* 493–501.

Garces, E., Thomas, D, & Currie, J. (2002). Longer-term effects of Head Start. *The American Economic Review, 92*(4), 999–1012.

Gorman-Smith, D., Tolan, P. H., Henry, D., Quintana, E., Lutovsky, K., & Leventhal, A. (2007). The SAFEChildren prevention program. In P. Tolan, J. Szapocznik, & S. Sombrano (Eds.), *Developmental approaches to prevention of substance abuse and related problems* (pp. 113–136). Washington DC: American Psychological Association.

Greenberg, M. T., Weissberg, R. P., O'Brien, M. U., Zins, J. E., Fredericks, L., Resnik, H., et al. (2003). Enhancing school-based prevention and youth development through coordinated social, emotional, and academic learning. *American Psychologist, 58*(6/7), 466–474.

Henry, D. B., Miller-Johnson, S, Simon, T. R., Schoeny, M. E. & The Multi-site Violence Prevention Project. (2006).Validity of teacher ratings in selecting influential aggressive adolescents for a targeted preventive intervention. *Prevention Science, 7,* 31–41.

Hill, N. E., & Taylor, L. C. (2004). Parental school involvement and children's academic achievement: Pragmatics and issues. *Current Directions in Psychological Science, 13,* 161–164.

Hoover-Dempsey, K. V., Walker J. M. T., & Sandler, H. M. (2003). What motivates parents to become involved in their children's education. *The LSS Review, 2*(1), 6–7.

Lareau, A. (1987). Social class differences in family-school relationships: The importance of cultural capital. *Sociology of Education 60*(2), 73–85.

Lareau, A., & Horvat, E. M. (1999). Moments of social inclusion and exclusion: Race, class, and cultural capital in family-school relationships. *Sociology of Education, 72*(1), 37–53.

Mangione, P. L., & Speth, T. (1998). The transition to elementary school: A framework for creating early childhood continuity through home, school, and community partnerships. *The Elementary School Journal, 98*(4), 381–397.

McDaniel, E., & Mack, V. H. (1992). *Involving minority parents of at-risk children. A parent/school partnership.* Durham, NC: Durham County Schools.

McDonald, L., & Frey, H. E. (1999). Families and school together: Building relationships. *Juvenile Justice Bulletin,* 1–19. U. S. Department of Justice. Washington, DC: U.S. Government Printing Office.

McDonald, L., & Sayger, T. V. (1998). Impact of a family and school based prevention program on protective factors for high risk youth. In J. Valentine, J. A. De Jong, & N. J. Kennedy (Eds.), *Substance abuse prevention in multicultural communities* (pp. 61–85). Haworth Press.

McGuire, D., Manghi, E., & Tolan, P. H. (1989). The family-school system: The critical focus for structural-strategic therapy with school behavior problems. *Journal of Psychotherapy and the Family, 6,* 107–127.

Michael, S., Dittus, P., & Epstein, J. (2007). Family and community involvement in schools: Results from the School Health Policies and Programs Study 2006. *Journal of School Health, 77*(8), 567–579.

Miedel, W. T., & Reynolds, A. J. (1999). Parent involvement in early intervention for disadvantaged children: Does it matter? *Journal of School Psychology, 37*(4), 379–402.

Minke, K. M., & Anderson, K. J. (2005). Family-school collaboration and positive behavior support. *Journal of Positive Behavior Interventions, 7*(3), 181–185.

Mizelle, N. B., & Irvin, J. L. (2000). Transition from middle school into high school. *Middle School Journal, 31*(5), 57–61.

Moles, O. (2003) School-family relations and learning: Federal education initiatives. *The LSS Review, 2*(1), 20–21.

National Network of Partnership Schools. Action Team for Partnerships. (n.d.). Available at http://www.csos.jhu.edu/P2000/nnps_model/school/atp.htm

Patrikakou, E. N., & Weissberg, R. P. (2000). Parents' perceptions of teacher outreach and parent involvement in children's education. *Journal of Prevention & Intervention in the Community, 20*(1–2), 103–119.

Patrikakou, E. N., Weissberg, R. P., Manning, J. B., Redding, S., & Walberg, H. J. (2003). School-family partnerships: Promoting the social, emotional, and academic growth of children. *The LSS Review, 2*(1), 1–3.

Pianta, R. C., Kraft-Sayre, M., Rimm-Kaufman, S., Gercke, N., & Higgins, T. (2001). Collaboration in building partnerships between families and schools: The National Center for Early Development and Learning's Kindergarten Transition Intervention. *Early Childhood Research Quarterly, 16,* 117–132.

Reid, J. B., Eddy, J. M., Fetrow, R. A., & Stoolmiller, M. (1999). Description and immediate impacts of a preventive intervention for conduct problems. *American Journal of Community Psychology, 27*(4), 483–517.

Reynolds, A. J., & Clements, M. (2003). Parental involvement and children's school success. *The LSS Review, 2*(1), 10–11.

Reynolds, A. J., Ou, S., & Topitzes, J. W. (2004). Paths of effects of early childhood intervention on educational attainment and juvenile arrest. A confirmatory analysis of the Chicago Child-Parent Centers. *Child Development, 75,* 1299–1328.

Reynolds, A. J., & Temple, J. A. (in press). Economic returns of investments in preschool. In E. Zigler, W. Gilliam, & S. Jones (Eds.), *A vision for universal prekindergarten.* New York: Cambridge University Press.

Reynolds, A. J., Temple, J. A., Robertson, D. L., & Mann, E. A. (2001). Long-term effects of an early childhood intervention on educational achievement and juvenile arrest: A 15-year follow-up of low-income children in public schools. *Journal of the American Medical Association, 285,* 2339–2346.

Rutter, M. (1987). Psychosocial resilience and protective mechanisms. *American Journal of Orthopsychiatry, 57,* 316–331.

SAMHSA Model Programs. (n.d.). Families and Schools Together (FAST). Available at http://www.modelprograms.samhsa.gov

Sheldon, S. B., & Van Voorhis, F. L. (2004). Partnership programs in U. S. schools: Their development and relationship to family involvement outcomes. *School Effectiveness and School Improvement, 15*(2), 125–148.

Simon, B. S. (2001). Family involvement in high school: Predictors and effects. *NASSP Bulletin, 85*(627), 8–19.

Simon, B. S. (2004). High school outreach and family involvement. *Social Psychology of Education, 7,* 185–209.

Smith, E. P., Gorman-Smith, D., Quinn, W., Rabiner, D., Tolan, P., Winn, D-M., & The Multi-Site Violence Prevention Project. (2004). Community-based multiple family groups to prevent and reduce violent and aggressive behavior. The GREAT Families Program. *American Journal of Preventive Medicine, 26,* 39–47.

Taylor, R. D. (2003). Economic and social correlates of the social-emotional adjustment of African American adolescents. *The LSS Review, 2*(1), 16–17.

Tolan, P. H., & Dodge, K. A. (2005). Children's mental health as a primary care and concern: A system for comprehensive support and service. *American Psychologist, 60,* 601–614.

Tolan, P. H., Gorman-Smith, D., & Henry, D. (2004). Supporting families in a high-risk setting: Proximal effects of the SAFEChildren prevention program. *Journal of Consulting and Clinical Psychology, 72,* 855–869.

Tolan, P. H., & Grant, K. (in press). How social and cultural context shapes the development of coping: Youth in the inner-city as an example. In E. Skinner & M. Zimmer-Gembeck (Eds.), *Coping and the Development of Regulation.* New Directions in Child Development (R. Larson, Series Ed.). New York: Josey-Bass.

Tolan, P. H., Sherrod, L., Gorman-Smith, D., & Henry, D. (2003). Building protection, support, and opportunity for inner youth and their families. In K. Maton, C. Schellenbach, B. Leadbeater, & A Solarz (Eds.), *Investing in children, youth, families, and communities: Strengths-based research and policy* (pp. 193–211). Washington, DC: American Psychological Association.

Tolan, P. H., Szapocznik, J., & Sambrano, S. (2007). Opportunities for development prevention of substance abuse. In P. Tolan, J. Szapocznik, & S. Sombrano (Eds.), *Preventing youth substance abuse: Science-based programs for children and adolescents* (pp. 241–252). Washington, DC: American Psychological Association.

U.S. Department of Education & U. S. Department of Health and Human Services. (1995). *Continuity in early childhood: A framework for home, school, and community linkages.* Washington, DC: U.S. Government Printing Office.

Weist, M. D. (2003). Challenges and opportunities in moving toward a public health approach in school mental health. *Journal of School Psychology, 41,* 77–82.

WestEd. (2007). *Engaging parents in education: Lesson from five parental information and resource centers.* U. S. Department of Education. Washington, DC: U.S. Government Printing Office.

# EPILOGUE

In the months following the submission of the *Handbook of School-Family Partnerships* to the publisher, we had an opportunity to reflect on the contents. First, it is clear that the 21 chapters speak to one common imperative: there is an inextricable link between home and school for enhancing optimal child competence. In doing so, the chapters illustrated that the school-family partnership improves varied child outcomes across developmental periods and is characterized by shared, mutual goals for child competence. Inherent in the chapters is the concise message that the process for creating the partnership—what we referred to as an engagement process in the prologue—is as critical as achieving improved child outcomes.

At the time of the writing of this *Handbook*, family and school are still two systems that are used to operating autonomously rather than recognizing their reciprocal interaction and impact on student outcomes. Additionally, the role of students themselves across development is often ill-defined or unclear. One could argue that students are a missing piece of the puzzle in family-school interactions and partnerships. A systems orientation demands that *engaged partnerships* include students; such conceptualizations are often visualized as the essential three-legged stool for improving educational performance and youth development.

Also at this time, initiatives in education and psychology, such as the evidence-based intervention movement, Response to Intervention reforms, and the desire to increase family involvement and promote family-school partnerships, are viewed as disparate movements or add-ons to practice, rather than as an integrated, cohesive reform. We surmise that a concerted effort to integrate these three movements offers promise to "raise the bar" for academic, social, behavioral, and emotional learning outcomes of students across preschool to high school. In reporting child outcome data, we can no longer fail to consider the effect of multiple contextual influences. Similarly, as interventions are designed and implemented, to advance our knowledge base of child competence there must be no debate that the school-family relationship be viewed and measured as a "separate phenomena from the perceptions and behavior of involved individuals" (see Beretvas, Keith, and Carlson, this volume).

Bronfenbrener (1992), in his infinite wisdom about children's learning and development, repeatedly described that the mesosystem—illustrated by the school-family relationship—was a separate and critical variable that differentiated child outcomes. To address educational disparities for children and enhance child competence for *all* children, policy makers, researchers, and practitioners must account for and intervene at the level of the mesosystem. It is our belief that this change is essential to ensure a bright future for education, and our students, in the United States.

We hope that this *Handbook* contributes to and facilitates the impetus for engaged partnerships among educators and families to improve student outcomes. Our vision is that 10 years from now, it will no longer be necessary to argue the importance of school-family partnerships or assessments and interventions that account for context, and within this timeframe, we will have compiled a much richer, more detailed research literature detailing effective partnership processes, practices, and interventions.

**S.L.C.**
**A.L.R.**

## REFERENCE

Bronfenbrenner, U. (1992). Ecological systems theory. In R. Vasta (Ed.), *Annals of child development. Six theories of child development: Revised formulations and current issues* (pp. 187–249). London: Jessica Kingsley.

# CONTRIBUTORS

**Michelle I. Albright** is a consultant for The Consultation Center at the Yale University School of Medicine, and the School of the 21st Century at the Zigler Center in Child Development and Social Policy at Yale University. Dr. Albright's areas of interest and expertise include school-based prevention and intervention programs for urban children and families, with a particular emphasis on school-family relationships, educator preparation and professional development, and evaluation. A primary focus of her work has been to facilitate the exchange of resources among educators, clinicians, and researchers, and enhance the capacity of schools to utilize evaluation data to inform program development and implementation.

**S. Natasha Beretvas** is an associate professor and Chair of the Quantitative Methods program in the Educational Psychology Department at The University of Texas at Austin. Her research interests entail evaluation and application of statistical and psychometric modeling techniques with a focus on multilevel modeling and meta-analysis.

**Gary E. Bingham** is Assistant Professor of Early Childhood Education at Georgia State University. His research examines contextual factors that impact children's learning and development in early childhood. Specifically, he is interested in parents' and teachers' beliefs and practices that affect children's development of language, social, and early literacy skills. Dr. Bingham received his bachelor of science degree and master's of science degree in Family and Human Development from Utah State University and his doctoral degree in Child Development and Family Studies from Purdue University.

**Cindy Carlson**, PhD, is Professor of Educational Psychology and Chair of the School Psychology Program at The University of Texas at Austin. Her teaching and scholarship focus on reciprocal family-school processes and evidence-based family-school intervention.

**Sandra L. Christenson**, PhD, is the Birkmaier Professor of Educational Leadership, a Professor of Educational and Child Psychology, and a faculty member in the School

Psychology Program at the University of Minnesota. Her research interests include interventions that enhance student engagement at school and with learning, identification of contextual factors that facilitate student engagement and increase the probability for student success in school, and the development of family-school relationships to enhance students' academic, social, and emotional learning.

**Brandy L. Clarke**, PhD, is a post-doctoral fellow in the Nebraska Center for Research on Children, Youth, Families and Schools at the University of Nebraska-Lincoln. Research interests include home-school partnerships, parent-child interactions, early intervention, and early childhood education and development.

**Lora Cohen-Vogel**, PhD, is an associate professor of educational policy at Florida State University. Her teaching and research focus on the political antecedents of education policy and the governance structures that influence policy adoption, implementation, and effectiveness.

**Eric Dearing** is Assistant Professor of Applied Developmental Psychology in the Lynch School of Education at Boston College. His research is centered on the study of child development within contexts of family, school, and community poverty. As part of this work, he studies the role that family educational involvement may play in mitigating the developmental consequences of poverty

**Thomas Dishion**, PhD, is a professor in both Clinical Psychology and School Psychology at the University of Oregon. He is the director of the Child and Family Center at the University of Oregon. His research interests include prevention of substance use, family-centered intervention models, and peer relationships.

**Jason T. Downer**, PhD, is a senior research scientist in the Center for Advanced Study of Teaching and Learning at the University of Virginia. His program of research focuses on the application of a developmental, ecological model to the advancement of social, emotional and academic competencies in young children from economically disadvantaged families. Dr. Downer's primary interests lie in the identification of classroom and family processes that serve as resources to children as they develop the self-regulatory abilities and basic academic skills necessary to adjust and succeed in increasingly structured and demanding classroom environments.

**Carl J. Dunst**, PhD (Developmental Psychology, George Peabody College), is a Research Scientist, Orelena Hawks Puckett Institute, Asheville, NC. His research interests include capacity-building helpgiving practices, strengths-based practices, and the influences of both types of practices on parenting competence, confidence, and enjoyment. He is currently conducting meta-analyses of the relationships between helpgiving practices and parenting behavior.

**Corrina Falkenstein**, MS, is a doctoral student in Counseling Psychology at the University of Oregon and an NIMH fellowship trainee at the Child and Family Center. Her research interests include prevention and intervention with adolescents, parent-child relationships, and teacher relationships.

**Marika Ginsburg-Block**, PhD, is Program Coordinator and Assistant Professor of School Psychology at the University of Delaware. Her research focuses primarily on investigating school-based, peer and parent mediated intervention programs for vulnerable urban youth, while also seeking to better understand the numerous mechanisms that lead to student achievement.

**Nancy E. Hill**, PhD, is Associate Professor in the Department of Psychology and Neurosciences at Duke University and Visiting Associate Professor at Harvard University, Graduate School of Education. Professor Hill's research focuses on how cultural, economic and community contexts influence family dynamics and family socialization patterns and in turn and shape children's developmental outcomes. In addition to family dynamics within the home, Professor Hill's research examines the role of interactions between families and schools for promoting academic and social development and how they are shaped by cultural and economic factors. Her most recent work identifies culturally inclusive, developmentally-appropriate strategies for family involvement in education for adolescents in middle and high school.

**Soo Hong**, EdD, is Assistant Professor in the Department of Education at Wellesley College. Her research examines the role of community organizing and community-based organizations in building and strengthening parent engagement in urban schools.

**Kathleen V. Hoover-Dempsey**, PhD, is Associate Professor of Psychology and Human Development at Peabody College, Vanderbilt University. Her model of the parental involvement process, developed with colleagues and her students, examines why parents become involved in their children's education, and how their involvement, once engaged, influences students' personal resources for learning and achievement. She and her colleagues have also developed and evaluated school-based interventions designed to increase the effectiveness of school invitations to involvement.

**Christa L. Ice**, PhD, is a Research Instructor with the Department of Pediatrics at West Virginia University, Health Sciences Center. She is currently assisting the Coronary Artery Risk Detection in Appalachian Communities Project with methodological issues and statistical analyses while maintaining an interest in the effects of parental involvement on many facets of children's development.

**Ann P. Kaiser**, PhD, is the Susan W. Gray Professor of Education and Human Development at Peabody College of Vanderbilt University. She is the author of more than 125 articles on early language and behavior interventions for young children with disabilities and children growing up in poverty. Dr. Kaiser has been the Principal Investigator on research from the U.S. Department of Education, the National Institute of Mental Health, the U.S. Department of Health and Human Services, the National Institute for Child Health and Human Development and the Administration on Children Youth and

Families. She has received numerous awards for her research and mentoring including the Harvey Branscomb Distinguished Professorship at Vanderbilt University.

**Timothy Z. Keith** is Professor of Educational Psychology in the School Psychology program at The University of Texas at Austin. His research focuses on the nature and measurement of intelligence and on understanding the influences on school learning. Tim also has methodological interests in multiple regression analysis and structural equation modeling.

**Jie-Eun Lee** is a second-year doctoral student in Educational Leadership and Policy in the Department of Leadership, Policy, and Organizations at Vanderbilt University. Her research interests focus on refugee student engagement in U.S. schools, the social context of education, and education policy in developing countries.

**Heather Libbey**, PhD, is a post-doctoral fellow at the Emily Program, an Eating Disorders Clinic in St. Paul, Minnesota. In addition to her clinical practice in eating disorders, Heather's research interests include a range of adolescent risk and protective factors as well as health issues; including school connectedness, depression, anxiety, eating disorders, and childhood obesity.

**Brenda J. Lohman**, PhD, is an Assistant Professor of Human Development and Family Studies and a Research Associate at the Institute for Social and Behavioral Research at Iowa State University. Her research interests focus on the successful academic, physical, psychosocial, and sexual adjustment of adolescents, especially economically disadvantaged minority adolescents. She directs her work so that it can inform prevention and intervention strategies, as well as local and national policies, that enhance the positive development of youth.

**Patricia H. Manz**, PhD, Assistant Professor of School Psychology at Lehigh University, has research and professional interests in the interface of family and school systems, with a particular focus on the roles of school psychologists in fostering family-school partnerships. Her research examining the measurement of families' involvement in young children's early learning as well as in interventions designed to promote family involvement in early literacy and language, concentrates on ethnic-minority and linguistically diverse children and families living in socioeconomic disadvantage.

**Karen L. Mapp**, EdD, is a Lecturer on Education and the Program Director for the Education Policy and Management Master's Concentration at the Harvard Graduate School of Education. Her research and practice expertise is in the areas of educational leadership and educational partnerships among schools, families and community members.

**Jennifer L. Matjasko**, PhD, is a Behavioral Scientist in Violence Prevention at the National Center for Injury Prevention and Control at the Centers for Disease Control and Prevention. Her research interests focus on the development of at-risk adolescents and the factors that promote their health and well-being. Her research emphasizes the use of ecological, lifecourse, and person-centered approaches in understanding the relationship between individual, family, school, and community factors and adolescent functioning in order to inform prevention and intervention efforts targeted to at-risk youth.

**Clea McNeely**, DrPH, is Assistant Professor and Deputy Director of the Center for Adolescent Health in the Department of Population, Family and Reproductive Health at Johns Hopkins University's Bloomberg School of Public Health. Her research focuses on how the social contexts of adolescents their schools, after-school programs, families and peer networks affect health.

**Christine McWayne**, PhD, is an Assistant Professor of Applied Psychology in the Steinhardt School of Culture, Education, and Human Development at New York University. Dr. McWayne's early childhood research has been focused primarily on the influence of factors, such as parenting, family involvement, and neighborhood context, on low-income children's early development of social and academic competencies.

**Sonya S. Myers**, PhD, is a research scientist in the Center for Advanced Study of Teaching and Learning at the University of Virginia. Her program of research focuses on utilizing a developmental psychopathology approach for understanding mechanisms of development and change for children from low-income families. Dr. Myers' primary interests lie in understanding the mechanisms by which self-regulatory abilities and contextual factors (i.e., parent-child, teacher-child relationships) contribute to children's socioemotional and academic adjustment over time.

**Lynn Okagaki** is Professor Emeritas of Child Development and Family Studies at Purdue University. Her research focuses on academic achievement as influenced by culture and family values. From 2002–2005, she served as the first Deputy Director for Science in the U.S. Department of Education's Institute of Education Sciences. In December 2005, she was appointed for a six-year term as Commissioner for Education Research at the Institute of Education Sciences. Dr. Okagaki received her bachelor of science degree in applied behavioral sciences from the University of California at Davis and her doctoral degree in developmental psychology from Cornell University.

**M. Jamila Reid**, PhD, is a clinical psychologist who works at the University of Washington Parenting Clinic. Her research and clinical work centers around prevention and intervention of early-onset conduct problems. She is involved in research, delivery, training, and dissemination of the Incredible Years parent, teacher, and child interventions.

**Amy L. Reschly**, PhD, is an assistant professor in the Department of Educational Psychology & Instructional Technology at the University of Georgia. Her research interests include student engagement and dropout prevention; working with families and schools to promote student success; and, Curriculum-Based Measurement (CBM) and Problem-Solving.

**Arthur J. Reynolds** is a professor in the Institute of Child Development at the University of Minnesota. His primary research interests are child development and social policy, including the impacts of early educational interventions on lifecourse well-being. Additional interests are prevention science, evaluation research methods, and quantitative methods.

**Susan M. Sheridan**, PhD, is Willa Cather Professor and Professor of Educational Psychology, and Director of the Nebraska Center for Research on Children, Youth, Families and Schools at the University of Nebraska-Lincoln. Research interests include strengthening competencies in families and caregivers to support children's social-emotional learning and mental health. Her primary research focus is a model of service delivery known as conjoint behavioral consultation, a data-based, cross-systemic model that creates consistent, effective intervention programs for children at risk of developing psychological and learning problems.

**Rebecca J. Shlafer** is a graduate student in the Institute of Child Development at the University of Minnesota. She is interested in children's developmental outcomes in the context of early risk and adversity and in the influence of parent- and caregiver-child relationships on children's social and emotional functioning.

**Claire Smrekar**, PhD, is an associate professor of education and public policy at Vanderbilt University. Her teaching and research focus on the social context of education and the social organization of schools, with specific references to the intersection of school communities and social policy.

**Alacia Trent Stainbrook**, PhD, BCBA, is a Research Associate at Vanderbilt University. Her primary research interests are in early childhood special education, early childhood language acquisition and intervention, early childhood behavioral intervention, siblings of children with disabilities, and family-implemented interventions.

**Naomi C. Stephen**, M.Phil, is Coordinator at the Harvard Family Research Project at the Harvard Graduate School of Education. Research interests include extra-school supports for children's learning, classroom instruction, composition, and English and American literature.

**Elizabeth Stormshak**, PhD, is an associate professor in the Counseling Psychology Program at the University of Oregon and the co-director of the Child and Family Center. Her research interests include the development of effective interventions to reduce problem behavior, school-based prevention, and family-centered intervention models.

**Sandra Tang** is a PhD student in the Counseling, Developmental, and Educational Psychology department in the Lynch School of Education at Boston College. Her research focuses on the role of family, school, and culture in shaping children's academic and social-emotional development. She is particularly interested in the multiple and interactive contexts in which immigrant and minority children grow up and the implications of those factors for their development.

**Patrick H. Tolan** is Director, Institute for Juvenile Research and Professor, Department of Psychiatry and School of Public Health at the University of Illinois at Chicago. He collaborates with colleagues in the Families and Community Research Group on longitudinal risk and prevention trial studies intended to help improve outcomes for children growing up in high-risk urban communities. He is a frequent contributor to the literature on these topics and related work focused on helping bring empirical approaches to practice and policy to improve children's mental health.

**Carol M. Trivette**, PhD (Child Development and Family Relations, University of North Carolina, Greensboro) is a Research Scientist, Orelena Hawks Puckett Institute, Morganton, NC. Her research interests include the study of characteristics of helpgiving practices that influence the self-efficacy beliefs of adolescents and parents, and helpgiving practices that both directly and indirectly influence other aspects of behavior and functioning.

**Carolyn Webster-Stratton** PhD, Professor University of Washington. Dr. Webster-Stratton is a clinical psychologist who has spent the past 30 years developing and evaluating the Incredible Years Parent, Teacher and Child Programs. The goal of these programs is to promote positive parenting and teacher classroom management strategies and curricula which enhance children's emotional and social competencies and reduce conduct disorders.

**Heather B. Weiss**, EdD, is the Founder and Director of the Harvard Family Research Project at the Harvard Graduate School of Education. Research interests include family involvement; afterschool and youth initiatives; assessment of foundation grant-making strategies; and evaluation in support of learning, continuous improvement, and accountability.

**Roger P. Weissberg** is a LAS Distinguished Professor of Psychology and Education at the University of Illinois at Chicago (UIC). He is also President of the Collaborative for Academic, Social, and Emotional Learning (CASEL), an international organization committed to making evidence-based social, emotional, and academic learning an essential part of preschool through high school education (www.casel.org). Professor Weissberg trains scholars and practitioners about innovative ways to design, implement, and evaluate family, school, and community interventions to promote positive behavior in children and youth.

**Manya C. Whitaker**, MS, is a PhD in Developmental Psychology currently working on her dissertation which addresses issues of family-child relationships and students' invitations to involvement during in early adolescence. Her interests extend to issues of diversity, social and cultural capital, and the development of parental role construction for involvement in children's education.

**Janis Whitlock**, MPH, PhD, is a Research Scientist and Lecturer in Human Development at Cornell University. She is also the director of the Cornell Research Program on Self-Injurious Behavior. Her research interests include the influence of context on adolescent development, adolescent social and emotional development, and adolescent mental health.

**Samantha C. Woo**, MPH, is a member of the Families and Community Research Group at the Institute for Juvenile Research at the University of Illinois at Chicago. She has primary interests in prevention efforts to address developmental and ecological contributors to risk for children and youth. Within that focus she has particular interest in relationship quality issues among late adolescents.

**Kathryn E. Woods** is a doctoral student in the school psychology program at the University of Nebraska-Lincoln. Her research interests include pediatric psychology, early intervention for at-risk children and families, and investigating factors that promote family-school partnerships.

# INDEX

Page numbers in italics refer to Figures or Tables.